THE OXFORD PAPERBACK
GERMAN DICTIONARY

Also available

The Oxford Paperback French Dictionary
The Oxford Paperback Spanish Dictionary
The Oxford Paperback Italian Dictionary

The OXFORD PAPERBACK GERMAN DICTIONARY

German–English
English–German
Deutsch–Englisch
Englisch–Deutsch

GUNHILD PROWE

JILL SCHNEIDER

Oxford   New York
OXFORD UNIVERSITY PRESS
1994

Oxford University Press, Walton Street, Oxford OX2 6DP

Oxford New York Toronto
Delhi Bombay Calcutta Madras Karachi
Kuala Lumpur Singapore Hong Kong Tokyo
Nairobi Dar es Salaam Cape Town
Melbourne Auckland Madrid

and associated companies in
Berlin Ibadan

Oxford is a trade mark of Oxford University Press

© Oxford University Press 1993

First published 1993 as The Oxford German Minidictionary
First issued as an Oxford University Press paperback 1994

British Library Cataloguing in Publication Data
Data available

Library of Congress Cataloging in Publication Data
Data available
ISBN 0–19–280011–6

1 3 5 7 9 10 8 6 4 2

Typeset by Latimer Trend & Company Ltd.
Printed in Great Britain by
Clays Ltd.
Bungay, Suffolk

Preface

This new dictionary is designed for both English and German users. It provides a handy and comprehensive reference work for tourists and business people, and covers the needs of the student for GCSE.

We should like to express our thanks to Dr Michael Clark of Oxford University Press for his advice and support, and to Roswitha and Neil Morris for reading the proofs.

G.P. & J.S.

Contents

Introduction

A swung dash ~ represents the headword or that part of the headword preceding a vertical bar |. The initial letter of a German headword is given to show whether or not it is a capital.

The vertical bar | follows the part of the headword which is not to be repeated in compounds or derivatives.

Square brackets [ ] are used for optional material.

Angled brackets ⟨ ⟩ are used after a verb translation to indicate the object; before a verb translation to indicate the subject; before an adjective to indicate a typical noun which it qualifies.

Round brackets ( ) are used for field or style labels (see list on page vi) and for explanatory matter.

A ● indicates a new part of speech within an entry.

od (oder) and *or* denote that words or portions of a phrase are synonymous. An oblique stroke / is used where there is a difference in usage or meaning.

≈ is used where no exact equivalent exists in the other language.

A dagger † indicates that a German verb is irregular and that the parts can be found in the verb table on page 551. Compound verbs are not listed there as they follow the pattern of the basic verb.

The stressed vowel is marked in a German headword by – (long) or · (short). A phonetic transcription is only given for words which do not follow the normal rules of pronunciation. These rules can be found on page 549.

Phonetics are given for all English headwords and for derivatives where there is a change of pronunciation or stress. In blocks of compounds, if no stress is shown, it falls on the first element.

A change in pronunciation or stress shown within a block of compounds applies only to that particular word (subsequent entries revert to the pronunciation and stress of the headword).

German headword nouns are followed by the gender and, with the exception of compound nouns, by the genitive and plural. These are only given at compound nouns if they present some difficulty. Otherwise the user should refer to the final element.

Nouns that decline like adjectives are entered as follows: **-e(r)** *m/f,* **-e(s)** *nt.*

Adjectives which have no undeclined form are entered in the feminine form with the masculine and neuter in brackets **-e(r,s).**

The reflexive pronoun **sich** is accusative unless marked (*dat*).

Proprietary terms

This dictionary includes some words which are, or are asserted to be, proprietary names or trade marks. Their inclusion does not imply that they have acquired for legal purposes a non-proprietary or general significance, nor is any other judgement implied concerning their legal status. In cases where the editor has some evidence that a word is used as a proprietary name or trade mark this is indicated by the letter (P), but no judgement concerning the legal status of such words is made or implied thereby.

Abbreviations/Abkürzungen

adjective	a	Adjektiv
abbreviation	abbr	Abkürzung
accusative	acc	Akkusativ
Administration	Admin	Administration
adverb	adv	Adverb
American	Amer	amerikanisch
Anatomy	Anat	Anatomie
Archaeology	Archaeol	Archäologie
Architecture	Archit	Architektur
Astronomy	Astr	Astronomie
attributive	attrib	attributiv
Austrian	Aust	österreichisch
Motor vehicles	Auto	Automobil
Aviation	Aviat	Luftfahrt
Biology	Biol	Biologie
Botany	Bot	Botanik
Chemistry	Chem	Chemie
collective	coll	Kollektivum
Commerce	Comm	Handel
conjunction	conj	Konjunktion
Cookery	Culin	Kochkunst
dative	dat	Dativ
definite article	def art	bestimmter Artikel
demonstrative	dem	Demonstrativ-
dialect	dial	Dialekt
Electricity	Electr	Elektrizität
something	etw	etwas
feminine	f	Femininum
familiar	fam	familiär
figurative	fig	figurativ
genitive	gen	Genitiv
Geography	Geog	Geographie
Geology	Geol	Geologie
Geometry	Geom	Geometrie
Grammar	Gram	Grammatik
Horticulture	Hort	Gartenbau
impersonal	impers	unpersönlich
indefinite article	indef art	unbestimmter Artikel
inseparable	insep	untrennbar

interjection	int	Interjektion
invariable	inv	unveränderlich
irregular	irreg	unregelmäßig
someone	jd	jemand
someone	jdm	jemandem
someone	jdn	jemanden
someone's	jds	jemandes
Journalism	Journ	Journalismus
Law	Jur	Jura
Language	Lang	Sprache
literary	liter	dichterisch
masculine	m	Maskulinum
Mathematics	Math	Mathematik
Medicine	Med	Medizin
Meteorology	Meteorol	Meteorologie
Military	Mil	Militär
Mineralogy	Miner	Mineralogie
Music	Mus	Musik
noun	n	Substantiv
Nautical	Naut	nautisch
North German	N Ger	Norddeutsch
nominative	nom	Nominativ
neuter	nt	Neutrum
or	od	oder
Proprietary term	P	Warenzeichen
pejorative	pej	abwertend
Photography	Phot	Fotografie
Physics	Phys	Physik
plural	pl	Plural
Politics	Pol	Politik
possessive	poss	Possessiv-
past participle	pp	zweites Partizip
predicative	pred	prädikativ
prefix	pref	Präfix
preposition	prep	Präposition
present	pres	Präsens
present participle	pres p	erstes Partizip
pronoun	pron	Pronomen
Psychology	Psych	Psychologie
past tense	pt	Präteritum
Railway	Rail	Eisenbahn
reflexive	refl	reflexiv
regular	reg	regelmäßig

relative	rel	Relativ-
Religion	Relig	Religion
see	s.	siehe
School	Sch	Schule
separable	sep	trennbar
singular	sg	Singular
South German	S Ger	Süddeutsch
slang	sl	Slang
someone	s.o.	jemand
something	sth	etwas
Technical	Techn	Technik
Telephone	Teleph	Telefon
Textiles	Tex	Textilien
Theatre	Theat	Theater
Television	TV	Fernsehen
Typography	Typ	Typographie
University	Univ	Universität
auxiliary verb	v aux	Hilfsverb
intransitive verb	vi	intransitives Verb
reflexive verb	vr	reflexives Verb
transitive verb	vt	transitives Verb
vulgar	vulg	vulgär
Zoology	Zool	Zoologie

Pronunciation of the alphabet
Aussprache des Alphabets

English/Englisch   *German/Deutsch*

English		German
eɪ	a	aː
biː	b	beː
siː	c	tseː
diː	d	deː
iː	e	eː
ef	f	ɛf
dʒiː	g	geː
eɪtʃ	h	haː
aɪ	i	iː
dʒeɪ	j	jɔt
keɪ	k	kaː
el	l	ɛl
em	m	ɛm
en	n	ɛn
əʊ	o	oː
piː	p	peː
kjuː	q	kuː
aː(r)	r	ɛr
es	s	ɛs
tiː	t	teː
juː	u	uː
viː	v	faʊ
ˈdʌbljuː	w	veː
eks	x	ɪks
waɪ	y	ˈʏpsilɔn
zed	z	tsɛt
eɪ umlaut	ä	ɛː
əʊ umlaut	ö	øː
juː umlaut	ü	yː
esˈzed	ß	ɛsˈtsɛt

GERMAN–ENGLISH
DEUTSCH—ENGLISCH

A

Aal *m* -[e]s,-e eel. **a~en (sich)** *vr* laze; ⟨*ausgestreckt*⟩ stretch out

Aas *nt* -es carrion; ⟨*sl*⟩ swine

ab *prep* (+ *dat*) from; **ab Montag** from Monday ● *adv* off; (*weg*) away; (*auf Fahrplan*) departs; **von jetzt ab** from now on; **ab und zu** now and then; **auf und ab** up and down

abändern *vt sep* alter; (*abwandeln*) modify

abarbeiten *vt sep* work off; **sich a~** slave away

Abart *f* variety. **a~ig** *a* abnormal

Abbau *m* dismantling; (*Kohlen-*) mining; (*fig*) reduction. **a~en** *vt sep* dismantle; mine ⟨*Kohle*⟩; (*fig*) reduce, cut

abbeißen† *vt sep* bite off

abbeizen *vt sep* strip

abberufen† *vt sep* recall

abbestellen *vt sep* cancel; **jdn a~** put s.o. off

abbiegen† *vi sep* (*sein*) turn off; **[nach] links a~** turn left

Abbild *nt* image. **a~en** *vt sep* depict, portray. **A~ung** *f* -,-en illustration

Abbitte *f* **A~ leisten** apologize

abblättern *vi sep* (*sein*) flake off

abblend|en *vt/i sep* (*haben*) [**die Scheinwerfer**] **a~en** dip one's headlights. **A~licht** *nt* dipped headlights *pl*

abbrechen† *v sep* ● *vt* break off; (*abreißen*) demolish ● *vi* (*sein/haben*) break off

abbrennen† *v sep* ● *vt* burn off; (*niederbrennen*) burn down; let off ⟨*Feuerwerkskörper*⟩ ● *vi* (*sein*) burn down

abbringen† *vt sep* dissuade (**von** from)

Abbruch *m* demolition; (*Beenden*) breaking off; **etw** (*dat*) **keinen A~ tun** do no harm to sth

abbuchen *vt sep* debit

abbürsten *vt sep* brush down; (*entfernen*) brush off

abdank|en *vi sep* (*haben*) resign; ⟨*Herrscher:*⟩ abdicate. **A~ung** *f* -,-en resignation; abdication

abdecken *vt sep* uncover; (*abnehmen*) take off; (*zudecken*) cover; **den Tisch a~** clear the table

abdichten *vt sep* seal

abdrehen *vt sep* turn off

Abdruck *m* (*pl* ⁼e) impression; (*Finger-*) print; (*Nachdruck*) reprint. **a~en** *vt sep* print

abdrücken *vt/i sep* (*haben*) fire; **sich a~** leave an impression

Abend *m* -s,-e evening; **am A~** in the evening. **a~** *adv* **heute a~** this evening, tonight; **gestern a~** yesterday evening, last night. **A~brot** *nt* supper. **A~essen** *nt* dinner; (*einfacher*) supper. **A~kurs[us]** *m* evening class. **A~mahl** *nt* (*Relig*) [Holy] Communion. **a~s** *adv* in the evening

Abenteuer *nt* -s,- adventure; (*Liebes-*) affair. **a~lich** *a* fantastic; (*gefährlich*) hazardous

Abenteurer *m* -s,- adventurer

aber *conj* but; **oder a~** or else ● *adv* (*wirklich*) really; **a~ ja!** but of course! **Tausende und a~ Tausende** thousands upon thousands

Aber|glaube *m* superstition. **a~gläubisch** *a* superstitious

abermals *adv* once again

abfahr|en† *v sep* (*sein*) leave; ⟨*Auto:*⟩ drive off ● *vt* take away; (*entlangfahren*) drive along; use ⟨*Fahrkarte*⟩; **abgefahrene Reifen** worn tyres. **A~t** *f* departure; (*Talfahrt*) descent; (*Piste*) run; (*Ausfahrt*) exit

Abfall *m* refuse, rubbish, (*Amer*) garbage; (*auf der Straße*) litter; (*Industrie-*) waste. **A~eimer** *m* rubbish-bin; litter-bin

abfallen† *vi sep* (*sein*) drop, fall; (*übrigbleiben*) be left (**für** for); (*sich neigen*) slope away; (*fig*) compare badly (**gegen** with); **vom Glauben a~** renounce one's faith. **a~d** *a* sloping

Abfallhaufen *m* rubbish-dump

abfällig *a* disparaging, *adv* -ly

abfangen† *vt sep* intercept; *(beherrschen)* bring under control

abfärben *vi sep* (haben) ⟨*Farbe:*⟩ run; ⟨*Stoff:*⟩ not be colour-fast; **a~ auf** (+*acc*) *(fig)* rub off on

abfassen *vt sep* draft

abfertigen *vt sep* attend to; *(zollamtlich)* clear; **jdn kurz a~** *(fam)* give s.o. short shrift

abfeuern *vt sep* fire

abfind|en† *vt sep* pay off; *(entschädigen)* compensate; **sich a~en mit** come to terms with. **A~ung** *f* -,-en compensation

abflauen *vi sep* (sein) decrease

abfliegen† *vi sep* (sein) fly off; *(Aviat)* take off

abfließen† *vi sep* (sein) drain *or* run away

Abflug *m* *(Aviat)* departure

Abfluß *m* drainage; *(Öffnung)* drain. **A~rohr** *nt* drain-pipe

abfragen *vt sep* jdn *od* jdm Vokabeln **a~** test s.o. on vocabulary

Abfuhr *f* - removal; *(fig)* rebuff

abführ|en *vt sep* take *or* lead away. **a~end** *a* laxative. **A~mittel** *nt* laxative

abfüllen *vt sep* **auf** *od* **in Flaschen a~** bottle

Abgabe *f* handing in; *(Verkauf)* sale; *(Fußball)* pass; *(Steuer)* tax

Abgang *m* departure; *(Theat)* exit; *(Schul-)* leaving

Abgase *ntpl* exhaust fumes

abgeben† *vt sep* hand in; *(abliefern)* deliver; *(verkaufen)* sell; *(zur Aufbewahrung)* leave; *(Fußball)* pass; *(ausströmen)* give off; *(abfeuern)* fire; *(verlauten lassen)* give; cast ⟨*Stimme*⟩; **jdm etw a~** give s.o. a share of sth; **sich a~ mit** occupy oneself with

abgedroschen *a* hackneyed

abgehen† *v sep* ● *vi* (sein) leave; *(Theat)* exit; *(sich lösen)* come off; *(abgezogen werden)* be deducted; *(abbiegen)* turn off; *(verlaufen)* go off; **ihr geht jeglicher Humor ab** she totally lacks a sense of humour ● *vt* walk along

abgehetzt *a* harassed. **abgelegen** *a* remote. **abgeneigt** *a* etw *(dat)* **nicht abgeneigt sein** not be averse to sth.

abgenutzt *a* worn. **Abgeordnete(r)** *m/f* deputy; *(Pol)* Member of Parliament. **abgepackt** *a* pre-packed. **abgerissen** *a* ragged

abgeschieden *a* secluded. **A~heit** *f* - seclusion

abgeschlossen *a* *(fig)* complete; ⟨*Wohnung*⟩ self-contained. **abgeschmackt** *a* *(fig)* tasteless. **abgesehen** *prep* apart (from **von**). **abgespannt** *a* exhausted. **abgestanden** *a* stale. **abgestorben** *a* dead; ⟨*Glied*⟩ numb. **abgetragen** *a* worn. **abgewetzt** *a* threadbare

abgewinnen† *vt sep* win (**jdm** from s.o.); **etw** *(dat)* **Geschmack a~** get a taste for sth

abgewöhnen *vt sep* **jdm/sich das Rauchen a~** cure s.o. of/give up smoking

abgezehrt *a* emaciated

abgießen† *vt sep* pour off; drain ⟨*Gemüse*⟩

abgleiten† *vi sep* (sein) slip

Abgott *m* idol

abgöttisch *adv* **a~ lieben** idolize

abgrenz|en *vt sep* divide off; *(fig)* define. **A~ung** *f* - demarcation

Abgrund *m* abyss; *(fig)* depths *pl*

abgucken *vt sep* *(fam)* copy

Abguß *m* cast

abhacken *vt sep* chop off

abhaken *vt sep* tick off

abhalten† *vt sep* keep off; *(hindern)* keep, prevent (**von** from); *(veranstalten)* hold

abhanden *adv* **a~ kommen** get lost

Abhandlung *f* treatise

Abhang *m* slope

abhängen[1] *vt sep* (reg) take down; *(abkuppeln)* uncouple

abhäng|en[2]† *vi sep* (haben) depend (**von** on). **a~ig** *a* dependent (**von** on). **A~igkeit** *f* - dependence

abhärten *vt sep* toughen up

abhauen† *v sep* ● *vt* chop off ● *vi* (sein) *(fam)* clear off

abheben† *v sep* ● *vt* take off; *(vom Konto)* withdraw; **sich a~** stand out (**gegen** against) ● *vi* (haben) ⟨*Cards*⟩ cut [the cards]; *(Aviat)* take off; ⟨*Rakete:*⟩ lift off

abheften *vt sep* file

abhelfen† *vt sep* (+*dat*) remedy

Abhilfe *f* remedy; **A~ schaffen** take [remedial] action

abholen *vt sep* collect; call for ⟨*Person*⟩; **jdn am Bahnhof a~** meet s.o. at the station

abhorchen vt sep (Med) sound

abhör|en vt sep listen to; (überwachen) tap; jdn od jdm Vokabeln a∼en test s.o. on vocabulary. **A∼gerät** nt bugging device

Abitur nt -s ≈ A levels pl. **A∼ient(in)** m -en,-en (f -,-nen) pupil taking the 'Abitur'

abkanzeln vt sep (fam) reprimand

abkaufen vt sep buy (dat from)

abkehren (sich) vr sep turn away

abkette[l]n vt/i sep (haben) cast off

abklingen† vi sep (sein) die away; (nachlassen) subside

abkochen vt sep boil

abkommen† vi sep (sein) a∼ von stray from; (aufgeben) give up; vom Thema a∼ digress. **A∼** nt -s,- agreement

abkömmlich a available

Abkömmling m -s,-e descendant

abkratzen v sep ● vt scrape off ● vi (sein) (sl) die

abkühlen vt/i sep (sein) cool; sich a∼ cool [down]; (Wetter:) turn cooler

Abkunft f - origin

abkuppeln vt sep uncouple

abkürz|en vt sep shorten; abbreviate (Wort). **A∼ung** f short cut; (Wort) abbreviation

abladen† vt sep unload

Ablage f shelf; (für Akten) tray

ablager|n vt sep deposit; sich a∼n be deposited. **A∼ung** f -,-en deposit

ablassen† v sep ● vt drain [off]; let off (Dampf); (vom Preis) knock off ● vi (haben) a∼ von give up; von jdm a∼ leave s.o. alone

Ablauf m drain; (Verlauf) course; (Ende) end; (einer Frist) expiry. **a∼en†** v sep ● vi (sein) run or drain off; (verlaufen) go off; (enden) expire; (Zeit:) run out; (Uhrwerk:) run down ● vt walk along; (absuchen) scour (nach for); (abnutzen) wear down

ableg|en v sep ● vt put down; discard (Karte); (abheften) file; (ausziehen) take off; (aufgeben) give up; sit, take (Prüfung); abgelegte Kleidung castoffs pl ● vi (haben) take off one's coat; (Naut) cast off. **A∼er** m -s,- (Bot) cutting; (Schößling) shoot

ablehn|en vt sep refuse; (mißbilligen) reject. **A∼ung** f -,-en refusal; rejection

ableit|en vt sep divert; sich a∼en be derived (von/aus from). **A∼ung** f derivation; (Wort) derivative

ablenk|en vt sep deflect; divert (Aufmerksamkeit); (zerstreuen) distract. **A∼ung** f -,-en distraction

ablesen† vt sep read; (absuchen) pick off

ableugnen vt sep deny

ablicht|en vt sep photocopy. **A∼ung** f photocopy

abliefern vt sep deliver

ablös|en vt sep detach; (abwechseln) relieve; sich a∼en come off; (sich abwechseln) take turns. **A∼ung** f relief

abmach|en vt sep remove; (ausmachen) arrange; (vereinbaren) agree; abgemacht! agreed! **A∼ung** f -,-en agreement

abmager|n vi sep (sein) lose weight. **A∼ungskur** f slimming diet

abmarschieren vi sep (sein) march off

abmelden vt sep cancel (Zeitung); sich a∼ report that one is leaving; (im Hotel) check out

abmess|en† vt sep measure. **A∼ungen** fpl measurements

abmühen (sich) vr sep struggle

abnäh|en vt sep take in. **A∼er** m -s,- dart

Abnahme f - removal; (Kauf) purchase; (Verminderung) decrease

abnehm|en† v sep ● vt take off, remove; pick up (Hörer); jdm etw a∼en take/(kaufen) buy sth from s.o. ● vi (haben) decrease; (nachlassen) decline; (Person:) lose weight; (Mond:) wane. **A∼er** m -s,- buyer

Abneigung f dislike (gegen of)

abnorm a abnormal, adv -ly

abnutz|en vt sep wear out; sich a∼en wear out. **A∼ung** f - wear [and tear]

Abon|nement /abonə'mã:/ nt -s,-s subscription. **A∼nent** m -en,-en subscriber. **a∼nieren** vt take out a subscription to

Abordnung f -,-en deputation

abpassen vt sep wait for; gut a∼ time well

abprallen vi sep (sein) rebound; (Geschoß:) ricochet

abraten† vi sep (haben) jdm von etw a∼ advise s.o. against sth

abräumen vt/i (haben) clear away; clear (Tisch)

abrechn|en v sep ● vt deduct ● vi (haben) settle up; (fig) get even. **A∼ung** f settlement [of accounts]; (Rechnung) account

Abreise f departure. **a~n** vi sep (sein) leave

abreißen† v sep ● vt tear off; (demolieren) pull down ● vi (sein) come off; (fig) break off

abrichten vt sep train

abriegeln vt sep bolt; (absperren) seal off

Abriß m demolition; (Übersicht) summary

abrufen† vt sep call away; (Computer) retrieve

abrunden vt sep round off; **nach unten/oben a~** round down/up

abrupt a abrupt, adv -ly

abrüst|en vi sep (haben) disarm. **A~ung** f disarmament

abrutschen vi sep (sein) slip

Absage f -,-n cancellation; (Ablehnung) refusal. **a~n** v sep ● vt cancel ● vi (haben) **[jdm] a~n** cancel an appointment [with s.o.]; (auf Einladung) refuse [s.o.'s invitation]

absägen vt sep saw off; (fam) sack

Absatz m heel; (Abschnitt) paragraph; (Verkauf) sale

abschaff|en vt sep abolish; get rid of ⟨Auto, Hund⟩. **A~ung** f abolition

abschalten vt/i sep (haben) switch off

abschätzig a disparaging, adv -ly

Abschaum m (fig) scum

Abscheu m - revulsion

abscheulich a revolting; (fam) horrible, adv -bly

abschicken vt sep send off

Abschied m -[e]s,-e farewell; (Trennung) parting; **A~ nehmen** say goodbye (**von** to)

abschießen† vt sep shoot down; (abtrennen) shoot off; (abfeuern) fire; launch ⟨Rakete⟩

abschirmen vt sep shield

abschlagen† vt sep knock off; (verweigern) refuse; (abwehren) repel

abschlägig a negative; **a~e Antwort** refusal

Abschlepp|dienst m breakdown service. **a~en** vt sep tow away. **A~seil** nt tow-rope. **A~wagen** m breakdown vehicle

abschließen† v sep ● vt lock; (beenden, abmachen) conclude; make ⟨Wette⟩; balance ⟨Bücher⟩; **sich a~** (fig) cut oneself off ● vi (haben) lock up; (enden) end. **a~d** adv in conclusion

Abschluß m conclusion. **A~prüfung** f final examination. **A~zeugnis** nt diploma

abschmecken vt sep season

abschmieren vt sep lubricate

abschneiden† v sep ● vt cut off; **den Weg a~** take a short cut ● vi (haben) **gut/schlecht a~** do well/badly

Abschnitt m section; (Stadium) stage; (Absatz) paragraph; (Kontroll-) counterfoil

abschöpfen vt sep skim off

abschrauben vt sep unscrew

abschreck|en vt sep deter; (Culin) put in cold water ⟨Ei⟩. **a~end** a repulsive, adv -ly; **a~endes Beispiel** warning. **A~ungsmittel** nt deterrent

abschreib|en† v sep ● vt copy; (Comm & fig) write off ● vi (haben) copy. **A~ung** f (Comm) depreciation

Abschrift f copy

Abschuß m shooting down; (Abfeuern) firing; (Raketen-) launch

abschüssig a sloping; (steil) steep

abschwächen vt sep lessen; **sich a~** lessen; (schwächer werden) weaken

abschweifen vi sep (sein) digress

abschwellen† vi sep (sein) go down

abschwören† vi sep (haben) (+dat) renounce

abseh|bar a **in a~barer Zeit** in the foreseeable future. **a~en†** vt/i sep (haben) copy; (voraussehen) foresee; **a~en von** disregard; (aufgeben) refrain from; **es abgesehen haben auf** (+acc) have one's eye on; (schikanieren) have it in for

absein† vi sep (sein) (fam) have come off; (erschöpft) be worn out

abseits adv apart; (Sport) offside ● prep (+gen) away from. **A~** nt - (Sport) offside

absend|en† vt sep send off. **A~er** m sender

absetzen v sep ● vt put or set down; (ablagern) deposit; (abnehmen) take off; (absagen) cancel; (abbrechen) stop; (entlassen) dismiss; (verkaufen) sell; (abziehen) deduct; **sich a~** be deposited; (fliehen) flee ● vi (haben) pause

Absicht f -,-en intention; **mit A~** intentionally, on purpose

absichtlich a intentional, adv -ly, deliberate, adv -ly

absitzen† v sep ● vi (sein) dismount ● vt (fam) serve ⟨Strafe⟩

absolut a absolute, adv -ly

Absolution /-'tsio:n/ f - absolution

absolvieren vt complete; (*bestehen*) pass

absonderlich a odd

absonder|n vt sep separate; (*ausscheiden*) secrete; **sich a~n** keep apart (**von** from). **A~ung** f -,-en secretion

absor|bieren vt absorb. **A~ption** /-'tsio:n/ f - absorption

abspeisen vt sep fob off (**mit** with)

abspenstig a **a~ machen** take (**jdm** from s.o.)

absperr|en vt sep cordon off; (*abstellen*) turn off; (*SGer*) lock. **A~ung** f -,-en barrier

abspielen vt sep play; (*Fußball*) pass; **sich a~** take place

Absprache f agreement

absprechen† vt sep arrange; **sich a~** agree; **jdm etw a~** deny s.o. sth

abspringen† vi sep (*sein*) jump off; (*mit Fallschirm*) parachute; (*abgehen*) come off; (*fam: zurücktreten*) back out

Absprung m jump

abspülen vt sep rinse; (*entfernen*) rinse off

abstamm|en vi sep (*haben*) be descended (**von** from). **A~ung** f - descent

Abstand m distance; (*zeitlich*) interval; **A~ halten** keep one's distance; **A~ nehmen von** (*fig*) refrain from

abstatten vt sep **jdm einen Besuch a~** pay s.o. a visit

abstauben vt sep dust

abstech|en† vi sep (*haben*) stand out. **A~er** m -s,- detour

abstehen† vi sep (*haben*) stick out; **a~ von** be away from

absteigen† vi sep (*sein*) dismount; (*niedersteigen*) descend; (*Fußball*) be relegated

abstell|en vt sep put down; (*lagern*) store; (*parken*) park; (*abschalten*) turn off; (*fig: beheben*) remedy. **A~gleis** nt siding. **A~raum** m box-room

absterben† vi sep (*sein*) die; (*gefühllos werden*) go numb

Abstieg m -[e]s,-e descent; (*Fußball*) relegation

abstimm|en v sep ● vi (*haben*) vote (**über** + acc on) ● vt coordinate (**auf** + acc with). **A~ung** f vote

Abstinenz /-st-/ f - abstinence. **A~ler** m -s,- teetotaller

abstoßen† vt sep knock off; (*abschieben*) push off; (*verkaufen*) sell; (*fig: ekeln*) repel. **a~d** a repulsive, adv -ly

abstrakt /-st-/ a abstract

abstreifen vt sep remove; slip off ⟨*Kleidungsstück, Schuhe*⟩

abstreiten† vt sep deny

Abstrich m (*Med*) smear; (*Kürzung*) cut

abstufen vt sep grade

Absturz m fall; (*Aviat*) crash

abstürzen vi sep (*sein*) fall; (*Aviat*) crash

absuchen vt sep search; (*ablesen*) pick off

absurd a absurd

Abszeß m -sses,-sse abscess

Abt m -[e]s,"-e abbot

abtasten vt sep feel; (*Techn*) scan

abtauen vt/i sep (*sein*) thaw; (*entfrosten*) defrost

Abtei f -,-en abbey

Abteil nt compartment

abteilen vt sep divide off

Abteilung f -,-en section; (*Admin, Comm*) department

abtragen† vt sep clear; (*einebnen*) level; (*abnutzen*) wear out; (*abzahlen*) pay off

abträglich a detrimental (*dat* to)

abtreib|en† v sep ● vt (*Naut*) drive off course; **ein Kind a~en lassen** have an abortion ● vi (*sein*) drift off course. **A~ung** f -,-en abortion

abtrennen vt sep detach; (*abteilen*) divide off

abtret|en† v sep ● vt cede (**an** + acc to); **sich** (*dat*) **die Füße a~en** wipe one's feet ● vi (*sein*) (*Theat*) exit; (*fig*) resign. **A~er** m -s,- doormat

abtrocknen vt/i sep (*haben*) dry; **sich a~** dry oneself

abtropfen vi sep (*sein*) drain

abtrünnig a renegade; **a~ werden** (+ *dat*) desert

abtun† vt sep (*fig*) dismiss

abverlangen vt sep demand (*dat* from)

abwägen† vt sep (*fig*) weigh

abwandeln vt sep modify

abwandern vi sep (*sein*) move away

abwarten v sep ● vt wait for ● vi (*haben*) wait [and see]

abwärts adv down[wards]

Abwasch m -s washing-up; (*Geschirr*) dirty dishes pl. **a~en†** v sep ● vt wash; wash up ⟨*Geschirr*⟩; (*entfernen*) wash off ● vi (*haben*) wash up. **A~lappen** m dishcloth

Abwasser *nt* **-s,-** sewage. **A~kanal** *m* sewer

abwechseln *vi/r sep* (*haben*) **[sich] a~** alternate; ⟨*Personen:*⟩ take turns. **a~d** *a* alternate, *adv* -ly

Abwechslung *f* -,-en change; **zur A~** for a change. **a~sreich** *a* varied

Abweg *m* **auf A~e geraten** (*fig*) go astray. **a~ig** *a* absurd

Abwehr *f* - defence; (*Widerstand*) resistance; (*Pol*) counter-espionage. **a~en** *vt sep* ward off; (*Mil*) repel; (*zurückweisen*) dismiss. **A~system** *nt* immune system

abweich|en† *vi sep* (*sein*) deviate/ (*von Regel*) depart (**von** from); (*sich unterscheiden*) differ (**von** from). **a~end** *a* divergent; (*verschieden*) different. **A~ung** *f* -,-en deviation; difference

abweis|en† *vt sep* turn down; turn away ⟨*Person*⟩; (*abwehren*) repel. **a~end** *a* unfriendly. **A~ung** *f* rejection; (*Abfuhr*) rebuff

abwenden† *vt sep* turn away; (*verhindern*) avert; **sich a~** turn away; **den Blick a~** look away

abwerfen† *vt sep* throw off; throw ⟨*Reiter*⟩; (*Aviat*) drop; ⟨*Kartenspiel*⟩ discard; shed ⟨*Haut, Blätter*⟩; yield ⟨*Gewinn*⟩

abwert|en *vt sep* devalue. **a~end** *a* pejorative, *adv* -ly. **A~ung** *f* -,-en devaluation

abwesen|d *a* absent; (*zerstreut*) absent-minded. **A~heit** *f* - absence; absent-mindedness

abwickeln *vt sep* unwind; (*erledigen*) settle

abwischen *vt sep* wipe; (*entfernen*) wipe off

abwürgen *vt sep* stall ⟨*Motor*⟩

abzahlen *vt sep* pay off

abzählen *vt sep* count

Abzahlung *f* instalment

abzapfen *vt sep* draw

Abzeichen *nt* badge

abzeichnen *vt sep* copy; (*unterzeichnen*) initial; **sich a~** stand out

Abzieh|bild *nt* transfer. **a~en†** *v sep* • *vt* pull off; take off ⟨*Laken*⟩; strip ⟨*Bett*⟩; (*häuten*) skin; (*Phot*) print; run off ⟨*Kopien*⟩; (*zurückziehen*) withdraw; (*abrechnen*) deduct • *vi* (*sein*) go away; ⟨*Rauch:*⟩ escape

abzielen *vi sep* (*haben*) **a~ auf** (+ *acc*) (*fig*) be aimed at

Abzug *m* withdrawal; (*Abrechnung*) deduction; (*Phot*) print; (*Korrektur-*)

proof; (*am Gewehr*) trigger; (*A~söffnung*) vent; **A~e** *pl* deductions

abzüglich *prep* (+ *gen*) less

Abzugshaube *f* [cooker] hood

abzweig|en *v sep* • *vi* (*sein*) branch off • *vt* divert. **A~ung** *f* -,-en junction; (*Gabelung*) fork

ach *int* oh; **a~ je!** oh dear! **a~ so** I see; **mit A~ und Krach** (*fam*) by the skin of one's teeth

Achse *f* -,-n axis; (*Rad-*) axle

Achsel *f* -,-n shoulder; **die A~n zucken** shrug one's shoulders. **A~höhle** *f* armpit. **A~zucken** *nt* -s shrug

acht *inv a*, **A~** *f* -,-en eight; **heute in a~ Tagen** a week today

acht² **außer a~ lassen** disregard; **sich in a~ nehmen** be careful

acht|e(r,s) *a* eighth. **a~eckig** *a* octagonal. **A~el** *nt* -s,- eighth. **A~elnote** *f* quaver, (*Amer*) eighth note

achten *vt* respect • *vi* (*haben*) **a~ auf** (+ *acc*) pay attention to; (*aufpassen*) look after; **darauf a~, daß** take care that

ächten *vt* ban; ostracize ⟨*Person*⟩

Achter|bahn *f* roller-coaster. **a~n** *adv* (*Naut*) aft

achtgeben† *vi sep* (*haben*) be careful; **a~ auf** (+ *acc*) look after

achtlos *a* careless, *adv* -ly

achtsam *a* careful, *adv* -ly

Achtung *f* - respect (**vor** + *dat* for); **A~!** look out! (*Mil*) attention! **'A~ Stufe'** 'mind the step'

acht|zehn *inv* *a* eighteen. **a~zehnte(r,s)** *a* eighteenth. **a~zig** *a* *inv* eighty. **a~zigste(r,s)** *a* eightieth

ächzen *vi* (*haben*) groan

Acker *m* **-s,-** field. **A~bau** *m* agriculture. **A~land** *nt* arable land

addieren *vt/i* (*haben*) add; (*zusammenzählen*) add up

Addition /-'tsio:n/ *f* -,-en addition

ade *int* goodbye

Adel *m* **-s** nobility

Ader *f* -,-n vein; **künstlerische A~** artistic bent

Adjektiv *nt* -s,-e adjective

Adler *m* -s,- eagle

adlig *a* noble. **A~e(r)** *m* nobleman

Administration /-'tsio:n/ *f* - administration

Admiral *m* -s,-e admiral

adop|tieren vt adopt. **A~tion** /-'tsjo:n/ f -,-en adoption. **A~tiveltern** pl adoptive parents. **A~tivkind** nt adopted child

Adrenalin nt -s adrenalin

Adres|se f -,-n address. **a~sieren** vt address

adrett a neat, adv -ly

Adria f - Adriatic

Advent m -s Advent. **A~skranz** m Advent wreath

Adverb nt -s,-ien /-jən/ adverb

Affäre f -,-n affair

Affe m -n,-n monkey; (Menschen-) ape

Affekt m -[e]s,-e im **A~** in the heat of the moment

affektiert a affected. **A~heit** f - affectation

affig a affected; (eitel) vain

Afrika nt -s Africa

Afrikan|er(in) m -s,- (f -,-nen) African. **a~isch** a African

After m -s,- anus

Agen|t(in) m -en,-en (f -,-nen) agent. **A~tur** f -,-en agency

Aggres|sion f -,-en aggression. **a~siv** a aggressive, adv -ly. **A~sivität** f - aggressiveness

Agitation /-'tsjo:n/ f - agitation

Agnostiker m -s,- agnostic

Ägypt|en /ɛ'gyptən/ nt -s Egypt. **Ä~er(in)** m -s,- (f -,-nen) Egyptian. **ä~isch** a Egyptian

ähneln vi (haben) (+dat) resemble; **sich ä~** be alike

ahnen vt have a presentiment of; (vermuten) suspect

Ahnen mpl ancestors. **A~forschung** f genealogy. **A~tafel** f family tree

ähnlich a similar, adv -ly; **jdm ä~sehen** resemble s.o.; (typisch sein) be just like s.o. **Ä~keit** f -,-en similarity; resemblance

Ahnung f -,-en premonition; (Vermutung) idea, hunch; **keine A~** (fam) no idea. **a~slos** a unsuspecting

Ahorn m -s,-e maple

Ähre f -,-n ear [of corn]

Aids /e:ts/ nt - Aids

Akademie f -,-n academy

Akadem|iker(in) m -s,- (f -,-nen) university graduate. **a~isch** a academic, adv -ally

akklimatisieren (sich) vr become acclimatized

Akkord m -[e]s,-e (Mus) chord; **im A~** arbeiten be on piece-work. **A~arbeit** f piece-work

Akkordeon nt -s,-s accordion

Akkumulator m -s,-en /-'to:rən/ (Electr) accumulator

Akkusativ m -s,-e accusative. **A~objekt** nt direct object

Akrobat|(in) m -en,-en (f -,-nen) acrobat. **a~isch** a acrobatic

Akt m -[e]s,-e act; (Kunst) nude

Akte f -,-n file; **A~n** documents. **A~ndeckel** m folder. **A~nkoffer** m attaché case. **A~nschrank** m filing cabinet. **A~ntasche** f briefcase

Aktie /'aktsiə/ f -,-n (Comm) share. **A~ngesellschaft** f joint-stock company

Aktion /ak'tsjo:n/ f -,-en action; (Kampagne) campaign. **A~är** m -s,-e shareholder

aktiv a active, adv -ly. **a~ieren** vt activate. **A~ität** f -,-en activity

Aktualität f -,-en topicality; **A~en** current events

aktuell a topical; (gegenwärtig) current; **nicht mehr a~** no longer relevant

Akupunktur f - acupuncture

Akust|ik f - acoustics pl. **a~isch** a acoustic, adv -ally

akut a acute

Akzent m -[e]s,-e accent

akzept|abel a acceptable. **a~ieren** vt accept

Alarm m -s alarm; (Mil) alert; **A~schlagen** raise the alarm. **a~ieren** vt alert; (beunruhigen) alarm. **a~ierend** a alarming

albern a silly ● adv in a silly way ● vi (haben) play the fool

Album nt -s,-ben album

Algebra f - algebra

Algen fpl algae

Algerien /-jən/ nt -s Algeria

Alibi nt -s,-s alibi

Alimente pl maintenance sg

Alkohol m -s alcohol. **a~frei** a non-alcoholic

Alkohol|iker(in) m -s,- (f -,-nen) alcoholic. **a~isch** a alcoholic. **A~ismus** m - alcoholism

all inv pron **all das/mein Geld** all the/my money; **all dies** all this

All nt -s universe

alle pred a finished, (fam) all gone; **a~ machen** finish up

all|e(r,s) pron all; (jeder) every; **a~es** everything, all; (alle Leute) everyone; **a~e** pl all; **a~es Geld** all the money; **a~e meine Freunde** all my friends; **a~e beide** both [of them/us]; **wir a∼e** we all; **a∼e Tage** every day; **a∼e drei Jahre** every three years; **in a∼er Unschuld** in all innocence; **ohne a∼en Grund** without any reason; **vor a∼em** above all; **a∼es in a∼em** all in all; **a∼es aussteigen!** all change! **a∼edem** *pron* **bei/trotz a∼edem** with/despite all that

Allee *f* -,-n avenue

Alleg|orie *f* -,-n allegory. **a∼orisch** *a* allegorical

allein *adv* alone; (*nur*) only; **a∼ der Gedanke** the mere thought; **von a∼[e]** of its/⟨*Person*⟩ one's own accord; (*automatisch*) automatically; **einzig und a∼** solely ● *conj* but. **A∼erziehende(r)** *m/f* single parent. **a∼ig** *a* sole. **a∼stehend** *a* single; **A∼stehende** *pl* single people

allemal *adv* every time; (*gewiß*) certainly; **ein für a∼** once and for all

allenfalls *adv* at most; (*eventuell*) possibly

aller|beste(r,s) *a* very best; **am a∼besten** best of all. **a∼dings** *adv* indeed; (*zwar*) admittedly. **a∼erste(r,s)** *a* very first

Allergie *f* -,-n allergy

allergisch *a* allergic (**gegen**)

aller|hand *inv a* all sorts of ● *pron* all sorts of things; **das ist a∼hand!** that's quite something! (*empört*) that's a bit much! **A∼heiligen** *nt* -s All Saints Day. **a∼höchstens** *adv* at the very most. **a∼lei** *inv a* all sorts of ● *pron* all sorts of things. **a∼letzte(r,s)** *a* very last. **a∼liebst** *a* enchanting. **a∼liebste(r,s)** *a* favourite ● *adv* **am a∼liebsten** for preference; **am a∼liebsten haben** like best of all. **a∼meiste(r,s)** *a* most ● *adv* **am a∼meisten** most of all. **A∼seelen** *nt* -s All Souls Day. **a∼seits** *adv* generally; **guten Morgen a∼seits!** good morning everyone! **a∼wenigste(r,s)** *a* very least ● *adv* **am a∼wenigsten** least of all

alle|s *s.* **alle(r,s)**. **a∼samt** *adv* all. **A∼swisser** *m* -s,- (*fam*) know-all

allgemein *a* general, *adv* -ly; **im a∼en** in general. **A∼heit** *f* - community; (*Öffentlichkeit*) general public

Allheilmittel *nt* panacea

Allianz *f* -,-en alliance

Alligator *m* -s,-en /-'to:rən/ alligator

alliiert *a* allied; **die A∼en** *pl* the Allies

all|jährlich *a* annual, *adv* -ly. **a∼mächtig** *a* almighty; **der A∼mächtige** the Almighty. **a∼mählich** *a* gradual, *adv* -ly

Alltag *m* working day; **der A∼** (*fig*) everyday life

alltäglich *a* daily; (*gewöhnlich*) everyday; ⟨*Mensch*⟩ ordinary ● *adv* daily

alltags *adv* on weekdays

allzu *adv* [far] too; **a∼ vorsichtig** over-cautious. **a∼bald** *adv* all too soon. **a∼oft** *adv* all too often. **a∼sehr** *adv* far too much. **a∼viel** *adv* far too much

Alm *f* -,-en alpine pasture

Almosen *ntpl* alms

Alpdruck *m* nightmare

Alpen *pl* Alps. **A∼veilchen** *nt* cyclamen

Alphabet *nt* -[e]s,-e alphabet. **a∼isch** *a* alphabetical, *adv* -ly

Alptraum *m* nightmare

als *conj* as; (*zeitlich*) when; (*mit Komparativ*) than; **nichts als** nothing but; **als ob** as if *or* though; **so tun als ob** (*fam*) pretend

also *adv & conj* so; **a∼ gut** all right then; **na a∼!** there you are!

alt *a* (**älter, ältest**) old; (*gebraucht*) second-hand; (*ehemalig*) former; **alt werden** grow old; **alles beim a∼en lassen** leave things as they are

Alt *m* -s (*Mus*) contralto

Altar *m* -s,-ͤe altar

Alte(r) *m/f* old man/woman; **die A∼en** old people. **A∼eisen** *nt* scrap iron. **A∼enheim** *nt* old people's home

Alter *nt* -s,- age; (*Bejahrtheit*) old age; **im A∼ von** at the age of; **im A∼ in** old age

älter *a* older; **mein ä∼er Bruder** my elder brother

altern *vi* (*sein*) age

Alternative *f* -,-n alternative

Alters|grenze *f* age limit. **A∼heim** *nt* old people's home. **A∼rente** *f* old-age pension. **a∼schwach** *a* old and infirm; ⟨*Ding*⟩ decrepit

Alter|tum *nt* -s,-ͤer antiquity. **a∼tümlich** *a* old; (*altmodisch*) old-fashioned

ältest|e(r,s) *a* oldest; **der ä∼e Sohn** the eldest son

althergebracht *a* traditional

altklug *a* precocious, *adv* -ly

ältlich *a* elderly

alt|modisch old-fashioned ● *adv* in an old-fashioned way. **A∼papier** *nt* waste paper. **A~stadt** f old [part of a] town. **A~warenhändler** m second-hand dealer. **A~weibermärchen** nt old wives' tale. **A~weibersommer** m Indian summer; (Spinnfäden) gossamer

Alufolie f [aluminium] foil

Aluminium nt -s aluminium, (Amer) aluminum

am prep = an dem; **am Montag** on Monday; **am Morgen** in the morning; **am besten/meisten** [the] best/most; **am teuersten sein** be the most expensive

Amateur /-'tø:ɐ̯/ m -s,-e amateur

Ambition /-'tsio:n/ f -,-en ambition

Amboß m -sses,-sse anvil

ambulan|t a out-patient ... ● adv **a~t behandeln** treat as an out-patient. **A~z** f -,-en out-patients' department; (Krankenwagen) ambulance

Ameise f -,-n ant

amen int, **A~** nt -s amen

Amerika nt -s America

Amerikan|er(in) m -s,- (f -,-nen) American. **a~isch** a American

Ami m -s,-s (fam) Yank

Ammoniak nt -s ammonia

Amnestie f -,-n amnesty

amoralisch a amoral

Ampel f -,-n traffic lights pl; (Blumen-) hanging basket

Amphib|ie /-iə/ f -,-n amphibian. **a~isch** a amphibious

Amphitheater nt amphitheatre

Amput|ation /-'tsio:n/ f -,-en amputation. **a~ieren** vt amputate

Amsel f -,-n blackbird

Amt nt -[e]s,¨er office; (Aufgabe) task; (Teleph) exchange. **a~ieren** (haben) hold office; **a~ierend** acting. **a~lich** a official, adv -ly. **A~szeichen** nt dialling tone

Amulett nt -[e]s,-e [lucky] charm

amüs|ant a amusing, adv -ly. **a~ieren** vt amuse; **sich a~ieren** be amused (über + acc at); (sich vergnügen) enjoy oneself

an prep (+ dat/acc) at; (haftend, berührend) on; (gegen) against; (+ acc) ⟨schicken⟩ to; **an der/die Universität** at/to university; **an dem Tag** on that day; **es ist an mir** it is up to me; **an [und für] sich** actually; **die Arbeit an sich** the work as such ● adv (angeschaltet) on; (auf Fahrplan) arriving; **an die zwanzig**

Mark/Leute about twenty marks/people; **von heute an** from today

analog a analogous; (Computer) analog. **A~ie** f -,-n analogy

Analphabet m -en,-en illiterate person. **A~entum** nt -s illiteracy

Analy|se f -,-n analysis. **a~sieren** vt analyse. **A~tiker** m -s,- analyst. **a~tisch** a analytical

Anämie f - anaemia

Ananas f -,-[se] pineapple

Anarch|ie f - anarchy. **A~ist** m -en,-en anarchist

Anat|omie f - anatomy. **a~omisch** a anatomical, adv -ly

anbahnen (sich) vr sep develop

Anbau m cultivation; (Gebäude) extension. **a~en** vt sep build on; (anpflanzen) cultivate, grow

anbehalten† vt sep keep on

anbei adv enclosed

anbeißen† v sep ● vt take a bite of ● vi (haben) ⟨Fisch:⟩ bite; (fig) take the bait

anbelangen vt sep = anbetreffen

anbellen vt sep bark at

anbeten vt sep worship

Anbetracht m **in A~** (+ gen) in view of

anbetreffen† vt sep **was mich/das anbetrifft** as far as I am/that is concerned

Anbetung f - worship

anbiedern (sich) vr sep ingratiate oneself (bei with)

anbieten† vt sep offer; **sich a~** offer (zu to)

anbinden† vt sep tie up

Anblick m sight. **a~en** vt sep look at

anbrechen† v sep ● vt start on; break into ⟨Vorräte⟩ ● vi (sein) begin; ⟨Tag:⟩ break; ⟨Nacht:⟩ fall

anbrennen† v sep ● vt light ● vi (sein) burn; (Feuer fangen) catch fire

anbringen† vt sep bring [along]; (befestigen) fix

Anbruch m (fig) dawn; **A~ des Tages/der Nacht** daybreak/nightfall

anbrüllen vt sep (fam) bellow at

Andacht f -,-en reverence; (Gottesdienst) prayers pl

andächtig a reverent, adv -ly; (fig) rapt, adv -ly

andauern vi sep (haben) last; (anhalten) continue. **a~d** a persistent, adv -ly; (ständig) constant, adv -ly

Andenken nt -s,- memory; (Souvenir) souvenir; **zum A~ an** (+ acc) in memory of

ander|e(r,s) *a* other; (*verschieden*) different; (*nächste*) next; **ein a~er, eine a~e** another ● *pron* **der a~e/ die a~en** the other/others; **ein a~er** another [one]; (*Person*) someone else; **kein a~er** no one else; **einer nach dem a~en** one after the other; **alles a~e/nichts a~es** everything/nothing else; **etwas ganz a~es** something quite different; **alles a~e als** anything but; **unter a~em** among other things. **a~enfalls** *adv* otherwise. **a~erseits** *adv* on the other hand. **a~mal** *adv* **ein a~mal** another time

ändern *vt* alter; (*wechseln*) change; **sich ä~** change

andernfalls *adv* otherwise

anders *pred a* different; **a~ werden** change ● *adv* differently; (*riechen, schmecken*) different; (*sonst*) else; **jemand/niemand/irgendwo a~** someone/no one/somewhere else

anderseits *adv* on the other hand

anders|herum *adv* the other way round. **a~wo** *adv* (*fam*) somewhere else

anderthalb *inv a* one and a half; **a~ Stunden** an hour and a half

Änderung *f* -,-**en** alteration; (*Wechsel*) change

anderweitig *a* other ● *adv* otherwise; (*anderswo*) elsewhere

andeut|en *vt sep* indicate; (*anspielen*) hint at. **A~ung** *f* -,-**en** indication; hint

andicken *vt sep* (*Culin*) thicken

Andrang *m* rush (**nach** for); (*Gedränge*) crush

andre *a & pron* = **andere**

andrehen *vt sep* turn on; **jdm etw a~** (*fam*) palm sth off on s.o.

andrerseits *adv* = **andererseits**

androhen *vt sep* **jdm etw a~** threaten s.o. with sth

aneignen *vt sep* **sich** (*dat*) **a~** appropriate; (*lernen*) learn

aneinander *adv & pref* together; (*denken*) of one another; **a~ vorbei** past one another. **a~geraten**† *vi sep* (*sein*) quarrel

Anekdote *f* -,-**n** anecdote

anekeln *vt sep* nauseate

anerkannt *a* acknowledged

anerkenn|en† *vt sep* acknowledge, recognize; (*würdigen*) appreciate. **a~end** *a* approving, *adv* -ly. **A~ung** *f* - acknowledgement, recognition; appreciation

anfahren† *v sep* ● *vt* deliver; (*streifen*) hit; (*schimpfen*) snap at ● *vi* (*sein*) start; **angefahren kommen** drive up

Anfall *m* fit, attack. **a~en**† *v sep* ● *vt* attack ● *vi* (*sein*) arise; (*Zinsen:*) accrue

anfällig *a* susceptible (**für** to); (*zart*) delicate. **A~keit** *f* - susceptibility (**für** to)

Anfang *m* -**s,-̈e** beginning, start; **zu od am A~** at the beginning; (*anfangs*) at first. **a~en**† *vt/i sep* (*haben*) begin, start; (*tun*) do

Anfäng|er(in) *m* -**s,-** (*f* -,-**nen**) beginner. **a~lich** *a* initial, *adv* -ly

anfangs *adv* at first. **A~buchstabe** *m* initial letter. **A~gehalt** *nt* starting salary. **A~gründe** *mpl* rudiments

anfassen *v sep* ● *vt* touch; (*behandeln*) treat; (*Arbeit*) tackle **a~** take s.o.'s hand; **sich a~** hold hands; **sich weich a~** feel soft ● *vi* (*haben*) **mit a~** lend a hand

anfechten† *vt sep* contest; (*fig: beunruhigen*) trouble

anfeinden *vt sep* be hostile to

anfertigen *vt sep* make

anfeuchten *vt sep* moisten

anfeuern *vt sep* spur on

anflehen *vt sep* implore, beg

Anflug *m* (*Aviat*) approach; (*fig: Spur*) trace

anforder|n *vt sep* demand; (*Comm*) order. **A~ung** *f* demand

Anfrage *f* enquiry. **a~n** *vi sep* (*haben*) enquire, ask

anfreunden (sich) *vr sep* make friends (**mit** with); (*miteinander*) become friends

anfügen *vt sep* add

anfühlen *vt sep* feel; **sich weich a~** feel soft

anführ|en *vt sep* lead; (*zitieren*) quote; (*angeben*) give; **jdn a~en** (*fam*) have s.o. on. **A~er** *m* leader. **A~ungszeichen** *ntpl* quotation marks

Angabe *f* statement; (*Anweisung*) instruction; (*Tennis*) service; (*fam: Angeberei*) showing-off; **nähere A~n** particulars

angeb|en *v sep* ● *vt* state; give (*Namen, Grund*); (*anzeigen*) indicate; set (*Tempo*) ● *vi* (*haben*) (*Tennis*) serve; (*fam: protzen*) show off. **A~er(in)** *m* -**s,-** (*f* -,-**nen**) (*fam*)

show-off. **A~erei** *f* - (*fam*)
showing-off

angeblich *a* alleged, *adv* -ly

angeboren *a* innate; (*Med*)
congenital

Angebot *nt* offer; (*Auswahl*) range;
A~ und Nachfrage supply and
demand

angebracht *a* appropriate

angebunden *a* kurz a~ curt

angegriffen *a* worn out; ⟨*Gesundheit*⟩ poor

angeheiratet *a* ⟨*Onkel, Tante*⟩ by
marriage

angeheitert *a* (*fam*) tipsy

angehen† *v sep* ● *vi* (*sein*) begin,
start; ⟨*Licht, Radio:*⟩ come on; (*anwachsen*) take root; a~ gegen fight
● *vt* attack; tackle ⟨*Arbeit*⟩; (*bitten*)
ask (**um** for); (*betreffen*) concern;
das geht dich nichts an it's none of
your business. **a~d** *a* future;
⟨*Künstler*⟩ budding

angehör|en *vi sep* (*haben*) (+*dat*)
belong to. **A~ige(r)** *m/f* relative;
(*Mitglied*) member

Angeklagte(r) *m/f* accused

Angel *f* -,-n fishing rod; (*Tür*-) hinge

Angelegenheit *f* matter; **auswärtige
A~en** foreign affairs

Angel|haken *m* fish-hook. **a~n** *vi*
(*haben*) fish (**nach** for); **a~n gehen**
go fishing ● *vt* (*fangen*) catch. **A~
rute** *f* fishing-rod

angelsächsisch *a* Anglo-Saxon

angemessen *a* commensurate (*dat*
with); (*passend*) appropriate, *adv*
-ly

angenehm *a* pleasant, *adv* -ly; (*bei
Vorstellung*) a~! delighted to meet
you!

angenommen *a* ⟨*Kind*⟩ adopted;
⟨*Name*⟩ assumed

angeregt *a* animated, *adv* -ly

angesehen *a* respected; ⟨*Firma*⟩
reputable

angesichts *prep* (+*gen*) in view of

angespannt *a* intent, *adv* -ly; ⟨*Lage*⟩
tense

Angestellte(r) *m/f* employee

angetan *a* a~ sein von be taken with

angetrunken *a* slightly drunk

angewandt *a* applied

angewiesen *a* dependent (**auf** +*acc*
on); **auf sich selbst** a~ on one's own

angewöhnen *vt sep* jdm etw a~ get
s.o. used to sth; **sich** (*dat*) **etw** a~ get
into the habit of doing sth

Angewohnheit *f* habit

Angina *f* - tonsillitis

angleichen† *vt sep* adjust (*dat* to)

Angler *m* -s,- angler

anglikanisch *a* Anglican

Anglistik *f* - English [language and
literature]

Angorakatze *f* Persian cat

angreif|en† *vt sep* attack; tackle
⟨*Arbeit*⟩; (*schädigen*) damage; (*anbrechen*) break into; (*anfassen*)
touch. **A~er** *m* -s,- attacker; (*Pol*)
aggressor

angrenzen *vi sep* (*haben*) adjoin (**an**
etw *acc* sth). **a~d** *a* adjoining

Angriff *m* attack; **in A~ nehmen**
tackle. **a~slustig** *a* aggressive

Angst *f* -,¨e fear; (*Psych*) anxiety;
(*Sorge*) worry (**um** about); **A~ haben**
be afraid (**vor** + *dat* of); (*sich sorgen*)
be worried (**um** about) ● **jdm** a~
machen frighten s.o.; **mir ist** a~ I am
frightened; I am worried (**um** about)

ängstigen *vt* frighten; (*Sorge
machen*) worry; **sich** ä~ be
frightened; be worried (**um** about)

ängstlich *a* nervous, *adv* -ly; (*scheu*)
timid, *adv* -ly; (*verängstigt*)
frightened, scared; (*besorgt*) anxious, *adv* -ly. **Ä~keit** *f* - nervous-
ness; timidity; anxiety

angstvoll *a* anxious, *adv* -ly; (*verängstigt*) frightened

angucken *vt sep* (*fam*) look at

angurten (sich) *vr sep* fasten one's
seat-belt

anhaben† *vt sep* have on; **er/es kann
mir nichts** a~ (*fig*) he/it cannot hurt
me

anhalt|en† *v sep* ● *vt* stop; hold
⟨*Atem*⟩; **jdn zur Arbeit/Ordnung**
a~en urge s.o. to work/be tidy ● *vi*
(*haben*) stop; (*andauern*) continue.
a~end *a* persistent, *adv* -ly; (*Beifall*) prolonged. **A~er(in)** *m* -s,- (*f* -,-
nen) hitch-hiker; **per A~er fahren**
hitch-hike. **A~spunkt** *m* clue

anhand *prep* (+*gen*) with the aid of

Anhang *m* appendix; (*fam: Ange-
hörige*) family

anhängen¹ *vt sep* (*reg*) hang up;
(*befestigen*) attach; (*hinzufügen*) add

anhäng|en²† *vi* (*haben*) be a follower
of. **A~er** *m* -s,- (*Auto*)
trailer; (*Schild*) [tie-on] label;
(*Schmuck*) pendant; (*Aufhänger*)
loop. **A~erin** *f* -,-nen follower.
A~erschaft *f* - following, followers
pl. **a~lich** *a* affectionate. **A~sel** *nt*
-s,- appendage

anhäufen *vt sep* pile up; **sich a~** pile up, accumulate

anheben† *vt sep* lift; (*erhöhen*) raise

Anhieb *m* **auf A~** straight away

Anhöhe *f* hill

anhören *vt sep* listen to; **mit a~** overhear; **sich gut a~** sound good

animieren *vt* encourage (**zu** to)

Anis *m* **-es** aniseed

Anker *m* **-s,-** anchor; **vor A~ gehen** drop anchor. **a~n** *vi* (*haben*) anchor; (*liegen*) be anchored

anketten *vt sep* chain up

Anklage *f* accusation; (*Jur*) charge; (*Ankläger*) prosecution. **A~bank** *f* dock. **a~n** *vt sep* accuse (*gen* of); (*Jur*) charge (*gen* with)

Ankläger *m* accuser; (*Jur*) prosecutor

anklammern *vt sep* clip on; peg on the line (*Wäsche*); **sich a~** cling (**an** + *acc* to)

Anklang *m* **bei jdm A~ finden** meet with s.o.'s approval

ankleben *v sep* ● *vt* stick on ● *vi* (*sein*) stick (**an** + *dat* to)

Ankleide|kabine *f* changing cubicle; (*zur Anprobe*) fitting-room. **a~n** *vt sep* dress; **sich a~n** dress

anklopfen *vi sep* (*haben*) knock

anknipsen *vt sep* (*fam*) switch on

anknüpfen *v sep* ● *vt* tie on; (*fig*) enter into (*Gespräch, Beziehung*) ● *vi* (*haben*) refer (**an** + *acc* to)

ankommen† *vi sep* (*sein*) arrive; (*sich nähern*) approach; **gut a~** arrive safely; (*fig*) go down well (**bei** with); **nicht a~ gegen** (*fig*) be no match for; **a~ auf** (+ *acc*) depend on; **es a~ lassen auf** (+ *acc*) risk; **das kommt darauf an** it [all] depends

ankreuzen *vt sep* mark with a cross

ankündig|en *vt sep* announce. **A~ung** *f* announcement

Ankunft *f* **-** arrival

ankurbeln *vt sep* (*fig*) boost

anlächeln *vt sep* smile at

anlachen *vt sep* smile at

Anlage *f* **-,-n** installation; (*Industrie-*) plant; (*Komplex*) complex; (*Geld-*) investment; (*Plan*) layout; (*Beilage*) enclosure; (*Veranlagung*) aptitude; (*Neigung*) predisposition; **[öffentliche] A~n** [public] gardens; **als A~** enclosed

Anlaß *m* **-sses,-̈sse** reason; (*Gelegenheit*) occasion; **A~ geben zu** give cause for

anlass|en† *vt sep* (*Auto*) start; (*fam*) leave on (*Licht*); keep on (*Mantel*); **sich gut/schlecht a~en** start off well/badly. **A~er** *m* **-s,-** starter

anläßlich *prep* (+ *gen*) on the occasion of

Anlauf *m* (*Sport*) run-up; (*fig*) attempt. **a~en**† *v sep* ● *vi* (*sein*) start; (*beschlagen*) mist up; (*Metall:*) tarnish; **rot a~en** go red; (*erröten*) blush; **angelaufen kommen** come running up ● *vt* (*Naut*) call at

anlegen *v sep* ● *vt* put (**an** + *acc* against); put on (*Kleidung, Verband*); lay back (*Ohren*); aim (*Gewehr*); (*investieren*) invest; (*ausgeben*) spend (**für** on); (*erstellen*) build; (*gestalten*) lay out; draw up (*Liste*); **[mit] Hand a~** lend a hand; **es darauf a~** (*fig*) aim (**zu** to); **sich a~ mit** quarrel with ● *vi* (*haben*) (*Schiff:*) moor; **a~ auf** (+ *acc*) aim at

anlehnen *vt sep* lean (**an** + *acc* against); **sich a~** lean (**an** + *acc* on); **eine Tür angelehnt lassen** leave a door ajar

Anleihe *f* **-,-n** loan

anleinen *vt sep* put on a lead

anleit|en *vt sep* instruct. **A~ung** *f* instructions *pl*

anlernen *vt sep* train

Anliegen *nt* **-s,-** request; (*Wunsch*) desire

anlieg|en† *vi sep* (*haben*) **[eng] a~en** fit closely; **[eng] a~end** close-fitting. **A~er** *mpl* residents; **'A~er frei'** 'access for residents only'

anlocken *vt sep* attract

anlügen† *vt sep* lie to

anmachen *vt sep* (*fam*) fix; (*anschalten*) turn on; (*anzünden*) light; (*Culin*) dress (*Salat*)

anmalen *vt sep* paint

Anmarsch *m* (*Mil*) approach

anmaß|en *vt sep* **sich** (*dat*) **a~en** presume (**zu** to); **sich** (*dat*) **ein Recht a~en** claim a right. **a~end** *a* presumptuous, *adv* -ly; (*arrogant*) arrogant, *adv* -ly. **A~ung** *f* **-** presumption; arrogance

anmeld|en *vt sep* announce; (*Admin*) register; **sich a~en** say that one is coming; (*Admin*) register; (*Sch*) enrol; (*im Hotel*) check in; (*beim Arzt*) make an appointment. **A~ung** *f* announcement; (*Admin*) registration; (*Sch*) enrolment; (*Termin*) appointment

anmerk|en vt sep mark; **sich** (dat) **etw a~en lassen** show sth. **A~ung** f -,-en note

Anmut f - grace; (Charme) charm

anmuten vt sep **es mutet mich seltsam/vertraut an** it seems odd/familiar to me

anmutig a graceful, adv -ly; (lieblich) charming, adv -ly

annähen vt sep sew on

annäher|nd a approximate, adv -ly. **A~ungsversuche** mpl advances

Annahme f -,-n acceptance; (Adoption) adoption; (Vermutung) assumption

annehm|bar a acceptable. **a~en†** vt sep accept; (adoptieren) adopt; acquire (Gewohnheit); (sich zulegen, vermuten) assume; **sich a~en** (+ gen) take care of; **angenommen, daß** assuming that. **A~lichkeiten** fpl comforts

annektieren vt annex

Anno adv **A~ 1920** in the year 1920

Annon|ce /a'nõ:sə/ f -,-n advertisement. **a~cieren** /-'si:-/ vt/i (haben) advertise

annullieren vt annul; cancel (Flug)

anöden vt sep (fam) bore

Anomalie f -,-n anomaly

anonym a anonymous, adv -ly

Anorak m -s,-s anorak

anordn|en vt sep arrange; (befehlen) order. **A~ung** f arrangement; order

anorganisch a inorganic

anormal a abnormal

anpacken v sep ● vt grasp; tackle (Arbeit, Problem) ● vi (haben) **mit a~** lend a hand

anpass|en vt sep try on; (angleichen) adapt (dat to); **sich a~** adapt (dat to). **A~ung** f - adaptation. **a~ungsfähig** a adaptable. **A~ungsfähigkeit** f adaptability

Anpfiff m (Sport) kick-off; (fam: Rüge) reprimand

anpflanzen vt sep plant; (anbauen) grow

Anprall m -[e]s impact. **a~en** vi sep (sein) strike (**an etw** acc sth)

anprangern vt sep denounce

anpreisen† vt sep commend

Anprob|e f fitting. **a~ieren** vt sep try on

anrechnen vt sep count (**als** as); (berechnen) charge for; (verrechnen) allow (Summe); **ich rechne ihm seine Hilfe hoch an** I very much appreciate his help

Anrecht nt right (**auf** + acc to)

Anrede f [form of] address. **a~n** vt sep address; (ansprechen) speak to

anreg|en vt sep stimulate; (ermuntern) encourage (**zu** to); (vorschlagen) suggest. **a~end** a stimulating. **A~ung** f stimulation; (Vorschlag) suggestion

anreichern vt sep enrich

Anreise f journey; (Ankunft) arrival. **a~n** vi sep (sein) arrive

Anreiz m incentive

anrempeln vt sep jostle

Anrichte f -,-n sideboard. **a~n** vt sep (Culin) prepare; (garnieren) garnish (**mit** with); (verursachen) cause

anrüchig a disreputable

Anruf m call. **A~beantworter** m -s,- answering machine. **a~en†** v sep ● vt call to; (bitten) call on (**um** for); (Teleph) ring ● vi (haben) ring (**bei jdm** s.o.)

anrühren vt sep touch; (verrühren) mix

ans prep = **an das**

Ansage f announcement. **a~n** vt sep announce; **sich a~n** say that one is coming. **A~r(in)** m -s,- (f -,-nen) announcer

ansamm|eln vt sep collect; (anhäufen) accumulate; **sich a~eln** collect; (sich häufen) accumulate; (Leute:) gather. **A~lung** f collection; (Menschen-) crowd

ansässig a resident

Ansatz m beginning; (Haar-) hairline; (Versuch) attempt; (Techn) extension

anschaff|en vt sep [**sich** dat] **etw a~en** acquire/(kaufen) buy sth. **A~ung** f -,-en acquisition; (Kauf) purchase

anschalten vt sep switch on

anschau|en vt sep look at. **a~lich** a vivid, adv -ly. **A~ung** f -,-en (fig) view

Anschein m appearance; **den A~ haben** seem. **a~end** adv apparently

anschicken (sich) vr sep be about (**zu** to)

anschirren vt sep harness

Anschlag m notice; (Vor-) estimate; (Überfall) attack (**auf** + acc on); (Mus) touch; (Techn) stop; **240 A~e in der Minute** ≈ 50 words per minute. **A~brett** nt notice board. **a~en†** v sep ● vt put up (Aushang); strike (Note, Taste); cast on (Masche); (beschädigen) chip ● vi (*haben*) strike/(*stoßen*) knock (**an** + *acc* against); ⟨*Hund:*⟩ bark; (*wirken*) be effective ● *vi* (*sein*) knock (**an** + *acc* against); **mit dem Kopf a~en** hit one's head. **A~zettel** *m* notice

anschließen† *v sep* ● *vt* connect (**an** + *acc* to); (*zufügen*) add; **sich a~ an** (+ *acc*) (*anstoßen*) adjoin; (*folgen*) follow; (*sich anfreunden*) become friendly with; **sich jdm a~** join s.o. ● *vi* (*haben*) **a~ an** (+ *acc*) adjoin; (*folgen*) follow. **a~d** *a* adjoining; (*zeitlich*) following ● *adv* afterwards; **a~d an** (+ *acc*) after

Anschluß *m* connection; (*Kontakt*) contact; **A~ finden** make friends; **im A~ an** (+ *acc*) after

anschmieg|en (sich) *vr sep* snuggle up/⟨*Kleid:*⟩ cling (**an** + *acc* to). **a~sam** *a* affectionate

anschmieren *vt sep* smear; (*fam: täuschen*) cheat

anschnallen *vt sep* strap on; **sich a~** fasten one's seat-belt

anschneiden† *vt sep* cut into; broach ⟨*Thema*⟩

anschreiben† *vt sep* write (**an** + *acc* on); (*Comm*) put on s.o.'s account; (*sich wenden*) write to; **bei jdm gut/ schlecht angeschrieben sein** be in s.o.'s good/ bad books

anschreien† *vt sep* shout at

Anschrift *f* address

anschuldig|en *vt sep* accuse. **A~ung** *f* -,-en accusation

anschwellen† *vi sep* (*sein*) swell

anschwemmen *vt sep* wash up

anschwindeln *vt sep* (*fam*) lie to

ansehen† *vt sep* look at; (*einschätzen*) regard (**als** as); [**sich** *dat*] **etw a~** look at sth; (*TV*) watch sth. **A~** *nt* -s respect; (*Ruf*) reputation

ansehnlich *a* considerable

ansetzen *v sep* ● *vt* join (**an** + *acc* to); (*festsetzen*) fix; (*veranschlagen*) estimate; **Rost a~** get rusty; **sich a~** form ● *vi* (*haben*) (*anbrennen*) burn; **zum Sprung a~** get ready to jump

Ansicht *f* view; **meiner A~ nach** in my view; **zur A~** (*Comm*) on approval. **A~s[post]karte** *f* picture postcard. **A~ssache** *f* matter of opinion

ansiedeln (sich) *vr sep* settle

ansonsten *adv* apart from that

anspannen *vt sep* hitch up; (*anstrengen*) strain; tense ⟨*Muskel*⟩

anspiel|en *vi sep* (*haben*) **a~en auf** (+ *acc*) allude to; (*versteckt*) hint at. **A~ung** *f* -,-en allusion; hint

Anspitzer *m* -s,- pencil-sharpener

Ansporn *m* (*fig*) incentive. **a~en** *vt sep* spur on

Ansprache *f* address

ansprechen† *v sep* ● *vt* speak to; (*fig*) appeal to ● *vi* respond (**auf** + *acc* to). **a~d** *a* attractive

anspringen† *v sep* ● *vt* jump at ● *vi* (*sein*) (*Auto*) start

Anspruch *m* claim/(*Recht*) right (**auf** + *acc* to); **A~ haben** be entitled (**auf** + *acc* to); **in A~ nehmen** make use of; (*erfordern*) demand; take up ⟨*Zeit*⟩; occupy ⟨*Person*⟩; **hohe A~e stellen** be very demanding. **a~slos** *a* undemanding; (*bescheiden*) unpretentious. **a~svoll** *a* demanding; (*kritisch*) discriminating; (*vornehm*) up-market

anspucken *vt sep* spit at

anstacheln *vt sep* (*fig*) spur on

Anstalt *f* -,-en institution; **A~en/ keine A~en machen** prepare/make no move (**zu** to)

Anstand *m* decency; (*Benehmen*) [good] manners *pl*

anständig *a* decent, *adv* -ly; (*ehrbar*) respectable, *adv* -bly; (*fam: beträchtlich*) considerable, *adv* -bly; (*richtig*) proper, *adv* -ly

Anstands|dame *f* chaperon. **a~los** *adv* without any trouble; (*bedenkenlos*) without hesitation

anstarren *vt sep* stare at

anstatt *conj & prep* (+ *gen*) instead of; **a~ zu arbeiten** instead of working

anstechen† *vt sep* tap ⟨*Faß*⟩

ansteck|en *v sep* ● *vt* pin (**an** + *acc* to/on); put on ⟨*Ring*⟩; (*anzünden*) light; (*in Brand stecken*) set fire to; (*Med*) infect; **sich a~en** catch an infection (**bei** from) ● *vi* (*haben*) be infectious. **a~end** *a* infectious, (*fam*) catching. **A~ung** *f* -,-en infection

anstehen† *vi sep* (*haben*) queue, (*Amer*) stand in line

ansteigen† *vi sep* (*sein*) climb; ⟨*Gelände, Preise:*⟩ rise

anstelle *prep* (+ *gen*) instead of

anstell|en *vt sep* put, stand (**an** + *acc* against); (*einstellen*) employ; (*anschalten*) turn on; (*tun*) do; **sich a~en** queue [up], (*Amer*) stand in

line; (*sich haben*) make a fuss.
A~ung *f* employment; (*Stelle*) job
Anstieg *m* -[e]s,-e climb; (*fig*) rise
anstiften *vt sep* cause; (*anzetteln*)
instigate; **jdn a~n** put s.o. up (**zu** to).
A~r *m* instigator
Anstoß *m* (*Anregung*) impetus;
(*Stoß*) knock; (*Fußball*) kick-off; **A~**
erregen/nehmen give/take offence
(**an** + *dat* at). **a~en†** *v sep* ● *vt*
knock; (*mit dem Ellbogen*) nudge
● *vi* (*sein*) knock (**an** + *acc* against)
● *vi* (*haben*) adjoin (**an etw** *acc* sth);
[**mit den Gläsern**] **a~en** clink
glasses; **a~en auf** (+ *acc*) drink to;
mit der Zunge a~en lisp
anstößig *a* offensive, *adv* -ly
anstrahlen *vt sep* floodlight; (*anla-*
chen) beam at
anstreiche|n† *vt sep* paint; (*anmer-*
ken) mark. **A~r** *m* -s,- painter
anstreng|en *vt sep* strain; (*ermüden*)
tire; **sich a~en** exert oneself; (*sich*
bemühen) make an effort (**zu** to).
a~end *a* strenuous; (*ermüdend*) tiring. **A~ung** *f* -,-en strain; (*Mühe*)
effort
Anstrich *m* coat [of paint]
Ansturm *m* rush; (*Mil*) assault
Ansuchen *nt* -s,- request
Antagonismus *m* - antagonism
Antarktis *f* - Antarctic
Anteil *m* share; **A~ nehmen** take an
interest (**an** + *dat* in); (*mitfühlen*)
sympathize. **A~nahme** *f* - interest
(**an** + *dat* in); (*Mitgefühl*) sympathy
Antenne *f* -,-n aerial
Anthologie *f* -,-n anthology
Anthropologie *f* - anthropology
Anti|alkoholiker *m* teetotaller.
A~biotikum *nt* -s,-ka antibiotic
antik *a* antique. **A~e** *f* - [classical]
antiquity
Antikörper *m* antibody
Antilope *f* -,-n antelope
Antipathie *f* - antipathy
Anti|quariat *nt* -[e]s,-e antiquarian
bookshop. **a~quarisch** *a* & *adv*
second-hand
Antiquitäten *fpl* antiques.
A~händler *m* antique dealer
Antisemitismus *m* - anti-Semitism
Antisept|ikum *nt* -s,-ka antiseptic.
a~isch *a* antiseptic
Antrag *m* -[e]s,-e proposal; (*Pol*)
motion; (*Gesuch*) application. **A~**
steller *m* -s,- applicant
antreffen† *vt sep* find

antreiben† *v sep* ● *vt* urge on;
(*Techn*) drive; (*anschwemmen*)
wash up ● *vi* (*sein*) be washed up
antreten† *v sep* ● *vt* start; take up
⟨*Amt*⟩ ● *vi* (*sein*) line up; (*Mil*) fall in
Antrieb *m* urge; (*Techn*) drive; **aus**
eigenem A~ of one's own accord
antrinken† *vt sep* **sich** (*dat*) **einen**
Rausch a~ get drunk; **sich** (*dat*) **Mut**
a~ give oneself Dutch courage
Antritt *m* start; **bei A~ eines Amtes**
when taking office. **A~srede** *f* inaugural address
antun† *vt sep* **jdm etw a~** do sth to
s.o.; **sich** (*dat*) **etwas a~** take one's
own life; **es jdm angetan haben** appeal to s.o.
Antwort *f* -,-en answer, reply
(**auf** + *acc* to). **a~en** *vt/i* (*haben*)
answer (**jdm** s.o.)
anvertrauen *vt sep* entrust/(*mittei-*
len) confide (**jdm** to s.o.); **sich jdm a~**
confide in s.o.
anwachsen† *vi sep* (*sein*) take root;
(*zunehmen*) grow
Anwalt *m* -[e]s,-e, **Anwältin** *f* -,-nen
lawyer; (*vor Gericht*) counsel
Anwandlung *f* -,-en fit (**von** of)
Anwärter(in) *m*(*f*) candidate
anweis|en† *vt sep* assign (*dat* to);
(*beauftragen*) instruct. **A~ung** *f* instruction; (*Geld-*) money order
anwend|en† *vt sep* apply (**auf** + *acc*
to); (*gebrauchen*) use. **A~ung** *f* application; use
anwerben† *vt sep* recruit
Anwesen *nt* -s,- property
anwesen|d *a* present (**bei** at); **die**
A~den those present. **A~heit** *f* -
presence
anwidern *vt sep* disgust
Anwohner *mpl* residents
Anzahl *f* number
anzahl|en *vt sep* pay a deposit on; pay
on account ⟨*Summe*⟩. **A~ung** *f*
deposit
anzapfen *vt sep* tap
Anzeichen *nt* sign
Anzeige *f* -,-n announcement;
(*Inserat*) advertisement; **A~ erstat-**
ten gegen jdn report s.o. to the
police. **a~n** *vt sep* announce; (*inse-*
rieren) advertise; (*melden*) report [to
the police]; (*angeben*) indicate,
show. **A~r** *m* indicator
anzieh|en† *vt sep* ● *vt* attract; (*fest-*
ziehen) tighten; put on ⟨*Kleider,*
Bremse⟩; draw up ⟨*Beine*⟩; (*anklei-*
den) dress; **sich a~en** get dressed;

was soll ich a~en? what shall I wear? **gut angezogen** well-dressed ● *vi* (*haben*) start pulling; ⟨*Preise:*⟩ go up. **a~end** *a* attractive. **A~ung** *f* - attraction. **A~ungskraft** *f* attraction; (*Phys*) gravity

Anzug *m* suit; **im A~ sein** (*fig*) imminent

anzüglich *a* suggestive; ⟨*Bemerkung*⟩ personal

anzünden *vt sep* light; (*in Brand stecken*) set fire to

anzweifeln *vt sep* question

apart *a* striking, *adv* -ly

Apathie *f* - apathy

apathisch *a* apathetic, *adv* -ally

Aperitif *m* -s,-s aperitif

Apfel *m* -s,- apple. **A~mus** *nt* apple purée

Apfelsine *f* -,-n orange

Apostel *m* -s,- apostle

Apostroph *m* -s,-e apostrophe

Apotheke *f* -,-n pharmacy. **A~er(in)** *m* -s,- (*f* -,-nen) pharmacist, [dispensing] chemist

Apparat *m* -[e]s,-e device; (*Phot*) camera; (*Radio, TV*) set; (*Teleph*) telephone; **am A~!** speaking! **A~ur** *f* -,-en apparatus

Appell *m* -s,-e appeal; (*Mil*) rollcall. **a~ieren** *vi* (*haben*) appeal (**an** + *acc* to)

Appetit *m* -s appetite; **guten A~!** enjoy your meal! **a~lich** *a* appetizing, *adv* -ly

applaudieren *vi* (*haben*) applaud

Applaus *m* -es applause

Aprikose *f* -,-n apricot

April *m* -[s] April; **in den A~ schicken** (*fam*) make an April fool of

Aquarell *nt* -s,-e water-colour

Aquarium *nt* -s,-ien aquarium

Äquator *m* -s equator

Ära *f* - era

Araber(in) *m* -s,- (*f* -,-nen) Arab

arabisch *a* Arab; (*Geog*) Arabian; ⟨*Ziffer*⟩ Arabic

Arbeit *f* -,-en work; (*Anstellung*) employment, job; (*Aufgabe*) task; (*Sch*) [written] test; (*Abhandlung*) treatise; (*Qualität*) workmanship; **bei der A~** at work; **zur A~ gehen** go to work; **an die A~ gehen, sich an die A~ machen** set to work; **sich** (*dat*) **viel A~ machen** go to a lot of trouble. **a~en** *v sep* ● *vi* (*haben*) work (**an** + *dat* on) ● *vt* make; **einen Anzug a~en lassen** have a suit made; **sich durch etw a~en** work one's way

through sth. **A~er(in)** *m* -s,- (*f* -,-nen) worker; (*Land-, Hilfs-*) labourer. **A~erklasse** *f* working class

Arbeit|geber *m* -s,- employer. **A~nehmer** *m* -s,- employee. **a~sam** *a* industrious

Arbeits|amt *nt* employment exchange. **A~erlaubnis, A~genehmigung** *f* work permit. **A~kraft** *f* worker; **Mangel an A~kräften** shortage of labour. **a~los** *a* unemployed; **a~los sein** be out of work. **A~lose(r)** *m/f* unemployed person; **die A~losen** the unemployed *pl*. **A~losenunterstützung** *f* unemployment benefit. **A~losigkeit** *f* - unemployment

arbeitsparend *a* labour-saving

Arbeits|platz *m* job. **A~tag** *m* working day. **A~zimmer** *nt* study

Archäo|loge *m* -n,-n archaeologist. **A~logie** *f* - archaeology. **a~logisch** *a* archaeological

Arche *f* - **die A~ Noah** Noah's Ark

Architek|t(in) *m* -en,-en (*f* -,-nen) architect. **a~tonisch** *a* architectural. **A~tur** *f* - architecture

Archiv *nt* -s,-e archives *pl*

Arena *f* -,-nen arena

arg *a* (**ärger, ärgst**) bad; (*groß*) terrible; **sein ärgster Feind** his worst enemy ● *adv* badly; (*sehr*) terribly

Argentin|ien /-jən/ *nt* -s Argentina. **a~isch** *a* Argentinian

Ärger *m* -s annoyance; (*Unannehmlichkeit*) trouble. **ä~lich** *a* annoyed; (*leidig*) annoying; **ä~lich sein** be annoyed. **ä~n** *vt* annoy; (*necken*) tease; **sich ä~n** get annoyed (**über jdn/etw** with s.o./ about sth). **Ä~nis** *nt* -ses, -se annoyance; **öffentliches Ä~nis** public nuisance

Arglist *f* - malice. **a~ig** *a* malicious, *adv* -ly

arglos *a* unsuspecting; (*unschuldig*) innocent, *adv* -ly

Argument *nt* -[e]s,-e argument. **a~ieren** *vi* (*haben*) argue (**daß** that)

Argwohn *m* -s suspicion

argwöhn|en *vt* suspect. **a~isch** *a* suspicious, *adv* -ly

Arie /'a:rjə/ *f* -,-n aria

Aristo|krat *m* -en,-en aristocrat. **A~kratie** *f* - aristocracy. **a~kratisch** *a* aristocratic

Arithmetik *f* - arithmetic

Arkt|is *f* - Arctic. **a~isch** *a* Arctic

arm *a* (**ärmer, ärmst**) poor; **arm und reich** rich and poor

Arm *m* -[e]s,-e arm; **jdn auf den Arm nehmen** (*fam*) pull s.o.'s leg

Armaturenbrett *nt* instrument panel; (*Auto*) dashboard

Armband *nt* (*pl* -**bänder**) bracelet; (*Uhr*-) watch-strap. **A~uhr** *f* wrist-watch

Arm|e(r) *m/f* poor man/woman; **die A~en** the poor *pl*; **du A~e** *od* **Ärmste!** you poor thing!

Armee *f* -,-n army

Ärmel *m* -s,- sleeve. **A~kanal** *m* [English] Channel. **a~los** *a* sleeveless

Arm|lehne *f* arm. **A~leuchter** *m* candelabra

ärmlich *a* poor, *adv* -ly; (*elend*) miserable, *adv* -bly

armselig *a* miserable, *adv* -bly

Armut *f* - poverty

Arom|a *nt* -s,-men & -mas aroma; (*Culin*) essence. **a~atisch** *a* aromatic

Arran|gement /arãʒəˈmã:/ *nt* -s,-s arrangement. **a~gieren** /-'ʒi:rən/ *vt* arrange; **sich a~gieren** come to an arrangement

Arrest *m* -[e]s (*Mil*) detention

arrogan|t *a* arrogant, *adv* -ly. **A~z** *f* - arrogance

Arsch *m* -[e]s,-̈e (*vulg*) arse

Arsen *nt* -s arsenic

Art *f* -,-en manner; (*Weise*) way; (*Natur*) nature; (*Sorte*) kind; (*Biol*) species; **auf diese Art** in this way. **a~en** *vi* (*sein*) **a~en nach** take after

Arterie /-ɪə/ *f* -,-n artery

Arthritis *f* - arthritis

artig *a* well-behaved; (*höflich*) polite, *adv* -ly; **sei a~!** be good!

Artikel *m* -s,- article

Artillerie *f* - artillery

Artischocke *f* -,-n artichoke

Artist(in) *m* -en,-en (*f* -,-nen) [circus] artiste

Arznei *f* -,-en medicine. **A~mittel** *nt* drug

Arzt *m* -[e]s,-̈e doctor

Ärzt|in *f* -,-nen [woman] doctor. **ä~lich** *a* medical

As *nt* -ses,-se ace

Asbest *m* -[e]s asbestos

Asche *f* - ash. **A~nbecher** *m* ashtray. **A~rmittwoch** *m* Ash Wednesday

Asiat(in) *m* -en,-en (*f* -,-nen) Asian. **a~isch** *a* Asian

Asien /ˈaːzjən/ *nt* -s Asia

asozial *a* antisocial

Aspekt *m* -[e]s,-e aspect

Asphalt *m* -[e]s asphalt. **a~ieren** *vt* asphalt

Assistent(in) *m* -en,-en (*f* -,-nen) assistant

Ast *m* -[e]s,-̈e branch

ästhetisch *a* aesthetic

Asth|ma *nt* -s asthma. **a~matisch** *a* asthmatic

Astro|loge *m* -n,-n astrologer. **A~logie** *f* - astrology. **A~naut** *m* -en,-en astronaut. **A~nom** *m* -en,-en astronomer. **A~nomie** *f* - astronomy. **a~nomisch** *a* astronomical

Asyl *nt* -s,-e home; (*Pol*) asylum. **A~ant** *m* -en,-en asylum-seeker

Atelier /-'lɪe:/ *nt* -s,-s studio

Atem *m* -s breath; **tief A~ holen** take a deep breath. **a~beraubend** *a* breath-taking. **a~los** *a* breathless, *adv* -ly. **A~pause** *f* breather. **A~zug** *m* breath

Atheist *m* -en,-en atheist

Äther *m* -s ether

Äthiopien /-ɪən/ *nt* -s Ethiopia

Athlet(in) *m* -en,-en (*f* -,-nen) athlete. **a~isch** *a* athletic

Atlant|ik *m* -s Atlantic. **a~isch** *a* Atlantic; **der A~ische Ozean** the Atlantic Ocean

Atlas *m* -lasses,-lanten atlas

atmen *vt/i* (*haben*) breathe

Atmosphär|e *f* -,-n atmosphere. **a~isch** *a* atmospheric

Atmung *f* - breathing

Atom *nt* -s,-e atom. **a~ar** *a* atomic. **A~bombe** *f* atom bomb. **A~krieg** *m* nuclear war

Atten|tat *nt* -[e]s,-e assassination attempt. **A~täter** *m* [would-be] assassin

Attest *nt* -[e]s,-e certificate

Attrak|tion /-'tsio:n/ *f* -,-en attraction. **a~tiv** *a* attractive, *adv* -ly

Attrappe *f* -,-n dummy

Attribut *nt* -[e]s,-e attribute. **a~iv** *a* attributive, *adv* -ly

ätzen *vt* corrode; (*Med*) cauterize; (*Kunst*) etch. **ä~d** *a* corrosive; ⟨*Spott*⟩ caustic

au *int* ouch; **au fein!** oh good!

Aubergine /obɛrˈʒiːnə/ *f* -,-n aubergine

auch *adv* & *conj* also, too; (*außerdem*) what's more; (*selbst*) even; **a~ wenn** even if; **ich mag ihn—ich a~** I like him—so do I; **ich bin nicht müde—ich a~ nicht** I'm not tired—nor *or* neither am I; **sie weiß es a~ nicht** she doesn't know either; **wer/**

wie/was a~ immer whoever/however/whatever; **ist das a~ wahr?** is that really true?

Audienz f -,-en audience

audiovisuell a audio-visual

Auditorium nt -s,-ien (Univ) lecture hall

auf prep (+dat) on; (+acc) on [to]; (bis) until, till; (Proportion) to; **auf deutsch/englisch** in German/English; **auf einer/eine Party** at/to a party; **auf der Straße** in the street; **auf seinem Zimmer** in one's room; **auf einem Ohr taub** deaf in one ear; **auf einen Stuhl steigen** climb on [to] a chair; **auf die Toilette gehen** go to the toilet; **auf ein paar Tage verreisen** go away for a few days; **auf 10 Kilometer zu sehen** visible for 10 kilometres ● adv open; (in die Höhe) up; **auf und ab** up and down; **sich auf und davon machen** make off; **Tür auf!** open the door!

aufarbeiten vt sep do up; **Rückstände a~** clear arrears [of work]

aufatmen vi sep (haben) heave a sigh of relief

aufbahren vt sep lay out

Aufbau m construction; (Struktur) structure. **a~en** v sep ● vt construct, build; (errichten) erect; (schaffen) build up; (arrangieren) arrange; **sich a~en** (fig) be based (auf+dat on) ● vi (haben) be based (auf+dat on)

aufbäumen (sich) vr sep rear [up]; (fig) rebel

aufbauschen vt sep puff out; (fig) exaggerate

aufbehalten† vt sep keep on

aufbekommen† vt sep get open; (Sch) be given [as homework]

aufbessern vt sep improve; (erhöhen) increase

aufbewahr|en vt sep keep; (lagern) store. **A~ung** f - safe keeping; storage; (Gepäck-) left-luggage office

aufbieten† vt sep mobilize; (fig) summon up

aufblas|bar a inflatable. **a~en**† vt sep inflate; **sich a~en (** fig) give oneself airs

aufbleiben† vi sep (sein) stay open; (Person:) stay up

aufblenden vt/i sep (haben) (Auto) switch to full beam

aufblicken vi sep (haben) look up (**zu** at/(fig) to)

aufblühen vi sep (sein) flower; (Knospe:) open

aufbocken vt sep jack up

aufbraten† vt sep fry up

aufbrauchen vt sep use up

aufbrausen vi sep (sein) (fig) flare up. **a~d** a quick-tempered

aufbrechen† v sep ● vt break open ● vi (sein) (Knospe:) open; (sich aufmachen) set out, start

aufbringen† vt sep raise (Geld); find (Kraft); (wütend machen) infuriate

Aufbruch m start, departure

aufbrühen vt sep make (Tee)

aufbürden vt sep **jdm etw a~** (fig) burden s.o. with sth

aufdecken vt sep (auflegen) put on; (abdecken) uncover; (fig) expose

aufdrängen vt sep force (dat on); **sich jdm a~** force one's company on s.o.

aufdrehen vt sep turn on

aufdringlich a persistent

aufeinander adv one on top of the other; (schießen) at each other; (warten) for each other. **a~folgen** vi sep (sein) follow one another. **a~folgend** a successive; (Tage) consecutive

Aufenthalt m stay; **10 Minuten A~ haben** (Zug:) stop for 10 minutes. **A~serlaubnis, A~sgenehmigung** f residence permit. **A~sraum** m recreation room; (im Hotel) lounge

auferlegen vt sep impose (dat on)

aufersteh|en† vi sep (sein) rise from the dead. **A~ung** f - resurrection

aufessen† vt sep eat up

auffahr|en† vi sep (sein) drive up; (aufprallen) crash, run (auf+acc into); (aufschrecken) start up; (aufbrausen) flare up. **A~t** f drive; (Autobahn-) access road, slip road; (Bergfahrt) ascent

auffallen† vi sep (sein) be conspicuous; **unangenehm a~** make a bad impression; **jdm a~** strike s.o. **a~d** a striking, adv -ly

auffällig a conspicuous, adv -ly; (grell) gaudy, adv -ily

auffangen† vt sep catch; pick up (Funkspruch)

auffass|en vt sep understand; (deuten) take; **falsch a~en** misunderstand. **A~ung** f understanding; (Ansicht) view. **A~ungsgabe** f grasp

aufforder|n vt sep ask; (einladen) invite; **jdn zum Tanz a~n** ask s.o. to dance. **A~ung** f request; invitation

auffrischen *v sep* ● *vt* freshen up; revive ⟨*Erinnerung*⟩; **seine Englischkenntnisse a~** brush up one's English

aufführ|en *vt sep* perform; (*angeben*) list; **sich a~en** behave. **A~ung** *f* performance

auffüllen *vt sep* fill up; **[wieder] a~** replenish

Aufgabe *f* task; (*Rechen-*) problem; (*Verzicht*) giving up; **A~n** (*Sch*) homework *sg*

Aufgang *m* way up; (*Treppe*) stairs *pl*; (*Astr*) rise

aufgeben† *v sep* ● *vt* give up; post ⟨*Brief*⟩; send ⟨*Telegramm*⟩; place ⟨*Bestellung*⟩; register ⟨*Gepäck*⟩; put in the paper ⟨*Annonce*⟩; **jdm eine Aufgabe/ein Rätsel a~** set s.o. a task/a riddle; **jdm Suppe a~** serve s.o. with soup ● *vi* (*haben*) give up

aufgeblasen *a* (*fig*) conceited

Aufgebot *nt* contingent (**an** + *dat* of); (*Relig*) banns *pl*; **unter A~ aller Kräfte** with all one's strength

aufgebracht *a* (*fam*) angry

aufgedunsen *a* bloated

aufgehen† *vi sep* (*sein*) open; (*sich lösen*) come undone; ⟨*Teig, Sonne:*⟩ rise; ⟨*Saat:*⟩ come up; (*Math*) come out exactly; **in Flammen a~** go up in flames; **in etw** (*dat*) **a~** (*fig*) be wrapped up in sth; **ihm ging auf** (*fam*) he realized (**daß** that)

aufgelegt *a* **a~ sein zu** be in the mood for; **gut/schlecht a~ sein** be in a good/bad mood

aufgelöst *a* (*fig*) distraught; **in Tränen a~** in floods of tears

aufgeregt *a* excited, *adv* -ly; (*erregt*) agitated, *adv* -ly

aufgeschlossen *a* (*fig*) open-minded

aufgesprungen *a* chapped

aufgeweckt *a* (*fig*) bright

aufgießen† *vt sep* pour on; (*aufbrühen*) make ⟨*Tee*⟩

aufgreifen† *vt sep* pick up; take up ⟨*Vorschlag, Thema*⟩

aufgrund *prep* (+ *gen*) on the strength of

Aufguß *m* infusion

aufhaben† *v sep* ● *vt* have on; **den Mund a~** have one's mouth open; **viel a~** (*Sch*) have a lot of homework ● *vi* (*haben*) be open

aufhalsen *vt sep* (*fam*) saddle with

aufhalten† *vt sep* hold up; (*anhalten*) stop; (*abhalten*) keep, detain; (*offenhalten*) hold open; hold out ⟨*Hand*⟩;

sich a~ stay; (*sich befassen*) spend one's time (**mit** on)

aufhäng|en *vt/i sep* (*haben*) hang up; (*henken*) hang; **sich a~en** hang oneself. **A~er** *m* -s,- loop. **A~ung** *f* - (*Auto*) suspension

aufheben† *vt sep* pick up; (*hochheben*) raise; (*aufbewahren*) keep; (*beenden*) end; (*rückgängig machen*) lift; (*abschaffen*) abolish; (*Jur*) quash ⟨*Urteil*⟩; repeal ⟨*Gesetz*⟩; (*ausgleichen*) cancel out; **sich a~** cancel each other out; **gut aufgehoben sein** be well looked after. **A~** *nt* **-s viel A~s machen** make a great fuss (**von** about)

aufheitern *vt sep* cheer up; **sich a~** ⟨*Wetter:*⟩ brighten up

aufhellen *vt sep* lighten; **sich a~** ⟨*Himmel:*⟩ brighten

aufhetzen *vt sep* incite

aufholen *v sep* ● *vt* make up ● *vi* (*haben*) catch up; (*zeitlich*) make up time

aufhorchen *vi sep* (*haben*) prick up one's ears

aufhören *vi sep* (*haben*) stop; **mit der Arbeit a~, a~ zu arbeiten** stop working

aufklappen *vt/i sep* (*sein*) open

aufklär|en *vt sep* solve; **jdn a~en** enlighten s.o.; (*sexuell*) tell s.o. the facts of life; **sich a~en** be solved; ⟨*Wetter:*⟩ clear up. **A~ung** *f* solution; enlightenment; (*Mil*) reconnaissance; **sexuelle A~ung** sex education

aufkleb|en *vt sep* stick on. **A~er** *m* -s,- sticker

aufknöpfen *vt sep* unbutton

aufkochen *v sep* ● *vt* bring to the boil ● *vi* (*sein*) come to the boil

aufkommen† *vi sep* (*sein*) start; ⟨*Wind:*⟩ spring up; ⟨*Mode:*⟩ come in; **a~ für** pay for

aufkrempeln *vt sep* roll up

aufladen† *vt sep* load; (*Electr*) charge

Auflage *f* impression; (*Ausgabe*) edition; (*Zeitungs-*) circulation; (*Bedingung*) condition; (*Überzug*) coating

auflassen† *vt sep* leave open; leave on ⟨*Hut*⟩

auflauern *vi sep* (*haben*) **jdm a~** lie in wait for s.o.

Auflauf *m* crowd; (*Culin*) ≈ soufflé. **a~en†** *vi sep* (*sein*) (*Naut*) run aground

auflegen *v sep* ● *vt* apply (**auf** +*acc* to); put down ⟨*Hörer*⟩; **neu a~** reprint ● *vi* (*haben*) ring off

auflehn|en (sich) *vr sep* ⟨*fig*⟩ rebel. **A~ung** *f* - rebellion

auflesen† *vt sep* pick up

aufleuchten *vi sep* (*haben*) light up

aufliegen† *vi sep* (*haben*) rest (**auf** +*dat* on)

auflisten *vt sep* list

auflockern *vt sep* break up; (*entspannen*) relax; (*fig*) liven up

auflös|en *vt sep* dissolve; close ⟨*Konto*⟩; **sich a~en** dissolve; ⟨*Nebel:*⟩ clear. **A~ung** *f* dissolution; (*Lösung*) solution

aufmach|en *v sep* ● *vt* open; (*lösen*) undo; **sich a~en** set out (**nach** for); (*sich schminken*) make oneself up ● *vi* (*haben*) open; **jdm a~en** open the door to s.o. **A~ung** *f* -,**-en** get-up; (*Comm*) presentation

aufmerksam *a* attentive, *adv* -ly; **a~ werden auf** (+*acc*) notice; **jdn a~ machen auf** (+*acc*) draw s.o.'s attention to. **A~keit** *f* -,**-en** attention; (*Höflichkeit*) courtesy

aufmucken *vi sep* (*haben*) rebel

aufmuntern *vt sep* cheer up

Aufnahme *f* -,**-n** acceptance; (*Empfang*) reception; (in *Klub, Krankenhaus*) admission; (*Einbeziehung*) inclusion; (*Beginn*) start; (*Foto*) photograph; (*Film-*) shot; (*Mus*) recording; (*Band-*) tape recording. **a~fähig** *a* receptive. **A~prüfung** *f* entrance examination

aufnehmen† *vt sep* pick up; (*absorbieren*) absorb; take ⟨*Nahrung, Foto*⟩; (*fassen*) hold; (*annehmen*) accept; (*leihen*) borrow; (*empfangen*) receive; (in *Klub, Krankenhaus*) admit; (*beherbergen, geistig erfassen*) take in; (*einbeziehen*) include; (*beginnen*) take up; (*niederschreiben*) take down; (*filmen*) film, shoot; (*Mus*) record; **mit Band a~** tape[-record]; **etw gelassen a~** take sth calmly; **es a~ können mit** (*fig*) be a match for

aufopfer|n *vt sep* sacrifice; **sich a~n** sacrifice oneself. **a~nd** *a* devoted, *adv* -ly. **A~ung** *f* self-sacrifice

aufpassen *vi sep* (*haben*) pay attention; (*sich vorsehen*) take care; **a~ auf** (+*acc*) look after

aufpflanzen (sich) *vr sep* (*fam*) plant oneself

aufplatzen *vi sep* (*sein*) split open

aufplustern (sich) *vr sep* ⟨*Vogel:*⟩ ruffle up its feathers

Aufprall *m* -[e]s impact. **a~en** *vi sep* (*sein*) **a~en auf** (+*acc*) hit

aufpumpen *vt sep* pump up, inflate

aufputsch|en *vt sep* incite; **sich a~en** take stimulants. **A~mittel** *nt* stimulant

aufquellen† *vi sep* (*sein*) swell

aufraffen *vt sep* pick up; **sich a~** pick oneself up; (*fig*) pull oneself together; (*sich aufschwingen*) find the energy (**zu** for)

aufragen *vi sep* (*sein*) rise [up]

aufräumen *vt/i sep* (*haben*) tidy up; (*wegräumen*) put away; **a~ mit** (*fig*) get rid of

aufrecht *a* & *adv* upright. **a~erhalten**† *vt sep* (*fig*) maintain

aufreg|en *vt sep* excite; (*beunruhigen*) upset; (*ärgern*) annoy; **sich a~en** get excited; (*sich erregen*) get worked up. **a~end** *a* exciting. **A~ung** *f* excitement

aufreiben† *vt sep* chafe; (*fig*) wear down; **sich a~** wear oneself out. **a~d** *a* trying, wearing

aufreißen† *v sep* ● *vt* tear open; dig up ⟨*Straße*⟩; open wide ⟨*Augen, Mund*⟩ ● *vi* (*sein*) split open

aufreizend *a* provocative, *adv* -ly

aufrichten *vt sep* erect; (*fig: trösten*) comfort; **sich a~** straighten up; (*sich setzen*) sit up

aufrichtig *a* sincere, *adv* -ly. **A~keit** *f* - sincerity

aufriegeln *vt sep* unbolt

aufrollen *vt sep* roll up; (*entrollen*) unroll

aufrücken *vi sep* (*sein*) move up; (*fig*) be promoted

Aufruf *m* appeal (**an** +*dat* to). **a~en**† *vt sep* call out ⟨*Namen*⟩; **jdn a~en** call s.o.'s name; (*fig*) call on s.o. (**zu** to)

Aufruhr *m* -s,**-e** turmoil; (*Empörung*) revolt

aufrühr|en *vt sep* stir up. **A~er** *m* -s,**-** rebel. **a~erisch** *a* inflammatory; (*rebellisch*) rebellious

aufrunden *vt sep* round up

aufrüsten *vt sep* (*haben*) arm

aufs *prep* = **auf das**

aufsagen *vt sep* recite

aufsammeln *vt sep* gather up

aufsässig *a* rebellious

Aufsatz *m* top; (*Sch*) essay

aufsaugen† *vt sep* soak up

aufschauen vi sep (haben) look up (**zu** at/(fig) to)

aufschichten vt sep stack up

aufschieben† vt sep slide open; (verschieben) put off, postpone

Aufschlag m impact; (Tennis) service; (Hosen-) turn-up; (Ärmel-) upturned cuff; (Revers) lapel; (Comm) surcharge. **a~en**† v sep • vt open; crack ⟨Ei⟩; (hochschlagen) turn up; (errichten) put up; (erhöhen) increase; cast on ⟨Masche⟩; **sich** (dat) **das Knie a~en** cut [open] one's knee • vi (haben) hit (**auf etw** acc/dat sth); (Tennis) serve; (teurer werden) go up

aufschließen† v sep • vt unlock • vi (haben) unlock the door

aufschlitzen vt sep slit open

Aufschluß m **A~ geben** give information (**über** + acc on). **a~reich** a revealing; (lehrreich) informative

aufschneid|en† v sep • vt cut open; (in Scheiben) slice; carve ⟨Braten⟩ • vi (haben) (fam) exaggerate. **A~er** m -s,- (fam) show-off

Aufschnitt m sliced sausage, cold meat [and cheese]

aufschrauben vt sep screw on; (abschrauben) unscrew

aufschrecken v sep • vt startle • vi† (sein) start up; **aus dem Schlaf a~** wake up with a start

Aufschrei m [sudden] cry

aufschreiben† vt sep write down; (fam: verschreiben) prescribe; **jdn a~** ⟨Polizist:⟩ book s.o.

aufschreien† vi sep (haben) cry out

Aufschrift f inscription; (Etikett) label

Aufschub m delay; (Frist) grace

aufschürfen vt sep **sich** (dat) **das Knie a~** graze one's knee

aufschwatzen vt sep **jdm etw a~** talk s.o. into buying sth

aufschwingen† (**sich**) vr sep find the energy (**zu** for)

Aufschwung m (fig) upturn

aufsehen† vi sep (haben) look up (**zu** at/(fig) to). **A~** nt -s **A~ erregen** cause a sensation. **a~erregend** a sensational

Aufseher(in) m -s,- (f -,-nen) supervisor; (Gefängnis-) warder

aufsein† vi sep (sein) be open; ⟨Person:⟩ be up

aufsetzen vt sep put on; (verfassen) draw up; (entwerfen) draft; **sich a~** sit up

Aufsicht f supervision; (Person) supervisor. **A~srat** m board of directors

aufsitzen† vi sep (sein) mount

aufspannen vt sep put up

aufsparen vt sep save, keep

aufsperren vt sep open wide

aufspielen v sep • vi (haben) play • vr **sich a~** show off; **sich als Held a~** play the hero

aufspießen vt sep spear

aufspringen† vi sep (sein) jump up; (aufprallen) bounce; (sich öffnen) burst open; ⟨Haut:⟩ become chapped; **a~ auf** (+ acc) jump on

aufspüren vt sep track down

aufstacheln vt sep incite

aufstampfen vi sep (haben) **mit dem Fuß a~** stamp one's foot

Aufstand m uprising, rebellion

aufständisch a rebellious. **A~e(r)** m rebel, insurgent

aufstapeln vt sep stack up

aufstauen vt sep dam [up]

aufstehen† vi sep (sein) get up; (offen sein) be open; (fig) rise up

aufsteigen† vi sep (sein) get on; ⟨Reiter:⟩ mount; ⟨Bergsteiger:⟩ climb up; (hochsteigen) rise [up]; (fig: befördert werden) rise (**zu** to); (Sport) be promoted

aufstell|en vt sep put up; (Culin) put on; (postieren) post; (in einer Reihe) line up; (nominieren) nominate; (Sport) select ⟨Mannschaft⟩; make out ⟨Liste⟩; lay down ⟨Regel⟩; make ⟨Behauptung⟩; set up ⟨Rekord⟩; **sich a~en** rise [up]; (in einer Reihe) line up. **A~ung** f nomination; (Liste) list

Aufstieg m ascent; (fig) rise; (Sport) promotion

aufstöbern vt sep flush out; (fig) track down

aufstoßen† v sep • vt push open • vi (haben) burp; **a~ auf** (+ acc) strike. **A~** nt -s burping

aufstrebend a (fig) ambitious

Aufstrich m [sandwich] spread

aufstützen vt sep rest (**auf** + acc on); **sich a~** lean (**auf** + acc on)

aufsuchen vt sep look for; (besuchen) go to see

Auftakt m (fig) start

auftauchen vi sep (sein) emerge; ⟨U-Boot:⟩ surface; (fig) turn up; ⟨Frage:⟩ crop up

auftauen vt/i sep (sein) thaw

aufteil|en vt sep divide [up]. **A~ung** f division

auftischen *vt sep* serve [up]

Auftrag *m* -[e]s, ⁻e task; (*Kunst*) commission; (*Comm*) order; **im A~** (+*gen*) on behalf of. **a~en†** *v sep* ● *vt* apply; (*servieren*) serve; (*abtragen*) wear out; **jdm a~en** instruct s.o. (**zu** to) ● *vi* (*haben*) **dick a~en** (*fam*) exaggerate. **A~geber** *m* -s,- client

auftreiben† *vt sep* distend; (*fam: beschaffen*) get hold of

auftrennen *vt sep* unpick, undo

auftreten† *v sep* ● *vi* (*sein*) tread; (*sich benehmen*) behave, act; (*Theat*) appear; (*die Bühne betreten*) enter; (*vorkommen*) occur ● *vt* kick open. **A~** *nt* -s occurrence; (*Benehmen*) manner

Auftrieb *m* buoyancy; (*fig*) boost

Auftritt *m* (*Theat*) appearance; (*auf die Bühne*) entrance; (*Szene*) scene

auftun† *vt sep* **jdm Suppe a~** serve s.o. with soup; **sich** (*dat*) **etw a~** help oneself to sth; **sich a~** open

aufwachen *vi sep* (*sein*) wake up

aufwachsen† *vi sep* (*sein*) grow up

Aufwand *m* -[e]s expenditure; (*Luxus*) extravagance; (*Mühe*) trouble; **A~ treiben** be extravagant

aufwärmen *vt sep* heat up; (*fig*) rake up; **sich a~** warm oneself; (*Sport*) warm up

Aufwartefrau *f* cleaner

aufwärts *adv* upwards; (*bergauf*) uphill. **a~gehen†** *vi sep* (*sein*) **es geht a~ mit jdm/etw** s.o./sth is improving

Aufwartung *f* - cleaner; **jdm seine A~ machen** call on s.o.

aufwaschen† *vt/i sep* (*haben*) wash up

aufwecken *vt sep* wake up

aufweichen *v sep* ● *vt* soften ● *vi* (*sein*) become soft

aufweisen† *vt sep* have, show

aufwenden|en *vt sep* spend; **Mühe a~en** take pains. **a~ig** *a* lavish, *adv* -ly; (*teuer*) expensive, *adv* -ly

aufwerfen† *vt sep* (*fig*) raise

aufwert|en *vt sep* revalue. **A~ung** *f* revaluation

aufwickeln *vt sep* roll up; (*auswickeln*) unwrap

aufwiegeln *vt sep* stir up

aufwiegen† *vt sep* compensate for

Aufwiegler *m* -s,- agitator

aufwirbeln *vt sep* **Staub a~** stir up dust; (*fig*) cause a stir

aufwisch|en *vt sep* wipe up; wash ⟨*Fußboden*⟩. **A~lappen** *m* floor-cloth

aufwühlen *vt sep* churn up; (*fig*) stir up

aufzähl|en *vt sep* enumerate, list. **A~ung** *f* list

aufzeichn|en *vt sep* record; (*zeichnen*) draw. **A~ung** *f* recording; **A~ungen** notes

aufziehen† *v sep* ● *vt* pull up; hoist ⟨*Segel*⟩; (*öffnen*) open; draw ⟨*Vorhang*⟩; (*großziehen*) bring up; rear ⟨*Tier*⟩; mount ⟨*Bild*⟩; thread ⟨*Perlen*⟩; wind up ⟨*Uhr*⟩; (*arrangieren*) organize; (*fam: necken*) tease ● *vi* (*sein*) approach

Aufzucht *f* rearing

Aufzug *m* hoist; (*Fahrstuhl*) lift, (*Amer*) elevator; (*Prozession*) procession; (*Theat*) act; (*fam: Aufmachung*) get-up

Augapfel *m* eyeball

Auge *nt* -s,-n eye; (*Punkt*) spot; **vier A~n werfen** throw a four; **gute A~n** good eyesight; **unter vier A~n** in private; **aus den A~n verlieren** lose sight of; **im A~ behalten** keep in sight; (*fig*) bear in mind

Augenblick *m* moment; **im/jeden A~** at the/at any moment; **A~!** just a moment! **a~lich** *a* immediate; (*derzeitig*) present ● *adv* immediately; (*derzeit*) at present

Augen|braue *f* eyebrow. **A~höhle** *f* eye socket. **A~licht** *nt* sight. **A~lid** *nt* eyelid. **A~schein** *m* in **A~schein nehmen** inspect. **A~zeuge** *m* eyewitness

August *m* -[s] August

Auktion /-'tsjo:n/ *f* -,-en auction. **A~ator** *m* -s,-en /-'to:rən/ auctioneer

Aula *f* -,-len (*Sch*) [assembly] hall

Au-pair-Mädchen /o'pɛːr-/ *nt* au-pair

aus *prep* (+*dat*) out of; (*von*) from; (*bestehend*) [made] of; **aus Angst** from *or* out of fear; **aus Spaß** for fun ● *adv* out; ⟨*Licht, Radio*⟩ off; **und ein** in and out; **nicht mehr aus noch ein wissen** be at one's wits' end; **von … aus** from …; **von sich aus** of one's own accord; **von mir aus** as far as I'm concerned

ausarbeiten *vt sep* work out

ausarten *vi sep* (*sein*) degenerate (**in**+*acc* into)

ausatmen *vt/i sep* (*haben*) breathe out

ausbaggern *vt sep* excavate; dredge ⟨*Fluß*⟩

ausbauen *vt sep* remove; (*vergrö-ßern*) extend; (*fig*) expand

ausbedingen† *vt sep* **sich** (*dat*) **a~** insist on; (*zur Bedingung machen*) stipulate

ausbesser|n *vt sep* mend, repair. **A~ung** *f* repair

ausbeulen *vt sep* remove the dents from; (*dehnen*) make baggy

Ausbeut|e *f* yield. **a~en** *vt sep* exploit. **A~ung** *f* - exploitation

ausbild|en *vt sep* train; (*formen*) form; (*entwickeln*) develop; **sich a~en** train (**als/zu** as); (*entstehen*) develop. **A~er** *m* -s,- instructor. **A~ung** *f* training; (*Sch*) education

ausbitten† *vt sep* **sich** (*dat*) **a~** ask for; (*verlangen*) insist on

ausblasen† *vt sep* blow out

ausbleiben† *vi sep* (*sein*) fail to appear;⟨*Erfolg:*⟩ materialize; (*nicht heimkommen*) stay out; **es konnte nicht a~** it was inevitable. **A~** *nt* -s absence

Ausblick *m* view

ausbrech|en† *vi sep* (*sein*) break out; ⟨*Vulkan:*⟩ erupt; (*fliehen*) escape; **in Tränen a~en** burst into tears. **A~er** *m* runaway

ausbreit|en *vt sep* spread [out]; **sich a~en** spread. **A~ung** *f* - spread

ausbrennen† *v sep* ● *vt* cauterize ● *vi* (*sein*) burn out; ⟨*Haus:*⟩ be gutted [by fire]

Ausbruch *m* outbreak; (*Vulkan-*) eruption; (*Wut-*) outburst; (*Flucht*) escape, break-out

ausbrüten *vt sep* hatch

Ausbund *m* **A~ der Tugend** paragon of virtue

ausbürsten *vt sep* brush; (*entfernen*) brush out

Ausdauer *f* perseverance; (*körper-lich*) stamina. **a~nd** *a* persevering; (*unermüdlich*) untiring; (*Bot*) perennial ● *adv* with perseverance; untiringly

ausdehn|en *vt sep* stretch; (*fig*) extend; **sich a~en** stretch; (*Phys & fig*) expand; (*dauern*) last. **A~ung** *f* expansion; (*Umfang*) extent

ausdenken† *vt sep* **sich** (*dat*) **a~** think up; (*sich vorstellen*) imagine

ausdrehen *vt sep* turn off

Ausdruck *m* expression; (*Fach-*) term; (*Computer*) printout. **a~en** *vt sep* print

ausdrück|en *vt sep* squeeze out; squeeze ⟨*Zitrone*⟩; stub out ⟨*Ziga-rette*⟩; (*äußern*) express; **sich a~en** express oneself. **a~lich** *a* express, *adv* -ly

ausdrucks|los *a* expressionless. **a~voll** *a* expressive

auseinander *adv* apart; (*entzwei*) in pieces. **a~falten** *vt sep* unfold. **a~gehen†** *vi sep* (*sein*) part; ⟨*Li-nien, Meinungen:*⟩ diverge; ⟨*Menge:*⟩ disperse; ⟨*Ehe:*⟩ break up; (*entzwei-gehen*) come apart. **a~halten†** *vt sep* tell apart. **a~nehmen†** *vt sep* take apart *or* to pieces. **a~setzen** *vt sep* explain (**jdm** to s.o.); **sich a~setzen** have it out (**mit jdm** with s.o.); come to grips (**mit einem Problem** with a problem). **A~setzung** *f* -,-en discussion; (*Streit*) argument

auserlesen *a* select, choice

ausfahr|en† *v sep* ● *vt* take for a drive; take out ⟨*Baby*⟩ [in the pram] ● *vi* (*sein*) go for a drive. **A~t** *f* drive; (*Autobahn-, Garagen-*) exit

Ausfall *m* failure; (*Absage*) cancellation; (*Comm*) loss. **a~en†** *vi sep* (*sein*) fall out; (*versagen*) fail; (*abgesagt werden*) be cancelled; **gut/schlecht a~en** turn out to be good/poor

ausfallend, ausfällig *a* abusive

ausfertig|en *vt sep* make out. **A~ung** *f* -,-en **in doppelter/drei-facher A~ung** in duplicate/triplicate

ausfindig *a* **a~ machen** find

ausflippen *vi* (*sein*) freak out

Ausflucht *f* -,¨e excuse

Ausflug *m* excursion, outing

Ausflügler *m* -s,- [day-]tripper

Ausfluß *m* outlet; (*Abfluß*) drain; (*Med*) discharge

ausfragen *vt sep* question

ausfransen *vi sep* (*sein*) fray

Ausfuhr *f* -,-en (*Comm*) export

ausführ|en *vt sep* take out; (*Comm*) export; (*durchführen*) carry out; (*erklären*) explain. **a~lich** *a* detailed ● *adv* in detail. **A~ung** *f* execution; (*Comm*) version; (*äußere*) finish; (*Qualität*) workmanship; (*Erklä-rung*) explanation

Ausgabe *f* issue; (*Buch-*) edition; (*Comm*) version

Ausgang *m* way out, exit; (*Flugsteig*) gate; (*Ende*) end; (*Ergebnis*) outcome, result; **A~ haben** have time

off. **A~spunkt** *m* starting-point.
A~ssperre *f* curfew
ausgeben† *vt sep* hand out; issue
⟨*Fahrkarten*⟩; spend ⟨*Geld*⟩; buy
⟨*Runde Bier*⟩; **sich a~ als** pretend to
be
ausgebeult *a* baggy
ausgebildet *a* trained
ausgebucht *a* fully booked; ⟨*Vorstellung*⟩ sold out
ausgedehnt *a* extensive; (*lang*) long
ausgedient *a* worn out; ⟨*Person*⟩
retired
ausgefallen *a* unusual
ausgefranst *a* frayed
ausgeglichen *a* [well-]balanced;
(*gelassen*) even-tempered
ausgeh|en† *vi sep* (*sein*) go out;
⟨*Haare:*⟩ fall out; ⟨*Vorräte, Geld:*⟩
run out; (*verblassen*) fade; (*herrühren*) come (**von** from); (*abzielen*) aim
(**auf** +*acc* at); **gut/schlecht a~en**
end well/badly; **leer a~en** come
away empty-handed; **davon a~en,
daß** assume that. **A~verbot** *nt*
curfew
ausgelassen *a* high-spirited; **a~
sein** be in high spirits
ausgelernt *a* [fully] trained
ausgemacht *a* agreed; (*fam: vollkommen*) utter
ausgenommen *conj* except; **a~
wenn** unless
ausgeprägt *a* marked
ausgerechnet *adv* **a~ heute** today of
all days; **a~ er/Rom** he of all
people/Rome of all places
ausgeschlossen *pred a* out of the
question
ausgeschnitten *a* low-cut
ausgesprochen *a* marked ● *adv*
decidedly
ausgestorben *a* extinct; **[wie] a~**
⟨*Straße:*⟩ deserted
Ausgestoßene(r) *m/f* outcast
ausgewachsen *a* fully-grown
ausgewogen *a* [well-]balanced
ausgezeichnet *a* excellent, *adv* -ly
ausgiebig *a* extensive, *adv* -ly; (*ausgedehnt*) long; **a~ Gebrauch machen
von** make full use of; **a~ frühstücken** have a really good breakfast
ausgießen† *vt sep* pour out; (*leeren*)
empty
Ausgleich *m* -[e]s balance; (*Entschädigung*) compensation. **a~en**† *v sep*
● *vt* balance; even out ⟨*Höhe*⟩; (*wettmachen*) compensate for; **sich a~en**
balance out ● *vi* (*haben*) (*Sport*)

equalize. **A~sgymnastik** *f* keep-fit
exercises *pl.* **A~streffer** *m*
equalizer
ausgleiten† *vi sep* (*sein*) slip
ausgrab|en† *vt sep* dig up;
(*Archaeol*) excavate. **A~ung** *f* -,-en
excavation
Ausguck *m* -[e]s,-e look-out post;
(*Person*) look-out
Ausguß *m* [kitchen] sink
aushaben† *vt sep* have finished
⟨*Buch*⟩; **wann habt ihr Schule aus?**
when do you finish school?
aushalten† *v sep* ● *vt* bear, stand;
hold ⟨*Note*⟩; (*Unterhalt zahlen für*)
keep; **nicht auszuhalten, nicht zum
A~** unbearable ● *vi* (*haben*) hold out
aushandeln *vt sep* negotiate
aushändigen *vt sep* hand over
Aushang *m* [public] notice
aushängen¹ *vt sep* (*reg*) display; take
off its hinges ⟨*Tür*⟩
aushäng|en²† *vi sep* (*haben*) be displayed. **A~eschild** *nt* sign
ausharren *vi sep* (*haben*) hold out
ausheben† *vt sep* excavate; take off
its hinges ⟨*Tür*⟩
aushecken *vt sep* (*fig*) hatch
aushelfen† *vi sep* (*haben*) help out
(**jdm** s.o.)
Aushilf|e *f* [temporary] assistant; **zur
A~e** to help out. **A~skraft** *f* temporary worker. **a~sweise** *adv*
temporarily
aushöhlen *vt sep* hollow out
ausholen *vi sep* (*haben*) **[zum
Schlag] a~** raise one's arm [ready to
strike]
aushorchen *vt sep* sound out
auskennen† (**sich**) *vr sep* know
one's way around; **sich mit/in etw**
(*dat*) **a~** know all about sth
auskleiden *vt sep* undress; (*Techn*)
line; **sich a~** undress
ausknipsen *vi sep* switch off
auskommen† *vi sep* (*sein*) manage
(**mit/ohne** with/without); (*sich vertragen*) get on (**gut** well). **A~** *nt* -s
sein A~/ein gutes A~ haben get
by/be well off
auskosten *vt sep* enjoy [to the full]
auskugeln *vt sep* **sich** (*dat*) **den Arm
a~** dislocate one's shoulder
auskühlen *vt/i sep* (*sein*) cool
auskundschaften *vt sep* spy out;
(*erfahren*) find out
Auskunft *f* -,-̈e information;
(*A~sstelle*) information desk/
(*Büro*) bureau; (*Teleph*) enquiries

pl; **eine A~** a piece of information. **A~sbüro** *nt* information bureau

auslachen *vt sep* laugh at

ausladen† *vt sep* unload; (*fam: absagen*) put off ‹*Gast*›. **a~d** *a* projecting

Auslage *f* [window] display; **A~n** expenses

Ausland *nt* **im/ins A~** abroad

Ausländ|er(in) *m* **-s,- (***f* **-,-nen)** foreigner. **a~isch** *a* foreign

Auslandsgespräch *nt* international call

auslass|en† *vt sep* let out; let down ‹*Saum*›; (*weglassen*) leave out; (*versäumen*) miss; (*Culin*) melt; (*fig*) vent ‹*Ärger*› **(an**+*dat* on); **sich a~en über** (+*acc*) go on about. **A~ungszeichen** *nt* apostrophe

Auslauf *m* run. **a~en†** *vi sep* (*sein*) run out; ‹*Farbe:*› run; (*Naut*) put to sea; (*leerlaufen*) run dry; (*enden*) end; ‹*Modell:*› be discontinued

Ausläufer *m* (*Geog*) spur; (*Bot*) runner, sucker

ausleeren *vt sep* empty [out]

ausleg|en *vt sep* lay out; display ‹*Waren*›; (*bedecken*) cover/(*auskleiden*) line (**mit** with); (*bezahlen*) pay; (*deuten*) interpret. **A~ung** *f* **-,-en** interpretation

ausleihen† *vt sep* lend; **sich** (*dat*) **a~** borrow

auslernen *vi sep* (*haben*) finish one's training

Auslese *f* - selection; (*fig*) pick; (*Elite*) elite. **a~n†** *vt sep* finish reading ‹*Buch*›; (*auswählen*) pick out, select

ausliefer|n *vt sep* hand over; (*Jur*) extradite; **ausgeliefert sein** (+*dat*) be at the mercy of. **A~ung** *f* handing over; (*Jur*) extradition; (*Comm*) distribution

ausliegen† *vi sep* (*haben*) be on display

auslöschen *vt sep* extinguish; (*abwischen*) wipe off; (*fig*) erase

auslosen *vt sep* draw lots for

auslös|en *vt sep* set off, trigger; (*fig*) cause; arouse ‹*Begeisterung*›; (*einlösen*) redeem; pay a ransom for ‹*Gefangene*›. **A~er** *m* **-s,-** trigger; (*Phot*) shutter release

Auslosung *f* draw

auslüften *vt/i sep* (*haben*)

ausmachen *vt sep* put out; (*abschalten*) turn off; (*abmachen*) arrange; (*erkennen*) make out; (*betragen*) amount to; (*darstellen*) represent;

(*wichtig sein*) matter; **das macht mir nichts aus** I don't mind

ausmalen *vt sep* paint; (*fig*) describe; **sich** (*dat*) **a~** imagine

Ausmaß *nt* extent; **A~e** dimensions

ausmerzen *vt sep* eliminate

ausmessen† *vt sep* measure

Ausnahm|e *f* **-,-n** exception. **A~ezustand** *m* state of emergency. **a~slos** *adv* without exception. **a~sweise** *adv* as an exception

ausnehmen† *vt sep* take out; gut ‹*Fisch*›; draw ‹*Huhn*›; (*ausschließen*) exclude; (*fam: schröpfen*) fleece; **sich gut a~** look good. **a~d** *adv* exceptionally

ausnutz|en, ausnütz|en *vt sep* exploit; make the most of ‹*Gelegenheit*›. **A~ung** *f* exploitation

auspacken *v sep* • *vt* unpack; (*auswickeln*) unwrap • *vi* (*haben*) (*fam*) talk

auspeitschen *vt sep* flog

auspfeifen *vt sep* whistle and boo

ausplaudern *vt sep* let out, blab

ausplündern *vt sep* loot; rob ‹*Person*›

ausprobieren *vt sep* try out

Auspuff *m* **-s** exhaust [system]. **A~gase** *ntpl* exhaust fumes. **A~rohr** *nt* exhaust pipe

auspusten *vt sep* blow out

ausradieren *vt sep* rub out

ausrangieren *vt sep* (*fam*) discard

ausrauben *vt sep* rob

ausräuchern *vt sep* smoke out; fumigate ‹*Zimmer*›

ausräumen *vt sep* clear out

ausrechnen *vt sep* work out, calculate

Ausrede *f* excuse. **a~n** *v sep* • *vi* (*haben*) finish speaking; **laß mich a~n!** let me finish! • *vt* **jdm etw a~n** talk s.o. out of sth

ausreichen *vi sep* (*haben*) be enough; **a~ mit** have enough. **a~d** *a* adequate, *adv* **-ly;** (*Sch*) ≈ pass

Ausreise *f* departure [from a country]. **a~n** *vi sep* (*sein*) leave the country. **A~visum** *nt* exit visa

ausreiß|en† *v sep* • *vt* pull *or* tear out • *vi* (*sein*) (*fam*) run away. **A~er** *m* (*fam*) runaway

ausrenken *vt sep* dislocate; **sich** (*dat*) **den Arm a~** dislocate one's shoulder

ausrichten *vt sep* align; (*bestellen*) deliver; (*erreichen*) achieve; **jdm a~** tell s.o. (**daß** that); **kann ich etwas**

a~? can I take a message? **ich soll Ihnen Grüße von X a~** X sends [you] his regards

ausrotten vt sep exterminate; (fig) eradicate

ausrücken vi sep (sein) (Mil) march off; (fam) run away

Ausruf m exclamation. **a~en†** vt sep exclaim; call out ⟨Namen⟩; (verkünden) proclaim; call ⟨Streik⟩; **jdn a~en lassen** have s.o. paged. **A~ezeichen** nt exclamation mark

ausruhen vt/i sep (haben) rest; **sich a~** have a rest

ausrüst|en vt sep equip. **A~ung** f equipment; (Mil) kit

ausrutschen vi sep (sein) slip

Aussage f -,-n statement; (Jur) testimony, evidence; (Gram) predicate. **a~n** vt/i sep (haben) state; (Jur) give evidence, testify

Aussatz m leprosy

Aussätzige(r) m/f leper

ausschachten vt sep excavate

ausschalten vt sep switch or turn off; (fig) eliminate

Ausschank m sale of alcoholic drinks; (Bar) bar

Ausschau f - **A~ halten nach** look out for. **a~en** vi sep (haben) (SGer) look; **a~en nach** look out for

ausscheiden† v sep ● vi sep (sein) leave; (Sport) drop out; (nicht in Frage kommen) be excluded; **aus dem Dienst a~** retire ● vt eliminate; (Med) excrete

ausschenken vt sep pour out; (verkaufen) sell

ausscheren vi sep (sein) (Auto) pull out

ausschildern vt sep signpost

ausschimpfen vt sep tell off

ausschlachten vt sep (fig) exploit

ausschlafen† v sep ● vi/r (haben) [sich] a~ get enough sleep; (morgens) sleep late; **nicht ausgeschlafen haben** od **sein** be still tired ● vt sleep off ⟨Rausch⟩

Ausschlag m (Med) rash; **den A~ geben** (fig) tip the balance. **a~en†** v sep ● vi (haben) kick [out]; (Bot) sprout; ⟨Baum:⟩ come into leaf ● vt knock out; (auskleiden) line; (ablehnen) refuse. **a~gebend** a decisive

ausschließ|en† vt sep lock out; (fig) exclude; (entfernen) expel. **a~lich** a exclusive, adv -ly

ausschlüpfen vi sep (sein) hatch

Ausschluß m exclusion; expulsion; **unter A~ der Öffentlichkeit** in camera

ausschmücken vt sep decorate; (fig) embellish

ausschneiden† vt sep cut out

Ausschnitt m excerpt, extract; (Zeitungs-) cutting; (Hals-) neckline

ausschöpfen vt sep ladle out; (Naut) bail out; exhaust ⟨Möglichkeiten⟩

ausschreiben† vt sep write out; (ausstellen) make out; (bekanntgeben) announce; put out to tender ⟨Auftrag⟩

Ausschreitungen fpl riots; (Exzesse) excesses

Ausschuß m committee; (Comm) rejects pl

ausschütten vt sep tip out; (verschütten) spill; (leeren) empty; **sich vor Lachen a~** (fam) be in stitches

ausschweif|end a dissolute. **A~ung** f -,-en debauchery; **A~ungen** excesses

ausschwenken vt sep rinse [out]

aussehen† vi sep (haben) look; **es sieht nach Regen aus** it looks like rain; **wie sieht er/es aus?** what does he/it look like? **A~** nt -s appearance

aussein† vi sep (sein) be out; ⟨Licht, Radio:⟩ be off; (zu Ende sein) be over; **a~ auf** (+acc) be after; **mit ihm ist es aus** he's had it

außen adv [on the] outside; **nach a~** outwards. **A~bordmotor** m outboard motor. **A~handel** m foreign trade. **A~minister** m Foreign Minister. **A~politik** f foreign policy. **A~seite** f outside. **A~seiter** m -s,- outsider; (fig) misfit. **A~stände** mpl outstanding debts. **A~stehende(r)** m/f outsider

außer prep (+dat) except [for], apart from; (außerhalb) out of; **a~ Atem/ Sicht** out of breath/sight; **a~ sich** (fig) beside oneself ● conj except; **a~ wenn** unless. **a~dem** adv in addition, as well ● conj moreover

äußer|e(r,s) a external; ⟨Teil, Schicht⟩ outer. **Ä~e(s)** nt exterior; (Aussehen) appearance

außer|ehelich a extra-marital. **a~gewöhnlich** a exceptional, adv -ly. **a~halb** prep (+gen) outside ● adv **a~halb wohnen** live outside town

äußer|lich a external, adv -ly; (fig) outward, adv -ly. **ä~n** vt express;

sich ä∼n comment; (*sich zeigen*) manifest itself

außerordentlich *a* extraordinary, *adv* -ily; (*außergewöhnlich*) exceptional, *adv* -ly

äußerst *adv* extremely

außerstande *adv* unable (**zu** to)

äußerste(r,s) *a* outermost; (*weiteste*) furthest; (*höchste*) utmost, extreme; (*letzte*) last; (*schlimmste*) worst; **am ä∼n Ende** at the very end; **aufs ä∼** extremely. **Ä∼(s)** *nt* **das Ä∼** the limit; (*Schlimmste*) the worst; **sein Ä∼s tun** do one's utmost

Äußerung *f* -,-en comment; (*Bemerkung*) remark

aussetzen *v sep* ● *vt* expose (*dat* to); abandon ⟨*Kind, Hund*⟩; launch ⟨*Boot*⟩; offer ⟨*Belohnung*⟩; **etwas auszusetzen haben an** (+*dat*) find fault with ● *vi* (*haben*) stop; ⟨*Motor:*⟩ cut out

Aussicht *f* -,-en view/(*fig*) prospect (**auf** + *acc* of); **in A∼ stellen** promise; **weitere A∼en** (*Meteorol*) further outlook *sg*. **a∼slos** *a* hopeless, *adv* -ly. **a∼sreich** *a* promising

aussöhnen *vt sep* reconcile; **sich a∼** become reconciled

aussortieren *vt sep* pick out; (*ausscheiden*) eliminate

ausspann|en *v sep* ● *vt* spread out; unhitch ⟨*Pferd*⟩; (*fam: wegnehmen*) take (*dat* from) ● *vi* (*haben*) rest. **A∼ung** *f* rest

aussperr|en *vt sep* lock out. **A∼ung** *f* -,-en lock-out

ausspielen *v sep* ● *vt* play ⟨*Karte*⟩; (*fig*) play off (**gegen** against) ● *vi* (*haben*) (*Kartenspiel*) lead

Aussprache *f* pronunciation; (*Sprechweise*) diction; (*Gespräch*) talk

aussprechen† *v sep* ● *vt* pronounce; (*äußern*) express; **sich a∼** talk; come out (**für/gegen** in favour of/against) ● *vi* (*haben*) finish [speaking]

Ausspruch *m* saying

ausspucken *v sep* ● *vt* spit out ● *vi* (*haben*) spit

ausspülen *vt sep* rinse out

ausstaffieren *vt sep* (*fam*) kit out

Ausstand *m* strike; **in den A∼ treten** go on strike

ausstatt|en *vt sep* equip; **mit Möbeln a∼en** furnish. **A∼ung** *f* -,-en equipment; (*Innen-*) furnishings *pl*; (*Theat*) scenery and costumes *pl*; (*Aufmachung*) get-up

ausstehen† *v sep* ● *vt* suffer; **Angst a∼** be frightened; **ich kann sie nicht a∼** I can't stand her ● *vi* (*haben*) be outstanding

aussteig|en† *vi sep* (*sein*) get out; (*aus Bus, Zug*) get off; (*fam: ausscheiden*) opt out; (*aus einem Geschäft*) back out; **alles a∼en!** all change! **A∼er(in)** *m* -s,- (*f* -,-nen) (*fam*) drop-out

ausstell|en *vt sep* exhibit; (*Comm*) display; (*ausfertigen*) make out; issue ⟨*Paß*⟩. **A∼er** *m* -s,- exhibitor. **A∼ung** *f* exhibition; (*Comm*) display. **A∼ungsstück** *nt* exhibit

aussterben† *vi sep* (*sein*) die out; (*Biol*) become extinct. **A∼** *nt* -s extinction

Aussteuer *f* trousseau

Ausstieg *m* -[e]s,-e exit

ausstopfen *vt sep* stuff

ausstoßen† *vt sep* emit; utter ⟨*Fluch*⟩; heave ⟨*Seufzer*⟩; (*ausschließen*) expel

ausstrahl|en *vt/i sep* (*sein*) radiate, emit; (*Radio, TV*) broadcast. **A∼ung** *f* radiation; (*fig*) charisma

ausstrecken *vt sep* stretch out; put out ⟨*Hand*⟩; **sich a∼** stretch out

ausstreichen† *vt sep* cross out

ausstreuen *vt sep* scatter; spread ⟨*Gerüchte*⟩

ausströmen *v sep* ● *vi* (*sein*) pour out; (*entweichen*) escape ● *vt* emit; (*ausstrahlen*) radiate

aussuchen *vt sep* pick, choose

Austausch *m* exchange. **a∼bar** *a* interchangeable. **a∼en** *vt sep* exchange; (*auswechseln*) replace

austeilen *vt sep* distribute; (*ausgeben*) hand out

Auster *f* -,-n oyster

austoben (sich) *vr sep* ⟨*Sturm:*⟩ rage; ⟨*Person:*⟩ let off steam; ⟨*Kinder:*⟩ romp about

austragen† *vt sep* deliver; hold ⟨*Wettkampf*⟩; play ⟨*Spiel*⟩

Austral|ien /-jən/ *nt* -s Australia. **A∼ier(in)** *m* -s,- (*f* -,-nen) Australian. **a∼isch** *a* Australian

austreiben† *v sep* ● *vt* drive out; (*Relig*) exorcize ● *vi* (*haben*) (*Bot*) sprout

austreten† *v sep* ● *vt* stamp out; (*abnutzen*) wear down ● *vi* (*sein*) come out; (*ausscheiden*) leave (**aus etw** sth); **[mal] a∼** (*fam*) go to the loo; (*Sch*) be excused

austrinken† *vt/i sep* (*haben*) drink up; (*leeren*) drain

Austritt *m* resignation

austrocknen *vt/i sep* (*sein*) dry out

ausüben *vt sep* practise; carry on ⟨*Handwerk*⟩; exercise ⟨*Recht*⟩; exert ⟨*Druck, Einfluß*⟩; have ⟨*Wirkung*⟩

Ausverkauf *m* [clearance] sale. **a~t** *a* sold out; **a~tes Haus** full house

auswachsen† *vt sep* outgrow

Auswahl *f* choice, selection; (*Comm*) range; (*Sport*) team

auswählen *vt sep* choose, select

Auswander|er *m* emigrant. **a~n** *vi sep* (*sein*) emigrate. **A~ung** *f* emigration

auswärt|ig *a* non-local; (*ausländisch*) foreign. **a~s** *adv* outwards; (*Sport*) away; **a~s essen** eat out; **a~s arbeiten** not work locally. **A~sspiel** *nt* away game

auswaschen† *vt sep* wash out

auswechseln *vt sep* change; (*ersetzen*) replace; (*Sport*) substitute

Ausweg *m* (*fig*) way out. **a~los** *a* (*fig*) hopeless

ausweich|en† *vi sep* (*sein*) get out of the way; **jdm/etw a~en** avoid/⟨*sich entziehen*⟩ evade s.o./sth. **a~end** *a* evasive, *adv* -ly

ausweinen *vt sep* **sich** (*dat*) **die Augen a~** cry one's eyes out; **sich a~** have a good cry

Ausweis *m* **-es,-e** pass; (*Mitglieds-, Studenten-*) card. **a~en†** *vt sep* deport; **sich a~en** prove one's identity. **A~papiere** *ntpl* identification papers. **A~ung** *f* deportation

ausweiten *vt sep* stretch; (*fig*) expand

auswendig *adv* by heart

auswerten *vt sep* evaluate; (*nutzen*) utilize

auswickeln *vt sep* unwrap

auswirk|en (sich) *vr sep* have an effect (**auf** + *acc* on). **A~ung** *f* effect; (*Folge*) consequence

auswischen *vt sep* wipe out; **jdm eins a~** (*fam*) play a nasty trick on s.o.

auswringen *vt sep* wring out

Auswuchs *m* excrescence; **Auswüchse** (*fig*) excesses

auszahlen *vt sep* pay out; (*entlohnen*) pay off; (*abfinden*) buy out; **sich a~** (*fig*) pay off

auszählen *vt sep* count; (*Boxen*) count out

Auszahlung *f* payment

auszeichn|en *vt sep* (*Comm*) price; (*ehren*) honour; (*mit einem Preis*) award a prize to; (*Mil*) decorate; **sich a~en** distinguish oneself. **A~ung** *f* honour; (*Preis*) award; (*Mil*) decoration; (*Sch*) distinction

ausziehen† *v sep* ● *vt* pull out; (*auskleiden*) undress; take off ⟨*Mantel, Schuhe*⟩; **sich a~** take off one's coat; (*sich entkleiden*) undress ● *vi* (*sein*) move out; (*sich aufmachen*) set out

Auszubildende(r) *m/f* trainee

Auszug *m* departure; (*Umzug*) move; (*Ausschnitt*) extract, excerpt; (*Bank-*) statement

authentisch *a* authentic

Auto *nt* **-s,-s** car; **A~ fahren** drive; (*mitfahren*) go in the car. **A~bahn** *f* motorway, (*Amer*) freeway

Autobiographie *f* autobiography

Auto|bus *m* bus. **A~fähre** *f* car ferry. **A~fahrer(in)** *m(f)* driver, motorist. **A~fahrt** *f* drive

Autogramm *nt* **-s,-e** autograph

autokratisch *a* autocratic

Automat *m* **-en,-en** automatic device; (*Münz-*) slot-machine; (*Verkaufs-*) vending-machine; (*Fahrkarten-*) machine; (*Techn*) robot. **A~ik** *f* - automatic mechanism; (*Auto*) automatic transmission

Auto|mation /-'tsio̱:n/ *f* - automation. **a~matisch** *a* automatic, *adv* -ally

autonom *a* autonomous. **A~ie** *f* - autonomy

Autonummer *f* registration number

Autopsie *f* **-,-n** autopsy

Autor *m* **-s,-en** /-'to:rən/ author

Auto|reisezug *m* Motorail. **A~rennen** *nt* motor race

Autorin *f* **-,-nen** author[ess]

Autori|sation /-'tsio̱:n/ *f* - authorization. **a~sieren** *vt* authorize. **a~tär** *a* authoritarian. **A~tät** *f* **-,-en** authority

Auto|schlosser *m* motor mechanic. **A~skooter** /-sku:tɐ/ *m* **-s,-** dodgem. **A~stopp** *m* **-s** per **A~stopp fahren** hitch-hike. **A~verleih** *m* car hire [firm]. **A~waschanlage** *f* car wash

autsch *int* ouch

Aversion *f* **-,-en** aversion (**gegen** to)

Axt *f* **-,⁓e** axe

B

B, b /be:/ *nt* - (*Mus*) B flat
Baby /'be:bi/ *nt* **-s,-s** baby. **B~aus-stattung** *f* layette. **B~sitter** /-sɪtɐ/ *m* **-s,-** babysitter
Bạch *m* **-[e]s,-ͤe** stream
Bạckbord *nt* **-[e]s** port [side]
Bạcke *f* **-,-n** cheek
bạcken *v* ● *vt/i* † (*haben*) bake; (*braten*) fry ● *vi* (*reg*) (*haben*) (*kleben*) stick (**an** + *dat* to)
Bạckenzahn *m* molar
Bạ̈cker *m* **-s,-** baker. **B~ei** *f* **-,-en,** **B~laden** *m* baker's shop
Bạck|form *f* baking tin. **B~obst** *nt* dried fruit. **B~ofen** *m* oven. **B~pfeife** *f* (*fam*) slap in the face. **B~pflaume** *f* prune. **B~pulver** *nt* baking-powder. **B~rohr** *nt* oven. **B~stein** *m* brick. **B~werk** *nt* cakes and pastries *pl*
Bad *nt* **-[e]s,-ͤer** bath; (*im Meer*) bathe; (*Zimmer*) bathroom; (*Schwimm-*) pool; (*Ort*) spa
Bade|anstalt *f* swimming baths *pl.* **B~anzug** *m* swim-suit. **B~hose** *f* swimming trunks *pl.* **B~kappe** *f* bathing-cap. **B~mantel** *m* bathrobe. **B~matte** *f* bath-mat. **B~mütze** *f* bathing-cap. **b~n** *vi* (*haben*) have a bath; (*im Meer*) bathe ● *vt* bath; (*waschen*) bathe. **B~ort** *m* seaside resort; (*Kurort*) spa. **B~tuch** *nt* bath-towel. **B~wanne** *f* bath[-tub]. **B~zimmer** *nt* bathroom
Bagatelle *f* **-,-n** trifle; (*Mus*) bagatelle
Bạgger *m* **-s,-** excavator; (*Naß-*) dredger. **b~n** *vt/i* (*haben*) excavate; dredge. **B~see** *m* flooded gravel-pit
Bahn *f* **-,-en** path; (*Astr*) orbit; (*Sport*) track; (*einzelne*) lane; (*Rodel-*) run; (*Stoff-, Papier-*) width; (*Rock-*) panel; (*Eisen-*) railway; (*Zug*) train; (*Straßen-*) tram; **auf die schiefe B~ kommen** (*fig*) get into bad ways. **b~brechend** *a* (*fig*) pioneering. **b~en** *vt* **sich** (*dat*) **einen Weg b~en** clear a way (**durch** through). **B~hof** *m* [railway] station. **B~steig** *m* **-[e]s,-e** platform. **B~übergang** *m* level crossing, (*Amer*) grade crossing
Bahre *f* **-,-n** stretcher; (*Toten-*) bier
Baiser /bɛ'ze:/ *nt* **-s,-s** meringue
Bajonẹtt *nt* **-[e]s,-e** bayonet
Bake *f* **-,-n** (*Naut, Aviat*) beacon
Baktẹrien /-i̯ən/ *fpl* bacteria

Balanc|e /ba'lã:sə/ *f* balance; **die B~e halten/verlieren** keep/lose one's balance. **b~ieren** *vt/i* (*haben/sein*) balance
bald *adv* soon; (*fast*) almost; **b~ ... b~ ...** now ... now ...
Baldachin /-xi:n/ *m* **-s,-e** canopy
bạld|ig *a* early; (*Besserung*) speedy. **b~möglichst** *adv* as soon as possible
Balg *nt* & *m* **-[e]s,-ͤer** (*fam*) brat. **b~en** (**sich**) *vr* tussle. **B~erei** *f* **-,-en** tussle
Balkan *m* **-s** Balkans *pl*
Bạlken *m* **-s,-** beam
Balkon /bal'kõ:/ *m* **-s,-s** balcony; (*Theat*) circle
Ball[1] *m* **-[e]s,-ͤe** ball
Ball[2] *m* **-[e]s,-ͤe** (*Tanz*) ball
Ballade *f* **-,-n** ballad
Bạllast *m* **-[e]s** ballast. **B~stoffe** *mpl* roughage *sg*
bạllen *vt* **die [Hand zur] Faust b~** clench one's fist; **sich b~** gather, mass. **B~** *m* **-s,-** bale; (*Anat*) ball of the hand/(*Fuß-*) foot; (*Med*) bunion
Ballerina *f* **-,-nen** ballerina
Ballẹtt *nt* **-s,-e** ballet
Ballẹttänzer(in) *m*(*f*) ballet dancer
ballịstisch *a* ballistic
Ballon /ba'lõ:/ *m* **-s,-s** balloon
Ball|saal *m* ballroom. **B~ungsgebiet** *nt* conurbation. **B~wechsel** *m* (*Tennis*) rally
Bạlsam *m* **-s** balm
Bạlt|ikum *nt* **-s** Baltic States *pl.* **b~isch** *a* Baltic
Balustrade *f* **-,-n** balustrade
Bạmbus *m* **-ses,-se** bamboo
banạl *a* banal. **B~ität** *f* **-,-en** banality
Banane *f* **-,-n** banana
Banạuse *m* **-n,-n** philistine
Band[1] *nt* **-[e]s,-ͤer** ribbon; (*Naht-, Ton-, Ziel-*) tape; (*Anat*) ligament; **auf B~ aufnehmen** tape; **laufendes B~** conveyor belt; **am laufenden B~** (*fam*) non-stop
Band[2] *m* **-[e]s,-ͤe** volume
Band[3] *nt* **-[e]s,-e** (*fig*) bond; **B~e der Freundschaft** bonds of friendship
Band[4] /bɛnt/ *f* **-,-s** [jazz] band
Bandag|e /ban'da:ʒə/ *f* **-,-n** bandage. **b~ieren** *vt* bandage
Bande *f* **-,-n** gang
bạ̈ndigen *vt* control, restrain; (*zähmen*) tame
Bandịt *m* **-en,-en** bandit
Band|maß *nt* tape-measure. **B~nudeln** *fpl* noodles. **B~scheibe** *f* (*Anat*)

disc. **B~scheibenvorfall** m slipped disc. **B~wurm** m tapeworm

bang|[e] a (**bänger, bängst**) anxious; **jdm b~e machen** frighten s.o. **B~e**f **B~e haben** be afraid. **b~en** vi (**haben**) fear (**um** for); **mir b~t davor** I dread it

Banjo nt -s,-s banjo

Bank¹ f -,ːe bench

Bank² f -,-en (**Comm**) bank. **B~einzug** m direct debit

Bankett nt -s,-e banquet

Bankier /baŋ'kjeː/ m -s,-s banker

Bank|konto nt bank account. **B~note** f banknote

Bankrott m -s,-s bankruptcy; **B~ machen** go bankrupt. **b~** a bankrupt

Bankwesen nt banking

Bann m -[e]s,-e (**fig**) spell; **in jds B~** under s.o.'s spell. **b~en** vt exorcize; (**abwenden**) avert; **[wie] gebannt** spellbound

Banner nt -s,- banner

Baptist(in) m -en,-en (f -,-nen) Baptist

bar a (**rein**) sheer; ⟨**Gold**⟩ pure; **b~es Geld** cash; **[in] bar bezahlen** pay cash; **etw für b~e Münze nehmen** (**fig**) take sth as gospel

Bar f -,-s bar

Bär m -en,-en bear; **jdm einen B~en aufbinden** (**fam**) pull s.o.'s leg

Baracke f -,-n (**Mil**) hut

Barb|ar m -en,-en barbarian. **b~arisch** a barbaric

bar|fuß adv barefoot. **B~geld** nt cash

Bariton m -s,-e /-'toːnə/ baritone

Barkasse f -,-n launch

Barmann m (**pl -männer**) barman

barmherzig a merciful. **B~keit** f - mercy

barock a baroque. **B~** nt & m -[s] baroque

Barometer nt -s,- barometer

Baron m -s,-e baron. **B~in** f -,-nen baroness

Barren m -s,- (**Gold-**) bar, ingot; (**Sport**) parallel bars pl. **B~gold** nt gold bullion

Barriere f -,-n barrier

Barrikade f -,-n barricade

barsch a gruff, adv -ly; (**kurz**) curt, adv -ly

Barsch m -[e]s,-e (**Zool**) perch

Barschaft f - **meine ganze B~** all I have/had on me

Bart m -[e]s,ːe beard; (**der Katze**) whiskers pl

bärtig a bearded

Barzahlung f cash payment

Basar m -s,-e bazaar

Base¹ f -,-n [female] cousin

Base² f -,-n (**Chem**) alkali, base

Basel nt -s Basle

basieren vi (**haben**) be based (**auf** +dat on)

Basilikum nt -s basil

Basis f -,**Basen** base; (**fig**) basis

basisch a (**Chem**) alkaline

Bask|enmütze f beret. **b~isch** a Basque

Baß m -sses,ːsse bass; (**Kontra-**) double-bass

Bassin /ba'sɛ̃ː/ nt -s,-s pond; (**Brunnen-**) basin; (**Schwimm-**) pool

Bassist m -en,-en bass player; (**Sänger**) bass

Baßstimme f bass voice

Bast m -[e]s raffia

basta int **[und damit] b~!** and that's that!

bast|eln vt make ● vi (**haben**) do handicrafts; (**herum-**) tinker (**an-** +dat with). **B~ler** m -s,- amateur craftsman; (**Heim-**) do-it-yourselfer

Bataillon /batal'joːn/ nt -s,-e battalion

Batterie f -,-n battery

Bau¹ m -[e]s,-e burrow; (**Fuchs-**) earth

Bau² m -[e]s,-ten construction; (**Gebäude**) building; (**Auf-**) structure; (**Körper-**) build; (**B~stelle**) building site; **im Bau** under construction. **B~arbeiten** fpl building work sg; (**Straßen-**) roadworks. **B~art** f design; (**Stil**) style

Bauch m -[e]s, **Bäuche** abdomen, belly; (**Magen**) stomach; (**Schmer-**) paunch; (**Bauchung**) bulge. **b~ig** a bulbous. **B~nabel** m navel. **B~redner** m ventriloquist. **B~schmerzen** mpl stomach-ache sg. **B~speicheldrüse** f pancreas. **B~weh** nt stomach-ache

bauen vt build; (**konstruieren**) construct; (**an-**) grow; **einen Unfall b~** (**fam**) have an accident ● vi (**haben**) build (**an etw** dat sth); **b~ auf** (+acc) (**fig**) rely on

Bauer¹ m -s,-n farmer; (**Schach**) pawn

Bauer² nt -s,- [bird]cage

Bäuer|in f -,-nen farmer's wife. **b~lich** a rustic

Bauern|haus nt farmhouse. **B~hof** m farm

bau|fällig a dilapidated. **B~geneh-migung** f planning permission. **B~gerüst** nt scaffolding. **B~jahr** nt year of construction; **B~jahr 1985** (Auto) 1985 model. **B~kasten** m box of building bricks; (Modell-) model kit. **B~klotz** m building brick. **B~kunst** f architecture. **b~lich** a structural, adv -ly. **B~lichkeiten** fpl buildings

Baum m -[e]s, **Bäume** tree

baumeln vi (haben) dangle; **die Beine b~ lassen** dangle one's legs

bäumen (sich) vr rear [up]

Baum|schule f [tree] nursery. **B~stamm** m tree-trunk. **B~wolle** f cotton. **b~wollen** a cotton

Bauplatz m building plot

bäurisch a rustic; (plump) uncouth

Bausch m -[e]s, **Bäusche** wad; **in B~ und Bogen** (fig) wholesale. **b~en** vt puff out; **sich b~en** billow [out]. **b~ig** a puffed [out]; ⟨Ärmel⟩ full

Bau|sparkasse f building society. **B~stein** m building brick; (fig) element. **B~stelle** f building site; (Straßen-) roadworks pl. **B~unter-nehmer** m building contractor. **B~werk** nt building. **B~zaun** m hoarding

Bayer|(in) m -s,-n (f -,-nen) Bavarian. **B~n** nt -s Bavaria

bay[e]risch a Bavarian

Bazillus m -,-len bacillus; (fam: Keim) germ

beabsichtig|en vt intend. **b~t** a intended; (absichtlich) intentional

beacht|en vt take notice of; (einhalten) observe; (folgen) follow; **nicht b~en** ignore. **b~lich** a consider-able. **B~ung** f - observance; **etw** (dat) **keine B~ung schenken** take no notice of sth

Beamte(r) m, **Beamtin** f -,-nen offi-cial; (Staats-) civil servant; (Schalter-) clerk

beängstigend a alarming

beanspruchen vt claim; (erfordern) demand; (brauchen) take up; (Techn) stress; **die Arbeit bean-sprucht ihn sehr** his work is very demanding

beanstand|en vt find fault with; (Comm) make a complaint about. **B~ung** f -,-en complaint

beantragen vt apply for

beantworten vt answer

bearbeiten vt work; (weiter-) pro-cess; (behandeln) treat (mit with); (Admin) deal with; (redigieren) edit; (Theat) adapt; (Mus) arrange; (fam: bedrängen) pester; (fam: schlagen) pummel

Beatmung f **künstliche B~** artificial respiration. **B~sgerät** nt ventilator

beaufsichtig|en vt supervise. **B~ung** f - supervision

beauftrag|en vt instruct; commis-sion ⟨Künstler⟩; **jdn mit einer Arbeit b~en** assign a task to s.o. **B~te(r)** m/f representative

bebauen vt build on; (bestellen) cultivate

beben vi (haben) tremble

bebildert a illustrated

Becher m -s,- beaker; (Henkel-) mug; (Joghurt-, Sahne-) carton

Becken nt -s,- basin; (Schwimm-) pool; (Mus) cymbals pl; (Anat) pelvis

bedacht a careful; **b~ auf** (+ acc) concerned about; **darauf b~ anxious (zu to)

bedächtig a careful, adv -ly; (lang-sam) slow, adv -ly

bedanken (sich) vr thank (**bei jdm** s.o.)

Bedarf m -s need/(Comm) demand (**an** + dat for); **bei B~** if required. **B~sartikel** mpl requisites. **B~s-haltestelle** f request stop

bedauer|lich a regrettable. **b~licherweise** adv unfortunately. **b~n** vt regret; (bemitleiden) feel sorry for; **bedaure!** sorry! **B~n** nt -s regret; (Mitgefühl) sympathy. **b~nswert** a pitiful; (bedauerlich) regrettable

bedeck|en vt cover; **sich b~en** ⟨Him-mel:⟩ cloud over. **b~t** a covered; ⟨Himmel⟩ overcast

bedenken† vt consider; (überlegen) think over; **jdn b~** give s.o. a pres-ent; **sich b~** consider. **B~** pl misgiv-ings; **ohne B~** without hesitation. **b~los** a unhesitating, adv -ly

bedenklich a doubtful; (verdächtig) dubious; (bedrohlich) worrying; (ernst) serious

bedeut|en vi (haben) mean; **jdm viel/nichts b~en** mean a lot/nothing to s.o.; **es hat nichts zu b~en** it is of no significance. **b~end** a import-ant; (beträchtlich) considerable. **b~sam** a = **b~ungsvoll**. **B~ung** f -,-en meaning; (Wichtigkeit) importance. **b~ungslos** a meaningless; (*unwichtig*) unimportant. **b~ungs-voll** a significant; (*vielsagend*) meaningful, adv -ly

bedien|en vt serve; (*betätigen*) operate; **sich [selbst] b~en** help oneself. **B~ung** f -,-en service; (*Betätigung*) operation; (*Kellner*) waiter; (*Kellnerin*) f waitress. **B~ungsgeld** nt, **B~ungszuschlag** m service charge

bedingt a conditional; (*eingeschränkt*) qualified

Bedingung f -,-en condition; **B~en** conditions; (*Comm*) terms. **b~slos** a unconditional, adv -ly; (*unbedingt*) unquestioning, adv -ly

bedrängen vt press; (*belästigen*) pester

bedroh|en vt threaten. **b~lich** a threatening. **B~ung** f threat

bedrück|en vt depress. **b~end** a depressing. **b~t** a depressed

bedruckt a printed

bedürf|en† vi (*haben*) (+ gen) need. **B~nis** nt -ses,-se need. **B~nisanstalt** f public convenience. **b~tig** a needy

Beefsteak /'bi:fste:k/ nt -s,-s steak; **deutsches B~** hamburger

beeilen (sich) vr hurry; hasten (**zu** to); **beeilt euch!** hurry up!

beeindrucken vt impress

beeinflussen vt influence

beeinträchtigen vt mar; (*schädigen*) impair

beend[ig]en vt end

beengen vt restrict; **beengt wohnen** live in cramped conditions

beerben vt jdn **b~** inherit s.o.'s property

beerdig|en vt bury. **B~ung** f -,-en funeral

Beere f -,-n berry

Beet nt -[e]s,-e (*Hort*) bed

Beete f -,-n **rote B~** beetroot

befähig|en vt enable; (*qualifizieren*) qualify. **B~ung** f - qualification; (*Fähigkeit*) ability

befahr|bar a passable. **b~en†** vt drive along; **stark b~ene Straße** busy road

befallen† vt attack; ⟨Angst:⟩ seize

befangen a shy; (*gehemmt*) self-conscious; (*Jur*) biased. **B~heit** f - shyness; self-consciousness; bias

befassen (sich) vr concern oneself/ (*behandeln*) deal (**mit** with)

Befehl m -[e]s,-e order; (*Leitung*) command (**über** + acc of). **b~en†** vt jdm etw **b~en** order s.o. to do sth

● vi (*haben*) give the orders. **b~igen** vt (*Mil*) command. **B~sform** f (*Gram*) imperative. **B~shaber** m -s,- commander

befestig|en vt fasten (**an** + dat to); (*stärken*) strengthen; (*Mil*) fortify. **B~ung** f -,-en fastening; (*Mil*) fortification

befeuchten vt moisten

befinden† (sich) vr be. **B~** nt -s [state of] health

beflecken vt stain

beflissen a assiduous, adv -ly

befolgen vt follow

beförder|n vt transport; (*im Rang*) promote. **B~ung** f -,-en transport; promotion

befragen vt question

befrei|en vt free; (*räumen*) clear (**von** of); (*freistellen*) exempt (**von** from); **sich b~en** free oneself. **B~er** m -s,- liberator. **b~t** a (*erleichtert*) relieved. **B~ung** f - liberation; exemption

befremd|en vt disconcert. **B~en** nt -s surprise. **b~lich** a strange

befreunden (sich) vr make friends; **befreundet sein** be friends

befriedig|en vt satisfy. **b~end** a satisfying; (*zufriedenstellend*) satisfactory. **B~ung** f - satisfaction

befrucht|en vt fertilize. **B~ung** f - fertilization; **künstliche B~ung** artificial insemination

Befug|nis f -,-se authority. **b~t** a authorized

Befund m result

befürcht|en vt fear. **B~ung** f -,-en fear

befürworten vt support

begab|t a gifted. **B~ung** f -,-en gift, talent

begatten (sich) vr mate

begeben† (sich) vr go; (*liter: geschehen*) happen; **sich in Gefahr b~** expose oneself to danger. **B~heit** f -,-en incident

begegn|en vi (*sein*) jdm/etw **b~en** meet s.o./sth; **sich b~en** meet. **B~ung** f -,-en meeting; (*Sport*) encounter

begehen† vt walk along; (*verüben*) commit; (*feiern*) celebrate

begehr|en vt desire. **b~enswert** a desirable. **b~t** a sought-after

begeister|n vt jdn **b~n** arouse s.o.'s enthusiasm; **sich b~n** be enthusiastic (**für** about). **b~t** a enthusiastic, *adv* -ally; (*eifrig*) keen. **B∼ung** *f* - enthusiasm

Begier|de *f* -,-n desire. **b∼ig** *a* eager (**auf** + *acc* for)

begießen† *vt* water; (*Culin*) baste; (*fam: feiern*) celebrate

Beginn *m* -s beginning; **zu B∼** at the beginning. **b∼en†** *vt/i* (*haben*) start, begin; (*anstellen*) do

beglaubigen *vt* authenticate

begleichen† *vt* settle

begleit|en *vt* accompany. **B∼er** *m* -s,-, **B∼erin** *f* -,-nen companion; (*Mus*) accompanist. **B∼ung** *f* -,-en company; (*Gefolge*) entourage; (*Mus*) accompaniment

beglück|en *vt* make happy. **b∼t** *a* happy. **b∼wünschen** *vt* congratulate (**zu** on)

begnadig|en *vt* (*Jur*) pardon. **B∼ung** *f* -,-en (*Jur*) pardon

begnügen (sich) *vr* content oneself (**mit** with)

Begonie /-jə/ *f* -,-n begonia

begraben† *vt* bury

Begräbnis *n* -ses,-se burial; (*Feier*) funeral

begreif|en† *vt* understand; **nicht zu b∼en** incomprehensible. **b∼lich** *a* understandable; **jdm etw b∼lich machen** make s.o. understand sth. **b∼licherweise** *adv* understandably

begrenz|en *vt* form the boundary of; (*beschränken*) restrict. **b∼t** *a* limited. **B∼ung** *f* -,-en restriction; (*Grenze*) boundary

Begriff *m* -[e]s,-e concept; (*Ausdruck*) term; (*Vorstellung*) idea; **für meine B∼e** to my mind; **im B∼ sein** *od* **stehen** be about (**zu** to); **schwer von B∼** (*fam*) slow on the uptake. **b∼sstutzig** *a* obtuse

begründ|en *vt* give one's reason for; (*gründen*) establish. **b∼et** *a* justified. **B∼ung** *f* -,-en reason

begrüß|en *vt* greet; (*billigen*) welcome. **b∼enswert** *a* welcome. **B∼ung** *f* - greeting; welcome

begünstigen *vt* favour; (*fördern*) encourage

begutachten *vt* give an opinion on; (*fam: ansehen*) look at

begütert *a* wealthy

begütigen *vt* placate

behaart *a* hairy

behäbig *a* portly; (*gemütlich*) comfortable, *adv* -bly

behag|en *vi* (*haben*) please (**jdm** s.o.). **B∼en** *nt* -s contentment; (*Genuß*)

enjoyment. **b∼lich** *a* comfortable, *adv* -bly. **B∼lichkeit** *f* - comfort

behalten† *vt* keep; (*sich merken*) remember; **etw für sich b∼** (*verschweigen*) keep sth to oneself

Behälter *m* -s,- container

behand|eln *vt* treat; (*sich befassen*) deal with. **B∼lung** *f* treatment

beharr|en *vi* (*haben*) persist (**auf** + *dat* in). **b∼lich** *a* persistent, *adv* -ly; (*hartnäckig*) dogged, *adv* -ly. **B∼lichkeit** *f* - persistence

behaupt|en *vt* maintain; (*vorgeben*) claim; (*sagen*) say; (*bewahren*) retain; **sich b∼en** hold one's own. **B∼ung** *f* -,-en assertion; claim; (*Äußerung*) statement

beheben† *vt* remedy; (*beseitigen*) remove

behelf|en† (sich) *vr* make do (**mit** with). **b∼smäßig** *a* makeshift ● *adv* provisionally

behelligen *vt* bother

behende *a* nimble, *adv* -bly

beherbergen *vt* put up

beherrsch|en *vt* rule over; (*dominieren*) dominate; (*meistern, zügeln*) control; (*können*) master; **sich b∼en** control oneself. **b∼t** *a* self-controlled. **B∼ung** *f* - control; (*Selbst-*) self-control; (*Können*) mastery

beherz|igen *vt* heed. **b∼t** *a* courageous, *adv* -ly

behilflich *a* **jdm b∼ sein** help s.o.

behinder|n *vt* hinder; (*blockieren*) obstruct. **b∼t** *a* handicapped; (*schwer*) disabled. **B∼te(r)** *m/f* handicapped/disabled person. **B∼ung** *f* -,-en obstruction; (*Med*) handicap; disability

Behörde *f* -,-n [public] authority

behüte|n *vt* protect; **Gott behüte!** heaven forbid! **b∼t** *a* sheltered

behutsam *a* careful, *adv* -ly; (*zart*) gentle, *adv* -ly

bei *prep* (+ *dat*) near; (*dicht*) by; at ⟨*Firma, Veranstaltung*⟩; **bei der Hand nehmen** take by the hand; **bei sich haben** have with one; **bei mir** at my place; (*in meinem Fall*) in my case; **Herr X bei Meyer** Mr X c/o Meyer; **bei Regen** when/(*falls*) if it rains; **bei Feuer** in case of fire; **bei Tag/Nacht** by day/night; **bei der Ankunft** on arrival; **bei Tisch/der Arbeit** at table/work; **bei guter Gesundheit** in good health; **bei der hohen Miete** [what] with the high rent;

bei all seiner Klugheit for all his cleverness

beibehalten† *vt sep* keep

beibringen† *vt sep* **jdm etw b~** teach s.o. sth; (*mitteilen*) break sth to s.o.; (*zufügen*) inflict sth on s.o.

Beicht|e *f* -,-n confession. **b~en** *vt/i* (*haben*) confess. **B~stuhl** *m* confessional

beide *a* & *pron* both; **die b~n Brüder** the two brothers; **b~s** both; **dreißig b~** (*Tennis*) thirty all. **b~rseitig** *a* mutual. **b~rseits** *adv* & *prep* (+ *gen*) on both sides (of)

beidrehen *vi sep* (*haben*) heave to

beieinander *adv* together

Beifahrer|(in) *m(f)* [front-seat] passenger; (*Lkw*) driver's mate; (*Motorrad*) pillion passenger. **B~sitz** *m* passenger seat

Beifall *m* -[e]s applause; (*Billigung*) approval; **B~ klatschen** applaud

beifällig *a* approving, *adv* -ly

beifügen *vt sep* add; (*beilegen*) enclose

beige /bɛːʒ/ *inv a* beige

beigeben† *v sep* ● *vt* add ● *vi* (*haben*) **klein b~** give in

Beigeschmack *m* [slight] taste

Beihilfe *f* financial aid; (*Studien-*) grant; (*Jur*) aiding and abetting

beikommen† *vi sep* (*sein*) **jdm b~** get the better of s.o.

Beil *nt* -[e]s,-e hatchet, axe

Beilage *f* supplement; (*Gemüse*) vegetable; **als B~ Reis** (*Culin*) served with rice

beiläufig *a* casual, *adv* -ly

beilegen *vt sep* enclose; (*schlichten*) settle

beileibe *adv* **b~ nicht** by no means

Beileid *nt* condolences *pl*. **B~sbrief** *m* letter of condolence

beiliegend *a* enclosed

beim *prep* = **bei dem**; **b~ Militär** in the army; **b~ Frühstück** at breakfast; **b~ Lesen** when reading; **b~ Lesen sein** be reading

beimessen† *vt sep* (*fig*) attach (*dat* to)

Bein *nt* -[e]s,-e leg; **jdm ein B~ stellen** trip s.o. up

beinah[e] *adv* nearly, almost

Beiname *m* epithet

beipflichten *vi sep* (*haben*) agree (*dat* with)

Beirat *m* advisory committee

beirren *vt* **sich nicht b~ lassen** not let oneself be put off

beisammen *adv* together. **b~sein**† *vi sep* (*sein*) be together. **B~sein** *nt* -s get-together

Beisein *nt* presence

beiseite *adv* aside; (*abseits*) apart; **b~ legen** put aside; (*sparen*) put by; **Spaß** *od* **Scherz b~** joking apart

beisetz|en *vt sep* bury. **B~ung** *f* -,-en funeral

Beispiel *nt* example; **zum B~** for example. **b~haft** *a* exemplary. **b~los** *a* unprecedented. **b~sweise** *adv* for example

beispringen† *vi sep* (*sein*) **jdm b~** come to s.o.'s aid

beiß|en† *vt* & *i* (*haben*) bite; (*brennen*) sting; **sich b~en** ⟨*Farben:*⟩ clash. **b~end** *a* (*fig*) biting; ⟨*Bemerkung*⟩ caustic. **B~zange** *f* pliers *pl*

Bei|stand *m* -[e]s help; **jdm B~stand leisten** help s.o. **b~stehen**† *vi sep* (*haben*) **jdm b~stehen** help s.o.

beisteuern *vt sep* contribute

beistimmen *vi sep* (*haben*) agree

Beistrich *m* comma

Beitrag *m* -[e]s,-̈e contribution; (*Mitglieds-*) subscription; (*Versicherungs-*) premium; (*Zeitungs-*) article. **b~en**† *vt/i sep* (*haben*) contribute

beitreten† *vi sep* (*sein*) (+ *dat*) join. **B~tritt** *m* joining

beiwohnen *vi sep* (*haben*) (+ *dat*) be present at

Beize *f* -,-n (*Holz-*) stain; (*Culin*) marinade

beizeiten *adv* in good time

beizen *vt* stain ⟨*Holz*⟩

bejahen *vt* answer in the affirmative; (*billigen*) approve of

bejahrt *a* aged, old

bejubeln *vt* cheer

bekämpf|en *vt* fight. **B~ung** *f* - fight (*gen* against)

bekannt *a* well-known; (*vertraut*) familiar; **jdm b~ sein** be known to s.o.; **jdn b~ machen** introduce s.o. **B~e(r)** *m/f* acquaintance; (*Freund*) friend. **B~gabe** *f* announcement. **b~geben**† *vt sep* announce. **b~lich** *adv* as is well known. **b~machen** *vt sep* announce. **B~machung** *f* -,-en announcement; (*Anschlag*) notice. **B~schaft** *f* - acquaintance; (*Leute*) acquaintances *pl*; (*Freunde*) friends *pl*. **b~werden**† *vi sep* (*sein*) become known

bekehr|en vt convert; **sich b~en** become converted. **B~ung** f -,-en conversion

bekenn|en† vt confess; profess ⟨Glauben⟩; **sich [für] schuldig b~en** admit one's guilt; **sich b~en zu** confess to ⟨Tat⟩; profess ⟨Glauben⟩; ⟨stehen zu⟩ stand by. **B~tnis** nt -ses,-se confession; (Konfession) denomination

beklag|en vt lament; (bedauern) deplore; **sich b~en** complain. **b~enswert** a unfortunate. **B~te(r)** m/f (Jur) defendant

beklatschen vt applaud

bekleid|en vt hold ⟨Amt⟩. **b~et** a dressed (mit in). **B~ung** f clothing

Beklemmung f -,-en feeling of oppression

beklommen a uneasy; (ängstlich) anxious, adv -ly

bekommen† vt get; have ⟨Baby⟩; catch ⟨Erkältung⟩; **Angst/Hunger b~** get frightened/hungry; **etw geliehen b~** be lent sth ● vi (sein) **jdm gut b~** do s.o. good; ⟨Essen:⟩ agree with s.o.

bekömmlich a digestible

beköstig|en vt feed; **sich selbst b~en** cater for oneself. **B~ung** f - board; (Essen) food

bekräftigen vt reaffirm; (bestätigen) confirm

bekreuzigen (sich) vr cross oneself

bekümmert a troubled; (besorgt) worried

bekunden vt show; (bezeugen) testify

belächeln vt laugh at

beladen† vt load ● a laden

Belag m -[e]s,¨e coating; (Fußboden-) covering; (Brot-) topping; (Zahn-) tartar; (Brems-) lining

belager|n vt besiege. **B~ung** f -,-en siege

Belang m von/ohne **B~** of/of no importance; **B~e** pl interests. **b~en** vt (Jur) sue. **b~los** a irrelevant; (unwichtig) trivial. **B~losigkeit** f -,-en triviality

belassen† vt leave; **es dabei b~** leave it at that

belasten vt load; (fig) burden; (beanspruchen) put a strain on; (Comm) debit; (Jur) incriminate

belästigen vt bother; (bedrängen) pester; (unsittlich) molest

Belastung f -,-en load; (fig) strain; (Last) burden; (Comm) debit.

B~smaterial nt incriminating evidence. **B~szeuge** m prosecution witness

belaufen† (sich) vr amount (auf + acc to)

belauschen vt eavesdrop on

beleb|en vt (fig) revive; (lebhaft machen) enliven; **sich b~en** revive; ⟨Stadt:⟩ come to life. **b~t** a lively; ⟨Straße⟩ busy

Beleg m -[e]s,-e evidence; (Beispiel) instance (für of); (Quittung) receipt. **b~en** vt cover/(garnieren) garnish (mit with); (besetzen) reserve; (Univ) enrol for; (nachweisen) provide evidence for; **den ersten Platz b~en** (Sport) take first place. **B~schaft** f -,-en work-force. **b~t** a occupied; ⟨Zunge⟩ coated; ⟨Stimme⟩ husky; **b~te Brote** open sandwiches; **der Platz ist b~t** this seat is taken

belehren vt instruct; (aufklären) inform

beleibt a corpulent

beleidig|en vt offend; (absichtlich) insult. **B~ung** f -,-en insult

belesen a well-read

beleucht|en vt light; (anleuchten) illuminate. **B~ung** f -,-en illumination; (elektrisch) lighting; (Licht) light

Belg|ien /-jən/ nt -s Belgium. **B~ier(in)** m -s,- (f -,-nen) Belgian. **b~isch** a Belgian

belicht|en vt (Phot) expose. **B~ung** f - exposure

Belieb|en nt -s nach **B~en** [just] as one likes; (Culin) if liked. **b~ig** a **eine b~ige Zahl/Farbe** any number/ colour you like ● adv **b~ig lange/ oft** as long/often as one likes. **b~t** a popular. **B~theit** f - popularity

beliefern vt supply (mit with)

bellen vi (haben) bark

belohn|en vt reward. **B~ung** f -,-en reward

belüften vt ventilate

belügen† vt lie to; **sich [selbst] b~** deceive oneself

belustig|en vt amuse. **B~ung** f -,-en amusement

bemächtigen (sich) vr (+ gen) seize

bemalen vt paint

bemängeln vt criticize

bemannt a manned

bemerk|bar a **sich b~bar machen** attract attention; ⟨Ding:⟩ become noticeable. **b~en** vt notice; (äußern) remark. **b~enswert** *a* remarkable, *adv* -bly. **B~ung** *f* -,-en remark

bemitleiden *vt* pity

bemittelt *a* well-to-do

bemüh|en *vt* trouble; **sich b~en** try (**zu** to; **um etw zu** get sth); (*sich kümmern*) attend (**um** to); **b~t sein** endeavour (**zu** to). **B~ung** *f* -,-en effort; (*Mühe*) trouble

bemuttern *vt* mother

benachbart *a* neighbouring

benachrichtig|en *vt* inform; (*amtlich*) notify. **B~ung** *f* -,-en notification

benachteilig|en *vt* discriminate against; (*ungerecht sein*) treat unfairly. **B~ung** *f* -,-en discrimination (*gen* against)

benehmen† (**sich**) *vr* behave. **B~** *nt* -s behaviour

beneiden *vt* envy (**um etw** sth). **b~swert** *a* enviable

Bengel *m* -s,- boy; (*Rüpel*) lout

benommen *a* dazed

benötigen *vt* need

benutz|en, (*SGer*) **benütz|en** *vt* use; take (*Bahn*). **B~er** *m* -s,- user. **b~erfreundlich** *a* user-friendly. **B~ung** *f* use

Benzin *nt* -s petrol, (*Amer*) gasoline. **B~tank** *m* petrol tank

beobacht|en *vt* observe. **B~er** *m* -s,- observer. **B~ung** *f* -,-en observation

bepacken *vt* load (**mit** with)

bepflanzen *vt* plant (**mit** with)

bequem *a* comfortable, *adv* -bly; (*mühelos*) easy, *adv* -ily; (*faul*) lazy. **b~en** (**sich**) *vr* deign (**zu** to). **B~lichkeit** *f* -,-en comfort; (*Faulheit*) laziness

berat|en† *vt* advise; (*überlegen*) discuss; **sich b~en** confer; **sich b~en lassen** get advice ● *vi* (*haben*) discuss (**über etw** *acc* sth); (*beratschlagen*) confer. **B~er** *m* -s,-, **B~erin** *f* -,-nen adviser. **b~schlagen** *vi* (*haben*) confer. **B~ung** *f* -,-en guidance; (*Rat*) advice; (*Besprechung*) discussion; (*Med, Jur*) consultation. **B~ungsstelle** *f* advice centre

berauben *vt* rob (*gen* of)

berauschen *vt* intoxicate. **b~d** *a* intoxicating, heady

berechn|en *vt* calculate; (*anrechnen*) charge for; (*abfordern*) charge. **b~end** *a* (*fig*) calculating. **B~ung** *f* calculation

berechtig|en *vt* entitle; (*befugen*) authorize; (*fig*) justify. **b~t** *a* justified, justifiable. **B~ung** *f* -,-en authorization; (*Recht*) right; (*Rechtmäßigkeit*) justification

bered|en *vt* talk about; (*klatschen*) gossip about; (*überreden*) talk round; **sich b~en** talk. **B~samkeit** *f* - eloquence

beredt *a* eloquent, *adv* -ly

Bereich *m* -[e]s,-e area; (*fig*) realm; (*Fach-*) field

bereichern *vi* enrich; **sich b~** grow rich (**an** + *dat* on)

Bereifung *f* - tyres *pl*

bereinigen *vt* (*fig*) settle

bereit *a* ready. **b~en** *vt* prepare; (*verursachen*) cause; give (*Überraschung*). **b~halten†** *vt sep* have/ (*ständig*) keep ready. **b~legen** *vt sep* put out [ready]. **b~machen** *vt sep* get ready; **sich b~machen** get ready. **b~s** *adv* already

Bereitschaft *f* -,-en readiness; (*Einheit*) squad. **B~sdienst** *m* **B~sdienst haben** (*Mil*) be on standby; 〈*Arzt:*〉 be on call; 〈*Apotheke:*〉 be open for out-of-hours dispensing. **B~spolizei** *f* riot police

bereit|stehen† *vi sep* (*haben*) be ready. **b~stellen** *vt sep* put out ready; (*verfügbar machen*) make available. **B~ung** *f* - preparation. **b~willig** *a* willing, *adv* -ly. **B~willigkeit** *f* - willingness

bereuen *vt* regret

Berg *m* -[e]s,-e mountain; (*Anhöhe*) hill; **in den B~en** in the mountains. **b~ab** *adv* downhill. **b~an** *adv* uphill. **B~arbeiter** *m* miner. **b~auf** *adv* uphill; **es geht b~auf** (*fig*) things are looking up. **B~bau** *m* -[e]s mining

bergen† *vt* recover; (*Naut*) salvage; (*retten*) rescue

Berg|führer *m* mountain guide. **b~ig** *a* mountainous. **B~kette** *f* mountain range. **B~mann** *m* (*pl* -leute) miner. **B~steigen** *nt* -s mountaineering. **B~steiger(in)** *m* -s,- (*f* -,-nen) mountaineer, climber. **B~-und-Talbahn** *f* roller-coaster

Bergung *f* - recovery; (*Naut*) salvage; (*Rettung*) rescue

Berg|wacht *f* mountain rescue service. **B~werk** *nt* mine

Bericht *m* -[e]s,-e report; (*Reise-*) account; **B~ erstatten** report (**über** + *acc* on). **b~en** *vt/i* (*haben*) report;

(erzählen) tell **(von** of**)**. **B⁓erstat-ter(in)** *m* **-s,-** *(f* **-,-nen)** reporter; *(Korrespondent)* correspondent

berichtig|en *vt* correct. **B⁓ung** *f* **-,-en** correction

beriesel|n *vt* irrigate. **B⁓ungsan-lage** *f* sprinkler system

beritten *a* ⟨*Polizei*⟩ mounted

Berlin *nt* **-s** Berlin. **B⁓er** *m* **-s,-** Berliner; *(Culin)* doughnut ● *a* Berlin ...

Bernhardiner *m* **-s,-** St Bernard

Bernstein *m* amber

bersten† *vi* (sein) burst

berüchtigt *a* notorious

berückend *a* entrancing

berücksichtig|en *vt* take into con-sideration. **B⁓ung** *f* - consideration

Beruf *m* profession; *(Tätigkeit)* occu-pation; *(Handwerk)* trade. **b⁓en†** *vt* appoint; **sich b⁓en** refer **(auf** + *acc* to); *(vorgeben)* plead **(auf etw** *acc* sth) ● *a* competent; **b⁓en sein** be destined **(zu** to). **b⁓lich** *a* profes-sional; ⟨*Ausbildung*⟩ vocational ● *adv* professionally; **b⁓lich tätig sein** work, have a job. **B⁓saussicht-en** *fpl* career prospects. **B⁓sbera-ter(in)** *m(f)* careers officer. **B⁓sberatung** *f* vocational guid-ance. **b⁓smäßig** *adv* professionally. **B⁓sschule** *f* vocational school. **B⁓ssoldat** *m* regular soldier. **b⁓stätig** *a* working; **b⁓stätig sein** work, have a job. **B⁓stätige(r)** *m|f* working man/woman. **B⁓sverkehr** *m* rush-hour traffic. **B⁓ung** *f* **-,-en** appointment; *(Bestimmung)* vo-cation; *(Jur)* appeal; **B⁓ung einle-gen** appeal. **B⁓ungsgericht** *nt* ap-peal court

beruhen *vi* (haben) be based **(auf** + *dat* on); **eine Sache auf sich b⁓ las-sen** let a matter rest

beruhig|en *vt* calm [down]; *(zuver-sichtlich machen)* reassure; **sich b⁓en** calm down. **b⁓end** *a* calming; *(tröstend)* reassuring; *(Med)* seda-tive. **B⁓ung** *f* - calming; reassur-ance; *(Med)* sedation. **B⁓ungsmit-tel** *nt* sedative; *(bei Psychosen)* tranquillizer

berühmt *a* famous. **B⁓heit** *f* **-,-en** fame; *(Person)* celebrity

berühr|en *vt* touch; *(erwähnen)* touch on; *(beeindrucken)* affect; **sich b⁓en** touch. **B⁓ung** *f* **-,-en** touch; *(Kontakt)* contact

besag|en *vt* say; *(bedeuten)* mean. **b⁓t** *a* [afore]said

besänftigen *vt* soothe; **sich b⁓** calm down

Besatz *m* **-es,⁓e** trimming

Besatzung *f* **-,-en** crew; *(Mil)* occupy-ing force

besaufen† (**sich**) *vr* *(sl)* get drunk

beschädig|en *vt* damage. **B⁓ung** *f* **-,-en** damage

beschaffen *vt* obtain, get ● *a* **so b⁓ sein, daß** be such that; **wie ist es b⁓ mit?** what about? **B⁓heit** *f* - consist-ency; *(Art)* nature

beschäftig|en *vt* occupy; ⟨*Arbeit-geber:*⟩ employ; **sich b⁓en** occupy oneself. **b⁓t** *a* busy; *(angestellt)* em-ployed **(bei** at). **B⁓te(r)** *m|f* em-ployee. **B⁓ung** *f* **-,-en** occupation; *(Anstellung)* employment. **b⁓ungs-los** *a* unemployed. **B⁓ungstherapie** *f* occupational therapy

beschäm|en *vt* make ashamed. **b⁓end** *a* shameful; *(demütigend)* humiliating. **b⁓t** *a* ashamed; *(verle-gen)* embarrassed

beschatten *vt* shade; *(überwachen)* shadow

beschau|en *vt* (SGer) [**sich** *(dat)*] **etw b⁓en** look at sth. **b⁓lich** *a* tranquil; *(Relig)* contemplative

Bescheid *m* **-[e]s** information; **jdm B⁓ sagen** *od* **geben** let s.o. know; **B⁓ wissen** know

bescheiden *a* modest, *adv* -ly. **B⁓heit** *f* - modesty

bescheinen† *vt* shine on; **von der Sonne beschienen** sunlit

bescheinig|en *vt* certify. **B⁓ung** *f* **-,-en** [written] confirmation; *(Schein)* certificate

beschenken *vt* give a present/pre-sents to

bescher|en *vt* **jdn b⁓en** give s.o. presents; **jdm etw b⁓en** give s.o. sth. **B⁓ung** *f* **-,-en** distribution of Christmas presents; *(fam: Schla-massel)* mess

beschießen† *vt* fire at; *(mit Artil-lerie)* shell, bombard

beschild|ern *vt* signpost

beschimpf|en *vt* abuse, swear at. **B⁓ung** *f* **-,-en** abuse

beschirmen *vt* protect

Beschlag *m* **in B⁓ nehmen, mit B⁓ belegen** monopolize. **b⁓en†** *vt* shoe ● *vi* (sein) steam *or* mist up ● *a* steamed *or* misted up; *(erfahren)* knowledgeable **(in** + *dat* about).

B∼nahme *f* -,-n confiscation; (*Jur*) seizure. **b∼nahmen** *vt* confiscate; (*Jur*) seize; (*fam*) monopolize

beschleunig|en *vt* hasten; (*schneller machen*) speed up; quicken ⟨*Schritt, Tempo*⟩; **sich b∼en** speed up; quicken ● *vi* (*haben*) accelerate. **B∼ung** *f* acceleration

beschließen† *vt* decide; (*beenden*) end ● *vi* (*haben*) decide (**über** + *acc* about)

Beschluß *m* decision

beschmieren *vt* smear/(*bestreichen*) spread (**mit** with)

beschmutzen *vt* make dirty; **sich b∼** get [oneself] dirty

beschneid|en† *vt* trim; (*Hort*) prune; (*fig: kürzen*) cut back; (*Relig*) circumcise. **B∼ung** *f* - circumcision

beschneit *a* snow-covered

beschnüffeln, beschnuppern *vt* sniff at

beschönigen *vt* (*fig*) gloss over

beschränken *vt* limit, restrict; **sich b∼ auf** (+ *acc*) confine oneself to; ⟨*Sache:*⟩ be limited to

beschrankt *a* ⟨*Bahnübergang*⟩ with barrier[s]

beschränk|t *a* limited; (*geistig*) dull-witted; (*borniert*) narrow-minded. **B∼ung** *f* -,-en limitation, restriction

beschreib|en† *vt* describe; (*schreiben*) write on. **B∼ung** *f* -,-en description

beschuldig|en *vt* accuse. **B∼ung** *f* -,-en accusation

beschummeln *vt* (*fam*) cheat

Beschuß *m* -sses (*Mil*) fire; (*Artillerie-*) shelling

beschütz|en *vt* protect. **B∼er** *m* -s,- protector

Beschwer|de *f* -,-n complaint; **B∼den** (*Med*) trouble *sg*. **b∼en** *vt* weight down; **sich b∼en** complain. **b∼lich** *a* difficult

beschwichtigen *vt* placate

beschwindeln *vt* cheat (**um** out of); (*belügen*) lie to

beschwingt *a* elated; (*munter*) lively

beschwipst *a* (*fam*) tipsy

beschwören† *vt* swear to; (*anflehen*) implore; (*herauf-*) invoke

besehen† *vt* look at

beseitig|en *vt* remove. **B∼ung** *f* - removal

Besen *m* -s,- broom. **B∼ginster** *m* (*Bot*) broom. **B∼stiel** *m* broomstick

besessen *a* obsessed (**von** by)

besetz|en *vt* occupy; fill ⟨*Posten*⟩; (*Theat*) cast ⟨*Rolle*⟩; (*verzieren*) trim (**mit** with). **b∼t** *a* occupied; ⟨*Toilette, Leitung*⟩ engaged; ⟨*Zug, Bus*⟩ full up; **der Platz ist b∼t** this seat is taken; **mit Perlen b∼t** set with pearls. **B∼tzeichen** *nt* engaged tone. **B∼ung** *f* -,-en occupation; (*Theat*) cast

besichtig|en *vt* look round ⟨*Stadt, Museum*⟩; (*prüfen*) inspect; (*besuchen*) visit. **B∼ung** *f* -,-en visit; (*Prüfung*) inspection; (*Stadt-*) sightseeing

besiedelt *a* **dünn/dicht b∼** sparsely/densely populated

besiegeln *vt* (*fig*) seal

besieg|en *vt* defeat; (*fig*) overcome. **B∼te(r)** *m*/*f* loser

besinn|en† (**sich**) *vr* think, reflect; (*sich erinnern*) remember (**auf jdn/etw** s.o./sth); **sich anders b∼en** change one's mind. **b∼lich** *a* contemplative; (*nachdenklich*) thoughtful. **B∼ung** *f* - reflection; (*Bewußtsein*) consciousness; **bei/ohne B∼ung** conscious/unconscious; **zur B∼ung kommen** regain consciousness; (*fig*) come to one's senses. **b∼ungslos** *a* unconscious

Besitz *m* possession; (*Eigentum, Land-*) property; (*Gut*) estate. **b∼anzeigend** *a* (*Gram*) possessive. **b∼en**† *vt* own, possess; (*haben*) have. **B∼er(in)** *m* -s,- (*f* -,-nen) owner; (*Comm*) proprietor. **B∼ung** *f* -,-en [landed] property; (*Gut*) estate

besoffen *a* (*sl*) drunken; **b∼ sein** be drunk

besohlen *vt* sole

besold|en *vt* pay. **B∼ung** *f* - pay

besonder|e(r,s) *a* special; (*bestimmt*) particular; (*gesondert*) separate; **nichts B∼es** nothing special. **B∼heit** *f* -,-en peculiarity. **b∼s** *adv* [e]specially, particularly; (*gesondert*) separately

besonnen *a* calm, *adv* -ly

besorg|en *vt* get; (*kaufen*) buy; (*erledigen*) attend to; (*versorgen*) look after. **B∼nis** *f* -,-se anxiety; (*Sorge*) worry. **b∼niserregend** *a* worrying. **b∼t** *a* worried/(*bedacht*) concerned (**um** about). **B∼ung** *f* -,-en errand; **B∼ungen machen** do shopping

bespielt *a* recorded

bespitzeln *vt* spy on

besprech|en† *vt* discuss; (*rezensieren*) review; **sich b∼en** confer;

ein Tonband b~en make a tape recording. **B~ung** f -,-en discussion; review; (Konferenz) meeting

bespritzen vt splash

besser a & adv better. **b~n** vt improve; **sich b~n** get better, improve. **B~ung** f - improvement; **gute B~ung!** get well soon! **B~wisser** m -s,- know-all

Bestand m -[e]s,-̈e existence; (Vorrat) stock (**an**+dat of); **B~ haben, von B~ sein** last

beständig a constant, adv -ly; ⟨Wetter⟩ settled; **b~ gegen** resistant to

Bestand|saufnahme f stock-taking. **B~teil** m part

bestärken vt (fig) strengthen

bestätig|en vt confirm; acknowledge ⟨Empfang⟩; **sich b~en** prove to be true. **B~ung** f -,-en confirmation

bestatt|en vt bury. **B~ung** f -,-en funeral. **B~ungsinstitut** nt [firm of] undertakers pl, (Amer) funeral home

bestäuben vt pollinate

bestaubt a dusty

Bestäubung f - pollination

bestaunen vt gaze at in amazement; (bewundern) admire

best|e(r,s) a best; **b~en Dank!** many thanks! **am b~en sein** be best; **zum b~en geben** recite ⟨Gedicht⟩; tell ⟨Geschichte, Witz⟩; sing ⟨Lied⟩; **jdn zum b~en halten** (fam) pull s.o.'s leg. **B~e(r,s)** m/f/nt best; **sein B~es tun** do one's best; **zum B~en der Armen** for the benefit of the poor

bestech|en† vt bribe; (bezaubern) captivate. **b~end** a captivating. **b~lich** a corruptible. **B~ung** f - bribery. **B~ungsgeld** nt bribe

Besteck nt -[e]s,-e [set of] knife, fork and spoon; (coll) cutlery

besteh|en† vi (haben) exist; (fortdauern) last; (bei Prüfung) pass; **b~ aus** consist/(gemacht sein) be made of; **b~ auf** (+dat) insist on ● vt pass ⟨Prüfung⟩. **B~** nt -s existence

bestehlen† vt rob

besteig|en† vt climb; (einsteigen) board; (aufsteigen) mount; ascend ⟨Thron⟩. **B~ung** f ascent

bestell|en vt order; (vor-) book; (ernennen) appoint; (bebauen) cultivate; (ausrichten) tell; **zu sich b~en** send for; **b~t sein** have an appointment; **kann ich etwas b~en?** can I take a message? **b~en Sie Ihrer Frau Grüße von mir** give my regards to your wife. **B~schein** m order form. **B~ung** f order; (Botschaft) message; (Bebauung) cultivation

besten|falls adv at best. **b~s** adv very well

besteuer|n vt tax. **B~ung** f - taxation

bestialisch /-st-/ a bestial

Bestie /'bɛstjə/ f -,-n beast

bestimm|en vt fix; (entscheiden) decide; (vorsehen) intend; (ernennen) appoint; (ermitteln) determine; (definieren) define; (Gram) qualify ● vi (haben) be in charge (**über**+acc of). **b~t** a definite, adv -ly; (gewiß) certain, adv -ly; (fest) firm, adv -ly. **B~theit** f- firmness; **mit B~theit** for certain. **B~ung** f fixing; (Vorschrift) regulation; (Ermittlung) determination; (Definition) definition; (Zweck) purpose; (Schicksal) destiny. **B~ungsort** m destination

Bestleistung f (Sport) record

bestraf|en vt punish. **B~ung** f -,-en punishment

bestrahl|en vt shine on; (Med) treat with radiotherapy; irradiate ⟨Lebensmittel⟩. **B~ung** f radiotherapy

Bestreb|en nt -s endeavour; (Absicht) aim. **b~t** a **b~t sein** endeavour (**zu** to). **B~ung** f -,-en effort

bestreichen† vt spread (**mit** with)

bestreikt a strike-hit

bestreiten† vt dispute; (leugnen) deny; (bezahlen) pay for

bestreuen vt sprinkle (**mit** with)

bestürmen vt (fig) besiege

bestürz|t a dismayed; (erschüttert) stunned. **B~ung** f - dismay, consternation

Bestzeit f (Sport) record [time]

Besuch m -[e]s,-e visit; (kurz) call; (Schul-) attendance; (Gast) visitor; (Gäste) visitors pl; **b~ haben** have a visitor/visitors; **bei jdm zu od auf B~ sein** be staying with s.o. **b~en** vt visit; (kurz) call on; (teilnehmen) attend; go to ⟨Schule, Ausstellung⟩; **gut b~t** well attended. **B~er(in)** m -s,- (f -,-nen) visitor; caller; (Theat) patron. **B~szeit** f visiting hours pl

betagt a aged, old

betasten vt feel

betätig|en vt operate; **sich b~en** work (**als** as); **sich politisch b~en** engage in politics. **B~ung** f -,-en operation; (Tätigkeit) activity

betäub|en vt stun; ⟨Lärm:⟩ deafen; (Med) anaesthetize; (lindern) ease; deaden ⟨Schmerz⟩; **wie b~t** dazed.

B~ung f - daze; (*Med*) anaesthesia; unter örtlicher **B~ung** under local anaesthetic. **B~ungsmittel** *nt* anaesthetic

Bete f -,-n rote **B~** beetroot

beteilig|en *vt* give a share to; **sich b~en** take part (**an** + *dat* in); (*beitragen*) contribute (**an** + *dat* to). **b~t** *a* **b~t sein** take part/(*an Unfall*) be involved/(*Comm*) have a share (**an** + *dat* in); **alle B~ten** all those involved. **B~ung** f -,-en participation; (*Anteil*) share

beten *vi* (*haben*) pray; (*bei Tisch*) say grace ● *vt* say

beteuer|n *vt* protest. **B~ung** f -,-en protestation

Beton /be'tõ/ *m* -s concrete

betonen *vt* stress, emphasize

betonieren *vt* concrete

beton|t *a* stressed; (*fig*) pointed, *adv* -ly. **B~ung** f -,-en stress, emphasis

betören *vt* bewitch

betr., Betr. *abbr* (**betreffs**) re

Betracht *m* in **B~ ziehen** consider; **außer B~ lassen** disregard; **nicht in B~ kommen** be out of the question. **b~en** *vt* look at; (*fig*) regard (**als** as)

beträchtlich *a* considerable, *adv* -bly

Betrachtung f -,-en contemplation; (*Überlegung*) reflection

Betrag *m*-[e]s,¨e amount. **b~en†** *vt* amount to; **sich b~en** behave. **B~en** *nt* -s behaviour; (*Sch*) conduct

betrauen *vt* entrust (**mit** with)

betrauern *vt* mourn

betreff|en† *vt* affect; (*angehen*) concern; **was mich betrifft** as far as I am concerned. **b~end** *a* relevant; **der b~ende Brief** the letter in question. **b~s** *prep* (+ *gen*) concerning

betreiben† *vt* (*leiten*) run; (*ausüben*) carry on; (*vorantreiben*) pursue; (*antreiben*) run (**mit** on)

betreten† *vt* step on; (*eintreten*) enter; 'B~ verboten' 'no entry'; (*bei Rasen*) 'keep off [the grass]' ● *a* embarrassed ● *adv* in embarrassment

betreu|en *vt* look after. **B~er(in)** *m* -s,- (f -,-nen) helper; (*Kranken-*) nurse. **B~ung** f - care

Betrieb *m* business; (*Firma*) firm; (*Treiben*) activity; (*Verkehr*) traffic; **in B~** working; (*in Gebrauch*) in use; **außer B~** not in use; (*defekt*) out of order

Betriebs|anleitung, B~anweisung f operating instructions pl.

B~ferien pl firm's holiday; 'B~ferien' 'closed for the holidays'. **B~leitung** f management. **B~rat** *m* works committee. **B~ruhe** f 'montags **B~ruhe**' 'closed on Mondays'. **B~störung** f breakdown

betrinken† (sich) *vr* get drunk

betroffen *a* disconcerted; **b~ sein** be affected (**von** by); **die B~en** those affected ● *adv* in consternation

betrüb|en *vt* sadden. **b~lich** *a* sad. **b~t** *a* sad, *adv* -ly

Betrug *m* -[e]s deception; (*Jur*) fraud

betrüg|en† *vt* cheat, swindle; (*Jur*) defraud; (*in der Ehe*) be unfaithful to; **sich selbst b~en** deceive oneself. **B~er(in)** *m* -s,- (f -,-nen) swindler. **B~erei** f -,-en fraud. **b~erisch** *a* fraudulent; (*Person*) deceitful

betrunken *a* drunken; **b~ sein** be drunk. **B~e(r)** *m* drunk

Bett *nt* -[e]s,-en bed; **im B~** in bed; **ins od zu B~ gehen** go to bed. **B~couch** f sofa-bed. **B~decke** f blanket; (*Tages-*) bedspread

bettel|arm *a* destitute. **B~ei** f - begging. **b~n** *vi* (*haben*) beg

bett|en *vt* lay, put; **sich b~en** lie down. **b~lägerig** *a* bedridden. **B~laken** *nt* sheet

Bettler(in) *m* -s,- (f -,-nen) beggar

Bettpfanne f bedpan

Bettuch *nt* sheet

Bett|vorleger *m* bedside rug. **B~wäsche** f bed linen. **B~zeug** *nt* bedding

betupfen *vt* dab (**mit** with)

beug|en *vt* bend; (*Gram*) decline; conjugate (*Verb*); **sich b~en** bend; (*lehnen*) lean; (*sich fügen*) submit (**dat** to). **B~ung** f -,-en (*Gram*) declension; conjugation

Beule f -,-n bump; (*Delle*) dent

beunruhig|en *vt* worry; **sich b~en** worry. **B~ung** f - worry

beurlauben *vt* give leave to; (*des Dienstes entheben*) suspend

beurteil|en *vt* judge. **B~ung** f -,-en judgement; (*Ansicht*) opinion

Beute f - booty, haul; (*Jagd-*) bag; (*B~tier*) quarry; (*eines Raubtiers*) prey

Beutel *m* -s,- bag; (*Geld-*) purse; (*Tabak-* & *Zool*) pouch. **B~tier** *nt* marsupial

bevölker|n *vt* populate. **B~ung** f -,-en population

bevollmächtig|en *vt* authorize. **B~te(r)** *m*/f [authorized] agent

bevor *conj* before; **b~ nicht** until
bevormunden *vt* treat like a child
bevorstehen† *vi sep* (*haben*) approach; (*unmittelbar*) be imminent; **jdm b~** be in store for s.o. **b~d** *a* approaching, forthcoming; **unmittelbar b~d** imminent
bevorzug|en *vt* prefer; (*begünstigen*) favour. **b~t** *a* privileged; ⟨*Behandlung*⟩ preferential; (*beliebt*) favoured
bewachen *vt* guard; **bewachter Parkplatz** car park with an attendant
bewachsen *a* covered (**mit** with)
Bewachung *f* - guard; **unter B~** under guard
bewaffn|en *vt* arm. **b~et** *a* armed. **B~ung** *f* - armament; (*Waffen*) arms *pl*
bewahren *vt* protect (**vor** + *dat* from); (*behalten*) keep; **die Ruhe b~** keep calm; **Gott bewahre!** heaven forbid!
bewähren (sich) *vr* prove one's/ ⟨*Ding:*⟩ its worth; (*erfolgreich sein*) prove a success
bewahrheiten (sich) *vr* prove to be true
bewähr|t *a* reliable; (*erprobt*) proven. **B~ung** *f* - (*Jur*) probation. **B~ungsfrist** *f* [period of] probation. **B~ungsprobe** *f* (*fig*) test
bewaldet *a* wooded
bewältigen *vt* cope with; (*überwinden*) overcome; (*schaffen*) manage
bewandert *a* knowledgeable
bewässer|n *vt* irrigate. **B~ung** *f* - irrigation
bewegen¹ *vt* (*reg*) move; **sich b~** move; (*körperlich*) take exercise
bewegen²† *vt* **jdn dazu b~,** **etw zu tun** induce s.o. to do sth
Beweg|grund *m* motive. **b~lich** *a* movable, mobile; (*wendig*) agile. **B~lichkeit** *f* - mobility; agility. **b~t** *a* moved; (*ereignisreich*) eventful; ⟨*See*⟩ rough. **B~ung** *f* -,-en movement; (*Phys*) motion; (*Rührung*) emotion; (*Gruppe*) movement; **körperliche B~ung** physical exercise; **sich in B~ung setzen** [start to] move. **B~ungsfreiheit** *f* freedom of movement/(*fig*) of action. **b~ungslos** *a* motionless
beweinen *vt* mourn
Beweis *m* -es,-e proof; (*Zeichen*) token; **B~e** evidence *sg.* **b~en†** *vt* prove; (*zeigen*) show; **sich b~en**

prove oneself/⟨*Ding:*⟩ itself. **B~material** *nt* evidence
bewenden *vi* **es dabei b~ lassen** leave it at that
bewerb|en† (**sich**) *vr* apply (**um** for; **bei** to). **B~er(in)** *m* -s,- (*f* -,-nen) applicant. **B~ung** *f* -,-en application
bewerkstelligen *vt* manage
bewerten *vt* value; (*einschätzen*) rate; (*Sch*) mark, grade
bewilligen *vt* grant
bewirken *vt* cause; (*herbeiführen*) bring about; (*erreichen*) achieve
bewirt|en *vt* entertain. **B~ung** *f* - hospitality
bewohn|bar *a* habitable. **b~en** *vt* inhabit, live in. **B~er(in)** *m* -s,- (*f* -,-nen) resident, occupant; (*Einwohner*) inhabitant
bewölk|en (**sich**) *vr* cloud over; **b~t** cloudy. **B~ung** *f* - clouds *pl*
bewunder|n *vt* admire. **b~nswert** *a* admirable. **B~ung** *f* - admiration
bewußt *a* conscious (*gen*); (*absichtlich*) deliberate, *adv* -ly; (*besagt*) said; **sich** (*dat*) **etw** (*gen*) **b~ sein/werden** be/become aware of sth. **b~los** *a* unconscious. **B~losigkeit** *f* - unconsciousness. **B~sein** *n* -s consciousness; (*Gewißheit*) awareness; **bei [vollem] B~sein** [fully] conscious; **mir kam zum B~sein** I realized (**daß** that)
bez. *abbr* (**bezahlt**) paid; (**bezüglich**) re
bezahl|en *vt/i* (*haben*) pay; pay for ⟨*Ware, Essen*⟩; **sich b~t machen** (*fig*) pay off. **B~ung** *f* - payment; (*Lohn*) pay
bezähmen *vt* control; (*zügeln*) restrain; **sich b~** restrain oneself
bezaubern *vt* enchant. **b~d** *a* enchanting
bezeichn|en *vt* mark; (*bedeuten*) denote; (*beschreiben, nennen*) describe (**als** as). **b~end** *a* typical. **B~ung** *f* marking; (*Beschreibung*) description (**als** as); (*Ausdruck*) term; (*Name*) name
bezeugen *vt* testify to
bezichtigen *vt* accuse (*gen* of)
bezieh|en† *vt* cover; (*einziehen*) move into; (*beschaffen*) obtain; (*erhalten*) get, receive; take ⟨*Zeitung*⟩; (*in Verbindung bringen*) relate (**auf** + *acc* to); **sich b~en** (*bewölken*) cloud over; **sich b~en auf** (+ *acc*) refer to; **das Bett frisch b~en** put clean sheets on the bed. **B~ung** *f*

-,-en relation; (*Verhältnis*) relationship; (*Bezug*) respect; **in dieser B~ung** in this respect; **[gute] B~ungen haben** have [good] connections. **b~ungsweise** *adv* respectively; (*vielmehr*) or rather

beziffern (sich) *vr* amount (**auf** + *acc* to)

Bezirk *m* -[e]s,-e district

Bezug *m* cover; (*Kissen-*) case; (*Beschaffung*) obtaining; (*Kauf*) purchase; (*Zusammenhang*) reference; **B~e** *pl* earnings; **B~ nehmen** refer (**auf** + *acc* to); **in b~ auf** (+ *acc*) regarding, concerning

bezüglich *prep* (+ *gen*) regarding, concerning ● *a* relating (**auf** + *acc* to); (*Gram*) relative

bezwecken *vt* (*fig*) aim at

bezweifeln *vt* doubt

bezwingen† *vt* conquer

BH /be:'ha:/ *m* -[s],-[s] bra

bibbern *vi* (*haben*) tremble; (*vor Kälte*) shiver

Bibel *f* -,-n Bible

Biber[1] *m* -s,- beaver

Biber[2] *m & nt* -s flannelette

Biblio|graphie *f* -,-n bibliography. **B~thek** *f* -,-en library. **B~thekar(in)** *m* -s,- (*f* -,-nen) librarian

biblisch *a* biblical

bieder *a* honest, upright; (*ehrenwert*) worthy; (*einfach*) simple

biegen† *vt* bend; **sich b~en** bend; **sich vor Lachen b~en** (*fam*) double up with laughter ● *vi* (*sein*) curve (**nach** to); **um die Ecke b~en** turn the corner. **b~sam** *a* flexible, supple. **B~ung** *f* -,-en bend

Biene *f* -,-n bee. **B~nhonig** *m* natural honey. **B~nstock** *m* beehive. **B~nwabe** *f* honeycomb

Bier *nt* -s,-e beer. **B~deckel** *m* beermat. **B~krug** *m* beer-mug

Biest *nt* -[e]s,-er (*fam*) beast

bieten† *vt* offer; (*bei Auktion*) bid; (*zeigen*) present; **das lasse ich mir nicht b~** I won't stand for that

Bifokalbrille *f* bifocals *pl*

Biga|mie *f* - bigamy. **B~mist** *m* -en,-en bigamist

bigott *a* over-pious

Bikini *m* -s,-s bikini

Bilanz *f* -,-en balance sheet; (*fig*) result; **die B~ ziehen** (*fig*) draw conclusions (**aus** from)

Bild *nt* -[e]s,-er picture; (*Theat*) scene; **jdn ins B~ setzen** put s.o. in the picture

bilden *vt* form; (*sein*) be; (*erziehen*) educate; **sich b~** form; (*geistig*) educate oneself

Bild|erbuch *nt* picture-book. **B~ergalerie** *f* picture gallery. **B~fläche** *f* screen; **von der B~fläche verschwinden** disappear from the scene. **B~hauer** *m* -s,- sculptor. **B~hauerei** *f* - sculpture. **b~hübsch** *a* very pretty. **b~lich** *a* pictorial; (*figurativ*) figurative, *adv* -ly. **B~nis** *nt* -ses,-se portrait. **B~schirm** *m* (*TV*) screen. **B~schirmgerät** *nt* visual display unit, VDU. **b~schön** *a* very beautiful

Bildung *f* - formation; (*Erziehung*) education; (*Kultur*) culture

Billard /'bɪljart/ *nt* -s billiards *sg*. **B~tisch** *m* billiard table

Billett /bɪl'jɛt/ *nt* -[e]s,-e & -s ticket

Billiarde *f* -,-n thousand million million

billig *a* cheap, *adv* -ly; (*dürftig*) poor; (*gerecht*) just; **recht und b~** right and proper. **b~en** *vt* approve. **B~ung** *f* - approval

Billion /bɪl'jo:n/ *f* -,-en million million, billion

bimmeln *vi* (*haben*) tinkle

Bimsstein *m* pumice stone

bin *s.* **sein; ich bin** I am

Binde *f* -,-n band; (*Verband*) bandage; (*Damen-*) sanitary towel. **B~hautentzündung** *f* conjunctivitis. **b~n†** *vt* tie (**an** + *acc* to); make ⟨*Strauß*⟩; bind ⟨*Buch*⟩; (*fesseln*) tie up; (*Culin*) thicken; **sich b~n** commit oneself. **b~nd** *a* (*fig*) binding. **B~strich** *m* hyphen. **B~wort** *nt* (*pl* -wörter) (*Gram*) conjunction

Bind|faden *m* string; **ein B~faden a** piece of string. **B~ung** *f* -,-en (*fig*) tie, bond; (*Beziehung*) relationship; (*Verpflichtung*) commitment; (*Ski-*) binding; (*Tex*) weave

binnen *prep* (+ *dat*) within; **b~ kurzem** shortly. **B~handel** *m* home trade

Binse *f* -,-n (*Bot*) rush. **B~nwahrheit, B~nweisheit** *f* truism

Bio- *pref* organic

Bio|chemie *f* biochemistry. **b~dynamisch** *m* organic

Bio|graphie *f* -,-n biography

Bio|hof *m* organic farm. **B~laden** *m* health-food store

Biolog|e *m* -n,-n biologist. **B~ie** *f* - biology. **b~isch** *a* biological, *adv* -ly;

b~ischer Anbau organic farming; **b~isch angebaut** organically grown

Birke f -,-n birch [tree]

Birm|a nt -s Burma. **b~anisch** a Burmese

Birn|baum m pear-tree. **B~e** f -,-n pear; (Electr) bulb

bis prep (+acc) as far as, [up] to; (zeitlich) until, till; (spätestens) by; **bis zu** up to; **bis jetzt** up to now, so far; **bis dahin** until/(spätestens) by then; **bis auf** (+acc) (einschließlich) [down] to; (ausgenommen) except [for]; **drei bis vier Mark** three to four marks; **bis morgen!** see you tomorrow! ● conj until

Bischof m -s,-̈e bishop

bisher adv so far, up to now. **b~ig** attrib a (Präsident) outgoing; **meine b~igen Erfahrungen** my experiences so far

Biskuit|rolle /bɪsˈkviːt-/ f Swiss roll. **B~teig** m sponge mixture

bislang adv so far, up to now

Biß m -sses,-sse bite

bißchen inv pron **ein b~** a bit, a little; **ein b~ Brot** a bit of bread; **kein b~** not a bit

Biss|en m -s,- bite, mouthful. **b~ig** a vicious; (fig) caustic

bist s. sein; **du b~** you are

Bistum nt -s,-̈er diocese, see

bisweilen adv from time to time

bitt|e adv please; (nach Klopfen) come in; (als Antwort auf 'danke') don't mention it, you're welcome; **wie b~e?** pardon? (empört) I beg your pardon? **möchten Sie Kaffee?—ja b~e** would you like some coffee?—yes please. **B~e** f -,-n request/(dringend) plea (um for). **b~en†** vt/i (haben) ask/(dringend) beg (um for); (einladen) invite, ask; **ich b~e dich!** I beg [of] you! (empört) I ask you! **b~end** a pleading, adv -ly

bitter a bitter, adv -ly. **B~keit** f - bitterness. **b~lich** adv bitterly

Bittschrift f petition

bizarr a bizarre, adv -ly

bläh|en vt swell; puff out (Vorhang); **sich b~en** swell; (Vorhang, Segel:) billow ● vi (haben) cause flatulence. **B~ungen** fpl flatulence sg, (fam) wind sg

Blamage /blaˈmaːʒə/ f -,-n humiliation; (Schande) disgrace

blamieren vt disgrace; **sich b~** disgrace oneself; (sich lächerlich machen) make a fool of oneself

blanchieren /blãˈʃiːrən/ vt (Culin) blanch

blank a shiny; (nackt) bare; **b~ sein** (fam) be broke. **B~oscheck** m blank cheque

Blase f -,-n bubble; (Med) blister; (Anat) bladder. **B~balg** m -[e]s,-̈e bellows pl. **b~n†** vt/i (haben) blow; play (Flöte). **B~nentzündung** f cystitis

Bläser m -s,- (Mus) wind player; **die B~** the wind section sg

blasiert a blasé

Blas|instrument nt wind instrument. **B~kapelle** f brass band

Blasphemie f - blasphemy

blaß a (blasser, blassest) pale; (schwach) faint; **b~ werden** turn pale

Blässe f - pallor

Blatt nt -[e]s,-̈er (Bot) leaf; (Papier) sheet; (Zeitung) paper; **kein B~ vor den Mund nehmen** (fig) not mince one's words

blätter|n vi (haben) **b~n in** (+dat) leaf through. **B~teig** m puff pastry

Blattlaus f greenfly

blau a, **B~** nt -s,- blue; **b~er Fleck** bruise; **b~es Auge** black eye; **b~ sein** (fam) be tight; **Fahrt ins B~e** mystery tour. **B~beere** f bilberry. **B~licht** nt blue flashing light. **b~machen** vi sep (haben) (fam) skive off work

Blech nt -[e]s,-e sheet metal; (Weiß-) tin; (Platte) metal sheet; (Back-) baking sheet; (Mus) brass; (fam: Unsinn) rubbish. **b~en** vt/i (haben) (fam) pay. **B~(blas)instrument** nt brass instrument. **B~schaden** m (Auto) damage to the bodywork

Blei nt -[e]s lead

Bleibe f - place to stay. **b~n†** vi (sein) remain, stay; (übrig-) be left; **ruhig b~n** keep calm; **bei etw b~n** (fig) stick to sth; **b~n Sie am Apparat** hold the line. **b~nd** a permanent; (anhaltend) lasting. **b~nlassen†** vt sep **etw b~nlassen** not do sth; (aufhören) stop doing sth

bleich a pale. **b~en†** vi (sein) bleach; (ver-) fade ● vt (reg) bleach. **B~mittel** nt bleach

blei|ern a leaden. **b~frei** a unleaded. **B~stift** m pencil. **B~stiftabsatz** m stiletto heel. **B~stiftspitzer** m -s,- pencil-sharpener

Blende f -,-n shade, shield; (Sonnen-) [sun] visor; (Phot) diaphragm; (Öffnung) aperture; (an Kleid) facing. **b~n** vt dazzle, blind. **b~nd** a (fig) dazzling; (prima) marvellous, adv -ly

Blick m -[e]s,-e look; (kurz) glance; (Aussicht) view; **auf den ersten B~** at first sight; **einen B~ für etw haben** (fig) have an eye for sth. **b~en** vi (haben) look/(kurz) glance (**auf** + acc at). **B~punkt** m (fig) point of view

blind a blind; (trübe) dull; **b~er Alarm** false alarm; **b~er Passagier** stowaway. **B~darm** m appendix. **B~darmentzündung** f appendicitis. **B~e(r)** m/f blind man/woman; **die B~en** the blind pl. **B~enhund** m guide-dog. **B~enschrift** f braille. **B~-gänger** m -s,- (Mil) dud. **B~heit** f - blindness. **b~lings** adv (fig) blindly

blink|en vi (haben) flash; (funkeln) gleam; (Auto) indicate. **B~er** m -s,- (Auto) indicator. **B~licht** nt flashing light

blinzeln vi (haben) blink

Blitz m -[e]s,-e [flash of] lightning; (Phot) flash; **ein B~ aus heiterem Himmel** (fig) a bolt from the blue. **B~ableiter** m lightning-conductor. **b~artig** a lightning ... ● adv like lightning. **B~birne** f flashbulb. **b~en** vi (haben) flash; (funkeln) sparkle; **es hat geblitzt** there was a flash of lightning. **B~gerät** nt flash [unit]. **B~licht** nt (Phot) flash. **b~sauber** a spick and span. **b~schnell** a lightning ... ● adv like lightning. **B~strahl** m flash of lightning

Block m -[e]s,⸚e block ● -[e]s,-s & ⸚e (Schreib-) [note-]pad; (Häuser-) block; (Pol) bloc

Blockade f -,-n blockade

Blockflöte f recorder

blockieren vt block; (Mil) blockade

Blockschrift f block letters pl

blöd[e] a feeble-minded; (dumm) stupid, adv -ly

Blödsinn m -[e]s idiocy; (Unsinn) nonsense. **b~ig** a feeble-minded; (verrückt) idiotic

blöken vi (haben) bleat

blond a fair-haired; ⟨Haar⟩ fair. **B~ine** f -,-n blonde

bloß a bare; (alleinig) mere; **mit b~em Auge** with the naked eye

● adv only, just; **was mache ich b~?** whatever shall I do?

Blöße f -,-n nakedness; **sich** (dat) **eine B~ geben** (fig) show a weakness

bloß|legen vt sep uncover; **b~stellen** vt sep compromise; **sich b~stellen** show oneself up

Bluff m -s,-s bluff. **b~en** vt/i (haben) bluff

blühen vi (haben) flower; (fig) flourish. **b~d** a flowering; (fig) flourishing, thriving; ⟨Phantasie⟩ fertile

Blume f -,-n flower; (vom Wein) bouquet. **B~nbeet** n flower-bed. **B~ngeschäft** nt flower-shop, florist's [shop]. **B~nkohl** m cauliflower. **B~nmuster** nt floral design. **B~nstrauß** m bunch of flowers. **B~ntopf** m flowerpot; (Pflanze) [flowering] pot plant. **B~nzwiebel** f bulb

blumig a (fig) flowery

Bluse f -,-n blouse

Blut nt -[e]s blood. **b~arm** a anaemic. **B~bahn** f bloodstream. **b~befleckt** a blood-stained. **B~bild** nt blood count. **B~buche** f copper beech. **B~druck** m blood pressure. **b~dürstig** a bloodthirsty

Blüte f -,-n flower, bloom; (vom Baum) blossom; (B~zeit) flowering period; (Baum-) blossom time; (fig) flowering; (Höhepunkt) peak, prime; (fam: Banknote) forged note, (fam) dud

Blut|egel m -s,- leech. **b~en** vi (haben) bleed

Blüten|blatt nt petal. **B~staub** m pollen

Blut|er m -s,- haemophiliac. **B~erguß** m bruise. **B~gefäß** nt blood-vessel. **B~gruppe** f blood group. **B~hund** m bloodhound. **b~ig** a bloody. **b~jung** a very young. **B~körperchen** nt -s,- [blood] corpuscle. **B~probe** f blood test. **b~rünstig** a (fig) bloody, gory; ⟨Person⟩ bloodthirsty. **B~schande** f incest. **B~spender** m blood donor. **B~sturz** m haemorrhage. **B~sverwandte(r)** m/f blood relation. **B~transfusion, B~übertragung** f blood transfusion. **B~ung** f -,-en bleeding; (Med) haemorrhage; (Regel-) period. **b~unterlaufen** a bruised; ⟨Auge⟩ bloodshot. **B~vergießen** nt -s bloodshed. **B~vergiftung** f blood-poisoning. **B~wurst** f black pudding

Bö *f* -,-en gust; (*Regen-*) squall

Bob *m* -s,-s bob[-sleigh]

Bock *m* -[e]s,-̈e buck; (*Ziege*) billy goat; (*Schaf*) ram; (*Gestell*) support; **einen B~ schießen** (*fam*) make a blunder. **b~en** *vi* (*haben*) ⟨*Pferd:*⟩ buck; ⟨*Kind:*⟩ be stubborn. **b~ig** *a* (*fam*) stubborn. **B~springen** *nt* leap-frog

Boden *m* -s,-̈ ground; (*Erde*) soil; (*Fuß-*) floor; (*Grundfläche*) bottom; (*Dach-*) loft, attic. **B~kammer** *f* attic [room]. **b~los** *a* bottomless; (*fam*) incredible. **B~satz** *m* sediment. **B~schätze** *mpl* mineral deposits. **B~see** (der) Lake Constance

Bogen *m* -s,- & -̈ curve; (*Geom*) arc; (*beim Skilauf*) turn; (*Archit*) arch; (*Waffe, Geigen-*) bow; (*Papier*) sheet; **einen großen B~ um jdn/etw machen** (*fam*) give s.o./sth a wide berth. **B~gang** *m* arcade. **B~schießen** *nt* archery

Bohle *f* -,-n [thick] plank

Böhm|en *nt* -s Bohemia. **b~isch** *a* Bohemian

Bohne *f* -,-n bean; **grüne B~n** French beans. **B~nkaffee** *m* real coffee

bohner|n *vt* polish. **B~wachs** *nt* floor-polish

bohr|en *vt/i* (*haben*) drill (**nach** for); drive ⟨*Tunnel*⟩; sink ⟨*Brunnen*⟩; ⟨*Insekt:*⟩ bore; **in der Nase b~en** pick one's nose. **B~er** *m* -s,- drill. **B~insel** *f* [offshore] drilling rig. **B~maschine** *f* electric drill. **B~turm** *m* derrick

Boje *f* -,-n buoy

Böllerschuß *m* gun salute

Bolzen *m* -s,- bolt; (*Stift*) pin

bombardieren *vt* bomb; (*fig*) bombard (**mit** with)

bombastisch *a* bombastic

Bombe *f* -,-n bomb. **B~nangriff** *m* bombing raid. **B~nerfolg** *m* huge success. **B~r** *m* -s,- (*Aviat*) bomber

Bon /bɔŋ/ *m* -s,-s voucher; (*Kassen-*) receipt

Bonbon /bɔŋ'bɔŋ/ *m* & *nt* -s,-s sweet

Bonus *m* -[sses],-[sse] bonus

Boot *nt* -[e]s,-e boat. **B~ssteg** *m* landing-stage

Bord[1] *nt* -[e]s,-e shelf

Bord[2] *m* (*Naut*) **an B~** aboard, on board; **über B~** overboard. **B~buch** *nt* log[-book]

Bordell *nt* -s,-e brothel

Bord|karte *f* boarding-pass. **B~stein** *m* kerb

borgen *vt* borrow; **jdm etw b~** lend s.o. sth

Borke *f* -,-n bark

borniert *a* narrow-minded

Börse *f* -,-n purse; (*Comm*) stock exchange. **B~nmakler** *m* stockbroker

Borst|e *f* -,-n bristle. **b~ig** *a* bristly

Borte *f* -,-n braid

bösartig *a* vicious; (*Med*) malignant

Böschung *f* -,-en embankment; (*Hang*) slope

böse *a* wicked, evil; (*unartig*) naughty; (*schlimm*) bad, *adv* -ly; (*zornig*) cross; **jdm** *od* **auf jdn b~ sein** be cross with s.o. **B~wicht** *m* -[e]s,-e villain; (*Schlingel*) rascal

bos|haft *a* malicious, *adv* -ly; (*gehässig*) spiteful, *adv* -ly. **B~heit** *f* -,-en malice; spite; (*Handlung*) spiteful act/(*Bemerkung*) remark

böswillig *a* malicious, *adv* -ly. **B~keit** *f* - malice

Botani|k *f* - botany. **B~ker(in)** *m* -s,-(*f* -,-nen) botanist. **b~sch** *a* botanical

Bot|e *m* -n,-n messenger. **B~engang** *m* errand. **B~schaft** *f* -,-en message; (*Pol*) embassy. **B~schafter** *m* -s,- ambassador

Bottich *m* -[e]s,-e vat; (*Wasch-*) tub

Bouillon /bʊl'jɔŋ/ *f* -,-s clear soup. **B~würfel** *m* stock cube

Bowle /'boːlə/ *f* -,-n punch

box|en *vi* (*haben*) box ● *vt* punch. **B~en** *nt* -s boxing. **B~er** *m* -s,- boxer. **B~kampf** *m* boxing match; (*Boxen*) boxing

Boykott *m* -[e]s,-s boycott. **b~ieren** *vt* boycott; (*Comm*) black

brachliegen† *vi sep* (*haben*) lie fallow

Branche /'brãːʃə/ *f* -,-n [line of] business. **B~nverzeichnis** *nt* (*Teleph*) classified directory

Brand *m* -[e]s,-̈e fire; (*Med*) gangrene; (*Bot*) blight; **in B~ geraten** catch fire; **in B~ setzen** *od* **stecken** set on fire. **B~bombe** *f* incendiary bomb

branden *vi* (*haben*) surge; (*sich brechen*) break

Brand|geruch *m* smell of burning. **b~marken** *vt* (*fig*) brand. **B~stifter** *m* arsonist. **B~stiftung** *f* arson

Brandung *f* - surf. **B~sreiten** *nt* surfing

Brand|wunde *f* burn. **B~zeichen** *nt* brand

Branntwein m spirit; (coll) spirits pl. **B~brennerei** f distillery

bras|ilianisch a Brazilian. **B~ilien** /-jən/ nt -s Brazil

Brat|apfel m baked apple. **b~en†** vt/i (haben) roast; (in der Pfanne) fry. **B~en** m -s,- roast; (B~stück) joint. **B~ensoße** f gravy. **b~fertig** a oven-ready. **B~hähnchen**, **B~huhn** nt roast/(zum Braten) roasting chicken. **B~kartoffeln** fpl fried potatoes. **B~klops** m rissole. **B~pfanne** f frying-pan

Bratsche f -,-n (Mus) viola

Brat|spieß m spit. **B~wurst** f sausage for frying; (gebraten) fried sausage

Brauch m -[e]s,"e custom. **b~bar** a usable; (nützlich) useful. **b~en** vt need; (ge-, verbrauchen) use; take ⟨Zeit⟩; **er b~t es nur zu sagen** he only has to say; **du b~st nicht zu gehen** you needn't go

Braue f -,-n eyebrow

brau|en vt brew. **B~er** m -s,- brewer. **B~erei** f -,-en brewery

braun a, **B~** nt -s,- brown; **b~ werden** ⟨Person:⟩ get a tan

Bräune f- [sun-]tan. **b~n** vt/i (haben) brown; (in der Sonne) tan

braungebrannt a [sun-]tanned

Braunschweig nt -s Brunswick

Brause f -,-n (Dusche) shower; (an Gießkanne) rose; (B~limonade) fizzy drink. **b~n** vi (haben) roar; (duschen) shower ● vi (sein) rush [along] ● vr **sich b~n** shower. **b~nd** a roaring; (sprudelnd) effervescent

Braut f -,"e bride; (Verlobte) fiancée

Bräutigam m -s,-e bridegroom; (Verlobter) fiancé

Brautkleid nt wedding dress

bräutlich a bridal

Brautpaar nt bridal couple; (Verlobte) engaged couple

brav a good, well-behaved; (redlich) honest ● adv dutifully; (redlich) honestly

bravo int bravo!

BRD abbr (Bundesrepublik Deutschland) FRG

Brech|eisen nt jemmy; (B~stange) crowbar. **b~en†** vt break; (Phys) refract ⟨Licht⟩; (erbrechen) vomit; **sich b~en** ⟨Wellen:⟩ break; ⟨Licht:⟩ be refracted; **sich** (dat) **den Arm b~en** break one's arm ● vi (sein) break ● vi (haben) vomit, be sick; **mit jdm b~en** (fig) break with s.o.

B~er m -s,- breaker. **B~reiz** m nausea. **B~stange** f crowbar

Brei m -[e]s,-e paste; (Culin) purée; (Grieß-) pudding; (Hafer-) porridge. **b~ig** a mushy

breit a wide; ⟨Schultern, Grinsen⟩ broad ● adv b~ grinsen grin broadly. **b~beinig** a & adv with legs apart. **B~e** f -,-n width; breadth; (Geog) latitude. **b~en** vt spread (über + acc over). **B~engrad** m [degree of] latitude. **B~enkreis** m parallel. **B~seite** f long side; (Naut) broadside

Bremse¹ f -,-n horsefly

Bremse² f -,-n brake. **b~n** vt slow down; (fig) restrain ● vi (haben) brake

Bremslicht nt brake-light

brenn|bar a combustible; **leicht b~bar** highly [in]flammable. **b~en†** vi (haben) burn; ⟨Licht:⟩ be on; ⟨Zigarette:⟩ be alight; (weh tun) smart, sting; **es b~t in X** there's a fire in X; **darauf b~en, etw zu tun** be dying to do sth ● vt burn; (rösten) roast; (im Brennofen) fire; (destillieren) distil. **b~end** a burning; (angezündet) lighted; (fig) fervent ● adv **ich würde b~end gern** ... I'd love to ... **B~erei** f -,-en distillery

Brennessel f -,-n stinging nettle

Brenn|holz nt firewood. **B~ofen** m kiln. **B~punkt** m (Phys) focus; **im B~punkt des Interesses stehen** be the focus of attention. **B~spiritus** m methylated spirits. **B~stoff** m fuel

brenzlig a (fam) risky; **b~er Geruch** smell of burning

Bresche f -,-n (fig) breach

Bretagne /bre'tanjə/ (die) - Brittany

Brett nt -[e]s,-er board; (im Regal) shelf; **schwarzes B~** notice board. **B~chen** nt -s,- slat; (Frühstücks-) small board (used as plate). **B~spiel** nt board game

Brezel f -,-n pretzel

Bridge /brɪtʃ/ nt - (Spiel) bridge

Brief m -[e]s,-e letter. **B~beschwerer** m -s,- paperweight. **B~block** m writing pad. **B~freund(in)** m(f) penfriend. **B~kasten** m letter-box, (Amer) mailbox. **B~kopf** m letterhead. **b~lich** a & adv by letter. **B~marke** f [postage] stamp. **B~öffner** m paper-knife. **B~papier** nt notepaper. **B~porto** nt letter rate. **B~tasche** f wallet. **B~träger** m

postman, (*Amer*) mailman.
B~umschlag *m* envelope. B~wahl *f*
postal vote. B~wechsel *m*
correspondence

Brigade *f* -,-n brigade

Brikett *nt* -s,-s briquette

brillant /bril'jant/ *a* brilliant, *adv* -ly.
B~t *m* -en,-en [cut] diamond. B~z *f*
- brilliance

Brille *f* -,-n glasses *pl*, spectacles *pl*;
(*Schutz-*) goggles *pl*; (*Klosett-*) toilet
seat

bringen† *vt* bring; (*fort-*) take; (*ein-*)
yield; (*veröffentlichen*) publish; (*im
Radio*) broadcast; show ⟨*Film*⟩; **ins
Bett b~** put to bed; **jdn nach Hause
b~** take/(*begleiten*) see s.o. home;
an sich (*acc*) **b~** get possession of;
mit sich b~ entail; **um etw b~** deprive of sth; **etw hinter sich** (*acc*) **b~**
get sth over [and done] with; **jdn
dazu b~, etw zu tun** get s.o. to do sth;
es weit b~ (*fig*) go far

brisant *a* explosive

Brise *f* -,-n breeze

Brit|e *m* -n,-n, B~in *f* -,-nen Briton.
b~isch *a* British

Bröck|chen *nt* -s,- (*Culin*) crouton.
b~elig *a* crumbly; (*Gestein*) friable.
b~eln *vt/i* (*haben/sein*) crumble

Brocken *m* -s,- chunk; (*Erde, Kohle*)
lump; **ein paar B~ Englisch** (*fam*) a
smattering of English

Brokat *m* -[e]s,-e brocade

Brokkoli *pl* broccoli *sg*

Brombeer|e *f* blackberry.
B~strauch *m* bramble [bush]

Bronchitis *f* - bronchitis

Bronze /'brõ:sə/ *f* -,-n bronze

Brosch|e *f* -,-n brooch. b~iert *a*
paperback. B~üre *f* -,-n brochure;
(*Heft*) booklet

Brösel *mpl* (*Culin*) breadcrumbs

Brot *n* -[e]s,-e bread; **ein B~** a loaf [of
bread]; (*Scheibe*) a slice of bread;
sein B~ verdienen (*fig*) earn one's
living (**mit** by)

Brötchen *n* -s,- [bread] roll

Brot|krümel *m* breadcrumb. B~ver-
diener *m* breadwinner

Bruch *m* -[e]s,ːe break; (*Brechen*)
breaking; (*Rohr-*) burst; (*Med*) fracture; (*Eingeweide-*) rupture, hernia;
(*Math*) fraction; (*fig*) breach; (*in
Beziehung*) break-up

brüchig *a* brittle

Bruch|landung *f* crash-landing.
B~rechnung *f* fractions *pl*. B~stück

nt fragment. b~stückhaft *a* fragmentary. B~teil *m* fraction

Brücke *f* -,-n bridge; (*Teppich*) rug

Bruder *m* -s,ː brother

brüderlich *a* brotherly, fraternal

Brügge *nt* -s Bruges

Brüh|e *f* -,-n broth; (*Knochen-*) stock;
klare B~e clear soup. b~en *vt* scald;
(*auf-*) make ⟨*Kaffee*⟩. B~würfel *m*
stock cube

brüllen *vt/i* (*haben*) roar; ⟨*Kuh:*⟩moo;
(*fam: schreien*) bawl

brumm|eln *vt/i* (*haben*) mumble.
b~en *vi* (*haben*) ⟨*Insekt:*⟩ buzz;
⟨*Bär:*⟩ growl; ⟨*Motor:*⟩ hum; (*murren*) grumble ● *vt* mutter. B~er *m* -
s,- (*fam*) bluebottle. b~ig *a* (*fam*)
grumpy, *adv* -ily

brünett *a* dark-haired. B~e *f* -,-n
brunette

Brunnen *m* -s,- well; (*Spring-*) fountain; (*Heil-*) spa water. B~kresse *f*
watercress

brüsk *a* brusque, *adv* -ly. b~ieren *vt*
snub

Brüssel *nt* -s Brussels

Brust *f* -,ːe chest; (*weibliche, Culin:
B~stück*) breast. B~bein *nt* breast-
bone. B~beutel *m* purse worn
round the neck

brüsten (sich) *vr* boast

Brust|fellentzündung *f* pleurisy.
B~schwimmen *nt* breast-stroke.
B~ung *f* -,-en parapet

Brustwarze *f* nipple

Brut *f* -,-en incubation; (*Junge*)
brood; (*Fisch-*) fry

brutal *a* brutal, *adv* -ly. B~ität *f* -,-en
brutality

brüten *vi* (*haben*) sit (*on eggs*); (*fig*)
ponder (**über** +*dat* over); b~de
Hitze oppressive heat

Brutkasten *m* (*Med*) incubator

brutto *adv*, B~- *pref* gross

brutzeln *vi* (*haben*) sizzle ● *vt* fry

Bub *m* -en,-en (*SGer*) boy. B~e *m*
-n,-n (*Karte*) jack, knave

Bubikopf *m* bob

Buch *nt* -[e]s,ːer book; B~ führen
keep a record (**über**+*acc* of); **die
B~er führen** keep the accounts.
B~drucker *m* printer

Buche *f* -,-n beech

buchen *vt* book; (*Comm*) enter

Bücher|bord, B~brett *nt* bookshelf.
B~ei *f* -,-en library. B~regal *nt*
bookcase, bookshelves *pl*.
B~schrank *m* bookcase. B~wurm
m bookworm

Buchfink *m* chaffinch
Buch|führung *f* bookkeeping.
B~halter(in) *m* -s,- (*f* -,-nen) book-
keeper, accountant. **B~haltung** *f*
bookkeeping, accountancy; (*Abteilung*) accounts department. **B~händ-
ler(in)** *m(f)* bookseller. **B~hand-
lung** *f* bookshop. **B~macher** *m* -s,-
bookmaker. **B~prüfer** *m* auditor
Büchse *f* -,-n box; (*Konserven-*) tin,
can; (*Gewehr*) [sporting] gun.
B~nmilch *f* evaporated milk.
B~nöffner *m* tin *or* can opener
Buch|stabe *m* -n,-n letter. **b~sta-
bieren** *vt* spell [out]. **b~stäblich** *adv*
literally
Buchstützen *fpl* book-ends
Bucht *f* -,-en (*Geog*) bay
Buchung *f* -,-en booking, reservation; (*Comm*) entry
Buckel *m* -s,- hump; (*Beule*) bump;
(*Hügel*) hillock; **einen B~ machen**
⟨*Katze:*⟩ arch its back
bücken (sich) *vr* bend down
bucklig *a* hunchbacked. **B~e(r)** *m/f*
hunchback
Bückling *m* -s,-e smoked herring;
(*fam: Verbeugung*) bow
buddeln *vt/i* (*haben*) (*fam*) dig
Buddhis|mus *m* - Buddhism. **B~t(in)**
m -en,-en (*f* -,-nen) Buddhist.
b~tisch *a* Buddhist
Bude *f* -,-n hut; (*Kiosk*) kiosk; (*Markt*)
stall; (*fam: Zimmer*) room; (*Studen-
ten-*) digs *pl*
Budget /bʏˈdʒeː/ *nt* -s,-s budget
Büfett *nt* -[e]s,-e sideboard; (*Theke*)
bar; **kaltes B~** cold buffet
Büffel *m* -s,- buffalo. **b~n** *vt/i* (*haben*)
(*fam*) swot
Bug *m* -[e]s,-e (*Naut*) bow[s *pl*]
Bügel *m* -s,- frame; (*Kleider-*) coat-
hanger; (*Steig-*) stirrup; (*Brillen-*)
sidepiece. **B~brett** *nt* ironing-
board. **B~eisen** *nt* iron. **B~falte** *f*
crease. **b~frei** *a* non-iron. **b~n**
vt/i (*haben*) iron
bugsieren *vt* (*fam*) manœuvre
buhen *vi* (*haben*) (*fam*) boo
Buhne *f* -,-n breakwater
Bühne *f* -,-n stage. **B~nbild** *nt* set.
B~neingang *m* stage door
Buhrufe *mpl* boos
Bukett *nt* -[e]s,-e bouquet
Bulette *f* -,-n [meat] rissole
Bulgarien /-jən/ *nt* -s Bulgaria
Bull|auge *nt* (*Naut*) porthole.
B~dogge *f* bulldog. **B~dozer**

/-doːzɐ/ *m* -s,- bulldozer. **B~e**
m -n,-n bull; (*sl: Polizist*) cop
Bummel|l *m* -s,- (*fam*) stroll. **B~lant**
m -en,-en (*fam*) dawdler; (*Faulenzer*) loafer. **B~lei** *f* - (*fam*) dawd-
ling; (*Nachlässigkeit*) carelessness
bummel|ig *a* (*fam*) slow; (*nachläs-
sig*) careless. **b~n** *vi* (*sein*) (*fam*)
stroll ● *vi* (*haben*) (*fam*) dawdle.
B~streik *m* go-slow. **B~zug** *m* (*fam*)
slow train
Bums *m* -es,-e (*fam*) bump, thump
Bund¹ *nt* -[e]s,-e bunch; (*Stroh-*)
bundle
Bund² *m* -[e]s,-̈e association; (*Bündnis*) alliance; (*Pol*) federation;
(*Rock-, Hosen-*) waistband; **im B~e
sein** be in league (**mit** with); **der B~**
the Federal Government; (*fam:
Bundeswehr*) the [German] Army
Bündel *nt* -s,- bundle. **b~n** *vt* bundle
[up]
Bundes|- *pref* Federal. **B~genosse** *m*
ally. **B~kanzler** *m* Federal Chancellor. **B~land** *nt* [federal] state; (*Aust*)
province. **B~liga** *f* German national
league. **B~rat** *m* Upper House of
Parliament. **B~regierung** *f* Federal
Government. **B~republik** *f* **die
B~republik Deutschland** the Federal Republic of Germany.
B~straße *f* ≈ A road. **B~tag** *m*
Lower House of Parliament.
B~wehr *f* [Federal German] Army
bünd|ig *a & adv* **kurz und b~ig** short
and to the point. **B~nis** *nt* -sses,-sse
alliance
Bunker *m* -s,- bunker; (*Luftschutz-*)
shelter
bunt *a* coloured; (*farbenfroh*) colour-
ful; (*grell*) gaudy; (*gemischt*) varied;
(*wirr*) confused; **b~er Abend** social
evening; **b~e Platte** assorted cold
meats ● *adv* **b~ durcheinander**
higgledy-piggledy; **es zu b~ treiben**
(*fam*) go too far. **B~stift** *m* crayon
Bürde *f* -,-n (*fig*) burden
Burg *f* -,-en castle
Bürge *m* -n,-n guarantor. **b~n** *vi*
(*haben*) **b~n für** vouch for; (*fig*)
guarantee
Bürger|(in) *m* -s,- (*f* -,-nen) citizen.
B~krieg *m* civil war. **b~lich** *a* civil;
⟨*Pflicht*⟩ civic; (*mittelständisch*)
middle-class; **b~liche Küche** plain
cooking. **B~liche(r)** *m/f* commoner.
B~meister *m* mayor. **B~rechte** *npl*
civil rights. **B~steig** *m* -[e]s,-e pavement, (*Amer*) sidewalk

Burggraben *m* moat
Bürgschaft *f* -,-en surety; **B~ leisten** stand surety
Burgunder *m* -s,- (*Wein*) Burgundy
Burleske *f* -,-n burlesque
Büro *nt* -s,-s office. **B~angestellte(r)** *m/f* office-worker. **B~klammer** *f* paper-clip. **B~krat** *m* -en,-en bureaucrat. **B~kratie** *f* -,-n bureaucracy. **b~kratisch** *a* bureaucratic
Bursch|e *m* -n,-n lad, youth; (*fam: Kerl*) fellow. **b~ikos** *a* hearty; (*männlich*) mannish
Bürste *f* -,-n brush. **b~n** *vt* brush. **B~nschnitt** *m* crew cut
Bus *m* -ses, -se bus; (*Reise-*) coach. **B~bahnhof** *m* bus and coach station
Busch *m* -[e]s,-e bush
Büschel *nt* -s,- tuft
buschig *a* bushy
Busen *m* -s,- bosom
Bussard *m* -s,-e buzzard
Buße *f* -,-n penance; (*Jur*) fine
büßen *vt/i* (*haben*) **[für] etw b~** atone for sth; (*fig: bezahlen*) pay for sth
bußfertig *a* penitent. **B~geld** *nt* (*Jur*) fine
Büste *f* -,-n bust; (*Schneider-*) dummy. **B~nhalter** *m* -s,- bra
Butter *f* - butter. **B~blume** *f* buttercup. **B~brot** *nt* slice of bread and butter. **B~brotpapier** *nt* greaseproof paper. **B~faß** *nt* churn. **B~milch** *f* buttermilk. **b~n** *vi* (*haben*) make butter ● *vt* butter
b.w. *abbr* (**bitte wenden**) PTO
bzgl. *abbr* s. **bezüglich**
bzw. *abbr* s. **beziehungsweise**

C

ca. *abbr* (**circa**) about
Café /ka'fe:/ *nt* -s,-s café
Cafeteria /kafete'ri:a/ *f* -,-s cafeteria
camp|en /'kɛmpən/ *vi* (*haben*) go camping. **C~ing** *nt* -s camping. **C~ingplatz** *m* campsite
Cape /ke:p/ *nt* -s,-s cape
Caravan /'ka[:]ravan/ *m* -s,-s (*Auto*) caravan; (*Kombi*) estate car
Cassette /ka'sɛta/ *f* -,-n cassette. **C~nrecorder** /-rekɔrdɐ/ *m* -s,- cassette recorder
CD /tse:'de:/ *f* -,-s compact disc, CD

Cell|ist(in) /tʃɛ'lɪst(ɪn)/ *m* -en,-en (*f* -,-nen) cellist. **C~o** /'tʃɛlo/ *nt* -,-los & -li cello
Celsius /'tsɛlzjʊs/ *inv* Celsius, centigrade
Cembalo /'tʃɛmbalo/ *nt* -s,-los & -li harpsichord
Champagner /ʃam'panjɐ/ *m* -s champagne
Champignon /'ʃampɪnjɔŋ/ *m* -s,-s [field] mushroom
Chance /'ʃã:s[ə]/ *f* -,-n chance
Chaos /'ka:ɔs/ *nt* - chaos
chaotisch /ka'o:tɪʃ/ *a* chaotic
Charakter /ka'raktɐ/ *m* -s,-e /-'te:rə/ character. **c~isieren** *vt* characterize. **c~istisch** *a* characteristic (**für** of), *adv* -ally
Charism|a /ka'rɪsma/ *nt* -s charisma. **c~atisch** *a* charismatic
charm|ant /ʃar'mant/ *a* charming, *adv* -ly. **C~e** /ʃarm/ *m* -s charm
Charter|flug /'tʃ-, 'ʃartɐ-/ *m* charter flight. **c~n** *vt* charter
Chassis /ʃa'si:/ *nt* -,- /-'si:[s], -'si:s/ chassis
Chauffeur /ʃɔ'fø:ɐ/ *m* -s,-e chauffeur; (*Taxi-*) driver
Chauvinis|mus /ʃovi'nɪsmʊs/ *m* - chauvinism. **C~t** *m* -en,-en chauvinist
Chef /ʃɛf/ *m* -s,-s head; (*fam*) boss
Chem|ie /çe'mi:/ *f* - chemistry. **C~ikalien** /-jən/ *fpl* chemicals
Chem|iker(in) /'çe:-/ *m* -s,- (*f* -,-nen) chemist. **c~isch** *a* chemical, *adv* -ly; **c~ische Reinigung** dry-cleaning; (*Geschäft*) dry-cleaner's
Chicorée /'ʃɪkore/ *m* -s chicory
Chiffr|e /'ʃɪfə, 'ʃɪfrə/ *f* -,-n cipher; (*bei Annonce*) box number. **c~iert** *a* coded
Chile /'çi:le/ *nt* -s Chile
Chin|a /'çi:na/ *nt* -s China. **C~ese** *m* -n,-n, **C~esin** *f* -,-nen Chinese. **c~esisch** *a* Chinese. **C~esisch** *nt* -[s] (*Lang*) Chinese
Chip /tʃɪp/ *m* -s,-s [micro]chip. **C~s** *pl* crisps, (*Amer*) chips
Chirurg /çi'rʊrk/ *m* -en,-en surgeon. **C~ie** /-'gi:/ *f* - surgery. **c~isch** /-g-/ *a* surgical, *adv* -ly
Chlor /klo:ɐ/ *nt* -s chlorine. **C~oform** /kloro'fɔrm/ *nt* -s chloroform
Choke /tʃo:k/ *m* -s,-s (*Auto*) choke
Cholera /'ko:lera/ *f* - cholera
cholerisch /ko'le:rɪʃ/ *a* irascible
Cholesterin /ço-, kolɛste'ri:n/ *nt* -s cholesterol

Chor /koːɐ̯/ *m* -[e]s,-̈e choir; (*Theat*) chorus; **im C~** in chorus
Choral /koˈraːl/ *m* -[e]s,-̈e chorale
Choreographie /koreograˈfiː/ *f* -,-n choreography
Chor|knabe /ˈkoːɐ̯-/ *m* choirboy. **C~musik** *f* choral music
Christ /krɪst/ *m* -en,-en Christian. **C~baum** *m* Christmas tree. **C~entum** *nt* -s Christianity. **C~in** *f* -,-nen Christian. **C~kind** *nt* Christ-child; (*als Geschenkbringer*) ≈ Father Christmas. **c~lich** *a* Christian
Christus /ˈkrɪstʊs/ *m* -ti Christ
Chrom /kroːm/ *nt* -s chromium
Chromosom /kromoˈzoːm/ *nt* -s,-en chromosome
Chronik /ˈkroːnɪk/ *f* -,-en chronicle
chron|isch /ˈkroːnɪʃ/ *a* chronic, *adv* -ally. **c~ologisch** *a* chronological, *adv* -ly
Chrysantheme /kryzanˈteːmə/ *f* -,-n chrysanthemum
circa /ˈtsɪrka/ *adv* about
Clique /ˈklɪkə/ *f* -,-n clique
Clou /kluː/ *m* -s,-s highlight, (*fam*) high spot
Clown /klaʊn/ *m* -s,-s clown. **c~en** *vi* (*haben*) clown
Club /klʊp/ *m* -s,-s club
Cocktail /ˈkɔktɛːl/ *m* -s,-s cocktail
Code /koːt/ *m* -s,-s code
Cola /ˈkoːla/ *f* -,- (*fam*) Coke (P)
Comic-Heft /ˈkɔmɪk-/ *nt* comic
Computer /kɔmˈpjuːtɐ/ *m* -s,- computer. **c~isieren** *vt* computerize
Conférencier /kõferɑˈsi̯eː/ *m* -s,-s compère
Cord /kɔrt/ *m* -s, **C~samt** *m* corduroy. **C~[samt]hose** *f* cords *pl*
Couch /kaʊtʃ/ *f* -,-es settee. **C~tisch** *m* coffee-table
Coupon /kuˈpõː/ *m* -s,-s = **Kupon**
Cousin /kuˈzɛː/ *m* -s,-s [male] cousin. **C~e** /-ˈziːnə/ *f* -,-n [female] cousin
Crem|e /kreːm/ *f* -s,-s cream; (*Speise*) cream dessert. **c~efarben** *a* cream. **c~ig** *a* creamy
Curry /ˈkari, ˈkœri/ *nt & m* -s curry powder ● *nt* -s,-s (*Gericht*) curry

D

da *adv* there; (*hier*) here; (*zeitlich*) then; (*in dem Fall*) in that case; **von da an** from then on ● *conj* as, since
dabehalten† *vt sep* keep there

dabei (*emphatic:* **dabei**) *adv* nearby; (*daran*) with it; (*eingeschlossen*) included; (*hinsichtlich*) about it; (*während dem*) during this; (*gleichzeitig*) at the same time; (*doch*) and yet; **dicht d~** close by; **d~ bleiben** (*fig*) remain adamant; **was ist denn d~?** (*fam*) so what? **d~sein†** *vi sep* (*sein*) be present; (*mitmachen*) be involved; **d~sein, etw zu tun** be just doing sth
dableiben† *vi sep* (*sein*) stay there
Dach *nt* -[e]s,-̈er roof. **D~boden** *m* loft. **D~gepäckträger** *m* roof-rack. **D~kammer** *f* attic room. **D~luke** *f* skylight. **D~rinne** *f* gutter
Dachs *m* -es,-e badger
Dach|sparren *m* -s,- rafter. **D~ziegel** *m* [roofing] tile
Dackel *m* -s,- dachshund
dadurch (*emphatic:* **dadurch**) *adv* through it/them; (*Ursache*) by it; (*deshalb*) because of that; **d~, daß** because
dafür (*emphatic:* **dafür**) *adv* for it/them; (*anstatt*) instead; (*als Ausgleich*) but [on the other hand]; **d~, daß** considering that. **d~können†** *vi sep* (*haben*) **ich kann nichts dafür** it's not my fault
dagegen (*emphatic:* **dagegen**) *adv* against it/them; (*Mittel, Tausch*) for it; (*verglichen damit*) by comparison; (*jedoch*) however; **hast du was d~?** do you mind? **d~halten†** *vt sep* argue (**daß** that)
daheim *adv* at home
daher (*emphatic:* **daher**) *adv* from there; (*deshalb*) for that reason; **das kommt d~, weil** that's because; **d~ meine Eile** hence my hurry ● *conj* that is why
dahin (*emphatic:* **dahin**) *adv* there; **bis d~** up to there; (*bis dann*) until; (*Zukunft*) by then; **jdn d~ bringen, daß er etw tut** get s.o. to do sth; **d~ sein** (*fam*) be gone. **d~gehen†** *vi sep* (*sein*) walk along; ⟨*Zeit:*⟩ pass. **d~gestellt** *a* **d~gestellt lassen** (*fig*) leave open; **das bleibt d~gestellt** that remains to be seen
dahinten *adv* back there
dahinter (*emphatic:* **dahinter**) *adv* behind it/them. **d~kommen†** *vi sep* (*sein*) (*fig*) get to the bottom of it
Dahlie /-i̯ə/ *f* -,-n dahlia
dalassen† *vt sep* leave there
daliegen† *vi sep* (*haben*) lie there

damalig *a* at that time; **der d~e Minister** the then minister

damals *adv* at that time

Damast *m* **-es,-e** damask

Dame *f* **-,-n** lady; (*Karte, Schach*) queen; (*D~spiel*) draughts *sg*, (*Amer*) checkers *sg*; (*Doppelstein*) king. **D~n-** *pref* ladies'/lady's ... **d~nhaft** *a* ladylike

damit (*emphatic:* **damit**) *adv* with it/them; (*dadurch*) by it; **hör auf d~!** stop it! ● *conj* so that

dämlich *a* (*fam*) stupid, *adv* -ly

Damm *m* **-[e]s,-e** dam; (*Insel-*) causeway; **nicht auf dem D~** (*fam*) under the weather

dämmer|ig *a* dim; **es wird d~ig** dusk is falling. **D~licht** *nt* twilight. **d~n** *vi* (*haben*) ⟨*Morgen:*⟩ dawn; **der Abend d~t** dusk is falling; **es d~t** it is getting light/(*abends*) dark. **D~ung** *f* - dawn; (*Abend-*) dusk

Dämon *m* **-s,-en** /-'mo:nən/ demon

Dampf *m* **-es,-e** steam; (*Chem*) vapour. **d~en** *vi* (*haben*) steam

dämpfen *vt* (*Culin*) steam; (*fig*) muffle ⟨*Ton*⟩; lower ⟨*Stimme*⟩; dampen ⟨*Enthusiasmus*⟩

Dampf|er *m* **-s,-** steamer. **D~koch-topf** *m* pressure-cooker. **D~ma-schine** *f* steam engine. **D~walze** *f* steamroller

Damwild *nt* fallow deer *pl*

danach (*emphatic:* **danach**) *adv* after it/them; ⟨*suchen*⟩ for it; ⟨*rie-chen*⟩ of it; (*später*) afterwards; (*ent-sprechend*) accordingly; **es sieht d~ aus** it looks like it

Däne *m* **-n,-n** Dane

daneben (*emphatic:* **daneben**) *adv* beside it/them; (*außerdem*) in addition; (*verglichen damit*) by comparison. **d~gehen†** *vi sep* (*sein*) miss; (*scheitern*) fail

Dän|emark *nt* **-s** Denmark. **D~in** *f* **-,-nen** Dane. **d~isch** *a* Danish

Dank *m* **-es** thanks *pl*; **vielen D~!** thank you very much! **d~** *prep* (+*dat or gen*) thanks to. **d~bar** *a* grateful, *adv* -ly; (*erleichtert*) thankful, *adv* -ly; (*lohnend*) rewarding. **D~barkeit** *f* - gratitude. **d~e** *adv* **d~e [schön** *od* **sehr]!** thank you [very much]! **[nein] d~e!** no thank you! **d~en** *vi* (*haben*) ⟨*jdm s.o.*⟩; (*ablehnen*) decline; **ich d~e!** no thank you! **nichts zu d~en!** don't mention it!

dann *adv* then; **d~ und wann** now and then; **nur/selbst d~, wenn** only/even if

daran (*emphatic:* **daran**) *adv* on it/them; at it/them; ⟨*denken*⟩ of it; **nahe d~** on the point (**etw zu tun** *od* doing sth); **denkt d~!** remember! **d~gehen†** *vi sep* (*sein*), **d~machen (sich)** *vr sep* set about (**etw zu tun** *od* doing sth). **d~setzen** *vt sep* **alles d~setzen** do one's utmost (**zu to**)

darauf (*emphatic:* **darauf**) *adv* on it/them; ⟨*warten*⟩ for it; ⟨*antworten*⟩ to it; (*danach*) after that; (*d~hin*) as a result; **am Tag d~** the day after. **d~folgend** *a* following. **d~hin** *adv* as a result

daraus (*emphatic:* **daraus**) *adv* out of or from it/them; **er macht sich nichts d~** he doesn't care for it; **was ist d~ geworden?** what has become of it?

Darbietung *f* **-,-en** performance; (*Nummer*) item

darin (*emphatic:* **darin**) *adv* in it/them

darlegen *vt sep* expound; (*erklären*) explain

Darlehen *nt* **-s,-** loan

Darm *m* **-[e]s,-e** intestine; (*Wurst-*) skin. **D~grippe** *f* gastric flu

darstell|en *vt sep* represent; (*bild-lich*) portray; (*Theat*) interpret; (*spielen*) play; (*schildern*) describe. **D~er** *m* **-s,-** actor. **D~erin** *f* **-,-nen** actress. **D~ung** *f* representation; interpretation; description; (*Bericht*) account

darüber (*emphatic:* **darüber**) *adv* over it/them; (*höher*) above it/them; ⟨*sprechen, lachen, sich freuen*⟩ about it; (*mehr*) more; (*inzwischen*) in the meantime; **d~ hinaus** beyond [it]; (*dazu*) on top of that

darum (*emphatic:* **darum**) *adv* round it/them; ⟨*bitten, kämpfen*⟩ for it; (*deshalb*) that is why; **d~, weil** because

darunter (*emphatic:* **darunter**) *adv* under it/them; (*tiefer*) below it/them; (*weniger*) less; (*dazwischen*) among them

das *def art & pron s.* **der**

dasein† *vi sep* (*sein*) be there/(*hier*) here; (*existieren*) exist; **wieder d~** be back; **noch nie dagewesen** unprecedented. **D~** *nt* **-s** existence

dasitzen† *vi sep* (*haben*) sit there

dasjenige *pron s.* **derjenige**

daß *conj* that; **daß du nicht fällst!** mind you don't fall!

dasselbe *pron s.* derselbe

dastehen† *vi sep* (*haben*) stand there; **allein d~** (*fig*) be alone

Daten|sichtgerät *nt* visual display unit, VDU. **D~verarbeitung** *f* data processing

datieren *vt/i* (*haben*) date

Dativ *m* -s,-e dative. **D~objekt** *nt* indirect object

Dattel *f* -,-n date

Datum *nt* -s,-ten date; **Daten** (*Angaben*) data

Dauer *f* - duration, length; (*Jur*) term; **von D~** lasting; **auf die D~** in the long run. **D~auftrag** *m* standing order. **d~haft** *a* lasting, enduring; (*fest*) durable. **D~karte** *f* season ticket. **D~lauf** *m* im **D~lauf** at a jog. **D~milch** *f* long-life milk. **d~n** *vi* (*haben*) last; **lange d~n** take a long time. **d~nd** *a* lasting; (*ständig*) constant, *adv* -ly; **d~nd fragen** keep asking. **D~stellung** *f* permanent position. **D~welle** *f* perm. **D~wurst** *f* salami-type sausage

Daumen *m* -s,- thumb; **jdm den D~ drücken** *od* **halten** keep one's fingers crossed for s.o.

Daunen *fpl* down *sg.* **D~decke** *f* [down-filled] duvet

davon (*emphatic:* **davon**) *adv* from it/them; (*dadurch*) by it; (*damit*) with it/them; (*darüber*) about it; (*Menge*) of it/them; **die Hälfte d~** half of it/them; **das kommt d~!** it serves you right! **d~kommen**† *vi sep* (*sein*) escape (**mit dem Leben** with one's life). **d~laufen**† *vi sep* (*sein*) run away. **d~machen** (**sich**) *vr sep* (*fam*) make off. **d~tragen**† *vt sep* carry off; (*erleiden*) suffer; (*gewinnen*) be

davor (*emphatic:* **davor**) *adv* in front of it/them; 〈*sich fürchten*〉 of it; (*zeitlich*) before it/them

dazu (*emphatic:* **dazu**) *adv* to it/them; (*damit*) with it/them; (*dafür*) for it; **noch d~** in addition to that; **jdn d~ bringen, etw zu tun** get s.o. to do sth; **ich kam nicht d~** I didn't get round to [doing] it. **d~gehören** *vi sep* (*haben*) belong to it/them; **alles, was d~gehört** everything that goes with it. **d~kommen**† *vi sep* (*sein*) arrive [on the scene]; (*hinzukommen*) be added; (*hinzukommen*) **d~ kommt, daß er krank ist** on top of that he is ill. **d~rechnen** *vt sep* add to it/them

dazwischen (*emphatic:* **dazwischen**) *adv* between them; in between; (*darunter*) among them. **d~fahren**† *vi sep* (*sein*) (*fig*) intervene. **d~kommen**† *vi sep* (*sein*) (*fig*) crop up; **wenn nichts d~kommt** if all goes well. **d~reden** *vi sep* (*haben*) interrupt. **d~treten**† *vi sep* (*sein*) (*fig*) intervene

DDR *f* - *abbr* (**Deutsche Demokratische Republik**) GDR

Debat|te *f* -,-n debate; **zur D~te stehen** be at issue. **d~tieren** *vt/i* (*haben*) debate

Debüt /de'by:/ *nt* -s,-s début

dechiffrieren /deʃɪ'fri:rən/ *vt* decipher

Deck *nt* -[e]s,-s (*Naut*) deck; **an D~** on deck. **D~bett** *nt* duvet

Decke *f* -,-n cover; (*Tisch-*) tablecloth; (*Bett-*) blanket; (*Reise-*) rug; (*Zimmer-*) ceiling; **unter einer D~ stecken** (*fam*) be in league

Deckel *m* -s,- lid; (*Flaschen-*) top; (*Buch-*) cover

decken *vt* cover; tile 〈*Dach*〉; lay 〈*Tisch*〉; (*schützen*) shield; (*Sport*) mark; meet 〈*Bedarf*〉; (*Sport*) cover up for s.o.; **sich d~** (*fig*) cover oneself (**gegen** against); (*übereinstimmen*) coincide

Deck|mantel *m* (*fig*) pretence. **D~name** *m* pseudonym

Deckung *f* - (*Mil*) cover; (*Sport*) defence; (*Mann-*) marking; (*Boxen*) guard; (*Sicherheit*) security; **in D~ gehen** take cover

Defekt *m* -[e]s,-e defect. **d~** *a* defective

defensiv *a* defensive. **D~e** *f* - defensive

defilieren *vi* (*sein/haben*) file past

defin|ieren *vt* define. **D~ition** /-'tsio:n/ *f* -,-en definition. **d~itiv** *a* definite, *adv* -ly

Defizit *nt* -s,-e deficit

Deflation /-'tsio:n/ *f* - deflation

deformiert *a* deformed

deftig *a* (*fam*) 〈*Mahlzeit*〉 hearty; 〈*Witz*〉 coarse

Degen *m* -s,- sword; (*Fecht-*) épée

degenerier|en *vi* (*sein*) degenerate. **d~t** *a* (*fig*) degenerate

degradieren *vt* (*Mil*) demote; (*fig*) degrade

dehn|bar *a* elastic. **d~en** *vt* stretch; lengthen 〈*Vokal*〉; **sich d~en** stretch

Deich *m* -[e]s,-e dike

Deichsel *f* -,-n pole; (*Gabel-*) shafts *pl*

dein *poss pron* your. **d~e(r,s)** *poss pron* yours; **die D~en** *pl* your family *sg*. **d~erseits** *adv* for your part. **d~etwegen** *adv* for your sake; (*wegen dir*) because of you, on your account. **d~etwillen** *adv* **um d~etwillen** for your sake. **d~ige** *poss pron* **der/die/das d~ige** yours. **d~s** *poss pron* yours

Deka *nt* -[s].- (*Aust*) = **Dekagramm**

dekaden|t *a* decadent. **D~z** *f* - decadence

Dekagramm *nt* (*Aust*) 10 grams; **10 D~** 100 grams

Dekan *m* -s,-e dean

Deklin|ation /-'tsio:n/ *f* -,-en declension. **d~ieren** *vt* decline

Dekolleté /dekol'te:/ *nt* -s,-s low neckline

Dekor *m* & *nt* -s decoration. **D~ateur** /-'tø:ɐ/ *m* -s,-e interior decorator; (*Schaufenster-*) window-dresser. **D~ation** /-'tsio:n/ *f* -,-en decoration; (*Schaufenster-*) window-dressing; (*Auslage*) display; **D~ationen** (*Theat*) scenery *sg*. **d~ativ** *a* decorative. **d~ieren** *vt* decorate; dress ⟨*Schaufenster*⟩

Deleg|ation /-'tsio:n/ *f* -,-en delegation. **d~ieren** *vt* delegate. **D~ierte(r)** *m/f* delegate

delikat *a* delicate; (*lecker*) delicious; (*taktvoll*) tactful, *adv* -ly. **D~esse** *f* -,-n delicacy. **D~essengeschäft** *nt* delicatessen

Delikt *nt* -[e]s,-e offence

Delinquent *m* -en,-en offender

Delirium *nt* -s delirium

Delle *f* -,-n dent

Delphin *m* -s,-e dolphin

Delta *nt* -s,-s delta

dem *def art* & *pron s.* der

Dement|i *nt* -s,-s denial. **d~ieren** *vt* deny

dem|entsprechend *a* corresponding; (*passend*) appropriate ● *adv* accordingly; (*passend*) appropriately. **d~gemäß** *adv* accordingly. **d~nach** *adv* according to that; (*folglich*) consequently. **d~nächst** *adv* soon; (*in Kürze*) shortly

Demokrat *m* -en,-en democrat. **D~ie** *f* -,-n democracy. **d~isch** *a* democratic, *adv* -ally

demolieren *vt* wreck

Demonstr|ant *m* -en,-en demonstrator. **D~ation** /-'tsio:n/ *f* -,-en demonstration. **d~ativ** *a* pointed, *adv* -ly; (*Gram*) demonstrative.

D~ativpronomen *nt* demonstrative pronoun. **d~ieren** *vt/i* (*haben*) demonstrate

demontieren *vt* dismantle

demoralisieren *vt* demoralize

Demoskopie *f* - opinion research

Demut *f* - humility

demütig *a* humble, *adv* -bly. **d~en** *vt* humiliate; **sich d~en** humble oneself. **D~ung** *f* -,-en humiliation

demzufolge *adv* = demnach

den *def art* & *pron s.* der. **d~en** *pron s.* der

denk|bar *a* conceivable. **d~en†** *vt/i* (*haben*) think (**an** + *acc* of); (*sich erinnern*) remember (**an etw** *acc* sth); **für jdn gedacht** meant for s.o.; **das kann ich mir d~en** I can imagine [that]; **ich d~e nicht daran** I have no intention of doing it; **d~t daran!** don't forget! **D~mal** *nt* memorial; (*Monument*) monument. **d~würdig** *a* memorable. **D~zettel** *m* jdm einen **D~zettel geben** (*fam*) teach s.o. a lesson

denn *conj* for; **besser/mehr d~** je better/more than ever ● *adv* **wie/wo d~?** but how/where? **warum d~ nicht?** why ever not? **es sei d~ [, daß]** unless

dennoch *adv* nevertheless

Denunz|iant *m* -en,-en informer. **d~ieren** *vt* denounce

Deodorant *nt* -s,-s deodorant

deplaciert /-'tsi:ɐt/ *a* (*fig*) out of place

Deponie *f* -,-n dump. **d~ren** *vt* deposit

deportieren *vt* deport

Depot /de'po:/ *nt* -s,-s depot; (*Lager*) warehouse; (*Bank-*) safe deposit

Depression *f* -,-en depression

deprimieren *vt* depress. **d~d** *a* depressing

Deputation /-'tsio:n/ *f* -,-en deputation

der, die, das, *pl* **die** *def art* (*acc* **den, die, das,** *pl* **die**; *gen* **des, der, des,** *pl* **der**; *dat* **dem, der, dem,** *pl* **den**) the; **der Mensch** man; **die Natur** nature; **das Leben** life; **das Lesen/Tanzen** reading/dancing; **sich** (*dat*) **das Gesicht/die Hände waschen** wash one's face/hands; **5 Mark das Pfund** 5 marks a pound ● *pron* (*acc* **den, die, das,** *pl* **die**; *gen* **dessen, deren, dessen,** *pl* **deren**; *dat* **dem, der, dem,** *pl* **denen**) ● *dem pron* that; (*pl*) those; (*substantivisch*) he, she, it; (*Ding*) it; (*betont*) that; (**d~jenige**) the one; (*pl*) they, those; (*Dinge*) those; (*diejenigen*) the ones; **der und der** such and such; **um die und die Zeit** at such and such a time; **das waren Zeiten!** those were the days! ● *rel pron* who; (*Ding*) which, that

derart *adv* so; (*so sehr*) so much. **d~ig** *a* such ● *adv* = **derart**

derb *a* tough; (*kräftig*) strong; (*grob*) coarse, *adv* -ly; (*unsanft*) rough, *adv* -ly

deren *pron* s. **der**

dergleichen *inv a* such ● *pron* such a thing/such things; **nichts d~** nothing of the kind; **und d~** and the like

der-/die-/dasjenige, *pl* **diejenigen** *pron* the one; (*Person*) he; she; (*Ding*) it; (*pl*) those, the ones

dermaßen *adv* = **derart**

der-/die-/dasselbe, *pl* **dieselben** *pron* the same; **ein- und dasselbe** one and the same thing

derzeit *adv* at present

des *def art* s. **der**

Desert|eur /-'tøːɐ̯/ *m* **-s,-e** deserter. **d~ieren** *vi* (*sein/haben*) desert

desgleichen *adv* likewise ● *pron* the like

deshalb *adv* for this reason; (*also*) therefore

Designer(in) /di'zaɪnɐ, -nərɪn/ *m* **-s,-** (*f* -,-nen) designer

Desin|fektion /dɛsʔɪnfɛktsi̯oːn/ *f* - disinfecting. **D~fektionsmittel** *nt* disinfectant. **d~fizieren** *vt* disinfect

Desodorant *nt* **-s,-s** deodorant

Despot *m* **-en,-en** despot

dessen *pron* s. **der**

Dessert /dɛ'seːɐ̯/ *nt* **-s,-s** dessert, sweet. **D~löffel** *m* dessertspoon

Destill|ation /-'tsi̯oːn/ *f* - distillation. **d~ieren** *vt* distil

desto *adv* **je mehr/eher, d~ besser** the more/sooner the better

destruktiv *a* (*fig*) destructive

deswegen *adv* = **deshalb**

Detail /de'tai̯/ *nt* **-s,-s** detail

Detektiv *m* **-s,-e** detective. **D~roman** *m* detective story

Deton|ation /-'tsi̯oːn/ *f* -,-en explosion. **d~ieren** *vi* (*sein*) explode

deut|en *vt* interpret; predict ⟨*Zukunft*⟩ ● *vi* (*haben*) point (**auf** + *acc* at/(*fig*) to). **d~lich** *a* clear, *adv* -ly; (*eindeutig*) plain, *adv* -ly. **D~lichkeit** *f* - clarity

deutsch *a* German; **auf d~** in German. **D~** *nt* **-[s]** (*Lang*) German.

D~e(r) *m/f* German. **D~land** *nt* **-s** Germany

Deutung *f* -,-en interpretation

Devise *f* -,-n motto. **D~n** *pl* foreign currency or exchange *sg*

Dezember *m* **-s,-** December

dezent *a* unobtrusive, *adv* -ly; (*diskret*) discreet, *adv* -ly

Dezernat *nt* **-[e]s,-e** department

Dezimal|system *nt* decimal system. **D~zahl** *f* decimal

dezimieren *vt* decimate

dgl. *abbr* s. **dergleichen**

d.h. *abbr* (**das heißt**) i.e.

Dia *nt* **-s,-s** (*Phot*) slide

Diabet|es *m* - diabetes. **D~iker** *m* **-s,-** diabetic

Diadem *nt* **-s,-e** tiara

Diagnos|e *f* -,-n diagnosis. **d~tizieren** *vt* diagnose

diagonal *a* diagonal, *adv* -ly. **D~e** *f* -,-n diagonal

Diagramm *nt* **-s,-e** diagram; (*Kurven-*) graph

Diakon *m* **-s,-e** deacon

Dialekt *m* **-[e]s,-e** dialect

Dialog *m* **-[e]s,-e** dialogue

Diamant *m* **-en,-en** diamond

Diameter *m* **-s,-** diameter

Diapositiv *nt* **-s,-e** (*Phot*) slide

Diaprojektor *m* slide projector

Diät *f* -,-en (*Med*) diet. **d~** *adv* **d~ leben** be on a diet. **D~assistent(in)** *m*(*f*) dietician

dich *pron* (*acc* **du**) you; (*refl*) yourself

dicht *a* dense; (*dick*) thick; (*undurchlässig*) airtight; (*wasser-*) watertight ● *adv* densely; thickly; (*nahe*) close (**bei** to). **D~e** *f* - density. **d~en**[1] *vt* make watertight; (*ab-*) seal

dicht|en[2] *vi* (*haben*) write poetry. ● *vt* write, compose. **D~er(in)** *m* **-s,-** (*f* -,-nen) poet. **d~erisch** *a* poetic. **D~ung**[1] *f* -,-en poetry; (*Gedicht*) poem

Dichtung[2] *f* -,-en seal; (*Ring*) washer; (*Auto*) gasket

dick *a* thick, *adv* -ly; (*beleibt*) fat; (*geschwollen*) swollen; (*fam: eng*) close; **d~ werden** get fat; **d~ machen** be fattening; **ein d~es Fell haben** (*fam*) be thick-skinned. **D~e** *f* -,-n thickness; (*D~leibigkeit*) fatness. **d~fellig** *a* (*fam*) thick-skinned. **d~flüssig** *a* thick; (*Phys*) viscous. **D~kopf** *m* (*fam*) stubborn person; **einen D~kopf haben** be

stubborn. **d∼köpfig** *a* (*fam*)
stubborn

didaktisch *a* didactic

die *def art & pron s.* **der**

Dieb|(in) *m* -[e]s,-e (*f* -,-nen) thief.
d∼isch *a* thieving; ⟨*Freude*⟩ malicious. **D∼stahl** *m* -[e]s,⁻e theft; (*geistig*) plagiarism

diejenige *pron s.* **derjenige**

Diele *f* -,-n floorboard; (*Flur*) hall

dien|en *vi* (*haben*) serve. **D∼er** *m* -s,-
servant; (*Verbeugung*) bow. **D∼erin**
f -,-nen maid, servant. **d∼lich** *a*
helpful

Dienst *m* -[e]s,-e service; (*Arbeit*)
work; (*Amtsausübung*) duty; **außer**
D∼ off duty; (*pensioniert*) retired;
D∼ haben work; ⟨*Soldat, Arzt:*⟩ be
on duty; **jdm einen schlechten D∼**
erweisen do s.o. a disservice

Dienstag *m* Tuesday. **d∼s** *adv* on
Tuesdays

Dienst|alter *nt* seniority. **d∼bereit** *a*
obliging; ⟨*Apotheke*⟩ open. **D∼bote**
m servant. **d∼eifrig** *a* zealous, *adv*
-ly. **d∼frei** *a* **d∼freier Tag** day off;
d∼frei haben have time off; ⟨*Soldat,*
Arzt:⟩ be off duty. **D∼grad** *m* rank.
d∼habend *a* duty ... **D∼leistung** *f*
service. **d∼lich** *a* official ● *adv*
d∼lich verreist away on business.
D∼mädchen *nt* maid. **D∼reise** *f*
business trip. **D∼stelle** *f* office.
D∼stunden *fpl* office hours.
D∼weg *m* official channels *pl*

dies *inv pron* this. **d∼bezüglich** *a*
relevant ● *adv* regarding this matter. **d∼e(r,s)** *pron* this; (*pl*) these;
(*substantivisch*) this [one]; (*pl*)
these; **d∼e Nacht** tonight; (*letzte*)
last night

Diesel *m* -[s],- (*fam*) diesel

dieselbe *pron s.* **derselbe**

Diesel|kraftstoff *m* diesel [oil].
D∼motor *m* diesel engine

diesig *a* hazy, misty

dies|mal *adv* this time. **d∼seits** *adv*
& *prep* (+*gen*) this side (of)

Dietrich *m* -s,-e skeleton key

Diffam|ation /-'tsi̯o:n/ *f* - defamation.
d∼ierend *a* defamatory

Differential /-'tsi̯a:l/ *nt* -s,-e
differential

Differenz *f* -,-en difference. **d∼ieren**
vt/i (*haben*) differentiate (**zwischen**
+ *dat* between)

Digital- *pref* digital. **D∼uhr** *f* digital
clock/watch

Dikt|at *nt* -[e]s,-e dictation. **D∼ator**
m -s,-en /-'to:rən/ dictator. **d∼atorisch**
a dictatorial. **D∼atur** *f* -,-en dictatorship. **d∼ieren** *vt/i* (*haben*)
dictate

Dilemma *nt* -s,-s dilemma

Dilettant|(in) *m* -en,-en (*f* -,-nen)
dilettante. **d∼isch** *a* amateurish

Dill *m* -s dill

Dimension *f* -,-en dimension

Ding *nt* -[e]s,-e & (*fam*) -er thing;
guter D∼e sein be cheerful; **vor al-**
len D∼en above all

Dinghi /'dɪŋgi/ *nt* -s,-s dinghy

Dinosaurier /-i̯ɐ/ *m* -s,- dinosaur

Diözese *f* -,-n diocese

Diphtherie *f* - diphtheria

Diplom *nt* -s,-e diploma; (*Univ*)
degree

Diplomat *m* -en,-en diplomat. **D∼ie**
f - diplomacy. **d∼isch** *a* diplomatic,
adv -ally

dir *pron* (*dat of* **du**) [to] you; (*refl*)
yourself; **ein Freund von dir** a friend
of yours

direkt *a* direct ● *adv* directly; (*wirklich*) really. **D∼ion** /-'tsi̯o:n/ *f* -
management; (*Vorstand*) board of
directors. **D∼or** *m* -s,-en /-'to:rən/,
D∼orin *f* -,-nen director; (*Bank-,
Theater-*) manager; (*Sch*) head; (*Gefängnis*) governor. **D∼übertragung**
f live transmission

Dirig|ent *m* -en,-en (*Mus*) conductor.
d∼ieren *vt* direct; (*Mus*) conduct

Dirndl *nt* -s,- dirndl [dress]

Dirne *f* -,-n prostitute

Diskant *m* -s,-e (*Mus*) treble

Diskette *f* -,-n floppy disc

Disko *f* -,-s (*fam*) disco. **D∼thek** *f*
-,-en discothèque

Diskrepanz *f* -,-en discrepancy

diskret *a* discreet, *adv* -ly. **D∼ion**
/-'tsi̯o:n/ *f* - discretion

diskriminier|en *vt* discriminate
against. **D∼ung** *f* - discrimination

Diskus *m* -,-se & **Disken** discus

Disku|ssion *f* -,-en discussion.
d∼tieren *vt/i* (*haben*) discuss

disponieren *vi* (*haben*) make arrangements; **d∼ [können] über**
(+*acc*) have at one's disposal

Disput *m* -[e]s,-e dispute

Disqualifi|kation /-'tsi̯o:n/ *f* disqualification. **d∼zieren** *vt* disqualify

Dissertation /-'tsi̯o:n/ *f* -,-en
dissertation

Dissident *m* -en,-en dissident

Dissonanz *f* -,-en dissonance

Distanz f -,-en distance. **d∼ieren (sich)** vr dissociate oneself (von from). **d∼iert** a aloof

Distel f -,-n thistle

distinguiert /dıstıŋ'gi:ɐt/ a distinguished

Disziplin f -,-en discipline. **d∼arisch** a disciplinary. **d∼iert** a disciplined

dito adv ditto

diverse attrib a pl various

Divid|ende f -,-n dividend. **d∼ieren** vt divide (durch by)

Division f -,-en division

DJH abbr (Deutsche Jugendherberge) [German] youth hostel

DM abbr (Deutsche Mark) DM

doch conj & adv but; (dennoch) yet; (trotzdem) after all; **wenn d∼ ...!** if only ...! **nicht d∼!** don't [do that]! **er kommt d∼?** he is coming, isn't he? **kommst du nicht?— d∼!** aren't you coming?—yes, I am!

Docht m -[e]s,-e wick

Dock nt -s,-s dock. **d∼en** vt/i (haben) dock

Dogge f -,-n Great Dane

Dogm|a nt -s,-men dogma. **d∼atisch** a dogmatic, adv -ally

Dohle f -,-n jackdaw

Doktor m -s,-en /-'to:rən/ doctor. **D∼arbeit** f [doctoral] thesis. **D∼würde** f doctorate

Doktrin f -,-en doctrine

Dokument nt -[e]s,-e document. **D∼arbericht** m documentary. **D∼arfilm** m documentary film

Dolch m -[e]s,-e dagger

doll a (fam) fantastic; (schlimm) awful ● adv beautifully; (sehr) very; (schlimm) badly

Dollar m -s,- dollar

dolmetsch|en vt/i (haben) interpret. **D∼er(in)** m -s,- (f -,-nen) interpreter

Dom m -[e]s,-e cathedral

domin|ant a dominant. **d∼ieren** vi (haben) dominate; (vorherrschen) predominate

Domino nt -s,-s dominoes sg. **D∼stein** m domino

Dompfaff m -en,-en bullfinch

Donau f - Danube

Donner m -s thunder. **d∼n** vi (haben) thunder

Donnerstag m Thursday. **d∼s** adv on Thursdays

Donnerwetter nt (fam) telling-off; (Krach) row ● int /'--'--/ wow! (Fluch) damn it!

doof a (fam) stupid, adv -ly

Doppel nt -s,- duplicate; (Tennis) doubles pl. **D∼bett** nt double bed. **D∼decker** m -s,- double-decker [bus]. **d∼deutig** a ambiguous. **D∼gänger** m -s,double. **D∼kinn** nt double chin. **D∼name** m double-barrelled name. **D∼punkt** m (Gram) colon. **D∼schnitte** f sandwich. **d∼sinnig** a ambiguous. **D∼stecker** m two-way adaptor. **d∼t** a double; ⟨Boden⟩ false; **in d∼ter Ausfertigung** in duplicate; **die d∼te Menge** twice the amount ● adv doubly; (zweimal) twice; **d∼t so viel** twice as much. **D∼zimmer** nt double room

Dorf nt -[e]s,-ͤer village. **D∼bewohner** m villager

dörflich a rural

Dorn m -[e]s,-en thorn. **d∼ig** a thorny

Dörrobst nt dried fruit

Dorsch m -[e]s,-e cod

dort adv there; **d∼ drüben** over there. **d∼her** adv [von] **d∼her** from there. **d∼hin** adv there. **d∼ig** a local

Dose f -,-n tin, can; (Schmuck-) box

dösen vi (haben) doze

Dosen|milch f evaporated milk. **D∼öffner** m tin or can opener

dosieren vt measure out

Dosis f -, Dosen dose

Dotter m & nt -s,- [egg] yolk

Dozent(in) m -en,-en (f -,-nen) (Univ) lecturer

Dr. abbr (Doktor) Dr

Drache m -n,-n dragon. **D∼n** m -s,- kite; (fam: Frau) dragon. **D∼nfliegen** nt hang-gliding. **D∼nflieger** m hang-glider

Draht m -[e]s,ͤe wire; **auf D∼** (fam) on the ball. **d∼ig** a (fig) wiry. **D∼seilbahn** f cable railway

drall a plump; ⟨Frau⟩ buxom

Dram|a nt -s,-men drama. **D∼atik** f - drama. **D∼atiker** m -s,- dramatist. **d∼atisch** a dramatic, adv -ally. **d∼atisieren** vt dramatize

dran adv (fam) = daran; **gut/schlecht d∼ sein** be well off/in a bad way; **ich bin d∼** it's my turn

Dränage /-'na:ʒə/ f - drainage

Drang m -[e]s,ͤe urge; (Druck) pressure

dräng|eln vt/i (haben) push; (bedrängen) pester. **d∼en** vt push; (bedrängen) urge; **sich d∼en** crowd (um round) ● vi (haben) push; (eilen) be urgent; ⟨Zeit:⟩ press; **d∼en auf** (+ acc) press for

dran|halten† (sich) *vr sep* hurry.
d~kommen† *vi sep* (*sein*) have
one's turn; **wer kommt dran?** whose
turn is it?

drapieren *vt* drape

drastisch *a* drastic, *adv* -ally

drauf *adv* (*fam*)=**darauf**; **d~ und
dran sein** be on the point (**etw zu tun**
of doing sth). **D~gänger** *m* -s,- dare-
devil. **d~gängerisch** *a* reckless

draus *adv* (*fam*)=**daraus**

draußen *adv* outside; (*im Freien*) out
of doors

drechseln *vt* (*Techn*) turn

Dreck *m* -s dirt; (*Morast*) mud; (*fam:
Kleinigkeit*) trifle; **in den D~ ziehen**
(*fig*) denigrate. **d~ig** *a* dirty; muddy

Dreh *m* -s (*fam*) knack; **den D~ her-
aushaben** have got the hang of it.
D~bank *f* lathe. **D~bleistift** *m* pro-
pelling pencil. **D~buch** *nt* screen-
play, script. **d~en** *vt* turn; (*im
Kreis*) rotate; (*verschlingen*) twist;
roll 〈*Zigarette*〉; shoot 〈*Film*〉;
lauter/ leiser d~en turn up/down;
sich d~en turn; (*im Kreis*) rotate;
(*schnell*) spin; 〈*Wind:*〉 change; **sich
d~en um** revolve around; (*sich handeln*) be about ● *vi* (*haben*) turn;
〈*Wind:*〉 change; **an etw** (*dat*) **d~en**
turn sth. **D~orgel** *f* barrel organ.
D~stuhl *m* swivel chair. **D~tür** *f*
revolving door. **D~ung** *f* -,-en turn;
(*im Kreis*) rotation. **D~zahl** *f*
number of revolutions

drei *inv a*, **D~** *f* -,-en three; (*Sch*) ≈
pass. **D~eck** *nt* -[e]s,-e triangle.
d~eckig *a* triangular. **D~einigkeit** *f*
- **die [Heilige] D~einigkeit** the [Holy]
Trinity. **d~erlei** *inv a* three kinds of
● *pron* three things. **d~fach** *a*
triple; **in d~facher Ausfertigung** in
triplicate. **D~faltigkeit** *f* - = **D~ei-
nigkeit**. **d~mal** *adv* three times.
D~rad *nt* tricycle

dreißig *inv a* thirty. **d~ste(r,s)** *a*
thirtieth

dreist *a* impudent, *adv* -ly; (*verwegen*)
audacious, *adv* -ly. **D~igkeit** *f* - impudence; audacity

dreiviertel *inv a* three-quarter.
D~stunde *f* three quarters of an
hour

dreizehn *inv a* thirteen. **d~te(r,s)** *a*
thirteenth

dreschen† *vt* thresh

dress|ieren *vt* train. **D~ur** *f* -
training

dribbeln *vi* (*haben*) dribble

Drill *m* -[e]s (*Mil*) drill. **d~en** *vt* drill

Drillinge *mpl* triplets

drin *adv* (*fam*)=**darin**; (*drinnen*)
inside

dring|en† *vi* (*sein*) penetrate (**in**+*acc*
into; **durch etw** sth); (*heraus-*) come
(**aus** out of); **d~en auf** (+*acc*) insist
on. **d~end** *a* urgent, *adv* -ly. **d~lich**
a urgent. **D~lichkeit** *f* - urgency

Drink *m* -[s],-s [alcoholic] drink

drinnen *adv* inside; (*im Haus*)
indoors

dritt *adv* **zu d~** in threes; **wir waren
zu d~** there were three of us.
d~e(r,s) *a* third; **ein D~er** a third
person. **D~el** *nt* -s,- third. **d~ens**
adv thirdly. **d~rangig** *a* third-rate

Drog|e *f* -,-n drug. **D~enabhän-
gige(r)** *m/f* drug addict. **D~erie** *f*
-,-n chemist's shop, (*Amer*) drug-
store. **D~ist** *m* -en,-en chemist

drohen *vi* (*haben*) threaten (**jdm**
s.o.). **d~d** *a* threatening; 〈*Gefahr*〉
imminent

dröhnen *vi* (*haben*) resound; (*tönen*)
boom

Drohung *f* -,-en threat

drollig *a* funny; (*seltsam*) odd

Drops *m* -,- [fruit] drop

Droschke *f* -,-n cab

Drossel *f* -,-n thrush

drosseln *vt* (*Techn*) throttle; (*fig*) cut
back

drüb|en *adv* over there. **d~er** *adv*
(*fam*)=**darüber**

Druck¹ *m* -[e]s,¨e pressure; **unter D~
setzen** (*fig*) pressurize

Druck² *m* -[e]s,-e printing; (*Schrift,
Reproduktion*) print. **D~buchstabe**
m block letter

Drückeberger *m* -s,- shirker

drucken *vt* print

drücken *vt/i* (*haben*) press; (*aus-*)
squeeze; 〈*Schuh:*〉 pinch; (*umarmen*)
hug; (*fig: belasten*) weigh down;
Preise d~ force down prices; (*an
Tür*) **d~** push; **sich d~** (*fam*) make
oneself scarce; **sich d~ vor** (+*dat*)
(*fam*) shirk. **d~d** *a* heavy; (*schwül*)
oppressive

Drucker *m* -s,- printer

Drücker *m* -s,- push-button; (*Tür-*)
door knob

Druckerei *f* -,-en printing works

Druck|fehler *m* misprint. **D~knopf**
m press-stud; (*Drücker*) push-button. **D~luft** *f* compressed air.
D~sache *f* printed matter.
D~schrift *f* type; (*Veröffentlichung*)

publication; **in D~schrift** in block letters *pl*

drucksen *vi* (*haben*) hum and haw

Druck|stelle *f* bruise. **D~taste** *f* push-button. **D~topf** *m* pressure-cooker

drum *adv* (*fam*)= **darum**

drunter *adv* (*fam*)= **darunter; alles geht d~ und drüber** (*fam*) everything is topsy-turvy

Drüse *f* -,-n (*Anat*) gland

Dschungel *m* -s,- jungle

du *pron* (*familiar address*) you; **auf du und du** on familiar terms

Dübel *m* -s,- plug

duck|en *vt* duck; (*fig: demütigen*) humiliate; **sich d~en** duck; (*fig*) cringe. **D~mäuser** *m* -s,- moral coward

Dudelsack *m* bagpipes *pl*

Duell *nt* -s,-e duel

Duett *nt* -s,-e [vocal] duet

Duft *m* -[e]s,ˉe fragrance, scent; (*Aroma*) aroma. **d~en** *vi* (*haben*) smell (**nach** of). **d~ig** *a* fine; (*zart*) delicate

duld|en *vt* tolerate; (*erleiden*) suffer ● *vi* (*haben*) suffer. **d~sam** *a* tolerant

dumm *a* (**dümmer, dümmst**) stupid, *adv* -ly; (*unklug*) foolish, *adv* -ly; (*fam: lästig*) awkward; **wie d~!** what a nuisance! **der D~e sein** (*fig*) be the loser. **d~erweise** *adv* stupidly; (*leider*) unfortunately. **D~heit** *f* -,-en stupidity; (*Torheit*) foolishness; (*Handlung*) folly. **D~kopf** *m* (*fam*) fool.

dumpf *a* dull, *adv* -y; (*muffig*) musty. **d~ig** *a* musty

Düne *f* -,-n dune

Dung *m* -s manure

Düng|emittel *nt* fertilizer. **d~en** *vt* fertilize. **D~er** *m* -s,- fertilizer

dunk|el *a* dark; (*vage*) vague, *adv* -ly; (*fragwürdig*) shady; **d~les Bier** brown ale; **im D~eln** in the dark

Dünkel *m* -s conceit

dunkel|blau *a* dark blue. **d~braun** *a* dark brown

dünkelhaft *a* conceited

Dunkel|heit *f* - darkness. **D~kammer** *f* dark-room. **d~n** *vi* (*haben*) get dark. **d~rot** *a* dark red

dünn *a* thin, *adv* -ly; ⟨*Buch*⟩ slim; (*spärlich*) sparse; (*schwach*) weak

Dunst *m* -es,ˉe mist, haze; (*Dampf*) vapour

dünsten *vt* steam

dunstig *a* misty, hazy

Dünung *f* - swell

Duo *nt* -s,-s [instrumental] duet

Duplikat *nt* -[e]s,-e duplicate

Dur *nt* - (*Mus*) major [key]; **in A-Dur** in A major

durch *prep* (+*acc*) through; (*mittels*) by; [*geteilt*] **d~** (*Math*) divided by ● *adv* **die Nacht d~** throughout the night; **sechs Uhr d~** (*fam*) gone six o'clock; **d~ und d~ naß** wet through

durcharbeiten *vt sep* work through; **sich d~** work one's way through

durchaus *adv* absolutely; **d~ nicht** by no means

durchbeißen† *vt sep* bite through

durchblättern *vt sep* leaf through

durchblicken *vi sep* (*haben*) look through; **d~ lassen** (*fig*) hint at

Durchblutung *f* circulation

durchbohren *vt insep* pierce

durchbrechen¹† *vt/i sep* (*haben*) break [in two]

durchbrechen²† *vt insep* break through; break ⟨*Schallmauer*⟩

durchbrennen† *vi sep* (*sein*) burn through; ⟨*Sicherung:*⟩ blow; (*fam: weglaufen*) run away

durchbringen† *vt sep* get through; (*verschwenden*) squander; (*versorgen*) support; **sich d~ mit** make a living by

Durchbruch *m* breakthrough

durchdacht *a* **gut d~** well thought out

durchdrehen *v sep* ● *vt* mince ● *vi* (*haben/sein*) (*fam*) go crazy

durchdringen¹† *vt insep* penetrate

durchdringen²† *vi sep* (*sein*) penetrate; (*sich durchsetzen*) get one's way. **d~d** *a* penetrating; ⟨*Schrei*⟩ piercing

durcheinander *adv* in a muddle; ⟨*Person*⟩ confused. **D~** *nt* -s muddle. **d~bringen†** *vt sep* muddle [up]; confuse ⟨*Person*⟩. **d~geraten†** *vi sep* (*sein*) get mixed up. **d~reden** *vi sep* (*haben*) all talk at once

durchfahren¹† *vi sep* (*sein*) drive through; ⟨*Zug:*⟩ go through

durchfahren²† *vt insep* drive/go through; **jdn d~** ⟨*Gedanke:*⟩ flash through s.o.'s mind

Durchfahrt *f* journey/drive through; **auf der D~** passing through; **'D~ verboten'** 'no thoroughfare'

Durchfall *m* diarrhoea; (*fam: Versagen*) flop. **d~en†** *vi sep* (*sein*) fall through; (*fam: versagen*) flop; (*bei Prüfung*) fail

durchfliegen¹† *vi sep* (*sein*) fly through; (*fam: durchfallen*) fail

durchfliegen²† *vt insep* fly through; (*lesen*) skim through

durchfroren *a* frozen

Durchfuhr *f* - (*Comm*) transit

durchführ|bar *a* feasible. **d∼en** *vt sep* carry out

Durchgang *m* passage; (*Sport*) round; **'D∼ verboten'** 'no entry'. **D∼sverkehr** *m* through traffic

durchgeben† *vt sep* pass through; (*übermitteln*) transmit; (*Radio, TV*) broadcast

durchgebraten *a* gut **d∼** well done

durchgehen† *v sep* ● *vi* (*sein*) go through; (*davonlaufen*) run away; ⟨*Pferd:*⟩ bolt; **jdm etw d∼ lassen** let s.o. get away with sth ● *vt* go through. **d∼d** *a* continuous, *adv* -ly; **d∼d geöffnet** open all day; **d∼der Wagen/Zug** through carriage/train

durchgreifen† *vi sep* (*haben*) reach through; (*vorgehen*) take drastic action. **d∼d** *a* drastic

durchhalte|n† *v sep* (*fig*) ● *vi* (*haben*) hold out ● *vt* keep up. **D∼vermögen** *nt* stamina

durchhängen† *vi sep* (*haben*) sag

durchkommen† *vi sep* (*sein*) come through; (*gelangen, am Telefon*) get through; (*bestehen*) pass; (*überleben*) pull through; (*finanziell*) get by (**mit** on)

durchkreuzen *vt insep* thwart

durchlassen† *vt sep* let through

durchlässig *a* permeable; (*undicht*) leaky

durchlaufen¹† *v sep* ● *vi* (*sein*) run through ● *vt* wear out

durchlaufen²† *vt insep* pass through

Durchlauferhitzer *m* -**s,**- geyser

durchleben *vt insep* live through

durchlesen† *vt sep* read through

durchleuchten *vt insep* X-ray

durchlöchert *a* riddled with holes

durchmachen *vt sep* go through; (*erleiden*) undergo; have ⟨*Krankheit*⟩

Durchmesser *m* -**s,**- diameter

durchnäßt *a* wet through

durchnehmen† *vt sep* (*Sch*) do

durchnumeriert *a* numbered consecutively

durchpausen *vt sep* trace

durchqueren *vt insep* cross

Durchreiche *f* -,-**n** [serving] hatch. **d∼n** *vt sep* pass through

Durchreise *f* journey through; **auf der D∼** passing through. **d∼n** *vi sep* (*sein*) pass through

durchreißen† *vt/i sep* (*sein*) tear

durchs *adv* = **durch das**

Durchsage *f* -,-**n** announcement. **d∼n** *vt sep* announce

durchschauen *vt insep* (*fig*) see through

durchscheinend *a* translucent

Durchschlag *m* carbon copy; (*Culin*) colander. **d∼en**¹† *v sep* ● *vt* (*Culin*) rub through a sieve; **sich d∼en** (*fig*) struggle through ● *vi* (*sein*) ⟨*Sicherung:*⟩ blow

durchschlagen²† *vt insep* smash

durchschlagend *a* (*fig*) effective; ⟨*Erfolg*⟩ resounding

durchschneiden† *vt sep* cut

Durchschnitt *m* average; **im D∼** on average. **d∼lich** *a* average ● *adv* on average. **D∼s-** *pref* average

Durchschrift *f* carbon copy

durchsehen† *v sep* ● *vi* (*haben*) see through ● *vt* look through

durchseihen† *vt sep* strain

durchsetzen¹ *vt sep* force through; **sich d∼** assert oneself; ⟨*Mode:*⟩ catch on

durchsetzen² *vt insep* intersperse; (*infiltrieren*) infiltrate

Durchsicht *f* check

durchsichtig *a* transparent

durchsickern *vi sep* (*sein*) seep through; ⟨*Neuigkeit:*⟩ leak out

durchsprechen† *vt sep* discuss

durchstehen† *vt sep* (*fig*) come through

durchstreichen† *vt sep* cross out

durchsuch|en *vt insep* search. **D∼ung** *f* -,-**en** search

durchtrieben *a* cunning

durchwachsen *a* ⟨*Speck*⟩ streaky; (*fam: gemischt*) mixed

durchwacht *a* sleepless ⟨*Nacht*⟩

durchwählen *vi sep* (*haben*) (*Teleph*) dial direct

durchweg *adv* without exception

durchweicht *a* soggy

durchwühlen *vt insep* rummage through; ransack ⟨*Haus*⟩

durchziehen† *v sep* ● *vt* pull through ● *vi* (*sein*) pass through

durchzucken *vt insep* (*fig*) shoot through; **jdn d∼** ⟨*Gedanke:*⟩ flash through s.o.'s mind

Durchzug *m* through draught

dürfen† *vt & v aux* etw [tun] **d~** be allowed to do sth; **darf ich?** may I? **sie darf es nicht sehen** she must not see it; **ich hätte es nicht tun/sagen d~** I ought not to have done/said it; **das dürfte nicht allzu schwer sein** that should not be too difficult

dürftig *a* poor; ⟨*Mahlzeit*⟩ scanty

dürr *a* dry; ⟨*Boden*⟩ arid; (*mager*) skinny. **D~e** *f* -,-n drought

Durst *m* -[e]s thirst; **D~ haben** be thirsty. **d~en** *vi* (*haben*) be thirsty. **d~ig** *a* thirsty

Dusche *f* -,-n shower. **d~n** *vi/r* (*haben*) [sich] **d~n** have a shower

Düse *f* -,-n nozzle. **D~nflugzeug** *nt* jet

düster *a* gloomy, *adv* -ily; (*dunkel*) dark

Dutzend *nt* -s,-e dozen. **d~weise** *adv* by the dozen

duzen *vt* jdn **d~** call s.o. 'du'

Dynam|ik *f* - dynamics *sg*; (*fig*) dynamism. **d~isch** *a* dynamic; ⟨*Rente*⟩ index-linked

Dynamit *nt* -es dynamite

Dynamo *m* -s,-s dynamo

Dynastie *f* -,-n dynasty

D-Zug /ˈdeː-/ *m* express [train]

E

Ebbe *f* -,-n low tide

eben *a* level; (*glatt*) smooth; **zu e~er Erde** on the ground floor ● *adv* just; (*genau*) exactly; **e~ noch** only just; (*gerade vorhin*) just now; **das ist es e~!** that's just it! [na] **e~!** exactly! **E~bild** *nt* image. **e~bürtig** *a* equal; **jdm e~bürtig sein** be s.o.'s equal

Ebene *f* -,-n (*Geog*) plain; (*Geom*) plane; (*fig: Niveau*) level

eben|falls *adv* also; **danke, e~falls** thank you, [the] same to you. **E~holz** *nt* ebony. **e~mäßig** *a* regular, *adv* -ly. **e~so** *adv* just the same; (*ebensosehr*) just as much; **e~so gut/teuer** just as good/expensive. **e~sogut** *adv* just as well. **e~sosehr** *adv* just as much. **e~soviel** *adv* just as much/many. **e~sowenig** *adv* just as little/few; (*noch*) no more

Eber *m* -s,- boar. **E~esche** *f* rowan

ebnen *vt* level; (*fig*) smooth

Echo *nt* -s,-s echo. **e~en** *vt/i* (*haben*) echo

echt *a* genuine, real; (*authentisch*) authentic; ⟨*Farbe*⟩ fast; (*typisch*) typical ● *adv* (*fam*) really; typically. **E~heit** *f* - authenticity

Eck|ball *m* (*Sport*) corner. **E~e** *f* -,-n corner; **um die E~e bringen** (*fam*) bump off. **e~ig** *a* angular; ⟨*Klammern*⟩ square; (*unbeholfen*) awkward. **E~stein** *m* corner-stone. **E~stoß** *m* = **E~ball**. **E~zahn** *m* canine tooth

Ecu, ECU /eˈkyː/ *m* -[s],-[s] ecu

edel *a* noble, *adv* -bly; (*wertvoll*) precious; (*fein*) fine. **E~mann** *m* (*pl* -leute) nobleman. **E~mut** *m* magnanimity. **e~mütig** *a* magnanimous, *adv* -ly. **E~stahl** *m* stainless steel. **E~stein** *m* precious stone

Efeu *m* -s ivy

Effekt *m* -[e]s,-e effect. **E~en** *pl* securities. **e~iv** *a* actual, *adv* -ly; (*wirksam*) effective, *adv* -ly. **e~voll** *a* effective

EG *f* - *abbr* (**Europäische Gemeinschaft**) EC

egal *a* **das ist mir e~** (*fam*) it's all the same to me ● *adv* **e~ wie/wo** no matter how/where. **e~itär** *a* egalitarian

Egge *f* -,-n harrow

Ego|ismus *m* - selfishness. **E~ist(in)** *m* -en,-en (*f* -,-nen) egoist. **e~istisch** *a* selfish, *adv* -ly. **e~zentrisch** *a* egocentric

eh *adv* (*Aust fam*) anyway; **seit eh und je** from time immemorial

ehe *conj* before; **ehe nicht** until

Ehe *f* -,-n marriage. **E~bett** *nt* double bed. **E~bruch** *m* adultery. **E~frau** *f* wife. **E~leute** *pl* married couple *sg*. **e~lich** *a* marital; ⟨*Recht*⟩ conjugal; ⟨*Kind*⟩ legitimate

ehemal|ig *a* former. **e~s** *adv* formerly

Ehe|mann *m* (*pl* -männer) husband. **E~paar** *nt* married couple

eher *adv* earlier, sooner; (*lieber, vielmehr*) rather; (*mehr*) more

Ehering *m* wedding ring

ehr|bar *a* respectable. **E~e** *f* -,-n honour; **jdm E~e machen** do credit to s.o. **e~en** *vt* honour. **e~enamtlich** *a* honorary ● *adv* in an honorary capacity. **E~endoktorat** *nt* honorary doctorate. **E~engast** *m* guest of honour. **e~enhaft** *a* honourable, *adv* -bly. **E~enmann** *m* (*pl*

-**männer**) man of honour. **E~enmit-glied** *nt* honorary member. **e~en-rührig** *a* defamatory. **E~enrunde** *f* lap of honour. **E~ensache** *f* point of honour. **e~enwert** *a* honourable. **E~enwort** *nt* word of honour. **e~erbietig** *a* deferential, *adv* -ly. **E~erbietung** *f* - deference. **E~furcht** *f* reverence; (*Scheu*) awe. **e~fürchtig** *a* reverent, *adv* -ly. **E~gefühl** *nt* sense of honour. **E~geiz** *m* ambition. **e~geizig** *a* ambitious. **e~lich** *a* honest, *adv* -ly; **e~lich gesagt** to be honest. **E~lich-keit** *f* - honesty. **e~los** *a* dishonourable. **e~sam** *a* respectable. **e~wür-dig** *a* venerable; (*als Anrede*) Reverend

Ei *nt* -[e]s,-er egg

Eibe *f* -,-n yew

Eiche *f* -,-n oak. **E~l** *f* -,-n acorn. **E~lhäher** *m* -s,- jay

eichen *vt* standardize

Eichhörnchen *nt* -s,- squirrel

Eid *m* -[e]s,-e oath

Eidechse *f* -,-n lizard

eidlich *a* sworn ● *adv* on oath

Eidotter *m* & *nt* egg yolk

Eier|becher *m* egg-cup. **E~kuchen** *m* pancake; (*Omelett*) omelette. **E~schale** *f* eggshell. **E~schnee** *m* beaten egg-white. **E~stock** *m* ovary. **E~uhr** *f* egg-timer

Eifer *m* -s eagerness; (*Streben*) zeal. **E~sucht** *f* jealousy. **e~süchtig** *a* jealous, *adv* -ly

eiförmig *a* egg-shaped; (*oval*) oval

eifrig *a* eager, *adv* -ly; (*begeistert*) keen, *adv* -ly

Eigelb *nt* -[e]s,-e [egg] yolk

eigen *a* own; (*typisch*) characteristic (*dat* of); (*seltsam*) odd, *adv* -ly; (*genau*) particular. **E~art** *f* peculiarity. **e~artig** *a* peculiar, *adv* -ly; (*seltsam*) odd. **E~brötler** *m* -s,- crank. **e~händig** *a* personal, *adv* -ly; (*Unterschrift*) own. **E~heit** *f* -,-en peculiarity. **e~mächtig** *a* high-handed; (*unbefugt*) unauthorized ● *adv* high-handedly; without authority. **E~name** *m* proper name. **E~nutz** *m* self-interest. **e~nützig** *a* selfish, *adv* -ly. **e~s** *adv* specially. **E~schaft** *f* -,-en quality; (*Phys*) property; (*Merkmal*) characteristic; (*Funktion*) capacity. **E~schafts-wort** *nt* (*pl* -wörter) adjective. **E~sinn** *m* obstinacy. **e~sinnig** *a* obstinate, *adv* -ly

eigentlich *a* actual, real; (*wahr*) true ● *adv* actually, really; (*streng genommen*) strictly speaking; **wie geht es ihm e~?** by the way, how is he?

Eigen|tor *nt* own goal. **E~tum** *nt* -s property. **E~tümer(in)** *m* -s,- (*f* -,-nen) owner. **e~tümlich** *a* odd, *adv* -ly; (*typisch*) characteristic. **E~tumswohnung** *f* freehold flat. **e~willig** *a* self-willed; (*Stil*) highly individual

eign|en (sich) *vr* be suitable. **E~ung** *f* - suitability

Eil|brief *m* express letter. **E~e** *f* - hurry; **E~e haben** be in a hurry; (*Sache:*) be urgent. **e~en** *vi* (*sein*) hurry ● (*haben*) (*drängen*) be urgent. **e~ends** *adv* hurriedly. **e~ig** *a* hurried, *adv* -ly; (*dringend*) urgent, *adv* -ly; **es e~ig haben** be in a hurry. **E~zug** *m* semi-fast train

Eimer *m* -s,- bucket; (*Abfall-*) bin

ein[1] *adj* one; **e~es Tages/Abends** one day/evening; **mit jdm in einem Zimmer schlafen** sleep in the same room as s.o. ● *indef art* a, (*vor Vokal*) an; **so ein such a**; **was für ein** (*Frage*) what kind of a? (*Ausruf*) what a!

ein[2] *adv* **ein und aus** in and out; **nicht mehr ein noch aus wissen** (*fam*) be at one's wits' end

einander *pron* one another

einarbeiten *vt sep* train

einäscher|n *vt sep* reduce to ashes; cremate (*Leiche*). **E~ung** *f* -,-en cremation

einatmen *vt/i sep* (*haben*) inhale, breathe in

ein|äugig *a* one-eyed. **E~bahn-straße** *f* one-way street

einbalsamieren *vt sep* embalm

Einband *m* binding

Einbau *m* installation; (*Montage*) fitting. **e~en** *vt sep* install; (*montieren*) fit. **E~küche** *f* fitted kitchen

einbegriffen *pred a* included

einberuf|en *vt sep* convene; (*Mil*) call up, (*Amer*) draft. **E~ung** *f* call-up, (*Amer*) draft

Einbettzimmer *nt* single room

einbeulen *vt sep* dent

einbeziehen† *vt sep* [mit] **e~** include; (*berücksichtigen*) take into account

einbiegen† *vi sep* (*sein*) turn

einbild|en *vt sep* **sich** (*dat*) **etw e~en** imagine sth; **sich** (*dat*) **viel e~en** be conceited. **E~ung** *f* imagination;

(*Dünkel*) conceit. **E~ungskraft** *f* imagination

einblenden *vt sep* fade in

einbleuen *vt sep* **jdm etw e~** (*fam*) drum sth into s.o.

Einblick *m* insight

einbrech|en† *vi sep* (*haben/sein*) break in; **bei uns ist eingebrochen worden** we have been burgled ● (*sein*) set in; ⟨*Nacht:*⟩ fall. **E~er** *m* burglar

einbring|en† *vt sep* get in; bring in ⟨*Geld*⟩; **das bringt nichts ein** it's not worth while. **e~lich** *a* profitable

Einbruch *m* burglary; **bei E~ der Nacht** at nightfall

einbürger|n *vt sep* naturalize; **sich e~n** become established. **E~ung** *f* - naturalization

Ein|buße *f* loss (**an**+*dat* of). **e~büßen** *vt sep* lose

einchecken /-tʃɛkən/ *vt/i sep* (*haben*) check in

eindecken (sich) *vr sep* stock up

eindeutig *a* unambiguous; (*deutlich*) clear, *adv* -ly

eindicken *vt sep* (*Culin*) thicken

eindring|en† *vi sep* (*sein*) **e~en in** (+*acc*) penetrate into; (*mit Gewalt*) force one's/⟨*Wasser:*⟩ its way into; (*Mil*) invade; **auf jdn e~en** (*fig*) press s.o.; (*bittend*) plead with s.o. **e~lich** *a* urgent, *adv* -ly. **E~ling** *m* -s,-e intruder

Eindruck *m* impression; **E~ machen** impress (**auf jdn** s.o.)

eindrücken *vt sep* crush

eindrucksvoll *a* impressive

ein|e(r,s) *pron* one; (*jemand*) someone; (*man*) one, you; **e~er von uns** one of us; **es macht e~en müde** it makes you tired

einebnen *vt sep* level

eineiig *a* ⟨*Zwillinge*⟩ identical

eineinhalb *inv a* one and a half; **e~ Stunden** an hour and a half

Eineiternfamilie *f* one-parent family

einengen *vt sep* restrict

Einer *m* -s,- (*Math*) unit. **e~** *pron s.* **eine(r,s).** **e~lei** *inv a* ● *attrib a* one kind of; (*eintönig, einheitlich*) the same ● *pred a* (*fam*) immaterial; **es ist mir e~lei** it's all the same to me. **E~lei** *nt* -s monotony. **e~seits** *adv* on the one hand

einfach *a* simple, *adv* -ly; ⟨*Essen*⟩ plain; ⟨*Faden, Fahrt, Fahrkarte*⟩ single; **e~er Soldat** private. **E~heit** *f* - simplicity

einfädeln *vt sep* thread; (*fig: arrangieren*) arrange; **sich e~** (*Auto*) filter in

einfahr|en† *v sep* ● *vi* (*sein*) arrive; ⟨*Zug:*⟩ pull in ● *vt* (*Auto*) run in; **die Ernte e~en** get in the harvest. **E~t** *f* arrival; (*Eingang*) entrance, way in; (*Auffahrt*) drive; (*Autobahn-*) access road; **keine E~t** no entry

Einfall *m* idea; (*Mil*) invasion. **e~en†** *vi sep* (*sein*) collapse; (*eindringen*) invade; (*einstimmen*) join in; **jdm e~en** occur to s.o.; **sein Name fällt mir nicht ein** I can't think of his name; **was fällt ihm ein!** what does he think he is doing! **e~sreich** *a* imaginative

Einfalt *f* - naïvety

einfältig *a* simple; (*naiv*) naïve

Einfaltspinsel *m* simpleton

einfangen† *vt sep* catch

einfarbig *a* of one colour; ⟨*Stoff, Kleid*⟩ plain

einfass|en *vt sep* edge; set ⟨*Edelstein*⟩. **E~ung** *f* border, edging

einfetten *vt sep* grease

einfinden† (sich) *vr sep* turn up

einfließen† *vi sep* (*sein*) flow in

einflößen *vt sep* **jdm etw e~** give s.o. sips of sth; **jdm Angst e~** (*fig*) frighten s.o.

Einfluß *m* influence. **e~reich** *a* influential

einförmig *a* monotonous, *adv* -ly. **E~keit** *f* - monotony

einfried[ig]en *vt sep* enclose. **E~ung** *f* -,-en enclosure

einfrieren† *vt/i sep* (*sein*) freeze

einfügen *vt sep* insert; (*einschieben*) interpolate; **sich e~** fit in

einfühl|en (sich) *vr sep* empathize (**in**+*acc* with). **e~sam** *a* sensitive

Einfuhr *f* -,-en import

einführ|en *vt sep* introduce; (*einstecken*) insert; (*einweisen*) initiate; (*Comm*) import. **e~end** *a* introductory. **E~ung** *f* introduction; (*Einweisung*) initiation

Eingabe *f* petition; (*Computer*) input

Eingang *m* entrance, way in; (*Ankunft*) arrival

eingebaut *a* built-in; ⟨*Schrank*⟩ fitted

eingeben† *vt sep* hand in; (*einflößen*) give (**jdm** s.o.); (*Computer*) feed in

eingebildet *a* imaginary; (*überheblich*) conceited

Eingeborene(r) *m/f* native

Eingebung *f* -,-en inspiration

eingedenk *prep* (+ *gen*) mindful of

eingefleischt *a* **e~er Junggeselle** confirmed bachelor

eingehakt *adv* arm in arm

eingehen† *v sep* ● *vi* (*sein*) come in; (*ankommen*) arrive; (*einlaufen*) shrink; (*sterben*) die; ⟨*Zeitung, Firma:*⟩ fold; **auf etw** (*acc*) **e~** go into sth; (*annehmen*) agree to sth ● *vt* enter into; contract ⟨*Ehe*⟩; make ⟨*Wette*⟩; take ⟨*Risiko*⟩. **e~d** *a* detailed; (*gründlich*) thorough, *adv* -ly

eingelegt *a* inlaid; (*Culin*) pickled; (*mariniert*) marinaded

eingemacht *a* (*Culin*) bottled

eingenommen *pred a* (*fig*) taken (**von** with); prejudiced (**gegen** against); **von sich e~** conceited

eingeschneit *a* snowbound

eingeschrieben *a* registered

Einge|ständnis *nt* admission. **e~stehen**† *vt sep* admit

eingetragen *a* registered

Eingeweide *pl* bowels, entrails

eingewöhnen (sich) *vr sep* settle in

eingießen† *vt sep* pour in; (*einschenken*) pour

eingleisig *a* single-track

einglieder|n *vt sep* integrate. **E~ung** *f* integration

eingraben† *vt sep* bury

eingravieren *vt sep* engrave

eingreifen† *vi sep* (*haben*) intervene. **E~** *nt* -s intervention

Eingriff *m* intervention; (*Med*) operation

einhaken *vt/r sep* jdn **e~** *od* **sich bei jdm e~** take s.o.'s arm

einhalten† *v sep* ● *vt* keep; (*befolgen*) observe ● *vi* (*haben*) stop

einhändigen *vt sep* hand in

einhängen *v sep* ● *vt* hang; put down ⟨*Hörer*⟩; **sich bei jdm e~** take s.o.'s arm ● *vi* (*haben*) hang up

einheimisch *a* local; (*eines Landes*) native; (*Comm*) home-produced. **E~e(r)** *m/f* local; native

Einheit *f* -,-en unity; (*Maß-, Mil*) unit. **e~lich** *a* uniform, *adv* -ly; (*vereinheitlicht*) standard. **E~spreis** *m* standard price; (*Fahrpreis*) flat fare

einhellig *a* unanimous, *adv* -ly

einholen *vt sep* catch up with; (*aufholen*) make up for; (*erbitten*) seek; (*einkaufen*) buy; **e~ gehen** go shopping

einhüllen *vt sep* wrap

einhundert *inv a* one hundred

einig *a* united; [**sich** (*dat*)] **e~ werden/sein** come to an/be in agreement

einig|e(r,s) *pron* some; (*ziemlich viel*) quite a lot of; (*substantivisch*) **e~e** *pl* some; (*mehrere*) several; (*ziemlich viele*) quite a lot; **e~es** *sg* some things; **vor e~er Zeit** some time ago. **e~emal** *adv* a few times

einigen *vt* unite; unify ⟨*Land*⟩; **sich e~** come to an agreement; (*ausmachen*) agree (**auf** + *acc* on)

einigermaßen *adv* to some extent; (*ziemlich*) fairly; (*ziemlich gut*) fairly well

Einig|keit *f* - unity; (*Übereinstimmung*) agreement. **E~ung** *f* - unification; (*Übereinkunft*) agreement

einjährig *a* one-year-old; (*ein Jahr dauernd*) one year's …; **e~e Pflanze** annual

einkalkulieren *vt sep* take into account

einkassieren *vt sep* collect

Einkauf *m* purchase; (*Einkaufen*) shopping; **Einkäufe machen** do some shopping. **e~en** *vt sep* buy; **e~en gehen** go shopping. **E~skorb** *m* shopping/(*im Geschäft*) wire basket. **E~stasche** *f* shopping bag. **E~swagen** *m* shopping trolley. **E~szentrum** *nt* shopping centre

einkehren *vi sep* (*sein*) [**in einem Lokal**] **e~** stop for a meal/drink [at an inn]

einklammern *vt sep* bracket

Einklang *m* harmony; **in E~ stehen** be in accord (**mit** with)

einkleben *vt sep* stick in

einkleiden *vt sep* fit out

einklemmen *vt sep* clamp; **sich** (*dat*) **den Finger in der Tür e~** catch one's finger in the door

einkochen *v sep* ● *vi* (*sein*) boil down ● *vt* preserve, bottle

Einkommen *nt* -s income. **E~[s]-steuer** *f* income tax

einkreisen *vt sep* encircle; **rot e~** ring in red

Einkünfte *pl* income *sg*; (*Einnahmen*) revenue *sg*

einlad|en† *vt sep* load; (*auffordern*) invite; (*bezahlen für*) treat. **e~end** *a* inviting. **E~ung** *f* invitation

Einlage *f* enclosure; (*Schuh-*) arch support; (*Zahn-*) temporary filling; (*Programm-*) interlude; (*Comm*) investment; (*Bank-*) deposit; **Suppe**

mit **E~** soup with noodles/dumplings

Ein|laß *m* **-sses** admittance. **e~las-sen†** *vt sep* let in; run ⟨*Bad, Wasser*⟩; **sich auf etw** (*acc*)/**mit jdm e~lassen** get involved in sth/with s.o.

einlaufen† *vi sep* (*sein*) come in; (*ankommen*) arrive; ⟨*Wasser:*⟩ run in; (*schrumpfen*) shrink; **[in den Hafen] e~** enter port

einleben (sich) *vr sep* settle in

Einlege|arbeit *f* inlaid work. **e~n** *vt sep* put in; lay in ⟨*Vorrat*⟩; lodge ⟨*Protest, Berufung*⟩; (*einfügen*) insert; (*Auto*) engage ⟨*Gang*⟩; (*verzieren*) inlay; (*Culin*) pickle; (*marinieren*) marinade; **eine Pause e~n** have a break. **E~sohle** *f* insole

einleit|en *vt sep* initiate; (*eröffnen*) begin. **e~end** *a* introductory. **E~ung** *f* introduction

einlenken *vi sep* (*haben*) (*fig*) relent

einleuchten *vi sep* (*haben*) be clear (*dat* to). **e~d** *a* convincing

einliefer|n *vt sep* take (**ins Krankenhaus** to hospital). **E~ung** *f* admission

einlösen *vt sep* cash ⟨*Scheck*⟩; redeem ⟨*Pfand*⟩; (*fig*) keep

einmachen *vt sep* preserve

einmal *adv* once; (*eines Tages*) one or some day; **noch/schon e~** again/before; **noch e~ so teuer** twice as expensive; **auf e~** at the same time; (*plötzlich*) suddenly; **nicht e~** not even; **es geht nun e~ nicht** it's just not possible. **E~eins** *nt* - [multiplication] tables *pl*. **e~ig** *a* single; (*einzigartig*) unique; (*fam: großartig*) fantastic, *adv* -ally

einmarschieren *vi sep* (*sein*) march in

einmisch|en (sich) *vr sep* interfere. **E~ung** *f* interference

einmütig *a* unanimous, *adv* -ly

Einnahme *f* -,-n taking; (*Mil*) capture; **E~n** *pl* income *sg*; (*Einkünfte*) revenue *sg*; (*Comm*) receipts; (*eines Ladens*) takings

einnehmen† *vt sep* take; have ⟨*Mahlzeit*⟩; (*Mil*) capture; take up ⟨*Platz*⟩; (*fig*) prejudice (**gegen** against); **jdn für sich e~** win s.o. over. **e~d** *a* engaging

einnicken *vi sep* (*sein*) nod off

Einöde *f* wilderness

einordnen *vt sep* put in its proper place; (*klassifizieren*) classify; **sich e~** fit in; (*Auto*) get in lane

einpacken *vt sep* pack; (*einhüllen*) wrap

einparken *vt sep* park

einpauken *vt sep* **jdm etw e~** (*fam*) drum sth into s.o.

einpflanzen *vt sep* plant; implant ⟨*Organ*⟩

einplanen *vt sep* allow for

einpräg|en *vt sep* impress (**jdm** [up]on s.o.); **sich** (*dat*) **etw e~en** memorize sth. **e~sam** *a* easy to remember; ⟨*Melodie*⟩ catchy

einquartieren *vt sep* (*Mil*) billet (**bei** on); **sich in einem Hotel e~** put up at a hotel

einrahmen *vt sep* frame

einrasten *vi sep* (*sein*) engage

einräumen *vt sep* put away; (*zugeben*) admit; (*zugestehen*) grant

einrechnen *vt sep* include

einreden *v sep* ● *vt* **jdm/sich** (*dat*) **etw e~** persuade s.o./oneself of sth ● *vi* (*haben*) **auf jdn e~** talk insistently to s.o.

einreib|en† *vt sep* rub (**mit** with). **E~mittel** *nt* liniment

einreichen *vt sep* submit; **die Scheidung e~** file for divorce

Einreih|er *m* -s,- single-breasted suit. **e~ig** *a* single-breasted

Einreise *f* entry. **e~n** *vi sep* (*sein*) enter (**nach Irland** Ireland). **E~visum** *nt* entry visa

einreißen† *v sep* ● *vt* tear; (*abreißen*) pull down ● *vi* (*sein*) tear; ⟨*Sitte:*⟩ become a habit

einrenken *vt sep* (*Med*) set

einricht|en *vt sep* fit out; (*möblieren*) furnish; (*anordnen*) arrange; (*Med*) set ⟨*Bruch*⟩; (*eröffnen*) set up; **sich e~en** furnish one's home; (*sich einschränken*) economize; (*sich vorbereiten*) prepare (**auf** + *acc* for). **E~ung** *f* furnishing; (*Möbel*) furnishings *pl*; (*Techn*) equipment; (*Vorrichtung*) device; (*Eröffnung*) setting up; (*Institution*) institution; (*Gewohnheit*) practice. **E~ungsgegenstand** *m* piece of equipment/ (*Möbelstück*) furniture

einrollen *vt sep* roll up; put in rollers ⟨*Haare*⟩

einrosten *vi sep* (*sein*) rust; (*fig*) get rusty

einrücken *v sep* ● *vi* (*sein*) (*Mil*) be called up; (*einmarschieren*) move in ● *vt* indent

eins *inv* *a* & *pron* one; **noch e~** one other thing; **mir ist alles e~** (*fam*) it's all the same to me. **E~** f -,-en one; (Sch) ≈ A

einsam a lonely; (allein) solitary; (abgelegen) isolated. **E~keit** f - loneliness; solitude; isolation

einsammeln vt sep collect

Einsatz m use; (Mil) mission; (Wett-) stake; (E~teil) insert; **im E~** in action. **e~bereit** a ready for action

einschalt|en vt sep switch on; (einschieben) interpolate; (fig: beteiligen) call in; **sich e~en** (fig) intervene. **E~quote** f (TV) viewing figures pl; ≈ ratings pl

einschärfen vt sep jdm etw e~ impress sth [up]on s.o.

einschätz|en vt sep assess; (bewerten) rate. **E~ung** f assessment; estimation

einschenken vt sep pour

einscheren vi sep (sein) pull in

einschicken vt sep send in

einschieben† vt sep push in; (einfügen) insert; (fig) interpolate

einschiff|en (sich) vr sep embark. **E~ung** f - embarkation

einschlafen† vi sep (sein) go to sleep; (aufhören) peter out

einschläfern vt sep lull to sleep; (betäuben) put out; (töten) put to sleep. **e~d** a soporific

Einschlag m impact; (fig: Beimischung) element. **e~en†** v sep ● vt knock in; (zerschlagen) smash; (einwickeln) wrap; (falten) turn up; (drehen) turn; take (Weg); take up (Laufbahn) ● vi (haben) hit/(Blitz:) strike (in etw acc sth); (zustimmen) shake hands [on a deal]; (Erfolg haben) be a hit; **auf jdn e~en** beat s.o.

einschlägig a relevant

einschleusen vt sep infiltrate

einschließ|en† vt sep lock in; (umgeben) enclose; (einkreisen) surround; (einbeziehen) include; **sich e~en** lock oneself in; **Bedienung eingeschlossen** service included. **e~lich** adv inclusive ● prep(+ gen) including

einschmeicheln (sich) vr sep ingratiate oneself (**bei** with)

einschnappen vi sep (sein) click shut; **eingeschnappt sein** (fam) be in a huff

einschneiden† vt/i sep (haben) [in] etw acc e~ cut into sth. **e~d** a (fig) drastic, adv -ally

Einschnitt m cut; (Med) incision; (Lücke) gap; (fig) decisive event

einschränk|en vt sep restrict; (reduzieren) cut back; **sich e~en** economize. **E~ung** f -,-en restriction; (Reduzierung) reduction; (Vorbehalt) reservation

Einschreib|[e]brief m registered letter. **e~en†** vt sep enter; register (Brief); **sich e~en** put one's name down; (sich anmelden) enrol. **E~en** nt registered letter/packet; **als** od **per E~en** by registered post

einschreiten† vi sep (sein) intervene

einschüchter|n vt sep intimidate. **E~ung** f - intimidation

einsehen† vt sep inspect; (lesen) consult; (begreifen) see. **E~** nt -s **ein E~ haben** show some understanding; (vernünftig sein) see reason

einseitig a one-sided; (Pol) unilateral ● adv on one side; (fig) one-sidedly; (Pol) unilaterally

einsenden† vt sep send in

einsetzen v sep ● vt put in; (einfügen) insert; (verwenden) use; put on (Zug); call out (Truppen); (Mil) deploy; (ernennen) appoint; (wetten) stake; (riskieren) risk; **sich e~ für** support ● vi (haben) start; (Winter, Regen:) set in

Einsicht f insight; (Verständnis) understanding; (Vernunft) reason; **zur E~ kommen** see reason. **e~ig** a understanding; (vernünftig) sensible

Einsiedler m hermit

einsilbig a monosyllabic; (Person) taciturn

einsinken† vi sep (sein) sink in

einspannen vt sep harness; jdn e~ (fam) rope s.o. in; **sehr eingespannt** (fam) very busy

einsparen vt sep save

einsperren vt sep shut/(im Gefängnis) lock up

einspielen (sich) vr sep warm up; **gut aufeinander eingespielt sein** work well together

einsprachig a monolingual

einspringen† vi sep (sein) step in (**für** for)

einspritzen vt sep inject

Einspruch m objection; **E~ erheben** object; (Jur) appeal

einspurig a single-track; (Auto) single-lane

einst adv once; (Zukunft) one day

Einstand m (Tennis) deuce

einstecken vt sep put in; post ⟨Brief⟩; (Electr) plug in; (fam: behalten) pocket; (fam: hinnehmen) take; suffer ⟨Niederlage⟩; **etw e∼** put sth in one's pocket

einstehen† vi sep (haben) **e∼ für** vouch for; answer for ⟨Folgen⟩

einsteigen† vi sep (sein) get in; (in Bus/Zug) get on

einstell|en vt sep put in; (anstellen) employ; (aufhören) stop; (regulieren) adjust, set; (Optik) focus; tune ⟨Motor, Zündung⟩; tune to ⟨Sender⟩; **sich e∼en** turn up; (ankommen) arrive; (eintreten) occur; ⟨Schwierigkeiten:⟩ arise; **sich e∼en auf** (+ acc) adjust to; (sich vorbereiten) prepare for. **E∼ung** f employment; (Aufhören) cessation; (Regulierung) adjustment; (Optik) focusing; (TV, Auto) tuning; (Haltung) attitude

Einstieg m -(e)s,-e entrance

einstig a former

einstimmen vi sep (haben) join in

einstimmig a unanimous, adv -ly. **E∼keit** f - unanimity

einstöckig a single-storey

einstudieren vt sep rehearse

einstufen vt sep classify

Ein|sturz m collapse. **e∼stürzen** vi sep (sein) collapse

einstweil|en adv for the time being; (inzwischen) meanwhile. **e∼ig** a temporary

eintasten vt sep key in

eintauchen vt/i sep (sein) dip in; (heftiger) plunge in

eintauschen vt sep exchange

eintausend inv a one thousand

einteil|en vt sep divide (in + acc into); (Biol) classify; **sich** (dat) **seine Zeit gut e∼en** organize one's time well. **e∼ig** a one-piece. **E∼ung** f division; classification

eintönig a monotonous, adv -ly. **E∼keit** f - monotony

Eintopf m, **E∼gericht** nt stew

Ein|tracht f - harmony. **e∼trächtig** a harmonious ● adv in harmony

Eintrag m -[e]s,-̈e entry. **e∼en**† vt sep enter; (Admin) register; (einbringen) bring in; **sich e∼en** put one's name down

einträglich a profitable

Eintragung f -,-en registration; (Eintrag) entry

eintreffen† vi sep (sein) arrive; (fig) come true; (geschehen) happen. **E∼** nt -s arrival

eintreiben† vt sep drive in; (einziehen) collect

eintreten† v sep ● vi (sein) enter; (geschehen) occur; **in einen Klub e∼** join a club; **e∼ für** (fig) stand up for ● vt kick in

Eintritt m entrance; (zu Veranstaltung) admission; (Beitritt) joining; (Beginn) beginning. **E∼skarte** f [admission] ticket

eintrocknen vi sep (sein) dry up

einüben vt sep practise

einundachtzig inv a eighty-one

einverleiben vt sep incorporate (dat into); **sich** (dat) **etw e∼** (fam) consume sth

Einvernehmen nt -s understanding; (Übereinstimmung) agreement; **in bestem E∼** on the best of terms

einverstanden a **e∼ sein** agree

Einverständnis nt agreement; (Zustimmung) consent

Einwand m -[e]s,-̈e objection

Einwander|er m immigrant. **e∼n** vi sep (sein) immigrate. **E∼ung** f immigration

einwandfrei a perfect, adv -ly; (untadelig) impeccable, adv -bly; (eindeutig) indisputable, adv -bly

einwärts adv inwards

einwechseln vt sep change

einwecken vt sep preserve, bottle

Einweg- pref non-returnable; ⟨Feuerzeug⟩ throw-away

einweichen vt sep soak

einweih|en vt sep inaugurate; (Relig) consecrate; (einführen) initiate; (fam) use for the first time; **in ein Geheimnis e∼en** let into a secret. **E∼ung** f -,-en inauguration; consecration; initiation

einweisen† vt sep direct; (einführen) initiate; **ins Krankenhaus e∼** send to hospital

einwenden† vt sep etwas **e∼** object (gegen to); **dagegen hätte ich nichts einzuwenden** (fam) I wouldn't say no

einwerfen† vt sep insert; post ⟨Brief⟩; (Sport) throw in; (vorbringen) interject; (zertrümmern) smash

einwickeln vt sep wrap [up]

einwillig|en vi sep (haben) consent, agree (in + acc to). **E∼ung** f - consent

einwirken vi sep (haben) **e∼ auf** (+ acc) have an effect on; (beeinflussen) influence

Einwohner|(in) *m* -s,- (*f* -,-nen) inhabitant. **E~zahl** *f* population

Einwurf *m* interjection; (*Einwand*) objection; (*Sport*) throw-in; (*Münz-*) slot

Einzahl *f* (*Gram*) singular

einzahl|en *vt sep* pay in. **E~ung** *f* payment; (*Einlage*) deposit

einzäunen *vt sep* fence in

Einzel *nt* -s,- (*Tennis*) singles *pl*. **E~bett** *nt* single bed. **E~fall** *m* individual/(*Sonderfall*) isolated case. **E~gänger** *m* -s,- loner. **E~haft** *f* solitary confinement. **E~handel** *m* retail trade. **E~händler** *m* retailer. **E~haus** *nt* detached house. **E~heit** *f* -,-en detail. **E~karte** *f* single ticket. **E~kind** *nt* only child

einzeln *a* single, *adv* -gly; (*individuell*) individual, *adv* -ly; (*gesondert*) separate, *adv* -ly; odd (*Handschuh, Socken*); **e~e Fälle** some cases. **e~e(r,s)** *pron* der/die **e~e** the individual; **ein e~er** a single one; **jeder e~e** every single one; **im e~en** in detail; **e~e** *pl* some

Einzel|person *f* single person. **E~teil** *nt* [component] part. **E~zimmer** *nt* single room

einziehen† *v sep* ● *vt* pull in; draw in (*Atem, Krallen*); (*Zool, Techn*) retract; indent (*Zeile*); (*aus dem Verkehr ziehen*) withdraw; (*beschlagnahmen*) confiscate; (*eintreiben*) collect; make (*Erkundigungen*); (*Mil*) call up; (*einfügen*) insert; (*einbauen*) put in; **den Kopf e~** duck [one's head] ● *vi* (*sein*) enter; (*umziehen*) move in; (*eindringen*) penetrate

einzig *a* only; (*einmalig*) unique; **eine/keine e~e Frage** a/not a single question; **ein e~es Mal** only once ● *adv* only; **e~ und allein** solely. **e~artig** *a* unique; (*unvergleichlich*) unparalleled. **e~e(r,s)** *pron* der/die/das **e~e** the only one; **ein/kein e~er** a/not a single one; **das e~e, was mich stört** the only thing that bothers me

Einzug *m* entry; (*Umzug*) move (in + *acc* into). **E~sgebiet** *nt* catchment area

Eis *nt* -es ice; (*Speise-*) ice-cream; **Eis am Stiel** ice lolly. **E~bahn** *f* ice rink. **E~bär** *m* polar bear. **E~becher** *m* ice-cream sundae. **E~bein** *nt* (*Culin*) knuckle of pork. **E~berg** *m* iceberg. **E~diele** *f* ice-cream parlour

Eisen *nt* -s,- iron. **E~bahn** *f* railway. **E~bahner** *m* -s,- railwayman

eisern *a* iron; (*fest*) resolute, *adv* -ly; **e~er Vorhang** (*Theat*) safety curtain; (*Pol*) Iron Curtain

Eis|fach *nt* freezer compartment. **e~gekühlt** *a* chilled. **e~ig** *a* icy. **E~kaffee** *m* iced coffee. **e~kalt** *a* ice cold; (*fig*) icy, *adv* -ily. **E~kunstlauf** *m* figure skating. **E~lauf** *m* skating. **e~laufen†** *vi sep* (*sein*) skate. **E~läufer(in)** *m*(*f*) skater. **E~pickel** *m* ice-axe. **E~scholle** *f* ice-floe. **E~schrank** *m* refrigerator. **E~vogel** *m* kingfisher. **E~würfel** *m* ice-cube. **E~zapfen** *m* icicle. **E~zeit** *f* ice age

eitel *a* vain; (*rein*) pure. **E~keit** *f* - vanity

Eiter *m* -s pus. **e~n** *vi* (*haben*) discharge pus

Eiweiß *nt* -es,-e egg-white; (*Chem*) protein

Ekel¹ *m* -s disgust; (*Widerwille*) revulsion

Ekel² *nt* -s,- (*fam*) beast

ekel|erregend *a* nauseating. **e~haft** *a* nauseating; (*widerlich*) repulsive. **e~n** *vt*/*i* (*haben*) **mich** *od* **mir e~t [es] davor** it makes me feel sick ● *vr* **sich e~n vor** (+ *dat*) find repulsive

eklig *a* disgusting, repulsive

Ekstase *f* - ecstasy. **e~tisch** *a* ecstatic, *adv* -ally

Ekzem *nt* -s,-e eczema

elasti|sch *a* elastic; (*federnd*) springy; (*fig*) flexible. **E~zität** *f* - elasticity; flexibility

Elch *m* -[e]s,-e elk

Elefant *m* -en,-en elephant

elegan|t *a* elegant, *adv* -ly. **E~z** *f* - elegance

elektrifizieren *vt* electrify

Elektri|ker *m* -s,- electrician. **e~sch** *a* electric, *adv* -ally

elektrisieren *vt* electrify; **sich e~** get an electric shock

Elektrizität *f* - electricity. **E~swerk** *nt* power station

Elektro|artikel *mpl* electrical appliances. **E~ode** *f* -,-n electrode. **E~oherd** *m* electric cooker. **E~on** *nt* -s,-en /-'troːnən/ electron. **E~onik** *f* - electronics *sg*. **e~onisch** *a* electronic

Element *nt* -[e]s,-e element; (*Anbau-*) unit. **e~ar** *a* elementary

Elend *nt* -s misery; (*Armut*) poverty. **e~** *a* miserable, *adv* -bly, wretched, *adv* -ly; (*krank*) poorly; (*gemein*) contemptible; (*fam: schrecklich*) dreadful, *adv* -ly. **E~sviertel** *nt* slum

elf *inv a*, **E~** *f* -,-en eleven

Elfe *f* -,-n fairy

Elfenbein *nt* ivory

Elfmeter *m* (*Fußball*) penalty

elfte(r,s) *a* eleventh

eliminieren *vt* eliminate

Elite *f* -,-n élite

Elixier *nt* -s,-e elixir

Ell[en]bogen *m* elbow

Ellip|se *f* -,-n ellipse. **e~tisch** *a* elliptical

Elsaß *nt* - Alsace

elsässisch *a* Alsatian

Elster *f* -,-n magpie

elter|lich *a* parental. **E~n** *pl* parents. **E~nhaus** *nt* [parental] home. **e~n-los** *a* orphaned. **E~nteil** *m* parent

Email /e'mai/ *nt* -s,-s, **E~le** /e'maljə/ *f* -,-n enamel. **e~lieren** /ema[l]'ji:rən/ *vt* enamel

Emanzi|pation /-'tsio:n/ *f* - emancipation. **e~piert** *a* emancipated

Embargo *nt*-s,-s embargo

Emblem *nt* -s,-e emblem

Embryo *m* -s,-s embryo

Emigr|ant(in) *m* -en,-en (*f* -,-nen) emigrant. **E~ation** /-'tsio:n/ *f* - emigration. **e~ieren** *vi* (*sein*) emigrate

eminent *a* eminent, *adv* -ly

Emission *f* -,-en emission; (*Comm*) issue

Emotion /-'tsio:n/ *f* -,-en emotion. **e~al** *a* emotional

Empfang *m* -[e]s,-̈e reception; (*Erhalt*) receipt; **in E~ nehmen** receive; (*annehmen*) accept. **e~en†** *vt* receive; (*Biol*) conceive

Empfäng|er *m* -s,- recipient; (*Post*-) addressee; (*Zahlungs*-) payee; (*Radio, TV*) receiver. **e~lich** *a* receptive/(*Med*) susceptible (**für** to). **E~nis** *f* - (*Biol*) conception

Empfängnisverhütung *f* contraception. **E~smittel** *nt* contraceptive

Empfangs|bestätigung *f* receipt. **E~chef** *m* reception manager. **E~dame** *f* receptionist. **E~halle** *f* [hotel] foyer

empfehl|en† *vt* recommend; **sich e~en** be advisable; (*verabschieden*) take one's leave. **e~enswert** *a* to be recommended; (*ratsam*) advisable. **E~ung** *f* -,-en recommendation; (*Gruß*) regards *pl*

empfind|en† *vt* feel. **e~lich** *a* sensitive (**gegen** to); (*zart*) delicate;

(*wund*) tender; (*reizbar*) touchy; (*hart*) severe, *adv* -ly. **E~lichkeit** *f* - sensitivity; delicacy; tenderness; touchiness. **e~sam** *a* sensitive; (*sentimental*) sentimental. **E~ung** *f* -,-en sensation; (*Regung*) feeling

emphatisch *a* emphatic, *adv* -ally

empor *adv* (*liter*) up[wards]

empören *vt* incense; **sich e~** be indignant; (*sich auflehnen*) rebel. **e~d** *a* outrageous

Empor|kömmling *m* -s,-e upstart. **e~ragen** *vi sep* (*haben*) rise [up]

empör|t *a* indignant, *adv* -ly. **E~ung** *f* - indignation; (*Auflehnung*) rebellion

emsig *a* busy, *adv* -ily

Ende *nt* -s,-n end; (*eines Films, Romans*) ending; (*fam: Stück*) bit; **E~ Mai** at the end of May; **zu E~ sein/gehen** be finished/come to an end; **etw zu E~ schreiben** finish writing sth; **am E~** at the end; (*schließlich*) in the end; (*fam: vielleicht*) perhaps; (*fam: erschöpft*) at the end of one's tether

end|en *vi* (*haben*) end. **e~gültig** *a* final, *adv* -ly; (*bestimmt*) definite, *adv* -ly

Endivie /-ịə/ *f* -,-n endive

end|lich *adv* at last, finally; (*schließlich*) in the end. **e~los** *a* endless, *adv* -ly. **E~resultat** *nt* final result. **E~spiel** *nt* final. **E~spurt** *m* -[e]s final spurt. **E~station** *f* terminus. **E~ung** *f* -,-en (*Gram*) ending

Energie *f* - energy

energisch *a* resolute, *adv* -ly; (*nachdrücklich*) vigorous, *adv* -ly; **e~ werden** put one's foot down

eng *a* narrow; (*beengt*) cramped; (*anliegend*) tight; (*nah*) close, *adv* -ly

Enga|gement /ãgaʒə'mã:/ *nt* -s,-s (*Theat*) engagement; (*fig*) commitment. **e~gieren** /-'ʒi:rən/ *vt* (*Theat*) engage; **sich e~gieren** become involved; **e~giert** committed

eng|anliegend *a* tight-fitting. **E~e** *f* - narrowness; **in die E~e treiben** (*fig*) drive into a corner

Engel *m* -s,- angel. **e~haft** *a* angelic

engherzig *a* petty

England *nt* -s England

Engländer *m* -s,- Englishman; (*Techn*) monkey-wrench; **die E~** the English *pl*. **E~in** *f* -,-nen Englishwoman

englisch *a* English; **auf e~** in English. **E~** *nt* -[s] (*Lang*) English

Engpaß m (fig) bottle-neck

en gros /ã'gro:/ adv wholesale

engstirnig a (fig) narrow-minded

Enkel m -s,- grandson; **E~** pl grandchildren. **E~in** f -,-nen granddaughter. **E~kind** nt grandchild. **E~sohn** m grandson. **E~tochter** f granddaughter

enorm a enormous, adv -ly; (fam: großartig) fantastic

Ensemble /ã'sã:bəl/ nt -s,-s ensemble; (Theat) company

entart|en vi (sein) degenerate. **e~et** a degenerate

entbehr|en vt do without; (vermissen) miss. **e~lich** a dispensable; (überflüssig) superfluous. **E~ung** f -,-en privation

entbind|en† vt release (von from); (Med) deliver (von of) ● vi (haben) give birth. **E~ung** f delivery. **E~ungsstation** f maternity ward

entblöß|en vt bare. **e~t** a bare

entdeck|en vt discover. **E~er** m -s,- discoverer; (Forscher) explorer. **E~ung** f -,-en discovery

Ente f -,-n duck

entehren vt dishonour

enteignen vt dispossess; expropriate ⟨Eigentum⟩

enterben vt disinherit

Enterich m -s,-e drake

entfachen vt kindle

entfallen† vi (sein) not apply; **jdm e~** slip from s.o.'s hand; (aus dem Gedächtnis) slip s.o.'s mind; **auf jdn e~** be s.o.'s share

entfalt|en vt unfold; (entwickeln) develop; (zeigen) display; **sich e~en** unfold; develop. **E~ung** f - development

entfern|en vt remove; **sich e~en** leave. **e~t** a distant; (schwach) vague, adv -ly; **2 Kilometer e~t** 2 kilometres away; **e~t verwandt** distantly related; **nicht im e~testen** not in the least. **E~ung** f -,-en removal; (Abstand) distance; (Reichweite) range. **E~ungsmesser** m range-finder

entfesseln vt (fig) unleash

entfliehen† vi (sein) escape

entfremd|en vt alienate. **E~ung** f - alienation

entfrosten vt defrost

entführ|en vt abduct, kidnap; hijack ⟨Flugzeug⟩. **E~er** m abductor, kidnapper; hijacker. **E~ung** f abduction, kidnapping; hijacking

entgegen adv towards ● prep (+dat) contrary to. **e~gehen†** vi sep (sein) (+dat) go to meet; (fig) be heading for. **e~gesetzt** a opposite; (gegensätzlich) opposing. **e~halten†** vt sep (fig) object. **e~kommen†** vi sep (sein) (+dat) come to meet; (zukommen auf) come towards; (fig) oblige. **E~kommen** nt -s helpfulness; (Zugeständnis) concession. **e~kommend** a approaching; ⟨Verkehr⟩ oncoming; (fig) obliging. **e~nehmen†** vt sep accept. **e~sehen†** vi sep (haben) (+dat) (fig) await; (freudig) look forward to. **e~setzen** vt sep **Widerstand e~setzen** (+dat) resist. **e~treten†** vi sep (sein) (+dat) (fig) confront; (bekämpfen) fight. **e~wirken** vi sep (haben) (+dat) counteract; (fig) oppose

entgegn|en vt reply (auf+acc to). **E~ung** f -,-en reply

entgehen† vi sep (sein) (+dat) escape; **jdm e~** (unbemerkt bleiben) escape s.o.'s notice; **sich (dat) etw e~ lassen** miss sth

entgeistert a flabbergasted

Entgelt nt -[e]s payment; **gegen E~** for money. **e~en** vt jdn etw **e~en lassen** (fig) make s.o. pay for sth

entgleis|en vi (sein) be derailed; (fig) make a gaffe. **E~ung** f -,-en derailment; (fig) gaffe

entgleiten† vi (sein) jdm **e~** slip from s.o.'s grasp

entgräten vt fillet, bone

Enthaarungsmittel nt depilatory

enthalt|en† vt contain; **in etw** (dat) **e~en sein** be contained/(eingeschlossen) included in sth; **sich der Stimme e~en** (Pol) abstain. **e~sam** a abstemious. **E~samkeit** f - abstinence. **E~ung** f (Pol) abstention

enthaupten vt behead

entheben† vt jdn seines Amtes **e~** relieve s.o. of his post

enthüll|en vt unveil; (fig) reveal. **E~ung** f -,-en revelation

Enthusias|mus m - enthusiasm. **E~t** m -en,-en enthusiast. **e~tisch** a enthusiastic, adv -ally

entkernen vt stone; core ⟨Apfel⟩

entkleid|en vt undress; **sich e~en** undress. **E~ungsnummer** f striptease [act]

entkommen† vi (sein) escape

entkorken vt uncork

entkräft|en vt weaken; (fig) invalidate. **E~ung** f - debility

entkrampfen *vt* relax; **sich e~** relax

entladen† *vt* unload; *(Electr)* discharge; **sich e~** discharge; *(Gewitter:)* break; *(Zorn:)* explode

entlang *adv & prep* (+ *preceding acc or following dat*) along; **die Straße e~, e~ der Straße** along the road; **an etw** *(dat)* **e~** along sth. **e~fahren**† *vi sep* (*sein*) drive along. **e~gehen**† *vi sep* (*sein*) walk along

entlarven *vt* unmask

entlass|en† *vt* dismiss; *(aus Krankenhaus)* discharge; *(aus der Haft)* release; **aus der Schule e~en werden** leave school. **E~ung** *f* -,-en dismissal; discharge; release

entlast|en *vt* relieve the strain on; ease *(Gewissen, Verkehr)*; relieve **(von** of); *(Jur)* exonerate. **E~ung** *f* - relief; exoneration. **E~ungszug** *m* relief train

entlaufen† *vi* (*sein*) run away

entledigen (sich) *vr* (+ *gen*) rid oneself of; *(ausziehen)* take off; *(erfüllen)* discharge

entleeren *vt* empty

entlegen *a* remote

entleihen† *vt* borrow **(von** from)

entlocken *vt* coax *(dat* from)

entlohnen *vt* pay

entlüft|en *vt* ventilate. **E~er** *m* -s,- extractor fan. **E~ung** *f* ventilation

entmündigen *vt* declare incapable of managing his own affairs

entmutigen *vt* discourage

entnehmen† *vt* take *(dat* from); *(schließen)* gather *(dat* from)

Entomologie *f* - entomology

entpuppen (sich) *vr* (*fig*) turn out **(als etw** to be sth)

entrahmt *a* skimmed

entreißen† *vt* snatch *(dat* from)

entrichten *vt* pay

entrinnen† *vi* (*sein*) escape

entrollen *vt* unroll; unfurl *(Fahne)*; **sich e~** unroll; unfurl

entrüst|en *vt* fill with indignation; **sich e~en** be indignant **(über** + *acc* at). **e~et** *a* indignant, *adv* -ly. **E~ung** *f* - indignation

entsaft|en *vt* extract the juice from. **E~er** *m* -s,- juice extractor

entsag|en *vi* (*haben*) (+ *dat*) renounce. **E~ung** *f* - renunciation

entschädig|en *vt* compensate. **E~ung** *f* -,-en compensation

entschärfen *vt* defuse

entscheid|en† *vt/i* (*haben*) decide; **sich e~en** decide; *(Sache:)* be decided. **e~end** *a* decisive, *adv* -ly; *(kritisch)* crucial. **E~ung** *f* decision

entschieden *a* decided, *adv* -ly; *(fest)* firm, *adv* -ly

entschlafen† *vi* (*sein*) *(liter)* pass away

entschließen† **(sich)** *vr* decide, make up one's mind; **sich anders e~** change one's mind

entschlossen *a* determined; *(energisch)* resolute, *adv* -ly; **kurz e~** without hesitation; *(spontan)* on the spur of the moment. **E~heit** *f* - determination

Entschluß *m* decision; **einen E~ fassen** make a decision

entschlüsseln *vt* decode

entschuld|bar *a* excusable. **e~igen** *vt* excuse; **sich e~igen** apologize **(bei** to); **e~igen Sie [bitte]!** sorry! *(bei Frage)* excuse me. **E~igung** *f* -,-en apology; *(Ausrede)* excuse; **[jdn] um E~igung bitten** apologize [to s.o.] **E~igung!** sorry! *(bei Frage)* excuse me

entsetz|en *vt* horrify. **E~en** *nt* -s horror. **e~lich** *a* horrible, *adv* -bly; *(schrecklich)* terrible, *adv* -bly. **e~t** *a* horrified

entsinnen† **(sich)** *vr* (+ *gen*) remember

Entsorgung *f* - waste disposal

entspann|en *vt* relax; **sich e~en** relax; *(Lage:)* ease. **E~ung** *f* - relaxation; easing; *(Pol)* détente

entsprech|en† *vi* (*haben*) (+ *dat*) correspond to; *(übereinstimmen)* agree with; *(nachkommen)* comply with. **e~end** *a* corresponding; *(angemessen)* appropriate; *(zuständig)* relevant ● *adv* correspondingly; appropriately; *(demgemäß)* accordingly ● *prep* (+ *dat*) in accordance with. **E~ung** *f* -,-en equivalent

entspringen† *vi* (*sein*) *(Fluß:)* rise; *(fig)* arise, spring *(dat* from); *(entfliehen)* escape

entstammen *vi* (*sein*) come/*(abstammen)* be descended *(dat* from)

entsteh|en† *vi* (*sein*) come into being; *(sich bilden)* form; *(sich entwickeln)* develop; *(Brand:)* start; *(stammen)* originate/*(sich ergeben)* result **(aus** from). **E~ung** *f* - origin; formation; development; *(fig)* birth

entsteinen *vt* stone

entstell|en vt disfigure; (verzerren) distort. **E~ung** f disfigurement; distortion

entstört a (Electr) suppressed

enttäusch|en vt disappoint. **E~ung** f disappointment

entvölkern vt depopulate

entwaffnen vt disarm. **e~d** a (fig) disarming

Entwarnung f all-clear [signal]

entwässer|n vt drain. **E~ung** f - drainage

entweder conj & adv either

entweichen† vi (sein) escape

entweih|en vt desecrate. **E~ung** f - desecration

entwenden vt steal (dat from)

entwerfen† vt design; (aufsetzen) draft; (skizzieren) sketch

entwert|en vt devalue; (ungültig machen) cancel. **E~er** m -s,- ticket-cancelling machine. **E~ung** f devaluation; cancelling

entwick|eln vt develop; **sich e~eln** develop. **E~lung** f -,-en development; (Biol) evolution. **E~lungs-land** nt developing country

entwinden† vt wrench (dat from)

entwirren vt disentangle; (fig) unravel

entwischen vi (sein) **jdm e~** (fam) give s.o. the slip

entwöhnen vt wean (gen from); cure ⟨Süchtige⟩

entwürdigend a degrading

Entwurf m design; (Konzept) draft; (Skizze) sketch

entwurzeln vt uproot

entzie|hen† vt take away (dat from); **jdm den Führerschein e~hen** disqualify s.o. from driving; **sich e~hen** (+ dat) withdraw from; (entgehen) evade. **E~hungskur** f treatment for drug/alcohol addiction

entziffern vt decipher

entzück|en vt delight. **E~** nt -s delight. **e~d** a delightful

Entzug m withdrawal; (Vorenthaltung) deprivation. **E~serscheinungen** fpl withdrawal symptoms

entzünd|en vt ignite; (anstecken) light; (fig: erregen) inflame; **sich e~en** ignite; (Med) become inflamed. **e~et** a (Med) inflamed. **e~lich** a inflammable. **E~ung** f (Med) inflammation

entzwei a broken. **e~en (sich)** vr quarrel. **e~gehen†** vi sep (sein) break

Enzian m -s,-e gentian

Enzyklo|pädie f -,-en encyclopaedia. **e~pädisch** a encyclopaedic

Enzym nt -s,-e enzyme

Epidemie f -,-n epidemic

Epi|lepsie f - epilepsy. **E~leptiker(in)** m -s,- (f -,-nen) epileptic. **e~leptisch** a epileptic

Epilog m -s,-e epilogue

episch a epic

Episode f -,-n episode

Epitaph nt -s,-e epitaph

Epoche f -,-n epoch. **e~machend** a epoch-making

Epos nt -,Epen epic

er pron he; (Ding, Tier) it

erachten vt consider (**für nötig** necessary). **E~** nt -s **meines E~s** in my opinion

erbarmen (sich) vr have pity/⟨Gott:⟩ mercy (gen on). **E~** nt -s pity; mercy

erbärmlich a wretched, adv -ly; (stark) terrible, adv -bly

erbarmungslos a merciless, adv -ly

erbau|en vt build; (fig) edify; **sich e~en** be edified (**an** + dat by); **nicht e~t von** (fam) not pleased about. **e~lich** a edifying

Erbe[1] m -n,-n heir

Erbe[2] nt -s inheritance; (fig) heritage. **e~n** vt inherit

erbeuten vt get; (Mil) capture

Erbfolge f (Jur) succession

erbieten† (sich) vr offer (**zu** to)

Erbin f -,-nen heiress

erbitten† vt ask for

erbittert a bitter; (heftig) fierce, adv -ly

erblassen vi (sein) turn pale

erblich a hereditary

erblicken vt catch sight of

erblinden vi (sein) go blind

erbost a angry, adv -ily

erbrechen† vt vomit ● vi/r [sich] e~ vomit. **E~** nt -s vomiting

Erbschaft f -,-en inheritance

Erbse f -,-n pea

Erb|stück nt heirloom. **E~teil** nt inheritance

Erd|apfel m (Aust) potato. **E~beben** nt -s,- earthquake. **E~beere** f strawberry. **E~boden** m ground

Erde f -,-n earth; (Erdboden) ground; (Fußboden) floor; **auf der E~** on earth; (auf dem Boden) on the ground/floor. **e~n** vt (Electr) earth

erdenklich a imaginable

Erdgas nt natural gas. **E~geschoß** nt ground floor, (Amer) first floor.

e~ig *a* earthy. **E~kugel** *f* globe. **E~kunde** *f* geography. **E~nuß** *f* peanut. **E~öl** *nt* [mineral] oil. **E~reich** *nt* soil

erdreisten (sich) *vr* have the audacity (**zu** to)

erdrosseln *vt* strangle

erdrücken *vt* crush to death. **e~d** *a* (*fig*) overwhelming

Erd|rutsch *m* landslide. **E~teil** *m* continent

erdulden *vt* endure

ereifern (sich) *vr* get worked up

ereignen (sich) *vr* happen

Ereignis *nt* **-ses,-se** event. **e~los** *a* uneventful. **e~reich** *a* eventful

Eremit *m* **-en,-en** hermit

ererbt *a* inherited

erfahr|en† *vt* learn, hear; (*erleben*) experience ● *a* experienced. **E~ung** *f* **-,-en** experience; **in E~ung bringen** find out

erfassen *vt* seize; (*begreifen*) grasp; (*einbeziehen*) include; (*aufzeichnen*) record; **von einem Auto erfaßt werden** be struck by a car

erfind|en† *vt* invent. **E~er** *m* **-s,-** inventor. **e~erisch** *a* inventive. **E~ung** *f* **-,-en** invention

Erfolg *m* **-[e]s,-e** success; (*Folge*) result; **E~ haben** be successful. **e~en** *vi* (*sein*) take place; (*geschehen*) happen. **e~los** *a* unsuccessful, *adv* -ly. **e~reich** *a* successful, *adv* -ly. **e~versprechend** *a* promising

erforder|lich *a* required, necessary. **e~n** *vt* require, demand. **E~nis** *nt* **-ses,-se** requirement

erforsch|en *vt* explore; (*untersuchen*) investigate. **E~ung** *f* exploration; investigation

erfreu|en *vt* please; **sich guter Gesundheit e~en** enjoy good health. **e~lich** *a* pleasing, gratifying; (*willkommen*) welcome. **e~licherweise** *adv* happily. **e~t** *a* pleased

erfrier|en† *vi* (*sein*) freeze to death; ⟨*Glied:*⟩ become frostbitten; ⟨*Pflanze:*⟩ be killed by the frost. **E~ung** *f* **-,-en** frostbite

erfrisch|en *vt* refresh; **sich e~en** refresh onself. **e~end** *a* refreshing. **E~ung** *f* **-,-en** refreshment

erfüll|en *vt* fill; (*nachkommen*) fulfil; serve ⟨*Zweck*⟩; discharge ⟨*Pflicht*⟩; **sich e~en** come true. **E~ung** *f* fulfilment; **in E~ung gehen** come true

erfunden invented; (*fiktiv*) fictitious

ergänz|en *vt* complement; (*nachtragen*) supplement; (*auffüllen*) replenish; (*vervollständigen*) complete; (*hinzufügen*) add; **sich e~en** complement each other. **E~ung** *f* complement; supplement; (*Zusatz*) addition. **E~ungsband** *m* supplement

ergeb|en† *vt* produce; (*zeigen*) show, establish; **sich e~en** result; ⟨*Schwierigkeit:*⟩ arise; (*kapitulieren*) surrender; (*sich fügen*) submit; **es ergab sich** it turned out (**daß** that) ● *a* devoted, *adv* -ly; (*resigniert*) resigned, *adv* -ly. **E~enheit** *f* - devotion

Ergebnis *nt* **-ses,-se** result. **e~los** *a* fruitless, *adv* -ly

ergehen† *vi* (*sein*) be issued; **etw über sich** (*acc*) **e~ lassen** submit to sth; **wie ist es dir ergangen?** how did you get on? ● *vr* **sich e~ in** (+ *dat*) indulge in

ergiebig *a* productive; (*fig*) rich

ergötzen *vt* amuse

ergreifen† *vt* seize; take ⟨*Maßnahme, Gelegenheit*⟩; take up ⟨*Beruf*⟩; (*rühren*) move; **die Flucht e~** flee. **e~d** *a* moving

ergriffen *a* deeply moved. **E~heit** *f* emotion

ergründen *vt* (*fig*) get to the bottom of

erhaben *a* raised; (*fig*) sublime; **über etw** (*acc*) **e~ sein** (*fig*) be above sth

Erhalt *m* **-[e]s** receipt. **e~en†** *vt* receive, get; (*gewinnen*) obtain; (*bewahren*) preserve, keep; (*instandhalten*) maintain; (*unterhalten*) support; **am Leben e~en** keep alive ● *a* **gut/schlecht e~en** in good/bad condition; **e~en bleiben** survive

erhältlich *a* obtainable

Erhaltung *f* - (*s.* **erhalten**) preservation; maintenance

erhängen (sich) *vr* hang oneself

erhärten *vt* (*fig*) substantiate

erheb|en† *vt* raise; levy ⟨*Steuer*⟩; charge ⟨*Gebühr*⟩; **Anspruch e~en** lay claim (**auf** + *acc* to); **Protest e~en** protest; **sich e~en** rise; ⟨*Frage:*⟩ arise; (*sich empören*) rise up. **e~lich** *a* considerable, *adv* -bly. **E~ung** *f* **-,-en** elevation; (*Anhöhe*) rise; (*Aufstand*) uprising; (*Ermittlung*) survey

erheiter|n *vt* amuse. **E~ung** *f* - amusement

erhitzen vt heat; **sich e~** get hot; (fig) get heated

erhoffen vt **sich (dat) etw e~** hope for sth

erhöh|en vt raise; (fig) increase; **sich e~en** rise, increase. **E~ung** f -,-en increase. **E~ungszeichen** nt (Mus) sharp

erhol|en (sich) vr recover (von from); (nach Krankheit) convalesce, recuperate; (sich ausruhen) have a rest. **e~sam** a restful. **E~ung** f - recovery; convalescence; (Ruhe) rest. **E~ungsheim** nt convalescent home

erhören vt (fig) answer

erinner|n vt remind (an + acc of); **sich e~n** remember (an jdn/etw s.o./sth). **E~ung** f -,-en memory; (Andenken) souvenir

erkält|en (sich) vr catch a cold; **e~et sein** have a cold. **E~ung** f -,-en cold

erkenn|bar a recognizable; (sichtbar) visible. **e~en†** vt recognize; (wahrnehmen) distinguish; (einsehen) realize. **e~tlich** a **sich e~tlich zeigen** show one's appreciation. **E~tnis** f -,-se recognition; realization; (Wissen) knowledge; **die neuesten E~tnisse** the latest findings

Erker m -s,- bay

erklär|en vt declare; (erläutern) explain; **sich bereit e~en** agree (zu to); **ich kann es mir nicht e~en** I can't explain it. **e~end** a explanatory. **e~lich** a explicable; (verständlich) understandable. **e~licherweise** adv understandably. **e~t** attrib a declared. **E~ung** f -,-en declaration; explanation; **öffentliche E~ung** public statement

erklingen† vi (sein) ring out

erkrank|en vi (sein) fall ill; be taken ill (an + dat with). **E~ung** f -,-en illness

erkunden vt explore; (Mil) reconnoitre

erkundig|en (sich) vr enquire (nach jdm/etw after s.o./about sth). **E~ung** f -,-en enquiry

erlahmen vi (sein) tire; ⟨Kraft, Eifer:⟩ flag

erlangen vt attain, get

Erlaß m -sses, ⁻sse (Admin) decree; (Befreiung) exemption; (Straf-) remission

erlassen† vt (Admin) issue; **jdm etw e~** exempt s.o. from sth; let s.o. off ⟨Strafe⟩

erlauben vt allow, permit; **sich e~, etw zu tun** take the liberty of doing sth; **ich kann es mir nicht e~** I can't afford it

Erlaubnis f - permission. **E~schein** m permit

erläuter|n vt explain. **E~ung** f -,-en explanation

Erle f -,-n alder

erleb|en vt experience; (mit-) see; have ⟨Überraschung, Enttäuschung⟩; **etw nicht mehr e~en** not live to see sth. **E~nis** nt -ses,-se experience

erledig|en vt do; (sich befassen mit) deal with; (beenden) finish; (entscheiden) settle; (töten) kill; **e~t sein** be done/settled/(fam: müde) worn out/(fam: ruiniert) finished

erleichter|n vt lighten; (vereinfachen) make easier; (befreien) relieve; (lindern) ease; **sich e~n** (fig) unburden oneself. **e~t** a relieved. **E~ung** f - relief

erleiden† vt suffer

erlernen vt learn

erlesen a exquisite; (auserlesen) choice, select

erleucht|en vt illuminate; **hell e~et** brightly lit. **E~ung** f -,-en (fig) inspiration

erliegen† vi (sein) succumb (dat to); **seinen Verletzungen e~** die of one's injuries

erlogen a untrue, false

Erlös m -es proceeds pl

erlöschen† vi (sein) go out; (vergehen) die; (aussterben) die out; (ungültig werden) expire; **erloschener Vulkan** extinct volcano

erlös|en vt save; (befreien) release (von from); (Relig) redeem. **e~t** a relieved. **E~ung** f release; (Erleichterung) relief; (Relig) redemption

ermächtig|en vt authorize. **E~ung** f -,-en authorization

ermahn|en vt exhort; (zurechtweisen) admonish. **E~ung** f exhortation; admonition

ermäßig|en vt reduce. **E~ung** f -,-en reduction

ermatten vi (sein) grow weary ● vt weary. **E~ung** f - weariness

ermessen† vt judge; (begreifen) appreciate. E~ nt -s discretion; (Urteil) judgement; **nach eigenem E~** at one's own discretion

ermitt|eln vt establish; (herausfinden) find out ● vi (haben) investigate (**gegen jdn** s.o.). **E~lungen** fpl investigations. **E~lungsverfahren** nt (Jur) preliminary inquiry

ermöglichen vt make possible

ermord|en vt murder. **E~ung** f -,-en murder

ermüd|en vt tire ● vi (sein) get tired. **E~ung** f - tiredness

ermunter|n vt encourage; **sich e~n** rouse oneself. **E~ung** f - encouragement

ermutigen vt encourage. **e~d** a encouraging

ernähr|en vt feed; (unterhalten) support, keep; **sich e~en von** live/ ⟨Tier:⟩ feed on. **E~er** m -s,- breadwinner. **E~ung** f - nourishment; nutrition; (Kost) diet

ernenn|en† vt appoint. **E~ung** f -,-en appointment

erneu|ern vt renew; (auswechseln) replace; change ⟨Verband⟩; (renovieren) renovate. **E~erung** f renewal; replacement; renovation. **e~t** a renewed; (neu) new ● adv again

erniedrig|en vt degrade; **sich e~en** lower oneself. **e~end** a degrading. **E~ungszeichen** nt (Mus) flat

ernst a serious, adv -ly; **e~ nehmen** take seriously. **E~** m -es seriousness; **im E~** seriously; **mit einer Drohung E~ machen** carry out a threat; **ist das dein E~?** are you serious? **E~fall** m **im E~fall** when the real thing happens. **e~haft** a serious, adv -ly. **e~lich** a serious, adv -ly

Ernte f -,-n harvest; (Ertrag) crop. **E~dankfest** nt harvest festival. **e~n** vt harvest; (fig) reap, win

ernüchter|n vt sober up; (fig) bring down to earth; (enttäuschen) disillusion. **e~nd** a (fig) sobering. **E~ung** f - disillusionment

Erober|er m -s,- conqueror. **e~n** vt conquer. **E~ung** f -,-en conquest

eröffn|en vt open; **jdm etw e~en** announce sth to s.o.; **sich jdm e~en** ⟨Aussicht:⟩ present itself to s.o. **E~ung** f opening; (Mitteilung) announcement. **E~ungsansprache** f opening address

erörter|n vt discuss. **E~ung** f -,-en discussion

Erosion f -,-en erosion

Erot|ik f - eroticism. **e~isch** a erotic

Erpel m -s,- drake

erpicht a **e~ auf** (+acc) keen on

erpress|en vt extort; blackmail ⟨Person⟩. **E~er** m -s,- blackmailer. **E~ung** f - extortion; blackmail

erprob|en vt test. **e~t** a proven

erquicken vt refresh

erraten† vt guess

erreg|bar a excitable. **e~en** vt excite; (hervorrufen) arouse; **sich e~en** get worked up. **e~end** a exciting. **E~er** m -s,- (Med) germ. **e~t** a agitated; (hitzig) heated. **E~ung** f - excitement; (Erregtheit) agitation

erreich|bar a within reach; ⟨Ziel⟩ attainable; ⟨Person⟩ available. **e~en** vt reach; catch ⟨Zug⟩; live to ⟨Alter⟩; (durchsetzen) achieve

erretten vt save

errichten vt erect

erringen† vt gain, win

erröten vi (sein) blush

Errungenschaft f -,-en achievement; (fam: Anschaffung) acquisition; **E~en der Technik** technical advances

Ersatz m -es replacement, substitute; (Entschädigung) compensation. **E~dienst** m = **Zivildienst**. **E~reifen** m spare tyre. **E~spieler(in)** m(f) substitute. **E~teil** nt spare part

ersäufen vt drown

erschaffen† vt create

erschallen† vi (sein) ring out

erschein|en† vi (sein) appear; ⟨Buch:⟩ be published; **jdm merkwürdig e~en** seem odd to s.o. **E~en** nt -s appearance; publication. **E~ung** f -,-en appearance; (Person) figure; (Phänomen) phenomenon; (Symptom) symptom; (Geist) apparition

erschieß|en† vt shoot [dead]. **E~ungskommando** nt firing squad

erschlaffen vi (sein) go limp; ⟨Haut, Muskeln:⟩ become flabby

erschlagen† vt beat to death; (tödlich treffen) strike dead; **vom Blitz e~ werden** be killed by lightning ● a (fam) (erschöpft) worn out; (fassungslos) stunned

erschließen† vt develop; (zugänglich machen) open up; (nutzbar machen) tap

erschöpf|en vt exhaust. **e~end** a exhausting; (fig: vollständig) exhaustive. **e~t** a exhausted. **E~ung** f - exhaustion

erschreck|en† vi (sein) get a fright ● vt (reg) startle; (beunruhigen) alarm; **du hast mich e~t** you gave me a fright ● vr (reg & irreg) sich **e~en** get a fright. **e~end** a alarming, adv -ly

erschrocken a frightened; (erschreckt) startled; (bestürzt) dismayed

erschütter|n vt shake; (ergreifen) upset deeply. **E~ung** f -,-en shock

erschweren vt make more difficult

erschwinglich a affordable

ersehen† vt (fig) see (aus from)

ersetzen vt replace; make good ⟨Schaden⟩; refund ⟨Kosten⟩; **jdm etw e~** compensate s.o. for sth

ersichtlich a obvious, apparent

erspar|en vt save; **jdm etw e~en** save/(fernhalten) spare s.o. sth. **E~nis** f -,-se saving; **E~nisse** savings

erst adv (zuerst) first; (noch nicht mehr als) only; (nicht vor) not until; **e~ dann** only then; **eben** od **gerade e~** [only] just; **das machte ihn e~ recht wütend** it made him all the more angry

erstarren vi (sein) solidify; (gefrieren) freeze; (steif werden) go stiff; (vor Schreck) be paralysed

erstatten vt (zurück-) refund; **Bericht e~** report (jdm to s.o.)

Erstaufführung f first performance, première

erstaun|en vt amaze, astonish. **E~en** nt amazement, astonishment. **e~lich** a amazing, adv -ly. **e~licherweise** adv amazingly

Erst|ausgabe f first edition. **e~e(r,s)** a first; (beste) best; **E~e Hilfe** first aid; **er kam als e~er** he arrived first; **als e~es** first of all; **fürs e~e** for the time being; **der e~e beste** the first one to come along; (fam) any Tom, Dick or Harry. **E~e(r)** m/f best; **er ist der/sie ist die E~e in Latein** he/she is top in Latin

erstechen† vt stab to death

erstehen† vt buy

ersteigern vt buy at an auction

erst|ens adv firstly, in the first place. **e~ere(r,s)** a the former; **der/die/das e~ere** the former

ersticken vt suffocate; smother ⟨Flammen⟩; (unterdrücken) suppress ● vi (sein) suffocate. **E~** nt -s suffocation; **zum E~** stifling

erst|klassig a first-class. **e~mals** adv for the first time

erstreben vt strive for. **e~swert** a desirable

erstrecken (sich) vr stretch; **sich e~ auf** (+ acc) (fig) apply to

ersuchen vt ask, request. **E~** nt -s request

ertappen vt (fam) catch

erteilen vt give (jdm s.o.)

ertönen vi (sein) sound; (erschallen) ring out

Ertrag m -[e]s,-̈e yield. **e~en**† vt bear

erträglich a bearable; (leidlich) tolerable

ertränken vt drown

ertrinken† vi (sein) drown

erübrigen (sich) vr be unnecessary

erwachen vi (sein) awake

erwachsen a grown-up. **E~e(r)** m/f adult, grown-up

erwäg|en† vt consider. **E~ung** f-,-en consideration; **in E~ung ziehen** consider

erwähn|en vt mention. **E~ung** f -,-en mention

erwärmen vt warm; **sich e~** warm up; (fig) warm (**für** to)

erwart|en vt expect; (warten auf) wait for. **E~ung** f -,-en expectation. **e~ungsvoll** a expectant, adv -ly

erwecken vt (fig) arouse; give ⟨Anschein⟩

erweichen vt soften; (fig) move; **sich e~ lassen** (fig) relent

erweisen† vt prove; (bezeigen) do ⟨Gefallen, Dienst, Ehre⟩; **sich e~ als** prove to be

erweitern vt widen; dilate ⟨Pupille⟩; (fig) extend, expand

Erwerb m -[e]s acquisition; (Kauf) purchase; (Brot-) livelihood; (Verdienst) earnings pl. **e~en**† vt acquire; (kaufen) purchase; (fig: erlangen) gain. **e~slos** a unemployed. **e~stätig** a [gainfully] employed. **E~ung** f -,-en acquisition

erwider|n vt reply; return ⟨Besuch, Gruß⟩. **E~ung** f -,-en reply

erwirken vt obtain

erwischen vt (fam) catch

erwünscht a desired

erwürgen vt strangle

Erz nt -es,-e ore

erzähl|en vt tell (**jdm** s.o.) ● vi (haben) talk (**von** about). **E~er** m -s,- narrator. **E~ung** f -,-en story, tale

Erzbischof m archbishop

erzeug|en vt produce; (Electr) generate; (fig) create. **E~er** m -s,- producer; (Vater) father. **E~nis** nt -ses, -se product; **landwirtschaftliche E~nisse** farm produce sg. **E~ung** f - production; generation

Erz|feind m arch-enemy. **E~herzog** m archduke

erzieh|en† vt bring up; (Sch) educate. **E~er** m -s,- [private] tutor. **E~erin** f -,-nen governess. **E~ung** f - upbringing; education

erzielen vt achieve; score ⟨Tor⟩

erzogen a **gut/schlecht e~** well/ badly brought up

erzürnt a angry

erzwingen† vt force

es pron it; (Mädchen) she; (acc) her; impers **es regnet** it is raining; **es gibt** there is/(pl) are; **ich hoffe es** I hope so

Esche f -,-n ash

Esel m -s,- donkey; (fam: Person) ass. **E~sohr** nt **E~sohren haben** ⟨Buch:⟩ be dog-eared

Eskal|ation /-'tsio:n/ f - escalation. **e~ieren** vt/i (haben) escalate

Eskimo m -[s],-[s] eskimo

Eskort|e f -,-n (Mil) escort. **e~ieren** vt escort

eßbar a edible. **Eßecke** f dining area

essen† vt/i (haben) eat; **zu Mittag/ Abend e~** have lunch/supper; [auswärts] **e~ gehen** eat out; **chinesisch e~** have a Chinese meal. **E~** nt -s,- food; (Mahl) meal; (festlich) dinner

Essenz f -,-en essence

Esser(in) m -s,- (f -,-nen) eater

Essig m -s vinegar. **E~gurke** f [pickled] gherkin

Eßkastanie f sweet chestnut. **Eßlöffel** m dessertspoon. **Eßstäbchen** ntpl chopsticks. **Eßtisch** m dining-table. **Eßwaren** fpl food sg; (Vorräte) provisions. **Eßzimmer** nt dining-room

Estland nt -s Estonia

Estragon m -s tarragon

etablieren (sich) vr establish oneself/⟨Geschäft:⟩ itself

Etage /e'ta:ʒə/ f -,-n storey. **E~nbett** nt bunk-beds pl. **E~nwohnung** f flat, (Amer) apartment

Etappe f -,-n stage

Etat /e'ta:/ m -s,-s budget

etepetete a (fam) fussy

Eth|ik f - ethic; (Sittenlehre) ethics sg. **e~isch** a ethical

Etikett nt -[e]s,-e[n] label; (Preis-) tag. **E~e** f -,-n etiquette; (Aust) = Etikett. **e~ieren** vt label

etlich|e(r,s) pron some; (mehrere) several; **e~es** a number of things; (ziemlich viel) quite a lot. **e~emal** adv several times

Etui /e'tvi:/ nt -s,-s case

etwa adv (ungefähr) about; (zum Beispiel) for instance; (womöglich) perhaps; **nicht e~, daß …** not that …; **denkt nicht e~ …** don't imagine …; **du hast doch nicht e~ Angst?** you're not afraid, are you? **e~ig** a possible

etwas pron something; (fragend/verneint) anything; (ein bißchen) some, a little; **ohne e~ zu sagen** without saying anything; **sonst noch e~?** anything else? **noch e~ Tee?** some more tea? **so e~ Ärgerliches!** what a nuisance! ● adv a bit

Etymologie f - etymology

euch pron (acc of **ihr** pl) you; (dat) [to] you; (refl) yourselves; (einander) each other; **ein Freund von e~** a friend of yours

euer poss pron pl your. **e~e**, **e~t-** s. eure, euret-

Eule f -,-n owl

Euphorie f - euphoria

eur|e poss pron pl your. **e~e(r,s)** poss pron yours. **e~erseits** adv for your part. **e~etwegen** adv for your sake; (wegen euch) because of you, on your account. **e~etwillen** adv **um e~etwillen** for your sake. **e~ige** poss pron **der/die/das e~ige** yours

Euro- pref Euro-

Europa nt -s Europe. **E~-** pref European

Europä|er(in) m -s,- (f -,-nen) European. **e~isch** a European; **E~ische Gemeinschaft** European Community

Euro|paß m Europasport. **E~scheck** m Eurocheque

Euter nt -s,- udder

evakuier|en vt evacuate. **E~ung** f - evacuation

evan|gelisch a Protestant. **E~gelist** m -en,-en evangelist. **E~gelium** nt -s,-ien gospel

evaporieren vt/i (sein) evaporate

Eventu|alität f -,-en eventuality. **e~ell** a possible ● adv possibly; (vielleicht) perhaps

Evolution /-'tsio:n/ f - evolution

evtl. abbr s. **eventuell**

ewig a eternal, adv -ly; (fam: ständig) constant, adv -ly; (endlos) never-ending; **e~ dauern** (fam) take ages. **E~keit** f - eternity; **eine E~keit** (fam) ages

exakt a exact, adv -ly. **E~heit** f - exactitude

Examen nt -s,- & -mina (Sch) examination

Exekutive f - (Pol) executive

Exempel nt -s,- example; **ein E~ an jdm statuieren** make an example of s.o.

Exemplar nt -s,-e specimen; (Buch) copy. **e~isch** a exemplary

exerzieren vt/i (haben) (Mil) drill; (üben) practise

exhumieren vt exhume

Exil nt -s exile

Existenz f -,-en existence; (Lebensgrundlage) livelihood; (pej: Person) individual

existieren vi (haben) exist

exklusiv a exclusive. **e~e** prep (+ gen) excluding

exkommunizieren vt excommunicate

Exkremente npl excrement sg

exotisch a exotic

expan|dieren vt/i (haben) expand. **E~sion** f - expansion

Expedition /-'tsio:n/ f -,-en expedition

Experiment nt -[e]s,-e experiment. **e~ell** a experimental. **e~ieren** vi (haben) experiment

Experte m -n,-n expert

explo|dieren vi (sein) explode. **E~sion** f -,-en explosion. **e~siv** a explosive

Expor|t m -[e]s,-e export. **E~teur** /-'tø:ɐ/ m -s,-e exporter. **e~tieren** vt export

Expreß m -sses,-sse express

extra adv separately; (zusätzlich) extra; (eigens) specially; (fam: absichtlich) on purpose

Extrakt m -[e]s,-e extract

Extras npl (Auto) extras

extravagan|t a flamboyant, adv -ly; (übertrieben) extravagant. **E~z** f -,-en flamboyance; extravagance; (Überspanntheit) folly

extravertiert a extrovert

extrem a extreme, adv -ly. **E~** nt -s,-e extreme. **E~ist** m -en,-en extremist. **E~itäten** fpl extremities

Exzellenz f - (title) Excellency

Exzentr|iker m -s,- eccentric. **e~isch** a eccentric

Exzeß m -sses,-sse excess

F

Fabel f -,-n fable. **f~haft** a (fam) fantastic, adv -ally

Fabrik f -,-en factory. **F~ant** m -en,-en manufacturer. **F~at** nt -[e]s,-e product; (Marke) make. **F~ation** /-'tsio:n/ f - manufacture

Facette /fa'sɛta/ f -,-n facet

Fach nt -[e]s,-̈er compartment; (Schub-) drawer; (Gebiet) field; (Sch) subject. **F~arbeiter** m skilled worker. **F~arzt** m, **F~ärztin** f specialist. **F~ausdruck** m technical term

fäch|eln (sich) vr fan oneself. **F~er** m -s,- fan

Fach|gebiet nt field. **f~gemäß, f~gerecht** a expert, adv -ly. **F~hochschule** f ≈ technical university. **f~kundig** a expert, adv -ly. **f~lich** a technical, adv -ly; (beruflich) professional. **F~mann** m (pl -leute) expert. **f~männisch** a expert, adv -ly. **F~schule** f technical college. **f~simpeln** vi (haben) (fam) talk shop. **F~werkhaus** nt half-timbered house. **F~wort** nt (pl -wörter) technical term

Fackel f -,-n torch. **F~zug** m torchlight procession

fade a insipid; (langweilig) dull

Faden m -s,-̈ thread; (Bohnen-) string; (Naut) fathom. **f~scheinig** a threadbare; ⟨Grund⟩ flimsy

Fagott nt -[e]s,-e bassoon

fähig a capable (zu/gen of); (tüchtig) able, competent. **F~keit** f -,-en ability; competence

fahl a pale

fahnd|en vi (haben) search (nach for). **F~ung** f -,-en search

Fahne f -,-n flag; (Druck-) galley [proof]; **eine F~ haben** (fam) reek of alcohol. **F~nflucht** f desertion. **f~nflüchtig** a **f~flüchtig werden** desert

Fahr|ausweis *m* ticket. **F~bahn** *f* carriageway; (*Straße*) road. **f~bar** *a* mobile
Fähre *f* **-,-n** ferry
fahr|en† *vi* (*sein*) go, travel; ⟨*Fahrer:*⟩ drive; ⟨*Radfahrer:*⟩ ride; (*verkehren*) run; (*ab-*) leave; ⟨*Schiff:*⟩ sail; **mit dem Auto/Zug f~en** go by car/train; **in die Höhe f~en** start up; **in die Kleider f~en** throw on one's clothes; **mit der Hand über etw** (*acc*) **f~en** run one's hand over sth; **was ist in ihn gefahren?** (*fam*) what has got into him? ● *vt* drive; ride ⟨*Fahrrad*⟩; take ⟨*Kurve*⟩. **f~end** *a* moving; (*f~bar*) mobile; (*nicht seßhaft*) travelling, itinerant. **F~er** *m* **-s,-** driver. **F~erflucht** *f* failure to stop after an accident. **F~erhaus** *nt* driver's cab. **F~erin** *f* **-,-nen** woman driver. **F~gast** *m* passenger; (*im Taxi*) fare. **F~geld** *nt* fare. **F~gestell** *nt* chassis; (*Aviat*) undercarriage. **f~ig** *a* nervy; (*zerstreut*) distracted. **F~karte** *f* ticket. **F~kartenausgabe** *f*, **F~kartenschalter** *m* ticket office. **f~lässig** *a* negligent, *adv* -ly. **F~lässigkeit** *f* **-** negligence. **F~lehrer** *m* driving instructor. **F~plan** *m* timetable. **f~planmäßig** *a* scheduled ● *adv* according to/(*pünktlich*) on schedule. **F~preis** *m* fare. **F~prüfung** *f* driving test. **F~rad** *nt* bicycle. **F~schein** *m* ticket
Fährschiff *nt* ferry
Fahr|schule *f* driving school. **F~schüler(in)** *m(f)* learner driver. **F~spur** *f* [traffic] lane. **F~stuhl** *m* lift, (*Amer*) elevator. **F~stunde** *f* driving lesson
Fahrt *f* **-,-en** journey; (*Auto*) drive; (*Ausflug*) trip; (*Tempo*) speed; **in voller F~** at full speed. **F~ausweis** *m* ticket
Fährte *f* **-,-n** track; (*Witterung*) scent; **auf der falschen F~** (*fig*) on the wrong track
Fahr|tkosten *pl* travelling expenses. **F~werk** *nt* undercarriage. **F~zeug** *nt* **-[e]s,-e** vehicle; (*Wasser-*) craft, vessel
fair /fɛːɐ̯/ *a* fair, *adv* -ly. **F~neß** *f* **-** fairness
Fakten *pl* facts
Faktor *m* **-s,-en** /-ˈtoːrən/ factor
Fakul|tät *f* **-,-en** faculty. **f~tativ** *a* optional
Falke *m* **-n,-n** falcon
Fall *m* **-[e]s,⸚e** fall; (*Jur, Med, Gram*) case; **im F~[e]** in case (*gen* of); **auf jeden F~, auf alle F⸚e** in any case; (*bestimmt*) definitely; **für alle F⸚e** just in case; **auf keinen F~** on no account
Falle *f* **-,-n** trap; **eine F~ stellen** set a trap (*dat* for)
fallen† *vi* (*sein*) fall; (*sinken*) go down; **[im Krieg] f~** be killed in the war; **f~ lassen** drop
fällen *vt* fell; (*fig*) pass ⟨*Urteil*⟩; make ⟨*Entscheidung*⟩
fallenlassen† *vt sep* (*fig*) drop; make ⟨*Bemerkung*⟩
fällig *a* due; ⟨*Wechsel*⟩ mature; **längst f~** long overdue. **F~keit** *f* **-** (*Comm*) maturity
Fallobst *nt* windfalls *pl*
falls *conj* in case; (*wenn*) if
Fallschirm *m* parachute. **F~jäger** *m* paratrooper. **F~springer** *m* parachutist
Falltür *f* trapdoor
falsch *a* wrong; (*nicht echt, unaufrichtig*) false; (*gefälscht*) forged; ⟨*Geld*⟩ counterfeit; ⟨*Schmuck*⟩ fake ● *adv* wrongly; falsely; ⟨*singen*⟩ out of tune; **f~ gehen** ⟨*Uhr:*⟩ be wrong
fälsch|en *vt* forge, fake. **F~er** *m* **-s,-** forger
Falsch|geld *nt* counterfeit money. **F~heit** *f* **-** falseness
fälschlich *a* wrong, *adv* -ly; (*irrtümlich*) mistaken, *adv* -ly. **f~erweise** *adv* by mistake
Falsch|meldung *f* false report; (*absichtlich*) hoax report. **F~münzer** *m* **-s,-** counterfeiter
Fälschung *f* **-,-en** forgery, fake; (*Fälschen*) forging
Falte *f* **-,-n** fold; (*Rock-*) pleat; (*Knitter-*) crease; (*im Gesicht*) line; (*Runzel*) wrinkle
falten *vt* fold; **sich f~** ⟨*Haut:*⟩ wrinkle. **F~rock** *m* pleated skirt
Falter *m* **-s,-** butterfly; (*Nacht-*) moth
faltig *a* creased; ⟨*Gesicht*⟩ lined; (*runzlig*) wrinkled
familiär *a* family ...; (*vertraut, zudringlich*) familiar; (*zwanglos*) informal
Familie /-i̯ə/ *f* **-,-n** family. **F~nanschluß** *m* **F~nanschluß haben** live as one of the family. **F~nforschung** *f* genealogy. **F~nleben** *nt* family life. **F~nname** *m* surname. **F~nplanung** *f* family planning. **F~nstand** *m* marital status

Fan /fɛn/ m -s,-s fan

Fana|tiker m -s,- fanatic. f~tisch a fanatical, adv -ly. F~tismus m - fanaticism

Fanfare f -,-n trumpet; (Signal) fanfare

Fang m -[e]s,ːe capture; (Beute) catch; F~e (Krallen) talons; (Zähne) fangs. F~arm m tentacle. f~en† vt catch; (ein-) capture; sich f~en get caught (in + dat in); (fig) regain one's balance/(seelisch) composure. F~en nt -s F~en spielen play tag. F~frage f catch question. F~zahn m fang

fantastisch a = phantastisch

Farb|aufnahme f colour photograph. F~band nt (pl -bänder) typewriter ribbon. F~e f -,-n colour; (Maler-) paint; (zum Färben) dye; (Karten) suit. f~echt a colour-fast

färben vt colour; dye (Textilien, Haare); (fig) slant (Bericht); sich [rot] f~ turn [red] ● vi (haben) not be colour-fast

farb|enblind a colour-blind. f~enfroh a colourful. F~fernsehen nt colour television. F~film m colour film. F~foto nt colour photo. f~ig a coloured ● adv in colour. F~ige(r) m/f coloured man/woman. F~kasten m box of paints. f~los a colourless. F~stift m crayon. F~stoff m dye; (Lebensmittel-) colouring. F~ton m shade

Färbung f -,-en colouring; (fig: Anstrich) bias

Farce /ˈfarsə/ f -,-n farce; (Culin) stuffing

Farn m -[e]s, -e, F~kraut nt fern

Färse f -,-n heifer

Fasan m -[e]s,-e[n] pheasant

Faschierte(s) nt (Aust) mince

Fasching m -s (SGer) carnival

Faschis|mus m - fascism. F~t m -en,-en fascist. f~tisch a fascist

faseln vt/i (haben) (fam) [Unsinn] f~ talk nonsense

Faser f -,-n fibre. f~n vi (haben) fray

Faß nt -sses,ːsser barrel, cask; Bier vom Faß draught beer; Faß ohne Boden (fig) bottomless pit

Fassade f -,-n façade

faßbar a comprehensible; (greifbar) tangible

fassen vt take [hold of], grasp; (ergreifen) seize; (fangen) catch; (ein-) set; (enthalten) hold; (fig: begreifen) take in, grasp; conceive (Plan); make (Entschluß); sich f~ compose oneself; sich kurz/in Geduld f~ be brief/patient; in Worte f~ put into words; nicht zu f~ (fig) unbelievable ● vi (haben) f~ an (+ acc) touch; f~ nach reach for

faßlich a comprehensible

Fasson /faˈsõ/ f - style; (Form) shape; (Weise) way

Fassung f -,-en mount; (Edelstein-) setting; (Electr) socket; (Version) version; (Beherrschung) composure; aus der F~ bringen disconcert. f~slos a shaken; (erstaunt) flabbergasted. F~svermögen nt capacity

fast adv almost, nearly; f~ nie hardly ever

fast|en vi (haben) fast. F~enzeit f Lent. F~nacht f Shrovetide; (Karneval) carnival. F~nachtsdienstag m Shrove Tuesday. F~tag m fast-day

Faszin|ation /-ˈtsi̯oːn/ f - fascination. f~ieren vt fascinate; f~ierend fascinating

fatal a fatal; (peinlich) embarrassing. F~ismus m - fatalism. F~ist m -en,-en fatalist

Fata Morgana f - -/- -nen mirage

fauchen vi (haben) spit, hiss ● vt snarl

faul a lazy; (verdorben) rotten, bad; (Ausrede) lame; (zweifelhaft) bad; (verdächtig) fishy

Fäule f - decay

faul|en vi (sein) rot; (Zahn:) decay; (verwesen) putrefy. f~enzen vi (haben) be lazy. F~enzer m -s,- lazybones sg. F~heit f - laziness. f~ig a rotting; (Geruch) putrid

Fäulnis f - decay

Faulpelz m (fam) lazy-bones sg

Fauna f - fauna

Faust f -,Fäuste fist; auf eigene F~ (fig) off one's own bat. F~handschuh m mitten. F~schlag m punch

Fauxpas /foˈpa/ m -,- /-[s],-s/ gaffe

Favorit(in) /favoˈriːt(ɪn)/ m -en,-en (f -,-nen) (Sport) favourite

Fax nt -,-[e] fax. f~en vt fax

Faxen fpl (fam) antics; F~ machen fool about; F~ schneiden pull faces

Faxgerät nt fax machine

Feber m -s,- (Aust) February

Februar m -s,-e February

fecht|en† vi (haben) fence. F~er m -s,- fencer

Feder f -,-n feather; (Schreib-) pen; (Spitze) nib; (Techn) spring. F~ball m shuttlecock; (Spiel) badminton.

F~busch m plume. **f~leicht** a as light as a feather. **F~messer** nt penknife. **f~n** vi (haben) be springy; (nachgeben) give; (hoch-) bounce; **f~nd** springy; (elastisch) elastic. **F~ung** f - (Techn) springs pl; (Auto) suspension

Fee f -,-n fairy

Fegefeuer nt purgatory

fegen vt sweep ● vi (sein) (rasen) tear

Fehde f -,-n feud

fehl a **f~ am Platze** out of place. **F~betrag** m deficit. **f~en** vi (haben) be missing/(ausbleiben) absent; (mangeln) be lacking; **es f~t an** (+ dat) there is a shortage of; **mir f~t die Zeit** I haven't got the time; **sie/es f~t mir sehr** I miss her/it very much; **was f~t ihm?** what's the matter with him? **es f~te nicht viel und er ... he** very nearly ...; **das hat uns noch gefehlt!** that's all we need! **f~end** a missing; (Sch) absent

Fehler m -s,- mistake, error; (Sport & fig) fault; (Makel) flaw. **f~frei** a faultless, adv -ly. **f~haft** a faulty. **f~los** a flawless, adv -ly

Fehl|geburt f miscarriage. **f~gehen†** vi sep (sein) go wrong; ⟨Schuß:⟩ miss; (fig) be mistaken. **F~griff** m mistake. **F~kalkulation** f miscalculation. **F~schlag** m failure. **f~schlagen†** vi sep (sein) fail. **F~start** m (Sport) false start. **F~tritt** m false step; (fig) [moral] lapse. **F~zündung** f (Auto) misfire

Feier f -,-n celebration; (Zeremonie) ceremony; (Party) party. **F~abend** m end of the working day; **F~abend machen** stop work, (fam) knock off; **nach F~abend** after work. **f~lich** a solemn, adv -ly; (förmlich) formal, adv -ly. **F~lichkeit** f -,-en solemnity; **F~lichkeiten** festivities. **f~n** vt celebrate; hold ⟨Fest⟩; (ehren) fête ● vi (haben) celebrate; (lustig sein) make merry. **F~tag** m [public] holiday; (kirchlicher) feast-day; **erster/ zweiter F~tag** Christmas Day / Boxing Day. **f~tags** adv on public holidays

feige a cowardly; **f~ sein** be a coward ● adv in a cowardly way

Feige f -,-n fig. **F~nbaum** m fig tree

Feig|heit f - cowardice. **F~ling** m -s,-e coward

Feile f -,-n file. **f~n** vt/i (haben) file

feilschen vi (haben) haggle

Feilspäne mpl filings

fein a fine, adv -ly; (zart) delicate, adv -ly; ⟨Strümpfe⟩ sheer; ⟨Unterschied⟩ subtle; (scharf) keen; (vornehm) refined; (elegant) elegant; (prima) great; **sich f~ machen** dress up. **F~arbeit** f precision work

Feind|(in) m -es,-e (f -,-nen) enemy. **f~lich** a enemy; (f~selig) hostile. **F~schaft** f -,-en enmity. **f~selig** a hostile. **F~seligkeit** f -,-en hostility

fein|fühlig a sensitive. **F~gefühl** nt sensitivity; (Takt) delicacy. **F~heit** f -,-en (s. fein) fineness; delicacy; subtlety; keenness; refinement; **F~heiten** subtleties. **F~kostgeschäft** nt delicatessen [shop]. **F~schmecker** m -s,- gourmet

feist a fat

feixen vi (haben) smirk

Feld nt -[e]s,-er field; (Fläche) ground; (Sport) pitch; (Schach-) square; (auf Formular) box. **F~bau** m agriculture. **F~bett** nt camp-bed, (Amer) cot. **F~forschung** f fieldwork. **F~herr** m commander. **F~marschall** m Field Marshal. **F~stecher** m -s,- field-glasses pl. **F~webel** m (Mil) sergeant. **F~zug** m campaign

Felge f -,-n [wheel] rim

Fell nt -[e]s,-e (Zool) coat; (Pelz) fur; (abgezogen) skin, pelt; **ein dickes F~ haben** (fam) be thick-skinned

Fels m -en,-en rock. **F~block** m boulder. **F~en** m -s,- rock. **f~enfest** a (fig) firm, adv -ly. **f~ig** a rocky

feminin a feminine; (weibisch) effeminate

Femininum nt -s,-na (Gram) feminine

Feminist|(in) m -en,-en (f -,-nen) feminist. **f~isch** a feminist

Fenchel m -s fennel

Fenster nt -s,- window. **F~brett** nt window-sill. **F~laden** m [window] shutter. **F~leder** nt chamois[-leather]. **F~putzer** m -s,- window-cleaner. **F~scheibe** f [window-]pane

Ferien /'fe:rjən/ pl holidays; (Univ) vacation sg; **F~ haben** be on holiday. **F~ort** m holiday resort

Ferkel nt -s,- piglet

fern a distant; **der F~e Osten** the Far East ● adv far away; **von f~** from a distance ● prep (+ dat) far [away] from. **F~bedienung** f remote control. **f~bleiben†** vi sep (sein) stay away (dat from). **F~e** f - distance;

in/aus der F~e in the/from a distance; **in weiter F~e** far away; (*zeitlich*) in the distant future. **f~er** *a* further ● *adv* (*außerdem*) furthermore; (*in Zukunft*) in future. **f~gelenkt** *a* remote-controlled; ⟨*Rakete*⟩ guided. **F~gespräch** *nt* long-distance call. **f~gesteuert** *a* = **f~gelenkt. F~glas** *nt* binoculars *pl.* **f~halten**† *vt sep* keep away; **sich f~halten** keep away. **F~kopierer** *m* **-s,-** fax machine. **F~kurs[us]** *m* correspondence course. **F~lenkung** *f* remote control. **F~licht** *nt* (*Auto*) full beam. **F~meldewesen** *nt* telecommunications *pl.* **F~rohr** *nt* telescope. **F~schreiben** *nt* telex. **F~schreiber** *m* **-s,-** telex [machine]

Fernseh|apparat *m* television set. **f~en**† *vi sep* (*haben*) watch television. **F~en** *nt* **-s** television. **F~er** *m* **-s,-** [television] viewer; (*Gerät*) television set. **F~gerät** *nt* television set

Fernsprech|amt *nt* telephone exchange, (*Amer*) central. **F~er** *m* telephone. **F~nummer** *f* telephone number. **F~zelle** *f* telephone box

Fernsteuerung *f* remote control

Ferse *f* **-,-n** heel. **F~ngeld** *nt* **F~ngeld geben** (*fam*) take to one's heels

fertig *a* finished; (*bereit*) ready; (*Comm*) ready-made; ⟨*Gericht*⟩ ready-to-serve; **f~ werden mit** finish; (*bewältigen*) cope with; **f~ sein** have finished; (*fig*) be through (**mit jdm** with s.o.); (*fam: erschöpft*) be all in/(*seelisch*) shattered ● *adv* **f~ essen/lesen** finish eating/reading. **F~bau** *m* (*pl* **-bauten**) prefabricated building. **f~bringen**† *vt sep* manage to do; (*beenden*) finish; **ich bringe es nicht f~** I can't bring myself to do it. **f~en** *vt* make. **F~gericht** *nt* ready-to-serve meal. **F~haus** *nt* prefabricated house. **F~keit** *f* **-,-en** skill. **f~kriegen** *vt sep* (*fam*) = **f~bringen. f~machen** *vt sep* finish; (*bereitmachen*) get ready; (*fam: erschöpfen*) wear out; (*seelisch*) shatter; (*fam: abkanzeln*) carpet; **sich f~machen** get ready. **f~stellen** *vt sep* complete. **F~stellung** *f* completion. **F~ung** *f* - manufacture

fesch *a* (*fam*) attractive; (*flott*) smart; (*Aust: nett*) kind

Fessel *f* **-,-n** ankle

fesseln *vt* tie up; tie (**an** + *acc* to); (*fig*) fascinate; **ans Bett gefesselt** confined to bed. **F~** *fpl* bonds. **f~d** *a* (*fig*) fascinating; (*packend*) absorbing

fest *a* firm; (*nicht flüssig*) solid; (*erstarrt*) set; (*haltbar*) strong; (*nicht locker*) tight; (*feststehend*) fixed; (*ständig*) steady; ⟨*Anstellung*⟩ permanent; ⟨*Schlaf*⟩ sound; ⟨*Blick, Stimme*⟩ steady; **f~ werden** harden; ⟨*Gelee:*⟩ set; **f~e Nahrung** solids *pl* ● *adv* firmly; tightly; steadily; soundly; (*kräftig, tüchtig*) hard; **f~ schlafen** be fast asleep

Fest *nt* **-[e]s,-e** celebration; (*Party*) party; (*Relig*) festival; **frohes F~!** happy Christmas!

fest|angestellt *a* permanent. **f~binden**† *vt sep* tie (**an** + *dat* to). **f~bleiben**† *vi sep* (*sein*) (*fig*) remain firm. **f~e** *adv* (*fam*) hard. **F~essen** *nt* = **F~mahl. f~fahren**† *vi/r sep* (*sein*) [sich] **f~fahren** get stuck; ⟨*Verhandlungen:*⟩ reach deadlock. **f~halten**† *v sep* ● *vt* hold on to; (*aufzeichnen*) record; **sich f~halten** hold on ● *vi* (*haben*) **f~halten an** (+ *dat*) (*fig*) stick to; cling to ⟨*Tradition*⟩. **f~igen** *vt* strengthen; **sich f~igen** grow stronger. **F~iger** *m* **-s,-** styling lotion/(*Schaum*) mousse. **F~igkeit** *f* (*s.* **fest**) firmness; solidity; strength; steadiness. **f~klammern** *vt sep* clip (**an** + *dat* to); **sich f~klammern** cling (**an** + *dat* to). **F~land** *nt* mainland; (*Kontinent*) continent. **f~legen** *vt sep* (*fig*) fix, settle; lay down ⟨*Regeln*⟩; tie up ⟨*Geld*⟩; **sich f~legen** commit oneself

festlich *a* festive, *adv* -ly. **F~keiten** *fpl* festivities

fest|liegen† *vi sep* (*haben*) be fixed, settled. **f~machen** *v sep* ● *vt* fasten; (*binden*) tie (**an** + *dat* to); (*f~legen*) fix, settle ● *vi* (*haben*) (*Naut*) moor. **F~mahl** *nt* feast; (*Bankett*) banquet. **F~nahme** *f* **-,-n** arrest. **f~nehmen**† *vt sep* arrest. **F~ordner** *m* steward. **f~setzen** *vt sep* fix, settle; (*inhaftieren*) gaol; **sich f~setzen** collect. **f~sitzen**† *vi sep* (*haben*) be firm/⟨*Schraube:*⟩ tight; (*haften*) stick; (*nicht weiterkommen*) be stuck. **F~spiele** *npl* festival *sg.* **f~stehen**† *vi sep* (*haben*) be certain. **f~stellen** *vt sep* fix; (*ermitteln*) establish; (*bemerken*) notice; (*sagen*) state. **F~stellung** *f* establishment;

(*Aussage*) statement; (*Erkenntnis*) realization. **F~tag** *m* special day

Festung *f* -,-en fortress

Fest|zelt *nt* marquee. **f~ziehen†** *vt sep* pull tight. **F~zug** *m* [grand] procession

Fete /'feːtə, 'fɛːtə/ *f* -,-n party

fett *a* fat; (*f~reich*) fatty; (*fettig*) greasy; (*üppig*) rich; ⟨*Druck*⟩ bold. **F~** *nt* -[e]s,-e fat; (*flüssig*) grease. **f~arm** *a* low-fat. **f~en** *vt* grease ● *vi* (*haben*) be greasy. **F~fleck** *m* grease mark. **f~ig** *a* greasy. **f~leibig** *a* obese. **F~näpfchen** *nt* ins **F~näpfchen treten** (*fam*) put one's foot in it

Fetzen *m* -s,- scrap; (*Stoff*) rag; **in F~** in shreds

feucht *a* damp, moist; ⟨*Luft*⟩ humid. **f~heiß** *a* humid. **F~igkeit** *f* - dampness; (*Nässe*) moisture; (*Luft*-) humidity. **F~igkeitscreme** *f* moisturizer

feudal *a* (*fam: vornehm*) sumptuous, *adv* -ly. **F~ismus** *m* - feudalism

Feuer *nt* -s,- fire; (*für Zigarette*) light; (*Begeisterung*) passion; **F~ machen** light a fire; **F~ fangen** catch fire; (*fam: sich verlieben*) be smitten; **jdm F~ geben** give s.o. a light. **F~alarm** *m* fire alarm. **F~bestattung** *f* cremation. **F~gefährlich** *a* [in]flammable. **F~leiter** *f* fire-escape. **F~löscher** *m* -s,- fire extinguisher. **F~melder** *m* -s,- fire alarm. **F~n** *vi* (*haben*) fire (**auf** + *acc* on) ● *vt* (*fam*) (*schleudern*) fling; (*entlassen*) fire. **F~probe** *f* (*fig*) test. **f~rot** *a* crimson. **f~speiend** *a* **f~speiender Berg** volcano. **F~stein** *m* flint. **F~stelle** *f* hearth. **F~treppe** *f* fire-escape. **F~wache** *f* fire station. **F~waffe** *f* firearm. **F~wehr** *f* -,-en fire brigade. **F~wehrauto** *nt* fire-engine. **F~wehrmann** *m* (*pl* -männer & -leute*) fireman. **F~werk** *nt* firework display, fireworks *pl*. **F~werkskörper** *m* firework. **F~zeug** *nt* lighter

feurig *a* fiery; (*fig*) passionate

Fiaker *m* -s,- (*Aust*) horse-drawn cab

Fichte *f* -,-n spruce

fidel *a* cheerful

Fieber *nt* -s [raised] temperature; **F~ haben** have a temperature. **f~haft** *a* (*fig*) feverish, *adv* -ly. **f~n** *vi* (*haben*) be feverish. **F~thermometer** *nt* thermometer

fiebrig *a* feverish

fies *a* (*fam*) nasty, *adv* -ily

Figur *f* -,-en figure; (*Roman*-, *Film*-) character; (*Schach*-) piece

Fik|tion /-'tsjoːn/ *f* -,-en fiction. **f~tiv** *a* fictitious

Filet /fi'leː/ *nt* -s,-s fillet

Filial|e *f* -,-n, **F~geschäft** *nt* (*Comm*) branch

Filigran *nt* -s filigree

Film *m* -[e]s,-e film; (*Kino*-) film, (*Amer*) movie; (*Schicht*) coating. **f~en** *vt/i* (*haben*) film. **F~kamera** *f* cine/(*für Kinofilm*) film camera

Filt|er *m* & (*Techn*) *nt* -s,- filter; (*Zigaretten*-) filter-tip. **f~ern** *vt* filter. **F~erzigarette** *f* filter-tipped cigarette. **f~rieren** *vt* filter

Filz *m* -es felt. **f~en** *vi* (*haben*) become matted ● *vt* (*fam*) (*durchsuchen*) frisk; (*stehlen*) steal. **F~schreiber** *m* -s,-, **F~stift** *m* felt-tipped pen

Fimmel *m* -s,- (*fam*) obsession

Fina|le *nt* -s,- (*Mus*) finale; (*Sport*) final. **F~list(in)** *m* -en,-en (*f* -,-nen) finalist

Finanz *f* -,-en finance. **F~amt** *nt* tax office. **f~iell** *a* financial, *adv* -ly. **f~ieren** *vt* finance. **F~minister** *m* minister of finance

find|en† *vt* find; (*meinen*) think; **den Tod f~en** meet one's death; **wie f~est du das?** what do you think of that? **f~est du?** do you think so? **es wird sich f~en** it'll turn up; (*fig*) it'll be all right ● *vi* (*haben*) find one's way. **F~er** *m* -s,- finder. **F~erlohn** *m* reward. **f~ig** *a* resourceful. **F~ling** *m* -s,-e boulder

Finesse *f* -,-n (*Kniff*) trick; **F~n** (*Techn*) refinements

Finger *m* -s,- finger; **die F~ lassen von** (*fam*) leave alone; **etw im kleinen F~ haben** (*fam*) have sth at one's fingertips. **F~abdruck** *m* finger-mark; (*Admin*) fingerprint. **F~hut** *m* thimble. **F~nagel** *m* finger-nail. **F~ring** *m* ring. **F~spitze** *f* finger-tip. **F~zeig** *m* -[e]s,-e hint

fingier|en *vt* fake. **f~t** *a* fictitious

Fink *m* -en,-en finch

Finn|e *m* -n,-n, **F~in** *f* -,-nen Finn. **f~isch** *a* Finnish. **F~land** *nt* -s Finland

finster *a* dark; (*düster*) gloomy; (*unheildrohend*) sinister; **im F~n** in the dark. **F~nis** *f* - darkness; (*Astr*) eclipse

Finte *f* -,-n trick; (*Boxen*) feint

Firma f -,-men firm, company

firmen vt (Relig) confirm

Firmen|wagen m company car.
F~zeichen nt trade mark, logo

Firmung f -,-en (Relig) confirmation

Firnis m -ses,-se varnish. f~sen vt
varnish

First m -[e]s,-e [roof] ridge

Fisch m -[e]s,-e fish; F~e (Astr)
Pisces. F~dampfer m trawler.
f~en vt/i (haben) fish; aus dem
Wasser f~en (fam) fish out of the
water. F~er m -s,- fisherman. F~e-
rei f -, F~fang m fishing. F~gräte f
fishbone. F~händler m fishmonger.
F~otter m otter. F~reiher m heron.
F~stäbchen nt -s,- fish finger.
F~teich m fish-pond

Fiskus m - der F~ the Treasury

Fisole f -,-n (Aust) French bean

fit a fit. F~neß f - fitness

fix a (fam) quick, adv -ly; (geistig)
bright; f~e Idee obsession; fix und
fertig all finished; (bereit) all ready;
(fam: erschöpft) shattered. F~er m
-s,- (sl) junkie

fixieren vt stare at; (Phot) fix

Fjord m -[e]s,-e fiord

FKK abbr (Freikörperkultur)
naturism

flach a flat; (eben) level; (niedrig) low;
(nicht tief) shallow; f~er Teller dinner plate; die f~e Hand the flat of the
hand

Fläche f -,-n area; (Ober-) surface;
(Seite) face. F~nmaß nt square
measure

Flachs m -es flax. f~blond a flaxen-
haired; (Haar) flaxen

flackern vi (haben) flicker

Flagg|e f -,-n flag

flagrant a flagrant

Flair /flɛːɐ̯/ nt -s air, aura

Flak f -,-[s] anti-aircraft artillery/
(Geschütz) gun

flämisch a Flemish

Flamme f -,-n flame; (Koch-) burner;
in F~n in flames

Flanell m -s (Tex) flannel

Flank|e f -,-n flank. f~ieren vt flank

Flasche f -,-n bottle. F~nbier nt
bottled beer. F~nöffner m
bottle-opener

flatter|haft a fickle. f~n vi (sein/
haben) flutter; (Segel:) flap

flau a (schwach) faint; (Comm) slack;
mir ist f~ I feel faint

Flaum m -[e]s down. f~ig a downy;
f~ig rühren (Aust Culin) cream

flauschig a fleecy; (Spielzeug) fluffy

Flausen fpl (fam) silly ideas; (Aus-
flüchte) silly excuses

Flaute f -,-n (Naut) calm; (Comm)
slack period; (Schwäche) low

fläzen (sich) vr (fam) sprawl

Flechte f -,-n (Med) eczema; (Bot)
lichen; (Zopf) plait. f~n† vt plait;
weave (Korb)

Fleck m -[e]s,-e[n] spot; (größer)
patch; (Schmutz-) stain, mark;
blauer F~ bruise; nicht vom F~
kommen (fam) make no progress.
f~en vi (haben) stain. F~en m -s,-
= Fleck; (Ortschaft) small town.
f~enlos a spotless. F~entferner m
-s,- stain remover. f~ig a stained;
(Haut) blotchy

Fledermaus f bat

Flegel m -s,- lout. f~haft a loutish.
F~jahre npl (fam) awkward age sg.
f~n (sich) vr loll

flehen vi (haben) beg (um for).
f~tlich a pleading, adv -ly

Fleisch nt -[e]s flesh; (Culin) meat;
(Frucht-) pulp. F~er m -s,- butcher.
F~erei f -,-en, F~erladen m
butcher's shop. f~fressend a carnivorous. F~fresser m -s,- carnivore.
F~hauer m -s,- (Aust) butcher. f~ig
a fleshy. f~lich a carnal. F~wolf m
mincer. F~wunde f flesh-wound

Fleiß m -es diligence; mit F~ dili-
gently; (absichtlich) on purpose.
f~ig a diligent, adv -ly; (arbeitsam)
industrious, adv -ly

flektieren vt (Gram) inflect

fletschen vt die Zähne f~ (Tier:)
bare its teeth

flexibel a flexible; (Einband) limp.
F~ibilität f - flexibility. F~ion f
-,-en (Gram) inflexion

flicken vt mend; (mit Flicken) patch.
F~ m -s,- patch

Flieder m -s lilac. f~farben a lilac

Fliege f -,-n fly; (Schleife) bow-tie;
zwei F~n mit einer Klappe schlagen
kill two birds with one stone. f~n†
vi (sein) fly; (geworfen werden) be
thrown; (fam: fallen) fall; (fam: entlassen werden) be fired/(von der
Schule) expelled; in die Luft f~n
blow up ● vt fly. f~nd a flying;
(Händler) itinerant; in f~nder Eile
in great haste. F~r m -s,- airman;
(Pilot) pilot; (fam: Flugzeug) plane.
F~rangriff m air raid

flieh|en† vi (sein) flee (vor + dat
from); (entweichen) escape ● vt

shun. **f~end** *a* fleeing; ⟨*Kinn, Stirn*⟩ receding. **F~kraft** *f* centrifugal force

Fliese *f* -,-n tile

Fließ|band *nt* assembly line. **f~en†** *vi* (*sein*) flow; (*aus Wasserhahn*) run. **f~end** *a* flowing; ⟨*Wasser*⟩ running; ⟨*Verkehr*⟩ moving; (*geläufig*) fluent, *adv* -ly. **F~heck** *nt* fastback. **F~wasser** *nt* running water

flimmern *vi* (*haben*) shimmer; (*TV*) flicker; **es flimmert mir vor den Augen** everything is dancing in front of my eyes

flink *a* nimble, *adv* -bly; (*schnell*) quick, *adv* -ly

Flinte *f* -,-n shotgun

Flirt /flœet/ *m* -s,-s flirtation. **f~en** *vi* (*haben*) flirt

Flitter *m* -s sequins *pl*; (*F~schmuck*) tinsel. **F~wochen** *fpl* honeymoon *sg*

flitzen *vi* (*sein*) (*fam*) dash; ⟨*Auto:*⟩ whizz

Flock|e *f* -,-n flake; (*Wolle*) tuft. **f~ig** *a* fluffy

Floh *m* -[e]s,-̈e flea. **F~markt** *m* flea market. **F~spiel** *nt* tiddly-winks *sg*

Flor *m* -s gauze; (*Trauer-*) crape; (*Samt-, Teppich-*) pile

Flora *f* - flora

Florett *nt* -[e]s,-e foil

florieren *vi* (*haben*) flourish

Floskel *f* -,-n [empty] phrase

Floß *nt* -es,-̈e raft

Flosse *f* -,-n fin; (*Seehund-, Gummi-*) flipper; (*sl: Hand*) paw

Flöt|e *f* -,-n flute; (*Block-*) recorder. **f~en** *vi* (*haben*) play the flute/recorder; (*fam: pfeifen*) whistle ● *vt* play on the flute/recorder. **F~ist(in)** *m* -en,-en (*f* -,-nen) flautist

flott *a* quick, *adv* -ly; (*lebhaft*) lively; (*schick*) smart, *adv* -ly; **f~ leben** live it up

Flotte *f* -,-n fleet

flottmachen *vt sep* **wieder f~** (*Naut*) refloat; get going again ⟨*Auto*⟩; put back on its feet ⟨*Unternehmen*⟩

Flöz *nt* -es,-e [coal] seam

Fluch *m* -[e]s,-̈e curse. **f~en** *vi* (*haben*) curse, swear

Flucht¹ *f* -,-en (*Reihe*) line; (*Zimmer-*) suite

Flucht² *f* - flight; (*Entweichen*) escape; **die F~ ergreifen** take flight. **f~artig** *a* hasty, *adv* -ily

flücht|en *vi* (*sein*) flee (**vor** + *dat* from); (*entweichen*) escape ● *vr* **sich**

f~en take refuge. **f~ig** *a* fugitive; (*kurz*) brief, *adv* -ly; ⟨*Blick, Gedanke*⟩ fleeting; ⟨*Bekanntschaft*⟩ passing; (*oberflächlich*) cursory, *adv* -ily; (*nicht sorgfältig*) careless, *adv* -ly; (*Chem*) volatile; **f~ig sein** be on the run; **f~ig kennen** know slightly. **F~igkeitsfehler** *m* slip. **F~ling** *m* -s,-e fugitive; (*Pol*) refugee

Fluchwort *nt* (*pl* **-wörter**) swearword

Flug *m* -[e]s,-̈e flight. **F~abwehr** *f* anti-aircraft defence. **F~ball** *m* (*Tennis*) volley. **F~blatt** *nt* pamphlet

Flügel *m* -s,- wing; (*Fenster-*) casement; (*Mus*) grand piano

Fluggast *m* [air] passenger

flügge *a* fully-fledged

Flug|gesellschaft *f* airline. **F~hafen** *m* airport. **F~lotse** *m* air-traffic controller. **F~platz** *m* airport; (*klein*) airfield. **F~preis** *m* air fare. **F~schein** *m* air ticket. **F~schneise** *f* flight path. **F~schreiber** *m* -s,- flight recorder. **F~schrift** *f* pamphlet. **F~steig** *m* -[e]s,-e gate. **F~wesen** *nt* aviation. **F~zeug** *nt* -[e]s,-e aircraft, plane

Fluidum *nt* -s aura

Flunder *f* -,-n flounder

flunkern *vi* (*haben*) (*fam*) tell fibs; (*aufschneiden*) tell tall stories

Flunsch *m* -[e]s,-e pout

fluoreszierend *a* fluorescent

Flur *m* -[e]s,-e (*entrance*) hall; (*Gang*) corridor

Flusen *fpl* fluff *sg*

Fluß *m* -sses, -̈sse river; (*Fließen*) flow; **im F~** (*fig*) in a state of flux. **f~abwärts** *adv* downstream. **f~aufwärts** *adv* upstream. **F~bett** *nt* river-bed

flüssig *a* liquid; ⟨*Lava*⟩ molten; (*fließend*) fluent, *adv* -ly; ⟨*Verkehr*⟩ freely moving. **F~keit** *f* -,-en liquid; (*Anat*) fluid

Flußpferd *nt* hippopotamus

flüstern *vt/i* (*haben*) whisper

Flut *f* -,-en high tide; (*fig*) flood; **F~en** waters. **F~licht** *nt* floodlight. **F~welle** *f* tidal wave

Föderation /-'tsio:n/ *f* -,-en federation

Fohlen *nt* -s,- foal

Föhn *m* -s föhn [wind]

Folg|e *f* -,-n consequence; (*Reihe*) succession; (*Fortsetzung*) instalment;

(*Teil*) part; F~e leisten (+*dat*) accept ⟨*Einladung*⟩; obey ⟨*Befehl*⟩. f~en *vi* (*sein*) follow (**jdm/etw** s.o./sth); (*zuhören*) listen (*dat* to); daraus f~t, daß it follows that; wie f~t as follows ● (*haben*) (*gehorchen*) obey (**jdm** s.o.). f~end *a* following; f~endes the following. f~endermaßen *adv* as follows

folger|n *vt* conclude (aus from). F~ung *f* -,-en conclusion

folg|lich *adv* consequently. f~sam *a* obedient, *adv* -ly

Folie /'fo:ljə/ *f* -,-n foil; (*Plastik-*) film

Folklore *f* - folklore

Folter *f* -,-n torture; auf die F~ spannen (*fig*) keep on tenterhooks. f~n *vt* torture

Fön (P) *m* -s,-e hair-drier

Fonds /fo:/ *m* -,- /-[s],-s/ fund

fönen *vt* [blow-]dry

Fontäne *f* -,-n jet; (*Brunnen*) fountain

Förder|band *nt* (*pl* -bänder) conveyor belt. f~lich *a* beneficial

fordern *vt* demand; (*beanspruchen*) claim; (*zum Kampf*) challenge; gefordert werden (*fig*) be stretched

fördern *vt* promote; (*unterstützen*) encourage; (*finanziell*) sponsor; (*gewinnen*) extract

Forderung *f* -,-en demand; (*Anspruch*) claim

Förderung *f* - (s. fördern) promotion; encouragement; (*Techn*) production

Forelle *f* -,-n trout

Form *f* -,-en form; (*Gestalt*) shape; (*Culin, Techn*) mould; (*Back-*) tin; [gut] in F~ in good form

Formalität *f* -,-en formality

Format *nt* -[e]s,-e format; (*Größe*) size; (*fig: Bedeutung*) stature

Formation /-'tsio:n/ *f* -,-en formation

Formel *f* -,-n formula

formell *a* formal, *adv* -ly

formen *vt* shape, mould; (*bilden*) form; sich f~ take shape

förmlich *a* formal, *adv* -ly; (*regelrecht*) virtual, *adv* -ly. F~keit *f* -,-en formality

form|los *a* shapeless; (*zwanglos*) informal, *adv* -ly. F~sache *f* formality

Formular *nt* -s,-e [printed] form

formulier|en *vt* formulate, word. F~ung *f* -,-en wording

forsch *a* brisk, *adv* -ly; (*schneidig*) dashing, *adv* -ly

forsch|en *vi* (*haben*) search (nach for). f~end *a* searching. F~er *m* -s,-

research scientist; (*Reisender*) explorer. F~ung *f* -,-en research.

F~ungsreisende(r) *m* explorer

Forst *m* -[e]s,-e forest

Förster *m* -s,- forester

Forstwirtschaft *f* forestry

Forsythie /-tsiə/ *f* -,-n forsythia

Fort *nt* -s,-s (*Mil*) fort

fort *adv* away; f~ sein be away; (*gegangen/verschwunden*) have gone; und so f~ and so on; in einem f~ continuously. f~bewegen *vt sep* move; sich f~bewegen move. F~bewegung *f* locomotion. F~bildung *f* further education/training. f~bleiben† *vi sep* (*sein*) stay away. f~bringen† *vt sep* take away. f~fahren† *vi sep* (*sein*) go away ● (*haben/sein*) continue (zu to). f~fallen† *vi sep* (*sein*) be dropped/ (*ausgelassen*) omitted; (*entfallen*) no longer apply; (*aufhören*) cease. f~führen *vt sep* continue. F~gang *m* departure; (*Verlauf*) progress. f~gehen† *vi sep* (*sein*) leave, go away; (*ausgehen*) go out; (*andauern*) go on. f~geschritten *a* advanced; (*spät*) late. F~geschrittene(r) *m/f* advanced student. f~gesetzt *a* constant, *adv* -ly. f~jagen *vt sep* chase away. f~lassen† *vt sep* let go; (*auslassen*) omit. f~laufen† *vi sep* (*sein*) run away; (*sich f~setzen*) continue. f~laufend *a* consecutive, *adv* -ly. f~nehmen† *vt sep* take away. f~pflanzen (sich) *vr sep* reproduce; ⟨*Ton, Licht:*⟩ travel. F~pflanzung *f* reproduction. F~pflanzungsorgan *nt* reproductive organ. f~reißen† *vt sep* carry away; (*entreißen*) tear away. f~schaffen *vt sep* take away. f~schicken *vt sep* send away; (*abschicken*) send off. f~schreiten† *vi sep* (*sein*) continue; (*Fortschritte machen*) progress, advance. f~schreitend *a* progressive; ⟨*Alter*⟩ advancing. F~schritt *m* progress; F~schritte machen make progress. f~schrittlich *a* progressive. f~setzen *vt sep* continue; sich f~setzen continue. F~setzung *f* -,-en continuation; (*Folge*) instalment; F~setzung folgt to be continued. F~setzungsroman *m* serialized novel, serial. f~während *a* constant, *adv* -ly. f~werfen† *vt sep* throw away. f~ziehen† *v sep* ● *vt* pull away ● *vi* (*sein*) move away

Fossil *nt* -,-ien /-jən/ fossil

Foto nt -s,-s photo. **F~apparat** m camera. **f~gen** a photogenic

Fotograf|(in) m -en,-en (f -,-nen) photographer. **F~ie** f -,-n photography; (*Bild*) photograph. **f~ieren** vt take a photo[graph] of; **sich f~ieren lassen** have one's photo[graph] taken ● vi (*haben*) take photographs. **f~isch** a photographic

Fotokopie f photocopy. **f~ren** vt photocopy. **F~rgerät** nt photocopier

Fötus m -,-ten foetus

Foul /faul/ nt -s,-s (*Sport*) foul. **f~en** vt foul

Foyer /foa'je:/ nt -s,-s foyer

Fracht f -,-en freight. **F~er** m -s,- freighter. **F~gut** nt freight. **F~schiff** nt cargo boat

Frack m -[e]s,⁓e & -s tailcoat; **im F~** in tails pl

Frage f -,-n question; **eine F~ stellen** ask a question; **etw in F~ stellen** question sth; (*ungewiß machen*) make sth doubtful; **ohne F~** undoubtedly; **nicht in F~ kommen** be out of the question. **F~bogen** m questionnaire. **f~n** vt/i (*haben*) ask; **sich f~n** wonder (**ob** whether). **f~nd** a questioning, adv -ly; (*Gram*) interrogative. **F~zeichen** nt question mark

frag|lich a doubtful; ⟨*Person, Sache*⟩ in question. **f~los** adv undoubtedly

Fragment nt -[e]s,-e fragment. **f~arisch** a fragmentary

fragwürdig a questionable; (*verdächtig*) dubious

fraisefarben /'frɛ:s-/ a strawberry-pink

Fraktion /-'tsjo:n/ f -,-en parliamentary party

Franken¹ m -s,- (*Swiss*) franc

Franken² nt -s Franconia

Frankfurter f -,- frankfurter

frankieren vt stamp, frank

Frankreich nt -s France

Fransen fpl fringe sg

Franz|ose m -n,-n Frenchman; **die F~osen** the French pl. **F~ösin** f -,-nen Frenchwoman. **f~ösisch** a French. **F~ösisch** nt -[s] (*Lang*) French

frapp|ant a striking. **f~ieren** vt (*fig*) strike; **f~ierend** striking

fräsen vt (*Techn*) mill

Fraß m -es feed; (*pej: Essen*) muck

Fratze f -,-n grotesque face; (*Grimasse*) grimace; (*pej: Gesicht*) face; **F~n schneiden** pull faces

Frau f -,-en woman; (*Ehe-*) wife; **F~ Thomas** Mrs/(*unverheiratet*) Miss/ (*Admin*) Ms Thomas; **Unsere Liebe F~** (*Relig*) Our Lady. **F~chen** nt -s,- mistress

Frauen|arzt m, **F~ärztin** f gynaecologist. **F~rechtlerin** f -,-nen feminist. **F~zimmer** nt woman

Fräulein nt -s,- single woman; (*jung*) young lady; (*Anrede*) Miss

fraulich a womanly

frech a cheeky, adv -ily; (*unverschämt*) impudent, adv -ly. **F~dachs** m (*fam*) cheeky monkey. **F~heit** f -,-en cheekiness; impudence; (*Äußerung, Handlung*) impertinence

frei a free; (*freischaffend*) freelance; ⟨*Künstler*⟩ independent; (*nicht besetzt*) vacant; (*offen*) open; (*bloß*) bare; **f~er Tag** day off; **sich** (*dat*) **f~ nehmen** take time off; **f~ machen** (*räumen*) clear; vacate ⟨*Platz*⟩; (*befreien*) liberate; (*entkleiden*) bare; **f~ lassen** leave free; **jdm f~e Hand lassen** give s.o. a free hand; **ist dieser Platz f~?** is this seat taken? **'Zimmer f~'** 'vacancies' ● adv freely; (*ohne Notizen*) without notes; (*umsonst*) free

Frei|bad nt open-air swimming pool. **f~bekommen†** vt sep get released; **einen Tag f~bekommen** get a day off. **f~beruflich** a & adv freelance. **F~e** nt im F~en in the open air, out of doors. **F~frau** f baroness. **F~gabe** f release. **f~geben†** v sep ● vt release; (*eröffnen*) open; **jdm einen Tag f~geben** give s.o. a day off ● vi (*haben*) **jdm f~geben** give s.o. time off. **f~gebig** a generous, adv -ly. **F~gebigkeit** f - generosity. **f~haben†** v sep ● vt eine Stunde **f~haben** have an hour off; (*Sch*) have a free period ● vi (*haben*) be off work/(*Sch*) school; (*beurlaubt sein*) have time off. **f~halten†** vt sep keep clear; (*belegen*) keep; **einen Tag/sich f~halten** keep a day/oneself free; **jdn f~halten** treat s.o. [to a meal/ drink]. **F~handelszone** f free-trade area. **f~händig** adv without holding on

Freiheit f -,-en freedom, liberty; **sich** (*dat*) **F~en erlauben** take liberties. **F~sstrafe** f prison sentence

freiheraus adv frankly

Frei|herr m baron. **F~karte** f free ticket. **F~körperkultur** f naturism. **f~lassen†** vt sep release, set free.

F∼lassung f - release. **F∼lauf** m free-wheel. **f∼legen** vt sep expose. **f∼lich** adv admittedly; (natürlich) of course. **F∼lichttheater** nt open-air theatre. **f∼machen** v sep ● vt (frankieren) frank ● vi/r (haben) [sich] **f∼machen** take time off. **F∼marke** f [postage] stamp. **F∼maurer** m Freemason. **f∼mütig** a candid, adv -ly. **F∼platz** m free seat; (Sch) free place. **f∼schaffend** a freelance. **f∼schwimmen†** (sich) vr sep pass one's swimming test. **f∼setzen** vt sep release; (entlassen) make redundant. **f∼sprechen†** vt sep acquit. **F∼spruch** m acquittal. **f∼stehen†** vi sep (haben) stand empty; **es steht ihm f∼** (fig) he is free (**zu** to). **f∼stellen** vt sep exempt (**von** from); **jdm etw f∼stellen** leave sth up to s.o. **f∼stempeln** vt sep frank. **F∼stil** m freestyle. **F∼stoß** m free kick. **F∼stunde** f (Sch) free period
Freitag m Friday. **f∼s** adv on Fridays
Frei|tod m suicide. **F∼übungen** fpl [physical] exercises. **F∼umschlag** m stamped envelope. **f∼weg** adv freely; (offen) openly. **f∼willig** a voluntary, adv -ily. **F∼willige(r)** m/f volunteer. **F∼zeichen** nt ringing tone; (Rufzeichen) dialling tone. **F∼zeit** f free or spare time; (Muße) leisure; (Tagung) [weekend/holiday] course. **F∼zeit-** pref leisure ... **F∼zeitbekleidung** f casual wear. **f∼zügig** a unrestricted; (großzügig) liberal; (moralisch) permissive
fremd a foreign; (unbekannt, ungewohnt) strange; (nicht das eigene) other people's; **ein f∼er Mann** a stranger; **f∼e Leute** strangers; **unter f∼em Namen** under an assumed name; **jdm f∼ sein** be unknown/(wesens-) alien to s.o.; **ich bin hier f∼** I'm a stranger here. **f∼artig** a strange, adv -ly; (exotisch) exotic. **F∼e** f - **in der F∼e** away from home; (im Ausland) in a foreign country. **F∼e(r)** m/f stranger; (Ausländer) foreigner; (Tourist) tourist. **F∼enführer** m [tourist] guide. **F∼enverkehr** m tourism. **F∼enzimmer** nt room [to let]; (Gäste-) guest room. **F∼gehen†** vi sep (sein) (fam) be unfaithful. **F∼körper** m foreign body. **f∼ländisch** a foreign; (exotisch) exotic. **F∼ling** m -s,-e

stranger. **F∼sprache** f foreign language. **F∼wort** nt (pl -wörter) foreign word
frenetisch a frenzied
frequ|entieren vt frequent. **F∼enz** f -,-en frequency
Freske f -,-n, **Fresko** nt -s,-ken fresco
Fresse f -,-n (sl) (Mund) gob; (Gesicht) mug; **halt die F∼!** shut your trap! **f∼n†** vt/i (haben) eat. **F∼n** nt -s feed; (sl: Essen) grub
Freßnapf m feeding bowl
Freud|e f -,-n pleasure; (innere) joy; **mit F∼en** with pleasure; **jdm eine F∼e machen** please s.o. **f∼ig** a joyful, adv -ly; (froher) happy event. **f∼los** a cheerless; (traurig) sad
freuen vt please; **sich f∼** be pleased (über+acc about); **sich f∼ auf** (+acc) look forward to; **es freut mich, ich freue mich** I'm glad or pleased (**daß** that)
Freund m -es,-e friend; (Verehrer) boyfriend; (Anhänger) lover (gen of). **F∼in** f -,-nen friend; (Liebste) girlfriend; (Anhängerin) lover (gen of). **f∼lich** a kind, adv -ly; (umgänglich) friendly; (angenehm) pleasant; **wären Sie so f∼lich?** would you be so kind? **f∼licherweise** adv kindly. **F∼lichkeit** f -,-en kindness; friendliness; pleasantness
Freundschaft f -,-en friendship; **F∼ schließen** become friends. **f∼lich** a friendly
Frevel /ˈfreːfəl/ m -s,- (liter) outrage. **f∼haft** a (liter) wicked
Frieden m -s peace; **F∼ schließen** make peace; **im F∼** in peacetime; **laß mich in F∼!** leave me alone! **F∼srichter** m ≈ magistrate. **F∼svertrag** m peace treaty
fried|fertig a peaceable. **F∼hof** m cemetery. **f∼lich** a peaceful, adv -ly; (verträglich) peaceable. **f∼liebend** a peace-loving
frieren† vi (haben) ⟨Person:⟩ be cold; impers **es friert/hat gefroren** it is freezing/there has been a frost; **frierst du? friert [es] dich?** are you cold? ● (sein) (gefrieren) freeze
Fries m -es,-e frieze
Frikadelle f -,-n [meat] rissole
frisch a fresh; (sauber) clean; (leuchtend) bright; (munter) lively; (rüstig) fit; **sich f∼ machen** freshen up ● adv freshly, newly; **f∼ gelegte**

Eier new-laid eggs; **ein Bett f~ beziehen** put clean sheets on a bed; **f~ gestrichen!** wet paint! **F~e** f - freshness; brightness; liveliness; fitness. **F~haltepackung** f vacuum pack. **F~käse** m ≈ cottage cheese. **f~weg** adv freely

Fri|seur /fri'zø:g/ m -s,-e hairdresser; (*Herren-*) barber. **F~seursalon** m hairdressing salon. **F~seuse** /-'zø:zə/ f -,-n hairdresser

frisier|en vt jdn/sich f~en do s.o.'s/ one's hair; **die Bilanz/einen Motor f~en** (*fam*) fiddle the accounts/soup up an engine. **F~kommode** f dressing-table. **F~salon** m = **Friseursalon**. **F~tisch** m dressing-table

Frisör m -s,-e = **Friseur**

Frist f -,-en period; (*Termin*) deadline; (*Aufschub*) time; **drei Tage F~** three days' grace. **f~en** vt **sein Leben f~en** eke out an existence. **f~los** a instant, adv -ly

Frisur f -,-en hairstyle

fritieren vt deep-fry

frivol /fri'vo:l/ a frivolous, adv -ly; (*schlüpfrig*) smutty

froh a happy; (*freudig*) joyful; (*erleichtert*) glad; **f~e Ostern!** happy Easter!

fröhlich a cheerful, adv -ly; (*vergnügt*) merry, adv -ily; **f~e Weihnachten!** merry Christmas! **F~keit** f - cheerfulness; merriment

frohlocken vi (*haben*) rejoice; (*schadenfroh*) gloat

Frohsinn m - cheerfulness

fromm a (**frömmer, frömmst**) devout, adv -ly; (*gutartig*) docile, adv -ly; **f~er Wunsch** idle wish

Frömm|igkeit f - devoutness, piety. **f~lerisch** a sanctimonious, adv -ly

frönen vi (*haben*) indulge (*dat* in)

Fronleichnam m Corpus Christi

Front f -,-en front. **f~al** a frontal; 〈*Zusammenstoß*〉 head-on ● adv from the front; 〈*zusammenstoßen*〉 head-on. **F~alzusammenstoß** m head-on collision

Frosch m -[e]s,-̈e frog. **F~laich** m frog-spawn. **F~mann** m (*pl* -**männer**) frogman

Frost m -[e]s,-̈e frost. **F~beule** f chilblain

frösteln vi (*haben*) shiver; **mich fröstelte [es]** I shivered/(*fror*) felt chilly

frost|ig a frosty, adv -ily. **F~schutzmittel** nt antifreeze

Frottee nt & m -s towelling

frottier|en vt rub down. **F~[hand]-tuch** nt terry towel

frotzeln vt/i (*haben*) [**über**] jdn f~ make fun of s.o.

Frucht f -,-̈e fruit; **F~ tragen** bear fruit. **f~bar** a fertile; (*fig*) fruitful. **F~barkeit** f - fertility. **f~en** vi (*haben*) **wenig/nichts f~en** have little/ no effect. **f~ig** a fruity. **f~los** a fruitless, adv -ly. **F~saft** m fruit juice

frugal a frugal, adv -ly

früh a early ● adv early; (*morgens*) in the morning; **heute/gestern/ morgen f~** this/yesterday/tomorrow morning; **von f~ an** from an early age. **f~auf** adv **von f~auf** from an early age. **F~aufsteher** m -s,- early riser. **F~e** f - in aller **F~e** bright and early; **in der F~e** (*SGer*) in the morning. **f~er** adv earlier; (*eher*) sooner; (*ehemals*) formerly; (*vor langer Zeit*) in the old days; **f~er oder später** sooner or later; **ich wohnte f~er in X** I used to live in X. **f~ere(r,s)** a earlier; (*ehemalig*) former; (*vorige*) previous; **in f~eren Zeiten** in former times. **f~estens** adv at the earliest. **F~geburt** f premature birth/(*Kind*) baby. **F~jahr** nt spring. **F~jahrsputz** m spring-cleaning. **F~kartoffeln** fpl new potatoes. **F~ling** m -s,-e spring. **f~morgens** adv early in the morning. **f~reif** a precocious

Frühstück nt breakfast. **f~en** vi (*haben*) have breakfast

frühzeitig a & adv early; (*vorzeitig*) premature, adv -ly

Frustr|ation /-'tsio:n/ f -,-en frustration. **f~ieren** vt frustrate; **f~ierend** frustrating

Fuchs m -es,-̈e fox; (*Pferd*) chestnut. **f~en** vt (*fam*) annoy

Füchsin f -,-nen vixen

fuchteln vi (*haben*) **mit etw f~** (*fam*) wave sth about

Fuder nt -s,- cart-load

Fuge¹ f -,-n joint; **aus den F~n gehen** fall apart

Fuge² f -,-n (*Mus*) fugue

füg|en vt fit (**in** + acc into); (*an-*) join (**an** + acc on to); (*dazu-*) add (**zu** to); (*fig: bewirken*) ordain; **sich f~en** fit (**in** + acc into); adjoin/(*folgen*) follow (**an etw** acc sth); (*fig: gehorchen*) submit (*dat* to); **sich in sein Schicksal f~en** resign oneself to one's fate; **es f~te sich** it so happened (**daß** that).

f∼sam *a* obedient, *adv* -ly. **F∼ung** *f*
-,-en eine **F∼ung des Schicksals** a
stroke of fate

fühl|bar *a* noticeable. **f∼en** *vt/i*
(*haben*) feel; **sich f∼en** feel (*krank/*
einsam ill/lonely); (*fam: stolz sein*)
fancy oneself; **sich [nicht] wohl**
f∼en [not] feel well. **F∼er** *m* -s,-
feeler. **F∼ung** *f* - contact; **F∼ung**
aufnehmen get in touch

Fuhre *f* -,-n load

führ|en *vt* lead; guide ⟨*Tourist*⟩;
(*geleiten*) take; (*leiten*) run; (*befehli-*
gen) command; (*verkaufen*) stock;
bear ⟨*Namen, Titel*⟩; keep ⟨*Liste,*
Bücher, Tagebuch⟩; **bei** *od* **mit sich**
f∼en carry; **sich gut/schlecht f∼en**
conduct oneself well/badly ● *vi* (*ha-*
ben) lead; (*verlaufen*) go, run; **zu etw**
f∼en lead to sth. **f∼end** *a* leading.
F∼er *m* -s,- leader; (*Fremden-*)
guide; (*Buch*) guide[book]. **F∼er-**
haus *nt* driver's cab. **F∼erschein** *m*
driving licence; **den F∼erschein ma-**
chen take one's driving test.
F∼erscheinentzug *m* disqualifica-
tion from driving. **F∼ung** *f* -,-en
leadership; (*Leitung*) management;
(*Mil*) command; (*Betragen*) conduct;
(*Besichtigung*) guided tour; (*Vor-*
sprung) lead; **in F∼ung gehen** go
into the lead

Fuhr|unternehmer *m* haulage con-
tractor. **F∼werk** *nt* cart

Fülle *f* -,-n abundance, wealth
(**an**+*dat* of); (*Körper-*) plumpness.
f∼n *vt* fill; (*Culin*) stuff; **sich f∼n** fill
[up]

Füllen *nt* -s,- foal

Füll|er *m* -s,- (*fam*), **F∼federhalter** *m*
fountain pen. **f∼ig** *a* plump; ⟨*Busen*⟩
ample. **F∼ung** *f* -,-en filling; (*Kis-*
sen-, Braten-) stuffing; (*Pralinen-*)
centre

fummeln *vi* (*haben*) fumble (**an**+*dat*
with)

Fund *m* -[e]s,-e find

Fundament *nt* -[e]s,-e foundations
pl. **f∼al** *a* fundamental

Fund|büro *nt* lost-property office.
F∼grube *f* (*fig*) treasure trove.
F∼sachen *fpl* lost property *sg*

fünf *inv a*, **F∼** *f* -,-en five; (*Sch*) ≈ fail
mark. **F∼linge** *mpl* quintuplets.
f∼te(r,s) *a* fifth. **f∼zehn** *inv a* fifteen. **f∼zehnte(r,s)** *a* fifteenth.
f∼zig *inv a* fifty. **F∼ziger** *m* -s,- man
in his fifties; (*Münze*) 50-pfennig
piece. **f∼zigste(r,s)** *a* fiftieth

fungieren *vi* (*haben*) act (**als** as)

Funk *m* -s radio; **über F∼** over the
radio. **F∼e** *m* -n,-n spark. **f∼eln** *vi*
(*haben*) sparkle; ⟨*Stern:*⟩ twinkle.
f∼elnagelneu *a* (*fam*) brand-new.
F∼en *m* -s,- spark. **f∼en** *vt* radio.
F∼er *m* -s,- radio operator.
F∼sprechgerät *nt* walkie-talkie.
F∼spruch *m* radio message. **F∼**
streife *f* [police] radio patrol

Funktion /-'tsio:n/ *f* -,-en function;
(*Stellung*) position; (*Funktionieren*)
working; **außer F∼** out of action.
F∼är *m* -s,-e official. **f∼ieren** *vi*
(*haben*) work

für *prep* (+*acc*) for; **Schritt für Schritt**
step by step; **was für [ein]** what [a]!
(*fragend*) what sort of [a]? **für sich**
by oneself/⟨*Ding:*⟩ itself. **Für** *nt* **das**
Für und Wider the pros and cons *pl*.
F∼bitte *f* intercession

Furche *f* -,-n furrow

Furcht *f* - fear (**vor**+*dat* of). **f∼bar** *a*
terrible, *adv* -ly

fürcht|en *vt/i* (*haben*) fear; **sich f∼en**
be afraid (**vor**+*dat* of); **ich f∼e, das**
geht nicht I'm afraid that's impossible. **f∼erlich** *a* dreadful, *adv* -ly.
furcht|erregend *a* terrifying. **f∼los**
a fearless, *adv* -ly. **f∼sam** *a* timid,
adv -ly

füreinander *adv* for each other

Furnier *nt* -s,-e veneer. **f∼t** *a*
veneered

fürs *prep* = **für das**

Fürsorg|e *f* care; (*Admin*) welfare;
(*fam: Geld*) ≈ social security. **F∼er**
(in) *m* -s,- (*f* -,-nen) social worker.
f∼lich *a* solicitous

Fürsprache *f* intercession; **F∼ einle-**
gen intercede

Fürsprecher *m* (*fig*) advocate

Fürst *m* -en,-en prince. **F∼entum** *nt*
-s,-̈er principality. **F∼in** *f* -,-nen
princess. **f∼lich** *a* princely; (*üppig*)
lavish, *adv* -ly

Furt *f* -,-en ford

Furunkel *m* -s,- (*Med*) boil

Fürwort *nt* (*pl* -wörter) pronoun

Furz *m* -es,-e (*vulg*) fart. **f∼en** *vi*
(*haben*) (*vulg*) fart

Fusion *f* -,-en fusion; (*Comm*) merger.
f∼ieren *vi* (*haben*) (*Comm*) merge

Fuß *m* -es,-̈e foot; (*Aust: Bein*) leg;
(*Lampen-*) base; (*von Weinglas*)
stem; **zu Fuß** on foot; **zu Fuß gehen**
walk; **auf freiem Fuß** free; **auf**
freundschaftlichem/großem Fuß on
friendly terms/in grand style.

F~abdruck *m* footprint. **F~abtreter** *m* -s,- doormat. **F~bad** *nt* footbath. **F~ball** *m* football. **F~ballspieler** *m* footballer. **F~balltoto** *nt* football pools *pl*. **F~bank** *f* footstool. **F~boden** *m* floor. **F~bremse** *f* footbrake

Fussel *f* -,-n & *m* -s,-[n] piece of fluff; **F~n** fluff *sg*. **f~n** *vi* (*haben*) shed fluff

fuß|en *vi* (*haben*) be based (**auf** + *dat* on). **F~ende** *nt* foot

Fußgänger|(in) *m* -s,- (*f* -,-nen) pedestrian. **F~brücke** *f* footbridge. **F~überweg** *m* pedestrian crossing. **F~zone** *f* pedestrian precinct

Fuß|geher *m* -s,- (*Aust*) = **F~gänger. F~gelenk** *nt* ankle. **F~hebel** *m* pedal. **F~nagel** *m* toenail. **F~note** *f* footnote. **F~pflege** *f* chiropody. **F~pfleger(in)** *m(f)* chiropodist. **F~rücken** *m* instep. **F~sohle** *f* sole of the foot. **F~stapfen** *pl* in jds **F~stapfen treten** (*fig*) follow in s.o.'s footsteps. **F~tritt** *m* kick. **F~weg** *m* footpath; **eine Stunde F~weg** an hour's walk

futsch *pred a* (*fam*) gone

Futter¹ *nt* -s feed; (*Trocken-*) fodder

Futter² *nt* -s,- (*Kleider-*) lining

Futteral *nt* -s,-e case

füttern¹ *vt* feed

füttern² *vt* line

Futur *nt* -s (*Gram*) future; **zweites F~** future perfect. **f~istisch** *a* futuristic

G

Gabe *f* -,-n gift; (*Dosis*) dose

Gabel *f* -,-n fork. **g~n (sich)** *vr* fork. **G~stapler** *m* -s,- fork-lift truck. **G~ung** *f* -,-en fork (*in road*)

gackern *vi* (*haben*) cackle

gaffen *vi* (*haben*) gape, stare

Gag /gɛk/ *m* -s,-s (*Theat*) gag

Gage /'gaːʒə/ *f* -,-n (*Theat*) fee

gähnen *vi* (*haben*) yawn. **G~** *nt* -s yawn; (*wiederholt*) yawning

Gala *f* - ceremonial dress

galant *a* gallant, *adv* -ly

Galavorstellung *f* gala performance

Galerie *f* -,-n gallery

Galgen *m* -s,- gallows *sg*. **G~frist** *f* (*fam*) reprieve

Galionsfigur *f* figurehead

Galle *f* - bile; (*G~nblase*) gall-bladder. **G~nblase** *f* gall-bladder. **G~nstein** *m* gallstone

Gallert *nt* -[e]s,-e, **Gallerte** *f* -,-n [meat] jelly

Galopp *m* -s gallop; **im G~** at a gallop. **g~ieren** *vi* (*sein*) gallop

galvanisieren *vt* galvanize

gamm|eln *vi* (*haben*) (*fam*) loaf around. **G~ler(in)** *m* -s,- (*f* -,-nen) drop-out

Gams *f* -,-en (*Aust*) chamois

gang *pred a* **g~ und gäbe** quite usual

Gang *m* -[e]s,̈e walk; (*G~art*) gait; (*Boten-*) errand; (*Funktionieren*) running; (*Verlauf, Culin*) course; (*Durch-*) passage; (*Korridor*) corridor; (*zwischen Sitzreihen*) aisle, gangway; (*Anat*) duct; (*Auto*) gear; **in G~ bringen/halten** get/keep going; **in G~ kommen** get going/(*fig*) under way; **im G~e/in vollem G~e sein** be in progress/in full swing; **Essen mit vier G~en** four-course meal. **G~art** *f* gait

gängig *a* common; (*Comm*) popular

Gangschaltung *f* gear change

Gangster /'gɛŋstɐ/ *m* -s,- gangster

Gangway /'gɛŋweː/ *f* -,-s gangway

Ganove *m* -n,-n (*fam*) crook

Gans *f* -,̈e goose

Gänse|blümchen *nt* -s,- daisy. **G~füßchen** *ntpl* inverted commas. **G~haut** *f* goose-pimples *pl*. **G~marsch** *m* **im G~marsch** in single file. **G~rich** *m* -s,-e gander

ganz *a* whole, entire; (*vollständig*) complete; (*fam: heil*) undamaged, intact; **die g~e Zeit** all the time, the whole time; **eine g~e Weile/Menge** quite a while/lot; **g~e zehn Mark** all of ten marks; **meine g~en Bücher** all my books; *inv* **g~ Deutschland** the whole of Germany; **g~ bleiben** (*fam*) remain intact; **wieder g~ machen** (*fam*) mend; **im g~en** in all, altogether; **im großen und g~en** on the whole ● *adv* quite; (*völlig*) completely, entirely; (*sehr*) very; **nicht g~** not quite; **g~ allein** all on one's own; **ein g~ alter Mann** a very old man; **g~ wie du willst** just as you like; **es war g~ nett** it was quite nice; **g~ und gar** completely, totally; **g~ und gar nicht** not at all. **G~e(s)** *nt* whole; **es geht ums G~e** it's all or nothing. **g~jährig** *adv* all the year round

gänzlich *adv* completely, entirely

ganz|tägig a & adv full-time; ⟨geöffnet⟩ all day. **g∼tags** adv all day; ⟨arbeiten⟩ full-time

gar¹ a done, cooked

gar² adv **gar nicht/nichts/niemand** not/nothing/no one at all; **oder gar** or even

Garage /ga'ra:ʒə/ f -,-n garage

Garantie f -,-n guarantee. **g∼ren** vt/i (haben) **[für]** etw **g∼ren** guarantee sth; **er kommt g∼rt zu spät** (fam) he's sure to be late. **G∼schein** m guarantee

Garbe f -,-n sheaf

Garderobe f -,-n (Kleider) wardrobe; (Ablage) cloakroom, (Amer) check-room; (Flur-) coat-rack; (Künstler-) dressing-room. **G∼nfrau** f cloak-room attendant

Gardine f -,-n curtain. **G∼nstange** f curtain rail

garen vt/i (haben) cook

gären† vi (haben) ferment; (fig) seethe

Garn nt -[e]s,-e yarn; (Näh-) cotton

Garnele f -,-n shrimp; (rote) prawn

garnieren vt decorate; (Culin) garnish

Garnison f -,-en garrison

Garnitur f -,-en set; (Wäsche) set of matching underwear; (Möbel-) suite; **erste/zweite G∼ sein** (fam) be first-rate/second best

garstig a nasty

Garten m -s,-̈ garden; **botanischer G∼** botanical gardens pl. **G∼arbeit** f gardening. **G∼bau** m horticulture. **G∼haus** nt, **G∼laube** f summer-house. **G∼lokal** nt open-air café. **G∼schere** f secateurs pl

Gärtner|(in) m -s,- (f -,-nen) gardener. **G∼ei** f -,-en nursery; (fam: Gartenarbeit) gardening

Gärung f - fermentation

Gas nt -es,-e gas; **Gas geben** (fam) accelerate. **G∼herd** m gas cooker. **G∼maske** f gas mask. **G∼pedal** nt (Auto) accelerator

Gasse f -,-n alley; (Aust) street

Gast m -[e]s,-̈e guest; (Hotel-, Urlaubs-) visitor; (im Lokal) patron; **zum Mittag G∼e haben** have people to lunch; **bei jdm zu G∼ sein** be staying with s.o. **G∼arbeiter** m foreign worker. **G∼bett** nt spare bed

Gäste|bett nt spare bed. **G∼buch** nt visitors' book. **G∼zimmer** nt [hotel] room; (privat) spare room; (Aufenthaltsraum) residents' lounge

gast|frei, g∼freundlich a hospitable, adv -bly. **G∼freundschaft** f hospitality. **G∼geber** m -s,- host. **G∼geberin** f -,-nen hostess. **G∼haus** nt, **G∼hof** m inn, hotel

gastieren vi (haben) make a guest appearance; ⟨Truppe, Zirkus:⟩ perform (in + dat in)

gastlich a hospitable, adv -bly. **G∼keit** f - hospitality

Gastro|nomie f - gastronomy. **g∼nomisch** a gastronomic

Gast|spiel nt guest performance. **G∼spielreise** f (Theat) tour. **G∼stätte** f restaurant. **G∼stube** f bar; (Restaurant) restaurant. **G∼wirt** m landlord. **G∼wirtin** f landlady. **G∼wirtschaft** f restaurant

Gas|werk nt gasworks sg. **G∼zähler** m gas-meter

Gatte m -n,-n husband

Gatter nt -s,- gate; (Gehege) pen

Gattin f -,-nen wife

Gattung f -,-en kind; (Biol) genus; (Kunst) genre. **G∼sbegriff** m generic term

Gaudi f - (Aust, fam) fun

Gaul m -[e]s, Gäule [old] nag

Gaumen m -s,- palate

Gauner m -s,- crook, swindler. **G∼ei** f -,-en swindle

Gaze /'ga:zə/ f - gauze

Gazelle f -,-n gazelle

geachtet a respected

geädert a veined

geartet a **gut g∼** good-natured; **anders g∼** different

Gebäck nt -s [cakes and] pastries pl; (Kekse) biscuits pl

Gebälk nt -s timbers pl

geballt a ⟨Faust⟩ clenched

Gebärde f -,-n gesture. **g∼n (sich)** vr behave (wie like)

Gebaren nt -s behaviour

gebär|en† vt give birth to, bear; **geboren werden** be born. **G∼mutter** f womb, uterus

Gebäude nt -s,- building

Gebeine ntpl [mortal] remains

Gebell nt -s barking

geben† vt give; (tun, bringen) put; (Karten) deal; (aufführen) perform; (unterrichten) teach; **etw verloren g∼** give sth up as lost; **von sich g∼** utter; (fam: erbrechen) bring up; **viel/wenig g∼ auf** (+ acc) set great/ little store by; **sich g∼** (nachlassen)

wear off; (*besser werden*) get better;
(*sich verhalten*) behave; **sich geschlagen g~** admit defeat ● *impers*
es gibt there is/are; **was gibt es Neues/
zum Mittag/im Kino?** what's the
news/for lunch/on at the cinema? **es
wird Regen g~** it's going to rain;
das gibt es nicht there's no such
thing ● *vi* (*haben*) (*Karten*) deal
Gebet *nt* -[e]s,-e prayer
Gebiet *nt* -[e]s,-e area; (*Hoheits-*) territory; (*Sach-*) field
gebiet|en† *vt* command; (*erfordern*)
demand ● *vi* (*haben*) rule. **G~er** *m*
-s,- master; (*Herrscher*) ruler. **g~e-
risch** *a* imperious, *adv* -ly; ⟨*Ton*⟩
peremptory
Gebilde *nt* -s,- structure
gebildet *a* educated; (*kultiviert*)
cultured
Gebirg|e *nt* -s,- mountains *pl.* **g~ig** *a*
mountainous
Gebiß *nt* -sses, -sse teeth *pl*; (*künstliches*) false teeth *pl*, dentures *pl*;
(*des Zaumes*) bit
geblümt *a* floral, flowered
gebogen *a* curved
geboren *a* born; **g~er Deutscher**
German by birth; **Frau X, g~e Y** Mrs
X, née Y
geborgen *a* safe, secure. **G~heit** *f* -
security
Gebot *nt* -[e]s,-e rule; (*Relig*) com-
mandment; (*bei Auktion*) bid
gebraten *a* fried
Gebrauch *m* use; (*Sprach-*) usage;
Gebräuche customs; **in G~** in use;
G~ machen von make use of. **g~en**
vt use; **ich kann es nicht/gut g~en** I
have no use for/can make good use
of it; **zu nichts zu g~en** useless
gebräuchlich *a* common; ⟨*Wort*⟩ in
common use
**Gebrauchs|anleitung, G~sanwei-
sung** *f* directions *pl* for use. **g~t** *a*
used; (*Comm*) second-hand. **G~twa-
gen** *m* used car
gebrechlich *a* frail, infirm
gebrochen *a* broken ● *adv* **g~ Englisch sprechen** speak broken English
Gebrüll *nt* -s roaring; (*fam: Schreien*)
bawling
Gebrumm *nt* -s buzzing; (*Motoren-*)
humming
Gebühr *f* -,-en charge, fee; **über G~**
excessively. **g~en** *vi* (*haben*) **ihm
g~t Respekt** he deserves respect;
wie es sich g~t as is right and
proper. **g~end** *a* due, *adv* duly;

(*geziemend*) proper, *adv* -ly. **g~en-
frei** *a* free ● *adv* free of charge.
g~enpflichtig *a* & *adv* subject to a
charge; **g~enpflichtige Straße** toll
road
gebunden *a* bound; ⟨*Suppe*⟩
thickened
Geburt *f* -,-en birth; **von G~** by birth.
G~enkontrolle, G~enregelung *f*
birth-control. **G~enziffer** *f*
birth-rate
gebürtig *a* native (**aus** of); **g~er
Deutscher** German by birth
Geburts|datum *nt* date of birth.
G~helfer *m* obstetrician. **G~hilfe** *f*
obstetrics *sg*. **G~ort** *m* place of
birth. **G~tag** *m* birthday. **G~ur-
kunde** *f* birth certificate
Gebüsch *nt* -[e]s,-e bushes *pl*
Gedächtnis *nt* -ses memory; **aus
dem G~** from memory
gedämpft *a* ⟨*Ton*⟩ muffled; ⟨*Stimme*⟩
hushed; ⟨*Musik*⟩ soft; ⟨*Licht, Stimmung*⟩ subdued
Gedanke *m* -ns,-n thought (**an**+*acc*
of); (*Idee*) idea; **sich** (*dat*) **G~n machen** worry (**über**+*acc* about).
G~nblitz *m* brainwave. **g~nlos** *a*
thoughtless, *adv* -ly; (*zerstreut*) ab-
sent-minded, *adv* -ly. **G~nstrich** *m*
dash. **G~nübertragung** *f* telepathy.
g~nvoll *a* pensive, *adv* -ly
Gedärme *ntpl* intestines; (*Tier-*)
entrails
Gedeck *nt* -[e]s,-e place setting; (*auf
Speisekarte*) set meal; **ein G~ auflegen** set a place. **g~t** *a* covered;
⟨*Farbe*⟩ muted
gedeihen† *vi* (*sein*) thrive, flourish
gedenken† *vi* (*haben*) propose (**etw
zu tun** to do sth); **jds/etw g~** remember s.o./sth. **G~** *nt* -s memory; **zum
G~ an** (+*acc*) in memory of
Gedenk|feier *f* commemoration.
G~gottesdienst *m* memorial service. **G~stätte** *f* memorial. **G~tafel**
f commemorative plaque. **G~tag** *m*
day of remembrance; (*Jahrestag*)
anniversary
Gedicht *nt* -[e]s,-e poem
gediegen *a* quality . . .; (*solide*) well-
made; ⟨*Charakter*⟩ upright; ⟨*Gold*⟩
pure ● *adv* **g~ gebaut** well built
Gedränge *nt* -s crush, crowd. **g~t** *a*
(*knapp*) concise ● *adv* **g~t voll**
packed
gedrückt *a* depressed
gedrungen *a* stocky

Geduld *f* - patience; **G~ haben** be patient. **g~en (sich)** *vr* be patient. **g~ig** *a* patient, *adv* -ly. **G~[s]spiel** *nt* puzzle

gedunsen *a* bloated

geehrt *a* honoured; **sehr g~er Herr X** dear Mr X

geeignet *a* suitable; **im g~en Moment** at the right moment

Gefahr *f* -,-en danger; **in/außer G~** in/out of danger; **auf eigene G~** at one's own risk; **G~ laufen** run the risk (**etw zu tun** of doing sth)

gefähr|den *vt* endanger; (*fig*) jeopardize. **g~lich** *a* dangerous, *adv* -ly; (*riskant*) risky

gefahrlos *a* safe

Gefährt *nt* -[e]s,-e vehicle

Gefährte *m* -n,-n, **Gefährtin** *f* -,-nen companion

gefahrvoll *a* dangerous, perilous

Gefälle *nt* -s,- slope; (*Straßen-*) gradient

gefallen† *vi* (*haben*) **jdm g~** please s.o.; **er/es gefällt mir** I like him/it; **sich** (*dat*) **etw g~ lassen** put up with sth

Gefallen¹ *m* -s,- favour

Gefallen² *nt* -s pleasure (**an** + *dat* in); **G~ finden an** (+ *dat*) like; **dir zu G~** to please you

Gefallene(r) *m* soldier killed in the war

gefällig *a* pleasing; (*hübsch*) attractive, *adv* -ly; (*hilfsbereit*) obliging; **jdm g~ sein** do s.o. a good turn; [**sonst**] **noch etwas g~?** will there be anything else? **G~keit** *f* -,-en favour; (*Freundlichkeit*) kindness. **g~st** *adv* (*fam*) kindly

Gefangen|e(r) *m/f* prisoner. **g~halten**† *vt sep* hold prisoner; keep in captivity ⟨*Tier*⟩. **G~nahme** *f* - capture. **g~nehmen**† *vt sep* take prisoner. **G~schaft** *f* - captivity; **in G~schaft geraten** be taken prisoner

Gefängnis *nt* -ses,-se prison; (*Strafe*) imprisonment. **G~strafe** *f* imprisonment; (*Urteil*) prison sentence. **G~wärter** *m* [prison] warder, (*Amer*) guard

Gefäß *nt* -es,-e container, receptacle; (*Blut-*) vessel

gefaßt *a* composed; (*ruhig*) calm, *adv* -ly; **g~ sein auf** (+ *acc*) be prepared for

Gefecht *nt* -[e]s,-e fight; (*Mil*) engagement; **außer G~ setzen** put out of action

gefedert *a* sprung

gefeiert *a* celebrated

Gefieder *nt* -s plumage. **g~t** *a* feathered

Geflecht *nt* -[e]s,-e network; (*Gewirr*) tangle; (*Korb-*) wickerwork

gefleckt *a* spotted

geflissentlich *adv* studiously

Geflügel *nt* -s poultry. **G~klein** *nt* -s giblets *pl*. **g~t** *a* winged; **g~tes Wort** familiar quotation

Geflüster *nt* - whispering

Gefolg|e *nt* -s retinue, entourage. **G~schaft** *f* - followers *pl*, following; (*Treue*) allegiance

gefragt *a* popular; **g~ sein** be in demand

gefräßig *a* voracious; ⟨*Mensch*⟩ greedy

Gefreite(r) *m* lance-corporal

gefrier|en† *vi* (*sein*) freeze. **G~fach** *nt* freezer compartment. **G~punkt** *m* freezing-point. **G~schrank** *m* upright freezer. **G~truhe** *f* chest freezer

gefroren *a* frozen. **G~e(s)** *nt* (*Aust*) ice-cream

Gefüge *nt* -s,- structure; (*fig*) fabric

gefügig *a* compliant; (*gehorsam*) obedient

Gefühl *nt* -[e]s,-e feeling; (*Empfindung*) sensation; (*G~sregung*) emotion; **im G~ haben** know instinctively. **g~los** *a* insensitive; (*herzlos*) unfeeling; (*taub*) numb. **G~sbetont** *a* emotional. **g~skalt** *a* (*fig*) cold. **g~smäßig** *a* emotional, *adv* -ly; (*instinktiv*) instinctive, *adv* -ly. **G~sregung** *f* emotion. **g~voll** *a* sensitive, *adv* -ly; (*sentimental*) sentimental, *adv* -ly

gefüllt *a* filled; (*voll*) full; (*Bot*) double; (*Culin*) stuffed; ⟨*Schokolade*⟩ with a filling

gefürchtet *a* feared, dreaded

gefüttert *a* lined

gegeben *a* given; (*bestehend*) present; (*passend*) appropriate; **zu g~er Zeit** at the proper time. **g~enfalls** *adv* if need be. **G~heiten** *fpl* realities, facts

gegen *prep* (+ *acc*) against; (*Sport*) versus; (*g~über*) to[wards]; (*Vergleich*) compared with; (*Richtung, Zeit*) towards; (*ungefähr*) around; **ein Mittel g~** a remedy for ● *adv* **g~ 100 Leute** about 100 people. **G~angriff** *m* counter-attack

Gegend f -,-en area, region; (*Umgebung*) neighbourhood

gegeneinander adv against/ (*gegenüber*) towards one another

Gegen|fahrbahn f opposite carriageway. **G~gift** nt antidote. **G~leistung** f **als G~leistung** in return. **G~maßnahme** f countermeasure. **G~satz** m contrast; (*Widerspruch*) contradiction; (*G~teil*) opposite; **im G~satz zu** unlike. **g~sätzlich** a contrasting; (*widersprüchlich*) opposing. **g~seitig** a mutual, adv -ly; **sich g~seitig hassen** hate one another. **G~spieler** m opponent. **G~sprechanlage** f intercom. **G~stand** m object; (*Gram, Gesprächs-*) subject. **g~standslos** a unfounded; (*überflüssig*) irrelevant; (*abstrakt*) abstract. **G~stück** nt counterpart; (*G~teil*) opposite. **G~teil** nt opposite, contrary; **im G~teil** on the contrary. **g~teilig** a opposite

gegenüber prep (+ dat) opposite; (*Vergleich*) compared with; **jdm g~ höflich sein** be polite to s.o. ● adv opposite. **G~** nt -s person opposite. **g~liegen†** vi sep (haben) be opposite (etw dat sth). **g~liegend** a opposite. **g~stehen†** vi sep (haben) (+ dat) face; **feindlich g~stehen** (+ dat) be hostile to s.o. **g~stellen** vt sep confront; (*vergleichen*) compare. **g~treten†** vi sep (sein) (+ dat) face

Gegen|verkehr m oncoming traffic. **G~vorschlag** m counter-proposal. **G~wart** f - present; (*Anwesenheit*) presence. **g~wärtig** a present ● adv at present. **G~wehr** f - resistance. **G~wert** m equivalent. **G~wind** m head wind. **g~zeichnen** vt sep countersign

geglückt a successful

Gegner|(in) m -s,- (f -,-nen) opponent. **g~isch** a opposing

Gehabe nt -s affected behaviour

Gehackte(s) nt mince, (*Amer*) ground meat

Gehalt¹ m -[e]s content

Gehalt² nt -[e]s,⁺er salary. **G~serhöhung** f rise, (*Amer*) raise

gehaltvoll a nourishing

gehässig a spiteful, adv -ly

gehäuft a heaped

Gehäuse nt -s,- case; (*TV, Radio*) cabinet; (*Schnecken-*) shell; (*Kern-*) core

Gehege nt -s,- enclosure

geheim a secret; **im g~en** secretly. **G~dienst** m Secret Service. **g~halten†** vt sep keep secret. **G~nis** nt -ses,-se secret. **g~nisvoll** a mysterious, adv -ly. **G~polizei** f secret police

gehemmt a (*fig*) inhibited

gehen† vi (sein) go; (*zu Fuß*) walk; (*fort-*) leave; (*funktionieren*) work; (*Teig:*) rise; **tanzen/einkaufen g~** go dancing/shopping; **an die Arbeit g~** set to work; **in Schwarz [gekleidet] g~** dress in black; **nach Norden g~** (*Fenster:*) face north; **wenn es nach mir ginge** if I had my way; **über die Straße g~** cross the road; **was geht hier vor sich?** what is going on here? **das geht zu weit** (*fam*) that's going too far; impers **wie geht es [Ihnen]?** how are you? **es geht mir gut/besser** I am well/better; **es geht nicht/nicht anders** it's impossible/there is no other way; **es ging ganz schnell** it was very quick; **es geht um** it concerns; **es geht ihr nur ums Geld** she is only interested in the money; **es geht [so]** (*fam*) not too bad ● vt walk. **g~lassen†** vr sep lose one's self-control; (*sich vernachlässigen*) let oneself go

geheuer a **nicht g~** eerie; (*verdächtig*) suspicious; **mir ist nicht g~** I feel uneasy

Geheul nt -s howling

Gehilfe m -n,-n, **Gehilfin** f -,-nen trainee; (*Helfer*) assistant

Gehirn nt -s brain; (*Verstand*) brains pl. **G~erschütterung** f concussion. **G~hautentzündung** f meningitis. **G~wäsche** f brainwashing

gehoben a (*fig*) superior; (*Sprache*) elevated

Gehöft nt -[e]s,-e farm

Gehölz nt -es,-e coppice, copse

Gehör nt -s hearing; **G~ schenken** (+ dat) listen to

gehorchen vi (haben) (+ dat) obey

gehören vi (haben) belong (dat to); **zu den Besten g~** be one of the best; **dazu gehört Mut** that takes courage; **sich g~** be [right and] proper; **es gehört sich nicht** it isn't done

gehörig a proper, adv -ly; **jdm g~ verprügeln** give s.o. a good hiding

gehörlos a deaf

Gehörn nt -s,-e horns pl; (*Geweih*) antlers pl

gehorsam a obedient, adv -ly. **G~** m -s obedience

Geh|steig m -[e]s,-e pavement, (*Amer*) sidewalk. **G~weg** m = Gehsteig; (*Fußweg*) footpath

Geier m -s,- vulture

Geig|e f -,-n violin. **g~en** vi (*haben*) play the violin ● vt play on the violin. **G~er(in)** m -s,- (f -,-nen) violinist

geil a lecherous; (*fam*) randy; (*fam: toll*) great

Geisel f -,-n hostage

Geiß f -,-en (*SGer*) [nanny-]goat. **G~blatt** nt honeysuckle

Geißel f -,-n scourge

Geist m -[e]s,-er mind; (*Witz*) wit; (*Gesinnung*) spirit; (*Gespenst*) ghost; **der Heilige G~** the Holy Ghost or Spirit; **im G~** in one's mind. **g~erhaft** a ghostly

geistes|abwesend a absent-minded, adv -ly. **G~blitz** m brainwave. **G~gegenwart** f presence of mind. **g~gegenwärtig** adv with great presence of mind. **g~gestört** a [mentally] deranged. **g~krank** a mentally ill. **G~krankheit** f mental illness. **G~wissenschaften** fpl arts. **G~zustand** m mental state

geist|ig a mental, adv -ly; (*intellektuell*) intellectual, adv -ly; **g~ige Getränke** spirits. **g~lich** a spiritual, adv -ly; (*religiös*) religious; ⟨*Musik*⟩ sacred; ⟨*Tracht*⟩ clerical. **G~liche(r)** m clergyman. **G~lichkeit** f clergy. **g~los** a uninspired. **g~reich** a clever; (*witzig*) witty

Geiz m -es meanness. **g~en** vi (*haben*) be mean (**mit** with). **G~hals** m (*fam*) miser. **g~ig** a mean, miserly. **G~kragen** m (*fam*) miser

Gekicher nt -s giggling

geknickt a (*fam*) dejected, adv -ly

gekonnt a accomplished ● adv expertly

Gekrakel nt -s scrawl

gekränkt a offended, hurt

Gekritzel nt -s scribble

gekünstelt a affected, adv -ly

Gelächter nt -s laughter

geladen a loaded; (*fam: wütend*) furious

Gelage nt -s,- feast

gelähmt a paralysed

Gelände nt -s,- terrain; (*Grundstück*) site. **G~lauf** m cross-country run

Geländer nt -s,- railings pl; (*Treppen*) banisters pl; (*Brücken-*) parapet

gelangen vi (*sein*) reach/(*fig*) attain (**zu etw/an etw** acc sth); **in jds Besitz g~** come into s.o.'s possession

gelassen a composed; (*ruhig*) calm, adv -ly. **G~heit** f- equanimity; (*Fassung*) composure

Gelatine /ʒela-/ f - gelatine

geläufig a common, current; (*fließend*) fluent, adv -ly; **jdm g~ sein** be familiar to s.o.

gelaunt a **gut/schlecht g~ sein** be in a good/bad mood

gelb a yellow; (*bei Ampel*) amber; **g~e Rübe** (*SGer*) carrot; **das G~e vom Ei** the yolk of the egg. **G~** nt -s,- yellow; **bei G~** (*Auto*) on [the] amber. **g~lich** a yellowish. **G~sucht** f jaundice

Geld nt -es,-er money; **öffentliche G~er** public funds. **G~beutel** m, **G~börse** f purse. **G~geber** m -s,- backer. **g~lich** a financial, adv -ly. **G~mittel** ntpl funds. **G~schein** m banknote. **G~schrank** m safe. **G~strafe** f fine. **G~stück** nt coin

Gelee /ʒe'le:/ nt -s,-s jelly

gelegen a situated; (*passend*) convenient; **jdm sehr g~ sein** od **kommen** suit s.o. well; **mir ist viel/wenig daran g~** I'm very/not keen on it; (*es ist wichtig*) it matters a lot/little to me

Gelegenheit f -,-en opportunity, chance; (*Anlaß*) occasion; (*Comm*) bargain; **bei G~** some time. **G~sarbeit** f casual work. **G~sarbeiter** m casual worker. **G~skauf** m bargain

gelegentlich a occasional ● adv occasionally; (*bei Gelegenheit*) some time ● prep (+ gen) on the occasion of

gelehrt a learned. **G~e(r)** m/f scholar

Geleise nt -s,- = **Gleis**

Geleit nt -[e]s escort; **freies G~** safe conduct. **g~en** vt escort. **G~zug** m (*Naut*) convoy

Gelenk nt -[e]s,-e joint. **g~ig** a supple; (*Techn*) flexible

gelernt a skilled

Geliebte(r) m/f lover; (*liter*) beloved

gelieren /ʒe-/ vi (*haben*) set

gelinde a mild, adv -ly; **g~ gesagt** to put it mildly

gelingen† vi (*sein*) succeed, be successful; **es gelang ihm, zu entkommen** he succeeded in escaping. **G~** nt -s success

gell int (*SGer*) = **gelt**

gellend a shrill, adv -y

geloben vt promise [solemnly]; **sich** (dat) **g~** vow (**zu** to); **das Gelobte Land** the Promised Land

Gelöbnis nt -ses,-se vow

gelöst a (fig) relaxed

Gelse f -,-n (Aust) mosquito

gelt int (SGer) **das ist schön, g~?** it's nice, isn't it? **ihr kommt doch, g~?** you are coming, aren't you?

gelten† vi (haben) be valid; ⟨Regel:⟩ apply; **g~ als** be regarded as; **etw nicht g~ lassen** not accept sth; **wenig/viel g~** be worth/(fig) count for little/a lot; **jdm g~** be meant for s.o.; **das gilt nicht** that doesn't count. **g~d** a valid; ⟨Preise⟩ current; ⟨Meinung⟩ prevailing; **g~d machen** assert ⟨Recht, Forderung⟩; bring to bear ⟨Einfluß⟩

Geltung f - validity; (Ansehen) prestige; **G~ haben** be valid; **zur G~ bringen/kommen** set off/show to advantage

Gelübde nt -s,- vow

gelungen a successful

Gelüst nt -[e]s,-e desire/(stark) craving (**nach** for)

gemächlich a leisurely ● adv in a leisurely manner

Gemahl m -s,-e husband. **G~in** f -,-nen wife

Gemälde nt -s,- painting. **G~galerie** f picture gallery

gemäß prep (+dat) in accordance with ● a **etw** (dat) **g~ sein** be in keeping with sth

gemäßigt a moderate; ⟨Klima⟩ temperate

gemein a common; (unanständig) vulgar; (niederträchtig) mean; **g~er Soldat** private; **etw g~ haben** have sth in common ● adv shabbily; (fam: schrecklich) terribly

Gemeinde f -,-n [local] community; (Admin) borough; (Pfarr-) parish; (bei Gottesdienst) congregation. **G~rat** m local council/ (Person) councillor. **G~wahlen** fpl local elections

gemein|gefährlich a dangerous. **G~heit** f -,-en (s. gemein) commonness; vulgarity; meanness; (Bemerkung, Handlung) mean thing [to say/do]; **so eine G~heit!** how mean! (wie ärgerlich) what a nuisance! **G~kosten** pl overheads. **g~nützig** a charitable. **G~platz** m platitude.

g~sam a common; **etw g~sam haben** have sth in common ● adv together

Gemeinschaft f -,-en community. **g~lich** a joint; ⟨Besitz⟩ communal ● adv jointly; (zusammen) together. **G~sarbeit** f team-work

Gemenge nt -s,- mixture

gemessen a measured; (würdevoll) dignified

Gemetzel nt -s,- carnage

Gemisch nt -[e]s,-e mixture. **g~t** a mixed

Gemme f -,-n engraved gem

Gemse f -,-n chamois

Gemurmel nt -s murmuring

Gemüse nt -s,- vegetable; (coll) vegetables pl. **G~händler** m greengrocer

gemustert a patterned

Gemüt nt -[e]s,-er nature, disposition; (Gefühl) feelings pl; (Person) soul

gemütlich a cosy; (gemächlich) leisurely; (zwanglos) informal; ⟨Person⟩ genial; **es sich** (dat) **g~ machen** make oneself comfortable ● adv cosily; in a leisurely manner; informally. **G~keit** f - cosiness; leisureliness

Gemüts|art f nature, disposition. **G~mensch** m (fam) placid person. **G~ruhe** f **in aller G~ruhe** (fam) calmly. **G~verfassung** f frame of mind

Gen nt -s,-e gene

genau a exact, adv -ly, precise, adv -ly; ⟨Waage, Messung⟩ accurate, adv -ly; (sorgfältig) meticulous, adv -ly; (ausführlich) detailed; **nichts G~es wissen** not know any details; **es nicht so g~ nehmen** not be too particular; **g~!** exactly! **g~genommen** adv strictly speaking. **G~igkeit** f - exactitude; precision; accuracy; meticulousness

genauso adv just the same; (g~sehr) just as much; **g~ gut/teuer** just as good/expensive. **g~gut** adv just as well. **g~sehr** adv just as much. **g~viel** adv just as much/many. **g~wenig** adv just as little/few; (noch) no more

Gendarm /ʒãˈdarm/ m -en,-en (Aust) policeman

Genealogie f - genealogy

genehmig|en vt grant; approve ⟨Plan⟩. **G~ung** f -,-en permission; (Schein) permit

geneigt *a* sloping, inclined; (*fig*) well-disposed (*dat* towards); [**nicht**] **g~ sein** (*fig*) [not] feel inclined (**zu** to)

General *m* -s,-̈e general. **G~direktor** *m* managing director. **g~isieren** *vi* (*haben*) generalize. **G~probe** *f* dress rehearsal. **G~streik** *m* general strike. **g~überholen** *vt insep* (*inf & pp only*) completely overhaul

Generation /-'tsio:n/ *f* -,-en generation

Generator *m* -s,-en /-'to:rən/ generator

generell *a* general, *adv* -ly

gene̱s|en† *vi* (*sein*) recover. **G~ung** *f* - recovery; (*Erholung*) convalescence

Gene̱t|ik *f* - genetics *sg*. **g~isch** *a* genetic, *adv* -ally

Genf *nt* -s Geneva. **G~er** *a* Geneva ...; **G~er See** Lake Geneva

genial *a* brilliant, *adv* -ly; **ein g~er Mann** a man of genius. **G~ität** *f* - genius

Genick *nt* -s,-e [back of the] neck; **sich** (*dat*) **das G~ brechen** break one's neck

Genie /ʒe'ni:/ *nt* -s,-s genius

genieren /ʒe'ni:rən/ *vt* embarrass; **sich g~** feel *or* be embarrassed

genieß|bar *a* fit to eat/drink. **g~en†** *vt* enjoy; (*verzehren*) eat/drink. **G~er** *m* -s,- gourmet. **g~erisch** *a* appreciative ● *adv* with relish

Genitiv *m* -s,-e genitive

Genosse *m* -n,-n (*Pol*) comrade. **G~nschaft** *f* -,-en co-operative

Genre /'ʒã:rə/ *nt* -s,-s genre

Gentechnologie *f* genetic engineering

genug *inv a & adv* enough

Genüge *f* **zur G~** sufficiently. **g~n** *vi* (*haben*) be enough; **jds Anforderungen g~n** meet s.o.'s requirements. **g~nd** *inv a* sufficient, enough; (*Sch*) fair ● *adv* sufficiently, enough

genügsam *a* frugal, *adv* -ly; (*bescheiden*) modest, *adv* -ly

Genugtuung *f* - satisfaction

Genuß *m* -sses, -̈sse enjoyment; (*Vergnügen*) pleasure; (*Verzehr*) consumption. **genüßlich** *a* pleasurable ● *adv* with relish

geöffnet *a* open

Geo|graphie *f* - geography. **g~graphisch** *a* geographical, *adv* -ly. **G~loge** *m* -n,-n geologist. **G~logie** *f* - geology. **g~logisch** *a* geological,

adv -ly. **G~meter** *m* -s,- surveyor. **G~metrie** *f* - geometry. **g~metrisch** *a* geometric[al]

geordnet *a* well-ordered; (*stabil*) stable; **alphabetisch g~** in alphabetical order

Gepäck *nt* -s luggage, baggage. **G~ablage** *f* luggage-rack. **G~aufbewahrung** *f* left-luggage office. **G~schalter** *m* luggage office. **G~schein** *m* left-luggage ticket; (*Aviat*) baggage check. **G~stück** *nt* piece of luggage. **G~träger** *m* porter; (*Fahrrad-*) luggage carrier; (*Dach-*) roof-rack. **G~wagen** *m* luggage-van

Gepard *m* -s,-e cheetah

gepflegt *a* well-kept; ⟨*Person*⟩ well-groomed; ⟨*Hotel*⟩ first-class

Gepflogenheit *f* -,-en practice; (*Brauch*) custom

Gepolter *nt* -s [loud] noise

gepunktet *a* spotted

gerade *a* straight; (*direkt*) direct; (*aufrecht*) upright; (*aufrichtig*) straightforward; ⟨*Zahl*⟩ even ● *adv* straight; directly; (*eben*) just; (*genau*) exactly; (*besonders*) especially; **nicht g~ billig** not exactly cheap; **g~ erst** only just; **g~ an dem Tag** on that very day. **G~f-,-n** straight line. **g~aus** *adv* straight ahead/on

gerade|biegen† *vt sep* straighten; (*fig*) straighten out. **g~halten†** (**sich**) *vr sep* hold oneself straight. **g~heraus** *adv* (*fig*) straight out. **g~sitzen†** *vi sep* (*haben*) sit [up] straight. **g~so** *adv* just the same; **g~so gut** just as good. **g~sogut** *adv* just as well. **g~stehen†** *vi sep* (*haben*) stand up straight; (*fig*) accept responsibility (**für** for). **g~wegs** *adv* directly, straight. **g~zu** *adv* virtually; (*wirklich*) absolutely

Geranie /-iə/ *f* -,-n geranium

Gerät *nt* -[e]s,-e tool; (*Acker-*) implement; (*Küchen-*) utensil; (*Elektro-*) appliance; (*Radio-, Fernseh-*) set; (*Turn-*) piece of apparatus; (*coll*) equipment

geraten† *vi* (*sein*) get; **in Brand g~** catch fire; **in Wut g~** get angry; **in Streit g~** start quarrelling; **gut/ schlecht g~** turn out well/badly; **nach jdm g~** take after s.o.

Geratewohl *nt* **aufs G~** at random

geräuchert *a* smoked

geräumig *a* spacious, roomy

Geräusch nt -[e]s,-e noise. **g~los** a noiseless, adv -ly. **g~voll** a noisy, adv -ily

gerben vt tan

gerecht a just, adv -ly; (fair) fair, adv -ly; **g~ werden** (+ dat) do justice to. **g~fertigt** a justified. **G~igkeit** f - justice; fairness

Gerede nt -s talk; (Klatsch) gossip

geregelt a regular

gereift a mature

gereizt a irritable, adv -bly. **G~heit** f - irritability

gereuen vt es gereut mich nicht I don't regret it

Geriatrie f - geriatrics sg

Gericht[1] nt -[e]s,-e (Culin) dish

Gericht[2] nt -[e]s,-e court [of law]; **vor G~** in court; **das Jüngste G~** the Last Judgement; **mit jdm ins G~ gehen** take s.o. to task. **g~lich** a judicial; ⟨Verfahren⟩ legal ● adv **g~lich vorgehen** take legal action. **G~sbarkeit** f - jurisdiction. **G~shof** m court of justice. **G~smedizin** f forensic medicine. **G~ssaal** m courtroom. **G~svollzieher** m -s,- bailiff

gerieben a grated; (fam: schlau) crafty

gering a small; (niedrig) low; (g~fügig) slight. **g~achten** vt sep have little regard for; (verachten) despise. **g~fügig** a slight, adv -ly. **g~schätzig** a contemptuous, adv -ly; ⟨Bemerkung⟩ disparaging. **g~ste(r,s)** a least; **nicht im g~sten** not in the least

gerinnen† vi (sein) curdle; ⟨Blut:⟩ clot

Gerippe nt -s,- skeleton; (fig) framework

gerissen a (fam) crafty

Germ m -[e]s (Aust) f - yeast

German|e m -n,-n [ancient] German. **g~isch** a Germanic. **G~ist(in)** m -en,-en (f -,-nen) Germanist. **G~istik** f - German [language and literature]

gern[e] adv gladly; **g~ haben** like; (lieben) be fond of; **ich tanze/ schwimme g~** I like dancing/swimming; **das kannst du g~ tun** you're welcome to do that; **willst du mit?— g~!** do you want to come?—I'd love to!

gerötet a red

Gerste f - barley. **G~nkorn** nt (Med) stye

Geruch m -[e]s,-̈e smell (von/nach of). **g~los** a odourless. **G~ssinn** m sense of smell

Gerücht nt -[e]s,-e rumour

geruhen vi (haben) deign (zu to)

gerührt a (fig) moved, touched

Gerümpel nt -s lumber, junk

Gerüst nt -[e]s,-e scaffolding; (fig) framework

gesalzen a salted; (fam: hoch) steep

gesammelt a collected; (gefaßt) composed

gesamt a entire, whole. **G~ausgabe** f complete edition. **G~betrag** m total amount. **G~eindruck** m overall impression. **G~heit** f - whole. **G~schule** f comprehensive school. **G~summe** f total

Gesandte(r) m/f envoy

Gesang m -[e]s,-̈e singing; (Lied) song; (Kirchen-) hymn. **G~buch** nt hymn-book. **G~verein** m choral society

Gesäß nt -es buttocks pl. **G~tasche** f hip pocket

Geschäft nt -[e]s,-e business; (Laden) shop, (Amer) store; (Transaktion) deal; (fam: Büro) office; **schmutzige G~e** shady dealings; **ein gutes G~ machen** do very well (mit out of); **sein G~ verstehen** know one's job. **g~ehalber** adv on business. **g~ig** a busy, adv -ily; ⟨Treiben⟩ bustling. **G~igkeit** f - activity. **g~lich** a business . . . ● adv on business

Geschäfts|brief m business letter. **G~führer** m manager; (Vereins-) secretary. **G~mann** m (pl -leute) businessman. **G~reise** f business trip. **G~stelle** f office; (Zweigstelle) branch. **g~tüchtig** a **g~tüchtig sein** be a good businessman/-woman. **G~viertel** nt shopping area. **G~zeiten** fpl hours of business

geschehen† vi (sein) happen (dat to); **es ist ein Unglück g~** there has been an accident; **es ist um uns g~** we are done for; **das geschieht dir recht!** it serves you right! **gern g~!** you're welcome! **G~** nt -s events pl

gescheit a clever; **daraus werde ich nicht g~** I can't make head or tail of it

Geschenk nt -[e]s,-e present, gift. **G~korb** m gift hamper

Geschicht|e f -,-n history; (Erzählung) story; (fam: Sache) business. **g~lich** a historical, adv -ly

Geschick *nt* -[e]s fate; (*Talent*) skill; **G~ haben** be good (**zu at**). **G~lichkeit** *f* - skilfulness, skill. **g~t** *a* skilful, *adv* -ly; (*klug*) clever, *adv* -ly

geschieden *a* divorced. **G~e(r)** *m*/*f* divorcee

Geschirr *nt* -s,-e (*coll*) crockery; (*Porzellan*) china; (*Service*) service; (*Pferde-*) harness; **schmutziges G~** dirty dishes *pl*. **G~spülmaschine** *f* dishwasher. **G~tuch** *nt* tea-towel

Geschlecht *nt* -[e]s,-er (*Gram*) gender; (*Familie*) family; (*Generation*) generation. **g~lich** *a* sexual, *adv* -ly. **G~skrankheit** *f* venereal disease. **G~steile** *ntpl* genitals. **G~sverkehr** *m* sexual intercourse. **G~swort** *nt* (*pl* -wörter) article

geschliffen *a* (*fig*) polished

geschlossen *a* closed ● *adv* unanimously; (*vereint*) in a body

Geschmack *m* -[e]s,-e taste; (*Aroma*) flavour; (*G~ssinn*) sense of taste; **einen guten G~ haben** (*fig*) have good taste; **G~ finden an** (+*dat*) acquire a taste for. **g~los** *a* tasteless, *adv* -ly; **g~los sein** (*fig*) be in bad taste. **G~ssache** *f* matter of taste. **g~voll** *a* (*fig*) tasteful, *adv* -ly

geschmeidig *a* supple; (*weich*) soft

Geschöpf *nt* -[e]s,-e creature

Geschoß *nt* -sses,-sse missile; (*Stockwerk*) storey, floor

geschraubt *a* (*fig*) stilted

Geschrei *nt* -s screaming; (*fig*) fuss

Geschütz *nt* -es,-e gun, cannon

geschützt *a* protected; ⟨*Stelle*⟩ sheltered

Geschwader *nt* -s,- squadron

Geschwätz *nt* -es talk. **g~ig** *a* garrulous

geschweift *a* curved

geschweige *conj* **g~ denn** let alone

geschwind *a* quick, *adv* -ly

Geschwindigkeit *f* -,-en speed; (*Phys*) velocity. **G~sbegrenzung**, **G~sbeschränkung** *f* speed limit

Geschwister *pl* brother[s] and sister[s]; siblings

geschwollen *a* swollen; (*fig*) pompous, *adv* -ly

Geschworene|(r) *m*/*f* juror; **die G~n** the jury *sg*

Geschwulst *f* -,-̈e swelling; (*Tumor*) tumour

geschwungen *a* curved

Geschwür *nt* -s,-e ulcer

Geselle *m* -n,-n fellow; (*Handwerks-*) journeyman

gesellig *a* sociable; (*Zool*) gregarious; (*unterhaltsam*) convivial; **g~er Abend** social evening. **G~keit** *f* -,-en entertaining; **die G~keit lieben** love company

Gesellschaft *f* -,-en company; (*Veranstaltung*) party; **die G~** society; **jdm G~ leisten** keep s.o. company. **g~lich** *a* social, *adv* -ly. **G~sreise** *f* group tour. **G~sspiel** *nt* party game

Gesetz *nt* -es,-e law. **G~entwurf** *m* bill. **g~gebend** *a* legislative. **G~gebung** *f* - legislation. **g~lich** *a* legal, *adv* -ly. **g~los** *a* lawless. **g~mäßig** *a* lawful, *adv* -ly; (*gesetzlich*) legal, *adv* -ly

gesetzt *a* staid; (*Sport*) seeded ● *conj* **g~ den Fall** supposing

gesetzwidrig *a* illegal, *adv* -ly

gesichert *a* secure

Gesicht *nt* -[e]s,-er face; (*Aussehen*) appearance; **zu G~ bekommen** set eyes on. **G~sausdruck** *m* [facial] expression. **G~sfarbe** *f* complexion. **G~spunkt** *m* point of view. **G~szüge** *mpl* features

Gesindel *nt* -s riff-raff

gesinnt *a* **gut/übel g~** well/ill disposed (*dat* towards)

Gesinnung *f* -,-en mind; (*Einstellung*) attitude; **politische G~** political convictions *pl*

gesittet *a* well-mannered; (*zivilisiert*) civilized

gesondert *a* separate, *adv* -ly

Gespann *nt* -[e]s,-e team; (*Wagen*) horse and cart/carriage

gespannt *a* taut; (*fig*) tense, *adv* -ly; ⟨*Beziehungen*⟩ strained; (*neugierig*) eager, *adv* -ly; (*erwartungsvoll*) expectant, *adv* -ly; **g~ sein, ob** wonder whether; **auf etw/jdn g~ sein** look forward eagerly to sth/to seeing s.o.

Gespenst *nt* -[e]s,-er ghost. **g~isch** *a* ghostly; (*unheimlich*) eerie

Gespött *nt* -[e]s mockery; **zum G~ werden** become a laughing-stock

Gespräch *nt* -[e]s,-e conversation; (*Telefon-*) call; **ins G~ kommen** get talking; **im G~ sein** be under discussion. **g~ig** *a* talkative. **G~sgegenstand** *m*, **G~sthema** *nt* topic of conversation

gesprenkelt *a* speckled

Gespür *nt* -s feeling; (*Instinkt*) instinct

Gestalt *f* -,-en figure; (*Form*) shape, form; **G~ annehmen** (*fig*) take shape. **g~en** *vt* shape; (*organisie-*

ren) arrange; (*schaffen*) create; (*entwerfen*) design; **sich g~en** turn out

geständ|ig *a* confessed; **g~ig sein** have confessed. **G~nis** *nt* -ses,-se confession

Gestank *m* -s stench, [bad] smell

gestatten *vt* allow, permit; **nicht gestattet** prohibited; **g~ Sie?** may I?

Geste /'gɛ-, 'geːstə/ *f* -,-n gesture

Gesteck *nt* -[e]s,-e flower arrangement

gestehen† *vt/i* (*haben*) confess; confess to ⟨*Verbrechen*⟩; **offen gestanden** to tell the truth

Gestein *nt* -[e]s,-e rock

Gestell *nt* -[e]s,-e stand; (*Flaschen-*) rack; (*Rahmen*) frame

gestellt *a* **gut/schlecht g~** well/badly off; **auf sich** (*acc*) **selbst g~ sein** be thrown on one's own resources

gestelzt *a* (*fig*) stilted

gesteppt *a* quilted

gestern *adv* yesterday; **g~ nacht** last night

Gestik /'gɛstɪk/ *f* - gestures *pl*. **g~ulieren** *vi* (*haben*) gesticulate

gestrandet *a* stranded

gestreift *a* striped

gestrichelt *a* ⟨*Linie*⟩ dotted

gestrichen *a* **g~er Teelöffel** level teaspoon[ful]

gestrig /'gɛstrɪç/ *a* yesterday's; **am g~en Tag** yesterday

Gestrüpp *nt* -s,-e undergrowth

Gestüt *nt* -[e]s,-e stud [farm]

Gesuch *nt* -[e]s,-e request; (*Admin*) application. **g~t** *a* sought-after; (*gekünstelt*) contrived

gesund *a* healthy, *adv* -ily; **g~ sein** be in good health; ⟨*Sport, Getränk:*⟩ be good for one; **wieder g~ werden** get well again

Gesundheit *f* - health; **G~!** (*bei Niesen*) bless you! **g~lich** *a* health . . .; **g~licher Zustand** state of health ● *adv* **es geht ihm g~lich gut/schlecht** he is in good/poor health. **g~shalber** *adv* for health reasons. **g~sschädlich** *a* harmful. **G~szustand** *m* state of health

getäfelt *a* panelled

getigert *a* tabby

Getöse *nt* -s racket, din

getragen *a* solemn, *adv* -ly

Getränk *nt* -[e]s,-e drink. **G~ekarte** *f* wine-list

getrauen *vt* **sich** (*dat*) **etw g~** dare [to] do sth; **sich g~** dare

Getreide *nt* -s (*coll*) grain

getrennt *a* separate, *adv* -ly; **g~ leben** live apart. **g~schreiben†** *vt sep* write as two words

getreu *a* faithful, *adv* -ly ● *prep* (+*dat*) true to; **der Wahrheit g~** truthfully. **g~lich** *adv* faithfully

Getriebe *nt* -s,- bustle; (*Techn*) gear; (*Auto*) transmission; (*Gehäuse*) gearbox

getrost *adv* with confidence

Getto *nt* -s,-s ghetto

Getue *nt* -s (*fam*) fuss

Getümmel *nt* -s tumult

getüpfelt *a* spotted

geübt *a* skilled; ⟨*Auge, Hand*⟩ practised

Gewächs *nt* -es,-e plant; (*Med*) growth

gewachsen *a* **jdm/etw g~ sein** be a match for s.o./be equal to sth

Gewächshaus *nt* greenhouse; (*Treibhaus*) hothouse

gewagt *a* daring

gewählt *a* refined

gewahr *a* **g~ werden** become aware (*acc/gen* of)

Gewähr *f* - guarantee

gewahren *vt* notice

gewähr|en *vt* grant; (*geben*) offer; **jdn g~en lassen** let s.o. have his way. **g~leisten** *vt* guarantee

Gewahrsam *m* -s safekeeping; (*Haft*) custody

Gewährsmann *m* (*pl* -**männer** & -**leute**) informant, source

Gewalt *f* -,-en power; (*Kraft*) force; (*Brutalität*) violence; **mit G~** by force; **G~ anwenden** use force; **sich in der G~ haben** be in control of oneself. **G~herrschaft** *f* tyranny. **g~ig** *a* powerful; (*fam: groß*) enormous, *adv* -ly; (*stark*) tremendous, *adv* -ly. **g~sam** *a* forcible, *adv* -bly; ⟨*Tod*⟩ violent. **g~tätig** *a* violent. **G~tätigkeit** *f* -,-en violence; (*Handlung*) act of violence

Gewand *nt* -[e]s,-̈er robe

gewandt *a* skilful, *adv* -ly; (*flink*) nimble, *adv* -bly. **G~heit** *f* - skill; nimbleness

Gewässer *nt* -s,- body of water; **G~** *pl* waters

Gewebe *nt* -s,- fabric; (*Anat*) tissue

Gewehr *nt* -s,-e rifle, gun

Geweih *nt* -[e]s,-e antlers *pl*

Gewerb|e *nt* -s,- trade. **g~lich** *a* commercial, *adv* -ly. **g~smäßig** *a* professional, *adv* -ly

Gewerkschaft f -,-en trade union. **G~ler(in)** m -s,- (f -,-nen) trade unionist

Gewicht nt -[e]s,-e weight; (Bedeutung) importance. **g~heben** nt -s weight-lifting. **g~ig** a important

gewieft a (fam) crafty

gewillt a g~ sein be willing

Gewinde nt -s,- [screw] thread

Gewinn m -[e]s,-e profit; (fig) gain, benefit; (beim Spiel) winnings pl; (Preis) prize; (Los) winning ticket. **G~beteiligung** f profit-sharing. **g~bringend** a profitable, adv -bly. **g~en†** vt win; (erlangen) gain; (fördern) extract; jdn für sich g~en win s.o. over ● vi (haben) win; **g~en an** (+ dat) gain in. **g~end** a engaging. **G~er(in)** m -s,- (f -,-nen) winner

Gewirr nt -s,-e tangle; (Straßen-) maze; **G~ von Stimmen** hubbub of voices

gewiß a (gewisser, gewissest) certain, adv -ly

Gewissen nt -s,- conscience. **g~haft** a conscientious, adv -ly. **g~los** a unscrupulous. **G~sbisse** mpl pangs of conscience

gewissermaßen adv to a certain extent; (sozusagen) as it were

Gewißheit f - certainty

Gewitt|er nt -s,- thunderstorm. **g~ern** vi (haben) es g~ert it is thundering. **g~rig** a thundery

gewogen a (fig) well-disposed (dat towards)

gewöhnen vt jdn/sich g~ an (+ acc) get s.o. used to/get used to; [an] jdn/ etw gewöhnt sein be used to s.o./sth

Gewohnheit f -,-en habit. **g~smäßig** a habitual, adv -ly. **G~srecht** nt common law

gewöhnlich a ordinary, adv -ily; (üblich) usual, adv -ly; (ordinär) common

gewohnt a customary; (vertraut) familiar; (üblich) usual; etw (acc) g~ sein be used to sth

Gewöhnung f - getting used (an + acc to); (Süchtigkeit) addiction

Gewölb|e nt -s,- vault. **g~t** a curved; (Archit) vaulted

gewollt a forced

Gewühl nt -[e]s crush

gewunden a winding

gewürfelt a check[ed]

Gewürz nt -es,-e spice. **G~nelke** f clove

gezackt a serrated

gezähnt a serrated; (Säge) toothed

Gezeiten fpl tides

gezielt a specific; (Frage) pointed

geziemend a proper, adv -ly

geziert a affected, adv -ly

gezwungen a forced ● adv g~ lachen give a forced laugh. **g~ermaßen** adv of necessity; etw g~ermaßen tun be forced to do sth

Gicht f - gout

Giebel m -s,- gable

Gier f - greed (nach for). **g~ig** a greedy, adv -ily

gieß|en† vt pour; water (Blumen, Garten); (Techn) cast ● v impers es g~t it is pouring [with rain]. **G~erei** f -,-en foundry. **G~kanne** f watering-can

Gift nt -[e]s,-e poison; (Schlangen-) venom; (Biol, Med) toxin. **g~ig** a poisonous; (Schlange) venomous; (Med, Chem) toxic; (fig) spiteful, adv -ly. **G~müll** m toxic waste. **G~pilz** m poisonous fungus, toadstool. **G~zahn** m [poison] fang

gigantisch a gigantic

Gilde f -,-n guild

Gimpel m -s,- bullfinch; (fam: Tölpel) simpleton

Gin /dʒɪn/ m -s gin

Ginster m -s (Bot) broom

Gipfel m -s,- summit, top; (fig) peak. **G~konferenz** f summit conference. **g~n** vi (haben) culminate (in + dat in)

Gips m -es plaster. **G~abguß** m plaster cast. **G~er** m -s,- plasterer. **G~verband** m (Med) plaster cast

Giraffe f -,-n giraffe

Girlande f -,-n garland

Girokonto /ˈʒiːro-/ nt current account

Gischt m -[e]s & f - spray

Gitar|re f -,-n guitar. **G~rist(in)** m -en,-en (f -,-nen) guitarist

Gitter nt -s,- bars pl; (Rost) grating, grid; (Geländer, Zaun) railings pl; (Fenster-) grille; (Draht-) wire screen; hinter G~n (fam) behind bars. **G~netz** nt grid

Glanz m -es shine; (von Farbe, Papier) gloss; (Seiden-) sheen; (Politur) polish; (fig) brilliance; (Pracht) splendour

glänzen vi (haben) shine. **g~d** a shining, bright; (Papier, Haar) glossy; (fig) brilliant, adv -ly

glanz|los a dull. **G~stück** nt masterpiece; (einer Sammlung) show-piece.

g~voll *a* (*fig*) brilliant, *adv* -ly; (*prachtvoll*) splendid, *adv* -ly. **G~zeit** *f* heyday

Glas *nt* **-es,-er** glass; (*Brillen-*) lens; (*Fern-*) binoculars *pl*; (*Marmeladen-*) [glass] jar. **G~er** *m* **-s,-** glazier

gläsern *a* glass ...

Glashaus *nt* greenhouse

glasieren *vt* glaze; ice ⟨*Kuchen*⟩

glas|ig *a* glassy; (*durchsichtig*) transparent. **G~scheibe** *f* pane

Glasur *f* **-,-en** glaze; (*Culin*) icing

glatt *a* smooth; (*eben*) even; ⟨*Haar*⟩ straight; (*rutschig*) slippery; (*einfach*) straightforward; (*eindeutig*) downright; ⟨*Absage*⟩ flat ● *adv* smoothly; evenly; (*fam: völlig*) completely; (*gerade*) straight; (*leicht*) easily; ⟨*ablehnen*⟩ flatly; **g~ verlaufen** go off smoothly; **das ist g~ gelogen** it's a downright lie

Glätte *f* - smoothness; (*Rutschigkeit*) slipperiness

Glatteis *nt* [black] ice; **aufs G~ führen** (*fam*) take for a ride

glätten *vt* smooth; **sich g~** become smooth; ⟨*Wellen:*⟩ subside

glatt|gehen† *vi sep* (*sein*) (*fig*) go off smoothly. **g~rasiert** *a* clean-shaven. **g~streichen†** *vt sep* smooth out. **g~weg** *adv* (*fam*) outright

Glatz|e *f* **-,-n** bald patch; (*Voll-*) bald head; **eine G~e bekommen** go bald. **g~köpfig** *a* bald

Glaube *m* **-ns** belief (**an**+*acc* in); (*Relig*) faith; **in gutem G~n** in good faith; **G~n schenken** (+ *dat*) believe. **g~n** *vt/i* (*haben*) believe (**an**+*acc* in); (*vermuten*) think; **jdm g~n** believe s.o.; **nicht zu g~n** unbelievable, incredible. **G~nsbekenntnis** *nt* creed

glaubhaft *a* credible; (*überzeugend*) convincing, *adv* -ly

gläubig *a* religious; (*vertrauend*) trusting, *adv* -ly. **G~e(r)** *m/f* (*Relig*) believer; **die G~en** the faithful. **G~er** *m* **-s,-** (*Comm*) creditor

glaub|lich *a* **kaum g~lich** scarcely believable. **g~würdig** *a* credible; (*Person*) reliable. **G~würdigkeit** *f* - credibilit ; reliability

gleich *a* same; (*identisch*) identical; (*g~wertig*) equal; **2 mal 5 [ist] g~ 10** two times 5 equals 10; **das ist mir g~** it's all the same to me; **ganz g~, wo/wer** no matter where/who ● *adv* equally; (*übereinstimmend*) identically, the same; (*sofort*) immediately; (*in Kürze*) in a minute; (*fast*) nearly; (*direkt*) right; **g~ alt/schwer sein** be the same age/weight. **g~altrig** *a* [of] the same age. **g~artig** *a* similar. **g~bedeutend** *a* synonymous. **g~berechtigt** *a* equal. **G~berechtigung** *f* equality. **g~bleibend** *a* constant

gleichen† *vi* (*haben*) **jdm/etw g~** be like *or* resemble s.o./sth; **sich g~** be alike

gleich|ermaßen *adv* equally. **g~falls** *adv* also, likewise; **danke g~falls** thank you, the same to you. **g~förmig** *a* uniform, *adv* -ly; (*eintönig*) monotonous, *adv* -ly. **G~förmigkeit** *f* - uniformity; monotony. **g~gesinnt** *a* like-minded. **G~gewicht** *nt* balance; (*Phys & fig*) equilibrium. **g~gültig** *a* indifferent, *adv* -ly; (*unwichtig*) unimportant. **G~gültigkeit** *f* indifference. **G~heit** *f* - equality; (*Ähnlichkeit*) similarity. **g~machen** *vt sep* make equal; **dem Erdboden g~machen** raze to the ground. **g~mäßig** *a* even, *adv* -ly, regular, *adv* -ly; (*beständig*) constant, *adv* -ly. **G~mäßigkeit** *f* - regularity. **G~mut** *m* equanimity. **g~mütig** *a* calm, *adv* -ly

Gleichnis *nt* **-ses, -se** parable

gleich|sam *adv* as it were. **G~schritt** *m* **im G~schritt** in step. **g~sehen†** *vi sep* (*haben*) **jdm g~sehen** look like s.o.; (*fam: typisch sein*) be just like s.o. **g~setzen** *vt sep* equate/ (*g~stellen*) place on a par (*dat/mit* with). **g~stellen** *vt sep* place on a par (*dat* with). **G~strom** *m* direct current. **g~tun†** *vi sep* (*haben*) **es jdm g~tun** emulate s.o.

Gleichung *f* **-,-en** equation

gleich|viel *adv* no matter (**ob/wer** whether/who). **g~wertig** *a* of equal value. **g~zeitig** *a* simultaneous, *adv* -ly

Gleis *nt* **-es,-e** track; (*Bahnsteig*) platform; **G~ 5** platform 5

gleiten† *vi* (*sein*) glide; (*rutschen*) slide. **g~d** *a* sliding; **g~de Arbeitszeit** flexitime

Gleitzeit *f* flexitime

Gletscher *m* **-s,-** glacier. **G~spalte** *f* crevasse

Glied *nt* **-[e]s,-er** limb; (*Teil*) part; (*Ketten-*) link; (*Mitglied*) member;

(*Mil*) rank. **g~ern** *vt* arrange; (*einteilen*) divide; **sich g~ern** (*in* + *acc* into). **G~maßen** *fpl* limbs

glimmen† *vi* (*haben*) glimmer

glimpflich *a* lenient, *adv* -ly; **g~ davonkommen** get off lightly

glitschig *a* slippery

glitzern *vi* (*haben*) glitter

global *a* global, *adv* -ly

Globus *m* -(busses), -ben & -busse globe

Glocke *f* -,-n bell. **G~nturm** *m* belltower, belfry

glorifizieren *vt* glorify

glorreich *a* glorious

Glossar *nt* -s,-e glossary

Glosse *f* -,-n comment

glotzen *vi* (*haben*) stare

Glück *nt* -[e]s [good] luck; (*Zufriedenheit*) happiness; **G~/kein G~ haben** be lucky/unlucky; **zum G~** luckily, fortunately; **auf gut G~** on the off chance; (*wahllos*) at random. **g~bringend** *a* lucky. **g~en** *vi* (*sein*) succeed; **es ist mir geglückt** I succeeded

gluckern *vi* (*haben*) gurgle

glücklich *a* lucky, fortunate; (*zufrieden*) happy; (*sicher*) safe ● *adv* happily; safely; (*fam: endlich*) finally. **g~erweise** *adv* luckily, fortunately

glückselig *a* blissfully happy. **G~keit** *f* bliss

glucksen *vi* (*haben*) gurgle

Glücksspiel *nt* game of chance; (*Spielen*) gambling

Glückwunsch *m* good wishes *pl*; (*Gratulation*) congratulations *pl*; **herzlichen G~!** congratulations! (*zum Geburtstag*) happy birthday! **G~karte** *f* greetings card

Glüh|birne *f* light-bulb. **g~en** *vi* (*haben*) glow. **g~end** *a* glowing; (*rot-*) red-hot; ⟨*Hitze*⟩ scorching; (*leidenschaftlich*) fervent, *adv* -ly. **G~faden** *m* filament. **G~wein** *m* mulled wine. **G~würmchen** *nt* -s,- glow-worm

Glukose *f* - glucose

Glut *f* - embers *pl*; (*Röte*) glow; (*Hitze*) heat; (*fig*) ardour

Glyzinie /-jə/ *f* -,-n wisteria

GmbH *abbr* (**Gesellschaft mit beschränkter Haftung**) ≈ plc

Gnade *f* - mercy; (*Gunst*) favour; (*Relig*) grace. **G~nfrist** *f* reprieve. **g~nlos** *a* merciless, *adv* -ly

gnädig *a* gracious, *adv* -ly; (*mild*) lenient, *adv* -ly; **g~e Frau** Madam

Gnom *m* -en,-en gnome

Gobelin /gobə'lɛ̃ː/ *m* -s,-s tapestry

Gold *nt* -[e]s gold. **g~en** *a* gold ...; (*g~farben*) golden; **g~ene Hochzeit** golden wedding. **G~fisch** *m* goldfish. **G~grube** *f* gold-mine. **g~ig** *a* sweet, lovely. **G~lack** *m* wallflower. **G~regen** *m* laburnum. **G~schmied** *m* goldsmith

Golf¹ *m* -[e]s,-e (*Geog*) gulf

Golf² *nt* -s golf. **G~platz** *m* golfcourse. **G~schläger** *m* golf-club. **G~spieler(in)** *m*(*f*) golfer

Gondel *f* -,-n gondola; (*Kabine*) cabin

Gong *m* -s,-s gong

gönnen *vt* jdm etw g~ not begrudge s.o. sth; **jdm etw nicht g~** begrudge s.o. sth; **sie gönnte sich** (*dat*) **keine Ruhe** she allowed herself no rest

Gönner *m* -s,- patron. **g~haft** *a* patronising, *adv* -ly

Gör *nt* -s,-en, **Göre** *f* -,-n (*fam*) kid

Gorilla *m* -s,-s gorilla

Gosse *f* -,-n gutter

Got|ik *f* - Gothic. **g~isch** *a* Gothic

Gott *m* -[e]s,ˉer God; (*Myth*) god

Götterspeise *f* jelly

Gottes|dienst *m* service. **g~lästerlich** *a* blasphemous, *adv* -ly. **G~lästerung** *f* blasphemy

Gottheit *f* -,-en deity

Göttin *f* -,-nen goddess

göttlich *a* divine, *adv* -ly

gott|los *a* ungodly; (*atheistisch*) godless. **g~verlassen** *a* God-forsaken

Götze *m* -n,-n, **G~nbild** *nt* idol

Gouver|nante /guvɛr'nantə/ *f* -,-n governess. **G~neur** /-'nøːɐ̯/ *m* -s,-e governor

Grab *nt* -[e]s,ˉer grave

graben† *vi* (*haben*) dig

Graben *m* -s,ˉ ditch; (*Mil*) trench

Grab|mal *nt* tomb. **G~stein** *m* gravestone, tombstone

Grad *m* -[e]s,-e degree

Graf *m* -en,-en count

Grafik *f* -,-en graphics *sg*; (*Kunst*) graphic arts *pl*; (*Druck*) print

Gräfin *f* -,-nen countess

grafisch *a* graphic; **g~e Darstellung** diagram

Grafschaft *f* -,-en county

Gram *m* -s grief

grämen (sich) *vr* grieve

grämlich *a* morose, *adv* -ly

Gramm *nt* -s,-e gram

Gram|matik *f* -,-en grammar. **g~matikalisch, g~matisch** *a* grammatical, *adv* -ly

Granat m -[e]s,-e (*Miner*) garnet. **G~apfel** m pomegranate. **G~e** f -,-n shell; (*Hand-*) grenade

Granit m -s,-e granite

Graph|ik f, **g~isch** a = **Grafik, grafisch**

Gras nt -es,⁻er grass. **g~en** vi (*haben*) graze. **G~hüpfer** m -s,- grasshopper

grassieren vi (*haben*) be rife

gräßlich a dreadful, adv -ly

Grat m -[e]s,-e [mountain] ridge

Gräte f -,-n fishbone

Gratifikation /-'tsjo:n/ f -,-en bonus

gratis adv free [of charge]. **G~probe** f free sample

Gratu|lant(in) m -en,-en (f -,-nen) well-wisher. **G~lation** /-'tsjo:n/ f -,-en congratulations pl; (*Glück-wünsche*) best wishes pl. **g~lieren** vi (*haben*) jdm **g~lieren** congratulate s.o. (**zu** on); (*zum Geburtstag*) wish s.o. happy birthday; [ich] **g~liere!** congratulations!

grau a, **G~** nt -s,- grey. **G~brot** nt mixed rye and wheat bread

grauen¹ vi (*haben*) **der Morgen** od **es graut** dawn is breaking

grauen² v impers **mir graut** [es] **davor** I dread it. **G~** nt -s dread. **g~haft, g~voll** a gruesome; (*gräß-lich*) horrible, adv -ly

gräulich a greyish

Graupeln fpl soft hail sg

grausam a cruel, adv -ly. **G~keit** f -,-en cruelty

graus|en v impers **mir graust davor** I dread it. **G~en** nt -s horror, dread. **g~ig** a gruesome

gravieren vt engrave. **g~d** a (*fig*) serious

Grazie /'gra:tsjə/ f - grace

graziös a graceful, adv -ly

greifbar a tangible; **in g~er Nähe** within reach

greifen† vt take hold of; (*fangen*) catch ● vi (*haben*) reach (**nach** for); **g~ zu** (*fig*) turn to; **um sich g~** (*fig*) spread. **G~** nt **G~ spielen** play tag

Greis m -es,-e old man. **G~enalter** nt extreme old age. **g~enhaft** a old. **G~in** f -,-nen old woman

grell a glaring; (*Farbe*) garish; (*schrill*) shrill, adv -y

Gremium nt -s,-ien committee

Grenz|e f -,-n border; (*Staats-*) frontier; (*Grundstücks-*) boundary; (*fig*) limit. **g~en** vi (*haben*) border (**an** + acc on). **g~enlos** a boundless;

(*maßlos*) infinite, adv -ly. **G~fall** m borderline case

Greuel m -s,- horror. **G~tat** f atrocity

greulich a horrible, adv -bly

Griech|e m -n,-n Greek. **G~enland** nt -s Greece. **G~in** f -,-nen Greek woman. **g~isch** a Greek. **G~isch** nt -[s] (*Lang*) Greek

griesgrämig a (*fam*) grumpy

Grieß m -es semolina

Griff m -[e]s,-e grasp, hold; (*Hand-*) movement of the hand; (*Tür-, Messer-*) handle; (*Schwert-*) hilt. **g~bereit** a handy

Grill m -s,-s grill; (*Garten-*) barbecue

Grille f -,-n (*Zool*) cricket; (*fig: Laune*) whim

grill|en vt grill; (*im Freien*) barbecue ● vi (*haben*) have a barbecue. **G~fest** nt barbecue. **G~gericht** nt grill

Grimasse f -,-n grimace; **G~n schnei-den** pull faces

grimmig a furious; ⟨*Kälte*⟩ bitter

grinsen vi (*haben*) grin. **G~** nt -s grin

Grippe f -,-n influenza, (*fam*) flu

grob a (**gröber, gröbst**) coarse, adv -ly; (*unsanft, ungefähr*) rough, adv -ly; (*unhöflich*) rude, adv -ly; (*schwer*) gross, adv -ly; (*Fehler*) bad; **g~e Arbeit** rough work; **g~ ge-schätzt** roughly. **G~ian** m -s,-e brute

gröblich a gross, adv -ly

grölen vt/i (*haben*) bawl

Groll m -[e]s resentment; **einen G~ gegen jdn hegen** bear s.o. a grudge. **g~en** vi (*haben*) be angry (*dat* with); ⟨*Donner:*⟩ rumble

Grönland nt -s Greenland

Gros¹ nt -ses,- (*Maß*) gross

Gros² /gro:/ nt -, majority, bulk

Groschen m -s,- (*Aust*) groschen; (*fam*) ten-pfennig piece; **der G~ ist gefallen** (*fam*) the penny's dropped

groß a (**größer, größt**) big; ⟨*Anzahl, Summe*⟩ large; (*bedeutend, stark*) great; (*g~artig*) grand; ⟨*Buchstabe*⟩ capital; **g~e Ferien** summer holidays; **g~e Angst haben** be very frightened; **der größte Teil** the majority or bulk; **g~ werden** ⟨*Person:*⟩ grow up; **g~ in etw** (*dat*) **sein** be good at sth; **g~ und klein** young and old; **im g~en und ganzen** on the whole ● adv ⟨*feiern*⟩ in style; (*fam: viel*) much; **jdn g~ ansehen** look at s.o. in amazement

groß|artig a magnificent, adv -ly. **G~aufnahme** f close-up. **G~britannien** nt -s Great Britain. **G~buchstabe** m capital letter. **G~e(r)** m/f unser **G~er** our eldest; die **G~en** the grown-ups; (fig) the great pl

Größe f -,-n size; (Ausmaß) extent; (Körper-) height; (Bedeutsamkeit) greatness; (Math) quantity; (Person) great figure

Groß|eltern pl grandparents. **g~enteils** adv largely

Größenwahnsinn m megalomania

Groß|handel m wholesale trade. **G~händler** m wholesaler. **g~herzig** a magnanimous, adv -ly. **G~macht** f superpower. **G~mut** f magnanimity. **g~mütig** a magnanimous, adv -ly. **G~mutter** f grandmother. **G~onkel** m great-uncle. **G~reinemachen** nt -s spring-clean. **G~schreibung** f capitalization. **g~sprecherisch** a boastful. **g~spurig** a pompous, adv -ly; (überheblich) arrogant, adv -ly. **G~stadt** f [large] city. **g~städtisch** a city ... **G~tante** f great-aunt. **G~teil** m large proportion; (Hauptteil) bulk

größtenteils adv for the most part

groß|tun† **(sich)** vr sep brag. **G~vater** m grandfather. **g~ziehen**† vt sep bring up; rear ⟨Tier⟩. **g~zügig** a generous, adv -ly; (weiträumig) spacious. **G~zügigkeit** f generosity

grotesk a grotesque, adv -ly

Grotte f -,-n grotto

Grübchen nt -s,- dimple

Grube f -,-n pit

grübeln vi (haben) brood

Gruft f -,-̈e [burial] vault

grün a green; im **G~en** out in the country; die **G~en** the Greens. **G~** nt -s,- green; (Laub, Zweige) greenery

Grund m -[e]s,-̈e ground; (Boden) bottom; (Hinter-) background; (Ursache) reason; **auf G~** (+ gen) on the strength of; aus diesem **G~e** for this reason; von **G~ auf** (fig) radically; im **G~e** [genommen] basically; auf **G~ laufen** (Naut) run aground. **G~begriffe** mpl basics. **G~besitz** m landed property. **G~besitzer** m landowner

gründ|en vt found, set up; start ⟨Familie⟩; (fig) base (**auf** + acc on);

sich **g~en** be based (**auf** + acc on). **G~er(in)** m -s,- (f -,-nen) founder

Grund|farbe f primary colour. **G~form** f (Gram) infinitive. **G~gesetz** nt (Pol) constitution. **G~lage** f basis, foundation. **g~legend** a fundamental, adv -ly

gründlich a thorough, adv -ly. **G~keit** f - thoroughness

grund|los a bottomless; (fig) groundless ● adv without reason. **G~mauern** fpl foundations

Gründonnerstag m Maundy Thursday

Grund|regel f basic rule. **G~riß** m ground-plan; (fig) outline. **G~satz** m principle. **g~sätzlich** a fundamental, adv -ly; (im allgemeinen) in principle; (prinzipiell) on principle. **G~schule** f primary school. **G~stein** m foundation-stone. **G~stück** nt plot [of land]

Gründung f -,-en foundation

grün|en vi (haben) become green. **G~gürtel** m green belt. **G~span** m verdigris. **G~streifen** m grass verge; (Mittel-) central reservation, (Amer) median strip

grunzen vi (haben) grunt

Gruppe f -,-n group; (Reise-) party

gruppieren vt group; sich **g~** form a group/groups

Grusel|geschichte f horror story. **g~ig** a creepy

Gruß m -es,-̈e greeting; (Mil) salute; einen schönen **G~ an** X give my regards to X; viele/herzliche **G~e** regards; Mit freundlichen **G~en** Yours sincerely/(Comm) faithfully

grüßen vt/i (haben) say hallo (jdn to s.o.); (Mil) salute; **g~ Sie X von mir** give my regards to X; **jdn g~ lassen** send one's regards to s.o.; **grüß Gott!** (SGer, Aust) good morning/afternoon/ evening!

guck|en vi (haben) (fam) look. **G~loch** nt peep-hole

Guerilla /ge'rɪlja/ f guerilla warfare. **G~kämpfer** m guerilla

Gulasch nt & m -s goulash

gültig a valid, adv -ly. **G~keit** f - validity

Gummi m & nt -s,-[s] rubber; (Harz) gum. **G~band** nt (pl -bänder) elastic or rubber band; (G~zug) elastic

gummiert a gummed

Gummi|knüppel m truncheon. **G~stiefel** m gumboot, wellington. **G~zug** m elastic

Gunst f - favour; **zu jds G∼en** in s.o.'s favour

günstig a favourable, adv -bly; (passend) convenient, adv -ly

Günstling m -s,-e favourite

Gurgel f -,-n throat. **g∼n** vi (haben) gargle. **G∼wasser** nt gargle

Gurke f -,-n cucumber; (Essig-) gherkin

gurren vi (haben) coo

Gurt m -[e]s,-e strap; (Gürtel) belt; (Auto) safety-belt. **G∼band** nt (pl -bänder) waistband

Gürtel m -s,- belt. **G∼linie** f waistline. **G∼rose** f shingles sg

GUS abbr (Gemeinschaft Unabhängiger Staaten) CIS

Guß m -sses,-sse (Techn) casting; (Strom) stream; (Regen-) downpour; (Torten-) icing. **G∼eisen** nt cast iron. **g∼eisern** a cast-iron

gut a (besser, best) good; (Gewissen) clear; (gütig) kind (**zu** to); **jdm gut sein** be fond of s.o.; **im g∼en** amicably; **zu g∼er Letzt** in the end; **schon gut** that's all right ● adv well; (schmecken, riechen) good; (leicht) easily; **es gut haben** be well off; (Glück haben) be lucky; **gut zu sehen** clearly visible; **gut drei Stunden** a good three hours; **du hast gut reden** it's easy for you to talk

Gut nt -[e]s,-er possession, property; (Land-) estate; **Gut und Böse** good and evil; **Güter** (Comm) goods

Gutacht|en nt -s,- expert's report. **G∼er** m -s,- expert

gut|artig a good-natured; (Med) benign. **g∼aussehend** a good-looking. **g∼bezahlt** a well-paid. **G∼dünken** nt -s nach eigenem G∼dünken at one's own discretion

Gute|(s) nt etwas/nichts **G∼s** something/nothing good; **G∼s tun** do good; **das G∼ daran** the good thing about it all; **alles G∼!** all the best!

Güte f -,-n goodness, kindness; (Qualität) quality; **du meine G∼!** my goodness!

Güterzug m goods/(Amer) freight train

gut|gehen† vi sep (sein) go well; **es geht mir gut** I am well/(geschäftlich) doing well. **g∼gehend** a flourishing, thriving. **g∼gemeint** a well-meant. **g∼gläubig** a trusting. **g∼haben**† vt sep **fünfzig Mark g∼haben** have fifty marks credit

(bei with). **G∼haben** nt -s,- [credit] balance; (Kredit) credit. **g∼heißen**† vt sep approve of

gütig a kind, adv -ly

gütlich a amicable, adv -bly

gut|machen vt sep make up for; make good (Schaden). **g∼mütig** a good-natured, adv -ly. **G∼mütigkeit** f - good nature. **G∼schein** m credit note; (Bon) voucher; (Geschenk-) gift token. **g∼schreiben**† vt sep credit. **G∼schrift** f credit

Guts|haus nt manor house. **G∼hof** m manor

gut|situiert a well-to-do. **g∼tun**† vi sep (haben) **jdm/etw g∼tun** do s.o./sth good. **g∼willig** a willing, adv -ly

Gymnasium nt -s,-ien ≈ grammar school

Gymnast|ik f - [keep-fit] exercises pl; (Turnen) gymnastics sg. **g∼isch** a **g∼ische Übung** exercise

Gynäko|loge m -n,-n gynaecologist. **G∼logie** f - gynaecology. **g∼logisch** a gynaecological

H

H, h /ha:/ nt -,- (Mus) B, b

Haar nt -[e]s,-e hair; **sich** (dat) **die Haare** od **das H∼ waschen** wash one's hair; **um ein H∼** (fam) very nearly. **H∼bürste** f hairbrush. **h∼en** vi (haben) shed hairs; (Tier:) moult ● vr **sich h∼en** moult. **h∼ig** a hairy; (fam) tricky. **H∼klammer, H∼klemme** f hair-grip. **H∼nadel** f hairpin. **H∼nadelkurve** f hairpin bend. **H∼schleife** f bow. **H∼schnitt** m haircut. **H∼spange** f slide. **h∼sträubend** a hair-raising; (empörend) shocking. **H∼trockner** m -s,- hair-drier. **H∼waschmittel** nt shampoo

Habe f - possessions pl

haben† vt have; **Angst/Hunger/ Durst h∼** be frightened/hungry/ thirsty; **ich hätte gern** I'd like; **sich h∼** (fam) make a fuss; **es gut/ schlecht h∼** be well/ badly off; **etw gegen jdn h∼** have sth against s.o.; **was hat er?** what's the matter with him? ● v aux have; **ich habe/hatte geschrieben** I have/had written; **er hätte ihr geholfen** he would have helped her

Habgier f greed. **h~ig** a greedy
Habicht m -[e]s,-e hawk
Hab|seligkeiten fpl belongings.
  H~sucht f = Habgier
Hachse f -,-n (Culin) knuckle
Hack|beil nt chopper. **H~braten** m
  meat loaf
Hacke¹ f -,-n hoe; (Spitz-) pick
Hacke² f -,-n, **Hacken** m -s,- heel
hack|en vt hoe; (schlagen, zerklei-
  nern) chop; ⟨Vogel:⟩ peck; **gehacktes
  Rindfleisch** minced/(Amer) ground
  beef. **H~fleisch** nt mince, (Amer)
  ground meat
Hafen m -s,- harbour; (See-) port.
  H~arbeiter m docker. **H~damm** m
  mole. **H~stadt** f port
Hafer m -s oats pl. **H~flocken** fpl
  [rolled] oats. **H~mehl** nt oatmeal
Haft f - (Jur) custody; (H~strafe)
  imprisonment. **h~bar** a (Jur) liable.
  H~befehl m warrant [of arrest]
haften vi (haben) cling; (kleben)
  stick; (bürgen) vouch/(Jur) be liable
  (für for)
Häftling m -s,-e detainee
Haftpflicht f (Jur) liability. **H~versi-
  cherung** f (Auto) third-party
  insurance
Haftstrafe f imprisonment
Haftung f - (Jur) liability
Hagebutte f -,-n rose-hip
Hagel m -s hail. **H~korn** nt hailstone.
  h~n vi (haben) hail
hager a gaunt
Hahn m -[e]s,-e cock; (Techn) tap,
  (Amer) faucet
Hähnchen nt -s,- (Culin) chicken
Hai[fisch] m -[e]s,-e shark
Häkchen nt -s,- tick
häkel|n vt/i (haben) crochet. **H~na-
  del** f crochet-hook
Haken m -s,- hook; (Häkchen) tick;
  (fam: Schwierigkeit) snag. **h~** vt
  hook (an+acc to). **H~kreuz** nt swastika. **H~nase** f hooked nose
halb a half; **eine h~e Stunde** half an
  hour; **zum h~en Preis** at half price;
  auf h~em Weg half-way ● adv half;
  h~ drei half past two; **fünf [Minu-
  ten] vor/nach h~ vier** twenty-five
  [minutes] past three/to four; **h~
  und h~** half and half; (fast ganz)
  more or less. **H~blut** nt half-breed.
  H~dunkel nt semi-darkness.
  H~e(r,s) f/m/nt half [a litre]
halber prep (+gen) for the sake of;
  Geschäfte h~ on business

Halb|finale nt semifinal. **H~heit** f
  -,-en (fig) half-measure
halbieren vt halve, divide in half;
  (Geom) bisect
Halb|insel f peninsula. **H~kreis** m
  semicircle. **H~kugel** f hemisphere.
  h~laut a low ● adv in an undertone.
  h~mast adv at half-mast.
  H~messer m -s,- radius. **H~mond**
  m half moon. **H~pension** f half-
  board. **h~rund** a semicircular.
  H~schuh m [flat] shoe. **h~stündlich**
  a & adv half-hourly. **h~tags** adv
  [for] half a day; **h~tags arbeiten** ≈
  work part-time. **H~ton** m semitone.
  h~wegs adv half-way; (ziemlich)
  more or less. **h~wüchsig** a adoles-
  cent. **H~zeit** f (Sport) half-time;
  (Spielzeit) half
Halde f -,-n dump, tip
Hälfte f -,-n half; zur **H~** half
Halfter¹ m & nt -s,- halter
Halfter² f -,-n & nt -s,- holster
Hall m -[e]s,-e sound
Halle f -,-n hall; (Hotel-) lobby; (Bahn-
  hofs-) station concourse
hallen vi (haben) resound; (wider-)
  echo
Hallen- pref indoor
hallo int hallo
Halluzination /-'tsi̯oːn/ f -,-en
  hallucination
Halm m -[e]s,-e stalk; (Gras-) blade
Hals m -es,-e neck; (Kehle) throat;
  aus vollem H~e at the top of one's
  voice; ⟨lachen⟩ out loud. **H~aus-
  schnitt** m neckline. **H~band** nt (pl -
  bänder) collar. **H~kette** f necklace.
  H~schmerzen mpl sore throat sg.
  h~starrig a stubborn. **H~tuch** nt
  scarf
halt¹ adv (SGer) just; **es geht h~
  nicht** it's just not possible
halt² int stop! (Mil) halt! (fam) wait a
  minute!
Halt m -[e]s,-e hold; (Stütze) support;
  (innerer) stability; (Anhalten) stop.
  h~bar a durable; (Tex) hard-
  wearing; (fig) tenable; **h~bar bis ...**
  (Comm) use by ...
halten† vt hold; make ⟨Rede⟩; give
  ⟨Vortrag⟩; (einhalten, bewahren)
  keep; [sich (dat)] **etw h~** keep
  ⟨Hund⟩; take ⟨Zeitung⟩; run ⟨Auto⟩;
  warm h~ keep warm; **h~ für** regard
  as; **viel/nicht viel h~ von** think high-
  ly/little of; **sich h~** hold on (an+dat
  to); (fig) hold out; ⟨Geschäft:⟩ keep
  going; (haltbar sein) keep; ⟨Wetter:⟩

hold; ⟨*Blumen:*⟩ last; **sich links h**∼ keep left; **sich gerade h**∼ hold oneself upright; **sich h**∼ **an** (+ *acc*) (*fig*) keep to ● *vi* (*haben*) hold; (*haltbar sein, bestehen bleiben*) keep; ⟨*Freundschaft, Blumen:*⟩ last; (*haltmachen*) stop; **h**∼ **auf** (+ *acc*) (*fig*) set great store by; **auf sich** (*acc*) **h**∼ take pride in oneself; **an sich** (*acc*) **h**∼ contain oneself; **zu jdm h**∼ be loyal to s.o.

Halter *m* -s,- holder

Halte|stelle *f* stop. **H**∼**verbot** *nt* waiting restriction; '**H**∼**verbot**' 'no waiting'

halt|los *a* (*fig*) unstable; (*unbegründet*) unfounded. **h**∼**machen** *vi sep* (*haben*) stop

Haltung *f* -,-en (*Körper-*) posture; (*Verhalten*) manner; (*Einstellung*) attitude; (*Fassung*) composure; (*Halten*) keeping; **H**∼ **annehmen** (*Mil*) stand to attention

Halunke *m* -n,-n scoundrel

Hamburger *m* -s,- hamburger

hämisch *a* malicious, *adv* -ly

Hammel *m* -s,- ram; (*Culin*) mutton. **H**∼**fleisch** *nt* mutton

Hammer *m* -s,̈ hammer

hämmern *vt/i* (*haben*) hammer; ⟨*Herz:*⟩ pound

Hämorrhoiden /hɛmɔrɔi'dən/ *fpl* haemorrhoids

Hamster *m* -s,- hamster. **h**∼**n** *vt/i* (*fam*) hoard

Hand *f* -,̈e hand; **jdm die H**∼ **geben** shake hands with s.o.; **rechter/linker H**∼ on the right/left; [aus] **zweiter H**∼ second-hand; **unter der H**∼ unofficially; (*geheim*) secretly; **an H**∼ **von** with the aid of; **H**∼ **und Fuß haben** (*fig*) be sound. **H**∼**arbeit** *f* manual work; (*handwerklich*) handicraft; (*Nadelarbeit*) needlework; (*Gegenstand*) hand-made article. **H**∼**ball** *m* [German] handball. **H**∼**besen** *m* brush. **H**∼**bewegung** *f* gesture. **H**∼**bremse** *f* handbrake. **H**∼**buch** *nt* handbook, manual

Händedruck *m* handshake

Handel *m* -s trade, commerce; (*Unternehmen*) business; (*Geschäft*) deal; **H**∼ **treiben** trade. **h**∼**n** *vi* (*haben*) act; (*Handel treiben*) trade (**mit** in); **von etw** *od* **über etw** (*acc*) **h**∼**n** deal with sth; **sich h**∼**n um** be about, concern. **H**∼**smarine** *f* merchant navy. **H**∼**sschiff** *nt* merchant vessel. **H**∼**sschule** *f* commercial college.

h∼**süblich** *a* customary. **H**∼**sware** *f* merchandise

Hand|feger *m* -s,- brush. **H**∼**fertigkeit** *f* dexterity. **h**∼**fest** *a* sturdy; (*fig*) solid. **H**∼**fläche** *f* palm. **h**∼**gearbeitet** *a* hand-made. **H**∼**gelenk** *nt* wrist. **h**∼**gemacht** *a* hand-made. **H**∼**gemenge** *nt* -s,- scuffle. **H**∼**gepäck** *nt* hand-luggage. **h**∼**geschrieben** *a* hand-written. **H**∼**granate** *f* hand-grenade. **h**∼**greiflich** *a* tangible; **h**∼**greiflich werden** become violent. **H**∼**griff** *m* handle; **mit einem H**∼**griff** with a flick of the wrist

handhaben *vt insep* (*reg*) handle

Handikap /'hɛndikɛp/ *nt* -s,-s handicap

Hand|kuß *m* kiss on the hand. **H**∼**lauf** *m* handrail

Händler *m* -s,- dealer, trader

handlich *a* handy

Handlung *f* -,-en act; (*Handeln*) action; (*Roman-*) plot; (*Geschäft*) shop. **H**∼**sweise** *f* conduct

Hand|schellen *fpl* handcuffs. **H**∼**schlag** *m* handshake. **H**∼**schrift** *f* handwriting; (*Text*) manuscript. **H**∼**schuh** *m* glove. **H**∼**schuhfach** *nt* glove compartment. **H**∼**stand** *m* handstand. **H**∼**tasche** *f* handbag. **H**∼**tuch** *nt* towel. **H**∼**voll** *f* -,- handful

Handwerk *nt* craft, trade; **sein H**∼ **verstehen** know one's job. **H**∼**er** *m* -s,- craftsman; (*Arbeiter*) workman

Hanf *m* -[e]s hemp

Hang *m* -[e]s,̈e slope; (*fig*) inclination, tendency

Hänge|brücke *f* suspension bridge. **H**∼**lampe** *f* [light] pendant. **H**∼**matte** *f* hammock

hängen[1] *vt* (*reg*) hang

hängen[2] *vi* (*haben*) hang; **h**∼ **an** (+ *dat*) (*fig*) be attached to. **h**∼**bleiben**† *vi sep* (*sein*) stick (**an** + *dat* to); ⟨*Kleid:*⟩ catch (**an** + *dat* on). **h**∼**lassen**† *vt sep* leave; **den Kopf h**∼**lassen** be downcast

Hannover *nt* -s Hanover

hänseln *vt* tease

hantieren *vi* (*haben*) busy oneself

hapern *vi* (*haben*) **es hapert** there's a lack (**an** + *dat* of)

Happen *m* -s,- mouthful; **einen H**∼ **essen** have a bite to eat

Harfe *f* -,-n harp

Harke *f* -,-n rake. **h**∼**n** *vt/i* (*haben*) rake

harmlos *a* harmless; (*arglos*) innocent, *adv* -ly. **H~igkeit** *f* -
harmlessness; innocence

Harmonie *f* -,-n harmony. **h~ren** *vi*
(*haben*) harmonize; (*gut auskommen*) get on well

Harmonika *f* -,-s accordion; (*Mund-*)
mouth-organ

harmonisch *a* harmonious, *adv* -ly

Harn *m* -[e]s urine. **H~blase** *f*
bladder

Harpune *f* -,-n harpoon

hart (härter, härtest) *a* hard; (*heftig*)
violent; (*streng*) harsh ● *adv* hard;
(*streng*) harshly

Härte *f* -,-n hardness; (*Strenge*)
harshness; (*Not*) hardship. **h~n** *vt*
harden

Hart|faserplatte *f* hardboard.
h~gekocht *a* hard-boiled. **h~her-
zig** *a* hard-hearted. **h~näckig** *a*
stubborn, *adv* -ly; (*ausdauernd*) persistent, *adv* -ly. **H~näckigkeit** *f* -
stubbornness; persistence

Harz *nt* -es,-e resin

Haschee *nt* -s,-s (*Culin*) hash

haschen *vi* (*haben*) **h~ nach** try to
catch

Haschisch *nt & m* -[s] hashish

Hase *m* -n,-n hare; **falscher H~** meat
loaf

Hasel *f* -,-n hazel. **H~maus** *f* dormouse. **H~nuß** *f* hazel-nut

Hasenfuß *m* (*fam*) coward

Haß *m* -sses hatred

hassen *vt* hate

häßlich *a* ugly; (*unfreundlich*) nasty,
adv -ily. **H~keit** *f* - ugliness;
nastiness

Hast *f* - haste. **h~en** *vi* (*sein*) hasten,
hurry. **h~ig** *a* hasty, *adv* -ily, hurried, *adv* -ly

hast, hat, hatte, hätte *s.* **haben**

Haube *f* -,-n cap; (*Trocken-*) drier;
(*Kühler-*) bonnet, (*Amer*) hood

Hauch *m* -[e]s breath; (*Luft-*) breeze;
(*Duft*) whiff; (*Spur*) tinge. **h~dünn** *a*
very thin; ⟨*Strümpfe*⟩ sheer. **h~en**
vt/i (*haben*) breathe

Haue *f* -,-n pick; (*fam: Prügel*) beating. **h~n†** *vt* beat; (*hämmern*)
knock; (*meißeln*) hew; **sich h~n**
fight; **übers Ohr h~n** (*fam*) cheat
● *vi* (*haben*) bang (**auf** + *acc* on); **jdm
ins Gesicht h~n** hit s.o. in the face

Haufen *m* -s,- heap, pile; (*Leute*)
crowd

häufen *vt* heap *or* pile [up]; **sich h~**
pile up; (*zunehmen*) increase

haufenweise *adv* in large numbers;
h~ Geld pots of money

häufig *a* frequent, *adv* -ly. **H~keit** *f* -
frequency

Haupt *nt* -[e]s, **Häupter** head.
H~bahnhof *m* main station.
H~darsteller *m*, **H~darstellerin** *f*
male/female lead. **H~fach** *nt* main
subject. **H~gericht** *nt* main course.
H~hahn *m* mains tap; (*Wasser-*)
stopcock

Häuptling *m* -s,-e chief

Haupt|mahlzeit *f* main meal.
H~mann *m* (*pl* -**leute**) captain.
H~person *f* most important person;
(*Theat*) principal character.
H~post *f* main post office. **H~quar-
tier** *nt* headquarters *pl*. **H~rolle** *f*
lead; (*fig*) leading role. **H~sache** *f*
main thing; **in der H~sache** in the
main. **h~sächlich** *a* main, *adv* -ly.
H~satz *m* main clause. **H~schlüssel**
m master key. **H~stadt** *f* capital.
H~straße *f* main street. **H~ver-
kehrsstraße** *f* main road. **H~ver-
kehrszeit** *f* rush-hour. **H~wort** *nt*
(*pl* -**wörter**) noun

Haus *nt* -es, **Häuser** house; (*Gebäude*)
building; (*Schnecken-*) shell; **zu H~e**
at home; **nach H~e** home. **H~an-
gestellte(r)** *m/f* domestic servant.
H~arbeit *f* housework; (*Sch*) homework. **H~arzt** *m* family doctor. **H~
aufgaben** *fpl* homework *sg*. **H~be-
setzer** *m* -s,- squatter. **H~besuch** *m*
house-call

hausen *vi* (*haben*) live; (*wüten*)
wreak havoc

Haus|frau *f* housewife. **H~gehilfin** *f*
domestic help. **h~gemacht** *a* home-
made. **H~halt** *m* -[e]s,-e household;
(*Pol*) budget. **h~halten†** *vi sep* (*haben*) **h~halten** with manage care-
fully; conserve ⟨*Kraft*⟩. **H~hälterin** *f*
-,-nen housekeeper. **H~haltsgeld** *nt*
housekeeping [money]. **H~halts-
plan** *m* budget. **H~herr** *m* head of
the household; (*Gastgeber*) host.
h~hoch *a* huge; (*fam*) big ● *adv*
(*fam*) vastly; (*verlieren*) by a wide
margin

hausier|en *vi* (*haben*) **h~en mit**
hawk. **H~er** *m* -s,- hawker

Hauslehrer *m* [private] tutor. **H~in** *f*
governess

häuslich *a* domestic; ⟨*Person*⟩
domesticated

Haus|meister *m* caretaker. **H~num-
mer** *f* house number. **H~ordnung** *f*

house rules *pl.* **H~putz** *m* cleaning.
H~rat *m* -[e]s household effects *pl.*
H~schlüssel *m* front-door key.
H~schuh *m* slipper. **H~stand** *m*
household. **H~suchung** *f* [police]
search. **H~suchungsbefehl** *m*
search-warrant. **H~tier** *nt* domestic
animal; (*Hund, Katze*) pet. **H~tür** *f*
front door. **H~wart** *m* -[e]s,-e caretaker. **H~wirt** *m* landlord. **H~wir-
tin** *f* landlady

Haut *f* -,Häute skin; (*Tier-*) hide; **aus
der H~ fahren** (*fam*) fly off the
handle. **H~arzt** *m* dermatologist
häuten *vt* skin; **sich h~** moult
haut|eng *a* skin-tight. **H~farbe** *f* col-
our; (*Teint*) complexion
Haxe *f* -,-n = Hachse
Hbf. *abbr s.* **Hauptbahnhof**
Hebamme *f* -,-n midwife
Hebel *m* -s,- lever. **H~kraft, H~wir-
kung** *f* leverage
heben† *vt* lift; (*hoch-, steigern*) raise;
sich h~ rise; (*Nebel:*) lift; (*sich ver-
bessern*) improve
hebräisch *a* Hebrew
hecheln *vi* (*haben*) pant
Hecht *m* -[e]s,-e pike
Heck *nt* -s,-s (*Naut*) stern; (*Aviat*) tail;
(*Auto*) rear
Hecke *f* -,-n hedge. **H~nschütze** *m*
sniper
Heck|fenster *nt* rear window.
H~motor *m* rear engine. **H~tür** *f*
hatchback
Heer *nt* -[e]s,-e army
Hefe *f* - yeast. **H~teig** *m* yeast dough.
H~teilchen *nt* Danish pastry
Heft¹ *nt* -[e]s,-e haft, handle
Heft² *nt* -[e]s,-e booklet; (*Sch*) exer-
cise book; (*Zeitschrift*) issue. **h~en**
vt (*nähen*) tack; (*stecken*) pin/(*klam-
mern*) clip/(*mit Heftmaschine*) staple
(**an** + *acc* to). **H~er** *m* -s,- file
heftig *a* fierce, *adv* -ly, violent, *adv*
-ly; (*Schlag, Regen*) heavy, *adv* -ily;
(*Schmerz, Gefühl*) intense, *adv* -ly;
(*Person*) quick-tempered. **H~keit** *f* -
fierceness, violence; intensity
Heft|klammer *f* staple; (*Büro-*)
paper-clip. **H~maschine** *f* stapler.
H~pflaster *nt* sticking plaster.
H~zwecke *f* -,-n drawing-pin
hegen *vt* care for; (*fig*) cherish (*Hoffnung*); harbour (*Verdacht*)
Hehl *nt & m* **kein[en] H~ machen aus**
make no secret of. **H~er** *m* -s,- receiver, fence
Heide¹ *m* -n,-n heathen

Heide² *f* -,-n heath; (*Bot*) heather.
H~kraut *nt* heather
Heidelbeere *f* bilberry, (*Amer*)
blueberry
Heid|in *f* -,-nen heathen. **h~nisch** *a*
heathen
heikel *a* difficult, tricky; (*delikat*)
delicate; (*dial*) (*Person*) fussy
heil *a* undamaged, intact; (*Person*)
unhurt; (*gesund*) well; **mit h~er
Haut** (*fam*) unscathed
Heil *nt* -s salvation; **sein H~ versuchen** try one's luck
Heiland *m* -s (*Relig*) Saviour
Heil|anstalt *f* sanatorium; (*Nerven-*)
mental hospital. **H~bad** *nt* spa.
h~bar *a* curable
Heilbutt *m* -[e]s,-e halibut
heilen *vt* cure; heal (*Wunde*) ● *vi*
(*sein*) heal
heilfroh *a* (*fam*) very relieved
Heilgymnastik *f* physiotherapy
heilig *a* holy; (*geweiht*) sacred; **der
H~e Abend** Christmas Eve; **die h~e
Anna** Saint Anne. **H~abend** *m*
Christmas Eve. **H~e(r)** *m/f* saint.
h~en *vt* keep, observe. **H~enschein**
m halo. **h~halten†** *vt sep* hold
sacred; keep (*Feiertag*). **H~keit** *f* -
sanctity, holiness. **h~sprechen†** *vt
sep* canonize. **H~tum** *nt* -s,-̈er
shrine
heil|kräftig *a* medicinal. **H~kräuter**
ntpl medicinal herbs. **h~los** *a* un-
holy. **H~mittel** *nt* remedy. **H~prak-
tiker** *m* -s,- practitioner of alternative medicine. **h~sam** *a* (*fig*) salutary. **H~sarmee** *f* Salvation Army.
H~ung *f* - cure
Heim *nt* -[e]s,-e home; (*Studenten-*)
hostel. **h~** *adv* home
Heimat *f* -,-en home; (*Land*) native
land. **H~abend** *m* folk evening.
h~los *a* homeless. **H~stadt** *f* home
town
heim|begleiten *vt sep* see home.
h~bringen† *vt sep* bring home; (*begleiten*) see home. **H~computer** *m*
home computer. **h~fahren†** *v sep* ●
vi (*sein*) go/drive home ● *vt* take/
drive home. **h~fahrt** *f* way home.
h~gehen† *vi sep* (*sein*) go home;
(*sterben*) die
heimisch *a* native, indigenous; (*Pol*)
domestic; **h~ sein/sich h~ fühlen**
be/feel at home
Heim|kehr *f* - return [home]. **h~keh-
ren** *vi sep* (*sein*) return home.

h~kommen† *vi sep* (*sein*) come home

heimlich *a* secret, *adv* -ly. **H~keit** *f* -,-en secrecy; **H~keiten** secrets. **H~tuerei** *f* - secretiveness

Heim|reise *f* journey home. **h~reisen** *vi sep* (*sein*) go home. **H~spiel** *nt* home game. **h~suchen** *vt sep* afflict. **h~tückisch** *a* treacherous; ⟨*Krankheit*⟩ insidious. **h~wärts** *adv* home. **H~weg** *m* way home. **H~weh** *nt* -s homesickness; **H~weh haben** be homesick. **H~werker** *m* -s,- [home] handyman. **h~zahlen** *vt sep* **jdm etw h~zahlen** (*fig*) pay s.o. back for sth

Heirat *f* -,-en marriage. **h~en** *vt/i* (*haben*) marry. **H~santrag** *m* proposal; **jdm einen H~santrag machen** propose to s.o. **h~sfähig** *a* marriageable

heiser *a* hoarse, *adv* -ly. **H~keit** *f* - hoarseness

heiß *a* hot, *adv* -ly; (*hitzig*) heated; (*leidenschaftlich*) fervent, *adv* -ly; **mir ist h~** I am hot

heißen† *vi* (*haben*) be called; (*bedeuten*) mean; **ich heiße ...** my name is **...; wie h~ Sie?** what is your name? **wie heißt ... auf englisch?** what's the English for ... ? **es heißt** it says; (*man sagt*) it is said; **das heißt** that is [to say]; **was soll das h~?** what does it mean? (*empört*) what is the meaning of this? ● *vt* call; **jdn etw tun h~** tell s.o. to do sth

heiß|geliebt *a* beloved. **h~hungrig** *a* ravenous. **H~wasserbereiter** *m* -s,- water heater

heiter *a* cheerful, *adv* -ly; ⟨*Wetter*⟩ bright; (*amüsant*) amusing; **aus h~em Himmel** (*fig*) out of the blue. **H~keit** *f* - cheerfulness; (*Gelächter*) mirth

Heiz|anlage *f* heating; (*Auto*) heater. **H~decke** *f* electric blanket. **h~en** *vt* heat; light ⟨*Ofen*⟩ ● *vi* (*haben*) put the heating on; ⟨*Ofen:*⟩ give out heat. **H~gerät** *nt* heater. **H~kessel** *m* boiler. **H~körper** *m* radiator. **H~lüfter** *m* -s,- fan heater. **H~material** *nt* fuel. **H~ofen** *m* heater. **H~ung** *f* -,-en heating; (*Heizkörper*) radiator

Hektar *nt & m* -s,- hectare

hektisch *a* hectic

Held *m* -en,-en hero. **h~enhaft** *a* heroic, *adv* -ally. **H~enmut** *m* heroism. **h~enmütig** *a* heroic, *adv* -ally.

H~entum *nt* -s heroism. **H~in** *f* -,-nen heroine

helf|en† *vi* (*haben*) help (**jdm** s.o.); (*nützen*) be effective; **sich** (*dat*) **nicht zu h~en wissen** not know what to do; **es hilft nichts** it's no use. **H~er** (**in**) *m* -s,- (*f* -,-nen) helper, assistant. **H~ershelfer** *m* accomplice

hell *a* light; (*Licht ausstrahlend, klug*) bright; ⟨*Stimme*⟩ clear; (*fam: völlig*) utter; **h~es Bier** ≈ lager ● *adv* brightly; **h~ begeistert** absolutely delighted. **h~hörig** *a* poorly soundproofed; **h~hörig werden** (*fig*) sit up and take notice

hellicht *a* **h~er Tag** broad daylight

Hell|igkeit *f* - brightness. **H~seher(in)** *m* -s,- (*f* -,-nen) clairvoyant. **h~wach** *a* wide awake

Helm *m* -[e]s,-e helmet

Hemd *nt* -[e]s,-en vest, (*Amer*) undershirt; (*Ober-*) shirt. **H~bluse** *f* shirt

Hemisphäre *f* -,-n hemisphere

hemm|en *vt* check; (*verzögern*) impede; (*fig*) inhibit. **H~ung** *f* -,-en (*fig*) inhibition; (*Skrupel*) scruple; **H~ungen haben** be inhibited. **h~ungslos** *a* unrestrained, *adv* -ly

Hendl *nt* -s,-[n] (*Aust*) chicken

Hengst *m* -[e]s,-e stallion. **H~fohlen** *nt* colt

Henkel *m* -s,- handle

henken *vt* hang

Henne *f* -,-n hen

her *adv* here; (*zeitlich*) ago; **her mit ...!** give me ...! **von oben/unten/ Norden/weit her** from above/below/the north/far away; **vor/hinter jdm/etw her** in front of/behind s.o./sth; **von der Farbe/vom Thema her** as far as the colour/subject is concerned

herab *adv* down [here]; **von oben h~** from above; (*fig*) condescending, *adv* -ly. **h~blicken** *vi sep* (*haben*) = **h~sehen**

herablass|en† *vt sep* let down; **sich h~en** condescend (**zu** to). **h~end** *a* condescending, *adv* -ly. **H~ung** *f* - condescension

herab|sehen† *vi sep* (*haben*) look down (**auf** + *acc* on). **h~setzen** *vt sep* reduce, cut; (*fig*) belittle. **h~setzend** *a* disparaging, *adv* -ly. **h~würdigen** *vt sep* belittle, disparage

Heraldik *f* - heraldry

heran *adv* near; **[bis] h~ an** (+ *acc*) up to. **h~bilden** *vt sep* train. **h~gehen**† *vi sep* (*sein*) **h~gehen an**

(+ *acc*) go up to; get down to ⟨*Arbeit*⟩.
h∼kommen† *vi sep* (*sein*) approach;
h∼kommen an (+ *acc*) come up to;
(*erreichen*) get at; (*fig*) measure up
to. **h∼machen (sich)** *vr sep* **sich
h∼machen an** (+ *acc*) approach; get
down to ⟨*Arbeit*⟩. **h∼reichen** *vi sep*
(*haben*) **h∼reichen an** (+ *acc*) reach;
(*fig*) measure up to. **h∼wachsen**† *vi
sep* (*sein*) grow up. **h∼ziehen** *v sep*
● *vt* pull up (**an** + *acc* to); (*züchten*)
raise; (*h∼bilden*) train; (*hinzuzie-
hen*) call in ● *vi* (*sein*) approach
herauf *adv* up [here]; **die Treppe h∼**
up the stairs. **h∼beschwören** *vt sep*
evoke; (*verursachen*) cause.
h∼kommen† *vi sep* (*sein*) come up.
h∼setzen *vt sep* raise, increase
heraus *adv* out (**aus** of); **h∼ damit** *od*
mit der Sprache! out with it! **h∼be-
kommen**† *vt sep* get out; (*ausfindig
machen*) find out; (*lösen*) solve; **Geld
h∼bekommen** get change. **h∼brin-
gen**† *vt sep* bring out; (*fam*) get
out. **h∼finden**† *v sep* ● *vt* find out
● *vi* (*haben*) find one's way out.
H∼forderer *m* -s,- challenger.
h∼fordern *vt sep* provoke; challenge ⟨*Person*⟩. **H∼forderung** *f* provocation; challenge. **H∼gabe** *f*
handing over; (*Admin*) issue; (*Veröffentlichung*) publication. **h∼geben**†
vt sep hand over; (*Admin*) issue;
(*veröffentlichen*) publish; edit
⟨*Zeitschrift*⟩; **jdm Geld h∼geben**
give s.o. change ● *vi* (*haben*) give
change (**auf** + *acc* for). **H∼geber** *m*
-s,- publisher; editor. **h∼gehen**† *vi
sep* (*sein*) ⟨*Fleck:*⟩ come out; **aus sich
h∼gehen** (*fig*) come out of one's
shell. **h∼halten**† (**sich**) *vr sep* (*fig*)
keep out (**aus** of). **h∼holen** *vt sep* get
out. **h∼kommen**† *vi sep* (*sein*) come
out; (*aus Schwierigkeit, Takt*) get
out; **auf eins** *od* **dasselbe h∼kom-
men** (*fam*) come to the same thing.
h∼lassen† *vt sep* let out. **h∼ma-
chen** *vt sep* get out; **sich gut h∼ma-
chen** (*fig*) do well. **h∼nehmen**† *vt
sep* take out; **sich zuviel h∼nehmen**
(*fig*) take liberties. **h∼platzen** *vi sep*
(*haben*) (*fam*) burst out laughing.
h∼putzen (sich) *vr sep* doll oneself
up. **h∼ragen** *vi sep* (*haben*) jut out;
(*fig*) stand out. **h∼reden (sich)** *vr
sep* make excuses. **h∼rücken** *v sep*
● *vt* move out; (*hergeben*) hand over
● *vi* (*sein*) **h∼rücken mit** hand over;

(*fig: sagen*) come out with. **h∼rut-
schen** *vi sep* (*sein*) slip out.
h∼schlagen† *vt sep* knock out; (*fig*)
gain. **h∼stellen** *vt sep* put out; **sich
h∼stellen** turn out (**als** to be; **daß**
that). **h∼suchen** *vt sep* pick out.
h∼ziehen† *vt sep* pull out
herb *a* sharp; ⟨*Wein*⟩ dry; ⟨*Landschaft*⟩ austere; (*fig*) harsh
herbei *adv* here. **h∼führen** *vt sep*
(*fig*) bring about. **h∼lassen**† (**sich**)
vr sep condescend (**zu** to). **h∼schaf-
fen** *vt sep* get. **h∼sehnen** *vt sep* long
for
Herberg|e *f* -,-n [youth] hostel;
(*Unterkunft*) lodging. **H∼svater** *m*
warden
herbestellen *vt sep* summon
herbitten† *vt sep* ask to come
herbringen† *vt sep* bring [here]
Herbst *m* -[e]s,-e autumn. **h∼lich** *a*
autumnal
Herd *m* -[e]s,-e stove, cooker; (*fig*)
focus
Herde *f* -,-n herd; (*Schaf*) flock
herein *adv* in [here]; **h∼!** come in!
h∼bitten† *vt sep* ask in. **h∼bre-
chen**† *vi sep* (*sein*) burst in; (*fig*) set
in; ⟨*Nacht:*⟩ fall; **h∼brechen über**
(+ *acc*) (*fig*) overtake. **h∼fallen**† *vi
sep* (*sein*) (*fam*) be taken in (**auf**
+ *acc* by). **h∼kommen**† *vi sep* (*sein*)
come in. **h∼lassen**† *vt sep* let in.
h∼legen *vt sep* (*fam*) take for a ride.
h∼rufen† *vt sep* call in
Herfahrt *f* journey/drive here
herfallen† *vi sep* (*sein*) **h∼ über**
(+ *acc*) attack; fall upon ⟨*Essen*⟩
hergeben† *vt sep* hand over; (*fig*)
give up; **sich h∼ zu** (*fig*) be a party to
hergebracht *a* traditional
hergehen† *vi sep* (*sein*) **h∼ vor/
neben/hinter** (+ *dat*) walk along in
front of/beside/behind; **es ging lustig her** (*fam*) there was a lot of
merriment
herhalten† *vt sep* (*haben*) hold out;
h∼ müssen be the one to suffer
herholen *vt sep* fetch; **weit hergeholt**
(*fig*) far-fetched
Hering *m* -s,-e herring; (*Zeltpflock*)
tent-peg
her|kommen† *vi sep* (*sein*) come
here; **wo kommt das her?** where
does it come from? **h∼kömmlich** *a*
traditional. **H∼kunft** *f* - origin
herlaufen† *vi sep* (*sein*) **h∼ vor/
neben/hinter** (+ *dat*) run/(*gehen*)
walk along in front of/beside/behind

herleiten *vt sep* derive

hermachen *vt sep* **viel/wenig h~** be impressive/unimpressive; *(wichtig nehmen)* make a lot of/little fuss **(von** of); **sich h~ über** (+*acc*) fall upon; tackle ⟨*Arbeit*⟩

Hermelin[1] *nt* **-s,-e** *(Zool)* stoat

Hermelin[2] *m* **-s,-e** *(Pelz)* ermine

hermetisch *a* hermetic, *adv* -ally

Hernie /'hɛrnjə/ *f* **-,-n** hernia

Heroin *nt* **-s** heroin

heroisch *a* heroic, *adv* -ally

Herr *m* **-en,-en** gentleman; *(Gebieter)* master **(über**+*acc* of); **[Gott,] der H~**the Lord [God]; **H~ Meier** Mr Meier; **Sehr geehrte H~en** Dear Sirs. **H~chen** *nt* **-s,-** master. **H~enhaus** *nt* manor [house]. **h~enlos** *a* ownerless; ⟨*Tier*⟩ stray. **H~ensitz** *m* manor

Herrgott *m* **der H~** the Lord; **H~ [noch mal]!** damn it!

herrichten *vt sep* prepare; **wieder h~** renovate

Herrin *f* **-,-nen** mistress

herrisch *a* imperious, *adv* -ly; ⟨*Ton*⟩ peremptory; *(herrschsüchtig)* overbearing

herrlich *a* marvellous, *adv* -ly; *(großartig)* magnificent, *adv* -ly. **H~keit** *f* **-,-en** splendour

Herrschaft *f* **-,-en** rule; *(Macht)* power; *(Kontrolle)* control; **meine H~en!** ladies and gentlemen!

herrsch|en *vi (haben)* rule; *(verbreitet sein)* prevail; **es h~te Stille/ große Aufregung** there was silence/ great excitement. **H~er(in)** *m* **-s,-** (*f* **-,-nen**) ruler. **h~süchtig** *a* domineering

herrühren *vi (haben)* stem **(von** from)

hersein† *vi sep (sein)* come **(von** from); **h~ hinter** (+*dat*) be after; **es ist schon lange/drei Tage her** it was a long time/three days ago

herstammen *vi sep (haben)* come **(aus/von** from)

herstell|en *vt sep* establish; *(Comm)* manufacture, make. **H~er** *m* **-s,-** manufacturer, maker. **H~ung** *f* **-** establishment; manufacture

herüber *adv* over [here]. **h~kommen†** *vi sep (sein)* come over [here]

herum *adv* **im Kreis h~** [round] in a circle; **falsch h~** the wrong way round; **um ... h~** round ... ; *(ungefähr)* [round] about ... **h~albern** *vi sep (haben)* fool around. **h~drehen**

vt sep turn round/*(wenden)* over; turn ⟨*Schlüssel*⟩; **sich h~drehen** turn round/over. **h~gehen†** *vi sep (sein)* walk around; ⟨*Zeit:*⟩ pass; **h~gehen um** go round. **h~kommen†** *vi sep (sein)* get about; **h~kommen um** get round; come round ⟨*Ecke*⟩; **um etw [nicht] h~kommen** *(fig)* [not] get out of sth. **h~kriegen** *vt sep* **jdn h~kriegen** *(fam)* talk s.o. round. **h~liegen†** *vi sep (sein)* lie around. **h~lungern** *vi sep (haben)* loiter. **h~schnüffeln** *vi sep (haben)* *(fam)* nose about. **h~sitzen†** *vi sep (haben)* sit around; **h~sitzen um** sit round. **h~sprechen†** **(sich)** *vr sep* ⟨*Gerücht:*⟩ get about. **h~stehen†** *vi sep (haben)* stand around; **h~stehen um** stand round. **h~treiben† (sich)** *vr sep* hang around. **h~ziehen†** *vi sep (sein)* move around; *(ziellos)* wander about

herunter *adv* down [here]; **die Treppe h~** down the stairs. **h~fallen†** *vi sep* fall off. **h~gehen†** *vi sep (sein)* come down; *(sinken)* go/come down. **h~gekommen** *a (fig)* run-down; ⟨*Gebäude*⟩ dilapidated; ⟨*Person*⟩ down-at-heel. **h~kommen†** *vi sep (sein)* come down; *(fig)* go to rack and ruin; ⟨*Firma, Person:*⟩ go downhill; *(gesundheitlich)* get run down. **h~lassen†** *vt sep* let down, lower. **h~machen** *vt sep (fam)* reprimand; *(herabsetzen)* run down. **h~spielen** *vt sep (fig)* play down. **h~ziehen†** *vt sep* pull down

hervor *adv* out **(aus** of). **h~bringen†** *vt sep* produce; utter ⟨*Wort*⟩. **h~gehen†** *vi sep (sein)* come/*(sich ergeben)* emerge/*(folgen)* follow **(aus** from). **h~heben†** *vt sep (fig)* stress, emphasize. **h~quellen†** *vi sep (sein)* stream out; *(h~treten)* bulge. **h~ragen** *vi sep (haben)* jut out; *(fig)* stand out. **h~ragend** *a (fig)* outstanding. **h~rufen†** *vt sep (fig)* cause. **h~stehen†** *vi sep (haben)* protrude. **h~treten†** *vi sep (sein)* protrude, bulge; *(fig)* stand out. **h~tun† (sich)** *vr sep (fig)* distinguish oneself; *(angeben)* show off

Herweg *m* way here

Herz *nt* **-ens,-en** heart; *(Kartenspiel)* hearts *pl*; **sich** *(dat)* **ein H~ fassen** pluck up courage. **H~anfall** *m* heart attack

herzeigen *vt sep* show

herz|en vt hug. **H~enslust** f nach **H~enslust** to one's heart's content. **h~haft** a hearty, adv -ily; (würzig) savoury

herziehen† v sep ● vt hinter sich (dat) **h~** pull along [behind one] ● vi (sein) hinter jdm **h~** follow along behind s.o.; über jdn **h~** (fam) run s.o. down

herz|ig a sweet, adorable. **H~infarkt** m heart attack. **H~klopfen** nt -s palpitations pl; **ich hatte H~klopfen** my heart was pounding

herzlich a cordial, adv -ly; (warm) warm, adv -ly; (aufrichtig) sincere, adv -ly; **h~en Dank!** many thanks! **h~e Grüße** kind regards; **h~ wenig** precious little. **H~keit** f - cordiality; warmth; sincerity

herzlos a heartless

Herzog m -s, ̈e duke. **H~in** f -,-nen duchess. **H~tum** nt -s, ̈er duchy

Herz|schlag m heartbeat; (Med) heart failure. **h~zerreißend** a heart-breaking

Hessen nt -s Hesse

heterosexuell a heterosexual

Hetze f - rush; (Kampagne) virulent campaign (gegen against). **h~n** vt chase; **sich h~n** hurry ● vi (haben) agitate; (sich beeilen) hurry ● vi (sein) rush

Heu nt -s hay; **Geld wie Heu haben** (fam) have pots of money

Heuchelei f - hypocrisy

heuch|eln vt feign ● vi (haben) pretend. **H~ler(in)** m -s,- (f -,-nen) hypocrite. **h~lerisch** a hypocritical, adv -ly

heuer adv (Aust) this year

Heuer f -,-n (Naut) pay. **h~n** vt hire; sign on ⟨Matrosen⟩

heulen vi (haben) howl; (fam: weinen) cry; ⟨Sirene:⟩ wail

Heurige(r) m (Aust) new wine

Heu|schnupfen m hay fever. **H~schober** m -s,- haystack. **H~schrecke** f -,-n grasshopper; (Wander-) locust

heut|e adv today; (heutzutage) nowadays; **h~e früh** od **morgen** this morning; **von h~e auf morgen** from one day to the next. **h~ig** a today's ...; (gegenwärtig) present; **der h~ige Tag** today. **h~zutage** adv nowadays

Hexe f -,-n witch. **h~n** vi (haben) work magic; **ich kann nicht h~n** (fam) I can't perform miracles.

H~njagd f witch-hunt. **H~nschuß** m lumbago. **H~rei** f - witchcraft

Hieb m -[e]s,-e blow; (Peitschen-) lash; **H~e** hiding sg

hier adv here; **h~ und da** here and there; (zeitlich) now and again

Hierarchie /hierar'çi:/ f -,-n hierarchy

hier|auf adv on this/these; (antworten) to this; (zeitlich) after this. **h~aus** adv out of or from this/these. **h~behalten†** vt sep keep here. **h~bleiben†** vi sep (sein) stay here. **h~durch** adv through this/these; (Ursache) as a result of this. **h~für** adv for this/these. **h~her** adv here. **h~hin** adv here. **h~in** adv in this/ these. **h~lassen†** vt sep leave here. **h~mit** adv with this/these; (Comm) herewith; (Admin) hereby. **h~nach** adv after this/ these; (demgemäß) according to this/these. **h~sein†** vi sep (sein) be here. **h~über** adv over/ (höher) above this/these; ⟨sprechen, streiten⟩ about this/these. **h~unter** adv under/(tiefer) below this/these; (dazwischen) among these. **h~von** adv from this/these; (h~über) about this/these; (Menge) of this/these. **h~zu** adv to this/these; (h~für) for this/these. **h~zulande** adv here

hiesig a local. **H~e(r)** m/f local

Hilfe f -,-n help, aid; **um H~e rufen** call for help; **jdm zu H~e kommen** come to s.o.'s aid. **h~los** a helpless, adv -ly. **H~losigkeit** f - helplessness. **h~reich** a helpful

Hilfs|arbeiter m unskilled labourer. **h~bedürftig** a needy; **h~bedürftig sein** be in need of help. **h~bereit** a helpful, adv -ly. **H~kraft** f helper. **H~mittel** nt aid. **H~verb, H~zeitwort** nt auxiliary verb

Himbeere f raspberry

Himmel m -s,- sky; (Relig & fig) heaven; (Bett-) canopy; **am H~** in the sky; **unter freiem H~** in the open air. **H~bett** nt four-poster [bed]. **H~fahrt** f Ascension; **Mariä H~fahrt** Assumption. **h~schreiend** a scandalous. **H~srichtung** f compass point; **in alle H~srichtungen** in all directions. **h~weit** a (fam) vast

himmlisch a heavenly

hin adv there; **hin und her** to and fro; **hin und zurück** there and back; (Rail) return; **hin und wieder** now and again; **an** (+dat) ... **hin** along; **auf** (+acc) ... **hin** in reply to ⟨Brief,

Anzeige); on ⟨*jds Rat*⟩; **zu** *od* **nach ... hin** towards; **vor sich hin reden** talk to oneself

hinab *adv* down [there]

hinauf *adv* up [there]; **die Treppe/ Straße h~** up the stairs/road. **h~gehen**† *vi sep* (*sein*) go up. **h~setzen** *vt sep* raise

hinaus *adv* out [there]; (*nach draußen*) outside; **zur Tür h~** out of the door; **auf Jahre h~** for years to come; **über etw** (*acc*) **h~** beyond sth; (*Menge*) [over and] above sth. **h~fliegen**† *v sep* ● *vi* (*sein*) fly out; (*fam*) get the sack ● *vt* fly out. **h~gehen**† *vi sep* (*sein*) go out; ⟨*Zimmer:*⟩ face (**nach Norden** north); **h~gehen über** (+*acc*) go beyond, exceed. **h~kommen**† *vi sep* (*sein*) get out; **h~kommen über** (+*acc*) get beyond. **h~laufen** *vi sep* (*sein*) run out; **h~laufen auf** (+*acc*) (*fig*) amount to. **h~lehnen** (**sich**) *vr sep* lean out. **h~ragen** *vi sep* (*haben*) **h~ragen über** (+*acc*) project beyond; (*in der Höhe*) rise above; (*fig*) stand out above. **h~schicken** *vt sep* send out. **h~schieben**† *vt sep* push out; (*fig*) put off. **h~sehen**† *vi sep* (*haben*) look out. **h~sein**† *vi sep* (*sein*) **über etw** (*acc*) **h~sein** (*fig*) be past sth. **h~werfen**† *vt sep* throw out; (*fam: entlassen*) fire. **h~wollen**† *vi sep* (*haben*) want to go out; **h~wollen auf** (+*acc*) (*fig*) aim at; **hoch h~wollen** (*fig*) be ambitious. **h~ziehen**† *v sep* ● *vt* pull out; (*in die Länge ziehen*) drag out; (*verzögern*) delay; **sich h~ziehen** drag on; be delayed ● *vi* (*sein*) move out. **h~zögern** *vt* delay; **sich h~zögern** be delayed

Hinblick *m* **im H~ auf** (+*acc*) in view of; (*hinsichtlich*) regarding

hinbringen† *vt sep* take there; (*verbringen*) spend

hinder|lich *a* awkward; **jdm h~lich sein** hamper s.o. **h~n** *vt* hamper; (*verhindern*) prevent. **H~nis** *nt* -ses,-se obstacle. **H~nisrennen** *nt* steeplechase

hindeuten *vi sep* (*haben*) point (**auf** + *acc* to)

Hindu *m* -s,-s Hindu. **H~ismus** *m* - Hinduism

hindurch *adv* through it/them; **den Sommer h~** throughout the summer

hinein *adv* in [there]; (*nach drinnen*) inside; **h~ in** (+*acc*) into. **h~fallen**† *vi sep* (*sein*) fall in. **h~gehen**† *vi sep* (*sein*) go in; **h~gehen in** (+*acc*) go into. **h~laufen**† *vi sep* (*sein*) run in; **h~laufen in** (+*acc*) run into. **h~reden** *vi sep* (*haben*) **jdm h~reden** interrupt s.o.; (*sich einmischen*) interfere in s.o.'s affairs. **h~versetzen** (**sich**) *vr sep* **sich in jds Lage h~versetzen** put oneself in s.o.'s position. **h~ziehen** *vt sep* pull in; **h~ziehen in** (+*acc*) pull into; **in etw** (*acc*) **h~gezogen werden** (*fig*) become involved in sth

hin|fahren† *v sep* ● *vi* (*sein*) go/drive there ● *vt* take/drive there. **H~fahrt** *f* journey/drive there; (*Rail*) outward journey. **h~fallen**† *vi sep* (*sein*) fall. **h~fällig** *a* (*gebrechlich*) frail; (*ungültig*) invalid. **h~fliegen**† *v sep* ● *vi* (*sein*) fly there; (*fam*) fall ● *vt* fly there. **H~flug** *m* flight there; (*Admin*) outward flight. **H~gabe** *f* - devotion; (*Eifer*) dedication

hingeb|en† *vt sep* give up; **sich h~en** (*fig*) devote oneself (**einer Aufgabe** to a task); abandon oneself (**dem Vergnügen** to pleasure). **H~ung** *f* - devotion. **h~ungsvoll** *a* devoted, *adv* -ly

hingegen *adv* on the other hand

hingehen† *vi sep* (*sein*) go/(*zu Fuß*) walk there; (*vergehen*) pass; **h~ zu** go up to; **wo gehst du hin?** where are you going? **etw h~ lassen** (*fig*) let sth pass

hingerissen *a* rapt, *adv* -ly; **h~ sein** be carried away (**von** by)

hin|halten† *vt sep* hold out; (*warten lassen*) keep waiting. **h~hocken** (**sich**) *vr sep* squat down. **h~kauern** (**sich**) *vr sep* crouch down

hinken *vi* (*haben/sein*) limp

hin|knien (**sich**) *vr sep* kneel down. **h~kommen**† *vi sep* (*sein*) get there; (*h~gehören*) belong, go; (*fam: auskommen*) manage (**mit** with); (*fam: stimmen*) be right. **h~länglich** *a* adequate, *adv* -ly. **h~laufen**† *vi sep* (*sein*) run/(*gehen*) walk there. **h~legen** *vt sep* lay *or* put down; **sich h~legen** lie down. **h~nehmen**† *vt sep* (*fig*) accept

hinreichen *v sep* ● *vt* hand (**dat** to) ● *vi* (*haben*) extend (**bis** to); (*ausreichen*) be adequate. **h~d** *a* adequate, *adv* -ly

Hinreise f journey there; (*Rail*) outward journey

hinreißen† vt sep (*fig*) carry away; **sich h~ lassen** get carried away. **h~d** a ravishing, adv -ly

hinricht|en vt sep execute. **H~ung** f execution

hinschicken vt sep send there

hinschleppen vt sep drag there; (*fig*) drag out; **sich h~** drag oneself along; (*fig*) drag on

hinschreiben† vt sep write there; (*aufschreiben*) write down

hinsehen† vi sep (*haben*) look

hinsein† vi sep (*sein*) (*fam*) be gone; (*kaputt, tot*) have had it; **[ganz] h~ von** be overwhelmed by; **es ist noch/ nicht mehr lange hin** it's a long time yet/not long to go

hinsetzen vt sep put down; **sich h~** sit down

Hinsicht f - **in dieser/gewisser H~** in this respect/in a certain sense; **in finanzieller H~** financially. **h~lich** prep (+ gen) regarding

hinstellen vt sep put or set down; park ⟨*Auto*⟩; (*fig*) make out (**als** to be); **sich h~** stand

hinstrecken vt sep hold out; **sich h~** extend

hintan|setzen, h~stellen vt sep ignore; (*vernachlässigen*) neglect

hinten adv at the back; **dort h~** back there; **nach/von h~** to the back/ from behind. **h~herum** adv round the back; (*fam*) by devious means; ⟨*erfahren*⟩ in a roundabout way

hinter prep (+ dat/acc) behind; (*nach*) after; **h~ jdm/etw herlaufen** run after s.o./sth; **h~ etw** (dat) **stecken** (*fig*) be behind sth; **h~ etw** (acc) **kommen** (*fig*) get to the bottom of sth; **etw h~ sich** (acc) **bringen** get sth over [and done] with. **H~bein** nt hind leg

Hinterbliebene pl (*Admin*) surviving dependants; **die H~n** the bereaved family sg

hinterbringen† vt tell (jdm s.o.)

hintere(r,s) a back, rear; **h~s Ende** far end

hintereinander adv one behind/(*zeitlich*) after the other; **dreimal h~** three times in succession/(*fam*) in a row

Hintergedanke m ulterior motive

hintergehen† vt deceive

Hinter|grund m background. **H~halt** m -[e]s,-e ambush; **aus dem**

H~halt überfallen ambush. **h~hältig** a underhand

hinterher adv behind, after; (*zeitlich*) afterwards. **h~gehen†** vi sep (*sein*) follow (jdm s.o.). **h~kommen†** vi sep (*sein*) follow [behind]. **h~laufen†** vi sep (*sein*) run after (jdm s.o.)

Hinter|hof m back yard. **H~kopf** m back of the head

hinterlassen† vt leave [behind]; (*Jur*) leave, bequeath (dat to). **H~schaft** f -,-en (*Jur*) estate

hinterlegen vt deposit

Hinter|leib m (*Zool*) abdomen. **H~list** f deceit. **h~listig** a deceitful, adv -ly. **h~m** prep = hinter dem. **H~mann** m (pl -männer) person behind. **h~n** prep = hinter den. **H~n** m -s,- (*fam*) bottom, backside. **H~rad** nt rear or back wheel. **h~rücks** adv from behind. **h~s** prep = hinter das. **h~ste(r,s)** a last; **h~ste Reihe** back row. **H~teil** nt (*fam*) behind

hintertreiben† vt (*fig*) block

Hinter|treppe f back stairs pl. **H~tür** f back door; (*fig*) loophole

hinterziehen† vt (*Admin*) evade

Hinterzimmer nt back room

hinüber adv over or across [there]. **h~gehen†** vi sep (*sein*) go over or across; **h~gehen über** (+ acc) cross

hinunter adv down [there]; **die Treppe/Straße h~** down the stairs/ road. **h~gehen†** vi sep (*sein*) go down. **h~schlucken** vt sep swallow

Hinweg m way there

hinweg adv away, off; **h~ über** (+ acc) over; **über eine Zeit h~** over a period. **h~gehen†** vi sep (*sein*) **h~gehen über** (+ acc) (*fig*) pass over. **h~kommen†** vi sep (*sein*) **h~kommen über** (+ acc) (*fig*) get over. **h~sehen†** vi sep (*haben*) **h~sehen über** (+acc) see over; (*fig*) overlook. **h~setzen (sich)** vr sep **sich h~setzen über** (+ acc) ignore

Hinweis m -es,-e reference; (*Andeutung*) hint; (*Anzeichen*) indication; **unter H~ auf** (+ acc) with reference to. **h~en†** v sep ● vi (*haben*) point (**auf** + acc to) ● vt jdn auf etw (acc) **h~en** point sth out to s.o. **h~end** a (*Gram*) demonstrative

hin|wenden† vt sep turn; **sich h~wenden** turn (**zu** to). **h~werfen†** vt sep throw down; drop ⟨*Bemerkung*⟩; (*schreiben*) jot down; (*zeichnen*) sketch; (*fam: aufgeben*) pack in

hinwieder adv on the other hand

hin|zeigen vi sep (haben) point (auf + acc to). **h~ziehen†** vt sep pull; (fig: in die Länge ziehen) drag out; (verzögern) delay; **sich h~ziehen** drag on; be delayed; **sich h~gezogen fühlen zu** (fig) feel drawn to

hinzu adv in addition. **h~fügen** vt sep add. **h~kommen†** vi sep (sein) be added; (ankommen) arrive [on the scene]; join (**zu jdm** s.o.). **h~rechnen** vt sep add. **h~ziehen†** vt sep call in

Hiobsbotschaft f bad news sg

Hirn nt -s brain; (Culin) brains pl. **H~gespinst** nt -[e]s,-e figment of the imagination. **H~hautentzündung** f meningitis. **h~verbrannt** a (fam) crazy

Hirsch m -[e]s,-e deer; (männlich) stag; (Culin) venison

Hirse f - millet

Hirt m -en,-en, **Hirte** m -n,-n shepherd

hissen vt hoist

Histor|iker m -s,- historian. **h~isch** a historical; (bedeutend) historic

Hit m -s,-s (Mus) hit

Hitz|e f - heat. **H~ewelle** f heat wave. **h~ig** a (fig) heated, adv -ly; (Person) hot-headed; (jähzornig) hot-tempered. **H~kopf** m hothead. **H~schlag** m heat-stroke

H-Milch /'ha:-/ f long-life milk

Hobby nt -s,-s hobby

Hobel m -s,- (Techn) plane; (Culin) slicer. **h~n** vt/i (haben) plane. **H~späne** mpl shavings

hoch a (höher, höchst; attrib hohe(r,s)) high; (Baum, Mast) tall; (Offizier) high-ranking; (Alter) great; (Summe) large; (Strafe) heavy; **hohe Schuhe** ankle boots ● adv high; (sehr) highly; **die Treppe/den Berg h~** up the stairs/hill; **sechs Mann h~** six of us/them. **H~** nt -s,-s cheer; (Meteorol) high

Hoch|achtung f high esteem. **H~achtungsvoll** adv Yours faithfully. **H~amt** nt High Mass. **h~arbeiten (sich)** vr sep work one's way up. **h~begabt** attrib a highly gifted. **H~betrieb** m great activity; **in den Geschäften herrscht H~betrieb** the shops are terribly busy. **H~burg** f (fig) stronghold. **H~deutsch** nt High German. **H~druck** m high pressure. **H~ebene** f plateau. **h~fahren†** vi sep (sein) go up; (auffahren) start up; (aufbrausen) flare up. **h~fliegend** a (fig) ambitious.

h~gehen† vi sep (sein) go up; (explodieren) blow up; (aufbrausen) flare up. **h~gestellt** attrib a high-ranking; (Zahl) superior. **h~gewachsen** a tall. **H~glanz** m high gloss. **h~gradig** a extreme, adv -ly. **h~hackig** a high-heeled. **h~halten†** vt sep hold up; (fig) uphold. **H~haus** nt high-rise building. **h~heben†** vt sep lift up; raise (Kopf, Hand). **h~herzig** a magnanimous, adv -ly. **h~kant** adv on end. **h~kommen†** vi sep (sein) come up; (aufstehen) get up; (fig) get on [in the world]. **H~konjunktur** f boom. **h~krempeln** vt sep roll up. **h~leben** vi sep (haben) **h~leben lassen** give three cheers for; … **lebe hoch!** three cheers for … ! **H~mut** m pride, arrogance. **h~mütig** a arrogant, adv -ly. **h~näsig** a (fam) snooty. **h~nehmen†** vt sep pick up; (fam) tease. **H~ofen** m blast-furnace. **h~ragen** vi sep rise [up]; (Turm:) soar. **H~ruf** m cheer. **H~saison** f high season. **H~schätzung** f high esteem. **h~schlagen†** vt sep turn up (Kragen). **h~schrecken†** vi sep (sein) start up. **H~schule** f university; (Musik-, Kunst-) academy. **h~sehen†** vi sep (haben) look up. **H~sommer** m midsummer. **H~spannung** f high/(fig) great tension. **h~spielen** vt sep (fig) magnify. **H~sprache** f standard language. **H~sprung** m high jump

höchst adv extremely, most

Hochstapler m -s,- confidence trickster

höchst|e(r,s) a highest; (Baum, Turm) tallest; (oberste, größte) top; **es ist h~e Zeit** it is high time. **h~ens** adv at most; (es sei denn) perhaps. **H~fall** m im **H~fall** at most. **H~geschwindigkeit** f top or maximum speed. **H~maß** nt maximum. **h~persönlich** adv in person. **H~preis** m top price. **H~temperatur** f maximum temperature. **h~wahrscheinlich** adv most probably

hoch|trabend a pompous, adv -ly. **h~treiben†** vt sep push up (Preis). **H~verrat** m high treason. **H~wasser** nt high tide; (Überschwemmung) floods pl. **h~würden** m -s Reverend; (Anrede) Father

Hochzeit f -,-en wedding; **H~ feiern** get married. **H~skleid** nt wedding

dress. H∼sreise *f* honeymoon [trip].
H∼stag *m* wedding day/(*Jahrestag*)
anniversary

hochziehen† *vt sep* pull up; (*hissen*)
hoist; raise ⟨*Augenbrauen*⟩

Hocke *f* - in der H∼ sitzen squat; **in
die H∼ gehen** squat down. **h∼n** *vi*
(*haben*) squat ● *vr* **sich h∼n** squat
down

Hocker *m* -s,- stool

Höcker *m* -s,- bump; (*Kamel*-) hump

Hockey /'hɔki/ *nt* -s hockey

Hode *f* -,-n, **Hoden** *m* -s,- testicle

Hof *m* -[e]s,-̈e [court]yard; (*Bauern*-)
farm; (*Königs*-) court; (*Schul*-) play-
ground; (*Astr*) halo

hoffen *vt/i* (*haben*) hope (**auf** + *acc*
for). **h∼tlich** *adv* I hope, let us hope;
(*als Antwort*) **h∼tlich/h∼tlich nicht**
let's hope so/not

Hoffnung *f* -,-en hope. **h∼slos** *a*
hopeless, *adv* -ly. **h∼svoll** *a* hopeful,
adv -ly

höflich *a* polite, *adv* -ly, courteous,
adv -ly. **H∼keit** *f* -,-en politeness,
courtesy; (*Äußerung*) civility

hohe(r,s) *a* s. **hoch**

Höhe *f* -,-n height; (*Aviat, Geog*) altitude; (*Niveau*) level; (*einer Summe*)
size; (*An*-) hill; **in die H∼ gehen** rise,
go up; **nicht auf der H∼** (*fam*) under
the weather; **das ist die H∼!** (*fam*)
that's the limit!

Hoheit *f* -,-en (*Staats*-) sovereignty;
(*Titel*) Highness. **H∼sgebiet** *nt* [sov-
ereign] territory. **H∼szeichen** *nt* national emblem

Höhe|nlinie *f* contour line.
H∼nsonne *f* sun-lamp. **H∼nzug** *m*
mountain range. **H∼punkt** *m* (*fig*)
climax, peak; (*einer Vorstellung*)
highlight. **h∼r** *a & adv* higher;
h∼re Schule secondary school

hohl *a* hollow; (*leer*) empty

Höhle *f* -,-n cave; (*Tier*-) den; (*Hohlraum*) cavity; (*Augen*-) socket

Hohl|maß *nt* measure of capacity.
H∼raum *m* cavity

Hohn *m* -s scorn, derision

höhn|en *vt* deride ● *vi* (*haben*) jeer.
h∼isch *a* scornful, *adv* -ly

holen *vt* fetch; get; (*kaufen*) buy;
(*nehmen*) take (**aus** from); **h∼ lassen**
send for; **[tief] Atem** *od* **Luft h∼** take
a [deep] breath; **sich** (*dat*) **etw h∼** get
sth; catch ⟨*Erkältung*⟩

Holland *nt* -s Holland

Holländ|er *m* -s,- Dutchman; **die
H∼er** the Dutch *pl*. **H∼erin** *f* -,-nen
Dutchwoman. **h∼isch** *a* Dutch

Höll|e *f* - hell. **h∼isch** *a* infernal;
(*schrecklich*) terrible, *adv* -bly

holpern *vi* (*sein*) jolt or bump along
● *vi* (*haben*) be bumpy

holp[e]rig *a* bumpy

Holunder *m* -s (*Bot*) elder

Holz *nt* -es,-̈er wood; (*Nutz*-) timber.
H∼blasinstrument *nt* woodwind
instrument

hölzern *a* wooden

Holz|hammer *m* mallet. **h∼ig** *a*
woody. **H∼kohle** *f* charcoal.
H∼schnitt *m* woodcut. **H∼schuh** *m*
[wooden] clog. **H∼wolle** *f* wood
shavings *pl*. **H∼wurm** *m* woodworm

homogen *a* homogeneous

Homöopathie *f* - homoeopathy

homosexuell *a* homosexual. **H∼e(r)**
m/f homosexual

Honig *m* -s honey. **H∼wabe** *f*
honeycomb

Hono|rar *nt* -s,-e fee. **h∼rieren** *vt*
remunerate; (*fig*) reward

Hopfen *m* -s hops *pl*; (*Bot*) hop

hopsen *vi* (*sein*) jump

Hör|apparat *m* hearing-aid. **h∼bar** *a*
audible, *adv* -bly

horchen *vi* (*haben*) listen (**auf** + *acc*
to); (*heimlich*) eavesdrop

Horde *f* -,-n horde; (*Gestell*) rack

hören *vt* hear; (*an*-) listen to ● *vi*
(*haben*) hear; (*horchen*) listen; (*gehorchen*) obey; **h∼ auf** (+ *acc*) listen
to. **H∼sagen** *nt* **vom H∼sagen** from
hearsay

Hör|er *m* -s,- listener; (*Teleph*)
receiver. **H∼funk** *m* radio. **H∼gerät**
nt hearing-aid

Horizon|t *m* -[e]s horizon. **h∼tal** *a*
horizontal, *adv* -ly

Hormon *nt* -s,-e hormone

Horn *nt* -s,-̈er horn. **H∼haut** *f* hard
skin; (*Augen*-) cornea

Hornisse *f* -,-n hornet

Horoskop *nt* -[e]s,-e horoscope

Hörrohr *nt* stethoscope

Horrorfilm *m* horror film

Hör|saal *m* (*Univ*) lecture hall.
H∼spiel *nt* radio play

Hort *m* -[e]s,-e (*Schatz*) hoard; (*fig*)
refuge. **h∼en** *vt* hoard

Hortensie /-iə/ *f* -,-n hydrangea

Hörweite *f* **in/außer H∼** within/out of
earshot

Hose *f* -,-n, **Hosen** *pl* trousers *pl*.
H∼nrock *m* culottes *pl*. **H∼nschlitz**

m fly, flies *pl.* H∼**nträger** *mpl*
braces, (*Amer*) suspenders

Hostess, Hosteß *f* -,-**tessen** hostess;
(*Aviat*) air hostess

Hostie /'hɔstjə/ *f* -,-**n** (*Relig*) host

Hotel *nt* -**s**,-**s** hotel; H∼ **garni** /gar'ni:/
bed-and-breakfast hotel. H∼**ier**
/-'lje:/ *m* -**s**,-**s** hotelier

hübsch *a* pretty, *adv* -ily; (*nett*) nice,
adv -ly; ⟨*Summe*⟩ tidy

Hubschrauber *m* -**s**,- helicopter

huckepack *adv* **jdn** h∼ **tragen** give
s.o. a piggyback

Huf *m* -[**e**]**s**,-**e** hoof. H∼**eisen** *nt*
horseshoe

Hüft|e *f* -,-**n** hip. H∼**gürtel**, H∼**halter**
m -**s**,- girdle

Hügel *m* -**s**,- hill. h∼**ig** *a* hilly

Huhn *nt* -**s**,-̈**er** chicken; (*Henne*) hen

Hühn|chen *nt* -**s**,- chicken. H∼**er-**
auge *nt* corn. H∼**erbrühe** *f* chicken
broth. H∼**erstall** *m* henhouse,
chicken-coop

huldig|en *vi* (*haben*) pay homage (*dat*
to). H∼**ung** *f* - homage

Hülle *f* -,-**n** cover; (*Verpackung*) wrap-
ping; (*Platten-*) sleeve; **in** H∼ **und**
Fülle in abundance. h∼**n** *vt* wrap

Hülse *f* -,-**n** (*Bot*) pod; (*Etui*) case.
H∼**nfrüchte** *fpl* pulses

human *a* humane, *adv* -ly. h∼**itär** *a*
humanitarian. H∼**ität** *f* - humanity

Hummel *f* -,-**n** bumble-bee

Hummer *m* -**s**,- lobster

Hum|or *m* -**s** humour; H∼**or haben**
have a sense of humour. h∼**oris-**
tisch *a* humorous. h∼**orvoll** *a* humorous, *adv* -ly

humpeln *vi* (*sein/haben*) hobble

Humpen *m* -**s**,- tankard

Hund *m* -[**e**]**s**,-**e** dog; (*Jagd-*) hound.
H∼**ehalsband** *nt* dog-collar. H∼**e-**
hütte *f* kennel. H∼**eleine** *f* dog lead

hundert *inv a* one/a hundred. H∼ *nt*
-**s**,-**e** hundred; H∼**e von** hundreds of.
H∼**jahrfeier** *f* centenary, (*Amer*)
centennial. h∼**prozentig** *a & adv*
one hundred per cent. h∼**ste(r,s)** *a*
hundredth. H∼**stel** *nt* -**s**,- hundredth

Hündin *f* -,-**nen** bitch

Hüne *m* -**n**,-**n** giant

Hunger *m* -**s** hunger; H∼ **haben** be
hungry. h∼**n** *vi* (*haben*) starve;
h∼**n nach** (*fig*) hunger for. H∼**snot** *f*
famine

hungrig *a* hungry, *adv* -ily

Hupe *f* -,-**n** (*Auto*) horn. h∼**n** *vi*
(*haben*) sound one's horn

hüpf|en *vi* (*sein*) skip; ⟨*Vogel,*
Frosch:⟩ hop; ⟨*Grashüpfer:*⟩ jump.
H∼**er** *m* -**s**,- skip, hop

Hürde *f* -,-**n** (*Sport & fig*) hurdle;
(*Schaf-*) pen, fold

Hure *f* -,-**n** whore

hurra *int* hurray. H∼ *nt* -**s**,-**s** hurray;
(*Beifallsruf*) cheer

Husche *f* -,-**n** [short] shower. h∼**n** *vi*
(*sein*) slip; ⟨*Eidechse:*⟩ dart; ⟨*Maus:*⟩
scurry; ⟨*Lächeln:*⟩ flit

hüsteln *vi* (*haben*) give a slight cough

husten *vi* (*haben*) cough. H∼ *m* -**s**
cough. H∼**saft** *m* cough mixture

Hut[1] *m* -[**e**]**s**,-̈**e** hat; (*Pilz-*) cap

Hut[2] *f* - **auf der** H∼ **sein** be on one's
guard (**vor** + *dat* against)

hüten *vt* watch over; tend ⟨*Tiere*⟩;
(*aufpassen*) look after; **das Bett** h∼
müssen be confined to bed; **sich** h∼
be on one's guard (**vor** + *dat*
against); **sich** h∼**, etw zu tun** take
care not to do sth

Hütte *f* -,-**n** hut; (*Hunde-*) kennel;
(*Techn*) iron and steel works.
H∼**nkäse** *m* cottage cheese.
H∼**nkunde** *f* metallurgy

Hyäne *f* -,-**n** hyena

Hybride *f* -,-**n** hybrid

Hydrant *m* -**en**,-**en** hydrant

hydraulisch *a* hydraulic, *adv* -ally

hydroelektrisch /hydroʔe'lɛktrɪʃ/ *a*
hydroelectric

Hygien|e /hy'gie:nə/ *f* - hygiene.
h∼**isch** *a* hygienic, *adv* -ally

hypermodern *a* ultra-modern

Hypno|se *f* - hypnosis. h∼**tisch** *a*
hypnotic. H∼**tiseur** /-'zøːɐ/ *m* -**s**,-**e**
hypnotist. h∼**tisieren** *vt* hypnotize

Hypochonder /hypo'xɔndɐ/ *m* -**s**,-
hypochondriac

Hypothek *f* -,-**en** mortgage

Hypothe|se *f* -,-**n** hypothesis.
h∼**tisch** *a* hypothetical, *adv* -ly

Hys|terie *f* - hysteria. h∼**terisch** *a*
hysterical, *adv* -ly

I

ich *pron* I; **ich bin's** it's me. **Ich** *nt*
-[**s**],-[**s**] self; (*Psych*) ego

IC-Zug /i'tse:-/ *m* inter-city train

ideal *a* ideal. I∼ *nt* -**s**,-**e** ideal.
i∼**isieren** *vt* idealize. I∼**ismus** *m* -
idealism. I∼**ist(in)** *m* -**en**,-**en** (*f*
-,-**nen**) idealist. i∼**istisch** *a* idealistic

Idee f -,-n idea; **fixe I~** obsession; **eine I~** (fam: wenig) a tiny bit
identifizieren vt identify
identi|sch a identical. **I~tät** f -,-en identity
Ideo|logie f -,-n ideology. **i~logisch** a ideological
idiomatisch a idiomatic
Idiot m -en,-en idiot. **i~isch** a idiotic, adv -ally
Idol nt -s,-e idol
idyllisch /i'dʏlɪʃ/ a idyllic
Igel m -s,- hedgehog
ignorieren vt ignore
ihm pron (dat of **er, es**) [to] him; (Ding, Tier) [to] it; **Freunde von ihm** friends of his
ihn pron (acc of **er**) him; (Ding, Tier) it. **i~en** pron (dat of **sie** pl) [to] them; **Freunde von i~en** friends of theirs. **I~en** pron (dat of **Sie**) [to] you; **Freunde von I~en** friends of yours
ihr pron (2nd pers pl) you ● (dat of **sie** sg) [to] her; (Ding, Tier) [to] it; **Freunde von ihr** friends of hers ● poss pron her; (Ding, Tier) its; (pl) their. **Ihr** poss pron your. **i~e(r,s)** poss pron hers; (pl) theirs. **I~e(r,s)** poss pron yours. **i~erseits** adv for her/(pl) their part. **I~erseits** adv on your part. **i~etwegen** adv for her/(Ding, Tier) its/(pl) their sake; (wegen) because of her/it/them, on her/its/their account. **I~etwegen** adv for your sake; (wegen) because of you, on your account. **i~etwillen** adv um **i~etwillen** for her/(Ding, Tier) its/(pl) their sake. **I~etwillen** adv um **I~etwillen** for your sake. **i~ige** poss pron **der/die/das i~ige** hers; (pl) theirs. **I~ige** poss pron **der/die/das I~ige** yours. **i~s** poss pron hers; (pl) theirs. **I~s** poss pron yours
Ikone f -,-n icon
illegal a illegal, adv -ly
Illus|ion f -,-en illusion; **sich** (dat) **I~ionen machen** delude oneself. **i~orisch** a illusory
Illustr|ation /-'tsio:n/ f -,-en illustration. **i~ieren** vt illustrate. **I~ierte** f -n,-[n] [illustrated] magazine
Iltis m -ses,-se polecat
im prep = **in dem**; **im Mai** in May; **im Kino** at the cinema
Image /'ɪmɪdʒ/ nt -[s],-s /-ɪs/ [public] image
Imbiß m snack. **I~halle, I~stube** f snack-bar

Imit|ation /-'tsio:n/ f -,-en imitation. **i~ieren** vt imitate
Imker m -s,- bee-keeper
Immatrikul|ation /-'tsio:n/ f - (Univ) enrolment. **i~ieren** vt (Univ) enrol; **sich i~ieren** enrol
immer adv always; **für i~** for ever; (endgültig) for good; **i~ noch** still; **i~ mehr/weniger/wieder** more and more/less and less/again and again; **wer/was [auch] i~** whoever/whatever. **i~fort** adv = **i~zu. i~grün** a evergreen. **i~hin** adv (wenigstens) at least; (trotzdem) all the same; (schließlich) after all. **i~zu** adv all the time
Immobilien /-iən/ pl real estate sg. **I~händler, I~makler** m estate agent, (Amer) realtor
immun a immune (**gegen** to). **i~isieren** vt immunize. **I~ität** f - immunity
Imperativ m -s,-e imperative
Imperfekt nt -s,-e imperfect
Imperialismus m - imperialism
impf|en vt vaccinate, inoculate. **I~stoff** m vaccine. **I~ung** f -,-en vaccination, inoculation
Implantat nt -[e]s,-e implant
imponieren vi (haben) impress (**jdm** s.o.)
Impor|t m -[e]s,-e import. **I~teur** /-'tø:ɐ̯/ m -s,-e importer. **i~tieren** vt import
imposant a imposing
impoten|t a (Med) impotent. **I~z** f - (Med) impotence
imprägnieren vt waterproof
Impressionismus m - impressionism
improvisieren vt/i (haben) improvise
Impuls m -es,-e impulse. **i~iv** a impulsive, adv -ly
imstande pred a able (**zu** to); capable (**etw zu tun** of doing sth)
in prep (+ dat) in; (+ acc) into, in; (bei Bus, Zug) on; **in der Schule/Oper** at school/the opera; **in die Schule** to school ● **a in sein** be in
Inbegriff m embodiment. **i~en** pred a included
Inbrunst f - fervour
inbrünstig a fervent, adv -ly
indem conj (während) while; (dadurch) by (+ -ing)
Inder(in) m -s,- (f -,-nen) Indian
indessen conj while ● adv (unterdessen) meanwhile; (jedoch) however

Indian *m* -s,-e (*Aust*) turkey

Indian|er(in) *m* -s,- (*f* -,-nen) (American) Indian. **i~isch** *a* Indian

Indien /'ɪndjən/ *nt* -s India

indigniert *a* indignant, *adv* -ly

Indikativ *m* -s,-e indicative

indirekt *a* indirect, *adv* -ly

indisch *a* Indian

indiskre|t *a* indiscreet. **I~tion** /-'tsjo:n/ *f* -,-en indiscretion

indiskutabel *a* out of the question

indisponiert *a* indisposed

Individu|alist *m* -en,-en individualist. **I~alität** *f* - individuality. **i~ell** *a* individual, *adv* -ly. **I~um** /-'vi:duom/ *nt* -s,-duen individual

Indizienbeweis /ɪn'di:tsjən-/ *m* circumstantial evidence

indoktrinieren *vt* indoctrinate

industr|ialisiert *a* industrialized. **I~ie** *f* -,-n industry. **i~iell** *a* industrial. **I~ielle(r)** *m* industrialist

ineinander *adv* in/into one another

Infanterie *f* - infantry

Infektion /-'tsjo:n/ *f* -,-en infection. **I~skrankheit** *f* infectious disease

Infinitiv *m* -s,-e infinitive

infizieren *vt* infect; **sich i~** become/⟨*Person:*⟩ be infected

Inflation /-'tsjo:n/ *f* - inflation. **i~är** *a* inflationary

infolge *prep* (+*gen*) as a result of. **i~dessen** *adv* consequently

Inform|atik *f* - information science. **I~ation** /-'tsjo:n/ *f* -,-en information; **I~ationen** information *sg*. **i~ieren** *vt* inform; **sich i~ieren** find out (**über** + *acc* about)

infrarot *a* infra-red

Ingenieur /ɪnʒe'njø:ɐ/ *m* -s,-e engineer

Ingwer *m* -s ginger

Inhaber(in) *m* -s,- (*f* -,-nen) holder; (*Besitzer*) proprietor; (*Scheck-*) bearer

inhaftieren *vt* take into custody

inhalieren *vt/i* (*haben*) inhale

Inhalt *m* -[e]s,-e contents *pl*; (*Bedeutung, Gehalt*) content; (*Geschichte*) story. **I~sangabe** *f* summary. **I~sverzeichnis** *nt* list/(*in Buch*) table of contents

Initiale /-'tsja:lə/ *f* -,-n initial

Initiative /initsja'ti:və/ *f* -,-n initiative

Injektion /-'tsjo:n/ *f* -,-en injection. **injizieren** *vt* inject

inklusive *prep* (+*gen*) including ● *adv* inclusive

inkognito *adv* incognito

inkonsequen|t *a* inconsistent, *adv* -ly. **I~z** *f* -,-en inconsistency

inkorrekt *a* incorrect, *adv* -ly

Inkubationszeit /-'tsjo:ns-/ *f* (*Med*) incubation period

Inland *nt* -[e]s home country; (*Binnenland*) interior. **I~sgespräch** *nt* inland call

inmitten *prep* (+*gen*) in the middle of; (*unter*) amongst ● *adv* **i~ von** amongst, amidst

inne|haben† *vt sep* hold, have. **i~halten†** *vi sep* (*haben*) pause

innen *adv* inside; **nach i~** inwards. **I~architekt(in)** *m(f)* interior designer. **I~minister** *m* Minister of the Interior; (*in UK*) Home Secretary. **I~politik** *f* domestic policy. **I~stadt** *f* town centre

inner|e(r,s) *a* inner; (*Med, Pol*) internal. **I~e(s)** *nt* interior; (*Mitte*) centre; (*fig: Seele*) inner being. **I~eien** *fpl* (*Culin*) offal *sg*. **i~halb** *prep* (+*gen*) inside; (*zeitlich & fig*) within; (*während*) during ● *adv* **i~halb von** within. **i~lich** *a* internal; (*seelisch*) inner; (*besinnlich*) introspective ● *adv* internally; (*im Inneren*) inwardly. **i~ste(r,s)** innermost; **im I~sten** (*fig*) deep down

innig *a* sincere, *adv* -ly; (*tief*) deep, *adv* -ly; (*eng*) intimate, *adv* -ly

Innung *f* -,-en guild

inoffiziell *a* unofficial, *adv* -ly

ins *prep* = **in das**; **ins Kino/Büro** to the cinema/office

Insasse *m* -n,-n inmate; (*im Auto*) occupant; (*Passagier*) passenger

insbesondere *adv* especially

Inschrift *f* inscription

Insekt *nt* -[e]s,-en insect. **I~envertilgungsmittel** *nt* insecticide

Insel *f* -,-n island

Inser|at *nt* -[e]s,-e [newspaper] advertisement. **I~ent** *m* -en,-en advertiser. **i~ieren** *vt/i* (*haben*) advertise

insge|heim *adv* secretly. **i~samt** *adv* [all] in all

Insignien /-jən/ *pl* insignia

insofern, insoweit *adv* /-'zo:-/ in this respect; **i~ als** in as much as ● *conj* /-zo'fɛrn, -'vaɪt/ **i~ als** in so far as

Insp|ektion /ɪnspɛk'tsjo:n/ *f* -,-en inspection. **I~ektor** *m* -en,-en /-'to:rən/ inspector

Inspir|ation /ɪnspira'tsjo:n/ *f* -,-en inspiration. **i~ieren** *vt* inspire

inspizieren /-sp-/ *vt* inspect

Install|ateur /ɪnstala'tøːɐ̯/ *m* -s,-e fitter; (*Klempner*) plumber. **i~ieren** *vt* install

instand *adv* ~ **halten** maintain; (*pflegen*) look after; (*reparieren*) repair. **I~haltung** *f* - maintenance, upkeep

inständig *a* urgent, *adv* -ly

Instandsetzung *f* - repair

Instant- /'ɪnstənt-/ *pref* instant

Instanz /-st-/ *f* -,-en authority

Instinkt /-st-/ *m* -[e]s,-e instinct. **i~iv** *a* instinctive, *adv* -ly

Institu|t /-st-/ *nt* -[e]s,-e institute. **I~tion** /-'tsi̯oːn/ *f* -,-en institution

Instrument /-st-/ *nt* -[e]s,-e instrument. **I~almusik** *f* instrumental music

Insulin *nt* -s insulin

inszenier|en *vt* (*Theat*) produce. **I~ung** *f* -,-en production

Integr|ation /-'tsi̯oːn/ *f* - integration. **i~ieren** *vt* integrate; **sich i~ieren** integrate. **I~ität** *f* - integrity

Intellekt *m* -[e]s intellect. **i~uell** *a* intellectual

intelligen|t *a* intelligent, *adv* -ly. **I~z** *f* - intelligence; (*Leute*) intelligentsia

Intendant *m* -en,-en director

Intens|ität *f* - intensity. **i~iv** *a* intensive, *adv* -ly. **i~ivieren** *vt* intensify. **I~ivstation** *f* intensive-care unit

inter|essant *a* interesting. **I~esse** *nt* -s,-n interest; **I~esse haben** be interested (**an** + *dat* in). **I~essengruppe** *f* pressure group. **I~essent** *m* -en,-en interested party; (*Käufer*) prospective buyer. **i~essieren** *vt* interest; **sich i~essieren** be interested (**für** in)

intern *a* (*fig*) internal, *adv* -ly

Inter|nat *nt* -[e]s,-e boarding school. **i~national** *a* international, *adv* -ly. **i~nieren** *vt* intern. **I~nierung** *f* - internment. **I~nist** *m* -en, -en specialist in internal diseases. **I~pretation** /-'tsi̯oːn/ *f* -,-en interpretation. **i~pretieren** *vt* interpret. **I~punktion** /-'tsi̯oːn/ *f* - punctuation. **I~rogativpronomen** *nt* interrogative pronoun. **I~vall** *nt* -s,-e interval. **I~vention** /-'tsi̯oːn/ *f* -,-en intervention

Interview /'ɪntɐvjuː/ *nt* -s,-s interview. **i~en** /-'vjuːən/ *vt* interview

intim *a* intimate, *adv* -ly. **I~ität** *f* -,-en intimacy

intoleran|t *a* intolerant. **I~z** *f* - intolerance

intransitiv *a* intransitive, *adv* -ly

intravenös *a* intravenous, *adv* -ly

Intrig|e *f* -,-n intrigue. **i~ieren** *vi* (*haben*) plot

introvertiert *a* introverted

Intui|tion /-'tsi̯oːn/ *f* -,-en intuition. **i~tiv** *a* intuitive, *adv* -ly

Invalidenrente *f* disability pension

Invasion *f* -,-en invasion

Inven|tar *nt* -s,-e furnishings and fittings *pl*; (*Techn*) equipment; (*Bestand*) stock; (*Liste*) inventory. **I~tur** *f* -,-en stock-taking

investieren *vt* invest

inwendig *a* & *adv* inside

inwiefern *adv* in what way. **i~weit** *adv* how far, to what extent

Inzest *m* -[e]s incest

inzwischen *adv* in the meantime

Irak (der) -[s] Iraq. **i~isch** *a* Iraqi

Iran (der) -[s] Iran. **i~isch** *a* Iranian

irdisch *a* earthly

Ire *m* -n,-n Irishman; **die I~n** the Irish *pl*

irgend *adv* **i~ jemand/etwas** someone/something; (*fragend, verneint*) anyone/anything; **wer/was/wann i~** whoever/whatever/whenever; **wenn i~ möglich** if at all possible. **i~ein** *indef art* some/any; **i~ein anderer** someone/anyone else. **i~eine(r,s)** *pron* any one; (*jemand*) someone/anyone. **i~wann** *pron* at some time [or other]/at any time. **i~was** *pron* (*fam*) something [or other]/anything. **i~welche(r,s)** *pron* any. **i~wer** *pron* someone/anyone. **i~wie** *adv* somehow [or other]. **i~wo** *adv* somewhere/anywhere; **i~wo anders** somewhere else

Irin *f* -,-nen Irishwoman

Iris *f* -,- (*Anat, Bot*) iris

irisch *a* Irish

Irland *nt* -s Ireland

Ironie *f* - irony

ironisch *a* ironic, *adv* -ally

irr *a* = **irre**

irrational *a* irrational

irre *a* mad, crazy; (*fam: gewaltig*) incredible, *adv* -bly; **i~ werden** get confused. **I~(r)** *m/f* lunatic. **i~führen** *vt sep* (*fig*) mislead. **i~gehen†** *vi sep* (*sein*) lose one's way; (*sich täuschen*) be wrong

irrelevant *a* irrelevant

irre|machen *vt sep* confuse. **i~n** *vi/r* (*haben*) [**sich**] **i~n** be mistaken; **wenn ich mich nicht i~** if I am not

mistaken ● *vi* (*sein*) wander. **I∼nanstalt** *f*, **I∼nhaus** *nt* lunatic asylum. **i∼reden** *vi sep* (*haben*) ramble

Irr|garten *m* maze. **i∼ig** *a* erroneous
irritieren *vt* irritate

Irr|sinn *m* madness, lunacy. **i∼sinnig** *a* mad; (*fam: gewaltig*) incredible, *adv* -bly. **I∼tum** *m* -s,ˑer mistake. **i∼tümlich** *a* mistaken, *adv* -ly

Ischias *m* & *nt* - sciatica

Islam (der) -[s] Islam. **islamisch** *a* Islamic

Island *nt* -s Iceland

Isolier|band *nt* insulating tape. **i∼en** *vt* isolate; (*Phys, Electr*) insulate; (*gegen Schall*) soundproof. **I∼ung** *f* - isolation; insulation; soundproofing

Israel /'ɪsraeːl/ *nt* -s Israel. **I∼eli** *m* -[s],-s & *f* -,-[s] Israeli. **i∼elisch** *a* Israeli

ist *s.* sein; **er ist** he is

Ital|ien /-jən/ *nt* -s Italy. **I∼iener(in)** *m* -s,- (*f* -,-nen) Italian. **i∼ienisch** *a* Italian. **I∼ienisch** *nt* -[s] (*Lang*) Italian

J

ja *adv* yes; **ich glaube ja** I think so; **'ja nicht!** not on any account! **seid 'ja vorsichtig!** whatever you do, be careful! **da seid ihr ja!** there you are! **das ist es ja** that's just it; **das mag ja wahr sein** that may well be true

Jacht *f* -,-en yacht

Jacke *f* -,-n jacket; (*Strick-*) cardigan

Jackett /ʒa'kɛt/ *nt* -s,-s jacket

Jade *m* -[s] & *f* - jade

Jagd *f* -,-en hunt; (*Schießen*) shoot; (*Jagen*) hunting; shooting; (*fig*) pursuit (**nach** of); **auf die J∼ gehen** go hunting/shooting. **J∼flugzeug** *nt* fighter aircraft. **J∼gewehr** *nt* sporting gun. **J∼hund** *m* gun-dog; (*Hetzhund*) hound

jagen *vt* hunt; (*schießen*) shoot; (*verfolgen, wegjagen*) chase; (*treiben*) drive; **sich j∼** chase each other; **in die Luft j∼** blow up ● *vi* (*haben*) hunt, go hunting/shooting; (*fig*) chase (**nach** after) ● *vi* (*sein*) race, dash

Jäger *m* -s,- hunter

jäh *a* sudden, *adv* -ly; (*steil*) steep, *adv* -ly

Jahr *nt* -[e]s,-e year. **J∼buch** *nt* yearbook. **j∼elang** *adv* for years. **J∼estag** *m* anniversary. **J∼eszahl** *f* year. **J∼eszeit** *f* season. **J∼gang** *m* year; (*Wein*) vintage. **J∼hundert** *nt* century. **J∼hundertfeier** *f* centenary, (*Amer*) centennial

jährlich *a* annual, yearly ● *adv* annually, yearly

Jahr|markt *m* fair. **J∼tausend** *nt* millennium. **J∼zehnt** *nt* -[e]s,-e decade

Jähzorn *m* violent temper. **j∼ig** *a* hot-tempered

Jalousie /ʒalu'ziː/ *f* -,-n venetian blind

Jammer *m* -s misery; (*Klagen*) lamenting; **es ist ein J∼** it is a shame

jämmerlich *a* miserable, *adv* -bly; (*mitleiderregend*) pitiful, *adv* -ly

jammer|n *vi* (*haben*) lament ● *vt* **jdn j∼n** arouse s.o.'s pity. **j∼schade** *a* **j∼schade sein** (*fam*) be a terrible shame

Jänner *m* -s,- (*Aust*) January

Januar *m* -s,-e January

Jap|an *nt* -s Japan. **J∼aner(in)** *m* -s,- (*f* -,-nen) Japanese. **j∼anisch** *a* Japanese. **J∼anisch** *nt* -[s] (*Lang*) Japanese

Jargon /ʒar'gõː/ *m* -s jargon

jäten *vt/i* (*haben*) weed

jauchzen *vi* (*haben*) (*liter*) exult

jaulen *vi* (*haben*) yelp

Jause *f* -,-n (*Aust*) snack

jawohl *adv* yes

Jawort *nt* **jdm sein J∼ geben** accept s.o.'s proposal [of marriage]

Jazz /jats, dʒɛs/ *m* - jazz

je *adv* (*jemals*) ever; (*jeweils*) each; (*pro*) per; **je nach** according to; **seit eh und je** always; **besser denn je** better than ever ● *conj* **je mehr, desto** *od* **um so besser** the more the better ● *prep* (+ *acc*) per

Jeans /dʒiːns/ *pl* jeans

jed|e(r,s) *pron* every; (*j∼ einzelne*) each; (*j∼ beliebige*) any; (*substantivisch*) everyone; each one; anyone; **ohne j∼en Grund** without any reason. **j∼enfalls** *adv* in any case; (*wenigstens*) at least. **j∼ermann** *pron* everyone. **j∼erzeit** *adv* at any time. **j∼esmal** *adv* every time; **j∼esmal wenn** whenever

jedoch *adv* & *conj* however

jeher *adv* **von** *od* **seit j∼** always

jemals *adv* ever

jemand *pron* someone, somebody; (*fragend, verneint*) anyone, anybody

jen|e(r,s) *pron* that; (*pl*) those; (*substantivisch*) that one; (*pl*) those. **j~seits** *prep* (+*gen*) [on] the other side of

jetzig *a* present; ⟨*Preis*⟩ current. **jetzt** *adv* now. **J~zeit** *f* present

jeweil|ig *a* respective. **j~s** *adv* at a time

jiddisch *a*, **J~** *nt* -[s] Yiddish

Job /dʒɔp/ *m* -s,-s job. **j~ben** *vi* (*haben*) (*fam*) work

Joch *nt* -[e]s,-e yoke

Jockei, Jockey /'dʒɔki/ *m* -s,-s jockey

Jod *nt* -[e]s iodine

jodeln *vi* (*haben*) yodel

Joga *m* & *nt* -[s] yoga

jogg|en /'dʒɔgən/ *vi* (*haben/sein*) jog. **J~ing** *nt* -[s] jogging

Joghurt *m* & *nt* -[s] yoghurt

Johannisbeere *f* redcurrant; **schwarze J~** blackcurrant

johlen *vi* (*haben*) yell; (*empört*) jeer

Joker *m* -s,- (*Karte*) joker

Jolle *f* -,-n dinghy

Jongl|eur /ʒõ'gløːɐ̯/ *m* -s,-e juggler. **j~ieren** *vi* (*haben*) juggle

Joppe *f* -,-n [thick] jacket

Jordanien /-jən/ *nt* -s Jordan

Journalis|mus /ʒʊrna'lɪsmʊs/ *m* - journalism. **J~t(in)** *m* -en,-en (*f* -,-nen) journalist

Jubel *m* -s rejoicing, jubilation. **j~n** *vi* (*haben*) rejoice

Jubil|ar(in) *m* -s,-e (*f* -,-nen) person celebrating an anniversary. **J~äum** *nt* -s,-äen jubilee; (*Jahrestag*) anniversary

juck|en *vi* (*haben*) itch; **sich j~en** scratch; **es j~t mich** I have an itch; (*fam: möchte*) I'm itching (**zu** to). **J~reiz** *m* itch[ing]

Jude *m* -n,-n Jew. **J~ntum** *nt* -s Judaism; (*Juden*) Jewry

Jüd|in *f* -,-nen Jewess. **j~isch** *a* Jewish

Judo *nt* -[s] judo

Jugend *f* - youth; (*junge Leute*) young people *pl*. **J~herberge** *f* youth hostel. **J~klub** *m* youth club. **J~kriminalität** *f* juvenile delinquency. **j~lich** *a* youthful. **J~liche(r)** *m/f* young man/woman; (*Admin*) juvenile; **J~liche** *pl* young people. **J~stil** *m* art nouveau. **J~zeit** *f* youth

Jugoslaw|ien /-jən/ *nt* -s Yugoslavia. **j~isch** *a* Yugoslav

Juli *m* -[s],-s July

jung *a* (jünger, jüngst) young; ⟨*Wein*⟩ new ● *pron* **j~** und **alt** young and old. **J~e** *m* -n,-n boy. **J~e(s)** *nt* young animal/bird; (*Katzen-*) kitten; (*Bären-, Löwen-*) cub; (*Hunde-, Seehund-*) pup; **die J~en** the young *pl*. **j~enhaft** *a* boyish

Jünger *m* -s,- disciple

Jungfer *f* -,-n **alte J~** old maid. **J~nfahrt** *f* maiden voyage

Jung|frau *f* virgin; (*Astr*) Virgo. **j~fräulich** *a* virginal. **J~geselle** *m* bachelor

Jüngling *m* -s,-e youth

jüngst|e(r,s) *a* youngest; (*neueste*) latest; **in j~er Zeit** recently

Juni *m* -[s],-s June

Junior *m* -s,-en /-'oːrən/ junior

Jura *pl* law *sg*

Jurist|(in) *m* -en,-en (*f* -,-nen) lawyer. **j~isch** *a* legal, *adv* -ly

Jury /ʒy'riː/ *f* -,-s jury; (*Sport*) judges *pl*

justieren *vt* adjust

Justiz *f* - **die J~** justice. **J~irrtum** *m* miscarriage of justice. **J~minister** *m* Minister of Justice

Juwel *nt* -s,-en & (*fig*) -e jewel. **J~ier** *m* -s,-e jeweller

Jux *m* -es,-e (*fam*) joke; **aus Jux** for fun

K

Kabarett *nt* -s,-s & -e cabaret

kabbelig *a* choppy

Kabel *nt* -s,- cable. **K~fernsehen** *nt* cable television

Kabeljau *m* -s,-e & -s cod

Kabine *f* -,-n cabin; (*Umkleide-*) cubicle; (*Telefon-*) booth; (*einer K~nbahn*) car. **K~nbahn** *f* cable-car

Kabinett *nt* -s,-e (*Pol*) Cabinet

Kabriolett *nt* -s,-s convertible

Kachel *f* -,-n tile. **k~n** *vt* tile

Kadaver *m* -s,- carcass

Kadenz *f* -,-en (*Mus*) cadence; (*für Solisten*) cadenza

Kadett *m* -en,-en cadet

Käfer *m* -s,- beetle

Kaff *nt* -s,-s (*fam*) dump

Kaffee /'kafe:, ka'fe:/ *m* -s,-s coffee; (*Mahlzeit*) afternoon coffee.

K∼grund *m* = K∼satz. K∼kanne *f* coffee-pot. K∼maschine *f* coffee-maker. K∼mühle *f* coffee-grinder. K∼satz *m* coffee-grounds *pl*

Käfig *m* -s,-e cage

kahl *a* bare; (*haarlos*) bald. k∼geschoren *a* shaven. k∼köpfig *a* bald-headed

Kahn *m* -s,-e boat; (*Last*-) barge

Kai *m* -s,-s quay

Kaiser *m* -s,- emperor. K∼in *f* -,-nen empress. k∼lich *a* imperial. K∼reich *nt* empire. K∼schnitt *m* Caesarean [section]

Kajüte *f* -,-n (*Naut*) cabin

Kakao /ka'kau/ *m* -s cocoa

Kakerlak *m* -s & -en,-en cockroach

Kaktee /kak'te:ə/ *f* -,-n, **Kaktus** *m* -,-teen /-'te:ən/ cactus

Kalb *nt* -[e]s,-er calf. K∼fleisch *nt* veal

Kalender *m* -s,- calendar; (*Taschen*-, *Termin*-) diary

Kaliber *nt* -s,- calibre; (*Gewehr*-) bore

Kalium *nt* -s potassium

Kalk *m* -[e]s,-e lime; (*Kalzium*) calcium. k∼en *vt* whitewash. K∼stein *m* limestone

Kalkul|ation /-'tsịo:n/ *f* -,-en calculation. k∼ieren *vt/i* (*haben*) calculate

Kalorie *f* -,-n calorie

kalt *a* (kälter, kältest) cold; es ist k∼ it is cold; mir ist k∼ I am cold. k∼blütig *a* cold-blooded, *adv* -ly; (*ruhig*) cool, *adv* -ly

Kälte *f* - cold; (*Gefühls*-) coldness; **10 Grad K∼** 10 degrees below zero. K∼welle *f* cold spell

kalt|herzig *a* cold-hearted. k∼schnäuzig *a* (*fam*) cold, *adv* -ly

Kalzium *nt* -s calcium

Kamel *nt* -s,-e camel; (*fam: Idiot*) fool

Kamera *f* -,-s camera

Kamerad|(in) *m* -en,-en (*f* -,-nen) companion; (*Freund*) mate; (*Mil, Pol*) comrade. K∼schaft *f* - comradeship

Kameramann *m* (*pl* -männer & -leute) cameraman

Kamille *f* - camomile

Kamin *m* -s,-e fireplace; (*SGer: Schornstein*) chimney. K∼feger *m* -s,- (*SGer*) chimney-sweep

Kamm *m* -[e]s,-e comb; (*Berg*-) ridge; (*Zool, Wellen*-) crest

kämmen *vt* comb; jdn/sich k∼ comb s.o.'s/one's hair

Kammer *f* -,-n small room; (*Techn, Biol, Pol*) chamber. K∼diener *m* valet. K∼musik *f* chamber music

Kammgarn *nt* (*Tex*) worsted

Kampagne /kam'panjə/ *f* -,-n (*Pol, Comm*) campaign

Kampf *m* -es,-e fight; (*Schlacht*) battle; (*Wett*-) contest; (*fig*) struggle; **schwere K∼e** heavy fighting *sg*; **den K∼ ansagen** (+*dat*) (*fig*) declare war on

kämpf|en *vi* (*haben*) fight; sich k∼en durch fight one's way through. K∼er(in) *m* -s,- (*f* -,-nen) fighter

kampf|los *adv* without a fight. K∼richter *m* (*Sport*) judge

kampieren *vi* (*haben*) camp

Kanada *nt* -s Canada

Kanad|ier(in) /-iɐ, -iərɪn/ *m* -s,- (*f* -,-nen) Canadian. k∼isch *a* Canadian

Kanal *m* -s,-e canal; (*Abfluß*-) drain, sewer; (*Radio, TV*) channel; der K∼ the [English] Channel

Kanalis|ation /-'tsịo:n/ *f* - sewerage system, drains *pl*. k∼ieren *vt* canalize; (*fig: lenken*) channel

Kanarienvogel /-iən-/ *m* canary

Kanarisch *a* K∼e Inseln Canaries

Kandi|dat(in) *m* -en,-en (*f* -,-nen) candidate. k∼dieren *vi* (*haben*) stand (für for)

kandiert *a* candied

Känguruh *nt* -s,-s kangaroo

Kaninchen *nt* -s,- rabbit

Kanister *m* -s,- canister; (*Benzin*-) can

Kännchen *nt* -s,- [small] jug; (*Kaffee*-) pot

Kanne *f* -,-n jug; (*Kaffee*-, *Tee*-) pot; (*Öl*-) can; (*große Milch*-) churn; (*Gieß*-) watering-can

Kannibal|e *m* -n,-n cannibal. K∼ismus *m* - cannibalism

Kanon *m* -s,-s canon; (*Lied*) round

Kanone *f* -,-n cannon, gun; (*fig: Könner*) ace

kanonisieren *vt* canonize

Kantate *f* -,-n cantata

Kante *f* -,-n edge; auf die hohe K∼ legen (*fam*) put by

Kanten *m* -s,- crust [of bread]

Kanter *m* -s,- canter

kantig *a* angular

Kantine *f* -,-n canteen

Kanton *m* -s,-e (*Swiss*) canton

Kantor *m* -s,-en /-'to:rən/ choirmaster and organist

Kanu *nt* -s,-s canoe

Kanzel *f* -,-n pulpit; (*Aviat*) cockpit

Kanzleistil m officialese
Kanzler m -s,- chancellor
Kap nt -s,-s (Geog) cape
Kapazität f -,-en capacity; (Experte) authority
Kapelle f -,-n chapel; (Mus) band
Kaper f -,-n (Culin) caper
kapern vt (Naut) seize
kapieren vt (fam) understand, (fam) get
Kapital nt -s capital; **K~ schlagen aus** (fig) capitalize on. **K~ismus** m - capitalism. **K~ist** m -en,-en capitalist. **k~istisch** a capitalist
Kapitän m -s,-e captain
Kapitel nt -s,- chapter
Kapitul|ation /-'tsjo:n/ f - capitulation. **k~ieren** vi (haben) capitulate
Kaplan m -s,-e curate
Kappe f -,-n cap. **k~n** vt cut
Kapsel f -,-n capsule; (Flaschen-) top
kaputt a (fam) broken; (zerrissen) torn; (defekt) out of order; (ruiniert) ruined; (erschöpft) worn out. **k~gehen**† vi sep (sein) (fam) break; (zerreißen) tear; (defekt werden) pack up; ⟨Ehe, Freundschaft:⟩ break up. **k~lachen (sich)** vr sep (fam) be in stitches. **k~machen** vt sep (fam) break; (zerreißen) tear; (defekt machen) put out of order; (erschöpfen) wear out; **sich k~machen** wear oneself out
Kapuze f -,-n hood
Kapuzinerkresse f nasturtium
Karaffe f -,-n carafe; (mit Stöpsel) decanter
Karambolage /karambo'la:ʒə/ f -,-n collision
Karamel m -s caramel. **K~bonbon** m & nt ≈ toffee
Karat nt -[e]s,-e carat
Karawane f -,-n caravan
Kardinal m -s,-e cardinal. **K~zahl** f cardinal number
Karfiol m -s (Aust) cauliflower
Karfreitag m Good Friday
karg a (kärger, kärgst) meagre; (frugal) frugal; (spärlich) sparse; (unfruchtbar) barren; (gering) scant. **k~en** vi (haben) be sparing (mit with)
kärglich a poor, meagre; (gering) scant
Karibik f - Caribbean
kariert a check[ed]; ⟨Papier⟩ squared; **schottisch k~** tartan

Karik|atur f -,-en caricature; (Journ) cartoon. **k~ieren** vt caricature
karitativ a charitable
Karneval m -s,-e & -s carnival
Karnickel nt -s,- (dial) rabbit
Kärnten nt -s Carinthia
Karo nt -s,- (Raute) diamond; (Viereck) square; (Muster) check; (Kartenspiel) diamonds pl. **K~muster** nt check
Karosserie f -,-n bodywork
Karotte f -,-n carrot
Karpfen m -s,- carp
Karre f -,-n = **Karren**
Karree nt -s,-s square; **ums K~** round the block
Karren m -s,- cart; (Hand-) barrow. **k~** vt cart
Karriere /ka'rjɛːrə/ f -,-n career; **K~ machen** get to the top
Karte f -,-n card; (Eintritts-, Fahr-) ticket; (Speise-) menu; (Land-) map
Kartei f -,-en card index. **K~karte** f index card
Karten|spiel nt card-game; (Spielkarten) pack/(Amer) deck of cards. **K~vorverkauf** m advance booking
Kartoffel f -,-n potato. **K~brei** m, **K~püree** nt mashed potatoes pl. **K~salat** m potato salad
Karton /kar'tɔŋ/ m -s,-s cardboard; (Schachtel) carton, cardboard box
Karussell nt -s,-s &-e roundabout
Karwoche f Holy Week
Käse m -s,- cheese. **K~kuchen** m cheesecake
Kaserne f -,-n barracks pl
Kasino nt -s,-s casino
Kasperle nt & m -s,- Punch. **K~theater** nt Punch and Judy show
Kasse f -,-n till; (Registrier-) cash register; (Zahlstelle) cash desk; (im Supermarkt) check-out; (Theater-) box-office; (Geld) pool [of money], (fam) kitty; (Kranken-) health insurance scheme; (Spar-) savings bank; **knapp/gut bei K~ sein** (fam) be short of cash/be flush. **K~npatient** m ≈ NHS patient. **K~nschlager** m box-office hit. **K~nwart** m -[e]s,-e treasurer. **K~nzettel** m receipt
Kasserolle f -,-n saucepan [with one handle]
Kassette f -,-n cassette; (Film-, Farbband-) cartridge; (Schmuck-) case; (Geld-) money-box. **K~nrecorder** /-rəkɔrdɐ/ m -s,- cassette recorder

kassier|en vi (haben) collect the money/(im Bus) the fares ● vt collect. **K~er(in)** m -s,- (f -,-nen) cashier

Kastagnetten /kastan'jɛtən/ pl castanets

Kastanie /kas'ta:niə/ f -,-n [horse] chestnut, (fam) conker. **k~nbraun** a chestnut

Kaste f -,-n caste

Kasten m -s,= box; (Brot-) bin; (Flaschen-) crate; (Brief-) letter-box; (Aust: Schrank) cupboard; (Kleider-) wardrobe

kastrieren vt castrate; neuter ⟨Tier⟩

Kasus m -,- /-u:s/ (Gram) case.

Katalog m -[e]s,-e catalogue. **k~isieren** vt catalogue

Katalysator m -s,-en /-'to:rən/ catalyst; (Auto) catalytic converter

Katapult nt -[e]s,-e catapult. **k~ieren** vt catapult

Katarrh m -s,-e catarrh

katastr|ophal a catastrophic. **K~ophe** f -,-n catastrophe

Katechismus m - catechism

Kateg|orie f -,-n category. **k~orisch** a categorical, adv -ly

Kater m -s,- tom-cat; (fam: Katzenjammer) hangover

Katheder nt -s,- [teacher's] desk

Kathedrale f -,-n cathedral

Kath|olik(in) m -en,-en (f -,-nen) Catholic. **k~olisch** a Catholic. **K~olizismus** m - Catholicism

Kätzchen nt -s,- kitten; (Bot) catkin

Katze f -,-n cat. **K~njammer** m (fam) hangover. **K~nsprung** m ein K~nsprung (fam) a stone's throw

Kauderwelsch nt -[s] gibberish

kauen vt/i (haben) chew; bite ⟨Nägel⟩

kauern vi (haben) crouch; sich k~ crouch down

Kauf m -[e]s, Käufe purchase; guter K~ bargain; in K~ nehmen (fig) put up with. **k~en** vt/i (haben) buy; k~en bei shop at

Käufer(in) m -s,- (f -,-nen) buyer; (im Geschäft) shopper

Kauf|haus nt department store. **K~kraft** f purchasing power. **K~laden** m shop

käuflich a saleable; (bestechlich) corruptible; k~ sein be for sale; k~ erwerben buy

Kauf|mann m (pl -leute) businessman; (Händler) dealer; (dial) grocer. **k~männisch** a commercial. **K~preis** m purchase price

Kaugummi m chewing-gum

Kaulquappe f -,-n tadpole

kaum adv hardly; k~ glaublich od zu glauben hard to believe

kauterisieren vt cauterize

Kaution /-'tsio:n/ f -,-en surety; (Jur) bail; (Miet-) deposit

Kautschuk m -s rubber

Kauz m -es, Käuze owl; komischer K~ (fam) odd fellow

Kavalier -s,-e gentleman

Kavallerie f - cavalry

Kaviar m -s caviare

keck a bold; (frech) cheeky

Kegel m -s,- skittle; (Geom) cone; mit Kind und K~ (fam) with all the family. **K~bahn** f skittle-alley. **k~förmig** a conical. **k~n** vi (haben) play skittles

Kehl|e f -,-n throat; aus voller K~e at the top of one's voice; etw in die falsche K~e bekommen (fam) take sth the wrong way. **K~kopf** m larynx. **K~kopfentzündung** f laryngitis

Kehr|e f -,-n [hairpin] bend. **k~en** vi (haben) (fegen) sweep ● vt sweep; (wenden) turn; den Rücken k~en turn one's back (dat on); sich k~en turn; sich nicht k~en an (+ acc) not care about. **K~icht** m -[e]s sweepings pl. **K~reim** m refrain. **K~seite** f (fig) drawback; die K~seite der Medaille the other side of the coin. **k~tmachen** vi sep (haben) turn back; (sich umdrehen) turn round. **K~twendung** f about-turn; (fig) U-turn

keifen vi (haben) scold

Keil m -[e]s,-e wedge

Keile f - (fam) hiding. **k~n (sich)** vr (fam) fight. **K~rei** f -,-en (fam) punch-up

Keil|kissen nt [wedge-shaped] bolster. **K~riemen** m fan belt

Keim m -[e]s,-e (Bot) sprout; (Med) germ; im K~ ersticken (fig) nip in the bud. **k~en** vi (haben) germinate; (austreiben) sprout. **k~frei** a sterile

kein pron no; not a; auf k~en Fall on no account; k~e fünf Minuten less than five minutes. **k~e(r,s)** pron no one, nobody; (Ding) none, not one. **k~esfalls** adv on no account. **k~eswegs** adv by no means. **k~mal** adv not once. **k~s** pron none, not one

Keks m -[es],-[e] biscuit, (Amer) cookie

Kelch m -[e]s,-e goblet, cup; (*Relig*) chalice; (*Bot*) calyx

Kelle f -,-n ladle; (*Maurer-, Pflanz-*) trowel

Keller m -s,- cellar. **K~ei** f -,-en winery. **K~geschoß** nt cellar; (*bewohnbar*) basement. **K~wohnung** f basement flat

Kellner m -s,- waiter. **K~in** f -,-nen waitress

keltern vt press

keltisch a Celtic

Kenia nt -s Kenya

kennen† vt know. **k~enlernen** vt sep get to know; (*treffen*) meet; **sich k~enlernen** meet; (*näher*) get to know one another. **K~er** m -s,-, **K~erin** f -,-nen connoisseur; (*Experte*) expert. **K~melodie** f signature tune. **k~tlich** a recognizable; **k~tlich machen** mark. **K~tnis** f -,-se knowledge; **zur K~tnis nehmen** take note of; **in K~tnis setzen** inform (*von* of). **K~wort** nt (*pl* -wörter) reference; (*geheimes*) password. **K~zeichen** nt distinguishing mark or feature; (*Merkmal*) characteristic; (*Markierung*) mark, marking; (*Abzeichen*) badge; (*Auto*) registration. **k~zeichnen** vt distinguish; (*markieren*) mark. **k~zeichnend** a typical (*für* of). **K~ziffer** f reference number

kentern vi (*sein*) capsize

Keramik f -,-en pottery, ceramics sg; (*Gegenstand*) piece of pottery

Kerbe f -,-n notch

Kerbholz nt **etwas auf dem K~ haben** (*fam*) have a record

Kerker m -s,- dungeon; (*Gefängnis*) prison

Kerl m -s,-e & -s (*fam*) fellow, bloke

Kern m -s,-e pip; (*Kirsch-*) stone; (*Nuß-*) kernel; (*Techn*) core; (*Atom-, Zell- & fig*) nucleus; (*Stadt-*) centre; (*einer Sache*) heart. **K~energie** f nuclear energy. **K~gehäuse** nt core. **k~gesund** a perfectly healthy. **k~ig** a robust; ⟨*Ausspruch*⟩ pithy. **k~los** a seedless. **K~physik** f nuclear physics sg

Kerze f -,-n candle. **k~ngerade** a & adv straight. **K~nhalter** m -s,- candlestick

keß a (**kesser, kessest**) pert

Kessel m -s,- kettle; (*Heiz-*) boiler. **K~stein** m fur

Kette f -,-n chain; (*Hals-*) necklace. **k~n** vt chain (**an**+acc to). **K~nladen** m chain store. **K~nraucher** m chain-smoker. **K~nreaktion** f chain reaction

Ketze|r(in) m -s,- (f -,-nen) heretic. **K~rei** f - heresy

keuch|en vi (*haben*) pant. **K~husten** m whooping cough

Keule f -,-n club; (*Culin*) leg; (*Hühner-*) drumstick

keusch a chaste. **K~heit** f - chastity

Kfz abbr s. **Kraftfahrzeug**

Khaki nt - khaki. **k~farben** a khaki

kichern vi (*haben*) giggle

Kiefer¹ f -,-n pine[-tree]

Kiefer² m -s,- jaw

Kiel m -s,-e (*Naut*) keel. **K~wasser** nt wake

Kiemen fpl gills

Kies m -es gravel. **K~el** m -s,-, **K~elstein** m pebble. **K~grube** f gravel pit

Kilo nt -s,-[s] kilo. **K~gramm** nt kilogram. **K~hertz** nt kilohertz. **K~meter** m kilometre. **K~meterstand** m ≈ mileage. **K~watt** nt kilowatt

Kind nt -es,-er child; **von K~ auf** from childhood

Kinder|arzt m, **K~ärztin** f paediatrician. **K~bett** nt child's cot. **K~ei** f -,-en childish prank. **K~garten** m nursery school. **K~gärtnerin** f nursery-school teacher. **K~geld** nt child benefit. **K~gottesdienst** m Sunday school. **K~lähmung** f polio. **k~leicht** a very easy. **k~los** a childless. **K~mädchen** nt nanny. **k~reich** a **k~reiche Familie** large family. **K~reim** m nursery rhyme. **K~spiel** nt children's game; **das ist ein/kein K~spiel** that is dead easy/not easy. **K~tagesstätte** f day nursery. **K~teller** m children's menu. **K~wagen** m pram, (*Amer*) baby carriage. **K~zimmer** nt child's/children's room; (*für Baby*) nursery

Kind|heit f - childhood. **k~isch** a childish, puerile. **k~lich** a childlike

kinetisch a kinetic

Kinn nt -[e]s,-e chin. **K~lade** f jaw

Kino nt -s,-s cinema

Kiosk m -[e]s,-e kiosk

Kippe f -,-n (*Müll-*) dump; (*fam: Zigaretten-*) fag-end; **auf der K~ stehen** (*fam*) be in a precarious position; (*unsicher sein*) hang in the balance. **k~lig** a wobbly. **k~ln** vi (*haben*) wobble. **k~n** vt tilt; (*schütten*) tip (**in**+acc into) ● vi (*sein*) topple

Kirch|e f -,-n church. **K~enbank** f pew. **K~endiener** m verger. **K~enlied** nt hymn. **K~enschiff** nt nave. **K~hof** m churchyard. **k~lich** a church ... ● adv **k~lich getraut werden** be married in church. **K~turm** m church tower, steeple. **K~weih** f -,-en [village] fair

Kirmes f -,-sen = Kirchweih

Kirsch|e f -,-n cherry. **K~wasser** nt kirsch

Kissen nt -s,- cushion; (*Kopf-*) pillow

Kiste f -,-n crate; (*Zigarren-*) box

Kitsch m -es sentimental rubbish; (*Kunst*) kitsch. **k~ig** a slushy; (*Kunst*) kitschy

Kitt m -s [adhesive] cement; (*Fenster*) putty

Kittel m -s,- overall, smock; (*Arzt-, Labor-*) white coat

kitten vt stick; (*fig*) cement

Kitz nt -es,-e (*Zool*) kid

Kitz|el m -s,- tickle; (*Nerven-*) thrill. **k~eln** vt/i (*haben*) tickle. **k~lig** a ticklish

Kladde f -,-n notebook

klaffen vi (*haben*) gape

kläffen vi (*haben*) yap

Klage f -,-n lament; (*Beschwerde*) complaint; (*Jur*) action. **k~n** vi (*haben*) lament; (*sich beklagen*) complain; (*Jur*) sue

Kläger(in) m -s,- (f -,-nen) (*Jur*) plaintiff

kläglich a pitiful, adv -ly; (*erbärmlich*) miserable, adv -bly

klamm a cold and damp; (*steif*) stiff. **K~** f -,-en (*Geog*) gorge

Klammer f -,-n (*Wäsche-*) peg; (*Büro-*) paper-clip; (*Heft-*) staple; (*Haar-*) grip; (*für Zähne*) brace; (*Techn*) clamp; (*Typ*) bracket. **k~n (sich)** vr cling (**an**+acc to)

Klang m -[e]s,ᵉe sound; (*K~farbe*) tone. **k~voll** a resonant; ⟨*Stimme*⟩ sonorous

Klapp|bett nt folding bed. **K~e** f -,-n flap; (*fam: Mund*) trap. **k~en** vt fold; (*hoch-*) tip up ● vi (*haben*) (*fam*) work out. **K~entext** m blurb

Klapper f -,-n rattle. **k~n** vi (*haben*) rattle. **K~schlange** rattlesnake

klapp|rig a rickety; (*schwach*) decrepit. **K~stuhl** m folding chair. **K~tisch** m folding table

Klaps m -es,-e pat; (*strafend*) smack. **k~en** vt smack

klar a clear; **sich** (*dat*) **k~** od im **k~en sein** realize ● adv clearly; (*fam: natürlich*) of course. **K~e(r)** m (*fam*) schnapps

klären vt clarify; **sich k~** clear; (*fig: sich lösen*) resolve itself

Klarheit f - clarity

Klarinette f -,-n clarinet

klar|machen vt sep make clear (*dat* to); **sich** (*dat*) **etw k~machen** understand sth. **K~sichtfolie** f transparent/(*haftend*) cling film. **k~stellen** vt sep clarify

Klärung f - clarification

klarwerden† vi sep (*sein*) (*fig*) become clear (*dat* to); **sich** (*dat*) **k~** make up one's mind; (*erkennen*) realize

Klasse f -,-n class; (*Sch*) class, form, (*Amer*) grade; (*Zimmer*) classroom; **erster/zweiter K~** first/second class. **k~** inv a (*fam*) super. **K~narbeit** f [written] test. **K~nbuch** nt ≈ register. **K~nkamerad(in)** m(f) class-mate. **K~nkampf** m class struggle. **K~nzimmer** nt classroom

klassifizier|en vt classify. **K~ung** f -,-en classification

Klass|ik f - classicism; (*Epoche*) classical period. **K~iker** m -s,- classical author/(*Mus*) composer. **k~isch** a classical; (*mustergültig, typisch*) classic

Klatsch m -[e]s gossip. **K~base** f (*fam*) gossip. **k~en** vt slap; Beifall **k~en** applaud ● vi (*haben*) make a slapping sound; (*im Wasser*) splash; (*tratschen*) gossip; (*applaudieren*) clap; [**in die Hände**] **k~en** clap one's hands ● vi (*haben/sein*) slap (**gegen** against). **K~maul** nt gossip. **k~naß** a (*fam*) soaking wet

klauben vt pick

Klaue f -,-n claw; (*fam: Schrift*) scrawl. **k~n** vt/i (*haben*) (*fam*) steal

Klausel f -,-n clause

Klaustrophobie f - claustrophobia

Klausur f -,-en (*Univ*) [examination] paper; (*Sch*) written test

Klaviatur f -,-en keyboard

Klavier nt -s,-e piano. **K~spieler(in)** m(f) pianist

kleb|en vt stick/(*mit Klebstoff*) glue (**an**+acc to) ● vi (*haben*) stick (**an** +dat to). **k~rig** a sticky. **K~stoff** m adhesive, glue. **K~streifen** m adhesive tape

kleckern vi (haben) (fam) =
klecksen
Klecks m -es,-e stain; (Tinten-) blot;
(kleine Menge) dab. **k∼en** vi (haben)
make a mess
Klee m -s clover. **K∼blatt** nt clover
leaf
Kleid nt -[e]s,-er dress; **K∼er** dresses;
(Kleidung) clothes. **k∼en** vt dress;
(gut stehen) suit; **sich k∼en** dress.
K∼erbügel m coat-hanger. **K∼er-
bürste** f clothes-brush. **K∼erhaken**
m coat-hook. **K∼errock** m pinafore
dress. **K∼erschrank** m wardrobe,
(Amer) closet. **k∼sam** a be-
coming. **K∼ung** f - clothes pl, clothing. **K∼ungsstück** nt garment
Kleie f - bran
klein a small, little; (von kleinem
Wuchs) short; **von k∼ auf** from
childhood. **K∼arbeit** f painstaking
work. **K∼bus** m minibus. **K∼e(r,s)**
m|f|nt little one. **K∼geld** nt [small]
change. **K∼hacken** vt sep chop up
small. **K∼handel** m retail trade.
K∼heit f - smallness; (Wuchs) short
stature. **K∼holz** nt firewood. **K∼ig-
keit** f -,-en trifle; (Mahl) snack.
K∼kind nt infant. **K∼kram** m (fam)
odds and ends pl; (Angelegenheiten)
trivia pl. **k∼laut** a subdued. **k∼lich**
a petty. **K∼lichkeit** f - pettiness.
k∼mütig a faint-hearted
Kleinod nt -[e]s,-e jewel
klein|schneiden† vt sep cut into
small pieces. **K∼stadt** f small town.
k∼städtisch a provincial. **K∼wa-
gen** m small car
Kleister m -s paste. **k∼n** vt paste
Klemme f -,-n [hair-]grip; **in der K∼
sitzen** (fam) be in a fix. **k∼n** vt jam;
sich (dat) **den Finger k∼n** get one's
finger caught ● vi (haben) jam, stick
Klempner m -s,- plumber
Klerus (der) - the clergy
Klette f -,-n burr; **wie eine K∼** (fig)
like a limpet
kletter|n vi (sein) climb. **K∼pflanze** f
climber. **K∼rose** f climbing rose
Klettverschluß m Velcro (P)
fastening
klicken vi (haben) click
Klient(in) /kli'ɛnt(ɪn)/ m -en,-en (f
-,-nen) (Jur) client
Kliff nt -[e]s,-e cliff
Klima m -s climate. **K∼anlage** f
air-conditioning
klimat|isch a climatic. **k∼isiert** a
air-conditioned

klimpern vi (haben) jingle; **k∼ auf**
(+dat) tinkle on ⟨Klavier⟩; strum
⟨Gitarre⟩
Klinge f -,-n blade
Klingel f -,-n bell. **k∼n** vi (haben)
ring; **es k∼t** there's a ring at the
door
klingen† vi (haben) sound
Klini|k f -,-en clinic. **k∼sch** a clinical,
adv -ly
Klinke f -,-n [door] handle
klipp pred a **k∼ und klar** quite plain,
adv -ly
Klipp m -s,-s = **Klips**
Klippe f -,-n [submerged] rock
Klips m -es,-e clip; (Ohr-) clip-on
ear-ring
klirren vi (haben) rattle; ⟨Geschirr,
Glas:⟩ chink
Klischee nt -s,-s cliché
Klo nt -s,-s (fam) loo, (Amer) john
klobig a clumsy
klönen vi (haben) (NGer fam) chat
klopf|en vi (haben) knock; (leicht)
tap; ⟨Herz:⟩ pound; **es k∼te** there
was a knock at the door ● vt beat;
(ein-) knock
Klops m -es,-e meatball; (Brat-)
rissole
Klosett nt -s,-s lavatory
Kloß m -es,-e dumpling; **ein K∼ im
Hals** (fam) a lump in one's throat
Kloster nt -s,- monastery; (Nonnen-)
convent
klösterlich a monastic
Klotz m -es,-e block
Klub m -s,-s club
Kluft[1] f -,-e cleft; (fig: Gegensatz) gulf
Kluft[2] f -,-en outfit; (Uniform)
uniform
klug a (klüger, klügst) intelligent, adv
-ly; (schlau) clever, adv -ly; **nicht k∼
werden aus** not understand. **K∼heit**
f - cleverness
Klump|en m -s,- lump. **k∼en** vi
(haben) go lumpy. **k∼ig** a lumpy
knabbern vt/i (haben) nibble
Knabe m -n,-n boy. **k∼nhaft** a boyish
Knäckebrot nt crispbread
knack|en vt/i (haben) crack. **K∼s** m
-es,-e crack; **einen K∼s haben** be
cracked/(fam: verrückt sein)
crackers
Knall m -[e]s,-e bang. **K∼bonbon** m
cracker. **k∼en** vi (haben) go bang;
⟨Peitsche:⟩ crack ● vt (fam: werfen)
chuck; **jdm eine k∼en** (fam) clout
s.o. **k∼ig** a (fam) gaudy. **k∼rot** a
bright red

knapp a (*gering*) scant; (*kurz*) short; (*mangelnd*) scarce; (*gerade ausreichend*) bare; (*eng*) tight; **ein k~es Pfund** just under a pound. **k~halten**† vt sep (*fam*) keep short (**mit** of). **K~heit** f - scarcity

Knarre f -,-n rattle. **k~n** vi (*haben*) creak

Knast m -[e]s (*fam*) prison

knattern vi (*haben*) crackle; ⟨*Gewehr:*⟩ stutter

Knäuel m & nt -s,- ball

Knauf m -[e]s, **Knäufe** knob

knauser|ig a (*fam*) stingy. **k~n** vi (*haben*) (*fam*) be stingy

knautschen vt (*fam*) crumple ● vi (*haben*) crease

Knebel m -s,- gag. **k~n** vt gag

Knecht m -[e]s,-e farm-hand; (*fig*) slave. **k~en** vt (*fig*) enslave. **K~schaft** f - (*fig*) slavery

kneif|en† vt pinch ● vi (*haben*) pinch; (*fam: sich drücken*) chicken out. **K~zange** f pincers pl

Kneipe f -,-n (*fam*) pub, (*Amer*) bar

knet|en vt knead; (*formen*) mould. **K~masse** f Plasticine (P)

Knick m -[e]s,-e bend; (*im Draht*) kink; (*Kniff*) crease. **k~en** vt bend; (*kniffen*) fold; **geknickt sein** (*fam*) be dejected. **k~[e]rig** a (*fam*) stingy

Knicks m -es,-e curtsy. **k~en** vi (*haben*) curtsy

Knie nt -s,- /'kni:ə/ knee. **K~bundhose** f knee-breeches pl. **K~kehle** f hollow of the knee

knien /'kni:ən/ vi (*haben*) kneel ● vr **sich k~** kneel [down]

Knie|scheibe f kneecap. **K~strumpf** m knee-length sock

Kniff m -[e]s,-e pinch; (*Falte*) crease; (*fam: Trick*) trick. **k~en** vt fold. **k~[e]lig** a (*fam*) tricky

knipsen vt (*lochen*) punch; (*Phot*) photograph ● vi (*haben*) `take a photograph/photographs

Knirps m -es,-e (*fam*) little chap; (P) (*Schirm*) telescopic umbrella

knirschen vi (*haben*) grate; ⟨*Schnee, Kies:*⟩ crunch; **mit den Zähnen k~** grind one's teeth

knistern vi (*haben*) crackle; ⟨*Papier:*⟩ rustle

Knitter|falte f crease. **k~frei** a crease-resistant. **k~n** vi (*haben*) crease

knobeln vi (*haben*) toss (**um** for); (*fam: überlegen*) puzzle

Knoblauch m -s garlic

Knöchel m -s,- ankle; (*Finger-*) knuckle

Knochen m -s,- bone. **K~mark** nt bone marrow. **k~trocken** a bone-dry

knochig a bony

Knödel m -s,- (*SGer*) dumpling

Knoll|e f -,-n tuber. **k~ig** a bulbous

Knopf m -[e]s,-e button; (*Kragen-*) stud; (*Griff*) knob

knöpfen vt button

Knopfloch nt buttonhole

Knorpel m -s gristle; (*Anat*) cartilage

knorrig a gnarled

Knospe f bud

Knötchen nt -s,- nodule

Knoten m -s,- knot; (*Med*) lump; (*Haar-*) bun, chignon. **k~** vt knot. **K~punkt** m junction

knotig a knotty; ⟨*Hände*⟩ gnarled

knuffen vt poke

knüll|en vt crumple ● vi (*haben*) crease. **K~er** m -s,- (*fam*) sensation

knüpfen vt knot; (*verbinden*) attach (**an** + acc to)

Knüppel m -s,- club; (*Gummi-*) truncheon

knurr|en vi (*haben*) growl; ⟨*Magen:*⟩ rumble; (*fam: schimpfen*) grumble. **k~ig** a grumpy

knusprig a crunchy, crisp

knutschen vi (*haben*) (*fam*) smooch

k.o. /ka:'?o:/ a k.o. **schlagen** knock out; **k.o. sein** (*fam*) be worn out. **K.o.** m -s,-s knock-out

Koalition /koali'tsio:n/ f -,-en coalition

Kobold m -[e]s,-e goblin, imp

Koch m -[e]s,-e cook; (*im Restaurant*) chef. **K~buch** nt cookery book, (*Amer*) cookbook. **k~en** vt cook; (*sieden*) boil; make ⟨*Kaffee, Tee*⟩ ● vi (*haben*) cook; (*sieden*) boil; (*fam*) seethe (**vor** + dat with). **K~en** nt -s cooking; (*Sieden*) boiling; **zum K~en bringen/kommen** bring/come to the boil. **k~end** a boiling ● adv **k~end heiß** boiling hot. **K~er** m -s,- cooker. **K~gelegenheit** f cooking facilities pl. **K~herd** m cooker, stove

Köchin f -,-nen [woman] cook

Koch|kunst f cookery. **K~löffel** m wooden spoon. **K~nische** f kitchenette. **K~platte** f hotplate. **K~topf** m saucepan

Kode /ko:t/ m -s,-s code

Köder m -s,- bait

Koexist|enz /'ko:'ɛksɪstɛnts/ f coexistence. **k~ieren** vi (*haben*) coexist

Koffein /kɔfeˈiːn/ *nt* **-s** caffeine. **k~frei** *a* decaffeinated

Koffer *m* **-s,-** suitcase. **K~kuli** *m* luggage trolley. **K~radio** *nt* portable radio. **K~raum** *m* (*Auto*) boot, (*Amer*) trunk

Kognak /ˈkɔnjak/ *m* **-s,-s** brandy

Kohl *m* **-[e]s** cabbage

Kohle *f* **-,-n** coal. **K~[n]hydrat** *nt* **-[e]s,-e** carbohydrate. **K~nbergwerk** *nt* coal-mine, colliery. **K~ndioxyd** *nt* carbon dioxide. **K~ngrube** *f* = **K~nbergwerk**. **K~nherd** *m* [kitchen] range. **K~nsäure** *f* carbon dioxide. **K~nstoff** *m* carbon. **K~papier** *nt* carbon paper

Kohl|kopf *m* cabbage. **K~rabi** *m* **-[s],-[s]** kohlrabi. **K~rübe** *f* swede

Koje *f* **-,-n** (*Naut*) bunk

Kokain /kokaˈiːn/ *nt* **-s** cocaine

kokett *a* flirtatious. **k~ieren** *vi* (*haben*) flirt

Kokon /koˈkõː/ *m* **-s,-s** cocoon

Kokosnuß *f* coconut

Koks *m* **-es** coke

Kolben *m* **-s,-** (*Gewehr-*) butt; (*Mais-*) cob; (*Techn*) piston; (*Chem*) flask

Kolibri *m* **-s,-s** humming-bird

Kolik *f* **-,-en** colic

Kollabora|teur /-ˈtøːɐ̯/ *m* **-s,-e** collaborator. **K~tion** /-ˈtsi̯oːn/ *f* **-** collaboration

Kolleg *nt* **-s,-s** & **-ien** /-i̯ən/ (*Univ*) course of lectures

Kolleg|e *m* **-n,-n**, **K~in** *f* **-,-nen** colleague. **K~ium** *nt* **-s,-ien** staff

Kollek|te *f* **-,-n** (*Relig*) collection. **K~tion** /-ˈtsi̯oːn/ *f* **-,-en** collection. **k~tiv** *a* collective. **K~tivum** *nt* **-s,-va** collective noun

kolli|dieren *vi* (*sein*) collide. **K~sion** *f* **-,-en** collision

Köln *nt* **-s** Cologne. **K~ischwasser**, **K~isch Wasser** *nt* eau-de-Cologne

Kolonialwaren *fpl* groceries

Kolon|ie *f* **-,-n** colony. **k~isieren** *vt* colonize

Kolonne *f* **-,-n** column; (*Mil*) convoy

Koloß *m* **-sses,-sse** giant

kolossal *a* enormous, *adv* **-ly**

Kolumne *f* **-,-n** (*Journ*) column

Koma *nt* **-s,-s** coma

Kombi *m* **-s,-s** = **K~wagen**. **K~nation** /-ˈtsi̯oːn/ *f* **-,-en** combination; (*Folgerung*) deduction; (*Kleidung*) co-ordinating outfit. **k~nieren** *vt*

combine; (*fig*) reason; (*folgern*) deduce. **K~wagen** *m* estate car, (*Amer*) station-wagon

Kombüse *f* **-,-n** (*Naut*) galley

Komet *m* **-en,-en** comet. **k~enhaft** *a* (*fig*) meteoric

Komfort /kɔmˈfoːɐ̯/ *m* **-s** comfort; (*Luxus*) luxury. **k~abel** /-ˈtaːbəl/ *a* comfortable, *adv* **-bly**; (*luxuriös*) luxurious, *adv* **-ly**

Komik *f* **-** humour. **K~er** *m* **-s,-** comic, comedian

komisch *a* funny; ⟨*Oper*⟩ comic; (*sonderbar*) odd, funny ● *adv* funnily; oddly. **k~erweise** *adv* funnily enough

Komitee *nt* **-s,-s** committee

Komma *nt* **-s,-s** & **-ta** comma; (*Dezimal-*) decimal point; **drei K~ fünf** three point five

Komman|dant *m* **-en,-en** commanding officer. **K~deur** /-ˈdøːɐ̯/ *m* **-s,-e** commander. **k~dieren** *vt* command; (*befehlen*) order; (*fam: herum-*) order about ● *vi* (*haben*) give the orders

Kommando *nt* **-s,-s** order; (*Befehlsgewalt*) command; (*Einheit*) detachment. **K~brücke** *f* bridge

kommen† *vi* (*sein*) come; (*eintreffen*) arrive; (*gelangen*) get (**nach** to); **k~ lassen** send for; **auf/hinter etw** (*acc*) **k~** think of/find out about sth; **um/ zu etw k~** lose/acquire sth; **wieder zu sich k~** come round; **wie kommt das?** why is that? **K~** *nt* **-s** coming; **K~ und Gehen** coming and going. **k~d** *a* coming; **k~den Montag** next Monday

Kommen|tar *m* **-s,-e** commentary; (*Bemerkung*) comment. **K~tator** *m* **-s,-en** /-ˈtoːrən/ commentator. **k~tieren** *vt* comment on

kommer|zialisieren *vt* commercialize. **k~ziell** *a* commercial, *adv* **-ly**

Kommili|tone *m* **-n,-n**, **K~tonin** *f* **-,-nen** fellow student

Kommiß *m* **-sses** (*fam*) army

Kommissar *m* **-s,-e** commissioner; (*Polizei-*) superintendent

Kommission *f* **-,-en** commission; (*Gremium*) committee

Kommode *f* **-,-n** chest of drawers

Kommunalwahlen *fpl* local elections

Kommunikation /-ˈtsi̯oːn/ *f* **-,-en** communication

Kommunion *f* **-,-en** [Holy] Communion

Kommuniqué /kɔmyni'ke:/ nt -s,-s communiqué

Kommun|ismus m -s Communism. **K~ist(in)** m -en,-en (f -,-nen) Communist. **k~istisch** a Communist

kommunizieren vi (haben) receive [Holy] Communion

Komödie /ko'mø:diə/ f -,-n comedy

Kompagnon /'kɔmpanjɔ:/ m -s,-s (Comm) partner

kompakt a compact. **K~schallplatte** f compact disc

Kompanie f -,-n (Mil) company

Komparativ m -s,-e comparative

Komparse m -n,-n (Theat) extra

Kompaß m -sses,-sse compass

kompatibel a compatible

kompeten|t a competent. **K~z** f -,-en competence

komplett a complete, adv -ly

Komplex m -es,-e complex. **k~** a complex

Komplikation /-'tsi̯o:n/ f -,-en complication

Kompliment nt -[es]s,-e compliment

Komplize m -n,-n accomplice

komplizier|en vt complicate. **k~t** a complicated

Komplott nt -[e]s,-e plot

kompo|nieren vt/i (haben) compose. **K~nist** m -en,-en composer. **K~sition** /-'tsi̯o:n/ f -,-en composition

Kompositum nt -s,-ta compound

Kompost m -[e]s compost

Kompott nt -[e]s,-e stewed fruit

Kompresse f -,-n compress

komprimieren vt compress

Kompromiß m -sses,-sse compromise; **einen K~ schließen** compromise. **k~los** a uncompromising

kompromittieren vt compromise

Konden|sation /-'tsi̯o:n/ f -condensation. **k~sieren** vt condense

Kondensmilch f evaporated/(gesüßt) condensed milk

Kondition /-'tsi̯o:n/ f - (Sport) fitness; **in K~** in form. **K~al** m -s,-e (Gram) conditional

Konditor m -s,-en /-'to:rən/ confectioner. **K~ei** f -,-en patisserie

Kondo|lenzbrief m letter of condolence. **k~lieren** vi (haben) express one's condolences

Kondom nt & m -s,-e condom

Konfekt nt -[e]s confectionery; (Pralinen) chocolates pl

Konfektion /-'tsi̯o:n/ f - ready-to-wear clothes pl

Konferenz f -,-en conference; (Besprechung) meeting

Konfession f -,-en [religious] denomination. **k~ell** a denominational. **k~slos** a non-denominational

Konfetti nt -s confetti

Konfirm|and(in) m -en,-en (f -,-nen) candidate for confirmation. **K~ation** /-'tsi̯o:n/ f -,-en (Relig) confirmation. **k~ieren** vt (Relig) confirm

Konfitüre f -,-n jam

Konflikt m -[e]s,-e conflict

Konföderation /-'tsi̯o:n/ f confederation

Konfront|ation /-'tsi̯o:n/ f -,-en confrontation. **k~ieren** vt confront

konfus a confused

Kongreß m -sses,-sse congress

König m -s,-e king. **K~in** f -,-nen queen. **k~lich** a royal, adv -ly; (hoheitsvoll) regal, adv -ly; (großzügig) handsome, adv -ly; (fam: groß) tremendous, adv -ly. **K~reich** nt kingdom

konisch a conical

Konjug|ation /-'tsi̯o:n/ f -,-en conjugation. **k~ieren** vt conjugate

Konjunktion /-'tsi̯o:n/ f -,-en (Gram) conjunction

Konjunktiv m -s,-e subjunctive

Konjunktur f - economic situation; (Hoch-) boom

konkav a concave

konkret a concrete

Konkurren|t(in) m -en,-en (f -,-nen) competitor, rival. **K~z** f - competition; **jdm K~z machen** compete with s.o. **k~zfähig** a (Comm) competitive. **K~zkampf** m competition, rivalry

konkurrieren vi (haben) compete

Konkurs m -es,-e bankruptcy; **K~ machen** go bankrupt

können† vt/i (haben) **etw k~** be able to do sth; (beherrschen) know sth; **k~ Sie Deutsch?** do you know any German? **das kann ich nicht** I can't do that; **er kann nicht mehr** he can't go on; **für etw nichts k~** not be to blame for sth □ v aux **lesen/ schwimmen k~** be able to read/ swim; **er kann/konnte es tun** he can/could do it; **das kann od könnte [gut] sein** that may [well] be. **K~** nt -s ability; (Wissen) knowledge

Könner(in) m -s,- (f -,-nen) expert

konsequen|t a consistent, adv -ly; (logisch) logical, adv -ly. **K~z** f -,-en consequence

konservativ *a* conservative

Konserv|e *fpl* tinned *or* canned food *sg*. **K~enbüchse, K~endose** *f* tin, can. **k~ieren** *vt* preserve; (*in Dosen*) tin, can. **K~ierungsmittel** *nt* preservative

Konsistenz *f* - consistency

konsolidieren *vt* consolidate

Konsonant *m* -en,-en consonant

konsterniert *a* dismayed

Konstitution /-'tsio:n/ *f* -,-en constitution. **k~ell** *a* constitutional

konstruieren *vt* construct; (*entwerfen*) design

Konstruk|tion /-'tsio:n/ *f* -,-en construction; (*Entwurf*) design. **k~tiv** *a* constructive

Konsul *m* -s,-n consul. **K~at** *nt* -[e]s,-e consulate

Konsult|ation /-'tsio:n/ *f* -,-en consultation. **k~ieren** *vt* consult

Konsum *m* -s consumption. **K~ent** *m* -en,-en consumer. **K~güter** *npl* consumer goods

Kontakt *m* -[e]s,-e contact. **K~linsen** *fpl* contact lenses. **K~person** *f* contact

kontern *vt/i* (*haben*) counter

Kontinent /'kɔn-, kɔnti'nɛnt/ *m* -s,-e continent

Kontingent *nt* -[e]s,-e (*Comm*) quota; (*Mil*) contingent

Kontinuität *f* - continuity

Konto *nt* -s,-s account. **K~auszug** *m* [bank] statement. **K~nummer** *f* account number. **K~stand** *m* [bank] balance

Kontrabaß *m* double-bass

Kontrast *m* -[e]s,-e contrast

Kontroll|abschnitt *m* counterfoil. **K~e** *f* -,-n control; (*Prüfung*) check. **K~eur** /-'løːɐ̯/ *m* -s,-e [ticket] inspector. **k~ieren** *vt* check; inspect ⟨*Fahrkarten*⟩; (*beherrschen*) control

Kontroverse *f* -,-n controversy

Kontur *f* -,-en contour

Konvention /-'tsio:n/ *f* -,-en convention. **k~ell** *a* conventional, *adv* -ly

Konversation /-'tsio:n/ *f* -,-en conversation. **K~slexikon** *nt* encyclopaedia

konvert|ieren *vi* (*haben*) (*Relig*) convert. **K~it** *m* -en,-en convert

konvex *a* convex

Konvoi /kɔn'vɔy/ *m* -s,-s convoy

Konzentration /-'tsio:n/ *f* -,-en concentration. **K~slager** *nt* concentration camp

konzentrieren *vt* concentrate; **sich k~** concentrate (**auf** + *acc* on)

Konzept *nt* -[e]s,-e [rough] draft; **jdn aus dem K~ bringen** put s.o. off his stroke. **K~papier** *nt* rough paper

Konzern *m* -s,-e (*Comm*) group [of companies]

Konzert *nt* -[e]s,-e concert; (*Klavier-, Geigen-*) concerto. **K~meister** *m* leader, (*Amer*) concert-master

Konzession *f* -,-en licence; (*Zugeständnis*) concession

Konzil *nt* -s,-e (*Relig*) council

Kooperation /ko'ɔpera'tsio:n/ *f* co-operation

Koordin|ation /ko'ɔrdina'tsio:n/ *f* - co-ordination. **k~ieren** *vt* co-ordinate

Kopf *m* -[e]s,ꞋꞋe head; **ein K~ Kohl/Salat** a cabbage/lettuce; **aus dem K~** from memory; (*auswendig*) by heart; **auf dem K~** (*verkehrt*) upside down; **K~ an K~** neck and neck; ⟨*stehen*⟩ shoulder to shoulder; **sich** (*dat*) **den K~ waschen** wash one's hair; **sich** (*dat*) **den K~ zerbrechen** rack one's brains. **K~ball** *m* header. **K~bedeckung** *f* head-covering

Köpf|chen *nt* -s,- little head; **K~chen haben** (*fam*) be clever. **k~en** *vt* behead; (*Fußball*) head

Kopf|ende *nt* head. **K~haut** *f* scalp. **K~hörer** *m* headphones *pl*. **K~kissen** *nt* pillow. **K~kissenbezug** *m* pillow-case. **k~los** *a* panic-stricken. **K~nicken** *nt* -s nod. **K~rechnen** *nt* mental arithmetic. **K~salat** *m* lettuce. **K~schmerzen** *mpl* headache *sg*. **K~schütteln** *nt* -s shake of the head. **K~sprung** *m* header, dive. **K~stand** *m* headstand. **K~steinpflaster** *nt* cobble-stones *pl*. **K~stütze** *f* head-rest. **K~tuch** *nt* headscarf. **k~über** *adv* head first; (*fig*) headlong. **K~wäsche** *f* shampoo. **K~weh** *nt* headache. **K~zerbrechen** *nt* -s **sich** (*dat*) **K~zerbrechen machen** rack one's brains; (*sich sorgen*) worry

Kopie *f* -,-n copy. **k~ren** *vt* copy

Koppel¹ *f* -,-n enclosure; (*Pferde-*) paddock

Koppel² *nt* -s,- (*Mil*) belt. **k~n** *vt* couple

Koralle *f* -,-n coral

Korb *m* -[e]s,ꞋꞋe basket; **jdm einen K~ geben** (*fig*) turn s.o. down. **K~ball** *m* [kind of] netball. **K~stuhl** *m* wicker chair

Kord m -s (*Tex*) corduroy
Kordel f -,-n cord
Korinthe f -,-n currant
Kork m -s cork. **K~en** m -s,- cork.
  K~enzieher m -s,- corkscrew
Korn[1] nt -[e]s,⸚er grain; (*Samen-*)
  seed; (*coll: Getreide*) grain, corn; (*am
  Visier*) front sight
Korn[2] m -[e]s,- (*fam*) grain schnapps
Körn|chen nt -s,- granule. **k~ig** a
  granular
Körper m -s,- body; (*Geom*) solid.
  K~bau m build, physique. **k~be-
  hindert** a physically disabled.
  k~lich a physical, adv -ly; ⟨*Strafe*⟩
  corporal. **K~pflege** f personal hygiene. **K~puder** m talcum powder.
  K~schaft f -,-en corporation, body.
  K~strafe f corporal punishment.
  K~teil m part of the body
Korps /koːɐ̯/ nt -,- /-[s],-s/ corps
korpulent a corpulent
korrekt a correct, adv -ly. **K~or** m
  -s,-en /-'toːrən/ proof-reader. **K~ur** f
  -,-en correction. **K~urabzug,
  K~urbogen** m proof
Korrespon|dent(in) m -en,-en (f
  -,-nen) correspondent. **K~denz** f -,-
  en correspondence. **k~dieren** vi
  (*haben*) correspond
Korridor m -s,-e corridor
korrigieren vt correct
Korrosion f - corrosion
korrumpieren vt corrupt
korrup|t a corrupt. **K~tion** /-'tsjoːn/ f
  - corruption
Korsett nt -[e]s,-e corset
koscher a kosher
Kose|name m pet name. **K~wort** nt
  (pl -wörter) term of endearment
Kosmet|ik f - beauty culture. **K~ika**
  ntpl cosmetics. **K~ikerin** f -,-nen
  beautician. **k~isch** a cosmetic;
  ⟨*Chirurgie*⟩ plastic
kosm|isch a cosmic. **K~onaut(in)** m
  -en,-en (f -,-nen) cosmonaut. **k~o-
  politisch** a cosmopolitan
Kosmos m - cosmos
Kost f - food; (*Ernährung*) diet; (*Verpflegung*) board
kostbar a precious. **K~keit** f -,-en
  treasure
kosten[1] vt/i (*haben*) [von] etw k~
  taste sth
kosten[2] vt cost; (*brauchen*) take; **wieviel kostet es?** how much is it? **K~** pl
  expense sg, cost sg; (*Jur*) costs; **auf**

meine K~ at my expense. **K~[vor]-
anschlag** m estimate. **k~los** a free
  ● adv free [of charge]
Kosthappen m taste
köstlich a delicious; (*entzückend*) de-
  lightful. **K~keit** f -,-en (*fig*) gem;
  (*Culin*) delicacy
Kost|probe f taste; (*fig*) sample.
  k~spielig a expensive, costly
Kostüm nt -s,-e (*Theat*) costume;
  (*Verkleidung*) fancy dress;
  (*Schneider-*) suit. **K~fest** nt fancy-
  dress party. **k~iert** a **k~iert sein** be
  in fancy dress
Kot m -[e]s excrement; (*Schmutz*) dirt
Kotelett /kɔt'let/ nt -s,-s chop, cutlet.
  K~en pl sideburns
Köter m -s,- (*pej*) dog
Kotflügel m (*Auto*) wing, (*Amer*)
  fender
kotzen vi (*haben*) (*sl*) throw up; **es
  ist zum K~** it makes you sick
Krabbe f -,-n crab; (*Garnele*) shrimp;
  (*rote*) prawn
krabbeln vi (*sein*) crawl
Krach m -[e]s,⸚e din, racket; (*Knall*)
  crash; (*fam: Streit*) row; (*fam: Ruin*)
  crash. **k~en** vi (*haben*) crash; **es hat
  gekracht** there was a bang/(*fam:
  Unfall*) a crash ● (*sein*) break,
  crack; (*auftreffen*) crash (**gegen**
  into)
krächzen vi (*haben*) croak
Kraft f -,⸚e strength; (*Gewalt*) force;
  (*Arbeits-*) worker; **in/außer K~**
  in/no longer in force; **in K~ treten**
  come into force. **k~** prep (+ gen) by
  virtue of. **K~ausdruck** m swear-
  word. **K~fahrer** m driver. **K~fahr-
  zeug** nt motor vehicle. **K~fahr-
  zeugbrief** m [vehicle] registration
  document
kräftig a strong; (*gut entwickelt*)
  sturdy; (*nahrhaft*) nutritious; (*heftig*) hard ● adv strongly; (*heftig*)
  hard. **k~en** vt strengthen
kraft|los a weak. **K~post** f post bus
  service. **K~probe** f trial of strength.
  K~rad nt motorcycle. **K~stoff** m
  (*Auto*) fuel. **k~voll** a strong, powerful. **K~wagen** m motor car.
  K~werk nt power station
Kragen m -s,- collar
Krähe f -,-n crow
krähen vi (*haben*) crow
krakeln vt/i (*haben*) scrawl
Kralle f -,-n claw. **k~n (sich)** vr clutch
  (**an** jdn/etw s.o./sth); ⟨*Katze:*⟩ dig its
  claws (**in** + acc into)

Kram m -s (fam) things pl, (fam) stuff; (Angelegenheiten) business; **wertloser K~** junk. **k~en** vi (haben) rummage about (**in** + dat in; **nach** for). **K~laden** m [small] general store

Krampf m -[e]s,∷e cramp. **K~adern** fpl varicose veins. **k~haft** a convulsive, adv -ly; (verbissen) desperate, adv -ly

Kran m -[e]s,∷e (Techn) crane

Kranich m -s,-e (Zool) crane

krank a (kränker, kränkst) sick; ⟨Knie, Herz⟩ bad; **k~ sein/werden/machen** be/fall/make ill; **sich k~ melden** report sick. **K~e(r)** m/f sick man/woman, invalid; **die K~en** the sick pl

kränkeln vi (haben) be in poor health. **k~d** a ailing

kranken vi (haben) (fig) suffer (**an** + dat from)

kränken vt offend, hurt

Kranken|bett nt sick-bed. **K~geld** nt sickness benefit. **K~gymnast(in)** m -en,-en (f -,-nen) physiotherapist. **K~gymnastik** f physiotherapy. **K~haus** nt hospital. **K~kasse** f health insurance scheme/(Amt) office. **K~pflege** f nursing. **K~pfleger(in)** m(f) nurse. **K~saal** m [hospital] ward. **K~schein** m certificate of entitlement to medical treatment. **K~schwester** f nurse. **K~urlaub** m sick-leave. **K~versicherung** f health insurance. **K~wagen** m ambulance. **K~zimmer** nt sick-room

krank|haft a morbid; (pathologisch) pathological. **K~heit** f -,-en illness, disease

kränk|lich a sickly. **K~ung** f -,-en slight

Kranz m -es,∷e wreath; (Ring) ring

Krapfen m -s,- doughnut

kraß a (krasser, krassest) glaring; (offensichtlich) blatant; (stark) gross; rank ⟨Außenseiter⟩

Krater m -s,- crater

kratz|bürstig a (fam) prickly. **k~en** vt/i (haben) scratch; **sich k~en** scratch oneself/⟨Tier:⟩ itself. **K~er** m -s,- scratch; (Werkzeug) scraper

Kraul nt -s (Sport) crawl. **k~en¹** vi (haben/sein) (Sport) do the crawl

kraulen² vt tickle; **sich am Kopf k~** scratch one's head

kraus a wrinkled; ⟨Haar⟩ frizzy; (verworren) muddled; **k~ ziehen**

wrinkle. **K~e** f -,-n frill, ruffle; (Haar) frizziness

kräuseln vt wrinkle; frizz ⟨Haar⟩; gather ⟨Stoff⟩; ripple ⟨Wasser⟩; **sich k~** wrinkle; (sich kringeln) curl; ⟨Haar:⟩ go frizzy; ⟨Wasser:⟩ ripple

krausen vt wrinkle; frizz ⟨Haar⟩; gather ⟨Stoff⟩; **sich k~** wrinkle; ⟨Haar:⟩ go frizzy

Kraut nt -[e]s, Kräuter herb; (SGer) cabbage; (Sauer-) sauerkraut; **wie K~ und Rüben** (fam) higgledy-piggledy

Krawall m -s,-e riot; (Lärm) row

Krawatte f -,-n [neck]tie

kraxeln vi (sein) (fam) clamber

krea|tiv /krea'ti:f/ a creative. **K~tur** f -,-en creature

Krebs m -es,-e crayfish; (Med) cancer; (Astr) Cancer. **k~ig** a cancerous

Kredit m -s,-e credit; (Darlehen) loan; **auf K~** on credit. **K~karte** f credit card

Kreid|e f -chalk. **k~ebleich** a deathly pale. **k~ig** a chalky

kreieren /kre'i:rən/ vt create

Kreis m -es,-e circle; (Admin) district

kreischen vt/i (haben) screech; (schreien) shriek

Kreisel m -s,- [spinning] top; (fam: Kreisverkehr) roundabout

kreis|en vi (haben) circle; revolve (**um** around). **k~förmig** a circular. **K~lauf** m cycle; (Med) circulation. **k~rund** a circular. **K~säge** f circular saw. **K~verkehr** m [traffic] roundabout, (Amer) traffic circle

Krem f -,-s & m -s,-e cream

Krematorium nt -s,-ien crematorium

Krempe f -,-n [hat] brim

Krempel m -s (fam) junk

krempeln vt turn (**nach oben** up)

Kren m -[e]s (Aust) horseradish

krepieren vi (sein) explode; (sl: sterben) die

Krepp m -s,-s & -e crêpe

Kreppapier nt crêpe paper

Kresse f -,-n cress; (Kapuziner-) nasturtium

Kreta nt -s Crete

Kreuz nt -es,-e cross; (Kreuzung) intersection; (Mus) sharp; (Kartenspiel) clubs pl; (Anat) small of the back; **über K~** crosswise; **das K~ schlagen** cross oneself. **k~ adv k~ und quer** in all directions. **k~en** vt cross; **sich k~en** cross; ⟨Straßen:⟩

intersect; ⟨*Meinungen:*⟩ clash ● *vi* (*haben/sein*) cruise; ⟨*Segelschiff:*⟩ tack. **K~er** *m* **-s,-** cruiser. **K~fahrt** *f* (*Naut*) cruise; (*K~zug*) crusade. **K~feuer** *nt* crossfire. **K~gang** *m* cloister

kreuzig|en *vt* crucify. **K~ung** *f* **-,-en** crucifixion

Kreuz|otter *f* adder, common viper. **K~ung** *f* **-,-en** intersection; (*Straßen-*) crossroads *sg*; (*Hybride*) cross. **K~verhör** *nt* cross-examination; (*K~verhör nehmen* cross-examine. **K~weg** *m* crossroads *sg*; (*Relig*) Way of the Cross. **k~weise** *adv* crosswise. **K~worträtsel** *nt* crossword [puzzle]. **K~zug** *m* crusade

kribbel|ig *a* (*fam*) edgy. **k~n** *vi* (*haben*) tingle; (*kitzeln*) tickle

kriech|en† *vi* (*sein*) crawl; (*fig*) grovel (**vor +** *dat* to). **k~erisch** *a* grovelling. **K~spur** *f* (*Auto*) crawler lane. **K~tier** *nt* reptile

Krieg *m* **-[e]s,-e** war

kriegen *vt* (*fam*) get; **ein Kind k~** have a baby

Krieger|denkmal *nt* war memorial. **k~isch** *a* warlike; (*militärisch*) military

kriegs|beschädigt *a* war-disabled. **K~dienstverweigerer** *m* **-s,-** conscientious objector. **K~gefangene(r)** *m* prisoner of war. **K~gefangenschaft** *f* captivity. **K~gericht** *nt* court martial. **K~list** *f* stratagem. **K~rat** *m* council of war. **K~recht** *nt* martial law. **K~schiff** *nt* warship. **K~verbrechen** *nt* war crime

Krimi *m* **-s,-s** (*fam*) crime story/film. **K~nalität** *f* - crime; (*Vorkommen*) crime rate. **K~nalpolizei** *f* criminal investigation department. **K~nalroman** *m* crime novel. **k~nell** *a* criminal. **K~nelle(r)** *m* criminal

kringeln (sich) *vr* curl [up]; (*vor Lachen*) fall about

Kripo *f* - = Kriminalpolizei

Krippe *f* **-,-n** manger; (*Weihnachts-*) crib; (*Kinder-*) crèche. **K~nspiel** *nt* Nativity play

Krise *f* **-,-n** crisis

Kristall¹ *nt* **-s** (*Glas*) crystal; (*geschliffen*) cut glass

Kristall² *m* **-s,-e** crystal. **k~isieren** *vi/r* (*haben*) [sich] **k~isieren** crystallize

Kriterium *nt* **-s,-ien** criterion

Kritik *f* **-,-en** criticism; (*Rezension*) review; **unter aller K~** (*fam*) abysmal

Kriti|ker *m* **-s,-** critic; (*Rezensent*) reviewer. **k~sch** *a* critical, *adv* -ly. **k~sieren** *vt* criticize; review

kritteln *vi* (*haben*) find fault (**an +** *acc* with)

kritzeln *vt/i* (*haben*) scribble

Krokette *f* **-,-n** (*Culin*) croquette

Krokodil *nt* **-s,-e** crocodile

Krokus *m* **-,-[se]** crocus

Krone *f* **-,-n** crown; (*Baum-*) top

krönen *vt* crown

Kron|leuchter *m* chandelier. **K~prinz** *m* crown prince

Krönung *f* **-,-en** coronation; (*fig: Höhepunkt*) crowning event/(*Leistung*) achievement

Kropf *m* **-[e]s,ᵉ** (*Zool*) crop; (*Med*) goitre

Kröte *f* **-,-n** toad

Krücke *f* **-,-n** crutch; (*Stock-*) handle; **an K~n** on crutches

Krug *m* **-[e]s,ᵉ** jug; (*Bier-*) tankard

Krume *f* **-,-n** soft part [of loaf]; (*Krümel*) crumb; (*Acker-*) topsoil

Krümel *m* **-s,-** crumb. **k~ig** *a* crumbly. **k~n** *vt* crumble ● *vi* (*haben*) be crumbly; ⟨*Person:*⟩ drop crumbs

krumm *a* crooked; (*gebogen*) curved; (*verbogen*) bent. **k~beinig** *a* bow-legged

krümmen *vt* bend; crook ⟨*Finger*⟩; **sich k~** bend; (*sich winden*) writhe; (*vor Schmerzen/Lachen*) double up

krummnehmen† *vt sep* (*fam*) take amiss

Krümmung *f* **-,-en** bend; (*Kurve*) curve

Krüppel *m* **-s,-** cripple

Kruste *f* **-,-n** crust; (*Schorf*) scab

Kruzifix *nt* **-es,-e** crucifix

Krypta /ˈkrypta/ *f* **-,-ten** crypt

Kub|a *nt* **-s** Cuba. **k~anisch** *a* Cuban

Kübel *m* **-s,-** tub; (*Eimer*) bucket; (*Techn*) skip

Kubik- *pref* cubic. **K~meter** *m* & *nt* cubic metre

Küche *f* **-,-n** kitchen; (*Kochkunst*) cooking; **kalte/warme K~** cold/hot food; **französische K~** French cuisine

Kuchen *m* **-s,-** cake

Küchen|herd *m* cooker, stove. **K~maschine** *f* food processor, mixer. **K~schabe** *f* **-,-n** cockroach. **K~zettel** *m* menu

Kuckuck m -s,-e cuckoo; **zum K~!** (*fam*) hang it! **K~suhr** f cuckoo clock

Kufe f -,-n [sledge] runner

Kugel f -,-n ball; (*Geom*) sphere; (*Gewehr-*) bullet; (*Sport*) shot. **k~förmig** a spherical. **K~lager** nt ball-bearing. **K~n** vt/i (haben) roll; **sich k~n** roll/(*vor Lachen*) fall about. **k~rund** a spherical; (*fam: dick*) tubby. **K~schreiber** m -s,- ballpoint [pen]. **k~sicher** a bullet-proof. **K~stoßen** nt -s shot-putting

Kuh f -,-e cow

kühl a cool, adv -ly; (*kalt*) chilly. **K~box** f -,-en cool-box. **K~e** f - coolness; chilliness. **k~en** vt cool; refrigerate (*Lebensmittel*); chill (*Wein*). **K~er** m -s,- ice-bucket; (*Auto*) radiator. **K~erhaube** f bonnet, (*Amer*) hood. **K~fach** nt frozenfood compartment. **K~raum** m cold store. **K~schrank** m refrigerator. **K~truhe** f freezer. **K~ung** f - cooling; (*Frische*) coolness. **K~wasser** nt [radiator] water

Kuhmilch f cow's milk

kühn a bold, adv -ly; (*wagemutig*) daring. **K~heit** f - boldness

Kuhstall m cowshed

Küken nt -s,- chick; (*Enten-*) duckling

Kukuruz m -[es] (*Aust*) maize

kulant a obliging

Kuli m -s,-s (*fam: Kugelschreiber*) ballpoint [pen], Biro (P)

kulinarisch a culinary

Kulissen fpl (*Theat*) scenery sg; (*seitlich*) wings; **hinter den K~** (*fig*) behind the scenes

kullern vt/i (sein) (*fam*) roll

Kult m -[e]s,-e cult

kultivier|en vt cultivate. **k~t** a cultured

Kultur f -,-en culture; **K~en** plantations. **K~beutel** m toilet-bag. **k~ell** a cultural. **K~film** m documentary film

Kultusminister m Minister of Education and Arts

Kümmel m -s caraway; (*Getränk*) kümmel

Kummer m -s sorrow, grief; (*Sorge*) worry; (*Ärger*) trouble

kümmer|lich a puny; (*dürftig*) meagre; (*armselig*) wretched. **k~n** vt concern; **sich k~n um** look after; (*sich befassen*) concern oneself with; (*beachten*) take notice of; **ich werde mich darum k~n** I shall see to

it; **k~e dich um deine eigenen Angelegenheiten!** mind your own business!

kummervoll a sorrowful

Kumpel m -s,- (*fam*) mate

Kunde m -n,-n customer. **K~ndienst** m [after-sales] service

Kund|gebung f -,-en (*Pol*) rally. **k~ig** a knowledgeable; (*sach-*) expert

kündig|en vt cancel (*Vertrag*); give notice of withdrawal for (*Geld*); give notice to quit (*Wohnung*); **seine Stellung k~en** give [in one's] notice ● vi (haben) give [in one's] notice; **jdm k~en** give s.o. notice [of dismissal/(*Vermieter:*) to quit]. **K~ung** f -,-en cancellation; notice [of withdrawal/dismissal/to quit]; (*Entlassung*) dismissal. **K~ungsfrist** f period of notice

Kund|in f -,-nen [woman] customer. **K~machung** f -,-en (*Aust*) [public] notice. **K~schaft** f - clientele, customers pl

künftig a future ● adv in future

Kunst f -,-e art; (*Können*) skill. **K~dünger** m artificial fertilizer. **K~faser** f synthetic fibre. **k~fertig** a skilful. **K~fertigkeit** f skill. **K~galerie** f art gallery. **k~gerecht** a expert, adv -ly. **K~geschichte** f history of art. **K~gewerbe** nt arts and crafts pl. **K~griff** m trick. **K~händler** m art dealer

Künstler m -s,- artist; (*Könner*) master. **K~in** f -,-nen [woman] artist. **k~isch** a artistic, adv -ally. **K~name** m pseudonym; (*Theat*) stage name

künstlich a artificial, adv -ly

kunst|los a simple. **K~maler** m painter. **K~stoff** m plastic. **K~stopfen** nt invisible mending. **K~stück** nt trick; (*große Leistung*) feat. **k~voll** a artistic; (*geschickt*) skilful, adv -ly; (*kompliziert*) elaborate, adv -ly. **K~werk** nt work of art

kunterbunt a multicoloured; (*gemischt*) mixed ● adv **k~ durcheinander** higgledy-piggledy

Kupfer nt -s copper. **k~n** a copper

kupieren vt crop

Kupon /ku'põ:/ m -s,-s voucher; (*Zins-*) coupon; (*Stoff-*) length

Kuppe f -,-n [rounded] top; (*Finger-*) end, tip

Kuppel f -,-n dome

kupp|eln vt couple (**an** + acc to) ● vi (haben) (Auto) operate the clutch. **K~lung** f -,-en coupling; (Auto) clutch

Kur f -,-en course of treatment; (im Kurort) cure

Kür f -,-en (Sport) free exercise; (Eislauf) free programme

Kurbel f -,-n crank. **k~n** vt wind (**nach oben/unten** up/down). **K~welle** f crankshaft

Kürbis m -ses,-se pumpkin; (Flaschen-) marrow

Kurgast m health-resort visitor

Kurier m -s,-e courier

kurieren vt cure

kurios a curious, odd. **K~ität** f -,-en oddness; (Objekt) curiosity; (Kunst) curio

Kur|ort m health resort; (Badeort) spa. **K~pfuscher** m quack

Kurs m -es,-e course; (Aktien-) price. **K~buch** nt timetable

kursieren vi (haben) circulate

kursiv a italic ● adv in italics. **K~schrift** f italics pl

Kursus m -,Kurse course

Kurswagen m through carriage

Kurtaxe f visitors' tax

Kurve f -,-n curve; (Straßen-) bend

kurz a (**kürzer, kürzest**) short; (knapp) brief; (rasch) quick; (schroff) curt; **k~e Hosen** shorts; **vor k~em** a short time ago; **seit k~em** lately; **binnen k~em** shortly; **den kürzeren ziehen** get the worst of it ● adv briefly; quickly; curtly; **k~ vor/nach** a little way/(zeitlich) shortly before/after; **sich k~ fassen** be brief; **k~ und gut** in short; **über k~ oder lang** sooner or later; **zu k~ kommen** get less than one's fair share. **K~arbeit** f short-time working. **k~ärmelig** a short-sleeved. **k~atmig** a **k~atmig sein** be short of breath

Kürze f - shortness; (Knappheit) brevity; **in K~** shortly. **k~n** vt shorten; (verringern) cut

kurz|erhand adv without further ado. **k~fristig** a short-term ● adv at short notice. **K~geschichte** f short story. **k~lebig** a short-lived

kürzlich adv recently

Kurz|meldung f newsflash. **K~nachrichten** fpl news headlines. **K~schluß** m short circuit; (fig) brainstorm. **K~schrift** f shorthand.

k~sichtig a short-sighted. **K~sichtigkeit** f - short-sightedness. **K~streckenrakete** f short-range missile. **k~um** adv in short

Kürzung f -,-en shortening; (Verringerung) cut (gen in)

Kurz|waren fpl haberdashery sg, (Amer) notions. **k~weilig** a amusing. **K~welle** f short wave

kuscheln (sich) vr snuggle (**an** + acc up to)

Kusine f -,-n [female] cousin

Kuß m -sses,ᴹsse kiss

küssen vt/i (haben) kiss; **sich k~** kiss

Küste f -,-n coast. **K~nwache, K~nwacht** f coastguard

Küster m -s,- verger

Kustos m -,-oden /-'to:-/ curator

Kutsch|e f -,-n [horse-drawn] carriage/(geschlossen) coach. **K~er** m -s,- coachman, driver. **k~ieren** vt/i (haben) drive

Kutte f -,-n (Relig) habit

Kutter m -s,- (Naut) cutter

Kuvert /ku've:ɐ̯/ nt -s,-s envelope

KZ /ka:'tsɛt/ nt -[s],-[s] concentration camp

L

labil a unstable

Labor nt -s,-s & -e laboratory. **L~ant(in)** m -en,-en (f -,-nen) laboratory assistant. **L~atorium** nt -s,-ien laboratory

Labyrinth nt -[e]s,-e maze, labyrinth

Lache f -,-n puddle; (Blut-) pool

lächeln vi (haben) smile. **L~** nt -s smile. **l~d** a smiling

lachen vi (haben) laugh. **L~** nt -s laugh; (Gelächter) laughter

lächerlich a ridiculous, adv -ly; **sich l~ machen** make a fool of oneself. **L~keit** f -,-en ridiculousness; (Kleinigkeit) triviality

lachhaft a laughable

Lachs m -es,-e salmon. **l~farben, l~rosa** a salmon-pink

Lack m -[e]s,-e varnish; (Japan-) lacquer; (Auto) paint. **l~en** vt varnish. **l~ieren** vt varnish; (spritzen) spray. **L~schuhe** mpl patent-leather shoes

Lade f -,-n drawer

laden† vt load; (Electr) charge; (Jur: vor-) summons

Laden m -s,ᴹ shop, (Amer) store; (Fenster-) shutter. **L~dieb** m shop-

lifter. **L∼diebstahl** *m* shop-lifting.
L∼schluß *m* [shop] closing-time.
L∼tisch *m* counter
Laderaum *m* (*Naut*) hold
lädieren *vt* damage
Ladung *f* -,-en load; (*Naut, Aviat*)
cargo; (*elektrische, Spreng-*) charge;
(*Jur: Vor-*) summons
Lage *f* -,-n position; (*Situation*) situation; (*Schicht*) layer; (*fam: Runde*)
round; **nicht in der L∼ sein** not be in
a position (**zu** to)
Lager *nt* -s,- camp; (*L∼haus*) warehouse; (*Vorrat*) stock; (*Techn*) bearing; (*Erz-, Ruhe-*) bed; (*eines Tieres*)
lair; **[nicht] auf L∼** [not] in stock.
L∼haus *nt* warehouse. **l∼n** *vt* store;
(*legen*) lay; **sich l∼n** settle; (*sich
legen*) lie down ● *vi* (*haben*) camp;
(*liegen*) lie; ⟨*Waren:*⟩ be stored.
L∼raum *m* store-room. **L∼stätte** *f*
(*Geol*) deposit. **L∼ung** *f* - storage
Lagune *f* -,-n lagoon
lahm *a* lame. **l∼en** *vi* (*haben*) be lame
lähmen *vt* paralyse
lahmlegen *vt sep* (*fig*) paralyse
Lähmung *f* -,-en paralysis
Laib *m* -[e]s,-e loaf
Laich *m* -[e]s (*Zool*) spawn. **l∼en** *vi*
(*haben*) spawn
Laie *m* -n,-n layman; (*Theat*) amateur. **l∼nhaft** *a* amateurish.
L∼nprediger *m* lay preacher
Lake *f* -,-n brine
Laken *nt* -s,- sheet
lakonisch *a* laconic, *adv* -ally
Lakritze *f* - liquorice
lallen *vt/i* (*haben*) mumble; ⟨*Baby:*⟩
babble
Lametta *nt* -s tinsel
Lamm *nt* -[e]s,¨er lamb
Lampe *f* -,-n lamp; (*Decken-, Wand-*)
light; (*Glüh-*) bulb. **L∼nfieber** *nt*
stage fright. **L∼nschirm** *m*
lampshade
Lampion /lamˈpiɔŋ/ *m* -s,-s Chinese
lantern
lancieren /lãˈsiːrən/ *vt* (*Comm*) launch
Land *nt* -[e]s,¨er country; (*Fest-*) land;
(*Bundes-*) state, Land; (*Aust*) province; **Stück L∼** piece of land; **auf dem
L∼e** in the country; **an L∼ gehen**
(*Naut*) go ashore. **L∼arbeiter** *m*
agricultural worker. **L∼ebahn** *f*
runway. **l∼einwärts** *adv* inland.
l∼en *vt/i* (*sein*) land; (*fam: gelangen*) end up
Ländereien *pl* estates
Länderspiel *nt* international

Landesteg *m* landing-stage
Landesverrat *m* treason
Land|karte *f* map. **l∼läufig** *a* popular
ländlich *a* rural
Land|maschinen *fpl* agricultural
machinery *sg*. **L∼schaft** *f* -,-en
scenery; (*Geog, Kunst*) landscape;
(*Gegend*) country[side]. **l∼schaft-
lich** *a* scenic; (*regional*) regional.
L∼smann *m* (*pl* -**leute**) fellow
countryman, compatriot. **L∼smän-
nin** *f* -,-nen fellow countrywoman.
L∼straße *f* country road; (*Admin*) ≈
B road. **L∼streicher** *m* -s,- tramp.
L∼tag *m* state/(*Aust*) provincial
parliament
Landung *f* -,-en landing. **L∼sbrücke** *f*
landing-stage
Land|vermesser *m* -s,- surveyor.
L∼weg *m* country lane; **auf dem
L∼weg** overland. **L∼wirt** *m* farmer.
L∼wirtschaft *f* agriculture; (*Hof*)
farm. **l∼wirtschaftlich** *a* agricultural
lang¹ *adv & prep* (+ *preceding acc or
preceding* **an** + *dat*) along; **den** *od* **am
Fluß l∼** along the river
lang² *a* (**länger, längst**) long; (*groß*)
tall; **seit l∼em** for a long time ● *adv*
eine Stunde/Woche l∼ for an hour/a
week; **mein Leben l∼** all my life.
l∼ärmelig *a* long-sleeved. **l∼atmig**
a long-winded. **l∼e** *adv* a long time;
⟨*schlafen*⟩ late; **wie/zu l∼e** how/ too
long; **schon l∼e** [for] a long time;
(*zurückliegend*) a long time ago; **l∼e
nicht** not for a long time; (*bei weitem
nicht*) nowhere near
Länge *f* -,-n length; (*Geog*) longitude;
der L∼ nach lengthways; ⟨*liegen,
fallen*⟩ full length
langen *vt* hand (*dat* to) ● *vi* (*haben*)
reach (**an etw** *acc* sth; **nach** for);
(*genügen*) be enough
Läng|engrad *m* degree of longitude.
L∼enmaß *nt* linear measure. **l∼er** *a
& adv* longer; (*längere Zeit*) [for]
some time
Langeweile *f* - boredom; **L∼ haben**
be bored
lang|fristig *a* long-term; ⟨*Vorher-
sage*⟩ long-range. **l∼jährig** *a* long-
standing; ⟨*Erfahrung*⟩ long. **l∼lebig**
a long-lived
länglich *a* oblong. **l∼rund** *a* oval
langmütig *a* long-suffering
längs *adv & prep* (+ *gen/dat*) along;
(*der Länge nach*) lengthways

lang|sam *a* slow, *adv* -ly. **L~samkeit**
f - slowness. **L~schläfer(in)** *m(f)*
(*fam*) late riser. **L~schrift** *f*
longhand

längst *adv* [**schon**] **I~** for a long time;
(*zurückliegend*) a long time ago; **I~**
nicht nowhere near

Lang|strecken- *pref* long-distance;
(*Mil, Aviat*) long-range. **I~weilen** *vt*
bore; **sich I~weilen** be bored.
I~weilig *a* boring, *adv* -ly. **L~welle** *f*
long wave. **I~wierig** *a* lengthy

Lanze *f* -,-n lance

Lappalie /la'pa:liə/ *f* -,-n trifle

Lappen *m* -s,- cloth; (*Anat*) lobe

läppisch *a* silly

Lapsus *m* -,- slip

Lärche *f* -,-n larch

Lärm *m* -s noise. **I~en** *vi* (*haben*)
make a noise. **I~end** *a* noisy

Larve /'larfə/ *f* -,-n larva; (*Maske*)
mask

lasch *a* listless; (*schlaff*) limp; (*fade*)
insipid

Lasche *f* -,-n tab; (*Verschluß-*) flap;
(*Zunge*) tongue

Laser /'le:-, 'la:zɐ/ *m* -s,- laser

lassen† *vt* leave; (*zulassen*) let; **jdm**
etw I~ let s.o. keep sth; **sein Leben**
I~ lose one's life; **etw** [**sein** *od* **blei-**
ben] **I~** not do sth; (*aufhören*) stop
[doing] sth; **laß das!** stop it! **jdn schla-**
fen/gewinnen I~ let s.o. sleep/win;
jdn warten I~ keep s.o. waiting; **etw**
machen/reparieren I~ have sth do-
ne/repaired; **etw verschwinden I~**
make sth disappear; **sich [leicht] bie-**
gen/öffnen I~ bend/open [easily];
sich gut waschen I~ wash well; **es**
läßt sich nicht leugnen it is undeniable; **laßt uns gehen!** let's go!

lässig *a* casual, *adv* -ly. **L~keit** *f* -
casualness

Lasso *nt* -s,-s lasso

Last *f* -,-en load; (*Gewicht*) weight;
(*fig*) burden; **L~en** charges;
(*Steuern*) taxes; **jdm zur L~ fallen** be
a burden on s.o. **L~auto** *nt* lorry.
I~en *vi* (*haben*) weigh heavily/(*lie-*
gen) rest (**auf** + *dat* on). **L~enaufzug**
m goods lift

Laster¹ *m* -s,- (*fam*) lorry, (*Amer*)
truck

Laster² *nt* -s,- vice. **I~haft** *a*
depraved; (*zügellos*) dissolute

läster|lich *a* blasphemous. **I~n** *vt*
blaspheme ● *vi* (*haben*) make disparaging remarks (**über** + *acc*
about). **L~ung** *f* -,-en blasphemy

lästig *a* troublesome; **I~ sein/wer-**
den be/become a nuisance

Last|kahn *m* barge. **L~[kraft]wagen**
m lorry, (*Amer*) truck. **L~zug** *m*
lorry with trailer[s]

Latein *nt* -[s] Latin. **L~amerika** *nt*
Latin America. **I~isch** *a* Latin

latent *a* latent

Laterne *f* -,-n lantern; (*Straßen-*)
street lamp. **L~npfahl** *m* lamp-post

latschen *vi* (*sein*) (*fam*) traipse;
(*schlurfen*) shuffle

Latte *f* -,-n slat; (*Tor-, Hochsprung-*)
bar

Latz *m* -es,ˆe bib

Lätzchen *nt* -s,- [baby's] bib

Latzhose *f* dungarees *pl*

lau *a* lukewarm; (*mild*) mild

Laub *nt* -[e]s leaves *pl*; (*L~werk*)
foliage. **L~baum** *m* deciduous tree

Laube *f* -,-n summer-house; (*ge-*
wachsen) arbour. **L~ngang** *m* per-
gola; (*Archit*) arcades *pl*

Laub|säge *f* fretsaw. **L~wald** *m* de-
ciduous forest

Lauch *m* -[e]s leeks *pl*

Lauer *f* **auf der L~ liegen** lie in wait.
I~n *vi* (*haben*) lurk; **I~n auf** (+ *acc*)
lie in wait for

Lauf *m* -[e]s, **Läufe** run; (*Laufen*) running; (*Verlauf*) course; (*Wett-*) race;
(*Sport: Durchgang*) heat; (*Gewehr-*)
barrel; **im L~[e]** (+ *gen*) in the
course of. **L~bahn** *f* career. **I~en†** *vi*
(*sein*) run; (*zu Fuß gehen*) walk;
(*gelten*) be valid; **Ski/Schlittschuh**
I~en ski/ skate. **I~end** *a* running;
(*gegenwärtig*) current; (*regelmäßig*)
regular; **I~ende Nummer** serial
number; **auf dem I~enden sein/jdn**
auf dem I~enden halten be/keep s.o.
up to date ● *adv* continually. **I~en-**
lassen† *vt sep* (*fam*) let go

Läufer *m* -s,- (*Person, Teppich*) runner; (*Schach*) bishop

Lauf|gitter *nt* play-pen. **L~masche** *f*
ladder. **L~rolle** *f* castor. **L~schritt**
m **im L~schritt** at a run; (*Mil*) at the
double. **L~stall** *m* play-pen. **L~zet-**
tel *m* circular

Lauge *f* -,-n soapy water

Laun|e *f* -,-n mood; (*Einfall*) whim;
guter L~e sein, gute L~e haben be
in a good mood. **I~enhaft** *a* capricious. **I~isch** *a* moody

Laus *f* -,**Läuse** louse; (*Blatt-*) greenfly.
L~bub *m* (*fam*) rascal

lauschen *vi* (*haben*) listen; (*heimlich*)
eavesdrop

lausig a (fam) lousy ● adv terribly

laut a loud, adv -ly; (geräuschvoll) noisy, adv -ily; l∼ **lesen** read aloud; l∼**er stellen** turn up ● prep (+gen/ dat) according to. **L∼** m -es,-e sound

Laute f -,-n (Mus) lute

lauten vi (haben) ⟨Text:⟩ run, read; **auf jds Namen l∼** be in s.o.'s name

läuten vt/i (haben) ring

lauter a pure; (ehrlich) honest; ⟨Wahrheit⟩ plain ● a inv sheer; (nichts als) nothing but. **L∼keit** f - integrity

läutern vt purify

laut|hals adv at the top of one's voice; ⟨lachen⟩ out loud. l∼**los** a silent, adv -ly; ⟨Stille⟩ hushed. **L∼schrift** f phonetics pl. **L∼sprecher** m loudspeaker. l∼**stark** a vociferous, adv -ly. **L∼stärke** f volume

lauwarm a lukewarm

Lava f -,-ven lava

Lavendel m -s lavender

lavieren vi (haben) manœuvre

Lawine f -,-n avalanche

lax a lax. **L∼heit** f - laxity

Lazarett nt -[e]s,-e military hospital

leasen /'li:sən/ vt rent

Lebehoch nt cheer

leben vt/i (haben) live (von on); **leb wohl!** farewell! **L∼** nt -s,- life; (Treiben) bustle; **am L∼** alive. l∼**d** a living

lebendig a live; (lebhaft) lively; (anschaulich) vivid, adv -ly; l∼ **sein** be alive. **L∼keit** f - liveliness; vividness

Lebens|abend m old age. **L∼alter** nt age. **L∼art** f manners pl. l∼**fähig** a viable. **L∼gefahr** f mortal danger; **in L∼gefahr** in mortal danger; ⟨Patient⟩ critically ill. l∼**gefährlich** a extremely dangerous; ⟨Verletzung⟩ critical ● adv critically. **L∼größe** f **in L∼größe** life-sized. **L∼haltungskosten** pl cost of living sg. l∼**lang** a lifelong. l∼**länglich** a life ... ● adv for life. **L∼lauf** m curriculum vitae. **L∼mittel** ntpl food sg. **L∼mittelgeschäft** nt food shop. **L∼mittelhändler** m grocer. l∼**notwendig** a vital. **L∼retter** m rescuer; (beim Schwimmen) life-guard. **L∼standard** m standard of living. **L∼unterhalt** m livelihood; **seinen L∼unterhalt verdienen** earn one's living. **L∼versicherung** f life assurance. **L∼wandel** m conduct. l∼**wichtig** a vital. **L∼zeichen** nt sign of life. **L∼zeit** f **auf L∼zeit** for life

Leber f -,-n liver. **L∼fleck** m mole. **L∼wurst** f liver sausage

Lebe|wesen nt living being. **L∼wohl** nt -s,-s & -e farewell

leb|haft a lively; ⟨Farbe⟩ vivid. **L∼haftigkeit** f - liveliness. **L∼kuchen** m gingerbread. l∼**los** a lifeless. **L∼tag** m **mein/dein L∼tag** all my/your life. **L∼zeiten** fpl **zu jds L∼zeiten** in s.o.'s lifetime

leck a leaking. **L∼** nt -s,-s leak. l∼**en¹** vi (haben) leak

lecken² vt/i (haben) lick

lecker a tasty. **L∼ bissen** m delicacy. **L∼ei** f -,-en sweet

Leder nt -s,- leather. l∼**n** a leather; (wie Leder) leathery

ledig a single. l∼**lich** adv merely

Lee f & nt - **nach Lee** (Naut) to leeward

leer a empty; (unbesetzt) vacant; l∼ **laufen** (Auto) idle. **L∼e** f - emptiness; (leerer Raum) void. l∼**en** vt empty; **sich l∼en** empty. **L∼lauf** m (Auto) neutral. **L∼ung** f -,-en (Post) collection

legal a legal, adv -ly. l∼**isieren** vt legalize. **L∼ität** f - legality

Legas|thenie f - dyslexia. **L∼theniker** m -s,- dyslexic

legen vt put; (hin-, ver-) lay; set ⟨Haare⟩; **Eier l∼** lay eggs; **sich l∼** lie down; ⟨Staub:⟩ settle; (nachlassen) subside

legendär a legendary

Legende f -,-n legend

leger /le'ʒe:ɐ/ a casual, adv -ly

legier|en vt alloy; (Culin) thicken. **L∼ung** f -,-en alloy

Legion f -,-en legion

Legislative f - legislature

legitim a legitimate, adv -ly. l∼**ieren** (sich) vr prove one's identity. **L∼ität** f - legitimacy

Lehm m -s clay. l∼**ig** a clayey

Lehn|e f -,-en (Rücken-) back; (Arm-) arm. l∼**en** vt lean (an +acc against); **sich l∼en** lean (an +acc against) ● vi (haben) be leaning (an +dat against). **L∼sessel**, **L∼stuhl** m armchair

Lehr|buch nt textbook. **L∼e** f -,-n apprenticeship; (Anschauung) doctrine; (Theorie) theory; (Wissenschaft) science; (Ratschlag) advice; (Erfahrung) lesson; **jdm eine L∼e erteilen** (fig) teach s.o. a lesson. l∼**en** vt/i (haben) teach. **L∼er** m -s,- teacher; (Fahr-, Ski-) instructor.

L~erin *f* -,-nen teacher. L~erzimmer *nt* staff-room. L~fach *nt* (*Sch*) subject. L~gang *m* course. L~kraft *f* teacher. L~ling *m* -s,-e apprentice; (*Auszubildender*) trainee. L~plan *m* syllabus. l~reich *a* instructive. L~stelle *f* apprenticeship. L~stuhl *m* (*Univ*) chair. L~zeit *f* apprenticeship

Leib *m* -es,-er body; (*Bauch*) belly. L~eserziehung *f* (*Sch*) physical education. L~eskraft *f* aus L~eskräften as hard/⟨*schreien*⟩ loud as one can. L~gericht *nt* favourite dish. l~haftig *a der* l~haftige Satan the devil incarnate ● *adv* in the flesh. l~lich *a* physical; (*blutsverwandt*) real, natural. L~speise *f* = L~gericht. L~wache *f* (*coll*) bodyguard. L~wächter *m* bodyguard. L~wäsche *f* underwear

Leiche *f* -,-n [dead] body; corpse. L~nbegängnis *nt* -ses,-se funeral. L~nbestatter *m* -s,- undertaker. l~nblaß *a* deathly pale. L~nhalle *f* mortuary. L~nwagen *m* hearse. L~nzug *m* funeral procession, cortège

Leichnam *m* -s,-e [dead] body

leicht *a* light, *adv* -ly; ⟨*Stoff, Anzug*⟩ lightweight; (*gering*) slight, *adv* -ly; (*mühelos*) easy, *adv* -ily. L~athletik *f* [track and field] athletics *sg*. l~fallen† *vi sep* (*sein*) be easy (*dat* for). l~fertig *a* thoughtless, *adv* -ly; (*vorschnell*) rash, *adv* -ly; (*frivol*) frivolous, *adv* -ly. L~gewicht *nt* (*Boxen*) lightweight. l~gläubig *a* gullible. l~hin *adv* casually. L~igkeit *f* - lightness; (*Mühelosigkeit*) ease; (*L~sein*) easiness; mit L~igkeit with ease. l~lebig *a* a happy-go-lucky. l~machen *vt sep* make easy (*dat* for); es sich (*dat*) l~machen take the easy way out. l~nehmen† *vt sep* (*fig*) take lightly. L~sinn *m* carelessness; recklessness; (*Frivolität*) frivolity. l~sinnig *a* careless, *adv* -ly; (*unvorsichtig*) reckless, *adv* -ly; (*frivol*) frivolous, *adv* -ly

Leid *nt* -[e]s sorrow, grief; (*Böses*) harm. l~ *a* jdn/etw l~ sein/werden be/get tired of s.o./sth; es tut mir l~ I am sorry; er tut mir l~ I feel sorry for him

Leide|form *f* passive. l~n† *vt/i* (*haben*) suffer (an + *dat* from); jdn [gut] l~n können like s.o.; jdn/etw nicht l~n können dislike s.o./sth.

L~n *nt* -s,- suffering; (*Med*) complaint; (*Krankheit*) disease. l~nd *a* suffering; l~nd sein be in poor health. L~nschaft *f* -,-en passion. l~nschaftlich *a* passionate, *adv* -ly

leid|er *adv* unfortunately; l~er ja/nicht I'm afraid so/not. l~ig *a* wretched. l~lich *a* tolerable, *adv* -bly. L~tragende(r) *m/f* person who suffers; (*Trauernde*) mourner. L~wesen *nt* zu meinem L~wesen to my regret

Leier *f* -,-n die alte L~ (*fam*) the same old story. L~kasten *m* barrel-organ. l~n *vt/i* (*haben*) wind; (*herunter-*) drone out

Leih|bibliothek, L~bücherei *f* lending library. l~en† *vt* loan. l~en† (*dat*) etw l~en borrow sth. L~gabe *f* loan. L~gebühr *f* rental; (*für Bücher*) lending charge. L~haus *nt* pawnshop. L~wagen *m* hire-car. l~weise *adv* on loan

Leim *m* -s glue. l~en *vt* glue

Leine *f* -,-n rope; (*Wäsche-*) line; (*Hunde-*) lead, leash

Lein|en *nt* -s linen. l~en *a* linen. L~tuch *nt* sheet. L~wand *f* linen; (*Kunst*) canvas; (*Film-*) screen

leise *a* quiet, *adv* -ly; ⟨*Stimme, Musik, Berührung*⟩ soft, *adv* -ly; (*schwach*) faint, *adv* -ly; (*leicht*) light, *adv* -ly; l~r stellen turn down

Leiste *f* -,-n strip; (*Holz-*) batten; (*Zier-*) moulding; (*Anat*) groin

Leisten *m* -s,- [shoemaker's] last

leist|en *vt* achieve, accomplish; sich (*dat*) etw l~en treat oneself to sth; (*fam: anstellen*) get up to sth; ich kann es mir nicht l~en I can't afford it. L~ung *f* -,-en achievement; (*Sport, Techn*) performance; (*Produktion*) output; (*Zahlung*) payment. l~ungsfähig *a* efficient. L~ungsfähigkeit *f* efficiency

Leit|artikel *m* leader, editorial. L~bild *nt* (*fig*) model. l~en *vt* run, manage; (*an-/hinführen*) lead; (*Mus, Techn, Phys*) conduct; (*lenken, schicken*) direct. l~end *a* leading; ⟨*Posten*⟩ executive

Leiter¹ *f* -,-n ladder

Leit|er² *m* -s,- director; (*Comm*) manager; (*Führer*) leader; (*Sch*) head; (*Mus, Phys*) conductor. L~erin *f* -,-nen director; manageress; leader; head. L~faden *m* manual. L~kegel *m* [traffic] cone. L~planke *f* crash barrier. L~spruch *m* motto.

L~ung f -,-en (*Führung*) direction; (*Comm*) management; (*Aufsicht*) control; (*Electr: Schnur*) lead, flex; (*Kabel*) cable; (*Telefon-*) line; (*Rohr-*) pipe; (*Haupt-*) main. **L~ungswasser** *nt* tap water

Lektion /-'tsio:n/ f -,-en lesson

Lekt|or *m* -s,-en /-'to:ran/, **L~orin** f -,-nen (*Univ*) assistant lecturer; (*Verlags-*) editor. **L~üre** f -,-n reading matter; (*Lesen*) reading

Lende f -,-n loin

lenk|bar *a* steerable; (*fügsam*) tractable. **l~en** *vt* guide; (*steuern*) steer; (*Aust*) drive; (*regeln*) control; **jds Aufmerksamkeit auf sich** (*acc*) **l~en** attract s.o.'s attention. **L~er** *m* -s,- driver; (*L~stange*) handlebars *pl.* **L~rad** *nt* steering-wheel. **L~stange** f handlebars *pl.* **L~ung** f - steering

Leopard *m* -en,-en leopard

Lepra f - leprosy

Lerche f -,-n lark

lernen *vt/i* (*haben*) learn; (*für die Schule*) study; **schwimmen l~** learn to swim

lesbar *a* readable; (*leserlich*) legible

Lesb|ierin /'lɛsbiərɪn/ f-,-nen lesbian. **l~isch** *a* lesbian

Lese f-,-n harvest. **L~buch** *nt* reader. **l~n†** *vt/i* (*haben*) read; (*Univ*) lecture ● *vt* pick, gather. **L~n** *nt* -s reading. **L~r(in)** *m* -s,- (f -,-nen) reader. **L~ratte** f (*fam*) bookworm. **l~rlich** *a* legible, *adv* -bly. **L~zeichen** *nt* bookmark

Lesung f -,-en reading

lethargisch *a* lethargic, *adv* -ally

Lettland *nt* -s Latvia

letzt|e(r,s) *a* last; (*neueste*) latest; **in l~er Zeit** recently; **l~en Endes** in the end. **l~emal** *adv* **das l~emal** the last time; **zum l~enmal** for the last time. **l~ens** *adv* recently; (*zuletzt*) lastly. **l~ere(r,s)** *a* the latter; **der/die/das l~ere** the latter

Leucht|e f -,-n light. **l~en** *vi* (*haben*) shine. **l~end** *a* shining. **L~er** *m* -s,- candlestick. **L~feuer** *nt* beacon. **L~kugel**, **L~rakete** f flare. **L~reklame** f neon sign. **L~[stoff]röhre** f fluorescent tube. **L~turm** *m* lighthouse. **L~zifferblatt** *nt* luminous dial

leugnen *vt* deny

Leukämie f - leukaemia

Leumund *m* -s reputation

Leute *pl* people; (*Mil*) men; (*Arbeiter*) workers

Leutnant *m* -s,-s second lieutenant

leutselig *a* affable, *adv* -bly

Levkoje /lɛf'ko:jə/ f -,-n stock

Lexikon *nt* -s,-ka encyclopaedia; (*Wörterbuch*) dictionary

Libanon (**der**) **-s** Lebanon

Libelle f -,-n dragonfly; (*Techn*) spirit-level; (*Haarspange*) slide

liberal *a* (*Pol*) Liberal

Libyen *nt* -s Libya

Licht *nt* -[e]s,-er light; (*Kerze*) candle; **L~ machen** turn on the light; **hinters L~ führen** (*fam*) dupe. **l~** *a* bright; (*Med*) lucid; (*spärlich*) sparse. **L~bild** *nt* [passport] photograph; (*Dia*) slide. **L~bildervortrag** *m* slide lecture. **L~blick** *m* (*fig*) ray of hope. **l~en** *vt* thin out; **den Anker l~en** (*Naut*) weigh anchor; **sich l~en** become less dense; ⟨*Haare:*⟩ thin. **L~hupe** f headlight flasher; **die L~hupe betätigen** flash one's headlights. **L~maschine** f dynamo. **L~schalter** *m* light-switch. **L~ung** f -,-en clearing

Lid *nt* -[e]s,-er [eye]lid. **L~schatten** *m* eye-shadow

lieb *a* dear; (*nett*) nice; (*artig*) good; **es ist mir l~** I'm glad (**daß** that); **es wäre mir l~er** I should prefer it (**wenn** if). **l~äugeln** *vi* (*haben*) **l~äugeln mit** fancy; toy with ⟨*Gedanken*⟩

Liebe f -,-n love. **L~lei** f -,-en flirtation. **l~n** *vt* love; (*mögen*) like; **sich l~n** love each other; (*körperlich*) make love. **l~nd** *a* loving ● *adv* **etw l~nd gern** love to do sth. **l~nswert** *a* lovable. **l~nswürdig** *a* kind. **l~nswürdigerweise** *adv* very kindly. **L~nswürdigkeit** f -,-en kindness

lieber *adv* rather; (*besser*) better; **l~ mögen** like better; **ich trinke l~ Tee** I prefer tea

Liebes|brief *m* love letter. **L~dienst** *m* favour. **L~geschichte** f love story. **L~kummer** *m* heartache; **L~kummer haben** be depressed over an unhappy love-affair. **L~paar** *nt* [pair of] lovers *pl*

lieb|evoll *a* loving, *adv* -ly; (*zärtlich*) affectionate, *adv* -ly. **l~gewinnen†** *vt sep* grow fond of. **l~haben†** *vt sep* be fond of; (*lieben*) love. **L~haber** *m* -s,- lover; (*Sammler*) collector. **L~haberei** f-,-en hobby. **l~kosen** *vt* caress. **L~kosung** f -,-en caress. **l~lich** *a* lovely; (*sanft*) gentle; (*süß*) sweet. **L∼ling** *m* **-s,-e** darling; (*Bevorzugte*) favourite. **L∼lings-** *pref* favourite. **l∼los** *a* loveless; ⟨*Eltern*⟩ uncaring; (*unfreundlich*) unkind ● *adv* unkindly; (*ohne Sorgfalt*) without care. **L∼schaft** *f* **-,-en** [love] affair. **l∼ste(r,s)** *a* dearest; (*bevorzugt*) favourite ● *adv* **am l∼sten** best [of all]; **jdn/etw am l∼sten mögen** like s.o./sth best [of all]; **ich hätte am l∼sten geweint** I felt like crying. **L∼ste(r)** *m/f* beloved; (*Schatz*) sweetheart

Lied *nt* **-[e]s,-er** song

liederlich *a* slovenly; (*unordentlich*) untidy; (*ausschweifend*) dissolute. **L∼keit** *f* - slovenliness; untidiness; dissoluteness

Lieferant *m* **-en,-en** supplier

liefer|bar *a* (*Comm*) available. **l∼n** *vt* supply; (*zustellen*) deliver; (*hervorbringen*) yield. **L∼ung** *f* **-,-en** delivery; (*Sendung*) consignment; (*per Schiff*) shipment. **L∼wagen** *m* delivery van

Liege *f* **-,-n** couch. **l∼n†** *vi* (*haben*) lie; (*gelegen sein*) be situated; **l∼n an** (+*dat*) ⟨*fig*⟩ be due to; (*abhängen*) depend on; **jdm [nicht] l∼n** [not] suit s.o.; (*ansprechen*) [not] appeal to s.o.; **mir liegt viel/nicht daran** it is very/not important to me. **l∼nbleiben†** *vi sep* (*sein*) remain lying [there]; (*im Bett*) stay in bed; ⟨*Ding:*⟩ be left; ⟨*Schnee:*⟩ settle; ⟨*Arbeit:*⟩ remain undone; (*zurückgelassen werden*) be left behind; (*Panne haben*) break down. **l∼nlassen†** *vt sep* leave lying [there]; (*zurücklassen*) leave behind; (*nicht fortführen*) leave undone. **L∼sitz** *m* reclining seat. **L∼stuhl** *m* deck-chair. **L∼stütz** *m* **-es,-e** press-up, (*Amer*) push-up. **L∼wagen** *m* couchette car. **L∼wiese** *f* lawn for sunbathing

Lift *m* **-[e]s,-e** & **-s** lift, (*Amer*) elevator

Liga *f* **-,-gen** league

Likör *m* **-s,-e** liqueur

lila *inv* *a* mauve; (*dunkel*) purple

Lilie /'li:liə/ *f* **-,-n** lily

Liliputaner(in) *m* **-s,-** / (*f* **-,-nen**) dwarf

Limo *f* **-,-[s]** (*fam*), **L∼nade** *f* **-,-n** fizzy drink, (*Amer*) soda; (*Zitronen-*) lemonade

Limousine /limu'zi:nə/ *f* **-,-n** saloon, (*Amer*) sedan; (*mit Trennscheibe*) limousine

lind *a* mild; (*sanft*) gentle

Linde *f* **-,-n** lime tree

linder|n *vt* relieve, ease. **L∼ung** *f* - relief

Line|al *nt* **-s,-e** ruler. **l∼ar** *a* linear

Linguistik *f* - linguistics *sg*

Linie /-iə/ *f* **-,-n** line; (*Zweig*) branch; (*Bus-*) route; **L∼ 4** number 4 [bus/tram]; **in erster L∼** primarily. **L∼nflug** *m* scheduled flight. **L∼nrichter** *m* linesman

lin[i]iert *a* lined, ruled

Link|e *f* **-n,-n** left side; (*Hand*) left hand; (*Boxen*) left; **die L∼e** (*Pol*) the left; **zu meiner L∼en** on my left. **l∼e(r,s)** *a* left; (*Pol*) left-wing; **l∼e Seite** left[-hand] side; (*von Stoff*) wrong side; **l∼e Masche** purl. **l∼isch** *a* awkward, *adv* -ly

links *adv* on the left; (*bei Stoff*) on the wrong side; (*verkehrt*) inside out; **von/nach l∼** from/to the left; **l∼ stricken** purl. **L∼händer(in)** *m* **-s,-** (*f* **-,-nen**) left-hander. **l∼händig** *a* & *adv* left-handed. **L∼verkehr** *m* driving on the left

Linoleum /-leʊm/ *nt* **-s** lino[leum]

Linse *f* **-,-n** lens; (*Bot*) lentil

Lippe *f* **-,-n** lip. **L∼nstift** *m* lipstick

Liquid|ation /-'tsio:n/ *f* **-,-en** liquidation. **l∼ieren** *vt* liquidate

lispeln *vt/i* (*haben*) lisp

List *f* **-,-en** trick, ruse; (*Listigkeit*) cunning

Liste *f* **-,-n** list

listig *a* cunning, crafty

Litanei *f* **-,-en** litany

Litauen *nt* **-s** Lithuania

Liter *m* & *nt* **-s,-** litre

liter|arisch *a* literary. **L∼atur** *f* - literature

Litfaßsäule *f* advertising pillar

Liturgie *f* **-,-n** liturgy

Litze *f* **-,-n** braid; (*Electr*) flex

live /laif/ *adv* (*Radio, TV*) live

Lizenz *f* **-,-en** licence

Lkw /ɛlka've:/ *m* **-[s],-s** = **Lastkraftwagen**

Lob *nt* **-[e]s** praise

Lobby /'lɔbi/ *f* - (*Pol*) lobby

loben *vt* praise. **l∼swert** *a* praiseworthy, laudable

löblich *a* praiseworthy

Lobrede *f* eulogy

Loch *nt* **-[e]s,ˉer** hole. **l∼en** *vt* punch a hole/holes in; punch ⟨*Fahrkarte*⟩. **L∼er** *m* **-s,-** punch

löcher|ig *a* full of holes. **l∼n** *vt* (*fam*) pester

Locke *f* **-,-n** curl. **l∼n¹** *vt* curl; **sich l∼n** curl

locken² *vt* lure, entice; (*reizen*) tempt. **l~d** *a* tempting

Lockenwickler *m* -s,- curler; (*Rolle*) roller

locker *a* loose, *adv* -ly; ⟨*Seil*⟩ slack; ⟨*Erde, Kuchen*⟩ light; (*zwanglos*) casual; (*zu frei*) lax; (*unmoralisch*) loose. **l~n** *vt* loosen; slacken ⟨*Seil, Zügel*⟩; break up ⟨*Boden*⟩; relax ⟨*Griff*⟩; **sich l~** become loose; ⟨*Seil:*⟩ slacken; (*sich entspannen*) relax. **L~ungsübungen** *fpl* limbering-up exercises

lockig *a* curly

Lock|mittel *nt* bait. **L~ung** *f* -,-en lure; (*Versuchung*) temptation. **L~vogel** *m* decoy

Loden *m* -s (*Tex*) loden

lodern *vi* (*haben*) blaze

Löffel *m* -s,- spoon; (*L~voll*) spoonful. **l~n** *vt* spoon up

Logarithmus *m* -,-men logarithm

Logbuch *nt* (*Naut*) log-book

Loge /'lo:ʒə/ *f* -,-n lodge; (*Theat*) box

Logierbesuch /lo'ʒiː:ʁ̩-/ *m* house guest/guests *pl*

Log|ik *f* - logic. **l~isch** *a* logical, *adv* -ly

Logo *nt* -s,-s logo

Lohn *m* -[e]s,⸚e wages *pl*, pay; (*fig*) reward. **L~empfänger** *m* wage-earner. **l~en** *vi/r* (*haben*) [**sich**] **l~en** be worth it *or* worth while • *vt* be worth; **jdm etw l~en** reward s.o. for sth. **l~end** *a* worthwhile; (*befriedigend*) rewarding. **L~erhöhung** *f* [pay] rise; (*Amer*) raise. **L~steuer** *f* income tax

Lok *f* -,-s (*fam*) = **Lokomotive**

Lokal *nt* -s,-e restaurant; (*Trink-*) bar. **l~** *a* local. **l~isieren** *vt* locate; (*begrenzen*) localize

Lokomotiv|e *f* -,-n engine, locomotive. **L~führer** *m* engine driver

London *nt* -s London. **L~er** *a* London ... • *m* -s,- Londoner

Lorbeer *m* -s,-en laurel; **Echter L~** bay. **L~blatt** *nt* (*Culin*) bay-leaf

Lore *f* -,-n (*Rail*) truck

Los *nt* -es,-e lot; (*Lotterie-*) ticket; (*Schicksal*) fate; **das Große Los ziehen** hit the jackpot

los *pred a* **los sein** be loose; **jdn/etw los sein** be rid of s.o./sth; **was ist [mit ihm] los?** what's the matter [with him]? • *adv* **los!** go on! **Achtung, fertig, los!** ready, steady, go!

lösbar *a* soluble

losbinden† *vt sep* untie

Lösch|blatt *nt* sheet of blotting-paper. **l~en¹** *vt* put out, extinguish; quench ⟨*Durst*⟩; blot ⟨*Tinte*⟩; (*tilgen*) cancel; (*streichen*) delete; erase ⟨*Aufnahme*⟩

löschen² *vt* (*Naut*) unload

Lösch|fahrzeug *nt* fire-engine. **L~gerät** *nt* fire extinguisher. **L~papier** *nt* blotting-paper

lose *a* loose, *adv* -ly

Lösegeld *nt* ransom

losen *vi* (*haben*) draw lots (**um** for)

lösen *vt* undo; (*lockern*) loosen; (*entfernen*) detach; (*klären*) solve; (*auflösen*) dissolve; cancel ⟨*Vertrag*⟩; break off ⟨*Beziehung, Verlobung*⟩; (*kaufen*) buy; **sich l~** come off; (*sich trennen*) detach oneself/itself; (*lose werden*) come undone; (*sich entspannen*) relax; (*sich klären*) resolve itself; (*sich auflösen*) dissolve

los|fahren† *vi sep* (*sein*) start; ⟨*Auto:*⟩ drive off; **l~fahren auf** (+ *acc*) head for; (*fig: angreifen*) go for. **l~gehen†** *vi sep* (*sein*) set off; (*fam: anfangen*) start; (*fam: abgehen*) come off; ⟨*Bombe, Gewehr:*⟩ go off; **l~gehen auf** (+ *acc*) head for; (*fig: angreifen*) go for. **l~kommen†** *vi sep* (*sein*) get away (**von** from); **l~kommen auf** (+ *acc*) come towards. **l~lachen** *vi sep* (*haben*) burst out laughing. **l~lassen†** *vt sep* let go of; (*freilassen*) release

löslich *a* soluble

los|lösen *vt sep* detach; **sich l~lösen** become detached; (*fig*) break away (**von** from). **l~machen** *vt sep* detach; (*losbinden*) untie; **sich l~machen** free oneself/itself. **l~platzen** *vi sep* (*sein*) (*fam*) burst out laughing. **l~reißen†** *vt sep* tear off; **sich l~reißen** break free; (*fig*) tear oneself away. **l~sagen** (**sich**) *vr sep* renounce (**von etw** sth). **l~schicken** *vt sep* send off. **l~sprechen†** *vt sep* absolve (**von** from). **l~steuern** *vi sep* (*sein*) head (**auf** + *acc* for)

Losung *f* -,-en (*Pol*) slogan; (*Mil*) password

Lösung *f* -,-en solution. **L~smittel** *nt* solvent

los|werden† *vt sep* get rid of. **l~ziehen†** *vi sep* (*sein*) set off; **l~ziehen gegen** *od* **über** (+ *acc*) (*beschimpfen*) run down

Lot *nt* -[e]s,-e perpendicular; (*Blei-*) plumb[-bob]; **im Lot sein** (*fig*) be all right. **l~en** *vt* plumb

löt|en vt solder. **L∼lampe** f blowlamp, (Amer) blowtorch. **L∼metall** nt solder

lotrecht a perpendicular, adv -ly

Lotse m -n,-n (Naut) pilot. **l∼n** vt (Naut) pilot; (fig) guide

Lotterie f -,-n lottery

Lotto nt -s,-s lotto; (Lotterie) lottery

Löw|e m -n,-n lion; (Astr) Leo. **L∼enanteil** m (fig) lion's share. **L∼enzahn** m (Bot) dandelion. **L∼in** f -,-nen lioness

loyal /loa'ja:l/ a loyal. **L∼ität** f -loyalty

Luchs m -es,-e lynx

Lücke f-,-n gap. **L∼nbüßer** m -s,-stopgap. **l∼nhaft** a incomplete; ⟨Wissen⟩ patchy. **l∼nlos** a complete; ⟨Folge⟩ unbroken

Luder nt -s,- (sl) (Frau) bitch; **armes L∼** poor wretch

Luft f -,¨e air; **tief L∼ holen** take a deep breath; **in die L∼ gehen** explode. **L∼angriff** m air raid. **L∼aufnahme** f aerial photograph. **L∼ballon** m balloon. **L∼bild** nt aerial photograph. **L∼blase** f air bubble

Lüftchen nt -s,- breeze

luft|dicht a airtight. **L∼druck** m atmospheric pressure

lüften vt air; raise ⟨Hut⟩; reveal ⟨Geheimnis⟩

Luft|fahrt f aviation. **L∼fahrtgesellschaft** f airline. **L∼gewehr** nt airgun. **L∼hauch** m breath of air. **l∼ig** a airy; ⟨Kleid⟩ light. **L∼kissenfahrzeug** nt hovercraft. **L∼krieg** m aerial warfare. **L∼kurort** m climatic health resort. **l∼leer** a **l∼leerer Raum** vacuum. **L∼linie** f **100 km L∼linie** 100 km as the crow flies. **L∼loch** nt air-hole; (Aviat) air pocket. **L∼matratze** f air-bed, inflatable mattress. **L∼pirat** m [aircraft] hijacker. **L∼post** f airmail. **L∼pumpe** f air pump; (Fahrrad-) bicyclepump. **L∼röhre** f windpipe. **L∼schiff** nt airship. **L∼schlange** f [paper] streamer. **L∼schlösser** ntpl castles in the air. **L∼schutzbunker** m air-raid shelter

Lüftung f - ventilation

Luft|veränderung f change of air. **L∼waffe** f air force. **L∼weg** m **auf dem L∼weg** by air. **L∼zug** m draught

Lüg|e f -,-n lie. **l∼en†** vt/i (haben) lie. **L∼ner(in)** m -s,- (f -,-nen) liar.

l∼nerisch a untrue; ⟨Person⟩ untruthful

Luke f -,-n hatch; (Dach-) skylight

Lümmel m -s,- lout; (fam: Schelm) rascal. **l∼n (sich)** vr loll

Lump m -en,-en scoundrel. **L∼en** m -s,- rag; **in L∼en** in rags. **l∼en** vt **sich nicht l∼en lassen** be generous. **L∼engesindel, L∼enpack** nt riffraff. **L∼ensammler** m rag-and-bone man. **l∼ig** a mean, shabby; (gering) measly

Lunchpaket /'lan[t]ʃ-/ nt packed lunch

Lunge f -,-n lungs pl; (L∼nflügel) lung. **L∼nentzündung** f pneumonia

lungern vi (haben) loiter

Lunte f **L∼ riechen** (fam) smell a rat

Lupe f -,-n magnifying glass

Lurch m -[e]s,-e amphibian

Lust f -,¨e pleasure; (Verlangen) desire; (sinnliche Begierde) lust; **L∼ haben** feel like (auf etw acc sth); **ich habe keine L∼** I don't feel like it; (will nicht) I don't want to

Lüster m -s,- lustre; (Kronleuchter) chandelier

lüstern a greedy (auf + acc for); (sinnlich) lascivious; (geil) lecherous

lustig a jolly; (komisch) funny; **sich l∼ machen über** (+ acc) make fun of

Lüstling m -s,-e lecher

lust|los a listless, adv -ly. **L∼mörder** m sex killer. **L∼spiel** nt comedy

lutherisch a Lutheran

lutsch|en vt/i (haben) suck. **L∼er** m -s,- lollipop; (Schnuller) dummy, (Amer) pacifier

lütt a (NGer) little

Lüttich nt -s Liège

Luv f & nt - **nach Luv** (Naut) to windward

luxuriös a luxurious, adv -ly

Luxus m - luxury. **L∼artikel** m luxury article. **L∼ausgabe** f de luxe edition. **L∼hotel** nt luxury hotel

Lymph|drüse /'lymf-/ f, **L∼knoten** m lymph gland

lynchen /'lynçən/ vt lynch

Lyr|ik f - lyric poetry. **L∼iker** m -s,- lyric poet. **l∼isch** a lyrical; ⟨Dichtung⟩ lyric

M

Mach|art f style. **m∼bar** a feasible. **m∼en** vt make; get ⟨Mahlzeit⟩; take

⟨*Foto*⟩; (*ausführen, tun, in Ordnung bringen*) do; (*Math: ergeben*) be; (*kosten*) come to; **sich** (*dat*) **etw m∼en lassen** have sth made; **was m∼st du da?** what are you doing? **was m∼t die Arbeit?** how is work? **das m∼t 6 Mark [zusammen]** that's 6 marks [altogether]; **das m∼t nichts** it doesn't matter; **sich** (*dat*) **wenig/ nichts m∼en aus** care little/ nothing for ● *vr* **sich m∼en** do well; **sich an die Arbeit m∼en** get down to work ● *vi* (*haben*) **ins Bett m∼en** (*fam*) wet the bed; **schnell m∼en** hurry. **M∼enschaften** *fpl* machinations

Macht *f* -,̈e power; **mit aller M∼** with all one's might. **M∼haber** *m* -s,- ruler

mächtig *a* powerful; (*groß*) enormous ● *adv* (*fam*) terribly

macht|los *a* powerless. **M∼wort** *nt* **ein M∼wort sprechen** put one's foot down

Mädchen *nt* -s,- girl; (*Dienst-*) maid. **m∼haft** *a* girlish. **M∼name** *m* girl's name; (*vor der Ehe*) maiden name

Made *f* -,-n maggot

Mädel *nt* -s,- girl

madig *a* maggoty; **jdn m∼ machen** (*fam*) run s.o. down

Madonna *f* -,-nen madonna

Magazin *nt* -s,-e magazine; (*Lager*) warehouse; (*Raum*) store-room

Magd *f* -,̈e maid

Magen *m* -s,̈ stomach. **M∼schmerzen** *mpl* stomach-ache *sg*. **M∼verstimmung** *f* stomach upset

mager *a* thin; ⟨*Fleisch*⟩ lean; ⟨*Boden*⟩ poor; (*dürftig*) meagre. **M∼keit** *f* - thinness; leanness. **M∼sucht** *f* anorexia

Magie *f* - magic

Mag|ier /ˈmaːgiɐ/ *m* -s,- magician. **m∼isch** *a* magic; (*geheimnisvoll*) magical

Magistrat *m* -s,-e city council

Magnesia *f* - magnesia

Magnet *m* -en & -[e]s, -e magnet. **m∼isch** *a* magnetic. **m∼isieren** *vt* magnetize. **M∼ismus** *m* - magnetism

Mahagoni *nt* -s mahogany

Mäh|drescher *m* -s,- combine harvester. **m∼en** *vt/i* (*haben*) mow

Mahl *nt* -[es]s,̈er meal

mahlen† *vt* grind

Mahlzeit *f* meal; **M∼!** enjoy your meal!

Mähne *f* -,-n mane

mahn|en *vt/i* (*haben*) remind (*wegen* about); (*ermahnen*) admonish; (*auffordern*) urge (**zu** to); **zur Vorsicht/Eile m∼en** urge caution/ haste. **M∼ung** *f* -,-en reminder; admonition; (*Aufforderung*) exhortation

Mai *m* -[e]s,-e May; **der Erste Mai** May Day. **M∼glöckchen** *nt* -s,- lily of the valley. **M∼käfer** *m* cockchafer

Mailand *nt* -s Milan

Mais *m* -es maize, (*Amer*) corn; (*Culin*) sweet corn. **M∼kolben** *m* corn-cob

Majestät *f* -,-en majesty. **m∼isch** *a* majestic, *adv* -ally

Major *m* -s,-e major

Majoran *m* -s marjoram

Majorität *f* -,-en majority

makaber *a* macabre

Makel *m* -s,- blemish; (*Defekt*) flaw; (*fig*) stain. **m∼los** *a* flawless; (*fig*) unblemished

mäkeln *vi* (*haben*) grumble

Makkaroni *pl* macaroni *sg*

Makler *m* -s,- (*Comm*) broker

Makrele *f* -,-n mackerel

Makrone *f* -,-n macaroon

mal *adv* (*Math*) times; (*bei Maßen*) by; (*fam: einmal*) once; (*eines Tages*) one day; **schon mal** once before; (*jemals*) ever; **nicht mal** not even; **hört/seht mal!** listen!/look!

Mal¹ *nt* -[e]s,-e time; **zum ersten Mal** for the first time; **mit einem Mal** all at once; **ein für alle Mal** once and for all

Mal² *nt* -[e]s,-e mark; (*auf der Haut*) mole; (*Mutter-*) birthmark

Mal|buch *nt* colouring book. **m∼en** *vt/i* (*haben*) paint. **M∼er** *m* -s,- painter. **M∼erei** *f* -,-en painting. **M∼erin** *f* -,-nen painter. **m∼erisch** *a* picturesque

Malheur /maˈløːɐ̯/ *nt* -s,-e & -s (*fam*) mishap; (*Ärger*) trouble

Mallorca /maˈlɔrka, -ˈjɔrka/ *nt* -s Majorca

malnehmen† *vt sep* multiply (**mit** by)

Malz *nt* -es malt. **M∼bier** *nt* malt beer

Mama /ˈmama, maˈma:/ *f* -s,-s mummy

Mammut *nt* -s,-e & -s mammoth

mampfen *vt* (*fam*) munch

man *pron* one, you; (*die Leute*) people, they; **man sagt** they say, it is said

Manager /ˈmɛnɪdʒɐ/ *m* -s,- manager

manch *inv pron* **m~ ein(e)** many a; **m~ einer/eine** many a man/woman. **m~e(r,s)** *pron* many a; **[so] m~es Mal** many a time; **m~e Leute** some people ● (*substantivisch*) **m~er/ m~e** many a man/woman; **m~e** *pl* some; (*Leute*) some people; (*viele*) many [people]; **m~es** some things; (*vieles*) many things. **m~erlei** *inv a* various ● *pron* various things

manchmal *adv* sometimes

Mandant(in) *m* -en,-en (*f* -,-nen) (*Jur*) client

Mandarine *f* -,-n mandarin

Mandat *nt* -[e]s,-e mandate; (*Jur*) brief; (*Pol*) seat

Mandel *f* -,-n almond; (*Anat*) tonsil. **M~entzündung** *f* tonsillitis

Manege /ma'ne:ʒə/ *f* -,-n ring; (*Reit-*) arena

Mangel[1] *m* -s,- lack; (*Knappheit*) shortage; (*Med*) deficiency; (*Fehler*) defect; **M~ leiden** go short

Mangel[2] *f* -,-n mangle

mangel|haft *a* faulty, defective; (*Sch*) unsatisfactory. **m~n**[1] *vi* (*haben*) **es m~t an** (+ *dat*) there is a lack/(*Knappheit*) shortage of

mangeln[2] *vt* put through the mangle

mangels *prep* (+ *gen*) for lack of

Mango *f* -,-s mango

Manie *f* -,-n mania; (*Sucht*) obsession

Manier *f* -,-en manner; **M~en** manners. **m~lich** *a* well-mannered ● *adv* properly

Manifest *nt* -[e]s,-e manifesto. **m~ieren (sich)** *vr* manifest itself

Maniküre *f* -,-n manicure; (*Person*) manicurist. **m~n** *vt* manicure

Manipul|ation /-'tsio:n/ *f* -,-en manipulation. **m~ieren** *vt* manipulate

Manko *nt* -s,-s disadvantage; (*Fehlbetrag*) deficit

Mann *m* -[e]s,"er man; (*Ehe-*) husband

Männchen *nt* -s,- little man; (*Zool*) male; **M~ machen** ⟨*Hund:*⟩ sit up

Mannequin /'manəkɛ̃/ *nt* -s,-s model

Männerchor *m* male voice choir

Mannes|alter *nt* manhood. **M~kraft** *f* virility

mannhaft *a* manful, *adv* -ly

mannigfaltig *a* manifold; (*verschieden*) diverse

männlich *a* male; (*Gram & fig*) masculine; (*mannhaft*) manly; ⟨*Frau*⟩ mannish. **M~keit** *f* - masculinity; (*fig*) manhood

Mannschaft *f* -,-en team; (*Naut*) crew. **M~sgeist** *m* team spirit

Manöv|er *nt* -s,- manoeuvre; (*Winkelzug*) trick. **m~rieren** *vt/i* (*haben*) manoeuvre

Mansarde *f* -,-n attic room; (*Wohnung*) attic flat

Manschette *f* -,-n cuff; (*Blumentopf-*) paper frill. **M~nknopf** *m* cuff-link

Mantel *m* -s,"- coat; (*dick*) overcoat; (*Reifen-*) outer tyre

Manuskript *nt* -[e]s,-e manuscript

Mappe *f* -,-n folder; (*Akten-*) briefcase; (*Schul-*) bag

Marathon *m* -s,-s marathon

Märchen *nt* -s,- fairy-tale. **m~haft** *a* fairy-tale ...; (*phantastisch*) fabulous

Margarine *f* - margarine

Marienkäfer /ma'ri:ən-/ *m* ladybird, (*Amer*) ladybug

Marihuana *nt* -s marijuana

Marille *f* -,-n (*Aust*) apricot

Marinade *f* -,-n marinade

Marine *f* marine; (*Kriegs-*) navy. **m~blau** *a* navy [blue]. **M~infanterist** *m* marine

marinieren *vt* marinade

Marionette *f* -,-n puppet, marionette

Mark[1] *f* -,- mark; **drei M~** three marks

Mark[2] *nt* -[e]s (*Knochen-*) marrow; (*Bot*) pith; (*Frucht-*) pulp; **bis ins M~ getroffen** (*fig*) cut to the quick

markant *a* striking

Marke *f* -,-n token; (*rund*) disc; (*Erkennungs-*) tag; (*Brief-*) stamp; (*Lebensmittel-*) coupon; (*Spiel-*) counter; (*Markierung*) mark; (*Fabrikat*) make; (*Tabak-*) brand. **M~nartikel** *m* branded article

markier|en *vt* mark; (*fam: vortäuschen*) fake. **M~ung** *f* -,-en marking

Markise *f* -,-n awning

Markstück *nt* one-mark piece

Markt *m* -[e]s, "e market; (*M~platz*) market-place. **M~forschung** *f* market research. **M~platz** *m* market-place

Marmelade *f* -,-n jam; (*Orangen-*) marmalade

Marmor *m* -s marble

Marokko *nt* -s Morocco

Marone *f* -,-n [sweet] chestnut

Marotte *f* -,-n whim

Marsch[1] *f* -,-en marsh

Marsch[2] *m* -[e]s, "e march. **m~** *int* (*Mil*) march! **m~ ins Bett!** off to bed!

Marschall *m* -s, "e marshal

marschieren vi (sein) march
Marter f -,-n torture. **m~n** vt torture
Martinshorn nt [police] siren
Märtyrer(in) m -s,- (f -,-nen) martyr
Martyrium nt -s martyrdom
Marxis|mus m - Marxism. **m~tisch** a Marxist
März m -,-e March
Marzipan nt -s marzipan
Masche f -,-n stitch; (im Netz) mesh; (fam: Trick) dodge. **M~ndraht** m wire netting
Maschin|e f -,-n machine; (Flugzeug) plane; (Schreib-) typewriter. **m~egeschrieben** a typewritten, typed. **m~ell** a machine ... ● adv by machine. **M~enbau** m mechanical engineering. **M~engewehr** nt machine-gun. **M~enpistole** f submachine-gun. **M~erie** f - machinery. **M~eschreiben** nt typing. **M~ist** m -en,-en machinist; (Naut) engineer
Masern pl measles sg
Maserung f -,-en [wood] grain
Maske f -,-n mask; (Theat) make-up. **M~rade** f -,-n disguise; (fig: Heuchelei) masquerade
maskieren vt mask; sich m~ dress up (als as)
Maskottchen nt -s,- mascot
maskulin a masculine
Maskulinum nt -s,-na (Gram) masculine
Masochis|mus /mazo'xısmʊs/ m - masochism. **M~t** m -en,-en masochist
Maß¹ nt -es,-e measure; (Abmessung) measurement; (Grad) degree; (Mäßigung) moderation; in od mit Maß[en] in moderation; in hohem Maße to a high degree
Maß² f -,- (SGer) litre [of beer]
Massage /ma'sa:ʒə/ f -,-n massage
Massaker nt -s,- massacre
Maß|anzug m made-to-measure suit. **M~band** nt (pl -bänder) tape-measure
Masse f -,-n mass; (Culin) mixture; (Menschen-) crowd; eine M~ Arbeit (fam) masses of work. **M~nartikel** m mass-produced article. **m~nhaft** adv in huge quantities. **M~nmedien** pl mass media. **M~nproduktion** f mass production. **m~nweise** adv in huge numbers
Masseu|r /ma'sø:ɐ̯/ m -s,-e masseur. **M~rin** f -,-nen, **M~se** /-'sø:zə/ f -,-n masseuse

maß|gebend a authoritative; (einflußreich) influential. **m~geblich** a decisive, adv -ly. **m~geschneidert** a made-to-measure. **m~halten**† vi sep (haben) exercise moderation
massieren¹ vt massage
massieren² (sich) vr mass
massig a massive
mäßig a moderate, adv -ly; (mittelmäßig) indifferent. **m~en** vt moderate; sich m~en moderate; (sich beherrschen) restrain oneself. **M~keit** f - moderation. **M~ung** f - moderation
massiv a solid; (stark) heavy
Maß|krug m beer mug. **m~los** a excessive; (grenzenlos) boundless; (äußerst) extreme, adv -ly. **M~nahme** f -,-n measure. **m~regeln** vt reprimand
Maßstab m scale; (Norm & fig) standard. **m~sgerecht**, **m~sgetreu** a scale ... ● adv to scale
maßvoll a moderate
Mast¹ m -[e]s,-en pole; (Überland-) pylon; (Naut) mast
Mast² f - fattening. **M~darm** m rectum
mästen vt fatten
Masturb|ation /-'tsio:n/ f - masturbation. **m~ieren** vi (haben) masturbate
Material nt -s,-ien /-jən/ material; (coll) materials pl. **M~ismus** m - materialism. **m~istisch** a materialistic
Mater|ie /ma'te:rjə/ f -,-n matter; (Thema) subject. **m~iell** a material
Mathe f - (fam) maths sg
Mathe|matik f - mathematics sg. **M~matiker** m -s,- mathematician. **m~matisch** a mathematical
Matinee f -,-n (Theat) morning performance
Matratze f -,-n mattress
Mätresse f -,-n mistress
Matrose m -n,-n sailor
Matsch m -[e]s mud; (Schnee-) slush. **m~ig** a muddy; slushy; (weich) mushy
matt a weak; (gedämpft) dim; (glanzlos) dull; ⟨Politur, Farbe⟩ matt; jdn m~ setzen checkmate s.o. **M~** nt -s (Schach) mate
Matte f -,-n mat
Mattglas nt frosted glass
Matt|igkeit f - weakness; (Müdigkeit) weariness. **M~scheibe** f (fam) television screen

Matura *f* - (*Aust*) ≈ A levels *pl*
Mauer *f* -,-n wall. **m~n** *vt* build ● *vi*
(*haben*) lay bricks. **M~werk** *nt*
masonry
Maul *nt* -[e]s,Mäuler (*Zool*) mouth;
halt's **M~**! (*fam*) shut up! **m~en** *vi*
(*haben*) (*fam*) grumble. **M~korb** *m*
muzzle. **M~tier** *nt* mule. **M~wurf**
m mole. **M~wurfshaufen, M~**
wurfshügel *m* molehill
Maurer *m* -s,- bricklayer
Maus *f* -,Mäuse mouse. **M~efalle** *f*
mousetrap
mausern (sich) *vr* moult; (*fam*) turn
(**zu** into)
Maut *f* -,-en (*Aust*) toll. **M~straße** *f*
toll road
maximal *a* maximum
Maximum *nt* -s,-ma maximum
Mayonnaise /majɔ'nɛːzə/ *f* -,-n
mayonnaise
Mäzen *m* -s,-e patron
Mechan|ik /me'çaːnɪk/ *f* - mechanics
sg; (*Mechanismus*) mechanism.
M~iker *m* -s,- mechanic. **m~isch** *a*
mechanical, *adv* -ly. **m~isieren** *vt*
mechanize. **M~ismus** *m* -,-men
mechanism
meckern *vi* (*haben*) bleat; (*fam*:
nörgeln) grumble
Medaill|e /me'daljə/ *f* -,-n medal.
M~on /-'jõː/ *nt* -s,-s medallion;
(*Schmuck*) locket
Medikament *nt* -[e]s,-e medicine
Medit|ation /-'tsi̯oːn/ *f* -,-en medi-
tation. **m~ieren** *vi* (*haben*) meditate
Medium *nt* -s,-ien medium; **die**
Medien the media
Medizin *f* -,-en medicine. **M~er** *m*
-s,- doctor; (*Student*) medical student. **m~isch** *a* medical; (*heilkräftig*) medicinal
Meer *nt* -[e]s,-e sea. **M~busen** *m*
gulf. **M~enge** *f* strait. **M~esspiegel**
m sea-level. **M~jungfrau** *f* mermaid. **M~rettich** *m* horseradish.
M~schweinchen *nt* -s,- guinea-pig
Megaphon *nt* -s,-e megaphone
Mehl *nt* -[e]s flour. **m~ig** *a* floury.
M~schwitze *f* (*Culin*) roux.
M~speise *f* (*Aust*) dessert; (*Kuchen*)
pastry. **M~tau** *m* (*Bot*) mildew
mehr *pron & adv* more; **m~ no**
more; (*zeitlich*) no longer; **nichts**
m~ no more; (*nichts weiter*) nothing
else; **nie m~** never again. **m~deu-**
tig *a* ambiguous. **m~en** *vt* increase;
sich m~en increase. **m~ere** *pron*
several. **m~eres** *pron* several

things *pl.* **m~fach** *a* multiple;
(*mehrmalig*) repeated ● *adv* several
times. **M~fahrtenkarte** *f* book of
tickets. **m~farbig** *a* [multi]col-
oured. **M~heit** *f* -,-en majority.
m~malig *a* repeated. **m~mals** *adv*
several times. **m~sprachig** *a* multi-
lingual. **m~stimmig** *a* (*Mus*) for several voices ● *adv* **m~stimmig**
singen sing in harmony. **M~wert-**
steuer *f* value-added tax, VAT.
M~zahl *f* majority; (*Gram*) plural.
M~zweck- *pref* multi-purpose
meiden† *vt* avoid, shun
Meierei *f* -,-en (*dial*) dairy
Meile *f* -,-n mile. **M~nstein** *m* mile-
stone. **m~nweit** *adv* [for] miles
mein *poss pron* my. **m~e(r,s)** *poss*
pron mine; **die M~en** *pl* my family
sg
Meineid *m* perjury; **einen M~ leisten**
perjure oneself
meinen *vt* mean; (*glauben*) think;
(*sagen*) say; **es gut m~** mean well
mein|erseits *adv* for my part.
m~etwegen *adv* for my sake; (*wegen mir*) because of me, on my account; (*fam: von mir aus*) as far as
I'm concerned. **m~etwillen** *adv* **um**
m~etwillen for my sake. **m~ige**
poss pron **der/die/das m~ige** mine.
m~s *poss pron* mine
Meinung *f* -,-en opinion; **jdm die M~**
sagen give s.o. a piece of one's mind.
M~sumfrage *f* opinion poll
Meise *f* -,-n (*Zool*) tit
Meißel *m* -s,- chisel. **m~n** *vt/i*
(*haben*) chisel
meist *adv* mostly; (*gewöhnlich*)
usually. **m~e** *a* **der/die/das m~e**
most; **die m~en Leute** most people;
die m~e Zeit most of the time; **am**
m~en [the] most ● *pron* **das m~e**
most [of it]; **die m~en** most. **m~ens**
adv mostly; (*gewöhnlich*) usually
Meister *m* -s,- master craftsman;
(*Könner*) master; (*Sport*) champion.
m~haft *a* masterly ● *adv* in
masterly fashion. **m~n** *vt* master.
M~schaft *f* -,-en mastery; (*Sport*)
championship. **M~stück, M~werk**
nt masterpiece
Melanch|olie /melaŋko'liː/ *f* - melan-
choly. **m~olisch** *a* melancholy
meld|en *vt* report; (*anmelden*) regis-
ter; (*ankündigen*) announce; **sich**
m~en report (**bei** to); (*zum Militär*)
enlist; (*freiwillig*) volunteer; (*Teleph*) answer; (*Sch*) put up one's

hand; (*von sich hören lassen*) get in touch (**bei** with); **sich krank m~en** report sick. **M~ung** *f* -,-en report; (*Anmeldung*) registration

meliert *a* mottled; **grau m~es Haar** hair flecked with grey

melken† *vt* milk

Melod|ie *f* -,-n tune, melody. **m~iös** *a* melodious

melodisch *a* melodic; (*melodiös*) melodious, tuneful

melodramatisch *a* melodramatic, *adv* -ally

Melone *f* -,-n melon; [**schwarze**] **M~** (*fam*) bowler [hat]

Membran *f* -,-en membrane

Memoiren |me'mǫa:rən|/ *pl* memoirs

Menge *f* -,-n amount, quantity; (*Menschen-*) crowd; (*Math*) set; **eine M~ Geld** a lot of money. **m~n** *vt* mix

Mensa *f* -,-sen (*Univ*) refectory

Mensch *m* -en,-en human being; **der M~** man; **die M~en** people; **jeder/kein M~** everybody/nobody. **M~enaffe** *m* ape. **M~enfeind** *m* misanthropist. **m~enfeindlich** *a* antisocial. **M~enfresser** *m* -s,- cannibal; (*Zool*) man-eater; (*fam*) ogre. **m~enfreundlich** *a* philanthropic. **M~enleben** *nt* human life; (*Lebenszeit*) lifetime. **m~enleer** *a* deserted. **M~enmenge** *f* crowd. **M~enraub** *m* kidnapping. **M~enrechte** *ntpl* human rights. **m~enscheu** *a* unsociable. **M~enskind** *int* (*fam*) good heavens! **M~enverstand** *m* **ge-sunder M~enverstand** common sense. **m~enwürdig** *a* humane, *adv* -ly. **M~heit** *f* - **die M~heit** mankind, humanity. **m~lich** *a* human; (*human*) humane, *adv* -ly. **M~lichkeit** *f* - humanity

Menstru|ation /-'tṣio:n/ *f* - menstruation. **m~ieren** *vi* (*haben*) menstruate

Mentalität *f* -,-en mentality

Menü *nt* -s,-s menu; (*festes M~*) set meal

Menuett *nt* -[e]s,-e minuet

Meridian *m* -s,-e meridian

merk|bar *a* noticeable. **M~blatt** *nt* [explanatory] leaflet. **m~en** *vt* notice; **sich** (*dat*) **etw m~en** remember sth. **m~lich** *a* noticeable, *adv* -bly. **M~mal** *nt* feature

merkwürdig *a* odd, *adv* -ly, strange, *adv* -ly. **m~erweise** *adv* oddly enough

meß|bar *a* measurable. **M~becher** *m* (*Culin*) measure

Messe¹ *f* -,-n (*Relig*) mass; (*Comm*) [trade] fair

Messe² *f* -,-n (*Mil*) mess

messen† *vt/i* (*haben*) measure; (*ansehen*) look at; [**bei jdm**] **Fieber m~** take s.o.'s temperature; **sich m~** compete (**mit** with); **sich mit jdm m~/nicht m~ können** be a/no match for s.o.

Messer *nt* -s,- knife

Messias *m* - Messiah

Messing *nt* -s brass

Messung *f* -,-en measurement

Metabolismus *m* - metabolism

Metall *nt* -s,-e metal. **m~en** *a* metal; (*metallisch*) metallic. **m~isch** *a* metallic

Metallurgie *f* - metallurgy

Metamorphose *f* -,-n metamorphosis

Metaph|er *f* -,-n metaphor. **m~orisch** *a* metaphorical, *adv* -ly

Meteor *m* -s,-e meteor. **M~ologe** *m* -n,-n meteorologist. **M~ologie** *f* - meteorology. **m~ologisch** *a* meteorological

Meter *m* & *nt* -s,- metre, (*Amer*) meter. **M~maß** *nt* tape-measure

Method|e *f* -,-n method. **m~isch** *a* methodical

metrisch *a* metric

Metropole *f* -,-n metropolis

metzeln *vt* (*fig*) massacre

Metzger *m* -s,- butcher. **M~ei** *f* -,-en butcher's shop

Meute *f* -,-n pack [of hounds]; (*fig: Menge*) mob

Meuterei *f* -,-en mutiny

meutern *vi* (*haben*) mutiny; (*fam: schimpfen*) grumble

Mexikan|er(in) *m* -s,- (*f* -,-nen) Mexican. **m~isch** *a* Mexican

Mexiko *nt* -s Mexico

miauen *vi* (*haben*) mew, miaow

mich *pron* (*acc of* **ich**) me; (*refl*) myself

Mieder *nt* -s,- bodice; (*Korsett*) corset

Miene *f* -,-n expression; **M~ machen** make as if (**zu** to)

mies *a* (*fam*) lousy; **mir ist m~** I feel rotten

Miet|e *f* -,-n rent; (*Mietgebühr*) hire charge; **zur M~e wohnen** live in rented accommodation. **m~en** *vt* rent ⟨*Haus, Zimmer*⟩; hire ⟨*Auto, Boot, Fernseher*⟩. **M~er(in)** *m* -s,- (*f* -,-nen) tenant. **m~frei** *a* & *adv* rent-free. **M~shaus** *nt* block of rented flats. **M~vertrag** *m* lease. **M~wagen** *m* hire-car. **M~wohnung** *f* rented flat; (*zu vermieten*) flat to let

Mieze *f* -,-n (*fam*) puss[y]

Migräne *f* -,-n migraine

Mikrobe *f* -,-n microbe

Mikro|chip *m* microchip. **M~computer** *m* microcomputer. **M~film** *m* microfilm

Mikro|fon, M~phon *nt* -s,-e microphone. **M~prozessor** *m* -s,-en /-'so:rən/ microprocessor. **M~skop** *nt* -s,-e microscope. **m~skopisch** *a* microscopic

Mikrowelle *f* microwave. **M~ngerät** *nt*, **M~nherd** *m* microwave oven

Milbe *f* -,-n mite

Milch *f* - milk. **M~bar** *f* milk bar. **M~geschäft** *nt* dairy. **M~glas** *nt* opal glass. **m~ig** *a* milky. **M~kuh** *f* dairy cow. **M~mann** *m* (*pl* -männer) milkman. **M~mixgetränk** *nt* milk shake. **M~straße** *f* Milky Way

mild *a* mild; (*nachsichtig*) lenient; **m~e Gaben** alms. **M~e** *f* - mildness; leniency. **m~ern** *vt* make milder; (*mäßigen*) moderate; (*lindern*) alleviate, ease; **sich m~ern** become milder; (*sich mäßigen*) moderate; (*nachlassen*) abate; ⟨*Schmerz:*⟩ ease; **m~ernde Umstände** mitigating circumstances. **m~tätig** *a* charitable

Milieu /mi'ljø:/ *nt* -s,-s [social] environment

militant *a* militant

Militär *nt* -s army; (*Soldaten*) troops *pl*; **beim M~** in the army. **m~isch** *a* military

Miliz *f* -,-en militia

Milliarde /mɪ'ljardə/ *f* -,-n thousand million, billion

Milli|gramm *nt* milligram. **M~meter** *m* & *nt* millimetre. **M~meterpapier** *nt* graph paper

Million /mɪ'ljo:n/ *f* -,-en million. **M~är** *m* -s,-e millionaire. **M~ärin** *f* -,-nen millionairess

Milz *f* - (*Anat*) spleen

mim|en *vt* (*fam: vortäuschen*) act. **M~ik** *f* - [expressive] gestures and facial expressions *pl*

Mimose *f* -,-n mimosa

minder *a* lesser ● *adv* less; **mehr oder m~** more or less. **M~heit** *f* -,-en minority

minderjährig *a* (*Jur*) under-age; **m~ sein** be under age. **M~e(r)** *m/f* (*Jur*) minor. **M~keit** *f* (*Jur*) minority

minder|n *vt* diminish; decrease ⟨*Tempo*⟩. **M~ung** *f* - decrease

minderwertig *a* inferior. **M~keit** *f* - inferiority. **M~keitskomplex** *m* inferiority complex

Mindest- *pref* minimum. **m~e** *a* & *pron* **der/die/das m~e** the least; **zum m~en** at least; **nicht im m~en** not in the least. **m~ens** *adv* at least. **M~lohn** *m* minimum wage. **M~maß** *nt* minimum

Mine *f* -,-n mine; (*Bleistift-*) lead; (*Kugelschreiber-*) refill. **M~nfeld** *nt* minefield. **M~nräumboot** *nt* minesweeper

Mineral *nt* -s,-e & -ien /-jən/ mineral. **m~isch** *a* mineral. **M~ogie** *f* - mineralogy. **M~wasser** *nt* mineral water

Miniatur *f* -,-en miniature

Minigolf *nt* miniature golf

minimal *a* minimal

Minimum *nt* -s,-ma minimum

Minirock *m* miniskirt

Mini|ster *m* -s,- minister. **m~steriell** *a* ministerial. **M~sterium** *nt* -s,-ien ministry

Minorität *f* -,-en minority

minus *conj, adv* & *prep* (+ *gen*) minus. **M~** *nt* - deficit; (*Nachteil*) disadvantage. **M~zeichen** *nt* minus [sign]

Minute *f* -,-n minute

mir *pron* (*dat of* ich) [to] me; (*refl*) myself; **mir nichts, dir nichts** without so much as a 'by your leave'

Misch|ehe *f* mixed marriage. **m~en** *vt* mix; blend ⟨*Tee, Kaffee*⟩; toss ⟨*Salat*⟩; shuffle ⟨*Karten*⟩; **sich m~en** mix; ⟨*Person:*⟩ mingle (**unter** + *acc* with); **sich m~en in** (+ *acc*) join in ⟨*Gespräch*⟩; meddle in ⟨*Angelegenheit*⟩ ● *vi* (*haben*) shuffle the cards. **M~ling** *m* -s,-e half-caste; (*Hund*) cross. **M~masch** *m* -[e]s,-e (*fam*) hotchpotch. **M~ung** *f* -,-en mixture; blend

miserabel *a* abominable; (*erbärmlich*) wretched

mißachten *vt* disregard

Miß|achtung *f* disregard. **M~behagen** *nt* [feeling of] unease. **M~bildung** *f* deformity

mißbilligen *vt* disapprove of

Miß|billigung *f* disapproval. **M~brauch** *m* abuse; **M~brauch treiben mit** abuse

miß|brauchen vt abuse; (vergewaltigen) rape. **m~deuten** vt misinterpret

missen vt do without; **ich möchte es nicht m~** I should not like to be without it

Miß|erfolg m failure. **M~ernte** f crop failure

Misse|tat f misdeed. **M~täter** m (fam) culprit

mißfallen† vi (haben) displease (**jdm** s.o.)

Miß|fallen nt -s displeasure; (Mißbilligung) disapproval. **m~gebildet** a deformed. **M~geburt** f freak; (fig) monstrosity. **M~geschick** nt mishap; (Unglück) misfortune. **m~gestimmt** a **m~gestimmt sein** be in a bad mood

miß|glücken vi (sein) fail. **m~gönnen** vt begrudge

Miß|griff m mistake. **M~gunst** f resentment. **m~günstig** a resentful

mißhandeln vt ill-treat

Miß|handlung f ill-treatment. **M~helligkeit** f -,-en disagreement

Mission f -,-en mission

Missionar(in) m -s,-e (f -,-nen) missionary

Miß|klang m discord. **M~kredit** m discredit; **in M~kredit bringen** discredit. **m~lich** a awkward. **m~liebig** a unpopular

mißlingen† vi (sein) fail; **es mißlang ihr** she failed. **M~** nt -s failure

Mißmut m ill humour. **m~ig** a morose, adv -ly

mißraten† vi (sein) turn out badly

Miß|stand m abuse; (Zustand) undesirable state of affairs. **M~stimmung** f discord; (Laune) bad mood. **M~ton** m discordant note

mißtrauen vi (haben) **jdm/etw m~** mistrust s.o./sth; (Argwohn hegen) distrust s.o./sth

Mißtrau|en nt -s mistrust; (Argwohn) distrust. **M~ensvotum** nt vote of no confidence. **m~isch** a distrustful; (argwöhnisch) suspicious

Miß|verhältnis nt disproportion. **M~verständnis** nt misunderstanding. **m~verstehen†** vt misunderstand. **M~wirtschaft** f mismanagement

Mist m -[e]s manure; (fam) rubbish

Mistel f -,-n mistletoe

Misthaufen m dungheap

mit prep (+ dat) with; ⟨sprechen⟩ to; (mittels) by; (inklusive) including; (bei) at; **mit Bleistift** in pencil; **mit lauter Stimme** in a loud voice; **mit drei Jahren** at the age of three ● adv (auch) as well; **mit anfassen** (fig) lend a hand; **es ist mit das ärmste Land der Welt** it is among the poorest countries in the world

Mitarbeit f collaboration. **m~en** vi sep collaborate (**an** + dat on). **M~er (in)** m(f) collaborator; (Kollege) colleague; (Betriebsangehörige) employee

Mitbestimmung f co-determination

mitbring|en† vt sep bring [along]; **jdm Blumen m~en** bring/(hinbringen) take s.o. flowers. **M~sel** nt -s,- present (brought back from holiday etc)

Mitbürger m fellow citizen

miteinander adv with each other

miterleben vt sep witness

Mitesser m (Med) blackhead

mitfahren† vi sep (sein) go/come along; **mit jdm m~** go with s.o.; (mitgenommen werden) be given a lift by s.o.

mitfühlen vi sep (haben) sympathize. **m~d** a sympathetic; (mitleidig) compassionate

mitgeben† vt sep **jdm etw m~** give s.o. sth to take with him

Mitgefühl nt sympathy

mitgehen† vi sep (sein) **mit jdm m~** go with s.o.; **etw m~ lassen** (fam) pinch sth

mitgenommen a worn; **m~ sein** be in a sorry state; (erschöpft) be exhausted

Mitgift f -,-en dowry

Mitglied nt member. **M~schaft** f - membership

mithalten† vi sep (haben) join in; **mit jdm nicht m~ können** not be able to keep up with s.o.

Mithilfe f assistance

mitkommen† vi sep (sein) come [along] too; (fig: folgen können) keep up; (verstehen) follow

Mitlaut m consonant

Mitleid nt pity, compassion. **M~enschaft** f **in M~enschaft ziehen** affect. **m~erregend** a pitiful. **m~ig** a pitying; (mitfühlend) compassionate. **m~slos** a pitiless

mitmachen v sep ● vt take part in; (erleben) go through ● vi (haben) join in

Mitmensch *m* fellow man

mitnehmen† *vt sep* take along; (*mitfahren lassen*) give a lift to; (*fig: schädigen*) affect badly; (*erschöpfen*) exhaust; '**zum M~n**' 'to take away', (*Amer*) 'to go'

mitnichten *adv* not at all

mitreden *vi sep* (*haben*) join in [the conversation]; (*mit entscheiden*) have a say (**bei** in)

mitreißen† *vt sep* sweep along; (*fig: begeistern*) carry away; **m~d** rousing

mitsamt *prep* (+ *dat*) together with

mitschneiden† *vt sep* record

mitschreiben† *vt sep* (*haben*) take down

Mitschuld *f* partial blame. **m~ig** *a* **m~ig sein** be partly to blame

Mitschüler(in) *m(f)* fellow pupil

mitspiel|en *vi sep* (*haben*) join in; (*Theat*) be in the cast; (*beitragen*) play a part; **jdm übel m~en** treat s.o. badly. **M~er** *m* fellow player; (*Mitwirkender*) participant

Mittag *m* midday, noon; (*Mahlzeit*) lunch; (*Pause*) lunch-break; [**zu**] **M~** essen have lunch. **M~** *adv* **heute m~** at lunch-time today. **M~essen** *nt* lunch. **m~s** *adv* at noon; (*als Mahlzeit*) for lunch; **um 12 Uhr m~s** at noon. **M~spause** *f* lunch-hour; (*Pause*) lunch-break. **M~sschlaf** *m* after-lunch nap. **M~stisch** *m* lunch table; (*Essen*) lunch. **M~szeit** *f* lunch-time

Mittäter(in) *m(f)* accomplice. **M~schaft** *f* complicity

Mitte *f* -,-n middle; (*Zentrum*) centre; **die goldene M~** the golden mean; **M~ Mai** in mid-May; **in unserer M~** in our midst

mitteil|en *vt sep* **jdm etw m~en** tell s.o. sth; (*amtlich*) inform s.o. of sth. **m~sam** *a* communicative. **M~ung** *f* -,-en communication; (*Nachricht*) piece of news

Mittel *nt* -s,- means *sg*; (*Heil-*) remedy; (*Medikament*) medicine; (*M~wert*) mean; (*Durchschnitt*) average; **M~** *pl* (*Geld-*) funds, resources. **m~** *pred a* medium; (*m~mäßig*) middling. **M~alter** *nt* Middle Ages *pl*. **m~alterlich** *a* medieval. **m~bar** *a* indirect, *adv* -ly. **M~ding** *nt* (*fig*) cross. **m~europäisch** *a* Central European. **M~finger** *m* middle finger. **m~groß** *a* medium-sized; (*Person*) of medium

height. **M~klasse** *f* middle range. **m~los** *a* destitute. **m~mäßig** *a* middling; [**nur**] **m~mäßig** mediocre. **M~meer** *nt* Mediterranean. **M~punkt** *m* centre; (*fig*) centre of attention

mittels *prep* (+ *gen*) by means of

Mittel|schule *f* = **Realschule**. **M~smann** *m* (*pl* -**männer**), **M~sperson** *f* intermediary, go-between. **M~stand** *m* middle class. **m~ste(r,s)** *a* middle. **M~streifen** *m* (*Auto*) central reservation, (*Amer*) median strip. **M~stürmer** *m* centreforward. **M~weg** *m* (*fig*) middle course; **goldener M~weg** happy medium. **M~welle** *f* medium wave. **M~wort** *nt* (*pl* -**wörter**) participle

mitten *adv* **m~ in/auf** (*dat/acc*) in the middle of; **m~ unter** (*dat/acc*) amidst. **m~durch** *adv* [right] through the middle

Mitternacht *f* midnight

mittler|e(r,s) *a* middle; ⟨*Größe, Qualität*⟩ medium; (*durchschnittlich*) mean, average. **m~weile** *adv* meanwhile; (*seitdem*) by now

Mittwoch *m* -s,-e Wednesday. **m~s** *adv* on Wednesdays

mitunter *adv* now and again

mitwirk|en *vi sep* (*haben*) take part; (*helfen*) contribute. **M~ung** *f* participation

mix|en *vt* mix. **M~er** *m* -s,- (*Culin*) liquidizer, blender. **M~tur** *f* -,-en (*Med*) mixture

Möbel *pl* furniture *sg*. **M~stück** *nt* piece of furniture. **M~tischler** *m* cabinet-maker. **M~wagen** *m* removal van

mobil *a* mobile; (*fam: munter*) lively; (*nach Krankheit*) fit [and well]; **m~ machen** mobilize

Mobile *nt* -s,-s mobile

Mobiliar *nt* -s furniture

mobilisier|en *vt* mobilize. **M~ung** *f* - mobilization

Mobilmachung *f* - mobilization

möblier|en *vt* furnish; **m~tes Zimmer** furnished room

mochte, möchte *s.* **mögen**

Modalverb *nt* modal auxiliary

Mode *f* -,-n fashion; **M~ sein** be fashionable

Modell *nt* -s,-e model; **M~ stehen** pose (**jdm** for s.o.). **m~ieren** *vt* model

Modenschau *f* fashion show

Modera|tor *m* **-s,-en** /-'to:rən/,
   M∼torin *f* **-,-nen** (*TV*) presenter
modern[1] *vi* (*haben*) decay
modern[2] *a* modern; (*modisch*)
   fashionable.   **m∼isieren**   *vt*
   modernize
Mode|schmuck *m* costume jewel-
   lery.   **M∼schöpfer** *m* fashion
   designer
Modifi|kation /-'tsio:n/ *f* **-,-en** modifi-
   cation. **m∼zieren** *vt* modify
modisch *a* fashionable
Modistin *f* **-,-nen** milliner
modrig *a* musty
modulieren *vt* modulate
Mofa *nt* **-s,-s** moped
mogeln *vi* (*haben*) (*fam*) cheat
mögen† *vt* like; **lieber m∼** prefer ● *v*
   aux **ich möchte** I'd like; **möchtest du
   nach Hause?** do you want to go
   home? **ich mag nicht mehr** I've had
   enough; **ich hätte weinen m∼** I
   could have cried; **ich mag mich irren**
   I may be wrong; **wer/was mag das
   sein?** whoever/whatever can it be?
   wie mag es ihm ergangen sein? I
   wonder how he got on; **[das] mag
   sein** that may well be; **mag kommen, was da will** come what may
möglich *a* possible; **alle m∼en** all
   sorts of. **m∼erweise** *adv* possibly.
   M∼keit *f* **-,-en** possibility. **M∼keits-
   form** *f* subjunctive. **m∼st** *adv* if
   possible; **m∼st viel/früh** as mu-
   ch/early as possible
Mohammedan|er(in)   *m*   **-s,-**   (*f*
   -,-nen) Muslim. **m∼isch** *a* Muslim
Mohn *m* **-s** poppy; (*Culin*) poppy-
   seed. **M∼blume** *f* poppy
Möhre, Mohrrübe *f* **-,-n** carrot
mokieren (sich) *vr* make fun (**über-**
   + *acc* of)
Mokka *m* **-s** mocha; (*Geschmack*)
   coffee
Molch *m* **-[e]s,-e** newt
Mole *f* **-,-n** (*Naut*) mole
Molekül *nt* **-s,-e** molecule
Molkerei *f* **-,-en** dairy
Moll *nt* **-** (*Mus*) minor
mollig *a* cosy; (*warm*) warm; (*rund-
   lich*) plump
Moment *m* **-s,-e** moment; **im/jeden
   M∼** at the/any moment; **M∼** [**mal**]!
   just a moment! **m∼an** *a* moment-
   ary, *adv* -ily; (*gegenwärtig*) at the
   moment
Momentaufnahme *f* snapshot
Monarch *m* **-en,-en** monarch. **M∼ie**
   f **-,-n** monarchy

Monat *m* **-s,-e** month. **m∼elang** *adv*
   for months. **m∼lich** *a* & *adv*
   monthly. **M∼skarte** *f* monthly season ticket
Mönch *m* **-[e]s,-e** monk
Mond *m* **-[e]s,-e** moon
mondän *a* fashionable, *adv* -bly
Mond|finsternis *f* lunar eclipse.
   m∼hell *a* moonlit. **M∼sichel** *f* crescent moon. **M∼schein** *m* moonlight
monieren *vt* criticize
Monitor *m* **-s,-en** /-'to:rən/ (*Techn*)
   monitor
Monogramm *nt* **-s,-e** monogram
Mono|log   *m*   **-s,-e**   monologue.
   M∼pol *nt* **-s,-e** monopoly. **m∼poli-
   sieren** *vt* monopolize. **m∼ton** *a*
   monotonous, *adv* -ly. **M∼tonie** *f* -
   monotony
Monster *nt* **-s,-** monster
monstr|ös *a* monstrous. **M∼osität** *f*
   -,-en monstrosity
Monstrum *nt* **-s,-stren** monster
Monsun *m* **-s,-e** monsoon
Montag *m* Monday
Montage /mɔn'ta:ʒə/ *f* **-,-n** fitting;
   (*Zusammenbau*) assembly; (*Film-*)
   editing; (*Kunst*) montage
montags *adv* on Mondays
Montanindustrie *f* coal and steel
   industry
Monteur /mɔn'tø:ɐ/ *m* **-s,-e** fitter.
   M∼anzug *m* overalls *pl*
montieren *vt* fit; (*zusammenbauen*)
   assemble
Monument *nt* **-[e]s,-e** monument.
   m∼al *a* monumental
Moor *nt* **-[e]s,-e** bog; (*Heide-*) moor
Moos *nt* **-es,-e** moss. **m∼ig** *a* mossy
Mop *m* **-s,-s** mop
Moped *nt* **-s,-s** moped
Mops *m* **-es,**ⁿ**e** pug [dog]
Moral *f* - morals *pl*; (*Selbstvertrauen*)
   morale; (*Lehre*) moral. **m∼isch** *a*
   moral, *adv* -ly. **m∼isieren** *vi* (*haben*)
   moralize
Morast *m* **-[e]s,-e** morass; (*Schlamm*)
   mud
Mord *m* **-[e]s,-e** murder; (*Pol*) assassination. **M∼anschlag** *m* murder/
   assassination attempt. **m∼en** *vt/i*
   (*haben*) murder, kill
Mörder *m* **-s,-** murderer; (*Pol*) assassin. **M∼in** *f* **-,-nen** murderess.
   m∼isch *a* murderous; (*fam:
   schlimm*) dreadful
Mords-   *pref*   (*fam*)   terrific.
   m∼mäßig *a* (*fam*) frightful, *adv* -ly

morgen *adv* tomorrow; **m~ früh/ nachmittag** tomorrow morning/ afternoon; **heute/gestern/Montag m~** this/yesterday/Monday morning

Morgen *m* -s,- morning; *(Maß)* ≈ acre; **am M~** in the morning. **M~dämmerung** *f* dawn. **m~dlich** *a* morning . . . **M~grauen** *nt* -s dawn; **im M~grauen** at dawn. **M~mantel**, **M~rock** *m* dressing-gown. **M~rot** *nt* red sky in the morning. **m~s** *a* in the morning

morgig *a* tomorrow's; **der m~e Tag** tomorrow

Morphium *nt* -s morphine

morsch *a* rotten

Morsealphabet *nt* Morse code

Mörtel *m* -s mortar

Mosaik /moza'i:k/ *nt* -s,-e[n] mosaic

Moschee *f* -,-n mosque

Mosel *f* - Moselle. **M~wein** *m* Moselle [wine]

Moskau *nt* -s Moscow

Moskito *m* -s,-s mosquito

Mos|lem *m* -s,-s Muslim. **m~lemisch** *a* Muslim

Most *m* -[e]s must; *(Apfel-)* ≈ cider

Mostrich *m* -s *(NGer)* mustard

Motel *nt* -s,-s motel

Motiv *nt* -s,-e motive; *(Kunst)* motif. **M~ation** /-'tsio:n/ *f* - motivation. **m~ieren** *vt* motivate

Motor /'mo:tɔr, mo'to:ɐ̯/ *m* -s,-en /-'to:rən/ engine; *(Elektro-)* motor. **M~boot** *nt* motor boat

motorisieren *vt* motorize

Motor|rad *nt* motor cycle. **M~radfahrer** *m* motor-cyclist. **M~roller** *m* motor scooter

Motte *f* -,-n moth. **M~nkugel** *f* mothball

Motto *nt* -s,-s motto

Möwe *f* -,-n gull

Mücke *f* -,-n gnat; *(kleine)* midge; *(Stech-)* mosquito

mucksen (sich) *vr* sich nicht m~ *(fam)* keep quiet

müd|e *a* tired; **nicht m~e werden/es m~e sein** not tire/be tired *(etw zu tun* of doing sth). **M~igkeit** *f* - tiredness

Muff *m* -s,-e muff

muffig *a* musty; *(fam: mürrisch)* grumpy

Mühe *f* -,-n effort; *(Aufwand)* trouble; **sich** *(dat)* **M~ geben** make an effort; *(sich bemühen)* try; **nicht der M~ wert** not worth while; **mit**

M~ und Not with great difficulty; *(gerade noch)* only just. **m~los** *a* effortless, *adv* -ly

muhen *vi (haben)* moo

mühe|n (sich) *vr* struggle. **m~voll** *a* laborious; *(anstrengend)* arduous

Mühl|e *f* -,-n mill; *(Kaffee-)* grinder. **M~stein** *m* millstone

Müh|sal *f* -,-e *(liter)* toil; *(Mühe)* trouble. **m~sam** *a* laborious, *adv* -ly; *(beschwerlich)* difficult, *adv* with difficulty. **m~selig** *a* laborious, *adv* -ly

Mulde *f* -,-n hollow

Müll *m* -s refuse, *(Amer)* garbage. **M~abfuhr** *f* refuse collection

Mullbinde *f* gauze bandage

Mülleimer *m* waste bin; *(Mülltonne)* dustbin, *(Amer)* garbage can

Müller *m* -s,- miller

Müll|halde *f* [rubbish] dump. **M~schlucker** *m* refuse chute. **M~tonne** *f* dustbin, *(Amer)* garbage can. **M~wagen** *m* dust-cart, *(Amer)* garbage truck

mulmig *a (fam)* dodgy; *(Gefühl)* uneasy; **ihm war m~ zumute** he felt uneasy/*(übel)* queasy

multi|national *a* multinational. **M~plikation** /-'tsio:n/ *f* -,-en multiplication. **m~plizieren** *vt* multiply

Mumie /'mu:mjə/ *f* -,-n mummy

mumifiziert *a* mummified

Mumm *m* -s *(fam)* energy

Mumps *m* - mumps

Mund *m* -[e]s,ˌ̈er mouth; **halt den M~!** be quiet! *(sl)* shut up! **M~art** *f* dialect. **m~artlich** *a* dialect

Mündel *nt* & *m* -s,- *(Jur)* ward. **m~sicher** *a* gilt-edged

münden *vi (sein)* flow/*(Straße:)* lead *(in + acc* into)

mund|faul *a* taciturn. **M~geruch** *m* bad breath. **M~harmonika** *f* mouth-organ

mündig *a* **m~ sein/werden** *(Jur)* be/ come of age. **M~keit** *f* - *(Jur)* majority

mündlich *a* verbal, *adv* -ly; **m~e Prüfung** oral

Mund|stück *nt* mouthpiece; *(Zigaretten-)* tip. **m~tot** *a* **m~tot machen** *(fig)* gag

Mündung *f* -,-en *(Fluß-)* mouth; *(Gewehr-)* muzzle

Mund|voll *m* -,- mouthful. **M~wasser** *nt* mouthwash.

M~werk nt **ein gutes M~werk haben** (fam) be very talkative. **M~winkel** m corner of the mouth

Munition /-'tsjo:n/ f - ammunition

munkeln vt/i (haben) talk (**von** of); **es wird gemunkelt** rumour has it (**daß** that)

Münster nt -s,- cathedral

munter a lively; (heiter) merry; **m~ sein** (wach) be wide awake/(aufgestanden, gesund) up and about; **gesund und m~** fit and well ● adv [immer] **m~** merrily

Münz|e f -,-n coin; (M~stätte) mint. **m~en** vt mint; **das war auf dich gemünzt** (fam) that was aimed at you. **M~fernsprecher** m coin-box telephone, payphone. **M~wäscherei** f launderette

mürbe a crumbly; ⟨Obst⟩ mellow; ⟨Fleisch⟩ tender; **jdn m~ machen** (fig) wear s.o. down. **M~teig** m short pastry

Murmel f -,-n marble

murmeln vt/i (haben) murmur; (undeutlich) mumble, mutter. **M~** nt -s murmur

Murmeltier nt marmot

murren vt/i (haben) grumble

mürrisch a surly

Mus nt -es purée

Muschel f -,-n mussel; (Schale) [sea] shell

Museum /mu'ze:om/ nt -s,-seen /-'ze:ən/ museum

Musik f - music. **M~alien** /-jən/ pl [printed] music sg. **m~alisch** a musical

Musikbox f juke-box

Musiker(in) m -s,- (f -,-nen) musician

Musik|instrument nt musical instrument. **M~kapelle** f band. **M~pavillon** m bandstand

musisch a artistic

musizieren vi (haben) make music

Muskat m -[e]s nutmeg

Muskel m -s,-n muscle. **M~kater** m stiff and aching muscles pl

Musku|latur f - muscles pl. **m~lös** a muscular

Müsli nt -s muesli

muß s. müssen. **Muß** nt - ein **Muß** a must

Muße f - leisure; **mit M~** at leisure

müssen† v aux **etw tun m~** have to/(fam) have got to do sth; **ich muß**

jetzt gehen I have to or must go now; **ich mußte lachen** I had to laugh; **ich muß es wissen** I need to know; **du müßtest es mal versuchen** you ought to or should try it; **muß das sein?** is that necessary?

müßig a idle; (unnütz) futile. **M~gang** m - idleness

mußte, müßte s. müssen

Muster nt -s,- pattern; (Probe) sample; (Vorbild) model. **M~beispiel** nt typical example; (Vorbild) perfect example. **M~betrieb** m model factory. **m~gültig, m~haft** a exemplary. **m~n** vt eye; (inspizieren) inspect. **M~schüler(in)** m(f) model pupil. **M~ung** f -,-en inspection; (Mil) medical; (Muster) pattern

Mut m -[e]s courage; **jdm Mut machen** encourage s.o.

Mutation /-'tsjo:n/ f -,-en (Biol) mutation

mut|ig a courageous, adv -ly. **m~los** a despondent; (entmutigt) disheartened

mutmaß|en vt presume; (Vermutungen anstellen) speculate. **m~lich** a probable, adv -bly; **der m~liche Täter** the suspect. **M~ung** f -,-en speculation, conjecture

Mutprobe f test of courage

Mutter¹ f -,- mother; **werdende M~** mother-to-be

Mutter² f -,-n (Techn) nut

Muttergottes f -,- madonna

Mutter|land nt motherland. **M~leib** m womb

mütterlich a maternal; (fürsorglich) motherly. **m~erseits** adv on one's/the mother's side

Mutter|mal nt birthmark; (dunkel) mole. **M~schaft** f - motherhood. **m~seelenallein** a & adv all alone. **M~sprache** f mother tongue. **M~tag** m Mother's Day

Mutti f -,-s (fam) mummy

Mutwill|e m wantonness. **m~ig** a wanton, adv -ly

Mütze f -,-n cap; **wollene M~** woolly hat

MwSt. abbr (Mehrwertsteuer) VAT

mysteriös a mysterious, adv -ly

Myst|ik /'mʏstɪk/ f - mysticism. **m~isch** a mystical

myth|isch a mythical. **M~ologie** f - mythology. **M~os** m -,-then myth

N

na *int* well; **na gut** all right then; **na ja** oh well; **na und?** so what?

Nabe *f* -,-n hub

Nabel *m* -s,- navel. **N~schnur** *f* umbilical cord

nach *prep* (+ *dat*) after; (*Uhrzeit*) past; (*Richtung*) to; ⟨greifen, rufen, sich sehnen⟩ for; (gemäß) according to; **meiner Meinung n~** in my opinion; **n~ oben** upwards ● *adv* **n~ und n~** gradually, bit by bit; **n~ wie vor** still

nachäffen *vt sep* mimic

nachahm|en *vt sep* imitate. **N~ung** *f* -,-en imitation

nacharbeiten *vt sep* make up for

nacharten *vi sep* (*sein*) **jdm n~** take after s.o.

Nachbar|(in) *m* -n,-n (*f* -,-nen) neighbour. **N~haus** *nt* house next door. **N~land** *nt* neighbouring country. **n~lich** *a* neighbourly; (*Nachbar-*) neighbouring. **N~schaft** *f* - neighbourhood; **gute N~schaft** neighbourliness

nachbestell|en *vt sep* reorder. **N~ung** *f* repeat order

nachbild|en *vt sep* copy, reproduce. **N~ung** *f* copy, reproduction

nachdatieren *vt sep* backdate

nachdem *conj* after; **je n~** it depends

nachdenk|en† *vi sep* (*haben*) think (über + *acc* about). **N~en** *nt* -s reflection, thought. **n~lich** *a* thoughtful, *adv* -ly

Nachdruck *m* (*pl* -e) reproduction; (*unveränderter*) reprint; (*Betonung*) emphasis

nachdrücklich *a* emphatic, *adv* -ally

nacheifern *vi sep* (*haben*) **jdm n~** emulate s.o.

nacheilen *vi sep* (*sein*) (+ *dat*) hurry after

nacheinander *adv* one after the other

Nachfahre *m* -n,-n descendant

Nachfolg|e *f* succession. **n~en** *vi sep* (*sein*) (+ *dat*) follow; (*im Amt*) succeed. **N~er(in)** *m* -s,- (*f* -,-nen) successor

nachforsch|en *vi sep* (*haben*) make enquiries. **N~ung** *f* enquiry; **N~ungen anstellen** make enquiries

Nachfrage *f* (*Comm*) demand. **n~n** *vi sep* (*haben*) enquire

nachfüllen *vt sep* refill ⟨Behälter⟩; **Wasser n~** fill up with water

nachgeben† *v sep* ● *vi* (*haben*) give way; (*sich fügen*) give in, yield ● *vt* **jdm Suppe n~** give s.o. more soup

Nachgebühr *f* surcharge

nachgehen† *vi sep* (*sein*) ⟨Uhr:⟩ be slow; **jdm/etw n~** follow s.o./sth; follow up ⟨Spur, Angelegenheit⟩; pursue ⟨Angelegenheit, Tätigkeit⟩; go about ⟨Arbeit⟩

nachgeraten† *vi sep* (*sein*) **jdm n~** take after s.o.

Nachgeschmack *m* after-taste

nachgiebig *a* indulgent; (*gefällig*) compliant. **N~keit** *f* - indulgence; compliance

nachgrübeln *vi sep* (*haben*) ponder (über + *acc* on)

nachhallen *vi sep* (*haben*) reverberate

nachhaltig *a* lasting

nachhelfen† *vi sep* (*haben*) help

nachher *adv* later; (*danach*) afterwards; **bis n~!** see you later!

Nachhilfeunterricht *m* coaching

nachhinein *adv* **im n~** afterwards

nachhinken *vi sep* (*sein*) (*fig*) lag behind

nachholen *vt sep* (*später holen*) fetch later; (*mehr holen*) get more; (*später machen*) do later; (*aufholen*) catch up on; make up for ⟨Zeit⟩

nachjagen *vi sep* (*haben*) (+ *dat*) chase after

Nachkomme *m* -n,-n descendant. **n~n†** *vi sep* (*sein*) follow [later], come later; (*Schritt halten*) keep up; **etw** (*dat*) **n~n** (*fig*) comply with ⟨Bitte, Wunsch⟩; carry out ⟨Versprechen, Pflicht⟩. **N~nschaft** *f* - descendants *pl*, progeny

Nachkriegszeit *f* post-war period

Nachlaß *m* -lasses,-lässe discount; (*Jur*) [deceased's] estate

nachlassen† *v sep* ● *vi* (*haben*) decrease; (*Regen, Hitze:*⟩ let up; ⟨Schmerz:⟩ ease; ⟨Sturm:⟩ abate; ⟨Augen, Kräfte, Leistungen:⟩ deteriorate; **er ließ nicht nach** [mit Fragen] he persisted [with his questions] ● *vt* **etw vom Preis n~** take sth off the price

nachlässig *a* careless, *adv* -ly; (*leger*) casual, *adv* -ly; (*unordentlich*) sloppy, *adv* -ily. **N~keit** *f* - carelessness; sloppiness

nachlaufen† *vi sep* (*sein*) (+ *dat*) run after

nachlegen *vt sep* Holz/Kohlen n~ put more wood/coal on the fire

nachlesen† *vt sep* look up

nachlöse|n *vi sep* (*haben*) pay one's fare on the train/on arrival. **N~schalter** *m* excess-fare office

nachmachen *vt sep* (*später machen*) do later; (*imitieren*) imitate, copy; (*fälschen*) forge; **jdm etw n~** copy sth from s.o.; repeat ⟨*Übung*⟩ after s.o.

Nachmittag *m* afternoon. **n~** *adv* **gestern/heute n~** yesterday/this afternoon. **n~s** *adv* in the afternoon

Nachnahme *f* **etw per N~ schicken** send sth cash on delivery or COD

Nachname *m* surname

Nachporto *nt* excess postage

nachprüfen *vt sep* check, verify

nachrechnen *vt sep* work out; (*prüfen*) check

Nachrede *f* üble N~ defamation

Nachricht *f* -,-en [piece of] news *sg*; **N~en** news *sg*; **eine N~ hinterlassen** leave a message; **jdm N~ geben** inform, notify s.o. **N~endienst** *m* (*Mil*) intelligence service. **N~ensendung** *f* news bulletin. **N~enwesen** *nt* communications *pl*

nachrücken *vi sep* (*sein*) move up

Nachruf *m* obituary

nachsagen *vt sep* repeat (**jdm** after s.o.); **jdm Schlechtes/Gutes n~** speak ill/well of s.o.; **man sagt ihm nach, daß er geizig ist** he is said to be stingy

Nachsaison *f* late season

Nachsatz *m* postscript

nachschicken *vt sep* (*später schicken*) send later; (*hinterher-*) send after (**jdm** s.o.); send on ⟨*Post*⟩ (**jdm** to s.o.)

nachschlag|en† *v sep* ● *vt* look up ● *vi* (*haben*) **in einem Wörterbuch n~en** consult a dictionary; **jdm n~en** take after s.o. **N~ewerk** *nt* reference book

Nachschlüssel *m* duplicate key

Nachschrift *f* transcript; (*Nachsatz*) postscript

Nachschub *m* (*Mil*) supplies *pl*

nachsehen† *v sep* ● *vt* (*prüfen*) check; (*nachschlagen*) look up; (*hinwegsehen über*) overlook ● *vi* (*haben*) have a look; (*prüfen*) check; **im Wörterbuch n~** consult a dictionary; **jdm/etw n~** gaze after s.o./sth. **N~** *nt* **das N~ haben** (*fam*) go empty-handed

nachsenden† *vt sep* forward ⟨*Post*⟩ (**jdm** to s.o.); **'bitte n~'** 'please forward'

Nachsicht *f* forbearance; (*Milde*) leniency; (*Nachgiebigkeit*) indulgence. **n~ig** *a* forbearing; lenient; indulgent

Nachsilbe *f* suffix

nachsitzen† *vi sep* (*haben*) **n~ müssen** be kept in [after school]; **jdn n~ lassen** give s.o. detention. **N~** *nt* -s (*Sch*) detention

Nachspeise *f* dessert, sweet

Nachspiel *nt* (*fig*) sequel

nachspionieren *vi sep* (*haben*) **jdm n~** spy on s.o.

nachsprechen† *vt sep* repeat (**jdm** after s.o.)

nachspülen *vt sep* rinse

nächst /-çst/ *prep* (+*dat*) next to. **n~beste(r,s)** *a* first [available]; (*zweitbeste*) next best. **n~e(r,s)** *a* next; (*nächstgelegene*) nearest; ⟨*Verwandte*⟩ closest; **n~e Woche** next week; **in n~er Nähe** close by; **am n~en sein** be nearest or closest ● *pron* **der/die/das n~e** the next; **der n~e bitte** next please; **als n~es** next; **fürs n~e** for the time being. **N~e(r)** *m* fellow man

nachstehend *a* following ● *adv* below

nachstellen *v sep* ● *vt* readjust; put back ⟨*Uhr*⟩ ● *vi* (*haben*) (+ *dat*) pursue

nächst|emal *adv* **das n~emal** [the] next time. **N~enliebe** *f* charity. **n~ens** *adv* shortly. **n~gelegen** *a* nearest. **n~liegend** *a* most obvious

nachstreben *vi sep* (*haben*) **jdm n~** emulate s.o.

nachsuchen *vi sep* (*haben*) search; **n~ um** request

Nacht *f* -,˸e night; **über/bei N~** overnight/at night. **n~** *adv* **Montag/morgen n~** Monday/tomorrow night; **heute n~** tonight; (*letzte Nacht*) last night; **gestern n~** last night; (*vorletzte Nacht*) the night before last. **N~dienst** *m* night duty

Nachteil *m* disadvantage; **zum N~** to the detriment (*gen* of). **n~ig** *a* adverse, *adv* -ly

Nacht|essen *nt* (*SGer*) supper. **N~falter** *m* moth. **N~hemd** *nt* night-dress; (*Männer-*) night-shirt

Nachtigall *f* -,-en nightingale

Nachtisch *m* dessert

Nacht|klub m night-club. **N~leben** nt night-life

nächtlich a nocturnal, night ...

Nacht|lokal nt night-club. **N~mahl** nt (Aust) supper

Nachtrag m postscript; (Ergänzung) supplement. **n~en†** vt sep add; **jdm etw n~en** walk behind s.o. carrying sth; (fig) bear a grudge against s.o. for sth. **n~end** a vindictive; **n~end sein** bear grudges

nachträglich a subsequent, later; (verspätet) belated ● adv later; (nachher) afterwards; (verspätet) belatedly

nachtrauern vi sep (haben) (+ dat) mourn the loss of

Nacht|ruhe f night's rest; **angenehme N~ruhe!** sleep well! **N~s** adv at night; **2 Uhr n~s** 2 o'clock in the morning. **N~schicht** f night-shift. **N~tisch** m bedside table. **N~tischlampe** f bedside lamp. **N~topf** m chamber-pot. **N~wächter** m nightwatchman. **N~zeit** f night-time

Nachuntersuchung f check-up

nachwachsen† vi sep (sein) grow again

Nachwahl f by-election

Nachweis m -es,-e proof. **n~bar** a demonstrable. **n~en†** vt sep prove; (aufzeigen) show; (vermitteln) give details of; **jdm nichts n~en können** have no proof against s.o. **n~lich** a demonstrable, adv -bly

Nachwelt f posterity

Nachwirkung f after-effect

Nachwort nt (pl -e) epilogue

Nachwuchs m new generation; (fam: Kinder) offspring. **N~spieler** m young player

nachzahlen vt/i sep (haben) pay extra; (später zahlen) pay later; **Steuern n~** pay tax arrears

nachzählen vt/i sep (haben) count again; (prüfen) check

Nachzahlung f extra/later payment; (Gehalts-) back-payment

nachzeichnen vt sep copy

Nachzügler m -s,- late-comer; (Zurückgebliebener) straggler

Nacken m -s,- nape or back of the neck

nackt a naked; (bloß, kahl) bare; (Wahrheit) plain. **N~baden** nt nude bathing. **N~heit** f - nakedness, nudity. **N~kultur** f nudism. **N~schnecke** f slug

Nadel f -,-n needle; (Häkel-) hook; (Schmuck-, Hut-) pin. **N~arbeit** f needlework. **N~baum** m conifer. **N~kissen** nt pincushion. **N~stich** m stitch; (fig) pinprick. **N~wald** m coniferous forest

Nagel m -s,̈ nail. **N~bürste** f nailbrush. **N~feile** f nail-file. **N~haut** f cuticle. **N~lack** m nail varnish. **n~n** vt nail. **n~neu** a brand-new. **N~schere** f nail scissors pl

nagen vt/i (haben) gnaw (**an**+ dat at); **n~d** (fig) nagging

Nagetier nt rodent

nah a, adv & prep = nahe; **von nah und fern** from far and wide

Näharbeit f sewing; **eine N~** a piece of sewing

Nahaufnahme f close-up

nahe a (näher, nächst) nearby; (zeitlich) imminent; (eng) close; **der N~ Osten** the Middle East; **in n~r Zukunft** in the near future; **von n~m** [from] close to; **n~ sein** be close (dat to); **den Tränen n~** close to tears ● adv near, close; (verwandt) closely; **n~ an** (+ acc/dat) near [to], close to; **n~ daran sein, etw zu tun** nearly do sth; **jdm zu n~ treten** (fig) offend s.o. ● prep (+ dat) near [to], close to

Nähe f - nearness, proximity; **aus der N~** [from] close to; **in der N~** near or close by; **in der N~ der Kirche** near the church

nahebei adv near or close by

nahe|gehen† vi sep (sein) **jdm n~gehen** (fig) affect s.o. deeply. **n~kommen†** vi sep (sein) (fig) come close (dat to); (vertraut werden) get close (dat to). **n~legen** vt sep recommend (dat to); **jdm n~legen, etw zu tun** urge s.o. to do sth. **n~liegen†** vi sep (haben) (fig) be highly likely. **n~liegend** a obvious

nahen vi (sein) (liter) approach

nähen vt/i (haben) sew; (anfertigen) make; (Med) stitch [up]

näher a closer; (Weg) shorter; (Einzelheiten) further ● adv closer; (genauer) more closely; **sich n~ erkundigen** make further enquiries; **n~ an** (+ acc/dat) nearer [to], closer to ● prep (+ dat) nearer [to], closer to. **N~e[s]** nt [further] details pl. **n~kommen†** vi sep (sein) come closer, approach; (fig) get closer (dat to). **n~n (sich)** vr approach

nahestehen† vi sep (haben) (fig) be close (dat to)

nahezu *adv* almost

Nähgarn *nt* [sewing] cotton

Nahkampf *m* close combat

Näh|maschine *f* sewing machine. **N~nadel** *f* sewing-needle

nähren *vt* feed; (*fig*) nurture; **sich n~ von** live on ● *vi* (*haben*) be nutritious

nahrhaft *a* nutritious

Nährstoff *m* nutrient

Nahrung *f* - food, nourishment. **N~smittel** *nt* food

Nährwert *m* nutritional value

Naht *f* -,-̈e seam; (*Med*) suture. **n~los** *a* seamless

Nahverkehr *m* local service. **N~szug** *m* local train

Nähzeug *nt* sewing; (*Zubehör*) sewing kit

naiv /na'i:f/ *a* naïve, *adv* -ly. **N~ität** /-vi'tɛ:t/ *f* - naïvety

Name *m* -ns,-n name; **im N~n** (+ *gen*) in the name of; ⟨*handeln*⟩ on behalf of; **das Kind beim rechten N~n nennen** (*fam*) call a spade a spade. **n~nlos** *a* nameless; (*unbekannt*) unknown, anonymous. **n~ns** *adv* by the name of ● *prep* (+ *gen*) on behalf of. **N~nstag** *m* name-day. **N~nsvetter** *m* namesake. **N~nszug** *m* signature. **n~ntlich** *adv* by name; (*besonders*) especially

namhaft *a* noted; (*ansehnlich*) considerable; **n~ machen** name

nämlich *adv* (*und zwar*) namely; (*denn*) because

nanu *int* hallo

Napf *m* -[e]s,-̈e bowl

Narbe *f* -,-n scar

Narkose *f* -,-n general anaesthetic. **N~arzt** *m* anaesthetist. **N~mittel** *nt* anaesthetic

Narkot|ikum *nt* -s,-ka narcotic; (*Narkosemittel*) anaesthetic. **n~isieren** *vt* anaesthetize

Narr *m* -en,-en fool; **zum N~en haben** *od* **halten** make a fool of. **n~en** *vt* fool. **n~ensicher** *a* foolproof. **N~heit** *f* -,-en folly

Närr|in *f* -,-nen fool. **n~isch** *a* foolish; (*fam: verrückt*) crazy (**auf** + *acc* about)

Narzisse *f* -,-n narcissus; **gelbe N~** daffodil

nasal *a* nasal

nasch|en *vt/i* (*haben*) nibble (**an** + *dat* at); **wer hat vom Kuchen genascht?** who's been at the cake? **n~haft** *a* sweet-toothed

Nase *f* -,-n nose; **an der N~ herumführen** (*fam*) dupe

näseln *vi* (*haben*) speak through one's nose; **n~d** nasal

Nasen|bluten *nt* -s nosebleed. **N~loch** *nt* nostril. **N~rücken** *m* bridge of the nose

Naseweis *m* -es,-e (*fam*) know-all

Nashorn *nt* rhinoceros

naß *a* (**nasser, nassest**) wet

Nässe *f* - wet; (*Naßsein*) wetness. **n~n** *vt* wet

naßkalt *a* cold and wet

Nation /na'tsjo:n/ *f* -,-en nation. **n~al** *a* national. **N~alhymne** *f* national anthem. **N~alismus** *m* - nationalism. **N~alität** *f* -,-en nationality. **N~alsozialismus** *m* National Socialism. **N~alspieler** *m* international

Natrium *nt* -s sodium

Natron *nt* -s **doppeltkohlensaures N~** bicarbonate of soda

Natter *f* -,-n snake; (*Gift*-) viper

Natur *f* -,-en nature; **von N~ aus** by nature. **N~alien** /-jən/ *pl* natural produce *sg*. **n~alisieren** *vt* naturalize. **N~alisierung** *f* -,-en naturalization

Naturell *nt* -s,-e disposition

Natur|erscheinung *f* natural phenomenon. **n~farben** *a* natural[-coloured]. **N~forscher** *m* naturalist. **N~kunde** *f* natural history. **N~lehrpfad** *m* nature trail

natürlich *a* natural ● *adv* naturally; (*selbstverständlich*) of course. **N~keit** *f* - naturalness

natur|rein *a* pure. **N~schutz** *m* nature conservation; **unter N~schutz stehen** be protected. **N~schutzgebiet** *nt* nature reserve. **N~wissenschaft** *f* [natural] science. **N~wissenschaftler** *m* scientist. **n~wissenschaftlich** *a* scientific; (*Sch*) science …

nautisch *a* nautical

Navigation /-'tsjo:n/ *f* - navigation

Nazi *m* -s,-s Nazi

n.Chr. *abbr* (**nach Christus**) AD

Nebel *m* -s,- fog; (*leicht*) mist. **n~haft** *a* hazy. **N~horn** *nt* fog-horn. **n~ig** *a* = **neblig**

neben *prep* (+ *dat/acc*) next to, beside; (+ *dat*) (*außer*) apart from; **n~ mir** next to me. **n~an** *adv* next door

Neben|anschluß *m* (*Teleph*) extension. **N~ausgaben** *fpl* incidental expenses

nebenbei *adv* in addition; (*beiläufig*) casually; **n~ bemerkt** incidentally

Neben|bemerkung f passing remark. **N~beruf** m second job. **N~beschäftigung** f spare-time occupation. **N~buhler(in)** m -s,- (f -,-nen) rival

nebeneinander adv next to each other, side by side

Neben|eingang m side entrance. **N~fach** nt (Univ) subsidiary subject. **N~fluß** m tributary. **N~gleis** nt siding. **N~haus** nt house next door

nebenher adv in addition. **n~gehen†** vi sep (sein) walk alongside

nebenhin adv casually

Neben|höhle f sinus. **N~kosten** pl additional costs. **N~mann** m (pl -männer) person next to one. **N~produkt** nt by-product. **N~rolle** f supporting role; (kleine) minor role; **eine N~rolle spielen** (fig) be unimportant. **N~sache** f unimportant matter. **n~sächlich** a unimportant. **N~satz** m subordinate clause. **N~straße** f minor road; (Seiten-) side street. **N~verdienst** m additional earnings pl. **N~wirkung** f side-effect. **N~zimmer** nt room next door

neblig a foggy; (leicht) misty

nebst prep (+ dat) [together] with

Necessaire /nesɛˈsɛːɐ̯/ nt -s,-s toilet bag; (Näh-, Nagel-) set

neck|en vt tease. **N~erei** f - teasing. **n~isch** a teasing; (keß) saucy

nee adv (fam) no

Neffe m -n,-n nephew

negativ a negative. **N~** nt -s,-e (Phot) negative

Neger m -s,- Negro

nehmen† vt take (dat from); **sich** (dat) **etw n~** take sth; help oneself to ⟨Essen⟩; **jdn zu sich n~** have s.o. to live with one

Neid m -[e]s envy, jealousy. **n~en** vt **jdm den Erfolg n~en** be jealous of s.o.'s success. **n~isch** a envious, jealous (**auf** + acc of); **auf jdn n~isch sein** envy s.o.

neig|en vt incline; (zur Seite) tilt; (beugen) bend; **sich n~en** incline; ⟨Boden:⟩ slope; ⟨Person:⟩ bend (über + acc over) ● vi (haben) **n~en zu** (fig) have a tendency towards; be prone to ⟨Krankheit⟩; incline towards ⟨Ansicht⟩; **dazu n~en, etw zu tun** tend to do sth. **N~ung** f -,-en inclination; (Gefälle) slope; (fig)

tendency; (Hang) leaning; (Herzens) affection

nein adv, **N~** nt -s no

Nektar m -s nectar

Nelke f -,-n carnation; (Feder-) pink; (Culin) clove

nenn|en† vt call; (taufen) name; (angeben) give; (erwähnen) mention; **sich n~en** call oneself. **n~enswert** a significant. **N~ung** f -,-en mention; (Sport) entry. **N~wert** m face value

Neofaschismus m neofascism

Neon nt -s neon. **N~beleuchtung** f fluorescent lighting

neppen vt (fam) rip off

Nerv m -s,-en /-fən/ nerve; **die N~en verlieren** lose control of oneself. **n~en** vt **jdn n~en** (sl) get on s.o.'s nerves. **N~enarzt** m neurologist. **n~enaufreibend** a nerve-racking. **N~enbündel** nt (fam) bundle of nerves. **N~enkitzel** m (fam) thrill. **N~ensystem** nt nervous system. **N~enzusammenbruch** m nervous breakdown

nervös a nervy, edgy; (Med) nervous; **n~ sein** be on edge

Nervosität f - nerviness, edginess

Nerz m -es,-e mink

Nessel f -,-n nettle

Nest nt -[e]s,-er nest; (fam: Ort) small place

nesteln vi (haben) fumble (**an** + dat with)

Nesthäkchen nt -s,- (fam) baby of the family

nett a nice, adv -ly; (freundlich) kind, adv -ly

netto adv net. **N~gewicht** nt net weight

Netz nt -es,-e net; (Einkaufs-) string bag; (Spinnen-) web; (auf Landkarte) grid; (System) network; (Electr) mains pl. **N~haut** f retina. **N~karte** f area season-ticket. **N~werk** nt network

neu a new; (modern) modern; **wie neu** as good as new; **das ist mir neu** it's news to me; **aufs n~e** [once] again; **von n~em** all over again ● adv newly; (gerade erst) only just; (erneut) again; **etw neu schreiben/ streichen** rewrite/repaint sth. **N~ankömmling** m -s,-e newcomer. **N~anschaffung** f recent acquisition. **n~artig** a new [kind of].

N~auflage f new edition; (*unverändert*) reprint. **N~bau** m (*pl* -ten) new house/building

Neu|e(r) m/f new person, newcomer; (*Schüler*) new boy/girl. **N~e(s)** nt das **N~e** the new; etwas **N~es** something new; (*Neuigkeit*) a piece of news; **was gibt's N~es?** what's the news?

neuer|dings adv [just] recently. **n~lich** a renewed, new ● adv again. **N~ung** f -,-en innovation

neuest|e(r,s) a newest; (*letzte*) latest; seit **n~em** just recently. **N~e** nt das **N~e** the latest thing; (*Neuigkeit*) the latest news sg

neugeboren a newborn

Neugier, Neugierde f - curiosity; (*Wißbegierde*) inquisitiveness

neugierig a curious (**auf** + acc about), adv -ly; (*wißbegierig*) inquisitive, adv -ly

Neuheit f -,-en novelty; (*Neusein*) newness; **die letzte N~** the latest thing

Neuigkeit f -,-en piece of news; **N~en** news sg

Neujahr nt New Year's Day; **über N~** over the New Year

neulich adv the other day

Neu|ling m -s,-e novice. **n~modisch** a newfangled. **N~mond** m new moon

neun inv a, **N~** f -,-en nine. **N~malkluge(r)** m (*fam*) clever Dick. **n~te(r,s)** a ninth. **n~zehn** inv a nineteen. **n~zehnte(r,s)** a nineteenth. **n~zig** inv a ninety. **n~zigste(r,s)** a ninetieth

Neuralgie f -,-n neuralgia

neureich a nouveau riche

Neurologe m -n,-n neurologist

Neuro|se f -,-n neurosis. **n~tisch** a neurotic

Neuschnee m fresh snow

Neuseeland nt -s New Zealand

neuste(r,s) a = **neueste(r,s)**

neutral a neutral. **n~isieren** vt neutralize. **N~ität** f - neutrality

Neutrum nt -s,-tra neuter noun

neu|vermählt a **n~vermähltes Paar** newly-weds pl. **N~zeit** f modern times pl

nicht adv not; **ich kann n~** I cannot or can't; **er ist n~ gekommen** he hasn't come; **n~ mehr/besser als** no more/better than; **bitte n~!** please don't! **n~ berühren!** do not touch! **du kommst doch auch, ~ [wahr]?** you

are coming too, aren't you? **du kennst ihn doch, n~?** you know him, don't you?

Nichtachtung f disregard; (*Geringschätzung*) disdain

Nichte f -,-n niece

nichtig a trivial; (*Jur*) [null and] void

Nichtraucher m non-smoker. **N~abteil** nt non-smoking compartment

nichts pron & a nothing; **n~ anderes/Besseres** nothing else/better; **n~ mehr** no more; **ich weiß n~** I know nothing or don't know anything. **N~** nt - nothingness; (*fig: Leere*) void; (*Person*) nonentity. **n~ahnend** a unsuspecting

Nichtschwimmer m non-swimmer

nichtsdesto|trotz adv all the same. **n~weniger** adv nevertheless

nichts|nutzig a good-for-nothing; (*fam: unartig*) naughty. **n~sagend** a meaningless; (*uninteressant*) nondescript. **N~tun** nt -s idleness

Nickel nt -s nickel

nicken vi (*haben*) nod. **N~** nt -s nod

Nickerchen nt -s,- (*fam*) nap; **ein N~ machen** have forty winks

nie adv never

nieder a low ● adv down. **n~brennen†** vt/i sep (*sein*) burn down. **N~deutsch** nt Low German. **N~gang** m (*fig*) decline. **n~gedrückt** a (*fig*) depressed. **n~gehen†** vi sep (*sein*) come down. **n~geschlagen** a dejected, despondent. **N~geschlagenheit** f - dejection, despondency. **N~kunft** f -,-̈e confinement. **N~lage** f defeat

Niederlande (die) pl the Netherlands

Niederländ|er m -s,- Dutchman; **die N~er** the Dutch pl. **N~erin** f -,-nen Dutchwoman. **n~isch** a Dutch

nieder|lassen† vt sep let down; **sich n~lassen** settle; (*sich setzen*) sit down. **N~lassung** f -,-en settlement; (*Zweigstelle*) branch. **n~legen** vt sep put or lay down; resign ⟨*Amt*⟩; **die Arbeit n~legen** go on strike; **sich n~legen** lie down. **n~machen, n~metzeln** vt sep massacre. **n~reißen†** vt sep tear down. **N~sachsen** nt Lower Saxony. **N~schlag** m precipitation; (*Regen*) rainfall; (*radioaktiver*) fall-out; (*Boxen*) knock-down. **n~schlagen†** vt sep knock down; lower ⟨*Augen*⟩; (*unterdrücken*) crush. **n~schmettern** vt sep (*fig*) shatter. **n~schreiben†** vt sep write down.

n~**schreien**† *vt sep* shout down.
n~**setzen** *vt sep* put *or* set down;
sich n~**setzen** sit down. n~**strecken**
vt sep fell; (*durch Schuß*) gun down
niederträchtig *a* base, vile
Niederung *f* -en low ground
nieder|walzen *vt sep* flatten.
n~**werfen**† *vt sep* throw down; (*unterdrücken*) crush; sich n~**werfen**
prostrate oneself
niedlich *a* pretty; (*goldig*) sweet;
(*Amer*) cute
niedrig *a* low; (*fig: gemein*) base
● *adv* low
niemals *adv* never
niemand *pron* nobody, no one
Niere *f* -,-n kidney; **künstliche N~**
kidney machine
nieseln *vi* (*haben*) drizzle; **es n~t** it
is drizzling. **N~regen** *m* drizzle
niesen *vi* (*haben*) sneeze. **N~** *nt* -s
sneezing; (*Nieser*) sneeze
Niet *m & nt* -[e]s,-e, **Niete**¹ *f* -,-n rivet;
(*an Jeans*) stud
Niete² *f* -,-n blank; (*fam*) failure
nieten *vt* rivet
Nikotin *nt* -s nicotine
Nil *m* -[s] Nile. **N~pferd** *nt*
hippopotamus
nimmer *adv* (*SGer*) not any more;
nie und n~ never. n~**müde** *a* tireless. n~**satt** *a* insatiable. **N~wiedersehen** *nt* **auf N~wiedersehen**
(*fam*) for good
nippen *vi* (*haben*) take a sip (**an** + *dat*
of)
nirgend|s, n~wo *adv* nowhere
Nische *f* -,-n recess, niche
nisten *vi* (*haben*) nest
Nitrat *nt* -[e]s,-e nitrate
Niveau /ni'vo:/ *nt* -s,-s level; (*geistig,
künstlerisch*) standard
nix *adv* (*fam*) nothing
Nixe *f* -,-n mermaid
nobel *a* noble; (*fam: luxuriös*) luxurious; (*fam: großzügig*) generous
noch *adv* still; (*zusätzlich*) as well;
(*mit Komparativ*) even; n~ **nicht** not
yet; **gerade** n~ only just; n~ **immer**
od **immer** n~ still; n~ **letzte Woche**
only last week; **es ist** n~ **viel Zeit**
there's plenty of time yet; **wer/was/
wo** n~? who/what/where else?
n~**jemand/etwas** someone/something
else; (*Frage*) anyone/anything
else? n~ **einmal** again; n~ **ein Bier**
another beer; n~ **größer** even bigger; n~ **so sehr/schön** however

much/beautiful ● *conj* **weder** ... n~
neither ... nor
nochmal|ig *a* further. n~s *adv* again
Nomad|e *m* -n,-n nomad. n~**isch** *a*
nomadic
Nominativ *m* -s,-e nominative
nominell *a* nominal, *adv* -ly
nominier|en *vt* nominate. **N~ung** *f*
-,-en nomination
nonchalant /nõʃa'lã:/ *a* nonchalant,
adv -ly
Nonne *f* -,-n nun. **N~nkloster** *nt*
convent
Nonstopflug *m* direct flight
Nord *m* -[e]s north. **N~amerika** *nt*
North America. n~**deutsch** *a* North
German
Norden *m* -s north; **nach N~** north
nordisch *a* Nordic
nördlich *a* northern; ⟨*Richtung*⟩
northerly ● *adv & prep* (+ *gen*) n~
[von] der Stadt [to the] north of the
town
Nordosten *m* north-east
Nord|pol *m* North Pole. **N~see** *f* -
North Sea. n~**wärts** *adv* northwards. **N~westen** *m* north-west
Nörgelei *f* -,-en grumbling
nörgeln *vi* (*haben*) grumble
Norm *f* -,-en norm; (*Techn*) standard;
(*Soll*) quota
normal *a* normal, *adv* -ly. n~**erweise** *adv* normally. n~**isieren** *vt*
normalize; **sich** n~**isieren** return to
normal
normen, normieren *vt* standardize
Norwe|gen *nt* -s Norway. **N~ger(in)**
m -s,- (*f* -,-nen) Norwegian. n~**gisch**
a Norwegian
Nost|algie *f* - nostalgia. n~**algisch** *a*
nostalgic
Not *f* -,ʺe need; (*Notwendigkeit*)
necessity; (*Entbehrung*) hardship;
(*seelisch*) trouble; **Not leiden** be in
need, suffer hardship; **mit knapper
Not** only just; **zur Not** if need be;
(*äußerstenfalls*) at a pinch
Notar *m* -s,-e notary public
Not|arzt *m* emergency doctor.
N~ausgang *m* emergency exit.
N~behelf *m* -[e]s,-e makeshift.
N~bremse *f* emergency brake.
N~dienst *m* **N~dienst haben** be on
call. n~**dürftig** *a* scant; (*behelfsmäßig*) makeshift
Note *f* -,-n note; (*Zensur*) mark;
ganze/halbe N~ (*Mus*) semibreve/
minim, (*Amer*) whole/half note;
N~n lesen read music; **persönliche**

N∼ personal touch. **N∼nblatt** *nt* sheet of music. **N∼nschlüssel** *m* clef. **N∼nständer** *m* music-stand

Notfall *m* emergency; **im N∼** in an emergency; (*notfalls*) if need be; **für den N∼** just in case. **n∼s** *adv* if need be

not|gedrungen *adv* of necessity. **N∼groschen** *m* nest-egg

notieren *vt* note down; (*Comm*) quote; **sich** (*dat*) **etw n∼** make a note of sth

nötig *a* necessary; **n∼ haben** need; **das N∼ste** the essentials *pl* ● *adv* urgently. **n∼en** *vt* force; (*auffordern*) press; **laßt euch nicht n∼en** help yourselves. **n∼enfalls** *adv* if need be. **N∼ung** *f* - coercion

Notiz *f* -,-en note; (*Zeitungs*-) item; [**keine**] **N∼ nehmen von** take [no] notice of. **N∼buch** *nt* notebook. **N∼kalender** *m* diary

Not|lage *f* plight. **n∼landen** *vi* (*sein*) make a forced landing. **N∼landung** *f* forced landing. **n∼leidend** *a* needy. **N∼lösung** *f* stopgap. **N∼lüge** *f* white lie

notorisch *a* notorious

Not|ruf *m* emergency call; (*Naut, Aviat*) distress call; (*Nummer*) emergency services number. **N∼signal** *nt* distress signal. **N∼stand** *m* state of emergency. **N∼unterkunft** *f* emergency accommodation. **N∼wehr** *f* - (*Jur*) self-defence

notwendig *a* necessary; (*unerläßlich*) essential ● *adv* urgently. **N∼keit** *f* -,-en necessity

Notzucht *f* - (*Jur*) rape

Nougat /'nuːgat/ *m* & *nt* -s nougat

Novelle *f* -,-n novella; (*Pol*) amendment

November *m* -s,- November

Novität *f* -,-en novelty

Novize *m* -n,-n, **Novizin** *f* -,-nen (*Relig*) novice

Nu *m* **im Nu** (*fam*) in a flash

Nuance /'nyãːsə/ *f* -,-n nuance; (*Spur*) shade

nüchtern *a* sober; (*sachlich*) matter-of-fact; (*schmucklos*) bare; (*ohne Würze*) bland; **auf n∼en Magen** on an empty stomach ● *adv* soberly

Nudel *f* -,-n piece of pasta; **N∼n** pasta *sg*; (*Band*-) noodles. **N∼holz** *nt* rolling-pin

Nudist *m* -en,-en nudist

nuklear *a* nuclear

null *inv* *a* zero, nought; (*Teleph*) 0; (*Sport*) nil; (*Tennis*) love; **n∼ Fehler** no mistakes; **n∼ und nichtig** (*Jur*) null and void. **N∼** *f* -,-en nought, zero; (*fig: Person*) nonentity; **drei Grad unter N∼** three degrees below zero. **N∼punkt** *m* zero

numerieren *vt* number

numerisch *a* numerical

Nummer *f* -,-n number; (*Ausgabe*) issue; (*Darbietung*) item; (*Zirkus*-) act; (*Größe*) size. **N∼nschild** *nt* number-/(*Amer*) license-plate

nun *adv* now; (*na*) well; (*halt*) just; **von nun an** from now on; **nun gut!** very well then! **das Leben ist nun mal so** life's like that

nur *adv* only, just; **wo kann sie nur sein?** wherever can she be? **alles, was ich nur will** everything I could possibly want; **er soll es nur versuchen!** (*drohend*) just let him try! **könnte/hätte ich nur ...!** if only I could/had ...! **nur Geduld!** just be patient!

Nürnberg *nt* -s Nuremberg

nuscheln *vt/i* (*haben*) mumble

Nuß *f* -,Nüsse nut. **N∼baum** *m* walnut tree. **N∼knacker** *m* -s,- nutcrackers *pl*. **N∼schale** *f* nutshell

Nüstern *fpl* nostrils

Nut *f* -,-en, **Nute** *f* -,-n groove

Nutte *f* -,-n (*sl*) tart (*sl*)

nutz|bar *a* usable; **n∼bar machen** utilize; cultivate 〈*Boden*〉. **n∼bringend** *a* profitable, *adv* -bly

nütze *a* **zu etwas/nichts n∼ sein** be useful/useless

nutzen *vt* use, utilize; (*aus*-) take advantage of ● *vi* (*haben*) = **nützen. N∼** *m* -s benefit; (*Comm*) profit; **N∼ ziehen aus** benefit from; **von N∼ sein** be useful

nützen *vi* (*haben*) be useful *or* of use (*dat* to); 〈*Mittel:*〉 be effective; **nichts n∼** be useless *or* no use; **was nützt mir das?** what good is that to me? ● *vt* = **nutzen**

Nutzholz *nt* timber

nützlich *a* useful; **sich n∼ machen** make oneself useful. **N∼keit** *f* - usefulness

nutz|los *a* useless; (*vergeblich*) vain. **N∼losigkeit** *f* - uselessness. **N∼nießer** *m* -s,- beneficiary. **N∼ung** *f* - use, utilization

Nylon /'nailɔn/ *nt* -s nylon

Nymphe /'nʏmfə/ *f* -,-n nymph

O

o *int* **o ja/nein!** oh yes/no! **o weh!** oh dear!

Oase *f -,-n* oasis

ob *conj* whether; **ob reich, ob arm** rich or poor; **ob sie wohl krank ist?** I wonder whether she is ill; **und ob!** (*fam*) you bet!

Obacht *f* **O∼ geben** pay attention; **O∼ geben auf** (+*acc*) look after; **O∼!** look out!

Obdach *nt* -[e]s shelter. **o∼los** *a* homeless. **O∼lose(r)** *m/f* homeless person; **die O∼losen** the homeless *pl*

Obduktion /-'tsio:n/ *f -,-en* post-mortem

O-Beine *ntpl* (*fam*) bow-legs, bandy legs. **O-beinig** *a* bandy-legged

oben *adv* at the top; (*auf der Oberseite*) on top; (*eine Treppe hoch*) upstairs; **da o∼** up there; **o∼ im Norden** up in the north; **siehe o∼** see above; **o∼ auf** (+*acc/dat*) on top of; **nach o∼** up[wards]; (*die Treppe hinauf*) upstairs; **von o∼** from above/ upstairs; **von o∼ bis unten** from top to bottom/⟨*Person*⟩ to toe; **jdn von o∼ bis unten mustern** look s.o. up and down. **o∼an** *adv* at the top. **o∼auf** *adv* on top; **o∼auf sein** (*fig*) be cheerful. **o∼drein** *adv* on top of that. **o∼erwähnt, o∼genannt** *a* above-mentioned. **o∼hin** *adv* casually

Ober *m* -s,- waiter

Ober|arm *m* upper arm. **O∼arzt** *m* ≈ senior registrar. **O∼befehlshaber** *m* commander-in-chief. **O∼begriff** *m* generic term. **O∼deck** *nt* upper deck. **o∼e(r,s)** *a* upper; (*höhere*) higher. **O∼fläche** *f* surface. **o∼flächlich** *a* superficial, *adv* -ly. **O∼geschoß** *nt* upper storey. **o∼halb** *adv & prep* (+*gen*) above; **o∼halb vom Dorf/des Dorfes** above the village. **O∼hand** *f* **die O∼hand gewinnen** gain the upper hand. **O∼haupt** *nt* (*fig*) head. **O∼haus** *nt* (*Pol*) upper house; (*in UK*) House of Lords. **O∼hemd** *nt* [man's] shirt

Oberin *f -,-nen* matron; (*Relig*) mother superior

ober|irdisch *a* surface ... ● *adv* above ground. **O∼kellner** *m* head waiter. **O∼kiefer** *m* upper jaw. **O∼körper** *m* upper part of the body. **O∼leutnant** *m* lieutenant. **O∼licht**

nt overhead light; (*Fenster*) skylight; (*über Tür*) fanlight. **O∼lippe** *f* upper lip

Obers *nt* - (*Aust*) cream

Ober|schenkel *m* thigh. **O∼schicht** *f* upper class. **O∼schule** *f* grammar school. **O∼schwester** *f* (*Med*) sister. **O∼seite** *f* upper/(*rechte Seite*) right side

Oberst *m* -en & -s,-en colonel

oberste(r,s) *a* top; (*höchste*) highest; ⟨*Befehlshaber, Gerichtshof*⟩ supreme; (*wichtigste*) first

Ober|stimme *f* treble. **O∼stufe** *f* upper school. **O∼teil** *nt* top. **O∼weite** *f* chest/(*der Frau*) bust size

obgleich *conj* although

Obhut *f* - care; **in guter O∼ sein** be well looked after

obig *a* above

Objekt *nt* -[e]s,-e object; (*Haus, Grundstück*) property; **O∼ der Forschung** subject of research

Objektiv *nt* -s,-e lens. **o∼** *a* objective, *adv* -ly. **O∼ität** *f* - objectivity

Oblate *f -,-n* (*Relig*) wafer

obliga|t *a* (*fam*) inevitable. **O∼tion** /-'tsio:n/ *f -,-en* obligation; (*Comm*) bond. **o∼torisch** *a* obligatory

Obmann *m* (*pl* -**männer**) [jury] foreman; (*Sport*) referee

Oboe /o'bo:ə/ *f -,-n* oboe

Obrigkeit *f* - authorities *pl*

obschon *conj* although

Observatorium *nt* -s,-ien observatory

obskur *a* obscure; (*zweifelhaft*) dubious

Obst *nt* -es (*coll*) fruit. **O∼baum** *m* fruit-tree. **O∼garten** *m* orchard. **O∼händler** *m* fruiterer. **O∼kuchen** *m* fruit flan. **O∼salat** *m* fruit salad

obszön *a* obscene. **O∼ität** *f -,-en* obscenity

O-Bus *m* trolley bus

obwohl *conj* although

Ochse *m* -n,-n ox. **o∼n** *vi* (*haben*) (*fam*) swot. **O∼nschwanzsuppe** *f* oxtail soup

öde *a* desolate; (*unfruchtbar*) barren; (*langweilig*) dull. **Öde** *f* - desolation; barrenness; dullness; (*Gegend*) waste

oder *conj* or; **du kennst ihn doch, o∼?** you know him, don't you?

Ofen *m* -s,-¨ stove; (*Heiz-*) heater; (*Back-*) oven; (*Techn*) furnace

offen *a* open, *adv* -ly; ⟨*Haar*⟩ loose; ⟨*Flamme*⟩ naked; (*o∼herzig*) frank, *adv* -ly; (o~ *gezeigt*) overt, *adv* -ly; (*unentschieden*) unsettled; **o~e Stelle** vacancy; **Tag der o~en Tür** open day; **Wein o~ verkaufen** sell wine by the glass; *adv* **o~ gesagt** *od* **gestanden** to be honest. **o~bar** *a* obvious ● *adv* apparently. **o~baren** *vt* reveal. **O~barung** *f* -,-en revelation. **o~bleiben†** *vi sep* (*sein*) remain open. **o~halten†** *vt sep* hold open ⟨*Tür*⟩; keep open ⟨*Mund, Augen*⟩. **O~heit** *f* - frankness, openness. **o~herzig** *a* frank, *adv* -ly. **O~herzigkeit** *f* - frankness. **o~kundig** *a* manifest, *adv* -ly. **o~lassen†** *vt sep* leave open; leave vacant ⟨*Stelle*⟩. **o~sichtlich** *a* obvious, *adv* -ly

offensiv *a* offensive. **O~e** *f* -,-n offensive

offenstehen† *vi sep* (*haben*) be open; ⟨*Rechnung:*⟩ be outstanding; **jdm o~** (*fig*) be open to s.o.

öffentlich *a* public, *adv* -ly. **Ö~keit** *f* - public; **an die Ö~keit gelangen** become public; **in aller Ö~keit** in public, publicly

Offerte *f* -,-n (*Comm*) offer

offiziell *a* official, *adv* -ly

Offizier *m* -s,-e (*Mil*) officer

öffn|en *vt/i* (*haben*) open; **sich ö~en** open. **Ö~er** *m* -s,- opener. **Ö~ung** *f* -,-en opening. **Ö~ungszeiten** *fpl* opening hours

oft *adv* often

öfter *adv* quite often. **ö~e(r,s)** *a* frequent; **des ö~en** frequently. **ö~s** *adv* (*fam*) quite often

oftmals *adv* often

oh *int* oh!

ohne *prep* (+ *acc*) without; **o~ mich!** count me out! **oben o~** topless; **nicht o~ sein** (*fam*) be not bad; (*nicht harmlos*) be quite nasty ● *conj* **o~ zu überlegen** without thinking; **o~ daß ich es merkte** without my noticing it. **o~dies** *adv* anyway. **o~gleichen** *pred a* unparalleled; **eine Frechheit o~gleichen** a piece of unprecedented insolence. **o~hin** *adv* anyway

Ohn|macht *f* -,-en faint; (*fig*) powerlessness; **in O~macht fallen** faint. **o~mächtig** *a* unconscious; (*fig*) powerless; **o~mächtig werden** faint

Ohr *nt* -[e]s,-en ear; **übers Ohr hauen** (*fam*) cheat

Öhr *nt* -[e]s,-e eye

ohren|betäubend *a* deafening. **O~schmalz** *nt* ear-wax. **O~**schmerzen *mpl* earache *sg*. **O~sessel** *m* wing-chair. **O~tropfen** *mpl* ear drops

Ohrfeige *f* slap in the face; **jdm eine O~ geben** slap s.o.'s face. **o~n** *od* **jdn o~n** slap s.o.'s face

Ohr|läppchen *nt* -s,- ear-lobe. **O~ring** *m* ear-ring. **O~wurm** *m* earwig

oje *int* oh dear!

okay /o'ke:/ *a & adv* (*fam*) OK

okkult *a* occult

Öko|logie *f* - ecology. **ö~logisch** *a* ecological. **Ö~nomie** *f* - economy (*Wissenschaft*) economics *sg*. **ö~nomisch** *a* economic; (*sparsam*) economical

Oktave *f* -,-n octave

Oktober *m* -s,- October

Okular *nt* -s,-e eyepiece

okulieren *vt* graft

ökumenisch *a* ecumenical

Öl *nt* -[e]s,-e oil; **in Öl malen** paint in oils. **Ölbaum** *m* olive-tree. **ölen** *vt* oil; **wie ein geölter Blitz** (*fam*) like greased lightning. **Ölfarbe** *f* oilpaint. **Ölfeld** *nt* oilfield. **Ölgemälde** *nt* oil-painting. **ölig** *a* oily

Oliv|e *f* -,-n olive. **O~enöl** *nt* olive oil. **o~grün** *a* olive[-green]

oll *a* (*fam*) old; (*fam: häßlich*) nasty

Ölmeßstab *m* dip-stick. **Ölsardinen** *fpl* sardines in oil. **Ölstand** *m* oillevel. **Öltanker** *m* oil-tanker. **Ölteppich** *m* oil-slick

Olympiade *f* -,-n Olympic Games *pl*, Olympics *pl*

Olymp|iasieger(in) /o'lympia-/ *m(f)* Olympic champion. **o~isch** *a* Olympic; **O~ische Spiele** Olympic Games

Ölzeug *nt* oilskins *pl*

Oma *f* -,-s (*fam*) granny

Omelett *nt* -[e]s,-e &-s omelette

Omen *nt* -s,- omen

ominös *a* ominous

Omnibus *m* bus; (*Reise-*) coach

onanieren *vi* (*haben*) masturbate

Onkel *m* -s,- uncle

Opa *m* -s,-s (*fam*) grandad

Opal *m* -s,-e opal

Oper *f* -,-n opera

Operation /-'tsio:n/ *f* -,-en operation. **O~ssaal** *m* operating-theatre

Operette *f* -,-n operetta

operieren *vt* operate on ⟨*Patient, Herz*⟩; **sich o~ lassen** have an operation ● *vi* (*haben*) operate

Opern|glas nt opera-glasses pl.
O∼haus nt opera-house. **O∼sänger(in)** m(f) opera-singer

Opfer nt -s,- sacrifice; (eines Unglücks) victim; **ein O∼ bringen** make a sacrifice; **jdm/etw zum O∼ fallen** fall victim to s.o./sth. **o∼n** vt sacrifice. **O∼ung** f -,-en sacrifice

Opium nt -s opium

opponieren vi (haben) **o∼ gegen** oppose

Opportun|ist m -en,-en opportunist. **o∼isch** a opportunist

Opposition /-'tsjo:n/ f - opposition. **O∼spartei** f opposition party

Optik f - optics sg; (fam: Objektiv) lens. **O∼er** m -s,- optician

optimal a optimum

Optim|ismus m - optimism. **O∼t** m -en,-en optimist. **o∼tisch** a optimistic, adv -ally

Optimum nt -s,-ma optimum

Option /ɔp'tsjo:n/ f -,-en option

optisch a optical; ⟨Eindruck⟩ visual

Orakel nt -s,- oracle

Orange /o'rã:ʒə/ f -,-n orange. **o∼** inv a orange. **O∼ade** /orã'ʒa:də/ f -,-n orangeade. **o∼nmarmelade** f [orange] marmalade. **O∼nsaft** m orange juice

Oratorium nt -s,-ien oratorio

Orchest|er /ɔr'kɛstɐ/ nt -s,- orchestra. **o∼rieren** vt orchestrate

Orchidee /ɔrçi'de:ə/ f -,-n orchid

Orden m -s,- (Ritter-, Kloster-) order; (Auszeichnung) medal, decoration; **jdm einen O∼ verleihen** decorate s.o. **O∼stracht** f (Relig) habit

ordentlich a neat, tidy; (anständig) respectable; (ordnungsgemäß, fam: richtig) proper; ⟨Mitglied, Versammlung⟩ ordinary; (fam: gut) decent; (fam: gehörig) good ● adv neatly, tidily; respectably; properly; (fam: gut, gehörig) well; (sehr) very; (regelrecht) really

Order f -,-s & -n order

ordinär a common

Ordin|ation /-'tsjo:n/ f -,-en (Relig) ordination; (Aust) surgery. **o∼ieren** vt (Relig) ordain

ordn|en vt put in order; (aufräumen) tidy; (an-) arrange; **sich zum Zug o∼en** form a procession. **O∼er** m -s,- steward; (Akten) file

Ordnung f - order; **O∼ halten** keep order; **O∼ machen** tidy up; **in O∼ bringen** put in order; (aufräumen) tidy; (reparieren) mend; (fig) put

right; **in O∼ sein** be in order; (ordentlich sein) be tidy; (fig) be all right; **ich bin mit dem Magen** od **mein Magen ist nicht ganz in O∼** I have a slight stomach upset; **[geht] in O∼!** OK! **o∼sgemäß** a proper, adv -ly. **O∼sstrafe** f (Jur) fine. **o∼swidrig** a improper, adv -ly

Ordonnanz f -,-en (Mil) orderly

Organ nt -s,-e organ; (fam: Stimme) voice

Organi|sation /-'tsjo:n/ f -,-en organization. **O∼sator** m -s,-en /-'to:rən/ organizer

organisch a organic, adv -ally

organisieren vt organize; (fam: beschaffen) get [hold of]

Organis|mus m -,-men organism; (System) system

Organist m -en,-en organist

Organspenderkarte f donor card

Orgasmus m -,-men orgasm

Orgel f -,-n (Mus) organ. **O∼pfeife** f organ-pipe

Orgie /'ɔrgjə/ f -,-n orgy

Orien|t /'o:rjɛnt/ m -s Orient. **o∼talisch** a Oriental

orientier|en /orjɛn'ti:rən/ vt inform (über + acc about); **sich o∼en** get one's bearings, orientate oneself; (unterrichten) inform oneself (über + acc about). **O∼ung** f - orientation; **die O∼ung verlieren** lose one's bearings

original a original. **O∼** nt -s,-e original; (Person) character. **O∼ität** f - originality. **O∼übertragung** f live transmission

originell a original; (eigenartig) unusual

Orkan m -s,-e hurricane

Ornament nt -[e]s,-e ornament

Ornat m -[e]s,-e robes pl

Ornithologie f - ornithology

Ort m -[e]s,-e place; (Ortschaft) [small] town; **am Ort** locally; **am Ort des Verbrechens** at the scene of the crime; **an Ort und Stelle** in the right place; (sofort) on the spot. **o∼en** vt locate

ortho|dox a orthodox. **O∼graphie** f - spelling. **o∼graphisch** a spelling ... **O∼päde** m -n,-n orthopaedic specialist. **o∼pädisch** a orthopaedic

örtlich a local, adv -ly. **Ö∼keit** f -,-en locality

Ortschaft f -,-en [small] town; (Dorf) village; **geschlossene O∼** (Auto) built-up area

orts|fremd *a* o∼fremd sein be a stranger. **O∼gespräch** *nt* (*Teleph*) local call. **O∼name** *m* place-name. **O∼sinn** *m* sense of direction. **O∼verkehr** *m* local traffic. **O∼zeit** *f* local time

Öse *f* -,-n eyelet; (*Schlinge*) loop; **Haken und Öse** hook and eye

Ost *m* -[e]s east. **o∼deutsch** *a* Eastern/(*Pol*) East German

Osten *m* -s east; **nach O∼** east

ostentativ *a* pointed, *adv* -ly

Osteopath *m* -en,-en osteopath

Oster|ei /'o:stɐʔai/ *nt* Easter egg. **O∼fest** *nt* Easter. **O∼glocke** *f* daffodil. **O∼montag** *m* Easter Monday. **O∼n** *nt* -,- Easter; **frohe O∼n!** happy Easter!

Österreich *nt* -s Austria. **Ö∼er** *m* -s,-, **Ö∼erin** *f* -,-nen Austrian. **ö∼isch** *a* Austrian

östlich *a* eastern; ⟨*Richtung*⟩ easterly ● *adv & prep* (+ *gen*) **ö∼ [von] der Stadt** [to the] east of the town

Ost|see *f* Baltic [Sea]. **o∼wärts** *adv* eastwards

oszillieren *vi* (*haben*) oscillate

Otter[1] *m* -s,- otter

Otter[2] *f* -,-n adder

Ouverture /uvɐr'ty:rə/ *f* -,-n overture

oval *a* oval. **O∼** *nt* -s,-e oval

Ovation /-'tsio:n/ *f* -,-en ovation

Ovulation /-'tsio:n/ *f* -,-en ovulation

Oxid, Oxyd *nt* -[e]s,-e oxide

Ozean *m* -s,-e ocean

Ozon *nt* -s ozone. **O∼loch** *nt* hole in the ozone layer. **O∼schicht** *f* ozone layer

P

paar *pron inv* **ein p∼** a few; **alle p∼ Tage** every few days. **P∼** *nt* -[e]s,-e pair; (*Ehe-, Liebes-, Tanz-*) couple. **p∼en** *vt* mate; (*verbinden*) combine; **sich p∼en** mate. **P∼ung** *f* -,-en mating. **p∼weise** *adv* in pairs, in twos

Pacht *f* -,-en lease; (*P∼summe*) rent. **p∼en** *vt* lease

Pächter *m* -s,- lessee; (*eines Hofes*) tenant

Pachtvertrag *m* lease

Pack[1] *m* -[e]s,-e bundle

Pack[2] *nt* -[e]s (*sl*) rabble

Päckchen *nt* -s,- package, small packet

pack|en *vt/i* (*haben*) pack; (*ergreifen*) seize; (*fig: fesseln*) grip; **p∼ dich!** (*sl*) beat it! **P∼en** *m* -s,- bundle. **p∼end** *a* (*fig*) gripping. **P∼papier** *nt* [strong] wrapping paper. **P∼ung** *f* -,-en packet; (*Med*) pack

Pädagog|e *m* -n,-n educationalist; (*Lehrer*) teacher. **P∼ik** *f* - educational science. **p∼isch** *a* educational

Paddel *nt* -s,- paddle. **P∼boot** *nt* canoe. **p∼n** *vt/i* (*haben/sein*) paddle. **P∼sport** *m* canoeing

Page /'pa:ʒə/ *m* -n,-n page

Paillette /pai'jɛtə/ *f* -,-n sequin

Paket *nt* -[e]s,-e packet; (*Post-*) parcel

Pakist|an *nt* -s Pakistan. **P∼aner(in)** *m* -s,- (*f* -,-nen) Pakistani. **p∼anisch** *a* Pakistani

Pakt *m* -[e]s,-e pact

Palast *m* -[e]s,-̈e palace

Palästina *nt* -s Palestine. **P∼inenser(in)** *m* -s,- (*f* -,-nen) Palestinian. **p∼inensisch** *a* Palestinian

Palette *f* -,-n palette

Palm|e *f* -,-n palm[-tree]; **jdn auf die P∼e bringen** (*fam*) drive s.o. up the wall. **P∼sonntag** *m* Palm Sunday

Pampelmuse *f* -,-n grapefruit

Panier|mehl *nt* (*Culin*) breadcrumbs *pl*. **p∼t** *a* (*Culin*) breaded

Panik *f* - panic; **in P∼ geraten** panic

panisch *a* **p∼e Angst** panic

Panne *f* -,-n breakdown; (*Reifen-*) flat tyre; (*Mißgeschick*) mishap. **P∼ndienst** *m* breakdown service

Panorama *nt* -s panorama

panschen *vt* adulterate ● *vi* (*haben*) splash about

Pantine *f* -,-n [wooden] clog

Pantoffel *m* -s,-n slipper; (*ohne Ferse*) mule. **P∼held** *m* (*fam*) henpecked husband

Pantomime[1] *f* -,-n mime

Pantomime[2] *m* -n,-n mime artist

pantschen *vt/i* = panschen

Panzer *m* -s,- armour; (*Mil*) tank; (*Zool*) shell. **p∼n** *vt* armour-plate. **P∼schrank** *m* safe

Papa /'papa, pa'pa:/ *m* -s,-s daddy

Papagei *m* -s & -en,-en parrot

Papier *nt* -[e]s,-e paper. **P∼korb** *m* waste-paper basket. **P∼schlange** *f* streamer. **P∼waren** *fpl* stationery *sg*

Pappe *f* - cardboard; (*dial: Kleister*) glue

Pappel *f* -,-n poplar

pappen *vt/i* (*haben*) (*fam*) stick

pappig *a* (*fam*) sticky

Papp|karton *m*, **P~schachtel** *f* cardboard box

Paprika *m* **-s,-[s]** [sweet] pepper; (*Gewürz*) paprika

Papst *m* **-[e]s,-̈e** pope

päpstlich *a* papal

Parade *f* **-,-n** parade

Paradeiser *m* **-s,-** (*Aust*) tomato

Paradies *nt* **-es,-e** paradise. **p~isch** *a* heavenly

Paradox *nt* **-es,-e** paradox. **p~** *a* paradoxical

Paraffin *nt* **-s** paraffin

Paragraph *m* **-en,-en** section

parallel *a* & *adv* parallel. **P~e** *f* **-,-n** parallel

Paranuß *f* Brazil nut

Parasit *m* **-en,-en** parasite

parat *a* ready

Pärchen *nt* **-s,-** pair; (*Liebes-*) couple

Parcours /par'kuːɐ̯/ *m* **-,-** /-[s],-s/ (*Sport*) course

Pardon /par'dõː/ *int* sorry!

Parfüm *nt* **-s,-e** & **-s** perfume, scent. **p~iert** *a* perfumed, scented

parieren¹ *vt* parry

parieren² *vi* (*haben*) (*fam*) obey

Parität *f* **-** parity; (*in Ausschuß*) equal representation

Park *m* **-s,-s** park. **p~en** *vt/i* (*haben*) park. **P~en** *nt* **-s** parking; '**P~en verboten**' 'no parking'

Parkett *nt* **-[e]s,-e** parquet floor; (*Theat*) stalls *pl*

Park|haus *nt* multi-storey car park. **P~lücke** *f* parking space. **P~platz** *m* car park, (*Amer*) parking-lot; (*für ein Auto*) parking space; (*Autobahn*) lay-by. **P~scheibe** *f* parking-disc. **P~schein** *m* car-park ticket. **P~uhr** *f* parking-meter. **P~verbot** *nt* parking ban; '**P~verbot**' 'no parking'

Parlament *nt* **-[e]s,-e** parliament. **p~arisch** *a* parliamentary

Parodie *f* **-,-n** parody. **p~ren** *vt* parody

Parole *f* **-,-n** slogan; (*Mil*) password

Part *m* **-s,-s** (*Theat, Mus*) part

Partei *f* **-,-en** (*Pol, Jur*) party; (*Miet-*) tenant; **für jdn P~ ergreifen** take s.o.'s part. **p~isch** *a* biased. **p~los** *a* independent

Parterre /par'tɛr/ *nt* **-s,-s** ground floor, (*Amer*) first floor; (*Theat*) rear stalls *pl*. **p~** *adv* on the ground floor

Partie *f* **-,-n** part; (*Tennis, Schach*) game; (*Golf*) round; (*Comm*) batch; **eine gute P~ machen** marry well

Partikel¹ *nt* **-s,-** particle

Partikel² *f* **-,-n** (*Gram*) particle

Partitur *f* **-,-en** (*Mus*) full score

Partizip *nt* **-s,-ien** /-iən/ participle; **erstes/zweites P~** present/past participle

Partner|(in) *m* **-s,-** (*f* **-,-nen**) partner. **P~schaft** *f* **-,-en** partnership. **P~stadt** *f* twin town

Party /'paːɐ̯ti/ *f* **-,-s** party

Parzelle *f* **-,-n** plot [of ground]

Paß *m* **-sses,-̈sse** passport; (*Geog, Sport*) pass

passabel *a* passable

Passage /pa'saːʒə/ *f* **-,-n** passage; (*Einkaufs-*) shopping arcade

Passagier /pasa'ʒiːɐ̯/ *m* **-s,-e** passenger

Paßamt *nt* passport office

Passant(in) *m* **-en,-en** (*f* **-,-nen**) passer-by

Paßbild *nt* passport photograph

Passe *f* **-,-n** yoke

passen *vi* (*haben*) fit; (*geeignet sein*) be right (**für** for); (*Sport*) pass the ball; (*aufgeben*) pass; **p~ zu** go [well] with; (*übereinstimmen*) match; **jdm p~** fit s.o.; (*gelegen sein*) suit s.o.; **seine Art paßt mir nicht** I don't like his manner; [**ich**] **passe** pass. **p~d** *a* suitable; (*angemessen*) appropriate; (*günstig*) convenient; (*übereinstimmend*) matching

passier|bar *a* passable. **p~en** *vt* pass; cross ⟨*Grenze*⟩; (*Culin*) rub through a sieve ● *vi* (*sein*) happen (**jdm** to s.o.); **es ist ein Unglück p~t** there has been an accident. **P~schein** *m* pass

Passion *f* **-,-en** passion. **p~iert** *a* very keen ⟨*Jäger, Angler*⟩

passiv *a* passive. **P~** *nt* **-s,-e** (*Gram*) passive

Paß|kontrolle *f* passport control. **P~straße** *f* pass

Paste *f* **-,-n** paste

Pastell *nt* **-[e]s,-e** pastel. **P~farbe** *f* pastel colour

Pastet|chen *nt* **-s,-** [individual] pie; (*Königin-*) vol-au-vent. **P~e** *f* **-,-n** pie; (*Gänseleber-*) paté

pasteurisieren /pastøri'ziːrən/ *vt* pasteurize

Pastille *f* **-,-n** pastille

Pastinake *f* **-,-n** parsnip

Pastor *m* **-s,-en** /-'toːrən/ pastor

Pate *m* **-n,-n** godfather; (*fig*) sponsor; **P~n** godparents. **P~nkind** *nt* godchild. **P~nschaft** *f* **-** sponsorship. **P~nsohn** *m* godson

Patent nt -[e]s,-e patent; (Offiziers-) commission. p~ a (fam) clever, adv -ly; ⟨Person⟩ resourceful. p~ieren vt patent

Patentochter f god-daughter

Pater m -s,- (Relig) Father

pathetisch a emotional ● adv with emotion

Patholog|e m -n,-n pathologist. p~isch a pathological, adv -ly

Pathos nt - emotion, feeling

Patience /pa'sjã:s/ f -,-n patience

Patient(in) /pa'tsjɛnt(ɪn)/ m -en,-en (f -,-nen) patient

Patin f -,-nen godmother

Patriot|(in) m -en,-en (f -,-nen) patriot. p~isch a patriotic. P~ismus m - patriotism

Patrone f -,-n cartridge

Patrouill|e /pa'trʊljə/ f -,-n patrol. p~ieren /-'ji:rən/ vi (haben/sein) patrol

Patsch|e f in der P~e sitzen (fam) be in a jam. p~en vi (haben/sein) splash ● vt slap. p~naß a (fam) soaking wet

Patt nt -s stalemate

Pätz|er m -s,- (fam) slip. p~ig a (fam) insolent

Pauk|e f -,-n kettledrum; auf die P~e hauen (fam) have a good time; (prahlen) boast. p~en vt/i (haben) (fam) swot. P~er m -s,- (fam: Lehrer) teacher

pausbäckig a chubby-cheeked

pauschal a all-inclusive; (einheitlich) flat-rate; (fig) sweeping ⟨Urteil⟩; p~e Summe lump sum ● adv in a lump sum; (fig) wholesale. P~e f -,-n lump sum. P~reise f package tour. P~summe f lump sum

Pause¹ f -,-n break; (beim Sprechen) pause; (Theat) interval; (im Kino) intermission; (Mus) rest; P~ machen have a break

Pause² f -,-n tracing. p~n vt trace

pausenlos a incessant, adv -ly

pausieren vi (haben) have a break; (ausruhen) rest

Pauspapier nt tracing-paper

Pavian m -s,-e baboon

Pavillon /'paviljõ/ m -s,-s pavilion

Pazifi|k m -s Pacific [Ocean]. p~sch a Pacific

Pazifist m -en,-en pacifist

Pech nt -s pitch; (Unglück) bad luck; P~ haben be unlucky. p~schwarz a pitch-black; ⟨Haare, Augen⟩ jet-black. P~strähne f run of bad luck. P~vogel m (fam) unlucky devil

Pedal nt -s,-e pedal

Pedant m -en,-en pedant. p~isch a pedantic, adv -ally

Pediküre f -,-n pedicure

Pegel m -s,- level; (Gerät) water-level indicator. P~stand m [water] level

peilen vt take a bearing on; über den Daumen gepeilt (fam) at a rough guess

Pein f - (liter) torment. p~igen vt torment

peinlich a embarrassing, awkward; (genau) scrupulous, adv -ly; es war mir sehr p~ I was very embarrassed

Peitsche f -,-n whip. p~n vt whip; (fig) lash ● vi (sein) lash (an + acc against). P~nhieb m lash

pekuniär a financial, adv -ly

Pelikan m -s,-e pelican

Pell|e f -,-n skin. p~en vt peel; shell ⟨Ei⟩; sich p~en peel. P~kartoffeln fpl potatoes boiled in their skins

Pelz m -es,-e fur. P~mantel m fur coat

Pendel nt -s,- pendulum. p~n vi (haben) swing ● vi (sein) commute. P~verkehr m shuttle-service; (für Pendler) commuter traffic

Pendler m -s,- commuter

penetrant a penetrating; (fig) obtrusive, adv -ly

penibel a fastidious, fussy; (pedantisch) pedantic

Penis m -,-se penis

Penne f -,-n (fam) school. p~n vi (haben) (fam) sleep. P~r m -s,- (sl) tramp

Pension /pã'zjo:n/ f -,-en pension; (Hotel) guest-house; bei voller/halber P~ with full/half board. P~är(in) m -s,-e (f -,-nen) pensioner. P~at nt -[e]s,-e boarding-school. p~ieren vt retire. p~iert a retired. P~ierung f - retirement

Pensum nt -s [allotted] work

Peperoni f -,- chilli

per prep (+ acc) by; per Luftpost by airmail

perfekt a perfect, adv -ly; p~ sein ⟨Vertrag:⟩ be settled

Perfekt nt -s (Gram) perfect

Perfektion /-'tsio:n/ f - perfection

perforiert a perforated

Pergament nt -[e]s,-e parchment. P~papier nt grease-proof paper

Period|e f -,-n period. p~isch a periodic, adv -ally

Perl|e f -,-n pearl; (Glas-, Holz-) bead; (Sekt-) bubble; (fam: Hilfe) treasure. **p~en** vi (haben) bubble. **P~mutt** nt -s, **P~mutter** f - & nt -s mother-of-pearl

perplex a (fam) perplexed

Perserkatze f Persian cat

Pers|ien /-jən/ nt -s Persia. **p~isch** a Persian

Person f -,-en person; (Theat) character; **ich für meine P~** [I] for my part; **für vier P~en** for four people

Personal nt -s personnel, staff. **P~ausweis** m identity card. **P~chef** m personnel manager. **P~ien** /-jən/ pl personal particulars. **P~mangel** m staff shortage. **P~pronomen** nt personal pronoun

Personen|kraftwagen m private car. **P~zug** m stopping train

personifizieren vt personify

persönlich a personal ● adv personally, in person. **P~keit** f -,-en personality

Perspektive f -,-n perspective; (Zukunfts-) prospect

Perücke f -,-n wig

pervers a [sexually] perverted. **P~ion** f -,-en perversion

Pessimis|mus m - pessimism. **P~t** m -en,-en pessimist. **p~tisch** a pessimistic, adv -ally

Pest f - plague

Petersilie /-jə/ f - parsley

Petroleum /-leʊm/ nt -s paraffin, (Amer) kerosene

Petze f -,-n (fam) sneak. **p~n** vi (haben) (fam) sneak

Pfad m -[e]s,-e path. **P~finder** m -s,- [Boy] Scout. **P~finderin** f -,-nen [Girl] Guide

Pfahl m -[e]s,̈e stake, post

Pfalz (die) - the Palatinate

Pfand nt -[e]s,̈er pledge; (beim Spiel) forfeit; (Flaschen-) deposit

pfänd|en vt (Jur) seize. **P~erspiel** nt game of forfeits

Pfand|haus nt pawnshop. **P~leiher** m -s,- pawnbroker

Pfändung f -,-en (Jur) seizure

Pfann|e f -,-n [frying-]pan. **P~kuchen** m pancake; **Berliner P~kuchen** doughnut

Pfarr|er m -s,- vicar, parson; (katholischer) priest. **P~haus** nt vicarage

Pfau m -s,-en peacock

Pfeffer m -s pepper. **P~kuchen** m gingerbread. **P~minzbonbon** m & nt [pepper]mint. **P~minze** f - (Bot)

peppermint. **P~minztee** m [pepper]mint tea. **p~n** vt pepper; (fam: schmeißen) chuck. **P~streuer** m -s,- pepper-pot

Pfeif|e f -,-n whistle; (Tabak-, Orgel-) pipe. **p~en†** vt/i (haben) whistle; (als Signal) blow the whistle; **ich p~e darauf!** (fam) I couldn't care less [about it]!

Pfeil m -[e]s,-e arrow

Pfeiler m -s,- pillar; (Brücken-) pier

Pfennig m -s,-e pfennig; **10 P~** 10 pfennigs

Pferch m -s,-e [sheep] pen. **p~en** vt (fam) cram (in + acc into)

Pferd nt -es,-e horse; **zu P~e** on horseback; **das P~ beim Schwanz aufzäumen** put the cart before the horse. **P~erennen** nt horse-race; (als Sport) [horse-]racing. **P~eschwanz** m horse's tail; (Frisur) pony-tail. **P~estall** m stable. **P~estärke** f horsepower. **P~ewagen** m horse-drawn cart

Pfiff m -[e]s,-e whistle; **P~ haben** (fam) have style

Pfifferling m -s,-e chanterelle

pfiffig a smart

Pfingst|en nt -s Whitsun. **P~montag** m Whit Monday. **P~rose** f peony

Pfirsich m -s,-e peach. **p~farben** a peach[-coloured]

Pflanz|e f -,-n plant. **p~en** vt plant. **P~enfett** nt vegetable fat. **p~lich** a vegetable; (Mittel) herbal. **P~ung** f -,-en plantation

Pflaster nt -s,- pavement; (Heft-) plaster. **p~n** vt pave. **P~stein** m paving-stone

Pflaume f -,-n plum

Pflege f - care; (Kranken-) nursing; **in P~ nehmen** look after; (Admin) foster ⟨Kind⟩. **p~bedürftig** a in need of care. **P~eltern** pl foster-parents. **P~kind** nt foster-child. **p~leicht** a easy-care. **P~mutter** f foster-mother. **p~n** vt look after, care for; nurse ⟨Kranke⟩; cultivate ⟨Künste, Freundschaft⟩. **P~r(in)** m -s,- (f -,-nen) nurse; (Tier-) keeper

Pflicht f -,-en duty; (Sport) compulsory exercise/routine. **p~bewußt** a conscientious, adv -ly. **p~eifrig** a zealous, adv -ly. **P~fach** nt (Sch) compulsory subject. **P~gefühl** nt sense of duty. **p~gemäß** a due ● adv duly

Pflock m -[e]s,̈e peg

pflücken *vt* pick
Pflug *m* -[e]s,-̈e plough
pflügen *vt/i* (*haben*) plough
Pforte *f* -,-n gate
Pförtner *m* -s,- porter
Pfosten *m* -s,- post
Pfote *f* -,-n paw
Pfropfen *m* -s,- stopper; (*Korken*) cork. **p~** *vt* graft (**auf** + *acc* on [to]); (*fam: pressen*) cram (**in** + *acc* into)
pfui *int* ugh; **p~ schäm dich!** you should be ashamed of yourself!
Pfund *nt* -[e]s,-e & - pound
Pfusch|arbeit *f* (*fam*) shoddy work. **p~en** *vi* (*haben*) (*fam*) botch one's work. **P~er** *m* -s,- (*fam*) shoddy worker. **P~erei** *f* -,-en (*fam*) botch-up
Pfütze *f* -,-n puddle
Phänomen *nt* -s,-e phenomenon. **p~al** *a* phenomenal
Phantasie *f* -,-n imagination; **P~n** fantasies; (*Fieber-*) hallucinations. **p~los** *a* unimaginative. **p~ren** *vi* (*haben*) fantasize; (*im Fieber*) be delirious. **p~voll** *a* imaginative, *adv* -ly
phant|astisch *a* fantastic, *adv* -ally. **P~om** *nt* -s,-e phantom
pharma|zeutisch *a* pharmaceutical. **P~zie** *f* - pharmacy
Phase *f* -,-n phase
Philanthrop *m* -en,-en philanthropist. **p~isch** *a* philanthropic
Philolo|ge *m* -n,-n teacher/student of language and literature. **P~gie** *f* - [study of] language and literature
Philosoph *m* -en,-en philosopher. **P~ie** *f* -,-n philosophy. **p~ieren** *vi* (*haben*) philosophize
philosophisch *a* philosophical, *adv* -ly
phlegmatisch *a* phlegmatic
Phobie *f* -,-n phobia
Phonet|ik *f* - phonetics *sg*. **p~isch** *a* phonetic, *adv* -ally
Phonotypistin *f* -,-nen audio typist
Phosphor *m* -s phosphorus
Photo *nt*, **Photo-** *s.* Foto, Foto-
Phrase *f* -,-n empty phrase
Physik *f* - physics *sg*. **p~alisch** *a* physical
Physiker(in) *m* -s,- (*f* -,-nen) physicist
Physio|logie *f* - physiology. **P~therapie** *f* physiotherapy
physisch *a* physical, *adv* -ly
Pianist(in) *m* -en,-en (*f* -,-nen) pianist

Pickel *m* -s,- pimple, spot; (*Spitzhacke*) pick. **p~ig** *a* spotty
picken *vt/i* (*haben*) peck (**nach** at); (*fam: nehmen*) pick (**aus** out of); (*Aust fam: kleben*) stick
Picknick *nt* -s,-s picnic. **p~en** *vi* (*haben*) picnic
piep[s]|en *vi* (*haben*) ⟨*Vogel:*⟩ cheep; ⟨*Maus:*⟩ squeak; (*Techn*) bleep. **P~er** *m* -s,- bleeper
Pier *m* -s,-e [harbour] pier
Pietät /pie'tɛːt/ *f* - reverence. **p~los** *a* irreverent, *adv* -ly
Pigment *nt* -[e]s,-e pigment. **P~ierung** *f* - pigmentation
Pik *nt* -s,-s (*Karten*) spades *pl*
pikant *a* piquant; (*gewagt*) racy
piken *vt* (*fam*) prick
pikiert *a* offended, hurt
piksen *vt* (*fam*) prick
Pilger|(in) *m* -s,- (*f* -,-nen) pilgrim. **P~fahrt** *f* pilgrimage. **p~n** *vi* (*sein*) make a pilgrimage
Pille *f* -,-n pill
Pilot *m* -en,-en pilot
Pilz *m* -es,-e fungus; (*eßbarer*) mushroom; **wie P~e aus dem Boden schießen** (*fig*) mushroom
pingelig *a* (*fam*) fussy
Pinguin *m* -s,-e penguin
Pinie /-iə/ *f* -,-n stone-pine
pink *pred a* shocking pink
pinkeln *vi* (*haben*) (*fam*) pee
Pinsel *m* -s,- [paint]brush
Pinzette *f* -,-n tweezers *pl*
Pionier *m* -s,-e (*Mil*) sapper; (*fig*) pioneer. **P~arbeit** *f* pioneering work
Pirat *m* -en,-en pirate
pirschen *vi* (*haben*) **p~ auf** (+ *acc*) stalk ● *vr* **sich p~** creep (**an** + *acc* up to)
pissen *vi* (*haben*) (*sl*) piss
Piste *f* -,-n (*Ski-*) run, piste; (*Renn-*) track; (*Aviat*) runway
Pistole *f* -,-n pistol
pitschnaß *a* (*fam*) soaking wet
pittoresk *a* picturesque
Pizza *f* -,-s pizza
Pkw /'peːkaveː/ *m* -s,-s (= **Personenkraftwagen**) [private] car
placieren /-'tsiːrən/ *vt* = plazieren
Plackerei *f* - (*fam*) drudgery
plädieren *vi* (*haben*) plead (**für** for); **auf Freispruch p~** (*Jur*) ask for an acquittal
Plädoyer /plɛdoa'jeː/ *nt* -s,-s (*Jur*) closing speech; (*fig*) plea

Plage *f* -,-n [hard] labour; (*Mühe*) trouble; (*Belästigung*) nuisance. **p~n** *vt* torment, plague; (*bedrängen*) pester; **sich p~n** struggle; (*arbeiten*) work hard

Plagi|at *nt* -[e]s,-e plagiarism. **p~ieren** *vt* plagiarize

Plakat *nt* -[e]s,-e poster

Plakette *f* -,-n badge

Plan *m* -[e]s,:e plan

Plane *f* -,-n tarpaulin; (*Boden-*) groundsheet

planen *vt/i* (*haben*) plan

Planet *m* -en,-en planet

planier|en *vt* level. **P~raupe** *f* bulldozer

Planke *f* -,-n plank

plan|los *a* unsystematic, *adv* -ally. **p~mäßig** *a* systematic; ⟨*Ankunft*⟩ scheduled ● *adv* systematically; (*nach Plan*) according to plan; ⟨*ankommen*⟩ on schedule

Plansch|becken *nt* paddling pool. **p~en** *vi* (*haben*) splash about

Plantage /plan'ta:ʒə/ *f* -,-n plantation

Planung *f* - planning

Plapper|maul *nt* (*fam*) chatterbox. **p~n** *vi* (*haben*) chatter ● *vt* talk ⟨*Unsinn*⟩

plärren *vi* (*haben*) bawl; ⟨*Radio:*⟩ blare

Plasma *nt* -s plasma

Plastik[1] *f* -,-en sculpture

Plast|ik[2] *nt* -s plastic. **p~isch** *a* three-dimensional; (*formbar*) plastic; (*anschaulich*) graphic, *adv* -ally. **p~ische Chirurgie** plastic surgery

Platane *f* -,-n plane [tree]

Plateau /pla'to:/ *nt* -s,-s plateau

Platin *nt* -s platinum

Platitüde *f* -,-n platitude

platonisch *a* platonic

platschen *vi* (*sein*) splash

plätschern *vi* (*haben*) splash; ⟨*Bach:*⟩ babble ● *vi* (*sein*) ⟨*Bach:*⟩ babble along

platt *a* & *adv* flat; **p~ sein** (*fam*) be flabbergasted. **P~** *nt* -[s] (*Lang*) Low German

Plättbrett *nt* ironing-board

Platte *f* -,-n slab; (*Druck-*) plate; (*Metall-, Glas-*) sheet; (*Fliese*) tile; (*Koch-*) hotplate; (*Tisch-*) top; (*Auszieh-*) leaf; (*Schall-*) record, disc; (*zum Servieren*) [flat] dish, platter; **kalte P~** assorted cold meats and cheeses *pl*

Plätt|eisen *nt* iron. **p~en** *vt/i* (*haben*) iron

Plattenspieler *m* record-player

Platt|form *f* -,-en platform. **P~füße** *mpl* flat feet. **P~heit** *f* -,-en platitude

Platz *m* -es,:e place; (*von Häusern umgeben*) square; (*Sitz-*) seat; (*Sport-*) ground; (*Fußball-*) pitch; (*Tennis-*) court; (*Golf-*) course; (*freier Raum*) room, space; **P~ nehmen** take a seat; **P~ machen/lassen** make/leave room; **vom P~ stellen** (*Sport*) send off. **P~angst** *f* agoraphobia; (*Klaustrophobie*) claustrophobia. **P~anweiserin** *f* -,-nen usherette

Plätzchen *nt* -s,- spot; (*Culin*) biscuit

platzen *vi* (*sein*) burst; (*auf-*) split; (*fam: scheitern*) fall through; ⟨*Verlobung:*⟩ be off; **vor Neugier p~** be bursting with curiosity

Platz|karte *f* seat reservation ticket. **P~konzert** *nt* open-air concert. **P~mangel** *m* lack of space. **P~patrone** *f* blank. **P~regen** *m* downpour. **P~verweis** *m* (*Sport*) sending off. **P~wunde** *f* laceration

Plauderei *f* -,-en chat

plaudern *vi* (*haben*) chat

Plausch *m* -[e]s,-e (*SGer*) chat. **p~en** *vi* (*haben*) (*SGer*) chat

plausibel *a* plausible

plazieren *vt* place, put; **sich p~** (*Sport*) be placed

pleite *a* (*fam*) **p~ sein** be broke; ⟨*Firma:*⟩ be bankrupt; **p~ gehen** go bankrupt. **P~** *f* -,-n (*fam*) bankruptcy; (*Mißerfolg*) flop; **P~ machen** go bankrupt

plissiert *a* [finely] pleated

Plomb|e *f* -,-n seal; (*Zahn-*) filling. **p~ieren** *vt* seal; fill ⟨*Zahn*⟩

plötzlich *a* sudden, *adv* -ly

plump *a* plump; (*ungeschickt*) clumsy, *adv* -ily

plumpsen *vi* (*sein*) (*fam*) fall

Plunder *m* -s (*fam*) junk, rubbish

plündern *vt/i* (*haben*) loot

Plunderstück *nt* Danish pastry

Plural *m* -s,-e plural

plus *adv, conj* & *prep* (+ *dat*) plus. **P~** *nt* - surplus; (*Gewinn*) profit; (*Vorteil*) advantage, plus. **P~punkt** *m* (*Sport*) point; (*fig*) plus. **P~quamperfekt** *nt* pluperfect. **P~zeichen** *nt* plus sign

Po *m* -s,-s (*fam*) bottom

Pöbel *m* -s mob, rabble. **p~haft** *a* loutish

pochen *vi* (*haben*) knock; ⟨*Herz:*⟩ pound; **p~ auf** (+ *acc*) (*fig*) insist on

pochieren /po'ʃi:rən/ *vt* poach

Pocken pl smallpox sg
Podest nt -[e]s,-e rostrum
Podium nt -s,-ien /-iən/ platform; (Podest) rostrum
Poesie /poe'zi:/ f - poetry
poetisch a poetic
Pointe /'poɛ̃:tə/ f -,-n point (of a joke)
Pokal m -s,-e goblet; (Sport) cup
pökeln vt (Culin) salt
Poker nt -s poker
Pol m -s,-e pole. **p∼ar** a polar
polarisieren vt polarize
Polarstern m pole-star
Pole m -n,-n Pole. **P∼n** nt -s Poland
Police /po'li:sə/ f -,-n policy
Polier m -s,-e foreman
polieren vt polish
Polin f -,-nen Pole
Politesse f -,-n [woman] traffic warden
Politik f - politics sg; (Vorgehen, Maßnahme) policy
Polit|iker(in) m -s,- (f -,-nen) politician. **p∼isch** a political, adv -ly
Politur f -,-en polish
Polizei f - police pl. **P∼beamte(r)** m police officer. **p∼lich** a police ... ● adv by the police; ⟨sich anmelden⟩ with the police. **P∼streife** f police patrol. **P∼stunde** f closing time. **P∼wache** f police station
Polizist m -en,-en policeman. **P∼in** f -,-nen policewoman
Pollen m -s pollen
polnisch a Polish
Polohemd nt polo shirt
Polster nt -s,- pad; (Kissen) cushion; (Möbel-) upholstery; (fam: Rücklage) reserves pl. **P∼er** m -s,- upholsterer. **P∼möbel** pl upholstered furniture sg. **p∼n** vt pad; upholster ⟨Möbel⟩. **P∼ung** f - padding; upholstery
Polter|abend m wedding-eve party. **p∼n** vi (haben) thump, bang; (schelten) bawl ● vi (sein) crash down; (gehen) clump [along]; (fahren) rumble [along]
Polyäthylen nt -s polythene
Polyester m -s polyester
Polyp m -en,-en polyp; (sl: Polizist) copper; **P∼en** adenoids pl
Pomeranze f -,-n Seville orange
Pommes pl (fam) French fries
Pommes frites /pom'fri:t/ pl chips; (dünner) French fries
Pomp m -s pomp
Pompon /põ'põ:/ m -s,-s pompon
pompös a ostentatious, adv -ly

Pony¹ nt -s,-s pony
Pony² m -s,-s fringe
Pop m -[s] pop. **P∼musik** f pop music
Popo m -s,-s (fam) bottom
popul|är a popular. **P∼arität** f - popularity
Pore f -,-n pore
Porno|graphie f - pornography. **p∼graphisch** a pornographic
porös a porous
Porree m -s leeks pl; **eine Stange P∼** a leek
Portal nt -s,-e portal
Portemonnaie /portmo'ne:/ nt -s,-s purse
Portier /por'tje:/ m -s,-s doorman, porter
Portion /-'tsio:n/ f -,-en helping, portion
Porto nt -s postage. **p∼frei** adv post free, post paid
Porträ|t /por'trɛ:/ nt -s,-s portrait. **p∼tieren** vt paint a portrait of
Portugal nt -s Portugal
Portugies|e m -n,-n, **P∼in** f -,-nen Portuguese. **p∼isch** a Portuguese
Portwein m port
Porzellan nt -s china, porcelain
Posaune f -,-n trombone
Pose f -,-n pose
posieren vi (haben) pose
Position /-'tsio:n/ f -,-en position
positiv a positive, adv -ly. **P∼** nt -s,-e (Phot) positive
Posse f -,-n (Theat) farce. **P∼n** m -s,- prank; **P∼n** pl tomfoolery sg
Possessivpronomen nt possessive pronoun
possierlich a cute
Post f - post office; (Briefe) mail, post; mit der **P∼** by post
postalisch a postal
Post|amt nt post office. **P∼anweisung** f postal money order. **P∼bote** m postman
Posten m -s,- post; (Wache) sentry; (Waren-) batch; (Rechnungs-) item, entry; **P∼ stehen** stand guard; **nicht auf dem P∼** (fam) under the weather
Poster nt & m -s,- poster
Postfach nt post-office or PO box
postieren vt post, station; **sich p∼** station oneself
Post|karte f postcard. **p∼lagernd** adv poste restante. **P∼leitzahl** f postcode, (Amer) Zip code. **P∼scheckkonto** nt ≈ National Girobank account. **P∼stempel** m postmark

postum a posthumous, adv -ly

post|wendend adv by return of post. **P~wertzeichen** nt [postage] stamp

Poten|tial /-'tsi̯a:l/ nt -s,-e potential. **p~tiell** /-'tsi̯ɛl/ a potential, adv -ly

Potenz f -,-en potency; (Math & fig) power

Pracht f - magnificence, splendour. **P~exemplar** nt magnificent specimen

prächtig a magnificent, adv -ly; (prima) splendid, adv -ly

prachtvoll a magnificent, adv -ly

Prädikat nt -[e]s,-e rating; (Comm) grade; (Gram) predicate. **p~iv** a (Gram) predicative, adv -ly. **P~swein** m high-quality wine

präge|n vt stamp (auf + acc on); emboss ⟨Leder, Papier⟩; mint ⟨Münze⟩; coin ⟨Wort, Ausdruck⟩; (fig) shape. **P~stempel** m die

pragmatisch a pragmatic, adv -ally

prägnant a succinct, adv -ly

prähistorisch a prehistoric

prahl|en vi (haben) boast, brag (mit about). **p~erisch** a boastful, adv -ly

Prakti|k f -,-en practice. **P~kant(in)** m -en,-en (f -,-nen) trainee

Prakti|kum nt -s,-ka practical training. **p~sch** a practical; (nützlich) handy; (tatsächlich) virtual; **p~scher Arzt** general practitioner ● adv practically; virtually; (in der Praxis) in practice; **p~sch arbeiten** do practical work. **p~zieren** vt/i (haben) practise; (anwenden) put into practice; (fam: bekommen) get

Praline f -,-n chocolate; **Schachtel P~n** box of chocolates

prall a bulging; (dick) plump; ⟨Sonne⟩ blazing ● adv **p~ gefüllt** full to bursting. **p~en** vi (sein) **p~ auf** (+ acc)/**gegen** collide with, hit; ⟨Sonne:⟩ blaze down on

Prämie /-i̯ə/ f -,-n premium; (Preis) award

präm[i]ieren vt award a prize to

Pranger m -s,- pillory

Pranke f -,-n paw

Präpar|at nt -[e]s,-e preparation. **p~ieren** vt prepare; (zerlegen) dissect; (ausstopfen) stuff

Präposition /-'tsi̯o:n/ f -,-en preposition

Präsens nt - (Gram) present

präsentieren vt present; **sich p~** present itself/⟨Person:⟩ oneself

Präsenz f - presence

Präservativ nt -s,-e condom

Präsident|(in) m -en,-en (f -,-nen) president. **P~schaft** f - presidency

Präsidium nt -s presidency; (Gremium) executive committee; (Polizei-) headquarters pl

prasseln vi (haben) ⟨Regen:⟩ beat down; ⟨Feuer:⟩ crackle ● vi (sein) **p~ auf** (+ acc)/**gegen** beat down on/beat against

prassen vi (haben) live extravagantly; (schmausen) feast

Präteritum nt -s imperfect

präventiv a preventive

Praxis f -,-xen practice; (Erfahrung) practical experience; (Arzt-) surgery; **in der P~** in practice

Präzedenzfall m precedent

präzis[e] a precise, adv -ly

Präzision f - precision

predig|en vt/i (haben) preach. **P~er** m -s,- preacher. **P~t** f -,-en sermon

Preis m -es,-e price; (Belohnung) prize; **um jeden/keinen P~** at any/not at any price. **P~ausschreiben** nt competition

Preiselbeere f (Bot) cowberry; (Culin) ≈ cranberry

preisen† vt praise; **sich glücklich p~** count oneself lucky

preisgeben† vt sep abandon (dat to); reveal ⟨Geheimnis⟩

preis|gekrönt a award-winning. **P~gericht** nt jury. **p~günstig** a reasonably priced ● adv at a reasonable price. **P~lage** f price range. **p~lich** a price ... ● adv in price. **P~richter** m judge. **P~schild** nt price-tag. **P~träger(in)** m(f) prizewinner. **p~wert** a reasonable, adv -bly; (billig) inexpensive, adv -ly

prekär a difficult; (heikel) delicate

Prell|bock m buffers pl. **p~en** vt bounce; (verletzen) bruise; (fam: betrügen) cheat. **P~ung** f -,-en bruise

Premiere /prə'mi̯e:rə/ f -,-n première

Premierminister(in) /prə'mi̯e:-/m(f) Prime Minister

Presse f -,-n press. **p~n** vt press; **sich p~n** press (an + acc against)

pressieren vi (haben) (SGer) be urgent

Preßluft f compressed air. **P~bohrer** m pneumatic drill

Prestige /prɛs'ti:ʒə/ nt -s prestige

Preuß|en nt -s Prussia. **p~isch** a Prussian

prickeln vi (haben) tingle

Priester m -s,- priest

prima *inv* *a* first-class, first-rate; (*fam: toll*) fantastic, *adv* fantastically well

primär *a* primary, *adv* -ily

Primel *f* -,-n primula; (*Garten-*) polyanthus

primitiv *a* primitive

Prinz *m* -en,-en prince. **P~essin** *f* -,-nen princess

Prinzip *nt* -s,-ien /-iən/ principle; **im/ aus P~** in/on principle. **p~iell** *a* ⟨*Frage*⟩ of principle ● *adv* on principle; (*im Prinzip*) in principle

Priorität *f* -,-en priority

Prise *f* -,-n **P~ Salz** pinch of salt

Prisma *nt* -s,-men prism

privat *a* private, *adv* -ly; (*persönlich*) personal. **P~adresse** *f* home address. **p~isieren** *vt* privatize

Privat|leben *nt* private life. **P~lehrer** *m* private tutor. **P~lehrerin** *f* governess. **P~patient(in)** *m*(*f*) private patient

Privileg *nt* -[e]s,-ien /-iən/ privilege. **p~iert** *a* privileged

pro *prep* (+ *dat*) per. **Pro** *nt* - **das Pro und Kontra** the pros and cons *pl*

Probe *f* -,-n test, trial; (*Menge, Muster*) sample; (*Theat*) rehearsal; **auf die P~ stellen** put to the test. **P~fahrt** *f* test drive. **p~n** *vt/i* (*haben*) (*Theat*) rehearse. **p~weise** *adv* on a trial basis. **P~zeit** *f* probationary period

probieren *vt/i* (*haben*) try; (*kosten*) taste; (*proben*) rehearse

Problem *nt* -s,-e problem. **p~atisch** *a* problematic

problemlos *a* problem-free ● *adv* without any problems

Produkt *nt* -[e]s,-e product

Produk|tion /-'tsɪoːn/ *f* -,-en production. **p~tiv** *a* productive. **P~tivität** *f* - productivity

Produ|zent *m* -en,-en producer. **p~zieren** *vt* produce; **sich p~zieren** (*fam*) show off

professionell *a* professional, *adv* -ly

Professor *m* -s,-en /-'soːrən/ professor

Profi *m* -s,-s (*Sport*) professional

Profil *nt* -s,-e profile; (*Reifen-*) tread; (*fig*) image. **p~iert** *a* (*fig*) distinguished

Profit *m* -[e]s,-e profit. **p~ieren** *vi* (*haben*) profit (**von** from)

Prognose *f* -,-n forecast; (*Med*) prognosis

Programm *nt* -s,-e programme; (*Computer-*) program; (*TV*) channel; (*Comm: Sortiment*) range. **p~ieren** *vt/i* (*haben*) (*Computer*) program. **P~ierer(in)** *m* -s,- (*f* -,-nen) [computer] programmer

progressiv *a* progressive

Projekt *nt* -[e]s,-e project

Projektor *m* -s,-en /-'toːrən/ projector

projizieren *vt* project

Proklam|ation /-'tsɪoːn/ *f* -,-en proclamation. **p~ieren** *vt* proclaim

Prolet *m* -en,-en boor. **P~ariat** *nt* -[e]s proletariat. **P~arier** /-iɐ/ *m* -s,- proletarian

Prolog *m* -s,-e prologue

Promenade *f* -,-n promenade. **P~nmischung** *f* (*fam*) mongrel

Promille *pl* (*fam*) alcohol level *sg* in the blood; **zuviel P~ haben** (*fam*) be over the limit

prominen|t *a* prominent. **P~z** *f* - prominent figures *pl*

Promiskuität *f* - promiscuity

promovieren *vi* (*haben*) obtain one's doctorate

prompt *a* prompt, *adv* -ly; (*fam: natürlich*) of course

Pronomen *nt* -s,- pronoun

Propag|anda *f* - propaganda; (*Reklame*) publicity. **p~ieren** *vt* propagate

Propeller *m* -s,- propeller

Prophet *m* -en,-en prophet. **p~isch** *a* prophetic

prophezei|en *vt* prophesy. **P~ung** *f* -,-en prophecy

Proportion /-'tsɪoːn/ *f* -,-en proportion. **p~al** *a* proportional. **p~iert** *a* **gut p~iert** well proportioned

Prosa *f* - prose

prosaisch *a* prosaic, *adv* -ally

prosit *int* cheers!

Prospekt *m* -[e]s,-e brochure; (*Comm*) prospectus

prost *int* cheers!

Prostitu|ierte *f* -n,-n prostitute. **P~tion** /-'tsɪoːn/ *f* - prostitution

Protest *m* -[e]s,-e protest

Protestant|(in) *m* -en,-en (*f* -,-nen) (*Relig*) Protestant. **p~isch** *a* (*Relig*) Protestant

protestieren *vi* (*haben*) protest

Prothese *f* -,-n artificial limb; (*Zahn-*) denture

Protokoll *nt* -s,-e record; (*Sitzungs-*) minutes *pl*; (*diplomatisches*) protocol; (*Strafzettel*) ticket

Prototyp *m* -s,-en prototype

protz|en *vi* (*haben*) show off (**mit etw** sth). **p~ig** *a* ostentatious

Proviant m -s provisions pl
Provinz f -,-en province. **p~iell** a provincial
Provision f -,-en (Comm) commission
provisorisch a provisional, adv -ly, temporary, adv -ily
Provokation /-'tsio:n/ f -,-en provocation
provozieren vt provoke. **p~d** a provocative, adv -ly
Prozedur f -,-en [lengthy] business
Prozent nt -[e]s,-e & - per cent; **5 P~** 5 per cent. **P~satz** m percentage. **p~ual** a percentage ...
Prozeß m -sses,-sse process; (Jur) lawsuit; (Kriminal-) trial
Prozession f -,-en procession
prüde a prudish
prüf|en vt test/(über-) check (auf + acc for); audit ⟨Bücher⟩; (Sch) examine; **p~ender Blick** searching look. **P~er** m -s,- inspector; (Buch-) auditor; (Sch) examiner. **P~ling** m -s,-e examination candidate. **P~ung** f -,-en examination; (Test) test; (Bücher-) audit; (fig) trial
Prügel m -s,- cudgel; **P~** pl hiding sg, beating sg. **P~ei** f -,-en brawl, fight. **p~n** vt beat, thrash; **sich p~n** fight, brawl
Prunk m -[e]s magnificence, splendour. **p~en** vi (haben) show off (**mit etw** sth). **p~voll** a magnificent, adv -ly
prusten vi (haben) splutter; (schnauben) snort
Psalm m -s,-en psalm
Pseudonym nt -s,-e pseudonym
pst int shush!
Psychi|ater m -s,- psychiatrist. **P~atrie** f - psychiatry. **p~atrisch** a psychiatric
psychisch a psychological, adv -ly; (Med) mental, adv -ly
Psycho|analyse f psychoanalysis. **P~loge** m -n,-n psychologist. **P~logie** f - psychology. **p~logisch** a psychological, adv -ly
Pubertät f - puberty
publik a **p~ werden/machen** become/make public
Publi|kum nt -s public; (Zuhörer) audience; (Zuschauer) spectators pl. **p~zieren** vt publish
Pudding m -s,-s blancmange; (im Wasserbad gekocht) pudding
Pudel m -s,- poodle
Puder m & (fam) nt -s,- powder; (Körper-) talcum [powder]. **P~dose**

f [powder] compact. **p~n** vt powder. **P~zucker** m icing sugar
Puff[1] m -[e]s,-e push, poke
Puff[2] m & nt -s,-s (sl) brothel
puffen vt (fam) poke ● vi (sein) puff along
Puffer m -s,- (Rail) buffer; (Culin) pancake. **P~zone** f buffer zone
Pull|i m -s,-s jumper. **P~over** m -s,- jumper; (Herren-) pullover
Puls m -es pulse. **P~ader** f artery. **p~ieren** vi (haben) pulsate
Pult nt -[e]s,-e desk; (Lese-) lectern
Pulver nt -s,- powder. **p~ig** a powdery. **p~isieren** vt pulverize
Pulver|kaffee m instant coffee. **P~schnee** m powder snow
pummelig a (fam) chubby
Pump m **auf P~** (fam) on tick
Pumpe f -,-n pump. **p~n** vt/i (haben) pump; (fam: leihen) lend; [sich (dat)] **etw p~n** (fam: borgen) borrow sth
Pumps /pœmps/ pl court shoes
Punkt m -[e]s,-e dot; (Tex) spot; (Geom, Sport & fig) point; (Gram) full stop, period; **P~ sechs Uhr** at six o'clock sharp; **nach P~en siegen** win on points. **p~iert** a ⟨Linie, Note⟩ dotted
pünktlich a punctual, adv -ly. **P~keit** f - punctuality
Punsch m -[e]s,-e [hot] punch
Pupille f -,-n (Anat) pupil
Puppe f -,-n doll; (Marionette) puppet; (Schaufenster-, Schneider-) dummy; (Zool) chrysalis
pur a pure; (fam: bloß) sheer; **Whisky pur** neat whisky
Püree nt -s,-s purée; (Kartoffel-) mashed potatoes pl
puritanisch a puritanical
purpurrot a crimson
Purzel|baum m (fam) somersault. **p~n** vi (sein) (fam) tumble
pusseln vi (haben) (fam) potter
Puste f - (fam) breath; **aus der P~** out of breath. **p~n** vt/i (haben) (fam) blow
Pute f -,-n turkey; (Henne) turkey hen. **P~r** m -s,- turkey cock
Putsch m -[e]s,-e coup
Putz m -es plaster; (Staat) finery. **p~en** vt clean; (Aust) dry-clean; (zieren) adorn; **sich p~en** dress up; **sich** (dat) **die Zähne/Nase p~en** clean one's teeth/blow one's nose. **P~frau** f cleaner, charwoman. **p~ig** a (fam) amusing, cute; (seltsam) odd. **P~macherin** f -,-nen milliner

Puzzlespiel /'pazl-/ *nt* jigsaw
Pyramide *f* -,-n pyramid

Q

Quacksalber *m* -s,- quack
Quadrat *nt* -[e]s,-e square. **q~isch** *a*
square. **Q~meter** *m* & *nt* square
metre
quaken *vi* (*haben*) quack; ⟨*Frosch:*⟩
croak
quäken *vi* (*haben*) screech; ⟨*Baby:*⟩
whine
Quäker(in) *m* -s,- (*f* -,-nen) Quaker
Qual *f* -,-en torment; (*Schmerz*) agony
quälen *vt* torment; (*foltern*) torture;
(*bedrängen*) pester; **sich q~** torment
oneself; (*leiden*) suffer; (*sich mühen*)
struggle. **q~d** *a* agonizing
Quälerei *f* -,-en torture; (*Qual*) agony
Quälgeist *m* (*fam*) pest
Qualifi|kation /-'tsio:n/ *f* -,-en qualifi-
cation. **q~zieren** *vt* qualify; **sich
q~zieren** qualify. **q~ziert** *a* quali-
fied; (*fähig*) competent; ⟨*Arbeit*⟩
skilled
Qualität *f* -,-en quality
Qualle *f* -,-n jellyfish
Qualm *m* -s [thick] smoke. **q~en** *vi*
(*haben*) smoke
qualvoll *a* agonizing
Quantität *f* -,-en quantity
Quantum *nt* -s,-ten quantity;
(*Anteil*) share, quota
Quarantäne *f* - quarantine
Quark *m* -s quark, ≈ curd cheese;
(*fam: Unsinn*) rubbish
Quartal *nt* -s,-e quarter
Quartett *nt* -[e]s,-e quartet
Quartier *nt* -s,-e accommodation;
(*Mil*) quarters *pl*; **ein Q~ suchen**
look for accommodation
Quarz *m* -es quartz
quasseln *vi* (*haben*) (*fam*) jabber
Quaste *f* -,-n tassel
Quatsch *m* -[e]s (*fam*) nonsense, rub-
bish; **Q~ machen** (*Unfug machen*)
fool around; (*etw falsch machen*) do
a silly thing. **q~en** (*fam*) *vi* (*haben*)
talk; (*schwatzen*) natter; ⟨*Wasser,
Schlamm:*⟩squelch ● *vt* talk. **q~naß**
a (*fam*) soaking wet
Quecksilber *nt* mercury
Quelle *f* -,-n spring; (*Fluß- & fig*)
source. **q~n†** *vi* (*sein*) well [up]/
(*fließen*) pour (**aus** from); (*aufquellen*) swell; (*hervortreten*) bulge

quengeln *vi* (*fam*) whine; ⟨*Baby:*⟩
grizzle
quer *adv* across, crosswise; (*schräg*)
diagonally
Quere *f* - **der Q~ nach** across, crosswise; **jdm in die Q~ kommen** get in
s.o.'s way
querfeldein *adv* across country
quer|gestreift *a* horizontally
striped. **q~köpfig** *a* (*fam*) awkward. **Q~latte** *f* crossbar. **Q~schiff**
nt transept. **Q~schnitt** *m* cross-sec-
tion. **q~schnittsgelähmt** *a* paraplegic. **Q~straße** *f* side-street; **die erste
Q~straße links** the first turning on
the left. **Q~verweis** *m*
cross-reference
quetsch|en *vt* squash; (*drücken*)
squeeze; (*zerdrücken*) crush; (*Culin*)
mash; **sich q~en in** (+ *acc*) squeeze
into; **sich** (*dat*) **den Arm q~en** bruise
one's arm. **Q~ung** *f* -,-en,
Q~wunde *f* bruise
Queue /kø:/ *nt* -s,-s cue
quicklebendig *a* very lively
quieken *vi* (*haben*) squeal; ⟨*Maus:*⟩
squeak
quietschen *vi* (*haben*) squeal; ⟨*Tür,
Dielen:*⟩ creak
Quintett *nt* -[e]s,-e quintet
Quirl *m* -[e]s,-e blender with a star-
shaped head. **q~en** *vt* mix
quitt *a* **q~sein** (*fam*) be quits
Quitte *f* -,-n quince
quittieren *vt* receipt ⟨*Rechnung*⟩;
sign for ⟨*Geldsumme, Sendung*⟩;
(*reagieren auf*) greet (**mit** with); **den
Dienst q~** resign
Quittung *f* -,-en receipt
Quiz /kvɪs/ *nt* -,- quiz
Quote *f* -,-n proportion

R

Rabatt *m* -[e]s,-e discount
Rabatte *f* -,-n (*Hort*) border
Rabattmarke *f* trading stamp
Rabbiner *m* -s,- rabbi
Rabe *m* -n,-n raven. **r~nschwarz** *a*
pitch-black
rabiat *a* violent, *adv* -ly; (*wütend*)
furious, *adv* -ly
Rache *f* - revenge, vengeance
Rachen *m* -s,- pharynx; (*Maul*) jaws
pl

rächen *vt* avenge; **sich r~** take revenge (**an** + *dat* on); ⟨Fehler, Leichtsinn:⟩ cost s.o. dear

Racker *m* -s,- (*fam*) rascal

Rad *nt* -[e]s,-̈er wheel; (*Fahr-*) bicycle, (*fam*) bike

Radar *m* & *nt* -s radar

Radau *m* -s (*fam*) din, racket

radebrechen *vt/i* (*haben*) [Deutsch/ Englisch] **r~** speak broken German/English

radeln *vi* (*sein*) (*fam*) cycle

Rädelsführer *m* ringleader

radfahr|en† *vi sep* (*sein*) cycle; **ich fahre gern Rad** I like cycling. **R~er (in)** *m(f)* -s,- (*f* -,-nen) cyclist

radier|en *vt/i* (*haben*) rub out; (*Kunst*) etch. **R~gummi** *m* eraser, rubber. **R~ung** *f* -,-en etching

Radieschen /-'di:sçən/ *nt* -s,- radish

radikal *a* radical, *adv* -ly; (*drastisch*) drastic, *adv* -ally. **R~e(r)** *m/f* (*Pol*) radical

Radio *nt* -s,-s radio

radioaktiv *a* radioactive. **R~ität** *f* - radioactivity

Radioapparat *m* radio [set]

Radius *m* -,-ien /-jən/ radius

Rad|kappe *f* hub-cap. **R~ler** *m* -s,- cyclist; (*Getränk*) shandy. **R~weg** *m* cycle track

raff|en *vt* grab; (*kräuseln*) gather; (*kürzen*) condense. **r~gierig** *a* avaricious

Raffin|ade *f* - refined sugar. **R~erie** *f* -,-n refinery. **R~esse** *f* -,-n refinement; (*Schlauheit*) cunning. **r~ieren** *vt* refine. **r~iert** *a* ingenious, *adv* -ly; (*durchtrieben*) crafty, *adv* -ily

Rage /'ra:ʒə/ *f* - (*fam*) fury

ragen *vi* (*haben*) rise [up]

Rahm *m* -s (*SGer*) cream

rahmen *vt* frame. **R~** *m* -s,- frame; (*fig*) framework; (*Grenze*) limits *pl*; (*einer Feier*) setting

Rain *m* -[e]s,-e grass verge

räkeln *v* = rekeln

Rakete *f* -,-n rocket; (*Mil*) missile

Rallye /'rali/ *nt* -s,-s rally

rammen *vt* ram

Rampe *f* -,-n ramp; (*Theat*) front of the stage. **R~nlicht** *nt* im **R~nlicht stehen** (*fig*) be in the limelight

ramponier|en *vt* (*fam*) damage; (*ruinieren*) ruin; **r~t** battered

Ramsch *m* -es junk. **R~laden** *m* junk-shop

ran *adv* = heran

Rand *m* -[e]s,-̈er edge; (*Teller-, Gläser-, Brillen-*) rim; (*Zier-*) border, edging; (*Buch-, Brief-*) margin; (*Stadt-*) outskirts *pl*; (*Ring*) ring; **am R~e des Ruins** on the brink of ruin; **am R~e erwähnen** mention in passing; **zu R~e kommen mit** (*fam*) cope with; **außer R~ und Band** (*fam: ausgelassen*) very boisterous

randalieren *vi* (*haben*) rampage

Rand|bemerkung *f* marginal note. **R~streifen** *m* (*Auto*) hard shoulder

Rang *m* -[e]s,-̈e rank; (*Theat*) tier; **erster/zweiter R~** (*Theat*) dress/upper circle; **ersten R~es** first-class

rangieren /raŋ'ʒi:rən/ *vt* shunt ● *vi* (*haben*) rank (**vor** + *dat* before); **an erster Stelle r~** come first

Rangordnung *f* order of importance; (*Hierarchie*) hierarchy

Ranke *f* -,-n tendril; (*Trieb*) shoot

ranken (sich) *vr* (*Bot*) trail; (*in die Höhe*) climb; **sich r~ um** twine around

Ranzen *m* -s,- (*Sch*) satchel

ranzig *a* rancid

Rappe *m* -n,-n black horse

rappeln *v* (*fam*) ● *vi* (*haben*) rattle ● *vr* **sich r~** pick oneself up; (*fig*) rally

Raps *m* -es (*Bot*) rape

rar *a* rare; **er macht sich rar** (*fam*) we don't see much of him. **R~ität** *f* -,-en rarity

rasant *a* fast; (*schnittig, schick*) stylish ● *adv* fast; stylishly

rasch *a* quick, *adv* -ly

rascheln *vi* (*haben*) rustle

Rasen *m* -s,- lawn

rasen *vi* (*sein*) tear [along]; ⟨Puls:⟩ race; ⟨Zeit:⟩ fly; **gegen eine Mauer r~** career into a wall ● *vi* (*haben*) rave; ⟨Sturm:⟩ rage; **vor Begeisterung r~** go wild with enthusiasm. **r~d** *a* furious; (*tobend*) raving; ⟨Sturm, Durst⟩ raging; ⟨Schmerz⟩ excruciating; ⟨Beifall⟩ tumultuous ● *adv* terribly

Rasenmäher *m* lawn-mower

Raserei *f* - speeding; (*Toben*) frenzy

Rasier|apparat *m* razor. **r~en** *vt* shave; **sich r~en** shave. **R~klinge** *f* razor blade. **R~pinsel** *m* shaving-brush. **R~wasser** *nt* aftershave [lotion]

Raspel *f* -,-n rasp; (*Culin*) grater. **r~n** *vt* grate

Rasse *f* -,-n race. **R~hund** *m* pedigree dog

Rassel f -,-n rattle. **r~n** vi (haben) rattle; ⟨Schlüssel:⟩ jangle; ⟨Kette:⟩ clank ● vi (sein) rattle [along]

Rassen|diskriminierung f racial discrimination. **R~trennung** f racial segregation

Rassepferd nt thoroughbred

rassisch a racial

Rassis|mus m - racism. **r~tisch** a racist

Rast f -,-en rest. **r~en** vi (haben) rest. **R~haus** nt motorway restaurant. **r~los** a restless, adv -ly; (ununterbrochen) ceaseless, adv -ly. **R~platz** m picnic area. **R~stätte** f motorway restaurant [and services]

Rasur f -,-en shave

Rat¹ m -[e]s [piece of] advice; **guter Rat** good advice; **zu Rat[e] ziehen** consult; **sich** (dat) **keinen Rat wissen** not know what to do

Rat² m -[e]s,-̈e (Admin) council; (Person) councillor

Rate f -,-n instalment

raten† vt guess; (empfehlen) advise ● vi (haben) guess; **jdm r~** advise s.o.

Ratenzahlung f payment by instalments

Rat|geber m -s,- adviser; (Buch) guide. **R~haus** nt town hall

ratifizier|en vt ratify. **R~ung** f -,-en ratification

Ration /ra'tsio:n/ f -,-en ration; **eiserne R~** iron rations pl. **r~al** a rational, adv -ly. **r~alisieren** vt/i (haben) rationalize. **r~ell** a efficient, adv -ly. **r~ieren** vt ration

rat|los a helpless, adv -ly; **r~los sein** not know what to do. **r~sam** pred a advisable; (klug) prudent. **R~schlag** m piece of advice; **R~schläge** advice sg

Rätsel nt -s,- riddle; (Kreuzwort-) puzzle; (Geheimnis) mystery. **r~haft** a puzzling, mysterious. **r~n** vi (haben) puzzle

Ratte f -,-n rat

rattern vi (haben) rattle ● vi (sein) rattle [along]

Raub m -[e]s robbery; (Menschen-) abduction; (Beute) loot, booty. **r~en** vt steal; abduct ⟨Menschen⟩; **jdm etw r~en** rob s.o. of sth

Räuber m -s,- robber

Raub|mord m robbery with murder. **R~tier** nt predator. **R~überfall** m robbery. **R~vogel** m bird of prey

Rauch m -[e]s smoke. **r~en** vt/i (haben) smoke. **R~en** nt -s smoking; '**R~en verboten**' 'no smoking'. **R~er** m -s,- smoker. **R~erabteil** nt smoking compartment

Räucher|lachs m smoked salmon. **r~n** vt (Culin) smoke

Rauch|fang m (Aust) chimney. **r~ig** a smoky. **R~verbot** nt smoking ban

räudig a mangy

rauf adv = herauf, hinauf

rauf|en vt pull; **sich** (dat) **die Haare r~en** (fig) tear one's hair ● vr/i (haben) **[sich] r~en** fight. **R~erei** f -,-en fight

rauh a rough, adv -ly; (unfreundlich) gruff, adv -ly; ⟨Klima, Wind⟩ harsh, raw; ⟨Landschaft⟩ rugged; (heiser) husky; ⟨Hals⟩ sore

Rauheit f - (s. rauh) roughness; gruffness; harshness; ruggedness

rauh|haarig a wire-haired. **R~reif** m hoar-frost

Raum m -[e]s, Räume room; (Gebiet) area; (Welt-) space

räumen vt clear; vacate ⟨Wohnung⟩; evacuate ⟨Gebäude, Gebiet, (Mil) Stellung⟩; (bringen) put (in/auf + acc into/on); (holen) get (aus out of); **beiseite r~** move/put to one side; **aus dem Weg r~** (fam) get rid of

Raum|fahrer m astronaut. **R~fahrt** f space travel. **R~fahrzeug** nt spacecraft. **R~flug** m space flight. **R~inhalt** m volume

räumlich a spatial. **R~keiten** fpl rooms

Raum|pflegerin f cleaner. **R~schiff** nt spaceship

Räumung f - (s. räumen) clearing; vacating; evacuation. **R~sverkauf** m clearance/closing-down sale

raunen vt/i (haben) whisper

Raupe f -,-n caterpillar

raus adv = heraus, hinaus

Rausch m -[e]s, Räusche intoxication; (fig) exhilaration; **einen R~ haben** be drunk

rauschen vi (haben) ⟨Wasser, Wind:⟩ rush; ⟨Bäume, Blätter:⟩ rustle ● vi (sein) rush [along]; **aus dem Zimmer r~** sweep out of the room. **r~d** a rushing; rustling; ⟨Applaus⟩ tumultuous

Rauschgift nt [narcotic] drug; (coll) drugs pl. **R~süchtige(r)** m/f drug addict

räuspern (sich) vr clear one's throat

rausschmeiß|en† *vt sep* (*fam*) throw out; (*entlassen*) sack. **R~er** *m* -s,- (*fam*) bouncer

Raute *f* -,-n diamond

Razzia *f* -,-ien /-ịən/ [police] raid

Reagenzglas *nt* test-tube

reagieren *vi* (*haben*) react (**auf**+*acc* to)

Reaktion /-'tsịo:n/ *f* -,-en reaction. **r~är** *a* reactionary

Reaktor *m* -s,-en /-'to:rən/ reactor

real *a* real; (*gegenständlich*) tangible; (*realistisch*) realistic, *adv* -ally. **r~i̠sieren** *vt* realize

Realis̠mus *m* - realism. **R~t** *m* -en, -en realist. **r~tisch** *a* realistic, *adv* -ally

Realität *f* -,-en reality

Realschule *f* ≈ secondary modern school

Rebe *f* -,-n vine

Rebell *m* -en,-en rebel. **r~ieren** *vi* (*haben*) rebel. **R~ion** *f* -,-en rebellion

rebellisch *a* rebellious

Rebhuhn *nt* partridge

Rebstock *m* vine

Rechen *m* -s,- rake. **r~** *vt*/*i* (*haben*) rake

Rechen|aufgabe *f* arithmetical problem; (*Sch*) sum. **R~fehler** *m* arithmetical error. **R~maschine** *f* calculator

Rechenschaft *f* - **R~ ablegen** give account (**über**+*acc* of); **jdn zur R~ ziehen** call s.o. to account

recherchieren /reʃɛr'ʃi:rən/ *vt*/*i* (*haben*) investigate; (*Journ*) research

rechnen *vi* (*haben*) do arithmetic; (*schätzen*) reckon; (*zählen*) count (**zu** among; **auf**+*acc* on); **r~ mit** reckon with; (*erwarten*) expect; **gut r~ können** be good at figures ● *vt* calculate, work out; do ⟨*Aufgabe*⟩; (*dazu-*) add (**zu** to); (*fig*) count (**zu** among). **R~** *nt* -s arithmetic

Rechner *m* -s,- calculator; (*Computer*) computer; **ein guter R~ sein** be good at figures

Rechnung *f* -,-en bill, (*Amer*) check; (*Comm*) invoice; (*Berechnung*) calculation; **R~ führen über** (+*acc*) keep account of; **etw** (*dat*) **R~ tragen** (*fig*) take sth into account. **R~sjahr** *nt* financial year. **R~sprüfer** *m* auditor

Recht *nt* -[e]s,-e law; (*Berechtigung*) right (**auf**+*acc* to); **im R~ sein** be in the right; **mit** *od* **zu R~** rightly; **von R~s wegen** by right; (*eigentlich*) by rights

recht *a* right; (*wirklich*) real; **ich habe keine r~e Lust** I don't really feel like it; **es jdm r~ machen** please s.o.; **jdm r~ sein** be all right with s.o. ● **r~ haben/behalten** be right; **r~ bekommen** be proved right; **jdm r~ geben** agree with s.o. ● *adv* correctly; (*ziemlich*) quite; (*sehr*) very; **r~ vielen Dank** many thanks

Recht|e *f* -n,-[n] right side; (*Hand*) right hand; (*Boxen*) right; **die R~e** (*Pol*) the right; **zu meiner R~en** on my right. **r~e(r,s)** *a* right; (*Pol*) right-wing; **r~e Masche** plain stitch. **R~e(r)** *m*/*f* der/die R~e the right man/woman; **du bist mir der/die R~e!** you're a fine one! **R~e(s)** *nt* **das R~e** the right thing; **etwas R~es lernen** learn something useful; **nach dem R~en sehen** see that everything is all right

Rechteck *nt* -[e]s,-e rectangle. **r~ig** *a* rectangular

rechtfertig|en *vt* justify; **sich r~en** justify oneself. **R~ung** *f* - justification

recht|haberisch *a* opinionated. **r~lich** *a* legal, *adv* -ly. **r~mäßig** *a* legitimate, *adv* -ly

rechts *adv* on the right; (*bei Stoff*) on the right side; **von/nach r~** from/to the right; **zwei r~, zwei links stricken** knit two, purl two. **R~anwalt** *m*, **R~anwältin** *f* lawyer

rechtschaffen *a* upright; (*ehrlich*) honest, *adv* -ly; **r~ müde** thoroughly tired

rechtschreib|en *vi* (*inf only*) spell correctly. **R~fehler** *m* spelling mistake. **R~ung** *f* - spelling

Rechts|händer(in) *m* -s,- (*f* -,-nen) right-hander. **r~händig** *a* & *adv* right-handed. **r~kräftig** *a* legal, *adv* -ly. **R~streit** *m* law suit. **R~verkehr** *m* driving on the right. **r~widrig** *a* illegal, *adv* -ly. **R~wissenschaft** *f* jurisprudence

recht|winklig *a* right-angled. **r~zeitig** *a* & *adv* in time

Reck *nt* -[e]s,-e horizontal bar

recken *vt* stretch; **sich r~** stretch; **den Hals r~** crane one's neck

Redakteur /redak'tø:ɐ̯/ *m* -s,-e editor; (*Radio, TV*) producer

Redaktion /-'tsịo:n/ *f* -,-en editing; (*Radio, TV*) production; (*Abteilung*)

editorial/production department. r~ell *a* editorial

Rede *f* -,-n speech; **zur R~ stellen** demand an explanation from; **davon ist keine R~** there's no question of it; **nicht der R~ wert** not worth mentioning. r~**gewandt** *a* eloquent, *adv* -ly

reden *vi* (haben) talk (**von** about; **mit** to); (eine Rede halten) speak ● *vt* talk; speak ⟨Wahrheit⟩; **kein Wort r~** not say a word. **R~sart** *f* saying; (Phrase) phrase

Redewendung *f* idiom

redigieren *vt* edit

redlich *a* honest, *adv* -ly

Red|ner *m* -s,- speaker. r~**selig** *a* talkative

reduzieren *vt* reduce

Reeder *m* -s,- shipowner. R~**ei** *f* -,-en shipping company

reell *a* real; (ehrlich) honest, *adv* -ly; ⟨Preis, Angebot⟩ fair

Refer|at *nt* -[e]s,-e report; (Abhandlung) paper; (Abteilung) section. R~**ent(in)** *m* -en,-en (*f* -,-nen) speaker; (Sachbearbeiter) expert. R~**enz** *f* -,-en reference. r~**ieren** *vi* (haben) deliver a paper; (berichten) report (**über** + *acc* on)

reflektieren *vt/i* (haben) reflect (**über** + *acc* on)

Reflex *m* -es,-e reflex; (Widerschein) reflection. R~**ion** *f* -,-en reflection. r~**iv** *a* reflexive. R~**ivpronomen** *nt* reflexive pronoun

Reform *f* -,-en reform. R~**ation** /-'tsjo:n/ *f* - (Relig) Reformation

Reform|haus *nt* health-food shop. r~**ieren** *vt* reform

Refrain /rə'frɛ̃:/ *m* -s,-s refrain

Regal *nt* -s,-e [set of] shelves *pl*

Regatta *f* -,-ten regatta

rege *a* active; (lebhaft) lively; (geistig) alert; ⟨Handel⟩ brisk ● *adv* actively

Regel *f* -,-n rule; (Monats-) period; **in der R~** as a rule. r~**mäßig** *a* regular, *adv* -ly. r~**n** *vt* regulate; direct ⟨Verkehr⟩; (erledigen) settle. r~**recht** *a* real, proper ● *adv* really. R~**ung** *f* -,-en regulation; settlement. r~**widrig** *a* irregular, *adv* -ly

regen *vt* move; **sich r~** move; (wach werden) stir

Regen *m* -s,- rain. R~**bogen** *m* rainbow. R~**bogenhaut** *f* iris

Regener|ation /-'tsjo:n/ *f* - regeneration. r~**ieren** *vt* regenerate; **sich r~ieren** regenerate

Regen|mantel *m* raincoat. R~**schirm** *m* umbrella. R~**tag** *m* rainy day. R~**tropfen** *m* raindrop. R~**wetter** *nt* wet weather. R~**wurm** *m* earthworm

Regie /re'ʒi:/ *f* - direction; **R~ führen** direct

regier|en *vt/i* (haben) govern, rule; ⟨Monarch:⟩ reign [over]; (Gram) take. r~**end** *a* ruling; reigning. R~**ung** *f* -,-en government; (Herrschaft) rule; (eines Monarchen) reign

Regime /re'ʒi:m/ *nt* -s,- /-mə/ regime

Regiment[1] *nt* -[e]s,-er regiment

Regiment[2] *nt* -[e]s,-e rule

Region *f* -,-en region. r~**al** *a* regional, *adv* -ly

Regisseur /reʒɪ'søːɐ̯/ *m* -s,-e director

Register *nt* -s,- register; (Inhaltsverzeichnis) index; (Orgel-) stop

registrier|en *vt* register; (Techn) record. R~**kasse** *f* cash register

Regler *m* -s,- regulator

reglos *a* & *adv* motionless

regn|en *vi* (haben) rain; **es r~et** it is raining. r~**erisch** *a* rainy

regul|är *a* normal, *adv* -ly; (rechtmäßig) legitimate, *adv* -ly. r~**ieren** *vt* regulate

Regung *f* -,-en movement; (Gefühls-) emotion. r~**slos** *a* & *adv* motionless

Reh *nt* -[e]s,-e roe-deer; (Culin) venison

Rehabilit|ation /-'tsjo:n/ *f* - rehabilitation. r~**ieren** *vt* rehabilitate

Rehbock *m* roebuck

Reib|e *f* -,-n grater. r~**en**† *vt* rub; (Culin) grate; **blank r~en** polish ● *vi* (haben) rub. R~**ereien** *fpl* (fam) friction *sg*. R~**ung** *f* - friction. r~**ungslos** *a* (fig) smooth, *adv* -ly

reich *a* rich (**an**+*dat* in), *adv* -ly; (r~haltig) abundant, *adv* -ly

Reich *nt* -[e]s,-e empire; (König-) kingdom; (Bereich) realm

Reich|e(r) *m/f* rich man/woman; **die R~en** the rich *pl*

reichen *vt* hand; (anbieten) offer ● *vi* (haben) be enough; (in der Länge) be long enough; **r~ bis zu** reach [up to]; (sich erstrecken) extend to; **mit dem Geld r~** have enough money; **mir reicht's!** I've had enough!

reich|haltig *a* extensive, large; ⟨Mahlzeit⟩ substantial. r~**lich** *a* ample; ⟨Vorrat⟩ abundant, plentiful;

eine r~liche Stunde a good hour ● *adv* amply; abundantly; (*fam: sehr*) very. **R~tum** *m* **-s,-tümer** wealth (**an**+*dat* of); **R~tümer** riches. **R~weite** *f* reach; (*Techn, Mil*) range

Reif *m* **-[e]s** [hoar-]frost

reif *a* ripe; (*fig*) mature; **r~ für** ready for. **R~e** *f* - ripeness; (*fig*) maturity. **r~en** *vi* (*sein*) ripen; ⟨*Wein, Käse & fig*⟩ mature

Reifen *m* **-s,-** hoop; (*Arm-*) bangle; (*Auto-*) tyre. **R~druck** *m* tyre pressure. **R~panne** *f* puncture, flat tyre

Reifeprüfung *f* ≈ A levels *pl*

reiflich *a* careful, *adv* -ly

Reihe *f* **-,-n** row; (*Anzahl & Math*) series; **der R~** nach in turn; **außer der R~** out of turn; **wer ist an der** *od* **kommt an die R~?** whose turn is it? **r~n (sich)** *vr* **sich r~n an** (+*acc*) follow. **R~nfolge** *f* order. **R~nhaus** *nt* terraced house. **r~nweise** *adv* in rows; (*fam*) in large numbers

Reiher *m* **-s,-** heron

Reim *m* **-[e]s,-e** rhyme. **r~en** *vt* rhyme; **sich r~en** rhyme

rein[1] *a* pure; (*sauber*) clean; ⟨*Unsinn, Dummheit*⟩ sheer; **ins r~e schreiben** make a fair copy of; **ins r~e bringen** (*fig*) sort out ● *adv* purely; (*fam*) absolutely

rein[2] *adv* = **herein, hinein**

Reineclaude /rɛ'nəˈkloːdə/ *f* **-,-n** greengage

Reinfall *m* (*fam*) let-down; (*Mißerfolg*) flop. **r~en**† *vi sep* (*sein*) fall in; (*fam*) be taken in (**auf**+*acc* by)

Rein|gewinn *m* net profit. **R~heit** *f* - purity

reinig|en *vt* clean; (*chemisch*) dry-clean. **R~ung** *f* **-,-en** cleaning; (*chemische*) dry-cleaning; (*Geschäft*) dry cleaner's

Reinkarnation /reˀɪnkarnaˈtsjoːn/ *f* **-,-en** reincarnation

reinlegen *vt sep* put in; (*fam*) dupe; (*betrügen*) take for a ride

reinlich *a* clean. **R~keit** *f* - cleanliness

Rein|machefrau *f* cleaner. **R~schrift** *f* fair copy. **r~seiden** *a* pure silk

Reis *m* **-es** rice

Reise *f* **-,-n** journey; (*See-*) voyage; (*Urlaubs-, Geschäfts-*) trip. **R~andenken** *nt* souvenir. **R~büro** *nt* travel agency. **R~bus** *m* coach. **R~führer** *m* tourist guide; (*Buch*)

guide. **R~gesellschaft** *f* tourist group. **R~leiter(in)** *m*(*f*) courier. **r~n** *vi* (*sein*) travel. **R~nde(r)** *m*/*f* traveller. **R~paß** *m* passport. **R~scheck** *m* traveller's cheque. **R~unternehmer, R~veranstalter** *m* **-s,-** tour operator. **R~ziel** *nt* destination

Reisig *nt* **-s** brushwood

Reißaus *m* **R~ nehmen** (*fam*) run away

Reißbrett *nt* drawing-board

reißen† *vt* tear; (*weg-*) snatch; (*töten*) kill; **Witze r~** crack jokes; **aus dem Schlaf r~** awaken rudely; **an sich** (*acc*) **r~** snatch; seize ⟨*Macht*⟩; **mit sich r~** sweep away; **sich r~ um** (*fam*) fight for; (*gern mögen*) be keen on; **hin und her gerissen sein** (*fig*) be torn ● *vi* (*haben*) **r~ an** (+*dat*) pull at. **r~d** *a* raging; ⟨*Tier*⟩ ferocious; ⟨*Schmerz*⟩ violent

Reißer *m* **-s,-** (*fam*) thriller; (*Erfolg*) big hit. **r~isch** *a* (*fam*) sensational

Reiß|nagel *m* = **R~zwecke. R~verschluß** *m* zip [fastener]. **R~wolf** *m* shredder. **R~zwecke** *f* **-,-n** drawing-pin, (*Amer*) thumbtack

reit|en† *vt*/*i* (*sein*) ride. **R~er(in)** *m* **-s,-** (*f* -,-nen) rider. **R~hose** *f* riding breeches *pl*. **R~pferd** *nt* saddle-horse. **R~schule** *f* riding-school. **R~weg** *m* bridle-path

Reiz *m* **-es,-e** stimulus; (*Anziehungskraft*) attraction, appeal; (*Charme*) charm. **r~bar** *a* irritable. **R~barkeit** *f* - irritability. **r~en** *vt* provoke; (*Med*) irritate; (*interessieren, locken*) appeal to; attract; arouse ⟨*Neugier*⟩; (*beim Kartenspiel*) bid. **r~end** *a* charming, *adv* -ly; (*entzückend*) delightful. **R~ung** *f* **-,-en** (*Med*) irritation. **r~voll** *a* attractive

rekapitulieren *vt*/*i* (*haben*) recapitulate

rekeln (sich) *vr* stretch; (*lümmeln*) sprawl

Reklamation /-'tsjoːn/ *f* **-,-en** (*Comm*) complaint

Reklam|e *f* **-,-n** advertising, publicity; (*Anzeige*) advertisement; (*TV, Radio*) commercial; **R~e machen** advertise (**für etw** sth). **r~ieren** *vt* complain about; (*fordern*) claim ● *vi* (*haben*) complain

rekonstru|ieren *vt* reconstruct. **R~ktion** /-'tsjoːn/ *f* **-,-en** reconstruction

Rekonvaleszenz f - convalescence
Rekord m -[e]s,-e record
Rekrut m -en,-en recruit. **r~ieren** vt recruit
Rek|tor m -s,-en /-'to:rən/ (Sch) head[master]; (Univ) vice-chancellor. **R~torin** f -,-nen head[mistress]; vice-chancellor
Relais /rə'lɛ:/ nt -,- /-s,-s/ (Electr) relay
relativ a relative, adv -ly. **R~pronomen** nt relative pronoun
relevan|t a relevant (für to). **R~z** f - relevance
Relief /rə'liɛf/ nt -s,-s relief
Religi|on f -,-en religion; (Sch) religious education. **r~ös** a religious
Reling f -,-s (Naut) rail
Reliquie /re'li:kvjə/ f -,-n relic
Remouladensoße /remu'la:dən-/ f ≈ tartar sauce
rempeln vt jostle; (stoßen) push
Ren nt -s,-s reindeer
Reneklode f -,-n greengage
Renn|auto nt racing car. **R~bahn** f race-track; (Pferde-) racecourse. **R~boot** nt speedboat. **r~en†** vt/i (sein) run; **um die Wette r~en** have a race. **R~en** nt -s,- race. **R~pferd** nt racehorse. **R~spor** m racing. **R~wagen** m racing car
renommiert a renowned; ⟨Hotel, Firma⟩ of repute
renovier|en vt renovate; redecorate ⟨Zimmer⟩. **R~ung** f - renovation; redecoration
rentabel a profitable, adv -bly
Rente f -,-n pension; **in R~ gehen** (fam) retire. **R~nversicherung** f pension scheme
Rentier nt reindeer
rentieren (sich) vr be profitable; (sich lohnen) be worth while
Rentner(in) m -s,- (f -,-nen) [old-age] pensioner
Reparatur f -,-en repair. **R~werkstatt** f repair workshop; (Auto) garage
reparieren vt repair, mend
repatriieren vt repatriate
Repertoire /reper'toa:ɐ̯/ nt -s,-s repertoire
Reportage /-'ta:ʒə/ f -,-n report
Reporter(in) m -s,- (f -,-nen) reporter
repräsent|ativ a representative (für of); (eindrucksvoll) imposing; (Prestige verleihend) prestigious. **r~ieren** vt represent ● vi (haben) perform official/social duties

Repress|alie /-ljə/ f -,-n reprisal. **r~iv** a repressive
Reprodu|ktion /-'tsjo:n/ f -,-en reproduction. **r~zieren** vt reproduce
Reptil nt -s,-ien /-jən/ reptile
Republik f -,-en republic. **r~anisch** a republican
requirieren vt (Mil) requisition
Requisiten pl (Theat) properties, (fam) props
Reservat nt -[e]s,-e reservation
Reserve f -,-n reserve; (Mil, Sport) reserves pl. **R~rad** nt spare wheel. **R~spieler** m reserve. **R~tank** m reserve tank
reservier|en vt reserve; **r~en lassen** book. **r~t** a reserved. **R~ung** f -,-en reservation
Reservoir /rezɛr'voa:ɐ̯/ nt -s,-s reservoir
Resid|enz f -,-en residence. **r~ieren** vi (haben) reside
Resign|ation /-'tsjo:n/ f - resignation. **r~ieren** vi (haben) (fig) give up. **r~iert** a resigned, adv -ly
resolut a resolute, adv -ly
Resolution /-'tsjo:n/ f -,-en resolution
Resonanz f -,-en resonance; (fig: Widerhall) response
Respekt /-sp-, -ʃp-/ m -[e]s respect (vor + dat for). **r~abel** a respectable. **r~ieren** vt respect
respekt|los a disrespectful, adv -ly. **r~voll** a respectful, adv -ly
Ressort /rɛ'so:ɐ̯/ nt -s,-s department
Rest m -[e]s,-e remainder, rest; **R~e** remains; (Essens-) leftovers
Restaurant /rɛsto'rã:/ nt -s,-s restaurant
Restaur|ation /rɛstaura'tsjo:n/ f - restoration. **r~ieren** vt restore
Rest|betrag m balance. **r~lich** a remaining. **r~los** a utter, adv -ly
Resultat nt -[e]s,-e result
Retorte f -,-n (Chem) retort. **R~nbaby** nt (fam) test-tube baby
rett|en vt save (vor + dat from); (aus Gefahr befreien) rescue; **sich r~en** save oneself; (flüchten) escape. **R~er** m -s,- rescuer; (fig) saviour
Rettich m -s,-e white radish
Rettung f -,-en rescue; (fig) salvation; **jds letzte R~** s.o.'s last hope. **R~sboot** nt lifeboat. **R~sdienst** m rescue service. **R~sgürtel** m lifebelt. **r~slos** adv hopelessly. **R~sring** m lifebelt. **R~swagen** m ambulance
retuschieren vt (Phot) retouch

Reu|e *f* - remorse; (*Relig*) repentance. **r~en** *vt* fill with remorse; **es reut mich nicht** I don't regret it. **r~ig** *a* penitent. **r~mütig** *a* contrite, *adv* -ly

Revanche /re'vã:ʃə/ *f* -,-n revenge; **R~e fordern** (*Sport*) ask for a return match. **r~ieren (sich)** *vr* take revenge; (*sich erkenntlich zeigen*) reciprocate (**mit** with); **sich für eine Einladung r~ieren** return an invitation

Revers /re've:ɐ̯/ *nt* -,- /-[s],-s/ lapel

revidieren *vt* revise; (*prüfen*) check

Revier *nt* -s,-e district; (*Zool & fig*) territory; (*Polizei-*) [police] station

Revision *f* -,-en revision; (*Prüfung*) check; (*Bücher-*) audit; (*Jur*) appeal

Revolte *f* -,-n revolt

Revolution /-'tsjo:n/ *f* -,-en revolution. **r~är** *a* revolutionary. **r~ieren** *vt* revolutionize

Revolver *m* -s,- revolver

Revue /rə'vy:/ *f* -,-n revue

Rezen|sent *m* -en,-en reviewer. **r~sieren** *vt* review. **R~sion** *f* -,-en review

Rezept *nt* -[e]s,-e prescription; (*Culin*) recipe

Rezeption /-'tsjo:n/ *f* -,-en reception

Rezession *f* -,-en recession

rezitieren *vt* recite

R-Gespräch *nt* reverse-charge call, (*Amer*) collect call

Rhabarber *m* -s rhubarb

Rhapsodie *f* -,-n rhapsody

Rhein *m* -s Rhine. **R~land** *nt* -s Rhineland. **R~wein** *m* hock

Rhetori|k *f* - rhetoric. **r~sch** *a* rhetorical

Rheum|a *nt* -s rheumatism. **r~atisch** *a* rheumatic. **R~atismus** *m* - rheumatism

Rhinozeros *nt* -[ses],-se rhinoceros

rhyth|misch /'ryt-/ *a* rhythmic[al], *adv* -ally. **R~mus** *m* -,-men rhythm

Ribisel *f* -,-n (*Aust*) redcurrant

richten *vt* direct (**auf** + *acc* at); address ⟨*Frage, Briefe*⟩ (**an** + *acc* to); aim, train ⟨*Waffe*⟩ (**auf** + *acc* at); (*einstellen*) set; (*vorbereiten*) prepare; (*reparieren*) mend; (*hinrichten*) execute; (*SGer: ordentlich machen*) tidy; **in die Höhe r~** raise [up]; **das Wort an jdn r~** address s.o.; **sich r~** be directed (**auf** + *acc* at; **gegen** against); ⟨*Blick:*⟩ turn (**auf** + *acc* on); **sich r~ nach** comply with ⟨*Vorschrift, jds Wünschen*⟩; fit in with

⟨*jds Plänen*⟩; (*befolgen*) go by; (*abhängen*) depend on ● *vi* (*haben*) **r~ über** (+ *acc*) judge

Richter *m* -s,- judge

Richtfest *nt* topping-out ceremony

richtig *a* right, correct; (*wirklich, echt*) real; **das R~e** the right thing ● *adv* correctly; really; **die Uhr geht r~** the clock is right. **R~keit** *f* - correctness. **r~stellen** *vt sep* (*fig*) correct

Richtlinien *fpl* guidelines

Richtung *f* -,-en direction; (*fig*) trend

riechen† *vt/i* (*haben*) smell (**nach** of; **an etw** *dat* sth)

Riegel *m* -s,- bolt; (*Seife*) bar

Riemen *m* -s,- strap; (*Ruder*) oar

Riese *m* -n,-n giant

rieseln *vi* (*sein*) trickle; ⟨*Schnee:*⟩ fall lightly

Riesen|erfolg *m* huge success. **r~groß** *a* huge, enormous

riesig *a* huge; (*gewaltig*) enormous ● *adv* (*fam*) terribly

Riff *nt* -[e]s,-e reef

rigoros *a* rigorous, *adv* -ly

Rille *f* -,-n groove

Rind *nt* -es,-er ox; (*Kuh*) cow; (*Stier*) bull; (*R~fleisch*) beef; **R~er** cattle *pl*

Rinde *f* -,-n bark; (*Käse-*) rind; (*Brot-*) crust

Rinderbraten *m* roast beef

Rind|fleisch *nt* beef. **R~vieh** *nt* cattle *pl*; (*fam: Idiot*) idiot

Ring *m* -[e]s,-e ring

ringeln (sich) *vr* curl; ⟨*Schlange:*⟩ coil itself (**um** round)

ring|en† *vi* (*haben*) wrestle; (*fig*) struggle (**um/nach** for) ● *vt* wring ⟨*Hände*⟩. **R~en** *nt* -s wrestling. **R~er** *m* -s,- wrestler. **R~kampf** *m* wrestling match; (*als Sport*) wrestling. **R~richter** *m* referee

rings *adv* **r~ im Kreis** in a circle; **r~ um jdn/etw** all around s.o./sth. **r~herum, r~um** *adv* all around

Rinn|e *f* -,-n channel; (*Dach-*) gutter. **r~en**† *vi* (*sein*) run; ⟨*Sand:*⟩ trickle. **R~stein** *m* gutter

Rippe *f* -,-n rib. **R~nfellentzündung** *f* pleurisy. **R~nstoß** *m* dig in the ribs

Risiko *nt* -s,-s & -ken risk; **ein R~ eingehen** take a risk

risk|ant *a* risky. **r~ieren** *vt* risk

Riß *m* -sses,-sse tear; (*Mauer-*) crack; (*fig*) rift

rissig *a* cracked; ⟨*Haut*⟩ chapped

Rist *m* -[e]s,-e instep

Ritt *m* -[e]s,-e ride

Ritter m -s,- knight. **r~lich** a chivalrous, adv -ly. **R~lichkeit** f - chivalry
rittlings adv astride
Ritu|al nt -s,-e ritual. **r~ell** a ritual
Ritz m -es,-e scratch. **R~e** f -,-n crack; (Fels-) cleft; (zwischen Betten, Vorhängen) gap. **r~en** vt scratch
Rival|e m -n,-n, **R~in** f -,-nen rival. **r~isieren** vi (haben) compete (mit with). **r~isierend** a rival ... **R~ität** f -,-en rivalry
Robbe f -,-n seal. **r~n** vi (sein) crawl
Robe f -,-n gown; (Talar) robe
Roboter m -s,- robot
robust a robust
röcheln vi (haben) breathe stertorously
Rochen m -s,- (Zool) ray
Rock¹ m -[e]s,ˉe skirt; (Jacke) jacket
Rock² m -[s] (Mus) rock
Rodel|bahn f toboggan run. **r~n** vi (sein/haben) toboggan. **R~schlitten** m toboggan
roden vt clear (Land); grub up (Stumpf)
Rogen m -s,- [hard] roe
Roggen m -s rye
roh a rough; (ungekocht) raw; (Holz) bare; (brutal) brutal; **r~e Gewalt** brute force ● adv roughly; brutally. **R~bau** m -[e]s,-ten shell. **R~kost** f raw [vegetarian] food. **R~ling** m -s,-e brute. **R~material** nt raw material. **R~öl** nt crude oil
Rohr nt -[e]s,-e pipe; (Geschütz-) barrel; (Bot) reed; (Zucker-, Bambus-) cane
Röhr|chen nt -s,- [drinking] straw; (Auto, fam) breathalyser (P). **R~e** f -,-n tube; (Radio-) valve; (Back-) oven
Rohstoff m raw material
Rokoko nt -s rococo
Rolladen m roller shutter
Rollbahn f taxiway; (Start-/Landebahn) runway
Rolle f -,-n roll; (Garn-) reel; (Draht-) coil; (Techn) roller; (Seil-) pulley; (Wäsche-) mangle; (Lauf-) castor; (Schrift-) scroll; (Theat) part, role; **das spielt keine R~** (fig) that doesn't matter. **r~n** vt roll; (auf-) roll up; roll out (Teig); put through the mangle (Wäsche); **sich r~n** roll; (sich ein-) curl up ● vi (sein) roll; (Flugzeug:) taxi ● vi (haben) (Donner:) rumble. **R~r** m -s,- scooter
Roll|feld nt airfield. **R~kragen** m polo-neck. **R~mops** m rollmop[s] sg
Rollo nt -s,-s [roller] blind

Roll|schuh m roller-skate; **R~schuh laufen** roller-skate. **R~splitt** m -s loose chippings pl. **R~stuhl** m wheelchair. **R~treppe** f escalator
Rom nt -s Rome
Roman m -s,-e novel. **r~isch** a Romanesque; (Sprache) Romance. **R~schriftsteller(in)** m(f) novelist
Romant|ik f - romanticism. **r~isch** a romantic, adv -ally
Romanze f -,-n romance
Röm|er(in) m -s,- (f -,-nen) Roman. **r~isch** a Roman
Rommé /'rɔmeː/ nt -s rummy
röntgen vt X-ray. **R~aufnahme** f, **R~bild** nt X-ray. **R~strahlen** mpl X-rays
rosa inv a, **R~** nt -[s],- pink
Rose f -,-n rose. **R~nkohl** m [Brussels] sprouts pl. **R~nkranz** m (Relig) rosary. **R~nmontag** m Monday before Shrove Tuesday
Rosette f -,-n rosette
rosig a rosy
Rosine f -,-n raisin
Rosmarin m -s rosemary
Roß nt Rosses, Rösser horse. **R~kastanie** f horse-chestnut
Rost¹ m -[e]s,-e grating; (Kamin-) grate; (Brat-) grill
Rost² m -[e]s rust. **r~en** vi (haben) rust
röst|en vt roast; toast (Brot). **R~er** m -s,- toaster
rostfrei a stainless
rostig a rusty
rot a (röter, rötest), **Rot** nt -s,- red; **rot werden** turn red; (erröten) go red, blush
Rotation /-'tsioːn/ f -,-en rotation
Röte f - redness; (Scham-) blush
Röteln pl German measles sg
röten vt redden; **sich r~** turn red
rothaarig a red-haired
rotieren vi (haben) rotate
Rot|kehlchen nt -s,- robin. **R~kohl** m red cabbage
rötlich a reddish
Rot|licht nt red light. **R~wein** m red wine
Rou|lade /ruˈlaːdə/ f -,-n beef olive. **R~leau** /-ˈloː/ nt -s,-s [roller] blind
Route /ˈruːtə/ f -,-n route
Routin|e /ruˈtiːnə/ f -,-n routine; (Erfahrung) experience. **r~emäßig** a routine ... ● adv routinely. **r~iert** a experienced
Rowdy /ˈraʊdi/ m -s,-s hooligan

Rübe f -,-n beet; **rote R~** beetroot; **gelbe R~** (SGer) carrot
rüber adv = **herüber, hinüber**
Rubin m -s,-e ruby
Rubrik f -,-en column; (Kategorie) category
Ruck m -[e]s,-e jerk
Rückantwort f reply
ruckartig a jerky, adv -ily
rück|bezüglich a (Gram) reflexive. **R~blende** f flashback. **R~blick** m (fig) review (**auf** + acc of). **r~blickend** adv in retrospect. **r~datieren** vt (inf & pp only) backdate
rücken vt/i (sein/haben) move; **an etw** (dat) **r~** move sth
Rücken m -s,- back; (Buch-) spine; (Berg-) ridge. **R~lehne** f back. **R~mark** nt spinal cord. **R~schwimmen** nt backstroke. **R~wind** m following wind; (Aviat) tail wind
rückerstatten vt (inf & pp only) refund
Rückfahr|karte f return ticket. **R~t** f return journey
Rück|fall m relapse. **r~fällig** a **r~fällig werden** (Jur) re-offend. **R~flug** m return flight. **R~frage** f [further] query. **r~fragen** vi (haben) (inf & pp only) check (**bei** with). **R~gabe** f return. **R~gang** m decline; (Preis-) drop, fall. **r~gängig** a **r~gängig machen** cancel; break off ⟨Verlobung⟩. **R~grat** nt -[e]s,-e spine, backbone. **R~halt** m (fig) support. **R~hand** f backhand. **R~kehr** return. **R~lagen** fpl reserves. **R~licht** nt rear-light. **r~lings** adv backwards; (von hinten) from behind. **R~reise** f return journey
Rucksack m rucksack
Rück|schau f review. **R~schlag** m (Sport) return; (fig) set-back. **R~schluß** m conclusion. **R~schritt** m (fig) retrograde step. **r~schrittlich** a retrograde. **R~seite** f back; (einer Münze) reverse
Rücksicht f -,-en consideration; **R~ nehmen auf** (+ acc) show consideration for; (berücksichtigen) take into consideration. **R~nahme** f - consideration. **r~slos** a inconsiderate, adv -ly; (schonungslos) ruthless, adv -ly. **r~svoll** a considerate, adv -ly
Rück|sitz m back seat; (Sozius) pillion. **R~spiegel** m rear-view mirror. **R~spiel** nt return match. **R~sprache** f consultation;

R~sprache nehmen mit consult. **R~stand** m (Chem) residue; (Arbeits-) backlog; **R~stände** arrears; **im R~stand sein** be behind. **r~ständig** a (fig) backward. **R~stau** m (Auto) tailback. **R~strahler** m -s,- reflector. **R~tritt** m resignation; (Fahrrad) back pedalling. **r~vergüten** vt (inf & pp only) refund. **R~wanderer** m repatriate
rückwärt|ig a back ..., rear ... **r~s** adv backwards. **R~sgang** m reverse [gear]
Rückweg m way back
ruckweise adv jerkily
rück|wirkend a retrospective, adv -ly. **R~wirkung** f retrospective force; **mit R~wirkung vom** backdated to. **R~zahlung** f repayment. **R~zug** m retreat
Rüde m -n,-n [male] dog
Rudel nt -s,- herd; (Wolfs-) pack; (Löwen-) pride
Ruder nt -s,- oar; (Steuer-) rudder; **am R~** (Naut & fig) at the helm. **R~boot** nt rowing boat. **R~er** m -s,- oarsman. **r~n** vt/i (haben/sein) row
Ruf m -[e]s,-e call; (laut) shout; (Telefon) telephone number; (Ansehen) reputation; **Künstler von Ruf** artist of repute. **r~en†** vt/i (haben) call (**nach** for); **r~en lassen** send for
Rüffel m -s,- (fam) telling-off. **r~n** vt (fam) tell off
Ruf|name m forename by which one is known. **R~nummer** f telephone number. **R~zeichen** nt dialling tone
Rüge f -,-n reprimand. **r~n** vt reprimand; (kritisieren) criticize
Ruhe f - rest; (Stille) quiet; (Frieden) peace; (innere) calm; (Gelassenheit) composure; **die R~ bewahren** keep calm; **in R~ lassen** leave in peace; **sich zur R~ setzen** retire; **R~ [da]!** quiet! **R~gehalt** nt [retirement] pension. **r~los** a restless, adv -ly. **r~n** vi (haben) rest (**auf** + dat on); ⟨Arbeit, Verkehr:⟩ have stopped; **hier ruht** ... here lies ... **R~pause** f rest, break. **R~stand** m retirement; **in den R~stand treten** retire; **im R~stand** retired. **R~störung** f disturbance of the peace. **R~tag** m day of rest; '**Montag R~tag**' 'closed on Mondays'
ruhig a quiet, adv -ly; (erholsam) restful; (friedlich) peaceful, adv -ly; (unbewegt, gelassen) calm, adv -ly; **r~ bleiben** remain calm; **sehen Sie**

sich r∼ **um** you're welcome to look round; **man kann r∼ darüber sprechen** there's no harm in talking about it

Ruhm *m* -[e]s fame; (*Ehre*) glory

rühmen *vt* praise; **sich r∼** boast (*gen* about)

ruhmreich *a* glorious

Ruhr *f* - (*Med*) dysentery

Rühr|ei *nt* scrambled eggs *pl*. **r∼en** *vt* move; (*Culin*) stir; **sich r∼en** move; **zu Tränen r∼en** move to tears; **r∼t euch!** (*Mil*) at ease! ● *vi* (*haben*) stir; **r∼en an** (+*acc*) touch; (*fig*) touch on; **r∼en von** (*fig*) come from. **r∼end** *a* touching, *adv* -ly

rühr|ig *a* active. **r∼selig** *a* sentimental. **R∼ung** *f* - emotion

Ruin *m* -s ruin. **R∼e** *f* -,-n ruin; ruins *pl* (*gen* of). **r∼ieren** *vt* ruin

rülpsen *vi* (*haben*) (*fam*) belch

Rum *m* -s rum

rum *adv* = **herum**

Rumän|ien /-jən/ *nt* -s Romania. **r∼isch** *a* Romanian

Rummel *m* -s (*fam*) hustle and bustle; (*Jahrmarkt*) funfair. **R∼platz** *m* fairground

rumoren *vi* (*haben*) make a noise; ⟨*Magen:*⟩

Rumpel|kammer *f* junk-room. **r∼n** *vi* (*haben*/*sein*) rumble

Rumpf *m* -[e]s,⸚e body, trunk; (*Schiffs-*) hull; (*Aviat*) fuselage

rümpfen *vt* **die Nase r∼** turn up one's nose (**über** + *acc* at)

rund *a* round ● *adv* approximately; **r∼ um** [a]round. **R∼blick** *m* panoramic view. **R∼brief** *m* circular [letter]

Runde *f* -,-n round; (*Kreis*) circle; (*eines Polizisten*) beat; (*beim Rennen*) lap; **eine R∼ Bier** a round of beer. **r∼n** *vt* round; **sich r∼n** become round; ⟨*Backen:*⟩ fill out

Rund|fahrt *f* tour. **R∼frage** *f* poll

Rundfunk *m* radio; **im R∼** on the radio. **R∼gerät** *nt* radio [set]

Rund|gang *m* round; (*Spaziergang*) walk (**durch** round). **r∼heraus** *adv* straight out. **r∼herum** *adv* all around. **r∼lich** *a* rounded; (*mollig*) plump. **R∼reise** *f* [circular] tour. **R∼schreiben** *nt* circular. **r∼um** *adv* all round. **R∼ung** *f* -,-en curve. **r∼weg** *adv* ⟨*ablehnen*⟩ flatly

runter *adv* = **herunter, hinunter**

Runzel *f* -,-n wrinkle. **r∼n** *vt* **die Stirn r∼n** frown

runzlig *a* wrinkled

Rüpel *m* -s,- (*fam*) lout. **r∼haft** *a* (*fam*) loutish

rupfen *vt* pull out; pluck ⟨*Geflügel*⟩; (*fam: schröpfen*) fleece

ruppig *a* rude, *adv* -ly

Rüsche *f* -,-n frill

Ruß *m* -es soot

Russe *m* -n,-n Russian

Rüssel *m* -s,- (*Zool*) trunk

rußen *vi* (*haben*) smoke. **r∼ig** *a* sooty

Russ|in *f* -,-nen Russian. **r∼isch** *a* Russian. **R∼isch** *nt* -[s] (*Lang*) Russian

Rußland *nt* -s Russia

rüsten *vi* (*haben*) prepare (**zu/für** for) ● *vr* **sich r∼** get ready; **gerüstet sein** be ready

rüstig *a* sprightly

rustikal *a* rustic

Rüstung *f* -,-en armament; (*Harnisch*) armour. **R∼skontrolle** *f* arms control

Rute *f* -,-n twig; (*Angel-, Wünschel-*) rod; (*zur Züchtigung*) birch; (*Schwanz*) tail

Rutsch *m* -[e]s,-e slide. **R∼bahn** *f* slide. **R∼e** *f* -,-n chute. **r∼en** *vt* slide; (*rücken*) move ● *vi* (*sein*) slide; (*aus-, ab-*) slip; (*Auto*) skid; (*rücken*) move [along]. **r∼ig** *a* slippery

rütteln *vt* shake ● *vi* (*haben*) **r∼ an** (+ *dat*) rattle

S

Saal *m* -[e]s, **Säle** hall; (*Theat*) auditorium; (*Kranken-*) ward

Saat *f* -,-en seed; (*Säen*) sowing; (*Gesätes*) crop. **S∼gut** *nt* seed

sabbern *vi* (*haben*) (*fam*) slobber; ⟨*Baby:*⟩ dribble; (*reden*) jabber

Säbel *m* -s,- sabre

Sabo|tage /zabo'ta:ʒə/ *f* - sabotage. **S∼teur** /-'tø:ɐ̯/ *m* -s,-e saboteur. **s∼tieren** *vt* sabotage

Sach|bearbeiter *m* expert. **S∼buch** *nt* non-fiction book. **s∼dienlich** *a* relevant

Sache *f* -,-n matter, business; (*Ding*) thing; (*fig*) cause; **zur S∼ kommen** come to the point

Sach|gebiet *nt* (*fig*) area, field. **s∼gemäß** *a* proper, *adv* -ly. **S∼kenntnis** *f* expertise. **s∼kundig** *a* expert, *adv* -ly. **s∼lich** *a* factual, *adv*

-ly; (*nüchtern*) matter-of-fact, *adv*
-ly; (*objektiv*) objective, *adv* -ly;
(*schmucklos*) functional

sächlich *a* (*Gram*) neuter

Sachse *m* -n,-n Saxon. **S~n** *nt* -s
Saxony

sächsisch *a* Saxon

sacht *a* gentle, *adv* -ly

Sach|verhalt *m* -[e]s facts *pl.* **s~ver-
ständig** *a* expert, *adv* -ly. **S~ver-
ständige(r)** *m/f* expert

Sack *m* -[e]s,¨e sack; **mit S~ und Pack**
with all one's belongings

sacken *vi* (*sein*) sink; (*zusammen-*) go
down; (*Person:*) slump

Sack|gasse *f* cul-de-sac; (*fig*) im-
passe. **S~leinen** *nt* sacking

Sadis|mus *m* - sadism. **S~t** *m*
-en, -en sadist. **s~tisch** *a* sadistic,
adv -ally

säen *vt/i* (*haben*) sow

Safe /zeːf/ *m* -s,-s safe

Saft *m* -[e]s,¨e juice; (*Bot*) sap. **s~ig** *a*
juicy; (*Wiese*) lush; (*Preis, Rech-
nung*) hefty; (*Witz*) coarse. **s~los** *a*
dry

Sage *f* -,-n legend

Säge *f* -,-n saw. **S~mehl** *nt* sawdust

sagen *vt* say; (*mitteilen*) tell; (*bedeuten*) mean; **das hat nichts zu s~** it
doesn't mean anything

sägen *vt/i* (*haben*) saw

sagenhaft *a* legendary; (*fam:
unglaublich*) fantastic, *adv* -ally

Säge|späne *mpl* wood shavings.
S~werk *nt* sawmill

Sahn|e *f* - cream. **S~ebonbon** *m* &
nt ≈ toffee. **s~ig** *a* creamy

Saison /zɛˈzõː/ *f* -,-s season

Saite *f* -,-n (*Mus, Sport*) string.
S~ninstrument *nt* stringed
instrument

Sakko *m* & *nt* -s,-s sports jacket

Sakrament *nt* -[e]s,-e sacrament

Sakrileg *nt* -s,-e sacrilege

Sakrist|an *m* -s,-e verger. **S~ei** *f* -,-en
vestry

Salat *m* -[e]s,-e salad; **ein Kopf S~** *a*
lettuce. **S~soße** *f* salad-dressing

Salbe *f* -,-n ointment

Salbei *m* -s & *f* - sage

salben *vt* anoint

Saldo *m* -s,-dos & -den balance

Salon /zaˈlõː/ *m* -s,-s salon; (*Naut*)
saloon

salopp *a* casual, *adv* -ly; (*Benehmen*)
informal, *adv* -ly; (*Ausdruck*) slangy

Salto *m* -s,-s somersault

Salut *m* -[e]s,-e salute. **s~ieren** *vi*
(*haben*) salute

Salve *f* -,-n volley; (*Geschütz-*) salvo;
(*von Gelächter*) burst

Salz *nt* -es,-e salt. **s~en†** *vt* salt.
S~faß *nt* salt-cellar. **s~ig** *a* salty.
S~kartoffeln *fpl* boiled potatoes.
S~säure *f* hydrochloric acid

Samen *m* -s,- seed; (*Anat*) semen,
sperm

sämig *a* (*Culin*) thick

Sämling *m* -s,-e seedling

Sammel|becken *nt* reservoir.
S~begriff *m* collective term. **s~n**
vt/i (*haben*) collect; (*suchen, versammeln*) gather; **sich s~n** collect; (*sich
versammeln*) gather; (*sich fassen*)
collect oneself. **S~name** *m* collective noun

Samm|ler(in) *m* -s,- (*f* -,-nen) collec-
tor. **S~lung** *f* -,-en collection; (*innere*) composure

Samstag *m* -s,-e Saturday. **s~s** *adv*
on Saturdays

samt *prep* (+*dat*) together with
● *adv* **s~ und sonders** without
exception

Samt *m* -[e]s velvet. **s~ig** *a* velvety

sämtlich *indef pron inv* all. **s~e(r,s)**
indef pron all the; **s~e Werke** complete works; **meine s~en Bücher** all
my books

Sanatorium *nt* -s,-ien sanatorium

Sand *m* -[e]s sand

Sandal|e *f* -,-n sandal. **S~ette** *f* -,-n
high-heeled sandal

Sand|bank *f* sandbank. **S~burg** *f*
sand-castle. **s~ig** *a* sandy. **S~kas-
ten** *m* sand-pit. **S~kuchen** *m* Madeira cake. **S~papier** *nt* sandpaper.
S~stein *m* sandstone

sanft *a* gentle, *adv* -ly. **s~mütig** *a*
meek

Sänger(in) *m* -s,- (*f* -,-nen) singer

sanieren *vt* clean up; redevelop
(*Gebiet*); (*modernisieren*) modernize; make profitable (*Industrie, Firma*); **sich s~** become profitable

sanitär *a* sanitary

Sanität|er *m* -s,- first-aid man;
(*Fahrer*) ambulance man; (*Mil*)
medical orderly. **S~swagen** *m*
ambulance

Sanktion /zaŋkˈtsi̯oːn/ *f* -,-en sanction. **s~ieren** *vt* sanction

Saphir *m* -s,-e sapphire

Sardelle *f* -,-n anchovy

Sardine *f* -,-n sardine

Sarg *m* -[e]s,¨e coffin

Sarkas|mus m - sarcasm. **s~tisch** a sarcastic, adv -ally

Sat|an m -s Satan; ⟨fam: Teufel⟩ devil. **s~anisch** a satanic

Satellit m -en,-en satellite. **S~enfernsehen** nt satellite television

Satin /za'tɛŋ/ m -s satin

Satir|e f -,-n satire. **s~isch** a satirical, adv -ly

satt a full; ⟨Farbe⟩ rich; **s~ sein** have had enough [to eat]; **sich s~ essen** eat as much as one wants; **s~ machen** feed; ⟨Speise:⟩ be filling; **etw s~ haben** (fam) be fed up with sth

Sattel m -s,⸚ saddle. **s~n** vt saddle. **S~schlepper** m tractor unit. **S~zug** m articulated lorry

sättigen vt satisfy; (Chem & fig) saturate ● vi (haben) be filling. **s~d** a filling

Satz m -es,⸚e sentence; (Teil-) clause; (These) proposition; (Math) theorem; (Mus) movement; (Tennis, Zusammengehöriges) set; (Boden-) sediment; (Kaffee-) grounds pl; (Steuer-, Zins-) rate; (Druck-) setting; (Schrift-) type; (Sprung) leap, bound. **S~aussage** f predicate. **S~gegenstand** m subject. **S~zeichen** nt punctuation mark

Sau f -,Säue sow; (sl: schmutziger Mensch) dirty pig

sauber a clean; (ordentlich) neat, adv -ly; (anständig) decent, adv -ly; (fam: nicht anständig) fine. **s~halten†** vt sep keep clean. **S~keit** f - cleanliness; neatness; decency

säuberlich a neat, adv -ly

saubermachen vt/i sep (haben) clean

säuber|n vt clean; (befreien) rid/(Pol) purge (von of). **S~ungsaktion** f (Pol) purge

Sauce /'zo:sə/ f -,-n sauce; (Braten-) gravy

Saudi-Arabien /-iən/ nt -s Saudi Arabia

sauer a sour; (Chem) acid; (eingelegt) pickled; (schwer) hard; **saurer Regen** acid rain; **s~ sein** (fam) be annoyed

Sauerei f -,-en = Schweinerei

Sauerkraut nt sauerkraut

säuerlich a slightly sour

Sauer|stoff m oxygen

saufen† vt/i (haben) drink; (sl) booze

Säufer m -s,- (sl) boozer

saugen† vt/i (haben) suck; (staub-) vacuum, hoover; **sich voll Wasser s~** soak up water

säugen vt suckle

Sauger m -s,- [baby's] dummy, (Amer) pacifier; (Flaschen-) teat

Säugetier nt mammal

saugfähig a absorbent

Säugling m -s,-e infant

Säule f -,-n column

Saum m -[e]s,Säume hem; (Rand) edge

säumen¹ vt hem; (fig) line

säum|en² vi (haben) delay. **s~ig** a dilatory

Sauna f -,-nas & -nen sauna

Säure f -,-n acidity; (Chem) acid

säuseln vi (haben) rustle [softly]

sausen vi (haben) rush; ⟨Ohren:⟩ buzz ● vi (sein) rush [along]

Sauwetter nt (sl) lousy weather

Saxophon nt -s,-e saxophone

SB- /ɛs'be:-/ pref (= Selbstbedienung) self-service ...

S-Bahn f city and suburban railway

sch int shush! (fort) shoo!

Schabe f -,-n cockroach

schaben vt/i (haben) scrape

schäbig a shabby, adv -ily

Schablone f -,-n stencil; (Muster) pattern; (fig) stereotype

Schach nt -s chess; **S~!** check! **in S~ halten** (fig) keep in check. **S~brett** nt chessboard

schachern vi (haben) haggle

Schachfigur f chess-man

schachmatt a **s~ setzen** checkmate; **s~!** checkmate!

Schachspiel nt game of chess

Schacht m -[e]s,⸚e shaft

Schachtel f -,-n box; (Zigaretten-) packet

Schachzug m move

schade a **s~ sein** be a pity or shame; **zu s~ für** too good for; **[wie] s~!** [what a] pity or shame!

Schädel m -s,- skull. **S~bruch** m fractured skull

schaden vi (haben) (+ dat) damage; (nachteilig sein) hurt; **das schadet nichts** that doesn't matter. **S~** m -s,⸚ damage; (Defekt) defect; (Nachteil) disadvantage; **zu S~ kommen** be hurt. **S~ersatz** m damages pl. **S~freude** f malicious glee. **s~froh** a gloating

schadhaft a defective

schädig|en vt damage, harm. **S~ung** f -,-en damage

schädlich *a* harmful

Schädling *m* -s,-e pest. **S~sbekämp-fungsmittel** *nt* pesticide

Schaf *nt* -[e]s,-e sheep; (*fam: Idiot*) idiot. **S~bock** *m* ram

Schäfchen *nt* -s,- lamb

Schäfer *m* -s,- shepherd. **S~hund** *m* sheepdog; **Deutscher S~hund** German shepherd, alsatian

Schaffell *nt* sheepskin

schaffen[1]† *vt* create; (*herstellen*) establish; make ⟨*Platz*⟩; **wie ge-schaffen für** made for

schaffen[2] *v* (*reg*) ● *vt* manage [to do]; pass ⟨*Prüfung*⟩; catch ⟨*Zug*⟩; (*bringen*) take; **jdm zu s~ machen** trouble s.o.; **sich** (*dat*) **zu s~ machen** busy oneself (**an** +*dat* with) ● *vi* (*haben*) (*SGer: arbeiten*) work. **S~** *nt* -s work

Schaffner *m* -s,- conductor; (*Zug-*) ticket-inspector

Schaffung *f* - creation

Schaft *m* -[e]s,ᵉe shaft; (*Gewehr-*) stock; (*Stiefel-*) leg. **S~stiefel** *m* high boot

Schal *m* -s,-s scarf

schal *a* insipid; (*abgestanden*) flat; (*fig*) stale

Schale *f* -,-n skin; (*abgeschält*) peel; (*Eier-, Nuß-, Muschel-*) shell; (*Schüssel*) dish

schälen *vt* peel; **sich s~** peel

schalkhaft *a* mischievous, *adv* -ly

Schall *m* -[e]s sound. **S~dämpfer** *m* silencer. **s~dicht** *a* soundproof. **s~en** *vi* (*haben*) ring out; (*nachhallen*) resound; **s~end lachen** roar with laughter. **S~mauer** *f* sound barrier. **S~platte** *f* record, disc

schalt|en *vt* switch ● *vi* (*haben*) switch/⟨*Ampel:*⟩ turn (**auf** +*acc* to); (*Auto*) change gear; (*fam: begreifen*) catch on. **S~er** *m* -s,- switch; (*Post-, Bank-*) counter; (*Fahrkarten-*) ticket window. **S~hebel** *m* switch; (*Auto*) gear-lever. **S~jahr** *nt* leap year. **S~kreis** *m* circuit. **S~ung** *f* -,-en circuit; (*Auto*) gear change

Scham *f* - shame; (*Anat*) private parts *pl*; **falsche S~** false modesty

schämen (**sich**) *vr* be ashamed; **schämt euch!** you should be ashamed of yourselves!

scham|haft *a* modest, *adv* -ly; (*schüchtern*) bashful, *adv* -ly. **s~los** *a* shameless, *adv* -ly

Schampon *nt* -s shampoo. **s~ieren** *vt* shampoo

Schande *f* - disgrace, shame; **s~ machen** (+*dat*) bring shame on

schänd|en *vt* dishonour; (*fig*) defile; (*Relig*) desecrate; (*sexuell*) violate. **s~lich** *a* disgraceful, *adv* -ly. **S~ung** *f* -,-en defilement; desecration; violation

Schanktisch *m* bar

Schanze *f* -,-n [ski-]jump

Schar *f* -,-en crowd; (*Vogel-*) flock; **in [hellen] S~en** in droves

Scharade *f* -,-n charade

scharen *vt* **um sich s~** gather round one; **sich s~ um** flock round. **s~weise** *adv* in droves

scharf *a* (**schärfer, schärfst**) sharp; (*stark*) strong; (*stark gewürzt*) hot; ⟨*Geruch*⟩ pungent; ⟨*Frost, Wind, Augen, Verstand*⟩ keen; (*streng*) harsh; ⟨*Galopp, Ritt*⟩ hard; ⟨*Munition*⟩ live; ⟨*Hund*⟩ fierce; **s~ einstellen** (*Phot*) focus; **s~ sein** (*Phot*) be in focus; **s~ sein auf** (+ *acc*) (*fam*) be keen on ● *adv* sharply; ⟨*hinsehen, nachdenken, bremsen, reiten*⟩ hard; (*streng*) harshly; **s~ schießen** fire live ammunition

Scharfblick *m* perspicacity

Schärfe *f* - (*s.* **scharf**) sharpness; strength; hotness; pungency; keenness; harshness. **s~n** *vt* sharpen

scharf|machen *vt* sep (*fam*) incite. **S~richter** *m* executioner. **S~schütze** *m* marksman. **s~sichtig** *a* perspicacious. **S~sinn** *m* astuteness. **s~sinnig** *a* astute, *adv* -ly

Scharlach *m* -s scarlet fever

Scharlatan *m* -s,-e charlatan

Scharnier *nt* -s,-e hinge

Schärpe *f* -,-n sash

scharren *vi* (*haben*) scrape; ⟨*Huhn:*⟩ scratch; ⟨*Pferd:*⟩ paw the ground ● *vt* scrape

Schart|e *f* -,-n nick. **s~ig** *a* jagged

Schaschlik *m* & *nt* -s,-s kebab

Schatten *m* -s,- shadow; (*schattige Stelle*) shade; **im S~** in the shade. **s~haft** *a* shadowy. **S~riß** *m* silhouette. **S~seite** *f* shady side; (*fig*) disadvantage

schattier|en *vt* shade. **S~ung** *f* -,-en shading; (*fig: Variante*) shade

schattig *a* shady

Schatz *m* -es,ᵉe treasure; (*Freund, Freundin*) sweetheart; (*Anrede*) darling

Schätzchen *nt* -s,- darling

schätzen *vt* estimate; (*taxieren*) value; (*achten*) esteem; (*würdigen*) appreciate; (*fam: vermuten*) reckon; **sich glücklich s~** consider oneself lucky

Schätzung *f* -,-en estimate; (*Taxierung*) valuation. **s~sweise** *adv* approximately

Schau *f* -,-en show; **zur S~ stellen** display. **S~bild** *nt* diagram

Schauder *m* -s shiver; (*vor Abscheu*) shudder. **s~haft** *a* dreadful, *adv* -ly. **s~n** *vi* (*haben*) shiver; (*vor Abscheu*) shudder; **mich s~te** I shivered/shuddered

schauen *vi* (*haben*) (*SGer, Aust*) look; **s~, daß** make sure that

Schauer *m* -s,- shower; (*Schauder*) shiver. **S~geschichte** *f* horror story. **s~lich** *a* ghastly. **s~n** *vi* (*haben*) shiver; **mich s~te** I shivered

Schaufel *f* -,-n shovel; (*Kehr-*) dustpan. **s~n** *vt* shovel; (*graben*) dig

Schaufenster *nt* shop-window. **S~bummel** *m* window-shopping. **S~puppe** *f* dummy

Schaukasten *m* display case

Schaukel *f* -,-n swing. **s~n** *vt* rock ● *vi* (*haben*) rock; (*auf einer Schaukel*) swing; (*schwanken*) sway. **S~pferd** *nt* rocking-horse. **S~stuhl** *m* rocking-chair

schaulustig *a* curious

Schaum *m* -[e]s foam; (*Seifen-*) lather; (*auf Bier*) froth; (*als Frisier-, Rasiermittel*) mousse

schäumen *vi* (*haben*) foam, froth; (*Seife:*) lather

Schaum|gummi *m* foam rubber. **s~ig** *a* frothy; **s~ig rühren** (*Culin*) cream. **S~krone** *f* white crest; (*auf Bier*) head. **S~speise** *f* mousse. **S~stoff** *m* [synthetic] foam. **S~wein** *m* sparkling wine

Schauplatz *m* scene

schaurig *a* dreadful, *adv* -ly; (*unheimlich*) eerie, *adv* eerily

Schauspiel *nt* play; (*Anblick*) spectacle. **S~er** *m* actor. **S~erin** *f* actress. **s~ern** *vi* (*haben*) act; (*sich verstellen*) play-act

Scheck *m* -s,-s cheque, (*Amer*) check. **S~buch**, **S~heft** *nt* cheque-book. **S~karte** *f* cheque card

Scheibe *f* -,-n disc; (*Schieß-*) target; (*Glas-*) pane; (*Brot-, Wurst-*) slice. **S~nwaschanlage** *f* windscreen washer. **S~nwischer** *m* -s,- windscreen-wiper

Scheich *m* -s,-e & -s sheikh

Scheide *f* -,-n sheath; (*Anat*) vagina

scheid|en† *vt* separate; (*unterscheiden*) distinguish; dissolve ⟨*Ehe*⟩; **sich s~en lassen** get divorced; **sich s~en** diverge; ⟨*Meinungen:*⟩ differ ● *vi* (*sein*) leave; (*voneinander*) part. **S~ung** *f* -,-en divorce

Schein *m* -[e]s,-e light; (*Anschein*) appearance; (*Bescheinigung*) certificate; (*Geld-*) note; **etw nur zum S~ tun** only pretend to do sth. **s~bar** *a* apparent, *adv* -ly. **s~en†** *vi* (*haben*) shine; (*den Anschein haben*) seem, appear; **mir s~t** it seems to me

scheinheilig *a* hypocritical, *adv* -ly. **S~keit** *f* hypocrisy

Scheinwerfer *m* -s,- floodlight; (*Such-*) searchlight; (*Auto*) headlight; (*Theat*) spotlight

Scheiß-, scheiß- *pref* (*vulg*) bloody. **S~e** *f* - (*vulg*) shit. **s~en†** *vi* (*haben*) (*vulg*) shit

Scheit *nt* -[e]s,-e log

Scheitel *m* -s,- parting. **s~n** *vt* part ⟨*Haar*⟩

scheitern *vi* (*sein*) fail

Schelle *f* -,-n bell. **s~n** *vi* (*haben*) ring

Schellfisch *m* haddock

Schelm *m* -s,-e rogue. **s~isch** *a* mischievous, *adv* -ly

Schelte *f* - scolding. **s~n†** *vi* (*haben*) grumble (**über** + *acc* about); **mit jdm s~n** scold s.o. ● *vt* scold; (*bezeichnen*) call

Schema *nt* -s,-mata model, pattern; (*Skizze*) diagram

Schemel *m* -s,- stool

Schenke *f* -,-n tavern

Schenkel *m* -s,- thigh; (*Geom*) side

schenken *vt* give [as a present]; **jdm Vertrauen/Glauben s~** trust/believe s.o.; **sich** (*dat*) **etw s~** give sth a miss

scheppern *vi* (*haben*) clank

Scherbe *f* -,-n [broken] piece

Schere *f* -,-n scissors *pl*; (*Techn*) shears *pl*; (*Hummer-*) claw. **s~n††** *vt* shear; crop ⟨*Haar*⟩; clip ⟨*Hund*⟩

scheren² *vt* (*reg*) (*fam*) bother; **sich nicht s~ um** not care about; **scher dich zum Teufel!** go to hell!

Scherenschnitt *m* silhouette

Scherereien *fpl* (*fam*) trouble *sg*

Scherz *m* -es,-e joke; **im/zum S~** as a joke. **s~en** *vi* (*haben*) joke. **S~frage** *f* riddle. **s~haft** *a* humorous

scheu *a* shy, *adv* -ly; ⟨*Tier*⟩ timid; **s~ werden** ⟨*Pferd:*⟩ shy; **s~ machen** startle. **S~** *f* - shyness; timidity; (*Ehrfurcht*) awe

scheuchen *vt* shoo

scheuen *vt* be afraid of; (*meiden*) shun; **keine Mühe/Kosten s~** spare no effort/expense; **sich s~** be afraid (**vor**+*dat* of); shrink (**etw zu tun** from doing sth) ● *vi* (*haben*) ⟨*Pferd:*⟩ shy

Scheuer|lappen *m* floor-cloth. **s~n** *vt* scrub; (*mit Scheuerpulver*) scour; (*reiben*) rub; **[wund] s~n** chafe ● *vi* (*haben*) rub, chafe. **S~tuch** *nt* floor-cloth

Scheuklappen *fpl* blinkers

Scheune *f* -,-n barn

Scheusal *nt* -s,-e monster

scheußlich *a* horrible, adv -bly

Schi *m* -s,-er ski; **S~ fahren** *od* **laufen** ski

Schicht *f* -,-en layer; (*Geol*) stratum; (*Gesellschafts-*) class; (*Arbeits-*) shift. **S~arbeit** *f* shift work. **s~en** *vt* stack [up]

schick *a* stylish, adv -ly; ⟨*Frau*⟩ chic; (*fam: prima*) great. **S~** *m* -[e]s style

schicken *vt/i* (*haben*) send; **s~ nach** send for; **sich s~ in** (+ *acc*) resign oneself to

schicklich *a* fitting, proper

Schicksal *nt* -s,-e fate. **s~haft** *a* fateful. **S~sschlag** *m* misfortune

Schieb|edach *nt* (*Auto*) sun-roof. **s~en†** *vt* push; (*gleitend*) slide; (*fam: handeln mit*) traffic in; **etw s~en auf** (+ *acc*) (*fig*) put sth down to; shift ⟨*Schuld, Verantwortung*⟩ on to ● *vi* (*haben*) push. **S~er** *m* -s,- slide; (*Person*) black marketeer. **S~etür** *f* sliding door. **S~ung** *f* -,-en (*fam*) illicit deal; (*Betrug*) rigging, fixing

Schieds|gericht *nt* panel of judges; (*Jur*) arbitration tribunal. **S~richter** *m* referee; (*Tennis*) umpire; (*Jur*) arbitrator

schief *a* crooked; (*unsymmetrisch*) lopsided; (*geneigt*) slanting, sloping; (*nicht senkrecht*) leaning; ⟨*Winkel*⟩ oblique; (*fig*) false; (*mißtrauisch*) suspicious ● *adv* not straight; **jdn s~ ansehen** look at s.o. askance

Schiefer *m* -s slate

schief|gehen† *vi sep* (*sei n*) (*fam*) go wrong. **s~lachen (sich)** *vr sep* double up with laughter

schielen *vi* (*haben*) squint

Schienbein *nt* shin; (*Knochen*) shinbone

Schiene *f* -,-n rail; (*Gleit-*) runner; (*Med*) splint. **s~n** *vt* (*Med*) put in a splint

schier¹ *adv* almost

schier² *a* pure; ⟨*Fleisch*⟩ lean

Schieß|bude *f* shooting-gallery. **s~en†** *vt* shoot; fire ⟨*Kugel*⟩; score ⟨*Tor*⟩ ● *vi* (*haben*) shoot, fire (**auf** + *acc* at) ● *vi* (*sein*) shoot [along]; (*strömen*) gush; **in die Höhe s~en** shoot up. **S~erei** *f* -,-en shooting. **S~scheibe** *f* target. **S~stand** *m* shooting-range

Schifahr|en *nt* skiing. **S~er(in)** *m(f)* skier

Schiff *nt* -[e]s,-e ship; (*Kirchen-*) nave; (*Seiten-*) aisle

Schiffahrt *f* shipping

schiff|bar *a* navigable. **S~bau** *m* shipbuilding. **S~bruch** *m* shipwreck. **s~brüchig** *a* shipwrecked. **S~chen** *nt* -s,- small boat; (*Tex*) shuttle. **S~er** *m* -s,- skipper

Schikan|e *f* -,-n harassment; **mit allen S~en** (*fam*) with every refinement. **s~ieren** *vt* harass; (*tyrannisieren*) bully

Schi|laufen *nt* -s skiing. **S~läufer(in)** *m(f)* skier

Schild¹ *m* -[e]s,-e shield; **etw im S~e führen** (*fam*) be up to sth

Schild² *nt* -[e]s,-er sign; (*Namens-, Nummern-*) plate; (*Mützen-*) badge; (*Etikett*) label

Schilddrüse *f* thyroid [gland]

schilder|n *vt* describe. **S~ung** *f* -,-en description⟩

Schild|kröte *f* tortoise; (*See-*) turtle. **S~patt** *nt* -[e]s tortoiseshell

Schilf *nt* -[e]s reeds *pl*

schillern *vi* (*haben*) shimmer

Schimmel *m* -s,- mould; (*Pferd*) white horse. **s~ig** *a* mouldy. **s~n** *vi* (*haben/sein*) go mouldy

Schimmer *m* -s gleam; (*Spur*) glimmer. **s~n** *vi* (*haben*) gleam

Schimpanse *m* -n,-n chimpanzee

schimpf|en *vi* (*haben*) grumble (**mit** at; **über**+*acc* about); scold (**mit jdm** s.o.) ● *vt* call. **S~name** *m* term of abuse. **S~wort** *nt* (*pl* -**wörter**) swear-word; (*Beleidigung*) insult

schind|en† *vt* work *or* drive hard; (*quälen*) ill-treat; **sich s~en** slave [away]; **Eindruck s~en** (*fam*) try to impress. **S~er** *m* -s,- slave-driver. **S~erei** *f* - slave-driving; (*Plackerei*) hard slog

Schinken *m* -s,- ham. **S~speck** *m* bacon

Schippe *f* -,-n shovel. **s~n** *vt* shovel

Schirm m -[e]s,-e umbrella; (*Sonnen-*) sunshade; (*Lampen-*) shade; (*Augen-*) visor; (*Mützen-*) peak; (*Ofen-, Bild-*) screen; (*fig: Schutz*) shield. **S~herr** m patron. **S~herrschaft** f patronage. **S~mütze** f peaked cap

schizophren a schizophrenic. **S~ie** f - schizophrenia

Schlacht f -,-en battle

schlachten vt slaughter, kill

Schlächter, Schlächter m -s,- (*NGer*) butcher

Schlacht|feld nt battlefield. **S~haus** nt, **S~hof** m abattoir. **S~platte** f plate of assorted cooked meats and sausages. **S~schiff** nt battleship

Schlacke f -,-n slag

Schlaf m -[e]s sleep; **im S~** in one's sleep. **S~anzug** m pyjamas pl, (*Amer*) pajamas pl. **S~couch** f sofa bed

Schläfe f -,-n (*Anat*) temple

schlafen† vi (*haben*) sleep; (*fam: nicht aufpassen*) be asleep; **s~ gehen** go to bed; **er schläft noch** he is still asleep. **S~szeit** f bedtime

Schläfer(in) m -s,- (f -,-nen) sleeper

schlaff a limp, adv -ly; (*Seil*) slack; (*Muskel*) flabby

Schlaf|lied nt lullaby. **s~los** a sleepless. **S~losigkeit** f - insomnia. **S~mittel** nt sleeping drug

schläfrig a sleepy, adv -ily

Schlaf|saal m dormitory. **S~sack** m sleeping-bag. **S~tablette** f sleeping-pill. **s~trunken** a [still] half asleep. **S~wagen** m sleeping-car, sleeper. **s~wandeln** vi (*haben/sein*) sleepwalk. **S~zimmer** nt bedroom

Schlag m -[e]s,¨e blow; (*Faust-*) punch; (*Herz-, Puls-, Trommel-*) beat; (*einer Uhr*) chime; (*Glocken-, Gong- & Med*) stroke; (*elektrischer*) shock; (*Portion*) helping; (*Art*) type; (*Aust*) whipped cream; **S~e bekommen** get a beating; **S~ auf S~** in rapid succession. **S~ader** f artery. **S~anfall** m stroke. **s~artig** a sudden, adv -ly. **S~baum** m barrier

schlagen† vt hit, strike; (*fällen*) fell; knock (*Loch, Nagel*) (in + acc into); (*prügeln, besiegen*) beat; (*Culin*) whisk (*Eiweiß*); whip (*Sahne*); (*legen*) throw; (*wickeln*) wrap; (*hinzufügen*) add (**zu** to); **sich s~** fight; **sich geschlagen geben** admit defeat ● vi (*haben*) beat; (*Tür:*) bang; (*Uhr:*) strike; (*melodisch*) chime; **mit den Flügeln s~** flap its wings; **um sich**

s~ lash out; **es schlug sechs** the clock struck six ● vi (*sein*) **in etw** (*acc*) **s~** (*Blitz, Kugel:*) strike sth; **s~ an** (+ *acc*) knock against; **nach jdm s~** (*fig*) take after s.o. **s~d** a (*fig*) conclusive, adv -ly

Schlager m -s,- pop song; (*Erfolg*) hit

Schläger m -s,- racket; (*Tischtennis-*) bat; (*Golf-*) club; (*Hockey-*) stick; (*fam: Raufbold*) thug. **S~ei** f -,-en fight, brawl

schlag|fertig a quick-witted. **S~instrument** nt percussion instrument. **S~loch** nt pot-hole. **S~sahne** f whipped cream; (*ungeschlagen*) whipping cream. **S~seite** f (*Naut*) list. **S~stock** m truncheon. **S~wort** nt (*pl -worte*) slogan. **S~zeile** f headline. **S~zeug** nt (*Mus*) percussion. **S~zeuger** m -s,- percussionist; (*in Band*) drummer

schlaksig a gangling

Schlamassel m & nt -s (*fam*) mess

Schlamm m -[e]s mud. **s~ig** a muddy

Schlamp|e f -,-n (*fam*) slut. **s~en** vi (*haben*) (*fam*) be sloppy (**bei** in). **S~erei** f -,-en sloppiness; (*Unordnung*) mess. **s~ig** a slovenly; (*Arbeit*) sloppy ● adv in a slovenly way; sloppily

Schlange f -,-n snake; (*Menschen-, Auto-*) queue; **S~ stehen** queue, (*Amer*) stand in line

schlängeln (sich) vr wind; (*Person:*) weave (**durch** through)

Schlangen|biß m snakebite. **S~linie** f wavy line

schlank a slim. **S~heit** f slimness. **S~heitskur** f slimming diet

schlapp a tired; (*schlaff*) limp, adv -ly. **S~e** f -,-n (*fam*) setback

schlau a clever, adv -ly; (*gerissen*) crafty, adv -ily; **ich werde nicht s~ daraus** I can't make head or tail of it

Schlauch m -[e]s,Schläuche tube; (*Wasser-*) hose[pipe]. **S~- boot** nt rubber dinghy. **s~en** vt (*fam*) exhaust

Schlaufe f -,-n loop

schlecht a bad; (*böse*) wicked; (*unzulänglich*) poor; **s~ werden** go bad; (*Wetter:*) turn bad; **s~er werden** get worse; **s~ aussehen** look bad/(*Person:*) unwell; **mir ist s~** I feel sick ● adv badly; poorly; (*kaum*) not really. **s~gehen**† vi sep (*sein*) (+ *dat*) **es geht ihm s~** he's doing badly; (*gesundheitlich*) he's not well. **s~gelaunt** attrib a bad-tempered.

s~**hin** *adv* quite simply. **S~igkeit** *f* - wickedness. s~**machen** *vt sep* (*fam*) run down

schlecken *vt/i* (*haben*) lick (**an etw** *dat* sth); (*auf-*) lap up

Schlegel *m* -s,- mallet; (*Trommel-*) stick; (*SGer: Keule*) leg; (*Hühner-*) drumstick

schleichen† *vi* (*sein*) creep; (*langsam gehen/fahren*) crawl ● *vr* **sich s~** creep. s~**d** *a* creeping; (*Krankheit*) insidious

Schleier *m* -s,- veil; (*fig*) haze. s~**haft** *a* **es ist mir s~haft** (*fam*) it's a mystery to me

Schleife *f* -,-n bow; (*Fliege*) bow-tie; (*Biegung*) loop

schleifen¹ *v* (*reg*) ● *vt* drag; (*zerstören*) raze to the ground ● *vi* (*haben*) trail, drag

schleifen²† *vt* grind; (*schärfen*) sharpen; cut (*Edelstein, Glas*); (*drillen*) drill

Schleim *m* -[e]s slime; (*Anat*) mucus; (*Med*) phlegm. s~**ig** *a* slimy

schlemm|en *vi* (*haben*) feast ● *vt* feast on. **S~er** *m* -s,- gourmet

schlendern *vi* (*sein*) stroll

schlenkern *vt/i* (*haben*) swing; s~ **mit** swing; dangle (*Beine*)

Schlepp|dampfer *m* tug. **S~e** *f* -,-n train. s~**en** *vt* drag; (*tragen*) carry; (*ziehen*) tow; (*sich hinziehen*) drag oneself; **sich s~en** drag on; **sich s~en mit** carry. s~**end** *a* slow, *adv* -ly. **S~er** *m* -s,- tug; (*Traktor*) tractor. **S~kahn** *m* barge. **S~lift** *m* T-bar lift. **S~tau** *nt* tow-rope; **ins S~tau nehmen** take in tow

Schleuder *f* -,-n catapult; (*Wäsche-*) spin-drier. s~**n** *vt* hurl; spin (*Wäsche*); extract (*Honig*) ● *vi* (*sein*) skid; **ins S~n geraten** skid. **S~preise** *mpl* knock-down prices. **S~sitz** *m* ejector seat

schleunigst *adv* hurriedly; (*sofort*) at once

Schleuse *f* -,-n lock; (*Sperre*) sluice[-gate]. s~**n** *vt* steer

Schliche *pl* tricks; **jdm auf die S~ kommen** (*fam*) get on to s.o.

schlicht *a* plain, *adv* -ly; (*einfach*) simple, *adv* -ply

schlicht|en *vt* settle ● *vi* (*haben*) arbitrate. **S~ung** *f* - settlement; (*Jur*) arbitration

Schlick *m* -[e]s silt

Schließe *f* -,-n clasp; (*Schnalle*) buckle

schließen† *vt* close; (*ab-*) lock; fasten (*Kleid, Verschluß*); (*stillegen*) close down; (*beenden, folgern*) conclude; enter into (*Vertrag*); **sich s~** close; **in die Arme s~** embrace; **etw s~ an** (+*acc*) connect sth to; **sich s~ an** (+*acc*) follow ● *vi* (*haben*) close; (*den Betrieb einstellen*) close down; (*den Schlüssel drehen*) turn the key; (*enden, folgern*) conclude; **s~ lassen auf** (+*acc*) suggest

Schließ|fach *nt* locker. s~**lich** *adv* finally, in the end; (*immerhin*) after all. **S~ung** *f* -,-en closure

Schliff *m* -[e]s cut; (*Schleifen*) cutting; (*fig*) polish; **der letzte S~** the finishing touches *pl*

schlimm *a* bad, *adv* -ly; s~**er werden** get worse; **nicht so s~!** it doesn't matter! s~**stenfalls** *adv* if the worst comes to the worst

Schlinge *f* -,-n loop; (*Henkers-*) noose; (*Med*) sling; (*Falle*) snare

Schlingel *m* -s,- (*fam*) rascal

schling|en† *vt* wind, wrap; tie (*Knoten*); **sich s~en um** coil around ● *vi* (*haben*) bolt one's food. **S~pflanze** *f* climber

Schlips *m* -es,-e tie

Schlitten *m* -s,- sledge; (*Rodel-*) toboggan; (*Pferde-*) sleigh; **S~ fahren** toboggan

schlittern *vi* (*haben/sein*) slide

Schlittschuh *m* skate; **S~ laufen** skate. **S~läufer(in)** *m*(*f*) skater

Schlitz *m* -es,-e slit; (*für Münze*) slot; (*Jacken-*) vent; (*Hosen-*) flies *pl*. s~**en** *vt* slit

Schloß *nt* -sses,"sser lock; (*Vorhänge-*) padlock; (*Verschluß*) clasp; (*Gebäude*) castle; (*Palast*) palace

Schlosser *m* -s,- locksmith; (*Auto-*) mechanic; (*Maschinen-*) fitter

Schlot *m* -[e]s,-e chimney

schlottern *vi* (*haben*) shake, tremble; (*Kleider:*) hang loose

Schlucht *f* -,-en ravine, gorge

schluchz|en *vi* (*haben*) sob. **S~er** *m* -s,- sob

Schluck *m* -[e]s,-e mouthful; (*klein*) sip

Schluckauf *m* -s hiccups *pl*

schlucken *vt/i* (*haben*) swallow. **S~** *m* -s hiccups *pl*

schlud|ern *vi* (*haben*) be sloppy (**bei** in). s~**rig** *a* sloppy, *adv* -ily; (*Arbeit*) slipshod

Schlummer *m* -s slumber. s~**n** *vi* (*haben*) slumber

Schlund m -[e]s [back of the] throat; (fig) mouth

schlüpf|en vi (sein) slip; [aus dem Ei] s~en hatch. S~er m -s,- knickers pl. s~rig a slippery; (anstößig) smutty

schlurfen vi (sein) shuffle

schlürfen vt/i (haben) slurp

Schluß m -sses,¨sse end; (S~folgerung) conclusion; **zum S~** finally; **S~ machen** stop (mit etw sth); finish (mit jdm with s.o.)

Schlüssel m -s,- key; (Schrauben-) spanner; (Geheim-) code; (Mus) clef. S~bein nt collar-bone. S~bund m & nt bunch of keys. S~loch nt keyhole. S~ring m key-ring

Schlußfolgerung f conclusion

schlüssig a conclusive, adv -ly; **sich** (dat) s~ werden make up one's mind

Schluß|licht nt rear-light. S~verkauf m [end of season] sale

Schmach f - disgrace

schmachten vi (haben) languish

schmächtig a slight

schmackhaft a tasty

schmal a narrow; (dünn) thin; (schlank) slender; (karg) meagre

schmälern vt diminish; (herabsetzen) belittle

Schmalz¹ nt -es lard; (Ohren-) wax

Schmalz² m -es (fam) schmaltz. s~ig a (fam) schmaltzy, slushy

schmarotz|en vi (haben) be parasitic (auf + acc on); ⟨Person:⟩ sponge (bei on). S~er m -s,- parasite; (Person) sponger

Schmarren m -s,- (Aust) pancake [torn into strips]; (fam: Unsinn) rubbish

schmatzen vi (haben) eat noisily

schmausen vi (haben) feast

schmecken vi (haben) taste (nach of); [gut] s~ taste good; **hat es dir geschmeckt?** did you enjoy it? ● vt taste

Schmeichelei f -,-en flattery; (Kompliment) compliment

schmeichel|haft a complimentary, flattering. **s~n** vi (haben) (+ dat) flatter

schmeißen† vt/i (haben) s~ [mit] (fam) chuck

Schmeißfliege f bluebottle

schmelz|en† vt/i (sein) melt; smelt ⟨Erze⟩. S~wasser nt melted snow

Schmerbauch m (fam) paunch

Schmerz m -es,-en pain; (Kummer) grief; S~en haben be in pain. s~en vt hurt; (fig) grieve ● vi (haben)

hurt, be painful. S~ensgeld nt compensation for pain and suffering. s~haft a painful. s~lich a (fig) painful; (traurig) sad, adv -ly. s~los a painless, adv -ly. s~stillend a pain-killing; s~stillendes Mittel analgesic, pain-killer. S~tablette f pain-killer

Schmetterball m (Tennis) smash

Schmetterling m -s,-e butterfly

schmettern vt hurl; (Tennis) smash; (singen) sing; (spielen) blare out ● vi (haben) sound; ⟨Trompeten:⟩ blare

Schmied m -[e]s,-e blacksmith

Schmiede f -,-n forge. s~eisen nt wrought iron. s~n vt forge; (fig) hatch; **Pläne s~n** make plans

schmieg|en vt press; sich s~en an (+ acc) nestle or snuggle up to; ⟨Kleid:⟩ cling to. s~sam a supple

Schmier|e f -,-n grease; (Schmutz) mess. s~en vt lubricate; (streichen) spread; (schlecht schreiben) scrawl; (sl: bestechen) bribe ● vi (schmieren) smudge; (schreiben) scrawl. S~fett nt grease. S~geld nt (fam) bribe. s~ig a greasy; (schmutzig) grubby; (anstößig) smutty; ⟨Person⟩ slimy. S~mittel nt lubricant

Schminke f -,-n make-up. s~n vt make up; sich s~n put on make-up; sich (dat) die Lippen s~n put on lipstick

schmirgel|n vt sand down. S~papier nt emery-paper

schmökern vt/i (haben) (fam) read

schmollen vi (haben) sulk; (s~d den Mund verziehen) pout

schmor|en vt/i (haben) braise; (fam: schwitzen) roast. S~topf m casserole

Schmuck m -[e]s jewellery; (Verzierung) ornament, decoration

schmücken vt decorate, adorn; **sich** s~ adorn oneself

schmuck|los a plain. S~stück nt piece of jewellery; (fig) jewel

schmuddelig a grubby

Schmuggel m -s smuggling. s~n vt smuggle. S~ware f contraband

Schmuggler m -s,- smuggler

schmunzeln vi (haben) smile

schmusen vi (haben) cuddle

Schmutz m -es dirt; in den S~ ziehen (fig) denigrate. s~en vi (haben) get dirty. S~fleck m dirty mark. s~ig a dirty

Schnabel m -s,¨ beak, bill; (eines Kruges) lip; (Tülle) spout

Schnake f -,-n mosquito; (Kohl-) daddy-long-legs

Schnalle f -,-n buckle. **s~n** vt strap; (zu-) buckle; **den Gürtel enger s~n** tighten one's belt

schnalzen vi (haben) **mit der Zunge/ den Fingern s~** click one's tongue/ snap one's fingers

schnapp|en vi (haben) **s~en nach** snap at; gasp for ⟨Luft⟩ ● vt snatch, grab; (fam: festnehmen) nab. **S~schloß** nt spring lock. **S~schuß** m snapshot

Schnaps m -es,"e schnapps

schnarchen vi (haben) snore

schnarren vi (haben) rattle; ⟨Klingel:⟩ buzz

schnattern vi (haben) cackle

schnauben vi (haben) snort ● vt **sich** (dat) **die Nase s~** blow one's nose

schnaufen vi (haben) puff, pant

Schnauze f -,-n muzzle; (eines Kruges) lip; (Tülle) spout

Schnecke f -,-n snail; (Nackt-) slug; (Spirale) scroll; (Gebäck) ≈ Chelsea bun. **S~nhaus** nt snail-shell

Schnee m -s snow; (Eier-) beaten egg-white. **S~ball** m snowball. **S~besen** m whisk. **S~brille** f snow-goggles pl. **S~fall** m snowfall. **S~flocke** f snow-flake. **S~glöckchen** nt -s,- snow-drop. **S~kette** f snow chain. **S~mann** m (pl -männer) snowman. **S~pflug** m snow-plough. **S~schläger** m whisk. **S~sturm** m snowstorm, blizzard. **S~wehe** f -,-n snow-drift

Schneid m -[e]s (SGer) courage

Schneide f -,-n [cutting] edge; (Klinge) blade

schneiden† vt cut; (in Scheiben) slice; (kreuzen) cross; (nicht beachten) cut dead; Gesichter **s~** pull faces; **sich s~** cut oneself; (über-) intersect; **sich** (dat/acc) **in den Finger s~** cut one's finger. **s~d** a cutting; (kalt) biting

Schneider m -s,- tailor. **S~in** f -,-nen dressmaker. **s~n** vt make ⟨Anzug, Kostüm⟩

Schneidezahn m incisor

schneidig a dashing, adv -ly

schneien vi (haben) snow; **es schneit** it is snowing

Schneise f -,-n path; (Feuer-) firebreak

schnell a quick; ⟨Auto, Tempo⟩ fast ● adv quickly; (in s~em Tempo) fast; (bald) soon; **mach s~!** hurry

up! **s~en** vi (sein) **in die Höhe s~en** shoot up. **S~igkeit** f - rapidity; (Tempo) speed. **S~imbiß** m snack-bar. **S~kochtopf** m pressure-cooker. **S~reinigung** f express cleaners. **s~stens** adv as quickly as possible. **S~zug** m express [train]

schnetzeln vt cut into thin strips

schneuzen (sich) vr blow one's nose

schnippen vt flick

schnippisch a pert, adv -ly

Schnipsel m & nt -s,- scrap

Schnitt m -[e]s,-e cut; (Film-) cutting; (S~muster) [paper] pattern; **im S~** (durchschnittlich) on average

Schnitte f -,-n slice [of bread]; (belegt) open sandwich

schnittig a stylish; (stromlinienförmig) streamlined

Schnitt|käse m hard cheese. **S~lauch** m chives pl. **S~muster** nt [paper] pattern. **S~punkt** m [point of] intersection. **S~wunde** f cut

Schnitzel nt -s,- scrap; (Culin) escalope. **s~n** vt shred

schnitz|en vt/i (haben) carve. **S~er** m -s,- carver; (fam: Fehler) blunder. **S~erei** f -,-en carving

schnodderig a (fam) brash

schnöde a despicable, adv -bly; (verächtlich) contemptuous, adv -ly

Schnorchel m -s,- snorkel

Schnörkel m -s,- flourish; (Kunst) scroll. **s~ig** a ornate

schnorren vt/i (haben) (fam) scrounge

schnüffeln vi (haben) sniff (**an etw** dat sth); (fam: spionieren) snoop [around]

Schnuller m -s,- [baby's] dummy, (Amer) pacifier

schnupf|en vt sniff; Tabak **s~en** take snuff. **S~en** m -s,- [head] cold. **S~tabak** m snuff

schnuppern vt/i (haben) sniff (**an etw** dat sth)

Schnur f -,"e string; (Kordel) cord; (Besatz-) braid; (Electr) flex; **eine S~** a piece of string

Schnür|chen nt -s,- **wie am S~-chen** (fam) like clockwork. **s~en** vt tie; lace [up] ⟨Schuhe⟩

schnurgerade a & adv dead straight

Schnurr|bart m moustache. **s~en** vi (haben) hum; ⟨Katze:⟩ purr

Schnür|schuh m lace-up shoe. **S~senkel** m [shoe-]lace

schnurstracks adv straight

Schock m -[e]s,-s shock. s~en vt (fam) shock; **geschockt sein** be shocked. s~ieren vt shock; s~ierend shocking

Schöffe m -n,-n lay judge

Schokolade f - chocolate

Scholle f -,-n clod [of earth]; (Eis-) [ice-]floe; (Fisch) plaice

schon adv already; (allein) just; (sogar) even; (ohnehin) anyway; s~ einmal before; (jemals) ever; s~ immer/oft/wieder always/often/again; hast du ihn s~ gesehen? have you seen him yet? s~ der Gedanke daran the mere thought of it; s~ deshalb for that reason alone; das ist s~ möglich that's quite possible; ja s~, aber well yes, but; nun geh/komm s~! go/come on then!

schön a beautiful; (Wetter) fine; (angenehm, nett) nice; (gut) good; (fam: beträchtlich) pretty; s~en Dank! thank you very much! s~ all right then ● adv beautifully; nicely; (gut) well; s~ langsam nice and slowly

schonen vt spare; (gut behandeln) look after; sich s~ take things easy. s~d a gentle, adv -tly

Schönheit f -,-en beauty. S~sfehler m blemish. S~skonkurrenz f, S~swettbewerb m beauty contest

schönmachen vt sep smarten up; sich s~ make oneself look nice

Schonung f -,-en gentle care; (nach Krankheit) rest; (Baum-) plantation. s~slos a ruthless, adv -ly

Schonzeit f close season

schöpf|en vt scoop [up]; ladle (Suppe); Mut s~en take heart; frische Luft s~en get some fresh air. S~er m -s,- creator; (Kelle) ladle. s~erisch a creative. S~kelle f, S~löffel m ladle. S~ung f -,-en creation

Schoppen m -s,- (SGer) ≈ pint

Schorf m -[e]s scab

Schornstein m chimney. S~feger m -s,- chimney-sweep

Schoß m -es,̈e lap; (Frack-) tail

Schote f -,-n pod; (Erbse) pea

Schotte m -n,-n Scot, Scotsman

Schotter m -s gravel; (für Gleise) ballast

schott|isch a Scottish, Scots. S~land nt -s Scotland

schraffieren vt hatch

schräg a diagonal, adv -ly; (geneigt) sloping; s~ halten tilt. S~e f -,-n slope. S~strich m oblique stroke

Schramme f -,-n scratch. s~n vt scrape, scratch

Schrank m -[e]s,̈e cupboard; (Kleider-) wardrobe; (Akten-, Glas-) cabinet

Schranke f -,-n barrier

Schraube f -,-n screw; (Schiffs-) propeller. s~n vt screw; (ab-) unscrew; (drehen) turn; sich in die Höhe s~n spiral upwards. S~nmutter f nut. S~nschlüssel m spanner. S~nzieher m -s,- screwdriver

Schraubstock m vice

Schrebergarten m ≈ allotment

Schreck m -[e]s,-e fright; jdm einen S~ einjagen give s.o. a fright. s~en m -s,- fright; (Entsetzen) horror. s~en vt (reg) frighten; (auf-) startle ● vi† (sein) in die Höhe s~en start up

Schreck|gespenst nt spectre. s~haft a easily frightened; (nervös) jumpy. s~lich a terrible, adv -bly. S~schuß m warning shot

Schrei m -[e]s,-e cry, shout; (gellend) scream; der letzte S~ (fam) the latest thing

Schreib|block m writing-pad. s~en† vt/i (haben) write; (auf der Maschine) type; richtig/falsch s~en spell right/wrong; sich s~en (Wort:) be spelt; (korrespondieren) correspond; sich krank s~en lassen get a doctor's certificate. S~en nt -s,- writing; (Brief) letter. S~fehler m spelling mistake. S~heft nt exercise book. S~kraft f clerical assistant; (für Maschineschreiben) typist. S~maschine f typewriter. S~papier nt writing-paper. S~schrift f script. S~tisch m desk. S~ung f -,-en spelling. S~waren fpl stationery sg. S~weise f spelling

schreien† vt/i (haben) cry; (gellend) scream; (rufen, laut sprechen) shout; zum S~ sein (fam) be a scream. s~d a (fig) glaring; (grell) garish

Schreiner m -s,- joiner

schreiten† vi (sein) walk

Schrift f -,-en writing; (Druck-) type; (Abhandlung) paper; die Heilige S~ the Scriptures pl. S~führer m secretary. s~lich a written ● adv in writing. S~sprache f written language. S~steller(in) m -s,- (f -,-nen) writer.

S∼**stück** *nt* document. S∼**zeichen** *nt* character

schrill *a* shrill, *adv* -y

Schritt *m* -[e]s,-e step; (*Entfernung*) pace; (*Gangart*) walk; (*der Hose*) crotch; **im S**∼ in step; (*langsam*) at walking pace; **S**∼ **halten mit** (*fig*) keep pace with. **S**∼**macher** *m* -s,- pace-maker. **s**∼**weise** *adv* step by step

schroff *a* precipitous, *adv* -ly; (*abweisend*) brusque, *adv* -ly; (*unvermittelt*) abrupt, *adv* -ly; ⟨*Gegensatz*⟩ stark

schröpfen *vt* (*fam*) fleece

Schrot *m & nt* -[e]s coarse meal; (*Blei-*) small shot. **s**∼**en** *vt* grind coarsely. **S**∼**flinte** *f* shotgun

Schrott *m* -[e]s scrap[-metal]; **zu S**∼ **fahren** (*fam*) write off. **S**∼**platz** *m* scrap-yard. **s**∼**reif** *a* ready for the scrap-heap

schrubb|en *vt/i* (*haben*) scrub. **S**∼**er** *m* -s,- [long-handled] scrubbing-brush

Schrull|e *f* -,-n whim; **alte S**∼**e** (*fam*) old crone. **s**∼**ig** *a* cranky

schrumpfen *vi* (*sein*) shrink; ⟨*Obst:*⟩ shrivel

schrump[e]lig *a* wrinkled

Schrunde *f* -,-n crack; (*Spalte*) crevasse

Schub *m* -[e]s,-e (*Phys*) thrust; (*S*∼*fach*) drawer; (*Menge*) batch. **S**∼**fach** *nt* drawer. **S**∼**karre** *f*, **S**∼**karren** *m* wheelbarrow. **S**∼**lade** *f* drawer

Schubs *m* -es,-e push, shove. **s**∼**en** *vt* push, shove

schüchtern *a* shy, *adv* -ly; (*zaghaft*) tentative, *adv* -ly. **S**∼**heit** *f* - shyness

Schuft *m* -[e]s,-e (*pej*) swine. **s**∼**en** *vi* (*haben*) (*fam*) slave away

Schuh *m* -[e]s,-e shoe. **S**∼**anzieher** *m* -s,- shoehorn. **S**∼**band** *nt* (*pl* -bänder) shoe-lace. **S**∼**creme** *f* shoe-polish. **S**∼**löffel** *m* shoehorn. **S**∼**macher** *m* -s,- shoemaker; (*zum Flicken*) [shoe] mender. **S**∼**werk** *nt* shoes *pl*

Schul|abgänger *m* -s,- school-leaver. **S**∼**arbeiten, S**∼**aufgaben** *fpl* homework *sg*. **S**∼**buch** *nt* school-book

Schuld *f* -,-en guilt; (*Verantwortung*) blame; (*Geld-*) debt; **S**∼**en machen** get into debt; **S**∼ **haben an** (+ *dat*) be to blame for ● **s**∼ **haben** *od* **sein** be to

blame (**an** + *dat* for); **jdm s**∼ **geben** blame s.o. **s**∼**en** *vt* owe

schuldig *a* guilty (*gen* of); (*gebührend*) due; **jdm etw s**∼ **sein** owe s.o. sth. **S**∼**keit** *f* - duty

schuld|los *a* innocent. **S**∼**ner** *m* -s,- debtor. **S**∼**spruch** *m* guilty verdict

Schule *f* -,-n school; **in der/die S**∼ at/to school. **s**∼**n** *vt* train

Schüler|(in) *m* -s,- (*f* -,-nen) pupil. **S**∼**lotse** *m* pupil acting as crossing warden

schul|frei *a* **s**∼**freier Tag** day without school; **wir haben morgen s**∼**frei** there's no school tomorrow. **S**∼**hof** *m* [school] playground. **S**∼**jahr** *nt* school year; (*Klasse*) form. **S**∼**junge** *m* schoolboy. **S**∼**kind** *nt* schoolchild. **S**∼**leiter(in)** *m(f)* head [teacher]. **S**∼**mädchen** *nt* schoolgirl. **S**∼**stunde** *f* lesson

Schulter *f* -,-n shoulder. **S**∼**blatt** *nt* shoulder-blade. **s**∼**n** *vt* shoulder. **S**∼**tuch** *nt* shawl

Schulung *f* - training

schummeln *vi* (*haben*) (*fam*) cheat

Schund *m* -[e]s trash. **S**∼**roman** *m* trashy novel

Schuppe *f* -,-n scale; **S**∼**n** *pl* dandruff *sg*. **s**∼**n** (*sich*) *vr* flake [off]

Schuppen *m* -s,- shed

Schur *f* - shearing

Schür|eisen *nt* poker. **s**∼**en** *vt* poke; (*fig*) stir up

schürf|en *vt* mine; **sich** (*dat*) **das Knie s**∼**en** graze one's knee ● *vi* (*haben*) **s**∼**en nach** prospect for. **S**∼**wunde** *f* abrasion, graze

Schürhaken *m* poker

Schurke *m* -n,-n villain

Schürze *f* -,-n apron. **s**∼**n** *vt* (*raffen*) gather [up]; tie ⟨*Knoten*⟩; purse ⟨*Lippen*⟩. **S**∼**njäger** *m* (*fam*) womanizer

Schuß *m* -sses,-sse shot; (*kleine Menge*) dash

Schüssel *f* -,-n bowl; (*TV*) dish

schusselig *a* (*fam*) scatter-brained

Schuß|fahrt *f* (*Ski*) schuss. **S**∼**waffe** *f* firearm

Schuster *m* -s,- = Schuhmacher

Schutt *m* -[e]s rubble. **S**∼**abladeplatz** *m* rubbish dump

Schüttel|frost *m* shivering fit. **s**∼**n** *vt* shake; **sich s**∼**n** shake oneself/itself; (*vor Ekel*) shudder; **jdm die Hand s**∼**n** shake s.o.'s hand

schütten *vt* pour; (*kippen*) tip; (*ver-*) spill ● *vi* (*haben*) **es schüttet** it is pouring [with rain]

Schutthaufen *m* pile of rubble

Schutz *m* -es protection; (*Zuflucht*) shelter; (*Techn*) guard; **S∼ suchen** take refuge; **unter dem S∼ der Dunkelheit** under cover of darkness. **S∼anzug** *m* protective suit. **S∼blech** *nt* mudguard. **S∼brille** goggles *pl*

Schütze *m* -n,-n marksman; (*Tor-*) scorer; (*Astr*) Sagittarius; **guter S∼** good shot

schützen *vt* protect/(*Zuflucht gewähren*) shelter (**vor** + *dat* from) ● *vi* (*haben*) give protection/shelter (**vor** + *dat* from). **s∼d** *a* protective, *adv* -ly

Schützenfest *nt* fair with shooting competition

Schutz|engel *m* guardian angel. **S∼heilige(r)** *m/f* patron saint

Schützling *m* -s,-e charge; (*Protégé*) protégé

schutz|los *a* defenceless, helpless. **S∼mann** *m* (*pl* -**männer** & -**leute**) policeman. **S∼umschlag** *m* dust-jacket

Schwaben *nt* -s Swabia

schwäbisch *a* Swabian

schwach *a* (**schwächer, schwächst**) weak, *adv* -ly; (*nicht gut; gering*) poor, *adv* -ly; (*leicht*) faint, *adv* -ly

Schwäche *f* -,-n weakness. **s∼n** *vt* weaken

Schwach|heit *f* - weakness. **S∼kopf** *m* (*fam*) idiot

schwäch|lich *a* delicate. **S∼ling** *m* - s,-e weakling

Schwachsinn *m* mental deficiency. **s∼ig** *a* mentally deficient; (*fam*) idiotic

Schwächung *f* - weakening

schwafeln (*fam*) *vi* (*haben*) waffle ● *vt* talk

Schwager *m* -s,- brother-in-law

Schwägerin *f* -,-nen sister-in-law

Schwalbe *f* -,-n swallow

Schwall *m* -[e]s torrent

Schwamm *m* -[e]s,-̈e sponge; (*SGer: Pilz*) fungus; (*eßbar*) mushroom. **s∼ig** *a* spongy; (*aufgedunsen*) bloated

Schwan *m* -[e]s,-̈e swan

schwanen *vi* (*haben*) (*fam*) **mir schwante, daß** I had a nasty feeling that

schwanger *a* pregnant

schwängern *vt* make pregnant

Schwangerschaft *f* -,-en pregnancy

Schwank *m* -[e]s,-̈e (*Theat*) farce

schwank|en *vi* (*haben*) sway; ⟨*Boot:*⟩ rock; (*sich ändern*) fluctuate; (*unentschieden sein*) be undecided ● (*sein*) stagger. **S∼ung** *f* -,-en fluctuation

Schwanz *m* -es,-̈e tail

schwänzen *vt* (*fam*) skip; **die Schule s∼** play truant

Schwarm *m* -[e]s,-̈e swarm; (*Fisch-*) shoal; (*fam: Liebe*) idol

schwärmen *vi* (*haben*) swarm; **s∼ für** (*fam*) adore; (*verliebt sein*) have a crush on; **s∼ von** (*fam*) rave about

Schwarte *f* -,-n (*Speck-*) rind; (*fam: Buch*) tome

schwarz *a* (**schwärzer, schwärzest**) black; (*fam: illegal*) illegal, *adv* -ly; **s∼er Markt** black market; **s∼ gekleidet** dressed in black; **s∼ auf weiß** in black and white; **ins S∼e treffen** score a bull's-eye. **S∼** *nt* -[e]s,- black. **S∼arbeit** *f* moonlighting. **s∼arbeiten** *vi sep* (*haben*) moonlight. **S∼brot** *nt* black bread. **S∼e(r)** *m/f* black

Schwärze *f* - blackness. **s∼n** *vt* blacken

Schwarz|fahrer *m* fare-dodger. **S∼handel** *m* black market (**mit** in). **S∼händler** *m* black marketeer. **S∼markt** *m* black market. **s∼sehen**† *vi sep* (*haben*) watch television without a licence; (*fig*) be pessimistic. **S∼wald** *m* Black Forest. **s∼weiß** *a* black and white

Schwatz *m* -es (*fam*) chat

schwatzen, (*SGer*) **schwätzen** *vi* (*haben*) chat; (*klatschen*) gossip; (*Sch*) talk [in class] ● *vt* talk

schwatzhaft *a* garrulous

Schwebe *f* - in **der S∼** (*fig*) undecided. **S∼bahn** *f* cable railway. **s∼n** *vi* (*haben*) float; (*fig*) be undecided; ⟨*Verfahren:*⟩ be pending; **in Gefahr s∼n** be in danger ● (*sein*) float

Schwed|e *m* -n,-n Swede. **S∼en** *nt* -s Sweden. **S∼in** *f* -,-nen Swede. **s∼isch** *a* Swedish

Schwefel *m* -s sulphur. **S∼säure** *f* sulphuric acid

schweigen† *vi* (*haben*) be silent; **ganz zu s∼ von** to say nothing of, let alone. **S∼** *nt* -s silence; **zum S∼ bringen** silence. **s∼d** *a* silent, *adv* -ly

schweigsam *a* silent; (*wortkarg*) taciturn

Schwein *nt* -[e]s,-e pig; (*Culin*) pork; (*sl*) (*schmutziger Mensch*) dirty pig; (*Schuft*) swine; **s∼ haben** (*fam*) be lucky. **S∼ebraten** *m* roast pork. **S∼efleisch** *nt* pork. **S∼ehund** *m* (*sl*) swine. **S∼erei** *f* -,-en (*sl*) [dirty] mess; (*Gemeinheit*) dirty trick. **S∼estall** *m* pigsty. **s∼isch** *a* lewd. **S∼sleder** *nt* pigskin

Schweiß *m* -es sweat

schweiß|en *vt* weld. **S∼er** *m* -s,- welder

Schweiz (die) - Switzerland. **S∼er** *a* & *m* -s,-, **S∼erin** *f* -,-nen Swiss. **s∼erisch** *a* Swiss

schwelen *vi* (*haben*) smoulder

schwelgen *vi* (*haben*) feast; **s∼ in** (+ *dat*) wallow in

Schwelle *f* -,-n threshold; (*Eisenbahn-*) sleeper

schwell|en† *vi* (*sein*) swell. **S∼ung** *f* -,-en swelling

Schwemme *f* -,-n watering-place; (*fig: Überangebot*) glut. **s∼n** *vt* wash; **an Land s∼n** wash up

Schwenk *m* -[e]s swing. **s∼en** *vt* swing; (*schwingen*) wave; (*spülen*) rinse; **in Butter s∼en** toss in butter ● *vi* (*sein*) turn

schwer *a* heavy; (*schwierig*) difficult; (*mühsam, streng*) hard; (*ernst*) serious; (*schlimm*) bad; **3 Pfund s∼** sein weigh 3 pounds ● *adv* heavily; with difficulty; (*mühsam, streng*) hard; (*schlimm, sehr*) badly, seriously; **s∼ hören** be hard of hearing; **s∼ arbeiten** work hard; **s∼ zu sagen** difficult *or* hard to say

Schwere *f* - heaviness; (*Gewicht*) weight; (*Schwierigkeit*) difficulty; (*Ernst*) gravity. **S∼losigkeit** *f* - weightlessness

schwer|fallen† *vi sep* (*sein*) be hard (*dat* for). **s∼fällig** *a* ponderous, *adv* -ly; (*unbeholfen*) clumsy, *adv* -ily. **S∼gewicht** *nt* heavyweight. **s∼hörig** *a* **s∼hörig sein** be hard of hearing. **S∼kraft** *f* (*Phys*) gravity. **s∼krank** *a* seriously ill. **s∼lich** *adv* hardly. **s∼machen** *vt sep* make difficult (*dat* for). **s∼mütig** *a* melancholic. **s∼nehmen†** *vt sep* take seriously. **S∼punkt** *m* centre of gravity; (*fig*) emphasis

Schwert *nt* -[e]s,-er sword. **S∼lilie** *f* iris

schwer|tun† (sich) *vr sep* have difficulty (**mit** with). **S∼verbrecher** *m* serious offender. **s∼verdaulich** *a* indigestible. **s∼verletzt** *a* seriously injured. **s∼wiegend** *a* weighty

Schwester *f* -,-n sister; (*Kranken-*) nurse. **s∼lich** *a* sisterly

Schwieger|eltern *pl* parents-in-law. **S∼mutter** *f* mother-in-law. **S∼sohn** *m* son-in-law. **S∼tochter** *f* daughter-in-law. **S∼vater** *m* father-in-law

Schwiele *f* -,-n callus

schwierig *a* difficult. **S∼keit** *f* -,-en difficulty

Schwimm|bad *nt* swimming-baths *pl*. **S∼becken** *nt* swimming-pool. **s∼en†** *vt/i* (*sein/haben*) swim; (*auf dem Wasser treiben*) float. **S∼er** *m* -s,- swimmer; (*Techn*) float. **S∼weste** *f* life-jacket

Schwindel *m* -s dizziness, vertigo; (*fam: Betrug*) fraud; (*Lüge*) lie. **S∼anfall** *m* dizzy spell. **s∼frei** *a* **s∼frei sein** have a good head for heights. **s∼n** *vi* (*haben*) (*lügen*) lie; **mir** *od* **mich s∼t** I feel dizzy

schwinden† *vi* (*sein*) dwindle; (*vergehen*) fade; (*nachlassen*) fail

Schwindl|er *m* -s,- liar; (*Betrüger*) fraud, con-man. **s∼ig** *a* dizzy; **mir ist** *od* **wird s∼ig** I feel dizzy

schwing|en† *vi* (*haben*) swing; (*Phys*) oscillate; (*vibrieren*) vibrate ● *vt* swing; wave ⟨*Fahne*⟩; (*drohend*) brandish. **S∼tür** *f* swing-door. **S∼ung** *f* -,-en oscillation; vibration

Schwips *m* -es,-e **einen S∼ haben** (*fam*) be tipsy

schwirren *vi* (*haben/sein*) buzz; (*surren*) whirr

Schwitz|e *f* -,-n (*Culin*) roux. **s∼en** *vi* (*haben*) sweat; **ich s∼e** *od* **mich s∼t** I am hot ● *vt* (*Culin*) sweat

schwören† *vt/i* (*haben*) swear (**auf** + *acc* by); **Rache s∼** swear revenge

schwul *a* (*fam: homosexuell*) gay

schwül *a* close. **S∼e** *f* - closeness

schwülstig *a* bombastic, *adv* -ally

Schwung *m* -[e]s,-e swing; (*Bogen*) sweep; (*Schnelligkeit*) momentum; (*Kraft*) vigour; (*Feuer*) verve; (*fam: Anzahl*) batch; **in S∼ kommen** gather momentum; (*fig*) get going. **s∼haft** *a* brisk, *adv* -ly. **s∼los** *a* dull. **s∼voll** *a* vigorous, *adv* -ly; ⟨*Bogen, Linie*⟩ sweeping; (*mitreißend*) spirited, lively

Schwur *m* -[e]s,-e vow; (*Eid*) oath. **S∼gericht** *nt* jury [court]

sechs *inv a*, **S∼** *f* -,-en six; (*Sch*) ≈ fail mark. **s∼eckig** *a* hexagonal. **s∼te(r,s)** *a* sixth

sech|zehn *inv* *a* sixteen.
s~zehnte(r,s) *a* sixteenth. **s~zig**
inv *a* sixty. **s~zigste(r,s)** *a* sixtieth
sedieren *vt* sedate
See[1] *m* -s,-n /'ze:ən/ lake
See[2] *f* - sea; **an die/der See** to/at the
seaside; **auf See** at sea. **S~bad** *nt*
seaside resort. **S~fahrt** *f* [sea]
voyage; (*Schiffahrt*) navigation.
S~gang *m* **schwerer S~gang** rough
sea. **S~hund** *m* seal. **s~krank** *a*
seasick
Seele *f* -,-n soul. **s~nruhig** *a* calm,
adv -ly
seelisch *a* psychological, *adv* -ly;
(*geistig*) mental, *adv* -ly
Seelsorger *m* -s,- pastor
See|luft *f* sea air. **S~macht** *f* mari-
time power. **S~mann** *m* (*pl* **-leute**)
seaman, sailor. **S~not** *f* **in S~not** in
distress. **S~räuber** *m* pirate.
S~reise *f* [sea] voyage. **S~rose** *f*
water-lily. **S~sack** *m* kitbag.
S~stern *m* starfish. **S~tang** *m*
seaweed. **s~tüchtig** *a* seaworthy.
S~weg *m* searoute; **auf dem
S~weg** by sea. **S~zunge** *f* sole
Segel *nt* -s,- sail. **S~boot** *nt* sailing-
boat. **S~fliegen** *nt* gliding.
S~flieger *m* glider pilot. **S~flug-
zeug** *nt* glider. **s~n** *vt/i* (*sein/haben*)
sail. **S~schiff** *nt* sailing-ship. **S~
sport** *m* sailing. **S~tuch** *nt* canvas
Segen *m* -s blessing. **s~sreich** *a*
beneficial; (*gesegnet*) blessed
Segler *m* -s,- yachtsman
Segment *nt* -[e]s,-e segment
segnen *vt* bless; **gesegnet mit**
blessed with
sehen† *vt* see; watch ⟨*Fernsehsen-
dung*⟩; **sich s~ lassen** show oneself
● *vi* (*haben*) see; (*blicken*) look (**auf**
+acc at); (*ragen*) show (**aus** above);
gut/schlecht s~ have good/bad eyesight; **vom S~ kennen** know by
sight; **s~ nach** keep an eye on; (*betreuen*) look after; (*suchen*) look for;
darauf s~, daß see [to it] that.
s~swert, s~swürdig *a* worth seeing. **S~swürdigkeit** *f* -,-en sight
Sehkraft *f* sight, vision
Sehne *f* -,-n tendon; (*eines Bogens*)
string
sehnen (sich) *vr* long (**nach** for)
sehnig *a* sinewy; (*zäh*) stringy
sehn|lich[st] *a* ⟨*Wunsch*⟩ dearest
● *adv* longingly. **S~sucht** *f* - longing
(**nach** for). **s~süchtig** *a* longing, *adv*
-ly; ⟨*Wunsch*⟩ dearest

sehr *adv* very; (*mit Verb*) very much
seicht *a* shallow
seid *s.* **sein**[1]; **ihr s~** you are
Seide *f* -,-n silk
Seidel *nt* -s,- beer-mug
seiden *a* silk ... **S~papier** *nt* tissue
paper. **S~raupe** *f* silkworm.
s~weich *a* silky-soft
seidig *a* silky
Seife *f* -,-n soap. **S~npulver** *nt* soap
powder. **S~nschaum** *m* lather
seifig *a* soapy
seihen *vt* strain
Seil *nt* -[e]s,-e rope; (*Draht-*) cable.
S~bahn *f* cable railway. **s~sprin-
gen†** *vi* (*sein*) (*inf* & *pp* only) skip.
S~tänzer(in) *m(f)* tightrope walker
sein[1]† *vi* (*sein*) be; **er ist Lehrer** he is a
teacher; **sei still!** be quiet! **mir ist
kalt/schlecht** I am cold/feel sick; **wie
dem auch sei** be that as it may ● *v
aux* have; **angekommen/gestorben
s~** have arrived/died; **er war/wäre
gefallen** he had/would have fallen;
es ist/war viel zu tun/nichts zu sehen
there is/was a lot to be done/nothing
to be seen
sein[2] *poss pron* his; (*Ding, Tier*) its;
(*nach man*) one's; **sein Glück versuchen** try one's luck. **s~e(r,s)** *poss
pron* his; (*nach man*) one's own; **das
S~e tun** do one's share. **s~erseits**
adv for his part. **s~erzeit** *adv* in
those days. **s~etwegen** *adv* for his
sake; (*wegen ihm*) because of him, on
his account. **s~etwillen** *adv* **um
s~etwillen** for his sake. **s~ige** *poss
pron* **der/die/das s~ige** his
seinlassen† *vt sep* leave; (*aufhören
mit*) stop
seins *poss pron* his; (*nach man*) one's
own
seit *conj* & *prep* (*+dat*) since; **s~
wann?** since when? **s~ einiger Zeit**
for some time [past]; **ich wohne s~
zehn Jahren hier** I've lived here for
ten years. **s~dem** *conj* since ● *adv*
since then
Seite *f* -,-n side; (*Buch-*) page; **S~ an
S~** side by side; **zur S~ legen/tre-
ten** put/step aside; **jds starke S~**
s.o.'s strong point; **von S~n** (*+gen*)
on the part of; **auf der einen/ande-
ren S~** (*fig*) on the one/other hand
seitens *prep* (*+gen*) on the part of
Seiten|schiff *nt* [side] aisle.
S~sprung *m* infidelity; **einen
S~sprung machen** be unfaithful.
S~stechen *nt* -s (*Med*) stitch.

S~straße f side-street. **S~streifen** m verge; (Autobahn-) hard shoulder

seither adv since then

seit|lich a side ... ● adv at/on the side; **s~lich von** to one side of ● prep (+ gen) to one side of. **s~wärts** adv on/to one side; (zur Seite) sideways

Sekret nt -[e]s,-e secretion

Sekret|är m -s,-e secretary; (Schrank) bureau. **S~ariat** nt -[e]s,-e secretary's office. **S~ärin** f -,-nen secretary

Sekt m -[e]s [German] sparkling wine

Sekte f -,-n sect

Sektion /-'tsio:n/ f -,-en section; (Sezierung) autopsy

Sektor m -s,-en /-'to:rən/ sector

Sekundant m -en,-en (Sport) second

sekundär a secondary

Sekunde f -,-n second

selber pron (fam) = selbst

selbst pron oneself; **ich/du/er/sie s~** I myself/you yourself/ he him-self/she herself; **wir/ihr/sie s~** we ourselves/you yourselves/they themselves; **ich schneide mein Haar s~** I cut my own hair; **von s~** of one's own accord; (automatisch) automatically ● adv even. **S~ach-tung** f self-esteem, self-respect

selbständig a independent, adv -ly; self-employed ⟨Handwerker⟩; **sich s~ machen** set up on one's own. **S~keit** f - independence

Selbstaufopferung f self-sacrifice

Selbstbedienung f self-service. **S~srestaurant** nt self-service res-taurant, cafeteria

Selbst|befriedigung f masturba-tion. **S~beherrschung** f self-con-trol. **S~bestimmung** f self-determi-nation. **s~bewußt** a self-confident. **S~bewußtsein** nt self-confidence. **S~bildnis** nt self-portrait. **S~erhal-tung** f self-preservation. **s~gefällig** a self-satisfied, smug, adv -ly. **s~ge-macht** a home-made. **s~gerecht** a self-righteous. **S~gespräch** nt soli-loquy; **S~gespräche führen** talk to oneself. **s~haftend** a self-adhesive. **s~herrlich** a autocratic, adv -ally. **S~hilfe** f self-help. **s~klebend** a self-adhesive. **S~kostenpreis** m cost price. **S~laut** m vowel. **s~los** a selfless, adv -ly. **S~mitleid** nt self-pity. **S~mord** m suicide. **S~mör-der(in)** m(f) suicide. **s~mörderisch**

a suicidal. **S~porträt** nt self-por-trait. **s~sicher** a self-assured. **S~si-cherheit** f self-assurance. **s~süchtig** a selfish, adv -ly. **S~tanken** nt self-service (for petrol). **s~tätig** a auto-matic, adv -ally. **S~versorgung** f self-catering

selbstverständlich a natural, adv -ly; **etw für s~ halten** take sth for granted; **das ist s~** that goes without saying; **s~!** of course! **S~keit** f - matter of course; **das ist eine S~keit** that goes without saying

Selbst|verteidigung f self-defence. **S~vertrauen** nt self-confidence. **S~verwaltung** f self-government. **s~zufrieden** a complacent, adv -ly

selig a blissfully happy; (Relig) blessed; (verstorben) late. **S~keit** f - bliss

Sellerie m -s,-s & f -,- celeriac; (Stan-gen-) celery

selten a rare ● adv rarely, seldom; (besonders) exceptionally. **S~heit** f -,-en rarity

Selterswasser nt seltzer [water]

seltsam a odd, adv -ly, strange, adv -ly. **s~erweise** adv oddly/strangely enough

Semester nt -s,- (Univ) semester

Semikolon nt -s,-s semicolon

Seminar nt -s,-e seminar; (Institut) department; (Priester-) seminary

Semmel f -,-n [bread] roll. **S~brösel** pl breadcrumbs

Senat m -[e]s,-e senate. **S~or** m -s,-en /-'to:rən/ senator

senden¹† vt send

sende|n² vt (reg) broadcast; (über Funk) transmit, send. **S~r** m -s,- [broadcasting] station; (Anlage) transmitter. **S~reihe** f series

Sendung f -,-en consignment, ship-ment; (Auftrag) mission; (Radio, TV) programme

Senf m -s mustard

sengend a scorching

senil a senile. **S~ität** f - senility

Senior m -s,-en /-'o:rən/ senior; **S~en** senior citizens. **S~enheim** nt old people's home. **S~enteller** m senior citizen's menu

Senke f -,-n dip, hollow

Senkel m -s,- [shoe-]lace

senken vt lower; bring down ⟨Fieber, Preise⟩; bow ⟨Kopf⟩; **sich s~** come down, fall; (absinken) subside; (ab-fallen) slope down

senkrecht *a* vertical, *adv* -ly. **S~e** *f* **-n,-n** perpendicular
Sensation /-'tsi̯o:n/ *f* -,-en sensation. **s~ell** *a* sensational, *adv* -ly
Sense *f* -,-n scythe
sensibel *a* sensitive, *adv* -ly. **S~ilität** *f* - sensitivity
sentimental *a* sentimental. **S~ität** *f* - sentimentality
separat *a* separate, *adv* -ly
September *m* -s,- September
Serenade *f* -,-n serenade
Serie /'ze:ri̯ə/ *f* -,-n series; (*Briefmarken*) set; (*Comm*) range. **S~nnummer** *f* serial number
seriös *a* respectable, *adv* -bly; (*zuverlässig*) reliable, *adv* -bly; (*ernstgemeint*) serious
Serpentine *f* -,-n winding road; (*Kehre*) hairpin bend
Serum *nt* -s,**Sera** serum
Service¹ /zer'vi:s/ *nt* -[s],-/-'vi:s[əs], -'vi:sə/ service, set
Service² /'zø:ɐvɪs/ *m* & *nt* -s /-vɪs[əs]/ (*Comm, Tennis*) service
servieren *vt/i* (*haben*) serve. **S~erin** *f* -,-nen waitress. **S~wagen** *m* trolley
Serviette *f* -,-n napkin, serviette
Servus *int* (*Aust*) cheerio; (*Begrüßung*) hallo
Sessel *m* -s,- armchair. **S~bahn** *f*, **S~lift** *m* chair-lift
seßhaft *a* settled; **s~ werden** settle down
Set /zɛt/ *nt* & *m* -[s],-s set; (*Deckchen*) place-mat
setzen *vt* put; (*abstellen*) set down; (*hin-*) sit down 〈*Kind*〉; move 〈*Spielstein*〉; (*pflanzen*) plant; (*schreiben, wetten*) put; **sich s~en** sit down; (*sinken*) settle ● *vi* (*sein*) leap ● *vi* (*haben*) **s~en auf** (+ *acc*) back. **S~ling** *m* -s,-e seedling
Seuche *f* -,-n epidemic
seufzen *vi* (*haben*) sigh. **S~er** *m* -s,- sigh
Sex /zɛks/ *m* -[es] sex. **s~istisch** *a* sexist
Sexualität *f* - sexuality. **s~ell** *a* sexual, *adv* -ly
sexy /'zɛksi/ *inv* *a* sexy
sezieren *vt* dissect
Shampoo /ʃam'pu:], **Shampoon** [ʃam'po:n] *nt* -s shampoo
siamesisch *a* Siamese
sich *refl pron* oneself; (*mit er/sie/es*) himself/herself/itself; (*mit sie pl*) themselves; (*mit Sie*) yourself; (*pl*)

yourselves; (*einander*) each other; **s~ kennen** know oneself/(*einander*) each other; **s~ waschen** have a wash; **s~** (*dat*) **die Zähne putzen/die Haare kämmen** clean one's teeth/comb one's hair; **s~** (*dat*) **das Bein brechen** break a leg; **s~ wundern/schämen** be surprised/ashamed; **s~ gut lesen/verkaufen** read/sell well; **von s~ aus** of one's own accord
Sichel *f* -,-n sickle
sicher *a* safe; (*gesichert*) secure; (*gewiß*) certain; (*zuverlässig*) reliable; sure 〈*Urteil, Geschmack*〉; steady 〈*Hand*〉; (*selbstbewußt*) self-confident; **sich** (*dat*) **etw** (*gen*) **s~ sein** be sure of sth; **bist du s~?** are you sure? ● *adv* safely; securely; certainly; reliably; self-confidently; (*wahrscheinlich*) most probably; **er kommt s~** he is sure to come; **s~!** certainly! **s~gehen†** *vi sep* (*sein*) be sure
Sicherheit *f* - safety; (*Pol, Psych, Comm*) security; (*Gewißheit*) certainty; (*Zuverlässigkeit*) reliability; (*des Urteils, Geschmacks*) surety; (*Selbstbewußtsein*) self-confidence. **S~sgurt** *m* safety-belt; (*Auto*) seatbelt. **s~shalber** *adv* to be on the safe side. **S~snadel** *f* safety-pin
sicherlich *adv* certainly; (*wahrscheinlich*) most probably
sichern *vt* secure; (*garantieren*) safeguard; (*schützen*) protect; put the safety-catch on 〈*Pistole*〉; **sich** (*dat*) **etw s~n** secure sth. **s~stellen** *vt sep* safeguard; (*beschlagnahmen*) seize. **S~ung** *f* -,-en safeguard, protection; (*Gewehr-*) safety-catch; (*Electr*) fuse
Sicht *f* - view; (**S~weite**) visibility; **in S~ kommen** come into view; **auf lange S~** in the long term. **s~bar** *a* visible, *adv* -bly. **s~en** *vt* sight; (*durchsehen*) sift through. **s~lich** *a* obvious, *adv* -ly. **S~vermerk** *m* visa. **S~weite** *f* visibility; **in/außer S~weite** within/out of sight
sickern *vi* (*sein*) seep
sie *pron* (*nom*) (*sg*) she; (*Ding, Tier*) it; (*pl*) they; (*acc*) (*sg*) her; (*Ding, Tier*) it; (*pl*) them
Sie *pron* you; **gehen/warten Sie!** go/wait!
Sieb *nt* -[e]s,-e sieve; (*Tee-*) strainer. **s~en¹** *vt* sieve, sift
sieben² *inv* *a*, **S~** *f* -,-en seven. **S~sachen** *fpl* (*fam*) belongings. **s~te(r,s)** *a* seventh

sieb|te(r,s) *a* seventh. **s~zehn** *inv a* seventeen. **s~zehnte(r,s)** *a* seventeenth. **s~zig** *inv a* seventy. **s~zigste(r,s)** *a* seventieth

siede|n† *vt/i* (*haben*) boil. **S~punkt** *m* boiling point

Siedl|er *m* -s,- settler. **S~ung** *f* -,-en [housing] estate; (*Niederlassung*) settlement

Sieg *m* -[e]s,-e victory

Siegel *nt* -s,- seal. **S~ring** *m* signet-ring

sieg|en *vi* (*haben*) win. **S~er(in)** *m* -s,- (*f* -,-nen) winner. **s~reich** *a* victorious

siezen *vt* jdn s~ call s.o. 'Sie'

Signal *nt* -s,-e signal. **s~isieren** *vt* signal

signieren *vt* sign

Silbe *f* -,-n syllable. **S~ntrennung** *f* word-division

Silber *nt* -s silver. **S~hochzeit** *f* silver wedding. **s~n** *a* silver. **S~papier** *nt* silver paper

Silhouette /zi'luɛta/ *f* -,-n silhouette

Silizium *nt* -s silicon

Silo *m* & *nt* -s,-s silo

Silvester *m* -s New Year's Eve

simpel *a* simple, *adv* -ply; (*einfältig*) simple-minded

Simplex *nt* -,-e simplex

Sims *m* & *nt* -es,-e ledge; (*Kamin-*) mantelpiece

Simul|ant *m* -en,-en malingerer. **s~ieren** *vt* feign; (*Techn*) simulate • *vi* (*haben*) pretend; (*sich krank stellen*) malinger

simultan *a* simultaneous, *adv* -ly

sind *s.* **sein¹**; **wir/sie s~** we/they are

Sinfonie *f* -,-n symphony

singen† *vt/i* (*haben*) sing

Singular *m* -s,-e singular

Singvogel *m* songbird

sinken† *vi* (*sein*) sink; (*nieder-*) drop; (*niedriger werden*) go down, fall; **den Mut s~ lassen** lose courage

Sinn *m* -[e]s,-e sense; (*Denken*) mind; (*Zweck*) point; **im S~ haben** have in mind; **in gewissem S~e** in a sense; **es hat keinen S~** it is pointless; **nicht bei S~en sein** be out of one's mind. **S~bild** *nt* symbol. **s~en†** *vi* (*haben*) think; **auf Rache s~en** plot one's revenge

sinnlich *a* sensory; (*sexuell*) sensual; (*Genüsse*) sensuous. **S~keit** *f* - sensuality; sensuousness

sinn|los *a* senseless, *adv* -ly; (*zwecklos*) pointless, *adv* -ly. **s~voll** *a* meaningful; (*vernünftig*) sensible, *adv* -bly

Sintflut *f* flood

Siphon /'zi:fõ/ *m* -s,-s siphon

Sipp|e *f* -,-n clan. **S~schaft** *f* - clan; (*Pack*) crowd

Sirene *f* -,-n siren

Sirup *m* -s,-e syrup; (*schwarzer*) treacle

Sitte *f* -,-n custom; **S~n** manners. **s~nlos** *a* immoral

sittlich *a* moral, *adv* -ly. **S~keit** *f* - morality. **S~keitsverbrecher** *m* sex offender

sittsam *a* well-behaved; (*züchtig*) demure, *adv* -ly

Situ|ation /-'tsjo:n/ *f* -,-en situation. **s~iert** *a* gut/schlecht s~iert well/ badly off

Sitz *m* -es,-e seat; (*Paßform*) fit

sitzen† *vi* (*haben*) sit; (*sich befinden*) be; (*passen*) fit; (*fam: treffen*) hit home; **s~ bleiben** remain seated; **[im Gefängnis] s~** (*fam*) be in jail. **s~bleiben†** *vi sep* (*sein*) (*fam*) (*Sch*) stay *or* be kept down; (*nicht heiraten*) be left on the shelf; **s~bleiben auf** (+ *dat*) be left with. **s~d** *a* seated; (*Tätigkeit*) sedentary. **s~lassen†** *vt sep* (*fam*) (*nicht heiraten*) jilt; (*im Stich lassen*) leave in the lurch; (*Sch*) keep down

Sitz|gelegenheit *f* seat. **S~platz** *m* seat. **S~ung** *f* -,-en session

Sizilien /-jən/ *nt* -s Sicily

Skala *f* -,-len scale; (*Reihe*) range

Skalpell *nt* -s,-e scalpel

skalpieren *vt* scalp

Skandal *m* -s,-e scandal. **s~ös** *a* scandalous

skandieren *vt* scan (*Verse*); chant (*Parolen*)

Skandinav|ien /-jən/ *nt* -s Scandinavia. **s~isch** *a* Scandinavian

Skat *m* -s skat

Skelett *nt* -[e]s,-e skeleton

Skep|sis *f* - scepticism. **s~tisch** *a* sceptical, *adv* -ly; (*mißtrauisch*) doubtful, *adv* -ly

Ski /ʃi:/ *m* -s,-er ski; **Ski fahren** *od* **laufen** ski. **S~fahrer(in), S~läufer(in)** *m*(*f*) skier. **S~sport** *m* skiing

Skizz|e *f* -,-n sketch. **s~enhaft** *a* sketchy, *adv* -ily. **s~ieren** *vt* sketch

Sklav|e *m* -n,-n slave. **S~erei** *f* - slavery. **S~in** *f* -,-nen slave. **s~isch** *a* slavish, *adv* -ly

Skorpion *m* -s,-e scorpion; (*Astr*) Scorpio

Skrupel *m* -s,- scruple. **s~los** *a* unscrupulous

Skulptur *f* -,-en sculpture

skurril *a* absurd, *adv* -ly

Slalom *m* -s,-s slalom

Slang /slɛŋ/ *m* -s slang

Slaw|e *m* -n,-n, **S~in** *f* -,-nen Slav. **s~isch** *a* Slav; (*Lang*) Slavonic

Slip *m* -s,-s briefs *pl*

Smaragd *m* -[e]s,-e emerald

Smoking *m* -s,-s dinner jacket, (*Amer*) tuxedo

Snob *m* -s,-s snob. **S~ismus** *m* - snobbery. **s~istisch** *a* snobbish

so *adv* so; (*so sehr*) so much; (*auf diese Weise*) like this/that; (*solch*) such; (*fam: sowieso*) anyway; (*fam: umsonst*) free; (*fam: ungefähr*) about; **nicht so schnell** not so fast; **so gut/bald wie** as good/soon as; **so ein Mann** a man like that; **so ein Zufall!** what a coincidence! **so nicht** not like that; **mir ist so, als ob** I feel as if; **so oder so** in any case; **eine Stunde oder so** an hour or so; **so um zehn Mark** (*fam*) about ten marks; **[es ist] gut so** that's fine; **so, das ist geschafft** there, that's done; **so?** really? **so kommt doch!** come on then! ● *conj* (*also*) so; (*dann*) then; so **daß** so that; **so gern ich auch käme** as much as I would like to come

sobald *conj* as soon as

Söckchen *nt* -s,- [ankle] sock

Socke *f* -,-n sock

Sockel *m* -s,- plinth, pedestal

Socken *m* -s,- sock

Soda *nt* -s soda. **S~wasser** *nt* soda water

Sodbrennen *nt* -s heartburn

soeben *adv* just [now]

Sofa *nt* -s,-s settee, sofa

sofern *adv* provided [that]

sofort *adv* at once, immediately; (*auf der Stelle*) instantly. **s~ig** *a* immediate

Software /'zɔftvɛːɐ̯/ *f* - software

sogar *adv* even

sogenannt *a* so-called

sogleich *adv* at once

Sohle *f* -,-n sole; (*Tal-*) bottom

Sohn *m* -[e]s,ᵉe son

Sojabohne *f* soya bean

solange *conj* as long as

solch *inv pron* such; **s~ ein(e)** such a; **s~ einer/eine/eins** one/ (*Person*) someone like that. **s~e(r,s)** *pron* such; **ein s~er Mann/eine s~e Frau** a man/woman

like that; **ich habe s~e Angst** I am so afraid ● (*substantivisch*) **ein s~er/eine s~e/ein s~es** one/ (*Person*) someone like that; **s~e** (*pl*) those; (*Leute*) people like that

Sold *m* -[e]s (*Mil*) pay

Soldat *m* -en,-en soldier

Söldner *m* -s,- mercenary

solidarisch *a* **s~e Handlung** act of solidarity; **sich s~ erklären** declare one's solidarity

Solidarität *f* - solidarity

solide *a* solid, *adv* -ly; (*haltbar*) sturdy, *adv* -ily; (*sicher*) sound, *adv* -ly; (*anständig*) respectable, *adv* -bly

Solist(in) *m* -en,-en (*f* -,-nen) soloist

Soll *nt* -s (*Comm*) debit; (*Produktions-*) quota

sollen† *v aux* **er soll warten** he is to wait; (*möge*) let him wait; **was soll ich machen?** what shall I do? **du sollst nicht lügen** you shouldn't tell lies; **du sollst nicht töten** (*liter*) thou shalt not kill; **ihr sollt jetzt still sein!** will you be quiet now! **du solltest dich schämen** you ought to *or* should be ashamed of yourself; **es hat nicht sein s~** it was not to be; **ich hätte es nicht tun s~** I ought not to *or* should not have done it; **er soll sehr nett/ reich sein** he is supposed to be very nice/rich; **sollte es regnen, so . . .** if it should rain then . . . ; **das soll man nicht [tun]** you're not supposed to [do that]; **soll ich [mal versuchen]?** shall I [try]? **soll er doch!** let him! **was soll's!** so what!

Solo *nt* -s,-los & -li solo. **s~** *adv* solo

somit *adv* therefore, so

Sommer *m* -s,- summer. **S~ferien** *pl* summer holidays. **s~lich** *a* summery; (*Sommer-*) summer . . . ● *adv* **s~lich warm** as warm as summer. **S~schlußverkauf** *m* summer sale. **S~sprossen** *fpl* freckles. **s~sprossig** *a* freckled

Sonate *f* -,-n sonata

Sonde *f* -,-n probe

Sonder|angebot *nt* special offer. **s~bar** *a* odd, *adv* -ly. **S~fahrt** *f* special excursion. **S~fall** *m* special case. **s~gleichen** *adv* **eine Gemeinheit/Grausamkeit s~gleichen** un-paralleled meanness/cruelty. **s~lich** *a* particular, *adv* -ly; (*sonderbar*) odd, *adv* -ly. **S~ling** *m* -s,-e crank. **S~marke** *f* special stamp

sondern / **Spalte**

sondern *conj* but; **nicht nur ... s~ auch** not only ... but also

Sonder|preis *m* special price. **S~schule** *f* special school. **S~zug** *m* special train

sondieren *vt* sound out

Sonett *nt* -[e]s,-e sonnet

Sonnabend *m* -s,-e Saturday. **s~s** *adv* on Saturdays

Sonne *f* -,-n sun. **s~n (sich)** *vr* sun oneself; (*fig*) bask (**in** + *dat* in)

Sonnen|aufgang *m* sunrise. **s~baden** *vi* (*haben*) sunbathe. **S~bank** *f* sun-bed. **S~blume** *f* sunflower. **S~brand** *m* sunburn. **S~brille** *f* sun-glasses *pl*. **S~energie** *f* solar energy. **S~finsternis** *f* solar eclipse. **S~milch** *f* sun-tan lotion. **S~öl** *nt* sun-tan oil. **S~schein** *m* sunshine. **S~schirm** *m* sunshade. **S~stich** *m* sunstroke. **S~uhr** *f* sundial. **S~untergang** *m* sunset. **S~wende** *f* solstice

sonnig *a* sunny

Sonntag *m* -s,-e Sunday. **s~s** *adv* on Sundays

sonst *adv* (*gewöhnlich*) usually; (*im übrigen*) apart from that; (*andernfalls*) otherwise, or [else]; **wer/was/wie/wo s~?** who/what/how/where else? **s~ niemand/nichts** no one/nothing else; **s~ noch jemand/etwas?** anyone/anything else? **s~ noch Fragen?** any more questions? **s~ig** *a* other. **s~jemand** *pron* (*fam*) someone/(*fragend, verneint*) anyone else. **s~wer** *pron* = **s~jemand**. **s~wie** *adv* (*fam*) some/any other way. **s~wo** *adv* (*fam*) somewhere/anywhere else

sooft *conj* whenever

Sopran *m* -s,-e soprano

Sorge *f* -,-n worry (**um** about); (*Fürsorge*) care; **in S~ sein** be worried; **sich** (*dat*) **S~n machen** worry; **keine S~!** don't worry! **s~n** *vi* (*haben*) **s~n für** look after, care for; (*vorsorgen*) provide for; (*sich kümmern*) see to; **dafür s~n, daß** see [to it] *or* make sure that ● *vr* **sich s~n** worry. **s~nfrei** *a* carefree. **s~nvoll** *a* worried, *adv* -ly. **S~recht** *nt* (*Jur*) custody

Sorg|falt *f* -care. **s~fältig** *a* careful, *adv* -ly. **s~los** *a* careless, *adv* -ly; (*unbekümmert*) carefree. **s~sam** *a* careful, *adv* -ly

Sorte *f* -,-n kind, sort; (*Comm*) brand

sort|ieren *vt* sort [out]; (*Comm*) grade. **S~iment** *nt* -[e]s,-e range

sosehr *conj* however much

Soße *f* -,-n sauce; (*Braten-*) gravy; (*Salat-*) dressing

Souffl|eur /zuˈfløːɐ̯/ *m* -s,-e, **S~euse** /-øːzə/ *f* -,-n prompter. **s~ieren** *vi* (*haben*) prompt

Souvenir /zuvəˈniːɐ̯/ *nt* -s,-s souvenir

souverän /zuvəˈrɛːn/ *a* sovereign; (*fig: überlegen*) expert, *adv* -ly. **S~ität** *f* - sovereignty

soviel *conj* however much; **s~ ich weiß** as far as I know ● *adv* as much (**wie** as); **s~ wie möglich** as much as possible

soweit *conj* as far as; (*insoweit*) [in] so far as ● *adv* on the whole; **s~ wie möglich** as far as possible; **s~ sein** be ready; **es ist s~** the time has come

sowenig *conj* however little ● *adv* no more (**wie** than); **s~ wie möglich** as little as possible

sowie *conj* as well as; (*sobald*) as soon as

sowieso *adv* anyway, in any case

sowjet|isch *a* Soviet. **S~union** *f* -Soviet Union

sowohl *adv* **s~ ... als** *od* **wie auch ...** ... as well as ...; **s~ er als auch seine Frau** both he and his wife

sozial *a* social, *adv* -ly; (*Einstellung, Beruf*) caring. **S~arbeit** *f* social work. **S~arbeiter(in)** *m(f)* social worker. **S~demokrat** *m* social democrat. **S~hilfe** *f* social security

Sozialis|mus *m* - socialism. **S~t** *m* -en,-en socialist. **s~tisch** *a* socialist

Sozial|versicherung *f* National Insurance. **S~wohnung** *f* ≈ council flat

Soziol|oge *m* -n,-n sociologist. **S~ogie** *f* - sociology

Sozius *m* -,-se (*Comm*) partner; (*Beifahrersitz*) pillion

sozusagen *adv* so to speak

Spachtel *m* -s,- & *f* -,-n spatula

Spagat *m* -[e]s,-e (*Aust*) string; **s~ machen** do the splits *pl*

Spaghetti *pl* spaghetti *sg*

spähen *vi* (*haben*) peer

Spalier *nt* -s,-e trellis; **S~ stehen** line the route

Spalt *m* -[e]s,-e crack; (*im Vorhang*) chink

Spalt|e *f* -,-n crack, crevice; (*Gletscher-*) crevasse; (*Druck-*) column; (*Orangen-*) segment. **s~en†** *vt*

split; **sich s∼en** split. **S∼ung** *f -,-en* splitting; (*Kluft*) split; (*Phys*) fission

Span *m* -[e]s,-̈e [wood] chip; (*Hobel-*) shaving

Spange *f -,-n* clasp; (*Haar-*) slide; (*Zahn-*) brace; (*Arm-*) bangle

Span|ien /-jən/ *nt* -s Spain. **S∼ier** *m* -s,-, **S∼ierin** *f* -,-nen Spaniard. **s∼isch** *a* Spanish. **S∼isch** *nt* -[s] (*Lang*) Spanish

Spann *m* -[e]s instep

Spanne *f -,-n* span; (*Zeit-*) space; (*Comm*) margin

spann|en *vt* stretch; put up ⟨*Leine*⟩; (*straffen*) tighten; (*an-*) harness (**an** + *acc* to); **den Hahn s∼en** cock the gun; **sich s∼en** tighten ● *vi* (*haben*) be too tight. **s∼end** *a* exciting. **S∼er** *m* -s,- (*fam*) Peeping Tom. **S∼ung** *f -,-en* tension; (*Erwartung*) suspense; (*Electr*) voltage

Spar|buch *nt* savings book. **S∼büchse** *f* money-box. **s∼en** *vt/i* (*haben*) save; (*sparsam sein*) economize (**mit/an** + *dat* on); **sich** (*dat*) **die Mühe s∼en** save oneself the trouble. **S∼er** *m* -s,- saver

Spargel *m* -s,- asparagus

Spar|kasse *f* savings bank. **S∼konto** *nt* deposit account

spärlich *a* sparse, *adv* -ly; (*dürftig*) meagre; (*knapp*) scanty, *adv* -ily

Sparren *m* -s,- rafter

sparsam *a* economical, *adv* -ly; ⟨*Person*⟩ thrifty. **S∼keit** *f* - economy; thrift

Sparschwein *nt* piggy bank

spartanisch *a* Spartan

Sparte *f -,-n* branch; (*Zeitungs-*) section; (*Rubrik*) column

Spaß *m* -es,-̈e fun; (*Scherz*) joke; **im/aus/zum S∼** for fun; **S∼ machen** be fun; ⟨*Person:*⟩ be joking; **es macht mir keinen S∼** I don't enjoy it; **viel S∼!** have a good time! **s∼en** *vi* (*haben*) joke. **s∼ig** *a* amusing, funny. **S∼vogel** *m* joker

Spast|iker *m* -s,- spastic. **s∼isch** *a* spastic

spät *a* & *adv* late; **wie s∼ ist es?** what time is it? **zu s∼** too late; **zu s∼ kommen** be late. **s∼abends** *adv* late at night

Spatel *m* -s,- & *f* -,-n spatula

Spaten *m* -s,- spade

später *a* later; (*zukünftig*) future ● *adv* later

spätestens *adv* at the latest

Spatz *m* -en,-en sparrow

Spätzle *pl* (*Culin*) noodles

spazieren *vi* (*sein*) stroll. **s∼gehen†** *vi sep* (*sein*) go for a walk

Spazier|gang *m* walk; **einen S∼gang machen** go for a walk. **S∼gänger(in)** *m* -s,- (*f* -,-nen) walker. **S∼stock** *m* walking-stick

Specht *m* -[e]s,-e woodpecker

Speck *m* -s bacon; (*fam: Fettpolster*) fat. **s∼ig** *a* greasy

Spedi|teur /ʃpedi'tøːɐ̯/ *m* -s,-e haulage/(*für Umzüge*) removals contractor. **S∼tion** /-'tsi̯oːn/ *f -,-en* carriage, haulage; (*Firma*) haulage/(*für Umzüge*) removals firm

Speer *m* -[e]s,-e spear; (*Sport*) javelin

Speiche *f -,-n* spoke

Speichel *m* -s saliva

Speicher *m* -s,- warehouse; (*dial: Dachboden*) attic; (*Computer*) memory. **s∼n** *vt* store

speien† *vt* spit; (*erbrechen*) vomit

Speise *f -,-n* food; (*Gericht*) dish; (*Pudding*) blancmange. **S∼eis** *nt* ice-cream. **S∼kammer** *f* larder. **S∼karte** *f* menu. **s∼n** *vi* (*haben*) eat; **zu Abend s∼n** have dinner ● *vt* feed. **S∼röhre** *f* oesophagus. **S∼saal** *m* dining-room. **S∼wagen** *m* dining-car

Spektakel *m* -s (*fam*) noise

spektakulär *a* spectacular

Spektrum *nt* -s,-tra spectrum

Spekul|ant *m* -en,-en speculator. **S∼ation** /-'tsi̯oːn/ *f -,-en* speculation. **s∼ieren** *vi* (*haben*) speculate; **s∼ieren auf** (+ *acc*) (*fam*) hope to get

Spelze *f -,-n* husk

spendabel *a* generous

Spende *f -,-n* donation. **s∼n** *vt* donate; give ⟨*Blut, Schatten*⟩; **Beifall s∼n** applaud. **S∼r** *m* -s,- donor; (*Behälter*) dispenser

spendieren *vt* pay for; **jdm etw/ein Bier s∼** treat s.o. to sth/stand s.o. a beer

Spengler *m* -s,- (*SGer*) plumber

Sperling *m* -s,-e sparrow

Sperre *f -,-n* barrier; (*Verbot*) ban; (*Comm*) embargo. **s∼n** *vt* close; (*ver-*) block; (*verbieten*) ban; cut off ⟨*Strom, Telefon*⟩; stop ⟨*Scheck, Kredit*⟩; **s∼n in** (+ *acc*) put in ⟨*Gefängnis, Käfig*⟩; **sich s∼n** balk (**gegen** at); **gesperrt gedruckt** (*Typ*) spaced

Sperr|holz *nt* plywood. **s∼ig** *a* bulky. **S∼müll** *m* bulky refuse. **S∼stunde** *f* closing time

Spesen *pl* expenses

spezial|isieren (sich) *vr* specialize (**auf**+*acc* in). **S~ist** *m* **-en,-en** specialist. **S~ität** *f* **-,-en** speciality
speziell *a* special, *adv* -ly
spezifisch *a* specific, *adv* -ally
Sphäre /'sfɛːrə/ *f* **-,-n** sphere
spicken *vt* (*Culin*) lard; **gespickt mit** (*fig*) full of ● *vi* (*haben*) (*fam*) crib (**bei** from)
Spiegel *m* **-s,-** mirror; (*Wasser-, Alkohol-*) level. **S~bild** *nt* reflection. **S~ei** *nt* fried egg. **s~n** *vt* reflect; **sich s~n** be reflected ● *vi* (*haben*) reflect [the light]; (*glänzen*) gleam. **S~ung** *f* **-,-en** reflection
Spiel *nt* **-[e]s,-e** game; (*Spielen*) playing; (*Glücks-*) gambling; (*Schau-*) play; (*Satz*) set; **ein S~ Karten** a pack/(*Amer*) deck of cards; **auf dem S~ stehen** be at stake; **aufs S~ setzen** risk. **S~art** *f* variety. **S~automat** *m* fruit machine. **S~bank** *f* casino. **S~dose** *f* musical box. **s~en** *vt/i* (*haben*) play; (*im Glücksspiel*) gamble; (*vortäuschen*) act; ⟨*Roman:*⟩ be set (**in**+*dat* in); **s~en mit** (*fig*) toy with. **s~end** *a* (*mühelos*) effortless, *adv* -ly
Spieler|(in) *m* **-s,-** (*f* **-,-nen**) player; (*Glücks-*) gambler. **S~ei** *f* **-,-en** amusement; (*Kleinigkeit*) trifle
Spiel|feld *nt* field, pitch. **S~gefährte** *m*, **S~gefährtin** *f* playmate. **S~karte** *f* playing-card. **S~marke** *f* chip. **S~plan** *m* programme. **S~platz** *m* playground. **S~raum** *m* (*fig*) scope; (*Techn*) clearance. **S~regeln** *fpl* rules [of the game]. **S~sachen** *fpl* toys. **S~verderber** *m* **-s,-** spoilsport. **S~waren** *fpl* toys. **S~warengeschäft** *nt* toyshop. **S~zeug** *nt* toy; (*S~sachen*) toys *pl*
Spieß *m* **-es,-e** spear; (*Brat-*) spit; (*für Schaschlik*) skewer; (*Fleisch-*) kebab; **den S~ umkehren** turn the tables on s.o. **S~bürger** *m* [petit] bourgeois. **s~bürgerlich** *a* bourgeois. **s~en** *vt* **etw auf etw** (*acc*) **s~en** spear sth with sth. **S~er** *m* **-s,-** [petit] bourgeois. **s~ig** *a* bourgeois. **S~ruten** *fpl* **S~ruten laufen** run the gauntlet
Spike[s]reifen /'ʃpaik[s]-/ *m* studded tyre
Spinat *m* **-s** spinach
Spind *m* & *nt* **-[e]s,-e** locker
Spindel *f* **-,-n** spindle
Spinne *f* **-,-n** spider

spinn|en† *vt/i* (*haben*) spin; **er spinnt** (*fam*) he's crazy. **S~ennetz** *nt* spider's web. **S~[en]gewebe** *nt*, **S~webe** *f* **-,-n** cobweb
Spion *m* **-s,-e** spy
Spionage /ʃpioˈnaːʒə/ *f* - espionage, spying; **S~ treiben** spy. **S~abwehr** *f* counter-espionage
spionieren *vi* (*haben*) spy
Spionin *f* **-,-nen** [woman] spy
Spiral|e *f* **-,-n** spiral. **s~ig** *a* spiral
Spiritis|mus *m* - spiritualism. **s~tisch** *a* spiritualist
Spirituosen *pl* spirits
Spiritus *m* - alcohol; (*Brenn-*) methylated spirits *pl*. **S~kocher** *m* spirit stove
Spital *nt* **-s,-̈er** (*Aust*) hospital
spitz *a* pointed; (*scharf*) sharp; (*schrill*) shrill; ⟨*Winkel*⟩ acute; **s~e Bemerkung** dig. **S~bube** *m* scoundrel; (*Schlingel*) rascal. **s~bübisch** *a* mischievous, *adv* -ly
Spitze *f* **-,-n** point; (*oberer Teil*) top; (*vorderer Teil*) front; (*Pfeil-, Finger-, Nasen-*) tip; (*Schuh-, Strumpf-*) toe; (*Zigarren-, Zigaretten-*) holder; (*Höchstleistung*) maximum; (*Tex*) lace; (*fam: Anspielung*) dig; **an der S~ liegen** be in the lead
Spitzel *m* **-s,-** informer
spitzen *vt* sharpen; purse ⟨*Lippen*⟩; prick up ⟨*Ohren*⟩; **sich s~ auf** (+*acc*) (*fam*) look forward to. **S~geschwindigkeit** *f* top speed
spitz|findig *a* over-subtle. **S~hacke** *f* pickaxe. **S~name** *m* nickname
Spleen /ʃpliːn/ *m* **-s,-e** obsession; **einen S~ haben** be crazy. **s~ig** *a* eccentric
Splitter *m* **-s,-** splinter. **s~n** *vi* (*sein*) shatter. **s~[faser]nackt** *a* (*fam*) stark naked
sponsern *vt* sponsor
spontan *a* spontaneous, *adv* -ly
sporadisch *a* sporadic, *adv* -ally
Spore *f* **-,-n** (*Biol*) spore
Sporn *m* **-[e]s,Sporen** spur; **einem Pferd die Sporen geben** spur a horse
Sport *m* **-[e]s** sport; (*Hobby*) hobby. **S~art** *f* sport. **S~fest** *nt* sports day. **S~ler** *m* **-s,-** sportsman. **S~lerin** *f* **-,-nen** sportswoman. **s~lich** *a* sports ...; (*fair*) sporting, *adv* -ly; (*flott, schlank*) sporty. **S~platz** *m* sports ground. **S~verein** *m* sports club. **S~wagen** *m* sports car; (*Kinder-*) push-chair, (*Amer*) stroller

Spott m -[e]s mockery. **s~billig** a & adv dirt cheap

spötteln vi (haben) mock; **s~ über** (+acc) poke fun at

spotten vi (haben) mock; **s~ über** (+acc) make fun of; (höhnend) ridicule

spöttisch a mocking, adv -ly

Sprach|e f -,-n language; (Sprechfähigkeit) speech; **zur S~e bringen** bring up. **S~fehler** m speech defect. **S~labor** nt language laboratory. **s~lich** a linguistic, adv -ally. **s~los** a speechless

Spray /ʃpreː/ nt & m -s,-s spray. **S~dose** f aerosol [can]

Sprech|anlage f intercom. **S~chor** m chorus; **im S~chor rufen** chant

sprechen† vi (haben) speak/(sich unterhalten) talk (über+acc/von about/of); **deutsch/englisch s~** speak German/English ● vt speak; (sagen, aufsagen) say; pronounce ⟨Urteil⟩; **schuldig s~** find guilty; **jdn s~** speak to s.o.; **Herr X ist nicht zu s~** Mr X is not available

Sprecher(in) m -s,- (f -,-nen) speaker; (Radio, TV) announcer; (Wortführer) spokesman, f spokeswoman

Sprechstunde f consulting hours pl; (Med) surgery. **S~nhilfe** f (Med) receptionist

Sprechzimmer nt consulting room

spreizen vt spread

Sprengel m -s,- parish

spreng|en vt blow up; blast ⟨Felsen⟩; (fig) burst; (begießen) water; (mit Sprenger) sprinkle; dampen ⟨Wäsche⟩. **S~er** m -s,- sprinkler. **S~kopf** m warhead. **S~körper** m explosive device. **S~stoff** m explosive

Spreu f - chaff

Sprich|wort nt (pl -wörter) proverb. **s~wörtlich** a proverbial

sprießen† vi (sein) sprout

Springbrunnen m fountain

spring|en† vi (sein) jump; (Schwimmsport) dive; ⟨Ball:⟩ bounce; (spritzen) spurt; (zer-) break; (rissig werden) crack; ⟨SGer: laufen⟩ run. **S~er** m -s,- jumper; (Kunst-) diver; (Schach) knight. **S~reiten** nt show-jumping. **S~seil** nt skipping-rope

Sprint m -s,-s sprint

Sprit m -s (fam) petrol

Spritz|e f -,-n syringe; (Injektion) injection; (Feuer-) hose. **s~en** vt spray; (be-, ver-) splash; (Culin) pipe; (Med) inject ● vi (haben) splash; ⟨Fett:⟩ spit ● vi (sein) splash; (hervor-) spurt; (fam: laufen) dash. **S~er** m -s,- splash; (Schuß) dash. **s~ig** a lively; ⟨Wein, Komödie⟩ sparkling. **S~tour** f (fam) spin

spröde a brittle; (trocken) dry; (rissig) chapped; ⟨Stimme⟩ harsh; (abweisend) aloof

Sproß m -sses,-sse shoot

Sprosse f -,-n rung. **S~nkohl** m (Aust) Brussels sprouts pl

Sprotte f -,-n sprat

Spruch m -[e]s,¨e saying; (Denk-) motto; (Zitat) quotation. **S~band** nt (pl -bänder) banner

Sprudel m -s,- sparkling mineral water. **s~n** vi (haben/sein) bubble

Sprüh|dose f aerosol [can]. **s~en** vt spray ● vi (sein) ⟨Funken:⟩ fly; (fig) sparkle. **S~regen** m fine drizzle

Sprung m -[e]s,¨e jump, leap; (Schwimmsport) dive; (fam: Katzen-) stone's throw; (Riß) crack; **auf einen S~** (fam) for a moment. **S~brett** nt springboard. **s~haft** a erratic; (plötzlich) sudden, adv -ly. **S~schanze** f ski-jump. **S~seil** nt skipping-rope

Spucke f - spit. **s~n** vt/i (haben) spit; (sich übergeben) be sick

Spuk m -[e]s,-e [ghostly] apparition. **s~en** vi (haben) ⟨Geist:⟩ walk; **in diesem Haus s~t es** this house is haunted

Spülbecken nt sink

Spule f -,-n spool

Spüle f -,-n sink unit; (Becken) sink

spulen vt spool

spül|en vt rinse; (schwemmen) wash; **Geschirr s~en** wash up ● vi (haben) flush [the toilet]. **S~kasten** m cistern. **S~mittel** nt washing-up liquid. **S~tuch** nt dishcloth

Spur f -,-en track; (Fahr-) lane; (Fährte) trail; (Anzeichen) trace; (Hinweis) lead; **keine od nicht die S~** (fam) not in the least

spürbar a noticeable, adv -bly

spuren vi (haben) (fam) toe the line

spür|en vt feel; (seelisch) sense. **S~hund** m tracker dog

spurlos adv without trace

spurten vi (sein) put on a spurt; (fam: laufen) sprint

sputen (sich) vr hurry

Staat *m* -[e]s,-en state; (*Land*) country; (*Putz*) finery. **s~lich** *a* state ... ● *adv* by the state

Staatsangehörig|e(r) *m/f* national. **S~keit** *f* - nationality

Staats|anwalt *m* state prosecutor. **S~beamte(r)** *m* civil servant. **S~besuch** *m* state visit. **S~bürger(in)** *m(f)* national. **S~mann** *m* (*pl* -männer) statesman. **S~streich** *m* coup

Stab *m* -[e]s,-e rod; (*Gitter-*) bar; (*Sport*) baton; (*Mitarbeiter-*) team; (*Mil*) staff

Stäbchen *ntpl* chopsticks

Stabhochsprung *m* pole-vault

stabil *a* stable; (*gesund*) robust; (*solide*) sturdy, *adv* -ily. **s~isieren** *vt* stabilize; **sich s~isieren** stabilize. **S~ität** *f* - stability

Stachel *m* -s,- spine; (*Gift-*) sting; (*Spitze*) spike. **S~beere** *f* gooseberry. **S~draht** *m* barbed wire. **s~ig** *a* prickly. **S~schwein** *nt* porcupine

Stadion *nt* -s,-ien stadium

Stadium *nt* -s,-ien stage

Stadt *f* -,-e town; (*Groß-*) city

Städt|chen *nt* -s,- small town. **s~isch** *a* urban; (*kommunal*) municipal

Stadt|mauer *f* city wall. **S~mitte** *f* town centre. **S~plan** *m* street map. **S~teil** *m* district. **S~zentrum** *nt* town centre

Staffel *f* -,-n team; (*S~lauf*) relay; (*Mil*) squadron

Staffelei *f* -,-en easel

Staffel|lauf *m* relay race. **s~n** *vt* stagger; (*abstufen*) grade

Stagn|ation /-'tsjo:n/ *f* - stagnation. **s~ieren** *vi* (*haben*) stagnate

Stahl *m* -s steel. **S~beton** *m* reinforced concrete

Stall *m* -[e]s,-e stable; (*Kuh-*) shed; (*Schweine-*) sty; (*Hühner-*) coop; (*Kaninchen-*) hutch

Stamm *m* -[e]s,-e trunk; (*Sippe*) tribe; (*Kern*) core; (*Wort-*) stem. **S~baum** *m* family tree; (*eines Tieres*) pedigree

stammeln *vt/i* (*haben*) stammer

stammen *vi* (*haben*) come/(*zeitlich*) date (**von/aus** from); **das Zitat stammt von Goethe** the quotation is from Goethe

Stamm|gast *m* regular. **S~halter** *m* son and heir

stämmig *a* sturdy

Stamm|kundschaft *f* regulars *pl.* **S~lokal** *nt* favourite pub. **S~tisch** *m* table reserved for the regulars; (*Treffen*) meeting of the regulars

stampf|en *vi* (*haben*) stamp; (*Maschine:*) pound; **mit den Füßen s~en** stamp one's feet ● *vi* (*sein*) tramp ● *vt* pound; mash (*Kartoffeln*). **S~kartoffeln** *fpl* mashed potatoes

Stand *m* -[e]s,-e standing position; (*Zustand*) state; (*Spiel-*) score; (*Höhe*) level; (*gesellschaftlich*) class; (*Verkaufs-*) stall; (*Messe-*) stand; (*Taxi-*) rank; **auf den neuesten S~ bringen** update

Standard *m* -s,-s standard. **s~isieren** *vt* standardize

Standarte *f* -,-n standard

Standbild *nt* statue

Ständchen *nt* -s,- serenade; **jdm ein S~ bringen** serenade s.o.

Ständer *m* -s,- stand; (*Geschirr-, Platten-*) rack; (*Kerzen-*) holder

Standesamt *nt* registry office. **S~beamte(r)** *m* registrar. **S~unterschied** *m* class distinction

stand|haft *a* steadfast, *adv* -ly. **s~halten†** *vi sep* (*haben*) stand firm; **etw** (*dat*) **s~halten** stand up to sth

ständig *a* constant, *adv* -ly; (*fest*) permanent, *adv* -ly

Stand|licht *nt* sidelights *pl.* **S~ort** *m* position; (*Firmen-*) location; (*Mil*) garrison. **S~pauke** *f* (*fam*) dressing-down. **S~punkt** *m* point of view. **S~spur** *f* hard shoulder. **S~uhr** *f* grandfather clock

Stange *f* -,-n bar; (*Holz-*) pole; (*Gardinen-*) rail; (*Hühner-*) perch; (*Zimt-*) stick; **von der S~** (*fam*) off the peg. **S~nbohne** *f* runner bean. **S~nbrot** *nt* French bread

Stanniol *nt* -s tin foil. **S~papier** *nt* silver paper

stanzen *vt* stamp; (*aus-*) stamp out; punch (*Loch*)

Stapel *m* -s,- stack, pile; **vom S~ laufen** be launched. **S~lauf** *m* launch[ing]. **s~n** *vt* stack *or* pile up; **sich s~n** pile up

stapfen *vi* (*sein*) tramp, trudge

Star¹ *m* -[e]s,-e starling

Star² *m* -[e]s (*Med*) [**grauer**] **S~** cataract; **grüner S~** glaucoma

Star³ *m* -s,-s (*Theat, Sport*) star

stark *a* (**stärker, stärkst**) strong; (*Motor*) powerful; (*Verkehr, Regen*) heavy; (*Hitze, Kälte*) severe; (*groß*) big; (*schlimm*) bad; (*dick*) thick;

(*korpulent*) stout ● *adv* strongly;
heavily; badly; (*sehr*) very much

Stärk|e *f* -,-n (*s. stark*) strength;
power; thickness; stoutness; (*Größe*)
size; (*Mais-, Wäsche-*) starch. **S~e-
mehl** *nt* cornflour. **s~en** *vt*
strengthen; starch (*Wäsche*); **sich
s~en** fortify oneself. **S~ung** *f* -,-en
strengthening; (*Erfrischung*)
refreshment

starr *a* rigid, *adv* -ly; (*steif*) stiff, *adv*
-ly; (*Blick*) fixed; (*unbeugsam*) in-
flexible, *adv* -bly

starren *vi* (*haben*) stare; **vor
Schmutz s~** be filthy

starr|köpfig *a* stubborn. **S~sinn** *m*
obstinacy. **s~sinnig** *a* obstinate, *adv*
-ly

Start *m* -s,-s start; (*Aviat*) take-off.
S~bahn *f* runway. **s~en** *vi* (*sein*)
start; (*Aviat*) take off; (*aufbrechen*)
set off; (*teilnehmen*) compete ● *vt*
start; (*fig*) launch

Station /-'tsjo:n/ *f* -,-en station; (*Haltestelle*) stop; (*Abschnitt*) stage;
(*Med*) ward; **S~ machen** break one's
journey; **bei freier S~** all found.
s~är *adv* as an in-patient. **s~ieren**
vt station

statisch *a* static

Statist(in) *m* -en,-en (*f* -,-nen)
(*Theat*) extra

Statisti|k *f* -,-en statistics *sg*; (*Auf-
stellung*) statistics *pl.* **s~sch** *a* stat-
istical, *adv* -ly

Stativ *nt* -s,-e (*Phot*) tripod

statt *prep* (+*gen*) instead of; **s~ dessen** instead ● *conj* **s~ etw zu tun**
instead of doing sth

Stätte *f* -,-n place

statt|finden† *vi sep* (*haben*) take
place. **s~haft** *a* permitted

stattlich *a* imposing; (*beträchtlich*)
considerable

Statue /'ʃta:tuə/ *f* -,-n statue

St ur *f* - build, stature

Status *m* - status. **S~symbol** *nt* status symbol

Statut *nt* -[e]s,-en statute

Stau *m* -[e]s,-s congestion; (*Auto*)
[traffic] jam; (*Rück-*) tailback

Staub *m* -[e]s dust; **S~ wischen** dust;
S~ saugen vacuum, hoover

Staubecken *nt* reservoir

staub|en *vi* (*haben*) raise dust; **es s~t**
it's dusty. **s~ig** *a* dusty. **s~saugen**
vt/i (*haben*) vacuum, hoover.
S~sauger *m* vacuum cleaner,
Hoover (P). **S~tuch** *nt* duster

Staudamm *m* dam

Staude *f* -,-n shrub

stauen *vt* dam up; **sich s~** accumulate; (*Autos:*) form a tailback

staunen *vi* (*haben*) be amazed *or*
astonished. **S~** *nt* -s amazement,
astonishment

Stau|see *m* reservoir. **S~ung** *f* -,-en
congestion; (*Auto*) [traffic] jam

Steak /ʃte:k, ste:k/ *nt* -s,-s steak

stechen† *vt* stick (**in** + *acc* in); (*verletzen*) prick; (*mit Messer*) stab; (*In-
sekt:*) sting; (*Mücke:*) bite; (*gravieren*) engrave ● *vi* (*haben*) prick; (*Insekt:*) sting; (*Mücke:*) bite; (*mit Stech-
uhr*) clock in/out; **in See s~** put to
sea. **s~d** *a* stabbing; (*Geruch*)
pungent

Stech|ginster *m* gorse. **S~kahn** *m*
punt. **S~mücke** *f* mosquito.
S~palme *f* holly. **S~uhr** *f* time clock

Steck|brief *m* 'wanted' poster.
S~dose *f* socket. **s~en** *vt* put; (*mit
Nadel, Reißzwecke*) pin; (*pflanzen*)
plant ● *vi* (*haben*) be; (*fest-*) be
stuck; **hinter etw** (*dat*) **s~en** (*fig*) be
behind sth

Stecken *m* -s,- (*SGer*) stick

stecken|bleiben† *vi sep* (*sein*) get
stuck. **s~lassen†** *vt sep* leave.
S~pferd *nt* hobby-horse

Steck|er *m* -s,- (*Electr*) plug. **S~ling**
m -s,-e cutting. **S~nadel** *f* pin.
S~rübe *f* swede

Steg *m* -[e]s,-e foot-bridge; (*Boots-*)
landing-stage; (*Brillen-*) bridge.
S~reif *m* **aus dem S~reif** extempore

stehen† *vi* (*haben*) stand; (*sich befinden*) be; (*still-*) be stationary; (*Maschine, Uhr:*) have stopped; **vor dem
Ruin s~** face ruin; **zu jdm/etw s~**
(*fig*) stand by s.o./sth; **gut s~** (*Getreide, Aktien:*) be doing well; (*Chancen:*) be good; **jdm [gut] s~** suit s.o.;
sich gut s~ be on good terms; **es
steht 3 zu 1** the score is 3–1; **es steht
schlecht um ihn** he is in a bad way.
S~ *nt* -s standing; **zum S~ bringen/
kommen** bring/come to a standstill.
s~bleiben† *vi sep* (*sein*) stop; (*Motor:*) stall; (*Zeit:*) stand still; (*Gebäude:*) be left standing. **s~d** *a*
standing; (*sich nicht bewegend*) stationary; (*Gewässer*) stagnant.
s~lassen† *vt sep* leave; **sich** (*dat*)
einen Bart s~lassen grow a beard

Steh|lampe *f* standard lamp.
S~leiter *f* step-ladder

stehlen† *vt/i* (*haben*) steal; **sich s~** steal, creep

Steh|platz *m* standing place. **S~vermögen** *nt* stamina, staying-power

steif *a* stiff, *adv* -ly. **S~heit** *f* - stiffness

Steig|bügel *m* stirrup. **S~eisen** *nt* crampon

steigen† *vi* (*sein*) climb; (*hochgehen*) rise, go up; ⟨*Schulden, Spannung:*⟩ mount; **s~ auf** (+ *acc*) climb on [to] ⟨*Stuhl*⟩; climb ⟨*Berg, Leiter*⟩; get on ⟨*Pferd, Fahrrad*⟩; **s~ in** (+ *acc*) climb into; get in ⟨*Auto*⟩; get on ⟨*Bus, Zug*⟩; **s~ aus** climb out of; get out of ⟨*Bett, Auto*⟩; get off ⟨*Bus, Zug*⟩; **einen Drachen s~ lassen** fly a kite; **s~de Preise** rising prices

steiger|n *vt* increase; **sich s~n** increase; (*sich verbessern*) improve. **S~ung** *f* -,-en increase; improvement; (*Gram*) comparison

Steigung *f* -,-en gradient; (*Hang*) slope

steil *a* steep, *adv* -ly. **S~küste** *f* cliffs *pl*

Stein *m* -[e]s,-e stone; (*Ziegel-*) brick; (*Spiel-*) piece. **s~alt** *a* ancient. **S~bock** *m* ibex; (*Astr*) Capricorn. **S~bruch** *m* quarry. **S~garten** *m* rockery. **S~gut** *nt* earthenware. **s~hart** *a* rock-hard. **s~ig** *a* stony. **s~igen** *vt* stone. **S~kohle** *f* [hard] coal. **s~reich** *a* (*fam*) very rich. **S~schlag** *m* rock fall

Stelle *f* -,-n place; (*Fleck*) spot; (*Abschnitt*) passage; (*Stellung*) job, post; (*Büro*) office; (*Behörde*) authority; **kahle s~** bare patch; **auf der S~** immediately; **an deiner S~** in your place

stellen *vt* put; (*aufrecht*) stand; set ⟨*Wecker, Aufgabe*⟩; ask ⟨*Frage*⟩; make ⟨*Antrag, Forderung, Diagnose*⟩; **zur Verfügung s~** provide; **lauter/leiser s~** turn up/down; **kalt/warm s~** chill/keep hot; **sich s~** [go and] stand; give oneself up (**der Polizei** to the police); **sich tot/schlafend s~** pretend to be dead/asleep; **gut gestellt sein** be well off

Stellen|anzeige *f* job advertisement. **S~vermittlung** *f* employment agency. **s~weise** *adv* in places

Stellung *f* -,-en position; (*Arbeit*) job; **S~ nehmen** make a statement (**zu** on). **s~slos** *a* jobless. **S~suche** *f* job-hunting

stellvertret|end *a* deputy … ● *adv* as a deputy; **s~end für jdn** on s.o.'s behalf. **S~er** *m* deputy

Stellwerk *nt* signal-box

Stelzen *fpl* stilts. **s~** *vi* (*sein*) stalk

stemmen *vt* press; lift ⟨*Gewicht*⟩; **sich s~ gegen** brace oneself against

Stempel *m* -s,- stamp; (*Post-*) postmark; (*Präge-*) die; (*Feingehalts-*) hallmark. **s~n** *vt* stamp; hallmark ⟨*Silber*⟩; cancel ⟨*Marke*⟩

Stengel *m* -s,- stalk, stem

Steno *f* - (*fam*) shorthand

Steno|gramm *nt* -[e]s,-e shorthand text. **S~graphie** *f* - shorthand. **s~graphieren** *vt* take down in shorthand ● *vi* (*haben*) do shorthand. **S~typistin** *f* -,-nen shorthand typist

Steppdecke *f* quilt

Steppe *f* -,-n steppe

Steptanz *m* tap-dance

sterben† *vi* (*sein*) die (**an** + *dat* of); **im s~ liegen** be dying

sterblich *a* mortal. **S~e(r)** *m*/*f* mortal. **S~keit** *f* - mortality

stereo *adv* in stereo. **S~anlage** *f* stereo [system]

stereotyp *a* stereotyped

steril *a* sterile. **s~isieren** *vt* sterilize. **S~ität** *f* - sterility

Stern *m* -[e]s,-e star. **S~bild** *nt* constellation. **S~chen** *nt* -s,- asterisk. **S~kunde** *f* astronomy. **S~schnuppe** *f* -,-n shooting star. **S~warte** *f* -,-n observatory

stetig *a* steady, *adv* -ily

stets *adv* always

Steuer¹ *nt* -s,- steering-wheel; (*Naut*) helm; **am S~** at the wheel

Steuer² *f* -,-n tax

Steuer|bord *nt* -[e]s starboard [side]. **S~erklärung** *f* tax return. **s~frei** *a* & *adv* tax-free. **S~mann** *m* (*pl* -leute) helmsman; (*beim Rudern*) cox. **s~n** *vt* steer; (*Aviat*) pilot; (*Techn*) control ● *vi* (*haben*) be at the wheel/(*Naut*) helm ● (*sein*) head (**nach** for). **s~pflichtig** *a* taxable. **S~rad** *nt* steering-wheel. **S~ruder** *nt* helm. **S~ung** *f* - steering; (*Techn*) controls *pl*. **S~zahler** *m* -s,- taxpayer

Stewardeß /ˈstjuːədɛs/ *f* -,-dessen air hostess, stewardess

Stich *m* -[e]s,-e prick; (*Messer-*) stab; (*S~wunde*) stab wound; (*Bienen-*) sting; (*Mücken-*) bite; (*Schmerz*) stabbing pain; (*Näh-*) stitch; (*Kupfer-*)

engraving; (*Kartenspiel*) trick; **S~ ins Rötliche** tinge of red; **jdn im S~ lassen** leave s.o. in the lurch; ⟨*Gedächtnis:*⟩ fail s.o. **s~eln** *vi* (*haben*) make snide remarks

Stich|flamme *f* jet of flame. **s~haltig** *a* valid. **S~probe** *f* spot check. **S~wort** *nt* (*pl* **-wörter**) headword; (*pl* **-worte**) (*Theat*) cue; **S~worte** notes

stick|en *vt/i* (*haben*) embroider. **S~erei** *f* - embroidery

stickig *a* stuffy

Stickstoff *m* nitrogen

Stiefbruder *m* stepbrother

Stiefel *m* **-s,-** boot

Stief|kind *nt* stepchild. **S~mutter** *f* stepmother. **S~mütterchen** *nt* **-s,-** pansy. **S~schwester** *f* stepsister. **S~sohn** *m* stepson. **S~tochter** *f* stepdaughter. **S~vater** *m* stepfather

Stiege *f* **-,-n** stairs *pl*

Stiel *m* **-[e]s,-e** handle; (*Blumen-, Gläser-*) stem; (*Blatt-*) stalk

Stier *m* **-[e]s,-e** bull; (*Astr*) Taurus

stieren *vi* (*haben*) stare

Stier|kampf *m* bullfight

Stift¹ *m* **-[e]s,-e** pin; (*Nagel*) tack; (*Blei-*) pencil; (*Farb-*) crayon

Stift² *nt* **-[e]s,-e** [endowed] foundation. **s~en** *vt* endow; (*spenden*) donate; create ⟨*Unheil, Verwirrung*⟩; bring about ⟨*Frieden*⟩. **S~er** *m* **-s,-** founder; (*Spender*) donor. **S~ung** *f* **-,-en** foundation; (*Spende*) donation

Stigma *nt* **-s** (*fig*) stigma

Stil *m* **-[e]s,-e** style; **in großem S~** in style. **s~isiert** *a* stylized. **s~istisch** *a* stylistic, *adv* **-ally**

still *a* quiet, *adv* **-ly**; ⟨*reglos, ohne Kohlensäure*⟩ still; (*heimlich*) secret, *adv* **-ly**; **der S~e Ozean** the Pacific; **im s~en** secretly; (*bei sich*) inwardly. **S~e** *f* - quiet; (*Schweigen*) silence

Stilleben *nt* still life

stilleg|en *vt sep* close down. **S~ung** *f* **-,-en** closure

stillen *vt* satisfy; quench ⟨*Durst*⟩; stop ⟨*Schmerzen, Blutung*⟩; breastfeed ⟨*Kind*⟩

stillhalten† *vi sep* (*haben*) keep still

Stillschweigen *nt* silence. **s~d** *a* silent, *adv* **-ly**; (*fig*) tacit, *adv* **-ly**

still|sitzen† *vi sep* (*haben*) sit still. **S~stand** *m* standstill; **zum S~stand bringen** stop. **s~stehen†** *vi sep* (*haben*) stand still; (*anhalten*) stop; ⟨*Verkehr:*⟩ be at a standstill

Stil|möbel *pl* reproduction furniture *sg.* **s~voll** *a* stylish, *adv* **-ly**

Stimm|bänder *ntpl* vocal cords. **s~berechtigt** *a* entitled to vote. **S~bruch** *m* **er ist im S~bruch** his voice is breaking

Stimme *f* **-,-n** voice; (*Wahl-*) vote

stimmen *vi* (*haben*) be right; (*wählen*) vote; **stimmt das?** is that right/ (*wahr*) true? ● *vt* tune; **jdn traurig/ fröhlich s~** make s.o. feel sad/happy

Stimm|enthaltung *f* abstention. **S~recht** *nt* right to vote

Stimmung *f* **-,-en** mood; (*Atmosphäre*) atmosphere. **s~svoll** *a* full of atmosphere

Stimmzettel *m* ballot-paper

stimulieren *vt* stimulate

stink|en† *vi* (*haben*) smell/(*stark*) stink (**nach** of). **S~tier** *nt* skunk

Stipendium *nt* **-s,-ien** scholarship; (*Beihilfe*) grant

Stirn *f* **-,-en** forehead; **die S~ bieten** (+*dat*) (*fig*) defy. **S~runzeln** *nt* **-s** frown

stöbern *vi* (*haben*) rummage

stochern *vi* (*haben*) **s~ in** (+ *dat*) poke ⟨*Feuer*⟩; pick at ⟨*Essen*⟩; pick ⟨*Zähne*⟩

Stock¹ *m* **-[e]s,̈e** stick; (*Ski-*) pole; (*Bienen-*) hive; (*Rosen-*) bush; (*Reb-*) vine

Stock² *m* **-[e]s,-** storey, floor. **S~bett** *nt* bunk-beds *pl*. **s~dunkel** *a* (*fam*) pitch-dark

stock|en *vi* (*haben*) stop; ⟨*Verkehr:*⟩ come to a standstill; ⟨*Person:*⟩ falter. **s~end** *a* hesitant, *adv* **-ly**. **s~taub** *a* (*fam*) stone-deaf. **S~ung** *f* **-,-en** hold-up

Stockwerk *nt* storey, floor

Stoff *m* **-[e]s,-e** substance; (*Tex*) fabric, material; (*Thema*) subject [matter]; (*Gesprächs-*) topic. **S~tier** *nt* soft toy. **S~wechsel** *m* metabolism

stöhnen *vi* (*haben*) groan, moan. **S~** *nt* **-s** groan, moan

stoisch *a* stoic, *adv* **-ally**

Stola *f* **-,-len** stole

Stollen *m* **-s,-** gallery; (*Kuchen*) stollen

stolpern *vi* (*sein*) stumble; **s~ über** (+ *acc*) trip over

stolz *a* proud (**auf** + *acc* of), *adv* **-ly**. **S~** *m* **-es** pride

stolzieren *vi* (*sein*) strut

stopfen *vt* stuff; (*stecken*) put; (*ausbessern*) darn ● *vi* (*haben*) be constipating; (*fam: essen*) guzzle

Stopp m -s,-s stop. **s~** int stop!
stoppel|ig a stubbly. **S~n** fpl stubble sg
stopp|en vt stop; (*Sport*) time • vi (*haben*) stop. **S~schild** nt stop sign. **S~uhr** f stop-watch
Stöpsel m -s,- plug; (*Flaschen-*) stopper
Storch m -[e]s,"e stork
Store /ʃtoːɐ̯/ m -s,-s net curtain
stören vt disturb; disrupt ⟨*Rede, Sitzung*⟩; jam ⟨*Sender*⟩; (*mißfallen*) bother; **stört es Sie, wenn ich rauche?** do you mind if I smoke? • vi (*haben*) be a nuisance; **entschuldigen Sie, daß ich störe** I'm sorry to bother you
stornieren vt cancel
störrisch a stubborn, adv -ly
Störung f -,-en (s. *stören*) disturbance; disruption; (*Med*) trouble; (*Radio*) interference; **technische S~** technical fault
Stoß m -es,"e push, knock; (*mit Ellbogen*) dig; (*Hörner-*) butt; (*mit Waffe*) thrust; (*Schwimm-*) stroke; (*Ruck*) jolt; (*Erd-*) shock; (*Stapel*) stack, pile. **S~dämpfer** m -s,- shock absorber
stoßen† vt push, knock; (*mit Füßen*) kick; (*mit Kopf, Hörnern*) butt; (*an-*) poke, nudge; (*treiben*) thrust; **sich s~** knock oneself; **sich** (*dat*) **den Kopf s~** hit one's head • vi (*haben*) push; **s~ an** (+*acc*) knock against; (*angrenzen*) adjoin • vi (*sein*) **s~ gegen** knock against; bump into ⟨*Tür*⟩; **s~ auf** (+*acc*) bump into; (*entdecken*) come across; strike ⟨*Öl*⟩; (*fig*) meet with ⟨*Ablehnung*⟩
Stoß|stange f bumper. **S~verkehr** m rush-hour traffic. **S~zahn** m tusk. **S~zeit** f rush-hour
stottern vt/i (*haben*) stutter, stammer
Str. abbr (**Straße**) St
Straf|anstalt f prison. **S~arbeit** f (*Sch*) imposition. **s~bar** a punishable; **sich s~bar machen** commit an offence
Strafe f -,-n punishment; (*Jur & fig*) penalty; (*Geld-*) fine; (*Freiheits-*) sentence. **s~n** vt punish
straff a tight, taut. **s~en** vt tighten; **sich s~en** tighten
Strafgesetz nt criminal law
sträf|lich a criminal, adv -ly. **S~ling** m -s,-e prisoner

Straf|mandat nt (*Auto*) [parking/speeding] ticket. **S~porto** nt excess postage. **S~predigt** f (*fam*) lecture. **S~raum** m penalty area. **S~stoß** m penalty. **S~tat** f crime. **S~zettel** m (*fam*) = **S~mandat**
Strahl m -[e]s,-en ray; (*einer Taschenlampe*) beam; (*Wasser-*) jet. **s~en** vi (*haben*) shine; (*funkeln*) sparkle; (*lächeln*) beam. **S~enbehandlung** f radiotherapy. **s~end** a shining; sparkling; beaming; radiant ⟨*Schönheit*⟩. **S~entherapie** f radiotherapy. **S~ung** f - radiation
Strähn|e f -,-n strand. **s~ig** a straggly
stramm a tight, adv -ly; (*kräftig*) sturdy; (*gerade*) upright
Strampel|höschen nt -s,- rompers pl. **s~n** vi (*haben*) ⟨*Baby:*⟩ kick
Strand m -[e]s,"e beach. **s~en** vi (*sein*) run aground; (*fig*) fail. **S~korb** m wicker beach-chair. **S~promenade** f promenade
Strang m -[e]s,"e rope
Strapaz|e f -,-n strain. **s~ieren** vt be hard on; tax ⟨*Nerven, Geduld*⟩. **s~ierfähig** a hard-wearing. **s~iös** a exhausting
Straß m -& -sses paste
Straße f -,-n road; (*in der Stadt auch*) street; (*Meeres-*) strait; **auf der S~** in the road/street. **S~nbahn** f tram, (*Amer*) streetcar. **S~nkarte** f roadmap. **S~nlaterne** f street lamp. **S~nsperre** f road-block
Strat|egie f -,-n strategy. **s~egisch** a strategic, adv -ally
sträuben vt ruffle up ⟨*Federn*⟩; **sich s~** ⟨*Fell, Haar:*⟩ stand on end; (*fig*) resist
Strauch m -[e]s,Sträucher bush
straucheln vi (*sein*) stumble
Strauß¹ m -es, Sträuße bunch [of flowers]; (*Bukett*) bouquet
Strauß² m -es,-e ostrich
Strebe f -,-n brace, strut
streben vi (*haben*) strive (**nach** for) • vi (*sein*) head (**nach/zu** for)
Streb|er m -s,- pushy person; (*Sch*) swot. **s~sam** a industrious
Strecke f -,-n stretch, section; (*Entfernung*) distance; (*Rail*) line; (*Route*) route
strecken vt stretch; (*aus-*) stretch out; (*gerade machen*) straighten; (*Culin*) thin down; **sich s~** stretch; (*sich aus-*) stretch out; **den Kopf aus**

dem Fenster s~ put one's head out of the window
Streich m -[e]s,-e prank, trick; **jdm einen S~ spielen** play a trick on s.o.
streicheln vt stroke
streichen† vt spread; (weg-) smooth; (an-) paint; (aus-) delete; (kürzen) cut ● vi (haben) s~ **über** (+acc) stroke
Streicher m -s,- string-player; **die S~** the strings
Streichholz nt match. **S~schachtel** f matchbox
Streich|instrument nt stringed instrument. **S~käse** m cheese spread. **S~orchester** nt string orchestra. **S~ung** f -,-en deletion; (Kürzung) cut
Streife f -,-n patrol
streifen vt brush against; (berühren) touch; (verletzen) graze; (fig) touch on ⟨Thema⟩; (ziehen) slip (**über** +acc over); **mit dem Blick s~** glance at ● vi (sein) roam
Streifen m -s,- stripe; (Licht-) streak; (auf der Fahrbahn) line; (schmales Stück) strip
Streif|enwagen m patrol car. **s~ig** a streaky. **S~schuß** m glancing shot; (Wunde) graze
Streik m -s,-s strike; **in den S~ treten** go on strike. **S~brecher** m strikebreaker, (pej) scab. **s~en** vi (haben) strike; (fam) refuse; (versagen) pack up. **S~ende(r)** m striker. **S~posten** m picket
Streit m -[e]s,-e quarrel; (Auseinandersetzung) dispute. **s~en†** vr/i (haben) [sich] **s~en** quarrel. **s~ig** a **jdm etw s~ig machen** dispute s.o.'s right to sth. **S~igkeiten** fpl quarrels. **S~kräfte** fpl armed forces. **s~süchtig** a quarrelsome
streng a strict, adv -ly; ⟨Blick, Ton⟩ stern, adv -ly; (rauh, nüchtern) severe, adv -ly; ⟨Geschmack⟩ sharp. **S~e** f - strictness; sternness; severity. **s~genommen** adv strictly speaking. **s~gläubig** a strict; (orthodox) orthodox. **s~stens** adv strictly
Streß m -sses,-sse stress
streßig a (fam) stressful
streuen vt spread; (ver-) scatter; sprinkle ⟨Zucker, Salz⟩; **die Straßen s~** grit the roads
streunen vi (sein) roam; **s~der Hund** stray dog
Strich m -[e]s,-e line; (Feder-, Pinsel-) stroke; (Morse-, Gedanken-) dash;

gegen den S~ the wrong way; (fig) against the grain. **S~kode** m bar code. **S~punkt** m semicolon
Strick m -[e]s,-e cord; (Seil) rope; (fam: Schlingel) rascal
strick|en vt/i (haben) knit. **S~jacke** f cardigan. **S~leiter** f rope-ladder. **S~nadel** f knitting-needle. **S~waren** fpl knitwear sg. **S~zeug** nt knitting
striegeln vt groom
strikt a strict, adv -ly
strittig a contentious
Stroh nt -[e]s straw. **S~blumen** fpl everlasting flowers. **S~dach** nt thatched roof. **s~gedeckt** a thatched. **S~halm** m straw
Strolch m -[e]s,-e (fam) rascal
Strom m -[e]s,-̈e river; (Menschen-, Auto-, Blut-) stream; (Tränen-) flood; (Schwall) torrent; (Electr) current, power; **gegen den S~** (fig) against the tide; **es regnet in Strömen** it is pouring with rain. **s~abwärts** adv downstream. **s~aufwärts** adv upstream
strömen vi (sein) flow; ⟨Menschen, Blut⟩ stream, pour; **s~der Regen** pouring rain
Strom|kreis m circuit. **s~linienförmig** a streamlined. **S~sperre** f power cut
Strömung f -,-en current
Strophe f -,-n verse
strotzen vi (haben) be full (**vor** +dat of); **vor Gesundheit s~d** bursting with health
Strudel m -s,- whirlpool; (SGer Culin) strudel
Struktur f -,-en structure; (Tex) texture
Strumpf m -[e]s,-̈e stocking; (Knie-) sock. **S~band** nt (pl -bänder) suspender, (Amer) garter. **S~bandgürtel** m suspender/(Amer) garter belt. **S~halter** m = **S~band**. **S~hose** f tights pl, (Amer) pantyhose
Strunk m -[e]s,-̈e stalk; (Baum-) stump
struppig a shaggy
Stube f -,-n room. **s~nrein** a house-trained
Stuck m -s stucco
Stück nt -[e]s,-e piece; (Zucker-) lump; (Seife) tablet; (Theater-) play; (Gegenstand) item; (Exemplar) specimen; **20 S~ Vieh** 20 head of cattle; **ein S~** (Entfernung) some way; **aus freien S~en** voluntarily. **S~chen** nt

-s,- [little] bit. **s~weise** adv bit by bit; (einzeln) singly

Student|(in) m -en,-en (f -,-nen) student. **s~isch** a student ...

Studie /-jə/ f -,-n study

studier|en vt/i (haben) study. **S~zimmer** nt study

Studio nt -s,-s studio

Studium nt -s,-ien studies pl

Stufe f -,-n step; (Treppen-) stair; (Raketen-) stage; (Niveau) level. **s~n** vt terrace; (staffeln) grade

Stuhl m -[e]s,ˇe chair; (Med) stools pl. **S~gang** m bowel movement

stülpen vt put (über+acc over)

stumm a dumb; (schweigsam) silent, adv -ly

Stummel m -s,- stump; (Zigaretten-) butt; (Bleistift-) stub

Stümper m -s,- bungler. **s~haft** a incompetent, adv -ly

stumpf a blunt; (Winkel) obtuse; (glanzlos) dull; (fig) apathetic, adv -ally. **S~** m -[e]s,ˇe stump

Stumpfsinn m apathy; (Langweiligkeit) tedium. **s~ig** a apathetic, adv -ally; (langweilig) tedious

Stunde f -,-n hour; (Sch) lesson

stunden vt jdm eine Schuld **s~** give s.o. time to pay a debt

Stunden|kilometer mpl kilometres per hour. **s~lang** adv for hours. **S~lohn** m hourly rate. **S~plan** m timetable. **s~weise** adv by the hour

stündlich a & adv hourly

Stups m -es,-e nudge; (Schubs) push. **s~en** vt nudge; (schubsen) push. **S~nase** f snub nose

stur a pigheaded; (phlegmatisch) stolid, adv -ly; (unbeirrbar) dogged, adv -ly

Sturm m -[e]s,ˇe gale; (schwer) storm; (Mil) assault

stürm|en vi (haben) (Wind:) blow hard; **es s~t** it's blowing a gale ● vi (sein) rush ● vt storm; (bedrängen) besiege. **S~er** m -s,- forward. **s~isch** a stormy; (Überfahrt) rough; (fig) tumultuous, adv -ly; (ungestüm) tempestuous, adv -ly

Sturz m -es,ˇe [heavy] fall; (Preis-, Kurs-) sharp drop; (Pol) overthrow

stürzen vi (sein) fall [heavily]; (in die Tiefe) plunge; (Preise, Kurse:) drop sharply; (Regierung:) fall; (eilen) rush ● vt throw; (umkippen) turn upside down; turn out (Speise, Kuchen); (Pol) overthrow, topple; **sich**

s~ throw oneself (aus/in+acc out of/into); **sich s~ auf** (+acc) pounce on

Sturz|flug m (Aviat) dive. **S~helm** m crash-helmet

Stute f -,-n mare

Stütze f -,-n support; (Kopf-, Arm-) rest

stutzen vi (haben) stop short ● vt trim; (Hort) cut back; (kupieren) crop

stützen vt support; (auf-) rest; **sich s~ auf** (+acc) lean on; (beruhen) be based on

Stutzer m -s,- dandy

stutzig a puzzled; (mißtrauisch) suspicious

Stützpunkt m (Mil) base

Subjekt nt -[e]s,-e subject. **s~iv** a subjective, adv -ly

Subskription /-'tsio:n/ f -,-en subscription

Substantiv nt -s,-e noun

Substanz f -,-en substance

subtil a subtle, adv -tly

subtra|hieren vt subtract. **S~ktion** /-'tsio:n/ f -,-en subtraction

Subvention /-'tsio:n/ f -,-en subsidy. **s~ieren** vt subsidize

subversiv a subversive

Such|e f - search; **auf der S~e nach** looking for. **s~en** vt look for; (intensiv) search for; seek (Hilfe, Rat); 'Zimmer gesucht' 'room wanted' ● vi (haben) look, search (nach for). **S~er** m -s,- (Phot) viewfinder

Sucht f -,ˇe addiction; (fig) mania

süchtig a addicted. **S~e(r)** m/f addict

Süd m -[e]s south. **S~afrika** nt South Africa. **S~amerika** nt South America. **s~deutsch** a South German

Süden m -s south; **nach S~** south

Süd|frucht f tropical fruit. **s~lich** a southern; (Richtung) southerly ● adv & prep (+gen) **s~lich [von] der Stadt** [to the] south of the town. **S~osten** m south-east. **S~pol** m South Pole. **s~wärts** adv southwards. **S~westen** m south-west

süffisant a smug, adv -ly

suggerieren vt suggest (dat to)

Suggest|ion /-'tjo:n/ f -,-en suggestion. **s~iv** a suggestive

Sühne f -,-n atonement; (Strafe) penalty. **s~n** vt atone for

Sultanine f -,-n sultana

Sülze *f* -,-n [meat] jelly; (*Schweins-kopf-*) brawn

Summe *f* -,-n sum

summ|en *vi* (*haben*) hum; ⟨*Biene:*⟩ buzz ● *vt* hum. **S~er** *m* -s,- buzzer

summieren (sich) *vr* add up; (*sich häufen*) increase

Sumpf *m* -[e]s,ͤe marsh, swamp. **s~ig** *a* marshy

Sünd|e *f* -,-n sin. **S~enbock** *m* scapegoat. **S~er(in)** *m* -s,- (*f* -,-nen) sinner. **s~haft** *a* sinful. **s~igen** *vi* (*haben*) sin

super *inv a* (*fam*) great. **S~lativ** *m* -s,-e superlative. **S~markt** *m* supermarket

Suppe *f* -,-n soup. **S~nlöffel** *m* soupspoon. **S~nteller** *m* soup-plate. **S~nwürfel** *m* stock cube

Surf|brett /'sø:ɐ̯f-/ *nt* surfboard. **S~en** *nt* -s surfing

surren *vi* (*haben*) whirr

süß *a* sweet, *adv* -ly. **S~e** *f* - sweetness. **s~en** *vt* sweeten. **S~igkeit** *f* -,-en sweet. **s~lich** *a* sweetish; (*fig*) sugary. **S~speise** *f* sweet. **S~stoff** *m* sweetener. **S~waren** *fpl* confectionery *sg*, sweets *pl*. **S~wasser-** *pref* freshwater . . .

Sylvester *nt* -s = Silvester

Symbol *nt* -s,-e symbol. **S~ik** *f* - symbolism. **s~isch** *a* symbolic, *adv* -ally. **s~isieren** *vt* symbolize

Sym|metrie *f* - symmetry. **s~metrisch** *a* symmetrical, *adv* -ly

Sympathie *f* -,-n sympathy

sympath|isch *a* agreeable; ⟨*Person*⟩ likeable. **s~isieren** *vi* (*haben*) be sympathetic (mit to)

Symphonie *f* -,-n = Sinfonie

Symptom *nt* -s,-e symptom. **s~atisch** *a* symptomatic

Synagoge *f* -,-n synagogue

synchronisieren /zʏnkroni'ziːrən/ *vt* synchronize; dub ⟨*Film*⟩

Syndikat *nt* -[e]s,-e syndicate

Syndrom *nt* -s,-e syndrome

synonym *a* synonymous, *adv* -ly. **S~** *nt* -s,-e synonym

Syntax /'zʏntaks/ *f* - syntax

Synthe|se *f* -,-n synthesis. **S~tik** *nt* -s synthetic material. **s~tisch** *a* synthetic, *adv* -ally

Syrien /-iən/ *nt* -s Syria

System *nt* -s,-e system. **s~atisch** *a* systematic, *adv* -ally

Szene *f* -,-n scene. **S~rie** *f* scenery

T

Tabak *m* -s,-e tobacco

Tabelle *f* -,-n table; (*Sport*) league table

Tablett *nt* -[e]s,-s tray

Tablette *f* -,-n tablet

tabu *a* taboo. **T~** *nt* -s,-s taboo

Tacho *m* -s,-s, **Tachometer** *m* & *nt* speedometer

Tadel *m* -s,- reprimand; (*Kritik*) censure; (*Sch*) black mark. **t~los** *a* impeccable, *adv* -bly. **t~n** *vt* reprimand; censure. **t~nswert** *a* reprehensible

Tafel *f* -,-n (*Tisch, Tabelle*) table; (*Platte*) slab; (*Anschlag-, Hinweis-*) board; (*Gedenk-*) plaque; (*Schiefer-*) slate; (*Wand-*) blackboard; (*Bild-*) plate; (*Schokolade*) bar. **t~n** *vi* (*haben*) feast

Täfelung *f* - panelling

Tag *m* -[e]s,-e day; **Tag für Tag** day by day; **am T~e** in the daytime; **eines T~es** one day; **unter T~e** underground; **es wird Tag** it is getting light; **guten Tag!** good morning/afternoon! **t~aus** *adv* **t~aus, t~ein** day in, day out

Tage|buch *nt* diary. **t~lang** *adv* for days

tagen *vi* (*haben*) meet; ⟨*Gericht:*⟩ sit; **es tagt** day is breaking

Tages|anbruch *m* daybreak. **T~ausflug** *m* day trip. **T~decke** *f* bedspread. **T~karte** *f* day ticket; (*Speise-*) menu of the day. **T~licht** *nt* daylight. **T~mutter** *f* child-minder. **T~ordnung** *f* agenda. **T~rückfahrkarte** *f* day return [ticket]. **T~zeit** *f* time of the day. **T~zeitung** *f* daily [news]paper

täglich *a* & *adv* daily; **zweimal t~** twice a day

tags *adv* by day; **t~ zuvor/darauf** the day before/after

tagsüber *adv* during the day

tag|täglich *a* daily ● *adv* every single day. **T~traum** *m* daydream. **T~undnachtgleiche** *f* -,-n equinox. **T~ung** *f* -,-en meeting; (*Konferenz*) conference

Taill|e /'taljə/ *f* -,-n waist. **t~iert** /ta'jiːɐ̯t/ *a* fitted

Takt *m* -[e]s,-e tact; (*Mus*) bar; (*Tempo*) time; (*Rhythmus*) rhythm; **im T~** in time [to the music]. **T~gefühl** *nt* tact

Takt|ik f - tactics pl. **t~isch** a tactical, adv -ly

takt|los a tactless, adv -ly. **T~losigkeit** f - tactlessness. **T~stock** m baton. **t~voll** a tactful, adv -ly

Tal nt -[e]s,"-er valley

Talar m -s,-e robe; (Univ) gown

Talent nt -[e]s,-e talent. **t~iert** a talented

Talg m -s tallow; (Culin) suet

Talsperre f dam

Tampon /tam'põ:/ m -s,-s tampon

Tang m -s seaweed

Tangente f -,-n tangent; (Straße) bypass

Tank m -s,-s tank. **t~en** vt fill up with ⟨Benzin⟩ ● vi (haben) fill up with petrol; (Aviat) refuel; **ich muß t~en** I need petrol. **T~er** m -s,- tanker. **T~stelle** f petrol/(Amer) gas station. **T~wart** m -[e]s,-e petrol-pump attendant

Tanne f -,-n fir [tree]. **T~nbaum** m fir tree; (Weihnachtsbaum) Christmas tree. **T~nzapfen** m fir cone

Tante f -,-n aunt

Tantiemen /tan'tie:mən/ pl royalties

Tanz m -es,"-e dance. **t~en** vt/i (haben) dance

Tänzer(in) m -s,- (f -,-nen) dancer

Tanz|lokal nt dance-hall. **T~musik** f dance music

Tapete f -,-n wallpaper. **T~nwechsel** m (fam) change of scene

tapezier|en vt paper. **T~er** m -s,- paperhanger, decorator

tapfer a brave, adv -ly. **T~keit** f - bravery

tappen vi (sein) walk hesitantly; (greifen) grope (nach for)

Tarif m -s,-e rate; (Verzeichnis) tariff

tarn|en vt disguise; (Mil) camouflage; **sich t~en** disguise/camouflage oneself. **T~ung** f - disguise; camouflage

Tasche f -,-n bag; (Hosen-, Mantel-) pocket. **T~nbuch** nt paperback. **T~ndieb** m pickpocket. **T~ngeld** nt pocket-money. **T~nlampe** f torch, (Amer) flashlight. **T~nmesser** nt penknife. **T~ntuch** nt handkerchief

Tasse f -,-n cup

Tastatur f -,-en keyboard

tast|bar a palpable. **T~e** f -,-n key; (Druck-) push-button. **t~en** vi (haben) feel, grope (nach for) ● vt key in ⟨Daten⟩; **sich t~en** feel one's way (zu to). **t~end** a tentative, adv -ly

Tat f -,-en action; (Helden-) deed; (Straf-) crime; **in der Tat** indeed; **auf frischer Tat ertappt** caught in the act. **t~enlos** adv passively

Täter(in) m -s,- (f -,-nen) culprit; (Jur) offender

tätig a active, adv -ly; **t~ sein** work. **T~keit** f -,-en activity; (Funktionieren) action; (Arbeit) work, job

Tatkraft f energy

tätlich a physical, adv -ly; **t~ werden** become violent. **T~keiten** fpl violence sg

Tatort m scene of the crime

tätowier|en vt tattoo. **T~ung** f -,-en tattooing; (Bild) tattoo

Tatsache f fact. **T~nbericht** m documentary

tatsächlich a actual, adv -ly

tätscheln vt pat

Tatze f -,-n paw

Tau[1] m -[e]s dew

Tau[2] nt -[e]s,-e rope

taub a deaf; (gefühllos) numb; ⟨Nuß⟩ empty; ⟨Gestein⟩ worthless

Taube f -,-n pigeon; (Turtel- & fig) dove. **T~nschlag** m pigeon-loft

Taub|heit f - deafness; (Gefühllosigkeit) numbness. **t~stumm** a deaf and dumb

tauch|en vt dip, plunge; (unter-) duck ● vi (haben/sein) dive/(ein-) plunge (in + acc into); (auf-) appear (aus out of). **T~er** m -s,- diver. **T~eranzug** m diving-suit. **T~sieder** m -s,- [small, portable] immersion heater

tauen vi (sein) melt, thaw ● impers **es taut** it is thawing

Tauf|becken nt font. **T~e** f -,-n christening, baptism. **t~en** vt christen, baptize. **T~pate** m godfather. **T~stein** m font

tauge|n vi (haben) **etwas/nichts t~n** be good/no good; **zu etw t~n/nicht t~n** be good/no good for sth. **T~nichts** m -es,-e good-for-nothing

tauglich a suitable; (Mil) fit. **T~keit** f - suitability; fitness

Taumel m -s daze; **wie im T~** in a daze. **t~n** vi (sein) stagger

Tausch m -[e]s,-e exchange, (fam) swap. **t~en** vt exchange/(handeln) barter (gegen for); **die Plätze t~en** change places ● vi (haben) swap (mit etw sth; mit jdm with s.o.)

täuschen vt deceive, fool; betray ⟨Vertrauen⟩; **sich t~** delude oneself; (sich irren) be mistaken ● vi (haben) be deceptive. **t~d** a deceptive; ⟨*Ähnlichkeit*⟩ striking

Tausch|geschäft nt exchange. **T~handel** m barter; (*T~geschäft*) exchange

Täuschung f -,-en deception; (*Irrtum*) mistake; (*Illusion*) delusion

tausend inv a one/a thousand. **T~** nt -s,-e thousand. **T~füßler** m -s,- centipede. **t~ste(r,s)** a thousandth. **T~stel** nt -s,- thousandth

Tau|tropfen m dewdrop. **T~wetter** nt thaw. **T~ziehen** nt -s tug of war

Taxe f -,-n charge; (*Kur*-) tax; (*Taxi*) taxi

Taxi nt -s,-s taxi, cab

taxieren vt estimate/(*im Wert*) value (**auf** + acc at); (*fam: mustern*) size up

Taxi|fahrer m taxi driver. **T~stand** m taxi rank

Teakholz /'ti:k-/ nt teak

Team /ti:m/ nt -s,-s team

Techni|k f -,-en technology; (*Methode*) technique. **T~ker** m -s,- technician. **t~sch** a technical, adv -ly; (*technologisch*) technological, adv -ly; **T~sche Hochschule** Technical University

Techno|logie f -,-n technology. **t~logisch** a technological

Teckel m -s,- dachshund

Teddybär m teddy bear

Tee m -s,-s tea. **T~beutel** m tea-bag. **T~kanne** f teapot. **T~kessel** m kettle. **T~löffel** m teaspoon

Teer m -s tar. **t~en** vt tar

Tee|sieb nt tea-strainer. **T~tasse** f teacup. **T~wagen** m [tea] trolley

Teich m -[e]s,-e pond

Teig m -[e]s,-e pastry; (*Knet*-) dough; (*Rühr*-) mixture; (*Pfannkuchen*-) batter. **T~rolle** f, **T~roller** m rolling-pin. **T~waren** fpl pasta sg

Teil m -[e]s,-e part; (*Bestand*-) component; (*Jur*) party; **der vordere T~** the front part; **zum T~** partly; **zum großen/größten T~** for the most part ● m & nt -[e]s (*Anteil*-) share; **sein[en] T~ beitragen** do one's share; **ich für mein[en] T~** for my part ● nt -[e]s,-e part; (*Ersatz*-) spare part; (*Anbau*-) unit

teil|bar a divisible. **T~chen** nt -s,- particle. **t~en** vt divide; (*auf*-) share out; (*gemeinsam haben*) share; (*Pol*) partition ⟨*Land* ⟩; **sich** (*dat*) **etw [mit jdm] t~en** share sth [with s.o.]; **sich t~en** divide; (*sich gabeln*) fork;

⟨*Vorhang:*⟩ open; ⟨*Meinungen:*⟩ differ ● vi (*haben*) share

teilhab|en† vi sep (*haben*) share (**an etw** dat sth). **T~er** m -s,- (*Comm*) partner

Teilnahm|e f - participation; (*innere*) interest; (*Mitgefühl*) sympathy. **t~slos** a apathetic, adv -ally

teilnehm|en† vi sep (*haben*) **t~en an** (+ dat) take part in; (*mitfühlen*) share [in]. **T~er(in)** m -s,- (f -,-nen) participant; (*an Wettbewerb*) competitor

teil|s adv partly. **T~ung** f -,-en division; (*Pol*) partition. **t~weise** a partial ● adv partially, partly; (*manchmal*) in some cases. **T~zahlung** f part-payment; (*Rate*) instalment. **T~zeitbeschäftigung** f part-time job

Teint /tɛ:/ m -s,-s complexion

Telefax nt fax

Telefon nt -s,-e [tele]phone. **T~anruf** m, **T~at** nt -[e]s,-e [tele]phone call. **T~buch** nt [tele]phone book. **t~ieren** vi (*haben*) [tele]phone

telefon|isch a [tele]phone . . . ● adv by [tele]phone. **T~ist(in)** m -en,-en (f -,-nen) telephonist. **T~karte** f phone card. **T~nummer** f [tele]phone number. **T~zelle** f [tele]phone box

Telegraf m -en,-en telegraph. **T~enmast** m telegraph pole. **t~ieren** vi (*haben*) send a telegram. **t~isch** a telegraphic ● adv by telegram

Telegramm nt -s,-e telegram

Telegraph m -en,-en = **Telegraf**

Teleobjektiv nt telephoto lens

Telepathie f - telepathy

Telephon nt -s,-e = **Telefon**

Teleskop nt -s,-e telescope. **t~isch** a telescopic

Telex nt -,-[e] telex. **t~en** vt telex

Teller m -s,- plate

Tempel m -s,- temple

Temperament nt -s,-e temperament; (*Lebhaftigkeit*) vivacity. **t~los** a dull. **t~voll** a vivacious; ⟨*Pferd*⟩ spirited

Temperatur f -,-en temperature

Tempo nt -s,-s speed; (*Mus: pl* -**pi**) tempo; **T~** [**T~**]! hurry up!

Tendenz f -,-en trend; (*Neigung*) tendency. **t~ieren** vi (*haben*) tend (**zu** towards)

Tennis nt - tennis. **T~platz** m tennis-court. **T~schläger** m tennis-racket

Tenor m -s,-̈e (*Mus*) tenor

Teppich m -s,-e carpet. **T~boden** m fitted carpet

Termin m -s,-e date; (*Arzt-*) appointment; **[letzter] T~** deadline. **T~kalender** m [appointments] diary

Terminologie f -,-n terminology

Terpentin nt -s turpentine

Terrain /tɛ'rɛ̃ː/ nt -s,-s terrain

Terrasse f -,-n terrace

Terrier /'tɛrɪɐ/ m -s,- terrier

Terrine f -,-n tureen

Territorium nt -s,-ien territory

Terror m -s terror. **t~isieren** vt terrorize. **T~ismus** m - terrorism. **T~ist** m -en,-en terrorist

Terzett nt -[e]s,-e [vocal] trio

Tesafilm (P) m ≈ Sellotape (P)

Test m -[e]s,-s & -e test

Testament nt -[e]s,-e will; **Altes/ Neues T~** Old/New Testament. **T~svollstrecker** m -s,- executor

testen vt test

Tetanus m - tetanus

teuer a expensive, adv -ly; (*lieb*) dear; **wie t~?** how much? **T~ung** f -,-en rise in prices

Teufel m -s,- devil; **zum T~!** (*sl*) damn [it]! **T~skreis** m vicious circle

teuflisch a fiendish

Text m -[e]s,-e text; (*Passage*) passage; (*Bild-*) caption; (*Lied-*) lyrics pl, words pl; (*Opern-*) libretto. **T~er** m -s,- copy-writer; (*Schlager-*) lyricist

Textil|ien /-jən/ pl textiles; (*Textilwaren*) textile goods. **T~industrie** f textile industry

Textverarbeitungssystem nt word processor

TH abbr = **Technische Hochschule**

Theater nt -s,- theatre; (*fam: Getue*) fuss, to-do; **T~ spielen** act; (*fam*) put on an act. **T~kasse** f box-office. **T~stück** nt play

theatralisch a theatrical, adv -ly

Theke f -,-n bar; (*Ladentisch*) counter

Thema nt -s,-men subject; (*Mus*) theme

Themse f - Thames

Theolo|ge m -n,-n theologian. **T~gie** f - theology

theor|etisch a theoretical, adv -ly. **T~ie** f -,-n theory

Therapeut|(in) m -en,-en (f -,-nen) therapist. **t~isch** a therapeutic

Therapie f -,-n therapy

Thermal|bad nt thermal bath; (*Ort*) thermal spa. **T~quelle** f thermal spring

Thermometer nt -s,- thermometer

Thermosflasche (P) f Thermos flask (P)

Thermostat m -[e]s,-e thermostat

These f -,-n thesis

Thrombose f -,-n thrombosis

Thron m -[e]s,-e throne. **t~en** vi (*haben*) sit [in state]. **T~folge** f succession. **T~folger** m -s,- heir to the throne

Thunfisch m tuna

Thymian m -s thyme

Tick m -s,-s (*fam*) quirk; **einen T~ haben** be crazy

ticken vi (*haben*) tick

tief a deep; (*t~liegend, niedrig*) low; (*t~gründig*) profound; **t~er Teller** soup-plate; **im t~sten Winter** in the depths of winter ● adv deep; low; (*sehr*) deeply, profoundly; (*schlafen*) soundly. **T~** nt -s,-s (*Meteorol*) depression. **T~bau** m civil engineering. **T~e** f -,-n depth

Tief|ebene f [lowland] plain. **T~garage** f underground car-park. **t~gekühlt** a [deep-]frozen. **t~greifend** a radical, adv -ly. **t~gründig** a (*fig*) profound

Tiefkühl|fach nt freezer compartment. **T~kost** f frozen food. **T~truhe** f deep-freeze

Tief|land nt lowlands pl. **T~punkt** m (*fig*) low. **t~schürfend** a (*fig*) profound. **t~sinnig** a (*fig*) profound; (*trübsinnig*) melancholy. **T~stand** m (*fig*) low

Tiefsttemperatur f minimum temperature

Tier nt -[e]s,-e animal. **T~arzt** m, **T~ärztin** f vet, veterinary surgeon. **T~garten** m zoo. **t~isch** a animal ...; (*fig: roh*) bestial. **T~kreis** m zodiac. **T~kreiszeichen** nt sign of the zodiac. **T~kunde** f zoology. **T~quälerei** f cruelty to animals

Tiger m -s,- tiger

tilgen vt pay off (*Schuld*); (*streichen*) delete; (*fig: auslöschen*) wipe out

Tinte f -,-n ink. **T~nfisch** m squid

Tip m -s,-s (*fam*) tip

tipp|en vt (*fam*) type ● vi (*haben*) (*berühren*) touch (**auf/an etw** acc sth); (*fam: maschineschreiben*) type; **t~en auf** (+ acc) (*fam: wetten*) bet on. **T~fehler** m (*fam*) typing error. **T~schein** m pools/lottery coupon

tipptopp a (*fam*) immaculate, adv -ly

Tirol nt -s [the] Tyrol

Tisch m -[e]s,-e table; (*Schreib-*) desk; **nach T~** after the meal. **T~decke** f table-cloth. **T~gebet** nt grace. **T~ler** m -s,- joiner; (*Möbel-*) cabinet-maker. **T~rede** f after-dinner speech. **T~tennis** nt table tennis. **T~tuch** nt table-cloth

Titel m -s,- title. **T~rolle** f title-role

Toast /to:st/ m -[e]s,-e toast; (*Scheibe*) piece of toast; **einen T~ ausbringen** propose a toast (**auf** + *acc* to). **T~er** m -s,- toaster

tob|en vi (*haben*) rave; (*Sturm:*) rage; (*Kinder:*) play boisterously ● vi (*sein*) rush. **t~süchtig** a raving mad

Tochter f -, - daughter. **T~gesellschaft** f subsidiary

Tod m -es death. **t~ernst** a deadly serious, adv -ly

Todes|angst f mortal fear. **T~anzeige** f death announcement; (*Zeitungs-*) obituary. **T~fall** m death. **T~opfer** nt fatality, casualty. **T~strafe** f death penalty. **T~urteil** nt death sentence

Tod|feind m mortal enemy. **t~krank** a dangerously ill

tödlich a fatal, adv -ly; (*Gefahr*) mortal, adv -ly; (*groß*) deadly; **t~ gelangweilt** bored to death

tod|müde a dead tired. **t~sicher** a (*fam*) dead certain ● adv for sure. **T~sünde** f deadly sin. **t~unglücklich** a desperately unhappy

Toilette /toa'lɛtə/ f -,-n toilet. **T~napier** nt toilet paper

toler|ant a tolerant. **T~anz** f - tolerance. **t~ieren** vt tolerate

toll a crazy, mad; (*fam: prima*) fantastic; (*schlimm*) awful ● adv beautifully; (*sehr*) very; (*schlimm*) badly. **t~en** vi (*haben/sein*) romp. **t~kühn** a foolhardy. **T~wut** f rabies. **t~wütig** a rabid

tolpatschig a clumsy, adv -ily

Tölpel m -s,- fool

Tomate f -,-n tomato. **T~nmark** nt tomato purée

Tombola f -,-s raffle

Ton¹ m -[e]s clay

Ton² m -[e]s,-e tone; (*Klang*) sound; (*Note*) note; (*Betonung*) stress; (*Farb-*) shade; **der gute Ton** (*fig*) good form. **T~abnehmer** m -s,- pick-up. **t~angebend** a (*fig*) leading. **T~art** f tone [of voice]; (*Mus*) key. **T~band** nt (pl **-bänder**) tape. **T~bandgerät** nt tape recorder

tönen vi (*haben*) sound ● vt tint

Ton|fall m tone [of voice]; (*Akzent*) intonation. **T~leiter** f scale. **t~los** a toneless, adv -ly

Tonne f -,-n barrel, cask; (*Müll-*) bin; (*Maß*) tonne, metric ton

Topf m -[e]s, -̈e pot; (*Koch-*) pan

Topfen m -s (*Aust*) ≈ curd cheese

Töpfer|(in) m -s,- (f -,-nen) potter. **T~ei** f -,-en pottery

Töpferwaren fpl pottery sg

Topf|lappen m oven-cloth. **T~pflanze** f potted plant

Tor¹ m -en,-en fool

Tor² nt -[e]s,-e gate; (*Einfahrt*) gateway; (*Sport*) goal. **T~bogen** m archway

Torf m -s peat

Torheit f -,-en folly

Torhüter m -s,- goalkeeper

töricht a foolish, adv -ly

torkeln vi (*sein/haben*) stagger

Tornister m -s,- knapsack; (*Sch*) satchel

torp|edieren vt torpedo. **T~edo** m -s,-s torpedo

Torpfosten m goal-post

Torte f -,-n gâteau; (*Obst-*) flan

Tortur f -,-en torture

Torwart m -s,-e goalkeeper

tosen vi (*haben*) roar; (*Sturm:*) rage

tot a dead; **einen t~en Punkt haben** (*fig*) be at a low ebb

total a total, adv -ly. **t~itär** a totalitarian. **T~schaden** m ≈ write-off

Tote|(r) m/f dead man/woman; (*Todesopfer*) fatality; **die T~n** the dead pl

töten vt kill

toten|blaß a deathly pale. **T~gräber** m -s,- grave-digger. **T~kopf** m skull. **T~schein** m death certificate. **T~stille** f deathly silence

tot|fahren† vt sep run over and kill. **t~geboren** a stillborn. **t~lachen (sich)** vr sep (*fam*) be in stitches

Toto nt & m -s football pools pl. **T~schein** m pools coupon

tot|schießen† vt sep shoot dead. **T~schlag** m (*Jur*) manslaughter. **t~schlagen†** vt sep kill. **t~schweigen†** vt sep (*fig*) hush up. **t~stellen (sich)** vr sep pretend to be dead

Tötung f -,-en killing; **fahrlässige T~** (*Jur*) manslaughter

Toupet /tu'pe:/ nt -s,-s toupee. **t~ieren** vt back-comb

Tour /tu:ɐ/ f -,-en tour; (*Ausflug*) trip; (*Auto-*) drive; (*Rad-*) ride; (*Strecke*)

distance; (*Techn*) revolution; (*fam: Weise*) way; **auf vollen T~en** at full speed; (*fam*) flat out

Touris|mus /tuˈrɪsmʊs/ *m* - tourism. **T~t** *m* -en,-en tourist

Tournee /tʊrˈneː/ *f* -,-n tour

Trab *m* -[e]s trot

Trabant *m* -en,-en satellite

traben *vi* (*haben/sein*) trot

Tracht *f* -,-en [national] costume; **eine T~ Prügel** a good hiding

trachten *vi* (*haben*) strive (**nach** for); **jdm nach dem Leben t~** be out to kill s.o.

trächtig *a* pregnant

Tradition /-ˈtsi̯oːn/ *f* -,-en tradition. **t~ell** *a* traditional, *adv* -ly

Trafik *f* -,-en (*Aust*) tobacconist's

Trag|bahre *f* stretcher. **t~bar** *a* portable; ⟨*Kleidung*⟩ wearable; (*erträglich*) bearable

träge *a* sluggish, *adv* -ly; (*faul*) lazy, *adv* -ily; (*Phys*) inert

tragen† *vt* carry; (*an-/aufhaben*) wear; (*fig*) bear ● *vi* (*haben*) carry; **gut t~** ⟨*Baum:*⟩ produce a good crop; **schwer t~** carry a heavy load; (*fig*) be deeply affected (**an** + *dat* by). **t~d** *a* (*Techn*) load-bearing; (*trächtig*) pregnant

Träger *m* -s,- porter; (*Inhaber*) bearer; (*eines Ordens*) holder; (*Bau-*) beam; (*Stahl-*) girder; (*Achsel-*) [shoulder] strap. **T~kleid** *nt* pinafore dress

Trag|etasche *f* carrier bag. **T~fläche** *f* (*Aviat*) wing; (*Naut*) hydrofoil. **T~flächenboot, T~flügelboot** *nt* hydrofoil

Trägheit *f* - sluggishness; (*Faulheit*) laziness; (*Phys*) inertia

Trag|ik *f* - tragedy. **t~isch** *a* tragic, *adv* -ally

Tragödie /-i̯ə/ *f* -,-n tragedy

Tragweite *f* range; (*fig*) consequence

Train|er /ˈtrɛːnɐ/ *m* -s,- trainer; (*Tennis-*) coach. **t~ieren** *vt/i* (*haben*) train

Training /ˈtrɛːnɪŋ/ *nt* -s training. **T~sanzug** *m* tracksuit. **T~sschuhe** *mpl* trainers

Trakt *m* -[e]s,-e section; (*Flügel*) wing

traktieren *vi* (*haben*) **mit Schlägen/ Tritten t~** hit/kick

Traktor *m* -s,-en /-ˈtoːrən/ tractor

trampeln *vi* (*haben*) stamp one's feet ● *vi* (*sein*) trample (**auf** + *acc* on) ● *vt* trample

trampen /ˈtrɛmpən/ *vi* (*sein*) (*fam*) hitch-hike

Trance /ˈtrãːsə/ *f* -,-n trance

Tranchier|messer /trãˈʃiːɐ̯-/ *nt* carving-knife. **t~en** *vt* carve

Träne *f* -,-n tear. **t~n** *vi* (*haben*) water. **T~ngas** *nt* tear-gas

Tränke *f* -,-n watering-place; (*Trog*) drinking-trough. **t~n** *vt* water ⟨*Pferd*⟩; (*nässen*) soak (**mit** with)

Trans|aktion *f* transaction. **T~fer** *m* -s,-s transfer. **T~formator** *m* -s,-en /-ˈtoːrən/ transformer. **T~fusion** *f* -,-en [blood] transfusion

Transistor *m* -,-en /-ˈtoːrən/ transistor

Transit /tranˈziːt/ *m* -s transit

transitiv *a* transitive, *adv* -ly

transparent *nt* -[e]s,-e banner; (*Bild*) transparency

transpirieren *vi* (*haben*) perspire

Transplantation /-ˈtsi̯oːn/ *f* -,-en transplant

Transport *m* -[e]s,-e transport; (*Güter-*) consignment. **T~ieren** *vt* transport. **T~mittel** *nt* means of transport

Trapez *nt* -es,-e trapeze; (*Geom*) trapezium

Tratsch *m* -[e]s (*fam*) gossip. **t~en** *vi* (*haben*) gossip

Tratte *f* -,-n (*Comm*) draft

Traube *f* -,-n bunch of grapes; (*Beere*) grape; (*fig*) cluster. **T~nzucker** *m* glucose

trauen *vi* (*haben*) (+ *dat*) trust; **ich traute kaum meinen Augen** I could hardly believe my eyes ● *vt* marry; **sich t~** dare (**etw zu tun** [to] do sth); venture (**in** + *acc*/**aus** into/out of)

Trauer *f* - mourning; (*Schmerz*) grief (**um** for); **T~ tragen** be [dressed] in mourning. **T~fall** *m* bereavement. **T~feier** *f* funeral service. **T~marsch** *m* funeral march. **t~n** *vi* (*haben*) grieve; **t~n um** mourn [for]. **T~spiel** *nt* tragedy. **T~weide** *f* weeping willow

traulich *a* cosy, *adv* -ily

Traum *m* -[e]s,Träume dream

Trau|ma *nt* -s,-men trauma. **t~matisch** *a* traumatic

träumen *vt/i* (*haben*) dream

traumhaft *a* dreamlike; (*schön*) fabulous, *adv* -ly

traurig *a* sad, *adv* -ly; (*erbärmlich*) sorry. **T~keit** *f* - sadness

Trau|ring *m* wedding-ring. **T~schein** *m* marriage certificate. **T~ung** *f* -,-en wedding [ceremony]

Treck m -s,-s trek

Trecker m -s,- tractor

Treff nt -s,-s ⟨Karten⟩ spades pl

treff|en† vt hit; ⟨Blitz:⟩ strike; ⟨fig: verletzen⟩ hurt; ⟨zusammenkommen mit⟩ meet; take ⟨Maßnahme⟩; **sich t~en** meet (**mit jdm** s.o.); **sich gut t~en** be convenient; **es traf sich, daß** it so happened that; **es gut/schlecht t~en** be lucky/unlucky ● vi ⟨haben⟩ hit the target; **t~en auf** (+acc) meet; ⟨fig⟩ meet with. **T~en** nt -s,- meeting. **t~end** a apt, adv -ly; ⟨Ähnlichkeit⟩ striking. **T~er** m -s,- hit; ⟨Los⟩ winner. **T~punkt** m meeting-place

treiben† vt drive; ⟨sich befassen mit⟩ do; carry on ⟨Gewerbe⟩; indulge in ⟨Luxus⟩; get up to ⟨Unfug⟩; **Handel t~** trade; **Blüten/Blätter t~** come into flower/leaf; **zur Eile t~** hurry [up]; **was treibt ihr da?** ⟨fam⟩ what are you up to? ● vi ⟨sein⟩ drift; ⟨schwimmen⟩ float ● vi ⟨haben⟩ ⟨Bot⟩ sprout. **T~** nt -s activity; ⟨Getriebe⟩ bustle

Treib|haus nt hothouse. **T~hauseffekt** m greenhouse effect. **T~holz** nt driftwood. **T~riemen** m transmission belt. **T~sand** m quicksand. **T~stoff** m fuel

Trend m -s,-s trend

trenn|bar a separable. **t~en** vt separate/⟨abmachen⟩ detach (**von** from); divide, split ⟨Wort⟩; **sich t~en** separate; ⟨auseinandergehen⟩ part; **sich t~en von** leave; ⟨fortgeben⟩ part with. **T~ung** f -,-en separation; ⟨Silben-⟩ division. **T~ungsstrich** m hyphen. **T~wand** f partition

trepp|ab adv downstairs. **t~auf** adv upstairs

Treppe f -,-n stairs pl; ⟨Außen-⟩ steps pl; **eine T~** a flight of stairs/steps. **T~nflur** m landing. **T~ngeländer** nt banisters pl. **T~nhaus** nt stairwell. **T~nstufe** f stair, step

Tresor m -s,-e safe

Tresse f -,-n braid

Treteimer m pedal bin

treten† vi ⟨sein/haben⟩ step; ⟨versehentlich⟩ tread; ⟨ausschlagen⟩ kick (**nach** at); **in Verbindung t~** get in touch ● vt tread; ⟨mit Füßen⟩ kick

treu a faithful, adv -ly; ⟨fest⟩ loyal, adv -ly. **T~e** f - faithfulness; loyalty; ⟨eheliche⟩ fidelity. **T~händer** m -s,- trustee. **t~herzig** a trusting, adv -ly;

⟨arglos⟩ innocent, adv -ly. **t~los** a disloyal, adv -ly; ⟨untreu⟩ unfaithful

Tribüne f -,-n platform; ⟨Zuschauer-⟩ stand

Tribut m -[e]s,-e tribute; ⟨Opfer⟩ toll

Trichter m -s,- funnel; ⟨Bomben-⟩ crater

Trick m -s,-s trick. **T~film** m cartoon. **t~reich** a clever

Trieb m -[e]s,-e drive, urge; ⟨Instinkt⟩ instinct; ⟨Bot⟩ shoot. **T~täter, T~verbrecher** m sex offender. **T~werk** nt ⟨Aviat⟩ engine; ⟨Uhr-⟩ mechanism

trief|en† vi ⟨haben⟩ drip; ⟨naß sein⟩ be dripping (**von/vor** +dat with). **t~naß** a dripping wet

triftig a valid

Trigonometrie f - trigonometry

Trikot /tri'ko:/ m -s ⟨Tex⟩ jersey

Trikot nt -s,-s ⟨Sport⟩ jersey; ⟨Fußball-⟩ shirt

Trimester nt -s,- term

Trimm-dich nt -s keep-fit

trimmen vt trim; ⟨fam⟩ train; tune ⟨Motor⟩; **sich t~** keep fit

trink|bar a drinkable. **t~en†** vt/i ⟨haben⟩ drink. **T~er(in)** m -s,- ⟨f -,-nen⟩ alcoholic. **T~geld** nt tip. **T~halm** m [drinking-]straw. **T~spruch** m toast. **T~wasser** nt drinking-water

Trio nt -s,-s trio

trippeln vi ⟨sein⟩ trip along

trist a dreary

Tritt m -[e]s,-e step; ⟨Fuß-⟩ kick. **T~brett** nt step. **T~leiter** f step-ladder

Triumph m -s,-e triumph. **t~ieren** vi ⟨haben⟩ rejoice; **t~ieren über** (+acc) triumph over. **t~ierend** a triumphant, adv -ly

trocken a dry, adv drily. **T~haube** f drier. **T~heit** f -,-en dryness; ⟨Dürre⟩ drought. **t~legen** vt sep change ⟨Baby⟩; drain ⟨Sumpf⟩. **T~milch** f powdered milk

trockn|en vt/i ⟨sein⟩ dry. **T~er** m -s,- drier

Troddel f -,-n tassel

Trödel m -s ⟨fam⟩ junk. **T~laden** m ⟨fam⟩ junk-shop. **T~markt** m ⟨fam⟩ flea market. **t~n** vi ⟨haben⟩ dawdle

Trödler m -s,- ⟨fam⟩ slowcoach; ⟨Händler⟩ junk-dealer

Trog m -[e]s,-e trough

Trommel f -,-n drum. **T~fell** nt eardrum. **t~n** vi ⟨haben⟩ drum

Trommler m -s,- drummer

Trompete *f* -,-n trumpet. **T~r** *m* -s,- trumpeter

Tropen *pl* tropics

Tropf *m* -[e]s,-e (*Med*) drip

tröpfeln *vt/i* (*sein/haben*) drip; **es tröpfelt** it's spitting with rain

tropfen *vt/i* (*sein/haben*) drip. **T~** *m* -s,- drop; (*fallend*) drip. **t~weise** *adv* drop by drop

tropf|naß *a* dripping wet. **T~stein** *m* stalagmite; (*hängend*) stalactite

Trophäe /troˈfɛːə/ *f* -,-n trophy

tropisch *a* tropical

Trost *m* -[e]s consolation, comfort

tröst|en *vt* console, comfort; **sich t~en** console oneself. **t~lich** *a* comforting

trost|los *a* desolate; (*elend*) wretched; (*reizlos*) dreary. **T~preis** *m* consolation prize. **t~reich** *a* comforting

Trott *m* -s amble; (*fig*) routine

Trottel *m* -s,- (*fam*) idiot

trotten *vi* (*sein*) traipse; ⟨*Tier:*⟩ amble

Trottoir /trɔˈtoaːɐ̯/ *nt* -s,-s pavement, (*Amer*) sidewalk

trotz *prep* (+ *gen*) despite, in spite of. **T~** *m* -es defiance. **t~dem** *adv* nevertheless. **t~en** *vi* (*haben*) (+ *dat*) defy. **t~ig** *a* defiant, *adv* -ly; ⟨*Kind*⟩ stubborn

trübe *a* dull; ⟨*Licht*⟩ dim; ⟨*Flüssigkeit*⟩ cloudy; (*fig*) gloomy

Trubel *m* -s bustle

trüben *vt* dull; make cloudy ⟨*Flüssigkeit*⟩; (*fig*) spoil; strain ⟨*Verhältnis*⟩; **sich t~** ⟨*Flüssigkeit:*⟩ become cloudy; ⟨*Himmel:*⟩ cloud over; ⟨*Augen:*⟩ dim; ⟨*Verhältnis, Erinnerung:*⟩ deteriorate

Trüb|sal *f* - misery; **T~sal blasen** (*fam*) mope. **t~selig** *a* miserable; (*trübe*) gloomy, *adv* -ily. **T~sinn** *m* melancholy. **t~sinnig** *a* melancholy

Trugbild *nt* illusion

trüg|en† *vt* deceive ● *vi* (*haben*) be deceptive. **t~erisch** *a* false; (*täuschend*) deceptive

Trugschluß *m* fallacy

Truhe *f* -,-n chest

Trümmer *pl* rubble *sg*; (*T~teile*) wreckage *sg*; (*fig*) ruins. **T~haufen** *m* pile of rubble

Trumpf *m* -[e]s,-̈e trump [card]; **T~ sein** be trumps. **t~en** *vi* (*haben*) play trumps

Trunk *m* -[e]s drink. **T~enbold** *m* -[e]s,-e drunkard. **T~enheit** *f* - drunkenness; **T~enheit am Steuer** drunken driving. **T~sucht** *f* alcoholism

Trupp *m* -s,-s group; (*Mil*) squad. **T~e** *f* -,-n (*Mil*) unit; (*Theat*) troupe; **T~en** troops

Truthahn *m* turkey

Tschech|e *m* -n,-n, **T~in** *f* -,-nen Czech. **t~isch** *a* Czech. **T~oslowakei (die)** - Czechoslovakia

tschüs *int* bye, cheerio

Tuba *f* -,-ben (*Mus*) tuba

Tube *f* -,-n tube

Tuberkulose *f* - tuberculosis

Tuch¹ *nt* -[e]s,-̈er cloth; (*Hals-, Kopf-*) scarf; (*Schulter-*) shawl

Tuch² *nt* -[e]s,-e (*Stoff*) cloth

tüchtig *a* competent; (*reichlich, beträchtlich*) good; (*groß*) big ● *adv* competently; (*ausreichend*) well; ⟨*regnen, schneien*⟩ hard. **T~keit** *f* - competence

Tück|e *f* -,-n malice; **T~en haben** be temperamental; (*gefährlich sein*) be treacherous. **t~isch** *a* malicious, *adv* -ly; (*gefährlich*) treacherous

tüfteln *vi* (*haben*) (*fam*) fiddle (**an** + *dat* with); (*geistig*) puzzle (**an** + *dat* over)

Tugend *f* -,-en virtue. **t~haft** *a* virtuous

Tülle *f* -,-n spout

Tulpe *f* -,-n tulip

tummeln (sich) *vr* romp [about]; (*sich beeilen*) hurry [up]

Tümmler *m* -s,- porpoise

Tumor *m* -s,-en /-ˈmoːrən/ tumour

Tümpel *m* -s,- pond

Tumult *m* -[e]s,-e commotion; (*Aufruhr*) riot

tun† *vt* do; take ⟨*Schritt, Blick*⟩; work ⟨*Wunder*⟩; (*bringen*) put (**in** + *acc* into); **sich tun** happen; **jdm etwas tun** hurt s.o.; **viel zu tun haben** have a lot to do; **das tut man nicht** it isn't done; **das tut nichts** it doesn't matter ● *vi* (*haben*) act (**als ob** as if); **überrascht tun** pretend to be surprised; **er tut nur so** he's just pretending; **zu tun haben** have things/work to do; [**es**] **zu tun haben mit** have to deal with; [**es**] **mit dem Herzen zu tun haben** have heart trouble. **Tun** *nt* -s actions *pl*

Tünche *f* -,-n whitewash; (*fig*) veneer. **t~n** *vt* whitewash

Tunesien /-ịən/ *nt* -s Tunisia

Tunke *f* -,-n sauce. **t~n** *vt/i* (*haben*) (*fam*) dip (**in** + *acc* into)

Tunnel *m* -s,- tunnel

tupf|en *vt* dab ● *vi* (*haben*) **t∼en an/ auf** (+ *acc*) touch. **T∼en** *m* -s,- spot. **T∼er** *m* -s,- spot; (*Med*) swab

Tür *f* -,-en door

Turban *m* -s,-e turban

Turbine *f* -,-n turbine

turbulen|t *a* turbulent. **T∼z** *f* -,-en turbulence

Türk|e *m* -n,-n Turk. **T∼ei** (**die**) - Turkey. **T∼in** *f* -,-nen Turk

türkis *inv a* turquoise. **T∼** *m* -es,-e turquoise

türkisch *a* Turkish

Turm *m* -[e]s,⸚e tower; (*Schach*) rook, castle

Türm|chen *nt* -s,- turret. **t∼en** *vt* tile [up]; **sich t∼en** pile up ● *vi* (*sein*) (*fam*) escape

Turmspitze *f* spire

turn|en *vi* (*haben*) do gymnastics. **T∼en** *nt* -s gymnastics *sg*; (*Sch*) physical education, (*fam*) gym. **T∼er(in)** *m* -s,- (*f* -,-nen) gymnast. **T∼halle** *f* gymnasium

Turnier *nt* -s,-e tournament; (*Reit-*) show

Turnschuhe *mpl* gym shoes

Türschwelle *f* doorstep, threshold

Tusch *m* -[e]s,-e fanfare

Tusche *f* -,-n [drawing] ink; (*Wasser-farbe*) watercolour

tuscheln *vt/i* (*haben*) whisper

Tüte *f* -,-n bag; (*Comm*) packet; (*Eis-*) cornet; **in die T∼ blasen** (*fam*) be breathalysed

tuten *vi* (*haben*) hoot; ⟨*Schiff:*⟩ sound its hooter; ⟨*Sirene:*⟩ sound

TÜV *m* - ≈ MOT [test]

Typ *m* -s,-en type; (*fam: Kerl*) bloke. **T∼e** *f* -,-n type; (*fam: Person*) character

Typhus *m* - typhoid

typisch *a* typical, *adv* -ly (**für** of)

Typographie *f* - typography

Typus *m* -,**Typen** type

Tyrann *m* -en,-en tyrant. **T∼ei** *f* - tyranny. **t∼isch** *a* tyrannical. **t∼i-sieren** *vt* tyrannize

U

u.a. *abbr* (**unter anderem**) amongst other things

U-Bahn *f* underground, (*Amer*) subway

übel *a* bad; (*häßlich*) nasty, *adv* -ily; **mir ist/wird ü∼** I feel sick. **Ü∼** *nt* -s,-

evil. **Ü∼keit** *f* - nausea. **ü∼neh-men†** *vt sep* take amiss; **jdm etw ü∼nehmen** hold sth against s.o. **Ü∼täter** *m* culprit

üben *vt/i* (*haben*) practise; **sich in etw** (*dat*) **ü∼** practise sth

über *prep* (+ *dat/acc*) over; (*höher als*) above; (*betreffend*) about; ⟨*Buch, Vortrag*⟩ on; ⟨*Scheck, Rech-nung*⟩ for; (*quer ü∼*) across; **ü∼ Köln fahren** go via Cologne; **ü∼ Ostern** over Easter; **die Woche ü∼** dur-ing the week; **heute ü∼ eine Woche** a week today; **Fehler ü∼ Fehler** mis-take after mistake ● *adv* **ü∼** all over; **jdm ü∼ sein** be better/ (*stärker*) stronger than s.o. ● *a* (*fam*) **ü∼ sein** be left over; **etw ü∼ sein** be fed up with sth

überall *adv* everywhere

überanstrengen *vt insep* overtax; strain ⟨*Augen*⟩; **sich ü∼** overexert oneself

überarbeit|en *vt insep* revise; **sich ü∼en** overwork. **Ü∼ung** *f* - re-vision; overwork

überaus *adv* extremely

überbewerten *vt insep* overrate

überbieten† *vt insep* outbid; (*fig*) outdo; (*übertreffen*) surpass

Überblick *m* overall view; (*Abriß*) summary

überblicken *vt insep* overlook; (*ab-schätzen*) assess

überbringen† *vt insep* deliver

überbrücken *vt insep* (*fig*) bridge

überdauern *vt insep* survive

überdenken† *vt insep* think over

überdies *adv* moreover

überdimensional *a* oversized

Überdosis *f* overdose

Überdruß *m* -sses surfeit; **bis zum Ü∼** ad nauseam

überdrüssig *a* **ü∼ sein/werden** be/grow tired (*gen* of)

übereignen *vt insep* transfer

übereilt *a* over-hasty, *adv* -ily

übereinander *adv* one on top of/ above the other; ⟨*sprechen*⟩ about each other. **ü∼schlagen†** *vt sep* cross ⟨*Beine*⟩; fold ⟨*Arme*⟩

überein|kommen† *vi sep* (*sein*) agree. **Ü∼kunft** *f* - agreement. **ü∼stimmen** *vi sep* (*haben*) agree; ⟨*Zah-len:*⟩ tally; ⟨*Ansichten:*⟩ coincide; ⟨*Farben:*⟩ match. **Ü∼stimmung** *f* agreement

überempfindlich *a* over-sensitive; (*Med*) hypersensitive

überfahren† *vt insep* run over
Überfahrt *f* crossing
Überfall *m* attack; (*Bank-*) raid
überfallen† *vt insep* attack; raid
⟨*Bank*⟩; (*bestürmen*) bombard (*mit*
with); (*überkommen*) come over;
(*fam: besuchen*) surprise
überfällig *a* overdue
überfliegen† *vt insep* fly over;
(*lesen*) skim over
überflügeln *vt insep* outstrip
Überfluß *m* abundance; (*Wohlstand*)
affluence
überflüssig *a* superfluous
überfluten *vt insep* flood
überfordern *vt insep* overtax
überführ|en *vt insep* transfer; (*Jur*)
convict (*gen* of). **Ü~ung** *f* transfer;
(*Straße*) flyover; (*Fußgänger-*)
foot-bridge
überfüllt *a* overcrowded
Übergabe *f* (*s.* **übergeben**) handing
over; transfer
Übergang *m* crossing; (*Wechsel*)
transition. **Ü~sstadium** *nt* trans-
itional stage
übergeben† *vt insep* hand over;
(*übereignen*) transfer; **sich ü~** be
sick
übergehen¹† *vi sep* (*sein*) pass over
(**an**+*acc* to); (*überwechseln*) go over
(**zu** to); (*werden zu*) turn (**in**+*acc*
into); **zum Angriff ü~** start the
attack
übergehen²† *vt insep* (*fig*) pass over;
(*nicht beachten*) ignore; (*auslassen*)
leave out
Übergewicht *nt* excess weight; (*fig*)
predominance; **Ü~ haben** be
overweight
übergießen† *vt insep* **mit Wasser ü~**
pour water over
überglücklich *a* overjoyed
über|greifen† *vi sep* (*haben*) spread
(**auf**+*acc* to). **Ü~griff** *m* infringement
über|groß *a* outsize; (*übertrieben*)
exaggerated. **Ü~größe** *f* outsize
überhaben† *vt sep* have on; (*fam:*
satthaben) be fed up with
überhandnehmen† *vi sep* (*haben*)
increase alarmingly
überhängen *v sep* ● *vi†* (*haben*)
overhang ● *vt* (*reg*) **sich** (*dat*) **etw**
ü~ sling over one's shoulder ⟨*Ge-*
wehr⟩; put round one's shoulders
⟨*Jacke*⟩
überhäufen *vt insep* inundate (**mit**
with)

überhaupt *adv* (*im allgemeinen*) altogether; (*eigentlich*) anyway; (*über-*
dies) besides; **ü~ nicht/ nichts** not/
nothing at all
überheblich *a* arrogant, *adv* -ly.
Ü~keit *f* - arrogance
überhol|en *vt insep* overtake; (*repa-*
rieren) overhaul. **ü~t** *a* outdated.
Ü~ung *f* -,-en overhaul. **Ü~verbot**
nt **'Ü~verbot'** 'no overtaking'
überhören *vt insep* fail to hear;
(*nicht beachten*) ignore
überirdisch *a* supernatural
überkochen *vi sep* (*sein*) boil over
überladen† *vt insep* overload ● *a*
over-ornate
überlassen† *vt insep* **jdm etw ü~**
leave sth to s.o.; (*geben*) let s.o. have
sth; **sich seinem Schmerz ü~** abandon oneself to one's grief; **sich** (*dat*)
selbst ü~ sein be left to one's own
devices
überlasten *vt insep* overload; overtax ⟨*Person*⟩
Überlauf *m* overflow
überlaufen¹† *vi sep* (*sein*) overflow;
(*Mil, Pol*) defect
überlaufen²† *vt insep* **jdn ü~**
⟨*Gefühl:*⟩ come over s.o. ● *a* overrun; ⟨*Kursus*⟩ over-subscribed
Überläufer *m* defector
überleben *vt/i insep* (*haben*) survive.
Ü~de(r) *m/f* survivor
überlegen¹ *vt sep* put over
überlegen² *v insep* ● *vt* [**sich** *dat*] **ü~**
think over, consider; **es sich** (*dat*)
anders ü~ change one's mind ● *vi*
(*haben*) think, reflect; **ohne zu ü~**
without thinking
überlegen³ *a* superior; (*herablas-*
send) supercilious, *adv* -ly. **Ü~heit**
f - superiority
Überlegung *f* -,-en reflection
überliefer|n *vt insep* hand down.
Ü~ung *f* tradition
überlisten *vt insep* outwit
überm *prep*= **über dem**
Über|macht *f* superiority. **ü~mäch-**
tig *a* superior; ⟨*Gefühl*⟩ over-
powering
übermannen *vt insep* overcome
Über|maß *nt* excess. **ü~mäßig** *a* ex-
cessive, *adv* -ly
Übermensch *m* superman. **ü~lich** *a*
superhuman
übermitteln *vt insep* convey; (*sen-*
den) transmit
übermorgen *adv* the day after
tomorrow

übermüdet *a* overtired

Über|mut *m* high spirits *pl.* **ü~mütig** *a* high-spirited ● *adv* in high spirits

übern *prep* = über den

übernächst|e(r,s) *a* next ... but one; **ü~es Jahr** the year after next

übernacht|en *vi insep* (*haben*) stay overnight. **Ü~ung** *f* -,-en overnight stay; **Ü~ung und Frühstück** bed and breakfast

Übernahme *f* - taking over; (*Comm*) take-over

übernatürlich *a* supernatural

übernehmen† *vt insep* take over; (*annehmen*) take on; **sich ü~** overdo things; (*finanziell*) overreach oneself

überprüf|en *vt insep* check. **Ü~ung** *f* check

überqueren *vt insep* cross

überragen *vt insep* tower above; (*fig*) surpass. **ü~d** *a* outstanding

überrasch|en *vt insep* surprise. **ü~end** *a* surprising, *adv* -ly; (*unerwartet*) unexpected, *adv* -ly. **Ü~ung** *f* -,-en surprise

überreden *vt insep* persuade

überreichen *vt insep* present

überreizt *a* overwrought

überrennen† *vt insep* overrun

Überreste *mpl* remains

überrumpeln *vt insep* take by surprise

übers *prep* = über das

Überschall- *pref* supersonic

überschatten *vt insep* overshadow

überschätzen *vt insep* overestimate

Überschlag *m* rough estimate; (*Sport*) somersault

überschlagen¹† *vt sep* cross ⟨*Beine*⟩

überschlagen²† *vt insep* estimate roughly; (*auslassen*) skip; **sich ü~** somersault; ⟨*Ereignisse:*⟩ happen fast ● *a* tepid

überschnappen *vi sep* (*sein*) (*fam*) go crazy

überschneiden† (**sich**) *vr insep* intersect, cross; (*zusammenfallen*) overlap

überschreiben† *vt insep* entitle; (*übertragen*) transfer

überschreiten† *vt insep* cross; (*fig*) exceed

Überschrift *f* heading; (*Zeitungs-*) headline

Über|schuß *m* surplus. **ü~-schüssig** *a* surplus

überschütten *vt insep* **ü~ mit** cover with; (*fig*) shower with

überschwemm|en *vt insep* flood; (*fig*) inundate. **Ü~ung** *f* -,-en flood

überschwenglich *a* effusive, *adv* -ly

Übersee in/nach ü~ overseas; **aus/von ü~** from overseas. **Ü~dampfer** *m* ocean liner. **ü~isch** *a* overseas

übersehen† *vt insep* look out over; (*abschätzen*) assess; (*nicht sehen*) overlook, miss; (*ignorieren*) ignore

übersenden† *vt insep* send

übersetzen¹ *vi sep* (*haben/sein*) cross [over]

übersetz|en² *vt insep* translate. **Ü~er(in)** *m* -s,- (*f* -,-nen) translator. **Ü~ung** *f* -,-en translation

Übersicht *f* overall view; (*Abriß*) summary; (*Tabelle*) table. **ü~lich** *a* clear, *adv* -ly

übersied|eln *vi sep* (*sein*), **übersied|eln** *vi insep* (*sein*) move (**nach** to). **Ü~lung** *f* move

übersinnlich *a* supernatural

überspannt *a* exaggerated; (*verschroben*) eccentric

überspielen *vt insep* (*fig*) cover up; **auf Band ü~** tape

überspitzt *a* exaggerated

überspringen† *vt insep* jump [over]; (*auslassen*) skip

überstehen¹† *vi sep* (*haben*) project, jut out

überstehen²† *vt insep* come through; get over ⟨*Krankheit*⟩; (*überleben*) survive

übersteigen† *vt insep* climb [over]; (*fig*) exceed

überstimmen *vt insep* outvote

überstreifen *vt sep* slip on

Überstunden *fpl* overtime *sg*; **ü~ machen** work overtime

überstürz|en *vt insep* rush; **sich ü~en** ⟨*Ereignisse:*⟩ happen fast; ⟨*Worte:*⟩ tumble out. **ü~t** *a* hasty, *adv* -ily

übertölpeln *vt insep* dupe

übertönen *vt insep* drown [out]

übertrag|bar *a* transferable; (*Med*) infectious. **ü~en†** *vt insep* transfer; (*übergeben*) assign (**dat** to); (*Techn, Med*) transmit; (*Radio, TV*) broadcast; (*übersetzen*) translate; (*anwenden*) apply (**auf** + *acc* to) ● *a* transferred, figurative. **Ü~ung** *f* -,-en transfer; transmission; broadcast; translation; application

übertreffen† vt insep surpass; (übersteigen) exceed; **sich selbst ü~** excel oneself

übertreib|en† vt insep exaggerate; (zu weit treiben) overdo. **Ü~ung** f -,-en exaggeration

übertreten¹† vi sep (sein) step over the line; (Pol) go over/(Relig) convert (zu to)

übertret|en²† vt insep infringe; break ⟨Gesetz⟩. **Ü~ung** f -,-en infringement; breach

übertrieben a exaggerated; (übermäßig) excessive, adv -ly

übervölkert a overpopulated

übervorteilen vt insep cheat

überwachen vt insep supervise; (kontrollieren) monitor; (bespitzeln) keep under surveillance

überwachsen a overgrown

überwältigen vt insep overpower; (fig) overwhelm. **ü~d** a overwhelming

überweis|en† vt insep transfer; refer ⟨Patienten⟩. **Ü~ung** f transfer; (ärztliche) referral

überwerfen¹† vt sep throw on ⟨Mantel⟩

überwerfen²† (sich) vr insep fall out (mit with)

überwiegen† v insep ● vi (haben) predominate ● vt outweigh. **ü~d** a predominant, adv -ly

überwind|en† vt insep overcome; **sich ü~en** force oneself. **Ü~ung** f effort

Überwurf m wrap; (Bett-) bedspread

Über|zahl f majority. **ü~zählig** a spare

überzeug|en vt insep convince; **sich [selbst] ü~en** satisfy oneself. **ü~end** a convincing, adv -ly. **Ü~ung** f -,-en conviction

überziehen¹† vt sep put on

überziehen²† vt insep cover; overdraw ⟨Konto⟩

Überzug m cover; (Schicht) coating

üblich a usual; (gebräuchlich) customary

U-Boot nt submarine

übrig a remaining; (andere) other; **alles ü~e** [all] the rest; **im ü~en** besides; (ansonsten) apart from that; **ü~ sein** be left [over]; **etw ü~ haben** have sth left [over]. **ü~behalten**† vt sep have left [over]. **ü~bleiben**† vi sep (sein) be left [over]; **uns blieb nichts anderes ü~** we had

no choice. **ü~ens** adv by the way. **ü~lassen**† vt sep leave [over]

Übung f -,-en exercise; (Üben) practice; **außer** od **aus der Ü~** out of practice

UdSSR f - USSR

Ufer nt -s,- shore; (Fluß-) bank

Uhr f -,-en clock; (Armband-) watch; (Zähler) meter; **um ein U~** at one o'clock; **wieviel U~ ist es?** what's the time? **U~armband** nt watch-strap. **U~macher** m -s,- watch and clockmaker. **U~werk** nt clock/watch mechanism. **U~zeiger** m [clock-/watch-]hand. **U~zeigersinn** m im/entgegen dem U~zeigersinn clockwise/ anticlockwise. **U~zeit** f time

Uhu m -s,-s eagle owl

UKW abbr (Ultrakurzwelle) VHF

Ulk m -s fun; (Streich) trick. **u~en** vi (haben) joke. **u~ig** a funny; (seltsam) odd, adv -ly

Ulme f -,-n elm

Ultimatum nt -s,-ten ultimatum

Ultrakurzwelle f very high frequency

Ultraschall m ultrasound

ultraviolett a ultraviolet

um prep (+ acc) [a]round; (Uhrzeit) at; ⟨bitten, kämpfen⟩ for; ⟨streiten⟩ over; ⟨sich sorgen⟩ about; ⟨betrügen⟩ out of (bei Angabe einer Differenz) by; **um [... herum]** around, [round] about; **Tag um Tag** day after day; **einen Tag um den andern** every other day; **um seinetwillen** for his sake ● adv (ungefähr) around, about ● conj **um zu** to; (Absicht) [in order] to; **zu müde, um zu...** too tired to...; **um so besser** all the better

umändern vt sep alter

umarbeiten vt sep alter; (bearbeiten) revise

umarm|en vt insep embrace, hug. **U~ung** f -,-en embrace, hug

Umbau m rebuilding; conversion (**zu** into). **u~en** vt sep rebuild; convert (**zu** into)

umbild|en vt sep change; (umgestalten) reorganize; reshuffle ⟨Kabinett⟩. **U~ung** f reorganisation; (Pol) reshuffle

umbinden† vt sep put on

umblättern v sep ● vt turn [over] ● vi (haben) turn the page

umblicken (sich) vr sep look round; (zurück-) look back

umbringen† *vt sep* kill; **sich u~** kill oneself

Umbruch *m* (*fig*) radical change

umbuchen *v sep* ● *vt* change; (*Comm*) transfer ● *vi* (*haben*) change one's booking

umdrehen *v sep* ● *vt* turn round/ (*wenden*) over; turn ⟨*Schlüssel*⟩; (*umkrempeln*) turn inside out; **sich u~** turn round; (*im Liegen*) turn over ● *vi* (*haben/sein*) turn back

Umdrehung *f* turn; (*Motor-*) revolution

umeinander *adv* around each other; **sich u~ sorgen** worry about each other

umfahren[1]† *vt sep* run over

umfahren[2]† *vt insep* go round; bypass ⟨*Ort*⟩

umfallen† *vi sep* (*sein*) fall over; ⟨*Person:*⟩ fall down

Umfang *m* girth; (*Geom*) circumference; (*Größe*) size; (*Ausmaß*) extent; (*Mus*) range

umfangen† *vt insep* embrace; (*fig*) envelop

umfangreich *a* extensive; (*dick*) big

umfassen *vt insep* consist of, comprise; (*umgeben*) surround. **u~d** *a* comprehensive

Umfrage *f* survey, poll

umfüllen *vt sep* transfer

umfunktionieren *vt sep* convert

Umgang *m* [social] contact; (*Umgehen*) dealing (**mit** with); **U~ haben mit** associate with

umgänglich *a* sociable

Umgangs|formen *fpl* manners. **U~sprache** *f* colloquial language. **u~sprachlich** *a* colloquial, *adv* -ly

umgeb|en† *vt/i insep* (*haben*) surround ● *a* **u~en von** surrounded by. **U~ung** *f* -,-en surroundings *pl*

umgehen[1]† *vi sep* (*sein*) go round; **u~ mit** treat, handle; (*verkehren*) associate with; **in dem Schloß geht ein Gespenst um** the castle is haunted

umgehen[2]† *vt insep* avoid; (*nicht beachten*) evade; ⟨*Straße:*⟩ bypass

umgehend *a* immediate, *adv* -ly

Umgehungsstraße *f* bypass

umgekehrt *a* inverse; ⟨*Reihenfolge*⟩ reverse; **es war u~** it was the other way round ● *adv* conversely; **und u~** and vice versa

umgraben† *vt sep* dig [over]

umhaben† *vt sep* have on

Umhang *m* cloak

umhauen† *vt sep* knock down; (*fällen*) chop down

umher *adv* **weit u~** all around. **u~gehen**† *vi sep* (*sein*) walk about

umhören (sich) *vr sep* ask around

Umkehr *f* - turning back. **u~en** *v sep* ● *vi* (*sein*) turn back ● *vt* turn round; turn inside out ⟨*Tasche*⟩; (*fig*) reverse. **U~ung** *f* - reversal

umkippen *v sep* ● *vt* tip over; (*versehentlich*) knock over ● *vi* (*sein*) fall over; ⟨*Boot:*⟩ capsize; (*fam: ohnmächtig werden*) faint

Umkleide|kabine *f* changing-cubicle. **u~n (sich)** *vr sep* change. **U~raum** *m* changing-room

umknicken *v sep* ● *vt* bend; (*falten*) fold ● *vi* (*sein*) bend; (*mit dem Fuß*) go over on one's ankle

umkommen† *vi sep* (*sein*) perish; **u~ lassen** waste ⟨*Lebensmittel*⟩

Umkreis *m* surroundings *pl*; **im U~ von** within a radius of

umkreisen *vt insep* circle; (*Astr*) revolve around; ⟨*Satellit:*⟩ orbit

umkrempeln *vt sep* turn up; (*von innen nach außen*) turn inside out; (*ändern*) change radically

Umlauf *m* circulation; (*Astr*) revolution. **U~bahn** *f* orbit

Umlaut *m* umlaut

umlegen *vt sep* lay *or* put down; flatten ⟨*Getreide*⟩; turn down ⟨*Kragen*⟩; put on ⟨*Schal*⟩; throw ⟨*Hebel*⟩; (*verlegen*) transfer; (*fam: niederschlagen*) knock down; (*töten*) kill

umleit|en *vt sep* divert. **U~ung** *f* diversion

umliegend *a* surrounding

umpflanzen *vt sep* transplant

umrahmen *vt insep* frame

umranden *vt insep* edge

umräumen *vt sep* rearrange

umrechn|en *vt sep* convert. **U~ung** *f* conversion

umreißen[1]† *vt sep* tear down; knock down ⟨*Person*⟩

umreißen[2]† *vt insep* outline

umringen *vt insep* surround

Umriß *m* outline

umrühren *vt/i sep* (*haben*) stir

ums *pron* = **um das**; **u~ Leben kommen** lose one's life

Umsatz *m* (*Comm*) turnover

umschalten *vt/i sep* (*haben*) switch over; **auf Rot u~** ⟨*Ampel:*⟩ change to red

Umschau f U∼ halten nach look out
for. **u∼en (sich)** vr sep look round/
(zurück) back

Umschlag m cover; (Schutz-) jacket;
(Brief-) envelope; (Med) compress;
(Hosen-) turn-up; (Wechsel) change.
u∼en v sep ● vt turn up; turn over
⟨Seite⟩; (fällen) chop down ● vi
(sein) topple over; ⟨Boot:⟩ capsize;
⟨Wetter:⟩ change; ⟨Wind:⟩ veer

umschließen† vt insep enclose

umschnallen vt sep buckle on

umschreiben¹† vt sep rewrite

umschreib|en²† vt insep define;
(anders ausdrücken) paraphrase.
U∼ung f definition; paraphrase

umschulen vt sep retrain; (Sch)
transfer to another school

Umschweife pl keine U∼ machen
come straight out with it; ohne U∼
straight out

Umschwung m (fig) change; (Pol)
U-turn

umsehen† (sich) vr sep look round;
(zurück) look back; sich u∼ nach
look for

umsein† vi sep (sein) (fam) be over;
⟨Zeit:⟩ be up

umseitig a & adv overleaf

umsetzen vt sep move; (umpflanzen)
transplant; (Comm) sell

Umsicht f circumspection. **u∼ig** a
circumspect, adv -ly

umsied|eln v sep ● vt resettle ● vi
(sein) move. **U∼lung** f resettlement

umsonst adv in vain; (grundlos)
without reason; (gratis) free

umspringen† vi sep (sein) change;
⟨Wind:⟩ veer; übel u∼ mit treat
badly

Umstand m circumstance; (Tatsache) fact; (Aufwand) fuss; (Mühe)
trouble; unter U∼en possibly; U∼e
machen make a fuss; jdm U∼e machen put s.o. to trouble; in andern
U∼en pregnant

umständlich a laborious, adv -ly;
(kompliziert) involved; ⟨Person⟩
fussy

Umstands|kleid nt maternity dress.
U∼wort nt (pl -wörter) adverb

umstehen† vi insep surround

Umstehende pl bystanders

umsteigen† vi sep (sein) change

umstellen¹ vt insep surround

umstell|en² vt sep rearrange; trans-
pose ⟨Wörter⟩; (anders einstellen)
reset; (Techn) convert; (ändern)
change; sich u∼en adjust. **U∼ung** f

rearrangement; transposition; re-
setting; conversion; change;
adjustment

umstimmen vt sep jdn u∼ change
s.o.'s mind

umstoßen† vt sep knock over; (fig)
overturn; upset ⟨Plan⟩

umstritten a controversial; (ungeklärt) disputed

umstülpen vt sep turn upside down;
(von innen nach außen) turn inside
out

Um|sturz m coup. **u∼stürzen** v sep
● vt overturn; (Pol) overthrow ● vi
(sein) fall over

umtaufen vt sep rename

Umtausch m exchange. **u∼en** vt sep
change; exchange (gegen for)

umwälzend a revolutionary

umwandeln vt sep convert; (fig)
transform

umwechseln vt sep change

Umweg m detour; auf U∼en in a
roundabout way

Umwelt f environment. **u∼freun-
dlich** a environmentally friendly.
U∼schutz m protection of the environment. **U∼schützer** m
environmentalist

umwenden† vt sep turn over; sich
u∼ turn round

umwerfen† vt sep knock over; (fig)
upset ⟨Plan⟩; (fam) bowl over
⟨Person⟩

umziehen† v sep ● vi (sein) move
● vt change; sich u∼ change

umzingeln vt insep surround

Umzug m move; (Prozession)
procession

unabänderlich a irrevocable; ⟨Tat-
sache⟩ unalterable

unabhängig a independent, adv -ly;
u∼ davon, ob irrespective of
whether. **U∼keit** f - independence

unabkömmlich pred a busy

unablässig a incessant, adv -ly

unabsehbar a incalculable

unabsichtlich a unintentional, adv
-ly

unachtsam a careless, adv -ly.
U∼keit f - carelessness

unangebracht a inappropriate

unangemeldet a unexpected, adv -ly

unangemessen a inappropriate,
adv -ly

unangenehm a unpleasant, adv -ly;
(peinlich) embarrassing

Unannehmlichkeiten fpl trouble sg

unansehnlich a shabby; ⟨Person⟩ plain

unanständig a indecent, adv -ly

unantastbar a inviolable

unappetitlich a unappetizing

Unart f -,-en bad habit. **u~ig** a naughty

unauffällig a inconspicuous, adv -ly, unobtrusive, adv -ly

unauffindbar a **u~ sein** be nowhere to be found

unaufgefordert adv without being asked

unauf|haltsam a inexorable, adv -bly. **u~hörlich** a incessant, adv -ly

unaufmerksam a inattentive

unaufrichtig a insincere

unausbleiblich a inevitable

unausgeglichen a unbalanced; ⟨Person⟩ unstable

unaus|löschlich a (fig) indelible, adv -bly. **u~sprechlich** a indescribable, adv -bly. **u~stehlich** a insufferable

unbarmherzig a merciless, adv -ly

unbeabsichtigt a unintentional, adv -ly

unbedacht a rash, adv -ly

unbedenklich a harmless ● adv without hesitation

unbedeutend a insignificant; (geringfügig) slight, adv -ly

unbedingt a absolute, adv -ly; **nicht u~** not necessarily

unbefangen a natural, adv -ly; (unparteiisch) impartial

unbefriedig|end a unsatisfactory. **u~t** a dissatisfied

unbefugt a unauthorized ● adv without authorization

unbegreiflich a incomprehensible

unbegrenzt a unlimited ● adv indefinitely

unbegründet a unfounded

Unbehag|en nt unease; (körperlich) discomfort. **u~lich** a uncomfortable, adv -bly

unbeholfen a awkward, adv -ly

unbekannt a unknown; (nicht vertraut) unfamiliar. **U~e(r)** m/f stranger

unbekümmert a unconcerned; (unbeschwert) carefree

unbeliebt a unpopular. **U~heit** f unpopularity

unbemannt a unmanned

unbemerkt a & adv unnoticed

unbenutzt a unused

unbequem a uncomfortable, adv -bly; (lästig) awkward

unberechenbar a unpredictable

unberechtigt a unjustified; (unbefugt) unauthorized

unberufen int touch wood!

unberührt a untouched; (fig) virgin; ⟨Landschaft⟩ unspoilt

unbescheiden a presumptuous

unbeschrankt a unguarded

unbeschränkt a unlimited ● adv without limit

unbeschreiblich a indescribable, adv -bly

unbeschwert a carefree

unbesiegbar a invincible

unbesiegt a undefeated

unbesonnen a rash, adv -ly

unbespielt a blank

unbeständig a inconsistent; ⟨Wetter⟩ unsettled

unbestechlich a incorruptible

unbestimmt a indefinite; ⟨Alter⟩ indeterminate; (ungewiß) uncertain; (unklar) vague ● adv vaguely

unbestreitbar a indisputable, adv -bly

unbestritten a undisputed ● adv indisputably

unbeteiligt a indifferent; **u~ an** (+ dat) not involved in

unbetont a unstressed

unbewacht a unguarded

unbewaffnet a unarmed

unbeweglich a & adv motionless, still

unbewohnt a uninhabited

unbewußt a unconscious, adv -ly

unbezahlbar a priceless

unbezahlt a unpaid

unbrauchbar a useless

und conj and; **und so weiter** and so on; **nach und nach** bit by bit

Undank m ingratitude. **u~bar** a ungrateful; (nicht lohnend) thankless. **U~barkeit** f ingratitude

undefinierbar a indefinable

undenk|bar a unthinkable. **u~lich** a **seit u~lichen Zeiten** from time immemorial

undeutlich a indistinct, adv -ly; (vage) vague, adv -ly

undicht a leaking; **u~e Stelle** leak

Unding nt absurdity

undiplomatisch a undiplomatic, adv -ally

unduldsam a intolerant

undurch|dringlich a impenetrable; ⟨Miene⟩ inscrutable. **u~führbar** a impracticable

undurch|lässig *a* impermeable. **u~sichtig** *a* opaque; (*fig*) doubtful

uneben *a* uneven, *adv* -ly. **U~heit** *f* -,-en unevenness; (*Buckel*) bump

unecht *a* false; **u~er Schmuck/ Pelz** imitation jewellery/fur

unehelich *a* illegitimate

unehr|enhaft *a* dishonourable, *adv* -bly. **u~lich** *a* dishonest, *adv* -ly. **U~lichkeit** *f* dishonesty

uneinig *a* (*fig*) divided; [sich (*dat*)] **u~ sein** disagree. **U~keit** *f* disagreement; (*Streit*) discord

uneins *a* **u~ sein** be at odds

unempfindlich *a* insensitive (**gegen** to); (*widerstandsfähig*) tough; (*Med*) immune

unendlich *a* infinite, *adv* -ly; (*endlos*) endless, *adv* -ly. **U~keit** *f* - infinity

unentbehrlich *a* indispensable

unentgeltlich *a* free; ⟨*Arbeit*⟩ unpaid ● *adv* free of charge; ⟨*arbeiten*⟩ without pay

unentschieden *a* undecided; (*Sport*) drawn; **u~ spielen** draw. **U~** *nt* -s,- draw

unentschlossen *a* indecisive; (*unentschieden*) undecided. **U~heit** *f* indecision

unentwegt *a* persistent, *adv* -ly; (*unaufhörlich*) incessant, *adv* -ly

unerbittlich *a* implacable, *adv* -bly; ⟨*Schicksal*⟩ inexorable

unerfahren *a* inexperienced. **U~heit** *f* - inexperience

unerfreulich *a* unpleasant, *adv* -ly

unergründlich *a* unfathomable

unerhört *a* enormous, *adv* -ly; (*empörend*) outrageous, *adv* -ly

unerklärlich *a* inexplicable

unerlässlich *a* essential

unerlaubt *a* unauthorized ● *adv* without permission

unermeßlich *a* immense, *adv* -ly

unermüdlich *a* tireless, *adv* -ly

unersättlich *a* insatiable

unerschöpflich *a* inexhaustible

unerschütterlich *a* unshakeable

unerschwinglich *a* prohibitive

unersetzlich *a* irreplaceable; ⟨*Verlust*⟩ irreparable

unerträglich *a* unbearable, *adv* -bly

unerwartet *a* unexpected, *adv* -ly

unerwünscht *a* unwanted; ⟨*Besuch*⟩ unwelcome

unfähig *a* incompetent; **u~, etw zu tun** incapable of doing sth; (*nicht in der Lage*) unable to do sth. **U~keit** *f* incompetence; inability (**zu** to)

unfair *a* unfair, *adv* -ly

Unfall *m* accident. **U~flucht** *f* failure to stop after an accident. **U~station** *f* casualty department

unfaßbar *a* incomprehensible; (*unglaublich*) unimaginable

unfehlbar *a* infallible. **U~keit** *f* - infallibility

unfolgsam *a* disobedient

unförmig *a* shapeless

unfreiwillig *a* involuntary, *adv* -ily; (*unbeabsichtigt*) unintentional, *adv* -ly

unfreundlich *a* unfriendly; (*unangenehm*) unpleasant, *adv* -ly. **U~keit** *f* unfriendliness; unpleasantness

Unfriede[n] *m* discord

unfruchtbar *a* infertile; (*fig*) unproductive. **U~keit** *f* infertility

Unfug *m* -s mischief; (*Unsinn*) nonsense

Ungar|(in) *m* -n,-n (*f* -,-nen) Hungarian. **u~isch** *a* Hungarian. **U~n** *nt* -s Hungary

ungastlich *a* inhospitable

ungeachtet *prep* (+ *gen*) in spite of.

ungebärdig *a* unruly. **ungebeugt** *a* (*Gram*) uninflected. **ungebraucht** *a* unused. **ungebührlich** *a* improper, *adv* -ly. **ungedeckt** *a* uncovered; (*Sport*) unmarked; ⟨*Tisch*⟩ unlaid

Ungeduld *f* impatience. **u~ig** *a* impatient, *adv* -ly

ungeeignet *a* unsuitable

ungefähr *a* approximate, *adv* -ly, rough, *adv* -ly

ungefährlich *a* harmless

ungehalten *a* angry, *adv* -ily

ungeheuer *a* enormous, *adv* -ly. **U~** *nt* -s,- monster

ungeheuerlich *a* outrageous

ungehobelt *a* uncouth

ungehörig *a* improper, *adv* -ly; (*frech*) impertinent, *adv* -ly

ungehorsam *a* disobedient. **U~** *m* disobedience

ungeklärt *a* unsolved; ⟨*Frage*⟩ unsettled; ⟨*Ursache*⟩ unknown

ungeladen *a* unloaded; ⟨*Gast*⟩ uninvited

ungelegen *a* inconvenient. **U~heiten** *fpl* trouble *sg*

ungelernt *a* unskilled. **ungemein** *a* tremendous, *adv* -ly

ungemütlich *a* uncomfortable, *adv* -bly; (*unangenehm*) unpleasant, *adv* -ly

ungenau a inaccurate, adv -ly; (vage) vague, adv -ly. **U~igkeit** f -,-en inaccuracy

ungeniert /'ʊnʒeni:ɐ̯t/ a uninhibited ● adv openly

ungenießbar a inedible; ⟨Getränk⟩ undrinkable. **ungenügend** a inadequate, adv -ly; (Sch) unsatisfactory. **ungepflegt** a neglected; ⟨Person⟩ unkempt. **ungerade** a ⟨Zahl⟩ odd

ungerecht a unjust, adv -ly. **U~igkeit** f -,-en injustice

ungern adv reluctantly

ungesalzen a unsalted

ungeschehen a u~ **machen** undo

Ungeschick|lichkeit f clumsiness. **u~t** a clumsy, adv -ily

ungeschminkt a without make-up; ⟨Wahrheit⟩ unvarnished. **ungeschrieben** a unwritten. **ungesehen** a & adv unseen. **ungesellig** a unsociable. **ungesetzlich** a illegal, adv -ly. **ungestört** a undisturbed. **ungestraft** adv with impunity. **ungestüm** a impetuous, adv -ly. **ungesund** a unhealthy. **ungesüßt** a unsweetened. **ungetrübt** a perfect

Ungetüm nt -s,-e monster

ungewiß a uncertain; **im ungewissen lassen** leave in the dark. **U~heit** f uncertainty

ungewöhnlich a unusual, adv -ly. **ungewohnt** a unaccustomed; (nicht vertraut) unfamiliar. **ungewollt** a unintentional, adv -ly; ⟨Schwangerschaft⟩ unwanted

Ungeziefer nt -s vermin

ungezogen a naughty, adv -ily

ungezwungen a informal, adv -ly; (natürlich) natural, adv -ly

ungläubig a incredulous

unglaublich a incredible, adv -bly, unbelievable, adv -bly

ungleich a unequal, adv -ly; (verschieden) different. **U~heit** f - inequality. **u~mäßig** a uneven, adv -ly

Unglück nt -s,-e misfortune; (Pech) bad luck; (Mißgeschick) mishap; (Unfall) accident; **U~ bringen** be unlucky. **u~lich** a unhappy, adv -ily; (ungünstig) unfortunate, adv -ly. **u~licherweise** adv unfortunately. **u~selig** a unfortunate. **U~sfall** m accident

ungültig a invalid; (Jur) void

ungünstig a unfavourable, adv -bly; (unpassend) inconvenient, adv -ly

ungut a ⟨Gefühl⟩ uneasy; **nichts für u~!** no offence!

unhandlich a unwieldy

Unheil nt -s disaster; **U~ anrichten** cause havoc

unheilbar a incurable, adv -bly

unheimlich a eerie; (gruselig) creepy; (fam: groß) terrific ● adv eerily; (fam: sehr) terribly

unhöflich a rude, adv -ly. **U~keit** f rudeness

unhörbar a inaudible, adv -bly

unhygienisch a unhygienic

Uni f -,-s (fam) university

uni /y'ni:/ inv a plain

Uniform f -,-en uniform

uninteress|ant a uninteresting. **u~iert** a uninterested; (unbeteiligt) disinterested

Union f -,-en union

universal a universal

universell a universal, adv -ly

Universität f -,-en university

Universum nt -s universe

unkennt|lich a unrecognizable. **U~nis** f ignorance

unklar a unclear; (ungewiß) uncertain; (vage) vague, adv -ly; **im u~en sein** be in the dark. **U~heit** f -,-en uncertainty

unklug a unwise, adv -ly

unkompliziert a uncomplicated

Unkosten pl expenses

Unkraut nt weed; (coll) weeds pl; **U~ jäten** weed. **U~vertilgungsmittel** nt weed-killer

unkultiviert a uncultured

unlängst adv recently

unlauter a dishonest; (unfair) unfair

unleserlich a illegible, adv -bly

unleugbar a undeniable, adv -bly

unlogisch a illogical, adv -ly

unlös|bar a (fig) insoluble. **u~lich** a (Chem) insoluble

unlustig a listless, adv -ly

unmäßig a excessive, adv -ly; (äußerst) extreme, adv -ly

Unmenge f enormous amount/(Anzahl) number

Unmensch m (fam) brute. **u~lich** a inhuman; (entsetzlich) appalling, adv -ly

unmerklich a imperceptible, adv -bly

unmißverständlich a unambiguous, adv -ly; (offen) unequivocal, adv -ly

unmittelbar a immediate, adv -ly; (direkt) direct, adv -ly

unmöbliert a unfurnished

unmodern a old-fashioned

unmöglich a impossible, adv -bly.
U~keit f - impossibility

Unmoral f immorality. **u~isch** a immoral, adv -ly

unmündig a under-age

Unmut m displeasure

unnachahmlich a inimitable

unnachgiebig a intransigent

unnatürlich a unnatural, adv -ly

unnormal a abnormal, adv -ly

unnötig a unnecessary, adv -ily

unnütz a useless ● adv needlessly

unord|entlich a untidy, adv -ily;
(nachlässig) sloppy, adv -ily. **U~
nung** f disorder; (Durcheinander)
muddle

unorganisiert a disorganized

unorthodox a unorthodox ● adv in
an unorthodox manner

unparteiisch a impartial, adv -ly

unpassend a inappropriate, adv -ly;
⟨Moment⟩ inopportune

unpäßlich a indisposed

unpersönlich a impersonal

unpraktisch a impractical

unpünktlich a unpunctual ● adv late

unrasiert a unshaven

Unrast f restlessness

unrealistisch a unrealistic, adv -ally

unrecht a wrong, adv -ly ● n **u~
haben** be wrong; **jdm u~ tun** do s.o.
an injustice; **jdm u~ geben** disagree
with s.o. **U~** nt wrong; **zu U~**
wrongly. **u~mäßig** a unlawful, adv
-ly

unregelmäßig a irregular, adv -ly.
U~keit f irregularity

unreif a unripe; (fig) immature

unrein a impure; ⟨Luft⟩ polluted;
⟨Haut⟩ bad; **ins u~e schreiben** make
a rough draft of

unrentabel a unprofitable, adv -bly

unrichtig a incorrect

Unruh|e f -,-n restlessness; (Erre-
gung) agitation; (Besorgnis) anxiety; **U~en** (Pol) unrest sg. **u~ig** a
restless, adv -ly; ⟨Meer⟩ agitated;
(laut) noisy, adv -ily; (besorgt)
anxious, adv -ly

uns pron (acc/dat of **wir**) us; (refl)
ourselves; (einander) each other;
ein Freund von uns a friend of ours

unsagbar, unsäglich a indescribable, adv -bly

unsanft a rough, adv -ly

unsauber a dirty; (nachlässig)
sloppy, adv -ily; (unlauter) dishonest, adv -ly

unschädlich a harmless

unscharf a blurred

unschätzbar a inestimable

unscheinbar a inconspicuous

unschicklich a improper, adv -ly

unschlagbar a unbeatable

unschlüssig a undecided

Unschuld f - innocence; (Jungfräu-
lichkeit) virginity. **u~ig** a innocent,
adv -ly

unselbständig a dependent ● adv
u~ denken not think for oneself

unser poss pron our. **u~e(r,s)** poss
pron ours. **u~erseits** adv for our
part. **u~twegen** adv for our sake;
(wegen uns) because of us, on our
account. **u~twillen** adv **um u~twil-
len** for our sake

unsicher a unsafe; (ungewiß) uncertain; (nicht zuverlässig) unreliable;
⟨Schritte, Hand⟩ unsteady; ⟨Person⟩
insecure ● adv unsteadily. **U~heit** f
uncertainty; unreliability; insecur-
ity

unsichtbar a invisible

Unsinn m nonsense. **u~ig** a nonsens-
ical, absurd

Unsitt|e f bad habit. **u~lich** a in-
decent, adv -ly

unsportlich a not sporty; (unfair)
unsporting, adv -ly

uns|re(r,s) poss pron = **unsere(r,s)**.
u~rige poss pron **der/die/das u~
rige** ours

unsterblich a immortal. **U~keit** f
immortality

unstet a restless, adv -ly; (unbeständig) unstable

Unstimmigkeit f -,-en inconsistency;
(Streit) difference

Unsumme f vast sum

unsymmetrisch a not symmetrical

unsympathisch a unpleasant; **er ist
mir u~** I don't like him

untätig a idle, adv idly. **U~keit** f -
idleness

untauglich a unsuitable; (Mil) unfit

unteilbar a indivisible

unten adv at the bottom; (auf der
Unterseite) underneath; (eine Treppe
tiefer) downstairs; **hier/da u~** down
here/there; **nach u~** down[wards]
(die Treppe hinunter) downstairs

unter prep (+ dat/acc) under; (niedriger als) below; (inmitten, zwischen)
among; **u~ anderem** among other
things; **u~ der Woche** during the
week; **u~ sich** by themselves; **u~
uns gesagt** between ourselves

Unter|arm *m* forearm. **U~bewußt-sein** *nt* subconscious

unterbieten† *vt insep* undercut; beat ⟨*Rekord*⟩

unterbinden† *vt insep* stop

unterbleiben† *vi insep* (sein) cease; **es hat zu u~** it must stop

unterbrech|en† *vt insep* interrupt; break ⟨*Reise*⟩. **U~ung** *f* -,-en interruption; break

unterbreiten *vt insep* present

unterbringen† *vt sep* put; (*beherbergen*) put up

unterdessen *adv* in the mean-time

unterdrück|en *vt insep* suppress; oppress ⟨*Volk*⟩. **U~ung** *f* - suppression; oppression

untere(r,s) *a* lower

untereinander *adv* one below the other; (*miteinander*) among ourselves/yourselves/themselves

unterernähr|t *a* undernourished. **U~ung** *f* malnutrition

Unterfangen *nt* -s,- venture

Unterführung *f* underpass; (*Fußgänger-*) subway

Untergang *m* (*Astr*) setting; (*Naut*) sinking; (*Zugrundegehen*) disappearance; (*der Welt*) end

Untergebene(r) *m/f* subordinate

untergehen† *vi sep* (sein) (*Astr*) set; (*versinken*) go under; ⟨*Schiff:*⟩ go down, sink; (*zugrunde gehen*) disappear; ⟨*Welt:*⟩ come to an end

untergeordnet *a* subordinate

Untergeschoß *nt* basement

untergraben† *vt insep* (fig) undermine

Untergrund *m* foundation; (*Hintergrund*) background; (*Pol*) underground. **U~bahn** *f* underground [railway], (*Amer*) subway

unterhaken *vt sep* jdn u~ take s.o.'s arm; **untergehakt** arm in arm

unterhalb *adv & prep* (+ *gen*) below

Unterhalt *m* maintenance

unterhalt|en† *vt insep* maintain; (*ernähren*) support; (*betreiben*) run; (*erheitern*) entertain; **sich u~en** talk; (*sich vergnügen*) enjoy oneself. **u~sam** *a* entertaining. **U~ung** *f* -,-en maintenance; (*Gespräch*) conversation; (*Zeitvertreib*) entertainment

unterhandeln *vi insep* (haben) negotiate

Unter|haus *nt* (*Pol*) lower house; (in UK) House of Commons. **U~hemd** *nt* vest. **U~holz** *nt* undergrowth.

U~hose *f* underpants *pl.* **u~irdisch** *a & adv* underground

unterjochen *vt insep* subjugate

Unterkiefer *m* lower jaw

unter|kommen† *vi sep* (sein) find accommodation; (*eine Stellung finden*) get a job. **u~kriegen** *vt sep* (*fam*) get down

Unterkunft *f* -,-künfte accommodation

Unterlage *f* pad; **U~n** papers

Unterlaß *m* ohne U~ incessantly

unterlass|en† *vt insep* **etw u~en** refrain from [doing] sth; **es u~en, etw zu tun** fail *or* omit to do sth. **U~ung** *f* -,-en omission

unterlaufen† *vi insep* (sein) occur; **mir ist ein Fehler u~** I made a mistake

unterlegen¹ *vt sep* put underneath

unterlegen² *a* inferior; (*Sport*) losing; **zahlenmäßig u~** outnumbered (*dat* by). **U~e(r)** *m/f* loser

Unterleib *m* abdomen

unterliegen† *vi insep* (sein) lose (*dat* to); (*unterworfen sein*) be subject (*dat* to)

Unterlippe *f* lower lip

unterm *prep* = unter dem

Untermiete *f* zur U~ wohnen be a lodger. **U~r(in)** *m(f)* lodger

unterminieren *vt insep* undermine

untern *prep* = unter den

unternehm|en† *vt insep* undertake; take ⟨*Schritte*⟩; **etw/nichts u~en** do sth/nothing. **U~en** *nt* -s,- undertaking, enterprise; (*Betrieb*) concern. **u~end** *a* enterprising. **U~er** *m* -s,- employer; (*Bau-*) contractor; (*Industrieller*) industrialist. **U~ung** *f* -,-en undertaking; (*Comm*) venture. **u~ungslustig** *a* enterprising; (*abenteuerlustig*) adventurous

Unteroffizier *m* non-commissioned officer

unterordnen *vt sep* subordinate; **sich u~** accept a subordinate role

Unterredung *f* -,-en talk

Unterricht *m* -[e]s teaching; (*Privat-*) tuition; (*U~sstunden*) lessons *pl*; **U~ geben/nehmen** give/have lessons

unterrichten *vt/i insep* (haben) teach; (*informieren*) inform; **sich u~** inform oneself

Unterrock *m* slip

unters *prep* = unter das

untersagen *vt insep* forbid

Untersatz m mat; (mit Füßen) stand; (Gläser-) coaster

unterschätzen vt insep underestimate

unterscheid|en† vt/i insep (haben) distinguish; (auseinanderhalten) tell apart; **sich u~en** differ. **U~ung** f -,-en distinction

Unterschied m -[e]s,-e difference; (Unterscheidung) distinction; **im U~ zu ihm** unlike him. **u~lich** a different; (wechselnd) varying; **das ist u~lich** it varies. **u~slos** a equal, adv -ly

unterschlag|en† vt insep embezzle; (verheimlichen) suppress. **U~ung** f -,-en embezzlement; suppression

Unterschlupf m -[e]s shelter; (Versteck) hiding-place

unterschreiben† vt/i insep (haben) sign

Unter|schrift f signature; (Bild-) caption. **U~seeboot** nt submarine. **U~setzer** m -s,- = Untersatz

untersetzt a stocky

Unterstand m shelter

unterste(r,s) a lowest, bottom

unterstehen¹† vi sep (haben) shelter

unterstehen²† v insep • vi (haben) be answerable (dat to); (unterliegen) be subject (dat to) • vr **sich u~** dare; **untersteh dich!** don't you dare!

unterstellen¹ vt sep put underneath; (abstellen) store; **sich u~** shelter

unterstellen² vt insep place under the control (dat of); (annehmen) assume; (fälschlich zuschreiben) impute (dat to)

unterstreichen† vt insep underline

unterstütz|en vt insep support; (helfen) aid. **U~ung** f -,-en support; (finanziell) aid; (regelmäßiger Betrag) allowance; (Arbeitslosen-) benefit

untersuch|en vt insep examine; (Jur) investigate; (prüfen) test; (überprüfen) check; (durchsuchen) search. **U~ung** f -,-en examination; investigation; test; check; search. **U~ungshaft** f detention on remand; **in U~ungshaft** on remand. **U~ungsrichter** m examining magistrate

Untertan m -s & -en,-en subject

Untertasse f saucer

untertauchen v sep • vt duck • vi (sein) go under; (fig) disappear

Unterteil nt bottom (part)

unterteilen vt insep subdivide; (aufteilen) divide

Untertitel m subtitle

Unterton m undertone

untervermieten vt/i insep (haben) sublet

unterwandern vt insep infiltrate

Unterwäsche f underwear

Unterwasser- pref underwater

unterwegs adv on the way; (außer Haus) out; (verreist) away

unterweisen† vt insep instruct

Unterwelt f underworld

unterwerfen† vt insep subjugate; **sich u~en** submit (dat to); **etw** (dat) **unterworfen sein** be subject to sth

unterwürfig a obsequious, adv -ly

unterzeichnen vt insep sign

unterziehen¹† vt sep put on underneath; (Culin) fold in

unterziehen²† vt insep **etw einer Untersuchung/Überprüfung u~** examine/ check sth; **sich einer Operation/Prüfung u~** have an operation/ take a test

Untier nt monster

untragbar a intolerable

untrennbar a inseparable

untreu a disloyal; (in der Ehe) unfaithful. **U~e** f disloyalty; infidelity

untröstlich a inconsolable

untrüglich a infallible

Untugend f bad habit

unüberlegt a rash, adv -ly

unüber|sehbar a obvious; (groß) immense. **u~troffen** a unsurpassed

unum|gänglich a absolutely necessary. **u~schränkt** a absolute. **u~wunden** adv frankly

ununterbrochen a incessant, adv -ly

unveränderlich a invariable; (gleichbleibend) unchanging

unverändert a unchanged

unverantwortlich a irresponsible, adv -bly

unverbesserlich a incorrigible

unverbindlich a non-committal; (Comm) not binding • adv without obligation

unverblümt a blunt • adv -ly

unverdaulich a indigestible

unver|einbar a incompatible. **u~geßlich** a unforgettable. **u~gleichlich** a incomparable

unver|hältnismäßig adv disproportionately. **u~heiratet** a unmarried. **u~hofft** a unexpected, adv -ly. **u~hohlen** a undisguised • adv openly. **u~käuflich** a not for sale; (Muster) free

unverkennbar a unmistakable, adv -bly

unverletzt a unhurt

unvermeidlich a inevitable

unver|mindert a & adv undiminished. **u~mittelt** a abrupt, adv -ly. **u~mutet** a unexpected, adv -ly

Unver|nunft f folly. **u~nünftig** a foolish, adv -ly

unverschämt a insolent, adv -ly; (fam: ungeheuer) outrageous, adv -ly. **U~heit** f -,-en insolence

unver|sehens adv suddenly. **u~sehrt** a unhurt; (unbeschädigt) intact. **u~söhnlich** a irreconcilable; ⟨Gegner⟩ implacable

unverständ|lich a incomprehensible; (undeutlich) indistinct. **U~nis** nt lack of understanding

unverträglich a incompatible; ⟨Person⟩ quarrelsome; (unbekömmlich) indigestible

unverwandt a fixed, adv -ly

unver|wundbar a invulnerable. **u~wüstlich** a indestructible; ⟨Person, Humor⟩ irrepressible; ⟨Gesundheit⟩ robust. **u~zeihlich** a unforgivable

unverzüglich a immediate, adv -ly

unvollendet a unfinished

unvollkommen a imperfect; (unvollständig) incomplete. **U~heit** f -,-en imperfection

unvollständig a incomplete

unvor|bereitet a unprepared. **u~eingenommen** a unbiased. **u~hergesehen** a unforeseen

unvorsichtig a careless, adv -ly. **U~keit** f - carelessness

unvorstellbar a unimaginable, adv -bly

unvorteilhaft a unfavourable; (nicht hübsch) unattractive; ⟨Kleid, Frisur⟩ unflattering

unwahr a untrue. **U~heit** f -,-en untruth. **u~scheinlich** a unlikely; (unglaublich) improbable; (fam: groß) incredible, adv -bly

unweigerlich a inevitable, adv -bly

unweit adv & prep (+ gen) not far; **u~** vom Fluß/des Flusses not far from the river

unwesentlich a unimportant ● adv slightly

Unwetter nt -s,- storm

unwichtig a unimportant

unwider|legbar a irrefutable. **u~ruflich** a irrevocable, adv -bly. **u~stehlich** a irresistible

Unwill|e m displeasure. **u~ig** a angry, adv -ily; (widerwillig) reluctant, adv -ly. **u~kürlich** a involuntary, adv -ily; (instinktiv) instinctive, adv -ly

unwirklich a unreal

unwirksam a ineffective

unwirsch a irritable, adv -bly

unwirtlich a inhospitable

unwirtschaftlich a uneconomic, adv -ally

unwissen|d a ignorant. **U~heit** f - ignorance

unwohl a unwell; (unbehaglich) uneasy. **U~sein** nt -s indisposition

unwürdig a unworthy (gen of); (würdelos) undignified

Unzahl f vast number. **unzählig** a innumerable, countless

unzerbrechlich a unbreakable

unzerstörbar a indestructible

unzertrennlich a inseparable

Unzucht f sexual offence; **gewerbsmäßige U~** prostitution

unzüchtig a indecent, adv -ly; ⟨Schriften⟩ obscene

unzufrieden a dissatisfied; (innerlich) discontented. **U~heit** f dissatisfaction; (Pol) discontent

unzulänglich a inadequate, adv -ly

unzulässig a inadmissible

unzumutbar a unreasonable

unzurechnungsfähig a insane. **U~keit** f insanity

unzusammenhängend a incoherent

unzutreffend a inapplicable; (falsch) incorrect

unzuverlässig a unreliable

unzweckmäßig a unsuitable, adv -bly

unzweideutig a unambiguous

unzweifelhaft a undoubted, adv -ly

üppig a luxuriant, adv -ly; (überreichlich) lavish, adv -ly; ⟨Busen, Figur⟩ voluptuous

uralt a ancient

Uran nt -s uranium

Uraufführung f first performance

urbar a **u~** machen cultivate

Ureinwohner mpl native inhabitants

Urenkel m great-grandson; (pl) great-grandchildren

Urgroß|mutter f great-grandmother. **U~vater** m great-grandfather

Urheber *m* -s,- originator; (*Verfasser*) author. **U~recht** *nt* copyright

Urin *m* -s,-e urine

Urkunde *f* -,-n certificate; (*Dokument*) document

Urlaub *m* -s holiday; (*Mil, Ad- min*) leave; **auf U~** on holiday/ leave; **U~haben** be on holiday/ leave. **U~er(in)** *m* -s,- (*f* -,-nen) holiday-maker. **U~sort** *m* holiday resort

Urne *f* -,-n urn; (*Wahl-*) ballot-box

Ursache *f* cause; (*Grund*) reason; **keine U~!** don't mention it!

Ursprung *m* origin

ursprünglich *a* original, *adv* -ly; (*anfänglich*) initial, *adv* -ly; (*natürlich*) natural

Urteil *nt* -s,-e judgement; (*Meinung*) opinion; (*U~sspruch*) verdict; (*Strafe*) sentence. **u~en** *vi* (*haben*) judge. **U~svermögen** *nt* [power of] judgement

Urwald *m* primeval forest; (*tropischer*) jungle

urwüchsig *a* natural; (*derb*) earthy·

Urzeit *f* primeval times *pl*; **seit U~en** from time immemorial

USA *pl* USA *sg*

usw. *abbr* (**und so weiter**) etc.

Utensilien /-i̯ən/ *ntpl* utensils

utopisch *a* Utopian

V

vage /'va:gə/ *a* vague, *adv* -ly

Vakuum /'va:kuʊm/ *nt* -s vacuum. **v~verpackt** *a* vacuum-packed

Vanille /va'nɪljə/ *f* - vanilla

vari|abel /va'ri̯a:bəl/ *a* variable. **V~ante** *f* -,-n variant. **V~ation** /-'tsi̯o:n/ *f* -,-en variation. **v~ieren** *vt/i* (*haben*) vary

Vase /'va:zə/ *f* -,-n vase

Vater *m* -s,‿ father. **V~land** *nt* fatherland

väterlich *a* paternal; (*fürsorglich*) fatherly. **v~erseits** *adv* on one's/the father's side

Vater|schaft *f* - fatherhood; (*Jur*) paternity. **V~unser** *nt* -s,- Lord's Prayer

Vati *m* -s,-s (*fam*) daddy

v. Chr. *abbr* (**vor Christus**) BC

Vegetar|ier(in) /vege'ta:ri̯ɐ, -i̯ərɪn/ *m(f)* -s,- (*f* -,-nen) vegetarian. **v~isch** *a* vegetarian

Vegetation /vegeta'tsi̯o:n/ *f* -,-en vegetation

Veilchen *nt* -s,- violet

Vene /'ve:nə/ *f* -,-n vein

Venedig /ve'ne:dɪç/ *nt* -s Venice

Ventil /vɛn'ti:l/ *nt* -s,-e valve. **V~ator** *m* -s,-en /-'to:rən/ fan

verabred|en *vt* arrange; **sich [mit jdm]** v~en arrange to meet [s.o.]. **V~ung** *f* -,-en arrangement; (*Treffen*) appointment

verabreichen *vt* administer

verabscheuen *vt* detest, loathe

verabschieden *vt* say goodbye to; (*aus dem Dienst*) retire; pass ⟨*Gesetz*⟩; **sich v~** say goodbye

verachten *vt* despise. **v~swert** *a* contemptible

verächtlich *a* contemptuous, *adv* -ly; (*unwürdig*) contemptible

Verachtung *f* - contempt

verallgemeiner|n *vt/i* (*haben*) generalize. **V~ung** *f* -,-en generalization

veralte|n *vi* (*sein*) become obsolete. **v~t** *a* obsolete

Veranda /ve'randa/ *f* -,-den veranda

veränder|lich *a* changeable; (*Math*) variable. **v~n** *vt* change; **sich v~n** change; (*beruflich*) change one's job. **V~ung** *f* change

verängstigt *a* frightened, scared

verankern *vt* anchor

veranlag|t *a* **künstlerisch/musikalisch v~t** sein have an artistic/a musical bent; **praktisch v~t** practically minded. **V~ung** *f* -,-en disposition; (*Neigung*) tendency; (*künstlerisch*) bent

veranlass|en *vt* (*reg*) arrange for; (*einleiten*) institute; **jdn v~en** prompt s.o. (**zu** to). **V~ung** *f* - reason; **auf meine V~ung** at my suggestion; (*Befehl*) on my orders

veranschaulichen *vt* illustrate

veranschlagen *vt* (*reg*) estimate

veranstalt|en *vt* organize; hold, give ⟨*Party*⟩; make ⟨*Lärm*⟩. **V~er** *m* -s,- organizer. **V~ung** *f* -,-en event

verantwort|en *vt* take responsibility for; **sich v~en** answer (**für** for). **v~lich** *a* responsible; **v~lich machen** hold responsible. **V~ung** *f* - responsibility. **V~ungsbewußt** *a* responsible, *adv* -bly. **v~ungslos** *a* irresponsible, *adv* -bly. **v~ungsvoll** *a* responsible

verarbeiten *vt* use; (*Techn*) process; (*verdauen & fig*) digest; **v~ zu** make into

verärgern vt annoy
verarmt a impoverished
verästeln (sich) vr branch out
verausgaben (sich) vr spend all
one's money; (körperlich) wear oneself out
veräußern vt sell
Verb /vɛrp/ nt -s,-en verb. **v~al**
/vɛr'baːl/ a verbal, adv -ly
Verband m -[e]s,ˆe association; (Mil)
unit; (Med) bandage; (Wund-) dressing. **V~szeug** nt first-aid kit
verbann|en vt exile; (fig) banish.
V~ung f - exile
verbarrikadieren vt barricade
verbeißen† vt suppress; **ich konnte
mir kaum das Lachen v~** I could
hardly keep a straight face
verbergen† vt hide; **sich v~** hide
verbesser|n vt improve; (berichti-
gen) correct. **V~ung** f -,-en improvement; correction
verbeug|en (sich) vr bow. **V~ung** f
bow
verbeulen vt dent
verbiegen† vt bend; **sich v~** bend
verbieten† vt forbid; (Admin) prohibit, ban
verbillig|en vt reduce [in price]. **v~t**
a reduced
verbinden† vt connect (**mit** to);
(zusammenfügen) join; (verknüpfen)
combine; (in Verbindung bringen)
associate; (Med) bandage; dress
⟨Wunde⟩; **sich v~** combine; (sich
zusammentun) join together; **jdm
die Augen v~** blindfold s.o.; **jdm
verbunden sein** (fig) be obliged to
s.o.
verbindlich a friendly; (bindend)
binding. **V~keit** f -,-en friendliness;
V~keiten obligations; (Comm)
liabilities
Verbindung f connection; (Ver-
knüpfung) combination; (Kontakt)
contact; (Vereinigung) association;
chemische V~ chemical compound;
in V~ stehen/sich in V~ setzen be/
get in touch
verbissen a grim, adv -ly; (zäh) dogged, adv -ly
verbitten† vt **sich** (dat) **etw v~** not
stand for sth
verbitter|n vt make bitter. **v~t** a
bitter. **V~ung** f - bitterness
verblassen vi (sein) fade
Verbleib m -s whereabouts pl.
v~en† vi (sein) remain
verbleichen† vi (sein) fade

verbleit a ⟨Benzin⟩ leaded
verblüff|en vt amaze, astound.
V~ung f - amazement
verblühen vi (sein) wither, fade
verbluten vi (sein) bleed to death
verborgen¹ a hidden
verborgen² vt lend
Verbot nt -[e]s,-e ban. **v~en** a forbidden; (Admin) prohibited; '**Rauchen
v~en**' 'no smoking'
Verbrauch m -[e]s consumption.
v~en vt use; consume ⟨Lebensmit-
tel⟩; (erschöpfen) use up, exhaust.
V~er m -s,- consumer. **v~t** a worn;
⟨Luft⟩ stale
verbrechen† vt (fam) perpetrate.
V~ nt -s,- crime
Verbrecher m -s,- criminal. **v~isch** a
criminal
verbreit|en vt spread; **sich v~en**
spread. **v~ern** vt widen; **sich v~ern**
widen. **v~et** a widespread. **V~ung**
f - spread; (Verbreiten) spreading
verbrenn|en† vt/i (sein) burn; cre-
mate ⟨Leiche⟩. **V~ung** f -,-en burning; cremation; (Wunde) burn
verbringen† vt spend
verbrühen vt scald
verbuchen vt enter; (fig) notch up
⟨Erfolg⟩
verbünd|en (sich) vr form an
alliance. **V~ete(r)** m/f ally
verbürgen vt guarantee; **sich v~ für**
vouch for
verbüßen vt serve ⟨Strafe⟩
Verdacht m -[e]s suspicion; **in** or **im
V~ haben** suspect
verdächtig a suspicious, adv -ly.
v~en vt suspect (gen of). **V~te(r)**
m/f suspect
verdamm|en vt condemn; (Relig)
damn. **V~nis** f - damnation. **v~t** a &
adv (sl) damned; **v~t!** damn!
verdampfen vt/i (sein) evaporate
verdanken vt owe (dat to)
verdau|en vt digest. **v~lich** a digest-
ible. **V~ung** f - digestion
Verdeck nt -[e]s,-e hood; (Oberdeck)
top deck. **v~en** vt cover; (verbergen)
hide, conceal
verdenken† vt **das kann man ihm
nicht v~** you can't blame him for it
verderb|en† vi (sein) spoil; ⟨Lebens-
mittel:⟩ go bad ● vt spoil; (zerstören)
ruin; (moralisch) corrupt; **ich habe
mir den Magen verdorben** I have an
upset stomach. **V~en** nt -s ruin.
v~lich a perishable; (schädlich)
pernicious

verdeutlichen vt make clear

verdichten vt compress; **sich v~** ⟨Nebel:⟩ thicken

verdien|en vt/i (haben) earn; (fig) deserve. **V~er** m -s,- wage-earner

Verdienst¹ m -[e]s earnings pl

Verdienst² nt -[e]s,-e merit

verdient a well-deserved; ⟨Person⟩ of outstanding merit. **v~ermaßen** adv deservedly

verdoppeln vt double; (fig) redouble; **sich v~** double

verdorben a spoilt, ruined; ⟨Magen⟩ upset; (moralisch) corrupt; (verkommen) depraved

verdorren vi (sein) wither

verdrängen vt force out; (fig) displace; (psychisch) repress

verdreh|en vt twist; roll ⟨Augen⟩; (fig) distort. **v~t** a (fam) crazy

verdreifachen vt treble, triple

verdreschen† vt (fam) thrash

verdrießlich a morose, adv -ly

verdrücken vt crumple; (fam: essen) polish off; **sich v~** (fam) slip away

Verdruß m -sses annoyance

verdunk|eln vt darken; black out ⟨Zimmer⟩; **sich v~eln** darken. **V~[e]lung** f - black-out

verdünnen vt dilute; **sich v~** taper off

verdunst|en vi (sein) evaporate. **V~ung** f - evaporation

verdursten vi (sein) die of thirst

verdutzt a baffled

veredeln vt refine; (Hort) graft

verehr|en vt revere; (Relig) worship; (bewundern) admire; (schenken) give. **V~er(in)** m -s,- (f -,-nen) admirer. **V~ung** f - veneration; worship; admiration

vereidigen vt swear in

Verein m -s,-e society; (Sport-) club

vereinbar a compatible. **v~en** vt arrange; **nicht zu v~en** incompatible. **V~ung** f -,-en agreement

vereinen vt unite; **sich v~** unite

vereinfachen vt simplify

vereinheitlichen vt standardize

vereinig|en vt unite; merge ⟨Firmen⟩; **sich v~** unite; **V~te Staaten [von Amerika]** United States sg [of America]. **V~ung** f -,-en union; (Organisation) organization

vereinsamt a lonely

vereinzelt a isolated ● adv occasionally

vereist a frozen; ⟨Straße⟩ icy

vereiteln vt foil, thwart

vereitert a septic

verenden vi (sein) die

verengen vt restrict; **sich v~** narrow; ⟨Pupille:⟩ contract

vererb|en vt leave (dat to); (Biol & fig) pass on (dat to). **V~ung** f - heredity

verewigen vt immortalize; **sich v~** (fam) leave one's mark

verfahren† vi (sein) proceed; **v~ mit** deal with ● vr **sich v~** lose one's way ● a muddled. **V~** nt -s,- procedure; (Techn) process; (Jur) proceedings pl

Verfall m decay; (eines Gebäudes) dilapidation; (körperlich & fig) decline; (Ablauf) expiry. **v~en**† vi (sein) decay; ⟨Person, Sitten:⟩ decline; (ablaufen) expire; **v~en in** (+acc) lapse into; **v~en auf** (+acc) hit on ⟨Idee⟩; **jdm/etw v~en sein** be under the spell of s.o./sth; be addicted to ⟨Alkohol⟩

verfälschen vt falsify; adulterate ⟨Wein, Lebensmittel⟩

verfänglich a awkward

verfärben (sich) vr change colour; ⟨Stoff:⟩ discolour

verfass|en vt write; (Jur) draw up; (entwerfen) draft. **V~er** m -s,- author. **V~ung** f (Pol) constitution; (Zustand) state

verfaulen vi (sein) rot, decay

verfechten† vt advocate

verfehlen vt miss

verfeinde|n (sich) vr become enemies; **v~t sein** be enemies

verfeinern vt refine; (verbessern) improve

verfilmen vt film

verfilzt a matted

verfliegen† vi (sein) evaporate; ⟨Zeit:⟩ fly

verflixt a (fam) awkward; (verdammt) blessed; **v~!** damn!

verfluch|en vt curse. **v~t** a & adv (fam) damned; **v~!** damn!

verflüchtigen (sich) vr evaporate

verflüssigen vt liquefy

verfolg|en vt pursue; (folgen) follow; (bedrängen) pester; (Pol) persecute; **strafrechtlich v~en** prosecute. **V~er** m -s,- pursuer. **V~ung** f - pursuit; persecution

verfrachten vt ship

verfrüht a premature

verfügbar a available

verfüg|en vt order; (Jur) decree ● vi (haben) **v~en über** (+acc) have at one's disposal. **V~ung** f -,-en order;

(*Jur*) decree; **jdm zur V~ung ste-hen/stellen** be/place at s.o.'s disposal

verführ|en *vt* seduce; (*verlocken*) tempt. **V~er** *m* seducer. **v~erisch** *a* seductive; tempting. **V~ung** *f* seduction; temptation

vergammelt *a* rotten; (*Gebäude*) decayed; (*Person*) scruffy

vergangen *a* past; (*letzte*) last. **V~heit** *f* - past; (*Gram*) past tense

vergänglich *a* transitory

vergas|en *vt* gas. **V~er** *m* -s,- carburettor

vergeb|en† *vt* award (**an**+*dat* to); (*weggeben*) give away; (*verzeihen*) forgive. **v~ens** *adv* in vain. **v~lich** *a* futile, vain ● *adv* in vain. **V~ung** *f* - forgiveness

vergehen† *vi* (*sein*) pass; **v~ vor** (+*dat*) nearly die of; **sich v~** violate (**gegen etw** sth); (*sexuell*) sexually assault (**an jdm** s.o.). **V~** *nt* -s,- offence

vergelt|en† *vt* repay. **V~ung** *f* - retaliation; (*Rache*) revenge. **V~ungs-maßnahme** *f* reprisal

vergessen† *vt* forget; (*liegenlassen*) leave behind. **V~heit** *f* - oblivion; **in V~heit geraten** be forgotten

vergeßlich *a* forgetful. **V~keit** *f* - forgetfulness

vergeuden *vt* waste, squander

vergewaltig|en *vt* rape. **V~ung** *f* -,-en rape

vergewissern (sich) *vr* make sure (*gen* of)

vergießen† *vt* spill; shed (*Tränen, Blut*)

vergift|en *vt* poison. **V~ung** *f* -,-en poisoning

Vergißmeinnicht *nt* -[e]s,-[e] forget-me-not

vergittert *a* barred

verglasen *vt* glaze

Vergleich *m* -[e]s,-e comparison; (*Jur*) settlement. **v~bar** *a* comparable. **v~en**† *vt* compare (**mit** with/to). **v~sweise** *adv* comparatively

vergnüg|en (sich) *vr* enjoy oneself. **V~en** *nt* -s,- pleasure; (*Spaß*) fun; **viel V~en!** have a good time! **v~lich** *a* enjoyable. **v~t** *a* cheerful, *adv* -ly; (*zufrieden*) happy, *adv* -ily; (*vergnüglich*) enjoyable. **V~ungen** *fpl* entertainments

vergolden *vt* gild; (*plattieren*) gold-plate

vergönnen *vt* grant

vergöttern *vt* idolize

vergraben† *vt* bury

vergreifen† **(sich)** *vr* **sich v~ an** (+*dat*) assault; (*stehlen*) steal

vergriffen *a* out of print

vergrößer|n *vt* enlarge; (*Linse:*) magnify; (*vermehren*) increase; (*erweitern*) extend; expand (*Geschäft*); **sich v~n** grow bigger; (*Firma:*) expand; (*zunehmen*) increase. **V~ung** *f* -,-en magnification; increase; expansion; (*Phot*) enlargement. **V~ungsglas** *nt* magnifying glass

Vergünstigung *f* -,-en privilege

vergüt|en *vt* pay for; **jdm etw v~en** reimburse s.o. for sth. **V~ung** *f* -,-en remuneration; (*Erstattung*) reimbursement

verhaft|en *vt* arrest. **V~ung** *f* -,-en arrest

verhalten† **(sich)** *vr* behave; (*handeln*) act; (*beschaffen sein*) be; **sich still v~** keep quiet. **V~** *nt* -s behaviour, conduct

Verhältnis *nt* -ses,-se relationship; (*Liebes-*) affair; (*Math*) ratio; **V~se** circumstances; (*Bedingungen*) conditions; **über seine V~se leben** live beyond one's means. **v~mäßig** *adv* comparatively, relatively

verhand|eln *vt* discuss; (*Jur*) try ● *vi* (*haben*) negotiate; **v~eln gegen** (*Jur*) try. **V~lung** *f* (*Jur*) trial; **V~lungen** negotiations

verhängen *vt* cover; (*fig*) impose

Verhängnis *nt* -ses fate, doom. **v~voll** *a* fatal, disastrous

verharmlosen *vt* play down

verharren *vi* (*haben*) remain

verhärten *vt/i* (*sein*) harden; **sich v~** harden

verhaßt *a* hated

verhätscheln *vt* spoil, pamper

verhauen† *vt* (*fam*) beat; make a mess of (*Prüfung*)

verheerend *a* devastating; (*fam*) terrible

verhehlen *vt* conceal

verheilen *vi* (*sein*) heal

verheimlichen *vt* keep secret

verheirat|en (sich) *vr* get married (**mit** to). **v~et** *a* married

verhelfen† *vi* (*haben*) **jdm zu etw v~** help s.o. get sth

verherrlichen *vt* glorify

verhexen *vt* bewitch; **es ist wie ver-hext** (*fam*) there is a jinx on it

verhinder|n vt prevent; **v∼t sein** be unable to come. **V∼ung** f - prevention
verhöhnen vt deride
Verhör nt -s,-e interrogation; **ins V∼ nehmen** interrogate. **v∼en** vt interrogate; **sich v∼en** mishear
verhüllen vt cover; (fig) disguise. **v∼d** a euphemistic, adv -ally
verhungern vi (sein) starve
verhüt|en vt prevent. **V∼ung** f - prevention. **V∼ungsmittel** nt contraceptive
verhutzelt a wizened
verirren (sich) vr get lost
verjagen vt chase away
verjüngen vt rejuvenate; **sich v∼** taper
verkalkt a (fam) senile
verkalkulieren (sich) vr miscalculate
Verkauf m sale; **zum V∼** for sale. **v∼en** vt sell; **zu v∼en** for sale
Verkäufer(in) m seller; (im Geschäft) shop assistant
Verkehr m -s traffic; (Kontakt) contact; (Geschlechts-) intercourse; **aus dem V∼ ziehen** take out of circulation. **v∼en** vi (haben) operate; ⟨Bus, Zug:⟩ run; (Umgang haben) associate, mix (mit with); (Gast sein) visit (bei jdm s.o.); frequent (in einem Lokal a restaurant); **brieflich v∼en** correspond ● vt **ins Gegenteil v∼en** turn round
Verkehrs|ampel f traffic lights pl. **V∼büro** nt = **V∼verein. V∼funk** m [radio] traffic information. **V∼unfall** m road accident. **V∼verein** m tourist office. **V∼zeichen** nt traffic sign
verkehrt a wrong, adv -ly. **v∼herum** adv the wrong way round; (links) inside out
verkennen† vt misjudge
verklagen vt sue (**auf**+acc for)
verkleid|en vt disguise; (Techn) line; **sich v∼en** disguise oneself; (für Kostümfest) dress up. **V∼ung** f -,-en disguise; (Kostüm) fancy dress; (Techn) lining
verkleiner|n vt reduce [in size]. **V∼ung** f-reduction. **V∼ungsform** f diminutive
verklemmt a jammed; (psychisch) inhibited
verkneifen† vt **sich** (dat) **etw v∼** do without sth; (verbeißen) suppress sth

verknittern vt/i (sein) crumple
verknüpfen vt knot together; (verbinden) connect, link; (zugleich tun) combine
verkommen† vi (sein) be neglected; (sittlich) go to the bad; (verfallen) decay; ⟨Haus:⟩ fall into disrepair; ⟨Gegend:⟩ become run-down; ⟨Lebensmittel:⟩ go bad ● a neglected; (sittlich) depraved; ⟨Haus⟩ dilapidated; ⟨Gegend⟩ run-down
verkörper|n vt embody, personify. **V∼ung** f -,-en embodiment, personification
verkraften vt cope with
verkrampft a (fig) tense
verkriechen† (**sich**) vr hide
verkrümmt a crooked, bent
verkrüppelt a crippled; ⟨Glied⟩ deformed
verkühl|en (**sich**) vr catch a chill. **V∼ung** f -,-en chill
verkümmer|n vi (sein) waste/ ⟨Pflanze:⟩ wither away. **v∼t** a stunted
verkünd|en vt announce; pronounce ⟨Urteil⟩. **v∼igen** vt announce; (predigen) preach
verkürzen vt shorten; (verringern) reduce; (abbrechen) cut short; while away ⟨Zeit⟩
verladen† vt load
Verlag m -[e]s,-e publishing firm
verlangen vt ask for; (fordern) demand; (berechnen) charge; **am Telefon verlangt werden** be wanted on the telephone. **V∼** nt -s desire; (Bitte) request; **auf V∼** on demand
verlänger|n vt extend; lengthen ⟨Kleid⟩; (zeitlich) prolong; renew ⟨Paß, Vertrag⟩; (Culin) thin down. **V∼ung** f -,-en extension; renewal. **V∼ungsschnur** f extension cable
verlangsamen vt slow down
Verlaß m -sses **auf ihn ist kein V∼** you cannot rely on him
verlassen† vt leave; (im Stich lassen) desert; **sich v∼ auf** (+acc) rely or depend on ● a deserted. **V∼heit** f - desolation
verläßlich a reliable
Verlauf m course; **im V∼** (+gen) in the course of. **v∼en**† vi (sein) run; (ablaufen) go; (zerlaufen) melt; **gut v∼en** go [off] well ● vr **sich v∼en** lose one's way; ⟨Menge:⟩ disperse; ⟨Wasser:⟩ drain away
verleben vt spend

verlegen vt move; (verschieben) postpone; (vor-) bring forward; (verlieren) mislay; (versperren) block; (legen) lay ⟨Teppich, Rohre⟩; (veröffentlichen) publish; **sich v~ auf** (+acc) take up ⟨Beruf, Fach⟩; resort to ⟨Taktik, Bitten⟩ ● a embarrassed; **nie v~ um** never at a loss for. **V~heit** f - embarrassment

Verleger m -s,- publisher

verleihen† vt lend; (gegen Gebühr) hire out; (überreichen) award, confer; (fig) give

verleiten vt induce/(verlocken) tempt (**zu** to)

verlernen vt forget

verlesen¹† vt read out; **ich habe mich v~** I misread it

verlesen²† vt sort out

verletz|en vt injure; (kränken) hurt; (verstoßen gegen) infringe; violate ⟨Grenze⟩. **v~end** a hurtful, wounding. **v~lich** a vulnerable. **V~te(r)** m/f injured person; (bei Unfall) casualty. **V~ung** f -,-en injury; (Verstoß) infringement; violation

verleugnen vt deny; disown ⟨Freund⟩

verleumd|en vt slander; (schriftlich) libel. **v~erisch** a slanderous; libellous. **V~ung** f-,-en slander; (schriftlich) libel

verlieben (sich) vr fall in love (**in**+acc with); **verliebt sein** be in love (**in**+acc with)

verlier|en† vt lose; shed ⟨Laub⟩; **sich v~en** disappear; (Weg:) peter out ● vi (haben) lose (**an etw** dat sth). **V~er** m -s,- loser

verlob|en (sich) vr get engaged (**mit** to); **v~t sein** be engaged. **V~te** f fiancée. **V~te(r)** m fiancé. **V~ung** f -,-en engagement

verlock|en vt tempt; **v~end** tempting. **V~ung** f -,-en temptation

verlogen a lying

verloren a lost; **v~e Eier** poached eggs. **v~gehen**† vi sep (sein) get lost

verlos|en vt raffle. **V~ung** f -,-en raffle; (Ziehung) draw

verlottert a run-down; ⟨Person⟩ scruffy; (sittlich) dissolute

Verlust m -[e]s,-e loss

vermachen vt leave, bequeath

Vermächtnis nt -ses,-se legacy

vermähl|en (sich) vr marry. **V~ung** f -,-en marriage

vermehren vt increase; propagate ⟨Pflanzen⟩; **sich v~** increase; (sich fortpflanzen) breed, multiply

vermeiden† vt avoid

vermeintlich a supposed, adv -ly

Vermerk m -[e]s,-e note. **v~en** vt note [down]; **übel v~en** take amiss

vermess|en† vt measure; survey ⟨Gelände⟩ ● a presumptuous. **V~enheit** f - presumption. **V~ung** f measurement; (Land-) survey

vermiet|en vt let, rent [out]; hire out ⟨Boot, Auto⟩; **zu v~en** to let; ⟨Boot:⟩ for hire. **V~er** m landlord. **V~erin** f landlady

verminder|n vt reduce, lessen. **V~ung** f - reduction, decrease

vermischen vt mix; **sich v~** mix

vermissen vt miss

vermißt a missing. **V~e(r)** m missing person/(Mil) soldier

vermittel|n vi (haben) mediate ● vt arrange; (beschaffen) find; place ⟨Arbeitskräfte⟩; impart ⟨Wissen⟩; convey ⟨Eindruck⟩. **v~s** prep (+gen) by means of

Vermittl|er m -s,- agent; (Schlichter) mediator. **V~ung** f -,-en arrangement; (Agentur) agency; (Teleph) exchange; (Schlichtung) mediation

vermögen† vt be able (**zu** to). **V~** nt -s,- fortune. **v~d** a wealthy

vermut|en vt suspect; (glauben) presume. **v~lich** a probable ● adv presumably. **V~ung** f -,-en supposition; (Verdacht) suspicion; (Mutmaßung) conjecture

vernachlässig|en vt neglect. **V~ung** f - neglect

vernehm|en† vt hear; (verhören) question; (Jur) examine. **V~ung** f -,-en questioning

verneig|en (sich) vr bow. **V~ung** f -,-en bow

vernein|en vt answer in the negative; (ablehnen) reject. **v~end** a negative. **V~ung** f -,-en negative answer; (Gram) negative

vernicht|en vt destroy; (ausrotten) exterminate. **v~end** a devastating; ⟨Niederlage⟩ crushing. **V~ung** f - destruction; extermination

Vernunft f - reason; **V~ annehmen** see reason

vernünftig a reasonable, sensible; (fam: ordentlich) decent ● adv sensibly; (fam) properly

veröffentlich|en vt publish. **V~ung** f -,-en publication

verordn|en *vt* prescribe (*dat* for).
V~ung *f* -,-en prescription; (*Verfügung*) decree

verpachten *vt* lease [out]

verpack|en *vt* pack; (*einwickeln*) wrap. **V~ung** *f* packaging; wrapping

verpassen *vt* miss; (*fam: geben*) give

verpfänden *vt* pawn

verpflanzen *vt* transplant

verpfleg|en *vt* feed; **sich selbst v~en** cater for oneself. **V~ung** *f* - board; (*Essen*) food; **Unterkunft und V~ung** board and lodging

verpflicht|en *vt* oblige; (*einstellen*) engage; (*Sport*) sign; **sich v~en** undertake/(*versprechen*) promise (**zu** to); (*vertraglich*) sign a contract; **jdm v~et sein** be indebted to s.o. **V~ung** *f* -,-en obligation, commitment

verpfuschen *vt* make a mess of

verpönt *a* **v~ sein** be frowned upon

verprügeln *vt* beat up, thrash

Verputz *m* -es plaster. **v~en** *vt* plaster; (*fam: essen*) polish off

Verrat *m* -[e]s betrayal, treachery. **v~en†** *vt* betray; give away (*Geheimnis*); (*fam: sagen*) tell; **sich v~en** give oneself away

Verräter *m* -s,- traitor. **v~isch** *a* treacherous; (*fig*) revealing

verräuchert *a* smoky

verrech|nen *vt* settle; clear (*Scheck*); **sich v~nen** make a mistake; (*fig*) miscalculate. **V~nungsscheck** *m* crossed cheque

verregnet *a* spoilt by rain; (*Tag*) rainy, wet

verreisen *vi* (*sein*) go away; **verreist sein** be away

verreißen† *vt* (*fam*) pan, slate

verrenken *vt* dislocate; **sich v~** contort oneself

verricht|en *vt* perform, do; say (*Gebet*). **V~ung** *f* -,-en task

verriegeln *vt* bolt

verringer|n *vt* reduce; **sich v~n** decrease. **V~ung** *f* - reduction; decrease

verrost|en *vi* (*sein*) rust. **v~et** *a* rusty

verrücken *vt* move

verrückt *a* crazy, mad; **v~ werden/machen** go/drive crazy. **V~e(r)** *m/f* lunatic. **V~heit** *f* -,-en madness; (*Torheit*) folly

Verruf *m* disrepute. **v~en** *a* disreputable

verrühren *vt* mix

verrunzelt *a* wrinkled

verrutschen *vi* (*sein*) slip

Vers /fɛrs/ *m* -es,-e verse

versag|en *vi* (*haben*) fail ● *vt* **jdm/sich etw v~en** deny s.o./oneself sth. **V~en** *nt* -s,- failure. **V~er** *m* -s,- failure

versalzen† *vt* put too much salt in/on; (*fig*) spoil

versamm|eln *vt* assemble; **sich v~eln** assemble, meet. **V~lung** *f* assembly, meeting

Versand *m* -[e]s dispatch. **V~haus** *nt* mail-order firm

versäum|en *vt* miss; lose (*Zeit*); (*unterlassen*) neglect; **[es] v~en, etw zu tun** fail *or* neglect to do sth. **V~nis** *nt* -ses,-se omission

verschaffen *vt* get; **sich** (*dat*) **v~** obtain; gain (*Respekt*)

verschämt *a* bashful, *adv* -ly

verschandeln *vt* spoil

verschärfen *vt* intensify; tighten (*Kontrolle*); increase (*Tempo*); aggravate (*Lage*); **sich v~** intensify; increase; (*Lage:*) worsen

verschätzen (sich) *vr* **sich v~** (+ *dat*) misjudge

verschenken *vt* give away

verscheuchen *vt* shoo/(*jagen*) chase away

verschicken *vt* send; (*Comm*) dispatch

verschieb|en† *vt* move; (*aufschieben*) put off, postpone; (*sl: handeln mit*) traffic in; **sich v~en** move, shift; (*verrutschen*) slip; (*zeitlich*) be postponed. **V~ung** *f* shift; postponement

verschieden *a* different; **v~e** (*pl*) different; (*mehrere*) various; **v~es** some things; (*dieses und jenes*) various things; **die v~sten Farben** a whole variety of colours; **das ist v~** it varies ● *adv* differently; **v~ groß/lang** of different sizes/lengths. **v~artig** *a* diverse. **V~heit** *f* - difference; (*Vielfalt*) diversity. **v~tlich** *adv* several times

verschimmel|n *vi* (*sein*) go mouldy. **v~t** *a* mouldy

verschlafen† *vi* (*haben*) oversleep ● *vt* sleep through (*Tag*); (*versäumen*) miss (*Zug, Termin*); **sich v~** oversleep ● *a* sleepy; **noch v~** still half asleep

Verschlag *m* -[e]s,-̈e shed

verschlagen† vt lose ⟨Seite⟩; **jdm die Sprache/den Atem v~** leave s.o. speechless/take s.o.'s breath away; **nach X v~ werden** end up in X ● a sly, adv -ly

verschlechter|n vt make worse; **sich v~n** get worse, deteriorate. **V~ung** f -,-en deterioration

verschleiern vt veil; (fig) hide

Verschleiß m -es wear and tear; (Verbrauch) consumption. **v~en**† vt/i (sein) wear out

verschleppen vt carry off; (entführen) abduct; spread ⟨Seuche⟩; neglect ⟨Krankheit⟩; (hinausziehen) delay

verschleudern vt sell at a loss; (verschwenden) squander

verschließen† vt close; (abschließen) lock; (einschließen) lock up

verschlimmer|n vt make worse; aggravate ⟨Lage⟩; **sich v~n** get worse, deteriorate. **V~ung** f -,-en deterioration

verschlingen† vt intertwine; (fressen) devour; (fig) swallow

verschlissen a worn

verschlossen a reserved. **V~heit** f - reserve

verschlucken vt swallow; **sich v~** choke (an + dat on)

Verschluß m -sses,-̈sse fastener, clasp; (Fenster-, Koffer-) catch; (Flaschen-) top; (luftdicht) seal; (Phot) shutter; **unter V~** under lock and key

verschlüsselt a coded

verschmähen vt spurn

verschmelzen† vt/i (sein) fuse

verschmerzen vt get over

verschmutz|en vt dirty; pollute ⟨Luft⟩ ● vi (sein) get dirty. **V~ung** f - pollution

verschnaufen vi/r (haben) [sich] **v~** get one's breath

verschneit a snow-covered

verschnörkelt a ornate

verschnüren vt tie up

verschollen a missing

verschonen vt spare

verschönern vt brighten up; (verbessern) improve

verschossen a faded

verschrammt a scratched

verschränken vt cross

verschreiben† vt prescribe; **sich v~** make a slip of the pen

verschrie[e]n a notorious

verschroben a eccentric

verschrotten vt scrap

verschulden vt be to blame for. **V~ nt** -s fault

verschuldet a **v~ sein** be in debt

verschütten vt spill; (begraben) bury

verschweigen† vt conceal, hide

verschwend|en† vt waste. **v~erisch** a extravagant, adv -ly; (üppig) lavish, adv -ly. **V~ung** f - extravagance; (Vergeudung) waste

verschwiegen a discreet; ⟨Ort⟩ secluded. **V~heit** f - discretion

verschwimmen† vi (sein) become blurred

verschwinden† vi (sein) disappear; [mal] **v~** (fam) spend a penny. **V~ nt** -s disappearance

verschwommen a blurred

verschwör|en† (sich) vr conspire. **V~ung** f -,-en conspiracy

versehen† vt perform; hold ⟨Posten⟩; keep ⟨Haushalt⟩; **v~ mit** provide with; **sich v~** make a mistake; **ehe man sich's versieht** before you know where you are. **V~ nt** -s,- oversight; (Fehler) slip; **aus V~** by mistake. **v~tlich** adv by mistake

Versehrte(r) m disabled person

versenden† vt send [out]

versengen vt singe; (stärker) scorch

versenken vt sink; **sich v~ in** (+ acc) immerse oneself in

versessen a keen (auf + acc on)

versetz|en vt move; transfer ⟨Person⟩; (Sch) move up; (verpfänden) pawn; (verkaufen) sell; (vermischen) blend; (antworten) reply; **jdn v~en** (fam: warten lassen) stand s.o. up; **jdm einen Stoß/Schreck v~en** give s.o. a push/fright; **jdm in Angst/Erstaunen v~en** frighten/astonish s.o.; **sich in jds Lage v~en** put oneself in s.o.'s place. **V~ung** f -,-en move; transfer; (Sch) move to a higher class

verseuch|en vt contaminate. **V~ung** f - contamination

versicher|n vt insure; (bekräftigen) affirm; **jdm v~n** assure s.o. (daß that). **V~ung** f -,-en insurance; assurance

versiegeln vt seal

versiegen vi (sein) dry up

versiert /vɛrˈziːɐt/ a experienced

versilbert a silver-plated

versinken† vi (sein) sink; **in Gedanken versunken** lost in thought

Version /vɛrˈzjoːn/ f -,-en version

Versmaß /ˈfɛrs-/ nt metre

versöhn|en *vt* reconcile; **sich v~en** become reconciled. **v~lich** *a* conciliatory. **V~ung** *f* -,-en reconciliation

versorg|en *vt* provide, supply (**mit** with); provide for ⟨*Familie*⟩; (*betreuen*) look after; keep ⟨*Haushalt*⟩. **V~ung** *f* - provision, supply; (*Betreuung*) care

verspät|en (sich) *vr* be late. **v~et** *a* late; ⟨*Zug*⟩ delayed; ⟨*Dank, Glückwunsch*⟩ belated ● *adv* late; belatedly. **V~ung** *f* - lateness; **V~ung haben** be late

versperren *vt* block; bar ⟨*Weg*⟩

verspiel|en *vt* gamble away; **sich v~en** play a wrong note. **v~t** *a* playful, *adv* -ly

verspotten *vt* mock, ridicule

versprech|en† *vt* promise; **sich v~en** make a slip of the tongue; **sich** (*dat*) **viel v~en von** have high hopes of. **V~en** *nt* -s,- promise. **V~ungen** *fpl* promises

verspüren *vt* feel

verstaatlich|en *vt* nationalize. **V~ung** *f* - nationalization

Verstand *m* -[e]s mind; (*Vernunft*) reason; **den V~ verlieren** go out of one's mind. **v~esmäßig** *a* rational, *adv* -ly

verständig *a* sensible, *adv* -bly; (*klug*) intelligent, *adv* -ly. **v~en** *vt* notify, inform; **sich v~en** communicate; (*sich verständlich machen*) make oneself understood; (*sich einigen*) reach agreement. **V~ung** *f* - notification; communication; (*Einigung*) agreement

verständlich *a* comprehensible, *adv* -bly; (*deutlich*) clear, *adv* -ly; (*begreiflich*) understandable; **sich v~ machen** make oneself understood. **v~erweise** *adv* understandably

Verständnis *nt* -ses understanding. **v~los** *a* uncomprehending, *adv* -ly. **v~voll** *a* understanding, *adv* -ly

verstärk|en *vt* strengthen, reinforce; (*steigern*) intensify, increase; amplify ⟨*Ton*⟩; **sich v~en** intensify. **V~er** *m* -s,- amplifier. **V~ung** *f* reinforcement; increase; amplification; (*Truppen*) reinforcements *pl*

verstaubt *a* dusty

verstauchen *vt* sprain

verstauen *vt* stow

Versteck *nt* -[e]s,-e hiding-place; **V~ spielen** play hide-and-seek. **v~en** *vt* hide; **sich v~en** hide. **v~t** *a* hidden;

(*heimlich*) secret; (*verstohlen*) furtive, *adv* -ly

verstehen† *vt* understand; (*können*) know; **falsch v~** misunderstand; **sich v~** understand one another; (*auskommen*) get on; **das versteht sich von selbst** that goes without saying

versteifen *vt* stiffen; **sich v~** stiffen; (*fig*) insist (**auf** + *acc* on)

versteiger|n *vt* auction. **V~ung** *f* auction

versteinert *a* fossilized

verstell|bar *a* adjustable. **v~en** *vt* adjust; (*versperren*) block; (*verändern*) disguise; **sich v~en** pretend. **V~ung** *f* - pretence

versteuern *vt* pay tax on

verstiegen *a* (*fig*) extravagant

verstimm|t *a* disgruntled; ⟨*Magen*⟩ upset; (*Mus*) out of tune. **V~ung** *f* - ill humour; (*Magen-*) upset

verstockt *a* stubborn, *adv* -ly

verstohlen *a* furtive, *adv* -ly

verstopf|en *vt* plug; (*versperren*) block; **v~t** blocked; ⟨*Person*⟩ constipated. **V~ung** *f* -,-en blockage; (*Med*) constipation

verstorben *a* late, deceased. **V~e(r)** *m/f* deceased

verstört *a* bewildered

Verstoß *m* infringement. **v~en**† *vt* disown ● *vi* (*haben*) **v~en gegen** contravene, infringe; offend against ⟨*Anstand*⟩

verstreichen† *vt* spread ● *vi* (*sein*) pass

verstreuen *vt* scatter

verstümmeln *vt* mutilate; garble ⟨*Text*⟩

verstummen *vi* (*sein*) fall silent; ⟨*Gespräch, Lärm:*⟩ cease

Versuch *m* -[e]s,-e attempt; (*Experiment*) experiment. **v~en** *vt/i* (*haben*) try; **sich v~en in** (+ *dat*) try one's hand at; **v~t sein** be tempted (**zu** to). **V~skaninchen** *nt* (*fig*) guinea-pig. **v~sweise** *adv* as an experiment. **V~ung** *f* -,-en temptation

versündigen (sich) *vr* sin (**an** + *dat* against)

vertagen *vt* adjourn; (*aufschieben*) postpone; **sich v~** adjourn

vertauschen *vt* exchange; (*verwechseln*) mix up

verteidig|en *vt* defend. **V~er** *m* -s,- defender; (*Jur*) defence counsel. **V~ung** *f* -,-en defence

verteil|en *vt* distribute; (*zuteilen*) allocate; (*ausgeben*) hand out; (*verstreichen*) spread; **sich v~en** spread out. **V~ung** *f* - distribution; allocation

vertief|en *vt* deepen; **v~t sein** in (*+acc*) be engrossed in. **V~ung** *f* -,-en hollow, depression

vertikal /vɛrti'ka:l/ *a* vertical, *adv* -ly

vertilgen *vt* exterminate; kill [off] ⟨*Unkraut*⟩; (*fam: essen*) demolish

vertippen (sich) *vr* make a typing mistake

vertonen *vt* set to music

Vertrag *m* -[e]s,:̈e contract; (*Pol*) treaty

vertragen† *vt* tolerate, stand; take ⟨*Kritik, Spaß*⟩; **sich v~** get on; (*passen*) go (**mit** with); **sich wieder v~** make it up ● *a* worn

vertraglich *a* contractual

verträglich *a* good-natured; (*bekömmlich*) digestible

vertrauen *vi* (*haben*) trust (**jdm/etw** s.o./sth; **auf**+*acc* in). **V~** *nt* -s trust, confidence (**zu** in); **im V~** in confidence. **V~smann** *m* (*pl* **-leute**) representative; (*Sprecher*) spokesman. **v~svoll** *a* trusting, *adv* -ly. **v~swürdig** *a* trustworthy

vertraulich *a* confidential, *adv* -ly; (*intim*) familiar, *adv* -ly

vertraut *a* intimate; (*bekannt*) familiar; **sich v~ machen mit** familiarize oneself with. **V~heit** *f* - intimacy; familiarity

vertreib|en† *vt* drive away; drive out ⟨*Feind*⟩; (*Comm*) sell; **sich** (*dat*) **die Zeit v~en** pass the time. **V~ung** *f* -,-en expulsion

vertret|en† *vt* represent; (*einspringen für*) stand in *or* deputize for; (*verfechten*) support; hold ⟨*Meinung*⟩; **sich** (*dat*) **den Fuß v~en** twist one's ankle; **sich** (*dat*) **die Beine v~en** stretch one's legs. **V~er** *m* -s,- representative; deputy; (*Arzt-*) locum; (*Verfechter*) supporter, advocate. **V~ung** *f* -,-en representation; (*Person*) deputy; (*eines Arztes*) locum; (*Handels-*) agency

Vertrieb *m* -[e]s (*Comm*) sale. **V~ene(r)** *m/f* displaced person

vertrocknen *vi* (*sein*) dry up

vertrösten *vt* **jdn auf später v~** put s.o. off until later

vertun† *vt* waste; **sich v~** (*fam*) make a mistake

vertuschen *vt* hush up

verübeln *vt* **jdm etw v~** hold sth against s.o.

verüben *vt* commit

verunglimpfen *vt* denigrate

verunglücken *vi* (*sein*) be involved in an accident; (*fam: mißglücken*) go wrong; **tödlich v~** be killed in an accident

verunreinigen *vt* pollute; (*verseuchen*) contaminate; (*verschmutzen*) soil

verunstalten *vt* disfigure

veruntreu|en *vt* embezzle. **V~ung** *f* - embezzlement

verursachen *vt* cause

verurteil|en *vt* condemn; (*Jur*) convict (**wegen** of); sentence (**zum Tode** to death). **V~ung** *f* - condemnation; (*Jur*) conviction

vervielfachen *vt* multiply

vervielfältigen *vt* duplicate

vervollkommnen *vt* perfect

vervollständigen *vt* complete

verwachsen *a* deformed

verwählen (sich) *vr* misdial

verwahren *vt* keep; (*verstauen*) put away; **sich v~** (*fig*) protest

verwahrlost *a* neglected; ⟨*Haus*⟩ dilapidated; (*sittlich*) depraved

Verwahrung *f* - keeping; **in V~ nehmen** take into safe keeping

verwaist *a* orphaned

verwalt|en *vt* administer; (*leiten*) manage; govern ⟨*Land*⟩. **V~er** *m* -s,- administrator; manager. **V~ung** *f* -,-en administration; management; government

verwand|eln *vt* transform, change (**in**+*acc* into); **sich v~eln** change, turn (**in**+*acc* into). **V~lung** *f* transformation

verwandt *a* related (**mit** to). **V~e(r)** *m/f* relative. **V~schaft** *f* - relationship; (*Menschen*) relatives *pl*

verwarn|en *vt* warn, caution. **V~ung** *f* warning, caution

verwaschen *a* washed out, faded

verwechs|eln *vt* mix up, confuse; (*halten für*) mistake (**mit** for). **V~lung** *f* -,-en mix-up

verwegen *a* audacious, *adv* -ly

Verwehung *f* -,-en [snow-]drift

verweichlicht *a* (*fig*) soft

verweiger|n *vt/i* (*haben*) refuse (**jdm etw** s.o sth); **den Gehorsam v~n** refuse to obey. **V~ung** *f* refusal

verweilen *vi* (*haben*) stay

Verweis *m* -es,-e reference (**auf**+*acc* to); (*Tadel*) reprimand. **v~en†** *vt*

refer (**auf/an** + *acc* to); (*tadeln*) reprimand; **von der Schule v~en** expel
verwelken *vi* (*sein*) wilt
verwend|en† *vt* use; spend ⟨*Zeit,*
Mühe⟩. **V~ung** *f* use
verwerf|en† *vt* reject; **sich v~en**
warp. **v~lich** *a* reprehensible
verwert|en *vt* utilize, use; (*Comm*)
exploit. **V~ung** *f* - utilization;
exploitation
verwesen *vi* (*sein*) decompose
verwick|eln *vt* involve (**in** + *acc* in);
sich v~eln get tangled up; **in etw**
(*acc*) **v~elt sein** (*fig*) be involved *or*
mixed up in sth. **v~elt** *a*
complicated
verwildert *a* wild; ⟨*Garten*⟩ overgrown; ⟨*Aussehen*⟩ unkempt
verwinden† *vt* (*fig*) get over
verwirken *vt* forfeit
verwirklichen *vt* realize; **sich v~** be
realized
verwirr|en *vt* tangle up; (*fig*) con-
fuse; **sich v~en** get tangled; (*fig*)
become confused. **v~t** *a* confused.
V~ung *f* - confusion
verwischen *vt* smudge
verwittert *a* weathered; ⟨*Gesicht*⟩
weather-beaten
verwitwet *a* widowed
verwöhn|en *vt* spoil. **v~t** *a* spoilt;
(*anspruchsvoll*) discriminating
verworren *a* confused
verwund|bar *a* vulnerable. **v~en** *vt*
wound
verwunder|lich *a* surprising. **v~n** *vt*
surprise; **sich v~n** be surprised.
V~ung *f* - surprise
Verwund|ete(r) *m* wounded soldier;
die V~eten the wounded *pl*. **V~ung**
f -,-en wound
verwünsch|en *vt* curse. **v~t** *a*
confounded
verwüst|en *vt* devastate, ravage.
V~ung *f* -,-en devastation
verzagen *vi* (*haben*) lose heart
verzählen (sich) *vr* miscount
verzärteln *vt* mollycoddle
verzauber|n *vt* bewitch; (*fig*)
enchant; **v~ in** (+ *acc*) turn into
Verzehr *m* -s consumption. **v~en** *vt*
eat; (*aufbrauchen*) use up; **sich v~en**
(*fig*) pine away
verzeich|nen *vt* list; (*registrieren*)
register. **V~nis** *nt* -ses,-se list; (*In-
halts-*) index
verzeih|en† *vt* forgive; **v~en Sie!**
excuse me! **V~ung** *f* - forgiveness;
um V~ung bitten apologize;

V~ung! sorry! (*bei Frage*) excuse
me!
verzerren *vt* distort; contort
⟨*Gesicht*⟩; pull ⟨*Muskel*⟩
Verzicht *m* -[e]s renunciation
(**auf** + *acc* of). **v~en** *vi* (*haben*) do
without; **v~en auf** (+ *acc*) give up;
renounce ⟨*Recht, Erbe*⟩
verziehen† *vt* pull out of shape; (*verwöhnen*) spoil; **sich v~** lose shape;
⟨*Holz:*⟩ warp; ⟨*Gesicht:*⟩ twist;
(*verschwinden*) disappear; ⟨*Nebel:*⟩
disperse; ⟨*Gewitter:*⟩ pass; **das Gesicht v~** pull a face ● *vi* (*sein*) move
[away]
verzier|en *vt* decorate. **V~ung** *f* -,-en
decoration
verzinsen *vt* pay interest on
verzöger|n *vt* delay; (*verlangsamen*)
slow down; **sich v~n** be delayed.
V~ung *f* -,-en delay
verzollen *vt* pay duty on; **haben Sie**
etwas zu v~? have you anything to
declare?
verzück|t *a* ecstatic, *adv* -ally.
V~ung *f* - rapture, ecstasy
Verzug *m* delay; **in V~** in arrears
verzweif|eln *vi* (*sein*) despair. **v~elt**
a desperate, *adv* -ly; **v~elt sein** be in
despair; (*ratlos*) be desperate.
V~lung *f* - despair; (*Ratlosigkeit*)
desperation
verzweigen (sich) *vr* branch [out]
verzwickt *a* (*fam*) tricky
Veto /'ve:to/ *nt* -s,-s veto
Vetter *m* -s,-n cousin. **V~nwirt-
schaft** *f* nepotism
vgl. *abbr* (**vergleiche**) cf
Viadukt /vja'dʊkt/ *nt* -[e]s,-e viaduct
vibrieren /vi'bri:rən/ *vi* (*haben*)
vibrate
Video /'vi:deo/ *nt* -s,-s video. **V~kas-
sette** *f* video cassette. **V~recorder**
/-rəkɔrdə/ *m* -s,video recorder
Vieh *nt* -[e]s livestock; (*Rinder*) cattle
pl; (*fam: Tier*) creature. **v~isch** *a*
brutal, *adv* -ly
viel *pron* a great deal/(*fam*) a lot of;
(*pl*) many, (*fam*) a lot of; (*substantivisch*) **v~[es]** much, (*fam*) a lot;
nicht/zu v~ not/too much; **v~e** *pl*
many; **das v~e Geld/Lesen** all that
money/reading ● *adv* much, (*fam*) a
lot; **v~ mehr/weniger** much more/
less; **v~ zu groß/klein** much *or* far
too big/small
viel|deutig *a* ambiguous. **v~erlei** *inv*
a many kinds of ● *pron* many
things. **v~fach** *a* multiple ● *adv*

many times; (*fam: oft*) frequently.
V~falt *f* - diversity, [great] variety.
v~fältig *a* diverse, varied

vielleicht *adv* perhaps, maybe; (*fam: wirklich*) really

vielmals *adv* very much; **danke v~!** thank you very much!

viel|mehr *adv* rather; (*im Gegenteil*) on the contrary. **v~sagend** *a* meaningful, *adv* -ly

vielseitig *a* varied; ⟨*Person*⟩ versatile ● *adv* **v~ begabt** versatile. **V~keit** *f* - versatility

vielversprechend *a* promising

vier *inv a*, **V~** *f* -,-en four; (*Sch*) ≈ fair. **V~eck** *nt* -[e]s,-e oblong, rectangle; (*Quadrat*) square. **v~eckig** *a* oblong, rectangular; square. **v~fach** *a* quadruple. **V~linge** *mpl* quadruplets

Viertel /'fɪrtəl/ *nt* -s,- quarter; (*Wein*) quarter litre; **V~ vor/nach sechs** [a] quarter to/past six; **V~ neun** [a] quarter past eight; **drei V~ neun** [a] quarter to nine. **V~finale** *nt* quarter-final. **V~jahr** *nt* three months *pl*; (*Comm*) quarter. **v~jährlich** *a & adv* quarterly. **v~n** *vt* quarter. **V~note** *f* crotchet, (*Amer*) quarter note. **V~stunde** *f* quarter of an hour

vier|zehn /'fɪr-/ *inv a* fourteen. **v~zehnte(r,s)** *a* fourteenth. **v~zig** *inv a* forty. **v~zigste(r,s)** *a* fortieth

Villa /'vɪla/ *f* -,-len villa

violett /vjo'lɛt/ *a* violet

Vio|line /vjo'li:nə/ *f* -,-n violin. **V~linschlüssel** *m* treble clef. **V~loncello** /-lɔn'tʃɛlo/ *nt* cello

Virtuose /vɪr'tuo:zə/ *m* -n,-n virtuoso

Virus /'vi:rʊs/ *nt* -,-ren virus

Visier /vi'zi:ɐ/ *nt* -s,-e visor

Vision /vi'zjo:n/ *f* -,-en vision

Visite /vi'zi:tə/ *f* -,-n round; **V~ machen** do one's round

visuell /vi'zuɛl/ *a* visual, *adv* -ly

Visum /'vi:zʊm/ *nt* -s,-sa visa

vital /vi'ta:l/ *a* vital; ⟨*Person*⟩ energetic. **V~ität** *f* - vitality

Vitamin /vita'mi:n/ *nt* -s,-e vitamin

Vitrine /vi'tri:nə/ *f* -,-n display cabinet/(*im Museum*) case

Vizepräsident /'fi:tsə-/ *m* vice president

Vogel *m* -s,- bird; **einen V~ haben** (*fam*) have a screw loose. **V~scheuche** *f* -,-n scarecrow

Vokab|eln /vo'ka:bəln/ *fpl* vocabulary *sg*. **V~ular** *nt* -s,-e vocabulary

Vokal /vo'ka:l/ *m* -s,-e vowel

Volant /vo'lã:/ *m* -s,-s flounce; (*Auto*) steering-wheel

Volk *nt* -[e]s,"er people *sg*; (*Bevölkerung*) people *pl*; (*Bienen-*) colony

Völker|kunde *f* ethnology. **V~mord** *m* genocide. **V~recht** *nt* international law

Volks|abstimmung *f* plebiscite. **V~fest** *nt* public festival. **V~hochschule** *f* adult education classes *pl*/(*Gebäude*) centre. **V~lied** *nt* folksong. **V~tanz** *m* folk-dance. **v~tümlich** *a* popular. **V~wirt** *m* economist. **V~wirtschaft** *f* economics *sg*. **V~zählung** *f* [national] census

voll *a* full (**von** *od* **mit** of); ⟨*Haar*⟩ thick; ⟨*Erfolg, Ernst*⟩ complete; ⟨*Wahrheit*⟩ whole; **v~ machen** fill up; **die Uhr schlug v~** (*fam*) the clock struck the hour ● *adv* (*ganz*) completely; ⟨*arbeiten*⟩ full-time; ⟨*auszahlen*⟩ in full; **v~ und ganz** completely

vollauf *adv* fully, completely

Voll|beschäftigung *f* full employment. **V~blut** *nt* thoroughbred

vollbringen† *vt insep* accomplish; work ⟨*Wunder*⟩

vollende|n *vt insep* complete. **v~t** *a* perfect, *adv* -ly; **v~te Gegenwart/Vergangenheit** perfect/pluperfect

vollends *adv* completely

Vollendung *f* completion; (*Vollkommenheit*) perfection

voller *inv a* full of; **v~ Angst/Freude** filled with fear/joy; **v~ Flecken** covered with stains

Völlerei *f* - gluttony

Volleyball /'vɔli-/ *m* volleyball

vollführen *vt insep* perform

vollfüllen *vt sep* fill up

Vollgas *nt* **v~ geben** put one's foot down; **mit v~** flat out

völlig *a* complete, *adv* -ly

volljährig *a* **v~ sein** (*Jur*) be of age. **V~keit** *f* - (*Jur*) majority

Vollkaskoversicherung *f* fully comprehensive insurance

vollkommen *a* perfect, *adv* -ly; (*völlig*) complete, *adv* -ly. **V~heit** *f* - perfection

Voll|kornbrot *nt* wholemeal bread. **V~macht** *f* -,-en authority; (*Jur*) power of attorney. **V~mond** *m* full moon. **V~pension** *f* full board. **v~schlank** *a* with a fuller figure

vollständig *a* complete, *adv* -ly

vollstrecken vt insep execute; carry out ⟨Urteil⟩

volltanken vi sep (haben) (Auto) fill up [with petrol]

Volltreffer m direct hit

vollzählig a complete; **sind wir v~?** are we all here?

vollziehen† vt insep carry out; perform ⟨Handlung⟩; consummate ⟨Ehe⟩; **sich v~** take place

Volt /vɔlt/ nt -[s],- volt

Volumen /voˈluːmən/ nt -s,- volume

vom prep = **von dem; vom Rauchen** from smoking

von prep (+ dat) of; (über) about; (Ausgangspunkt, Ursache) from; (beim Passiv) by; **Musik von Mozart** music by Mozart; **einer von euch** one of you; **von hier/heute an** from here/ today; **von mir aus** I don't mind

voneinander adv from each other; ⟨abhängig⟩ on each other

vonstatten adv **v~ gehen** take place; **gut v~ gehen** go [off] well

vor prep (+ dat/acc) in front of; (zeitlich, Reihenfolge) before; (+ dat) (bei Uhrzeit) to; ⟨warnen, sich fürchten, schämen⟩ of; ⟨schützen, davonlaufen⟩ from; ⟨Respekt haben⟩ for; **vor Angst/ Kälte zittern** tremble with fear/ cold; **vor drei Tagen/Jahren** three days/years ago; **vor sich** (acc) **hin murmeln** mumble to oneself; **vor allen Dingen** above all ● adv forward; **vor und zurück** backwards and forwards

Vor|abend m eve. **V~ahnung** f premonition

voran adv at the front; (voraus) ahead; (vorwärts) forward ● im (Fortschritte machen) make progress; **jdm/etw v~gehen** precede s.o./sth. **v~kommen†** vi sep (sein) make progress; (fig) get on

Vor|anschlag m estimate. **V~anzeige** f advance notice. **V~arbeit** f preliminary work. **V~arbeiter** m foreman

voraus adv ahead (dat of); (vorn) at the front; (vorwärts) forward ● im **voraus** in advance. **v~bezahlen** vt sep pay in advance. **v~gehen†** vi sep (sein) go on ahead; **jdm/etw v~gehen** precede s.o./sth. **v~sage** f -,-n prediction. **v~sagen** vt sep predict. **v~sehen†** vt sep foresee

voraussetz|en vt sep take for granted; (erfordern) require; **vorausgesetzt, daß** provided that. **V~ung** f -,-en assumption; (Erfordernis) prerequisite; **unter der V~ung, daß** on condition that

Voraussicht f foresight; **aller V~ nach** in all probability. **v~lich** a anticipated, expected ● adv probably

Vorbehalt m -[e]s,-e reservation. **v~en†** vt sep sich (dat) **v~en** reserve ⟨Recht⟩; **jdm v~en sein/bleiben** be left to s.o. **v~los** a unreserved, adv -ly

vorbei adv past (**an** jdm/etw s.o./ sth); (zu Ende) over. **v~fahren†** vi sep (sein) drive/go past. **v~gehen†** vi sep (sein) go past; (verfehlen) miss; (vergehen) pass; (fam: besuchen) drop in (**bei** on). **v~kommen†** vi sep (sein) pass/(v~können) get past (**an** jdm/etw s.o./sth); (fam: besuchen) drop in (**bei** on)

vorbereit|en vt sep prepare; prepare for ⟨Reise⟩; **sich v~en** prepare [oneself] (**auf** + acc for). **V~ung** f -,-en preparation

vorbestellen vt sep order/(im Theater, Hotel) book in advance

vorbestraft a **v~ sein** have a [criminal] record

vorbeug|en v sep ● vt bend forward; **sich v~en** bend or lean forward ● vi (haben) prevent (etw dat sth); **v~end** preventive. **V~ung** f -prevention

Vorbild nt model. **v~lich** a exemplary, model ● adv in an exemplary manner

vorbringen† vt sep put forward; offer ⟨Entschuldigung⟩

vordatieren vt sep post-date

Vorder|bein nt foreleg. **v~e(r,s)** a front. **V~grund** m foreground. **V~mann** m (pl -männer) person in front; **auf V~mann bringen** (fam) lick into shape; (aufräumen) tidy up. **V~rad** nt front wheel. **V~seite** f front; (einer Münze) obverse. **v~ste(r,s)** a front, first. **V~teil** nt front

vor|drängeln (sich) vr sep (fam) jump the queue. **v~drängen (sich)** vr sep push forward. **v~dringen†** vi sep (sein) advance

vor|ehelich a pre-marital. **v~eilig** a rash, adv -ly

voreingenommen a biased, prejudiced. **V~heit** f - bias

vorenthalten† *vt sep* withhold

vorerst *adv* for the time being

Vorfahr *m* -en,-en ancestor

vorfahren† *vi sep* (*sein*) drive up; (*vorwärts-*) move forward; (*voraus-*) drive on ahead

Vorfahrt *f* right of way; 'V~ beachten' 'give way'. **V~sstraße** *f* ≈ major road

Vorfall *m* incident. **v~en**† *vi sep* (*sein*) happen

vorfinden† *vt sep* find

Vorfreude *f* [happy] anticipation

vorführ|en *vt sep* present, show; (*demonstrieren*) demonstrate; (*aufführen*) perform. **V~ung** *f* presentation; demonstration; performance

Vor|gabe *f* (*Sport*) handicap. **V~gang** *m* occurrence; (*Techn*) process. **V~gänger(in)** *m* -s,- (*f* -,-nen) predecessor. **V~garten** *m* front garden

vorgeben† *vt sep* pretend

vor|gefaßt *a* preconceived. **v~gefertigt** *a* prefabricated

vorgehen† *vi sep* (*sein*) go forward; (*voraus-*) go on ahead; ⟨*Uhr:*⟩ be fast; (*wichtig sein*) take precedence; (*verfahren*) act, proceed; (*geschehen*) happen, go on. **V~** *nt* -s action

vor|geschichtlich *a* prehistoric. **V~geschmack** *m* foretaste. **V~gesetzte(r)** *m/f* superior. **v~gestern** *adv* the day before yesterday

vorhaben† *vt sep* propose, intend (**zu** to); **etw v~** have sth planned; **nichts v~** have no plans. **V~** *nt* -s,- plan; (*Projekt*) project

vorhalt|en *v sep* ● *vt* hold up; **jdm etw v~en** reproach s.o. for sth ● *vi* (*haben*) last. **V~ungen** *fpl* **jdm V~ungen machen** reproach s.o. (**wegen** for)

Vorhand *f* (*Sport*) forehand

vorhanden *a* existing; **v~ sein** exist; (*verfügbar sein*) be available. **V~sein** *nt* -s existence

Vorhang *m* curtain

Vorhängeschloß *nt* padlock

vorher *adv* before[hand]

vorhergehend *a* previous

vorherig *a* prior; (*vorhergehend*) previous

Vorherrsch|aft *f* supremacy. **v~en** *vi sep* (*haben*) predominate. **v~end** *a* predominant

Vorher|sage *f* -,-n prediction; (*Wetter-*) forecast. **v~sagen** *vt sep* predict; forecast ⟨*Wetter*⟩. **v~sehen**† *vt sep* foresee

vorhin *adv* just now

vorige(r,s) *a* last, previous

Vor|kämpfer *m* (*fig*) champion. **V~kehrungen** *fpl* precautions. **V~kenntnisse** *fpl* previous knowledge *sg*

vorkommen† *vi sep* (*sein*) happen; (*vorhanden sein*) occur; (*nach vorn kommen*) come forward; (*hervorkommen*) come out; (*zu sehen sein*) show; **jdm bekannt/verdächtig v~** seem familiar/suspicious to s.o.; **sich** (*dat*) **dumm/alt v~** feel stupid/old. **V~** *nt* -s,- occurrence; (*Geol*) deposit

Vorkriegszeit *f* pre-war period

vorlad|en† *vt sep* (*Jur*) summons. **V~ung** *f* summons

Vorlage *f* model; (*Muster*) pattern; (*Gesetzes-*) bill

vorlassen† *vt sep* admit; **jdn v~** (*fam*) let s.o. pass; (*den Vortritt lassen*) let s.o. go first

Vor|lauf *m* (*Sport*) heat. **V~läufer** *m* forerunner. **v~läufig** *a* provisional, *adv* -ly; (*zunächst*) for the time being. **v~laut** *a* forward. **V~leben** *nt* past

vorleg|en *vt sep* put on ⟨*Kette*⟩; (*unterbreiten*) present; (*vorzeigen*) show; **jdm Fleisch v~en** serve s.o. with meat. **V~er** *m* -s,- mat; (*Bett-*) rug

vorles|en† *vt sep* read [out]; **jdm v~en** read to s.o. **V~ung** *f* lecture

vorletzt|e(r,s) *a* last ... but one; ⟨*Silbe*⟩ penultimate; **v~es Jahr** the year before last

Vorliebe *f* preference

vorliebnehmen† *vt sep* make do (**mit** with)

vorliegen† *vi sep* (*haben*) be present/(*verfügbar*) available; (*bestehen*) exist, be; **es muß ein Irrtum v~** there must be some mistake. **v~d** *a* present; ⟨*Frage*⟩ at issue

vorlügen† *vt sep* lie (**dat** to)

vorm *prep* = **vor dem**

vormachen *vt sep* put up; put on ⟨*Kette*⟩; push ⟨*Riegel*⟩; (*zeigen*) demonstrate; **jdm etwas v~** (*fam: täuschen*) kid s.o.

Vormacht *f* supremacy

vormals *adv* formerly

Vormarsch *m* (*Mil & fig*) advance

vormerken vt sep make a note of; (reservieren) reserve

Vormittag m morning. **v~** adv gestern/heute **v~** yesterday/this morning. **v~s** adv in the morning

Vormund m -[e]s,-munde & -münder guardian

vorn adv at the front; **nach v~** to the front; **von v~** from the front/ (vom Anfang) beginning; **von v~ anfangen** start afresh

Vorname m first name

vorne adv = vorn

vornehm a distinguished; (elegant) smart, adv -ly

vornehmen† vt sep carry out; **sich** (dat) **v~, etw zu tun** plan/(beschließen) resolve to do sth

vorn|herein adv von **v~herein** from the start. **v~über** adv forward

Vor|ort m suburb. **V~rang** m priority, precedence (**vor** + dat over). **V~rat** m -[e]s,-e supply, stock (**an** + dat of). **v~rätig** a available; **v~rätig haben** have in stock. **V~ratskammer** f larder. **V~raum** m ante-room. **V~recht** nt privilege. **V~richtung** f device

vorrücken vt/i sep (sein) move forward; (Mil) advance

Vorrunde f qualifying round

vors prep = vor das

vorsagen vt/i sep (haben) recite; **jdm [die Antwort] v~** tell s.o. the answer

Vor|satz m resolution. **v~sätzlich** a deliberate, adv -ly; (Jur) premeditated

Vorschau f preview; (Film-) trailer

Vorschein m **zum V~ kommen** appear

vorschießen† vt sep advance (Geld)

Vorschlag m suggestion, proposal. **v~en†** vt sep suggest, propose

vorschnell a rash, adv -ly

vorschreiben† vt sep lay down; dictate (dat to); **vorgeschriebene Dosis** prescribed dose

Vorschrift f regulation; (Anweisung) instruction; **jdm V~en machen** tell s.o. what to do; **Dienst nach V~** work to rule. **v~smäßig** a correct, adv -ly

Vorschule f nursery school

Vorschuß m advance

vorschützen vt sep plead [as an excuse]; feign (Krankheit)

vorseh|en† v sep ● vt intend (**für/ als** for/as); (planen) plan; **sich v~en** be careful (**vor** + dat of) ● vi (haben) peep out. **V~ung** f - providence

vorsetzen vt sep move forward; **jdm etw v~** serve s.o. sth

Vorsicht f - care; (bei Gefahr) caution; **V~!** careful! (auf Schild) 'caution'. **v~ig** a careful, adv -ly; cautious, adv -ly. **v~shalber** adv to be on the safe side. **V~smaßnahme** f precaution

Vorsilbe f prefix

Vorsitz m chairmanship; **den V~ führen** be in the chair. **v~en†** vi sep (haben) preside (dat over). **V~ende(r)** m/f chairman

Vorsorge f **V~ treffen** take precautions; make provisions (**für** for). **v~n** vi sep (haben) provide (**für** for). **V~untersuchung** f check-up

vorsorglich adv as a precaution

Vorspeise f starter

Vorspiel nt prelude. **v~en** v sep ● vt perform/ (Mus) play (dat for) ● vi (haben) audition

vorsprechen† v sep ● vt recite; (zum Nachsagen) say (dat to) ● vi (haben) (Theat) audition; **bei jdm v~** call on s.o.

vorspringen† vi sep (sein) jut out; **v~des Kinn** prominent chin

Vor|sprung m projection; (Fels-) ledge; (Vorteil) lead (**vor** + dat over). **V~stadt** f suburb. **v~städtisch** a suburban. **V~stand** m board [of directors]; (Vereins-) committee; (Partei-) executive

vorsteh|en† vi sep (haben) project, protrude; **einer Abteilung v~en** be in charge of a department; **v~end** protruding; (Augen) bulging. **V~er** m -s,- head; (Gemeinde-) chairman

vorstell|bar a imaginable, conceivable. **v~en** vt sep put forward (Bein, Uhr); (darstellen) represent; (bekanntmachen) introduce; **sich v~en** introduce oneself; (als Bewerber) go for an interview; **sich** (dat) **etw v~en** imagine sth. **V~ung** f introduction; (bei Bewerbung) interview; (Aufführung) performance; (Idee) idea; (Phantasie) imagination. **V~ungsgespräch** nt interview. **V~ungskraft** f imagination

Vorstoß m advance

Vorstrafe f previous conviction

Vortag m day before

vortäuschen vt sep feign, fake

Vorteil m advantage. **v~haft** a advantageous, adv -ly; (Kleidung, Farbe) flattering

Vortrag m -[e]s,ᵉe talk; (*wissenschaftlich*) lecture; (*Klavier-*, *Gedicht-*) recital. **v~en†** vt sep perform; (*aufsagen*) recite; (*singen*) sing; (*darlegen*) present (*dat* to); express (*Wunsch*)

vortrefflich a excellent, adv -ly

vortreten† vi sep (*sein*) step forward; (*hervor-*) protrude

Vortritt m precedence; **jdm den V~ lassen** let s.o. go first

vorüber adv **v~ sein** be over; **an etw** (*dat*) **v~** past sth. **v~gehen†** vi sep (*sein*) walk past; (*vergehen*) pass. **v~gehend** a temporary, adv -ily

Vor|urteil nt prejudice. **V~verkauf** m advance booking

vorverlegen vt sep bring forward

Vor|wahl[nummer] f dialling code. **V~wand** m -[e]s,ᵉe pretext; (*Ausrede*) excuse

vorwärts adv forward[s]. **v~kommen†** vi sep (*sein*) make progress; (*fig*) get on

vorweg adv beforehand; (*vorn*) in front; (*voraus*) ahead. **v~nehmen†** vt sep anticipate

vorweisen† vt sep show

vorwerfen† vt sep throw (*dat* to); **jdm etw v~** reproach s.o. with sth; (*beschuldigen*) accuse s.o. of sth

vorwiegend adv predominantly

Vorwort nt (*pl* -worte) preface

Vorwurf m reproach; **jdm Vorwürfe machen** reproach s.o. **v~svoll** a reproachful, adv -ly

Vorzeichen nt sign; (*fig*) omen

vorzeigen vt sep show

vorzeitig a premature, adv -ly

vorziehen† vt sep pull forward; draw (*Vorhang*); (*vorverlegen*) bring forward; (*lieber mögen*) prefer; (*bevorzugen*) favour

Vor|zimmer nt ante-room; (*Büro*) outer office. **V~zug** m preference; (*gute Eigenschaft*) merit, virtue; (*Vorteil*) advantage

vorzüglich a excellent, adv -ly

vorzugsweise adv preferably

vulgär /vʊlˈgɛː@/ a vulgar ● adv in a vulgar way

Vulkan /vʊlˈkaːn/ m -s,-e volcano

W

Waage f -,-n scales pl; (*Astr*) Libra. **w~recht** a horizontal, adv -ly

Wabe f -,-n honeycomb

wach a awake; (*aufgeweckt*) alert; **w~ werden** wake up

Wach|e f -,-n guard; (*Posten*) sentry; (*Dienst*) guard duty; (*Naut*) watch; (*Polizei-*) station; **w~e halten** keep watch; **W~e stehen** stand guard. **w~en** vi (*haben*) be awake; **w~en über** (+*acc*) watch over. **W~hund** m guard-dog

Wacholder m -s juniper

Wachposten m sentry

Wachs nt -es wax

wachsam a vigilant, adv -ly. **W~keit** f - vigilance

wachsen†¹ vi (*sein*) grow

wachs|en² vt (*reg*) wax. **W~figur** f waxwork. **W~tuch** nt oilcloth

Wachstum nt -s growth

Wächter m -s,- guard; (*Park-*) keeper; (*Parkplatz-*) attendant

Wacht|meister m [police] constable. **W~posten** m sentry

Wachturm m watch-tower

wackel|ig a wobbly; (*Stuhl*) rickety; (*Person*) shaky. **w~kontakt** m loose connection. **w~n** vi (*haben*) wobble; (*zittern*) shake ● vi (*sein*) totter

wacklig a = **wackelig**

Wade f -,-n (*Anat*) calf

Waffe f -,-n weapon; **w~n** arms

Waffel f -,-n waffle; (*Eis-*) wafer

Waffen|ruhe f cease-fire. **W~schein** m firearms licence. **W~stillstand** m armistice

Wagemut m daring. **w~ig** a daring, adv -ly

wagen vt risk; **es w~,** etw zu tun dare [to] do sth; **sich w~** (*gehen*) venture

Wagen m -s,- cart; (*Eisenbahn-*) carriage, coach; (*Güter-*) wagon; (*Kinder-*) pram; (*Auto*) car. **W~heber** m -s,- jack

Waggon /vaˈgõː/ m -s,-s wagon

waghalsig a daring, adv -ly

Wagnis nt -ses,-se risk

Wahl f -,-en choice; (*Pol*, *Admin*) election; (*geheime*) ballot; **zweite W~** (*Comm*) seconds pl

wähl|en vt/i (*haben*) choose; (*Pol*, *Admin*) elect; (*stimmen*) vote; (*Teleph*) dial. **W~er(in)** m -s,- (f -,-nen) voter. **w~erisch** a choosy, fussy

Wahl|fach nt optional subject. **w~frei** a optional. **W~kampf** m

election campaign. **W~kreis** m constituency. **W~lokal** nt polling-station. **w~los** a indiscriminate, adv -ly. **W~recht** nt [right to] vote
Wählscheibe f (Teleph) dial
Wahl|spruch m motto. **W~urne** f ballot-box
Wahn m -[e]s delusion; (Manie) mania
wähnen vt believe
Wahnsinn m madness. **w~ig** a mad, insane; (fam: unsinnig) crazy; (fam: groß) terrible; **w~ig werden** go mad ● adv (fam) terribly. **W~ige(r)** m/f maniac
wahr a true; (echt) real; **w~ werden** come true; **du kommst doch, nicht w~?** you are coming, aren't you?
wahren vt keep; (verteidigen) safeguard; **den Schein w~** keep up appearances
währen vi (haben) last
während prep (+ gen) during ● conj while; (wohingegen) whereas. **w~dessen** adv in the meantime
wahrhaben vt etw nicht w~ wollen refuse to admit sth
wahrhaftig adv really, truly
Wahrheit f -,-en truth. **w~sgemäß** a truthful, adv -ly
wahrnehm|bar a perceptible. **w~en†** vt sep notice; (nutzen) take advantage of; exploit ⟨Vorteil⟩; look after ⟨Interessen⟩. **W~ung** f -,-en perception
wahrsag|en v sep ● vt predict ● vi (haben) **jdm w~en** tell s.o.'s fortune. **W~erin** f -,-nen fortune-teller
wahrscheinlich a probable, adv -bly. **W~keit** f - probability
Währung f -,-en currency
Wahrzeichen nt symbol
Waise f -,-n orphan. **W~nhaus** nt orphanage. **W~nkind** nt orphan
Wal m -[e]s,-e whale
Wald m -[e]s,¨er wood; (groß) forest. **w~ig** a wooded
Walis|er m -s,- Welshman. **w~isch** a Welsh
Wall m -[e]s,¨e mound; (Mil) rampart
Wallfahr|er(in) m(f) pilgrim. **W~t** f pilgrimage
Walnuß f walnut
Walze f -,-n roller. **w~n** vt roll
wälzen vt roll; pore over ⟨Bücher⟩; mull over ⟨Probleme⟩; **sich w~** roll [about]; (schlaflos) toss and turn
Walzer m -s,- waltz

Wand f -,¨e wall; (Trenn-) partition; (Seite) side; (Fels-) face
Wandel m -s change. **w~bar** a changeable. **w~n** vi (sein) stroll ● vr **sich w~n** change
Wander|er m -s,-, **W~in** f -,-nen hiker, rambler. **w~n** vi (sein) hike, ramble; (ziehen) travel; (gemächlich gehen) wander; (ziellos) roam. **W~schaft** f - travels pl. **W~ung** f -,-en hike, ramble; (länger) walking tour. **W~weg** m footpath
Wandgemälde nt mural
Wandlung f -,-en change, transformation
Wand|malerei f mural. **W~tafel** f blackboard. **W~teppich** m tapestry
Wange f -,-n cheek
wank|elmütig a fickle. **w~en** vi (haben) sway; ⟨Person:⟩ stagger; (fig) waver ● vi (sein) stagger
wann adv when
Wanne f -,-n tub
Wanze f -,-n bug
Wappen nt -s,- coat of arms. **W~kunde** f heraldry
war, wäre s. sein[1]
Ware f -,-n article; (Comm) commodity; (coll) merchandise; **W~n** goods. **W~nhaus** nt department store. **W~nprobe** f sample. **W~nzeichen** nt trademark
warm a (wärmer, wärmst) warm; ⟨Mahlzeit⟩ hot; **w~ machen** heat ● adv warmly; **w~ essen** have a hot meal
Wärm|e f - warmth; (Phys) heat; **10 Grad W~e** 10 degrees above zero. **w~en** vt warm; heat ⟨Essen, Wasser⟩. **W~flasche** f hot-water bottle
warmherzig a warm-hearted
Warn|blinkanlage f hazard [warning] lights pl. **w~en** vt/i (haben) warn (vor + dat of). **W~ung** f -,-en warning
Warteliste f waiting list
warten vi (haben) wait (auf + acc for); **auf sich** (acc) **w~ lassen** take one's/ its time ● vt service
Wärter(in) m -s,- (f -,-nen) keeper; (Museums-) attendant; (Gefängnis-) warder, (Amer) guard; (Kranken-) orderly
Warte|raum, W~saal m waiting-room. **W~zimmer** nt (Med) waiting-room
Wartung f - (Techn) service
warum adv why

Warze *f* -,-n wart

was *pron* what; **was für [ein]?** what kind of [a]? **was für ein Pech!** what bad luck! **das gefällt dir, was?** you like that, don't you? ● *rel pron* that; **alles, was ich brauche** all [that] I need ● *indef pron* (*fam: etwas*) something; (*fragend, verneint*) anything; **was zu essen** something to eat; **so was Ärgerliches!** what a nuisance! ● *adv* (*fam*) (*warum*) why; (*wie*) how

wasch|bar *a* washable. **W~becken** *nt* wash-basin. **W~beutel** *m* sponge-bag

Wäsche *f* - washing; (*Unter-*) underwear; **in der W~** in the wash

waschecht *a* colour-fast; (*fam*) genuine

Wäsche|klammer *f* clothes-peg. **W~leine** *f* clothes-line

waschen† *vt* wash; **sich w~** have a wash; **sich** (*dat*) **die Hände w~** wash one's hands; **W~ und Legen** shampoo and set ● *vi* (*haben*) do the washing

Wäscherei *f* -,-en laundry

Wäsche|schleuder *f* spin-drier. **W~trockner** *m* tumble-drier

Wasch|küche *f* laundry-room. **W~lappen** *m* face-flannel, (*Amer*) washcloth; (*fam: Feigling*) sissy. **W~maschine** *f* washing machine. **W~mittel** *nt* detergent. **W~pulver** *nt* washing-powder. **W~raum** *m* wash-room. **W~salon** *m* launderette. **W~zettel** *m* blurb

Wasser *nt* -s water; (*Haar-*) lotion; **ins W~ fallen** (*fam*) fall through; **mir lief das W~ im Mund zusammen** my mouth was watering. **W~ball** *m* beach-ball; (*Spiel*) water polo. **w~dicht** *a* watertight; ⟨*Kleidung*⟩ waterproof. **W~fall** *m* waterfall. **W~farbe** *f* watercolour. **W~hahn** *m* tap, (*Amer*) faucet. **W~kasten** *m* cistern. **W~kraft** *f* water-power. **W~kraftwerk** *nt* hydroelectric power-station. **W~leitung** *f* watermain; aus der **W~leitung** from the tap. **W~mann** *m* (*Astr*) Aquarius

wässern *vt* soak; (*begießen*) water ● *vi* (*haben*) water

Wasser|scheide *f* watershed. **W~ski** *nt* -s water-skiing. **W~stoff** *m* hydrogen. **W~straße** *f* waterway. **W~waage** *f* spirit-level. **W~werfer** *m* -s,- water-cannon. **W~zeichen** *nt* watermark

wäßrig *a* watery

waten *vi* (*sein*) wade

watscheln *vi* (*sein*) waddle

Watt¹ *nt* -[e]s mud-flats *pl*

Watt² *nt* -s,- (*Phys*) watt

Watt|e *f* - cotton wool. **w~iert** *a* padded; (*gesteppt*) quilted

WC /ve'tse:/ *nt* -s,-s WC

web|en *vt/i* (*haben*) weave. **W~er** *m* -s,- weaver. **W~stuhl** *m* loom

Wechsel *m* -s,- change; (*Tausch*) exchange; (*Comm*) bill of exchange. **W~geld** *nt* change. **w~haft** *a* changeable. **W~jahre** *npl* menopause *sg*. **W~kurs** *m* exchange rate. **w~n** *vt* change; (*tauschen*) exchange ● *vi* (*haben*) change; (*ab-*) alternate; (*verschieden sein*) vary. **w~nd** *a* changing; (*verschieden*) varying. **w~seitig** *a* mutual, *adv* -ly. **W~strom** *m* alternating current. **W~stube** *f* bureau de change. **w~weise** *adv* alternately. **W~wirkung** *f* interaction

weck|en *vt* wake [up]; (*fig*) awaken ● *vi* (*haben*) ⟨*Wecker:*⟩ go off. **W~er** *m* -s,- alarm [clock]

wedeln *vi* (*haben*) wave; **mit dem Schwanz w~** wag its tail

weder *conj* **w~ ... noch** neither ... nor

Weg *m* -[e]s,-e way; (*Fuß-*) path; (*Fahr-*) track; (*Gang*) errand; **auf dem Weg** on the way (**nach** to); **sich auf den Weg machen** set off; **im Weg sein** be in the way

weg *adv* away, off; (*verschwunden*) gone; **weg sein** be away; (*gegangen/ verschwunden*) have gone; (*fam: schlafen*) be asleep; **Hände weg!** hands off! **w~bleiben†** *vi sep* (*sein*) stay away. **w~bringen†** *vt sep* take away

wegen *prep* (+ *dat*) because of; (*um ... willen*) for the sake of; (*bezüglich*) about

weg|fahren† *vi sep* (*sein*) go away; (*abfahren*) leave. **w~fallen†** *vi sep* (*sein*) be dropped/(*ausgelassen*) omitted; (*entfallen*) no longer apply; (*aufhören*) cease. **w~geben†** *vt sep* give away; send to the laundry ⟨*Wäsche*⟩. **w~gehen†** *vi sep* (*sein*) leave, go away; (*ausgehen*) go out; ⟨*Fleck:*⟩ come out. **w~jagen** *vt sep* chase away. **w~kommen†** *vi sep* (*sein*) get away; (*verlorengehen*) disappear. **w~lassen†** *vt sep* let go; (*auslassen*) omit. **w~laufen†** *vi sep*

(sein) run away. **w~machen** *vt sep*
remove. **w~nehmen**† *vt sep* take
away. **w~räumen** *vt sep* put away;
(entfernen) clear away. **w~schicken**
vt sep send away; *(abschicken)* send
off. **w~tun**† *vt sep* put away; *(wegwerfen)* throw away

Wegweiser *m* -s,- signpost

weg|werfen† *vt sep* throw away.
w~ziehen† *v sep* • *vt* pull away • *vi*
(sein) move away

weh *a* sore; **weh tun** hurt; *(Kopf,
Rücken:)* ache; **jdm weh tun** hurt s.o.
• *int* oh weh! oh dear!

wehe *int* alas; **w~** **[dir/euch]!** *(drohend)* don't you dare!

wehen *vi* *(haben)* blow; *(flattern)*
flutter • *vt* blow

Wehen *fpl* contractions; **in den W~
liegen** be in labour

weh|leidig *a* soft; *(weinerlich)* whin-
ing. **W~mut** *f* - wistfulness. **w~mü-
tig** *a* wistful, *adv* -ly

Wehr[1] *nt* -[e]s,-e weir

Wehr[2] *f* **sich zur W~ setzen** resist.
W~dienst *m* military service.
W~dienstverweigerer *m* -s,- con-
scientious objector

wehren (sich) *vr* resist; *(gegen An-
schuldigung)* protest; *(sich sträuben)* refuse

wehr|los *a* defenceless. **W~macht** *f*
armed forces *pl*. **W~pflicht** *f*
conscription

Weib *nt* -[e]s,-er woman; *(Ehe-)* wife.
W~chen *nt* -s,- *(Zool)* female.
W~erheld *m* womanizer. **w~isch** *a*
effeminate. **w~lich** *a* feminine;
(Biol) female. **W~lichkeit** *f* -
femininity

weich *a* soft, *adv* -ly; *(gar)* done; *(Ei)*
soft-boiled; *(Mensch)* soft-hearted;
w~ werden *(fig)* relent

Weiche *f* -,-n *(Rail)* points *pl*

weichen[1] *vi* *(sein)* *(reg)* soak

weichen[2]† *vi* *(sein)* give way *(dat* to);
nicht von jds Seite w~ not leave
s.o.'s side

Weich|heit *f* - softness. **w~herzig** *a*
soft-hearted. **w~lich** *a* soft; *(Charakter)* weak. **W~spüler** *m* -s,- *(Tex)*
conditioner. **W~tier** *nt* mollusc

Weide[1] *f* -,-n *(Bot)* willow

Weide[2] *f* -,-n pasture. **w~n** *vt/i*
(haben) graze; **sich w~n an** (+ *dat*)
enjoy; *(schadenfroh)* gloat over

weiger|n (sich) *vr* refuse. **W~ung** *f*
-,-en refusal

Weihe *f* -,-n consecration; *(Priester-)*
ordination. **w~n** *vt* consecrate;
(zum Priester) ordain; dedicate
(Kirche) *(dat* to)

Weiher *m* -s,- pond

Weihnacht|en *nt* -s & *pl* Christmas.
w~lich *a* Christmassy. **W~sbaum**
m Christmas tree. **W~sfest** *nt*
Christmas. **W~slied** *nt* Christmas
carol. **W~smann** *m* *(pl* -männer)
Father Christmas. **W~stag** *m* **er-
ster/zweiter W~stag** Christmas Day/
Boxing Day

Weih|rauch *m* incense. **W~wasser**
nt holy water

weil *conj* because; *(da)* since

Weile *f* - while

Wein *m* -[e]s,-e wine; *(Bot)* vines *pl*;
(Trauben) grapes *pl*. **W~bau** *m*
wine-growing. **W~beere** *f* grape.
W~berg *m* vineyard. **W~brand** *m*
-[e]s brandy

wein|en *vt/i* *(haben)* cry, weep.
w~erlich *a* tearful, *adv* -ly

Wein|glas *nt* wineglass. **W~karte** *f*
wine-list. **W~keller** *m* wine-cellar.
W~lese *f* grape harvest. **W~liste** *f*
wine-list. **W~probe** *f* wine-tasting.
W~rebe *f*, **W~stock** *m* vine.
W~stube *f* wine-bar. **W~traube** *f*
bunch of grapes; *(W~beere)* grape

weise *a* wise, *adv* -ly

Weise *f* -,-n way; *(Melodie)* tune; **auf
diese W~** in this way

weisen† *vt* show; **von sich w~** *(fig)*
reject • *vi* *(haben)* point (**auf** + *acc*
at)

Weisheit *f* -,-en wisdom. **W~szahn** *m*
wisdom tooth

weiß *a*, **W~** *nt* -,- white

weissag|en *vt/i insep* *(haben)* pro-
phesy. **W~ung** *f* -,-en prophecy

Weiß|brot *nt* white bread. **W~e(r)**
m/f white man/woman. **w~en** *vt*
whitewash. **W~wein** *m* white wine

Weisung *f* -,-en instruction; *(Befehl)*
order

weit *a* wide; *(ausgedehnt)* extensive;
(lang) long • *adv* widely; *(offen, öffnen)* wide; *(lang)* far; **von w~em**
from a distance; **bei w~em** by far;
w~ und breit far and wide; **ist es
noch w~?** is it much further? **ich
bin so w~** I'm ready; **zu w~ gehen**
(fig) go too far. **w~aus** *adv* far.
W~blick *m* *(fig)* far-sightedness.
w~blickend *a* *(fig)* far-sighted

Weite *f* -,-n expanse; (*Entfernung*) distance; (*Größe*) width. **w~n** *vt* widen; stretch ⟨*Schuhe*⟩; **sich w~n** widen; stretch; ⟨*Pupille*⟩ dilate

weiter *a* further • *adv* further; (*außerdem*) in addition; (*anschließend*) then; **etw w~ tun** go on doing sth; **w~ nichts/niemand** nothing/no one else; **und so w~** and so on. **w~arbeiten** *vi sep* (*haben*) go on working

weiter|e(r,s) *a* further; **im w~en Sinne** in a wider sense; **ohne w~es** just like that; (*leicht*) easily; **bis auf w~es** until further notice; (*vorläufig*) for the time being

weiter|erzählen *vt sep* go on with; (*w~sagen*) repeat. **w~fahren**† *vi sep* (*sein*) go on. **w~geben**† *vt sep* pass on. **w~gehen**† *vi sep* (*sein*) go on. **w~hin** *adv* (*immer noch*) still; (*in Zukunft*) in future; (*außerdem*) furthermore; **etw w~hin tun** go on doing sth. **w~kommen**† *vi sep* (*sein*) get on. **w~machen** *vi sep* (*haben*) carry on. **w~sagen** *vt sep* pass on; (*verraten*) repeat

weit|gehend *adv* extensive • *adv* to a large extent. **w~hin** *adv* a long way; (*fig*) widely. **w~läufig** *a* spacious; (*entfernt*) distant, *adv* -ly; (*ausführlich*) lengthy, *adv* at length. **w~reichend** *a* far-reaching. **w~schweifig** *a* long-winded. **w~sichtig** *a* long-sighted; (*fig*) farsighted. **W~sprung** *m* long jump. **w~verbreitet** *a* widespread

Weizen *m* -s wheat

welch *inv pron* what; **w~ ein(e)** what a. **w~e(r,s)** *pron* which; **um w~e Zeit?** at what time? • *rel pron* which; (*Person*) who • *indef pron* some; (*fragend*) any; **was für w~e?** what sort of?

welk *a* wilted; ⟨*Laub*⟩ dead. **w~en** *vi* (*haben*) wilt; (*fig*) fade

Wellblech *nt* corrugated iron

Well|e *f* -,-n wave; (*Techn*) shaft. **W~enlänge** *f* wavelength. **W~enlinie** *f* wavy line. **W~enreiten** *nt* surfing. **W~ensittich** *m* -s,-e budgerigar. **w~ig** *a* wavy

Welt *f* -,-en world; **auf der W~** in the world; **auf die** *od* **zur W~ kommen** be born. **W~all** *nt* universe. **w~berühmt** *a* worldfamous. **w~fremd** *a* unworldly. **w~gewandt** *a* sophisticated. **W~kugel** *f*

globe. **w~lich** *a* worldly; (*nicht geistlich*) secular

Weltmeister|(in) *m*(*f*) world champion. **W~schaft** *f* world championship

Weltraum *m* space. **W~fahrer** *m* astronaut

Welt|rekord *m* world record. **w~weit** *a & adv* world-wide

wem *pron* (*dat of* **wer**) to whom

wen *pron* (*acc of* **wer**) whom

Wende *f* -,-n change. **W~kreis** *m* (*Geog*) tropic

Wendeltreppe *f* spiral staircase

wenden¹ *vt* (*reg*) turn; **sich zum Guten w~** take a turn for the better • *vi* (*haben*) turn [round]

wenden²† (*& reg*) *vt* turn; **sich w~** turn; **sich an jdn w~** turn/(*schriftlich*) write to s.o.

Wend|epunkt *m* (*fig*) turning-point. **w~ig** *a* nimble; ⟨*Auto*⟩ manœuvrable. **W~ung** *f* -,-en turn; (*Biegung*) bend; (*Veränderung*) change

wenig *pron* little; (*pl*) few; **w~e** *pl* few • *adv* little; (*kaum*) not much. **w~er** *pron* less; (*pl*) fewer; **immer w~er** less and less • *adv & conj* less. **w~ste(r,s)** least; **am w~sten** least [of all]. **w~stens** *adv* at least

wenn *conj* if; (*sobald*) when; **immer w~** whenever; **w~ nicht** *od* **außer w~** unless; **w~ auch** even though

wer *pron* who; (*fam: jemand*) someone; (*fragend*) anyone; **ist da wer?** is anyone there?

Werbe|agentur *f* advertising agency. **w~n**† *vt* recruit; attract ⟨*Kunden, Besucher*⟩ • *vi* (*haben*) **w~n für** advertise; canvass for ⟨*Partei*⟩; **w~n um** try to attract ⟨*Besucher*⟩; court ⟨*Frau, Gunst*⟩. **W~spot** /-sp-/ *m* -s,-s commercial

Werbung *f* - advertising

werden† *vi* (*sein*) become; ⟨*müde, alt, länger*⟩ get, grow; ⟨*blind, wahnsinnig*⟩ go; **blaß w~** turn pale; **krank w~** fall ill; **es wird warm/dunkel** it is getting warm/ dark; **mir wurde schlecht/schwindlig** I felt sick/dizzy; **er will Lehrer w~** he wants to be a teacher; **was ist aus ihm geworden?** what has become of him? • *v aux* (*Zukunft*) shall; **wir w~ sehen** we shall see; **es wird bald regnen** it's going to rain soon; **würden Sie so nett sein?** would you be so kind? ● (*Passiv; pp* **worden**) be; **ge-liebt/geboren w~** be loved/born; **es wurde gemunkelt** it was rumoured

werfen† *vt* throw; cast ⟨*Blick, Schatten*⟩; **sich w~** ⟨*Holz:*⟩ warp ● *vi* (*haben*) **w~ mit** throw

Werft *f* -,-**en** shipyard

Werk *nt* -[e]s,-e work; (*Fabrik*) works *sg*, factory; (*Trieb-*) mechanism. **W~en** *nt* -s (*Sch*) handicraft. **W~statt** *f* -,-̈**en** workshop; (*Auto-*) garage; (*Künstler-*) studio. **W~tag** *m* weekday. **w~tags** *adv* on weekdays. **w~tätig** *a* working. **W~unterricht** *m* (*Sch*) handicraft

Werkzeug *nt* tool; (*coll*) tools *pl*. **W~maschine** *f* machine tool

Wermut *m* -s vermouth

wert *a* **viel/50 Mark w~** worth a lot/50 marks; **nichts w~ sein** be worthless; **jds/etw** (*gen*) **w~ sein** be worthy of s.o./sth. **W~** *m* -[e]s,-e value; (*Nenn-*) denomination; **im W~ von** worth; **W~ legen auf** (+*acc*) set great store by. **w~en** *vt* rate

Wert|gegenstand *m* object of value; **W~gegenstände** valuables. **w~los** *a* worthless. **W~minderung** *f* depreciation. **W~papier** *nt* (*Comm*) security. **W~sachen** *fpl* valuables. **w~voll** *a* valuable

Wesen *nt* -s,- nature; (*Lebe-*) being; (*Mensch*) creature

wesentlich *a* essential; (*grundlegend*) fundamental; (*erheblich*) considerable; **im w~en** essentially ● *adv* considerably, much

weshalb *adv* why

Wespe *f* -,-n wasp

wessen *pron* (*gen of* **wer**) whose

westdeutsch *a* West German

Weste *f* -,-n waistcoat, (*Amer*) vest

Westen *m* -s west; **nach W~** west

Western *m* -[s],- western

Westfalen *nt* -s Westphalia

Westindien *nt* West Indies *pl*

west|lich *a* western; ⟨*Richtung*⟩ westerly ● *adv* & *prep* (+ *gen*) **w~lich [von] der Stadt** [to the] west of the town. **w~wärts** *adv* westwards

weswegen *adv* why

wett *a* **w~ sein** be quits

Wett|bewerb *m* -s,-e competition. **W~büro** *nt* betting shop

Wette *f* -,-n bet; **um die W~ laufen** race (**mit jdm** s.o.)

wetteifern *vi* (*haben*) compete

wetten *vt/i* (*haben*) bet (**auf** + *acc* on); **mit jdm w~** have a bet with s.o.

Wetter *nt* -s,- weather; (*Un-*) storm. **W~bericht** *m* weather report. **W~hahn** *m* weathercock. **W~lage** *f* weather conditions *pl*. **W~vorhersage** *f* weather forecast. **W~warte** *f* -,-n meteorological station

Wett|kampf *m* contest. **W~kämpfer(in)** *m(f)* competitor. **W~lauf** *m* race. **w~machen** *vt sep* make up for. **W~rennen** *nt* race. **W~streit** *m* contest

wetzen *vt* sharpen ● *vi* (*sein*) (*fam*) dash

Whisky *m* -s whisky

wichsen *vt* polish

wichtig *a* important; **w~ nehmen** take seriously. **W~keit** *f* - importance. **w~tuerisch** *a* self-important

Wicke *f* -,-n sweet pea

Wickel *m* -s,- compress

wick|eln *vt* wind; (*ein-*) wrap; (*bandagieren*) bandage; **ein Kind frisch w~eln** change a baby. **W~ler** *m* -s,- curler

Widder *m* -s,- ram; (*Astr*) Aries

wider *prep* (+ *acc*) against; (*entgegen*) contrary to; **w~ Willen** against one's will

widerfahren† *vi insep* (*sein*) **jdm w~** happen to s.o.

widerhallen *vi sep* (*haben*) echo

widerlegen *vt insep* refute

wider|lich *a* repulsive; (*unangenehm*) nasty, *adv* -ily. **w~rechtlich** *a* unlawful, *adv* -ly. **W~rede** *f* contradiction; **keine W~rede!** don't argue!

widerrufen† *vt/i insep* (*haben*) retract; revoke ⟨*Befehl*⟩

Widersacher *m* -s,- adversary

widersetzen (sich) *vr insep* resist (**jdm/etw** s.o./sth)

wider|sinnig *a* absurd. **w~spenstig** *a* unruly; (*störrisch*) stubborn

widerspiegeln *vt sep* reflect; **sich w~** be reflected

widersprechen† *vi insep* (*haben*) contradict (**jdm/etw** s.o./sth)

Wider|spruch *m* contradiction; (*Protest*) protest. **w~sprüchlich** *a* contradictory. **w~spruchslos** *adv* without protest

Widerstand *m* resistance; **W~ leisten** resist. **w~sfähig** *a* resistant; (*Bot*) hardy

widerstehen† *vi insep* (*haben*) resist (**jdm/etw** s.o./sth); (*anwidern*) be repugnant (**jdm** to s.o.)

widerstreben *vi insep (haben)* es **widerstrebt mir** I am reluctant (**zu** to). **W~** *nt* -**s** reluctance. **w~d** *a* reluctant, *adv* -ly

widerwärtig *a* disagreeable, unpleasant; (*ungünstig*) adverse

Widerwill|e *m* aversion, repugnance. **w~ig** *a* reluctant, *adv* -ly

widm|en *vt* dedicate (*dat* to); (*verwenden*) devote (*dat* to); **sich w~en** (+ *dat*) devote oneself to. **W~ung** *f* -,-**en** dedication

widrig *a* adverse, unfavourable

wie *adv* how; **wie viele?** how many? **wie ist Ihr Name?** what is your name? **wie ist das Wetter?** what is the weather like? ● *conj* as; (*gleich wie*) like; (*sowie*) as well as; (*als*) when, as; **genau wie du** just like you; **so gut/ reich wie** as good/rich as; **nichts wie** nothing but; **größer wie ich** (*fam*) bigger than me

wieder *adv* again; **er ist w~ da** he is back

Wiederaufbau *m* reconstruction. **w~en** *vt sep* reconstruct

wiederauf|nehmen† *vt sep* resume. **W~aufrüstung** *f* rearmament

wieder|bekommen† *vt sep* get back. **w~beleben** *vt sep* revive. **W~belebung** *f* - resuscitation. **w~bringen**† *vt sep* bring back. **w~erkennen**† *vt sep* recognize. **W~gabe** *f* (*s.* **w~geben**) return; portrayal; rendering; reproduction. **w~geben**† *vt sep* give back, return; (*darstellen*) portray; (*ausdrücken, übersetzen*) render; (*zitieren*) quote; (*Techn*) reproduce. **W~geburt** *f* reincarnation

wiedergutmach|en *vt sep* (*fig*) make up for; redress (*Unrecht*); (*bezahlen*) pay for. **W~ung** *f* - reparation; (*Entschädigung*) compensation

wiederher|stellen *vt sep* re-establish; restore (*Gebäude*); restore to health (*Kranke*); **w~gestellt sein** be fully recovered. **W~stellung** *f* re-establishment; restoration; (*Genesung*) recovery

wiederholen¹ *vt sep* get back

wiederhol|en² *vt insep* repeat; (*Sch*) revise; **sich w~en** recur; (*Person:*) repeat oneself. **w~t** *a* repeated, *adv* -ly. **W~ung** *f* -,-**en** repetition; (*Sch*) revision

Wieder|hören *nt* **auf W~hören!** goodbye! **W~käuer** *m* -**s**,- ruminant.

W~kehr *f* - return; (*W~holung*) recurrence. **w~kehren** *vi sep* (*sein*) return; (*sich wiederholen*) recur. **w~kommen**† *vi sep* (*sein*) come back

wiedersehen† *vt sep* see again. **W~** *nt* -**s**,- reunion; **auf W~!** goodbye!

wiederum *adv* again; (*andererseits*) on the other hand

wiedervereinig|en *vt sep* reunify (*Land*). **W~ung** *f* reunification

wieder|verheiraten (sich) *vr sep* remarry. **w~verwenden**† *vt sep* reuse. **w~verwerten** *vt sep* recycle. **w~wählen** *vt sep* re-elect

Wiege *f* -,-**n** cradle

wiegen¹† *vt/i (haben)* weigh

wiegen² *vt (reg)* rock; **sich w~** sway; (*schaukeln*) rock. **W~lied** *nt* lullaby

wiehern *vi (haben)* neigh

Wien *nt* -**s** Vienna. **W~er** *a* Viennese; **W~er Schnitzel** Wiener schnitzel ● *m* -**s**,- Viennese ● *f* -,- ≈ frankfurter. **w~erisch** *a* Viennese

Wiese *f* -,-**n** meadow

Wiesel *nt* -**s**,- weasel

wieso *adv* why

wieviel *pron* how much/(*pl*) many; **um w~ Uhr?** at what time? **w~te(r,s)** *a* which; **der W~te ist heute?** what is the date today?

wieweit *adv* how far

wild *a* wild, *adv* -ly; (*Stamm*) savage; **w~er Streik** wildcat strike; **w~ wachsen** grow wild. **W~** *nt* -[**e**]**s** game; (*Rot-*) deer; (*Culin*) venison. **W~dieb** *m* poacher. **W~e(r)** *m/f* savage

Wilder|er *m* -**s**,- poacher. **w~n** *vt/i (haben)* poach

wildfremd *a* totally strange; **w~e Leute** total strangers

Wild|heger, W~hüter *m* -**s**,- gamekeeper. **W~leder** *nt* suede. **w~ledern** *a* suede. **W~nis** *f* - wilderness. **W~schwein** *nt* wild boar. **W~westfilm** *m* western

Wille *m* -**ns** will; **Letzter W~** will; **seinen W~n durchsetzen** get one's [own] way; **mit W~n** intentionally

willen *prep* (+ *gen*) **um ... w~** for the sake of . . .

Willens|kraft *f* will-power. **w~stark** *a* strong-willed

willig *a* willing, *adv* -ly

willkommen *a* welcome; **w~ heißen** welcome. **W~** *nt* -**s** welcome

willkürlich *a* arbitrary, *adv* -ily

wimmeln *vi (haben)* swarm

wimmern *vi* (*haben*) whimper

Wimpel *m* -s,- pennant

Wimper *f* -,-n [eye]lash; **nicht mit der W** ∼ **zucken** (*fam*) not bat an eyelid. **W**∼**ntusche** *f* mascara

Wind *m* -[e]s,-e wind

Winde *f* -,-n (*Techn*) winch

Windel *f* -,-n nappy, (*Amer*) diaper

winden† *vt* wind; make ⟨*Kranz*⟩; **in die Höhe w**∼ winch up; **sich w**∼ wind (*um* round); (*sich krümmen*) writhe

Wind|hund *m* greyhound. **w**∼**ig** *a* windy. **W**∼**mühle** *f* windmill. **W**∼**pocken** *fpl* chickenpox *sg*. **W**∼**schutzscheibe** *f* windscreen, (*Amer*) windshield. **w**∼**still** *a* calm. **W**∼**stille** *f* calm. **W**∼**stoß** *m* gust of wind. **W**∼**surfen** *nt* windsurfing

Windung *f* -,-en bend; (*Spirale*) spiral

Wink *m* -[e]s,-e sign; (*Hinweis*) hint

Winkel *m* -s,- angle; (*Ecke*) corner. **W**∼**messer** *m* -s,- protractor

winken *vi* (*haben*) wave; **jdm w**∼ wave/(*herbei*∼) beckon to s.o.

winseln *vi* (*haben*) whine

Winter *m* -s,- winter. **w**∼**lich** *a* wintry; (*Winter-*) winter... **W**∼**schlaf** *m* hibernation; **W**∼**schlaf halten** hibernate. **W**∼**sport** *m* winter sports *pl*

Winzer *m* -s,- winegrower

winzig *a* tiny, minute

Wipfel *m* -s,- [tree-]top

Wippe *f* -,-n see-saw. **w**∼**n** *vi* (*haben*) bounce; (*auf Wippe*) play on the see-saw

wir *pron* we; **wir sind es** it's us

Wirbel *m* -s,- eddy; (*Drehung*) whirl; (*Trommel-*) roll; (*Anat*) vertebra; (*Haar-*) crown; (*Aufsehen*) fuss. **w**∼**n** *vt/i* (*sein/haben*) whirl. **W**∼**säule** *f* spine. **W**∼**sturm** *m* cyclone. **W**∼**tier** *nt* vertebrate. **W**∼**wind** *m* whirlwind

wird *s.* **werden**

wirken *vi* (*haben*) have an effect (**auf** + *acc* on); (*zur Geltung kommen*) be effective; (*tätig sein*) work; (*scheinen*) seem ● *vt* (*Tex*) knit; **Wunder w**∼ work miracles

wirklich *a* real, *adv* -ly. **W**∼**keit** *f* -,-en reality

wirksam *a* effective, *adv* -ly. **W**∼**keit** *f* - effectiveness

Wirkung *f* -,-en effect. **w**∼**slos** *a* ineffective, *adv* -ly. **w**∼**svoll** *a* effective, *adv* -ly

wirr *a* tangled; ⟨*Haar*⟩ tousled; (*verwirrt, verworren*) confused. **W**∼**warr** *m* -s tangle; (*fig*) confusion; (*von Stimmen*) hubbub

Wirt *m* -[e]s,-e landlord. **W**∼**in** *f* -,-nen landlady

Wirtschaft *f* -,-en economy; (*Gast-*) restaurant; (*Kneipe*) pub. **w**∼**en** *vi* (*haben*) manage one's finances; (*sich betätigen*) busy oneself; **sie kann nicht w**∼**en** she's a bad manager. **W**∼**erin** *f* -,-nen housekeeper. **w**∼**lich** *a* economic, *adv* -ally; (*sparsam*) economical, *adv* -ly. **W**∼**sgeld** *nt* housekeeping [money]. **W**∼**sprüfer** *m* auditor

Wirtshaus *nt* inn; (*Kneipe*) pub

Wisch *m* -[e]s,-e (*fam*) piece of paper

wisch|en *vt/i* (*haben*) wipe; wash ⟨*Fußboden*⟩ ● *vi* (*sein*) slip; ⟨*Maus:*⟩ scurry. **W**∼**lappen** *m* cloth; (*Aufwisch-*) floor-cloth

wispern *vt/i* (*haben*) whisper

wissen† *vt/i* (*haben*) know; **weißt du noch?** do you remember? **nichts w**∼ **wollen** not want anything to do with. **W**∼ *nt* -s knowledge; **meines W**∼**s** to my knowledge

Wissenschaft *f* -,-en science. **W**∼**ler** *m* -s,- academic; (*Natur-*) scientist. **w**∼**lich** *a* academic, *adv* -ally; scientific, *adv* -ally

wissen|swert *a* worth knowing. **w**∼**tlich** *a* deliberate ● *adv* knowingly

witter|n *vt* scent; (*ahnen*) sense. **W**∼**ung** *f* - scent; (*Wetter*) weather

Witwe *f* -,-n widow. **W**∼**r** *m* -s,- widower

Witz *m* -es,-e joke; (*Geist*) wit. **W**∼**bold** *m* -[e]s,-e joker. **w**∼**ig** *a* funny; (*geistreich*) witty

wo *adv* where; (*als*) when; (*irgendwo*) somewhere; **wo immer** wherever ● *conj* seeing that; (*obwohl*) although; (*wenn*) if

woanders *adv* somewhere else

wobei *adv* how; (*relativ*) during the course of which

Woche *f* -,-n week. **W**∼**nende** *nt* weekend. **W**∼**nkarte** *f* weekly ticket. **w**∼**nlang** *adv* for weeks. **W**∼**ntag** *m* day of the week; (*Werktag*) weekday. **w**∼**tags** *adv* on weekdays

wöchentlich *a* & *adv* weekly

Wodka *m* -s vodka

wodurch adv how; (relativ) through/ (Ursache) by which; (Folge) as a result of which

wofür adv what ... for; (relativ) for which

Woge f -,-n wave

wogegen adv what ... against; (relativ) against which ● conj whereas. **woher** adv where from; **woher weißt du das?** how do you know that?. **wohin** adv where [to]; **wohin gehst du?** where are you going? **wohingegen** conj whereas

wohl adv well; (vermutlich) probably; (etwa) about; (zwar) perhaps; **w~ kaum** hardly; **w~ oder übel** willy-nilly; **sich w~ fühlen** feel well/ (behaglich) comfortable; **der ist w~ verrückt!** he must be mad! **W~** nt -[e]s welfare, well-being; **auf jds W~ trinken** drink s.o.'s health; **zum W~** (+gen) for the good of; **zum W~!** cheers!

wohlauf a **w~ sein** be well

Wohl|befinden nt well-being. **W~behagen** nt feeling of well-being. **w~behalten** a safe, adv -ly. **W~ergehen** nt -s welfare. **w~erzogen** a well brought-up

Wohlfahrt f - welfare. **W~sstaat** m Welfare State

Wohl|gefallen nt -s pleasure. **W~geruch** m fragrance. **w~gesinnt** a well disposed (dat towards). **w~habend** a prosperous, well-to-do. **w~ig** a comfortable, adv -bly. **w~klingend** a melodious. **w~riechend** a fragrant. **w~schmeckend** a tasty

Wohlstand m prosperity. **W~sgesellschaft** f affluent society

Wohltat f [act of] kindness; (Annehmlichkeit) treat; (Genuß) bliss

Wohltät|er m benefactor. **w~ig** a charitable

wohl|tuend a agreeable, adv -bly. **w~tun†** vi sep (haben) **jdm w~tun** do s.o. good. **w~verdient** a well-deserved. **w~weislich** adv deliberately

Wohlwollen nt -s goodwill; (Gunst) favour. **w~d** a benevolent, adv -ly

Wohn|anhänger m = Wohnwagen. **W~block** m block of flats. **w~en** vi (haben) live; (vorübergehend) stay. **W~gegend** f residential area. **w~haft** a resident. **W~haus** nt

[dwelling]-house. **W~heim** nt hostel; (Alten-) home. **w~lich** a comfortable, adv -bly. **W~mobil** nt -s,-e camper. **W~ort** m place of residence. **W~raum** m living space; (Zimmer) living-room. **W~sitz** m place of residence

Wohnung f -,-en flat, (Amer) apartment; (Unterkunft) accommodation. **W~snot** f housing shortage

Wohn|wagen m caravan, (Amer) trailer. **W~zimmer** nt living-room

wölb|en vt curve; arch ⟨Rücken⟩. **W~ung** f -,-en curve; (Archit) vault

Wolf m -[e]s,ʺe wolf; (Fleisch-) mincer; (Reiß-) shredder

Wolk|e f -,-n cloud. **W~enbruch** m cloudburst. **W~enkratzer** m skyscraper. **w~enlos** a cloudless. **w~ig** a cloudy

Woll|decke f blanket. **W~e** f -,-n wool

wollen¹† vt/i (haben) & v aux want; **etw tun w~** want to do sth; (beabsichtigen) be going to do sth; **ich will nach Hause** I want to go home; **wir wollten gerade gehen** we were just going; **ich wollte, ich könnte dir helfen** I wish I could help you; **der Motor will nicht anspringen** the engine won't start

woll|en² a woollen. **w~ig** a woolly. **W~sachen** fpl woollens

wollüstig a sensual, adv -ly

womit adv what ... with; (relativ) with which. **womöglich** adv possibly. **wonach** adv what ... after/ ⟨suchen⟩ for/⟨riechen⟩ of; (relativ) after/ for/of which

Wonn|e f -,-n bliss; (Freude) joy. **w~ig** a sweet

woran adv what ... on/⟨denken, sterben⟩ of; (relativ) on/of which; **woran hast du ihn erkannt?** how did you recognize him? **worauf** adv what ... on/⟨warten⟩ for; (relativ) on/for which; (woraufhin) whereupon. **woraufhin** adv whereupon. **woraus** adv what ... from; (relativ) from which. **worin** adv what ... in; (relativ) in which

Wort nt -[e]s,ʺer & -e word; **jdm ins W~ fallen** interrupt s.o.; **ein paar W~e sagen** say a few words. **w~brüchig** a **w~brüchig werden** break one's word

Wörterbuch nt dictionary

Wort|führer m spokesman. **w~getreu** a & adv word-for-word.

w~gewandt *a* eloquent, *adv* -ly.
w~karg *a* taciturn. W~laut *m* wording

wörtlich *a* literal, *adv* -ly; *(wortgetreu)* word-for-word

wort|los *a* silent ● *adv* without a word. W~schatz *m* vocabulary. W~spiel *nt* pun, play on words. W~wechsel *m* exchange of words; *(Streit)* argument. w~wörtlich *a & adv* = wörtlich

worüber *adv* what ... over/⟨*lachen, sprechen*⟩ about; *(relativ)* over/ about which. worum *adv* what... round/⟨*bitten, kämpfen*⟩ for; *(relativ)* round/for which; worum geht es? what is it about?. worunter *adv* what...under/⟨*wozwischen*⟩ among; *(relativ)* under/among which. wovon *adv* what ... from/ ⟨*sprechen*⟩about; *(relativ)* from/about which. wovor *adv* what ... in front of; ⟨*sich fürchten*⟩ what ... of; *(relativ)* in front of which; of which. wozu *adv* what ... to/⟨*brauchen, benutzen*⟩ for; *(relativ)* to/for which; wozu? what for?

Wrack *nt* -s,-s wreck

wringen† *vt* wring

wucher|n *vi (haben/sein)* grow profusely. W~preis *m* extortionate price. W~ung *f* -,-en growth

Wuchs *m* -es growth; *(Gestalt)* stature

Wucht *f* - force. w~en *vt* heave. w~ig *a* massive

wühlen *vi (haben)* rummage; *(in der Erde)* burrow ● *vt* dig

Wulst *m* -[e]s,¨e bulge; *(Fett-)* roll. w~ig *a* bulging; ⟨*Lippen*⟩ thick

wund *a* sore; w~ reiben chafe. W~brand *m* gangrene

Wunde *f* -,-n wound

Wunder *nt* -s,- wonder, marvel; *(übernatürliches)* miracle; kein W~! no wonder! w~bar *a* miraculous; *(herrlich)* wonderful, *adv* -ly, marvellous, *adv* -ly. W~kind *nt* infant prodigy. w~lich *a* odd, *adv* -ly. w~n *vt* surprise; sich w~n be surprised *(über + acc* at). w~schön *a* beautiful, *adv* -ly. w~voll *a* wonderful, *adv* -ly

Wundstarrkrampf *m* tetanus

Wunsch *m* -[e]s,¨e wish; *(Verlangen)* desire; *(Bitte)* request

wünschen *vt* want; sich *(dat)* etw w~ want sth; *(bitten um)* ask for sth; jdm Glück/gute Nacht w~ wish s.o.

luck/good night; ich wünschte, ich könnte . . . I wish I could . . .; Sie w~? can I help you? w~swert *a* desirable

Wunsch|konzert *nt* musical request programme. W~traum *m (fig)* dream

wurde, würde *s.* werden

Würde *f* -,-n dignity; *(Ehrenrang)* honour. w~los *a* undignified. W~nträger *m* dignitary. w~voll *a* dignified ● *adv* with dignity

würdig *a* dignified; *(wert)* worthy. w~en *vt* recognize; *(schätzen)* appreciate; keines Blickes w~en not deign to look at

Wurf *m* -[e]s,¨e throw; *(Junge)* litter

Würfel *m* -s,- cube; *(Spiel-)* dice; *(Zucker-)* lump. w~n *vi (haben)* throw the dice; w~n um play dice for ● *vt* throw; *(in Würfel schneiden)* dice. W~zucker *m* cube sugar

würgen *vt* choke ● *vi (haben)* retch; choke (an+*dat* on)

Wurm *m* -[e]s,¨er worm; *(Made)* maggot. w~en *vi (haben)* jdn w~en *(fam)* rankle [with s.o.]. w~stichig *a* worm-eaten

Wurst *f* -,¨e sausage; das ist mir W~ *(fam)* I couldn't care less

Würstchen *nt* -s,- small sausage; Frankfurter W~ frankfurter

Würze *f* -,-n spice; *(Aroma)* aroma

Wurzel *f* -,-n root; W~n schlagen take root. w~n *vi (haben)* root

würz|en *vt* season. w~ig *a* tasty; *(aromatisch)* aromatic; *(pikant)* spicy

wüst *a* chaotic; *(wirr)* tangled; *(öde)* desolate; *(wild)* wild, *adv* -ly; *(schlimm)* terrible, *adv* -bly

Wüste *f* -,-n desert

Wut *f* - rage, fury. W~anfall *m* fit of rage

wüten *vi (haben)* rage. w~d *a* furious, *adv* -ly; w~d machen infuriate

X

x /ıks/ *inv a (Math)* x; *(fam)* umpteen. X-Beine *ntpl* knock-knees. x-beinig *a* knock-kneed. x-beliebig *a (fam)* any; eine x-beliebige Zahl any number [you like]. x-mal *adv (fam)* umpteen times

Y

Yoga /'jo:ga/ *m* & *nt* -[s] yoga

Z

Zack|e *f* -,-n point; (*Berg-*) peak; (*Gabel-*) prong. **z∼ig** *a* jagged; (*gezackt*) serrated; (*fam: schneidig*) smart, *adv* -ly

zaghaft *a* timid, *adv* -ly; (*zögernd*) tentative, *adv* -ly

zäh *a* tough; (*hartnäckig*) tenacious, *adv* -ly; (*zähflüssig*) viscous; (*schleppend*) sluggish, *adv* -ly. **z∼flüssig** *a* viscous; ⟨*Verkehr*⟩ slow-moving. **Z∼igkeit** *f* - toughness; tenacity

Zahl *f* -,-en number; (*Ziffer, Betrag*) figure

zahl|bar *a* payable. **z∼en** *vt/i* (*haben*) pay; (*bezahlen*) pay for; **bitte z∼en!** the bill please!

zählen *vi* (*haben*) count; **z∼ zu** (*fig*) be one/(*pl*) some of; **z∼ auf** (+*acc*) count on ● *vt* count; **z∼ zu** add to; (*fig*) count among; **die Stadt zählt 5000 Einwohner** the town has 5000 inhabitants

zahlenmäßig *a* numerical, *adv* -ly

Zähler *m* -s,- meter

Zahl|grenze *f* fare-stage. **Z∼karte** *f* paying-in slip. **z∼los** *a* countless. **z∼reich** *a* numerous; ⟨*Anzahl, Gruppe*⟩ large ● *adv* in large numbers. **Z∼ung** *f* -,-en payment; **in Z∼ung nehmen** take in part-exchange

Zählung *f* -,-en count

zahlungsunfähig *a* insolvent

Zahlwort *nt* (*pl* -wörter) numeral

zahm *a* tame

zähmen *vt* tame; (*fig*) restrain

Zahn *m* -[e]s,ᵉe tooth; (*am Zahnrad*) cog. **Z∼arzt** *m*, **Z∼ärztin** *f* dentist. **Z∼belag** *m* plaque. **Z∼bürste** *f* toothbrush. **z∼en** *vi* (*haben*) be teething. **Z∼fleisch** *nt* gums *pl*. **z∼los** *a* toothless. **Z∼pasta** *f* -,-en toothpaste. **Z∼rad** *nt* cog-wheel. **Z∼schmelz** *m* enamel. **Z∼schmerzen** *mpl* toothache *sg*. **Z∼spange** *f* brace. **Z∼stein** *m* tartar. **Z∼stocher** *m* -s,- toothpick

Zange *f* -,-n pliers *pl*; (*Kneif-*) pincers *pl*; (*Kohlen-, Zucker-*) tongs *pl*; (*Geburts-*) forceps *pl*

Zank *m* -[e]s squabble. **z∼en** *vr* sich **z∼en** squabble ● *vi* (*haben*) scold (**mit jdm** s.o.)

zänkisch *a* quarrelsome

Zäpfchen *nt* -s,- (*Anat*) uvula; (*Med*) suppository

Zapfen *m* -s,- (*Bot*) cone; (*Stöpsel*) bung; (*Eis-*) icicle. **z∼** *vt* tap, draw. **Z∼streich** *m* (*Mil*) tattoo

Zapf|hahn *m* tap. **Z∼säule** *f* petrol-pump

zappel|ig *a* fidgety; (*nervös*) jittery. **z∼n** *vi* (*haben*) wriggle; ⟨*Kind:*⟩ fidget

zart *a* delicate, *adv* -ly; (*weich, zärtlich*) tender, *adv* -ly; (*sanft*) gentle, *adv* -ly. **Z∼gefühl** *nt* tact. **Z∼heit** *f* - delicacy; tenderness; gentleness

zärtlich *a* tender, *adv* -ly; (*liebevoll*) loving, *adv* -ly. **Z∼keit** *f* -,-en tenderness; (*Liebkosung*) caress

Zauber *m* -s magic; (*Bann*) spell. **Z∼er** *m* -s,- magician. **z∼haft** *a* enchanting. **Z∼künstler** *m* conjurer. **Z∼kunststück** *nt* = **Z∼trick**. **z∼n** *vi* (*haben*) do magic; (*Zaubertricks ausführen*) do conjuring tricks ● *vt* produce as if by magic. **Z∼stab** *m* magic wand. **Z∼trick** *m* conjuring trick

zaudern *vi* (*haben*) delay; (*zögern*) hesitate

Zaum *m* -[e]s,Zäume bridle; **im Z∼ halten** (*fig*) restrain

Zaun *m* -[e]s,Zäune fence. **Z∼könig** *m* wren

z.B. *abbr* (**zum Beispiel**) e.g.

Zebra *nt* -s,-s zebra. **Z∼streifen** *m* zebra-crossing

Zeche *f* -,-n bill; (*Bergwerk*) pit

zechen *vi* (*haben*) (*fam*) drink

Zeder *f* -,-n cedar

Zeh *m* -[e]s,-en toe. **Z∼e** *f* -,-n toe; (*Knoblauch-*) clove. **Z∼ennagel** *m* toenail

zehn *inv a*, **Z∼** *f* -,-en ten. **z∼te(r,s)** *a* tenth. **Z∼tel** *nt* -s,- tenth

Zeichen *nt* -s,- sign; (*Signal*) signal. **Z∼setzung** *f* - punctuation. **Z∼trickfilm** *m* cartoon [film]

zeichn|en *vt/i* (*haben*) draw; (*kenn-*) mark; (*unter-*) sign. **Z∼er** *m* -s,- draughtsman. **Z∼ung** *f* -,-en drawing; (*auf Fell*) markings *pl*

Zeige|finger *m* index finger. **z~n** *vt* show; **sich z~n** appear; *(sich herausstellen)* become clear; **das wird sich z~n** we shall see ● *vi (haben)* point **(auf** + *acc* to). **Z~r** *m* -s,- pointer; *(Uhr-)* hand

Zeile *f* -,-n line; *(Reihe)* row

zeit *prep* (+*gen*) **z~ meines/ seines Lebens** all my/his life

Zeit *f* -,-en time; **sich** *(dat)* **Z~ lassen** take one's time; **es hat Z~** there's no hurry; **mit der Z~** in time; **in nächster Z~** in the near future; **die erste Z~** at first; **von Z~ zu Z~** from time to time; **zur Z~** at present; *(rechtzeitig)* in time; **[ach] du liebe Z~!** *(fam)* good heavens!

Zeit|alter *nt* age, era. **Z~arbeit** *f* temporary work. **Z~bombe** *f* time bomb. **z~gemäß** *a* modern, up-to-date. **Z~genosse** *m,* **Z~genossin** *f* contemporary. **z~genössisch** *a* contemporary. **z~ig** *a* & *adv* early. **Z~lang** *f* **eine Z~lang** for a time *or* while. **z~lebens** *adv* all one's life

zeitlich *a* *(Dauer)* in time; *(Folge)* chronological ● *adv* **z~ begrenzt** for a limited time

zeit|los *a* timeless. **Z~lupe** *f* slow motion. **Z~punkt** *m* time. **Z~raubend** *a* time-consuming. **Z~raum** *m* period. **Z~schrift** *f* magazine, periodical

Zeitung *f* -,-en newspaper. **Z~spapier** *nt* newspaper

Zeit|verschwendung *f* waste of time. **Z~vertreib** *m* pastime; **zum Z~vertreib** to pass the time. **z~weilig** *a* temporary ● *adv* temporarily; *(hin und wieder)* at times. **z~weise** *adv* at times. **Z~wort** *nt* *(pl* -wörter) verb. **Z~zünder** *m* time fuse

Zelle *f* -,-n cell; *(Telefon-)* box

Zelt *nt* -[e]s,-e tent; *(Fest-)* marquee. **z~en** *vi (haben)* camp. **Z~en** *nt* -s camping. **Z~plane** *f* tarpaulin. **Z~platz** *m* campsite

Zement *m* -[e]s cement. **z~ieren** *vt* cement

zen|sieren *vt (Sch)* mark; censor *(Presse, Film)*. **Z~sur** *f* -,-en *(Sch)* mark, *(Amer)* grade; *(Presse-)* censorship

Zentimeter *m* & *nt* centimetre. **Z~maß** *nt* tape-measure

Zentner *m* -s,- [metric] hundred-weight *(50 kg)*

zentral *a* central, *adv* -ly. **Z~e** *f* -,-n central office; *(Partei-)* head-quarters *pl*; *(Teleph)* exchange. **Z~heizung** *f* central heating. **z~isieren** *vt* centralize

Zentrum *nt* -s,-tren centre

zerbrech|en† *vt/i (sein)* break; **sich** *(dat)* **den Kopf z~en** rack one's brains. **z~lich** *a* fragile

zerdrücken *vt* crush; mash *(Kartoffeln)*

Zeremonie *f* -,-n ceremony

Zeremoniell *nt* -s,-e ceremonial. **z~** *a* ceremonial, *adv* -ly

Zerfall *m* disintegration; *(Verfall)* decay. **z~en†** *vi (sein)* disintegrate; *(verfallen)* decay; **in drei Teile z~en** be divided into three parts

zerfetzen *vt* tear to pieces

zerfließen† *vi (sein)* melt; *(Tinte:)* run

zergehen† *vi (sein)* melt; *(sich auflösen)* dissolve

zergliedern *vt* dissect

zerkleinern *vt* chop/*(schneiden)* cut up; *(mahlen)* grind

zerknirscht *a* contrite

zerknüllen *vt* crumple [up]

zerkratzen *vt* scratch

zerlassen† *vt* melt

zerlegen *vt* take to pieces, dismantle; *(zerschneiden)* cut up; *(tranchieren)* carve

zerlumpt *a* ragged

zermalmen *vt* crush

zermürb|en *vt (fig)* wear down. **Z~ungskrieg** *m* war of attrition

zerplatzen *vi (sein)* burst

zerquetschen *vt* squash, crush, mash *(Kartoffeln)*

Zerrbild *nt* caricature

zerreißen† *vt* tear; *(in Stücke)* tear up; break *(Faden, Seil)* ● *vi (sein)* tear; break

zerren *vt* drag; pull *(Muskel)* ● *vi (haben)* pull **(an** + *dat* at)

zerrinnen† *vi (sein)* melt

zerrissen *a* torn

zerrütten *vt* ruin, wreck; shatter *(Nerven)*; **zerrüttete Ehe** broken marriage

zerschlagen† *vt* smash; smash up *(Möbel)*; **sich z~** *(fig)* fall through; *(Hoffnung:)* be dashed ● *a (erschöpft)* worn out

zerschmettern *vt/i (sein)* smash

zerschneiden† *vt* cut; *(in Stücke)* cut up

zersetzen *vt* corrode; undermine ⟨*Moral*⟩; **sich z~** decompose

zersplittern *vi* (sein) splinter; ⟨*Glas:*⟩ shatter ● *vt* shatter

zerspringen† *vi* (sein) shatter; (*bersten*) burst

Zerstäuber *m* -s,- atomizer

zerstör|en *vt* destroy; (*zunichte machen*) wreck. **Z~er** *m* -s,- destroyer. **Z~ung** *f* destruction

zerstreu|en *vt* scatter; disperse ⟨*Menge*⟩; dispel ⟨*Zweifel*⟩; **sich z~en** disperse; (*sich unterhalten*) amuse oneself. **z~t** *a* absent-minded, *adv* -ly. **Z~ung** *f* -,-en (*Unterhaltung*) entertainment

zerstückeln *vt* cut up into pieces

zerteilen *vt* divide up

Zertifikat *nt* -[e]s,-e certificate

zertreten† *vt* stamp on; (*zerdrücken*) crush

zertrümmern *vt* smash [up]; wreck ⟨*Gebäude, Stadt*⟩

zerzaus|en *vt* tousle. **z~t** *a* dishevelled; ⟨*Haar*⟩ tousled

Zettel *m* -s,- piece of paper; (*Notiz*) note; (*Bekanntmachung*) notice; (*Reklame:*) leaflet

Zeug *nt* -s (*fam*) stuff; (*Sachen*) things *pl*; (*Ausrüstung*) gear; **dummes Z~** nonsense; **das Z~ haben zu** have the makings of

Zeuge *m* -n,-n witness. **z~n** *vi* (*haben*) testify; **z~n von** (*fig*) show ● *vt* father. **Z~naussage** *f* testimony. **Z~nstand** *m* witness box/ (*Amer*) stand

Zeugin *f* -,-nen witness

Zeugnis *nt* -ses,-se certificate; (*Sch*) report; (*Referenz*) reference; (*fig: Beweis*) evidence

Zickzack *m* -[e]s,-e zigzag

Ziege *f* -,-n goat

Ziegel *m* -s,- brick; (*Dach-*) tile. **Z~stein** *m* brick

ziehen† *vt* pull; (*sanfter; zücken; zeichnen*) draw; (*heraus-*) pull out; extract ⟨*Zahn*⟩; raise ⟨*Hut*⟩; put on ⟨*Bremse*⟩; move ⟨*Schachfigur*⟩; put up ⟨*Leine, Zaun*⟩; (*dehnen*) stretch; make ⟨*Grimasse, Scheitel*⟩; (*züchten*) breed; grow ⟨*Rosen, Gemüse*⟩; **nach sich z~** (*fig*) entail ● *vr* **sich z~** (*sich erstrecken*) run; (*sich verziehen*) warp ● *vi* (*haben*) pull (**an** + *dat* on/at); ⟨*Tee, Ofen:*⟩ draw; (*Culin*) simmer; **es zieht** there is a draught; **solche Filme z~ nicht mehr** films like that are no longer popular

● *vi* (sein) (*um-*) move (**nach** to); ⟨*Menge:*⟩ march; ⟨*Vögel:*⟩ migrate; ⟨*Wolken, Nebel:*⟩ drift. **Z~ nt -s** ache

Ziehharmonika *f* accordion

Ziehung *f* -,-en draw

Ziel *nt* -[e]s,-e destination; (*Sport*) finish; (*Z~scheibe & Mil*) target; (*Zweck*) aim, goal. **z~bewußt** *a* purposeful, *adv* -ly. **z~en** *vi* (*haben*) aim (**auf** + *acc* at). **z~end** *a* (*Gram*) transitive. **z~los** *a* aimless, *adv* -ly. **Z~scheibe** *f* target; (*fig*) butt. **z~strebig** *a* single-minded, *adv* -ly

ziemen (**sich**) *vr* be seemly

ziemlich *a* (*fam*) fair ● *adv* rather, fairly; (*fast*) pretty well

Zier|de *f* -,-n ornament. **z~en** *vt* adorn; **sich z~en** make a fuss; (*sich bitten lassen*) need coaxing

zierlich *a* dainty, *adv* -ily; (*fein*) delicate, *adv* -ly; ⟨*Frau*⟩ petite

Ziffer *f* -,-n figure, digit; (*Zahlzeichen*) numeral. **Z~blatt** *nt* dial

zig *inv* *a* (*fam*) umpteen

Zigarette *f* -,-n cigarette

Zigarre *f* -,-n cigar

Zigeuner(in) *m* -s,- (*f* -,-nen) gypsy

Zimmer *nt* -s,- room. **Z~mädchen** *nt* chambermaid. **Z~mann** *m* (*pl* -leute) carpenter. **z~n** *vt* make ● *vi* (*haben*) do carpentry. **Z~nachweis** *m* accommodation bureau. **Z~pflanze** *f* house plant

zimperlich *a* squeamish; (*wehleidig*) soft; (*prüde*) prudish

Zimt *m* -[e]s cinnamon

Zink *nt* -s zinc

Zinke *f* -,-n prong; (*Kamm-*) tooth

Zinn *m* -s tin; (*Gefäße*) pewter

Zins|en *mpl* interest *sg*; **Z~en tragen** earn interest. **Z~eszins** *m* -es,-en compound interest. **Z~fuß, Z~satz** *m* interest rate

Zipfel *m* -s,- corner; (*Spitze*) point; (*Wurst-*) [tail-]end

zirka *a* *v* a out

Zirkel *m* -s,- [pair of] compasses *pl*; (*Gruppe*) circle

Zirkul|ation /-'tsio:n/ *f* - circulation. **z~ieren** *vi* (*sein*) circulate

Zirkus *m* -,-se circus

zirpen *vi* (*haben*) chirp

zischen *vi* (*haben*) hiss; ⟨*Fett:*⟩ sizzle ● *vt* hiss

Zit|at *nt* -[e]s,-e quotation. **z~ieren** *vt/i* (*haben*) quote; (*rufen*) summon

Zitr|onat *nt* -[e]s candied lemon-peel. **Z~one** *f* -,-n lemon. **Z~onenlimonade** *f* lemonade

zittern vi (haben) tremble; (vor Kälte) shiver; (beben) shake

zittrig a shaky, adv ·ily

Zitze f -,-n teat

zivil a civilian; ⟨Ehe, Recht, Luftfahrt⟩ civil; (mäßig) reasonable. **Z∼** nt -s civilian clothes pl. **Z∼courage** /-kura:ʒə/ f - courage of one's convictions. **Z∼dienst** m community service

Zivili|sation /-'tsio:n/ f -,-en civilization. **z∼sieren** vt civilize. **z∼siert** a civilized ● adv in a civilized manner

Zivilist m -en,-en civilian

zögern vi (haben) hesitate. **Z∼** nt -s hesitation. **z∼d** a hesitant, adv ·ly

Zoll[1] m -[e]s,- inch

Zoll[2] m -[e]s,∼e [customs] duty; (Behörde) customs pl. **Z∼abfertigung** f customs clearance. **Z∼beamte(r)** m customs officer. **z∼frei** a & adv duty-free. **Z∼kontrolle** f customs check

Zone f -,-n zone

Zoo m -s,-s zoo

Zoo|loge /tsoo'lo:gə/ m -n,-n zoologist. **Z∼logie** f - zoology. **z∼logisch** a zoological

Zopf m -[e]s,∼e plait

Zorn m -[e]s anger. **z∼ig** a angry, adv ·ily

zotig a smutty, dirty

zottig a shaggy

z.T. abbr (zum Teil) partly

zu prep (+ dat) to; (dazu) with; (zeitlich, preislich) at; (Zweck) for; (über) about; **zu ... hin** towards; **zu Hause** at home; **zu Fuß/Pferde** on foot/horseback; **zu beiden Seiten** on both sides; **zu Ostern** at Easter; **zu diesem Zweck** for this purpose; **zu meinem Erstaunen/Entsetzen** to my surprise/horror; **zu Dutzenden** by the dozen; **eine Marke zu 60 Pfennig** a 60-pfennig stamp; **das Stück zu zwei Mark** at two marks each; **wir waren zu dritt/ viert** there were three/four of us; **es steht 5 zu 3** the score is 5–3; **zu etw werden** turn into sth ● adv (allzu) too; (Richtung) towards; (geschlossen) closed; (an Schalter, Hahn) off; **zu groß/weit** too big/far; **nach dem Fluß zu** towards the river; **Augen zu!** close your eyes! **Tür zu!** shut the door! **nur zu!** go on! **mach zu!** (fam) hurry up! ● conj to; **etwas zu essen** something to eat; **nicht zu**

glauben unbelievable; **zu erörternde Probleme** problems to be discussed

zuallererst adv first of all. **z∼letzt** adv last of all

Zubehör nt -s accessories pl

zubereit|en vt sep prepare. **Z∼ung** f - preparation; (in Rezept) method

zubilligen vt sep grant

zubinden† vt sep tie [up]

zubring|en† vt sep spend. **Z∼er** m -s,- access road; (Bus) shuttle

Zucchini /tsu'ki:ni/ pl courgettes

Zucht f -,-en breeding; (Pflanzen-) cultivation; (Art, Rasse) breed; (von Pflanzen) strain; (Z∼farm) farm; (Pferde-) stud; (Disziplin) discipline

zücht|en vt breed; cultivate, grow ⟨Rosen, Gemüse⟩. **Z∼er** m -s,- breeder; grower

Zuchthaus nt prison

züchtigen vt chastise

Züchtung f -,-en breeding; (Pflanzen-) cultivation; (Art, Rasse) breed; (von Pflanzen) strain

zucken vi (haben) twitch; (sich z∼d bewegen) jerk; ⟨Blitz:⟩ flash; ⟨Flamme:⟩ flicker ● vt **die Achseln z∼** shrug one's shoulders

zücken vt draw ⟨Messer⟩

Zucker m -s sugar. **Z∼dose** f sugar basin. **Z∼guß** m icing. **z∼krank** a diabetic. **Z∼krankheit** f diabetes. **z∼n** vt sugar. **Z∼rohr** nt sugar cane. **Z∼rübe** f sugar beet. **z∼süß** a sweet; (fig) sugary. **Z∼watte** f candyfloss. **Z∼zange** f sugar tongs pl

zuckrig a sugary

zudecken vt sep cover up; (im Bett) tuck up; cover ⟨Topf⟩

zudem adv moreover

zudrehen vt sep turn off; **jdm den Rücken z∼** turn one's back on s.o.

zudringlich a pushing, (fam) pushy

zudrücken vt sep press or push shut; close ⟨Augen⟩

zueinander adv to one another; **z∼ passen** go together. **z∼halten**† vi sep (haben) (fig) stick together

zuerkennen† vt sep award (dat to)

zuerst adv first; (anfangs) at first; **mit dem Kopf z∼** head first

zufahr|en† vi sep (sein) **z∼en auf** (+ acc) drive towards. **Z∼t** f access; (Einfahrt) drive

Zufall m chance; (Zusammentreffen) coincidence; **durch Z∼** by chance/coincidence. **z∼en**† vi sep (sein)

close, shut; **jdm z~en** ⟨*Aufgabe:*⟩ fall/⟨*Erbe:*⟩ go to s.o.

zufällig a chance, accidental ● adv by chance; **ich war z~ da** I happened to be there

Zuflucht f refuge; ⟨*Schutz*⟩ shelter. **Z~sort** m refuge

zufolge prep (+ dat) according to

zufrieden a contented, adv -ly; ⟨*befriedigt*⟩ satisfied. **z~geben**† **(sich)** vr sep be satisfied. **Z~heit** f - contentment; satisfaction. **z~lassen**† vt sep leave in peace. **z~stellen** vt sep satisfy. **z~stellend** a satisfactory, adv -ly

zufrieren† vi sep (sein) freeze over

zufügen vt sep inflict (dat on); do ⟨*Unrecht*⟩ (dat to)

Zufuhr f - supply

zuführen vt sep ● vt supply ● vi (haben) **z~ auf** (+ acc) lead to

Zug m -[e]s, ⁻e train; ⟨*Kolonne*⟩ column; ⟨*Um-*⟩ procession; ⟨*Mil*⟩ platoon; ⟨*Vogelschar*⟩ flock; ⟨*Ziehen, Zugkraft*⟩ pull; ⟨*Wandern, Ziehen*⟩ migration; ⟨*Schluck, Luft-*⟩ draught; ⟨*Atem-*⟩ breath; ⟨*beim Rauchen*⟩ puff; ⟨*Schach-*⟩ move; ⟨*beim Schwimmen, Rudern*⟩ stroke; ⟨*Gesichts-*⟩ feature; ⟨*Wesens-*⟩ trait; **etw in vollen Zügen genießen** enjoy sth to the full; **in einem Zug[e]** at one go

Zugabe f ⟨*Geschenk*⟩ [free] gift; ⟨*Mus*⟩ encore

Zugang m access

zugänglich a accessible; ⟨*Mensch:*⟩ approachable; ⟨*fig*⟩ amenable (dat/ **für** to)

Zugbrücke f drawbridge

zugeben† vt sep add; ⟨*gestehen*⟩ admit; ⟨*erlauben*⟩ allow. **zugegebenermaßen** adv admittedly

zugegen a **z~ sein** be present

zugehen† vi sep (sein) close; **jdm z~** be sent to s.o.; **z~ auf** (+ acc) go towards; **dem Ende z~** draw to a close; ⟨*Vorräte:*⟩ run low; **auf der Party ging es lebhaft zu** the party was pretty lively

Zugehörigkeit f - membership

Zügel m -s,- rein

zugelassen a registered

zügel|los a unrestrained, adv -ly; ⟨*sittenlos*⟩ licentious. **z~n** vt rein in; ⟨*fig*⟩ curb

Zuge|ständnis nt concession. **z~stehen**† vt sep grant

zugetan a fond ⟨*dat* of⟩

zugig a draughty

zügig a quick, adv -ly

Zug|kraft f pull; ⟨*fig*⟩ attraction. **z~kräftig** a effective; ⟨*anreizend*⟩ popular; ⟨*Titel*⟩ catchy

zugleich adv at the same time

Zug|luft f draught. **Z~pferd** nt draught-horse; ⟨*fam*⟩ draw

zugreifen† vi sep (haben) grab it/ them; ⟨*bei Tisch*⟩ help oneself; ⟨*bei Angebot:*⟩ jump at it; ⟨*helfen*⟩ lend a hand

zugrunde adv **z~ richten** destroy; **z~ gehen** be destroyed; ⟨*Ehe:*⟩ founder; ⟨*sterben*⟩ die; **z~ liegen** form the basis ⟨*dat* of⟩

zugucken vi sep (haben) = **zusehen**

zugunsten prep (+ gen) in favour of; ⟨*Sammlung*⟩ in aid of

zugute adv **jdm/etw z~ kommen** benefit s.o./sth; **jdm seine Jugend z~ halten** make allowances for s.o.'s youth

Zugvogel m migratory bird

zuhalten† v sep ● vt keep closed; ⟨*bedecken*⟩ cover; **sich** ⟨*dat*⟩ **die Nase z~** hold one's nose ● vi (haben) **z~ auf** (+ acc) head for

Zuhälter m -s,- pimp

Zuhause nt -s,- home

zuhör|en vi sep (haben) listen ⟨*dat* to⟩. **Z~er(in)** m(f) listener

zujubeln vi sep (haben) **jdm z~** cheer s.o.

zukehren vt sep turn ⟨*dat* to⟩

zukleben vt sep seal

zuknallen vt/i sep (sein) slam

zuknöpfen vt sep button up

zukommen† vi sep (sein) **z~ auf** (+ acc) come towards; ⟨*sich nähern*⟩ approach; **z~ lassen** send (**jdm** s.o.); devote ⟨*Pflege*⟩ (dat to); **jdm z~** be s.o.'s right

Zukunft f - future. **zukünftig** a future ● adv in future

zulächeln vi sep (haben) smile ⟨*dat* at⟩

Zulage f -,-n extra allowance

zulangen vi sep (haben) help oneself; **tüchtig z~** tuck in

zulassen† vt sep allow, permit; ⟨*teilnehmen lassen*⟩ admit; ⟨*Admin*⟩ license, register; ⟨*geschlossen lassen*⟩ leave closed; leave unopened ⟨*Brief*⟩

zulässig a permissible

Zulassung f -,-en admission; registration; ⟨*Lizenz*⟩ licence

zulaufen† vi sep (sein) **z~en auf** (+ acc) run towards; **spitz z~en** taper to a point

zulegen vt sep add; **sich** (dat) **etw z~** get sth; grow ⟨Bart⟩

zuleide adv **jdm etwas z~ tun** hurt s.o.

zuletzt adv last; (schließlich) in the end; **nicht z~** not least

zuliebe adv **jdm/etw z~** for the sake of s.o./sth

zum prep = **zu dem; zum Spaß** for fun; **etw zum Lesen** sth to read

zumachen v sep ● vt close, shut; do up ⟨Jacke⟩; seal ⟨Umschlag⟩; turn off ⟨Hahn⟩; (stillegen) close down ● vi (haben) close, shut; (stillgelegt werden) close down

zumal adv especially ● conj especially since

zumeist adv for the most part

zumindest adv at least

zumutbar a reasonable

zumute adv **mir ist traurig/elend z~** I feel sad/wretched; **mir ist nicht danach z~** I don't feel like it

zumut|en vt sep **jdm etw z~en** ask or expect sth of s.o.; **sich** (dat) **zuviel z~en** overdo things. **Z~ung** f - imposition; **eine Z~ung sein** be unreasonable

zunächst adv first [of all]; (anfangs) at first; (vorläufig) for the moment ● prep (+ dat) nearest to

Zunahme f -,-n increase

Zuname m surname

zünd|en vt/i (haben) ignite; **z~ende Rede** rousing speech. **Z~er** m -s,- detonator, fuse. **Z~holz** nt match. **Z~kerze** f sparking-plug. **Z~schlüssel** m ignition key. **Z~schnur** f fuse. **Z~ung** f -,-en ignition

zunehmen† vi sep (haben) increase (an + dat in); ⟨Mond:⟩ wax; (an Gewicht) put on weight. **z~d** a increasing, adv -ly

Zuneigung f - affection

Zunft f -,⁻e guild

zünftig a proper, adv -ly

Zunge f -,-n tongue. **Z~nbrecher** m tongue-twister

zunichte a **z~ machen** wreck; **z~ werden** come to nothing

zunicken vi sep (haben) nod (dat to)

zunutze a **sich** (dat) **etw z~ machen** make use of sth; (ausnutzen) take advantage of sth

zuoberst adv right at the top

zuordnen vt sep assign (dat to)

zupfen vt/i (haben) pluck (an + dat at); pull out ⟨Unkraut⟩

zur prep = **zu der; zur Schule/Arbeit** to school/work; **zur Zeit** at present

zurechnungsfähig a of sound mind

zurecht|finden† (sich) vr sep find one's way. **z~kommen**† vi sep (sein) cope (mit with); (rechtzeitig kommen) be in time. **z~legen** vt sep put out ready; **sich** (dat) **eine Ausrede z~legen** have an excuse all ready. **z~machen** vt sep get ready; **sich z~machen** get ready. **z~weisen**† vt sep reprimand. **Z~weisung** f reprimand

zureden vi sep (haben) **jdm z~** try to persuade s.o.

zurichten vt sep prepare; (beschädigen) damage; (verletzen) injure

zuriegeln vt sep bolt

zurück adv back; **Berlin, hin und z~** return to Berlin. **z~behalten**† vt sep keep back; be left with ⟨Narbe⟩. **z~bekommen**† vt sep get back; **20 Pfennig z~bekommen** get 20 pfennigs change. **z~bleiben**† vi sep (sein) stay behind; (nicht mithalten) lag behind. **z~blicken** vi sep (haben) look back. **z~bringen**† vt sep bring back; (wieder hinbringen) take back. **z~erobern** vt sep recapture; (fig) regain. **z~erstatten** vt sep refund. **z~fahren** v sep ● vt drive back ● vi (sein) return, go back; (im Auto) drive back; (z~weichen) recoil. **z~finden**† vi sep (haben) find one's way back. **z~führen** v sep ● vt take back; (fig) attribute (auf + acc to) ● vi (haben) lead back. **z~geben**† vt sep give back, return. **z~geblieben** a retarded. **z~gehen**† vi sep (sein) go back, return; (abnehmen) go down; **z~gehen auf** (+ acc) (fig) go back to

zurückgezogen a secluded. **Z~heit** f - seclusion

zurückhalt|en† vt sep hold back; (abhalten) stop; **sich z~en** restrain oneself. **z~end** a reserved. **Z~ung** f - reserve

zurück|kehren vi sep (sein) return. **z~kommen**† vi sep (sein) come back, return; (ankommen) get back; **z~kommen auf** (+ acc) (fig) come back to. **z~lassen**† vt sep leave behind; (z~kehren lassen) allow back. **z~legen** vt sep put back; (reservieren) keep; (sparen) put by; cover ⟨Strecke⟩. **z~lehnen (sich)** vr sep lean back. **z~liegen**† vi sep (haben) be in the past; (*Sport*) be behind; **das liegt lange zurück** that was long ago. **z~melden (sich)** *vr sep* report back. **z~nehmen†** *vt sep* take back. **z~rufen†** *vt/i sep* (*haben*) call back. **z~scheuen** *vi sep* (*sein*) shrink (**vor** + *dat* from). **z~schicken** *vt sep* send back. **z~schlagen†** *v sep* ● *vi* (*haben*) hit back ● *vt* hit back; (*abwehren*) beat back; (*umschlagen*) turn back. **z~schneiden†** *vt sep* cut back. **z~schrecken†** *vi sep* (*sein*) shrink back, recoil; (*fig*) shrink (**vor** + *dat* from). **z~setzen** *v sep* ● *vt* put back; (*Auto*) reverse, back; (*herabsetzen*) reduce; (*fig*) neglect ● *vi* (*haben*) reverse, back. **z~stellen** *vt sep* put back; (*reservieren*) keep; (*fig*) put aside; (*aufschieben*) postpone. **z~stoßen†** *v sep* ● *vt* push back ● *vi* (*sein*) reverse, back. **z~treten†** *vi sep* (*sein*) step back; (*vom Amt*) resign; (*verzichten*) withdraw. **z~weichen†** *vi sep* (*sein*) draw back; (*z~schrecken*) shrink back. **z~weisen†** *vt sep* turn away; (*fig*) reject. **z~werfen†** *vt* throw back; (*reflektieren*) reflect. **z~zahlen** *vt sep* pay back. **z~ziehen†** *vt sep* draw back; (*fig*) withdraw; **sich z~ziehen** withdraw; (*vom Beruf*) retire; (*Mil*) retreat

Zuruf *m* shout. **r~en†** *vt sep* shout (*dat* to)

Zusage *f* -,-n acceptance; (*Versprechen*) promise. **z~n** *v sep* ● *vt* promise ● *vi* (*haben*) accept; **jdm z~n** appeal to s.o.

zusammen *adv* together; (*insgesamt*) altogether. **Z~arbeit** *f* co-operation. **z~arbeiten** *vi sep* (*haben*) co-operate. **z~bauen** *vt sep* assemble. **z~beißen†** *vt sep* **die Zähne z~beißen** clench/ (*fig*) grit one's teeth. **z~bleiben†** *vi sep* (*sein*) stay together. **z~brechen†** *vi sep* (*sein*) collapse. **z~bringen†** *vt sep* bring together; (*beschaffen*) raise. **Z~bruch** *m* collapse; (*Nerven- & fig*) breakdown. **z~fahren†** *vi sep* (*sein*) collide; (*z~zucken*) start. **z~fallen†** *vi sep* (*sein*) collapse; (*zeitlich*) coincide. **z~falten** *vt sep* fold up. **z~fassen** *vt sep* summarize, sum up. **Z~fassung** *f* summary. **z~fügen** *vt sep* fit together. **z~führen** *vt sep* bring together. **z~gehören** *vi sep* (*haben*) belong together; (*z~passen*) go together. **z~gesetzt** *a*

(*Gram*) compound. **z~halten†** *v sep* ● *vt* hold together; (*beisammenhalten*) keep together ● *vi* (*haben*) (*fig*) stick together. **Z~hang** *m* connection; (*Kontext*) context. **z~hängen†** *vi sep* (*haben*) be connected. **z~hanglos** *a* incoherent, *adv* -ly. **z~klappen** *v sep* ● *vt* fold up ● *vi* (*sein*) collapse. **z~kommen†** *vi sep* (*sein*) meet; (*sich sammeln*) accumulate. **Z~kunft** *f* -,-ẽe meeting. **z~laufen†** *vi sep* (*sein*) gather; (*Flüssigkeit:*) collect; (*Linien:*) converge. **z~leben** *vi sep* (*haben*) live together. **z~legen** *v sep* ● *vt* put together; (*z~falten*) fold up; (*vereinigen*) amalgamate; pool (*Geld*) ● *vi* (*haben*) club together. **z~nehmen†** *vt sep* gather up; summon up (*Mut*); collect (*Gedanken*); **sich z~nehmen** pull oneself together. **z~passen** *vi sep* (*haben*) go together, match; (*Personen:*) be well matched. **Z~prall** *m* collision. **z~prallen** *vi sep* (*sein*) collide. **z~rechnen** *vt sep* add up. **z~reißen†** (**sich**) *vr sep* (*fam*) pull oneself together. **z~rollen** *vt sep* roll up; **sich z~rollen** curl up. **z~schlagen†** *vt sep* smash up; (*prügeln*) beat up. **z~schließen†** (**sich**) *vr sep* join together; (*Firmen:*) merge. **Z~schluß** *m* union; (*Comm*) merger. **z~schreiben†** *vt sep* write as one word

zusammensein† *vi sep* (*sein*) be together. **Z~** *nt* -s get-together

zusammensetz|en *vt sep* put together; (*Techn*) assemble; **sich z~en** sit [down] together; (*bestehen*) be made up (**aus** from). **Z~ung** *f* -,-en composition; (*Techn*) assembly; (*Wort*) compound

zusammen|stellen *vt sep* put together; (*gestalten*) compile. **Z~stoß** *m* collision; (*fig*) clash. **z~stoßen†** *vi sep* (*sein*) collide. **z~treffen†** *vi sep* (*sein*) meet; (*zeitlich*) coincide. **Z~treffen** *nt* meeting; coincidence. **z~zählen** *vt sep* add up. **z~ziehen†** *v sep* ● *vt* draw together; (*addieren*) add up; (*konzentrieren*) mass; **sich z~ziehen** contract; (*Gewitter:*) gather ● *vi* (*sein*) move in together; move in (**mit** with). **z~zucken** *vi sep* (*sein*) start; (*vor Schmerz*) wince

Zusatz *m* addition; (*Jur*) rider; (*Lebensmittel-*) additive. **Z~gerät** *nt*

siv/ *a* Scheuer-; ⟨re-
...d ● *n* Scheuermittel
...eifmittel *nt*
... *adv* nebeneinander;
...itt halten mit
.../ *vt* kürzen
... *adv* im Ausland; **go**
...fahren
.../ *a*, **-ly** *adv* abrupt;
...ch; (*curt*) schroff
... *n* Abszeß *m*
...nd/ *vi* entfliehen
...s/ *n* Abwesenheit *f*
.../*a*, **-ly** *adv* abwesend;
...ent/ *vt* **~** **oneself**
...n'ti:/ *n* Abwesende(r)
...d /æbsənt'maindid/ *a*,
...bwesend; (*forgetful*)
...lu:t/*a*, **-ly** *adv* absolut
...bsə'lu:ʃn/ *n* Absolu-
.../ *vt* lossprechen
.../ *vt* absorbieren, auf-
...n vertieft in (+ *acc*)
...saugfähig
...so:pʃn/*n* Absorption *f*
...n/ *vi* sich enthalten
...from voting sich der
...lten
...sti:mɪəs/ *a* enthaltsam
...stenʃn/ *n* (*Pol*) [Stim-
...*f*
...ebstɪnəns/ *n* Enthalt-
...rækt/ *a* abstrakt ● *n*
...riß *m*
.../ *a*, **-ly** *adv* absurd.
...dität *f*
...'bʌndəns/ *n* Fülle *f* (**of**
...*a* reichlich
.../ *vt* mißbrauchen; (*in-*
...pfen
...s/ *n* Mißbrauch *m*; (*in-*
...pfungen *pl*. **~ive** /-ɪv
...pt/pp **abutted**) angren-
...+ *acc*)
...zml/ *a* (*fam*) kata-
...Abgrund *m*
...ə'demɪk/ *a*, **-ally** *adv*
...● *n* Akademiker(in)
...edəmɪ/ *n* Akademie *f*

accede /ək'si:d/ *vi* **~ to** zustimmen (+ *dat*); besteigen ⟨*throne*⟩

accelerat|e /ək'selərət/ *vt* beschleunigen ● *vi* die Geschwindigkeit erhöhen. **~ion** /-'reɪʃn/ *n* Beschleunigung *f*. **~or** *n* (*Auto*) Gaspedal *nt*

accent¹ /'æksənt/ *n* Akzent *m*

accent² /æk'sent/ *vt* betonen

accentuate /ək'sentjʊeɪt/ *vt* betonen

accept /ək'sept/ *vt* annehmen; (*fig*) akzeptieren ● *vi* zusagen. **~able** /-əbl/ *a* annehmbar. **~ance** *n* Annahme *f*; (*of invitation*) Zusage *f*

access /'ækses/ *n* Zugang *m*; (*road*) Zufahrt *f*. **~ible** /ək'sesəbl/ *a* zugänglich

accession /ək'seʃn/ *n* (*to throne*) Thronbesteigung *f*

accessor|y /ək'sesərɪ/ *n* (*Jur*) Mitschuldige(r) *m/f*; **~ies** *pl* (*fashion*) Accessoires *pl*; (*Techn*) Zubehör *nt*

accident /'æksɪdənt/ *n* Unfall *m*; (*chance*) Zufall *m*; **by ~** zufällig; (*unintentionally*) versehentlich. **~al** /-'dentl/ *a*, **-ly** *adv* zufällig; (*unintentional*) versehentlich

acclaim /ə'kleɪm/ *n* Beifall *m* ● *vt* feiern (**as** als)

acclimate /'æklɪmeɪt/ *vt* (*Amer*) = **acclimatize**

acclimatize /ə'klaɪmətaɪz/ *vt* **become ~d** sich akklimatisieren

accolade /'ækəleɪd/ *n* Auszeichnung *f*

accommodat|e /ə'kɒmədeɪt/ *vt* unterbringen; (*oblige*) entgegenkommen (+ *dat*). **~ing** *a* entgegenkommend. **~ion** /-'deɪʃn/ *n* (*rooms*) Unterkunft *f*

accompan|iment /ə'kʌmpənɪmənt/ *n* Begleitung *f*. **~ist** *n* (*Mus*) Begleiter(in) *m(f)*

accompany /ə'kʌmpənɪ/ *vt* (*pt/pp* **-ied**) begleiten

accomplice /ə'kʌmplɪs/ *n* Komplize/ zin *m/f*

accomplish /ə'kʌmplɪʃ/ *vt* erfüllen ⟨*task*⟩; (*achieve*) erreichen. **~ed** *a* fähig. **~ment** *n* Fertigkeit *f*; (*achievement*) Leistung *f*

accord /ə'kɔ:d/ *n* (*treaty*) Abkommen *nt*; **of one ~** einmütig; **of one's own ~** aus eigenem Antrieb ● *vt* gewähren. **~ance** *n* **in ~ance with** entsprechend (+ *dat*)

according /ə'kɔ:dɪŋ/ *adv* **~ to** nach (+ *dat*). **~ly** *adv* entsprechend

accordion /ə'kɔ:dɪən/ *n* Akkordeon *nt*

accost /ə'kɒst/ *vt* ansprechen

attachment. **zusätzlich** *a* additional ● *adv* in addition

zuschanden *adv* **z~ machen** ruin, wreck; **z~ fahren** wreck

zuschau|en *vi sep* (*haben*) watch. **Z~er(in)** *m* -s,- (*f* -,-nen) spectator; (*TV*) viewer. **Z~erraum** *m* auditorium

zuschicken *vt sep* send (*dat* to)

Zuschlag *m* surcharge; (*D-Zug-*) supplement. **z~en†** *v sep* ● *vt* shut; (*heftig*) slam; (*bei Auktion*) knock down (**jdm** to s.o.) ● *vi* (*haben*) hit out; ⟨*Feind:*⟩ strike ● *vi* (*sein*) slam shut. **z~pflichtig** *a* for which a supplement is payable

zuschließen† *v sep* ● *vt* lock ● *vi* (*haben*) lock up

zuschneiden† *vt sep* cut out; cut to size ⟨*Holz*⟩

zuschreiben† *vt sep* attribute (*dat* to); **jdm die Schuld z~** blame s.o.

Zuschrift *f* letter; (*auf Annonce*) reply

zuschulden *adv* **sich** (*dat*) **etwas z~ kommen lassen** do wrong

Zuschuß *m* contribution; (*staatlich*) subsidy

zusehen† *vi sep* (*haben*) watch; **z~, daß** see [to it] that

zusehends *adv* visibly

zusein† *vi sep* (*sein*) be closed

zusenden† *vt sep* send (*dat* to)

zusetzen *v sep* ● *vt* add; (*einbüßen*) lose ● *vi* (*haben*) **jdm z~** pester s.o.; ⟨*Hitze:*⟩ take it out of s.o.

zusicher|n *vt sep* promise. **Z~ung** *f* promise

Zuspätkommende(r) *m/f* latecomer

zuspielen *vt sep* (*Sport*) pass

zuspitzen (sich) *vr sep* (*fig*) become critical

zusprechen† *v sep* ● *vt* award (**jdm** s.o.); **jdm Trost/Mut z~** comfort/encourage s.o. ● *vi* (*haben*) **dem Essen z~** eat heartily

Zustand *m* condition, state

zustande *adv* **z~ bringen/kommen** bring/come about

zuständig *a* competent; (*verantwortlich*) responsible. **Z~keit** *f* - competence; responsibility

zustehen† *vi sep* (*haben*) **jdm z~** be s.o.'s right; ⟨*Urlaub:*⟩ be due to s.o.; **es steht ihm nicht zu** he is not entitled to it; (*gebührt*) it is not for him (**zu** to)

zusteigen† *vi sep* (*sein*) get on; **noch jemand zugestiegen?** tickets please; (*im Bus*) any more fares please?

zustell|en *vt sep* block; (*bringen*) deliver. **Z~ung** *f* delivery

zusteuern *v sep* ● *vi* (*sein*) head (**auf** + *acc* for) ● *vt* contribute

zustimm|en *vi sep* (*haben*) agree. (*billigen*) approve (*dat* of). **Z~ung** *f* consent; approval

zustoßen† *vi sep* (*sein*) happen (*dat* to)

Zustrom *m* influx

zutage *adv* **z~ treten** *od* **kommen/ bringen** come/bring to light

Zutat *f* (*Culin*) ingredient

zuteil|en *vt sep* allocate; assign ⟨*Aufgabe*⟩. **Z~ung** *f* allocation

zutiefst *adv* deeply

zutragen† *vt sep* carry/(*fig*) report (*dat* to); **sich z~** happen

zutrau|en *vt sep* **jdm etw z~** believe s.o. capable of sth. **Z~en** *nt* -s confidence. **z~lich** *a* trusting, *adv* -ly; ⟨*Tier*⟩ friendly

zutreffen† *vi sep* (*haben*) be correct; **z~ auf** (+*acc*) apply to. **z~d** *a* applicable (**auf** + *acc* to); (*richtig*) correct, *adv* -ly

zutrinken† *vi sep* (*haben*) **jdm z~** drink to s.o.

Zutritt *m* admittance

zuunterst *adv* right at the bottom

zuverlässig *a* reliable, *adv* -bly. **Z~keit** *f* - reliability

Zuversicht *f* - confidence. **z~lich** *a* confident, *adv* -ly

zuviel *pron & adv* too much; (*pl*) too many

zuvor *adv* before; (*erst*) first

zuvorkommen† *vi sep* (*sein*) (+*dat*) anticipate; **jdm z~** beat s.o. to it. **z~d** *a* obliging, *adv* -ly

Zuwachs *m* -es increase

zuwege *adv* **z~ bringen** achieve

zuweilen *adv* now and then

zuweisen† *vt sep* assign; (*zuteilen*) allocate

zuwend|en† *vt sep* turn (*dat* to); **sich z~en** (+*dat*) turn to; (*fig*) devote oneself to. **Z~ung** *f* donation; (*Fürsorge*) care

zuwenig *pron & adv* too little; (*pl*) too few

zuwerfen† *vt sep* slam ⟨*Tür*⟩; **jdm etw z~** throw s.o. sth; give s.o. ⟨*Blick, Lächeln*⟩

zuwider *adv* **jdm z~ sein** be repugnant to s.o. ● *prep* (+*dat*) contrary to. **z~handeln** *vi sep* (*haben*) contravene (**etw** *dat* sth)

zuzahlen *vt sep* pay extra

zuziehen† *v sep* ● *vt* pull tight; draw ⟨*Vorhänge*⟩; (*hinzu-*) call in; **sich** (*dat*) *etw* **z**~ contract ⟨*Krankheit*⟩; sustain ⟨*Verletzung*⟩; incur ⟨*Zorn*⟩ ● *vi* (*sein*) move into the area

zuzüglich *prep* (+ *gen*) plus

Zwang *m* -[e]s,ⁿe compulsion; (*Gewalt*)force;(*Verpflichtung*)obligation

zwängen *vt* squeeze

zwanglos *a* informal, *adv* -ly; ⟨*Benehmen*⟩free and easy. **Z**~**igkeit** *f* - informality

Zwangs|jacke *f* straitjacket. **Z**~**lage** *f* predicament. **z**~**läufig** *a* inevitable, *adv* -bly

zwanzig *inv a* twenty. **z**~**ste(r,s)** *a* twentieth

zwar *adv* admittedly; **und z**~ to be precise

Zweck *m* -[e]s,-e purpose; (*Sinn*) point; **es hat keinen Z**~ there is no point. **z**~**dienlich** *a* appropriate; ⟨*Information*⟩ relevant. **z**~**los** *a* pointless. **z**~**mäßig** *a* suitable, *adv* -bly; (*praktisch*) functional, *adv* -ly. **z**~**s** *prep* (+ *gen*) for the purpose of

zwei *inv a*, **Z**~ *f* -,-en two; (*Sch*) ≈ B. **Z**~**bettzimmer** *nt* twinbedded room

zweideutig *a* ambiguous, *adv* -ly; (*schlüpfrig*) suggestive, *adv* -ly. **Z**~**keit** *f* -,-en ambiguity

zwei|erlei *inv a* two kinds of ● *pron* two things. **z**~**fach** *a* double

Zweifel *m* -s,- doubt. **z**~**haft** *a* doubtful; (*fragwürdig*) dubious. **z**~**los** *adv* undoubtedly. **z**~**n** *vi* (*haben*) doubt (**an etw** *dat* sth)

Zweig *m* -[e]s,-e branch. **Z**~**geschäft** *nt* branch. **Z**~**stelle** *f* branch [office]

Zwei|kampf *m* duel. **z**~**mal** *adv* twice. **z**~**reihig** *a* double-breasted. **z**~**sprachig** *a* bilingual

zweit *adv* zu **z**~ in twos; **wir waren zu z**~ there were two of us. **z**~**beste(r,s)** *a* second-best. **z**~**e(r,s)** *a* second

zwei|teilig *a* two-piece; ⟨*Film, Programm*⟩ two-part. **z**~**tens** *adv* secondly

zweitklassig *a* second-class

Zwerchfell *nt* diaphragm

Zwerg *m* -[e]s,-e dwarf

Zwetsch[g]e *f* -,-n quetsche

Zwickel *m* -s,- gusset

zwicken *vt/i* (*haben*) pinch

Zwieback *m* -[e]s,ⁿe rusk

Zwiebel *f* -,-n onion; (*Blumen-*) bulb

Zwielicht *nt* half-light; (*Dämmerlicht*) twilight. **z**~**ig** *a* shady

Zwie|spalt *m* conflict. **z**~**spältig** *a* conflicting. **Z**~**tracht** *f* - discord

Zwilling *m* -s,-e twin; **Z**~**e** (*Astr*) Gemini

zwingen† *vt* force; **sich z**~ force oneself. **z**~**d** *a* compelling

Zwinger *m* -s,- run; (*Zucht-*) kennels *pl*

zwinkern *vi* (*haben*) blink; (*als Zeichen*) wink

Zwirn *m* -[e]s button thread

zwischen *prep* (+ *dat/acc*) between; (*unter*) among[st]. **Z**~**bemerkung** *f* interjection. **Z**~**ding** *nt* (*fam*) cross. **z**~**durch** *adv* in between; (*in der Z*~*zeit*) in the meantime; (*ab und zu*) now and again. **Z**~**fall** *m* incident. **Z**~**händler** *m* middleman. **Z**~**landung** *f* stop-over. **Z**~**raum** *m* gap, space. **Z**~**ruf** *m* interjection. **Z**~**stecker** *m* adaptor. **Z**~**wand** *f* partition. **Z**~**zeit** *f* **in der Z**~**zeit** in the meantime

Zwist *m* -[e]s,-e discord; (*Streit*) feud. **Z**~**igkeiten** *fpl* quarrels

zwitschern *vi* (*haben*) chirp

zwo *inv a* two

zwölf *inv a* twelve. **z**~**te(r,s)** *a* twelfth

zwote(r,s) *a* second

Zyklus *m* -,-klen cycle

Zylind|er *m* -s,- cylinder; (*Hut*) top hat. **z**~**risch** *a* cylindrical

Zyn|iker *m* -s,- cynic. **z**~**isch** *a* cynical, *adv* -ly. **Z**~**ismus** *m* - cynicism

Zypern *nt* -s Cyprus

Zypresse *f* -,-n cypress

Zyste /ˈtsʏstə/ *f* -,-n cyst

z.Zt. *abbr* (**zur Zeit**) at present

---

a /ə, *betont* eɪ/ (*vor einem Vokal* a *indef art* ein(e); (*each*) pro; **not kein(e)**

aback /əˈbæk/ *adv* **be taken** ~ ve blüfft sein

abandon /əˈbændən/ *vt* verlasse (*give up*) aufgeben ● *n* Hingabe ~**ed** *a* verlassen; ⟨*behaviou* hemmungslos

abase /əˈbeɪs/ *vt* demütigen

abashed /əˈbæʃt/ *a* beschäm verlegen

abate /əˈbeɪt/ *vi* nachlassen

abattoir /ˈæbətwɑː(r)/ *n* Schlachtho *m*

abb|ey /ˈæbɪ/ *n* Abtei *f*. ~**ot** *n* Abt *m*

abbreviat|e /əˈbriːvɪeɪt/ *vt* abkürzen ~**ion** /-ˈeɪʃn/ *n* Abkürzung *f*

abdicat|e /ˈæbdɪkeɪt/ *vi* abdanken ~**ion** /-ˈkeɪʃn/ *n* Abdankung *f*

abdom|en /ˈæbdəmən/ *n* Unterleib *m*. ~**inal** /-ˈdemɪnl/ *a* Unterleibs-

abduct /əbˈdʌkt/ *vt* entführen. ~**ion** /-ˈʌkʃn/ *n* Entführung *f*. ~**or** *n* Entführer *m*

aberration /æbəˈreɪʃn/ *n* Abweichung *f*; (*mental*) Verwirrung *f*

abet /əˈbet/ *vt* (*pt/pp* **abetted**) aid and ~ (*Jur*) Beihilfe leisten (+ *dat*)

abeyance /əˈbeɪəns/ *n* **in** ~ [zeitweilig] außer Kraft; **fall into** ~ außer Kraft kommen

abhor /əbˈhɔː(r)/ *vt* (*pt/pp* **abhorred**) verabscheuen. ~**rence** /-ˈherəns/ *n* Abscheu *f*. ~**rent** /-ˈherənt/ *a* abscheulich

abid|e /əˈbaɪd/ *vt* (*pt/pp* **abided**) (*tolerate*) aushalten; ausstehen ⟨*person*⟩ ● *vi* ~**e by** sich halten an (+ *acc*). ~**ing** *a* bleibend

ability /əˈbɪlətɪ/ *n* Fähigkeit *f*; (*talent*) Begabung *f*

abject /ˈæbdʒekt/ *a* erbärmlich; (*humble*) demütig

ablaze /əˈbleɪz/ *a* in Flammen; **be** ~ in Flammen stehen

---

abrasive /əˈbreɪ mark⟩ verletze *nt*; (*Techn*) Sch

abreast /əˈbrest **keep** ~ **of** Sch

abridge /əˈbrɪdʒ

abroad /əˈbrɔːd ~ **ins Ausland**

abrupt /əˈbrʌp (*sudden*) plötzl

abscess /ˈæbsɛs

abscond /əbˈsk

absence /ˈæbsə

absent[1] /ˈæbsən **be** ~ **fehlen**

absent[2] /æbˈs fernbleiben

absentee /æbs *m*/*f*

absent-minde -**ly** *adv* geistes zerstreut

absolute /ˈæbs

absolution /æ tion *f*

absolve /əbˈsɔ

absorb /əbˈsɔ saugen; ~**ed** ~**ent** /-ənt/ *a*

absorption /əb

abstain /əbˈste (**from** *gen*); ~ Stimme entha

abstemious /əb

abstention /əb m]enthaltung

abstinence /ˈ samkeit *f*

abstract /ˈæbs (*summary*) A

absurd /əbˈsɜː ~**ity** *n* Absur

abundan|ce /ə an + *dat*). ~

abuse[1] /əˈbjuː *sult*) beschim

abus|e[2] /əˈbjuː *sults*) Beschi ausfallend

abut /əˈbʌt/ *vi* zen (**on to** *a*

abysmal /əˈb strophal

abyss /əˈbɪs/ *n*

academic /æ akademisch *m*(*f*)

academy /əˈk

account /ə'kaʊnt/ n Konto nt; (bill) Rechnung f; (description) Darstellung f; (report) Bericht m; ~s pl (Comm) Bücher pl; on ~ of wegen (+ gen); on no ~ auf keinen Fall; on this ~ deshalb; on my ~ meinetwegen; of no ~ ohne Bedeutung; take into ~ in Betracht ziehen, berücksichtigen ● vi ~ for Rechenschaft ablegen für; (explain) erklären

accountant /ə'kaʊntənt/ n Buchhalter(in) m(f); (chartered) Wirtschaftsprüfer m; (for tax) Steuerberater m

accoutrements /ə'ku:trəmənts/ npl Ausrüstung f

accredited /ə'kredtid/ a akkreditiert

accrue /ə'kru:/ vi sich ansammeln

accumulat|e /ə'kju:mjʊleɪt/ vt ansammeln, anhäufen ● vi sich ansammeln, sich anhäufen. ~ion /-'leɪʃn/ n Ansammlung f, Anhäufung f. ~or n (Electr) Akkumulator m

accura|cy /'ækjʊrəsɪ/ n Genauigkeit f. ~te /-rət/ a, -ly adv genau

accusation /ækju:'zeɪʃn/ n Anklage f

accusative /ə'kju:zətɪv/ a & n ~ [case] (Gram) Akkusativ m

accuse /ə'kju:z/ vt (Jur) anklagen (of gen); ~ s.o. of doing sth jdn beschuldigen, etw getan zu haben. ~d n the ~d der/die Angeklagte

accustom /ə'kʌstəm/ vt gewöhnen (to an + dat); grow or get ~ed to sich gewöhnen an (+ acc). ~ed a gewohnt

ace /eɪs/ n (Cards, Sport) As nt

ache /eɪk/ n Schmerzen pl ● vi weh tun, schmerzen

achieve /ə'tʃi:v/ vt leisten; (gain) erzielen; (reach) erreichen. ~ment n (feat) Leistung f

acid /'æsɪd/ a sauer; (fig) beißend ● n Säure f. ~ity /ə'sɪdətɪ/ n Säure f. ~ 'rain n saurer Regen m

acknowledge /ək'nɒlɪdʒ/ vt anerkennen; (admit) zugeben; erwidern ⟨greeting⟩; ~ receipt of den Empfang bestätigen (+ gen). ~ment n Anerkennung f; (of letter) Empfangsbestätigung f

acne /'æknɪ/ n Akne f

acorn /'eɪkɔ:n/ n Eichel f

acoustic /ə'ku:stɪk/ a, -ally adv akustisch. ~s npl Akustik f

acquaint /ə'kweɪnt/ vt ~ s.o. with jdn bekannt machen mit; be ~ed with kennen; vertraut sein mit ⟨fact⟩. ~ance n Bekanntschaft f; (person)

Bekannte(r) m/f; make s.o.'s ~ance jdn kennenlernen

acquiesce /ækwɪ'es/ vi einwilligen (to in + acc). ~nce n Einwilligung f

acquire /ə'kwaɪə(r)/ vt erwerben

acquisit|ion /ækwɪ'zɪʃn/ n Erwerb m; (thing) Erwerbung f. ~ive /ə'kwɪzɪtɪv/ a habgierig

acquit /ə'kwɪt/ vt (pt/pp acquitted) freisprechen; ~ oneself well seiner Aufgabe gerecht werden. ~tal n Freispruch m

acre /'eɪkə(r)/ n ≈ Morgen m

acrid /'ækrɪd/ a scharf

acrimon|ious /ækrɪ'məʊnɪəs/ a bitter. ~y /'ækrɪmənɪ/ n Bitterkeit f

acrobat /'ækrəbæt/ n Akrobat(in) m(f). ~ic /-'bætɪk/ a akrobatisch

across /ə'krɒs/ adv hinüber/herüber; (wide) breit; (not lengthwise) quer; (in crossword) waagerecht; come ~ sth auf etw (acc) stoßen; go ~ hinübergehen; bring ~ herüberbringen ● prep über (+ acc); (crosswise) quer über (+ acc/dat); (on the other side of) auf der anderen Seite (+ gen)

act /ækt/ n Tat f; (action) Handlung f; (law) Gesetz nt; (Theat) Akt m; (item) Nummer f; put on an ~ (fam) sich verstellen ● vi handeln; (behave) sich verhalten; (Theat) spielen; (pretend) sich verstellen; ~ as fungieren als ● vt spielen ⟨role⟩. ~ing a (deputy) stellvertretend ● n (Theat) Schauspielerei f. ~ing profession n Schauspielerberuf m

action /'ækʃn/ n Handlung f; (deed) Tat f; (Mil) Einsatz m; (Jur) Klage f; (effect) Wirkung f; (Techn) Mechanismus m; out of ~ ⟨machine:⟩ außer Betrieb; take ~ handeln; killed in ~ gefallen. ~ 'replay n (TV) Wiederholung f

activate /'æktɪveɪt/ vt betätigen; (Chem, Phys) aktivieren

activ|e /'æktɪv/ a, -ly adv aktiv; on ~e service im Einsatz. ~ity /-'tɪvətɪ/ n Aktivität f

act|or /'æktə(r)/ n Schauspieler m. ~ress n Schauspielerin f

actual /'æktʃʊəl/ a, -ly adv eigentlich; (real) tatsächlich. ~ity /-'ælətɪ/ n Wirklichkeit f

acumen /'ækjʊmən/ n Scharfsinn m

acupuncture /'ækjʊ-/ n Akupunktur f

acute /ə'kju:t/ a scharf; ⟨angle⟩ spitz; ⟨illness⟩ akut. ~ly adv sehr

ad /æd/ n (fam) = **advertisement**

AD abbr (**Anno Domini**) n.Chr.

adamant /'ædəmənt/ a **be ~ that** darauf bestehen, daß

adapt /ə'dæpt/ vt anpassen; bearbeiten ⟨play⟩ ● vi sich anpassen. **~ability** /ə'bɪləti/ n Anpassungsfähigkeit f. **~able** /-əbl/ a anpassungsfähig

adaptation /ædæp'teɪʃn/ n (Theat) Bearbeitung f

adapter, adaptor /ə'dæptə(r)/ n (Techn) Adapter m; (Electr) (two-way) Doppelstecker m

add /æd/ vt hinzufügen; (Math) addieren ● vi zusammenzählen, addieren; **~ to** hinzufügen zu; (fig: increase) steigern; (compound) verschlimmern. **~ up** vt zusammenzählen ⟨figures⟩ ● vi zusammenzählen, aufmachen; **~ up to** zu machen; **it doesn't ~ up** (fig) da stimmt etwas nicht

adder /'ædə(r)/ n Kreuzotter f

addict /'ædɪkt/ n Süchtige(r) m/f

addict|ed /ə'dɪktɪd/ a süchtig; **~ed to drugs** drogensüchtig. **~ion** /-ɪkʃn/ n Sucht f. **~ive** /-ɪv/ a **be ~ive** zur Süchtigkeit führen

addition /ə'dɪʃn/ n Hinzufügung f; (Math) Addition f; (thing added) Ergänzung f; **in ~** zusätzlich. **~al** a, **-ly** adv zusätzlich

additive /'ædɪtɪv/ n Zusatz m

address /ə'dres/ n Adresse f, Anschrift f; (speech) Ansprache f; **form of ~** Anrede f ● vt adressieren (**to** an + acc); (speak to) anreden ⟨person⟩; sprechen vor (+ dat) ⟨meeting⟩. **~ee** /ædre'si:/ n Empfänger m

adenoids /'ædənɔɪdz/ npl [Rachen] polypen pl

adept /'ædept/ a geschickt (**at** in + dat)

adequate /'ædɪkwət/ a, **-ly** adv ausreichend

adhere /əd'hɪə(r)/ vi kleben/(fig) festhalten (**to** an + dat). **~nce** n Festhalten n

adhesive /əd'hi:sɪv/ a klebend ● n Klebstoff m

adjacent /ə'dʒeɪsnt/ a angrenzend

adjective /'ædʒɪktɪv/ n Adjektiv nt

adjoin /ə'dʒɔɪn/ vt angrenzen an (+ acc). **~ing** a angrenzend

adjourn /ə'dʒɜ:n/ vt vertagen (**until** auf + acc) ● vi sich vertagen. **~ment** n Vertagung f

adjudicate /ə'dʒu:dɪkeɪt/ vi entscheiden; (in competition) Preisrichter sein

adjust /ə'dʒʌst/ vt einstellen; (alter) verstellen ● vi sich anpassen (**to** dat). **~able** /-əbl/ a verstellbar. **~ment** n Einstellung f; Anpassung f

ad lib /æd'lɪb/ adv aus dem Stegreif ● vi (pt/pp **ad libbed**) (fam) improvisieren

administer /əd'mɪnɪstə(r)/ vt verwalten; verabreichen ⟨medicine⟩

administrat|ion /ədmɪnɪ'streɪʃn/ n Verwaltung f; (Pol) Regierung f. **~or** /əd'mɪnɪstreɪtə(r)/ n Verwaltungsbeamte(r) m /-beamtin f

admirable /'ædmərəbl/ a bewundernswert

admiral /'ædmərəl/ n Admiral m

admiration /ædmə'reɪʃn/ n Bewunderung f

admire /əd'maɪə(r)/ vt bewundern. **~r** n Verehrer(in) m(f)

admissible /əd'mɪsəbl/ a zulässig

admission /əd'mɪʃn/ n Eingeständnis nt; (entry) Eintritt m

admit /əd'mɪt/ vt (pt/pp **admitted**) (let in) hereinlassen; (acknowledge) zugeben; **~ to sth** etw zugeben. **~tance** n Eintritt m. **~tedly** adv zugegebenermaßen

admoni|sh /əd'mɒnɪʃ/ vt ermahnen. **~tion** /ædmə'nɪʃn/ n Ermahnung f

ado /ə'du:/ n **without more ~** ohne weiteres

adolescen|ce /ædə'lesns/ n Jugend f, Pubertät f. **~t** a Jugend-; ⟨boy, girl⟩ halbwüchsig ● n Jugendliche(r) m/f

adopt /ə'dɒpt/ vt adoptieren; ergreifen ⟨measure⟩; (Pol) annehmen ⟨candidate⟩. **~ion** /-ɒpʃn/ n Adoption f. **~ive** /-ɪv/ a Adoptiv-

ador|able /ə'dɔ:rəbl/ a bezaubernd. **~ation** /ædə'reɪʃn/ n Anbetung f

adore /ə'dɔ:(r)/ vt (worship) anbeten; (fam: like) lieben

adorn /ə'dɔ:n/ vt schmücken. **~ment** n Schmuck m

adrenalin /ə'drenəlɪn/ n Adrenalin nt

Adriatic /eɪdrɪ'ætɪk/ a & n **~** [Sea] Adria f

adrift /ə'drɪft/ a **be ~** treiben; **come ~** sich losreißen

adroit /ə'drɔɪt/ a, **-ly** adv gewandt, geschickt

adulation /ædjʊ'leɪʃn/ n Schwärmerei f

adult /'ædʌlt/ n Erwachsene(r) m/f

adulterate /ə'dʌltəreɪt/ vt verfälschen; panschen ⟨wine⟩

adultery /ə'dʌltərɪ/ n Ehebruch m

advance /əd'vɑːns/ n Fortschritt m; (Mil) Vorrücken nt; (payment) Vorschuß m; **in ~** im voraus ● vi vorankommen; (Mil) vorrücken; (make progress) Fortschritte machen ● vt fördern ⟨cause⟩; vorbringen ⟨idea⟩; vorschießen ⟨money⟩. **~ booking** n Kartenvorverkauf m. **~d** a fortgeschritten; (progressive) fortschrittlich. **~ment** n Förderung f; (promotion) Beförderung f

advantage /əd'vɑːntɪdʒ/ n Vorteil m; **take ~ of** ausnutzen. **~ous** /ædvən'teɪdʒəs/ a vorteilhaft

advent /'ædvent/ n Ankunft f; **A~** (season) Advent m

adventur|e /əd'ventʃə(r)/ n Abenteuer nt. **~er** n Abenteurer m. **~ous** /-rəs/ a abenteuerlich; ⟨person⟩ abenteuerlustig

adverb /'ædvɜːb/ n Adverb nt

adversary /'ædvəsərɪ/ n Widersacher m

advers|e /'ædvɜːs/ a ungünstig. **~ity** /əd'vɜːsətɪ/ n Not f

advert /'ædvɜːt/ n (fam) = **advertisement**

advertise /'ædvətaɪz/ vt Reklame machen für; (by small ad) inserieren ● vi Reklame machen; inserieren; **~ for** per Anzeige suchen

advertisement /əd'vɜːtɪsmənt/ n Anzeige f; (publicity) Reklame f; (small ad) Inserat nt

advertis|er /'ædvətaɪzə(r)/ n Inserent m. **~ing** n Werbung f ● attrib Werbe-

advice /əd'vaɪs/ n Rat m. **~ note** n Benachrichtigung f

advisable /əd'vaɪzəbl/ a ratsam

advis|e /əd'vaɪz/ vt raten (s.o. jdm); (counsel) beraten; (inform) benachrichtigen; **~e s.o. against sth** jdm von etw abraten ● vi raten. **~er** n Berater(in) m(f). **~ory** a beratend

advocate¹ /'ædvəkət/ n [Rechts]anwalt m/-anwältin f; (supporter) Befürworter m

advocate² /'ædvəkeɪt/ vt befürworten

aerial /'eərɪəl/ a Luft- ● n Antenne f

aerobics /eə'rəubɪks/ n Aerobic nt

aero|drome /'eərədrəum/ n Flugplatz m. **~plane** n Flugzeug nt

aerosol /'eərəsɒl/ n Spraydose f

aesthetic /iːs'θetɪk/ a ästhetisch

afar /ə'fɑː(r)/ adv **from ~** aus der Ferne

affable /'æfəbl/ a, **-bly** adv freundlich

affair /ə'feə(r)/ n Angelegenheit f, Sache f; (scandal) Affäre f; **[love-] ~** [Liebes]verhältnis nt

affect /ə'fekt/ vt sich auswirken auf (+ acc); (concern) betreffen; (move) rühren; (pretend) vortäuschen. **~ation** /æfek'teɪʃn/ n Affektiertheit f. **~ed** a affektiert

affection /ə'fekʃn/ n Liebe f. **~ate** /-ət/ a, **-ly** adv liebevoll

affiliated /ə'fɪlɪeɪtɪd/ a angeschlossen (to dat)

affinity /ə'fɪnətɪ/ n Ähnlichkeit f; (attraction) gegenseitige Anziehung f

affirm /ə'fɜːm/ vt behaupten; (Jur) eidesstattlich erklären

affirmative /ə'fɜːmətɪv/ a bejahend ● n Bejahung f

affix /ə'fɪks/ vt anbringen (to dat); (stick) aufkleben (to auf + acc); setzen ⟨signature⟩ (to unter + acc)

afflict /ə'flɪkt/ vt **be ~ed with** behaftet sein mit. **~ion** /-ɪkʃn/ n Leiden nt

affluen|ce /'æfluəns/ n Reichtum m. **~t** a wohlhabend. **~t society** n Wohlstandsgesellschaft f

afford /ə'fɔːd/ vt (provide) gewähren; **be able to ~ sth** sich (dat) etw leisten können. **~able** /-əbl/ a erschwinglich

affray /ə'freɪ/ n Schlägerei f

affront /ə'frʌnt/ n Beleidigung f ● vt beleidigen

afield /ə'fiːld/ adv **further ~** weiter weg

afloat /ə'fləut/ a **be ~** ⟨ship:⟩ flott sein; **keep ~** ⟨person:⟩ sich über Wasser halten

afoot /ə'fut/ a im Gange

aforesaid /ə'fɔːsed/ a (Jur) obenerwähnt

afraid /ə'freɪd/ a **be ~** Angst haben (of vor + dat); **I'm ~ not** leider nicht; **I'm ~ so** [ja] leider; **I'm ~ I can't help you** ich kann Ihnen leider nicht helfen

afresh /ə'freʃ/ adv von vorne

Africa /'æfrɪkə/ n Afrika nt. **~n** a afrikanisch ● n Afrikaner(in) m(f)

after /'ɑːftə(r)/ adv danach ● prep nach (+ dat); **~ that** danach; **~ all** schließlich; **the day ~ tomorrow** übermorgen; **be ~** aussein auf (+ acc) ● conj nachdem

after: ~-effect n Nachwirkung f. **~math** /-mɑːθ/ n Auswirkungen pl.

~'**noon** *n* Nachmittag *m*; **good**
~**noon!** guten Tag! ~**sales service** *n*
Kundendienst *m.* ~**shave** *n* Rasier-
wasser *nt.* ~**thought** *n* nachträg-
licher Einfall *m.* ~**wards** *adv*
nachher

again /ə'geɪn/ *adv* wieder; (*once more*)
noch einmal; (*besides*) außerdem; ~
and ~ immer wieder

against /ə'geɪnst/ *prep* gegen (+ *acc*)

age /eɪdʒ/ *n* Alter *nt*; (*era*) Zeitalter *nt*;
~**s** (*fam*) ewig; **under** ~ minderjährig; **of** ~ volljährig; **two years of** ~
zwei Jahre alt ● *v* (*pres p* **ageing**)
● *vt* älter machen ● *vi* altern; (*mature*) reifen

aged¹ /eɪdʒd/ *a* ~ **two** zwei Jahre alt
aged² /'eɪdʒɪd/ *a* betagt ● *n* **the** ~ *pl*
die Alten

ageless /'eɪdʒlɪs/ *a* ewig jung

agency /'eɪdʒənsɪ/ *n* Agentur *f*; (*office*)
Büro *nt*; **have the** ~ **for** die Vertre-
tung haben für

agenda /ə'dʒendə/ *n* Tagesordnung *f*;
on the ~ auf dem Programm

agent /'eɪdʒənt/ *n* Agent(in) *m*(*f*);
(*Comm*) Vertreter(in) *m*(*f*); (*substance*) Mittel *nt*

aggravat|e /'ægrəveɪt/ *vt* verschlim-
mern; (*fam: annoy*) ärgern. ~**ion**
/-'veɪʃn/ *n* (*fam*) Ärger *m*

aggregate /'ægrɪgət/ *a* gesamt ● *n* Gesamtzahl *f*; (*sum*) Gesamtsumme *f*

aggress|ion /ə'greʃn/ *n* Aggression *f*.
~**ive** /- sɪv/ *a*, -**ly** *adv* aggressiv.
~**iveness** *n* Aggressivität *f*. ~**or** *n*
Angreifer(in) *m*(*f*)

aggrieved /ə'griːvd/ *a* verletzt

aggro /'ægrəʊ/ *n* (*fam*) Ärger *m*

aghast /ə'gɑːst/ *a* entsetzt

agil|e /'ædʒaɪl/ *a* flink, behende;
⟨*mind*⟩ wendig. ~**ity** /ə'dʒɪlətɪ/ *n*
Flinkheit *f*, Behendigkeit *f*

agitat|e /'ædʒɪteɪt/ *vt* bewegen;
(*shake*) schütteln ● *vi* (*fig*) ~ **for**
agitieren für. ~**ed** *a* erregt.
~**ion** /-'teɪʃn/ *n* Erregung *f*; (*Pol*)
Agitation *f*. ~**or** *n* Agitator *m*

agnostic /æg'nɒstɪk/ *n* Agnostiker *m*

ago /ə'gəʊ/ *adv* vor (+ *dat*); **a month**
~ vor einem Monat; **a long time** ~
vor langer Zeit; **how long** ~ **is it?** wie
lange ist es her?

agog /ə'gɒg/ *a* gespannt

agoniz|e /'ægənaɪz/ *vi* [innerlich]
ringen. ~**ing** *a* qualvoll

agony /'ægənɪ/ *n* Qual *f*; **be in** ~
furchtbare Schmerzen haben

agree /ə'griː/ *vt* vereinbaren; (*admit*)
zugeben; ~ **to do sth** sich bereit
erklären, etw zu tun ● *vi* ⟨*people,
figures:*⟩ übereinstimmen; (*reach
agreement*) sich einigen; (*get on*) gut
miteinander auskommen; (*consent*)
einwilligen (**to** in + *acc*); **I** ~ der
Meinung bin ich auch; ~ **with s.o.**
jdm zustimmen; ⟨*food:*⟩ jdm bekommen; ~ **with sth** (*approve of*) mit etw
einverstanden sein

agreeable /ə'griːəbl/ *a* angenehm; **be**
~ einverstanden sein (**to** mit)

agreed /ə'griːd/ *a* vereinbart

agreement /ə'griːmənt/ *n* Übereinstimmung *f*; (*consent*) Einwilligung
f; (*contract*) Abkommen *nt*; **reach** ~
sich einigen

agricultur|al /ægrɪ'kʌltʃərəl/ *a* land-
wirtschaftlich. ~**e** /'ægrɪkʌltʃə(r)/ *n*
Landwirtschaft *f*

aground /ə'graʊnd/ *a* gestrandet; **run**
~ ⟨*ship:*⟩ stranden

ahead /ə'hed/ *adv* **straight** ~ geradeaus; **be** ~ **of s.o./sth** vor jdm/etw
sein; (*fig*) voraus sein; **draw** ~ nach
vorne ziehen; **go on** ~ vorgehen;
get ~ vorankommen; **go** ~! (*fam*)
bitte! **look/plan** ~ vorausblicken/
-planen

aid /eɪd/ *n* Hilfe *f*; (*financial*) Unterstützung *f*; **in** ~ **of** zugunsten (+
gen) ● *vt* helfen (+ *dat*)

aide /eɪd/ *n* Berater *m*

Aids /eɪdz/ *n* Aids *nt*

ail|ing /'eɪlɪŋ/ *a* kränkelnd. ~**ment** *n*
Leiden *nt*

aim /eɪm/ *n* Ziel *nt*; **take** ~ zielen ● *vt*
richten (**at** auf + *acc*); ~ **at** zielen (at
auf + *acc*); ~ **to do sth** beabsichtigen, etw zu tun. ~**less** *a*, -**ly** *adv*
ziellos

air /eə(r)/ *n* Luft *f*; (*tune*) Melodie *f*;
(*expression*) Miene *f*; (*appearance*)
Anschein *m*; **be on the** ~ ⟨*programme:*⟩ gesendet werden; ⟨*person:*⟩ senden, auf Sendung sein; **put
on** ~**s** vornehm tun; **by** ~ auf dem
Luftweg; (*airmail*) mit Luftpost ● *vt*
lüften; vorbringen ⟨*views*⟩

air: ~**-bed** *n* Luftmatratze *f*. ~**-con-
ditioned** *a* klimatisiert. ~**-condi-
tioning** *n* Klimaanlage *f*. ~**craft** *n*
Flugzeug *nt*. ~ **fare** *n* Flugpreis *m*.
~**field** *n* Flugplatz *m*. ~ **force** *n*
Luftwaffe *f*. ~ **freshener** *n* Raum-
spray *nt*. ~**gun** *n* Luftgewehr *nt*. ~
hostess *n* Stewardeß *f*. ~ **letter** *n*

Aerogramm *nt*. ~**line** *n* Fluggesell-
schaft *f*. ~**lock** *n* Luftblase *f*. ~**mail**
n Luftpost *f*. ~**man** *n* Flieger *m*.
~**plane** *n* (*Amer*) Flugzeug *nt*. ~
pocket *n* Luftloch *nt*. ~**port** *n* Flug-
hafen *m*. ~**raid** *n* Luftangriff *m*. ~
raid shelter *n* Luftschutzbunker *m*.
~**ship** *n* Luftschiff *nt*. ~ **ticket** *n*
Flugschein *m*. ~**tight** *a* luftdicht. ~
traffic *n* Luftverkehr *m*. ~**-traffic
controller** *n* Fluglotse *m*. ~**worthy** *a*
flugtüchtig

airy /'eərɪ/ *a* (**-ier, -iest**) lüftig; ⟨*manner*⟩ nonchalant

aisle /aɪl/ *n* Gang *m*

ajar /ə'dʒɑ:(r)/ *a* angelehnt

akin /ə'kɪn/ *a* ~ **to** verwandt mit;
(*similar*) ähnlich (**to** *dat*)

alabaster /'æləbɑ:stə(r)/ *n* Alabaster
m

alacrity /ə'lækrətɪ/ *n* Bereitfertigkeit *f*

alarm /ə'lɑ:m/ *n* Alarm *m*; (*device*)
Alarmanlage *f*; (*clock*) Wecker *m*;
(*fear*) Unruhe *f* ● *vt* erschrecken;
alarmieren. ~ **clock** *n* Wecker *m*

alas /ə'læs/ *int* ach!

album /'ælbəm/ *n* Album *nt*

alcohol /'ælkəhɒl/ *n* Alkohol *m*. ~**ic**
/-'hɒlɪk/ *a* alkoholisch ● *n* Alkohol-
iker(in) *m*(*f*). ~**ism** *n* Alkoholismus
m

alcove /'ælkəʊv/ *n* Nische *f*

alert /ə'lɜ:t/ *a* aufmerksam ● *n* Alarm
m; **on the** ~ auf der Hut ● *vt*
alarmieren

algae /'ældʒɪ/ *npl* Algen *pl*

algebra /'ældʒɪbrə/ *n* Algebra *f*

Algeria /æl'dʒɪərɪə/ *n* Algerien *nt*

alias /'eɪlɪəs/ *n* Deckname *m* ● *adv*
alias

alibi /'ælɪbaɪ/ *n* Alibi *nt*

alien /'eɪlɪən/ *a* fremd ● *n* Ausländ-
er(in) *m*(*f*)

alienat|e /'eɪlɪəneɪt/ *vt* entfremden.
~**ion** /-'neɪʃn/ *n* Entfremdung *f*

alight[1] /ə'laɪt/ *vi* aussteigen (**from**
aus); ⟨*bird*:⟩ sich niederlassen

alight[2] *a* **be** ~ brennen; **set** ~
anzünden

align /ə'laɪn/ *vt* ausrichten. ~**ment** *n*
Ausrichtung *f*; **out of** ~**ment** nicht
richtig ausgerichtet

alike /ə'laɪk/ *a* & *adv* ähnlich; (*same*)
gleich; **look** ~ sich (*dat*) ähnlich
sehen

alimony /'ælɪmənɪ/ *n* Unterhalt *m*

alive /ə'laɪv/ *a* lebendig; **be** ~ leben;
be ~ **with** wimmeln von

alkali /'ælkəlaɪ/ *n* Base *f*, Alkali *nt*

all /ɔ:l/ *a* alle *pl*; (*whole*) ganz; ~ [**the**]
children alle Kinder; ~ **our children**
alle unsere Kinder; ~ **the others** alle
anderen; ~ **day** den ganzen Tag; ~
the wine der ganze Wein; **for** ~ **that**
(*nevertheless*) trotzdem; **in** ~ **innocence** in aller Unschuld ● *pron* alle
pl; (*everything*) alles; ~ **of** you/
them Sie/sie alle; ~ **of the town** die
ganze Stadt; **not at** ~ gar nicht; **in** ~
insgesamt; ~ **in** ~ alles in allem;
most of ~ am meisten; **once and for**
~ ein für allemal ● *adv* ganz; ~ **but**
fast; ~ **at once** auf einmal; ~ **too
soon** viel zu früh; ~ **the same** (*nevertheless*) trotzdem; ~ **the better** um
so besser; **be** ~ **in** (*fam*) völlig erledigt sein; **four** ~ (*Sport*) vier zu vier

allay /ə'leɪ/ *vt* zerstreuen

allegation /ælɪ'geɪʃn/ *n* Behauptung
f

allege /ə'ledʒ/ *vt* behaupten. ~**d** *a*, **-ly**
/-ɪdlɪ/ *adv* angeblich

allegiance /ə'li:dʒəns/ *n* Treue *f*

allegor|ical /ælɪ'gɒrɪkl/ *a* allegorisch.
~**y** /'ælɪgərɪ/ *n* Allegorie *f*

allerg|ic /ə'lɜ:dʒɪk/ *a* allergisch (**to**
gegen). ~**y** /'ælədʒɪ/ *n* Allergie *f*

alleviate /ə'li:vɪeɪt/ *vt* lindern

alley /'ælɪ/ *n* Gasse *f*; (*for bowling*)
Bahn *f*

alliance /ə'laɪəns/ *n* Verbindung *f*;
(*Pol*) Bündnis *nt*

allied /'ælaɪd/ *a* alliiert; (*fig: related*)
verwandt (**to** mit)

alligator /'ælɪgeɪtə(r)/ *n* Alligator *m*

allocat|e /'æləkeɪt/ *vt* zuteilen; (*share
out*) verteilen. ~**ion** /-'keɪʃn/ *n* Zu-
teilung *f*

allot /ə'lɒt/ *vt* (*pt/pp* **allotted**) zuteilen
(**s.o.** jdm). ~**ment** *n* ≈ Schrebergarten *m*

allow /ə'laʊ/ *vt* erlauben; (*give*) geben;
(*grant*) gewähren; (*reckon*) rechnen;
(*agree, admit*) zugeben; ~ **for** berücksichtigen; ~ **s.o. to do sth** jdm
erlauben, etw zu tun; **be** ~**ed to do
sth** etw tun dürfen

allowance /ə'laʊəns/ *n* [finanzielle]
Unterstützung *f*; ~ **for petrol** Ben-
zingeld *nt*; **make** ~**s for**
berücksichtigen

alloy /'ælɔɪ/ *n* Legierung *f*

allude /ə'lu:d/ *vi* anspielen (**to** auf +
acc)

allure /ə'lʊə(r)/ *n* Reiz *m*

allusion /ə'lu:ʒn/ *n* Anspielung *f*

ally[1] /'ælaɪ/ *n* Verbündete(r) *m*/*f*; **the
Allies** *pl* die Alliierten

ally² /ə'laɪ/ vt (pt/pp **-ied**) verbinden; ~ **oneself with** sich verbünden mit

almighty /ɔ:l'maɪtɪ/ a allmächtig; (fam: big) Riesen- ● n **the A**~ der Allmächtige

almond /'ɑ:mənd/ n (Bot) Mandel f

almost /'ɔ:lməʊst/ adv fast, beinahe

alms /ɑ:mz/ npl (liter) Almosen pl

alone /ə'ləʊn/ a & adv allein; **leave me** ~ laß mich in Ruhe; **leave that** ~! laß die Finger davon! **let** ~ ganz zu schweigen von

along /ə'lɒŋ/ prep entlang (+ acc); ~ **the river** den Fluß entlang ● adv ~ **with** zusammen mit; **all** ~ die ganze Zeit; **come** ~ komm doch; **I'll bring it** ~ ich bringe es mit; **move** ~ weitergehen

along'side adv daneben ● prep neben (+ dat)

aloof /ə'lu:f/ a distanziert

aloud /ə'laʊd/ adv laut

alphabet /'ælfəbet/ n Alphabet nt. ~**ical** /-'betɪkl/ a, **-ly** adv alphabetisch

alpine /'ælpaɪn/ a alpin; **A**~ Alpen-

Alps /ælps/ npl Alpen pl

already /ɔ:l'redɪ/ adv schon

Alsace /æl'sæs/ n Elsaß nt

Alsatian /æl'seɪʃn/ n (dog) [deutscher] Schäferhund m

also /'ɔ:lsəʊ/ adv auch

altar /'ɔ:ltə(r)/ n Altar m

alter /'ɔ:ltə(r)/ vt ändern ● vi sich verändern. ~**ation** /-'reɪʃn/ n Änderung f

alternate¹ /'ɔ:ltəneɪt/ vi [sich] abwechseln ● vt abwechseln

alternate² /ɔ:l'tɜ:nət/ a, **-ly** adv abwechselnd; (Amer: alternative) andere(r,s); **on** ~ **days** jeden zweiten Tag

'alternating current n Wechselstrom m

alternative /ɔ:l'tɜ:nətɪv/ a andere(r,s) ● n Alternative f. ~**ly** adv oder aber

although /ɔ:l'ðəʊ/ conj obgleich, obwohl

altitude /'æltɪtju:d/ n Höhe f

altogether /ɔ:ltə'geðə(r)/ adv insgesamt; (on the whole) alles in allem

altruistic /æltru:'ɪstɪk/ altruistisch

aluminium /æljʊ'mɪnɪəm/ n, (Amer) **aluminum** /ə'lu:mɪnəm/ n Aluminium nt

always /'ɔ:lweɪz/ adv immer

am /æm/ see **be**

a.m. abbr (**ante meridiem**) vormittags

amalgamate /ə'mælgəmeɪt/ vt vereinigen; (Chem) amalgamieren ● vi sich vereinigen; (Chem) sich amalgamieren

amass /ə'mæs/ vt anhäufen

amateur /'æmətə(r)/ n Amateur m ● attrib Amateur-; (Theat) Laien-. ~**ish** a laienhaft

amaze /ə'meɪz/ vt erstaunen. ~**d** a erstaunt. ~**ment** n Erstaunen nt

amazing /ə'meɪzɪŋ/ a, **-ly** adv erstaunlich

ambassador /æm'bæsədə(r)/ n Botschafter m

amber /'æmbə(r)/ n Bernstein m ● a (colour) gelb

ambidextrous /æmbɪ'dekstrəs/ a be ~ mit beiden Händen gleich geschickt sein

ambience /'æmbɪəns/ n Atmosphäre f

ambigu|ity /æmbɪ'gju:ətɪ/ n Zweideutigkeit f. ~**ous** /-'bɪgjʊəs/ a, **-ly** adv zweideutig

ambiti|on /æm'bɪʃn/ n Ehrgeiz m; (aim) Ambition f. ~**ous** /-ʃəs/ a ehrgeizig

ambivalent /æm'bɪvələnt/ a zwiespältig; **be/feel** ~ im Zwiespalt sein

amble /'æmbl/ vi schlendern

ambulance /'æmbjʊləns/ n Krankenwagen m. ~ **man** n Sanitäter m

ambush /'æmbʊʃ/ n Hinterhalt m ● vt aus dem Hinterhalt überfallen

amen /ɑ:'men/ int amen

amenable /ə'mi:nəbl/ a ~ **to** zugänglich (**to** dat)

amend /ə'mend/ vt ändern. ~**ment** n Änderung f. ~**s** npl **make** ~**s for sth** etw wiedergutmachen

amenities /ə'mi:nətɪz/ npl Einrichtungen pl

America /ə'merɪkə/ n Amerika nt. ~**n** a amerikanisch ● n Amerikaner(in) m(f). ~**nism** n Amerikanismus m

amiable /'eɪmɪəbl/ a nett

amicable /'æmɪkəbl/ a, **-bly** adv freundschaftlich; ⟨agreement⟩ gütlich

amid[st] /ə'mɪd[st]/ prep inmitten (+ gen)

amiss /ə'mɪs/ a be ~ nicht stimmen ● adv **not come** ~ nicht unangebracht sein; **take sth** ~ etw übelnehmen

ammonia /ə'məʊnɪə/ n Ammoniak nt

ammunition /æmjʊ'nɪʃn/ n Munition f

amnesia /æm'ni:zɪə/ n Amnesie f

amnesty /'æmnəstɪ/ n Amnestie f

among[st] /ə'mʌŋ[st]/ *prep* unter (+ *dat*/*acc*); ~ **yourselves** untereinander

amoral /eɪ'mɒrəl/ *a* amoralisch

amorous /'æmərəs/ *a* zärtlich

amount /ə'maʊnt/ *n* Menge *f*; (*sum of money*) Betrag *m*; (*total*) Gesamtsumme *f* ● *vi* ~ **to** sich belaufen auf (+ *acc*); (*fig*) hinauslaufen auf (+ *acc*)

amp /æmp/ *n* Ampere *nt*

amphibi|an /æm'fɪbɪən/ *n* Amphibie *f*. ~**ous** /-ɪəs/ *a* amphibisch

amphitheatre /'æmfɪ-/ *n* Amphitheater *nt*

ample /'æmpl/ *a* (-r, -st), -ly *adv* reichlich; (*large*) füllig

amplif|ier /'æmplɪfaɪə(r)/ *n* Verstärker *m*. ~**y** /-faɪ/ *vt* (*pt*/*pp* -ied) weiter ausführen; verstärken ⟨*sound*⟩

amputat|e /'æmpjʊteɪt/ *vt* amputieren. ~**ion** /-'teɪʃn/ *n* Amputation *f*

amuse /ə'mjuːz/ *vt* amüsieren, belustigen; (*entertain*) unterhalten. ~**ment** *n* Belustigung *f*; Unterhaltung *f*. ~**ment arcade** *n* Spielhalle *f*

amusing /ə'mjuːzɪŋ/ *a* amüsant

an /ən/, *betont* æn/ *see* **a**

anaem|ia /ə'niːmɪə/ *n* Blutarmut *f*, Anämie *f*. ~**ic** *a* blutarm

anaesthesia /ænəs'θiːzɪə/ *n* Betäubung *f*

anaesthetic /ænəs'θetɪk/ *n* Narkosemittel *nt*, Betäubungsmittel *nt*; **under [an]** ~ in Narkose; **give s.o. an** ~ jdm eine Narkose geben

anaesthet|ist /ə'niːsθətɪst/ *n* Narkosearzt *m*. ~**ize** /-taɪz/ *vt* betäuben

analog[ue] /'ænəlɒg/ *a* Analog-

analogy /ə'nælədʒɪ/ *n* Analogie *f*

analyse /'ænəlaɪz/ *vt* analysieren

analysis /ə'næləsɪs/ *n* Analyse *f*

analyst /'ænəlɪst/ *n* Chemiker(in) *m(f)*; (*Psych*) Analytiker *m*

analytical /ænə'lɪtɪkl/ *a* analytisch

anarch|ist /'ænəkɪst/ *n* Anarchist *m*. ~**y** *n* Anarchie *f*

anathema /ə'næθəmə/ *n* Greuel *m*

anatom|ical /ænə'tɒmɪkl/ *a*, -ly *adv* anatomisch. ~**y** /ə'nætəmɪ/ *n* Anatomie *f*

ancest|or /'ænsestə(r)/ *n* Vorfahr *m*. ~**ry** *n* Abstammung *f*

anchor /'æŋkə(r)/ *n* Anker *m* ● *vi* ankern ● *vt* verankern

anchovy /'æntʃəvɪ/ *n* Sardelle *f*

ancient /'eɪnʃənt/ *a* alt

ancillary /æn'sɪlərɪ/ *a* Hilfs-

and /ənd/, *betont* ænd/ *conj* und; ~ **so on** und so weiter; **six hundred** ~ **two** sechshundertzwei; **more** ~ **more** immer mehr; **nice** ~ **warm** schön warm; **try** ~ **come** versuche zu kommen

anecdote /'ænɪkdəʊt/ *n* Anekdote *f*

anew /ə'njuː/ *adv* von neuem

angel /'eɪndʒl/ *n* Engel *m*. ~**ic** /æn'dʒelɪk/ *a* engelhaft

anger /'æŋgə(r)/ *n* Zorn *m* ● *vt* zornig machen

angle¹ /'æŋgl/ *n* Winkel *m*; (*fig*) Standpunkt *m*; **at an** ~ schräg

angle² *vi* angeln; ~ **for** (*fig*) fischen nach. ~**r** *n* Angler *m*

Anglican /'æŋglɪkən/ *a* anglikanisch ● *n* Anglikaner(in) *m(f)*

Anglo-Saxon /æŋgləʊ'sæksn/ *a* angelsächsisch ● *n* Angelsächsisch *nt*

angry /'æŋgrɪ/ *a* (-ier, -iest), -ily *adv* zornig; **be** ~ **with** böse sein auf (+ *acc*)

anguish /'æŋgwɪʃ/ *n* Qual *f*

angular /'æŋgjʊlə(r)/ *a* eckig; ⟨*features*⟩ kantig

animal /'ænɪml/ *n* Tier *nt* ● *a* tierisch

animate¹ /'ænɪmət/ *a* lebendig

animat|e² /'ænɪmeɪt/ *vt* beleben. ~**ed** *a* lebhaft. ~**ion** /-'meɪʃn/ *n* Lebhaftigkeit *f*

animosity /ænɪ'mɒsətɪ/ *n* Feindseligkeit *f*

aniseed /'ænɪsiːd/ *n* Anis *m*

ankle /'æŋkl/ *n* [Fuß]knöchel *m*

annex /ə'neks/ *vt* annektieren

annex[e] /'æneks/ *n* Nebengebäude *nt*; (*extension*) Anbau *m*

annihilat|e /ə'naɪəleɪt/ *vt* vernichten. ~**ion** /-'leɪʃn/ *n* Vernichtung *f*

anniversary /ænɪ'vɜːsərɪ/ *n* Jahrestag *m*

annotate /'ænəteɪt/ *vt* kommentieren

announce /ə'naʊns/ *vt* bekanntgeben; (*over loudspeaker*) durchsagen; (*at reception*) ankündigen; (*Radio, TV*) ansagen; (*in newspaper*) anzeigen. ~**ment** *n* Bekanntgabe *f*, Bekanntmachung *f*; Durchsage *f*; Ansage *f*; Anzeige *f*. ~**r** *n* Ansager(in) *m(f)*

annoy /ə'nɔɪ/ *vt* ärgern; (*pester*) belästigen; **get** ~**ed** sich ärgern. ~**ance** *n* Ärger *m*. ~**ing** *a* ärgerlich

annual /'ænjʊəl/ *a*, -ly *adv* jährlich ● *n* (*Bot*) einjährige Pflanze *f*; (*book*) Jahresalbum *nt*

annuity /ə'njuːətɪ/ *n* [Leib]rente *f*

annul /ə'nʌl/ vt (pt/pp **annulled**) annullieren

anoint /ə'nɔɪnt/ vt salben

anomaly /ə'nɒmǝlɪ/ n Anomalie f

anonymous /ə'nɒnɪməs/ a, **-ly** adv anonym

anorak /'ænǝræk/ n Anorak m

anorexia /ænǝ'reksɪǝ/ n Magersucht f

another /ə'nʌðǝ(r)/ a & pron ein anderer/eine andere/ein anderes; (additional) noch ein(e); ~ **[one]** noch einer/eine/eins; ~ **day** an einem anderen Tag; **in ~ way** auf andere Weise; ~ **time** ein andermal; **one** ~ einander

answer /'ɑ:nsǝ(r)/ n Antwort f; (solution) Lösung f ● vt antworten (s.o. jdm); beantworten ⟨question, letter⟩; ~ **the door/telephone** an die Tür/ ans Telefon gehen ● vi antworten; (Teleph) sich melden; ~ **back** eine freche Antwort geben; ~ **for** verantwortlich sein für. ~**able** /-ǝbl/ a verantwortlich. ~**ing machine** n (Teleph) Anrufbeantworter m

ant /ænt/ n Ameise f

antagonis|m /æn'tægǝnɪzm/ n Antagonismus m. ~**tic** /-'nɪstɪk/ a feindselig

antagonize /æn'tægǝnaɪz/ vt gegen sich aufbringen

Antarctic /ænt'ɑ:ktɪk/ n Antarktis f

antelope /'æntɪlǝup/ n Antilope f

antenatal /æntɪ'neɪtl/ a ~ **care** Schwangerschaftsfürsorge f

antenna /æn'tenǝ/ n Fühler m; (Amer: aerial) Antenne f

ante-room /'æntɪ-/ n Vorraum m

anthem /'ænθǝm/ n Hymne f

anthology /æn'θɒlǝdʒɪ/ n Anthologie f

anthropology /ænθrǝ'pɒlǝdʒɪ/ n Anthropologie f

anti-'aircraft /æntɪ-/ a Flugabwehr-

antibiotic /æntɪbaɪ'ɒtɪk/ n Antibiotikum nt

'antibody n Antikörper m

anticipat|e /æn'tɪsɪpeɪt/ vt vorhersehen; (forestall) zuvorkommen (+ dat); (expect) erwarten. ~**ion** /-'peɪʃn/ n Erwartung f

anti'climax n Enttäuschung f

anti'clockwise a & adv gegen den Uhrzeigersinn

antics /'æntɪks/ npl Mätzchen pl

anti'cyclone n Hochdruckgebiet nt

antidote /'æntɪdǝut/ n Gegengift nt

'antifreeze n Frostschutzmittel nt

antipathy /æn'tɪpǝθɪ/ n Abneigung f, Antipathie f

antiquarian /æntɪ'kweǝrɪǝn/ a antiquarisch. ~ **bookshop** n Antiquariat nt

antiquated /'æntɪkweɪtɪd/ a veraltet

antique /æn'ti:k/ a antik ● n Antiquität f. ~ **dealer** n Antiquitätenhändler m

antiquity /æn'tɪkwǝtɪ/ n Altertum nt

anti-Semitic /æntɪsɪ'mɪtɪk/ a antisemitisch

anti'septic a antiseptisch ● n Antiseptikum nt

anti'social a asozial; (fam) ungesellig

antithesis /æn'tɪθǝsɪs/ n Gegensatz m

antlers /'æntlǝz/ npl Geweih nt

anus /'eɪnǝs/ n After m

anvil /'ænvɪl/ n Amboß m

anxiety /æŋ'zaɪǝtɪ/ n Sorge f

anxious /'æŋkʃǝs/ a, **-ly** adv ängstlich; (worried) besorgt; **be ~ to do sth** etw gerne machen wollen

any /'enɪ/ a irgendein(e); pl irgendwelche; (every) jede(r,s); pl alle; (after negative) kein(e); pl keine; ~ **colour/number you like** eine beliebige Farbe/Zahl; **have you ~ wine/apples?** haben Sie Wein/Äpfel? **for ~ reason** aus irgendeinem Grund ● pron [irgend]einer/eine/ eins; pl [irgend]welche; (some) welche(r,s); pl welche; (all) alle pl; (negative) keiner/keine/keins; pl keine; **I don't want ~ of it** ich will nichts davon; **there aren't ~** es gibt eine; **I need wine/apples/money— have we ~?** ich brauche Wein /Äpfel/Geld—haben wir welchen /welche/welches? ● adv noch; ~ **quicker/slower** noch schneller/langsamer; **is it ~ better?** geht es etwas besser? **would you like ~ more?** möchten Sie noch [etwas]? **I can't eat ~ more** ich kann nichts mehr essen; **I can't go ~ further** ich kann nicht mehr weiter

'anybody pron [irgend] jemand; (after negative) niemand; ~ **can do that** das kann jeder

'anyhow adv jedenfalls; (nevertheless) trotzdem; (badly) irgendwie

'anyone pron = **anybody**

'anything pron [irgend] etwas; (after negative) nichts; (everything) alles

'anyway adv jedenfalls; (in any case) sowieso

'**anywhere** adv irgendwo; (after negative) nirgendwo; ⟨be, live⟩ überall; **I'd go** ~ ich würde überallhin gehen

apart /ə'pɑːt/ adv auseinander; **live** ~ getrennt leben; ~ **from** abgesehen von

apartment /ə'pɑːtmənt/ n Zimmer nt; (Amer: flat) Wohnung f

apathy /'æpəθɪ/ n Apathie f

ape /eɪp/ n [Menschen]affe m ● vt nachäffen

aperitif /ə'perətɪf/ n Aperitif m

aperture /'æpətʃə(r)/ n Öffnung f; (Phot) Blende f

apex /'eɪpeks/ n Spitze f; (fig) Gipfel m

apiece /ə'piːs/ adv pro Person; (thing) pro Stück

apologetic /əpɒlə'dʒetɪk/ a, **-ally** adv entschuldigend; **be** ~ sich entschuldigen

apologize /ə'pɒlədʒaɪz/ vi sich entschuldigen (**to** bei)

apology /ə'pɒlədʒɪ/ n Entschuldigung f

apostle /ə'pɒsl/ n Apostel m

apostrophe /ə'pɒstrəfɪ/ n Apostroph m

appal /ə'pɔːl/ vt (pt/pp **appalled**) entsetzen. ~**ling** a entsetzlich

apparatus /æpə'reɪtəs/ n Apparatur f; (Sport) Geräte pl; (single piece) Gerät nt

apparel /ə'pærəl/ n Kleidung f

apparent /ə'pærənt/ a offenbar; (seeming) scheinbar. ~**ly** adv offenbar, anscheinend

apparition /æpə'rɪʃn/ n Erscheinung f

appeal /ə'piːl/ n Appell m, Aufruf m; (request) Bitte f; (attraction) Reiz m; (Jur) Berufung f ● vi appellieren (**to** an + acc); (ask) bitten (**for** um); (be attractive) zusagen (**to** dat); (Jur) Berufung einlegen. ~**ing** a ansprechend

appear /ə'pɪə(r)/ vi erscheinen; (seem) scheinen; (Theat) auftreten. ~**ance** n Erscheinen nt; (look) Aussehen nt; **to all** ~**ances** allem Anschein nach

appease /ə'piːz/ vt beschwichtigen

append /ə'pend/ vt nachtragen; setzen ⟨signature⟩ (**to** unter + acc). ~**age** /-ɪdʒ/ n Anhängsel nt

appendicitis /əpendɪ'saɪtɪs/ n Blinddarmentzündung f

appendix /ə'pendɪks/ n (pl **-ices** /-ɪsɪːz/) (of book) Anhang m ● (pl **-es**) (Anat) Blinddarm m

appertain /æpə'teɪn/ vi ~ **to** betreffen

appetite /'æpɪtaɪt/ n Appetit m

appetizing /'æpɪtaɪzɪŋ/ a appetitlich

applau|d /ə'plɔːd/ vt/i Beifall klatschen (+ dat). ~**se** n Beifall m

apple /'æpl/ n Apfel m

appliance /ə'plaɪəns/ n Gerät nt

applicable /'æplɪkəbl/ a anwendbar (**to** auf + acc); (on form) **not** ~ nicht zutreffend

applicant /'æplɪkənt/ n Bewerber(in) m(f)

application /æplɪ'keɪʃn/ n Anwendung f; (request) Antrag m; (for job) Bewerbung f; (diligence) Fleiß m

applied /ə'plaɪd/ a angewandt

apply /ə'plaɪ/ vt (pt/pp **-ied**) auftragen ⟨paint⟩; anwenden ⟨force, rule⟩ ● vi zutreffen (**to** auf + acc); (**for** beantragen; sich bewerben um ⟨job⟩

appoint /ə'pɔɪnt/ vt ernennen; (fix) festlegen; **well** ~**ed** gut ausgestattet. ~**ment** n Ernennung f; (meeting) Verabredung f; (at doctor's, hairdresser's) Termin m; (job) Posten m; **make an** ~**ment** sich anmelden

apposite /'æpəzɪt/ a treffend

appraise /ə'preɪz/ vt abschätzen

appreciable /ə'priːʃəbl/ a merklich; (considerable) beträchtlich

appreciat|e /ə'priːʃɪeɪt/ vt zu schätzen wissen; (be grateful for) dankbar sein für; (enjoy) schätzen; (understand) verstehen ● vi (increase in value) im Wert steigen. ~**ion** /-'eɪʃn/ n (gratitude) Dankbarkeit f; **in** ~**ion** als Dank (**of** für). ~**ive** /-ətɪv/ a dankbar

apprehend /æprɪ'hend/ vt festnehmen

apprehens|ion /æprɪ'henʃn/ n Festnahme f; (fear) Angst f. ~**ive** /-sɪv/ a ängstlich

apprentice /ə'prentɪs/ n Lehrling m. ~**ship** n Lehre f

approach /ə'prəʊtʃ/ n Näherkommen nt; (of time) Nahen nt; (access) Zugang m; (road) Zufahrt f ● vi sich nähern; ⟨time:⟩ nahen ● vt sich nähern (+ dat); (with request) herantreten an (+ acc); (set about) sich heranmachen an (+ acc). ~**able** /-əbl/ a zugänglich

approbation /æprə'beɪʃn/ n Billigung f

appropriate¹ /ə'prəupriət/ a angebracht, angemessen

appropriate² /ə'prəuprieit/ vt sich (dat) aneignen

approval /ə'pru:vl/ n Billigung f; **on** ~ zur Ansicht

approv|e /ə'pru:v/ vt billigen ● vi ~**e of sth/s.o.** mit etw/jdm einverstanden sein. ~**ing** a, -**ly** adv anerkennend

approximate¹ /ə'prɒksimeit/ vi ~ **to** nahekommen (+ dat)

approximate² /ə'prɒksimət/ a ungefähr. ~**ly** adv ungefähr, etwa

approximation /əprɒksi'meiʃn/ n Schätzung f

apricot /'eiprikɒt/ n Aprikose f

April /'eiprəl/ n April m; **make an** ~ **fool of** in den April schicken

apron /'eiprən/ n Schürze f

apropos /'æprəpəu/ adv ~ **[of]** betreffs (+ gen)

apt /æpt/ a, -**ly** adv passend; ⟨pupil⟩ begabt; **be** ~ **to do sth** dazu neigen, etw zu tun

aptitude /'æptitju:d/ n Begabung f

aqualung /'ækwəlʌŋ/ n Tauchgerät nt

aquarium /ə'kweəriəm/ n Aquarium nt

Aquarius /ə'kweəriəs/ n (Astr) Wassermann m

aquatic /ə'kwætik/ a Wasser-

Arab /'ærəb/ a arabisch ● n Araber(in) m(f). ~**ian** /ə'reibiən/ a arabisch

Arabic /'ærəbik/ a arabisch

arable /'ærəbl/ a ~ **land** Ackerland nt

arbitrary /'a:bitrəri/ a, -**ily** adv willkürlich

arbitrat|e /'a:bitreit/ vi schlichten. ~**ion** /-'treiʃn/ n Schlichtung f

arc /a:k/ n Bogen m

arcade /a:'keid/ n Laubengang m; ⟨shops⟩ Einkaufspassage f

arch /a:tʃ/ n Bogen m; (of foot) Gewölbe nt ● vt ~ **its back** ⟨cat:⟩ einen Buckel machen

archaeological /a:kiə'lɒdʒikl/ a archäologisch

archaeolog|ist /a:ki'ɒlədʒist/ n Archäologe m/-login f. ~**y** n Archäologie f

archaic /a:'keiik/ a veraltet

arch'bishop /a:tʃ-/ n Erzbischof m

arch-'enemy n Erzfeind m

archer /'a:tʃə(r)/ n Bogenschütze m. ~**y** n Bogenschießen nt

architect /'a:kitekt/ n Architekt(in) m(f). ~**ural** /a:ki'tektʃərəl/ a, -**ly** adv architektonisch

architecture /'a:kitektʃə(r)/ n Architektur f

archives /'a:kaivz/ npl Archiv nt

archway /'a:tʃwei/ n Torbogen m

Arctic /'a:ktik/ a arktisch ● n **the** ~ die Arktis

ardent /'a:dənt/ a, -**ly** adv leidenschaftlich

ardour /'a:də(r)/ n Leidenschaft f

arduous /'a:djuəs/ a mühsam

are /a:(r)/ see **be**

area /'eəriə/ n (surface) Fläche f; (Geom) Flächeninhalt m; (region) Gegend f; (fig) Gebiet nt. ~ **code** n Vorwahlnummer f

arena /ə'ri:nə/ n Arena f

aren't /a:nt/ = **are not**. See **be**

Argentina /a:dʒən'ti:nə/ n Argentinien nt

Argentin|e /'a:dʒəntain/, ~**ian** /-'tiniən/ a argentinisch

argue /'a:gju:/ vi streiten (**about** über + acc); ⟨two people:⟩ sich streiten; (debate) diskutieren; **don't** ~! keine Widerrede! ● vt (debate) diskutieren; (reason) ~ **that** argumentieren, daß

argument /'a:gjumənt/ n Streit m, Auseinandersetzung f; (reasoning) Argument nt; **have an** ~ sich streiten. ~**ative** /-'mentətiv/ a streitlustig

aria /'a:riə/ n Arie f

arid /'ærid/ a dürr

Aries /'eəri:z/ n (Astr) Widder m

arise /ə'raiz/ vi (pt arose, pp arisen) sich ergeben (**from** aus)

aristocracy /æri'stɒkrəsi/ n Aristokratie f

aristocrat /'æristəkræt/ n Aristokrat (in) m(f). ~**ic** /-'krætik/ a aristokratisch

arithmetic /ə'riθmətik/ n Rechnen nt

ark /a:k/ n **Noah's A**~ die Arche Noah

arm /a:m/ n Arm m; (of chair) Armlehne f; ~**s** pl (weapons) Waffen pl; (Heraldry) Wappen nt; **up in** ~**s** (fam) empört ● vt bewaffnen

armament /'a:məmənt/ n Bewaffnung f; ~**s** pl Waffen pl

'armchair n Sessel m

armed /a:md/ a bewaffnet; ~ **forces** Streitkräfte pl

armistice /'a:mistis/ n Waffenstillstand m

armour /'a:mə(r)/ n Rüstung f. ~**ed** a Panzer-

'armpit n Achselhöhle f

army /'ɑːmɪ/ n Heer nt; (specific) Armee f; **join the** ~ zum Militär gehen

aroma /ə'rəʊmə/ n Aroma nt, Duft m. ~**tic** /ærə'mætɪk/ a aromatisch

arose /ə'rəʊz/ see **arise**

around /ə'raʊnd/ adv [all]~ rings herum; **he's not** ~ er ist nicht da; **look/turn** ~ sich umsehen/umdrehen; **travel** ~ herumreisen ● prep um (+ acc) ... herum; (approximately) gegen

arouse /ə'raʊz/ vt aufwecken; (excite) erregen

arrange /ə'reɪndʒ/ vt arrangieren; anordnen (furniture, books); (settle) abmachen; **I have** ~**d to go there** ich habe abgemacht, daß ich dahingehe. ~**ment** n Anordnung f; (agreement) Vereinbarung f; (of flowers) Gesteck nt; **make** ~**ments** Vorkehrungen treffen

arrears /ə'rɪəz/ npl Rückstände pl; **in** ~ im Rückstand

arrest /ə'rest/ n Verhaftung f; **under** ~ verhaftet ● vt verhaften

arrival /ə'raɪvl/ n Ankunft f; **new** ~**s** pl Neuankömmlinge pl

arrive /ə'raɪv/ vi ankommen; ~ **at** (fig) gelangen zu

arroganc|e /'ærəgəns/ n Arroganz f. ~**t** a, **-ly** adv arrogant

arrow /'ærəʊ/ n Pfeil m

arse /ɑːs/ n (vulg) Arsch m

arsenic /'ɑːsənɪk/ n Arsen nt

arson /'ɑːsn/ n Brandstiftung f. ~**ist** /-sənɪst/ n Brandstifter m

art /ɑːt/ n Kunst f; **work of** ~ Kunstwerk nt; ~**s and crafts** pl Kunstgewerbe nt; **A**~**s** pl (Univ) Geisteswissenschaften pl

artery /'ɑːtərɪ/ n Schlagader f, Arterie f

artful /'ɑːtfl/ a gerissen

'art gallery n Kunstgalerie f

arthritis /ɑː'θraɪtɪs/ n Arthritis f

artichoke /'ɑːtɪtʃəʊk/ n Artischocke f

article /'ɑːtɪkl/ n Artikel m; (object) Gegenstand m; ~ **of clothing** Kleidungsstück nt

articulate¹ /ɑː'tɪkjʊlət/ a deutlich; **be** ~ sich gut ausdrücken können

articulate² /ɑː'tɪkjʊleɪt/ vt aussprechen. ~**d lorry** n Sattelzug m

artifice /'ɑːtɪfɪs/ n Arglist f

artificial /ɑːtɪ'fɪʃl/ a, **-ly** adv künstlich

artillery /ɑː'tɪlərɪ/ n Artillerie f

artist /'ɑːtɪst/ n Künstler(in) m(f)

artiste /ɑː'tiːst/ n (Theat) Artist(in) m(f)

artistic /ɑː'tɪstɪk/ a, **-ally** adv künstlerisch

artless /'ɑːtlɪs/ a unschuldig

as /æz/ conj (because) da; (when) als; (while) während ● prep als; **as a child/foreigner** als Kind/Ausländer ● adv as well auch; **as soon as** sobald; **as much as** soviel wie; **as quick as you** so schnell wie du; **as you know** wie Sie wissen; **as far as I'm concerned** was mich betrifft

asbestos /æz'bestəs/ n Asbest m

ascend /ə'send/ vi [auf]steigen ● vt besteigen (throne)

Ascension /ə'senʃn/ n (Relig) [Christi] Himmelfahrt f

ascent /ə'sent/ n Aufstieg m

ascertain /æsə'teɪn/ vt ermitteln

ascribe /ə'skraɪb/ vt zuschreiben (**to** dat)

ash¹ /æʃ/ n (tree) Esche f

ash² n Asche f

ashamed /ə'ʃeɪmd/ a beschämt; **be** ~ sich schämen (**of** über + acc)

ashore /ə'ʃɔː(r)/ adv an Land

ash: ~**tray** n Aschenbecher m. **A**~ **'Wednesday** n Aschermittwoch m

Asia /'eɪʃə/ n Asien nt. ~**n** a asiatisch ● n Asiat(in) m(f). ~**tic** /eɪʃɪ'ætɪk/ a asiatisch

aside /ə'saɪd/ adv beiseite; ~ **from** (Amer) außer (+ dat)

ask /ɑːsk/ vt/i fragen; stellen (question); (invite) einladen; ~ **for** bitten um; verlangen (s.o.); ~ **after** sich erkundigen nach; ~ **s.o. in** jdn hereinbitten; ~ **s.o. to do sth** jdn bitten, etw zu tun

askance /ə'skɑːns/ adv look ~ **at** schief ansehen

askew /ə'skjuː/ a & adv schief

asleep /ə'sliːp/ a be ~ schlafen; **fall** ~ einschlafen

asparagus /ə'spærəgəs/ n Spargel m

aspect /'æspekt/ n Aspekt m

aspersions /ə'spɜːʃnz/ npl cast ~ **on** schlechtmachen

asphalt /'æsfælt/ n Asphalt m

asphyxia /æ'sfɪksɪə/ n Erstickung f. ~**te** /æ'sfɪksɪeɪt/ vt/i ersticken. ~**tion** /-'eɪʃn/ n Erstickung f

aspirations /æspə'reɪʃnz/ npl Streben nt

aspire /ə'spaɪə(r)/ vi ~ **to** streben nach

ass /æs/ n Esel m

assail /ə'seɪl/ vt bestürmen. ~**ant** n Angreifer(in) m(f)

assassin /ə'sæsɪn/ n Mörder(in) m(f).
~**ate** vt ermorden. ~**ation** /-'neɪʃn/
n [politischer] Mord m

assault /ə'sɔːlt/ n (Mil) Angriff m;
(Jur) Körperverletzung f ● vt [tät-
lich] angreifen

assemble /ə'sembl/ vi sich versammeln ● vt versammeln; (Techn)
montieren

assembly /ə'semblɪ/ n Versammlung
f; (Sch) Andacht f; (Techn) Montage
f. ~ **line** n Fließband m

assent /ə'sent/ n Zustimmung f ● vi
zustimmen (**to** dat)

assert /ə'sɜːt/ vt behaupten; ~ **oneself**
sich durchsetzen. ~**ion** /-ʃn/ n Behauptung f. ~**ive** /-tɪv/ a be ~**ive**
sich durchsetzen können

assess /ə'ses/ vt bewerten; (fig & for
tax purposes) einschätzen; schätzen
⟨value⟩. ~**ment** n Einschätzung f;
(of tax) Steuerbescheid m

asset /'æset/ n Vorteil m; ~**s** pl
(money) Vermögen nt; (Comm) Akti-
va pl

assiduous /ə'sɪdjʊəs/ a, -**ly** adv fleißig

assign /ə'saɪn/ vt zuweisen (**to** dat).
~**ment** n (task) Aufgabe f

assimilate /ə'sɪmɪleɪt/ vt aufnehmen;
(integrate) assimilieren

assist /ə'sɪst/ vt/i helfen (+ dat).
~**ance** n Hilfe f. ~**ant** a Hilfs- ●n
Assistent(in) m(f); (in shop)
Verkäufer(in) m(f)

associat|e[1] /ə'səʊʃɪeɪt/ vt verbinden;
(Psych) assoziieren ● vi ~ **with** verkehren mit. ~**ion** /-'eɪʃn/ n Verband
m. **A~ion 'football** n Fußball m

associate[2] /ə'səʊʃɪət/ a assoziiert ● n
Kollege m/-gin f

assort|ed /ə'sɔːtɪd/ a gemischt.
~**ment** n Mischung f

assum|e /ə'sjuːm/ vt annehmen; über-
nehmen ⟨office⟩; ~**ing that** angenommen, daß

assumption /ə'sʌmpʃn/ n Annahme
f; **on the** ~ in der Annahme (**that**
daß)

assurance /ə'ʃʊərəns/ n Versiche-
rung f; (confidence) Selbstsicherheit
f

assure /ə'ʃʊə(r)/ vt versichern (s.o.
jdm); **I** ~ **you** [**of that**] das versi-
chere ich Ihnen. ~**d** a sicher

asterisk /'æstərɪsk/ n Sternchen nt

astern /ə'stɜːn/ adv achtern

asthma /'æsmə/ n Asthma nt. ~**tic**
/-'mætɪk/ a asthmatisch

astonish /ə'stɒnɪʃ/ vt erstaunen.
~**ing** a erstaunlich. ~**ment** n Erstaunen nt

astound /ə'staʊnd/ vt in Erstaunen
setzen

astray /ə'streɪ/ adv **go** ~ verlorengehen; ⟨person:⟩ sich verlaufen; (fig)
vom rechten Weg abkommen; **lead**
~ verleiten

astride /ə'straɪd/ adv rittlings ● prep
rittlings auf (+ dat/acc)

astringent /ə'strɪndʒənt/ a adstrin-
gierend; (fig) beißend

astrolog|er /ə'strɒlədʒə(r)/ n Astro-
loge m/-gin f. ~**y** n Astrologie f

astronaut /'æstrənɔːt/ n Astronaut
(in) m(f)

astronom|er /ə'strɒnəmə(r)/ n Astro-
nom m. ~**ical** /æstrə'nɒmɪkl/ a astro-
nomisch. ~**y** n Astronomie f

astute /ə'stjuːt/ a scharfsinnig.
~**ness** n Scharfsinn m

asylum /ə'saɪləm/ n Asyl nt; [**lunatic**]
~ Irrenanstalt f

at /ət, betont æt/ prep an (+ dat/acc);
(with town) in; (price) zu; (speed)
mit; **at the station** am Bahnhof; **at
the beginning/end** am Anfang/
Ende; **at home** zu Hause; **at John's**
bei John; **at work/the hairdresser's**
bei der Arbeit/beim Friseur; **at
school/the office** in der Schule/im
Büro; **at a party/wedding** auf einer
Party/Hochzeit; **at one o'clock** um
ein Uhr; **at Christmas/Easter** zu
Weihnachten/Ostern; **at the age of**
im Alter von; **not at all** gar nicht; **at
times** manchmal; **two at a time** zwei
auf einmal; **good/bad at languages**
gut/schlecht in Sprachen

ate /et/ see **eat**

atheist /'eɪθɪɪst/ n Atheist(in) m(f)

athlet|e /'æθliːt/ n Athlet(in) m(f).
~**ic** /-'letɪk/ a sportlich. ~**ics**
/-'letɪks/ n Leichtathletik f

Atlantic /ət'læntɪk/ a & n **the** ~
[**Ocean**] der Atlantik

atlas /'ætləs/ n Atlas m

atmospher|e /'ætməsfɪə(r)/ n Atmo-
sphäre f. ~**ic** /-'ferɪk/ a atmo-
sphärisch

atom /'ætəm/ n Atom nt. ~ **bomb** n
Atombombe f

atomic /ə'tɒmɪk/ a Atom-

atone /ə'təʊn/ vi büßen (**for** für).
~**ment** n Buße f

atrocious /ə'trəʊʃəs/ a abscheulich

atrocity /ə'trɒsətɪ/ n Greueltat f

attach /ə'tætʃ/ *vt* befestigen (**to** an + *dat*); beimessen ⟨*importance*⟩ (**to** *dat*); **be** ~**ed to** (*fig*) hängen an (+ *dat*)

attaché /ə'tæʃeɪ/ *n* Attaché *m*. ~ **case** *n* Aktenkoffer *m*

attachment /ə'tætʃmənt/ *n* Bindung *f*; (*tool*) Zubehörteil *nt*; (*additional*) Zusatzgerät *nt*

attack /ə'tæk/ *n* Angriff *m*; (*Med*) Anfall *m* ● *vt/i* angreifen. ~**er** *n* Angreifer *m*

attain /ə'teɪn/ *vt* erreichen; (*get*) erlangen. ~**able** /-əbl/ *a* erreichbar

attempt /ə'tempt/ *n* Versuch *m* ● *vt* versuchen

attend /ə'tend/ *vt* anwesend sein bei; (*go regularly to*) besuchen; (*take part in*) teilnehmen an (+ *dat*); (*accompany*) begleiten; ⟨*doctor:*⟩ behandeln ● *vi* anwesend sein; (*pay attention*) aufpassen; ~ **to** sich kümmern um; (*in shop*) bedienen. ~**ance** *n* Anwesenheit *f*; (*number*) Besucherzahl *f*. ~**ant** *n* Wärter(in) *m(f)*; (*in car park*) Wächter *m*

attention /ə'tenʃn/ *n* Aufmerksamkeit *f*; ~**!** (*Mil*) stillgestanden! **pay** ~ aufpassen; **pay** ~ **to** beachten, achten auf (+ *acc*); **need** ~ reparaturbedürftig sein; **for the** ~ **of** zu Händen von

attentive /ə'tentɪv/ *a*, **-ly** *adv* aufmerksam

attest /ə'test/ *vt/i* ~**[to]** bezeugen

attic /'ætɪk/ *n* Dachboden *m*

attire /ə'taɪə(r)/ *n* Kleidung *f* ● *vt* kleiden

attitude /'ætɪtjuːd/ *n* Haltung *f*

attorney /ə'tɜːnɪ/ *n* (*Amer: lawyer*) Rechtsanwalt *m*; **power of** ~ Vollmacht *f*

attract /ə'trækt/ *vt* anziehen; erregen ⟨*attention*⟩; ~ **s.o.'s attention** jds Aufmerksamkeit auf sich (*acc*) lenken. ~**ion** /-ækʃn/ *n* Anziehungskraft *f*; (*charm*) Reiz *m*; (*thing*) Attraktion *f*. ~**ive** /-tɪv/ *a*, **-ly** *adv* attraktiv

attribute[1] /'ætrɪbjuːt/ *n* Attribut *nt*

attribute[2] /ə'trɪbjuːt/ *vt* zuschreiben (**to** *dat*). ~**ive** /-tɪv/ *a*, **-ly** *adv* attributiv

attrition /ə'trɪʃn/ *n* **war of** ~ Zermürbungskrieg *m*

aubergine /'əʊbəʒiːn/ *n* Aubergine *f*

auburn /'ɔːbən/ *a* kastanienbraun

auction /'ɔːkʃn/ *n* Auktion *f*, Versteigerung *f* ● *vt* versteigern. ~**eer** /-ʃə'nɪə(r)/ *n* Auktionator *m*

audaci|ous /ɔː'deɪʃəs/ *a*, **-ly** *adv* verwegen. ~**ty** /-'dæsətɪ/ *n* Verwegenheit *f*; (*impudence*) Dreistigkeit *f*

audible /'ɔːdəbl/ *a*, **-bly** *adv* hörbar

audience /'ɔːdɪəns/ *n* Publikum *nt*; (*Theat, TV*) Zuschauer *pl*; (*Radio*) Zuhörer *pl*; (*meeting*) Audienz *f*

audio /'ɔːdɪəʊ/: ~ **typist** *n* Phonotypistin *f*. ~'**visual** *a* audiovisuell

audit /'ɔːdɪt/ *n* Bücherrevision *f* ● *vt* (*Comm*) prüfen

audition /ɔː'dɪʃn/ *n* (*Theat*) Vorsprechen *nt*; (*Mus*) Vorspielen *nt*; (*for singer*) Vorsingen *nt* ● *vi* vorsprechen; vorspielen; vorsingen

auditor /'ɔːdɪtə(r)/ *n* Buchprüfer *m*

auditorium /ɔːdɪ'tɔːrɪəm/ *n* Zuschauerraum *m*

augment /ɔːg'ment/ *vt* vergrößern

augur /'ɔːgə(r)/ *vi* ~ **well/ill** etwas/ nichts Gutes verheißen

august /ɔː'gʌst/ *a* hoheitsvoll

August /'ɔːgəst/ *n* August *m*

aunt /ɑːnt/ *n* Tante *f*

au pair /əʊ'peə(r)/ *n* ~ **[girl]** Au-pair-Mädchen *nt*

aura /'ɔːrə/ *n* Fluidum *nt*

auspices /'ɔːspɪsɪz/ *npl* (*protection*) Schirmherrschaft *f*

auspicious /ɔː'spɪʃəs/ *a* günstig; ⟨*occasion*⟩ freudig

auster|e /ɒ'stɪə(r)/ *a* streng; (*simple*) nüchtern. ~**ity** /-terətɪ/ *n* Strenge *f*; (*hardship*) Entbehrung *f*

Australia /ɒ'streɪlɪə/ *n* Australien *nt*. ~**n** *a* australisch ● *n* Australier(in) *m(f)*

Austria /'ɒstrɪə/ *n* Österreich *nt*. ~**n** *a* österreichisch ● *n* Österreicher(in) *m(f)*

authentic /ɔː'θentɪk/ *a* echt, authentisch. ~**ate** *vt* beglaubigen. ~**ity** /-'tɪsətɪ/ *n* Echtheit *f*

author /'ɔːθə(r)/ *n* Schriftsteller *m*, Autor *m*; (*of document*) Verfasser *m*

authoritarian /ɔːθerɪ'teərɪən/ *a* autoritär

authoritative /ɔː'θerɪtətɪv/ *a* maßgebend; **be** ~ Autorität haben

authority /ɔː'θerətɪ/ *n* Autorität *f*; (*public*) Behörde *f*; **in** ~ verantwortlich

authorization /ɔːθəraɪ'zeɪʃn/ *n* Ermächtigung *f*

authorize /'ɔ:θəraɪz/ vt ermächtigen ⟨s.o.⟩; genehmigen ⟨sth⟩

autobi'ography /ɔ:tə-/ n Autobiographie f

autocratic /ɔ:tə'krætɪk/ a autokratisch

autograph /'ɔ:tə-/ n Autogramm nt

automatic /ɔ:tə'mætɪk/ a, **-ally** adv automatisch ● n (car) Fahrzeug nt mit Automatikgetriebe; (washing machine) Waschautomat m

automation /ɔ:tə'meɪʃn/ n Automation f

automobile /'ɔ:təməbi:l/ n Auto nt

autonom|ous /ɔ:'tɒnəməs/ a autonom. **~y** n Autonomie f

autopsy /'ɔ:tɒpsɪ/ n Autopsie f

autumn /'ɔ:təm/ n Herbst m. **~al** /-'tʌmnl/ a herbstlich

auxiliary /ɔ:g'zɪlɪərɪ/ a Hilfs- ● n Helfer(in) m(f), Hilfskraft f

avail /ə'veɪl/ n to no **~** vergeblich ● vi **~ oneself of** Gebrauch machen von

available /ə'veɪləbl/ a verfügbar; (obtainable) erhältlich

avalanche /'ævəla:nʃ/ n Lawine f

avaric|e /'ævərɪs/ n Habsucht f. **~ious** /-'rɪʃəs/ a habgierig, habsüchtig

avenge /ə'vendʒ/ vt rächen

avenue /'ævənju:/ n Allee f

average /'ævərɪdʒ/ a Durchschnitts-, durchschnittlich ● n Durchschnitt m; **on ~** im Durchschnitt, durchschnittlich ● vt durchschnittlich schaffen ● vi **~ out at** im Durchschnitt ergeben

avers|e /ə'vɜ:s/ a **not be ~e to sth** etw (dat) nicht abgeneigt sein. **~ion** /-ɜ:ʃn/ n Abneigung f (**to** gegen)

avert /ə'vɜ:t/ vt abwenden

aviary /'eɪvɪərɪ/ n Vogelhaus nt

aviation /eɪvɪ'eɪʃn/ n Luftfahrt f

avid /'ævɪd/ a gierig (**for** nach); (keen) eifrig

avocado /ævə'ka:dəʊ/ n Avocado f

avoid /ə'vɔɪd/ vt vermeiden; **~ s.o.** jdm aus dem Weg gehen. **~able** /-əbl/ a vermeidbar. **~ance** n Vermeidung f

await /ə'weɪt/ vt warten auf (+ acc)

awake /ə'weɪk/ a wach; **wide ~** hellwach ● vi (pt **awoke**, pp **awoken**) erwachen

awaken /ə'weɪkn/ vt wecken ● vi erwachen. **~ing** n Erwachen nt

award /ə'wɔ:d/ n Auszeichnung f; (prize) Preis m ● vt zuerkennen (**to s.o.** dat); verleihen ⟨prize⟩

aware /ə'weə(r)/ a **become ~** gewahr werden (**of** gen); **be ~ that** wissen, daß. **~ness** n Bewußtsein nt

awash /ə'wɒʃ/ a **be ~** unter Wasser stehen

away /ə'weɪ/ adv weg, fort; (absent) abwesend; **be ~** nicht da sein; **far ~** weit weg; **four kilometres ~** vier Kilometer entfernt; **play ~** (Sport) auswärts spielen; **go/stay ~** weggehen/-bleiben. **~ game** n Auswärtsspiel nt

awe /ɔ:/ n Ehrfurcht f

awful /'ɔ:fl/ a, **-ly** adv furchtbar

awhile /ə'waɪl/ adv eine Weile

awkward /'ɔ:kwəd/ a schwierig; (clumsy) ungeschickt; (embarrassing) peinlich; (inconvenient) ungünstig. **~ly** adv ungeschickt; (embarrassedly) verlegen

awning /'ɔ:nɪŋ/ n Markise f

awoke(n) /ə'wəʊk(ən)/ see **awake**

awry /ə'raɪ/ adv schief

axe /æks/ n Axt f ● vt (pres p **axing**) streichen; (dismiss) entlassen

axis /'æksɪs/ n (pl **axes** /-si:z/) Achse f

axle /'æksl/ n (Techn) Achse f

ay[e] /aɪ/ adv ja ● n Jastimme f

B

B /bi:/ n (Mus) H nt

BA abbr of **Bachelor of Arts**

babble /'bæbl/ vi plappern; ⟨stream:⟩ plätschern

baboon /bə'bu:n/ n Pavian m

baby /'beɪbɪ/ n Baby nt; (Amer, fam) Schätzchen nt

baby: **~ carriage** n (Amer) Kinderwagen m. **~ish** a kindisch. **~minder** n Tagesmutter f. **~sit** vi babysitten. **~-sitter** n Babysitter m

bachelor /'bætʃələ(r)/ n Junggeselle m; **B~ of Arts/Science** Bakkalaureus Artium/Scientium

bacillus /bə'sɪləs/ n (pl **-lli**) Bazillus m

back /bæk/ n Rücken m; (reverse) Rückseite f; (of chair) Rückenlehne f; (Sport) Verteidiger m; **at**/(Auto) **in the ~** hinten; **on the ~** auf der Rückseite; **~ to front** verkehrt; **at the ~ of beyond** am Ende der Welt ● a Hinter- ● adv zurück; **~ here/there** hier/da hinten; **~ at home** zu Hause; **go/pay ~** zurückgehen/-zahlen ● vt (support) unterstützen; (with money) finanzieren; (Auto) zurücksetzen; (*Betting*) [Geld] setzen auf (+ *acc*); (*cover the back of*) mit einer Verstärkung versehen ● *vi* (*Auto*) zurücksetzen. ~ **down** *vi* klein beigeben. ~ **in** *vi* rückwärts hineinfahren. ~ **out** *vi* rückwärts hinaus-/herausfahren; (*fig*) aussteigen (**of** aus). ~ **up** *vt* unterstützen; (*confirm*) bestätigen ● *vi* (*Auto*) zurücksetzen

back: ~**ache** *n* Rückenschmerzen *pl*. ~**biting** *n* gehässiges Gerede *nt*. ~**bone** *n* Rückgrat *nt*. ~**chat** *n* Widerrede *f*. ~**comb** *vt* toupieren. ~**date** *vt* rückdatieren; ~**dated** to rückwirkend von. ~ **'door** *n* Hintertür *f*

backer /'bækə(r)/ *n* Geldgeber *m*

back: ~**'fire** *vi* (*Auto*) fehlzünden; (*fig*) fehlschlagen. ~**ground** *n* Hintergrund *m*; **family** ~**ground** Familienverhältnisse *pl*. ~**hand** *n* (*Sport*) Rückhand *f*. ~**'handed** *a* (*compliment*) zweifelhaft. ~**'hander** *n* (*Sport*) Rückhandschlag *m*; (*fam: bribe*) Schmiergeld *nt*

backing /'bækɪŋ/ *n* (*support*) Unterstützung *f*; (*material*) Verstärkung *f*

back: ~**lash** *n* (*fig*) Gegenschlag *m*. ~**log** *n* Rückstand *m* (**of** an + *dat*). ~ **'seat** *n* Rücksitz *m*. ~**side** *n* (*fam*) Hintern *m*. ~**stage** *adv* hinter der Bühne. ~**stroke** *n* Rückenschwimmen *nt*. ~**up** *n* · Unterstützung *f*; (*Amer: traffic jam*) Stau *m*

backward /'bækwəd/ *a* zurückgeblieben; (*country*) rückständig ● *adv* rückwärts. ~**s** *adv* rückwärts; ~**s and forwards** hin und her

back: ~**water** *n* (*fig*) unberührtes Fleckchen *nt*. ~ **'yard** *n* Hinterhof *m*; **not in my** ~ **yard** (*fam*) nicht vor meiner Haustür

bacon /'beɪkn/ *n* [Schinken]speck *m*

bacteria /bæk'tɪərɪə/ *npl* Bakterien *pl*

bad /bæd/ *a* (**worse, worst**) schlecht; (*serious*) schwer, schlimm; (*naughty*) unartig; ~ **language** gemeine Ausdrucksweise *f*; **feel** ~ sich schlecht fühlen; (*feel guilty*) ein schlechtes Gewissen haben; **go** ~ schlecht werden

bade /bæd/ *see* **bid²**

badge /bædʒ/ *n* Abzeichen *nt*

badger /'bædʒə(r)/ *n* Dachs *m* ● *vt* plagen

badly /'bædlɪ/ *adv* schlecht; (*seriously*) schwer; ~ **off** schlecht gestellt; ~ **behaved** unerzogen; **want** ~

sich (*dat*) sehnsüchtig wünschen; **need** ~ dringend brauchen

bad-'mannered *a* mit schlechten Manieren

badminton /'bædmɪntən/ *n* Federball *m*

bad-'tempered *a* schlecht gelaunt

baffle /'bæfl/ *vt* verblüffen

bag /bæg/ *n* Tasche *f*; (*of paper*) Tüte *f*; (*pouch*) Beutel *m*; ~**s of** (*fam*) jede Menge ● *vt* (*fam: reserve*) in Beschlag nehmen

baggage /'bægɪdʒ/ *n* [Reise]gepäck *nt*

baggy /'bægɪ/ *a* (*clothes*) ausgebeult

'bagpipes *npl* Dudelsack *m*

bail /beɪl/ *n* Kaution *f*; **on** ~ gegen Kaution ● *vt* ~ **s.o. out** jdn gegen Kaution freibekommen; (*fig*) jdm aus der Patsche helfen. ~ **out** *vt* (*Naut*) ausschöpfen ● *vi* (*Aviat*) abspringen

bailiff /'beɪlɪf/ *n* Gerichtsvollzieher *m*; (*of estate*) Gutsverwalter *m*

bait /beɪt/ *n* Köder *m* ● *vt* mit einem Köder versehen; (*fig: torment*) reizen

bake /beɪk/ *vt/i* backen

baker /'beɪkə(r)/ *n* Bäcker *m*; ~**'s** **[shop]** Bäckerei *f*. ~**y** *n* Bäckerei *f*

baking /'beɪkɪŋ/ *n* Backen *nt*. ~**powder** *n* Backpulver *nt*. ~**tin** *n* Backform *f*

balance /'bæləns/ *n* (*equilibrium*) Gleichgewicht *nt*, Balance *f*; (*scales*) Waage *f*; (*Comm*) Saldo *m*; (*outstanding sum*) Restbetrag *m*; **[bank]** ~ Kontostand *m*; **in the** ~ (*fig*) in der Schwebe ● *vt* balancieren; (*equalize*) ausgleichen; (*Comm*) abschließen (*books*) ● *vi* balancieren; (*fig & Comm*) sich ausgleichen. ~**d** *a* ausgewogen. ~ **sheet** *n* Bilanz *f*

balcony /'bælkənɪ/ *n* Balkon *m*

bald /bɔːld/ *a* (**-er, -est**) kahl; (*person*) kahlköpfig; **go** ~ eine Glatze bekommen

balderdash /'bɔːldədæʃ/ *n* Unsinn *m*

bald|ing /'bɔːldɪŋ/ *a* **be** ~**ing** eine Glatze bekommen. ~**ly** *adv* unverblümt. ~**ness** *n* Kahlköpfigkeit *f*

bale /beɪl/ *n* Ballen *m*

baleful /'beɪlfl/ *a*, **-ly** *adv* böse

balk /bɔːk/ *vt* vereiteln ● *vi* ~ **at** zurückschrecken vor (+ *dat*)

Balkans /'bɔːlkənz/ *npl* Balkan *m*

ball¹ /bɔːl/ *n* Ball *m*; (*Billiards, Croquet*) Kugel *f*; (*of yarn*) Knäuel *m* & *nt*; **on the** ~ (*fam*) auf Draht

ball² n (dance) Ball m
ballad /'bæləd/ n Ballade f
ballast /'bæləst/ n Ballast m
ball-'bearing n Kugellager nt
ballerina /bælə'ri:nə/ n Ballerina f
ballet /'bæleɪ/ m Ballett nt. ~ **dancer** n Ballettänzer(in) m(f)
ballistic /bə'lɪstɪk/ a ballistisch. ~**s** n Ballistik f
balloon /bə'lu:n/ n Luftballon m; (Aviat) Ballon m
ballot /'bælət/ n [geheime] Wahl f; (on issue) [geheime] Abstimmung f. ~-**box** n Wahlurne f. ~-**paper** n Stimmzettel m
ball: ~-**point** ['pen] n Kugelschreiber m. ~**room** n Ballsaal m
balm /bɑ:m/ n Balsam m
balmy /'bɑ:mɪ/ a (-ier, -iest) a sanft; (fam: crazy) verrückt
Baltic /'bɔ:ltɪk/ a & n the ~ [Sea] die Ostsee
balustrade /bælə'streɪd/ n Balustrade f
bamboo /bæm'bu:/ n Bambus m
bamboozle /bæm'bu:zl/ vt (fam) übers Ohr hauen
ban /bæn/ n Verbot nt ● vt (pt/pp banned) verbieten
banal /bə'nɑ:l/ a banal. ~**ity** /-'ælətɪ/ n Banalität f
banana /bə'nɑ:nə/ n Banane f
band /bænd/ n Band nt; (stripe) Streifen m; (group) Schar f; (Mus) Kapelle f ● vi ~ **together** sich zusammenschließen
bandage /'bændɪdʒ/ n Verband m; (for support) Bandage f ● vt verbinden; bandagieren ⟨limb⟩
b. & b. abbr of bed and breakfast
bandit /'bændɪt/ n Bandit m
band: ~**stand** n Musikpavillon m. ~**wagon** n jump on the ~**wagon** (fig) sich einer erfolgreichen Sache anschließen
bandy¹ /'bændɪ/ vt (pt/pp -ied) wechseln ⟨words⟩
bandy² a (-ier, -iest) be ~ O-Beine haben. ~-**legged** a O-beinig
bang /bæŋ/ n Knall m; (blow) Schlag m ● adv go ~ knallen ● int bums! peng! ● vt knallen; (shut noisily) zuknallen; (strike) schlagen auf (+ acc); ~ **one's head** sich (dat) den Kopf stoßen (**on** an + acc) ● vi schlagen; ⟨door:⟩ zuknallen
banger /'bæŋə(r)/ n (firework) Knallfrosch m; (fam: sausage) Wurst f; **old** ~ (fam: car) Klapperkiste f

bangle /'bæŋgl/ n Armreifen m
banish /'bænɪʃ/ vt verbannen
banisters /'bænɪstəz/ npl [Treppen]geländer nt
banjo /'bændʒəʊ/ n Banjo nt
bank¹ /bæŋk/ n (of river) Ufer nt; (slope) Hang m ● vi (Aviat) in die Kurve gehen
bank² n Bank f ● vt einzahlen; ~ **with** ein Konto haben bei. ~ **on** vt sich verlassen auf (+ acc)
'**bank account** n Bankkonto nt
banker /'bæŋkə(r)/ n Bankier m
bank: ~ '**holiday** n gesetzlicher Feiertag m. ~**ing** n Bankwesen nt. ~**note** n Banknote f
bankrupt /'bæŋkrʌpt/ a bankrott; **go** ~ bankrott machen ● n Bankrotteur m ● vt bankrott machen. ~**cy** n Bankrott m
banner /'bænə(r)/ n Banner nt; (carried by demonstrators) Transparent nt, Spruchband nt
banns /bænz/ npl (Relig) Aufgebot nt
banquet /'bæŋkwɪt/ n Bankett nt
banter /'bæntə(r)/ n Spötterei f
bap /bæp/ n weiches Brötchen nt
baptism /'bæptɪzm/ n Taufe f
Baptist /'bæptɪst/ n Baptist(in) m(f)
baptize /bæp'taɪz/ vt taufen
bar /bɑ:(r)/ n Stange f; (of cage) [Gitter]stab m; (of gold) Barren m; (of chocolate) Tafel f; (of soap) Stück nt; (long) Riegel m; (café) Bar f; (counter) Theke f; (Mus) Takt m; (fig: obstacle) Hindernis nt; **parallel** ~**s** (Sport) Barren m; **be called to the** ~ (Jur) als plädierender Anwalt zugelassen werden; **behind** ~**s** (fam) hinter Gittern ● vt (pt/pp barred) versperren ⟨way, door⟩; ausschließen ⟨person⟩ ● prep außer; **none** ohne Ausnahme
barbarian /bɑ:'beərɪən/ n Barbar m
barbar|ic /bɑ:'bærɪk/ a barbarisch. ~**ity** n Barbarei f. ~**ous** /'bɑ:bərəs/ a barbarisch
barbecue /'bɑ:bɪkju:/ n Grill m; (party) Grillfest nt ● vt [im Freien] grillen
barbed /'bɑ:bd/ a ~ **wire** Stacheldraht m
barber /'bɑ:bə(r)/ n [Herren]friseur m
barbiturate /bɑ:'bɪtjʊrət/ n Barbiturat nt
'**bar code** n Strichkode m
bare /beə(r)/ a (-r, -st) nackt, bloß; ⟨tree⟩ kahl; (empty) leer; (mere) bloß ● vt entblößen; fletschen ⟨teeth⟩

bare: ~**back** adv ohne Sattel. ~**faced** a schamlos. ~**foot** adv barfuß. ~'**headed** a mit unbedecktem Kopf

barely /'beəlɪ/ adv kaum

bargain /'bɑːgɪn/ n (agreement) Geschäft nt; (good buy) Gelegenheitskauf m; **into the** ~ noch dazu; **make a** ~ sich einigen ● vi handeln; (haggle) feilschen; ~ **for** (expect) rechnen mit

barge /bɑːdʒ/ n Lastkahn m; (towed) Schleppkahn m ● vi ~ **in** (fam) hereinplatzen

baritone /'bærɪtəʊn/ n Bariton m

bark[1] /bɑːk/ n (of tree) Rinde f

bark[2] n Bellen nt ● vi bellen

barley /'bɑːlɪ/ n Gerste f

bar: ~**maid** n Schankmädchen nt. ~**man** Barmann m

barmy /'bɑːmɪ/ a (fam) verrückt

barn /bɑːn/ n Scheune f

barometer /bə'rɒmɪtə(r)/ n Barometer nt

baron /'bærn/ n Baron m. ~**ess** n Baronin f

baroque /bə'rɒk/ a barock ● n Barock nt

barracks /'bærəks/ npl Kaserne f

barrage /'bærɑːʒ/ n (in river) Wehr nt; (Mil) Sperrfeuer nt; (fig) Hagel m

barrel /'bærl/ n Faß nt; (of gun) Lauf m; (of cannon) Rohr nt. ~-**organ** n Drehorgel f

barren /'bærn/ a unfruchtbar; ⟨landscape⟩ öde

barricade /bærɪ'keɪd/ n Barrikade f ● vt verbarrikadieren

barrier /'bærɪə(r)/ n Barriere f; (across road) Schranke f; (Rail) Sperre f; (fig) Hindernis nt

barring /'bɑːrɪŋ/ prep ~ **accidents** wenn alles gutgeht

barrister /'bærɪstə(r)/ n [plädierender] Rechtsanwalt m

barrow /'bærəʊ/ n Karre f, Karren m. ~ **boy** n Straßenhändler m

barter /'bɑːtə(r)/ vt tauschen (for gegen)

base /beɪs/ n Fuß m; (fig) Basis f; (Mil) Stützpunkt m ● a gemein; ⟨metal⟩ unedel ● vt stützen (on auf + acc); **be** ~**d on** basieren auf (+ dat)

base: ~**ball** n Baseball m. ~**less** a unbegründet. ~**ment** n Kellergeschoß nt. ~**ment flat** n Kellerwohnung f

bash /bæʃ/ n Schlag m; **have a** ~! (fam) probier es mal! ● vt hauen; (dent) einbeulen; ~**ed in** verbeult

bashful /'bæʃfl/ a, -**ly** adv schüchtern

basic /'beɪsɪk/ a Grund-; (fundamental) grundlegend; (essential) wesentlich; (unadorned) einfach; **the** ~**s** das Wesentliche. ~**ally** adv grundsätzlich

basil /'bæzɪl/ n Basilikum nt

basilica /bə'zɪlɪkə/ n Basilika f

basin /'beɪsn/ n Becken nt; (for washing) Waschbecken nt; (for food) Schüssel f

basis /'beɪsɪs/ n (pl -**ses** /-siːz/) Basis f

bask /bɑːsk/ vi sich sonnen

basket /'bɑːskɪt/ n Korb m. ~**ball** n Basketball m

Basle /bɑːl/ n Basel nt

bass /beɪs/ a Baß-; ~ **voice** Baßstimme f ● n Baß m; (person) Bassist m

bassoon /bə'suːn/ n Fagott nt

bastard /'bɑːstəd/ n (sl) Schuft m

baste[1] /beɪst/ vt (sew) heften

baste[2] vt (Culin) begießen

bastion /'bæstɪən/ n Bastion f

bat[1] /bæt/ n Schläger m; **off one's own** ~ (fam) auf eigene Faust ● vt (pt/pp **batted**) schlagen; **not** ~ **an eyelid** (fig) nicht mit der Wimper zucken

bat[2] n (Zool) Fledermaus f

batch /bætʃ/ n (of people) Gruppe f; (of papers) Stoß m; (of goods) Sendung f; (of bread) Schub m

bated /'beɪtɪd/ a **with** ~ **breath** mit angehaltenem Atem

bath /bɑːθ/ n (pl ~**s** /bɑːðz/) Bad nt; (tub) Badewanne f; ~**s** pl Badeanstalt f; **have a** ~ baden ● vt/i baden

bathe /beɪð/ n Bad nt ● vt/i baden. ~**r** n Badende(r) m/f

bathing /'beɪðɪŋ/ n Baden nt. ~-**cap** n Bademütze f. ~-**costume** n Badeanzug m

bath: ~-**mat** n Bademattef. ~**robe** n (Amer) Bademantel m. ~-**room** n Badezimmer nt. ~-**towel** n Badetuch nt

baton /'bætn/ n (Mus) Taktstock m; (Mil) Stab m

battalion /bə'tælɪən/ n Bataillon nt

batten /'bætn/ n Latte f

batter /'bætə(r)/ n (Culin) flüssiger Teig m ● vt schlagen. ~**ed** a ⟨car⟩ verbeult; ⟨wife⟩ mißhandelt

battery /'bætərɪ/ n Batterie f

battle /'bætl/ n Schlacht f; (fig) Kampf m ● vi (fig) kämpfen (for um)

battle: ~**axe** n (fam) Drachen m. ~**field** n Schlachtfeld nt. ~**ship** n Schlachtschiff nt

batty /'bætɪ/ a (fam) verrückt

Bavaria /bə'veərɪə/ n Bayern nt. ~**n** a bayrisch ● n Bayer(in) m(f)

bawdy /'bɔːdɪ/ a (-ier, -iest) derb

bawl /bɔːl/ vt/i brüllen

bay¹ /beɪ/ n (Geog) Bucht f; (Archit) Erker m

bay² n keep at ~ fernhalten

bay³ n (horse) Braune(r) m

bay⁴ n (Bot) [echter] Lorbeer m. ~**leaf** n Lorbeerblatt nt

bayonet /'beɪənet/ n Bajonett nt

bay 'window n Erkerfenster nt

bazaar /bə'zɑː(r)/ n Basar m

BC abbr (before Christ) v. Chr.

be /biː/ vi (pres am, are, is, pl are; pt was, pl were; pp been) sein; (lie) liegen; (stand) stehen; (cost) kosten; **he is a teacher** er ist Lehrer; **be quiet!** sei still! **I am cold/hot** mir ist kalt/heiß; **how are you?** wie geht es Ihnen? **I am well** mir geht es gut; **there is/are** es gibt; **what do you want to be?** was willst du werden? **I have been to Vienna** ich bin in Wien gewesen; **has the postman been?** war der Briefträger schon da? **it's hot, isn't it?** es ist heiß, nicht [wahr]? **you are coming too, aren't you?** du kommst mit, nicht [wahr]? **it's yours, is it?** das gehört also Ihnen? **yes he is/I am** ja; (negating previous statement) doch; **three and three are six** drei und drei macht sechs ● v aux ~ **reading/going** lesen/gehen; **I am coming/staying** ich komme/ bleibe; **what is he doing?** was macht er? **I am being lazy** ich faulenze; **I was thinking of you** ich dachte an dich; **you were going to . . .** du wolltest . . .; **I am to stay** ich soll bleiben; **you are not to . . .** du darfst nicht . . .; **you are to do that immediately** das mußt du sofort machen ● passive werden; **be attacked/deceived** überfallen/betrogen werden

beach /biːtʃ/ n Strand m. ~**wear** n Strandkleidung f

beacon /'biːkn/ n Leuchtfeuer nt; (Naut, Aviat) Bake f

bead /biːd/ n Perle f

beak /biːk/ n Schnabel m

beaker /'biːkə(r)/ n Becher m

beam /biːm/ n Balken m; (of light) Strahl m ● vi strahlen. ~**ing** a [freude]strahlend

bean /biːn/ n Bohne f; **spill the** ~**s** (fam) alles ausplaudern

bear¹ /beə(r)/ n Bär m

bear² vt/i (pt bore, pp borne) tragen; (endure) ertragen; gebären ⟨child⟩; ~ **right** sich rechts halten. ~**able** /-əbl/ a erträglich

beard /bɪəd/ n Bart m. ~**ed** a bärtig

bearer /'beərə(r)/ n Träger m; (of news, cheque) Überbringer m; (of passport) Inhaber(in) m(f)

bearing /'beərɪŋ/ n Haltung f; (Techn) Lager nt; **have a** ~ **on** von Belang sein für; **get one's** ~**s** sich orientieren; **lose one's** ~**s** die Orientierung verlieren

beast /biːst/ n Tier nt; (fam: person) Biest nt

beastly /'biːstlɪ/ a (-ier, -iest) (fam) scheußlich; ⟨person⟩ gemein

beat /biːt/ n Schlag m; (of policeman) Runde f; (rhythm) Takt m ● vt/i (pt beat, pp beaten) schlagen; (thrash) verprügeln; klopfen ⟨carpet⟩; (hammer) hämmern (on an + acc); ~ **a retreat** (Mil) sich zurückziehen; ~ **it!** (fam) hau ab! **it** ~**s me** (fam) das begreife ich nicht. ~ **up** vt zusammenschlagen

beat|en /'biːtn/ a off the ~**en track** abseits. ~**ing** n Prügel pl

beautician /bjuː'tɪʃn/ n Kosmetikerin f

beauti|ful /'bjuːtɪfl/ a, **-ly** adv schön. ~**fy** /-faɪ/ vt (pt/pp -ied) verschönern

beauty /'bjuːtɪ/ n Schönheit f. ~ **parlour** n Kosmetiksalon m. ~ **spot** n Schönheitsfleck m; (place) landschaftlich besonders reizvolle Stelle f

beaver /'biːvə(r)/ n Biber m

became /bɪ'keɪm/ see **become**

because /bɪ'kɒz/ conj weil ● adv ~ **of** wegen (+ gen)

beckon /'bekn/ vt/i ~ **[to]** herbeiwinken

becom|e /bɪ'kʌm/ vt/i (pt **became**, pp **become**) werden. ~**ing** a ⟨clothes⟩ kleidsam

bed /bed/ n Bett nt; (layer) Schicht f; (of flowers) Beet nt; **in** ~ im Bett; **go to** ~ ins od zu Bett gehen; ~ **and breakfast** Zimmer mit Frühstück. ~**clothes** npl, ~**ding** n Bettzeug nt

bedlam /'bedləm/ n Chaos nt

'bedpan n Bettpfanne f

bedraggled /bɪ'drægld/ *a* naß und verschmutzt

bed: ~**ridden** *a* bettlägerig. ~**room** *n* Schlafzimmer *nt*

'bedside *n* at his ~ an seinem Bett. ~ **'lamp** *n* Nachttischlampe *f*. ~ **'rug** *n* Bettvorleger *m*. ~ **'table** *n* Nachttisch *m*

bed: ~**'sitter** *n*, ~**'sitting-room** *n* Wohnschlafzimmer *nt*. ~**spread** *n* Tagesdecke *f*. ~**time** *n* at ~**time** vor dem Schlafengehen

bee /biː/ *n* Biene *f*

beech /biːtʃ/ *n* Buche *f*

beef /biːf/ *n* Rindfleisch *nt*. ~**burger** *n* Hamburger *m*

bee: ~**hive** *n* Bienenstock *m*. ~**keeper** *n* Imker(in) *m(f)*. ~**keeping** *n* Bienenzucht *f*. ~**line** *n* make a ~**line for** (*fam*) zusteuern auf (+ *acc*)

been /biːn/ *see* **be**

beer /bɪə(r)/ *n* Bier *nt*

beet /biːt/ *n* (*Amer: beetroot*) rote Bete *f*; **[sugar]** ~ Zuckerrübe *f*

beetle /'biːtl/ *n* Käfer *m*

'beetroot *n* rote Bete *f*

before /bɪ'fɔː(r)/ *prep* vor (+ *dat/acc*); **the day** ~ **yesterday** vorgestern; ~ **long** bald ● *adv* vorher; (*already*) schon; **never** ~ noch nie; ~ **that** davor ● *conj* (*time*) ehe, bevor. ~**hand** *adv* vorher, im voraus

befriend /bɪ'frend/ *vt* sich anfreunden mit

beg /beg/ *v* (*pt/pp* **begged**) ● *vi* betteln ● *vt* (*entreat*) anflehen; (*ask*) bitten (**for** um)

began /bɪ'gæn/ *see* **begin**

beggar /'begə(r)/ *n* Bettler(in) *m(f)*; (*fam*) Kerl *m*

begin /bɪ'gɪn/ *vt/i* (*pt* **began**, *pp* **begun**, *pres p* **beginning**) anfangen, beginnen; **to** ~ **with** anfangs. ~**ner** *n* Anfänger(in) *m(f)*. ~**ning** *n* Anfang *m*, Beginn *m*

begonia /bɪ'gəʊnɪə/ *n* Begonie *f*

begrudge /bɪ'grʌdʒ/ *vt* mißgönnen

beguile /bɪ'gaɪl/ *vt* betören

begun /bɪ'gʌn/ *see* **begin**

behalf /bɪ'hɑːf/ *n* **on** ~ **of** im Namen von; **on my** ~ meinetwegen

behave /bɪ'heɪv/ *vi* sich verhalten; ~ **oneself** sich benehmen

behaviour /bɪ'heɪvjə(r)/ *n* Verhalten *nt*; **good/bad** ~ gutes/schlechtes Benehmen *nt*; ~ **pattern** Verhaltensweise *f*

behead /bɪ'hed/ *vt* enthaupten

beheld /bɪ'held/ *see* **behold**

behind /bɪ'haɪnd/ *prep* hinter (+ *dat/acc*); **be** ~ **sth** hinter etw (*dat*) stecken ● *adv* hinten; (*late*) im Rückstand; **a long way** ~ weit zurück; **in the car** ~ im Wagen dahinter ● *n* (*fam*) Hintern *m*. ~**hand** *adv* im Rückstand

behold /bɪ'həʊld/ *vt* (*pt/pp* **beheld**) (*liter*) sehen

beholden /bɪ'həʊldn/ *a* verbunden (**to** *dat*)

beige /beɪʒ/ *a* beige

being /'biːɪŋ/ *n* Dasein *nt*; **living** ~ Lebewesen *nt*; **come into** ~ entstehen

belated /bɪ'leɪtɪd/ *a*, **-ly** *adv* verspätet

belch /beltʃ/ *vi* rülpsen ● *vt* ~ **out** ausstoßen ⟨*smoke*⟩

belfry /'belfrɪ/ *n* Glockenstube *f*; (*tower*) Glockenturm *m*

Belgian /'beldʒən/ *a* belgisch ● *n* Belgier(in) *m(f)*

Belgium /'beldʒəm/ *n* Belgien *nt*

belief /bɪ'liːf/ *n* Glaube *m*

believable /bɪ'liːvəbl/ *a* glaubhaft

believe /bɪ'liːv/ *vt/i* glauben (**s.o.** jdm; **in** an + *acc*). ~**r** *n* (*Relig*) Gläubige(r) *m/f*

belittle /bɪ'lɪtl/ *vt* herabsetzen

bell /bel/ *n* Glocke *f*; (*on door*) Klingel *f*

belligerent /bɪ'lɪdʒərənt/ *a* kriegführend; (*aggressive*) streitlustig

bellow /'beləʊ/ *vt/i* brüllen

bellows /'beləʊz/ *npl* Blasebalg *m*

belly /'belɪ/ *n* Bauch *m*

belong /bɪ'lɒŋ/ *vi* gehören (**to** *dat*); (*be member*) angehören (**to** *dat*). ~**ings** *npl* Sachen *pl*

beloved /bɪ'lʌvɪd/ *a* geliebt ● *n* Geliebte(r) *m/f*

below /bɪ'ləʊ/ *prep* unter (+ *dat/acc*) ● *adv* unten; (*Naut*) unter Deck

belt /belt/ *n* Gürtel *m*; (*area*) Zone *f*; (*Techn*) [Treib]riemen *m* ● *vi* (*fam: rush*) rasen ● *vt* (*fam: hit*) hauen

bemused /bɪ'mjuːzd/ *a* verwirrt

bench /bentʃ/ *n* Bank *f*; (*work-*) Werkbank *f*; **the B**~ (*Jur*) ≈ die Richter *pl*

bend /bend/ *n* Biegung *f*; (*in road*) Kurve *f*; **round the** ~ (*fam*) verrückt ● *v* (*pt/pp* **bent**) ● *vt* biegen; beugen ⟨*arm, leg*⟩ ● *vi* sich bücken; ⟨*thing*⟩ sich biegen; ⟨*road:*⟩ eine Biegung machen. ~ **down** *vi* sich bücken. ~ **over** *vi* sich vornüberbeugen

beneath /bɪ'ni:θ/ *prep* unter (+ *dat/acc*); ~ **him** (*fig*) unter seiner Würde; ~ **contempt** unter aller Würde ● *adv* darunter

benediction /benɪ'dɪkʃn/ *n* (*Relig*) Segen *m*

benefactor /'benɪfæktə(r)/ *n* Wohltäter(in) *m(f)*

beneficial /benɪ'fɪʃl/ *a* nützlich

beneficiary /benɪ'fɪʃərɪ/ *n* Begünstigte(r) *m/f*

benefit /'benɪfɪt/ *n* Vorteil *m*; (*allowance*) Unterstützung *f*; (*insurance*) Leistung *f*; **sickness** ~ Krankengeld *nt* ● *v* (*pt/pp* -**fited**, *pres p* -**fiting**) ● *vt* nützen (+ *dat*) ● *vi* profitieren (**from** von)

benevolen|ce /bɪ'nevələns/ *n* Wohlwollen *nt*. ~**t** *a*, -**ly** *adv* wohlwollend

benign /bɪ'naɪn/ *a*, -**ly** *adv* gütig; (*Med*) gutartig

bent /bent/ *see* **bend** ● *a* ⟨person⟩ gebeugt; (*distorted*) verbogen; (*fam: dishonest*) korrupt; **be** ~ **on doing sth** darauf erpicht sein, etw zu tun ● *n* Hang *m*, Neigung *f* (**for** zu); **artistic** ~ künstlerische Ader *f*

be|queath /bɪ'kwi:ð/ *vt* vermachen (**to** *dat*). ~**quest** /-'kwest/ *n* Vermächtnis *nt*

bereave|d /bɪ'ri:vd/ *n* **the** ~**d** *pl* die Hinterbliebenen. ~**ment** *n* Trauerfall *m*; (*state*) Trauer *f*

bereft /bɪ'reft/ *a* ~ **of** beraubt (+ *gen*)

beret /'bereɪ/ *n* Baskenmütze *f*

Berne /bɜ:n/ *n* Bern *nt*

berry /'berɪ/ *n* Beere *f*

berserk /bə'sɜ:k/ *a* **go** ~ wild werden

berth /bɜ:θ/ *n* (*on ship*) [Schlaf]koje *f*; (*ship's anchorage*) Liegeplatz *m*; **give a wide** ~ **to** (*fam*) einen großen Bogen machen um ● *vi* anlegen

beseech /bɪ'si:tʃ/ *vt* (*pt/pp* **beseeched** *or* **besought**) anflehen

beside /bɪ'saɪd/ *prep* neben (+ *dat/acc*); ~ **oneself** außer sich (*dat*)

besides /bɪ'saɪdz/ *prep* außer (+ *dat*) ● *adv* außerdem

besiege /bɪ'si:dʒ/ *vt* belagern

besought /bɪ'sɔ:t/ *see* **beseech**

bespoke /bɪ'spəʊk/ *a* ⟨suit⟩ maßgeschneidert

best /best/ *a & n* beste(r,s); **the** ~ der/die/das Beste; **at** ~ bestenfalls; **all the** ~! alles Gute! **do one's** ~ sein Bestes tun; **the** ~ **part of a year** fast ein Jahr; **to the** ~ **of my knowledge** soviel ich weiß; **make the** ~ **of it** das

Beste daraus machen ● *adv* am besten; **as** ~ **I could** so gut ich konnte. ~ '**man** *n* ≈ Trauzeuge *m*

bestow /bɪ'stəʊ/ *vt* schenken (**on** *dat*)

best'seller *n* Bestseller *m*

bet /bet/ *n* Wette *f* ● *v* (*pt/pp* **bet** *or* **betted**) ● *vt* ~ **s.o. £5** mit jdm um £5 wetten ● *vi* wetten; ~ **on** [Geld] setzen auf (+ *acc*)

betray /bɪ'treɪ/ *vt* verraten. ~**al** *n* Verrat *m*

better /'betə(r)/ *a* besser; **get** ~ sich bessern; (*after illness*) sich erholen ● *adv* besser; ~ **off** besser dran; ~ **not** lieber nicht; **all the** ~ um so besser; **the sooner the** ~ je eher, desto besser; **think** ~ **of sth** sich eines Besseren besinnen; **you'd** ~ **stay** du bleibst am besten hier ● *vt* verbessern; (*do better than*) übertreffen; ~ **oneself** sich verbessern

'**betting shop** *n* Wettbüro *nt*

between /bɪ'twi:n/ *prep* zwischen (+ *dat/acc*); ~ **you and me** unter uns; ~ **us** (*together*) zusammen ● *adv* [**in**] ~ dazwischen

beverage /'bevərɪdʒ/ *n* Getränk *nt*

bevy /'bevɪ/ *n* Schar *f*

beware /bɪ'weə(r)/ *vi* sich in acht nehmen (**of** vor + *dat*); ~ **of the dog!** Vorsicht, bissiger Hund!

bewilder /bɪ'wɪldə(r)/ *vt* verwirren. ~**ment** *n* Verwirrung *f*

bewitch /bɪ'wɪtʃ/ *vt* verzaubern; (*fig*) bezaubern

beyond /bɪ'jɒnd/ *prep* über (+ *acc*) ... hinaus; (*further*) weiter als; ~ **reach** außer Reichweite; ~ **doubt** ohne jeden Zweifel; **it's** ~ **me** (*fam*) das geht über meinen Horizont ● *adv* darüber hinaus

bias /'baɪəs/ *n* Voreingenommenheit *f*; (*preference*) Vorliebe *f*; (*Jur*) Befangenheit *f*; **cut on the** ~ schräg geschnitten ● *vt* (*pt/pp* **biased**) (*influence*) beeinflussen. ~**ed** *a* voreingenommen; (*Jur*) befangen

bib /bɪb/ *n* Lätzchen *nt*

Bible /'baɪbl/ *n* Bibel *f*

biblical /'bɪblɪkl/ *a* biblisch

bibliography /bɪblɪ'ɒgrəfɪ/ *n* Bibliographie *f*

bicarbonate /baɪ'kɑ:bəneɪt/ *n* ~ **of soda** doppeltkohlensaures Natron *nt*

bicker /'bɪkə(r)/ *vi* sich zanken

bicycle /'baɪsɪkl/ *n* Fahrrad *nt* ● *vi* mit dem Rad fahren

bid¹ /bɪd/ n Gebot nt; (attempt) Versuch m ● vt/i (pt/pp bid, pres p bidding) bieten (for auf + acc); (Cards) reizen

bid² vt (pt bade or bid, pp bidden or bid, pres p bidding) (liter) heißen; ~ s.o. welcome jdn willkommen heißen

bidder /ˈbɪdə(r)/ n Bieter(in) m(f)

bide /baɪd/ vt ~ one's time den richtigen Moment abwarten

biennial /baɪˈenɪəl/ a zweijährlich; (lasting two years) zweijährig

bier /bɪə(r)/ n [Toten]bahre f

bifocals /baɪˈfəʊklz/ npl [pair of] ~ Bifokalbrille f

big /bɪg/ a (bigger, biggest) groß ● adv talk ~ (fam) angeben

bigam|ist /ˈbɪgəmɪst/ n Bigamist m. ~y n Bigamie f

big-'headed a (fam) eingebildet

bigot /ˈbɪgət/ n Eiferer m. ~ed a engstirnig

'bigwig n (fam) hohes Tier nt

bike /baɪk/ n (fam) [Fahr]rad nt

bikini /bɪˈkiːnɪ/ n Bikini m

bilberry /ˈbɪlbərɪ/ n Heidelbeere f

bile /baɪl/ n Galle f

bilingual /baɪˈlɪŋgwəl/ a zweisprachig

bilious /ˈbɪljəs/ a (Med) ~ attack verdorbener Magen m

bill¹ /bɪl/ n Rechnung f; (poster) Plakat nt; (Pol) Gesetzentwurf m; (Amer: note) Banknote f; ~ of exchange Wechsel m ● vt eine Rechnung schicken (+ dat)

bill² n (beak) Schnabel m

billet /ˈbɪlɪt/ n (Mil) Quartier nt ● vt (pt/pp billeted) einquartieren (on bei)

'billfold n (Amer) Brieftasche f

billiards /ˈbɪljədz/ n Billard nt

billion /ˈbɪljən/ n (thousand million) Milliarde f; (million million) Billion f

billy-goat /ˈbɪlɪ-/ n Ziegenbock m

bin /bɪn/ n Mülleimer m; (for bread) Kasten m

bind /baɪnd/ vt (pt/pp bound) binden (to an + acc); (bandage) verbinden; (Jur) verpflichten; (cover the edge of) einfassen. ~ing a verbindlich ● n Einband m; (braid) Borte f; (on ski) Bindung f

binge /bɪndʒ/ n (fam) go on the ~ eine Sauftour machen

binoculars /bɪˈnɒkjʊləz/ npl [pair of] ~ Fernglas nt

bio|'chemistry /baɪəʊ-/ n Biochemie f. ~degradable /-dɪˈgreɪdəbl/ a biologisch abbaubar

biograph|er /baɪˈɒgrəfə(r)/ n Biograph(in) m(f). ~y n Biographie f

biological /baɪəˈlɒdʒɪkl/ a biologisch

biolog|ist /baɪˈɒlədʒɪst/ n Biologe m. ~y n Biologie f

birch /bɜːtʃ/ n Birke f; (whip) Rute f

bird /bɜːd/ n Vogel m; (fam: girl) Mädchen nt; kill two ~s with one stone zwei Fliegen mit einer Klappe schlagen

Biro (P) /ˈbaɪrəʊ/ n Kugelschreiber m

birth /bɜːθ/ n Geburt f

birth: ~ certificate n Geburtsurkunde f. ~-control n Geburtenregelung f. ~day n Geburtstag m. ~mark n Muttermal nt. ~-rate n Geburtenziffer f. ~right n Geburtsrecht nt

biscuit /ˈbɪskɪt/ n Keks m

bisect /baɪˈsekt/ vt halbieren

bishop /ˈbɪʃəp/ n Bischof m; (Chess) Läufer m

bit¹ /bɪt/ n Stückchen nt; (for horse) Gebiß nt; (Techn) Bohreinsatz m; a ~ ein bißchen; ~ by ~ nach und nach; a ~ of bread ein bißchen Brot; do one's ~ sein Teil tun

bit² see bite

bitch /bɪtʃ/ n Hündin f; (sl) Luder nt. ~y a gehässig

bit|e /baɪt/ n Biß m; [insect] ~ Stich m; (mouthful) Bissen m ● vt/i (pt bit, pp bitten) beißen; ⟨insect:⟩ stechen; kauen ⟨one's nails⟩. ~ing a beißend

bitter /ˈbɪtə(r)/ a, -ly adv bitter; cry ~ly bitterlich weinen; ~ly cold bitterkalt ● n bitteres Bier nt. ~ness n Bitterkeit f

bitty /ˈbɪtɪ/ a zusammengestoppelt

bizarre /bɪˈzɑː(r)/ a bizarr

blab /blæb/ vi (pt/pp blabbed) alles ausplaudern

black /blæk/ a (-er, -est) schwarz; be ~and blue grün und blau sein ● n Schwarz nt; (person) Schwarze(r) m/f ● vt schwärzen; boykottieren ⟨goods⟩. ~ out vt verdunkeln ● vi (lose consciousness) das Bewußtsein verlieren

black: ~berry n Brombeere f. ~bird n Amsel f. ~board n (Sch) [Wand]tafel f. ~currant n schwarze Johannisbeere f

blacken vt/i schwärzen

black: ~ 'eye n blaues Auge nt. B~ 'Forest n Schwarzwald m. ~ 'ice n

Glatteis *nt*. ~leg *n* Streikbrecher *m*. ~list *vt* auf die schwarze Liste setzen. ~mail *n* Erpressung *f* ● *vt* erpressen. ~mailer *n* Erpresser(in) *m(f)*. ~ 'market *n* schwarzer Markt *m*. ~out *n* Verdunkelung *f*; have a ~out (*Med*) das Bewußtsein verlieren. ~ 'pudding *n* Blutwurst *f*. ~smith *n* [Huf]schmied *m*

bladder /'blædə(r)/ *n* (*Anat*) Blase *f*

blade /bleɪd/ *n* Klinge *f*; (*of grass*) Halm *m*

blame /bleɪm/ *n* Schuld *f* ● *vt* die Schuld geben (+ *dat*); no one is to ~ keiner ist schuld daran. ~less *a* schuldlos

blanch /blɑːntʃ/ *vi* blaß werden ● *vt* (*Culin*) blanchieren

blancmange /blə'mɒnʒ/ *n* Pudding *m*

bland /blænd/ *a* (-er, -est) mild

blank /blæŋk/ *a* leer; ⟨*look*⟩ ausdruckslos ● *n* Lücke *f*; (*cartridge*) Platzpatrone *f*. ~ 'cheque *n* Blankoscheck *m*

blanket /'blæŋkɪt/ *n* Decke *f*; wet ~ (*fam*) Spielverderber(in) *m(f)*

blank 'verse *n* Blankvers *m*

blare /bleə(r)/ *vt/i* schmettern

blasé /'blɑːzeɪ/ *a* blasiert

blaspheme /blæs'fiːm/ *vi* lästern

blasphem|ous /'blæsfəməs/ *a* [gottes]lästerlich. ~y *n* [Gottes]lästerung *f*

blast /blɑːst/ *n* (*gust*) Luftstoß *m*; (*sound*) Stoß *m* ● *vt* sprengen ● *int* (*sl*) verdammt. ~ed *a* (*sl*) verdammt

blast: ~-furnace *n* Hochofen *m*. ~-off *n* (*of missile*) Start *m*

blatant /'bleɪtənt/ *a* offensichtlich

blaze /bleɪz/ *n* Feuer *nt* ● *vi* brennen

blazer /'bleɪzə(r)/ *n* Blazer *m*

bleach /bliːtʃ/ *n* Bleichmittel *nt* ● *vt/i* bleichen

bleak /bliːk/ *a* (-er, -est) öde; (*fig*) trostlos

bleary-eyed /'blɪərɪ-/ *a* mit trüben/ (*on waking up*) verschlafenen Augen

bleat /bliːt/ *vi* blöken; ⟨*goat:*⟩ meckern

bleed /bliːd/ *v* (*pt/pp* bled) ● *vi* bluten ● *vt* entlüften ⟨*radiator*⟩

bleep /bliːp/ *n* Piepton *m* ● *vi* piepsen ● *vt* mit dem Piepser rufen. ~er *n* Piepser *m*

blemish /'blemɪʃ/ *n* Makel *m*

blend /blend/ *n* Mischung *f* ● *vt* mischen ● *vi* sich vermischen. ~er *n* (*Culin*) Mixer *m*

bless /bles/ *vt* segnen. ~ed /'blesɪd/ *a* heilig; (*sl*) verflixt. ~ing *n* Segen *m*

blew /bluː/ *see* blow²

blight /blaɪt/ *n* (*Bot*) Brand *m* ● *vt* (*spoil*) vereiteln

blind /blaɪnd/ *a* blind; ⟨*corner*⟩ unübersichtlich; ~ man/woman Blinde(r) *m/f* ● *n* [roller] ~ Rouleau *nt* ● *vt* blenden

blind: ~ 'alley *n* Sackgasse *f*. ~fold *a* & *adv* mit verbundenen Augen ● *n* Augenbinde *f* ● *vt* die Augen verbinden (+ *dat*). ~ly *adv* blindlings. ~ness *n* Blindheit *f*

blink /blɪŋk/ *vi* blinzeln; ⟨*light:*⟩ blinken

blinkers /'blɪŋkəz/ *npl* Scheuklappen *pl*

bliss /blɪs/ *n* Glückseligkeit *f*. ~ful *a* glücklich

blister /'blɪstə(r)/ *n* (*Med*) Blase *f* ● *vi* ⟨*paint:*⟩ Blasen werfen

blitz /blɪts/ *n* Luftangriff *m*; (*fam*) Großaktion *f*

blizzard /'blɪzəd/ *n* Schneesturm *m*

bloated /'bləʊtɪd/ *a* aufgedunsen

blob /blɒb/ *n* Klecks *m*

bloc /blɒk/ *n* (*Pol*) Block *m*

block /blɒk/ *n* Block *m*; (*of wood*) Klotz *m*; (*of flats*) [Wohn]block *m* ● *vt* blockieren. ~ up *vt* zustopfen

blockade /blɒ'keɪd/ *n* Blockade *f* ● *vt* blockieren

blockage /'blɒkɪdʒ/ *n* Verstopfung *f*

block: ~head *n* (*fam*) Dummkopf *m*. ~ 'letters *npl* Blockschrift *f*

bloke /bləʊk/ *n* (*fam*) Kerl *m*

blonde /blɒnd/ *a* blond ● *n* Blondine *f*

blood /blʌd/ *n* Blut *nt*

blood: ~ count *n* Blutbild *nt*. ~-curdling *a* markerschütternd. ~ donor *n* Blutspender *m*. ~ group *n* Blutgruppe *f*. ~hound *n* Bluthund *m*. ~-poisoning *n* Blutvergiftung *f*. ~ pressure *n* Blutdruck *m*. ~ relative *n* Blutsverwandte(r) *m/f*. ~shed *n* Blutvergießen *nt*. ~shot *a* blutunterlaufen. ~ sports *npl* Jagdsport *m*. ~-stained *a* blutbefleckt. ~stream *n* Blutbahn *f*. ~ test *n* Blutprobe *f*. ~thirsty *a* blutdürstig. ~ transfusion *n* Blutübertragung *f*. ~-vessel *n* Blutgefäß *nt*

bloody /'blʌdɪ/ *a* (-ier, -iest) blutig; (*sl*) verdammt. ~-'minded *a* (*sl*) stur

bloom /bluːm/ n Blüte f ● vi blühen
bloom|er /'bluːmə(r)/ n (fam) Schnitzer m. ~**ing** a (fam) verdammt
blossom /'blɒsəm/ n Blüte f ● vi blühen. ~ **out** vi (fig) aufblühen
blot /blɒt/ n [Tinten]klecks m; (fig) Fleck m ● vt (pt/pp **blotted**) löschen. ~ **out** vt (fig) auslöschen
blotch /blɒtʃ/ n Fleck m. ~**y** a fleckig
'**blotting-paper** n Löschpapier nt
blouse /blaʊz/ n Bluse f
blow¹ /bləʊ/ n Schlag m
blow² v (pt **blew**, pp **blown**) ● vt blasen; (fam: squander) verpulvern; ~ **one's nose** sich (dat) die Nase putzen ● vi blasen; ⟨fuse:⟩ durchbrennen. ~ **away** vt wegblasen ● vi wegfliegen. ~ **down** vt umwehen ● vi umfallen. ~ **out** vt (extinguish) ausblasen. ~ **over** vi umfallen; (fig: die down) vorübergehen. ~ **up** vt (inflate) aufblasen; (enlarge) vergrößern; (shatter by explosion) sprengen ● vi explodieren
blow: ~-**dry** vt fönen. ~**fly** n Schmeißfliege f. ~**lamp** n Lötlampe f
blown /bləʊn/ see **blow**²
'**blowtorch** n (Amer) Lötlampe f
blowy /'bləʊɪ/ a windig
bludgeon /'blʌdʒn/ vt (fig) zwingen
blue /bluː/ a (-r, -st) blau; **feel** ~ deprimiert sein ● n Blau nt; **have the** ~**s** deprimiert sein; **out of the** ~ aus heiterem Himmel
blue: ~**bell** n Sternhyazinthe f. ~**berry** n Heidelbeere f. ~**bottle** n Schmeißfliege f. ~ **film** n Pornofilm m. ~**print** n (fig) Entwurf m
bluff /blʌf/ n Bluff m ● vi bluffen
blunder /'blʌndə(r)/ n Schnitzer m ● vi einen Schnitzer machen
blunt /blʌnt/ a stumpf; ⟨person⟩ geradeheraus. ~**ly** adv unverblümt, geradeheraus
blur /blɜː(r)/ n **it's all a** ~ alles ist verschwommen ● vt (pt/pp **blurred**) verschwommen machen; ~**red** verschwommen
blurb /blɜːb/ n Klappentext m
blurt /blɜːt/ vt ~ **out** herausplatzen mit
blush /blʌʃ/ n Erröten nt ● vi erröten
bluster /'blʌstə(r)/ n Großtuerei f. ~**y** a windig
boar /bɔː(r)/ n Eber m
board /bɔːd/ n Brett nt; (for notices) schwarzes Brett nt; (committee)

Ausschuß m; (of directors) Vorstand m; **on** ~ an Bord; **full** ~ Vollpension f; ~ **and lodging** Unterkunft und Verpflegung pl; **go by the** ~ (fam) unter den Tisch fallen ● vt einsteigen in (+ acc); (Naut, Aviat) besteigen ● vi an Bord gehen; ~ **with** in Pension wohnen bei. ~ **up** vt mit Brettern verschlagen
boarder /'bɔːdə(r)/ n Pensionsgast m; (Sch) Internatsschüler(in) m(f)
board: ~-**game** n Brettspiel nt. ~**ing-house** n Pension f. ~**ing-school** n Internat nt
boast /bəʊst/ vt sich rühmen (+ gen) ● vi prahlen (about mit). ~**ful** a, -**ly** adv prahlerisch
boat /bəʊt/ n Boot nt; (ship) Schiff nt. ~**er** n (hat) flacher Strohhut m
bob /bɒb/ n Bubikopf m ● vi (pt/pp **bobbed**) (curtsy) knicksen; ~ **up and down** sich auf und ab bewegen
bobbin /'bɒbɪn/ n Spule f
'**bob-sleigh** n Bob m
bode /bəʊd/ vi ~ **well/ill** etwas/nichts Gutes verheißen
bodice /'bɒdɪs/ n Mieder nt
bodily /'bɒdɪlɪ/ a körperlich ● adv (forcibly) mit Gewalt
body /'bɒdɪ/ n Körper m; (corpse) Leiche f; (corporation) Körperschaft f; **the main** ~ der Hauptanteil. ~**guard** n Leibwächter m. ~**work** n (Auto) Karosserie f
bog /bɒg/ n Sumpf m ● vt (pt/pp **bogged**) **get** ~**ged down** steckenbleiben
boggle /'bɒgl/ vi **the mind** ~**s** es ist kaum vorstellbar
bogus /'bəʊgəs/ a falsch
boil¹ /bɔɪl/ n Furunkel m
boil² n **bring/come to the** ~ zum Kochen bringen/kommen ● vt/i kochen; ~**ed potatoes** Salzkartoffeln pl. ~ **down** vi (fig) hinauslaufen (to auf + acc). ~ **over** vi überkochen. ~ **up** vt aufkochen
boiler /'bɔɪlə(r)/ n Heizkessel m. ~**suit** n Overall m
'**boiling point** n Siedepunkt m
boisterous /'bɔɪstərəs/ a übermütig
bold /bəʊld/ a (-er, -est), -**ly** adv kühn; (Typ) fett. ~**ness** n Kühnheit f
bollard /'bɒlɑːd/ n Poller m
bolster /'bəʊlstə(r)/ n Nackenrolle f ● vt ~ **up** Mut machen (+ dat)
bolt /bəʊlt/ n Riegel m; (Techn) Bolzen m; **nuts and** ~**s** Schrauben und Muttern pl ● vt schrauben (to an + acc);

verriegeln ⟨door⟩; hinunterschlingen ⟨food⟩ ● vi abhauen; ⟨horse:⟩ durchgehen ● adv ~ **upright** adv kerzengerade

bomb /bɒm/ n Bombe f ● vt bombardieren

bombard /bɒmˈbɑːd/ vt beschießen; (fig) bombardieren

bombastic /bɒmˈbæstɪk/ a bombastisch

bomb|er /ˈbɒmə(r)/ n (Aviat) Bomber m; (person) Bombenleger(in) m(f). **~shell** n be a ~shell (fig) wie eine Bombe einschlagen

bond /bɒnd/ n (fig) Band nt; (Comm) Obligation f; **be in ~** unter Zollverschluß stehen

bondage /ˈbɒndɪdʒ/ n (fig) Sklaverei f

bone /bəʊn/ n Knochen m; (of fish) Gräte f ● vt von den Knochen lösen ⟨meat⟩; entgräten ⟨fish⟩. **~-'dry** a knochentrocken

bonfire /ˈbɒn-/ n Gartenfeuer nt; (celebratory) Freudenfeuer nt

bonnet /ˈbɒnɪt/ n Haube f

bonus /ˈbəʊnəs/ n Prämie f; (gratuity) Gratifikation f; (fig) Plus nt

bony /ˈbəʊnɪ/ a (-ier, -iest) knochig; ⟨fish⟩ grätig

boo /buː/ int buh! ● vt ausbuhen ● vi buhen

boob /buːb/ n (fam: mistake) Schnitzer m ● vi (fam) einen Schnitzer machen

book /bʊk/ n Buch nt; (of tickets) Heft nt; **keep the ~s** (Comm) die Bücher führen ● vt/i buchen; (reserve) [vor]bestellen; (for offence) aufschreiben. **~able** /-əbl/ a im Vorverkauf erhältlich

book: **~case** n Bücherregal nt. **~ends** npl Buchstützen pl. **~ing-office** n Fahrkartenschalter m. **~keeping** n Buchführung f. **~let** n Broschüre f. **~maker** n Buchmacher m. **~mark** n Lesezeichen nt. **~seller** n Buchhändler(in) m(f). **~shop** n Buchhandlung f. **~stall** n Bücherstand m. **~worm** n Bücherwurm m

boom /buːm/ n (Comm) Hochkonjunktur f; (upturn) Aufschwung m ● vi dröhnen; (fig) blühen

boon /buːn/ n Segen m

boor /bʊə(r)/ n Flegel m. **~ish** a flegelhaft

boost /buːst/ n Auftrieb m ● vt Auftrieb geben (+ dat). **~er** n (Med) Nachimpfung f

boot /buːt/ n Stiefel m; (Auto) Kofferraum m

booth /buːð/ n Bude f; (cubicle) Kabine f

booty /ˈbuːtɪ/ n Beute f

booze /buːz/ n (fam) Alkohol m ● vi (fam) saufen

border /ˈbɔːdə(r)/ n Rand m; (frontier) Grenze f; (in garden) Rabatte f ● vi ~ **on** grenzen an (+ acc). **~line** n Grenzlinie f. **~line case** n Grenzfall m

bore¹ /bɔː(r)/ see **bear²**

bore² vt/i (Techn) bohren

bor|e³ n (of gun) Kaliber nt; (person) langweiliger Mensch m; (thing) langweilige Sache f ● vt langweilen; **be ~ed** sich langweilen. **~edom** n Langeweile f. **~ing** a langweilig

born /bɔːn/ pp **be ~** geboren werden ● a geboren

borne /bɔːn/ see **bear²**

borough /ˈbʌrə/ n Stadtgemeinde f

borrow /ˈbɒrəʊ/ vt [sich (dat)] borgen od leihen (**from** von)

bosom /ˈbʊzm/ n Busen m

boss /bɒs/ n (fam) Chef m ● vt herumkommandieren. **~y** a herrschsüchtig

botanical /bəˈtænɪkl/ a botanisch

botan|ist /ˈbɒtənɪst/ n Botaniker(in) m(f). **~y** n Botanik f

botch /bɒtʃ/ vt verpfuschen

both /bəʊθ/ a & pron beide; **~[of] the children** beide Kinder; **~ of them** beide [von ihnen] ● adv ~ **men and women** sowohl Männer als auch Frauen

bother /ˈbɒðə(r)/ n Mühe f; (minor trouble) Ärger m ● int (fam) verflixt! ● vt belästigen; (disturb) stören ● vi sich kümmern (**about** um); **don't ~** nicht nötig

bottle /ˈbɒtl/ n Flasche f ● vt auf Flaschen abfüllen; (preserve) einmachen. **~ up** vt (fig) in sich (dat) aufstauen

bottle: **~-neck** n (fig) Engpaß m. **~-opener** n Flaschenöffner m

bottom /ˈbɒtəm/ a unterste(r,s) ● n (of container) Boden m; (of river) Grund m; (of page, hill) Fuß m; (buttocks) Hintern m; **at the ~** unten; **get to the ~ of sth** (fig) hinter etw (acc) kommen. **~less** a bodenlos

bough /baʊ/ n Ast m

bought /bɔːt/ see **buy**

boulder /'bəʊldə(r)/ n Felsblock m

bounce /baʊns/ vi [auf]springen; ⟨cheque:⟩ (fam) nicht gedeckt sein ● vt aufspringen lassen ⟨ball⟩

bouncer /'baʊnsə(r)/ n (fam) Rausschmeißer m

bouncing /'baʊnsɪŋ/ a ~ **baby** strammer Säugling m

bound¹ /baʊnd/ n Sprung m ● vi springen

bound² see **bind** ● a ~ **for** ⟨ship⟩ mit Kurs auf (+ acc); **be** ~ **to do sth** etw bestimmt machen; (obliged) verpflichtet sein, etw zu machen

boundary /'baʊndərɪ/ n Grenze f

'boundless a grenzenlos

bounds /baʊndz/ npl (fig) Grenzen pl; **out of** ~ verboten

bouquet /bʊ'keɪ/ n [Blumen]strauß m; (of wine) Bukett nt

bourgeois /'bʊəʒwɑː/ a (pej) spießbürgerlich

bout /baʊt/ n (Med) Anfall m; (Sport) Kampf m

bow¹ /bəʊ/ n (weapon & Mus) Bogen m; (knot) Schleife f

bow² /baʊ/ n Verbeugung f ● vi sich verbeugen ● vt neigen ⟨head⟩

bow³ /baʊ/ n (Naut) Bug m

bowel /'baʊəl/ n Darm m; ~ **movement** Stuhlgang m. ~**s** pl Eingeweide pl; (digestion) Verdauung f

bowl¹ /bəʊl/ n Schüssel f; (shallow) Schale f; (of pipe) Kopf m; (of spoon) Schöpfteil m

bowl² n (ball) Kugel f ● vt/i werfen. ~ **over** vt umwerfen

bow-legged /bəʊ'legd/ a O-beinig

bowler¹ /'bəʊlə(r)/ n (Sport) Werfer m

bowler² n ~ [**hat**] Melone f

bowling /'bəʊlɪŋ/ n Kegeln nt. ~**-alley** n Kegelbahn f

bowls /bəʊlz/ n Bowlsspiel nt

bow-'tie /bəʊ-/ n Fliege f

box¹ /bɒks/ n Schachtel f; (wooden) Kiste f; (cardboard) Karton m; (Theat) Loge f

box² vt/i (Sport) boxen; ~ **s.o.'s ears** jdn ohrfeigen

box|er /'bɒksə(r)/ n Boxer m. ~**ing** n Boxen nt. **B**~**ing Day** n zweiter Weihnachtstag m

box: ~**-office** n (Theat) Kasse f. ~**room** n Abstellraum m

boy /bɔɪ/ n Junge m

boycott /'bɔɪkɒt/ n Boykott m ● vt boykottieren

boy: ~**friend** n Freund m. ~**ish** a jungenhaft

bra /brɑː/ n BH m

brace /breɪs/ n Strebe f, Stütze f; (dental) Zahnspange f; ~**s** npl Hosenträger mpl ● vt ~ **oneself** sich stemmen (**against** gegen); (fig) sich gefaßt machen (**for** auf + acc)

bracelet /'breɪslɪt/ n Armband nt

bracing /'breɪsɪŋ/ a stärkend

bracken /'brækn/ n Farnkraut nt

bracket /'brækɪt/ n Konsole f; (group) Gruppe f; (Typ) **round/square** ~**s** runde/eckige Klammern ● vt einklammern

brag /bræg/ vi (pt/pp **bragged**) prahlen (**about** mit)

braid /breɪd/ n Borte f

braille /breɪl/ n Blindenschrift f

brain /breɪn/ n Gehirn nt; ~**s** (fig) Intelligenz f

brain: ~**child** n geistiges Produkt nt. ~**less** a dumm. ~**wash** vt einer Gehirnwäsche unterziehen. ~**wave** n Geistesblitz m

brainy /'breɪnɪ/ a (-ier, -iest) klug

braise /breɪz/ vt schmoren

brake /breɪk/ n Bremse f ● vt/i bremsen. ~**light** n Bremslicht nt

bramble /'bræmbl/ n Brombeerstrauch m

bran /bræn/ n Kleie f

branch /brɑːntʃ/ n Ast m; (fig) Zweig m; (Comm) Zweigstelle f; (shop) Filiale f ● vi sich gabeln. ~ **off** vi abzweigen. ~ **out** vi ~ **out into** sich verlegen auf (+ acc)

brand /brænd/ n Marke f; (on animal) Brandzeichen nt ● vt mit dem Brandeisen zeichnen ⟨animal⟩; (fig) brandmarken als

brandish /'brændɪʃ/ vt schwingen

brand-'new a nagelneu

brandy /'brændɪ/ n Weinbrand m

brash /bræʃ/ a naßforsch

brass /brɑːs/ n Messing nt; (Mus) Blech nt; **get down to** ~ **tacks** (fam) zur Sache kommen; **top** ~ (fam) hohe Tiere pl. ~ **band** n Blaskapelle f

brassiere /'bræzɪə(r)/ n Büstenhalter m

brassy /'brɑːsɪ/ a (-ier, -iest) (fam) ordinär

brat /bræt/ n (pej) Balg nt

bravado /brə'vɑːdəʊ/ n Forschheit f

brave /breɪv/ a (-r, -st), -**ly** adv tapfer ● vt die Stirn bieten (+ dat). ~**ry** /-ərɪ/ n Tapferkeit f

bravo /braːˈvəʊ/ *int* bravo!

brawl /brɔːl/ *n* Schlägerei *f* ● *vi* sich schlagen

brawn /brɔːn/ *n* (*Culin*) Sülze *f*

brawny /ˈbrɔːnɪ/ *a* muskulös

bray /breɪ/ *vi* iahen

brazen /ˈbreɪzn/ *a* unverschämt

brazier /ˈbreɪzɪə(r)/ *n* Kohlenbecken *nt*

Brazil /brəˈzɪl/ *n* Brasilien *nt*. **~ian** *a* brasilianisch. **~ nut** *n* Paranuß *f*

breach /briːtʃ/ *n* Bruch *m*; (*Mil & fig*) Bresche *f*; **~ of contract** Vertragsbruch *m* ● *vt* durchbrechen; brechen ⟨*contract*⟩

bread /bred/ *n* Brot *nt*; **slice of ~ and butter** Butterbrot *nt*

bread: **~crumbs** *npl* Brotkrümel *pl*; (*Culin*) Paniermehl *nt*. **~line** *n* **be on the ~line** gerade genug zum Leben haben

breadth /bredθ/ *n* Breite *f*

'bread-winner *n* Brotverdiener *m*

break /breɪk/ *n* Bruch *m*; (*interval*) Pause *f*; (*interruption*) Unterbrechung *f*; (*fam: chance*) Chance *f* ● *v* (*pt* **broke**, *pp* **broken**) ● *vt* brechen; (*smash*) zerbrechen; (*damage*) kaputtmachen (*fam*); (*interrupt*) unterbrechen; **~ one's arm** sich ⟨*dat*⟩ den Arm brechen ● *vi* brechen; ⟨*day:*⟩ anbrechen; ⟨*storm:*⟩ losbrechen; ⟨*thing:*⟩ kaputtgehen (*fam*); ⟨*rope, thread:*⟩ reißen; ⟨*news:*⟩ bekanntwerden; **his voice is ~ing** er ist im Stimmbruch. **~ away** *vi* sich losreißen/(*fig*) sich absetzen (**from** von). **~ down** *vi* zusammenbrechen; (*Techn*) eine Panne haben; ⟨*negotiations:*⟩ scheitern ● *vt* aufbrechen ⟨*door*⟩; aufgliedern ⟨*figures*⟩. **~ in** *vi* einbrechen. **~ off** *vt*/*i* abbrechen; lösen ⟨*engagement*⟩. **~ out** *vi* ausbrechen. **~ up** *vt* zerbrechen ● *vi* ⟨*crowd:*⟩ sich zerstreuen; ⟨*marriage, couple:*⟩ auseinandergehen; (*Sch*) Ferien bekommen

'break|able /ˈbreɪkəbl/ *a* zerbrechlich. **~age** /-ɪdʒ/ *n* Bruch *m*. **~down** *n* (*Techn*) Panne *f*; (*Med*) Zusammenbruch *m*; (*of figures*) Aufgliederung *f*. **~er** *n* (*wave*) Brecher *m*

breakfast /ˈbrekfəst/ *n* Frühstück *nt*

break: **~through** *n* Durchbruch *m*. **~water** *n* Buhne *f*

breast /brest/ *n* Brust *f*. **~bone** *n* Brustbein *nt*. **~-feed** *vt* stillen. **~-stroke** *n* Brustschwimmen *nt*

breath /breθ/ *n* Atem *m*; **out of ~** außer Atem; **under one's ~** vor sich (*acc*) hin

breathalyse /ˈbreθəlaɪz/ *vt* ins Röhrchen blasen lassen. **~r (P)** *n* Röhrchen *nt*. **~r test** *n* Alcotest (P) *m*

breathe /briːð/ *vt*/*i* atmen. **~ in** *vt*/*i* einatmen. **~ out** *vt*/*i* ausatmen

breath|er /ˈbriːðə(r)/ *n* Atempause *f*. **~ing** *n* Atmen *nt*

breath /breθ/: **~less** *a* atemlos. **~-taking** *a* atemberaubend. **~ test** *n* Alcotest (P) *m*

bred /bred/ *see* **breed**

breeches /ˈbrɪtʃɪz/ *npl* Kniehose *f*; (*for riding*) Reithose *f*

breed /briːd/ *n* Rasse *f* ● *v* (*pt*/*pp* **bred**) ● *vt* züchten; (*give rise to*) erzeugen ● *vi* sich vermehren. **~er** *n* Züchter *m*. **~ing** *n* Zucht *f*; (*fig*) [gute] Lebensart *f*

breez|e /briːz/ *n* Lüftchen *nt*; (*Naut*) Brise *f*. **~y** *a* [leicht] windig

brevity /ˈbrevətɪ/ *n* Kürze *f*

brew /bruː/ *n* Gebräu *nt* ● *vt* brauen; kochen ⟨*tea*⟩ ● *vi* (*fig*) sich zusammenbrauen. **~er** *n* Brauer *m*. **~ery** *n* Brauerei *f*

bribe /braɪb/ *n* (*money*) Bestechungsgeld *nt* ● *vt* bestechen. **~ry** /-ərɪ/ *n* Bestechung *f*

brick /brɪk/ *n* Ziegelstein *m*, Backstein *m* ● *vt* **~ up** zumauern

'bricklayer *n* Maurer *m*

bridal /ˈbraɪdl/ *a* Braut-

bride /braɪd/ *n* Braut *f*. **~groom** *n* Bräutigam *m*. **~smaid** *n* Brautjungfer *f*

bridge¹ /brɪdʒ/ *n* Brücke *f*; (*of nose*) Nasenrücken *m*; (*of spectacles*) Steg *m* ● *vt* (*fig*) überbrücken

bridge² (*Cards*) Bridge *nt*

bridle /ˈbraɪdl/ *n* Zaum *m*. **~-path** *n* Reitweg *m*

brief¹ /briːf/ *a* (**-er, -est**) kurz; **be ~** ⟨*person:*⟩ sich kurz fassen

brief² *n* Instruktionen *pl*; (*Jur: case*) Mandat *nt* ● *vt* Instruktionen geben (+ *dat*); (*Jur*) beauftragen. **~case** *n* Aktentasche *f*

brief|ing /ˈbriːfɪŋ/ *n* Informationsgespräch *nt*. **~ly** *adv* kurz. **~ness** *n* Kürze *f*

briefs /briːfs/ *npl* Slip *m*

brigad|e /brɪˈgeɪd/ *n* Brigade *f*. **~ier** /-əˈdɪə(r)/ *n* Brigadegeneral *m*

bright /braɪt/ a (-er, -est), -ly adv hell; ⟨day⟩ heiter; ~ **red** hellrot

bright|en /'braɪtn/ v ~**en** [**up**] ● vt aufheitern ● vi sich aufheitern. ~**ness** n Helligkeit f

brilliance /'brɪljəns/ n Glanz m; (of person) Genialität f

brilliant /'brɪljənt/ a, -ly adv glänzend; ⟨person⟩ genial

brim /brɪm/ n Rand m; (of hat) Krempe f ● vi (pt/pp **brimmed**) ~ **over** überfließen

brine /braɪn/ n Salzwasser nt; (Culin) [Salz]lake f

bring /brɪŋ/ vt (pt/pp **brought**) bringen; ~ **them with you** bring sie mit. ~ **about** vt verursachen. ~ **along** vt mitbringen. ~ **back** vt zurückbringen. ~ **down** vt herunterbringen; senken ⟨price⟩. ~ **off** vt vollbringen. ~ **on** vt (cause) verursachen. ~ **out** vt herausbringen. ~ **round** vt vorbeibringen; (persuade) überreden; wieder zum Bewußtsein bringen ⟨unconscious person⟩. ~ **up** vt heraufbringen; (vomit) erbrechen; aufziehen ⟨children⟩; erwähnen ⟨question⟩

brink /brɪŋk/ n Rand m

brisk /brɪsk/ a (-er, -est), -ly adv lebhaft; (quick) schnell

brist|le /'brɪsl/ n Borste f. ~**ly** a borstig

Brit|ain /'brɪtn/ n Großbritannien nt. ~**ish** a britisch; **the** ~**ish** die Briten pl. ~**on** n Brite m/Britin f

Brittany /'brɪtəni/ n die Bretagne

brittle /'brɪtl/ a brüchig, spröde

broach /brəʊtʃ/ vt anzapfen; anschneiden ⟨subject⟩

broad /brɔːd/ a (-er, -est) breit; ⟨hint⟩ deutlich; **in** ~ **daylight** am hellichten Tag. ~ **beans** npl dicke Bohnen pl

'broadcast n Sendung f ● vt/i (pt/pp -**cast**) senden. ~**er** n Rundfunk- und Fernsehpersönlichkeit f. ~**ing** n Funk und Fernsehen pl

broaden /'brɔːdn/ vt verbreitern; (fig) erweitern ● vi sich verbreitern

broadly /'brɔːdli/ adv breit; ~ **speaking** allgemein gesagt

broad'minded a tolerant

brocade /brə'keɪd/ n Brokat m

broccoli /'brɒkəlɪ/ n inv Brokkoli pl

brochure /'brəʊʃə(r)/ n Broschüre f

brogue /brəʊg/ n (shoe) Wanderschuh m; **Irish** ~ irischer Akzent m

broke /brəʊk/ see **break** ● a (fam) pleite

broken /'brəʊkn/ see **break** ● a zerbrochen, (fam) kaputt; ~ **English** gebrochenes Englisch nt. ~-**hearted** a untröstlich

broker /'brəʊkə(r)/ n Makler m

brolly /'brɒlɪ/ n (fam) Schirm m

bronchitis /brɒŋ'kaɪtɪs/ n Bronchitis f

bronze /brɒnz/ n Bronze f

brooch /brəʊtʃ/ n Brosche f

brood /bruːd/ n Brut f ● vi brüten; (fig) grübeln

brook¹ /brʊk/ n Bach m

brook² vt dulden

broom /bruːm/ n Besen m; (Bot) Ginster m. ~**stick** n Besenstiel m

broth /brɒθ/ n Brühe f

brothel /'brɒθl/ n Bordell nt

brother /'brʌðə(r)/ n Bruder m

brother: ~-**in-law** n (pl -**s-in-law**) Schwager m. ~**ly** a brüderlich

brought /brɔːt/ see **bring**

brow /braʊ/ n Augenbraue f; ⟨forehead⟩ Stirn f; (of hill) [Berg]kuppe f

'browbeat vt (pt -**beat**, pp -**beaten**) einschüchtern

brown /braʊn/ a (-er, -est) braun; ~ **'paper** Packpapier nt ● n Braun nt ● vt bräunen ● vi braun werden

Brownie /'braʊnɪ/ n Wichtel m

browse /braʊz/ vi (read) schmökern; (in shop) sich umsehen

bruise /bruːz/ n blauer Fleck m ● vt beschädigen ⟨fruit⟩; ~ **one's arm** sich (dat) den Arm quetschen

brunch /brʌntʃ/ n Brunch m

brunette /bruː'net/ n Brünette f

Brunswick /'brʌnzwɪk/ n Braunschweig nt

brunt /brʌnt/ n **the** ~ **of** die volle Wucht (+ gen)

brush /brʌʃ/ n Bürste f; (with handle) Handfeger m; (for paint, pastry) Pinsel m; (bushes) Unterholz nt; (fig: conflict) Zusammenstoß m ● vt bürsten; putzen ⟨teeth⟩; ~ **against** streifen [gegen]; ~ **aside** (fig) abtun. ~ **off** vt abbürsten; (reject) zurückweisen. ~ **up** vt/i (fig) ~**up** [**on**] auffrischen

brusque /brʊsk/ a, -ly adv brüsk

Brussels /'brʌslz/ n Brüssel nt. ~ **sprouts** npl Rosenkohl m

brutal /'bruːtl/ a, -ly adv brutal. ~**ity** /-'tælətɪ/ n Brutalität f

brute /bruːt/ n Unmensch m. ~ **force** n rohe Gewalt f

B.Sc. *abbr of* **Bachelor of Science**
bubble /'bʌbl/ *n* [Luft]blase *f* ● *vi*
sprudeln
buck¹ /bʌk/ *n* (*deer & Gym*) Bock *m*;
(*rabbit*) Rammler *m* ● *vi* ⟨*horse:*⟩
bocken. ∼ **up** *vi* (*fam*) sich aufheitern; (*hurry*) sich beeilen
buck² *n* (*Amer, fam*) Dollar *m*
buck³ *n* **pass the** ∼ die Verantwortung abschieben
bucket /'bʌkɪt/ *n* Eimer *m*
buckle /'bʌkl/ *n* Schnalle *f* ● *vt* zu-
schnallen ● *vi* sich verbiegen
bud /bʌd/ *n* Knospe *f* ● *vi* (*pt/pp*
budded) knospen
Buddhis|m /'budɪzm/ *n* Buddhismus
m. ∼**t** *a* buddhistisch ● *n* Buddhist
(in) *m*(*f*)
buddy /'bʌdɪ/ *n* (*fam*) Freund *m*
budge /bʌdʒ/ *vt* bewegen ● *vi* sich
[von der Stelle] rühren
budgerigar /'bʌdʒərɪgɑ:(r)/ *n* Wellen-
sittich *m*
budget /'bʌdʒɪt/ *n* Budget *nt*; (*Pol*)
Haushaltsplan *m*; (*money available*)
Etat *m* ● *vi* (*pt/pp* **budgeted**) ∼ **for**
sth etw einkalkulieren
buff /bʌf/ *a* (*colour*) sandfarben ● *n*
Sandfarbe *f*; (*Amer, fam*) Fan *m* ● *vt*
polieren
buffalo /'bʌfələʊ/ *n* (*inv or pl* **-es**)
Büffel *m*
buffer /'bʌfə(r)/ *n* (*Rail*) Puffer *m*; **old**
∼ (*fam*) alter Knacker *m*; ∼ **zone**
Pufferzone *f*
buffet¹ /'bʊfeɪ/ *n* Büfett *nt*; (*on
station*) Imbißstube *f*
buffet² /'bʌfɪt/ *vt* (*pt/pp* **buffeted**) hin
und her werfen
buffoon /bə'fu:n/ *n* Narr *m*
bug /bʌg/ *n* Wanze *f*; (*fam: virus*)
Bazillus *m*; (*fam: device*) Abhörger-
ät *nt*, (*fam*) Wanze *f* ● *vt* (*pt/pp*
bugged) (*fam*) verwanzen ⟨*room*⟩;
abhören ⟨*telephone*⟩; (*Amer: annoy*)
ärgern
buggy /'bʌgɪ/ *n* [Kinder]sportwagen
m
bugle /'bju:gl/ *n* Signalhorn *nt*
build /bɪld/ *n* (*of person*) Körperbau
m ● *vt*/*i* (*pt/pp* **built**) bauen. ∼ **on** *vt*
anbauen (**to** an + *acc*). ∼ **up** *vt*
aufbauen ● *vi* zunehmen; ⟨*traffic:*⟩
sich stauen
builder /'bɪldə(r)/ *n* Bauunternehmer
m
building /'bɪldɪŋ/ *n* Gebäude *nt*. ∼
site *n* Baustelle *f*. ∼ **society** *n* Bau-
sparkasse *f*

built /bɪlt/ *see* **build**. ∼**-in** *a*
eingebaut. ∼**-in 'cupboard** *n* Einbauschrank *m*. ∼**-up area** *n* be-
bautes Gebiet *nt*; (*Auto*) geschlossene Ortschaft *f*
bulb /bʌlb/ *n* [Blumen]zwiebel *f*;
(*Electr*) [Glüh]birne *f*
bulbous /'bʌlbəs/ *a* bauchig
Bulgaria /bʌl'geərɪə/ *n* Bulgarien *nt*
bulg|e /bʌldʒ/ *n* Ausbauchung *f* ● *vi*
sich ausbauchen. ∼**ing** *a* prall;
⟨*eyes*⟩ hervorquellend; ∼**ing with**
prall gefüllt mit
bulk /bʌlk/ *n* Masse *f*; (*greater part*)
Hauptteil *m*; **in** ∼ en gros; (*loose*)
lose. ∼**y** *a* sperrig; (*large*) massig
bull /bʊl/ *n* Bulle *m*, Stier *m*
'bulldog *n* Bulldogge *f*
bulldozer /'bʊldəʊzə(r)/ *n* Planier-
raupe *f*
bullet /'bʊlɪt/ *n* Kugel *f*
bulletin /'bʊlɪtɪn/ *n* Bulletin *nt*
'bullet-proof *a* kugelsicher
'bullfight *n* Stierkampf *m*. ∼**er** *n*
Stierkämpfer *m*
'bullfinch *n* Dompfaff *m*
bullion /'bʊlɪən/ *n* **gold** ∼ Barrengold
nt
bullock /'bʊlək/ *n* Ochse *m*
bull: ∼**ring** *n* Stierkampfarena *f*.
∼**'s-eye** *n* **score a** ∼**'s-eye** ins
Schwarze treffen
bully /'bʊlɪ/ *n* Tyrann *m* ● *vt*
tyrannisieren
bum¹ /bʌm/ *n* (*sl*) Hintern *m*
bum² *n* (*Amer, fam*) Landstreicher *m*
bumble-bee /'bʌmbl-/ *n* Hummel *f*
bump /bʌmp/ *n* Bums *m*; (*swelling*)
Beule *f*; (*in road*) holperige Stelle *f*
● *vt* stoßen; ∼ **into** stoßen gegen;
(*meet*) zufällig treffen. ∼ **off** *vt*
(*fam*) um die Ecke bringen
bumper /'bʌmpə(r)/ *a* Rekord- ● *n*
(*Auto*) Stoßstange *f*
bumpkin /'bʌmpkɪn/ *n* **country** ∼
Tölpel *m*
bumptious /'bʌmpʃəs/ *a* aufgeblasen
bumpy /'bʌmpɪ/ *a* holperig
bun /bʌn/ *n* Milchbrötchen *nt*; (*hair*)
[Haar]knoten *m*
bunch /bʌntʃ/ *n* (*of flowers*) Strauß
m; (*of radishes, keys*) Bund *m*; (*of
people*) Gruppe *f*; ∼ **of grapes**
[ganze] Weintraube *f*
bundle /'bʌndl/ *n* Bündel *nt* ● *vt*
∼**[up]** bündeln
bung /bʌŋ/ *vt* (*fam*) (*throw*)
schmeißen. ∼ **up** *vt* (*fam*)
verstopfen

bungalow /'bʌŋgələʊ/ n Bungalow m

bungle /'bʌŋgl/ vt verpfuschen

bunion /'bʌnjən/ n (Med) Ballen m

bunk /bʌŋk/ n [Schlaf]koje f. **~-beds** npl Etagenbett nt

bunker /'bʌŋkə(r)/ n Bunker m

bunkum /'bʌŋkəm/ n Quatsch m

bunny /'bʌnɪ/ n (fam) Kaninchen nt

buoy /bɔɪ/ n Boje f. **~ up** vt (fig) stärken

buoyan|cy /'bɔɪənsɪ/ n Auftrieb m. **~t** a be **~t** schwimmen; ⟨water:⟩ gut tragen

burden /'bɜːdn/ n Last f ● vt belasten. **~some** /-səm/ a lästig

bureau /bjʊəˈrəʊ/ n (pl **-x** /-əʊz/ or **~s**) (desk) Sekretär m; (office) Büro nt

bureaucracy /bjʊəˈrɒkrəsɪ/ n Bürokratie f

bureaucrat /'bjʊərəkræt/ n Bürokrat m. **~ic** /-'krætɪk/ a bürokratisch

burger /'bɜːgə(r)/ n Hamburger m

burglar /'bɜːglə(r)/ n Einbrecher m. **~ alarm** n Alarmanlage f

burglar|ize /'bɜːgləraɪz/ vt (Amer) einbrechen in (+ acc). **~y** n Einbruch m

burgle /'bɜːgl/ vt einbrechen in (+ acc); **they have been ~d** bei ihnen ist eingebrochen worden

Burgundy /'bɜːgəndɪ/ n Burgund nt; **b~** (wine) Burgunder m

burial /'berɪəl/ n Begräbnis nt

burlesque /bɜː'lesk/ n Burleske f

burly /'bɜːlɪ/ a (-ier, -iest) stämmig

Burm|a /'bɜːmə/ n Birma nt. **~ese** /-'miːz/ a birmanisch

burn /bɜːn/ n Verbrennung f; (on skin) Brandwunde f; (on material) Brandstelle f ● v (pt/pp burnt or burned) ● vt verbrennen ● vi brennen; ⟨food:⟩ anbrennen. **~ down** vt/i niederbrennen

burnish /'bɜːnɪʃ/ vt polieren

burnt /bɜːnt/ see burn

burp /bɜːp/ vi (fam) aufstoßen

burrow /'bʌrəʊ/ n Bau m ● vi wühlen

bursar /'bɜːsə(r)/ n Rechnungsführer m. **~y** n Stipendium nt

burst /bɜːst/ n Bruch m; (surge) Ausbruch m ● v (pt/pp burst) ● vt platzen machen ● vi platzen; ⟨bud:⟩ aufgehen; **~ into tears** in Tränen ausbrechen

bury /'berɪ/ vt (pt/pp -ied) begraben; (hide) vergraben

bus /bʌs/ n [Auto]bus m ● vt/i (pt/pp bussed) mit dem Bus fahren

bush /bʊʃ/ n Strauch m; (land) Busch m. **~y** a (-ier, -iest) buschig

busily /'bɪzɪlɪ/ adv eifrig

business /'bɪznɪs/ n Angelegenheit f; (Comm) Geschäft nt; **on ~** geschäftlich; **he has no ~ to** er hat kein Recht, zu; **mind one's own ~** sich um seine eigenen Angelegenheiten kümmern; **that's none of your ~** das geht Sie nichts an. **~-like** a geschäftsmäßig. **~man** n Geschäftsmann m

busker /'bʌskə(r)/ n Straßenmusikant m

'bus-stop n Bushaltestelle f

bust¹ /bʌst/ n Büste f. **~ size** n Oberweite f

bust² a (fam) kaputt; **go ~** pleite machen ● v (pt/pp busted or bust) (fam) ● vt kaputtmachen ● vi kaputtgehen

bustl|e /'bʌsl/ n Betrieb m, Getriebe nt ● vi **~e about** geschäftig hin und her laufen. **~ing** a belebt

'bust-up n (fam) Streit m, Krach m

busy /'bɪzɪ/ a (-ier, -iest) beschäftigt; ⟨day⟩ voll; ⟨street⟩ belebt; (with traffic) stark befahren; (Amer Teleph) besetzt; **be ~** zu tun haben ● vt **~ oneself** sich beschäftigen (with mit)

'busybody n Wichtigtuer(in) m(f)

but /bʌt, unbetont bət/ conj aber; (after negative) sondern ● prep außer (+ dat); **~ for** (without) ohne (+ acc); **the last ~ one** der/die/das vorletzte; **the next ~ one** der/die/das übernächste ● adv nur

butcher /'bʊtʃə(r)/ n Fleischer m, Metzger m; **~'s [shop]** Fleischerei f, Metzgerei f ● vt [ab]schlachten

butler /'bʌtlə(r)/ n Butler m

butt /bʌt/ n (of gun) [Gewehr]kolben m; (fig: target) Zielscheibe f; ⟨of cigarette⟩ Stummel m; (for water) Regentonne f ● vt mit dem Kopf stoßen ● vi **~ in** unterbrechen

butter /'bʌtə(r)/ n Butter f ● vt mit Butter bestreichen. **~ up** vt (fam) schmeicheln (+ dat)

butter: **~cup** a Butterblume f, Hahnenfuß m. **~fly** n Schmetterling m

buttocks /'bʌtəks/ npl Gesäß nt

button /'bʌtn/ n Knopf m ● vt **~[up]** zuknöpfen ● vi geknöpft werden. **~hole** n Knopfloch m

buttress /'bʌtrɪs/ n Strebepfeiler m; **flying ~** Strebebogen m

buxom /'bʌksəm/ a drall

buy /baɪ/ n Kauf m ● vt (pt/pp
bought) kaufen. ~er n Käufer(in)
m(f)

buzz /bʌz/ n Summen nt ● vi summen. ~ **off** vi (fam) abhauen

buzzard /'bʌzəd/ n Bussard m

buzzer /'bʌzə(r)/ n Summer m

by /baɪ/ prep (close to) bei (+ dat);
(next to) neben (+ dat/acc); (past) an
(+ dat) ... vorbei; (to the extent of)
um (+ acc); (at the latest) bis; (by
means of) durch; by Mozart/Dickens
von Mozart/Dickens; ~ oneself allein; ~ the sea am Meer; ~ car/bus
mit dem Auto/Bus; ~ sea mit dem
Schiff; ~ day/night bei Tag/Nacht;
~ the hour pro Stunde; ~ the metre
meterweise; six metres ~ four sechs
mal vier Meter; win ~ a length mit
einer Länge Vorsprung gewinnen;
miss the train ~ a minute den Zug
um eine Minute verpassen ● adv ~
and ~ mit der Zeit; ~ and large im
großen und ganzen; put ~ beiseite
legen; go/pass ~ vorbeigehen

bye /baɪ/ int (fam) tschüs

by: ~-election n Nachwahl f. ~gone
a vergangen. ~-law n Verordnung f.
~pass n Umgehungsstraße f; (Med)
Bypass m ● vt umfahren. ~-pro-
duct n Nebenprodukt m. ~-road n
Nebenstraße f. ~stander n Zu-
schauer(in) m(f)

Byzantine /bɪ'zæntaɪn/ a
byzantinisch

C

cab /kæb/ n Taxi nt; (of lorry, train)
Führerhaus nt

cabaret /'kæbəreɪ/ n Kabarett nt

cabbage /'kæbɪdʒ/ n Kohl m

cabin /'kæbɪn/ n Kabine f; (hut) Hütte
f

cabinet /'kæbɪnɪt/ n Schrank m; [dis-
play] ~ Vitrine f; (TV, Radio) Gehäuse nt; **C**~ (Pol) Kabinett nt. ~-
maker n Möbeltischler m

cable /'keɪbl/ n Kabel nt; (rope) Tau
nt. ~ 'railway n Seilbahn f. ~ 'television n Kabelfernsehen nt

cache /kæʃ/ n Versteck nt; ~ of arms
Waffenlager nt

cackle /'kækl/ vi gackern

cactus /'kæktəs/ n (pl -ti /-taɪ/ or
-tuses) Kaktus m

caddie /'kædɪ/ n Caddie m

caddy /'kædɪ/ n [tea-]~ Teedose f

cadet /kə'det/ n Kadett m

cadge /kædʒ/ vt/i (fam) schnorren

Caesarean /sɪ'zeərɪən/ a & n ~ [sec-
tion] Kaiserschnitt m

café /'kæfeɪ/ n Café nt

cafeteria /kæfə'tɪərɪə/ n Selbstbedie-
nungsrestaurant nt

caffeine /'kæfi:n/ n Koffein nt

cage /keɪdʒ/ n Käfig m

cagey /'keɪdʒɪ/ a (fam) be ~ mit der
Sprache nicht herauswollen

cajole /kə'dʒəʊl/ vt gut zureden
(+ dat)

cake /keɪk/ n Kuchen m; (of soap)
Stück nt. ~d a verkrustet (with mit)

calamity /kə'læmətɪ/ n Katastrophe f

calcium /'kælsɪəm/ n Kalzium nt

calculat|e /'kælkjʊleɪt/ vt berechnen;
(estimate) kalkulieren. ~ing a (fig)
berechnend. ~ion /-'leɪʃn/ n Rechnung f, Kalkulation f. ~or n
Rechner m

calendar /'kælɪndə(r)/ n Kalender m

calf[1] /kɑ:f/ n (pl calves) Kalb nt

calf[2] n (pl calves) (Anat) Wade f

calibre /'kælɪbə(r)/ n Kaliber nt

calico /'kælɪkəʊ/ n Kattun m

call /kɔ:l/ n Ruf m; (Teleph) Anruf m;
(visit) Besuch m; be on ~ ⟨doctor:⟩
Bereitschaftsdienst haben ● vt rufen; (Teleph) anrufen; (wake)
wecken; (summon) ausrufen ⟨strike⟩; (name)
nennen; be ~ed heißen ● vi rufen;
~ [in or round] vorbeikommen. ~
back vt zurückrufen ● vi noch einmal vorbeikommen. ~ for vt rufen
nach; (demand) verlangen; (fetch)
abholen. ~ off vt zurückrufen
⟨dog⟩; (cancel) absagen. ~ on vt
bitten (for um); (appeal to) appellier-
en an (+ acc); (visit) besuchen. ~
out vt rufen; aufrufen ⟨names⟩ ● vi
rufen. ~ up vt (Mil) einberufen;
(Teleph) anrufen

call: ~-box n Telefonzelle f. ~er n
Besucher m; (Teleph) Anrufer m.
~ing n Berufung f

callous /'kæləs/ a gefühllos

'call-up n (Mil) Einberufung f

calm /kɑ:m/ a (-er, -est), -ly adv ruhig
● n Ruhe f ● vt ~ [down] beruhigen
● vi ~ down sich beruhigen. ~ness
n Ruhe f; (of sea) Stille f

calorie /'kælərɪ/ n Kalorie f

calves /kɑ:vz/ npl see calf[1] & [2]

camber /'kæmbə(r)/ n Wölbung f

came /keɪm/ see come

camel /'kæml/ n Kamel nt

camera /'kæmərə/ n Kamera f. ~-man n Kameramann m

camouflage /'kæməflɑːʒ/ n Tarnung f ● vt tarnen

camp /kæmp/ n Lager nt ● vi campen; (Mil) kampieren

campaign /kæm'peɪn/ n Feldzug m; (Comm, Pol) Kampagne f ● vi kämpfen; (Pol) im Wahlkampf arbeiten

camp: ~-bed n Feldbett nt. ~er n Camper m; (Auto) Wohnmobil nt. ~ing n Camping nt. ~site n Campingplatz m

campus /'kæmpəs/ n (pl -puses) (Univ) Campus m

can¹ /kæn/ n (for petrol) Kanister m; (tin) Dose f, Büchse f; a ~ of beer eine Dose Bier ● vt in Dosen od Büchsen konservieren

can² /kæn, unbetont kən/ v aux (pres can; pt could) können; **I cannot/ can't go** ich kann nicht gehen; **he could not go** er konnte nicht gehen; **if I could go** wenn ich gehen könnte

Canad|a /'kænədə/ n Kanada nt. ~ian /kə'neɪdɪən/ a kanadisch ● n Kanadier(in) m(f)

canal /kə'næl/ n Kanal m

Canaries /kə'neərɪz/ npl Kanarische Inseln pl

canary /kə'neərɪ/ n Kanarienvogel m

cancel /'kænsl/ vt/i (pt/pp cancelled) absagen; entwerten ⟨stamp⟩; (annul) rückgängig machen; (Comm) stornieren; abbestellen ⟨newspaper⟩; be ~led ausfallen. ~lation /-ə'leɪʃn/ n Absage f

cancer /'kænsə(r)/ n, & (Astr) C~ Krebs m. ~ous /-rəs/ a krebsig

candelabra /kændə'lɑːbrə/ n Armleuchter m

candid /'kændɪd/ a, -ly adv offen

candidate /'kændɪdət/ n Kandidat(in) m(f)

candied /'kændɪd/ a kandiert

candle /'kændl/ n Kerze f. ~stick n Kerzenständer m, Leuchter m

candour /'kændə(r)/ n Offenheit f

candy /'kændɪ/ n (Amer) Süßigkeiten pl; **[piece of]** ~ Bonbon m. ~floss /-flɒs/ n Zuckerwatte f

cane /keɪn/ n Rohr nt; (stick) Stock m ● vt mit dem Stock züchtigen

canine /'keɪnaɪn/ a Hunde-. ~ tooth n Eckzahn m

canister /'kænɪstə(r)/ n Blechdose f

cannabis /'kænəbɪs/ n Haschisch nt

canned /kænd/ a Dosen-, Büchsen-; ~ **music** (fam) Musik f aus der Konserve

cannibal /'kænɪbl/ n Kannibale m. ~ism n Kannibalismus m

cannon /'kænən/ n inv Kanone f. ~-ball n Kanonenkugel f

cannot /'kænɒt/ see can²

canny /'kænɪ/ a schlau

canoe /kə'nuː/ n Paddelboot nt; (Sport) Kanu nt ● vi paddeln; (Sport) Kanu fahren

canon /'kænən/ n Kanon m; (person) Kanonikus m. ~ize /-aɪz/ vt kanonisieren

'can-opener n Dosenöffner m, Büchsenöffner m

canopy /'kænəpɪ/ n Baldachin m

cant /kænt/ n Heuchelei f

can't /kɑːnt/ = cannot. See can²

cantankerous /kæn'tæŋkərəs/ a zänkisch

canteen /kæn'tiːn/ n Kantine f; ~ **of cutlery** Besteckkasten m

canter /'kæntə(r)/ n Kanter m ● vi kantern

canvas /'kænvəs/ n Segeltuch nt; (Art) Leinwand f; (painting) Gemälde nt

canvass /'kænvəs/ vi um Stimmen werben

canyon /'kænjən/ n Cañon m

cap /kæp/ n Kappe f, Mütze f; (nurse's) Haube f; (top, lid) Verschluß m ● vt (pt/pp capped) (fig) übertreffen

capability /keɪpə'bɪlətɪ/ n Fähigkeit f

capable /'keɪpəbl/ a, -bly adv fähig; be ~ **of doing sth** fähig sein, etw zu tun

capacity /kə'pæsətɪ/ n Fassungsvermögen nt; (ability) Fähigkeit f; in my ~ **as** in meiner Eigenschaft als

cape¹ /keɪp/ n (cloak) Cape nt

cape² n (Geog) Kap nt

caper¹ /'keɪpə(r)/ vi herumspringen

caper² n (Culin) Kaper f

capital /'kæpɪtl/ a ⟨letter⟩ groß ● n (town) Hauptstadt f; (money) Kapital nt; (letter) Großbuchstabe m

capital|ism /'kæpɪtəlɪzm/ n Kapitalismus m. ~ist /-ɪst/ a kapitalistisch ● n Kapitalist m. ~ize /-aɪz/ vi ~ize **on** (fig) Kapital schlagen aus. ~ **letter** n Großbuchstabe m. ~ 'punishment n Todesstrafe f

capitulat|e /kə'pɪtjʊleɪt/ vi kapitulieren. ~ion /-'leɪʃn/ n Kapitulation f

capricious /kə'prɪʃəs/ a launisch

Capricorn /'kæprɪkɔːn/ n (Astr) Steinbock m

capsize /kæp'saɪz/ *vi* kentern • *vt* zum Kentern bringen

capsule /'kæpsjʊl/ *n* Kapsel *f*

captain /'kæptɪn/ *n* Kapitän *m*; (*Mil*) Hauptmann *m* • *vt* anführen ⟨*team*⟩

caption /'kæpʃn/ *n* Überschrift *f*; (*of illustration*) Bildtext *m*

captivate /'kæptɪveɪt/ *vt* bezaubern

captiv|e /'kæptɪv/ *a* **hold/take ∼e** gefangenhalten/-nehmen • *n* Gefangene(r) *m/f.* ∼**ity** /-'tɪvətɪ/ *n* Gefangenschaft *f*

capture /'kæptʃə(r)/ *n* Gefangennahme *f* • *vt* gefangennehmen; [ein]fangen ⟨*animal*⟩; (*Mil*) einnehmen ⟨*town*⟩

car /kɑː(r)/ *n* Auto *nt*, Wagen *m*; **by ∼** mit dem Auto *od* Wagen

carafe /kə'ræf/ *n* Karaffe *f*

caramel /'kærəmel/ *n* Karamel *m*

carat /'kærət/ *n* Karat *nt*

caravan /'kærəvæn/ *n* Wohnwagen *m*; (*procession*) Karawane *f*

carbohydrate /kɑːbə'haɪdreɪt/ *n* Kohlenhydrat *nt*

carbon /'kɑːbən/ *n* Kohlenstoff *m*; (*paper*) Kohlepapier *nt*; (*copy*) Durchschlag *m*

carbon: ∼ **copy** *n* Durchschlag *m*. ∼ **di'oxide** *n* Kohlendioxyd *nt*; (*in drink*) Kohlensäure *f*. ∼ **paper** *n* Kohlepapier *nt*

carburettor /kɑːbjʊ'retə(r)/ *n* Vergaser *m*

carcass /'kɑːkəs/ *n* Kadaver *m*

card /kɑːd/ *n* Karte *f*

'cardboard *n* Pappe *f*, Karton *m*. ∼ **'box** *n* Pappschachtel *f*; (*large*) [Papp]karton *m*

'card-game *n* Kartenspiel *nt*

cardiac /'kɑːdɪæk/ *a* Herz-

cardigan /'kɑːdɪgən/ *n* Strickjacke *f*

cardinal /'kɑːdɪnl/ *a* Kardinal-; ∼ **number** Kardinalzahl *f* • *n* (*Relig*) Kardinal *m*

card 'index *n* Kartei *f*

care /keə(r)/ *n* Sorgfalt *f*; (*caution*) Vorsicht *f*; (*protection*) Obhut *f*; (*looking after*) Pflege *f*; (*worry*) Sorge *f*; ∼ **of** (*on letter abbr* **c/o**) bei; **take ∼** vorsichtig sein; **take into ∼** in Pflege nehmen; **take ∼ of** sich kümmern um • *vi* ∼ **about** sich kümmern um; ∼ **for** (*like*) mögen; (*look after*) betreuen; **I don't ∼** das ist mir gleich

career /kə'rɪə(r)/ *n* Laufbahn *f*; (*profession*) Beruf *m* • *vi* rasen

care: ∼**free** *a* sorglos. ∼**ful** *a*, **-ly** *adv* sorgfältig; (*cautious*) vorsichtig. ∼**less** *a*, **-ly** *adv* nachlässig. ∼**lessness** *n* Nachlässigkeit *f*

caress /kə'res/ *n* Liebkosung *f* • *vt* liebkosen

'caretaker *n* Hausmeister *m*

'car ferry *n* Autofähre *f*

cargo /'kɑːgəʊ/ *n* (*pl* **-es**) Ladung *f*

Caribbean /kærɪ'biːən/ *n* **the ∼** die Karibik

caricature /'kærɪkətjʊə(r)/ *n* Karikatur *f* • *vt* karikieren

caring /'keərɪŋ/ *a* ⟨*parent*⟩ liebevoll; ⟨*profession, attitude*⟩ sozial

carnage /'kɑːnɪdʒ/ *n* Gemetzel *nt*

carnal /'kɑːnl/ *a* fleischlich

carnation /kɑː'neɪʃn/ *n* Nelke *f*

carnival /'kɑːnɪvl/ *n* Karneval *m*

carnivorous /kɑː'nɪvərəs/ *a* fleischfressend

carol /'kærəl/ *n* **[Christmas]** ∼ Weihnachtslied *nt*

carp[1] /kɑːp/ *n inv* Karpfen *m*

carp[2] *vi* nörgeln; ∼ **at** herumnörgeln an (+ *dat*)

'car park *n* Parkplatz *m*; (*multistorey*) Parkhaus *nt*; (*underground*) Tiefgarage *f*

carpent|er /'kɑːpɪntə(r)/ *n* Zimmermann *m*; (*joiner*) Tischler *m*. ∼**ry** *n* Tischlerei *f*

carpet /'kɑːpɪt/ *n* Teppich *m* • *vt* mit Teppich auslegen

carriage /'kærɪdʒ/ *n* Kutsche *f*; (*Rail*) Wagen *m*; (*of goods*) Beförderung *f*; (*cost*) Frachtkosten *pl*; (*bearing*) Haltung *f*. ∼**way** *n* Fahrbahn *f*

carrier /'kærɪə(r)/ *n* Träger(in) *m(f)*; (*Comm*) Spediteur *m*; ∼**[-bag]** *n* Tragetasche *f*

carrot /'kærət/ *n* Möhre *f*, Karotte *f*

carry /'kærɪ/ *vt/i* (*pt/pp* **-ied**) tragen; **be carried away** (*fam*) hingerissen sein. ∼ **off** *vt* wegtragen; gewinnen ⟨*prize*⟩. ∼ **on** *vi* weitermachen; ∼ **on at** (*fam*) herumnörgeln an (+ *dat*); ∼ **on with** (*fam*) eine Affäre haben mit • *vt* führen; (*continue*) fortführen. ∼ **out** *vt* hinaus-/heraustragen; (*perform*) ausführen

'carry-cot *n* Babytragetasche *f*

cart /kɑːt/ *n* Karren *m*; **put the ∼ before the horse** das Pferd beim Schwanz aufzäumen • *vt* karren; (*fam: carry*) schleppen

cartilage /'kɑːtɪlɪdʒ/ *n* (*Anat*) Knorpel *m*

carton /'kɑːtn/ n [Papp]karton m; (for drink) Tüte f; (of cream, yoghurt) Becher m

cartoon /kɑː'tuːn/ n Karikatur f; (joke) Witzzeichnung f; (strip) Comic Strips pl; (film) Zeichentrickfilm m; (Art) Karton m. **~ist** n Karikaturist m

cartridge /'kɑːtrɪdʒ/ n Patrone f; (for film, typewriter ribbon) Kassette f; (of record player) Tonabnehmer m

carve /kɑːv/ vt schnitzen; (in stone) hauen; (Culin) aufschneiden

carving /'kɑːvɪŋ/ n Schnitzerei f. **~-knife** n Tranchiermesser nt

'car wash n Autowäsche f; (place) Autowaschanlage f

case¹ /keɪs/ n Fall m; **in any ~** auf jeden Fall; **just in ~** für alle Fälle; **in ~ he comes** falls er kommt

case² n Kasten m; (crate) Kiste f; (for spectacles) Etui nt; (suitcase) Koffer m; (for display) Vitrine f

cash /kæʃ/ n Bargeld nt; **pay [in]~** [in] bar bezahlen; **~ on delivery** per Nachnahme ● vt einlösen ⟨cheque⟩. **~ desk** n Kasse f

cashier /kæ'ʃɪə(r)/ n Kassierer(in) m(f)

'cash register n Registrierkasse f

casino /kə'siːnəʊ/ n Kasino nt

cask /kɑːsk/ n Faß nt

casket /'kɑːskɪt/ n Kasten m; (Amer: coffin) Sarg m

casserole /'kæsərəʊl/ n Schmortopf m; (stew) Eintopf m

cassette /kə'set/ n Kassette f. **~ recorder** n Kassettenrecorder m

cast /kɑːst/ n (throw) Wurf m; (mould) Form f; (model) Abguß m; (Theat) Besetzung f; **[plaster] ~** (Med) Gipsverband m ● vt (pt/pp cast) (throw) werfen; (shed) abwerfen; abgeben ⟨vote⟩; gießen ⟨metal⟩; (Theat) besetzen ⟨role⟩; **~ a glance at** einen Blick werfen auf (+ acc). **~ off** vi (Naut) ablegen ● vt (Knitting) abketten. **~ on** vt (Knitting) anschlagen

castanets /kæstə'nets/ npl Kastagnetten pl

castaway /'kɑːstəweɪ/ n Schiffbrüchige(r) m/f

caste /kɑːst/ n Kaste f

cast 'iron n Gußeisen nt

cast-'iron a gußeisern

castle /'kɑːsl/ n Schloß nt; (fortified) Burg f; (Chess) Turm m

'cast-offs npl abgelegte Kleidung f

castor /'kɑːstə(r)/ n (wheel) [Lauf] rolle f

'castor sugar n Streuzucker m

castrat|e /kæ'streɪt/ vt kastrieren. **~ion** /-eɪʃn/ n Kastration f

casual /'kæʒʊəl/ a, **-ly** adv (chance) zufällig; (offhand) lässig; (informal) zwanglos; (not permanent) Gelegenheits-; **~ wear** Freizeitbekleidung f

casualty /'kæʒʊəltɪ/ n [Todes]opfer nt; (injured person) Verletzte(r) m/f; **~[department]** Unfallstation f

cat /kæt/ n Katze f

catalogue /'kætəlɒg/ n Katalog m ● vt katalogisieren

catalyst /'kætəlɪst/ n (Chem & fig) Katalysator m

catalytic /kætə'lɪtɪk/ a **~ converter** (Auto) Katalysator m

catapult /'kætəpʌlt/ n Katapult nt ● vt katapultieren

cataract /'kætərækt/ n (Med) grauer Star m

catarrh /kə'tɑː(r)/ n Katarrh m

catastroph|e /kə'tæstrəfɪ/ n Katastrophe f. **~ic** /kætə'strɒfɪk/ a katastrophal

catch /kætʃ/ n (of fish) Fang m; (fastener) Verschluß m; (on door) Klinke f; (fam: snag) Haken m (fam) ● v (pt/pp caught) ● vt fangen; (be in time for) erreichen; (travel by) fahren mit; bekommen ⟨illness⟩; **~ a cold** sich erkälten; **~ sight of** erblicken; **~ s.o. stealing** jdn beim Stehlen erwischen; **~ one's finger in the door** sich (dat) den Finger in der Tür [ein]klemmen ● vi (burn) anbrennen; (get stuck) klemmen. **~ on** vi (fam) (understand) kapieren; (become popular) sich durchsetzen. **~ up** vt einholen ● vi aufholen; **~ up with** einholen ⟨s.o.⟩; nachholen ⟨work⟩

catching /'kætʃɪŋ/ a ansteckend

catch: **~-phrase** n, **~word** n Schlagwort nt

catchy /'kætʃɪ/ a (-ier, -iest) einprägsam

catechism /'kætɪkɪzm/ n Katechismus m

categor|ical /kætɪ'gɒrɪkl/ a, **-ly** adv kategorisch. **~y** /'kætɪgərɪ/ n Kategorie f

cater /'keɪtə(r)/ vi **~ for** beköstigen; ⟨firm:⟩ das Essen liefern für ⟨party⟩; (fig) eingestellt sein auf (+ acc). **~ing** n (trade) Gaststättengewerbe nt

caterpillar /'kætəpɪlə(r)/ n Raupe f

cathedral /kə'θi:drl/ n Dom m, Kathedrale f

Catholic /'kæθəlɪk/ a katholisch ● n Katholik(in) m(f). **C~ism** /kə'θɛlɪsɪzm/ n Katholizismus m

catkin /'kætkɪn/ n (Bot) Kätzchen nt

cattle /'kætl/ npl Vieh nt

catty /'kætɪ/ a (-ier, -iest) boshaft

caught /kɔ:t/ see **catch**

cauldron /'kɔ:ldrən/ n [großer] Kessel m

cauliflower /'kɛlɪ-/ n Blumenkohl m

cause /kɔ:z/ n Ursache f; (reason) Grund m; **good ~** gute Sache f ● vt verursachen; **~ s.o. to do sth** jdn veranlassen, etw zu tun

'**causeway** n [Insel]damm m

caustic /'kɔ:stɪk/ a ätzend; (fig) beißend

cauterize /'kɔ:təraɪz/ vt kauterisieren

caution /'kɔ:ʃn/ n Vorsicht f; (warning) Verwarnung f ● vt (Jur) verwarnen

cautious /'kɔ:ʃəs/ a, **-ly** adv vorsichtig

cavalry /'kævəlrɪ/ n Kavallerie f

cave /keɪv/ n Höhle f ● vi **~ in** einstürzen

cavern /'kævən/ n Höhle f

caviare /'kævɪɑ:(r)/ n Kaviar m

caving /'keɪvɪŋ/ n Höhlenforschung f

cavity /'kævətɪ/ n Hohlraum m; (in tooth) Loch nt

cavort /kə'vɔ:t/ vi tollen

cease /si:s/ n **without ~** unaufhörlich ● vt/i aufhören. **~-fire** n Waffenruhe f. **~less** a, **-ly** adv unaufhörlich

cedar /'si:də(r)/ n Zeder f

cede /si:d/ vt abtreten (**to** an + acc)

ceiling /'si:lɪŋ/ n [Zimmer]decke f; (fig) oberste Grenze f

celebrat|e /'selɪbreɪt/ vt/i feiern. **~ed** a berühmt (**for** wegen). **~ion** /-'breɪʃn/ n Feier f

celebrity /sɪ'lebrətɪ/ n Berühmtheit f

celery /'selərɪ/ n [Stangen]sellerie m & f

celiba|cy /'selɪbəsɪ/ n Zölibat nt. **~te** a **be ~te** im Zölibat leben

cell /sel/ n Zelle f

cellar /'selə(r)/ n Keller m

cellist /'tʃelɪst/ n Cellist(in) m(f)

cello /'tʃeləu/ n Cello nt

Celsius /'selsɪəs/ a Celsius

Celt /kelt/ n Kelte m/ Keltin f. **~ic** a keltisch

cement /sɪ'ment/ n Zement m; (adhesive) Kitt m ● vt zementieren; (stick) kitten

cemetery /'semətrɪ/ n Friedhof m

censor /'sensə(r)/ n Zensor m ● vt zensieren. **~ship** n Zensur f

censure /'senʃə(r)/ n Tadel m ● vt tadeln

census /'sensəs/ n Volkszählung f

cent /sent/ n (coin) Cent m

centenary /sen'ti:nərɪ/ n, (Amer) **centennial** /sen'tenɪəl/ n Hundertjahrfeier f

center /'sentə(r)/ n (Amer) = **centre**

centi|grade /'sentɪ-/ a Celsius-; 5° **~** 5° Celsius. **~metre** n Zentimeter m & nt. **~pede** /-pi:d/ n Tausendfüßler m

central /'sentrəl/ a, **-ly** adv zentral. **~ 'heating** n Zentralheizung f. **~ize** vt zentralisieren. **~ reser'vation** n (Auto) Mittelstreifen m

centre /'sentə(r)/ n Zentrum nt; (middle) Mitte f ● v (pt/pp **centred**) ● vt zentrieren; **~ on** (fig) sich drehen um. **~-'forward** n Mittelstürmer m

centrifugal /sentrɪ'fju:gl/ a **~ force** Fliehkraft f

century /'sentʃərɪ/ n Jahrhundert nt

ceramic /sɪ'ræmɪk/ a Keramik-. **~s** n Keramik f

cereal /'sɪərɪəl/ n Getreide nt; (breakfast food) Frühstücksflocken pl

cerebral /'serɪbrl/ a Gehirn-

ceremon|ial /serɪ'məunɪəl/ a, **-ly** adv zeremoniell, feierlich ● n Zeremoniell nt. **~ious** /-ɪəs/ a, **-ly** adv formell

ceremony /'serɪmənɪ/ n Zeremonie f, Feier f; **without ~** ohne weitere Umstände

certain /'sɜ:tn/ a sicher; (not named) gewiß; **for ~** mit Bestimmtheit; **make ~** (check) sich vergewissern (**that** daß); (ensure) dafür sorgen (**that** daß); **he is ~ to win** er wird ganz bestimmt siegen. **~ly** adv bestimmt, sicher; **~ly not!** auf keinen Fall! **~ty** n Sicherheit f, Gewißheit f; **it's a ~ty** es ist sicher

certificate /sə'tɪfɪkət/ n Bescheinigung f; (Jur) Urkunde f; (Sch) Zeugnis nt

certify /'sɜ:tɪfaɪ/ vt (pt/pp **-ied**) bescheinigen; (declare insane) für geisteskrank erklären

cessation /se'seɪʃn/ n Ende nt

cesspool /'sespu:l/ n Senkgrube f

cf abbr (compare) vgl

chafe /tʃeɪf/ vt wund reiben

chaff /tʃɑːf/ n Spreu f
chaffinch /'tʃæfɪntʃ/ n Buchfink m
chain /tʃeɪn/ n Kette f ● vt ketten (**to an** + acc). ~ **up** vt anketten
chain: ~ **re'action** n Kettenreaktion f. ~**smoker** n Kettenraucher m. ~ **store** n Kettenladen m
chair /tʃeə(r)/ n Stuhl m; (Univ) Lehrstuhl m ● vt den Vorsitz führen bei. ~**-lift** n Sessellift m. ~**man** n Vorsitzende(r) m/f
chalet /'ʃæleɪ/ n Chalet nt
chalice /'tʃælɪs/ n (Relig) Kelch m
chalk /tʃɔːk/ n Kreide f. ~**y** a kreidig
challeng|e /'tʃælɪndʒ/ n Herausforderung f; (Mil) Anruf m ● vt herausfordern; (Mil) anrufen; (fig) anfechten ⟨statement⟩. ~**er** n Herausforderer m. ~**ing** a herausfordernd; (demanding) anspruchsvoll
chamber /'tʃeɪmbə(r)/ n Kammer f; ~**s** pl (Jur) [Anwalts]büro nt; **C~ of Commerce** Handelskammer f
chamber: ~**maid** n Zimmermädchen nt. ~ **music** n Kammermusik f. ~**-pot** n Nachttopf m
chamois¹ /'ʃæmwɑː/ n inv (animal) Gemse f
chamois² /'ʃæmɪ/ n ~**[-leather]** Ledertuch nt
champagne /ʃæm'peɪn/ n Champagner m
champion /'tʃæmpɪən/ n (Sport) Meister(in) m(f); (of cause) Verfechter m ● vt sich einsetzen für. ~**ship** n (Sport) Meisterschaft f
chance /tʃɑːns/ n Zufall m; (prospect) Chancen pl; (likelihood) Aussicht f; (opportunity) Gelegenheit f; **by** ~ zufällig; **take a** ~ ein Risiko eingehen; **give s.o. a** ~ jdm eine Chance geben ● attrib zufällig ● vt ~ **it** es riskieren
chancellor /'tʃɑːnsələ(r)/ n Kanzler m; (Univ) Rektor m; **C~ of the Exchequer** Schatzkanzler m
chancy /'tʃɑːnsɪ/ a riskant
chandelier /ʃændə'lɪə(r)/ n Kronleuchter m
change /tʃeɪndʒ/ n Veränderung f; (alteration) Änderung f; (money) Wechselgeld nt; **for a** ~ zur Abwechslung ● vt wechseln; (alter) ändern; (exchange) umtauschen (**for** gegen); (transform) verwandeln; **trocken legen** ⟨baby⟩; ~ **one's clothes** sich umziehen; ~ **trains** umsteigen ● vi sich verändern; (~

clothes) sich umziehen; (~ trains) umsteigen; **all** ~! alles aussteigen!
changeable /'tʃeɪndʒəbl/ a wechselhaft
'changing-room n Umkleideraum m
channel /'tʃænl/ n Rinne f; (Radio, TV) Kanal m; (fig) Weg m; **the [English] C~** der Ärmelkanal; **the C~ Islands** die Kanalinseln ● vt (pt/pp **channelled**) leiten; (fig) lenken
chant /tʃɑːnt/ n liturgischer Gesang m ● vt singen; ⟨demonstrators:⟩ skandieren
chao|s /'keɪɒs/ n Chaos nt. ~**tic** /-'ɒtɪk/ a chaotisch
chap /tʃæp/ n (fam) Kerl m
chapel /'tʃæpl/ n Kapelle f
chaperon /'ʃæpərəʊn/ n Anstandsdame f ● vt begleiten
chaplain /'tʃæplɪn/ n Geistliche(r) m
chapped /tʃæpt/ a ⟨skin⟩ aufgesprungen
chapter /'tʃæptə(r)/ n Kapitel nt
char¹ /tʃɑː(r)/ n (fam) Putzfrau f
char² vt (pt/pp **charred**) (burn) verkohlen
character /'kærɪktə(r)/ n Charakter m; (in novel, play) Gestalt f; (Typ) Schriftzeichen nt; **out of** ~ uncharakteristisch; **quite a** ~ (fam) ein Original
characteristic /kærɪktə'rɪstɪk/ a, **-ally** adv charakteristisch (**of** für) ● n Merkmal nt
characterize /'kærɪktəraɪz/ vt charakterisieren
charade /ʃə'rɑːd/ n Scharade f
charcoal /'tʃɑː-/ n Holzkohle f
charge /tʃɑːdʒ/ n (price) Gebühr f; (Electr) Ladung f; (attack) Angriff m; (Jur) Anklage f; **free of** ~ kostenlos; **be in** ~ verantwortlich sein (**of** für); **take** ~ die Aufsicht übernehmen (**of** über + acc) ● vt berechnen ⟨fee⟩; (Electr) laden; (attack) angreifen; (Jur) anklagen (**with** gen); ~ **s.o. for sth** jdm etw berechnen ● vi (attack) angreifen
chariot /'tʃærɪət/ n Wagen m
charisma /kə'rɪzmə/ n Charisma nt. ~**tic** /kærɪz'mætɪk/ a charismatisch
charitable /'tʃærɪtəbl/ a wohltätig; (kind) wohlwollend
charity /'tʃærətɪ/ n Nächstenliebe f; (organization) wohltätige Einrichtung f; **for** ~ für Wohltätigkeitszwecke; **live on** ~ von Almosen leben
charlatan /'ʃɑːlətən/ n Scharlatan m

charm /tʃɑːm/ n Reiz m; (of person) Charme f; (object) Amulett nt • vt bezaubern. **~ing** a, **-ly** adv reizend; ⟨person, smile⟩ charmant

chart /tʃɑːt/ n Karte f; (table) Tabelle f

charter /'tʃɑːtə(r)/ n ~ **[flight]** Charterflug m • vt chartern; **~ed accountant** Wirtschaftsprüfer(in) m(f)

charwoman /'tʃɑː-/ n Putzfrau f

chase /tʃeɪs/ n Verfolgungsjagd f • vt jagen, verfolgen. **~ away** or **off** vt wegjagen

chasm /'kæzm/ n Kluft f

chassis /'ʃæsɪ/ n (pl **chassis** /-sɪz/) Chassis nt

chaste /tʃeɪst/ a keusch

chastise /tʃæ'staɪz/ vt züchtigen

chastity /'tʃæstətɪ/ n Keuschheit f

chat /tʃæt/ n Plauderei f; **have a ~ with** plaudern mit • vi (pt/pp **chatted**) plaudern. **~ show** n Talk-Show f

chatter /'tʃætə(r)/ n Geschwätz nt • vi schwatzen; ⟨child:⟩ plappern; ⟨teeth:⟩ klappern. **~box** n (fam) Plappermaul nt

chatty /'tʃætɪ/ a (**-ier**, **-iest**) geschwätzig

chauffeur /'ʃəʊfə(r)/ n Chauffeur m

chauvin|ism /'ʃəʊvɪnɪzm/ n Chauvinismus m. **~ist** n Chauvinist m; **male ~ist** (fam) Chauvi m

cheap /tʃiːp/ a & adv (**-er**, **-est**), **-ly** adv billig. **~en** vt entwürdigen; **~en oneself** sich erniedrigen

cheat /tʃiːt/ n Betrüger(in) m(f); (at games) Mogler m • vt betrügen • vi (at games) mogeln (fam)

check¹ /tʃek/ a (squared) kariert • n Karo nt

check² n Überprüfung f; (inspection) Kontrolle f; (Chess) Schach nt; (Amer: bill) Rechnung f; (Amer: cheque) Scheck m; (Amer: tick) Haken m; **keep a ~ on** kontrollieren • vt [über]prüfen; (inspect) kontrollieren; (restrain) hemmen; (stop) aufhalten • vi **[go and] ~** nachsehen. **~ in** vi sich anmelden; (Aviat) einchecken • vt abfertigen; einchecken. **~ out** vi sich abmelden. **~ up** vi prüfen, kontrollieren; **~ up on** überprüfen

check|ed /tʃekt/ a kariert. **~ers** n (Amer) Damespiel nt

check: **~mate** int schachmatt! **~out** n Kasse f. **~room** n (Amer)

Garderobe f. **~up** n (Med) [Kontroll]untersuchung f

cheek /tʃiːk/ n Backe f; (impudence) Frechheit f. **~y** a, **-ily** adv frech

cheep /tʃiːp/ vi piepen

cheer /tʃɪə(r)/ n Beifallsruf m; **three ~s** ein dreifaches Hoch (**for** auf + acc); **~s!** prost! (goodbye) tschüs! • vt zujubeln (+ dat) • vi jubeln. **~ up** vt aufmuntern; aufheitern • vi munterer werden. **~ful** a, **-ly** adv fröhlich. **~fulness** n Fröhlichkeit f

cheerio /tʃɪərɪ'əʊ/ int (fam) tschüs!

'cheerless a trostlos

cheese /tʃiːz/ n Käse m. **~cake** n Käsekuchen m

cheetah /'tʃiːtə/ n Gepard m

chef /ʃef/ n Koch m

chemical /'kemɪkl/ a, **-ly** adv chemisch • n Chemikalie f

chemist /'kemɪst/ n (pharmacist) Apotheker(in) m(f); (scientist) Chemiker(in) m(f); **~'s [shop]** Drogerie f; (dispensing) Apotheke f. **~ry** n Chemie f

cheque /tʃek/ n Scheck m. **~-book** n Scheckbuch nt. **~ card** n Scheckkarte f

cherish /'tʃerɪʃ/ vt lieben; (fig) hegen

cherry /'tʃerɪ/ n Kirsche f • attrib Kirsch-

cherub /'tʃerəb/ n Engelchen nt

chess /tʃes/ n Schach nt

chess: **~board** n Schachbrett nt. **~man** n Schachfigur f

chest /tʃest/ n Brust f; (box) Truhe f

chestnut /'tʃesnʌt/ n Eßkastanie f, Marone f; (horse-) [Roß]kastanie f

chest of 'drawers n Kommode f

chew /tʃuː/ vt kauen. **~ing-gum** n Kaugummi m

chic /ʃiːk/ a schick

chick /tʃɪk/ n Küken nt

chicken /'tʃɪkɪn/ n Huhn nt • attrib Hühner- • a (fam) feige • vi **~ out** (fam) kneifen. **~pox** n Windpocken pl

chicory /'tʃɪkərɪ/ n Chicorée f; (in coffee) Zichorie f

chief /tʃiːf/ a Haupt- • n Chef m; (of tribe) Häuptling m. **~ly** adv hauptsächlich

chilblain /'tʃɪlbleɪn/ n Frostbeule f

child /tʃaɪld/ n (pl **~ren**) Kind nt

child: **~birth** n Geburt f. **~hood** n Kindheit f. **~ish** a kindisch. **~less** a kinderlos. **~like** a kindlich. **~minder** n Tagesmutter f

children /'tʃɪldrən/ npl see **child**

Chile /'tʃɪlɪ/ n Chile nt

chill /tʃɪl/ n Kälte f; (illness) Erkältung f ● vt kühlen

chilli /'tʃɪlɪ/ n (pl -es) Chili m

chilly /'tʃɪlɪ/ a kühl; **I felt** ~ mich fröstelte [es]

chime /tʃaɪm/ vi läuten; ⟨clock:⟩ schlagen

chimney /'tʃɪmnɪ/ n Schornstein m. ~-**pot** n Schornsteinaufsatz m. ~-**sweep** n Schornsteinfeger m

chimpanzee /tʃɪmpæn'ziː/ n Schimpanse m

chin /tʃɪn/ n Kinn nt

china /'tʃaɪnə/ n Porzellan nt

Chin|a n China nt. ~**ese** /-'niːz/ a chinesisch ● n (Lang) Chinesisch nt; **the** ~**ese** pl die Chinesen. ~**ese 'lantern** n Lampion m

chink¹ /tʃɪnk/ n (slit) Ritze f

chink² n Geklirr nt ● vi klirren; ⟨coins:⟩ klimpern

chip /tʃɪp/ n (fragment) Span m; (in china, paintwork) angeschlagene Stelle f; (Computing, Gambling) Chip m; ~**s** pl (Culin) Pommes frites pl; (Amer: crisps) Chips pl ● vt (pt/pp **chipped**) (damage) anschlagen. ~**ped** a angeschlagen

chiropod|ist /kɪ'rɒpədɪst/ n Fußpfleger(in) m(f). ~**y** n Fußpflege f

chirp /tʃɜːp/ vi zwitschern; ⟨cricket:⟩ zirpen. ~**y** a (fam) munter

chisel /'tʃɪzl/ n Meißel m ● vt/i (pt/pp **chiselled**) meißeln

chit /tʃɪt/ n Zettel m

chival|rous /'ʃɪvlrəs/ a, -**ly** adv ritterlich. ~**ry** n Ritterlichkeit f

chives /tʃaɪvz/ npl Schnittlauch m

chlorine /'klɔːriːn/ n Chlor nt

chloroform /'klɒrəfɔːm/ n Chloroform nt

chocolate /'tʃɒkələt/ n Schokolade f; (sweet) Praline f

choice /tʃɔɪs/ n Wahl f; (variety) Auswahl f ● a auserlesen

choir /'kwaɪə(r)/ n Chor m. ~**boy** n Chorknabe m

choke /tʃəʊk/ n (Auto) Choke m ● vt würgen; (to death) erwürgen ● vi sich verschlucken; ~ **on** [fast] ersticken an (+ dat)

cholera /'kɒlərə/ n Cholera f

cholesterol /kə'lestərəl/ n Cholesterin nt

choose /tʃuːz/ vt/i (pt **chose**, pp **chosen**) wählen; (select) sich (dat) aussuchen; ~ **to do/go** [freiwillig] tun/gehen; **as you** ~ wie Sie wollen

choos[e]y /'tʃuːzɪ/ a (fam) wählerisch

chop /tʃɒp/ n (blow) Hieb m; (Culin) Kotelett nt ● vt (pt/pp **chopped**) hacken. ~ **down** vt abhacken; fällen ⟨tree⟩. ~ **off** vt abhacken

chop|per /'tʃɒpə(r)/ n Beil nt; (fam) Hubschrauber m. ~**py** a kabbelig

'chopsticks npl Eßstäbchen pl

choral /'kɔːrəl/ a Chor-; ~ **society** Gesangverein m

chord /kɔːd/ n (Mus) Akkord m

chore /tʃɔː(r)/ n lästige Pflicht f; **[household]** ~**s** Hausarbeit f

choreography /kɒrɪ'ɒgrəfɪ/ n Choreographie f

chortle /'tʃɔːtl/ vi [vor Lachen] glucksen

chorus /'kɔːrəs/ n Chor m; (of song) Refrain m

chose, chosen /tʃəʊz, 'tʃəʊzn/ see **choose**

Christ /kraɪst/ n Christus m

christen /'krɪsn/ vt taufen. ~**ing** n Taufe f

Christian /'krɪstʃən/ a christlich ● n Christ(in) m(f). ~**ity** /-stɪ'ænətɪ/ n Christentum nt. ~ **name** n Vorname m

Christmas /'krɪsməs/ n Weihnachten nt. ~ **card** n Weihnachtskarte f. ~ **'Day** n erster Weihnachtstag m. ~ **'Eve** n Heiligabend m. ~ **tree** n Weihnachtsbaum m

chrome /krəʊm/ n, **chromium** /'krəʊmɪəm/ n Chrom nt

chromosome /'krəʊməsəʊm/ n Chromosom nt

chronic /'krɒnɪk/ a chronisch

chronicle /'krɒnɪkl/ n Chronik f

chronological /krɒnə'lɒdʒɪkl/ a, -**ly** adv chronologisch

chrysalis /'krɪsəlɪs/ n Puppe f

chrysanthemum /krɪ'sænθəməm/ n Chrysantheme f

chubby /'tʃʌbɪ/ a (-ier, -iest) mollig

chuck /tʃʌk/ vt (fam) schmeißen. ~ **out** vt (fam) rausschmeißen

chuckle /'tʃʌkl/ vi in sich (acc) hineinlachen

chum /tʃʌm/ n Freund(in) m(f)

chunk /tʃʌnk/ n Stück nt

church /tʃɜːtʃ/ n Kirche f. ~**yard** n Friedhof m

churlish /'tʃɜːlɪʃ/ a unhöflich

churn /tʃɜːn/ n Butterfaß nt; (for milk) Milchkanne f ● vt ~ **out** am laufenden Band produzieren

chute /ʃuːt/ n Rutsche f; (for rubbish) Müllschlucker m

CID abbr (**Criminal Investigation Department**) Kripo f

cider /'saɪdə(r)/ n Apfelwein m

cigar /sɪ'gɑː(r)/ n Zigarre f

cigarette /sɪgə'ret/ n Zigarette f

cine-camera /'sɪnɪ-/ n Filmkamera f

cinema /'sɪnɪmə/ n Kino nt

cinnamon /'sɪnəmən/ n Zimt m

cipher /'saɪfə(r)/ n (code) Chiffre f; (numeral) Ziffer f; (fig) Null f

circle /'sɜːkl/ n Kreis m; (Theat) Rang m • vt umkreisen • vi kreisen

circuit /'sɜːkɪt/ n Runde f; (race-track) Rennbahn f; (Electr) Stromkreis m. ~**ous** /sə'kjuːɪtəs/ a ~ **route** Umweg m

circular /'sɜːkjələ(r)/ a kreisförmig • n Rundschreiben nt. ~ '**saw** n Kreissäge f. ~ '**tour** n Rundfahrt f

circulat|e /'sɜːkjəleɪt/ vt in Umlauf setzen • vi zirkulieren. ~**ion** /-'leɪʃn/ n Kreislauf m; (of newspaper) Auflage f

circumcis|e /'sɜːkəmsaɪz/ vt beschneiden. ~**ion** /-'sɪʒn/ n Beschneidung f

circumference /sə'kʌmfərəns/ n Umfang m

circumspect /'sɜːkəmspekt/ a, **-ly** adv umsichtig

circumstance /'sɜːkəmstəns/ n Umstand m; ~**s** pl Umstände pl; (financial) Verhältnisse pl

circus /'sɜːkəs/ n Zirkus m

CIS abbr (**Commonwealth of Independent States**) GUS f

cistern /'sɪstən/ n (tank) Wasserbehälter m; (of WC) Spülkasten m

cite /saɪt/ vt zitieren

citizen /'sɪtɪzn/ n Bürger(in) m(f). ~**ship** n Staatsangehörigkeit f

citrus /'sɪtrəs/ n ~ [**fruit**] Zitrusfrucht f

city /'sɪtɪ/ n [Groß]stadt f

civic /'sɪvɪk/ a Bürger-

civil /'sɪvl/ a bürgerlich; ⟨aviation, defence⟩ zivil; (polite) höflich. ~ **engineering** n Hoch- und Tiefbau m

civilian /sɪ'vɪljən/ a Zivil-; **in** ~ **clothes** in Zivil • n Zivilist m

civility /sɪ'vɪlətɪ/ n Höflichkeit f

civiliz|ation /sɪvəlaɪ'zeɪʃn/ n Zivilisation f. ~**e** /'sɪvəlaɪz/ vt zivilisieren

civil: ~'**servant** n Beamte(r) m/Beamtin f. **C**~ '**Service** n Staatsdienst m

clad /klæd/ a gekleidet (**in** in + acc)

claim /kleɪm/ n Anspruch m; (application) Antrag m; (demand) Forderung f; (assertion) Behauptung f • vt beanspruchen; (apply for) beantragen; (demand) fordern; (assert) behaupten; (collect) abholen. ~**ant** n Antragsteller m

clairvoyant /kleə'vɔɪənt/ n Hellseher(in) m(f)

clam /klæm/ n Klaffmuschel f

clamber /'klæmbə(r)/ vi klettern

clammy /'klæmɪ/ a (**-ier, -iest**) feucht

clamour /'klæmə(r)/ n Geschrei nt • vi ~ **for** schreien nach

clamp /klæmp/ n Klammer f • vt [ein]spannen • vi (fam) ~ **down** durchgreifen; ~ **down on** vorgehen gegen

clan /klæn/ n Clan m

clandestine /klæn'destɪn/ a geheim

clang /klæŋ/ n Schmettern nt. ~**er** n (fam) Schnitzer m

clank /klæŋk/ vi klirren

clap /klæp/ n **give s.o. a** ~ jdm Beifall klatschen; ~ **of thunder** Donnerschlag m • vt/i (pt/pp clapped) Beifall klatschen (+ dat); ~ **one's hands** [in die Hände] klatschen

claret /'klærət/ n roter Bordeaux m

clari|fication /klærɪfɪ'keɪʃn/ n Klärung f. ~**fy** /'klærɪfaɪ/ vt/i (pt/pp -ied) klären

clarinet /klærɪ'net/ n Klarinette f

clarity /'klærətɪ/ n Klarheit f

clash /klæʃ/ n Geklirr nt; (fig) Konflikt m • vi klirren; ⟨colours:⟩ sich beißen; ⟨events:⟩ ungünstig zusammenfallen

clasp /klɑːsp/ n Verschluß m • vt ergreifen; (hold) halten

class /klɑːs/ n Klasse f; **first/second** ~ erster/zweiter Klasse • vt einordnen

classic /'klæsɪk/ a klassisch • n Klassiker m; ~**s** pl (Univ) Altphilologie f. ~**al** a klassisch

classi|fication /klæsɪfɪ'keɪʃn/ n Klassifikation f. ~**fy** /'klæsɪfaɪ/ vt (pt/pp -ied) klassifizieren

'**classroom** n Klassenzimmer nt

classy /'klɑːsɪ/ a (**-ier, -iest**) (fam) schick

clatter /'klætə(r)/ n Geklapper nt • vi klappern

clause /klɔːz/ n Klausel f; (Gram) Satzteil m

claustrophobia /klɔːstrə'fəʊbɪə/ n Klaustrophobie f, (fam) Platzangst m

claw /klɔ:/ n Kralle f; (of bird of prey & Techn) Klaue f; (of crab, lobster) Schere f ● vt kratzen

clay /kleɪ/ n Lehm m; (pottery) Ton m

clean /kli:n/ a (-er, -est) sauber ● adv glatt ● vt saubermachen; putzen ⟨shoes, windows⟩; ~ one's teeth sich (dat) die Zähne putzen; have sth ~ed etw reinigen lassen. ~ up vt saubermachen

cleaner /'kli:nə(r)/ n Putzfrau f; (substance) Reinigungsmittel nt; [dry] ~'s chemische Reinigung f

cleanliness /'klenlɪnɪs/ n Sauberkeit f

cleanse /klenz/ vt reinigen. ~r n Reinigungsmittel nt

clean-shaven a glattrasiert

cleansing cream /'klenz-/ n Reinigungscreme f

clear /klɪə(r)/ a (-er, -est), -ly adv klar; (obvious) eindeutig; (distinct) deutlich; ⟨conscience⟩ rein; (without obstacles) frei; make sth ~ etw klarmachen (to dat) ● adv stand ~ zurücktreten; keep ~ of aus dem Wege gehen (+ dat) ● vt räumen; abräumen ⟨table⟩; (acquit) freisprechen; (authorize) genehmigen; (jump over) überspringen; ~ one's throat sich räuspern ● vi ⟨fog:⟩ sich auflösen. ~ away vt wegräumen. ~ off vi (fam) abhauen. ~ out vt ausräumen ● vi (fam) abhauen. ~ up vt (tidy) aufräumen; (solve) aufklären ● vi ⟨weather:⟩ sich aufklären

clearance /'klɪərəns/ n Räumung f; (authorization) Genehmigung f; (customs) [Zoll]abfertigung f; (Techn) Spielraum m. ~ sale n Räumungsverkauf m

clear|ing /'klɪərɪŋ/ n Lichtung f. ~way n (Auto) Straße f mit Halteverbot

cleavage /'kli:vɪdʒ/ n Spaltung f; (woman's) Dekolleté nt

clef /klef/ n Notenschlüssel m

cleft /kleft/ n Spalte f

clemen|cy /'klemənsɪ/ n Milde f. ~t a mild

clench /klentʃ/ vt ~ one's fist die Faust ballen; ~ one's teeth die Zähne zusammenbeißen

clergy /'klɜ:dʒɪ/ npl Geistlichkeit f. ~man n Geistliche(r) m

cleric /'klerɪk/ n Geistliche(r) m. ~al a Schreib-; (Relig) geistlich

clerk /klɑ:k, Amer: klɜ:k/ n Büroangestellte(r) m/f; (Amer: shop assistant) Verkäufer(in) m(f)

clever /'klevə(r)/ a (-er, -est), -ly adv klug; (skilful) geschickt

cliché /'kli:ʃeɪ/ n Klischee nt

click /klɪk/ vi klicken

client /'klaɪənt/ n Kunde m/Kundin f; (Jur) Klient(in) m(f)

clientele /kli:ɒn'tel/ n Kundschaft f

cliff /klɪf/ n Kliff nt

climat|e /'klaɪmət/ n Klima nt. ~ic /-'mætɪk/ a klimatisch

climax /'klaɪmæks/ n Höhepunkt m

climb /klaɪm/ n Aufstieg m ● vt besteigen ⟨mountain⟩; steigen auf (+ acc) ⟨ladder, tree⟩ ● vi klettern; ⟨rise⟩ steigen; ⟨road:⟩ ansteigen. ~ down vi hinunter-/herunterklettern; (from ladder, tree) heruntersteigen; (fam) nachgeben.

climber /'klaɪmə(r)/ n Bergsteiger m; (plant) Kletterpflanze f

clinch /klɪntʃ/ vt perfekt machen ⟨deal⟩ ● vi (boxing) clinchen

cling /klɪŋ/ vi (pt/pp clung) sich klammern (to an + acc); (stick) haften (to an + dat). ~ film n Sichtfolie f mit Hafteffekt

clinic /'klɪnɪk/ n Klinik f. ~al a, -ly adv klinisch

clink /klɪŋk/ n Klirren nt; (fam: prison) Knast m ● vi klirren

clip¹ /klɪp/ n Klammer f; (jewellery) Klipp m ● vt (pt/pp clipped) anklammern (to an + acc)

clip² (extract) Ausschnitt m ● vt schneiden; knipsen ⟨ticket⟩. ~board n Klemmbrett nt. ~pers npl Schere f. ~ping n (extract) Ausschnitt m

clique /kli:k/ n Clique f

cloak /kləʊk/ n Umhang m. ~room n Garderobe f; (toilet) Toilette f

clobber /'klɒbə(r)/ n (fam) Zeug nt ● vt (fam: hit, defeat) schlagen

clock /klɒk/ n Uhr f; (fam: speedometer) Tacho m ● vi ~ in/out stechen

clock: ~ tower n Uhrenturm m. ~wise a & adv im Uhrzeigersinn. ~work n Uhrwerk nt; (of toy) Aufziehmechanismus m; like ~work (fam) wie am Schnürchen

clod /klɒd/ n Klumpen m

clog /klɒg/ n Holzschuh m ● vt/i (pt/pp clogged) ~ [up] verstopfen

cloister /'klɔɪstə(r)/ n Kreuzgang m

close¹ /kləʊs/ a (-r, -st) nah[e] (to dat); ⟨friend⟩ eng; ⟨weather⟩ schwül;

have a ~ shave (*fam*) mit knapper Not davonkommen ● *adv* nahe; **~ by** nicht weit weg ● *n* (*street*) Sackgasse *f*

close² /kləuz/ *n* Ende *nt*; **draw to a ~** sich dem Ende nähern ● *vt* zumachen, schließen; (*bring to an end*) beenden; sperren ⟨*road*⟩ ● *vi* sich schließen; ⟨*shop*:⟩ schließen, zumachen; (*end*) enden. **~ down** *vt* schließen; stillegen ⟨*factory*⟩ ● *vi* schließen; ⟨*factory*:⟩ stillgelegt werden

closed 'shop /kləuzd-/ *n* ≈ Gewerkschaftszwang *m*

closely /'kləuslɪ/ *adv* eng, nah[e]; (*with attention*) genau

close season /'kləus-/ *n* Schonzeit *f*

closet /'klezɪt/ *n* (*Amer*) Schrank *m*

close-up /'kləus-/ *n* Nahaufnahme *f*

closure /'kləuʒə(r)/ *n* Schließung *f*; (*of factory*) Stillegung *f*; (*of road*) Sperrung *f*

clot /klɒt/ *n* [Blut]gerinnsel *nt*; (*fam: idiot*) Trottel *m* ● *vi* (*pt/pp* **clotted**) ⟨*blood*:⟩ gerinnen

cloth /klɒθ/ *n* Tuch *nt*

clothe /kləuð/ *vt* kleiden

clothes /kləuðz/ *npl* Kleider *pl*. **~brush** *n* Kleiderbürste *f*. **~-line** *n* Wäscheleine *f*

clothing /'kləuðɪŋ/ *n* Kleidung *f*

cloud /klaud/ *n* Wolke *f* ● *vi* ~ **over** sich bewölken. **~burst** *n* Wolkenbruch *m*

cloudy /'klaudɪ/ *a* (**-ier, -iest**) wolkig, bewölkt; ⟨*liquid*⟩ trübe

clout /klaut/ *n* (*fam*) Schlag *m*; (*influence*) Einfluß *m* ● *vt* (*fam*) hauen

clove /kləuv/ *n* [Gewürz]nelke *f*; ~ **of garlic** Knoblauchzehe *f*

clover /'kləuvə(r)/ *n* Klee *m*. ~ **leaf** *n* Kleeblatt *nt*

clown /klaun/ *n* Clown *m* ● *vi* ~ **[about]** herumalbern

club /klʌb/ *n* Klub *m*; (*weapon*) Keule *f*; (*Sport*) Schläger *m*; **~s** *pl* (*Cards*) Kreuz *nt*, Treff *nt* ● *v* (*pt/pp* **clubbed**) ● *vt* knüppeln ● *vi* ~ **together** zusammenlegen

cluck /klʌk/ *vi* glucken

clue /klu:/ *n* Anhaltspunkt *m*; (*in crossword*) Frage *f*; **I haven't a ~** (*fam*) ich habe keine Ahnung

clump /klʌmp/ *n* Gruppe *f*

clumsiness /'klʌmzɪnɪs/ *n* Ungeschicklichkeit *f*

clumsy /'klʌmzɪ/ *a* (**-ier, -iest**), **-ily** *adv* ungeschickt; (*unwieldy*) unförmig

clung /klʌŋ/ *see* **cling**

cluster /'klʌstə(r)/ *n* Gruppe *f*; (*of flowers*) Büschel *nt* ● *vi* sich scharen (**round um**)

clutch /klʌtʃ/ *n* Griff *m*; (*Auto*) Kupplung *f*; **be in s.o.'s ~es** (*fam*) in jds Klauen sein ● *vt* festhalten; (*grab*) ergreifen ● *vi* ~ **at** greifen nach

clutter /'klʌtə(r)/ *n* Kram *m* ● *vt* **~[up]** vollstopfen

c/o *abbr* (**care of**) bei

coach /kəutʃ/ *n* [Reise]bus *m*; (*Rail*) Wagen *m*; (*horse-drawn*) Kutsche *f*; (*Sport*) Trainer *m* ● *vt* Nachhilfestunden geben (+ *dat*); (*Sport*) trainieren

coagulate /kəu'ægjuleɪt/ *vi* gerinnen

coal /kəul/ *n* Kohle *f*

coalition /kəuə'lɪʃn/ *n* Koalition *f*

'coal-mine *n* Kohlenbergwerk *nt*

coarse /kɔ:s/ *a* (**-r, -st**), **-ly** *adv* grob

coast /kəust/ *n* Küste *f* ● *vi* (*free-wheel*) im Freilauf fahren; (*Auto*) im Leerlauf fahren. **~al** *a* Küsten-. **~er** *n* (*mat*) Untersatz *m*

coast: ~guard *n* Küstenwache *f*. **~line** *n* Küste *f*

coat /kəut/ *n* Mantel *m*; (*of animal*) Fell *nt*; (*of paint*) Anstrich *m*; ~ **of arms** Wappen *nt* ● *vt* überziehen; (*with paint*) [an]streichen. **~-hanger** *n* Kleiderbügel *m*. **~-hook** *n* Kleiderhaken *m*

coating /'kəutɪŋ/ *n* Überzug *m*, Schicht *f*; (*of paint*) Anstrich *m*

coax /kəuks/ *vt* gut zureden (+ *dat*)

cob /kɒb/ *n* (*of corn*) [Mais]kolben *m*

cobble¹ /'kɒbl/ *n* Kopfstein *m*; **~s** *pl* Kopfsteinpflaster *nt*

cobble² *vt* flicken. **~r** *m* Schuster *m*

'cobblestones *npl* = **cobbles**

cobweb /'kɒb-/ *n* Spinnengewebe *nt*

cocaine /kə'keɪn/ *n* Kokain *nt*

cock /kɒk/ *n* Hahn *m*; (*any male bird*) Männchen *nt* ● *vt* ⟨*animal*:⟩ ~ **its ears** die Ohren spitzen; ~ **the gun** den Hahn spannen. **~-and-'bull story** *n* (*fam*) Lügengeschichte *f*

cockerel /'kɒkərəl/ *n* [junger] Hahn *m*

cock-'eyed *a* (*fam*) schief; (*absurd*) verrückt

cockle /'kɒkl/ *n* Herzmuschel *f*

cockney /'kɒknɪ/ *n* (*dialect*) Cockney *nt*; (*person*) Cockney *m*

cock: ~pit *n* (*Aviat*) Cockpit *nt*. **~roach** /-rəutʃ/ *n* Küchenschabe *f*.

∼**tail** n Cocktail m. ∼**-up** n (sl)
make a ∼**-up** Mist bauen (**of** bei)

cocky /'kɒkɪ/ a (**-ier, -iest**) (fam)
eingebildet

cocoa /'kəʊkəʊ/ n Kakao m

coconut /'kəʊkənʌt/ n Kokosnuß f

cocoon /kə'ku:n/ n Kokon m

cod /kɒd/ n inv Kabeljau m

COD abbr (**cash on delivery**) per
Nachnahme

coddle /'kɒdl/ vt verhätscheln

code /kəʊd/ n Kode m; (Computing)
Code m; (set of rules) Kodex m. ∼**d** a
verschlüsselt

coedu'cational /kəʊ-/ a gemischt. ∼
school n Koedukationsschule f

coerc|e /kəʊ'ɜ:s/ vt zwingen. ∼**ion**
/-'ɜ:ʃn/ n Zwang m

coe'xist vi koexistieren. ∼**ence** n
Koexistenz f

coffee /'kɒfɪ/ n Kaffee m

coffee: ∼**-grinder** n Kaffeemühle f.
∼**-pot** n Kaffeekanne f. ∼**-table** n
Couchtisch m

coffin /'kɒfɪn/ n Sarg m

cog /kɒg/ n (Techn) Zahn m

cogent /'kəʊdʒənt/ a überzeugend

cog-wheel n Zahnrad nt

cohabit /kəʊ'hæbɪt/ vi (Jur)
zusammenleben

coherent /kəʊ'hɪərənt/ a zusammenhängend; (comprehensible) verständlich

coil /kɔɪl/ n Rolle f; (Electr) Spule f;
(one ring) Windung f ● vt ∼[**up**]
zusammenrollen

coin /kɔɪn/ n Münze f ● vt prägen

coincide /kəʊɪn'saɪd/ vi zusammenfallen; (agree) übereinstimmen

coinciden|ce /kəʊ'ɪnsɪdəns/ n Zufall
m. ∼**tal** /-'dentl/ a, **-ly** adv zufällig

coke /kəʊk/ n Koks m

Coke (P) n (drink) Cola f

colander /'kʌləndə(r)/ n (Culin)
Durchschlag m

cold /kəʊld/ a (**-er, -est**) kalt; **I am** or
feel ∼ mir ist kalt ● n Kälte f; (Med)
Erkältung f

cold: ∼**-'blooded** a kaltblütig. ∼
'hearted a kaltherzig. ∼**ly** adv (fig)
kalt, kühl. ∼**ness** n Kälte f

coleslaw /'kəʊlslɔ:/ n Krautsalat m

colic /'kɒlɪk/ n Kolik f

collaborat|e /kə'læbəreɪt/ vi zusam-
menarbeiten (**with** mit); ∼**e on sth**
mitarbeiten bei etw. ∼**ion** /-'reɪʃn/ n
Zusammenarbeit f, Mitarbeit f;
(with enemy) Kollaboration f. ∼**or** n

Mitarbeiter(in) m(f); Kollaborateur
m

collaps|e /kə'læps/ n Zusam-
menbruch m; Einsturz m ● vi zusammenbrechen; ⟨roof, building:⟩
einstürzen. ∼**ible** a zusammen-
klappbar

collar /'kɒlə(r)/ n Kragen m; (for
animal) Halsband nt. ∼**-bone** n
Schlüsselbein nt

colleague /'kɒli:g/ n Kollege m/Kolle-
gin f

collect /kə'lekt/ vt sammeln; (fetch)
abholen; einsammeln ⟨tickets⟩; einziehen ⟨taxes⟩ ● vi sich [an]sam-
meln ● adv **call** ∼ (Amer) ein R-
Gespräch führen. ∼**ed** /-ɪd/ a gesammelt; (calm) gefaßt

collection /kə'lekʃn/ n Sammlung f;
(in church) Kollekte f; (of post) Lee-
rung f; (designer's) Kollektion f

collective /kə'lektɪv/ a gemeinsam;
(Pol) kollektiv. ∼ '**noun** n Kollekti-
vum nt

collector /kə'lektə(r)/ n Sammler(in)
m(f)

college /'kɒlɪdʒ/ n College nt

collide /kə'laɪd/ vi zusammenstoßen

colliery /'kɒlɪərɪ/ n Kohlengrube f

collision /kə'lɪʒn/ n Zusammenstoß m

colloquial /kə'ləʊkwɪəl/ a, **-ly** adv
umgangssprachlich. ∼**ism** n um-
gangssprachlicher Ausdruck m

Cologne /kə'ləʊn/ n Köln nt

colon /'kəʊlən/ n Doppelpunkt m;
(Anat) Dickdarm m

colonel /'kɜ:nl/ n Oberst m

colonial /kə'ləʊnɪəl/ a Kolonial-

colon|ize /'kɒlənaɪz/ vt kolonisieren.
∼**y** n Kolonie f

colossal /kə'lɒsl/ a riesig

colour /'kʌlə(r)/ n Farbe f; (complexion) Gesichtsfarbe f; (race) Haut-
farbe f; ∼**s** pl (flag) Fahne f. **off** ∼
(fam) nicht ganz auf der Höhe ● vt
färben; ∼ [**in**] ausmalen ● vi (blush)
erröten

colour: ∼ **bar** n Rassenschranke f.
∼**-blind** a farbenblind. ∼**ed** a farbig
● n (person) Farbige(r) m/f. ∼**-fast**
a farbecht. ∼ **film** n Farbfilm m.
∼**ful** a farbenfroh. ∼**less** a farblos.
∼ **photo[graph]** n Farbaufnahme f.
∼ **television** n Farbfernsehen nt

colt /kəʊlt/ n junger Hengst m

column /'kɒləm/ n Säule f; (of sol-
diers, figures) Kolonne f; (Typ)
Spalte f; (Journ) Kolumne f. ∼**ist**
/-nɪst/ n Kolumnist m

coma /'kəʊmə/ n Koma nt

comb /kəʊm/ n Kamm m ● vt kämmen; (search) absuchen; ~ one's
hair sich (dat) [die Haare] kämmen

combat /'kɒmbæt/ n Kampf m ● vt
(pt/pp combated) bekämpfen

combination /kɒmbɪ'neɪʃn/ n Verbindung f; (for lock) Kombination f

combine¹ /kəm'baɪn/ vt verbinden
● vi sich verbinden; ⟨people:⟩ sich
zusammenschließen

combine² /'kɒmbaɪn/ n (Comm) Konzern m. ~ [harvester] n Mäh-
drescher m

combustion /kəm'bʌstʃn/ n Verbrennung f

come /kʌm/ vi (pt came, pp come)
kommen; (reach) reichen (to an +
acc); that ~s to £10 das macht £10;
~ into money zu Geld kommen; ~
true wahr werden; ~ in two sizes in
zwei Größen erhältlich sein; the
years to ~ die kommenden Jahre;
how ~? (fam) wie das? ~ about vi
geschehen. ~ across vi herüber-
kommen; (fam) klar werden ● vt
stoßen auf (+ acc). ~ apart vi
sich auseinandernehmen lassen;
(accidentally) auseinandergehen. ~
away vi weggehen; ⟨thing:⟩ abgehen. ~ back vi zurückkommen. ~
by vi vorbeikommen ● vt (obtain)
bekommen. ~ in vi hereinkommen.
~ off vi abgehen; (take place) stattfinden; (succeed) klappen (fam). ~
out vi herauskommen; ⟨book:⟩ erscheinen; ⟨stain:⟩ herausgehen. ~
round vi vorbeikommen; (after
fainting) [wieder] zu sich kommen;
(change one's mind) sich umstimmen lassen. ~ to vi [wieder] zu sich
kommen. ~ up vi heraufkommen;
⟨plant:⟩ aufgehen; (reach) reichen
(to bis); ~ up with sich (dat) einfallen lassen

'come-back n Comeback nt

comedian /kə'miːdɪən/ n Komiker m

'come-down n Rückschritt m

comedy /'kɒmədɪ/ n Komödie f

comet /'kɒmɪt/ n Komet m

come-uppance /kʌm'ʌpəns/ n get
one's ~ (fam) sein Fett abkriegen

comfort /'kʌmfət/ n Bequemlichkeit
f; (consolation) Trost m ● vt trösten

comfortable /'kʌmfətəbl/ a, -bly adv
bequem

'comfort station n (Amer) öffentliche Toilette f

comfy /'kʌmfɪ/ a (fam) bequem

comic /'kɒmɪk/ a komisch ● n
Komiker m; (periodical) Comic-Heft
nt. ~al a, -ly adv komisch. ~ strip n
Comic Strips pl

coming /'kʌmɪŋ/ a kommend ● n
Kommen nt; ~s and goings Kommen und Gehen nt

comma /'kɒmə/ n Komma nt

command /kə'mɑːnd/ n Befehl m;
(Mil) Kommando nt; (mastery) Beherrschung f ● vt befehlen (+ dat);
kommandieren ⟨army⟩

commandeer /kɒmən'dɪə(r)/ vt
beschlagnahmen

command|er /kə'mɑːndə(r)/ n Be-
fehlshaber m; (of unit) Komman-
deur m; (of ship) Kommandant m.
~ing a ⟨view⟩ beherrschend. ~ing
officer n Befehlshaber m. ~ment n
Gebot nt

commemorat|e /kə'meməreɪt/ vt
gedenken (+ gen). ~ion /-'reɪʃn/ n
Gedenken nt. ~ive /-ətɪv/ a Gedenk-

commence /kə'mens/ vt/i anfangen,
beginnen. ~ment n Anfang m, Beginn m

commend /kə'mend/ vt loben;
(recommend) empfehlen (to dat).
~able /-əbl/ a lobenswert. ~ation
/kɒmen'deɪʃn/ n Lob nt

commensurate /kə'menʃərət/ a
angemessen; be ~ with entsprechen
(+ dat)

comment /'kɒment/ n Bemerkung f;
no ~! kein Kommentar! ● vi sich
äußern (on zu); ~ on (Journ)
kommentieren

commentary /'kɒməntrɪ/ n Kommentar m; [running] ~ (Radio, TV) Reportage f

commentator /'kɒmənteɪtə(r)/ n
Kommentator m; (Sport) Reporter
m

commerce /'kɒmɜːs/ n Handel m

commercial /kə'mɜːʃl/ a, -ly adv kom-
merziell ● n (Radio, TV) Werbespot
m. ~ize vt kommerzialisieren

commiserate /kə'mɪzəreɪt/ vi sein
Mitleid ausdrücken (with dat)

commission /kə'mɪʃn/ n (order for
work) Auftrag m; (body of people)
Kommission f; (payment) Provision
f; (Mil) [Offiziers]patent nt; out of
~ außer Betrieb ● vt beauftragen
⟨s.o.⟩; in Auftrag geben ⟨thing⟩;
(Mil) zum Offizier ernennen

commissionaire /kəmɪʃə'neə(r)/ n
Portier m

commissioner /kəˈmɪʃənə(r)/ n Kommissar m; ~ **for oaths** Notar m

commit /kəˈmɪt/ vt (pt/pp **committed**) begehen; (entrust) anvertrauen (**to** dat); (consign) einweisen (**to** in + acc); ~ **oneself** sich festlegen; (involve oneself) sich engagieren; ~ **sth to memory** sich (dat) etw einprägen. ~**ment** n Verpflichtung f; (involvement) Engagement nt. ~**ted** a engagiert

committee /kəˈmɪtɪ/ n Ausschuß m, Komitee nt

commodity /kəˈmɒdətɪ/ n Ware f

common /ˈkɒmən/ a (-**er**, -**est**) gemeinsam; (frequent) häufig; (ordinary) gewöhnlich; (vulgar) ordinär ● n Gemeindeland nt; **have in** ~ gemeinsam haben; **House of C~s** Unterhaus nt. ~**er** n Bürgerliche(r) m/f

common: ~**law** n Gewohnheitsrecht nt. ~**ly** adv allgemein. **C~ 'Market** n Gemeinsamer Markt m. ~**place** a häufig. ~-**room** n Aufenthaltsraum m. ~ **'sense** n gesunder Menschenverstand m

commotion /kəˈməʊʃn/ n Tumult m

communal /ˈkɒmjʊnl/ a gemeinschaftlich

communicable /kəˈmjuːnɪkəbl/ a ⟨disease⟩ übertragbar

communicate /kəˈmjuːnɪkeɪt/ vt mitteilen (**to** dat); übertragen ⟨disease⟩ ● vi sich verständigen; (be in touch) Verbindung haben

communication /kəmjuːnɪˈkeɪʃn/ n Verständigung f; (contact) Verbindung f; (of disease) Übertragung f; (message) Mitteilung f; ~**s** pl (technology) Nachrichtenwesen nt. ~ **cord** n Notbremse f

communicative /kəˈmjuːnɪkətɪv/ a mitteilsam

Communion /kəˈmjuːnɪən/ n [Holy] ~ das [heilige] Abendmahl; (Roman Catholic) die [heilige] Kommunion

communiqué /kəˈmjuːnɪkeɪ/ n Kommuniqué nt

Communis|m /ˈkɒmjʊnɪzm/ n Kommunismus m. ~**t** /-ɪst/ a kommunistisch ● n Kommunist(in) m(f)

community /kəˈmjuːnətɪ/ n Gemeinschaft f; **local** ~ Gemeinde f. ~ **centre** n Gemeinschaftszentrum nt

commute /kəˈmjuːt/ vi pendeln ● vt (Jur) umwandeln. ~**r** n Pendler(in) m(f)

compact¹ /kəmˈpækt/ a kompakt

compact² /ˈkɒmpækt/ n Puderdose f. ~ **disc** n CD f

companion /kəmˈpænjən/ n Begleiter(in) m(f). ~**ship** n Gesellschaft f

company /ˈkʌmpənɪ/ n Gesellschaft f; (firm) Firma f; (Mil) Kompanie f; (fam: guests) Besuch m. ~ **car** n Firmenwagen m

comparable /ˈkɒmpərəbl/ a vergleichbar

comparative /kəmˈpærətɪv/ a vergleichend; (relative) relativ ● n (Gram) Komparativ m. ~**ly** adv verhältnismäßig

compare /kəmˈpeə(r)/ vt vergleichen (**with/to** mit) ● vi sich vergleichen lassen

comparison /kəmˈpærɪsn/ n Vergleich m

compartment /kəmˈpɑːtmənt/ n Fach nt; (Rail) Abteil nt

compass /ˈkʌmpəs/ n Kompaß m. ~**es** npl **pair of** ~**es** Zirkel m

compassion /kəmˈpæʃn/ n Mitleid nt. ~**ate** /-ʃənət/ a mitfühlend

compatible /kəmˈpætəbl/ a vereinbar; ⟨drugs⟩ verträglich; (Techn) kompatibel; **be** ⟨people:⟩ [gut] zueinander passen

compatriot /kəmˈpætrɪət/ n Landsmann m /-männin f

compel /kəmˈpel/ vt (pt/pp **compelled**) zwingen

compensat|e /ˈkɒmpənseɪt/ vt entschädigen ● vi ~**e for** (fig) ausgleichen. ~**ion** /-ˈseɪʃn/ n Entschädigung f; (fig) Ausgleich m

compère /ˈkɒmpeə(r)/ n Conférencier m

compete /kəmˈpiːt/ vi konkurrieren; (take part) teilnehmen (**in** an + dat)

competen|ce /ˈkɒmpɪtəns/ n Tüchtigkeit f; (ability) Fähigkeit f; (Jur) Kompetenz f. ~**t** a tüchtig; fähig; (Jur) kompetent

competition /kɒmpəˈtɪʃn/ n Konkurrenz f; (contest) Wettbewerb m; (in newspaper) Preisausschreiben nt

competitive /kəmˈpetɪtɪv/ a (Comm) konkurrenzfähig

competitor /kəmˈpetɪtə(r)/ n Teilnehmer m; (Comm) Konkurrent m

compile /kəmˈpaɪl/ vt zusammenstellen; verfassen ⟨dictionary⟩

complacen|cy /kəmˈpleɪsənsɪ/ n Selbstzufriedenheit f. ~**t** a, -**ly** adv selbstzufrieden

complain /kəm'pleɪn/ vi klagen (**about/of** über + acc); (formally) sich beschweren. ~**t** n Klage f; (formal) Beschwerde f; (Med) Leiden nt

complement¹ /'kɒmplɪmənt/ n Ergänzung f; **full** ~ volle Anzahl f

complement² /'kɒmplɪment/ vt ergänzen; ~ **each other** sich ergänzen. ~**ary** /-'mentərɪ/ a sich ergänzend; **be** ~**ary** sich ergänzen

complete /kəm'pli:t/ a vollständig; (finished) fertig; (utter) völlig ● vt vervollständigen; (finish) abschließen; (fill in) ausfüllen. ~**ly** adv völlig

completion /kəm'pli:ʃn/ n Vervollständigung f; (end) Abschluß m

complex /'kɒmpleks/ a komplex ● n Komplex m

complexion /kəm'plekʃn/ n Teint m; (colour) Gesichtsfarbe f; (fig) Aspekt m

complexity /kəm'pleksətɪ/ n Komplexität f

compliance /kəm'plaɪəns/ n Einverständnis nt; **in** ~ **with** gemäß (+ dat)

complicat|e /'kɒmplɪkeɪt/ vt komplizieren. ~**ed** a kompliziert. ~**ion** /-'keɪʃn/ n Komplikation f

complicity /kəm'plɪsətɪ/ n Mittäterschaft f

compliment /'kɒmplɪmənt/ n Kompliment nt; ~**s** pl Grüße pl ● vt ein Kompliment machen (+ dat). ~**ary** /-'mentərɪ/ a schmeichelhaft; (given free) Frei-

comply /kəm'plaɪ/ vi (pt/pp -ied) ~ **with** nachkommen (+ dat)

component /kəm'pəʊnənt/ a & n ~ [**part**] Bestandteil m, Teil nt

compose /kəm'pəʊz/ vt verfassen; (Mus) komponieren; ~ **oneself** sich fassen; **be** ~**d of** sich zusammensetzen aus. ~**d** a (calm) gefaßt. ~**r** n Komponist m

composition /kɒmpə'zɪʃn/ n Komposition f; (essay) Aufsatz m

compost /'kɒmpɒst/ n Kompost m

composure /kəm'pəʊʒə(r)/ n Fassung f

compound¹ /kəm'paʊnd/ vt (make worse) verschlimmern

compound² /'kɒmpaʊnd/ a zusammengesetzt; (fracture) kompliziert ● n (Chem) Verbindung f; (Gram) Kompositum nt; (enclosure) Einfriedigung f. ~ '**interest** n Zinseszins m

comprehen|d /kɒmprɪ'hend/ vt begreifen, verstehen; (include) umfassen. ~**sible** a, -**bly** adv verständlich. ~**sion** /-'henʃn/ n Verständnis nt

comprehensive /kɒmprɪ'hensɪv/ a & n umfassend; ~ [**school**] Gesamtschule f. ~ **insurance** n (Auto) Vollkaskoversicherung f

compress¹ /'kɒmpres/ n Kompresse f

compress² /kəm'pres/ vt zusammenpressen; ~**ed air** Druckluft f

comprise /kəm'praɪz/ vt umfassen, bestehen aus

compromise /'kɒmprəmaɪz/ n Kompromiß m ● vt kompromittieren ⟨person⟩ ● vi einen Kompromiß schließen

compuls|ion /kəm'pʌlʃn/ n Zwang m. ~**ive** /-sɪv/ a zwanghaft; ~**ive eating** Eßzwang m. ~**ory** /-sərɪ/ a obligatorisch; ~**ory subject** Pflichtfach nt

compunction /kəm'pʌŋkʃn/ n Gewissensbisse pl

comput|er /kəm'pju:tə(r)/ n Computer m. ~**erize** vt computerisieren ⟨data⟩; auf Computer umstellen ⟨firm⟩. ~**ing** n Computertechnik f

comrade /'kɒmreɪd/ n Kamerad m; (Pol) Genosse m/Genossin f. ~**ship** n Kameradschaft f

con¹ /kɒn/ see **pro**

con² n (fam) Schwindel m ● vt (pt/pp **conned**) (fam) beschwindeln

concave /'kɒnkeɪv/ a konkav

conceal /kən'si:l/ vt verstecken; (keep secret) verheimlichen

concede /kən'si:d/ vt zugeben; (give up) aufgeben

conceit /kən'si:t/ n Einbildung f. ~**ed** a eingebildet

conceivable /kən'si:vəbl/ a denkbar

conceive /kən'si:v/ vt (Biol) empfangen; (fig) sich (dat) ausdenken ● vi schwanger werden. ~ **of** (fig) sich (dat) vorstellen

concentrat|e /'kɒnsəntreɪt/ vt konzentrieren ● vi sich konzentrieren. ~**ion** /-'treɪʃn/ n Konzentration f. ~**ion camp** n Konzentrationslager nt

concept /'kɒnsept/ n Begriff m. ~**ion** /kən'sepʃn/ n Empfängnis f; (idea) Vorstellung f

concern /kən'sɜ:n/ n Angelegenheit f; (worry) Sorge f; (Comm) Unternehmen nt ● vt (be about, affect) betreffen; (worry) kümmern; **be** ~**ed about** besorgt sein um; ~ **oneself with** sich beschäftigen mit; **as far as I am** ~**ed**

was mich angeht *od* betrifft. **∼ing**
prep bezüglich (+ *gen*)

concert /'kɒnsət/ *n* Konzert *nt*; **in ∼** im
Chor. **∼ed** /kən'sɜːtɪd/ *a* gemeinsam

concertina /kɒnsə'tiːnə/ *n* Konzertina *f*

'**concert-master** *n* (*Amer*) Konzertmeister *m*

concerto /kən'tʃeətəʊ/ *n* Konzert *nt*

concession /kən'seʃn/ *n* Zugeständnis
nt; (*Comm*) Konzession *f*; (*reduction*)
Ermäßigung *f*. **∼ary** *a* (*reduced*)
ermäßigt

conciliation /kənsɪlɪ'eɪʃn/ *n* Schlich-
tung *f*

concise /kən'saɪs/ *a*, **-ly** *adv* kurz

conclude /kən'kluːd/ *vt/i* schließen

conclusion /kən'kluːʒn/ *n* Schluß *m*; **in
∼** abschließend, zum Schluß

conclusive /kən'kluːsɪv/ *a* schlüssig

concoct /kən'kɒkt/ *vt* zusammenstellen; (*fig*) fabrizieren. **∼ion** /-ək ʃn/ *n*
Zusammenstellung *f*; (*drink*) Gebräu
nt

concourse /'kɒŋkɔːs/ *n* Halle *f*

concrete /'kɒŋkriːt/ *a* konkret ● *n*
Beton *m* ● *vt* betonieren

concur /kən'kɜː(r)/ *vi* (*pt/pp* **concurred**)
übereinstimmen

concurrently /kən'kʌrəntlɪ/ *adv*
gleichzeitig

concussion /kən'kʌʃn/ *n* Gehirner-
schütterung *f*

condemn /kən'dem/ *vt* verurteilen;
(*declare unfit*) für untauglich erklär-
en. **∼ation** /kɒndem'neɪʃn/ *n* Verurteilung *f*

condensation /kɒnden'seɪʃn/ *n* Kon-
densation *f*

condense /kən'dens/ *vt* zusammenfassen; (*Phys*) kondensieren ● *vi* sich
kondensieren. **∼d milk** *n* Kondensmilch *f*

condescend /kɒndɪ'send/ *vi* sich herablassen (**to** zu). **∼ing** *a*, **-ly** *adv*
herablassend

condiment /'kɒndɪmənt/ *n* Gewürz *nt*

condition /kən'dɪʃn/ *n* Bedingung *f*;
(*state*) Zustand *m*; **∼s** *pl* Verhältnisse *pl*; **on ∼ that** unter der Bedingung, daß ● *vt* (*Psych*) konditio-
nieren. **∼al** *a* bedingt; **be ∼al on**
abhängen von ● *n* (*Gram*) Konditio-
nal *m*. **∼er** *n* Haarkur *f*; (*for fabrics*)
Weichspüler *m*

condolences /kən'dəʊlənsɪz/ *npl*
Beileid *nt*

condom /'kɒndəm/ *n* Kondom *nt*

condominium /kɒndə'mɪnɪəm/ *n*
(*Amer*) ≈ Eigentumswohnung *f*

condone /kən'dəʊn/ *vt* hinwegsehen
über (+ *acc*)

conducive /kən'djuːsɪv/ *a* förderlich
(**to** *dat*)

conduct[1] /'kɒndʌkt/ *n* Verhalten *nt*;
(*Sch*) Betragen *nt*

conduct[2] /kən'dʌkt/ *vt* führen; (*Phys*)
leiten; (*Mus*) dirigieren. **∼or** *n* Diri-
gent *m*; (*of bus*) Schaffner *m*; (*Phys*)
Leiter *m*. **∼ress** *n* Schaffnerin *f*

cone /kəʊn/ *n* Kegel *m*; (*Bot*) Zapfen
m; (*for ice-cream*) [Eis]tüte *f*; (*Auto*)
Leitkegel *m*

confectioner /kən'fekʃənə(r)/ *n* Konditor *m*. **∼y** *n* Süßwaren *pl*

confederation /kənfedə'reɪʃn/ *n*
Bund *m*; (*Pol*) Konföderation *f*

confer /kən'fɜː(r)/ *v* (*pt/pp* **conferred**)
● *vt* verleihen (**on** *dat*) ● *vi* sich
beraten

conference /'kɒnfərəns/ *n* Konferenz
f

confess /kən'fes/ *vt/i* gestehen;
(*Relig*) beichten. **∼ion** /-eʃn/ *n*
Geständnis *nt*; (*Relig*) Beichte *f*.
∼ional /-eʃənəl/ *n* Beichtstuhl *m*.
∼or *n* Beichtvater *m*

confetti /kən'fetɪ/ *n* Konfetti *nt*

confide /kən'faɪd/ *vt* anvertrauen ● *vi*
∼ in s.o. sich jdm anvertrauen

confidence /'kɒnfɪdəns/ *n* (*trust*) Vertrauen *nt*; (*self-assurance*) Selbstvertrauen *nt*; (*secret*) Geheimnis *nt*;
in ∼ im Vertrauen. **∼ trick** *n*
Schwindel *m*

confident /'kɒnfɪdənt/ *a*, **-ly** *adv* zu-
versichtlich; (*self-assured*) selbstsicher

confidential /kɒnfɪ'denʃl/ *a*, **-ly** *adv*
vertraulich

confine /kən'faɪn/ *vt* beschränken;
(*keep shut up*) einsperren; **∼ oneself to** sich beschränken auf (+ *acc*);
be ∼d to bed das Bett hüten müssen. **∼d** *a* (*narrow*) eng. **∼ment** *n*
Haft *f*

confines /'kɒnfaɪnz/ *npl* Grenzen *pl*

confirm /kən'fɜːm/ *vt* bestätigen;
(*Relig*) konfirmieren; (*Roman Catholic*) firmen. **∼ation** /kɒnfə'meɪʃn/ *n*
Bestätigung *f*; Konfirmation *f*; Firmung *f*. **∼ed** *a* **∼ed bachelor** einge-
fleischter Junggeselle *m*

confiscat|e /'kɒnfɪskeɪt/ *vt* beschlag-
nahmen. **∼ion** /-'keɪʃn/ *n* Beschlagnahme *f*

conflict[1] /'kɒnflɪkt/ *n* Konflikt *m*

conflict² /kən'flɪkt/ vi im Widerspruch stehen (**with** zu). **~ing** a widersprüchlich

conform /kən'fɔːm/ vi ⟨person:⟩ sich anpassen; ⟨thing:⟩ entsprechen (**to** dat). **~ist** n Konformist m

confounded /kən'faʊndɪd/ a (fam) verflixt

confront /kən'frʌnt/ vt konfrontieren. **~ation** /kɒnfrən'teɪʃn/ n Konfrontation f

confus|e /kən'fjuːz/ vt verwirren; (mistake for) verwechseln (**with** mit). **~ing** a verwirrend. **~ion** /-juːʒn/ n Verwirrung f; (muddle) Durcheinander nt

congeal /kən'dʒiːl/ vi fest werden; ⟨blood:⟩ gerinnen

congenial /kən'dʒiːnɪəl/ a angenehm

congenital /kən'dʒenɪtl/ a angeboren

congest|ed /kən'dʒestɪd/ a verstopft; (with people) überfüllt. **~ion** /-estʃn/ n Verstopfung f; Überfüllung f

congratulat|e /kən'grætjʊleɪt/ vt gratulieren (+ dat) (**on** zu). **~ions** /-'leɪʃnz/ npl Glückwünsche pl; **~ions!** [ich] gratuliere!

congregat|e /'kɒŋgrɪgeɪt/ vi sich versammeln. **~ion** /-'geɪʃn/ n (Relig) Gemeinde f

congress /'kɒŋgres/ n Kongreß m. **~man** n Kongreßabgeordnete(r) m

conical /'kɒnɪkl/ a kegelförmig

conifer /'kɒnɪfə(r)/ n Nadelbaum m

conjecture /kən'dʒektʃə(r)/ n Mutmaßung f ● vt/i mutmaßen

conjugal /'kɒndʒʊgl/ a ehelich

conjugat|e /'kɒndʒʊgeɪt/ vt konjugieren. **~ion** /-'geɪʃn/ n Konjugation f

conjunction /kən'dʒʌŋkʃn/ n Konjunktion f; **in ~ with** zusammen mit

conjunctivitis /kəndʒʌŋktɪ'vaɪtɪs/ n Bindehautentzündung f

conjur|e /'kʌndʒə(r)/ vi zaubern ● vt **~e up** heraufbeschwören. **~or** n Zauberkünstler m

conk /kɒŋk/ vi **~ out** (fam) ⟨machine:⟩ kaputtgehen; ⟨person:⟩ zusammenklappen

conker /'kɒŋkə(r)/ n (fam) [Roß]kastanie f

'con-man n (fam) Schwindler m

connect /kə'nekt/ vt verbinden (**to** mit); (Electr) anschließen (**to** an + acc) ● vi verbunden sein; ⟨train:⟩ Anschluß haben (**with** an + acc); **be**

~ed with zu tun haben mit; (be related to) verwandt sein mit

connection /kə'nekʃn/ n Verbindung f; (Rail, Electr) Anschluß m; **in ~ with** in Zusammenhang mit. **~s** npl Beziehungen pl

conniv|ance /kə'naɪvəns/ n stillschweigende Duldung f. **~e** vi **~e at** stillschweigend dulden

connoisseur /kɒnə'sɜː(r)/ n Kenner m

connotation /kɒnə'teɪʃn/ n Assoziation f

conquer /'kɒŋkə(r)/ vt erobern; (fig) besiegen. **~or** n Eroberer m

conquest /'kɒŋkwest/ n Eroberung f

conscience /'kɒnʃəns/ n Gewissen nt

conscientious /kɒnʃɪ'enʃəs/ a, **-ly** adv gewissenhaft. **~ ob'jector** n Kriegsdienstverweigerer m

conscious /'kɒnʃəs/ a, **-ly** adv bewußt; **[fully] ~** bei [vollem] Bewußtsein; **be/become ~ of sth** (dat) etw (gen) bewußt sein/werden. **~ness** n Bewußtsein nt

conscript¹ /'kɒnskrɪpt/ n Einberufene(r) m

conscript² /kən'skrɪpt/ vt einberufen. **~ion** /-ɪpʃn/ n allgemeine Wehrpflicht f

consecrat|e /'kɒnsɪkreɪt/ vt weihen; einweihen ⟨church⟩. **~ion** /-'kreɪʃn/ n Weihe f; Einweihung f

consecutive /kən'sekjʊtɪv/ a aufeinanderfolgend. **~ly** adv fortlaufend

consensus /kən'sensəs/ n Übereinstimmung f

consent /kən'sent/ n Einwilligung f, Zustimmung f ● vi einwilligen (**to** in + acc), zustimmen (**to** dat)

consequen|ce /'kɒnsɪkwəns/ n Folge f; (importance) Bedeutung f. **~t** a daraus folgend. **~tly** adv folglich

conservation /kɒnsə'veɪʃn/ n Erhaltung f, Bewahrung f. **~ist** n Umweltschützer m

conservative /kən'sɜːvətɪv/ a konservativ; ⟨estimate⟩ vorsichtig. **C~** (Pol) a konservativ ● n Konservative(r) m/f

conservatory /kən'sɜːvətrɪ/ n Wintergarten m

conserve /kən'sɜːv/ vt erhalten, bewahren; sparen ⟨energy⟩

consider /kən'sɪdə(r)/ vt erwägen; (think over) sich (dat) überlegen; (take into account) berücksichtigen; (regard as) betrachten als; **~doing sth** erwägen, etw zu tun. **~able** /-əbl/ a, **-bly** adv erheblich

consider|ate /kən'sɪdərət/ a, **-ly** adv rücksichtsvoll. ~**ation** /-'reɪʃn/ n Erwägung f; (thoughtfulness) Rücksicht f; (payment) Entgelt nt; take **into** ~**ation** berücksichtigen. ~**ing** prep wenn man bedenkt (**that**, daß); ~**ing the circumstances** unter den Umständen

consign /kən'saɪn/ vt übergeben (**to** dat). ~**ment** n Lieferung f

consist /kən'sɪst/ vi ~**of** bestehen aus

consisten|cy /kən'sɪstənsɪ/ n Konsequenz f; (density) Konsistenz f. ~**t** a konsequent; (unchanging) gleichbleibend; **be ~t with** entsprechen (+ dat). ~**tly** adv konsequent; (constantly) ständig

consolation /kɒnsə'leɪʃn/ n Trost m. ~ **prize** n Trostpreis m

console /kən'səʊl/ vt trösten

consolidate /kən'sɒlɪdeɪt/ vt konsolidieren

consonant /'kɒnsənənt/ n Konsonant m

consort /'kɒnsɔːt/ n Gemahl(in) m(f)

conspicuous /kən'spɪkjʊəs/ a auffällig

conspiracy /kən'spɪrəsɪ/ n Verschwörung f

conspire /kən'spaɪə(r)/ vi sich verschwören

constable /'kʌnstəbl/ n Polizist m

constant /'kɒnstənt/ a, **-ly** adv beständig; (continuous) ständig

constellation /kɒnstə'leɪʃn/ n Sternbild nt

consternation /kɒnstə'neɪʃn/ n Bestürzung f

constipat|ed /'kɒnstɪpeɪtɪd/ a verstopft. ~**ion** /-'peɪʃn/ n Verstopfung f

constituency /kən'stɪtjʊənsɪ/ n Wahlkreis m

constituent /kən'stɪtjʊənt/ n Bestandteil m; (Pol) Wähler(in) m(f)

constitut|e /'kɒnstɪtjuːt/ vt bilden. ~**ion** /-'tjuːʃn/ n (Pol) Verfassung f; (of person) Konstitution f. ~**ional** /-'tjuːʃənl/ a Verfassungs- ● n Verdauungsspaziergang m

constrain /kən'streɪn/ vt zwingen. ~**t** n Zwang m; (restriction) Beschränkung f; (strained manner) Gezwungenheit f

constrict /kən'strɪkt/ vt einengen

construct /kən'strʌkt/ vt bauen. ~**ion** /-ʌkʃn/ n Bau m; (Gram) Konstruktion f; (interpretation) Deutung f; **under** ~**ion** im Bau. ~**ive** /-ɪv/ a konstruktiv

construe /kən'struː/ vt deuten

consul /'kɒnsl/ n Konsul m. ~**ate** /'kɒnsjʊlət/ n Konsulat nt

consult /kən'sʌlt/ vt [um Rat] fragen; konsultieren ⟨doctor⟩; nachschlagen in (+ dat) ⟨book⟩. ~**ant** n Berater m; (Med) Chefarzt m. ~**ation** /kɒnsl'teɪʃn/ n Beratung f; (Med) Konsultation f

consume /kən'sjuːm/ vt verzehren; (use) verbrauchen. ~**r** n Verbraucher m. ~**r goods** npl Konsumgüter pl

consummat|e /'kɒnsəmeɪt/ vt vollziehen. ~**ion** /-'meɪʃn/ n Vollzug m

consumption /kən'sʌmpʃn/ n Konsum m; (use) Verbrauch m

contact /'kɒntækt/ n Kontakt m; (person) Kontaktperson f ● vt sich in Verbindung setzen mit. ~ '**lenses** npl Kontaktlinsen pl

contagious /kən'teɪdʒəs/ a direkt übertragbar

contain /kən'teɪn/ vt enthalten; (control) beherrschen. ~**er** n Behälter m; (Comm) Container m

contaminat|e /kən'tæmɪneɪt/ vt verseuchen. ~**ion** /-'neɪʃn/ n Verseuchung f

contemplat|e /'kɒntəmpleɪt/ vt betrachten; (meditate) nachdenken über (+ acc); ~**e doing sth** daran denken, etw zu tun. ~**ion** /-'pleɪʃn/ n Betrachtung f; Nachdenken nt

contemporary /kən'tempərərɪ/ a zeitgenössisch ● n Zeitgenosse m /-genossin f

contempt /kən'tempt/ n Verachtung f; **beneath** ~ verabscheuungswürdig; ~ **of court** Mißachtung f des Gerichts. ~**ible** /-əbl/ a verachtenswert. ~**uous** /-tjʊəs/ a, **-ly** adv verächtlich

contend /kən'tend/ vi kämpfen (**with** mit) ● vt (assert) behaupten. ~**er** n Bewerber(in) m(f); (Sport) Wettkämpfer(in) m(f)

content[1] /'kɒntent/ n & **contents** pl Inhalt m

content[2] /kən'tent/ a zufrieden ● n **to one's heart's** ~ nach Herzenslust ● vt ~ **oneself** sich begnügen (**with** mit). ~**ed** a, **-ly** adv zufrieden

contention /kən'tenʃn/ n (assertion) Behauptung f

contentment /kən'tentmənt/ n Zufriedenheit f

contest[1] /'kɒntest/ n Kampf m; (competition) Wettbewerb m

contest² /kən'test/ vt (dispute) bestreiten; (Jur) anfechten; (Pol) kandidieren in (+ dat). **~ant** n Teilnehmer m

context /'kɒntekst/ n Zusammenhang m

continent /'kɒntɪnənt/ n Kontinent m

continental /kɒntɪ'nentl/ a Kontinental-. **~ breakfast** n kleines Frühstück nt. **~ quilt** n Daunendecke f

contingen|cy /kən'tɪndʒənsɪ/ n Eventualität f. **~t** a be **~t** upon abhängen von ● n (Mil) Kontingent nt

continual /kən'tɪnjʊəl/ a, **-ly** adv dauernd

continuation /kəntɪnjʊ'eɪʃn/ n Fortsetzung f

continue /kən'tɪnju:/ vt fortsetzen; **~ doing** or **to do sth** fortfahren, etw zu tun; **to be ~d** Fortsetzung folgt ● vi weitergehen; (doing sth) weitermachen; (speaking) fortfahren; ⟨weather:⟩ anhalten

continuity /kɒntɪ'nju:ətɪ/ n Kontinuität f

continuous /kən'tɪnjʊəs/ a, **-ly** adv anhaltend, ununterbrochen

contort /kən'tɔ:t/ vt verzerren. **~ion** /-ɔ:ʃn/ n Verzerrung f

contour /'kɒntʊə(r)/ n Kontur f; (line) Höhenlinie f

contraband /'kɒntrəbænd/ n Schmuggelware f

contracep|tion /kɒntrə'sepʃn/ n Empfängnisverhütung f. **~tive** /-tɪv/ a empfängnisverhütend ● n Empfängnisverhütungsmittel nt

contract¹ /'kɒntrækt/ n Vertrag m

contract² /kən'trækt/ vi sich zusammenziehen ● vt zusammenziehen; sich (dat) zuziehen ⟨illness⟩. **~ion** /-ækʃn/ n Zusammenziehung f; (abbreviation) Abkürzung f; (in childbirth) Wehe f. **~or** n Unternehmer m

contradict /kɒntrə'dɪkt/ vt widersprechen (+ dat). **~ion** /-ɪkʃn/ n Widerspruch m. **~ory** a widersprüchlich

contra-flow /'kɒntrə-/ n Umleitung f [auf die entgegengesetzte Fahrbahn]

contralto /kən'træltəʊ/ n Alt m; (singer) Altistin f

contraption /kən'træpʃn/ n (fam) Apparat m

contrary¹ /'kɒntrərɪ/ a & adv entgegengesetzt; **~ to** entgegen (+ dat)

● n Gegenteil nt; **on the ~** im Gegenteil

contrary² /kən'treərɪ/ a widerspenstig

contrast¹ /'kɒntrɑ:st/ n Kontrast m

contrast² /kən'trɑ:st/ vt gegenüberstellen (with dat) ● vi einen Kontrast bilden (with zu). **~ing** a gegensätzlich; ⟨colour⟩ Kontrast-

contraven|e /kɒntrə'vi:n/ vt verstoßen gegen. **~tion** /-'venʃn/ n Verstoß m (of gegen)

contribut|e /kən'trɪbju:t/ vt/i beitragen; beisteuern ⟨money⟩; (donate) spenden. **~ion** /kɒntrɪ'bju:ʃn/ n Beitrag m; (donation) Spende f. **~or** n Beitragende(r) m/f

contrite /kən'traɪt/ a reuig

contrivance /kən'traɪvəns/ n Vorrichtung f

contrive /kən'traɪv/ vt verfertigen; **~ to do sth** es fertigbringen, etw zu tun

control /kən'trəʊl/ n Kontrolle f; (mastery) Beherrschung f; (Techn) Regler m; **~s** pl (of car, plane) Steuerung f; **get out of ~** außer Kontrolle geraten ● vt (pt/pp **controlled**) kontrollieren; (restrain) unter Kontrolle halten; **~ oneself** sich beherrschen

controvers|ial /kɒntrə'vɜ:ʃl/ a umstritten. **~y** /'kɒntrəvɜ:sɪ/ n Kontroverse f

conundrum /kə'nʌndrəm/ n Rätsel nt

conurbation /kɒnɜ:'beɪʃn/ n Ballungsgebiet nt

convalesce /kɒnvə'les/ vi sich erholen. **~nce** n Erholung f

convalescent /kɒnvə'lesnt/ a be **~** noch erholungsbedürftig sein. **~ home** n Erholungsheim nt

convector /kən'vektə(r)/ n **~ [heater]** Konvektor m

convene /kən'vi:n/ vt einberufen ● vi sich versammeln

convenience /kən'vi:nɪəns/ n Bequemlichkeit f; **[public] ~** öffentliche Toilette f; **with all modern ~s** mit allem Komfort

convenient /kən'vi:nɪənt/ a, **-ly** adv günstig; **be ~ for s.o.** jdm gelegen sein od jdm passen; **if it is ~ [for you]** wenn es Ihnen paßt

convent /'kɒnvənt/ n [Nonnen]kloster nt

convention /kən'venʃn/ n (custom) Brauch m, Sitte f; (agreement) Konvention f; (assembly) Tagung f. **~al** a, **-ly** adv konventionell

converge /kən'vɜːdʒ/ vi zusammenlaufen

conversant /kən'vɜːsənt/ a ~ **with** vertraut mit

conversation /kɒnvə'seɪʃn/ n Gespräch nt; (Sch) Konversation f

converse¹ /kən'vɜːs/ vi sich unterhalten

converse² /'kɒnvɜːs/ n Gegenteil nt. ~ly adv umgekehrt

conversion /kən'vɜːʃn/ n Umbau m; (Relig) Bekehrung f; (calculation) Umrechnung f

convert¹ /'kɒnvɜːt/ n Bekehrte(r) m/f, Konvertit m

convert² /kən'vɜːt/ vt bekehren ⟨person⟩; (change) umwandeln (**into** in + acc); umbauen ⟨building⟩; (calculate) umrechnen; (Techn) umstellen. ~**ible** /-əbl/ a verwandelbar ● n (Auto) Kabriolett nt

convex /'kɒnveks/ a konvex

convey /kən'veɪ/ vt befördern; vermitteln ⟨idea, message⟩. ~**ance** n Beförderung f; (vehicle) Beförderungsmittel nt. ~**or belt** n Förderband f

convict¹ /'kɒnvɪkt/ n Sträfling m

convict² /kən'vɪkt/ vt verurteilen (**of** wegen). ~**ion** /-ɪkʃn/ n Verurteilung f; (belief) Überzeugung f; **previous** ~**ion** Vorstrafe f

convinc|e /kən'vɪns/ vt überzeugen. ~**ing** a, -**ly** adv überzeugend

convivial /kən'vɪvɪəl/ a gesellig

convoluted /'kɒnvəluːtɪd/ a verschlungen; (fig) verwickelt

convoy /'kɒnvɔɪ/ n Konvoi m

convuls|e /kən'vʌls/ vt be ~**ed** sich krümmen (**with** vor + dat). ~**ion** /-ʌlʃn/ n Krampf m

coo /kuː/ vi gurren

cook /kʊk/ n Koch m/ Köchin f ● vt/i kochen; **is it** ~**ed?** ist es gar? ~ **the books** (fam) die Bilanz frisieren. ~**book** n (Amer) Kochbuch n

cooker /'kʊkə(r)/ n [Koch]herd m; (apple) Kochapfel m. ~**y** n Kochen nt. ~**y book** n Kochbuch nt

cookie /'kʊkɪ/ n (Amer) Keks m

cool /kuːl/ a (-er, -est), -**ly** adv kühl ● n Kühle f ● vt kühlen ● vi abkühlen. ~**-box** n Kühlbox f. ~**ness** n Kühle f

coop /kuːp/ n [Hühner]stall m ● vt ~ **up** einsperren

co-operat|e /kəʊ'ɒpəreɪt/ vi zusammenarbeiten. ~**ion** /-'reɪʃn/ n Kooperation f

co-operative /kəʊ'ɒpərətɪv/ a hilfsbereit ● n Genossenschaft f

co-opt /kəʊ'ɒpt/ vt hinzuwählen

co-ordinat|e /kəʊ'ɔːdɪneɪt/ vt koordinieren. ~**ion** /-'neɪʃn/ n Koordination f

cop /kɒp/ n (fam) Polizist m

cope /kəʊp/ vi (fam) zurechtkommen; ~ **with** fertig werden mit

copious /'kəʊpɪəs/ a reichlich

copper¹ /'kɒpə(r)/ n Kupfer nt; ~**s** pl Kleingeld nt ● a kupfern

copper² n (fam) Polizist m

copper 'beech n Blutbuche f

coppice /'kɒpɪs/ n, **copse** /kɒps/ n Gehölz nt

copulate /'kɒpjʊleɪt/ vi sich begatten

copy /'kɒpɪ/ n Kopie f; (book) Exemplar nt ● vt (pt/pp -**ied**) kopieren; (imitate) nachahmen; (Sch) abschreiben

copy: ~**right** n Copyright nt. ~**writer** n Texter m

coral /'kɒrəl/ n Koralle f

cord /kɔːd/ n Schnur f; (fabric) Cordsamt m; ~**s** pl Cordhose f

cordial /'kɔːdɪəl/ a, -**ly** adv herzlich ● n Fruchtsirup m

cordon /'kɔːdn/ n Kordon m ● vt ~ **off** absperren

corduroy /'kɔːdərɔɪ/ n Cordsamt m

core /kɔː(r)/ n Kern m; (of apple, pear) Kerngehäuse nt

cork /kɔːk/ n Kork m; (for bottle) Korken m. ~**screw** n Korkenzieher m

corn¹ /kɔːn/ n Korn nt; (Amer: maize) Mais m

corn² n (Med) Hühnerauge nt

cornea /'kɔːnɪə/ n Hornhaut f

corned beef /kɔːnd'biːf/ n Corned beef nt

corner /'kɔːnə(r)/ n Ecke f; (bend) Kurve f; (football) Eckball m ● vt (fig) in die Enge treiben; (Comm) monopolisieren ⟨market⟩. ~**stone** n Eckstein m

cornet /'kɔːnɪt/ n (Mus) Kornett nt; (for ice-cream) [Eis]tüte f

corn: ~**flour** n, (Amer) ~**starch** n Stärkemehl nt

corny /'kɔːnɪ/ a (fam) abgedroschen

coronary /'kɒrənərɪ/ a & n ~ **[thrombosis]** Koronarthrombose f

coronation /kɒrə'neɪʃn/ n Krönung f

coroner /'kɒrənə(r)/ n Beamte(r) m, der verdächtige Todesfälle untersucht

coronet /'kɒrənɪt/ n Adelskrone f

corporal¹ /'kɔːpərəl/ n (Mil) Stabs-unteroffizier m

corporal² a körperlich; ~ **punishment** körperliche Züchtigung f

corporate /'kɔːpərət/ a gemein-schaftlich

corporation /kɔːpə'reɪʃn/ n Körper-schaft f; (of town) Stadtverwaltung f

corps /kɔː(r)/ n (pl corps /kɔːz/) Korps nt

corpse /kɔːps/ n Leiche f

corpulent /'kɔːpjʊlənt/ a korpulent

corpuscle /'kɔːpʌsl/ n Blutkörper-chen nt

correct /kə'rekt/ a, -ly adv richtig; (proper) korrekt ● vt verbessern; (Sch, Typ) korrigieren. ~**ion** /-ekʃn/ n Verbesserung f; (Typ) Korrektur f

correlation /kɒrə'leɪʃn/ n Wechselbe-ziehung f

correspond /kɒrɪ'spɒnd/ vi entspre-chen (to dat); ⟨two things:⟩ sich entsprechen; (write) korrespondie-ren. ~**ence** n Briefwechsel m; (Comm) Korrespondenz f. ~**ent** n Korrespondent(in) m(f). ~**ing** a, -ly adv entsprechend

corridor /'kɒrɪdɔː(r)/ n Gang m; (Pol, Aviat) Korridor m

corroborate /kə'rɒbəreɪt/ vt bestätigen

corro|de /kə'rəʊd/ vt zerfressen ● vi rosten. ~**sion** /-'rəʊʒn/ n Korrosion f

corrugated /'kɒrəgeɪtɪd/ a gewellt. ~ **iron** n Wellblech nt

corrupt /kə'rʌpt/ a korrupt ● vt kor-rumpieren; (spoil) verderben. ~**ion** /-ʌpʃn/ n Korruption f

corset /'kɔːsɪt/ n & -s pl Korsett nt

Corsica /'kɔːsɪkə/ n Korsika nt

cortège /kɔː'teɪʒ/ n [funeral] ~ Lei-chenzug m

cosh /kɒʃ/ n Totschläger m

cosmetic /kɒz'metɪk/ a kosmetisch ● n ~s pl Kosmetika pl

cosmic /'kɒzmɪk/ a kosmisch

cosmonaut /'kɒzmənɔːt/ n Kosmo-naut(in) m(f)

cosmopolitan /kɒzmə'pɒlɪtən/ a kosmopolitisch

cosmos /'kɒzmɒs/ n Kosmos m

cosset /'kɒsɪt/ vt verhätscheln

cost /kɒst/ n Kosten pl; ~s pl (Jur) Kosten; at all ~s um jeden Preis; I learnt to my ~es ist mich teuer zu stehen gekommen ● vt (pt/pp cost) kosten; it ~ me £20 es hat mich £20 gekostet ● vt (pt/pp costed) ~ [out] die Kosten kalkulieren für

costly /'kɒstlɪ/ a (-ier, -iest) teuer

cost: ~ **of 'living** n Lebenshaltungs-kosten pl. ~ **price** n Selbstkosten-preis m

costume /'kɒstjuːm/ n Kostüm nt; (national) Tracht f. ~ **jewellery** n Modeschmuck m

cosy /'kəʊzɪ/ a (-ier, -iest) gemütlich ● n (tea-, egg-) Wärmer m

cot /kɒt/ n Kinderbett nt; (Amer: camp-bed) Feldbett nt

cottage /'kɒtɪdʒ/ n Häuschen nt. ~ **'cheese** n Hüttenkäse m

cotton /'kɒtn/ n Baumwolle f; (thread) Nähgarn nt ● a baumwol-len ● vi ~ **on** (fam) kapieren

cotton 'wool n Watte f

couch /kaʊtʃ/ n Liege f

couchette /kuː'ʃet/ n (Rail) Liege-platz m

cough /kɒf/ n Husten m ● vi husten. ~ **up** vt/i husten; (fam: pay) blechen

'cough mixture n Hustensaft m

could /kʊd, unbetont kəd/ see **can²**

council /'kaʊnsl/ n Rat m; (Admin) Stadtverwaltung f; (rural) Gemein-deverwaltung f. ~ **house** n ≈ Sozial-wohnung f

councillor /'kaʊnsələ(r)/ n Stadtver-ordnete(r) m/f

'council tax n Gemeindesteuer f

counsel /'kaʊnsl/ n Rat m; (Jur) Anwalt m ● vt (pt/pp counselled) beraten. ~**lor** n Berater(in) m(f)

count¹ /kaʊnt/ n Graf m

count² n Zählung f; keep ~ zählen ● vt/i zählen. ~ **on** vt rechnen auf (+ acc)

countenance /'kaʊntənəns/ n Ge-sicht nt ● vt dulden

counter¹ /'kaʊntə(r)/ n (in shop) Ladentisch m; (in bank) Schalter m; (in café) Theke f; (Games) Spiel-marke f

counter² adv ~ **to** gegen (+ acc) ● a Gegen- ● vt/i kontern

counter'act vt entgegenwirken (+ dat)

'counter-attack n Gegenangriff m

counter-'espionage n Spionageab-wehr f

'counterfeit /-fɪt/ a gefälscht ● n Fälschung f ● vt fälschen

'counterfoil n Kontrollabschnitt m

'counterpart n Gegenstück nt

counter-pro'ductive a be ~ das Gegenteil bewirken

'countersign vt gegenzeichnen

countess /'kaʊntɪs/ n Gräfin f

countless /'kauntlis/ *a* unzählig

countrified /'kʌntrɪfaɪd/ *a* ländlich

country /'kʌntrɪ/ *n* Land *nt*; (*native land*) Heimat *f*; (*countryside*) Landschaft *f*; **in the** ~ auf dem Lande. ~**man** *n* [**fellow**] ~**man** Landsmann *m*. ~**side** *n* Landschaft *f*

county /'kauntɪ/ *n* Grafschaft *f*

coup /ku:/ *n* (*Pol*) Staatsstreich *m*

couple /'kʌpl/ *n* Paar *nt*; **a** ~ **of** (*two*) zwei ● *vt* verbinden; (*Rail*) koppeln

coupon /'ku:pɒn/ *n* Kupon *m*; (*voucher*) Gutschein *m*; (*entry form*) Schein *m*

courage /'kʌrɪdʒ/ *n* Mut *m*. ~**ous** /kə'reɪdʒəs/ *a*, **-ly** *adv* mutig

courgettes /kʊə'ʒets/ *npl* Zucchini *pl*

courier /'kʊrɪə(r)/ *n* Bote *m*; (*diplomatic*) Kurier *m*; (*for tourists*) Reiseleiter(in) *m(f)*

course /kɔ:s/ *n* (*Naut, Sch*) Kurs *m*; (*Culin*) Gang *m*; (*for golf*) Platz *m*; ~ **of treatment** (*Med*) Kur *f*; **of** ~ natürlich, selbstverständlich; **in the** ~ **of** im Lauf[e] (+ *gen*)

court /kɔ:t/ *n* Hof *m*; (*Sport*) Platz *m*; (*Jur*) Gericht *nt* ● *vt* werben um; herausfordern (*danger*)

courteous /'kɜ:tɪəs/ *a*, **-ly** *adv* höflich

courtesy /'kɜ:təsɪ/ *n* Höflichkeit *f*

court: ~'**martial** *n* (*pl* ~**s martial**) Militärgericht *nt*. ~ **shoes** *npl* Pumps *pl*. ~**yard** *n* Hof *m*

cousin /'kʌzn/ *n* Vetter *m*, Cousin *m*; (*female*) Kusine *f*

cove /kəʊv/ *n* kleine Bucht *f*

cover /'kʌvə(r)/ *n* Decke *f*; (*of cushion*) Bezug *m*; (*of umbrella*) Hülle *f*; (*of typewriter*) Haube *f*; (*of book, lid*) Deckel *m*; (*of magazine*) Umschlag *m*; (*protection*) Deckung *f*, Schutz *m*; **take** ~ Deckung nehmen; **under separate** ~ mit getrennter Post ● *vt* bedecken; beziehen (*cushion*); decken (*costs, needs*); zurücklegen (*distance*); (*Journ*) berichten über (+ *acc*); (*insure*) versichern. ~ **up** *vt* zudecken; (*fig*) vertuschen

coverage /'kʌvərɪdʒ/ *n* (*Journ*) Berichterstattung *f* (**of** über + *acc*)

cover: ~ **charge** *n* Gedeck *nt*. ~**ing** *n* Decke *f*; (*for floor*) Belag *m*. ~**-up** *n* Vertuschung *f*

covet /'kʌvɪt/ *vt* begehren

cow /kau/ *n* Kuh *f*

coward /'kauəd/ *n* Feigling *m*. ~**ice** /-ɪs/ *n* Feigheit *f*. ~**ly** *a* feige

'**cowboy** *n* Cowboy *m*; (*fam*) unsolider Handwerker *m*

cower /'kauə(r)/ *vi* sich [ängstlich] ducken

'**cowshed** *n* Kuhstall *m*

cox /kɒks/ *n*, **coxswain** /'kɒksn/ *n* Steuermann *m*

coy /kɔɪ/ *a* (**-er, -est**) gespielt schüchtern

crab /kræb/ *n* Krabbe *f*. ~**-apple** *n* Holzapfel *m*

crack /kræk/ *n* Riß *m*; (*in china, glass*) Sprung *m*; (*noise*) Knall *m*; (*fam: joke*) Witz *m*; (*fam: attempt*) Versuch *m* ● *a* (*fam*) erstklassig ● *vt* knacken (*nut, code*); einen Sprung machen in (+ *acc*) (*china, glass*); (*fam*) reißen (*joke*); (*fam*) lösen (*problem*) ● *vi* (*china, glass:*) springen; (*whip:*) knallen. ~ **down** *vi* (*fam*) durchgreifen

cracked /krækt/ *a* gesprungen; (*rib*) angebrochen; (*fam: crazy*) verrückt

cracker /'krækə(r)/ *n* (*biscuit*) Kräcker *m*; (*firework*) Knallkörper *m*; [**Christmas**] ~ Knallbonbon *m*. ~**s** *a* **be** ~**s** (*fam*) einen Knacks haben

crackle /'krækl/ *vi* knistern

cradle /'kreɪdl/ *n* Wiege *f*

craft[1] /krɑ:ft/ *n* *inv* (*boat*) [Wasser]fahrzeug *nt*

craft[2] *n* Handwerk *nt*; (*technique*) Fertigkeit *f*. ~**sman** *n* Handwerker *m*

crafty /'krɑ:ftɪ/ *a* (**-ier, -iest**), **-ily** *adv* gerissen

crag /kræg/ *n* Felszacken *m*. ~**gy** *a* felsig; (*face*) kantig

cram /kræm/ *v* (*pt/pp* **crammed**) ● *vt* hineinstopfen (**into** in + *acc*); vollstopfen (**with** mit) ● *vi* (*for exams*) pauken

cramp /kræmp/ *n* Krampf *m*. ~**ed** *a* eng

crampon /'kræmpən/ *n* Steigeisen *nt*

cranberry /'krænbərɪ/ *n* (*Culin*) Preiselbeere *f*

crane /kreɪn/ *n* Kran *m*; (*bird*) Kranich *m* ● *vt* ~ **one's neck** den Hals recken

crank[1] /kræŋk/ *n* (*fam*) Exzentriker *m*

crank[2] *n* (*Techn*) Kurbel *f*. ~**shaft** *n* Kurbelwelle *f*

cranky /'kræŋkɪ/ *a* exzentrisch; (*Amer: irritable*) reizbar

cranny /'krænɪ/ *n* Ritze *f*

crash /kræʃ/ *n* (*noise*) Krach *m*; (*Auto*) Zusammenstoß *m*; (*Aviat*) Absturz *m* ● *vi* krachen (**into** gegen);

⟨*cars:*⟩ zusammenstoßen; ⟨*plane:*⟩ abstürzen ● *vt* einen Unfall haben mit ⟨*car*⟩
crash: ∼ **course** *n* Schnellkurs *m.* ∼**helmet** *n* Sturzhelm *m.* ∼**-landing** *n* Bruchlandung *f*
crate /kreɪt/ *n* Kiste *f*
crater /'kreɪtə(r)/ *n* Krater *m*
cravat /krə'væt/ *n* Halstuch *nt*
crav|e /kreɪv/ *vi* ∼**e for** sich sehnen nach. ∼**ing** *n* Gelüst *nt*
crawl /krɔːl/ *n* (*Swimming*) Kraul *nt*; **do the** ∼ kraulen; **at a** ∼ im Kriechtempo ● *vi* kriechen; ⟨*baby:*⟩ krabbeln; ∼ **with** wimmeln von. ∼**er lane** *n* (*Auto*) Kriechspur *f*
crayon /'kreɪən/ *n* Wachsstift *m*; (*pencil*) Buntstift *m*
craze /kreɪz/ *n* Mode *f*
crazy /'kreɪzɪ/ *a* (**-ier, -iest**) verrückt; **be** ∼ **about** verrückt sein nach
creak /kriːk/ *n* Knarren *nt* ● *vi* knarren
cream /kriːm/ *n* Sahne *f*; (*Cosmetic, Med, Culin*) Creme *f* ● *a* (*colour*) cremefarben ● *vt* (*Culin*) cremig rühren. ∼ '**cheese** *n* ≈ Quark *m.* ∼**y** *a* sahnig; (*smooth*) cremig
crease /kriːs/ *n* Falte *f*; (*unwanted*) Knitterfalte *f* ● *vt* falten; (*accidentally*) zerknittern ● *vi* knittern. ∼**-resistant** *a* knitterfrei
creat|e /kriː'eɪt/ *vt* schaffen. ∼**ion** /-'eɪʃn/ *n* Schöpfung *f.* ∼**ive** /-tɪv/ *a* schöpferisch. ∼**or** *n* Schöpfer *m*
creature /'kriːtʃə(r)/ *n* Geschöpf *nt*
crèche /kreʃ/ *n* Kinderkrippe *f*
credentials /krɪ'denʃlz/ *npl* Beglaubigungsschreiben *nt*
credibility /kredə'bɪlətɪ/ *n* Glaubwürdigkeit *f*
credible /'kredəbl/ *a* glaubwürdig
credit /'kredɪt/ *n* Kredit *m*; (*honour*) Ehre *f* ● *vt* glauben; ∼ **s.o. with sth** (*Comm*) jdm etw gutschreiben; (*fig*) jdm etw zuschreiben. ∼**able** /-əbl/ *a* lobenswert
credit: ∼ **card** *n* Kreditkarte *f.* ∼**or** *n* Gläubiger *m*
creed /kriːd/ *n* Glaubensbekenntnis *nt*
creek /kriːk/ *n* enge Bucht *f*; (*Amer: stream*) Bach *m*
creep /kriːp/ *vi* (*pt/pp* **crept**) schleichen ● *n* (*fam*) fieser Kerl *m*; **it gives me the** ∼**s** es ist mir unheimlich. ∼**er** *n* Kletterpflanze *f.* ∼**y** *a* gruselig

cremat|e /krɪ'meɪt/ *vt* einäschern. ∼**ion** /-eɪʃn/ *n* Einäscherung *f*
crematorium /kremə'tɔːrɪəm/ *n* Krematorium *nt*
crêpe /kreɪp/ *n* Krepp *m.* ∼ **paper** *n* Kreppapier *nt*
crept /krept/ *see* **creep**
crescent /'kresənt/ *n* Halbmond *m*
cress /kres/ *n* Kresse *f*
crest /krest/ *n* Kamm *m*; (*coat of arms*) Wappen *nt*
Crete /kriːt/ *n* Kreta *nt*
crevasse /krɪ'væs/ *n* [Gletscher]-spalte *f*
crevice /'krevɪs/ *n* Spalte *f*
crew /kruː/ *n* Besatzung *f*; (*gang*) Bande *f.* ∼ **cut** *n* Bürstenschnitt *m*
crib¹ /krɪb/ *n* Krippe *f*
crib² *vt/i* (*pt/pp* **cribbed**) (*fam*) abschreiben
crick /krɪk/ *n* ∼ **in the neck** steifes Genick *nt*
cricket¹ /'krɪkɪt/ *n* (*insect*) Grille *f*
cricket² *n* Kricket *nt.* ∼**er** *n* Kricketspieler *m*
crime /kraɪm/ *n* Verbrechen *nt*; (*rate*) Kriminalität *f*
criminal /'krɪmɪnl/ *a* kriminell, verbrecherisch; (*law, court*) Straf- ● *n* Verbrecher *m*
crimson /'krɪmzn/ *a* purpurrot
cringe /krɪndʒ/ *vi* sich [ängstlich] ducken
crinkle /'krɪŋkl/ *vt/i* knittern
cripple /'krɪpl/ *n* Krüppel *m* ● *vt* zum Krüppel machen; (*fig*) lahmlegen. ∼**d** *a* verkrüppelt
crisis /'kraɪsɪs/ *n* (*pl* **-ses** /-siːz/) Krise *f*
crisp /krɪsp/ *a* (**-er, -est**) knusprig. ∼**bread** *n* Knäckebrot *nt.* ∼**s** *npl* Chips *pl*
criss-cross /'krɪs-/ *a* schräg gekreuzt
criterion /kraɪ'tɪərɪən/ *n* (*pl* **-ria** /-rɪə/) Kriterium *nt*
critic /'krɪtɪk/ *n* Kritiker *m.* ∼**al** *a* kritisch. ∼**ally** *adv* kritisch; ∼**ally ill** schwer krank
criticism /'krɪtɪsɪzm/ *n* Kritik *f*
criticize /'krɪtɪsaɪz/ *vt* kritisieren
croak /krəʊk/ *vi* krächzen; ⟨*frog:*⟩ quaken
crochet /'krəʊʃeɪ/ *n* Häkelarbeit *f* ● *vt/i* häkeln. ∼**-hook** *n* Häkelnadel *f*
crock /krɒk/ *n* (*fam*) **old** ∼ (*person*) Wrack *m*; (*car*) Klapperkiste *f*
crockery /'krɒkərɪ/ *n* Geschirr *nt*
crocodile /'krɒkədaɪl/ *n* Krokodil *nt*
crocus /'krəʊkəs/ *n* (*pl* **-es**) Krokus *m*

crony /'krəʊni/ n Kumpel m

crook /krʊk/ n (stick) Stab m; (fam: criminal) Schwindler m, Gauner m

crooked /'krʊkɪd/ a schief; (bent) krumm; (fam: dishonest) unehrlich

crop /krɒp/ n Feldfrucht f; (harvest) Ernte f; (of bird) Kropf m ● v (pt/pp cropped) ● vt stutzen ● vi ~ up (fam) zur Sprache kommen; (occur) dazwischenkommen

croquet /'krəʊkeɪ/ n Krocket nt

croquette /krəʊ'ket/ n Krokette f

cross /krɒs/ a, -ly adv (annoyed) böse (with auf + acc); talk at ~ purposes aneinander vorbeireden ● n Kreuz nt; (Bot, Zool) Kreuzung f; on the ~ schräg ● vt kreuzen ⟨cheque, animals⟩; überqueren ⟨road⟩; ~ oneself sich bekreuzigen; ~ one's arms die Arme verschränken; ~ one's legs die Beine übereinanderschlagen; keep one's fingers ~ed for s.o. jdm die Daumen drücken; it ~ed my mind es fiel mir ein ● vi (go across) hinübergehen/ -fahren; ⟨lines:⟩ sich kreuzen. ~ out vt durchstreichen

cross: ~bar n Querlatte f; (on bicycle) Stange f. ~-'country n (Sport) Crosslauf m. ~-ex'amine vt ins Kreuzverhör nehmen. ~-exami'nation n Kreuzverhör nt. ~-'eyed a schielend; be ~-eyed schielen. ~fire n Kreuzfeuer nt. ~ing n Übergang m; (sea journey) Überfahrt f. ~-'reference n Querverweis m. ~roads n [Straßen]kreuzung f. ~-'section n Querschnitt m. ~-stitch n Kreuzstich m. ~wise adv quer. ~word n ~word [puzzle] Kreuzworträtsel nt

crotchet /'krɒtʃɪt/ n Viertelnote f

crotchety /'krɒtʃɪtɪ/ a griesgrämig

crouch /kraʊtʃ/ vi kauern

crow /krəʊ/ n Krähe f; as the ~ flies Luftlinie ● vi krähen. ~bar n Brechstange f

crowd /kraʊd/ n [Menschen]menge f ● vi sich drängen. ~ed /'kraʊdɪd/ a [gedrängt] voll

crown /kraʊn/ n Krone f ● vt krönen; überkronen ⟨tooth⟩

crucial /'kruːʃl/ a höchst wichtig; (decisive) entscheidend (to für)

crucifix /'kruːsɪfɪks/ n Kruzifix nt

cruci|fixion /'kruːsɪ'fɪkʃn/ n Kreuzigung f. ~y /'kruːsɪfaɪ/ vt (pt/pp -ied) kreuzigen

crude /kruːd/ a (-r, -st) (raw) roh

cruel /'kruːəl/ a (crueller, cruellest), -ly adv grausam (to gegen). ~ty n Grausamkeit f; ~ty to animals Tierquälerei f

cruis|e /kruːz/ n Kreuzfahrt f ● vi kreuzen; ⟨car:⟩ fahren. ~er n (Mil) Kreuzer m; (motor boat) Kajütboot nt. ~ing speed n Reisegeschwindigkeit f

crumb /krʌm/ n Krümel m

crumb|le /'krʌmbl/ vt/i krümeln; (collapse) einstürzen. ~ly a krümelig

crumple /'krʌmpl/ vt zerknittern ● vi knittern

crunch /krʌntʃ/ n (fam) when it comes to the ~ wenn es [wirklich] drauf ankommt ● vt mampfen ● vi knirschen

crusade /kruː'seɪd/ n Kreuzzug m; (fig) Kampagne f. ~r n Kreuzfahrer m; (fig) Kämpfer m

crush /krʌʃ/ n (crowd) Gedränge nt ● vt zerquetschen; zerknittern ⟨clothes⟩; (fig: subdue) niederschlagen

crust /krʌst/ n Kruste f

crutch /krʌtʃ/ n Krücke f

crux /krʌks/ n (fig) springender Punkt m

cry /kraɪ/ n Ruf m; (shout) Schrei m; a far ~ from (fig) weit entfernt von ● vi (pt/pp cried) (weep) weinen; ⟨baby:⟩ schreien; (call) rufen

crypt /krɪpt/ n Krypta f. ~ic a rätselhaft

crystal /'krɪstl/ n Kristall m; (glass) Kristall nt. ~lize vi [sich] kristallisieren

cub /kʌb/ n (Zool) Junge(s) nt; C~ [Scout] Wölfling m

Cuba /'kjuːbə/ n Kuba nt

cubby-hole /'kʌbɪ-/ n Fach nt

cub|e /kjuːb/ n Würfel m. ~ic a Kubik-

cubicle /'kjuːbɪkl/ n Kabine f

cuckoo /'kʊkuː/ n Kuckuck m. ~ clock n Kuckucksuhr f

cucumber /'kjuːkʌmbə(r)/ n Gurke f

cuddl|e /'kʌdl/ vt herzen ● vi ~e up to sich kuscheln an (+ acc). ~y a kuschelig. ~y 'toy n Plüschtier nt

cudgel /'kʌdʒl/ n Knüppel m

cue¹ /kjuː/ n Stichwort nt

cue² n (Billiards) Queue nt

cuff /kʌf/ n Manschette f; (Amer: turn-up) [Hosen]aufschlag m; (blow) Klaps m; off the ~ (fam) aus dem Stegreif ● vt einen Klaps geben (+ dat). ~-link n Manschettenknopf m

cul-de-sac /'kʌldəsæk/ n Sackgasse f

culinary /'kʌlɪnərɪ/ a kulinarisch

cull /kʌl/ vt pflücken ⟨flowers⟩; (kill) ausmerzen

culminat|e /'kʌlmɪneɪt/ vi gipfeln (in in + dat). ~ion /-'neɪʃn/ n Gipfelpunkt m

culottes /kju:'lɒts/ npl Hosenrock m

culprit /'kʌlprɪt/ n Täter m

cult /kʌlt/ n Kult m

cultivate /'kʌltɪveɪt/ vt anbauen ⟨crop⟩; bebauen ⟨land⟩

cultural /'kʌltʃərəl/ a kulturell

culture /'kʌltʃə(r)/ n Kultur f. ~d a kultiviert

cumbersome /'kʌmbəsəm/ a hinderlich; (unwieldy) unhandlich

cumulative /'kju:mjʊlətɪv/ a kumulativ

cunning /'kʌnɪŋ/ a listig ● n List f

cup /kʌp/ n Tasse f; (prize) Pokal m

cupboard /'kʌbəd/ n Schrank m

Cup 'Final n Pokalendspiel nt

Cupid /'kju:pɪd/ n Amor m

curable /'kjʊərəbl/ a heilbar

curate /'kjʊərət/ n Vikar m; (Roman Catholic) Kaplan m

curator /kjʊə'reɪtə(r)/ n Kustos m

curb /kɜ:b/ vt zügeln

curdle /'kɜ:dl/ vi gerinnen

cure /kjʊə(r)/ n [Heil]mittel nt ● vt heilen; (salt) pökeln; (smoke) räuchern; gerben ⟨skin⟩

curfew /'kɜ:fju:/ n Ausgangssperre f

curio /'kjʊərɪəʊ/ n Kuriosität f

curiosity /kjʊərɪ'ɒsətɪ/ n Neugier f; (object) Kuriosität f

curious /'kjʊərɪəs/ a, -ly adv neugierig; (strange) merkwürdig, seltsam

curl /kɜ:l/ n Locke f ● vt locken ● vi sich locken. ~up vi sich zusammenrollen

curler /'kɜ:lə(r)/ n Lockenwickler m

curly /'kɜ:lɪ/ a (-ier, -iest) lockig

currant /'kʌrənt/ n (dried) Korinthe f

currency /'kʌrənsɪ/ n Geläufigkeit f; (money) Währung f; **foreign ~** Devisen pl

current /'kʌrənt/ a augenblicklich, gegenwärtig; (in general use) geläufig, gebräuchlich ● n Strömung f; (Electr) Strom m. **~ affairs** or **events** npl Aktuelle(s) nt. **~ly** adv zur Zeit

curriculum /kə'rɪkjʊləm/ n Lehrplan m. **~ vitae** /-'vi:taɪ/ n Lebenslauf m

curry /'kʌrɪ/ n Curry nt & m; (meal) Currygericht nt ● vt (pt/pp -ied) ~

favour sich einschmeicheln (with bei)

curse /kɜ:s/ n Fluch m ● vt verfluchen ● vi fluchen

cursory /'kɜ:sərɪ/ a flüchtig

curt /kɜ:t/ a, -ly adv barsch

curtail /kɜ:'teɪl/ vt abkürzen

curtain /'kɜ:tn/ n Vorhang m

curtsy /'kɜ:tsɪ/ n Knicks m ● vi (pt/pp -ied) knicksen

curve /kɜ:v/ n Kurve f ● vi einen Bogen machen; **~ to the right/left** nach rechts/links biegen. **~d** a gebogen

cushion /'kʊʃn/ n Kissen nt ● vt dämpfen; (protect) beschützen

cushy /'kʊʃɪ/ a (-ier, -iest) (fam) bequem

custard /'kʌstəd/ n Vanillesoße f

custodian /kʌ'stəʊdɪən/ n Hüter m

custody /'kʌstədɪ/ n Obhut f; (of child) Sorgerecht nt; (imprisonment) Haft f

custom /'kʌstəm/ n Brauch m; (habit) Gewohnheit f; (Comm) Kundschaft f. **~ary** a üblich; (habitual) gewohnt. **~er** n Kunde m/Kundin f

customs /'kʌstəmz/ npl Zoll m. **~ officer** n Zollbeamte(r) m

cut /kʌt/ n Schnitt m; (Med) Schnittwunde f; (reduction) Kürzung f; (in price) Senkung f; **~[of meat]** [Fleisch]stück nt ● vt/i (pt/pp cut, pres p **cutting**) schneiden; (mow) mähen; abheben ⟨cards⟩; (reduce) kürzen; senken ⟨price⟩; **~ one's finger** sich in den Finger schneiden; **~ s.o.'s hair** jdm die Haare schneiden; **~ short** abkürzen. **~ back** vt zurückschneiden; (fig) einschränken, kürzen. **~ down** vt fällen; (fig) einschränken. **~ off** vt abschneiden; (disconnect) abstellen; **be ~ off** (Teleph) unterbrochen werden. **~ out** vt ausschneiden; (delete) streichen; **be ~ out for** (fam) geeignet sein zu. **~ up** vt zerschneiden; (slice) aufschneiden

'cut-back n Kürzung f, Einschränkung f

cute /kju:t/ a (-r, -st) (fam) niedlich

cut 'glass n Kristall nt

cuticle /'kju:tɪkl/ n Nagelhaut f

cutlery /'kʌtlərɪ/ n Besteck nt

cutlet /'kʌtlɪt/ n Kotelett nt

'cut-price a verbilligt

cutting /'kʌtɪŋ/ a ⟨remark⟩ bissig ● n (from newspaper) Ausschnitt m; (of plant) Ableger m

CV *abbr of* **curriculum vitae**

cyclamen /ˈsɪkləmən/ n Alpenveilchen nt

cycl|e /ˈsaɪkl/ n Zyklus m; (bicycle) [Fahr]rad nt ● vi mit dem Rad fahren. ~**ing** n Radfahren nt. ~**ist** n Radfahrer(in) m(f)

cyclone /ˈsaɪkləʊn/ n Wirbelsturm m

cylind|er /ˈsɪlɪndə(r)/ n Zylinder m. ~**rical** /-ˈlɪndrɪkl/ a zylindrisch

cymbals /ˈsɪmblz/ npl (Mus) Becken nt

cynic /ˈsɪnɪk/ n Zyniker m. ~**al** a, -**ly** adv zynisch. ~**ism** /-sɪzm/ n Zynismus m

cypress /ˈsaɪprəs/ n Zypresse f

Cyprus /ˈsaɪprəs/ n Zypern nt

cyst /sɪst/ n Zyste f. ~**itis** /-ˈtaɪtɪs/ n Blasenentzündung f

Czech /tʃek/ a tschechisch ● n Tscheche m/ Tschechin f

Czechoslovak /tʃekəˈsləʊvæk/ atschechoslowakisch. ~**ia** /-ˈvækɪə/ n die Tschechoslowakei. ~**ian** /-ˈvækɪən/ a tschechoslowakisch

D

dab /dæb/ n Tupfer m; (of butter) Klecks m; a ~ of ein bißchen ● vt (pt/pp **dabbed**) abtupfen; betupfen (with mit)

dabble /ˈdæbl/ vi ~ **in sth** (fig) sich nebenbei mit etw befassen

dachshund /ˈdækshʊnd/ n Dackel m

dad[dy] /ˈdæd[i]/ n (fam) Vati m

daddy-ˈlong-legs n [Kohl]schnake f; (Amer: spider) Weberknecht m

daffodil /ˈdæfədɪl/ n Osterglocke f, gelbe Narzisse f

daft /dɑːft/ a (-er, -est) dumm

dagger /ˈdægə(r)/ n Dolch m; (Typ) Kreuz nt; **be at** ~**s drawn** (fam) auf Kriegsfuß stehen

dahlia /ˈdeɪlɪə/ n Dahlie f

daily /ˈdeɪlɪ/ a & adv täglich ● n (newspaper) Tageszeitung f; (fam: cleaner) Putzfrau f

dainty /ˈdeɪntɪ/ a (-ier, -iest) zierlich

dairy /ˈdeərɪ/ n Molkerei f; (shop) Milchgeschäft nt. ~ **cow** n Milchkuh f. ~ **products** pl Milchprodukte pl

dais /ˈdeɪɪs/ n Podium nt

daisy /ˈdeɪzɪ/ n Gänseblümchen nt

dale /deɪl/ n (liter) Tal nt

dally /ˈdælɪ/ vi (pt/pp -**ied**) trödeln

dam /dæm/ n [Stau]damm m ● vt (pt/pp **dammed**) eindämmen

damag|e /ˈdæmɪdʒ/ n Schaden m (**to** an + dat); ~**es** pl (Jur) Schadenersatz m ● vt beschädigen; (fig) beeinträchtigen. ~**ing** a schädlich

damask /ˈdæməsk/ n Damast m

dame /deɪm/ n (liter) Dame f; (Amer sl) Weib nt

damn /dæm/ a, int & adv (fam) verdammt ● n **I don't care** or **give a** ~ (fam) ich schere mich einen Dreck darum ● vt verdammen. ~**ation** /-ˈneɪʃn/ n Verdammnis f ● int (fam) verdammt!

damp /dæmp/ a (-er, -est) feucht ● n Feuchtigkeit f ● vt = **dampen**

damp|en vt anfeuchten; (fig) dämpfen. ~**ness** n Feuchtigkeit f

dance /dɑːns/ n Tanz m; (function) Tanzveranstaltung f ● vt/i tanzen. ~**-hall** n Tanzlokal nt. ~ **music** n Tanzmusik f

dancer /ˈdɑːnsə(r)/ n Tänzer(in) m(f)

dandelion /ˈdændɪlaɪən/ n Löwenzahn m

dandruff /ˈdændrʌf/ n Schuppen pl

Dane /deɪn/ n Däne m/ Dänin f; **Great** ~ [deutsche] Dogge f

danger /ˈdeɪndʒə(r)/ n Gefahr f; **in/ out of** ~ in/außer Gefahr. ~**ous** /-rəs/ a, -**ly** adv gefährlich; ~**ously ill** schwer erkrankt

dangle /ˈdæŋgl/ vi baumeln ● vt baumeln lassen

Danish /ˈdeɪnɪʃ/ a dänisch. ~ **ˈpastry** n Hefeteilchen nt, Plunderstück nt

dank /dæŋk/ a (-er, -est) naßkalt

Danube /ˈdænjuːb/ n Donau f

dare /deə(r)/ n Mutprobe f ● vt/i (challenge) herausfordern (**to** zu); ~ **[to] do sth** [es] wagen, etw zu tun; **I** ~ **say!** das mag wohl sein! ~**devil** n Draufgänger m

daring /ˈdeərɪŋ/ a verwegen ● n Verwegenheit f

dark /dɑːk/ a (-er, -est) dunkel; ~ **blue/brown** dunkelblau/ -braun; ~ **horse** (fig) stilles Wasser nt; **keep sth** ~ (fig) etw geheimhalten ● n Dunkelheit f; **after** ~ nach Einbruch der Dunkelheit; **in the** ~ im Dunkeln; **keep in the** ~ (fig) im dunkeln lassen

dark|en /ˈdɑːkn/ vt verdunkeln ● vi dunkler werden. ~**ness** n Dunkelheit f

ˈdark-room n Dunkelkammer f

darling /'dɑːlɪŋ/ *a* allerliebst ● *n* Liebling *m*

darn /dɑːn/ *vt* stopfen. **~ing-needle** *n* Stopfnadel *f*

dart /dɑːt/ *n* Pfeil *m*; (*Sewing*) Abnäher *m*; **~s** *sg* (*game*) [Wurf]pfeil *m* ● *vi* flitzen

dash /dæʃ/ *n* (*Typ*) Gedankenstrich *m*; (*in Morse*) Strich *m*; **a ~ of milk** ein Schuß Milch; **make a ~** losstürzen (**for** auf + *acc*) ● *vi* rennen ● *vt* schleudern. **~ off** *vi* losstürzen ● *vt* (*write quickly*) hinwerfen

'dashboard *n* Armaturenbrett *nt*

dashing /'dæʃɪŋ/ *a* schneidig

data /'deɪtə/ *npl* & *sg* Daten *pl*. **~ processing** *n* Datenverarbeitung *f*

date¹ /deɪt/ *n* (*fruit*) Dattel *f*

date² *n* Datum *nt*; (*fam*) Verabredung *f*; **to ~** bis heute; **out of ~** überholt; (*expired*) ungültig; **be up to ~** auf dem laufenden sein ● *vt/i* datieren; (*Amer, fam: go out with*) ausgehen mit; **~ back to** zurückgehen auf (+ *acc*)

dated /'deɪtɪd/ *a* altmodisch

'date-line *n* Datumsgrenze *f*

dative /'deɪtɪv/ *a & n* (*Gram*) **~ [case]** Dativ *m*

daub /dɔːb/ *vt* beschmieren (**with** mit); schmieren ⟨*paint*⟩

daughter /'dɔːtə(r)/ *n* Tochter *f*. **~-in-law** *n* (*pl* **~s-in-law**) Schwiegertochter *f*

daunt /dɔːnt/ *vt* entmutigen; **nothing ~ed** unverzagt. **~less** *a* furchtlos

dawdle /'dɔːdl/ *vi* trödeln

dawn /dɔːn/ *n* Morgendämmerung *f*; **at ~** bei Tagesanbruch ● *vi* anbrechen; **it ~ed on me** (*fig*) es ging mir auf

day /deɪ/ *n* Tag *m*; **~ by ~** Tag für Tag; **~ after ~** Tag um Tag; **these ~s** heutzutage; **in those ~s** zu der Zeit; **it's had its ~** (*fam*) es hat ausgedient

day: ~break *n* **at ~break** bei Tagesanbruch *m*. **~-dream** *n* Tagtraum *m* ● *vi* [mit offenen Augen] träumen. **~light** *n* Tageslicht *nt*. **~ re'turn** *n* (*ticket*) Tagesrückfahrkarte *f*. **~time** *n* **in the ~time** am Tage

daze /deɪz/ *n* **in a ~** wie benommen. **~d** *a* benommen

dazzle /'dæzl/ *vt* blenden

deacon /'diːkn/ *n* Diakon *m*

dead /ded/ *a* tot; ⟨*flower*⟩ verwelkt; (*numb*) taub; **~ body** Leiche *f*; **be ~ on time** auf die Minute pünktlich kommen; **~ centre** genau in der Mitte ● *adv* **~ tired** todmüde; **~ slow** sehr langsam; **stop ~** stehenbleiben ● *n* **the ~** *pl* die Toten; **in the ~ of night** mitten in der Nacht

deaden /'dedn/ *vt* dämpfen ⟨*sound*⟩; betäuben ⟨*pain*⟩

dead: ~ 'end *n* Sackgasse *f*. **~ 'heat** *n* totes Rennen *nt*. **~-line** *n* [letzter] Termin *m*. **~lock** *n* **reach ~lock** (*fig*) sich festfahren

deadly /'dedlɪ/ *a* (**-ier, -iest**) tödlich; (*fam: dreary*) sterbenslangweilig; **~ sins** *pl* Todsünden *pl*

deaf /def/ *a* (**-er, -est**) taub; **~ and dumb** taubstumm. **~-aid** *n* Hörgerät *nt*

deaf|en /'defn/ *vt* betäuben; (*permanently*) taub machen. **~ening** *a* ohrenbetäubend. **~ness** *n* Taubheit *f*

deal /diːl/ *n* (*transaction*) Geschäft *nt*; **who's ~?** (*Cards*) wer gibt? **a good** *or* **great ~** eine Menge; **get a raw ~** (*fam*) sehr schlecht abschneiden ● *v* (*pt/pp* **dealt** /delt/) ● *vt* (*Cards*) geben; **~ out** austeilen; **~ s.o. a blow** jdm einen Schlag versetzen ● *vi* **~ in** handeln mit; **~ with** zu tun haben mit; (*handle*) sich befassen mit; (*cope with*) fertig werden mit; (*be about*) handeln von; **that's been dealt with** das ist schon erledigt

deal|er /'diːlə(r)/ *n* Händler *m*; (*Cards*) Kartengeber *m*. **~ings** *npl* **have ~ings with** zu tun haben mit

dean /diːn/ *n* Dekan *m*

dear /dɪə(r)/ *a* (**-er, -est**) lieb; (*expensive*) teuer; (*in letter*) liebe(r,s)/ (*formal*) sehr geehrte(r,s) ● *n* Liebe(r) *m/f* ● *int* **oh ~!** oje! **~ly** *adv* ⟨*love*⟩ sehr; ⟨*pay*⟩ teuer

dearth /dɜːθ/ *n* Mangel *m* (**of** an + *dat*)

death /deθ/ *n* Tod *m*; **three ~s** drei Todesfälle. **~ certificate** *n* Sterbeurkunde *f*. **~ duty** *n* Erbschaftssteuer *f*

deathly *a* **~ silence** Totenstille *f* ● *adv* **~ pale** totenblaß

death: ~ penalty *n* Todesstrafe *f*. **~'s head** *n* Totenkopf *m*. **~-trap** *n* Todesfalle *f*

debar /dɪ'bɑː(r)/ *vt* (*pt/pp* **debarred**) ausschließen

debase /dɪ'beɪs/ *vt* erniedrigen

debatable /dɪ'beɪtəbl/ *a* strittig

debate /dɪ'beɪt/ *n* Debatte *f* ● *vt/i* debattieren

debauchery /dɪˈbɔːtʃərɪ/ n Ausschweifung f

debility /dɪˈbɪlətɪ/ n Entkräftung f

debit /ˈdebɪt/ n Schuldbetrag m; ~ [side] Soll nt ● vt (pt/pp **debited**) (Comm) belasten; abbuchen ⟨sum⟩

debris /ˈdebriː/ n Trümmer pl

debt /det/ n Schuld f; **in** ~ verschuldet. ~**or** n Schuldner m

début /ˈdeɪbuː/ n Debüt nt

decade /ˈdekeɪd/ n Jahrzehnt nt

decaden|ce /ˈdekədəns/ n Dekadenz f. ~**t** a dekadent

decaffeinated /dɪˈkæfɪneɪtɪd/ a koffeinfrei

decant /dɪˈkænt/ vt umfüllen. ~**er** n Karaffe f

decapitate /dɪˈkæpɪteɪt/ vt köpfen

decay /dɪˈkeɪ/ n Verfall m; (rot) Verwesung f; (of tooth) Zahnfäule f ● vi verfallen; (rot) verwesen; ⟨tooth:⟩ schlecht werden

decease /dɪˈsiːs/ n Ableben nt. ~**d** a verstorben ● n **the** ~**d** der/die Verstorbene

deceit /dɪˈsiːt/ n Täuschung f. ~**ful** a, -ly adv unaufrichtig

deceive /dɪˈsiːv/ vt täuschen; (be unfaithful to) betrügen

December /dɪˈsembə(r)/ n Dezember m

decency /ˈdiːsənsɪ/ n Anstand m

decent /ˈdiːsənt/ a, -ly adv anständig

decentralize /diːˈsentrəlaɪz/ vt dezentralisieren

decept|ion /dɪˈsepʃn/ n Täuschung f; (fraud) Betrug m. ~**ive** /-tɪv/ a, -ly adv täuschend

decibel /ˈdesɪbel/ n Dezibel nt

decide /dɪˈsaɪd/ vt entscheiden ● vi sich entscheiden (**on** für)

decided /dɪˈsaɪdɪd/ a, -ly adv entschieden

deciduous /dɪˈsɪdjʊəs/ a ~ **tree** Laubbaum m

decimal /ˈdesɪml/ a Dezimal- ● n Dezimalzahl f. ~ '**point** n Komma nt. ~ **system** n Dezimalsystem nt

decimate /ˈdesɪmeɪt/ vt dezimieren

decipher /dɪˈsaɪfə(r)/ vt entziffern

decision /dɪˈsɪʒn/ n Entscheidung f; (firmness) Entschlossenheit f

decisive /dɪˈsaɪsɪv/ a ausschlaggebend; (firm) entschlossen

deck[1] /dek/ vt schmücken

deck[2] n (Naut) Deck nt; **on** ~ an Deck; **top** ~ (of bus) Oberdeck nt; ~ **of cards** (Amer) [Karten]spiel nt. ~**chair** n Liegestuhl m

declaration /dekləˈreɪʃn/ n Erklärung f

declare /dɪˈkleə(r)/ vt erklären; angeben ⟨goods⟩; **anything to** ~? etwas zu verzollen?

declension /dɪˈklenʃn/ n Deklination f

decline /dɪˈklaɪn/ n Rückgang m; (in health) Verfall m ● vt ablehnen; (Gram) deklinieren ● vi ablehnen; (fall) sinken; (decrease) nachlassen

decode /diːˈkəʊd/ vt entschlüsseln

decompos|e /diːkəmˈpəʊz/ vi sich zersetzen

décor /ˈdeɪkɔː(r)/ n Ausstattung f

decorat|e /ˈdekəreɪt/ vt (adorn) schmücken; verzieren ⟨cake⟩; (paint) streichen; (wallpaper) tapezieren; (award medal to) einen Orden verleihen (+ dat). ~**ion** /-ˈreɪʃn/ n Verzierung f; (medal) Orden m; ~**ions** pl Schmuck m. ~**ive** /-rətɪv/ a dekorativ. ~**or** n **painter and** ~**or** Maler und Tapezierer m

decorous /ˈdekərəs/ a, -ly adv schamhaft

decorum /dɪˈkɔːrəm/ n Anstand m

decoy[1] /ˈdiːkɔɪ/ n Lockvogel m

decoy[2] /dɪˈkɔɪ/ vt locken

decrease[1] /ˈdiːkriːs/ n Verringerung f; (in number) Rückgang m; **be on the** ~ zurückgehen

decrease[2] /dɪˈkriːs/ vt verringern; herabsetzen ⟨price⟩ ● vi sich verringern; ⟨price:⟩ sinken

decree /dɪˈkriː/ n Erlaß m ● vt (pt/pp **decreed**) verordnen

decrepit /dɪˈkrepɪt/ a altersschwach

dedicat|e /ˈdedɪkeɪt/ vt widmen; (Relig) weihen. ~**ed** a hingebungsvoll; ⟨person⟩ aufopfernd. ~**ion** /-ˈkeɪʃn/ n Hingabe f; (in book) Widmung f

deduce /dɪˈdjuːs/ vt folgern (**from** aus)

deduct /dɪˈdʌkt/ vt abziehen

deduction /dɪˈdʌkʃn/ n Abzug m; (conclusion) Folgerung f

deed /diːd/ n Tat f; (Jur) Urkunde f

deem /diːm/ vt halten für

deep /diːp/ a (-er, -est), -ly adv tief; **go off the** ~ **end** (fam) auf die Palme gehen ● adv tief

deepen /ˈdiːpn/ vt vertiefen ● vi tiefer werden; (fig) sich vertiefen

deep-'freeze /diːp-/ n Gefriertruhe f; (upright) Gefrierschrank m

deer /dɪə(r)/ n inv Hirsch m; (roe) Reh nt

deface /dɪ'feɪs/ vt beschädigen

defamat|ion /defə'meɪʃn/ n Verleumdung f. ~ory /dɪ'fæmətərɪ/ a verleumderisch

default /dɪ'fɔ:lt/ n (Jur) Nichtzahlung f; (failure to appear) Nichterscheinen nt; **win by ~** (Sport) kampflos gewinnen ● vi nicht zahlen; nicht erscheinen

defeat /dɪ'fi:t/ n Niederlage f; (defeating) Besiegung f; (rejection) Ablehnung f ● vt besiegen; ablehnen; (frustrate) vereiteln

defect¹ /dɪ'fekt/ vi (Pol) überlaufen

defect² /'di:fekt/ n Fehler m; (Techn) Defekt m. ~**ive** /dɪ'fektɪv/ a fehlerhaft; (Techn) defekt

defence /dɪ'fens/ n Verteidigung f. ~**less** a wehrlos

defend /dɪ'fend/ vt verteidigen; (justify) rechtfertigen. ~**ant** n (Jur) Beklagte(r) m/f; (in criminal court) Angeklagte(r) m/f

defensive /dɪ'fensɪv/ a defensiv ● n Defensive f

defer /dɪ'fɜ:(r)/ vt (pt/pp deferred) (postpone) aufschieben; ~ **to s.o.** sich jdm fügen

deferen|ce /'defərəns/ n Ehrerbietung f. ~**tial** /-'renʃl/ a, -ly adv ehrerbietig

defian|ce /dɪ'faɪəns/ n Trotz m; **in ~ce of** zum Trotz (+ dat). ~**t** a, -ly adv aufsässig

deficien|cy /dɪ'fɪʃənsɪ/ n Mangel m. ~**t** a mangelhaft; **he is ~t in ...** ihm mangelt es an ... (dat)

deficit /'defɪsɪt/ n Defizit nt

defile /dɪ'faɪl/ vt (fig) schänden

define /dɪ'faɪn/ vt bestimmen; definieren (word)

definite /'defɪnɪt/ a, -ly adv bestimmt; (certain) sicher

definition /defɪ'nɪʃn/ n Definition f; (Phot, TV) Schärfe f

definitive /dɪ'fɪnətɪv/ a endgültig; (authoritative) maßgeblich

deflat|e /dɪ'fleɪt/ vt die Luft auslassen aus. ~**ion** /-eɪʃn/ n (Comm) Deflation f

deflect /dɪ'flekt/ vt ablenken

deform|ed /dɪ'fɔ:md/ a mißgebildet. ~**ity** n Mißbildung f

defraud /dɪ'frɔ:d/ vt betrügen (**of** um)

defray /dɪ'freɪ/ vt bestreiten

defrost /di:'frɒst/ vt entfrosten; abtauen (fridge); auftauen (food)

deft /deft/ a (-er, -est), -ly adv geschickt. ~**ness** n Geschicklichkeit f

defunct /dɪ'fʌŋkt/ a aufgelöst; (law) außer Kraft gesetzt

defuse /di:'fju:z/ vt entschärfen

defy /dɪ'faɪ/ vt (pt/pp -ied) trotzen (+ dat); widerstehen (+ dat) (attempt)

degenerate¹ /dɪ'dʒenəreɪt/ vi degenerieren; ~ **into** (fig) ausarten in (+ acc)

degenerate² /dɪ'dʒenərət/ a degeneriert

degrading /dɪ'greɪdɪŋ/ a entwürdigend

degree /dɪ'gri:/ n Grad m; (Univ) akademischer Grad m; **20 ~s** 20 Grad

dehydrate /di:'haɪdreɪt/ vt Wasser entziehen (+ dat). ~**d** /-ɪd/ a ausgetrocknet

de-ice /di:'aɪs/ vt enteisen

deign /deɪn/ vi ~ **to do sth** sich herablassen, etw zu tun

deity /'di:ɪtɪ/ n Gottheit f

dejected /dɪ'dʒektɪd/ a, -ly adv niedergeschlagen

delay /dɪ'leɪ/ n Verzögerung f; (of train, aircraft) Verspätung f; **without ~** unverzüglich ● vt aufhalten; (postpone) aufschieben; **be ~ed** (person:) aufgehalten werden; (train, aircraft:) Verspätung haben ● vi zögern

delegate¹ /'delɪgət/ n Delegierte(r) m/f

delegat|e² /'delɪgeɪt/ vt delegieren. ~**ion** /-'geɪʃn/ n Delegation f

delet|e /dɪ'li:t/ vt streichen. ~**ion** /-i:ʃn/ n Streichung f

deliberate¹ /dɪ'lɪbərət/ a, -ly adv absichtlich; (slow) bedächtig

deliberat|e² /dɪ'lɪbəreɪt/ vt/i überlegen. ~**ion** /-'reɪʃn/ n Überlegung f; **with ~ion** mit Bedacht

delicacy /'delɪkəsɪ/ n Feinheit f; Zartheit f; (food) Delikatesse f

delicate /'delɪkət/ a fein; (fabric, health) zart; (situation) heikel; (mechanism) empfindlich

delicatessen /delɪkə'tesn/ n Delikatessengeschäft nt

delicious /dɪ'lɪʃəs/ a köstlich

delight /dɪ'laɪt/ n Freude f ● vt entzücken ● vi ~ **in** sich erfreuen an (+ dat). ~**ed** a hocherfreut; **be ~ed** sich sehr freuen. ~**ful** a reizend

delinquen|cy /dɪ'lɪŋkwənsɪ/ n Kriminalität f. ~**t** a straffällig ● n Straffällige(r) m/f

deli|rious /dɪ'lɪrɪəs/ a **be ~rious** im Delirium sein. **~rium** /-rɪəm/ n Delirium nt

deliver /dɪ'lɪvə(r)/ vt liefern; zustellen ⟨post, newspaper⟩; halten ⟨speech⟩; überbringen ⟨message⟩; versetzen ⟨blow⟩; (set free) befreien; **~ a baby** ein Kind zur Welt bringen. **~ance** n Erlösung f. **~y** n Lieferung f; (of post) Zustellung f; (Med) Entbindung f; **cash on ~y** per Nachnahme

delta /'deltə/ n Delta nt

delude /dɪ'lu:d/ vt täuschen; **~ oneself** sich (dat) Illusionen machen

deluge /'delju:dʒ/ n Flut f; (heavy rain) schwerer Guß m • vt überschwemmen

delusion /dɪ'lu:ʒn/ n Täuschung f

de luxe /də'lʌks/ a Luxus-

delve /delv/ vi hineingreifen (**into** in + acc); (fig) eingehen (**into** auf + acc)

demand /dɪ'mɑ:nd/ n Forderung f; (Comm) Nachfrage f; **in ~** gefragt; **on ~** auf Verlangen • vt verlangen, fordern (**of/from** von). **~ing** a anspruchsvoll

demarcation /di:mɑ:'keɪʃn/ n Abgrenzung f

demean /dɪ'mi:n/ vt **~ oneself** sich erniedrigen

demeanour /dɪ'mi:nə(r)/ n Verhalten nt

demented /dɪ'mentɪd/ a verrückt

demise /dɪ'maɪz/ n Tod m

demister /di:'mɪstə(r)/ n (Auto) Defroster m

demo /'deməʊ/ n (pl **~s**) (fam) Demonstration f

demobilize /di:'məʊbəlaɪz/ vt (Mil) entlassen

democracy /dɪ'mekrəsɪ/ n Demokratie f

democrat /'deməkræt/ n Demokrat m. **~ic** /-'krætɪk/ a, **-ally** adv demokratisch

demo|lish /dɪ'melɪʃ/ vt abbrechen; (destroy) zerstören. **~lition** /demə'lɪʃn/ n Abbruch m

demon /'di:mən/ n Dämon m

demonstrat|e /'demənstreɪt/ vt beweisen; vorführen ⟨appliance⟩ • vi (Pol) demonstrieren. **~ion** /-'streɪʃn/ n Vorführung f; (Pol) Demonstration f

demonstrative /dɪ'menstrətɪv/ a (Gram) demonstrativ; **be ~** seine Gefühle zeigen

demonstrator /'demənstreɪtə(r)/ n Vorführer m; (Pol) Demonstrant m

demoralize /dɪ'merəlaɪz/ vt demoralisieren

demote /dɪ'məʊt/ vt degradieren

demure /dɪ'mjʊə(r)/ a, **-ly** adv sittsam

den /den/ n Höhle f; (room) Bude f

denial /dɪ'naɪəl/ n Leugnen nt; **official ~** Dementi nt

denigrate /'denɪgreɪt/ vt herabsetzen

denim /'denɪm/ n Jeansstoff m; **~s** pl Jeans pl

Denmark /'denmɑ:k/ n Dänemark nt

denomination /dɪnɒmɪ'neɪʃn/ n (Relig) Konfession f; (money) Nennwert m

denote /dɪ'nəʊt/ vt bezeichnen

denounce /dɪ'naʊns/ vt denunzieren; (condemn) verurteilen

dens|e /dens/ a (**-r, -st**), **-ly** adv dicht; (fam: stupid) blöd[e]. **~ity** n Dichte f

dent /dent/ n Delle f, Beule f • vt einbeulen; **~ed** /-ɪd/ verbeult

dental /'dentl/ a Zahn-; ⟨treatment⟩ zahnärztlich. **~ floss** /flɒs/ n Zahnseide f. **~ surgeon** n Zahnarzt m

dentist /'dentɪst/ n Zahnarzt m/-ärztin f. **~ry** n Zahnmedizin f

denture /'dentʃə(r)/ n Zahnprothese f; **~s** pl künstliches Gebiß nt

denude /dɪ'nju:d/ vt entblößen

denunciation /dɪnʌnsɪ'eɪʃn/ n Denunziation f; (condemnation) Verurteilung f

deny /dɪ'naɪ/ vt (pt/pp **-ied**) leugnen; (officially) dementieren; **~ s.o. sth** jdm etw verweigern

deodorant /di:'əʊdərənt/ n Deodorant nt

depart /dɪ'pɑ:t/ vi abfahren; (Aviat) abfliegen; (go away) weggehen/-fahren; (deviate) abweichen (**from** von)

department /dɪ'pɑ:tmənt/ n Abteilung f; (Pol) Ministerium nt. **~ store** n Kaufhaus nt

departure /dɪ'pɑ:tʃə(r)/ n Abfahrt f; (Aviat) Abflug m; (from rule) Abweichung f; **new ~** Neuerung f

depend /dɪ'pend/ vi abhängen (**on** von); (rely) sich verlassen (**on** auf + acc); **it all ~s** das kommt darauf an. **~able** /-əbl/ a zuverlässig. **~ant** n Abhängige(r) m/f. **~ence** n Abhängigkeit f. **~ent** a abhängig (**on** von)

depict /dɪ'pɪkt/ vt darstellen

depilatory /dɪ'pɪlətərɪ/ n Enthaarungsmittel nt

deplete /dɪ'pliːt/ vt verringern

deplor|able /dɪ'plɔːrəbl/ a bedauerlich. ～e vt bedauern

deploy /dɪ'plɔɪ/ vt (Mil) einsetzen ● vi sich aufstellen

depopulate /diː'pɒpjʊleɪt/ vt entvölkern

deport /dɪ'pɔːt/ vt deportieren, ausweisen. ～ation /diːpɔː'teɪʃn/ n Ausweisung f

deportment /dɪ'pɔːtmənt/ n Haltung f

depose /dɪ'pəʊz/ vt absetzen

deposit /dɪ'pɒzɪt/ n Anzahlung f; (against damage) Kaution f; (on bottle) Pfand nt; (sediment) Bodensatz m; (Geol) Ablagerung f ● vt (pt/pp **deposited**) legen; (for safety) deponieren; (Geol) ablagern. ～ **account** n Sparkonto nt

depot /'depəʊ/ n Depot nt; (Amer: railway station) Bahnhof m

deprav|e /dɪ'preɪv/ vt verderben. ～ed a verkommen. ～ity /-'prævətɪ/ n Verderbtheit f

deprecate /'deprəkeɪt/ vt mißbilligen

depreciat|e /dɪ'priːʃɪeɪt/ vi an Wert verlieren. ～ion /-'eɪʃn/ n Wertminderung f; (Comm) Abschreibung f

depress /dɪ'pres/ vt deprimieren; (press down) herunterdrücken. ～ed a deprimiert; ～ed area Notstandsgebiet nt. ～ing a deprimierend. ～ion /-eʃn/ n Vertiefung f; (Med) Depression f; (Meteorol) Tief nt

deprivation /deprɪ'veɪʃn/ n Entbehrung f

deprive /dɪ'praɪv/ vt entziehen; ～ s.o. of sth jdm etw entziehen. ～d a benachteiligt

depth /depθ/ n Tiefe f; in ～ gründlich; in the ～s of winter im tiefsten Winter

deputation /depjʊ'teɪʃn/ n Abordnung f

deputize /'depjʊtaɪz/ vi ～ for vertreten

deputy /'depjʊtɪ/ n Stellvertreter m ● attrib stellvertretend

derail /dɪ'reɪl/ vt be ～ed entgleisen. ～ment n Entgleisung f

deranged /dɪ'reɪndʒd/ a geistesgestört

derelict /'derəlɪkt/ a verfallen; (abandoned) verlassen

deri|de /dɪ'raɪd/ vt verhöhnen. ～sion /-'rɪʒn/ n Hohn m

derisive /dɪ'raɪsɪv/ a, **-ly** adv höhnisch

derisory /dɪ'raɪsərɪ/ a höhnisch; ⟨offer⟩ lächerlich

derivation /derɪ'veɪʃn/ n Ableitung f

derivative /dɪ'rɪvətɪv/ a abgeleitet ● n Ableitung f

derive /dɪ'raɪv/ vt/i (obtain) gewinnen (**from** aus); **be ～d from** ⟨word:⟩ hergeleitet sein aus

dermatologist /dɜːmə'tɒlədʒɪst/ n Hautarzt m /-ärztin f

derogatory /dɪ'rɒgətrɪ/ a abfällig

derrick /'derɪk/ n Bohrturm m

derv /dɜːv/ n Diesel[kraftstoff] m

descend /dɪ'send/ vt/i hinunter-/heruntergehen; ⟨vehicle, lift:⟩ hinunter-/herunterfahren; **be ～ed from** abstammen von. ～ant n Nachkomme m

descent /dɪ'sent/ n Abstieg m; (lineage) Abstammung f

describe /dɪ'skraɪb/ vt beschreiben

descrip|tion /dɪ'skrɪpʃn/ n Beschreibung f; (sort) Art f. ～tive /-tɪv/ a beschreibend; (vivid) anschaulich

desecrat|e /'desɪkreɪt/ vt entweihen. ～ion /-'kreɪʃn/ n Entweihung f

desert[1] /'dezət/ n Wüste f ● a Wüsten-; ～ **island** verlassene Insel f

desert[2] /dɪ'zɜːt/ vt verlassen ● vi desertieren. ～ed a verlassen. ～er n (Mil) Deserteur m. ～ion /-ɜːʃn/ n Fahnenflucht f

deserts /dɪ'zɜːts/ npl **get one's ～** seinen verdienten Lohn bekommen

deserv|e /dɪ'zɜːv/ vt verdienen. ～edly /-ɪdlɪ/ adv verdientermaßen. ～ing a verdienstvoll; ～ing cause guter Zweck m

design /dɪ'zaɪn/ n Entwurf m; (pattern) Muster nt; (construction) Konstruktion f; (aim) Absicht f ● vt entwerfen; (construct) konstruieren; **be ～ed for** bestimmt sein für

designat|e /'dezɪgneɪt/ vt bezeichnen; (appoint) ernennen. ～ion /-'neɪʃn/ n Bezeichnung f

designer /dɪ'zaɪnə(r)/ n Designer m; (Techn) Konstrukteur m; (Theat) Bühnenbildner m

desirable /dɪ'zaɪrəbl/ a wünschenswert; (sexually) begehrenswert

desire /dɪ'zaɪə(r)/ n Wunsch m; (longing) Verlangen nt (**for** nach); (sexual) Begierde f ● vt [sich (dat)] wünschen; (sexually) begehren

desk /desk/ n Schreibtisch m; (Sch)
Pult nt; (Comm) Kasse f; (in hotel)
Rezeption f

desolat|e /'desələt/ a trostlos. ~ion
/-'leɪʃn/ n Trostlosigkeit f

despair /dɪ'speə(r)/ n Verzweiflung f;
in ~ verzweifelt ● vi verzweifeln

desperat|e /'despərət/ a, -ly adv ver-
zweifelt; (urgent) dringend; be ~e
⟨criminal:⟩ zum Äußersten entschlossen sein; be ~e for dringend
brauchen. ~ion /-'reɪʃn/ n Verzweiflung f; in ~ion aus Verzweiflung

despicable /dɪ'spɪkəbl/ a verachtenswert

despise /dɪ'spaɪz/ vt verachten

despite /dɪ'spaɪt/ prep trotz (+ gen)

despondent /dɪ'spɒndənt/ a
niedergeschlagen

despot /'despɒt/ n Despot m

dessert /dɪ'zɜːt/ n Dessert nt, Nachtisch m. ~ spoon n Dessertlöffel m

destination /destɪ'neɪʃn/ n [Reise]-
ziel nt; (of goods) Bestimmungsort m

destine /'destɪn/ vt bestimmen

destiny /'destɪnɪ/ n Schicksal nt

destitute /'destɪtjuːt/ a völlig
mittellos

destroy /dɪ'strɔɪ/ vt zerstören; (totally) vernichten. ~er n (Naut) Zer-
störer m

destruc|tion /dɪ'strʌkʃn/ n Zerstö-
rung f; Vernichtung f. **-tive** /-tɪv/ a
zerstörerisch; (fig) destruktiv

detach /dɪ'tætʃ/ vt abnehmen; (tear
off) abtrennen. ~able /-əbl/ a abnehmbar. ~ed a (fig) distanziert;
~ed house Einzelhaus nt

detachment /dɪ'tætʃmənt/ n Distanz
f; (objectivity) Abstand m; (Mil) Sonderkommando nt

detail /'diːteɪl/ n Einzelheit f, Detail
nt; in ~ ausführlich ● vt einzeln
aufführen; (Mil) abkommandieren.
~ed a ausführlich

detain /dɪ'teɪn/ vt aufhalten; ⟨police:⟩
in Haft behalten; (take into custody)
in Haft nehmen. ~ee /diːteɪ'niː/ n
Häftling m

detect /dɪ'tekt/ vt entdecken; (perceive) wahrnehmen. ~ion /-ekʃn/ n
Entdeckung f

detective /dɪ'tektɪv/ n Detektiv m. ~
story n Detektivroman m

detector /dɪ'tektə(r)/ n Suchgerät nt;
(for metal) Metalldetektor m

detention /dɪ'tenʃn/ n Haft f; (Sch)
Nachsitzen nt

deter /dɪ'tɜː(r)/ vt (pt/pp **deterred**)
abschrecken; (prevent) abhalten

detergent /dɪ'tɜːdʒənt/ n Wasch-
mittel nt

deteriorat|e /dɪ'tɪərɪəreɪt/ vi sich
verschlechtern. ~ion /-'reɪʃn/ n
Verschlechterung f

determination /dɪtɜːmɪ'neɪʃn/ n
Entschlossenheit f

determine /dɪ'tɜːmɪn/ vt bestimmen;
~ to (resolve) sich entschließen zu.
~d a entschlossen

deterrent /dɪ'terənt/ n Abschreckungsmittel nt

detest /dɪ'test/ vt verabscheuen.
~able /-əbl/ a abscheulich

detonat|e /'detəneɪt/ vt zünden ● vi
explodieren. ~or n Zünder m

detour /'diːtʊə(r)/ n Umweg m; (for
traffic) Umleitung f

detract /dɪ'trækt/ vi ~ from
beeinträchtigen

detriment /'detrɪmənt/ n to the ~
zum Schaden (of gen). ~al /-'mentl/
a schädlich (to dat)

deuce /djuːs/ n (Tennis) Einstand m

devaluation /diːvæljʊ'eɪʃn/ n Abwer-
tung f

de'value vt abwerten ⟨currency⟩

devastat|e /'devəsteɪt/ vt verwüsten.
~ed /-ɪd/ a (fam) erschüttert. ~ing
a verheerend. ~ion /-'steɪʃn/ n Verwüstung f

develop /dɪ'veləp/ vt entwickeln; bekommen ⟨illness⟩; erschließen
⟨area⟩ ● vi sich entwickeln (into zu).
~er n [property] ~er Bodenspeku-
lant m

de'veloping country n Entwick-
lungsland nt

development /dɪ'veləpmənt/ n
Entwicklung f

deviant /'diːvɪənt/ a abweichend

deviat|e /'diːvɪeɪt/ vi abweichen.
~ion /-'eɪʃn/ n Abweichung f

device /dɪ'vaɪs/ n Gerät nt; (fig) Mittel nt; **leave s.o. to his own** ~s jdn
sich (dat) selbst überlassen

devil /'devl/ n Teufel m. ~ish a
teuflisch

devious /'diːvɪəs/ a verschlagen; ~
route Umweg m

devise /dɪ'vaɪz/ vt sich (dat)
ausdenken

devoid /dɪ'vɔɪd/ a ~ of ohne

devolution /diːvə'luːʃn/ n Dezentrali-
sierung f; (of power) Übertragung f

devot|e /dɪ'vəʊt/ vt widmen (**to** dat).
~**ed** a, **-ly** adv ergeben; ⟨care⟩ liebevoll; **be** ~**ed to** s.o. sehr an jdm hängen. ~**ee** /devə'tiː/ n Anhänger(in) m(f)

devotion /dɪ'vəʊʃn/ n Hingabe f; ~**s** pl (Relig) Andacht f

devour /dɪ'vaʊə(r)/ vt verschlingen

devout /dɪ'vaʊt/ a fromm

dew /djuː/ n Tau m

dexterity /dek'sterətɪ/ n Geschicklichkeit f

diabet|es /daɪə'biːtiːz/ n Zuckerkrankheit f. ~**ic** /-'betɪk/ a zuckerkrank ● n Zuckerkranke(r) m/f, Diabetiker(in) m(f)

diabolical /daɪə'bɒlɪkl/ a teuflisch

diagnose /daɪəg'nəʊz/ vt diagnostizieren

diagnosis /daɪəg'nəʊsɪs/ n (pl **-oses** /-siːz/) Diagnose f

diagonal /daɪ'ægənl/ a, **-ly** adv diagonal ● n Diagonale f

diagram /'daɪəgræm/ n Diagramm nt

dial /'daɪəl/ n (of clock) Zifferblatt nt; (Techn) Skala f; (Teleph) Wählscheibe f ● vt/i (pt/pp **dialled**) (Teleph) wählen; ~ **direct** durchwählen

dialect /'daɪəlekt/ n Dialekt m

dialling: ~ **code** n Vorwahlnummer f. ~ **tone** n Amtszeichen nt

dialogue /'daɪəlɒg/ n Dialog m

'dial tone n (Amer, Teleph) Amtszeichen nt

diameter /daɪ'æmɪtə(r)/ n Durchmesser m

diametrically /daɪə'metrɪkəlɪ/ adv ~ **opposed** genau entgegengesetzt (**to** dat)

diamond /'daɪəmənd/ n Diamant m; (cut) Brillant m; (shape) Raute f; ~**s** pl (Cards) Karo nt

diaper /'daɪəpə(r)/ n (Amer) Windel f

diaphragm /'daɪəfræm/ n (Anat) Zwerchfell nt; (Phot) Blende f

diarrhoea /daɪə'rɪə/ n Durchfall m

diary /'daɪərɪ/ n Tagebuch nt; (for appointments) [Termin]kalender m

dice /daɪs/ n inv Würfel m ● vt (Culin) in Würfel schneiden

dicey /'daɪsɪ/ a (fam) riskant

dictat|e /dɪk'teɪt/ vt/i diktieren. ~**ion** /-eɪʃn/ n Diktat nt

dictator /dɪk'teɪtə(r)/ n Diktator m. ~**ial** /-tə'tɔːrɪəl/ a diktatorisch. ~**ship** n Diktatur f

diction /'dɪkʃn/ n Aussprache f

dictionary /'dɪkʃənrɪ/ n Wörterbuch nt

did /dɪd/ see **do**

didactic /dɪ'dæktɪk/ a didaktisch

diddle /'dɪdl/ vt (fam) übers Ohr hauen

didn't /'dɪdnt/ = **did not**

die¹ /daɪ/ n (Techn) Prägestempel m; (metal mould) Gußform f

die² vi (pres p **dying**) sterben (**of** an + dat); ⟨plant, animal:⟩ eingehen; ⟨flower:⟩ verwelken; **be dying to do sth** (fam) darauf brennen, etw zu tun; **be dying for sth** (fam) sich nach etw sehnen. ~ **down** vi nachlassen; ⟨fire:⟩ herunterbrennen. ~ **out** vi aussterben

diesel /'diːzl/ n Diesel m. ~ **engine** n Dieselmotor m

diet /'daɪət/ n Kost f; (restricted) Diät f; (for slimming) Schlankheitskur f; **be on a** ~ diät leben; eine Schlankheitskur machen ● vi diät leben; eine Schlankheitskur machen

dietician /daɪə'tɪʃn/ n Diätassistent(in) m(f)

differ /'dɪfə(r)/ vi sich unterscheiden; (disagree) verschiedener Meinung sein

differen|ce /'dɪfrəns/ n Unterschied m; (disagreement) Meinungsverschiedenheit f. ~**t** a andere(r,s); (various) verschiedene; **be** ~**t** anders sein (**from** als)

differential /dɪfə'renʃl/ a Differential- ● n Unterschied m; (Techn) Differential nt

differentiate /dɪfə'renʃɪeɪt/ vt/i unterscheiden (**between** zwischen + dat)

differently /'dɪfrəntlɪ/ adv anders

difficult /'dɪfɪkəlt/ a schwierig, schwer. ~**y** n Schwierigkeit f

diffiden|ce /'dɪfɪdəns/ n Zaghaftigkeit f. ~**t** a zaghaft

diffuse¹ /dɪ'fjuːs/ a ausgebreitet; (wordy) langatmig

diffuse² /dɪ'fjuːz/ vt (Phys) streuen

dig /dɪg/ n (poke) Stoß m; (remark) spitze Bemerkung f; (Archaeol) Ausgrabung f; ~**s** pl (fam) möbliertes Zimmer nt ● vt/i (pt/pp **dug**, pres p **digging**) graben; umgraben ⟨garden⟩; ~ s.o. **in the ribs** jdm einen Rippenstoß geben. ~ **out** vt ausgraben. ~ **up** vt ausgraben; umgraben ⟨garden⟩; aufreißen ⟨street⟩

digest¹ /'daɪdʒest/ n Kurzfassung f

digest² /dɪ'dʒest/ vt verdauen. ~**ible** a verdaulich. ~**ion** /-estʃn/ n Verdauung f

digger /'dɪgə(r)/ n (Techn) Bagger m

digit /'dɪdʒɪt/ n Ziffer f; (finger) Finger m; (toe) Zehe f

digital /'dɪdʒɪtl/ a Digital-; ~ **clock** Digitaluhr f

dignified /'dɪgnɪfaɪd/ a würdevoll

dignitary /'dɪgnɪtərɪ/ n Würdenträger m

dignity /'dɪgnɪtɪ/ n Würde f

digress /daɪ'gres/ vi abschweifen. ~**ion** /-eʃn/ n Abschweifung f

dike /daɪk/ n Deich m; (ditch) Graben m

dilapidated /dɪ'læpɪdeɪtɪd/ a baufällig

dilate /daɪ'leɪt/ vt erweitern ● vi sich erweitern

dilatory /'dɪlətərɪ/ a langsam

dilemma /dɪ'lemə/ n Dilemma nt

dilettante /dɪlɪ'tæntɪ/ n Dilettant(in) m(f)

diligen|ce /'dɪlɪdʒəns/ n Fleiß m. ~**t** a, -**ly** adv fleißig

dill /dɪl/ n Dill m

dilly-dally /'dɪlɪdælɪ/ vi (pt/pp -ied) (fam) trödeln

dilute /daɪ'luːt/ vt verdünnen

dim /dɪm/ a (**dimmer, dimmest**), -**ly** adv (weak) schwach; (dark) trüb[e]; (indistinct) undeutlich; (fam: stupid) dumm, (fam) doof ● v (pt/pp **dimmed**) ● vt dämpfen ● vi schwächer werden

dime /daɪm/ n (Amer) Zehncentstück nt

dimension /daɪ'menʃn/ n Dimension f; ~**s** pl Maße pl

diminish /dɪ'mɪnɪʃ/ vt verringern ● vi sich verringern

diminutive /dɪ'mɪnjʊtɪv/ a winzig ● n Verkleinerungsform f

dimple /'dɪmpl/ n Grübchen nt

din /dɪn/ n Krach m, Getöse nt

dine /daɪn/ vi speisen. ~**r** n Speisende(r) m/f; (Amer: restaurant) Eßlokal nt

dinghy /'dɪŋɪ/ n Dinghi nt; (inflatable) Schlauchboot nt

dingy /'dɪndʒɪ/ a (-ier, -iest) trübe

dining /'daɪnɪŋ/: ~-**car** n Speisewagen m. ~-**room** n Eßzimmer nt. ~-**table** n Eßtisch m

dinner /'dɪnə(r)/ n Abendessen nt; (at midday) Mittagessen nt; (formal) Essen nt. ~-**jacket** n Smoking m

dinosaur /'daɪnəsɔː(r)/ n Dinosaurier m

dint /dɪnt/ n by ~ of durch (+ acc)

diocese /'daɪəsɪs/ n Diözese f

dip /dɪp/ n (in ground) Senke f; (Culin) Dip m; **go for a** ~ kurz schwimmen gehen ● v (pt/pp **dipped**) vt [ein]tauchen; ~ **one's headlights** (Auto) [die Scheinwerfer] abblenden ● vt sich senken

diphtheria /dɪf'θɪərɪə/ n Diphtherie f

diphthong /'dɪfθɒŋ/ n Diphthong m

diploma /dɪ'pləʊmə/ n Diplom nt

diplomacy /dɪ'pləʊməsɪ/ n Diplomatie f

diplomat /'dɪpləmæt/ n Diplomat m. ~**ic** /-'mætɪk/ a, -**ally** adv diplomatisch

'dip-stick n (Auto) Ölmeßstab m

dire /'daɪə(r)/ a (-r, -st) bitter; ⟨situation, consequences⟩ furchtbar

direct /dɪ'rekt/ a & adv direkt ● vt (aim) richten (**at** auf / (fig) an + acc); (control) leiten; (order) anweisen; ~ **s.o.** (show the way) jdm den Weg sagen; ~ **a film/ play** bei einem Film/Theaterstück Regie führen. ~ '**current** n Gleichstrom m

direction /dɪ'rekʃn/ n Richtung f; (control) Leitung f; (of play, film) Regie f; ~**s** pl Anweisungen pl; ~**s for use** Gebrauchsanweisung f

directly /dɪ'rektlɪ/ adv direkt; (at once) sofort ● conj (fam) sobald

director /dɪ'rektə(r)/ n (Comm) Direktor m; (of play, film) Regisseur m

directory /dɪ'rektərɪ/ n Verzeichnis nt; (Teleph) Telefonbuch nt

dirt /dɜːt/ n Schmutz m; ⟨soil⟩ Erde f; ~ **cheap** (fam) spottbillig

dirty /'dɜːtɪ/ a (-ier, -iest) schmutzig ● vt schmutzig machen

dis|a'bility /dɪs-/ n Behinderung f. ~**abled** /dɪ'seɪbld/ a [körper]behindert

disad'van|tage n Nachteil m; **at a** ~**tage** im Nachteil. ~**taged** a benachteiligt. ~**tageous** a nachteilig

disaf'fected a unzufrieden; (disloyal) illoyal

disa'gree vi nicht übereinstimmen (**with** mit); **I** ~ ich bin anderer Meinung; **we** ~ wir sind verschiedener Meinung; **oysters** ~ **with me** Austern bekommen mir nicht

disa'greeable a unangenehm

disa'greement n Meinungsverschiedenheit f

disap'pear vi verschwinden. ~**ance** n Verschwinden nt

disap'point vt enttäuschen. ~**ment** n Enttäuschung f

disap'proval n Mißbilligung f

disap'prove *vi* dagegen sein; ~ **of** mißbilligen

dis'arm *vt* entwaffnen ● *vi* (*Mil*) abrüsten. ~**ament** *n* Abrüstung *f*. ~**ing** *a* entwaffnend

disar'ray *n* Unordnung *f*

disast|er /dɪˈzɑːstə(r)/ *n* Katastrophe *f*; (*accident*) Unglück *nt*. ~**rous** /-rəs/ *a* katastrophal

dis'band *vt* auflösen ● *vi* sich auflösen

disbe'lief *n* Ungläubigkeit *f*; **in** ~ ungläubig

disc /dɪsk/ *n* Scheibe *f*; (*record*) [Schall]platte *f*; (*CD*) CD *f*

discard /dɪˈskɑːd/ *vt* ablegen; (*throw away*) wegwerfen

discern /dɪˈsɜːn/ *vt* wahrnehmen. ~**ible** *a* wahrnehmbar. ~**ing** *a* anspruchsvoll

'discharge¹ *n* Ausstoßen *nt*; (*Naut, Electr*) Entladung *f*; (*dismissal*) Entlassung *f*; (*Jur*) Freispruch *m*; (*Med*) Ausfluß *m*

dis'charge² *vt* ausstoßen; (*Naut, Electr*) entladen; (*dismiss*) entlassen; (*Jur*) freisprechen ⟨*accused*⟩; ~ **a duty** seiner Pflicht entledigen

disciple /dɪˈsaɪpl/ *n* Jünger *m*; (*fig*) Schüler *m*

disciplinary /ˈdɪsɪplɪnəri/ *a* disziplinarisch

discipline /ˈdɪsɪplɪn/ *n* Disziplin *f* ● *vt* Disziplin beibringen (+ *dat*); (*punish*) bestrafen

'disc jockey *n* Diskjockey *m*

dis'claim *vt* abstreiten. ~**er** *n* Verzichterklärung *f*

dis'clos|e *vt* enthüllen. ~**ure** *n* Enthüllung *f*

disco /ˈdɪskəʊ/ *n* (*fam*) Disko *f*

dis'colour *vt* verfärben ● *vi* sich verfärben

dis'comfort *n* Beschwerden *pl*; (*fig*) Unbehagen *nt*

disconcert /dɪskənˈsɜːt/ *vt* aus der Fassung bringen

discon'nect *vt* trennen; (*Electr*) ausschalten; (*cut supply*) abstellen

disconsolate /dɪsˈkɒnsələt/ *a* untröstlich

discon'tent *n* Unzufriedenheit *f*. ~**ed** *a* unzufrieden

discon'tinue *vt* einstellen; (*Comm*) nicht mehr herstellen

'discord *n* Zwietracht *f*; (*Mus & fig*) Mißklang *m*. ~**ant** /dɪˈskɔːdənt/ *a* ~**ant note** Mißklang *m*

discothèque /ˈdɪskətek/ *n* Diskothek *f*

'discount¹ *n* Rabatt *m*

dis'count² *vt* außer acht lassen

dis'courage *vt* entmutigen; (*dissuade*) abraten (+ *dat*)

'discourse *n* Rede *f*

dis'courteous *a*, **-ly** *adv* unhöflich

discover /dɪˈskʌvə(r)/ *vt* entdecken. ~**y** *n* Entdeckung *f*

dis'credit *n* Mißkredit *m* ● *vt* in Mißkredit bringen

discreet /dɪˈskriːt/ *a*, **-ly** *adv* diskret

discrepancy /dɪˈskrepənsi/ *n* Diskrepanz *f*

discretion /dɪˈskreʃn/ *n* Diskretion *f*; (*judgement*) Ermessen *nt*

discriminat|e /dɪˈskrɪmɪneɪt/ *vi* unterscheiden (**between** zwischen + *dat*); ~**e against** diskriminieren. ~**ing** *a* anspruchsvoll. ~**ion** /-ˈneɪʃn/ *n* Diskriminierung *f*; (*quality*) Urteilskraft *f*

discus /ˈdɪskəs/ *n* Diskus *m*

discuss /dɪˈskʌs/ *vt* besprechen; (*examine critically*) diskutieren. ~**ion** /-ʌʃn/ *n* Besprechung *f*; Diskussion *f*

disdain /dɪsˈdeɪn/ *n* Verachtung *f* ● *vt* verachten. ~**ful** *a* verächtlich

disease /dɪˈziːz/ *n* Krankheit *f*. ~**d** *a* krank

disem'bark *vi* an Land gehen

disen'chant *vt* ernüchtern. ~**ment** *n* Ernüchterung *f*

disen'gage *vt* losmachen; ~ **the clutch** (*Auto*) auskuppeln

disen'tangle *vt* entwirren

dis'favour *n* Ungnade *f*; (*disapproval*) Mißfallen *nt*

dis'figure *vt* entstellen

dis'gorge *vt* ausspeien

dis'grace *n* Schande *f*; **in** ~ in Ungnade ● *vt* Schande machen (+ *dat*). ~**ful** *a* schändlich

disgruntled /dɪsˈgrʌntld/ *a* verstimmt

disguise /dɪsˈgaɪz/ *n* Verkleidung *f*; **in** ~ verkleidet ● *vt* verkleiden; verstellen ⟨*voice*⟩; (*conceal*) verhehlen

disgust /dɪsˈgʌst/ *n* Ekel *m*; **in** ~ empört ● *vt* anekeln; (*appal*) empören. ~**ing** *a* eklig; (*appalling*) abscheulich

dish /dɪʃ/ *n* Schüssel *f*; (*shallow*) Schale *f*; (*small*) Schälchen *nt*; (*food*) Gericht *nt*. ~ **out** *vt* austeilen. ~ **up** *vt* auftragen

'dishcloth *n* Spültuch *nt*

dis'hearten vt entmutigen. ~**ing** a entmutigend

dishevelled /dɪ'ʃevld/ a zerzaust

dis'honest a, **-ly** adv unehrlich. ~**y** n Unehrlichkeit f

dis'honour n Schande f ● vt entehren; nicht honorieren ⟨cheque⟩. ~**able** a, **-bly** adv unehrenhaft

'dishwasher n Geschirrspülmaschine f

disil'lusion vt ernüchtern. ~**ment** n Ernüchterung f

disin'fect vt desinfizieren. ~**ant** n Desinfektionsmittel nt

disin'herit vt enterben

dis'integrate vi zerfallen

dis'interested a unvoreingenommen; (uninterested) uninteressiert

dis'jointed a unzusammenhängend

disk /dɪsk/ n = **disc**

dis'like n Abneigung f ● vt nicht mögen

dislocate /'dɪsləkeɪt/ vt ausrenken; ~ **one's shoulder** sich (dat) den Arm auskugeln

dis'lodge vt entfernen

dis'loyal a, **-ly** adv illoyal. ~**ty** n Illoyalität f

dismal /'dɪzməl/ a trüb[e]; ⟨person⟩ trübselig; (fam: poor) kläglich

dismantle /dɪs'mæntl/ vt auseinandernehmen; (take down) abbauen

dis'may n Bestürzung f. ~**ed** a bestürzt

dis'miss vt entlassen; (reject) zurückweisen. ~**al** n Entlassung f; Zurückweisung f

dis'mount vi absteigen

diso'bedien|ce n Ungehorsam m. ~**t** a ungehorsam

diso'bey vt/i nicht gehorchen (+ dat); nicht befolgen ⟨rule⟩

dis'order n Unordnung f; (Med) Störung f. ~**ly** a unordentlich; ~**ly conduct** ungebührliches Benehmen nt

dis'organized a unorganisiert

dis'orientate vt verwirren; **be** ~**d** die Orientierung verloren haben

dis'own vt verleugnen

disparaging /dɪ'spærɪdʒɪŋ/ a, **-ly** adv abschätzig

disparity /dɪ'spærətɪ/ n Ungleichheit f

dispassionate /dɪ'spæʃənət/ a, **-ly** adv gelassen; (impartial) unparteiisch

dispatch /dɪ'spætʃ/ n (Comm) Versand m; (Mil) Nachricht f; (report) Bericht m; **with** ~ prompt ● vt [ab]senden; (deal with) erledigen; (kill) töten. ~**-rider** n Meldefahrer m

dispel /dɪ'spel/ vt (pt/pp **dispelled**) vertreiben

dispensable /dɪ'spensəbl/ a entbehrlich

dispensary /dɪ'spensərɪ/ n Apotheke f

dispense /dɪ'spens/ vt austeilen; ~ **with** verzichten auf (+ acc). ~**r** n Apotheker(in) m(f); (device) Automat m

dispers|al /dɪ'spɜ:sl/ n Zerstreuung f. ~**e** /dɪ'spɜ:s/ vt zerstreuen ● vi sich zerstreuen

dispirited /dɪ'spɪrɪtɪd/ a entmutigt

dis'place vt verschieben; ~**d person** Vertriebene(r) m/f

display /dɪ'spleɪ/ n Ausstellung f; (Comm) Auslage f; (performance) Vorführung f ● vt zeigen; ausstellen ⟨goods⟩

dis'please vt mißfallen (+ dat)

dis'pleasure n Mißfallen nt

disposable /dɪ'spəʊzəbl/ a Wegwerf-; ⟨income⟩ verfügbar

disposal /dɪ'spəʊzl/ n Beseitigung f; **be at s.o.'s** ~ jdm zur Verfügung stehen

dispose /dɪ'spəʊz/ vi ~ **of** beseitigen; (deal with) erledigen; **be well** ~**d** wohlgesinnt sein (**to** dat)

disposition /dɪspə'zɪʃn/ n Veranlagung f; (nature) Wesensart f

disproportionate /dɪsprə'pɔ:ʃənət/ a, **-ly** adv unverhältnismäßig

dis'prove vt widerlegen

dispute /dɪ'spju:t/ n Disput m; (quarrel) Streit m ● vt bestreiten

disquali'fication n Disqualifikation f

dis'qualify vt disqualifizieren; ~ **s.o. from driving** jdm den Führerschein entziehen

disquieting /dɪs'kwaɪətɪŋ/ a beunruhigend

disre'gard n Nichtbeachtung f ● vt nicht beachten, ignorieren

disre'pair n **fall into** ~ verfallen

dis'reputable a verrufen

disre'pute n Verruf m

disre'spect n Respektlosigkeit f. ~**ful** a, **-ly** adv respektlos

disrupt /dɪs'rʌpt/ vt stören. ~**ion** /-ʌpʃn/ n Störung f. ~**ive** /-tɪv/ a störend

dissatis'faction n Unzufriedenheit f

dis'satisfied a unzufrieden

dissect /dɪ'sekt/ vt zergliedern; (Med) sezieren. ~**ion** /-ekʃn/ n Zergliederung f; (Med) Sektion f

disseminat|e /dɪ'semɪneɪt/ *vt* verbreiten. **∼ion** /-'neɪʃn/ *n* Verbreitung *f*

dissent /dɪ'sent/ *n* Nichtübereinstimmung *f* ● *vi* nicht übereinstimmen

dissertation /dɪsə'teɪʃn/ *n* Dissertation *f*

dis'service *n* schlechter Dienst *m*

dissident /'dɪsɪdənt/ *n* Dissident *m*

dis'similar *a* unähnlich (**to** *dat*)

dissociate /dɪ'səʊʃɪeɪt/ *vt* trennen; **∼ oneself** sich distanzieren (**from** von)

dissolute /'dɪsəluːt/ *a* zügellos; ⟨*life*⟩ ausschweifend

dissolution /dɪsə'luːʃn/ *n* Auflösung *f*

dissolve /dɪ'zɒlv/ *vt* auflösen ● *vi* sich auflösen

dissuade /dɪ'sweɪd/ *vt* abbringen (**from** von)

distance /'dɪstəns/ *n* Entfernung *f*; **long/short ∼** lange/kurze Strecke *f*; **in the/from a ∼** in/aus der Ferne

distant /'dɪstənt/ *a* fern; (*aloof*) kühl; ⟨*relative*⟩ entfernt

dis'taste *n* Abneigung *f*. **∼ful** *a* unangenehm

distend /dɪ'stend/ *vi* sich [auf]blähen

distil /dɪ'stɪl/ *vt* (*pt/pp* **distilled**) brennen; (*Chem*) destillieren. **∼lation** /-'leɪʃn/ *n* Destillation *f*. **∼lery** /-əri/ *n* Brennerei *f*

distinct /dɪ'stɪŋkt/ *a* deutlich; (*different*) verschieden. **∼ion** /-ɪŋkʃn/ *n* Unterschied *m*; (*Sch*) Auszeichnung *f*. **∼ive** /-tɪv/ *a* kennzeichnend; (*unmistakable*) unverwechselbar. **∼ly** *adv* deutlich

distinguish /dɪ'stɪŋgwɪʃ/ *vt/i* unterscheiden; (*make out*) erkennen; **∼ oneself** sich auszeichnen. **∼ed** *a* angesehen; ⟨*appearance*⟩ distinguiert

distort /dɪ'stɔːt/ *vt* verzerren; (*fig*) verdrehen. **∼ion** /-ɔːʃn/ *n* Verzerrung *f*; (*fig*) Verdrehung *f*

distract /dɪ'strækt/ *vt* ablenken. **∼ed** /-ɪd/ *a* [völlig] aufgelöst. **∼ion** /-ækʃn/ *n* Ablenkung *f*; (*despair*) Verzweiflung *f*

distraught /dɪ'strɔːt/ *a* [völlig] aufgelöst

distress /dɪ'stres/ *n* Kummer *m*; (*pain*) Schmerz *m*; (*poverty, danger*) Not *f* ● *vt* Kummer/Schmerz bereiten (+ *dat*); (*sadden*) bekümmern; (*shock*) erschüttern. **∼ing** *a* schmerzlich; (*shocking*) erschütternd. **∼ signal** *n* Notsignal *nt*

distribut|e /dɪ'strɪbjuːt/ *vt* verteilen; (*Comm*) vertreiben. **∼ion** /-'bjuːʃn/ *n* Verteilung *f*; Vertrieb *m*. **∼or** *n* Verteiler *m*

district /'dɪstrɪkt/ *n* Gegend *f*; (*Admin*) Bezirk *m*. **∼ nurse** *n* Gemeindeschwester *f*

dis'trust *n* Mißtrauen *nt* ● *vt* mißtrauen (+ *dat*). **∼ful** *a* mißtrauisch

disturb /dɪ'stɜːb/ *vt* stören; (*perturb*) beunruhigen; (*touch*) anrühren. **∼ance** *n* Unruhe *f*; (*interruption*) Störung *f*. **∼ed** *a* beunruhigt; **[mentally] ∼ed** geistig gestört. **∼ing** *a* beunruhigend

dis'used *a* stillgelegt; (*empty*) leer

ditch /dɪtʃ/ *n* Graben *m* ● *vt* (*fam: abandon*) fallenlassen ⟨*plan*⟩; wegschmeißen ⟨*thing*⟩

dither /'dɪðə(r)/ *vi* zaudern

ditto /'dɪtəʊ/ *n* dito; (*fam*) ebenfalls

divan /dɪ'væn/ *n* Polsterbett *nt*

dive /daɪv/ *n* [Kopf]sprung *m*; (*Aviat*) Sturzflug *m*; (*fam: place*) Spelunke *f* ● *vi* einen Kopfsprung machen; (*when in water*) tauchen; (*Aviat*) einen Sturzflug machen; (*fam: rush*) stürzen

diver /'daɪvə(r)/ *n* Taucher *m*; (*Sport*) [Kunst]springer *m*

diver|ge /daɪ'vɜːdʒ/ *vi* auseinandergehen. **∼gent** /-ənt/ *a* abweichend

diverse /daɪ'vɜːs/ *a* verschieden

diversify /daɪ'vɜːsɪfaɪ/ *vt/i* (*pt/pp* **-ied**) variieren; (*Comm*) diversifizieren

diversion /daɪ'vɜːʃn/ *n* Umleitung *f*; (*distraction*) Ablenkung *f*

diversity /daɪ'vɜːsəti/ *n* Vielfalt *f*

divert /daɪ'vɜːt/ *vt* umleiten; ablenken ⟨*attention*⟩; (*entertain*) unterhalten

divest /daɪ'vest/ *vt* sich entledigen (**of** + *gen*); (*fig*) entkleiden

divide /dɪ'vaɪd/ *vt* teilen; (*separate*) trennen; (*Math*) dividieren (**by** durch) ● *vi* sich teilen

dividend /'dɪvɪdend/ *n* Dividende *f*

divine /dɪ'vaɪn/ *a* göttlich

diving /'daɪvɪŋ/ *n* (*Sport*) Kunstspringen *nt*. **∼-board** *n* Sprungbrett *nt*. **∼-suit** *n* Taucheranzug *m*

divinity /dɪ'vɪnəti/ *n* Göttlichkeit *f*; (*subject*) Theologie *f*

divisible /dɪ'vɪzɪbl/ *a* teilbar (**by** durch)

division /dɪ'vɪʒn/ *n* Teilung *f*; (*separation*) Trennung *f*; (*Math, Mil*) Division *f*; (*Parl*) Hammelsprung *m*;

(*line*) Trennlinie *f*; (*group*) Abteilung *f*

divorce /dɪ'vɔːs/ *n* Scheidung *f* ● *vt* sich scheiden lassen von. ∼**d** *a* geschieden; **get** ∼**d** sich scheiden lassen

divorcee /dɪvɔː'siː/ *n* Geschiedene(r) *m/f*

divulge /daɪ'vʌldʒ/ *vt* preisgeben

DIY *abbr of* do-it-yourself

dizziness /'dɪzɪnɪs/ *n* Schwindel *m*

dizzy /'dɪzɪ/ *a* (-ier, -iest) schwindlig; **I feel** ∼ mir ist schwindlig

do /duː/ *n* (*pl* **dos** *or* **do's**) (*fam*) Veranstaltung *f* ● *v* (*3 sg pres tense* **does**; *pt* **did**; *pp* **done**) ● *vt/i* tun, machen; (*be suitable*) passen; (*be enough*) reichen, genügen; (*cook*) kochen; (*clean*) putzen; (*Sch: study*) durchnehmen; (*fam: cheat*) beschwindeln (**out of** um); **do without** auskommen ohne; **do away with** abschaffen; **be done** (*Culin*) gar sein; **well done** gut gemacht! (*Culin*) gut durchgebraten; **done in** (*fam*) kaputt, fertig; **done for** (*fam*) verloren, erledigt; **do the flowers** die Blumen arrangieren; **do the potatoes** die Kartoffeln schälen; **do the washing up** abwaschen, spülen; **do one's hair** sich frisieren; **do well/badly** gut/schlecht abschneiden; **how is he doing?** wie geht es ihm? **this won't do** das geht nicht; **are you doing anything today?** haben Sie heute etwas vor? **I could do with a spanner** ich könnte einen Schraubenschlüssel gebrauchen ● *v aux* **do you speak German?** sprechen Sie deutsch? **yes, I do** ja; (*emphatic*) doch; **no, I don't** nein; **I don't smoke** ich rauche nicht; **don't you/doesn't he?** nicht [wahr]? **so do I** ich auch; **do come in** kommen Sie doch herein; **how do you do?** guten Tag. **do in** *vt* (*fam*) um die Ecke bringen. **do up** *vt* (*fasten*) zumachen; (*renovate*) renovieren; (*wrap*) einpacken

docile /'dəʊsaɪl/ *a* fügsam

dock¹ /dɒk/ *n* (*Jur*) Anklagebank *f*

dock² *n* Dock *nt* ● *vi* anlegen, docken ● *vt* docken. ∼**er** *n* Hafenarbeiter *m*. ∼**yard** *n* Werft *f*

doctor /'dɒktə(r)/ *n* Arzt *m*/ Ärztin *f*; (*Univ*) Doktor *m* ● *vt* kastrieren; (*spay*) sterilisieren. ∼**ate** /-ət/ *n* Doktorwürde *f*

doctrine /'dɒktrɪn/ *n* Lehre *f*, Doktrin *f*

document /'dɒkjʊmənt/ *n* Dokument *nt*. ∼**ary** /-'mentərɪ/ *a* Dokumentar- ● *n* Dokumentarbericht *m*; (*film*) Dokumentarfilm *m*

doddery /'dɒdərɪ/ *a* (*fam*) tatterig

dodge /dɒdʒ/ *n* (*fam*) Trick *m*, Kniff *m* ● *vt/i* ausweichen (+ *dat*); ∼ **out of the way** zur Seite springen

dodgems /'dɒdʒəmz/ *npl* Autoskooter *pl*

dodgy /'dɒdʒɪ/ *a* (-ier, -iest) (*fam*) (*awkward*) knifflig; (*dubious*) zweifelhaft

doe /dəʊ/ *n* Ricke *f*; (*rabbit*) [Kaninchen]weibchen *nt*

does /dʌz/ *see* do

doesn't /dʌznt/ = does not

dog /dɒg/ *n* Hund *m* ● *vt* (*pt/pp* **dogged**) verfolgen

dog: ∼**-biscuit** *n* Hundekuchen *m*. ∼**-collar** *n* Hundehalsband *nt*; (*Relig, fam*) Kragen *m* eines Geistlichen. ∼**-eared** *a* **be** ∼**-eared** Eselsohren haben

dogged /'dɒgɪd/ *a*, -**ly** *adv* beharrlich

dogma /'dɒgmə/ *n* Dogma *nt*. ∼**tic** /-'mætɪk/ *a* dogmatisch

'dogsbody *n* (*fam*) Mädchen *nt* für alles

doily /'dɔɪlɪ/ *n* Deckchen *nt*

do-it-yourself /duːɪtjə'self/ *n* Heimwerken *nt*. ∼ **shop** *n* Heimwerkerladen *m*

doldrums /'dɒldrəmz/ *npl* **be in the** ∼ niedergeschlagen sein; ⟨*business:*⟩ darniederliegen

dole /dəʊl/ *n* (*fam*) Stempelgeld *nt*; **be on the** ∼ arbeitslos sein ● *vt* ∼ **out** austeilen

doleful /'dəʊlfl/ *a*, -**ly** *adv* trauervoll

doll /dɒl/ *n* Puppe *f* ● *vt* (*fam*) ∼ **oneself up** sich herausputzen

dollar /'dɒlə(r)/ *n* Dollar *m*

dollop /'dɒləp/ *n* (*fam*) Klecks *m*

dolphin /'dɒlfɪn/ *n* Delphin *m*

domain /də'meɪn/ *n* Gebiet *nt*

dome /dəʊm/ *n* Kuppel *m*

domestic /də'mestɪk/ *a* häuslich; (*Pol*) Innen-; (*Comm*) Binnen-. ∼ **animal** *n* Haustier *nt*

domesticated /də'mestɪkeɪtɪd/ *a* häuslich; ⟨*animal*⟩ zahm

domestic: ∼ **flight** *n* Inlandflug *m*. ∼ **'servant** *n* Hausangestellte(r) *m/f*

dominant /'dɒmɪnənt/ *a* vorherrschend

dominat|e /'dɒmɪneɪt/ vt beherrschen ● vi dominieren; **~e over** beherrschen. **~ion** /-'neɪʃn/ n Vorherrschaft f

domineer /dɒmɪ'nɪə(r)/ vi ~ **over** tyrannisieren. **~ing** a herrschsüchtig

dominion /də'mɪnjən/ n Herrschaft f

domino /'dɒmɪnəʊ/ n (pl **-es**) Dominostein m; **~es** sg (game) Domino nt

don¹ /dɒn/ vt (pt/pp **donned**) (liter) anziehen

don² n [Universitäts]dozent m

donat|e /dəʊ'neɪt/ vt spenden. **~ion** /-eɪʃn/ n Spende f

done /dʌn/ see **do**

donkey /'dɒŋkɪ/ n Esel m; **~'s years** (fam) eine Ewigkeit. **~-work** n Routinearbeit f

donor /'dəʊnə(r)/ n Spender(in) m(f)

don't /dəʊnt/ = **do not**

doodle /'duːdl/ vi kritzeln

doom /duːm/ n Schicksal nt; (ruin) Verhängnis nt ● vt be **~ed to** failure zum Scheitern verurteilt sein

door /dɔː(r)/ n Tür f; **out of ~s** im Freien

door: **~man** n Portier m. **~mat** n [Fuß]abtreter m. **~step** n Türschwelle f; **on the ~step** vor der Tür. **~way** n Türöffnung f

dope /dəʊp/ n (fam) Drogen pl; (fam: information) Informationen pl; (fam: idiot) Trottel m ● vt betäuben; (Sport) dopen

dopey /'dəʊpɪ/ a (fam) benommen; (stupid) blöd[e]

dormant /'dɔːmənt/ a ruhend

dormer /'dɔːmə(r)/ n ~ **[window]** Mansardenfenster nt

dormitory /'dɔːmɪtərɪ/ n Schlafsaal m

dormouse /'dɔː-/ n Haselmaus f

dosage /'dəʊsɪdʒ/ n Dosierung f

dose /dəʊs/ n Dosis f

doss /dɒs/ vi (sl) pennen. **~er** n Penner m. **~-house** n Penne f

dot /dɒt/ n Punkt m; **on the ~** pünktlich

dote /dəʊt/ vi **~on** vernarrt sein in (+ acc)

dotted /'dɒtɪd/ a ~ **line** punktierte Linie f; **be ~ with** bestreut sein mit

dotty /'dɒtɪ/ a (**-ier, -iest**) (fam) verdreht

double /'dʌbl/ a & adv doppelt; ⟨bed, chin⟩ Doppel-; ⟨flower⟩ gefüllt ● n das Doppelte; (person) Doppelgänger m; **~s** pl (Tennis) Doppel nt;

at the ~ im Laufschritt ● vt verdoppeln; (fold) falten ● vi sich verdoppeln. **~ back** vi zurückgehen. **~ up** vi sich krümmen (**with** vor + dat)

double: **~-'bass** n Kontrabaß m. **~-breasted** a zweireihig. **~-'cross** vt ein Doppelspiel treiben mit. **~-'decker** n Doppeldecker m. **~ 'Dutch** n (fam) Kauderwelsch nt. **~ 'glazing** n Doppelverglasung f. **~ 'room** n Doppelzimmer nt

doubly /'dʌblɪ/ adv doppelt

doubt /daʊt/ n Zweifel m ● vt bezweifeln. **~ful** a, **-ly** adv zweifelhaft; (disbelieving) skeptisch. **~less** adv zweifellos

dough /dəʊ/ n [fester] Teig m; (fam: money) Pinke f. **~nut** n Berliner [Pfannkuchen] m, Krapfen m

douse /daʊs/ vt übergießen; ausgießen ⟨flames⟩

dove /dʌv/ n Taube f. **~tail** n (Techn) Schwalbenschwanz m

dowdy /'daʊdɪ/ a (**-ier, -iest**) unschick

down¹ /daʊn/ n (feathers) Daunen pl

down² adv unten; (with movement) nach unten; **go ~** hinuntergehen; **come ~** herunterkommen; **~ there** da unten; **£50 ~** £50 Anzahlung; **~!** (to dog) Platz! **~ with...!** nieder mit...! ● prep **~ the road/stairs** die Straße/Treppe hinunter; **~ the river** den Fluß abwärts; **be ~ the pub** (fam) in der Kneipe sein ● vt (fam) (drink) runterkippen; **~ tools** die Arbeit niederlegen

down: **~-and-'out** n Penner m. **~cast** a niedergeschlagen. **~fall** n Sturz m; (ruin) Ruin m. **~'grade** vt niedriger einstufen. **~'hearted** a entmutigt. **~hill** adv bergab. **~ payment** n Anzahlung f. **~pour** n Platzregen m. **~right** a & adv ausgesprochen. **~'stairs** adv unten; ⟨go⟩ nach unten ● a /'--/ im Erdgeschoß. **~'stream** adv stromabwärts. **~-to-'earth** a sachlich. **~town** adv (Amer) im Stadtzentrum. **~trodden** a unterdrückt. **~ward** a nach unten; ⟨slope⟩ abfallend ● adv & **~wards** abwärts, nach unten

downy /'daʊnɪ/ a (**-ier, -iest**) flaumig

dowry /'daʊrɪ/ n Mitgift f

doze /dəʊz/ n Nickerchen nt ● vi dösen. **~ off** vi einnicken

dozen /'dʌzn/ n Dutzend nt

Dr abbr of **doctor**

draft¹ /drɑːft/ n Entwurf m; (Comm) Tratte f; (Amer Mil) Einberufung f

● *vt* entwerfen; (*Amer Mil*) einberufen

draft² *n* (*Amer*) = **draught**

drag /dræg/ *n* (*fam*) Klotz *m* am Bein; **in ~** (*fam*) ⟨*man*⟩ als Frau gekleidet ● *vt* (*pt/pp* **dragged**) schleppen; absuchen ⟨*river*⟩. **~ on** *vi* sich in die Länge ziehen

dragon /'drægən/ *n* Drache *m*. **~-fly** *n* Libelle *f*

'drag show *n* Transvestitenshow *f*

drain /dreɪn/ *n* Abfluß *m*; (*underground*) Kanal *m*; **the ~s** die Kanalisation ● *vt* entwässern ⟨*land*⟩; ablassen ⟨*liquid*⟩; das Wasser ablassen aus ⟨*tank*⟩; abgießen ⟨*vegetables*⟩; austrinken ⟨*glass*⟩ ● *vi* **~** [**away**] ablaufen; **leave sth to ~** etw abtropfen lassen

drain|age /'dreɪnɪdʒ/ *n* Kanalisation *f*; (*of land*) Dränage *f*. **~ing board** *n* Abtropfbrett *nt*. **~-pipe** *n* Abflußrohr *nt*

drake /dreɪk/ *n* Enterich *m*

drama /'drɑːmə/ *n* Drama *nt*; (*quality*) Dramatik *f*

dramatic /drə'mætɪk/ *a*, **-ally** *adv* dramatisch

dramat|ist /'dræmətɪst/ *n* Dramatiker *m*. **~ize** *vt* für die Bühne bearbeiten; (*fig*) dramatisieren

drank /dræŋk/ *see* **drink**

drape /dreɪp/ *n* (*Amer*) Vorhang *m* ● *vt* drapieren

drastic /'dræstɪk/ *a*, **-ally** *adv* drastisch

draught /drɑːft/ *n* [Luft]zug *m*; **~s** *sg* (*game*) Damespiel *nt*; **there is a ~** es zieht

draught: ~ beer *n* Bier *nt* vom Faß. **~sman** *n* technischer Zeichner *m*

draughty /'drɑːftɪ/ *a* zugig; **it's ~** es zieht

draw /drɔː/ *n* Attraktion *f*; (*Sport*) Unentschieden *nt*; (*in lottery*) Ziehung *f* ● *v* (*pt* **drew**, *pp* **drawn**) ● *vt* ziehen; (*attract*) anziehen; zeichnen ⟨*picture*⟩; abheben ⟨*money*⟩; holen ⟨*water*⟩; **~ the curtains** die Vorhänge zuziehen/(*back*) aufziehen; **~ lots** losen (**for** um) ● *vi* ⟨*tea:*⟩ ziehen; (*Sport*) unentschieden spielen. **~ back** *vt* zurückziehen ● *vi* (*recoil*) zurückweichen. **~ in** *vt* einziehen ● *vi* einfahren; ⟨*days:*⟩ kürzer werden. **~ out** *vt* herausziehen; abheben ⟨*money*⟩ ● *vi* ausfahren; ⟨*days:*⟩ länger werden. **~ up** *vt* aufsetzen ⟨*document*⟩; herrücken ⟨*chair*⟩; **~**

oneself up sich aufrichten ● *vi* [an]halten

draw: ~back *n* Nachteil *m*. **~bridge** *n* Zugbrücke *f*

drawer /drɔː(r)/ *n* Schublade *f*

drawing /'drɔːɪŋ/ *n* Zeichnung *f*

drawing: ~-board *n* Reißbrett *nt*. **~-pin** *n* Reißzwecke *f*. **~-room** *n* Wohnzimmer *nt*

drawl /drɔːl/ *n* schleppende Aussprache *f*

drawn /drɔːn/ *see* **draw**

dread /dred/ *n* Furcht *f* (**of** vor + *dat*) ● *vt* fürchten

dreadful *a*, **-ly** *adv* fürchterlich

dream /driːm/ *n* Traum *m* ● *attrib* Traum- ● *vt/i* (*pt/pp* **dreamt** /dremt/ *or* **dreamed**) träumen (**about/of** von)

dreary /'drɪərɪ/ *a* (**-ier, -iest**) trüb[e]; (*boring*) langweilig

dredge /dredʒ/ *vt/i* baggern. **~r** *n* [Naß]bagger *m*

dregs /dregz/ *npl* Bodensatz *m*

drench /drentʃ/ *vt* durchnässen

dress /dres/ *n* Kleid *nt*; (*clothing*) Kleidung *f* ● *vt* anziehen; (*decorate*) schmücken; (*Culin*) anmachen; (*Med*) verbinden; **~ oneself, get ~ed** sich anziehen ● *vi* sich anziehen. **~ up** *vi* sich schön anziehen; (*in disguise*) sich verkleiden (**as** als)

dress: ~ circle *n* (*Theat*) erster Rang *m*. **~er** *n* (*furniture*) Anrichte *f*; (*Amer: dressing-table*) Frisiertisch *m*

dressing *n* (*Culin*) Soße *f*; (*Med*) Verband *m*

dressing: ~ 'down *n* (*fam*) Standpauke *f*. **~-gown** *n* Morgenmantel *m*. **~-room** *n* Ankleidezimmer *nt*; (*Theat*) [Künstler]garderobe *f*. **~-table** *n* Frisiertisch *m*

dress: ~maker *n* Schneiderin *f*. **~making** *n* Damenschneiderei *f*. **~ rehearsal** *n* Generalprobe *f*

dressy /'dresɪ/ *a* (**-ier, -iest**) schick

drew /druː/ *see* **draw**

dribble /'drɪbl/ *vi* sabbern; (*Sport*) dribbeln

dried /draɪd/ *a* getrocknet; **~ fruit** Dörrobst *nt*

drier /'draɪə(r)/ *n* Trockner *m*

drift /drɪft/ *n* Abtrift *f*; (*of snow*) Schneewehe *f*; (*meaning*) Sinn *m* ● *vi* treiben; (*off course*) abtreiben; ⟨*snow:*⟩ Wehen bilden; (*fig*) ⟨*person:*⟩ sich treiben lassen; **~ apart**

⟨persons:⟩ sich auseinanderleben.
∼**wood** n Treibholz nt

drill /drɪl/ n Bohrer m; (Mil) Drill m
● vt/i bohren (**for** nach); (Mil)
drillen

drily /'draɪlɪ/ adv trocken

drink /drɪŋk/ n Getränk nt; (alcoholic) Drink m; (alcohol) Alkohol m;
have a ∼ etwas trinken ● vt/i (pt
drank, pp **drunk**) trinken. ∼ **up** vt/i
austrinken

drink|able /'drɪŋkəbl/ a trinkbar. ∼**er**
n Trinker m

'**drinking-water** n Trinkwasser nt

drip /drɪp/ n Tropfen nt; (drop) Tropfen m; (Med) Tropf m; (fam: person)
Niete f ● vi (pt/pp **dripped**) tropfen.
∼-'**dry** a bügelfrei. ∼**ping** n
Schmalz nt

drive /draɪv/ n [Auto]fahrt f; (entrance) Einfahrt f; (energy) Elan m;
(Psych) Trieb m; (Pol) Aktion f;
(Sport) Treibschlag m; (Techn) Antrieb m ● v (pt **drove**, pp **driven**) ● vt
treiben; fahren ⟨car⟩; (Sport: hit)
schlagen; (Techn) antreiben; ∼ **s.o.**
mad (fam) jdn verrückt machen;
what are you driving at? (fam) worauf willst du hinaus? ● vi fahren. ∼
away vt vertreiben ● vi abfahren.
∼ **in** vi hinein-/hereinfahren. ∼ **off**
vt vertreiben ● vi abfahren. ∼ **on** vi
weiterfahren. ∼ **up** vi vorfahren

'**drive-in** a ∼ **cinema** Autokino nt

drivel /'drɪvl/ n (fam) Quatsch m

driven /'drɪvn/ see **drive**

driver /'draɪvə(r)/ n Fahrer(in) m(f);
(of train) Lokführer m

driving /'draɪvɪŋ/ a ⟨rain⟩ peitschend; ⟨force⟩ treibend

driving: ∼ **lesson** n Fahrstunde f. ∼
licence n Führerschein m. ∼ **school**
n Fahrschule f. ∼ **test** Fahrprüfung
f; **take one's** ∼ **test** den Führerschein machen

drizzle /'drɪzl/ n Nieselregen m ● vi
nieseln

drone /drəʊn/ n Drohne f; (sound)
Brummen nt

droop /druːp/ vi herabhängen;
⟨flowers:⟩ die Köpfe hängen lassen

drop /drɒp/ n Tropfen m; (fall) Fall
m; (in price, temperature) Rückgang
m ● v (pt/pp **dropped**) ● vt fallen
lassen; abwerfen ⟨bomb⟩; (omit) auslassen; (give up) aufgeben ● vi fallen;
(fall lower) sinken; ⟨wind:⟩ nachlassen. ∼ **in** vi vorbeikommen. ∼ **off** vt
absetzen ⟨person⟩ ● vi abfallen; (fall

asleep) einschlafen. ∼ **out** vi herausfallen; (give up) aufgeben

'**drop-out** n Aussteiger m

droppings /'drɒpɪŋz/ npl Kot m

drought /draʊt/ n Dürre f

drove /drəʊv/ see **drive**

droves /drəʊvz/ npl **in** ∼ in Scharen

drown /draʊn/ vi ertrinken ● vt
ertränken; übertönen ⟨noise⟩; **be**
∼**ed** ertrinken

drowsy /'draʊzɪ/ a schläfrig

drudgery /'drʌdʒərɪ/ n Plackerei f

drug /drʌg/ n Droge f ● vt (pt/pp
drugged) betäuben

drug: ∼ **addict** n Drogenabhängige(r) m/f. ∼**gist** n (Amer) Apotheker m. ∼**store** n (Amer) Drogerie
f; (dispensing) Apotheke f

drum /drʌm/ n Trommel f; (for oil)
Tonne f ● v (pt/pp **drummed**) ● vi
trommeln ● vt ∼**sth into s.o.** (fam)
jdm etw einbleuen. ∼**mer** n
Trommler m; (in pop-group) Schlagzeuger m. ∼**stick** n Trommelschlegel m; (Culin) Keule f

drunk /drʌŋk/ see **drink** ● a betrunken; **get** ∼ sich betrinken ● n Betrunkene(r) m

drunk|ard /'drʌŋkəd/ n Trinker m.
∼**en** a betrunken; ∼**en driving**
Trunkenheit f am Steuer

dry /draɪ/ a (**drier**, **driest**) trocken
● vt/i trocknen; ∼ **one's eyes** sich
dat die Tränen abwischen. ∼ **up** vi
austrocknen; (fig) versiegen ● vt
austrocknen; abtrocknen ⟨dishes⟩

dry: -'**clean** vt chemisch reinigen. ∼-
'**cleaner's** n (shop) chemische Reinigung f. ∼**ness** n Trockenheit f

dual /'djuːəl/ a doppelt

dual: ∼ '**carriageway** n ≈ Schnellstraße f. ∼-'**purpose** a zweifach
verwendbar

dub /dʌb/ vt (pt/pp **dubbed**) synchronisieren ⟨film⟩; kopieren ⟨tape⟩;
(name) nennen

dubious /'djuːbɪəs/ a zweifelhaft; **be**
∼ **about** Zweifel haben über (+ acc)

duchess /'dʌtʃɪs/ n Herzogin f

duck /dʌk/ n Ente f ● vt (in water)
untertauchen; ∼ **one's head** den
Kopf einziehen ● vi sich ducken.
∼**ling** n Entchen nt; (Culin) Ente f

duct /dʌkt/ n Rohr nt; (Anat) Gang m

dud /dʌd/ a (fam) nutzlos; ⟨coin⟩
falsch; ⟨cheque⟩ ungedeckt; (forged)
gefälscht ● n (fam) (banknote) Blüte
f; (Mil: shell) Blindgänger m

due /dju:/ *a* angemessen; **be ~** fällig sein; ⟨baby:⟩ erwartet werden; ⟨train:⟩ planmäßig ankommen; **~ to** ⟨owing to⟩ wegen (+ gen); zurückzuführen sein auf (+ acc); **in ~ course** im Laufe der Zeit; ⟨write⟩ zu gegebener Zeit ● *adv* **~west** genau westlich

duel /'dju:əl/ *n* Duell *nt*

dues /dju:z/ *npl* Gebühren *pl*

duet /dju:'et/ *n* Duo *nt*; ⟨vocal⟩ Duett *nt*

dug /dʌg/ *see* **dig**

duke /dju:k/ *n* Herzog *m*

dull /dʌl/ *a* (-er, -est) ⟨overcast, not bright⟩ trüb[e]; ⟨not shiny⟩ matt; ⟨sound⟩ dumpf; ⟨boring⟩ langweilig; ⟨stupid⟩ schwerfällig ● *vt* betäuben; abstumpfen ⟨mind⟩

duly /'dju:lɪ/ *adv* ordnungsgemäß

dumb /dʌm/ *a* (-er, -est) stumm; ⟨fam: stupid⟩ dumm. **~founded** *a* sprachlos

dummy /'dʌmɪ/ *n* ⟨tailor's⟩ [Schneider]puppe *f*; ⟨for baby⟩ Schnuller *m*; ⟨Comm⟩ Attrappe *f*

dump /dʌmp/ *n* Abfallhaufen *m*; ⟨for refuse⟩ Müllhalde *f*, Deponie *f*; ⟨fam: town⟩ Kaff *nt*; **be down in the ~s** ⟨fam⟩ deprimiert sein ● *vt* abladen; ⟨fam: put down⟩ hinwerfen (**on** auf + acc)

dumpling /'dʌmplɪŋ/ *n* Kloß *m*, Knödel *m*

dunce /dʌns/ *n* Dummkopf *m*

dune /dju:n/ *n* Düne *f*

dung /dʌŋ/ *n* Mist *m*

dungarees /dʌŋgə'ri:z/ *npl* Latzhose *f*

dungeon /'dʌndʒən/ *n* Verlies *nt*

dunk /dʌŋk/ *vt* eintunken

duo /'dju:əʊ/ *n* Paar *nt*; ⟨Mus⟩ Duo *nt*

dupe /dju:p/ *n* Betrogene(r) *m/f* ● *vt* betrügen

duplicate¹ /'dju:plɪkət/ *a* Zweit● *n* Doppel *nt*; ⟨document⟩ Duplikat *nt*; **in ~** in doppelter Ausfertigung *f*

duplicate² /'dju:plɪkeɪt/ *vt* kopieren; ⟨do twice⟩ zweimal machen. **~or** *n* Vervielfältigungsapparat *m*

durable /'djʊərəbl/ *a* haltbar

duration /djʊə'reɪʃn/ *n* Dauer *f*

duress /djʊə'res/ *n* Zwang *m*

during /'djʊərɪŋ/ *prep* während (+ gen)

dusk /dʌsk/ *n* [Abend]dämmerung *f*

dust /dʌst/ *n* Staub *m* ● *vt* abstauben; ⟨sprinkle⟩ bestäuben (**with** mit) ● *vi* Staub wischen

dust: **~bin** *n* Mülltonne *f*. **~cart** *n* Müllwagen *m*. **~er** *n* Staubtuch *nt*. **~-jacket** *n* Schutzumschlag *m*. **~man** *n* Müllmann *m*. **~pan** *n* Kehrschaufel *f*

dusty /'dʌstɪ/ *a* (-ier, -iest) staubig

Dutch /dʌtʃ/ *a* holländisch; **go ~** ⟨fam⟩ getrennte Kasse machen ● *n* ⟨Lang⟩ Holländisch *nt*; **the ~** *pl* die Holländer. **~man** *n* Holländer *m*

dutiable /'dju:tɪəbl/ *a* zollpflichtig

dutiful /'dju:tɪfl/ *a*, **-ly** *adv* pflichtbewußt; ⟨obedient⟩ gehorsam

duty /'dju:tɪ/ *n* Pflicht *f*; ⟨task⟩ Aufgabe *f*; ⟨tax⟩ Zoll *m*; **be on ~** Dienst haben. **~-free** *a* zollfrei

duvet /'du:veɪ/ *n* Steppdecke *f*

dwarf /dwɔ:f/ *n* (pl **-s** or **dwarves**) Zwerg *m*

dwell /dwel/ *vi* (pt/pp **dwelt**) ⟨liter⟩ wohnen; **~ on** ⟨fig⟩ verweilen bei. **~ing** *n* Wohnung *f*

dwindle /'dwɪndl/ *vi* abnehmen, schwinden

dye /daɪ/ *n* Farbstoff *m* ● *vt* (pres p **dyeing**) färben

dying /'daɪɪŋ/ *see* **die²**

dynamic /daɪ'næmɪk/ *a* dynamisch. **~s** *n* Dynamik *f*

dynamite /'daɪnəmaɪt/ *n* Dynamit *nt*

dynamo /'daɪnəməʊ/ *n* Dynamo *m*

dynasty /'dɪnəstɪ/ *n* Dynastie *f*

dysentery /'dɪsəntrɪ/ *n* Ruhr *f*

dyslex|ia /dɪs'leksɪə/ *n* Legasthenie *f*. **~ic** *a* legasthenisch; **be ~ic** Legastheniker sein

E

each /i:tʃ/ *a & pron* jede(r,s); ⟨per⟩ je; **~ other** einander; **£1~** £1 pro Person; ⟨for thing⟩ pro Stück

eager /'i:gə(r)/ *a*, **-ly** *adv* eifrig; **be ~ to do sth** etw gerne machen wollen. **~ness** *n* Eifer *m*

eagle /'i:gl/ *n* Adler *m*

ear¹ /ɪə(r)/ *n* ⟨of corn⟩ Ähre *f*

ear² *n* Ohr *nt*. **~ache** *n* Ohrenschmerzen *pl*. **~drum** *n* Trommelfell *nt*

earl /ɜ:l/ *n* Graf *m*

early /'ɜ:lɪ/ *a & adv* (-ier, -iest) früh; ⟨reply⟩ baldig; **be ~** früh dran sein; **~ in the morning** früh am Morgen

'earmark *vt* **~ for** bestimmen für

earn /ɜ:n/ *vt* verdienen

earnest /'ɜːnɪst/ a, **-ly** adv ernsthaft
● n in ~ im Ernst

earnings /'ɜːnɪŋz/ npl Verdienst m

ear: ~**phones** npl Kopfhörer pl. ~-
ring n Ohrring m; (clip-on) Ohrklips
m. ~**shot** n within/out of ~shot
in/außer Hörweite

earth /ɜːθ/ n Erde f; (of fox) Bau m;
where/what on ~? wo/was in aller
Welt? ● vt (Electr) erden

earthenware /'ɜːθn-/ n Tonwaren pl

earthly /'ɜːθlɪ/ a irdisch; **be no** ~ **use**
(fam) völlig nutzlos sein

'earthquake n Erdbeben nt

earthy /'ɜːθɪ/ a erdig; (coarse) derb

earwig /'ɪəwɪg/ n Ohrwurm m

ease /iːz/ n Leichtigkeit f; **at** ~**!** (Mil)
rührt euch! **be/feel ill at** ~ sich un-
gutes Gefühl haben ● vt erleichtern;
lindern ⟨pain⟩ ● vi ⟨pain:⟩ nachlassen; ⟨situation:⟩ sich entspannen

easel /'iːzl/ n Staffelei f

easily /'iːzɪlɪ/ adv leicht, mit
Leichtigkeit

east /iːst/ n Osten m; **to the** ~ **of**
östlich von ● a Ost-, ost- ● adv nach
Osten

Easter /'iːstə(r)/ n Ostern nt ● attrib
Oster-. ~ **egg** n Osterei nt

east|erly /'iːstəlɪ/ a östlich. ~**ern** a
östlich. ~**ward[s]** /-wəd[z]/ adv nach
Osten

easy /'iːzɪ/ a (-ier, -iest) leicht; **take it**
~ (fam) sich schonen; **take it** ~**!**
beruhige dich! **go** ~ **with** (fam)
sparsam umgehen mit

easy: ~ **chair** n Sessel m. ~'**going** a
gelassen; **too** ~**going** lässig

eat /iːt/ vt/i (pt ate, pp eaten) essen;
⟨animal:⟩ fressen. ~ **up** vt aufessen

eat|able /'iːtəbl/ a genießbar. ~**er** n
(apple) Eßapfel m

eau-de-Cologne /əʊdəkə'ləʊn/ n
Kölnisch Wasser nt

eaves /iːvz/ npl Dachüberhang m.
~**drop** vi (pt/pp ~dropped) [heim-
lich] lauschen; ~**drop on** belauschen

ebb /eb/ n (tide) Ebbe f; **at a low** ~
(fig) auf einem Tiefstand ● vi zurückgehen; (fig) verebben

ebony /'ebənɪ/ n Ebenholz nt

ebullient /ɪ'bʌlɪənt/ a überschwenglich

EC abbr (European Community) EG f

eccentric /ɪk'sentrɪk/ a exzentrisch
● n Exzentriker m

ecclesiastical /ɪkliːzɪ'æstɪkl/ a kirch-
lich

echo /'ekəʊ/ n (pl -es) Echo nt, Widerhall m ● v (pt/pp echoed, pres p
echoing) zurückwerfen; (imitate)
nachsagen ● vi widerhallen (with
von)

eclipse /ɪ'klɪps/ n (Astr) Finsternis f
● vt (fig) in den Schatten stellen

ecolog|ical /iːkə'lɒdʒɪkl/ a ökologisch.
~**y** /iː'kɒlədʒɪ/ n Ökologie f

economic /iːkə'nɒmɪk/ a wirtschaftlich. ~**al** a sparsam. ~**ally** adv
wirtschaftlich; (thriftily) sparsam.
~**s** n Volkswirtschaft f

economist /ɪ'kɒnəmɪst/ n Volkswirt
m; (Univ) Wirtschaftswissen-
schaftler m

economize /ɪ'kɒnəmaɪz/ vi sparen
(on an + dat)

economy /ɪ'kɒnəmɪ/ n Wirtschaft f;
(thrift) Sparsamkeit f

ecstasy /'ekstəsɪ/ n Ekstase f

ecstatic /ɪk'stætɪk/ a, **-ally** adv
ekstatisch

ecu /'eɪkjuː/ n Ecu m

ecumenical /iːkjʊ'menɪkl/ a ökumenisch

eczema /'eksɪmə/ n Ekzem nt

eddy /'edɪ/ n Wirbel m

edge /edʒ/ n Rand m; (of table, lawn)
Kante f; (of knife) Schneide f; **on** ~
(fam) nervös; **have the** ~ **on** (fam)
etwas besser sein als ● vt einfassen.
~ **forward** vi sich nach vorn
schieben

edging /'edʒɪŋ/ n Einfassung f

edgy /'edʒɪ/ a (fam) nervös

edible /'edɪbl/ a eßbar

edict /'iːdɪkt/ n Erlaß m

edifice /'edɪfɪs/ n [großes] Gebäude nt

edify /'edɪfaɪ/ vt (pt/pp -ied) erbauen.
~**ing** a erbaulich

edit /'edɪt/ vt (pt/pp edited) redigieren; herausgeben ⟨anthology,
dictionary⟩; schneiden ⟨film, tape⟩

edition /ɪ'dɪʃn/ n Ausgabe f; (impression) Auflage f

editor /'edɪtə(r)/ n Redakteur m; (of
anthology, dictionary) Herausgeber
m; (of newspaper) Chefredakteur m;
(of film) Cutter(in) m(f)

editorial /edɪ'tɔːrɪəl/ a redaktionell,
Redaktions- ● n (Journ) Leitartikel
m

educate /'edjʊkeɪt/ vt erziehen; **be**
~**d at X** auf die X-Schule gehen. ~**d**
a gebildet

education /edjʊ'keɪʃn/ n Erziehung
f; (culture) Bildung f. ~**al** a pädago-
gisch; ⟨visit⟩ kulturell

eel /iːl/ n Aal m

eerie /ˈɪərɪ/ a (-ier, -iest) unheimlich

effect /ɪˈfekt/ n Wirkung f, Effekt m; **in** ~ in Wirklichkeit; **take** ~ in Kraft treten • vt bewirken

effective /ɪˈfektɪv/ a, **-ly** adv wirksam, effektiv; (striking) wirkungsvoll, effektvoll; (actual) tatsächlich. ~**ness** n Wirksamkeit f

effeminate /ɪˈfemɪnət/ a unmännlich

effervescent /efəˈvesnt/ a sprudelnd

efficiency /ɪˈfɪʃənsɪ/ n Tüchtigkeit f; (of machine, organization) Leistungsfähigkeit f

efficient /ɪˈfɪʃənt/ a tüchtig; (machine, organization) leistungsfähig; (method) rationell. ~**ly** adv gut; (function) rationell

effigy /ˈefɪdʒɪ/ n Bildnis nt

effort /ˈefət/ n Anstrengung f; **make an** ~ sich (dat) Mühe geben. ~**less** a, **-ly** adv mühelos

effrontery /ɪˈfrʌntərɪ/ n Unverschämtheit f

effusive /ɪˈfjuːsɪv/ a, **-ly** adv überschwenglich

e.g. abbr (exempli gratia) z.B.

egalitarian /ɪɡælɪˈteərɪən/ a egalitär

egg¹ /eɡ/ vt ~**on** (fam) anstacheln

egg² n Ei nt. ~**-cup** n Eierbecher m. ~**shell** n Eierschale f. ~**-timer** n Eieruhr f

ego /ˈiːɡəʊ/ n Ich nt. ~**centric** /-ˈsentrɪk/ a egozentrisch. ~**ism** n Egoismus m. ~**ist** n Egoist m. ~**tism** n Ichbezogenheit f. ~**tist** n ichbezogener Mensch m

Egypt /ˈiːdʒɪpt/ n Ägypten nt. ~**ian** /ɪˈdʒɪpʃn/ a ägyptisch • n Ägypter(in) m(f)

eiderdown /ˈaɪdə-/ n (quilt) Daunendecke f

eigh|t /eɪt/ a acht • n Acht f; (boat) Achter m. ~**teen** a achtzehn. ~**teenth** a achtzehnte(r,s)

eighth /eɪtθ/ a achte(r,s) • n Achtel nt

eightieth /ˈeɪtɪɪθ/ a achtzigste(r,s)

eighty /ˈeɪtɪ/ a achtzig

either /ˈaɪðə(r)/ a & pron ~ **[of them]** einer von [den] beiden; (both) beide; **on** ~ **side** auf beiden Seiten • adv **I don't** ~ ich auch nicht • conj ~... **or** entweder ... oder

eject /ɪˈdʒekt/ vt hinauswerfen

eke /iːk/ vt ~ **out** strecken; (increase) ergänzen; ~ **out a living** sich kümmerlich durchschlagen

elaborate¹ /ɪˈlæbərət/ a, **-ly** adv kunstvoll; (fig) kompliziert

elaborate² /ɪˈlæbəreɪt/ vi ausführlicher sein; ~ **on** näher ausführen

elapse /ɪˈlæps/ vi vergehen

elastic /ɪˈlæstɪk/ a elastisch • n Gummiband nt. ~ **'band** n Gummiband nt

elasticity /ɪlæsˈtɪsətɪ/ n Elastizität f

elated /ɪˈleɪtɪd/ a überglücklich

elbow /ˈelbəʊ/ n Ellbogen m

elder¹ /ˈeldə(r)/ n Holunder m

eld|er² a ältere(r,s) • n **the** ~ der/die Ältere. ~**erly** a alt. ~**est** a älteste(r,s) • n **the** ~**est** der/die Älteste

elect /ɪˈlekt/ a **the president** ~ der designierte Präsident • vt wählen; ~ **to do sth** sich dafür entscheiden, etw zu tun. ~**ion** /-ekʃn/ n Wahl f

elector /ɪˈlektə(r)/ n Wähler(in) m(f). ~**al** a Wahl-; ~**al roll** Wählerverzeichnis nt. ~**ate** /-rət/ n Wählerschaft f

electric /ɪˈlektrɪk/ a, **-ally** adv elektrisch

electrical /ɪˈlektrɪkl/ a elektrisch; ~ **engineering** Elektrotechnik f

electric: ~ **'blanket** n Heizdecke f. ~ **'fire** n elektrischer Heizofen m

electrician /ɪlekˈtrɪʃn/ n Elektriker m

electricity /ɪlekˈtrɪsətɪ/ n Elektrizität f; (supply) Strom m

electrify /ɪˈlektrɪfaɪ/ vt (pt/pp -ied) elektrifizieren. ~**ing** a (fig) elektrisierend

electrocute /ɪˈlektrəkjuːt/ vt durch einen elektrischen Schlag töten; (execute) auf dem elektrischen Stuhl hinrichten

electrode /ɪˈlektrəʊd/ n Elektrode f

electron /ɪˈlektrɒn/ n Elektron nt

electronic /ɪlekˈtrɒnɪk/ a elektronisch. ~**s** n Elektronik f

elegance /ˈelɪɡəns/ n Eleganz f

elegant /ˈelɪɡənt/ a, **-ly** adv elegant

elegy /ˈelɪdʒɪ/ n Elegie f

element /ˈelɪmənt/ n Element nt. ~**ary** /-ˈmentərɪ/ a elementar

elephant /ˈelɪfənt/ n Elefant m

elevat|e /ˈelɪveɪt/ vt heben; (fig) erheben. ~**ion** /-ˈveɪʃn/ n Erhebung f

elevator /ˈelɪveɪtə(r)/ n (Amer) Aufzug m, Fahrstuhl m

eleven /ɪˈlevn/ a elf • n Elf f. ~**th** a elfte(r,s); **at the** ~**th hour** (fam) in letzter Minute

elf /elf/ n (pl elves) Elfe f

elicit /ɪˈlɪsɪt/ vt herausbekommen

eligible /'elɪdʒəbl/ a berechtigt; ~ **young man** gute Partie f

eliminate /ɪ'lɪmɪneɪt/ vt ausschalten; (excrete) ausscheiden

élite /er'li:t/ n Elite f

ellip|se /ɪ'lɪps/ n Ellipse f. ~**tical** a elliptisch

elm /elm/ n Ulme f

elocution /elə'kju:ʃn/ n Sprecherziehung f

elongate /'i:lɒŋgeɪt/ vt verlängern

elope /ɪ'ləʊp/ vi durchbrennen (fam)

eloquen|ce /'eləkwəns/ n Beredsamkeit f. ~**t** a, **-ly** adv beredt

else /els/ adv sonst; **who** ~? wer sonst? **nothing** ~ sonst nichts; **or** ~ oder; (otherwise) sonst; **someone/ somewhere** ~ jemand/irgendwo anders; **anyone** ~ jeder andere; (as question) sonst noch jemand? **anything** ~ alles andere; (as question) sonst noch etwas? ~**where** adv woanders

elucidate /ɪ'lu:sɪdeɪt/ vt erläutern

elude /ɪ'lu:d/ vt entkommen (+ dat); (avoid) ausweichen (+ dat)

elusive /ɪ'lu:sɪv/ a **be** ~ schwer zu fassen sein

emaciated /ɪ'meɪsɪeɪtɪd/ a abgezehrt

emanate /'eməneɪt/ vi ausgehen (from von)

emancipat|ed /ɪ'mænsɪpeɪtɪd/ emanzipiert. ~**ion** /-'peɪʃn/ n Emanzipation f; (of slaves) Freilassung f

embalm /ɪm'bɑ:m/ vt einbalsamieren

embankment /ɪm'bæŋkmənt/ n Böschung f; (of railway) Bahndamm m

embargo /em'bɑ:gəʊ/ n (pl **-es**) Embargo nt

embark /ɪm'bɑ:k/ vi sich einschiffen; ~ **on** anfangen mit. ~**ation** /emba:'keɪʃn/ n Einschiffung f

embarrass /ɪm'bærəs/ vt in Verlegenheit bringen. ~**ed** a verlegen. ~**ing** a peinlich. ~**ment** n Verlegenheit f

embassy /'embəsɪ/ n Botschaft f

embedded /ɪm'bedɪd/ a **be deeply** ~ **in** tief stecken in (+ dat)

embellish /ɪm'belɪʃ/ vt verzieren; (fig) ausschmücken

embers /'embəz/ npl Glut f

embezzle /ɪm'bezl/ vt unterschlagen. ~**ment** n Unterschlagung f

embitter /ɪm'bɪtə(r)/ vt verbittern

emblem /'embləm/ n Emblem nt

embodiment /ɪm'bɒdɪmənt/ n Verkörperung f

embody /ɪm'bɒdɪ/ vt (pt/pp **-ied**) verkörpern; (include) enthalten

emboss /ɪm'bɒs/ vt prägen

embrace /ɪm'breɪs/ n Umarmung f ● vt umarmen; (fig) umfassen ● vi sich umarmen

embroider /ɪm'brɔɪdə(r)/ vt besticken; sticken ⟨design⟩; (fig) ausschmücken ● vi sticken. ~**y** n Stickerei f

embroil /ɪm'brɔɪl/ vt **become** ~**ed in sth** in etw (acc) verwickelt werden

embryo /'embrɪəʊ/ n Embryo m

emerald /'emərəld/ n Smaragd m

emer|ge /ɪ'mɜ:dʒ/ vi auftauchen (from aus); (become known) sich herausstellen; (come into being) entstehen. ~**gence** /-əns/ n Auftauchen nt; Entstehung f

emergency /ɪ'mɜ:dʒənsɪ/ n Notfall m; **in an** ~ im Notfall. ~ **exit** n Notausgang m

emery-paper /'emərɪ-/ n Schmirgelpapier nt

emigrant /'emɪgrənt/ n Auswanderer m

emigrat|e /'emɪgreɪt/ vi auswandern. ~**ion** /-'greɪʃn/ n Auswanderung f

eminent /'emɪnənt/ a, **-ly** adv eminent

emission /ɪ'mɪʃn/ n Ausstrahlung f; (of pollutant) Emission f

emit /ɪ'mɪt/ vt (pt/pp **emitted**) ausstrahlen ⟨light, heat⟩; ausstoßen ⟨smoke, fumes, cry⟩

emotion /ɪ'məʊʃn/ n Gefühl nt. ~**al** a emotional; **become** ~**al** sich erregen

emotive /ɪ'məʊtɪv/ a emotional

empath|ize /'empəθaɪz/ vi ~**ize with s.o.** sich in jdn einfühlen. ~**y** n Einfühlungsvermögen nt

emperor /'empərə(r)/ n Kaiser m

emphasis /'emfəsɪs/ n Betonung f

emphasize /'emfəsaɪz/ vt betonen

emphatic /ɪm'fætɪk/ a, **-ally** adv nachdrücklich

empire /'empaɪə(r)/ n Reich nt

empirical /em'pɪrɪkl/ a empirisch

employ /ɪm'plɔɪ/ vt beschäftigen; (appoint) einstellen; (fig) anwenden. ~**ee** /emplɔɪ'i:/ n Beschäftigte(r) m/f; (in contrast to employer) Arbeitnehmer m. ~**er** n Arbeitgeber m. ~**ment** n Beschäftigung f; (work) Arbeit f. ~**ment agency** n Stellenvermittlung f

empower /ɪm'paʊə(r)/ vt ermächtigen

empress /'emprɪs/ n Kaiserin f

empties /'emptɪz/ npl leere Flaschen pl

emptiness /'emptɪnɪs/ n Leere f

empty /'emptɪ/ *a* leer ● *vt* leeren; ausleeren ⟨*container*⟩ ● *vi* sich leeren

emulate /'emjʊleɪt/ *vt* nacheifern (+ *dat*)

emulsion /ɪ'mʌlʃn/ *n* Emulsion *f*

enable /ɪ'neɪbl/ *vt* ~ **s.o. to** es jdm möglich machen, zu

enact /ɪ'nækt/ *vt* (*Theat*) aufführen

enamel /ɪ'næml/ *n* Email *nt*; (*on teeth*) Zahnschmelz *m*; (*paint*) Lack *m* ● *vt* (*pt/pp* **enamelled**) emaillieren

enamoured /ɪ'næməd/ *a* **be** ~ **of** sehr angetan sein von

enchant /ɪn'tʃɑ:nt/ *vt* bezaubern. ~**ing** *a* bezaubernd. ~**ment** *n* Zauber *m*

encircle /ɪn'sɜ:kl/ *vt* einkreisen

enclave /'enkleɪv/ *n* Enklave *f*

enclos|e /ɪn'kləʊz/ *vt* einschließen; (*in letter*) beilegen (**with** *dat*). ~**ure** /-ʒə(r)/ *n* (*at zoo*) Gehege *nt*; (*in letter*) Anlage *f*

encompass /ɪn'kʌmpəs/ *vt* umfassen

encore /'ɒŋkɔ:(r)/ *n* Zugabe *f* ● *int* bravo!

encounter /ɪn'kaʊntə(r)/ *n* Begegnung *f*; (*battle*) Zusammenstoß *m* ● *vt* begegnen (+ *dat*); (*fig*) stoßen auf (+ *acc*)

encourag|e /ɪn'kʌrɪdʒ/ *vt* ermutigen; (*promote*) fördern. ~**ement** *n* Ermutigung *f*. ~**ing** *a* ermutigend

encroach /ɪn'krəʊtʃ/ *vt* ~ **on** eindringen in (+ *acc*) ⟨*land*⟩; beanspruchen ⟨*time*⟩

encumb|er /ɪn'kʌmbə(r)/ *vt* belasten (**with** mit). ~**rance** /-rəns/ *n* Belastung *f*

encyclopaed|ia /ɪnsaɪklə'pi:dɪə/ *n* Enzyklopädie *f*, Lexikon *nt*. ~**ic** *a* enzyklopädisch

end /end/ *n* Ende *nt*; (*purpose*) Zweck *m*; **in the** ~ schließlich; **at the** ~ **of May** Ende Mai; **on** ~ hochkant; **for days on** ~ tagelang; **make** ~**s meet** (*fam*) [gerade] auskommen; **no** ~ **of** (*fam*) unheimlich viel[e] ● *vt* beenden ● *vi* enden; ~ **up in** (*fam: arrive at*) landen in (+ *dat*)

endanger /ɪn'deɪndʒə(r)/ *vt* gefährden

endear|ing /ɪn'dɪərɪŋ/ *a* liebenswert. ~**ment** *n* term of ~**ment** Kosewort *nt*

endeavour /ɪn'devə(r)/ *n* Bemühung *f* ● *vi* sich bemühen (**to** zu)

ending /'endɪŋ/ *n* Schluß *m*, Ende *nt*; (*Gram*) Endung *f*

endive /'endaɪv/ *n* Endivie *f*

endless /'endlɪs/ *a*, **-ly** *adv* endlos

endorse /en'dɔ:s/ *vt* (*Comm*) indossieren; (*confirm*) bestätigen. ~**ment** *n* (*Comm*) Indossament *nt*; (*fig*) Bestätigung *f*; (*on driving licence*) Strafvermerk *m*

endow /ɪn'daʊ/ *vt* stiften; **be** ~**ed with** (*fig*) haben. ~**ment** *n* Stiftung *f*

endur|able /ɪn'djʊərəbl/ *a* erträglich. ~**ance** /-rəns/ *n* Durchhaltevermögen *nt*; **beyond** ~**ance** unerträglich

endur|e /ɪn'djʊə(r)/ *vt* ertragen ● *vi* [lange] bestehen. ~**ing** *a* dauernd

enemy /'enəmɪ/ *n* Feind *m* ● *attrib* feindlich

energetic /enə'dʒetɪk/ *a* tatkräftig; **be** ~ voller Energie sein

energy /'enədʒɪ/ *n* Energie *f*

enforce /ɪn'fɔ:s/ *vt* durchsetzen. ~**d** *a* unfreiwillig

engage /ɪn'geɪdʒ/ *vt* einstellen ⟨*staff*⟩; (*Theat*) engagieren; (*Auto*) einlegen ⟨*gear*⟩ ● *vi* sich beteiligen (**in** an + *dat*); (*Techn*) ineinandergreifen. ~**d** *a* besetzt; ⟨*person*⟩ beschäftigt; (*to be married*) verlobt; **get** ~**d** sich verloben (**to** mit). ~**ment** *n* Verlobung *f*; (*appointment*) Verabredung *f*; (*Mil*) Gefecht *nt*

engaging /ɪn'geɪdʒɪŋ/ *a* einnehmend

engender /ɪn'dʒendə(r)/ *vt* (*fig*) erzeugen

engine /'endʒɪn/ *n* Motor *m*; (*Naut*) Maschine *f*; (*Rail*) Lokomotive *f*; (*of jet-plane*) Triebwerk *nt*. ~**-driver** *n* Lokomotivführer *m*

engineer /endʒɪ'nɪə(r)/ *n* Ingenieur *m*; (*service, installation*) Techniker *m*; (*Naut*) Maschinist *m*; (*Amer*) Lokomotivführer *m* ● *vt* (*fig*) organisieren. ~**ing** *n* [**mechanical**] ~**ing** Maschinenbau *m*

England /'ɪŋglənd/ *n* England *nt*

English /'ɪŋglɪʃ/ *a* englisch; **the** ~ **Channel** der Ärmelkanal ● *n* (*Lang*) Englisch *nt*; **in** ~ auf englisch; **into** ~ ins Englische; **the** ~ *pl* die Engländer. ~**man** *n* Engländer *m*. ~**woman** *n* Engländerin *f*

engrav|e /ɪn'greɪv/ *vt* eingravieren. ~**ing** *n* Stich *m*

engross /ɪn'grəʊs/ *vt* **be** ~**ed in** vertieft sein in (+ *acc*)

engulf /ɪn'gʌlf/ *vt* verschlingen

enhance /ɪn'hɑ:ns/ *vt* verschönern; (*fig*) steigern

enigma /ɪˈnɪgmə/ n Rätsel nt. ~tic /enɪgˈmætɪk/ a rätselhaft

enjoy /ɪnˈdʒɔɪ/ vt genießen; ~ oneself sich amüsieren; ~ cooking/painting gern kochen/malen; I ~ed it es hat mir gut gefallen/ ⟨food:⟩ geschmeckt. ~able /-əbl/ a angenehm, nett. ~ment n Vergnügen nt

enlarge /ɪnˈlɑːdʒ/ vt vergrößern ● vi ~ upon sich näher auslassen über (+ acc). ~ment n Vergrößerung f

enlighten /ɪnˈlaɪtn/ vt aufklären. ~ment n Aufklärung f

enlist /ɪnˈlɪst/ vt (Mil) einziehen; ~ s.o.'s help jdn zur Hilfe heranziehen ● vi (Mil) sich melden

enliven /ɪnˈlaɪvn/ vt beleben

enmity /ˈenmətɪ/ n Feindschaft f

enormity /ɪˈnɔːmətɪ/ n Ungeheuerlichkeit f

enormous /ɪˈnɔːməs/ a, -ly adv riesig

enough /ɪˈnʌf/ a, adv & n genug; be ~ reichen; funnily ~ komischerweise; I've had ~! (fam) jetzt reicht's mir aber!

enquir|e /ɪnˈkwaɪə(r)/ vi sich erkundigen (about nach) ● vt sich erkundigen nach. ~y n Erkundigung f; (investigation) Untersuchung f

enrage /ɪnˈreɪdʒ/ vt wütend machen

enrich /ɪnˈrɪtʃ/ vt bereichern; (improve) anreichern

enrol /ɪnˈrəʊl/ v (pt/pp -rolled) ● vt einschreiben ● vi sich einschreiben. ~ment n Einschreibung f

ensemble /ɒnˈsɒmbl/ n (clothing & Mus) Ensemble nt

ensign /ˈensaɪn/ n Flagge f

enslave /ɪnˈsleɪv/ vt versklaven

ensue /ɪnˈsjuː/ vi folgen; (result) sich ergeben (from aus)

ensure /ɪnˈʃʊə(r)/ vt sicherstellen; ~ that dafür sorgen, daß

entail /ɪnˈteɪl/ vt erforderlich machen; what does it ~? was ist damit verbunden?

entangle /ɪnˈtæŋgl/ vt get ~d sich verfangen (in in + dat); (fig) sich verstricken (in in + acc)

enter /ˈentə(r)/ vt eintreten/⟨vehicle:⟩ einfahren in (+ acc); einreisen in (+ acc) ⟨country⟩; (register) eintragen; sich anmelden zu ⟨competition⟩ ● vi eintreten; ⟨vehicle:⟩ einfahren; (Theat) auftreten; (register as competitor) sich anmelden; (take part) sich beteiligen (in an + dat)

enterpris|e /ˈentəpraɪz/ n Unternehmen nt; (quality) Unternehmungsgeist m. ~ing a unternehmend

entertain /entəˈteɪn/ vt unterhalten; (invite) einladen; (to meal) bewirten ⟨guest⟩; (fig) in Erwägung ziehen ● vi unterhalten; (have guests) Gäste haben. ~er n Unterhalter m. ~ment n Unterhaltung f

enthral /ɪnˈθrɔːl/ vt (pt/pp enthralled) be ~led gefesselt sein (by von)

enthuse /ɪnˈθjuːz/ vi ~ over schwärmen von

enthusias|m /ɪnˈθjuːzɪæzm/ n Begeisterung f. ~t n Enthusiast m. ~tic /-ˈæstɪk/ a, -ally adv begeistert

entice /ɪnˈtaɪs/ vt locken. ~ment n Anreiz m

entire /ɪnˈtaɪə(r)/ a ganz. ~ly adv ganz, völlig. ~ty /-rətɪ/ n in its ~ty in seiner Gesamtheit

entitle /ɪnˈtaɪtl/ vt berechtigen; ~d... mit dem Titel...; be ~d to sth das Recht auf etw (acc) haben. ~ment n Berechtigung f; (claim) Anspruch m (to auf + acc)

entity /ˈentətɪ/ n Wesen nt

entomology /entəˈmɒlədʒɪ/ n Entomologie f

entourage /ˈɒntʊrɑːʒ/ n Gefolge nt

entrails /ˈentreɪlz/ npl Eingeweide pl

entrance¹ /ɪnˈtrɑːns/ vt bezaubern

entrance² /ˈentrəns/ n Eintritt m; (Theat) Auftritt m; (way in) Eingang m; (for vehicle) Einfahrt f. ~ examination n Aufnahmeprüfung f. ~ fee n Eintrittsgebühr f

entrant /ˈentrənt/ n Teilnehmer(in) m(f)

entreat /ɪnˈtriːt/ vt anflehen (for um)

entrench /ɪnˈtrentʃ/ vt be ~ed in verwurzelt sein in (+ dat)

entrust /ɪnˈtrʌst/ vt ~ s.o. with sth, ~ sth to s.o. jdm etw anvertrauen

entry /ˈentrɪ/ n Eintritt m; (into country) Einreise f; (on list) Eintrag m; no ~ Zutritt/(Auto) Einfahrt verboten. ~ form n Anmeldeformular nt. ~ visa n Einreisevisum nt

enumerate /ɪˈnjuːməreɪt/ vt aufzählen

enunciate /ɪˈnʌnsɪeɪt/ vt [deutlich] aussprechen; (state) vorbringen

envelop /ɪnˈveləp/ vt (pt/pp enveloped) einhüllen

envelope /ˈenvələʊp/ n [Brief]umschlag m

enviable /ˈenvɪəbl/ a beneidenswert

envious /'enviəs/ *a*, **-ly** *adv* neidisch (**of** auf + *acc*)

environment /ɪn'vaɪərənmənt/ *n* Umwelt *f*

environmental /ɪnvaɪərən'mentl/ *a* Umwelt-. **~ist** *n* Umweltschützer *m*. **~ly** *adv* **~ly friendly** umweltfreundlich

envisage /ɪn'vɪzɪdʒ/ *vt* sich (*dat*) vorstellen

envoy /'envɔɪ/ *n* Gesandte(r) *m*

envy /'envɪ/ *n* Neid *m* ● *vt* (*pt/pp* -ied) **~ s.o. sth** jdn um etw beneiden

enzyme /'enzaɪm/ *n* Enzym *nt*

epic /'epɪk/ *a* episch ● *n* Epos *nt*

epidemic /epɪ'demɪk/ *n* Epidemie *f*

epilep|sy /'epɪlepsɪ/ *n* Epilepsie *f*. **~tic** /-'leptɪk/ *a* epileptisch ● *n* Epileptiker(in) *m(f)*

epilogue /'epɪlɒg/ *n* Epilog *m*

episode /'epɪsəʊd/ *n* Episode *f*; (*instalment*) Folge *f*

epistle /ɪ'pɪsl/ *n* (*liter*) Brief *m*

epitaph /'epɪtɑːf/ *n* Epitaph *nt*

epithet /'epɪθet/ *n* Beiname *m*

epitom|e /ɪ'pɪtəmɪ/ *n* Inbegriff *m*. **~ize** *vt* verkörpern

epoch /'iːpɒk/ *n* Epoche *f*. **~-making** *a* epochemachend

equal /'iːkwl/ *a* gleich (**to** *dat*); **be ~ to a task** einer Aufgabe gewachsen sein ● *n* Gleichgestellte(r) *m/f* ● *vt* (*pt/pp* **equalled**) gleichen (+ *dat*); (*fig*) gleichkommen (+ *dat*). **~ity** /ɪ'kwɒlətɪ/ *n* Gleichheit *f*

equalize /'iːkwəlaɪz/ *vt/i* ausgleichen. **~r** *n* (*Sport*) Ausgleich[streffer] *m*

equally /'iːkwəlɪ/ *adv* gleich; (*divide*) gleichmäßig; (*just as*) genauso

equanimity /ekwə'nɪmətɪ/ *n* Gleichmut *f*

equat|e /ɪ'kweɪt/ *vt* gleichsetzen (**with** mit). **~ion** /-eɪʒn/ *n* (*Math*) Gleichung *f*

equator /ɪ'kweɪtə(r)/ *n* Äquator *m*. **~ial** /ekwə'tɔːrɪəl/ *a* Äquator-

equestrian /ɪ'kwestrɪən/ *a* Reit-

equilibrium /iːkwɪ'lɪbrɪəm/ *n* Gleichgewicht *nt*

equinox /'iːkwɪnɒks/ *n* Tagundnachtgleiche *f*

equip /ɪ'kwɪp/ *vt* (*pt/pp* **equipped**) ausrüsten; (*furnish*) ausstatten. **~ment** *n* Ausrüstung *f*; Ausstattung *f*

equitable /'ekwɪtəbl/ *a* gerecht

equity /'ekwɪtɪ/ *n* Gerechtigkeit *f*

equivalent /ɪ'kwɪvələnt/ *a* gleichwertig; (*corresponding*) entsprechend

● *n* Äquivalent *nt*; (*value*) Gegenwert *m*; (*counterpart*) Gegenstück *nt*

equivocal /ɪ'kwɪvəkl/ *a* zweideutig

era /'ɪərə/ *n* Ära *f*, Zeitalter *nt*

eradicate /ɪ'rædɪkeɪt/ *vt* ausrotten

erase /ɪ'reɪz/ *vt* ausradieren; (*from tape*) löschen; (*fig*) auslöschen. **~r** *n* Radiergummi *m*

erect /ɪ'rekt/ *a* aufrecht ● *vt* errichten. **~ion** /-ekʃn/ *n* Errichtung *f*; (*building*) Bau *m*; (*Biol*) Erektion *f*

ermine /'ɜːmɪn/ *n* Hermelin *m*

ero|de /ɪ'rəʊd/ *vt* (*water:*) auswaschen; (*acid:*) angreifen. **~sion** /-əʊʒn/ *n* Erosion *f*

erotic /ɪ'rɒtɪk/ *a* erotisch. **~ism** /-tɪsɪzm/ *n* Erotik *f*

err /ɜː(r)/ *vi* sich irren; (*sin*) sündigen

errand /'erənd/ *n* Botengang *m*

erratic /ɪ'rætɪk/ *a* unregelmäßig; (*person*) unberechenbar

erroneous /ɪ'rəʊnɪəs/ *a* falsch; (*belief, assumption*) irrig. **~ly** *adv* fälschlich; irrigerweise

error /'erə(r)/ *n* Irrtum *m*; (*mistake*) Fehler *m*; **in ~** irrtümlicherweise

erudit|e /'erʊdaɪt/ *a* gelehrt. **~ion** /-'dɪʃn/ *n* Gelehrsamkeit *f*

erupt /ɪ'rʌpt/ *vi* ausbrechen. **~ion** /-ʌpʃn/ *n* Ausbruch *m*

escalat|e /'eskəleɪt/ *vt/i* eskalieren. **~ion** /-'leɪʃn/ *n* Eskalation *f*. **~or** *n* Rolltreppe *f*

escapade /'eskəpeɪd/ *n* Eskapade *f*

escape /ɪ'skeɪp/ *n* Flucht *f*; (*from prison*) Ausbruch *m*; **have a narrow ~** gerade noch davonkommen ● *vi* flüchten; (*prisoner:*) ausbrechen; entkommen (**from** aus; **from s.o.** jdm); (*gas:*) entweichen ● *vt* **~ notice** unbemerkt bleiben; **the name ~s me** der Name entfällt mir

escapism /ɪ'skeɪpɪzm/ *n* Flucht *f* vor der Wirklichkeit, Eskapismus *m*

escort¹ /'eskɔːt/ *n* (*of person*) Begleiter *m*; (*Mil*) Eskorte *f*; **under ~** unter Bewachung

escort² /ɪ'skɔːt/ *vt* begleiten; (*Mil*) eskortieren

Eskimo /'eskɪməʊ/ *n* Eskimo *m*

esoteric /esə'terɪk/ *a* esoterisch

especial /ɪ'speʃl/ *a* besondere(r,s). **~ly** *adv* besonders

espionage /'espɪənɑːʒ/ *n* Spionage *f*

essay /'eseɪ/ *n* Aufsatz *m*

essence /'esns/ *n* Wesen *nt*; (*Chem, Culin*) Essenz *f*; **in ~** im wesentlichen

essential /ɪ'senʃl/ *a* wesentlich; (*indispensable*) unentbehrlich ● *n* the ~s das Wesentliche; (*items*) das Nötigste. ~ly *adv* im wesentlichen

establish /ɪ'stæblɪʃ/ *vt* gründen; (*form*) bilden; (*prove*) beweisen. ~ment *n* (*firm*) Unternehmen *nt*

estate /ɪ'steɪt/ *n* Gut *nt*; (*possessions*) Besitz *m*; (*after death*) Nachlaß *m*; (*housing*) [Wohn]siedlung *f*. ~ agent *n* Immobilienmakler *m*. ~ car *n* Kombi[wagen] *m*

esteem /ɪ'stiːm/ *n* Achtung *f* ● *vt* hochschätzen

estimate¹ /'estɪmət/ *n* Schätzung *f*; (*Comm*) [Kosten]voranschlag *m*; at a rough ~ grob geschätzt

estimat|e² /'estɪment/ *vt* schätzen. ~ion /-'meɪʃn/ *n* Einschätzung *f*; (*esteem*) Achtung *f*; in my ~ion meiner Meinung nach

estuary /'estʊərɪ/ *n* Mündung *f*

etc. /et'setərə/ *abbr* (**et cetera**) und so weiter, usw.

etching /'etʃɪŋ/ *n* Radierung *f*

eternal /ɪ'tɜːnl/ *a*, **-ly** *adv* ewig

eternity /ɪ'tɜːnətɪ/ *n* Ewigkeit *f*

ether /'iːθə(r)/ *n* Äther *m*

ethic /'eθɪk/ *n* Ethik *f*. ~al *a* ethisch; (*morally correct*) moralisch einwandfrei. ~s *n* Ethik *f*

Ethiopia /iːθɪ'əʊpɪə/ *n* Äthiopien *nt*

ethnic /'eθnɪk/ *a* ethnisch

etiquette /'etɪket/ *n* Etikette *f*

etymology /etɪ'mɒlədʒɪ/ *n* Etymologie *f*

eucalyptus /juːkə'lɪptəs/ *n* Eukalyptus *m*

eulogy /'juːlədʒɪ/ *n* Lobrede *f*

euphemis|m /'juːfəmɪzm/ *n* Euphemismus *m*. ~tic /-'mɪstɪk/ *a*, **-ally** *adv* verhüllend

euphoria /juː'fɔːrɪə/ *n* Euphorie *f*

Euro-: /'jʊərəʊ-/ *pref* ~cheque *n* Euroscheck *m*. ~passport *n* Europaß *m*

Europe /'jʊərəp/ *n* Europa *nt*

European /jʊərə'piːən/ *a* europäisch; ~ Community Europäische Gemeinschaft *f* ● *n* Europäer(in) *m*(*f*)

evacuat|e /ɪ'vækjʊeɪt/ *vt* evakuieren; räumen ⟨*building, area*⟩. ~ion /-'eɪʃn/ *n* Evakuierung *f*; Räumung *f*

evade /ɪ'veɪd/ *vt* sich entziehen (+ *dat*); hinterziehen ⟨*taxes*⟩; ~ the issue ausweichen

evaluate /ɪ'væljʊeɪt/ *vt* einschätzen

evange|lical /iːvæn'dʒelɪkl/ *a* evangelisch. ~list /ɪ'vændʒəlɪst/ *n* Evangelist *m*

evaporat|e /ɪ'væpəreɪt/ *vi* verdunsten; ~ed milk Kondensmilch *f*, Dosenmilch *f*. ~ion /-'reɪʃn/ *n* Verdampfung *f*

evasion /ɪ'veɪʒn/ *n* Ausweichen *nt*; ~ of taxes Steuerhinterziehung *f*

evasive /ɪ'veɪsɪv/ *a*, **-ly** *adv* ausweichend; be ~ ausweichen

eve /iːv/ *n* (*liter*) Vorabend *m*

even /'iːvn/ *a* (*level*) eben; (*same, equal*) gleich; (*regular*) gleichmäßig; ⟨*number*⟩ gerade; get ~ with (*fam*) es jdm heimzahlen ● *adv* sogar, selbst; ~ so trotzdem; not ~ nicht einmal ● *vt* ~ the score ausgleichen. ~ up *vt* ausgleichen ● *vi* sich ausgleichen

evening /'iːvnɪŋ/ *n* Abend *m*; this ~ heute abend; in the ~ abends, am Abend. ~ class *n* Abendkurs *m*

evenly /'iːvnlɪ/ *adv* gleichmäßig

event /ɪ'vent/ *n* Ereignis *nt*; (*function*) Veranstaltung *f*; (*Sport*) Wettbewerb *m*; in the ~ of im Falle (+ *gen*); in the ~ wie es sich ergab. ~ful *a* ereignisreich

eventual /ɪ'ventjʊəl/ *a* his ~ success der Erfolg, der ihm schließlich zuteil wurde. ~ity /-'ælətɪ/ *n* Eventualität *f*, Fall *m*. ~ly *adv* schließlich

ever /'evə(r)/ *adv* je[mals]; not ~ nie; for ~ für immer; hardly ~ fast nie; ~ since seitdem; ~ so (*fam*) sehr, furchtbar (*fam*)

'evergreen *n* immergrüner Strauch *m*/ (*tree*) Baum *m*

ever'lasting *a* ewig

every /'evrɪ/ *a* jede(r,s); ~ one jede(r,s) einzelne; ~ other day jeden zweiten Tag

every: ~body *pron* jeder[mann]; alle *pl*. ~day *a* alltäglich. ~one *pron* jeder[mann]; alle *pl*. ~thing *pron* alles. ~where *adv* überall

evict /ɪ'vɪkt/ *vt* [aus der Wohnung] hinausweisen. ~ion /-ɪkʃn/ *n* Ausweisung *f*

eviden|ce /'evɪdəns/ *n* Beweise *pl*; (*Jur*) Beweismaterial *nt*; (*testimony*) Aussage *f*; give ~ce aussagen. ~t *a*, **-ly** *adv* offensichtlich

evil /'iːvl/ *a* böse ● *n* Böse *nt*

evocative /ɪ'vɒkətɪv/ *a* be ~ of heraufbeschwören

evoke /ɪ'vəʊk/ *vt* heraufbeschwören

evolution /iːvə'luːʃn/ *n* Evolution *f*

evolve /ɪ'vɒlv/ *vt* entwickeln ● *vi* sich entwickeln

ewe /juː/ *n* Schaf *nt*

355

exacerbate /ek'sæsəbeɪt/ *vt* verschlimmern; verschärfen ⟨situation⟩

exact /ɪg'zækt/ *a*, **-ly** *adv* genau; **not ~ly** nicht gerade. ● *vt* erzwingen. **~ing** *a* anspruchsvoll. **~itude** /-ɪtjuːd/ *n*, **~ness** *n* Genauigkeit *f*

exaggerat|e /ɪg'zædʒəreɪt/ *vt/i* übertreiben. **~ion** /-'reɪʃn/ *n* Übertreibung *f*

exalt /ɪg'zɔːlt/ *vt* erheben; (*praise*) preisen

exam /ɪg'zæm/ *n* (*fam*) Prüfung *f*

examination /ɪgzæmɪ'neɪʃn/ *n* Untersuchung *f*; (*Sch*) Prüfung *f*

examine /ɪg'zæmɪn/ *vt* untersuchen; (*Sch*) prüfen; (*Jur*) verhören. **~r** *n* (*Sch*) Prüfer *m*

example /ɪg'zɑːmpl/ *n* Beispiel *nt* (**of** für); **for ~** zum Beispiel; **make an ~ of** ein Exempel statuieren an (+ *dat*)

exasperat|e /ɪg'zæspəreɪt/ *vt* zur Verzweiflung treiben. **~ion** /-'reɪʃn/ *n* Verzweiflung *f*

excavat|e /'ekskəveɪt/ *vt* ausschachten; (*Archaeol*) ausgraben. **~ion** /-'veɪʃn/ *n* Ausgrabung *f*

exceed /ɪk'siːd/ *vt* übersteigen. **~ingly** *adv* äußerst

excel /ɪk'sel/ *v* (*pt/pp* **excelled**) *vi* sich auszeichnen ● *vt* **~ oneself** sich selbst übertreffen

excellen|ce /'eksələns/ *n* Vorzüglichkeit *f*. **E~cy** *n* (*title*) Exzellenz *f*. **~t** *a*, **-ly** *adv* ausgezeichnet, vorzüglich

except /ɪk'sept/ *prep* außer (+ *dat*); **~ for** abgesehen von ● *vt* ausnehmen. **~ing** *prep* außer (+ *dat*)

exception /ɪk'sepʃn/ *n* Ausnahme *f*; **take ~ to** Anstoß nehmen an (+ *dat*). **~al** *a*, **-ly** *adv* außergewöhnlich

excerpt /'eksɜːpt/ *n* Auszug *m*

excess /ɪk'ses/ *n* Übermaß *nt* (**of** an + *dat*); (*surplus*) Überschuß *m*; **~es** *pl* Exzesse *pl*; **in ~ of** über (+ *dat*)

excess 'fare /'ekses-/ *n* Nachlösegebühr *f*

excessive /ɪk'sesɪv/ *a*, **-ly** *adv* übermäßig

exchange /ɪks'tʃeɪndʒ/ *n* Austausch *m*; (*Teleph*) Fernsprechamt *nt*; (*Comm*) [Geld]wechsel *m*; **[stock] ~** Börse *f*; **in ~** dafür ● *vt* austauschen (**for** gegen); tauschen ⟨*places, greetings, money*⟩. **~ rate** *n* Wechselkurs *m*

exchequer /ɪks'tʃekə(r)/ *n* (*Pol*) Staatskasse *f*

excise¹ /'eksaɪz/ *n* **~ duty** Verbrauchssteuer *f*

excise² /ek'saɪz/ *vt* herausschneiden

excitable /ɪk'saɪtəbl/ *a* [leicht] erregbar

excit|e /ɪk'saɪt/ *vt* aufregen; (*cause*) erregen. **~ed** *a*, **-ly** *adv* aufgeregt; **get ~ed** sich aufregen. **~ement** *n* Aufregung *f*; Erregung *f*. **~ing** *a* aufregend; ⟨*story*⟩ spannend

exclaim /ɪk'skleɪm/ *vt/i* ausrufen

exclamation /eksklə'meɪʃn/ *n* Ausruf *m*. **~ mark** *n*, (*Amer*) **~ point** *n* Ausrufezeichen *nt*

exclu|de /ɪk'skluːd/ *vt* ausschließen. **~ding** *pron* ausschließlich (+ *gen*). **~sion** /-ʒn/ *n* Ausschluß *m*

exclusive /ɪk'skluːsɪv/ *a*, **-ly** *adv* ausschließlich; (*select*) exklusiv; **~ of** ausschließlich (+ *gen*)

excommunicate /ekskə'mjuːnɪkeɪt/ *vt* exkommunizieren

excrement /'ekskrɪmənt/ *n* Kot *m*

excrete /ɪk'skriːt/ *vt* ausscheiden

excruciating /ɪk'skruːʃɪeɪtɪŋ/ *a* gräßlich

excursion /ɪk'skɜːʃn/ *n* Ausflug *m*

excusable /ɪk'skjuːzəbl/ *a* entschuldbar

excuse¹ /ɪk'skjuːs/ *n* Entschuldigung *f*; (*pretext*) Ausrede *f*

excuse² /ɪk'skjuːz/ *vt* entschuldigen; **~ from** freistellen von; **~ me!** Entschuldigung!

ex-di'rectory *a* **be ~** nicht im Telefonbuch stehen

execute /'eksɪkjuːt/ *vt* ausführen; (*put to death*) hinrichten

execution /eksɪ'kjuːʃn/ *n* (*see execute*) Ausführung *f*; Hinrichtung *f*. **~er** *n* Scharfrichter *m*

executive /ɪg'zekjʊtɪv/ *a* leitend ● *n* leitende(r) Angestellte(r) *m/f*; (*Pol*) Exekutive *f*

executor /ɪg'zekjʊtə(r)/ *n* (*Jur*) Testamentsvollstrecker *m*

exemplary /ɪg'zemplərɪ/ *a* beispielhaft; (*as a warning*) exemplarisch

exemplify /ɪg'zemplɪfaɪ/ *vt* (*pt/pp* **-ied**) veranschaulichen

exempt /ɪg'zempt/ *a* befreit ● *vt* befreien (**from** von). **~ion** /-empʃn/ *n* Befreiung *f*

exercise /'eksəsaɪz/ *n* Übung *f*; **physical ~** körperliche Bewegung *f*; **take ~** sich bewegen ● *vt* (*use*) ausüben; bewegen ⟨*horse*⟩; spazierenführen

⟨*dog*⟩ ● *vi* sich bewegen. ~ **book** *n* [Schul]heft *nt*

exert /ɪgˈzɜːt/ *vt* ausüben; ~ **oneself** sich anstrengen. ~**ion** /-ɜːʃn/ *n* Anstrengung *f*

exhale /eksˈheɪl/ *vt/i* ausatmen

exhaust /ɪgˈzɔːst/ *n* (*Auto*) Auspuff *m*; (*pipe*) Auspuffrohr *nt*; (*fumes*) Abgase *pl* ● *vt* erschöpfen. ~**ed** *a* erschöpft. ~**ing** *a* anstrengend. ~**ion** /-ɔːstʃn/ *n* Erschöpfung *f*. ~**ive** /-ɪv/ *a* (*fig*) erschöpfend

exhibit /ɪgˈzɪbɪt/ *n* Ausstellungsstück *nt*; (*Jur*) Beweisstück *nt* ● *vt* ausstellen; (*fig*) zeigen

exhibition /eksɪˈbɪʃn/ *n* Ausstellung *f*; (*Univ*) Stipendium *nt*. ~**ist** *n* Exhibitionist(in) *m(f)*

exhibitor /ɪgˈzɪbɪtə(r)/ *n* Aussteller *m*

exhilarat|ed /ɪgˈzɪləreɪtɪd/ *a* beschwingt. ~**ing** *a* berauschend. ~**ion** /-ˈreɪʃn/ *n* Hochgefühl *nt*

exhort /ɪgˈzɔːt/ *vt* ermahnen

exhume /ɪgˈzjuːm/ *vt* exhumieren

exile /ˈeksaɪl/ *n* Exil *nt*; (*person*) im Exil Lebende(r) *m/f* ● *vt* ins Exil schicken

exist /ɪgˈzɪst/ *vi* bestehen, existieren. ~**ence** /-əns/ *n* Existenz *f*; **be in** ~**ence** existieren

exit /ˈeksɪt/ *n* Ausgang *m*; (*Auto*) Ausfahrt *f*; (*Theat*) Abgang *m* ● *vi* (*Theat*) abgehen. ~ **visa** *n* Ausreisevisum *nt*

exonerate /ɪgˈzɒnəreɪt/ *vt* entlasten

exorbitant /ɪgˈzɔːbɪtənt/ *a* übermäßig hoch

exorcize /ˈeksɔːsaɪz/ *vt* austreiben

exotic /ɪgˈzɒtɪk/ *a* exotisch

expand /ɪkˈspænd/ *vt* ausdehnen; (*explain better*) weiter ausführen ● *vi* sich ausdehnen; (*Comm*) expandieren; ~ **on** (*fig*) weiter ausführen

expans|e /ɪkˈspæns/ *n* Weite *f*. ~**ion** /-ænʃn/ *n* Ausdehnung *f*; (*Techn, Pol, Comm*) Expansion *f*. ~**ive** /-ɪv/ *a* mitteilsam

expatriate /eksˈpætrɪət/ *n* **be an** ~ im Ausland leben

expect /ɪkˈspekt/ *vt* erwarten; (*suppose*) annehmen; **I** ~ **so** wahrscheinlich; **we** ~ **to arrive on Monday** wir rechnen damit, daß wir am Montag ankommen

expectan|cy /ɪkˈspektənsɪ/ *n* Erwartung *f*. ~**t** *a*, -**ly** *adv* erwartungsvoll; ~**t mother** werdende Mutter *f*

expectation /ekspekˈteɪʃn/ *n* Erwartung *f*; ~ **of life** Lebenserwartung *f*

expedient /ɪkˈspiːdɪənt/ *a* zweckdienlich

expedite /ˈekspɪdaɪt/ *vt* beschleunigen

expedition /ekspɪˈdɪʃn/ *n* Expedition *f*. ~**ary** *a* (*Mil*) Expeditions-

expel /ɪkˈspel/ *vt* (*pt/pp* **expelled**) ausweisen (**from** aus); (*from school*) von der Schule verweisen

expend /ɪkˈspend/ *vt* aufwenden. ~**able** /-əbl/ *a* entbehrlich

expenditure /ɪkˈspendɪtʃə(r)/ *n* Ausgaben *pl*

expense /ɪkˈspens/ *n* Kosten *pl*; **business** ~**s** *pl* Spesen *pl*; **at my** ~ auf meine Kosten; **at the** ~ **of** (*fig*) auf Kosten (+ *gen*)

expensive /ɪkˈspensɪv/ *a*, -**ly** *adv* teuer

experience /ɪkˈspɪərɪəns/ *n* Erfahrung *f*; (*event*) Erlebnis *nt* ● *vt* erleben. ~**d** *a* erfahren

experiment /ɪkˈsperɪmənt/ *n* Versuch *m*, Experiment *nt* ● /-ment/ *vi* experimentieren. ~**al** /-ˈmentl/ *a* experimentell

expert /ˈekspɜːt/ *a*, -**ly** *adv* fachmännisch ● *n* Fachmann *m*, Experte *m*

expertise /ekspɜːˈtiːz/ *n* Sachkenntnis *f*; (*skill*) Geschick *nt*

expire /ɪkˈspaɪə(r)/ *vi* ablaufen

expiry /ɪkˈspaɪərɪ/ *n* Ablauf *m*. ~ **date** *n* Verfallsdatum *nt*

explain /ɪkˈspleɪn/ *vt* erklären

explana|tion /ekspləˈneɪʃn/ *n* Erklärung *f*. ~**tory** /ɪkˈsplænətərɪ/ *a* erklärend

expletive /ɪkˈspliːtɪv/ *n* Kraftausdruck *m*

explicit /ɪkˈsplɪsɪt/ *a*, -**ly** *adv* deutlich

explode /ɪkˈspləʊd/ *vi* explodieren ● *vt* zur Explosion bringen

exploit¹ /ˈeksplɔɪt/ *n* [Helden]tat *f*

exploit² /ɪkˈsplɔɪt/ *vt* ausbeuten. ~**ation** /eksplɔɪˈteɪʃn/ *n* Ausbeutung *f*

explora|tion /ekspləˈreɪʃn/ *n* Erforschung *f*. ~**tory** /ɪkˈsplɒrətərɪ/ *a* Probe-

explore /ɪkˈsplɔː(r)/ *vt* erforschen. ~**r** *n* Forschungsreisende(r) *m*

explos|ion /ɪkˈspləʊʒn/ *n* Explosion *f*. ~**ive** /-sɪv/ *a* explosiv ● *n* Sprengstoff *m*

exponent /ɪkˈspəʊnənt/ *n* Vertreter *m*

export¹ /ˈekspɔːt/ *n* Export *m*, Ausfuhr *f*

export² /ɪk'spɔːt/ vt exportieren, ausführen. **~er** n Exporteur m

expos|e /ɪk'spəʊz/ vt freilegen; (to danger) aussetzen (**to** dat); (reveal) aufdecken; (Phot) belichten. **~ure** /-ʒə(r)/ n Aussetzung f; (Med) Unterkühlung f; (Phot) Belichtung f; **24 ~ures** 24 Aufnahmen

expound /ɪk'spaʊnd/ vt erläutern

express /ɪk'spres/ a ausdrücklich; ⟨purpose⟩ fest ● adv ⟨send⟩ per Eilpost ● n (train) Schnellzug m ● vt ausdrücken; **~ oneself** sich ausdrücken. **~ion** /-ʃn/ n Ausdruck m. **~ive** /-ɪv/ a ausdrucksvoll. **~ly** adv ausdrücklich

expulsion /ɪk'spʌlʃn/ n Ausweisung f; (Sch) Verweisung f von der Schule

expurgate /'ekspəgeɪt/ vt zensieren

exquisite /ek'skwɪzɪt/ a erlesen

ex-'serviceman n Veteran m

extempore /ɪk'stempərɪ/ adv ⟨speak⟩ aus dem Stegreif

extend /ɪk'stend/ vt verlängern; ⟨stretch out⟩ ausstrecken; ⟨enlarge⟩ vergrößern ● vi sich ausdehnen; ⟨table:⟩ sich ausziehen lassen

extension /ɪk'stenʃn/ n Verlängerung f; (to house) Anbau m; (Teleph) Nebenanschluß m; **~ 7** Apparat 7

extensive /ɪk'stensɪv/ a weit; (fig) umfassend. **~ly** adv viel

extent /ɪk'stent/ n Ausdehnung f; (scope) Ausmaß nt, Umfang m; **to a certain ~** in gewissem Maße

extenuating /ɪk'stenʊeɪtɪŋ/ a mildernd

exterior /ɪk'stɪərɪə(r)/ a äußere(r,s) ● n **the ~** das Äußere

exterminat|e /ɪk'stɜːmɪneɪt/ vt ausrotten. **~ion** /-'neɪʃn/ n Ausrottung f

external /ɪk'stɜːnl/ a äußere(r,s); **for ~ use only** (Med) nur äußerlich. **~ly** adv äußerlich

extinct /ɪk'stɪŋkt/ a ausgestorben; ⟨volcano⟩ erloschen. **~ion** /-ɪŋkʃn/ n Aussterben nt

extinguish /ɪk'stɪŋgwɪʃ/ vt löschen. **~er** n Feuerlöscher m

extol /ɪk'stəʊl/ vt (pt/pp **extolled**) preisen

extort /ɪk'stɔːt/ vt erpressen. **~ion** /-ɔːʃn/ n Erpressung f

extortionate /ɪk'stɔːʃənət/ a übermäßig hoch

extra /'ekstrə/ a zusätzlich ● adv extra; (especially) besonders; **~ strong** extrastark ● n (Theat) Statist

extract¹ /'ekstrækt/ n Auszug m; (Culin) Extrakt m

extract² /ɪk'strækt/ vt herausziehen; ziehen ⟨tooth⟩; (fig) erzwingen. **~or** [**fan**] n Entlüfter m

extradit|e /'ekstrədaɪt/ vt (Jur) ausliefern. **~ion** /-'dɪʃn/ n (Jur) Auslieferung f

extra'marital a außerehelich

extraordinary /ɪk'strɔːdɪnərɪ/a, **-ily** adv außerordentlich; (strange) seltsam

extravagan|ce /ɪk'strævəgəns/ n Verschwendung f; **an ~ce** ein Luxus m. **~t** a verschwenderisch; (exaggerated) extravagant

extrem|e /ɪk'striːm/ a äußerste(r,s); (fig) extrem ● n Extrem nt; **in the ~e** im höchsten Grade. **~ely** adv äußerst. **~ist** n Extremist m

extremit|y /ɪk'stremətɪ/ n (distress) Not f; **the ~ies** pl die Extremitäten pl

extricate /'ekstrɪkeɪt/ vt befreien

extrovert /'ekstrəvɜːt/ n extravertierter Mensch m

exuberant /ɪg'zjuːbərənt/ a überglücklich

exude /ɪg'zjuːd/ vt absondern; (fig) ausstrahlen

exult /ɪg'zʌlt/ vi frohlocken

eye /aɪ/ n Auge nt; (of needle) Öhr nt; (for hook) Öse f; **keep an ~ on** aufpassen auf (+ acc); **see ~ to ~** einer Meinung sein ● vt (pt/pp **eyed**, pres p **ey[e]ing**) ansehen

eye: ~ball n Augapfel m. **~brow** n Augenbraue f. **~lash** n Wimper f. **~let** /-lɪt/ n Öse f. **~lid** n Augenlid nt. **~-shadow** n Lidschatten m. **~sight** n Sehkraft f. **~sore** n (fam) Schandfleck m. **~-tooth** n Eckzahn m. **~witness** n Augenzeuge m

F

fable /'feɪbl/ n Fabel f

fabric /'fæbrɪk/ n Stoff m; (fig) Gefüge nt

fabrication /fæbrɪ'keɪʃn/ n Erfindung f

fabulous /'fæbjʊləs/ a (fam) phantastisch

façade /fə'sɑːd/ n Fassade f

face /feɪs/ n Gesicht nt; (grimace) Grimasse f; (surface) Fläche f; (of clock) Zifferblatt nt; **pull** ∼s Gesichter schneiden; **in the** ∼ **of** angesichts (+ gen); **on the** ∼ **of it** allem Anschein nach ● vt/i gegenüberstehen (+ dat); ∼ **north** ⟨house:⟩ nach Norden liegen; ∼ **me!** sieh mich an! ∼ **the fact that** sich damit abfinden, daß; ∼ **up to s.o.** jdm die Stirn bieten

face: ∼-**flannel** n Waschlappen m. ∼**less** a anonym. ∼-**lift** n Gesichtsstraffung f

facet /'fæsɪt/ n Facette f; (fig) Aspekt m

facetious /fə'si:ʃəs/ a, **-ly** adv spöttisch

'face value n Nennwert m

facial /'feɪʃl/ a Gesichts-

facile /'fæsaɪl/ a oberflächlich

facilitate /fə'sɪlɪteɪt/ vt erleichtern

facilit|y /fə'sɪlətɪ/ n Leichtigkeit f; (skill) Gewandtheit f; ∼**ies** pl Einrichtungen pl

facing /'feɪsɪŋ/ n Besatz m

facsimile /fæk'sɪmǝlɪ/ n Faksimile nt

fact /fækt/ n Tatsache f; **in** ∼ tatsächlich; (actually) eigentlich

faction /'fækʃn/ n Gruppe f

factor /'fæktǝ(r)/ n Faktor m

factory /'fæktǝrɪ/ n Fabrik f

factual /'fæktʃʊǝl/ a, **-ly** adv sachlich

faculty /'fækǝltɪ/ n Fähigkeit f; (Univ) Fakultät f

fad /fæd/ n Fimmel m

fade /feɪd/ vi verblassen; ⟨material:⟩ verbleichen; ⟨sound:⟩ abklingen; ⟨flower:⟩ verwelken. ∼ **in/out** vt (Radio, TV) ein-/ausblenden

fag /fæg/ n (chore) Plage f; (fam: cigarette) Zigarette f; (Amer sl) Homosexuelle(r) m

fagged /fægd/ a ∼ **out** (fam) völlig erledigt

Fahrenheit /'færǝnhaɪt/ a Fahrenheit

fail /feɪl/ n **without** ∼ unbedingt ● vi ⟨attempt:⟩ scheitern; (grow weak) nachlassen; (break down) versagen; (in exam) durchfallen; ∼ **to do sth** etw nicht tun; **he** ∼**ed to break the record** es gelang ihm nicht, den Rekord zu brechen ● vt nicht bestehen ⟨exam⟩; durchfallen lassen ⟨candidate⟩; (disappoint) enttäuschen; **words** ∼ **me** ich weiß nicht, was ich sagen soll

failing /'feɪlɪŋ/ n Fehler m ● prep ∼ **that** andernfalls

failure /'feɪljǝ(r)/ n Mißerfolg m; (breakdown) Versagen nt; (person) Versager m

faint /feɪnt/ a (-er, -est), **-ly** adv schwach; **I feel**∼ mir ist schwach ● n Ohnmacht f ● vi ohnmächtig werden

faint: ∼-'**hearted** a zaghaft. ∼**ness** n Schwäche f

fair[1] /feǝ(r)/ n Jahrmarkt m; (Comm) Messe f

fair[2] a (-er, -est) ⟨hair⟩ blond; ⟨skin⟩ hell; ⟨weather⟩ heiter; (just) gerecht, fair; (quite good) ziemlich gut; (Sch) genügend; **a** ∼ **amount** ziemlich viel ● adv **play** ∼ fair sein. ∼**ly** adv gerecht; (rather) ziemlich. ∼**ness** n Blondheit f; Helle f; Gerechtigkeit f; (Sport) Fairneß f

fairy /'feǝrɪ/ n Elfe f; **good/wicked** ∼ gute/böse Fee f. ∼ **story,** ∼-**tale** n Märchen nt

faith /feɪθ/ n Glaube m; (trust) Vertrauen nt (**in** zu); **in good** ∼ in gutem Glauben

faithful /'feɪθfl/ a, **-ly** adv treu; (exact) genau; **Yours** ∼**ly** Hochachtungsvoll. ∼**ness** n Treue f; Genauigkeit f

'faith-healer n Gesundbeter(in) m(f)

fake /feɪk/ a falsch ● n Fälschung f; (person) Schwindler m ● vt fälschen; (pretend) vortäuschen

falcon /'fɔ:lkǝn/ n Falke m

fall /fɔ:l/ n Fall m; (heavy) Sturz m; (in prices) Fallen nt; (Amer: autumn) Herbst m; **have a** ∼ fallen ● vi (pt **fell,** pp **fallen**) fallen; (heavily) stürzen; ⟨night:⟩ anbrechen; ∼ **in love** sich verlieben; ∼ **back on** zurückgreifen auf (+ acc); ∼ **for s.o.** (fam) sich in jdn verlieben; ∼ **for sth** (fam) auf etw (acc) hereinfallen. ∼ **about** vi (with laughter) sich [vor Lachen] kringeln. ∼ **down** vi umfallen; ⟨thing:⟩ herunterfallen; ⟨building:⟩ einstürzen. ∼ **in** vi hineinfallen; (collapse) einfallen; (Mil) antreten; ∼ **in with** sich anschließen (+ dat). ∼ **off** vi herunterfallen; (diminish) abnehmen. ∼ **out** vi herausfallen; ⟨hair:⟩ ausfallen; (quarrel) sich überwerfen. ∼ **over** vi hinfallen. ∼ **through** vi durchfallen; ⟨plan:⟩ ins Wasser fallen

fallacy /'fælǝsɪ/ n Irrtum m

fallible /'fælǝbl/ a fehlbar

'fall-out n [radioaktiver] Niederschlag m

fallow /'fæləʊ/ *a* lie ∼ brachliegen

false /fɔːls/ *a* falsch; (*artificial*) künstlich; ∼ **start** (*Sport*) Fehlstart *m*. ∼**hood** *n* Unwahrheit *f*. ∼**ly** *adv* falsch. ∼**ness** *n* Falschheit *f*

false 'teeth *npl* [künstliches] Gebiß *nt*

falsify /'fɔːlsɪfaɪ/ *vt* (*pt/pp* -ied) fälschen; (*misrepresent*) verfälschen

falter /'fɔːltə(r)/ *vi* zögern; (*stumble*) straucheln

fame /feɪm/ *n* Ruhm *m*. ∼**d** *a* berühmt

familiar /fə'mɪljə(r)/ *a* vertraut; (*known*) bekannt; **too** ∼ familiär. ∼**ity** /-lɪ'ærətɪ/ *n* Vertrautheit *f*. ∼**ize** *vt* vertraut machen (**with** mit)

family /'fæməlɪ/ *n* Familie *f*

family: ∼ **al'lowance** *n* Kindergeld *nt*. ∼ **'doctor** *n* Hausarzt *m*. ∼ **'life** *n* Familienleben *nt*. ∼ **'planning** *n* Familienplanung *f*. ∼ **'tree** *n* Stammbaum *m*

famine /'fæmɪn/ *n* Hungersnot *f*

famished /'fæmɪʃt/ *a* sehr hungrig

famous /'feɪməs/ *a* berühmt

fan¹ /fæn/ Fächer *m*; (*Techn*) Ventilator *m* ● *v* (*pt/pp* **fanned**) ∼ fächeln; ∼ **oneself** sich fächeln ● *vi* ∼ **out** sich fächerförmig ausbreiten

fan² *m* (*admirer*) Fan *m*

fanatic /fə'nætɪk/ *n* Fanatiker *m*. ∼**al** *a*, **-ly** *adv* fanatisch. ∼**ism** /-sɪzm/ *n* Fanatismus *m*

'fan belt *n* Keilriemen *m*

fanciful /'fænsɪfl/ *a* phantastisch; (*imaginative*) phantasiereich

fancy /'fænsɪ/ *n* Phantasie *f*; **have a** ∼ **to** Lust haben, zu; **I have taken a real** ∼ **to him** er hat es mir angetan ● *a* ausgefallen; ∼ **cakes and biscuits** Feingebäck *nt* ● *vt* (*believe*) meinen; (*imagine*) sich (*dat*) einbilden; (*fam: want*) Lust haben auf (+ *acc*); ∼ **that!** stell dir vor! (*really*) tatsächlich! ∼ **'dress** *n* Kostüm *nt*

fanfare /'fænfeə(r)/ *n* Fanfare *f*

fang /fæŋ/ *n* Fangzahn *m*; (*of snake*) Giftzahn *m*

fan: ∼ **heater** *n* Heizlüfter *m*. ∼**light** *n* Oberlicht *nt*

fantasize /'fæntəsaɪz/ *vi* phantasieren. ∼**tic** /-'tæstɪk/ *a* phantastisch. ∼**y** *n* Phantasie *f*; (*Mus*) Fantasie *f*

far /fɑː(r)/ *adv* weit; (*much*) viel; **by** ∼ bei weitem; ∼ **away** weit weg; **as** ∼ **as I know** soviel ich weiß; **as** ∼ **as the church** bis zur Kirche ● *a* **at the**

∼ **end** am anderen Ende; **the F**∼ **East** der Ferne Osten

farc|e /fɑːs/ *n* Farce *f*. ∼**ical** *a* lächerlich

fare /feə(r)/ *n* Fahrpreis *m*; (*money*) Fahrgeld *nt*; (*food*) Kost *f*; **air** ∼ Flugpreis *m*. ∼**-dodger** /-dɒdʒə(r)/ *n* Schwarzfahrer *m*

farewell /feə'wel/ *int* (*liter*) lebe wohl! ● *n* Lebewohl *nt*; ∼ **dinner** Abschiedsessen *nt*

far-'fetched *a* weit hergeholt; **be** ∼ an den Haaren herbeigezogen sein

farm /fɑːm/ *n* Bauernhof *m* ● *vi* Landwirtschaft betreiben ● *vt* bewirtschaften ⟨*land*⟩. ∼**er** *n* Landwirt *m*

farm: ∼**house** *n* Bauernhaus *nt*. ∼**ing** *n* Landwirtschaft *f*. ∼**yard** *n* Hof *m*

far: ∼**-'reaching** *a* weitreichend. ∼**-'sighted** *a* (*fig*) umsichtig; (*Amer: long-sighted*) weitsichtig

fart /fɑːt/ *n* (*vulg*) Furz *m* ● *vi* (*vulg*) furzen

farther /'fɑːðə(r)/ *adv* weiter; ∼ **off** weiter entfernt ● *a* **at the** ∼ **end** am anderen Ende

fascinat|e /'fæsɪneɪt/ *vt* faszinieren. ∼**ing** *a* faszinierend. ∼**ion** /-'neɪʃn/ *n* Faszination *f*

fascis|m /'fæʃɪzm/ *n* Faschismus *m*. ∼**t** *n* Faschist *m* ● *a* faschistisch

fashion /'fæʃn/ *n* Mode *f*; (*manner*) Art *f* ● *vt* machen; (*mould*) formen. ∼**able** /-əbl/ *a*, **-bly** *adv* modisch; **be** ∼**able** Mode sein

fast¹ /fɑːst/ *a & adv* (**-er, -est**) schnell; (*firm*) fest; ⟨*colour*⟩ waschecht; **be** ∼ ⟨*clock:*⟩ vorgehen; **be** ∼ **asleep** fest schlafen

fast² *n* Fasten *nt* ● *vi* fasten

'fastback *n* (*Auto*) Fließheck *nt*

fasten /'fɑːsn/ *vt* zumachen; (*fix*) befestigen (**to an** + *dat*); ∼ **one's seatbelt** sich anschnallen. ∼**er** *n*, ∼**ing** *n* Verschluß *m*

fastidious /fə'stɪdɪəs/ *a* wählerisch; (*particular*) penibel

fat /fæt/ *a* (**fatter, fattest**) dick; ⟨*meat*⟩ fett ● *n* Fett *nt*

fatal /'feɪtl/ *a* tödlich; ⟨*error*⟩ verhängnisvoll. ∼**ism** /-təlɪzm/ *n* Fatalismus *m*. ∼**ist** /-təlɪst/ *n* Fatalist *m*. ∼**ity** /fə'tælətɪ/ *n* Todesopfer *nt*. ∼**ly** *adv* tödlich

fate /feɪt/ *n* Schicksal *nt*. ∼**ful** *a* verhängnisvoll

'fat-head *n* (*fam*) Dummkopf *m*

father /'fɑːðə(r)/ n Vater m; F~ Christmas der Weihnachtsmann ● vt
zeugen
father: ~**hood** n Vaterschaft f. ~-
in-law n (pl ~s-in-law) Schwieger-
vater m. ~**ly** a väterlich
fathom /'fæðəm/ n (Naut) Faden m
● vt verstehen; ~ **out** ergründen
fatigue /fə'tiːg/ n Ermüdung f ● vt
ermüden
fatten /'fætn/ vt mästen ⟨animal⟩.
~**ing** a cream is ~ing Sahne macht
dick
fatty /'fætɪ/ a fett; ⟨foods⟩ fetthaltig
fatuous /'fætjʊəs/ a, **-ly** adv albern
faucet /'fɔːsɪt/ n (Amer) Wasserhahn
m
fault /fɔːlt/ n Fehler m; (Techn)
Defekt m; (Geol) Verwerfung f; **at** ~
im Unrecht; **find** ~ **with** etwas auszusetzen haben an (+ dat); **it's your**
~ du bist schuld ✗ wir etwas auszusetzen haben an (+ dat). ~**less** a, **-ly**
adv fehlerfrei
faulty /'fɔːltɪ/ a fehlerhaft
fauna /'fɔːnə/ n Fauna f
favour /'feɪvə(r)/ n Gunst f; **I am in** ~
ich bin dafür; **do s.o. a** ~ jdm einen
Gefallen tun ● vt begünstigen;
(prefer) bevorzugen. ~**able** /-əbl/ a,
-bly adv günstig; ⟨reply⟩ positiv
favourit|e /'feɪvərɪt/ a Lieblings- ● n
Liebling m; (Sport) Favorit(in)
m(f). ~**ism** n Bevorzugung f
fawn¹ /fɔːn/ a rehbraun ● n Hirsch-
kalb nt
fawn² vi sich einschmeicheln (**on**
bei)
fax /fæks/ vt faxen (**s.o.** jdm). ~
machine n Faxgerät nt
fear /fɪə(r)/ n Furcht f, Angst f (**of** vor
+ dat); **no** ~! (fam) keine Angst!
● vt/i fürchten
fear|ful /'fɪəfl/ a besorgt; (awful)
furchtbar. ~**less** a, **-ly** adv furchtlos.
~**some** /-səm/ a furchterregend
feas|ibility /fiːzə'bɪlətɪ/ n Durchführ-
barkeit f. ~**ible** a durchführbar;
(possible) möglich
feast /fiːst/ n Festmahl nt; (Relig)
Fest nt ● vi ~ [**on**] schmausen
feat /fiːt/ n Leistung f
feather /'feðə(r)/ n Feder f
feature /'fiːtʃə(r)/ n Gesichtszug m;
(quality) Merkmal nt; (Journ)
Feature nt ● vt darstellen; ⟨film:⟩ in
der Hauptrolle zeigen. ~ **film** n
Hauptfilm m
February /'februərɪ/ n Februar m

feckless /'feklɪs/ a verantwortungslos
fed /fed/ see **feed** ● a **be** ~ **up** (fam)
die Nase voll haben (**with** von)
federal /'fedərəl/ a Bundes-
federation /fedə'reɪʃn/ n Föderation f
fee /fiː/ n Gebühr f; (professional)
Honorar nt
feeble /'fiːbl/ a (**-r**, **-st**), **-bly** adv
schwach
feed /fiːd/ n Futter nt; (for baby)
Essen nt ● v (pt/pp fed) ● vt füttern;
(support) ernähren; (into machine)
eingeben; speisen ⟨computer⟩ ● vi
sich ernähren (**on** von)
'**feedback** n Feedback nt
feel /fiːl/ v (pt/pp felt) ● vt fühlen;
(experience) empfinden; (think) meinen ● vi sich fühlen; ~ **soft/hard**
sich weich/hart anfühlen; **I** ~ **hot/ill**
mir ist heiß/schlecht; **I don't** ~ **like it**
ich habe keine Lust dazu. ~**er** n
Fühler m. ~**ing** n Gefühl nt; **no**
hard ~**ings** nichts für ungut
feet /fiːt/ see **foot**
feign /feɪn/ vt vortäuschen
feint /feɪnt/ n Finte f
feline /'fiːlaɪn/ a Katzen-; (catlike)
katzenartig
fell¹ /fel/ vt fällen
fell² see **fall**
fellow /'feləʊ/ n (of society) Mitglied
nt; (fam: man) Kerl m
fellow: ~'**countryman** n Landsmann
m. ~ **men** pl Mitmenschen pl.
~**ship** n Kameradschaft f; (group)
Gesellschaft f
felony /'felənɪ/ n Verbrechen nt
felt¹ /felt/ see **feel**
felt² n Filz m. ~[**-tipped**] '**pen** n
Filzstift m
female /'fiːmeɪl/ a weiblich ● nt
Weibchen nt; (pej: woman) Weib nt
femin|ine /'femɪnɪn/ a weiblich ● n
(Gram) Femininum nt. ~**inity**
/-'nɪnətɪ/ n Weiblichkeit f. ~**ist** a
feministisch ● n Feminist(in) m(f)
fenc|e /fens/ n Zaun m; (fam: person)
Hehler m ● vi (Sport) fechten ● vt
~**e in** einzäunen. ~**er** n Fechter m.
~**ing** n Zaun m; (Sport) Fechten nt
fend /fend/ vi ~ **for oneself** sich
allein durchschlagen. ~ **off** vt
abwehren
fender /'fendə(r)/ n Kaminvorsetzer
m; (Naut) Fender m; (Amer: wing)
Kotflügel m
fennel /'fenl/ n Fenchel m
ferment¹ /'fɜːment/ n Erregung f

ferment² /fə'ment/ *vi* gären ● *vt*
gären lassen. **~ation** /fɜ:men'teɪʃn/
n Gärung *f*

fern /fɜ:n/ *n* Farn *m*

feroc|ious /fə'rəʊʃəs/ *a* wild. **~ity**
/-'rɒsətɪ/ *n* Wildheit *f*

ferret /'ferɪt/ *n* Frettchen *nt*

ferry /'ferɪ/ *n* Fähre *f* ● *vt* ~ [across]
übersetzen

fertil|e /'fɜ:taɪl/ *a* fruchtbar. **~ity**
/fə'tɪlətɪ/ *n* Fruchtbarkeit *f*

fertilize /'fɜ:təlaɪz/ *vt* befruchten;
düngen ⟨*land*⟩. **~r** *n* Dünger *m*

fervent /'fɜ:vənt/ *a* leidenschaftlich

fervour /'fɜ:və(r)/ *n* Leidenschaft *f*

fester /'festə(r)/ *vi* eitern

festival /'festɪvl/ *n* Fest *nt*; (*Mus,
Theat*) Festspiele *pl*

festiv|e /'festɪv/ *a* festlich; **~e season**
Festzeit *f*. **~ities** /fe'stɪvətɪz/ *npl*
Feierlichkeiten *pl*

festoon /fe'stu:n/ *vi* behängen (**with**
mit)

fetch /fetʃ/ *vt* holen; (*collect*) abholen;
(*be sold for*) einbringen

fetching /'fetʃɪŋ/ *a* anziehend

fête /feɪt/ *n* Fest *nt* ● *vt* feiern

fetish /'fetɪʃ/ *n* Fetisch *m*

fetter /'fetə(r)/ *vt* fesseln

fettle /'fetl/ *n* **in fine ~** in bester Form

feud /fju:d/ *n* Fehde *f*

feudal /'fju:dl/ *a* Feudal-

fever /'fi:və(r)/ *n* Fieber *nt*. **~ish** *a*
fiebrig; (*fig*) fieberhaft

few /fju:/ *a* (**-er, -est**) wenige; **every
~ days** alle paar Tage ● *n a* ~ ein
paar; **quite a** ~ ziemlich viele

fiancé /fɪ'ɒnseɪ/ *n* Verlobte(r) *m*.
fiancée *n* Verlobte *f*

fiasco /fɪ'æskəʊ/ *n* Fiasko *nt*

fib /fɪb/ *n* kleine Lüge; **tell a ~**
schwindeln

fibre /'faɪbə(r)/ *n* Faser *f*

fickle /'fɪkl/ *a* unbeständig

fiction /'fɪkʃn/ *n* Erfindung *f*; [**works
of**] ~ Erzählungsliteratur *f*. **~al** *a*
erfunden

fictitious /fɪk'tɪʃəs/ *a* [frei] erfunden

fiddle /'fɪdl/ *n* (*fam*) Geige *f*;
(*cheating*) Schwindel *m* ● *vi*
herumspielen (**with** mit) ● *vt* (*fam*)
frisieren ⟨*accounts*⟩; (*arrange*)
arrangieren

fiddly /'fɪdlɪ/ *a* knifflig

fidelity /fɪ'delətɪ/ *n* Treue *f*

fidget /'fɪdʒɪt/ *vi* zappeln. **~y** *a*
zappelig

field /fi:ld/ *n* Feld *nt*; (*meadow*) Wiese
f; (*subject*) Gebiet *nt*

field: ~ events *npl* Sprung- und
Wurfdisziplinen *pl*. **~glasses** *npl*
Feldstecher *m*. **F~** '**Marshal** *n* Feld-
marschall *m*. **~work** *n* Feldfor-
schung *f*

fiend /fi:nd/ *n* Teufel *m*. **~ish** *a*
teuflisch

fierce /fɪəs/ *a* (**-r, -st**), **-ly** *adv* wild;
(*fig*) heftig. **~ness** *n* Wildheit *f*;
(*fig*) Heftigkeit *f*

fiery /'faɪərɪ/ *a* (**-ier, -iest**) feurig

fifteen /fɪf'ti:n/ *a* fünfzehn ● *n* Fünfzehn *f*. **~th** *a* fünfzehnte(r,s)

fifth /fɪfθ/ *a* fünfte(r,s)

fiftieth /'fɪftɪɪθ/ *a* fünfzigste(r,s)

fifty /'fɪftɪ/ *a* fünfzig

fig /fɪg/ *n* Feige *f*

fight /faɪt/ *n* Kampf *m*; (*brawl*) Schlägerei *f*; (*between children, dogs*) Rauferei *f* ● *v* (*pt/pp* **fought**) ● *vt* kämpfen gegen; (*fig*) bekämpfen ● *vi*
kämpfen; (*brawl*) sich schlagen;
⟨*children, dogs:*⟩ sich raufen. **~er** *n*
Kämpfer *m*; (*Aviat*) Jagdflugzeug *nt*.
~ing *n* Kampf *m*

figment /'fɪgmənt/ *n* ~ **of the imagination** Hirngespinst *nt*

figurative /'fɪgjərətɪv/ *a*, **-ly** *adv* bildlich, übertragen

figure /'fɪgə(r)/ *n* (*digit*) Ziffer *f*;
(*number*) Zahl *f*; (*sum*) Summe *f*;
(*carving, sculpture, woman's*) Figur
f; (*form*) Gestalt *f*; (*illustration*) Ab-
bildung *f*; ~ **of speech** Redefigur *f*;
good at ~s gut im Rechnen ● *vi*
(*appear*) erscheinen ● *vt* (*Amer:
think*) glauben. ~ **out** *vt* ausrechnen

figure: ~head *n* Galionsfigur *f*;
(*fig*) Repräsentationsfigur *f*. ~
skating *n* Eiskunstlauf *m*

filament /'fɪləmənt/ *n* Faden *m*;
(*Electr*) Glühfaden *m*

filch /fɪltʃ/ *vt* (*fam*) klauen

file¹ /faɪl/ *n* Akte *f*; (*for documents*)
[Akten]ordner *m* ● *vt* ablegen ⟨*documents*⟩; (*Jur*) einreichen

file² *n* (*line*) Reihe *f*; **in single ~** im
Gänsemarsch

file³ *n* (*Techn*) Feile *f* ● *vt* feilen

filigree /'fɪlɪgri:/ *n* Filigran *nt*

filings /'faɪlɪŋz/ *npl* Feilspäne *pl*

fill /fɪl/ *n* **eat one's ~** sich satt essen
● *vt* füllen; plombieren ⟨*tooth*⟩ ● *vi*
sich füllen. ~ **in** *vt* auffüllen; ausfüllen ⟨*form*⟩. ~ **out** *vt* ausfüllen
⟨*form*⟩. ~ **up** *vi* sich füllen ● *vt*
vollfüllen; (*Auto*) volltanken; ausfüllen ⟨*form*⟩

fillet /'fılıt/ *n* Filet *nt* ● *vt* (*pt/pp* **fil-leted**) entgräten

filling /'fılıŋ/ *n* Füllung *f*; (*of tooth*) Plombe *f*. ~ **station** *n* Tankstelle *f*

filly /'fılı/ *n* junge Stute *f*

film /fılm/ *n* Film *m*; (*Culin*) [**cling**] ~ Klarsichtfolie *f* ● *vt/i* filmen; verfilmen ⟨*book*⟩. ~ **star** *n* Filmstar *m*

filter /'fıltə(r)/ *n* Filter *m* ● *vt* filtern. ~ **through** *vi* durchsickern. ~ **tip** *n* Filter *m*; (*cigarette*) Filterzigarette *f*

filth /fılθ/ *n* Dreck *m*. ~**y** *a* (**-ier, -iest**) dreckig

fin /fın/ *n* Flosse *f*

final /'faınl/ *a* letzte(r,s); (*conclusive*) endgültig; ~ **result** Endresultat *nt* ● *n* (*Sport*) Finale *nt*, Endspiel *nt*; ~**s** *pl* (*Univ*) Abschlußprüfung *f*

finale /fı'nɑːlı/ *n* Finale *nt*

final|ist /'faınəlıst/ *n* Finalist(in) *m(f)*. ~**ity** /-'nælətı/ *n* Endgültigkeit *f*

final|ize /'faınəlaız/ *vt* endgültig festlegen. ~**ly** *adv* schließlich

finance /faı'næns/ *n* Finanz *f* ● *vt* finanzieren

financial /faı'nænʃl/ *a*, **-ly** *adv* finanziell

finch /fıntʃ/ *n* Fink *m*

find /faınd/ *n* Fund *m* ● *vt* (*pt/pp* **found**) finden; (*establish*) feststellen; **go and** ~ holen; **try to** ~ suchen; ~ **guilty** (*Jur*) schuldig sprechen. ~ **out** *vt* herausfinden; (*learn*) erfahren ● *vi* (*enquire*) sich erkundigen

findings /'faındıŋz/ *npl* Ergebnisse *pl*

fine¹ /faın/ *n* Geldstrafe *f* ● *vt* zu einer Geldstrafe verurteilen

fine² *a* (**-r, -st**), **-ly** *adv* fein; ⟨*weather*⟩ schön; **he's** ~ es geht ihm gut ● *adv* gut; **cut it** ~ (*fam*) sich (*dat*) wenig Zeit lassen. ~ **arts** *npl* schöne Künste *pl*

finery /'faınərı/ *n* Putz *m*, Staat *m*

finesse /fı'nes/ *n* Gewandtheit *f*

finger /'fıŋgə(r)/ *n* Finger *m* ● *vt* anfassen

finger: ~**-mark** *n* Fingerabdruck *m*. ~**-nail** *n* Fingernagel *m*. ~**print** *n* Fingerabdruck *m*. ~**tip** *n* Fingerspitze *f*; **have sth at one's** ~**tips** etw im kleinen Finger haben

finicky /'fınıkı/ *a* knifflig; (*choosy*) wählerisch

finish /'fınıʃ/ *n* Schluß *m*; (*Sport*) Finish *nt*; (*line*) Ziel *nt*; (*of product*) Ausführung *f* ● *vt* beenden; (*use up*)

aufbrauchen; ~ **one's drink** austrinken; ~ **reading** zu Ende lesen ● *vi* fertig werden; ⟨*performance:*⟩ zu Ende sein; ⟨*runner:*⟩ durchs Ziel gehen

finite /'faınaıt/ *a* begrenzt

Finland /'fınlənd/ *n* Finnland *nt*

Finn /fın/ *n* Finne *m*/ Finnin *f*. ~**ish** *a* finnisch

fiord /fjɔːd/ *n* Fjord *m*

fir /fɜː(r)/ *n* Tanne *f*

fire /'faıə(r)/ *n* Feuer *nt*; (*forest, house*) Brand *m*; **be on** ~ brennen; **catch** ~ Feuer fangen; **set** ~ **to** anzünden; ⟨*arsonist:*⟩ in Brand stecken; **under** ~ unter Beschuß ● *vt* brennen ⟨*pottery*⟩; abfeuern ⟨*shot*⟩; schießen mit ⟨*gun*⟩; (*fam: dismiss*) feuern ● *vi* schießen (**at** auf + *acc*); ⟨*engine:*⟩ anspringen

fire: ~ **alarm** *n* Feueralarm *m*; (*apparatus*) Feuermelder *m*. ~**arm** *n* Schußwaffe *f*. ~ **brigade** *n* Feuerwehr *f*. ~**-engine** *n* Löschfahrzeug *nt*. ~**-escape** *n* Feuertreppe *f*. ~ **extinguisher** *n* Feuerlöscher *m*. ~**man** *n* Feuerwehrmann *m*. ~**place** *n* Kamin *m*. ~**side** *n* **by** *or* **at the** ~**side** am Kamin. ~ **station** *n* Feuerwache *f*. ~**wood** *n* Brennholz *nt*. ~**work** *n* Feuerwerkskörper *m*; ~**works** *pl* (*display*) Feuerwerk *nt*

'firing squad *n* Erschießungskommando *nt*

firm¹ /fɜːm/ *n* Firma *f*

firm² *a* (**-er, -est**), **-ly** *adv* fest; (*resolute*) entschlossen; (*strict*) streng

first /fɜːst/ *a* & *n* erste(r,s); **at** ~ zuerst; **who's** ~? wer ist der erste? **at** ~ **sight** auf den ersten Blick; **for the** ~ **time** zum ersten Mal; **from the** ~ von Anfang an ● *adv* zuerst; (*firstly*) erstens

first: ~ **'aid** *n* Erste Hilfe. ~**'aid kit** *n* Verbandkasten *m*. ~**-class** *a* erstklassig; (*Rail*) erster Klasse ● /-'-/ *adv* ⟨*travel*⟩ erster Klasse. ~ **e'dition** *n* Erstausgabe *f*. ~ **'floor** *n* erster Stock; (*Amer: ground floor*) Erdgeschoß *nt*. ~**ly** *adv* erstens. ~**name** *n* Vorname *m*. ~**-rate** *a* erstklassig

fish /fıʃ/ *n* Fisch *m* ● *vt/i* fischen; (*with rod*) angeln. ~ **out** *vt* herausfischen

fish: ~**bone** *n* Gräte *f*. ~**erman** *n* Fischer *m*. ~**-farm** *n* Fischzucht *f*. ~ **'finger** *n* Fischstäbchen *nt*

fishing /'fɪʃɪŋ/ n Fischerei f. ~ **boat** n Fischerboot nt. ~**-rod** n Angel[rute] f

fish: ~**monger** /-mʌŋgə(r)/ n Fischhändler m. ~**-slice** n Fischheber m. ~**y** a Fisch-; (fam: suspicious) verdächtig

fission /'fɪʃn/ n (Phys) Spaltung f

fist /fɪst/ n Faust f

fit¹ /fɪt/ n (attack) Anfall m

fit² a (**fitter, fittest**) (suitable) geeignet; (healthy) gesund; (Sport) fit; ~ **to eat** eßbar; **keep** ~ sich fit halten; **see** ~ es für angebracht halten (to zu)

fit³ n (of clothes) Sitz m; **be a good** ~ gut passen • v (pt/pp fitted) • vi (be the right size) passen • vt anbringen (**to an** + dat); (install) einbauen; ⟨clothes:⟩ passen (+ dat); ~ **with** versehen mit. ~ **in** vi hineinpassen; (adapt) sich einfügen (**with** in + acc) • vt (accommodate) unterbringen

fit|ful /'fɪtfl/ a, **-ly** adv ⟨sleep⟩ unruhig. ~**ment** n Einrichtungsgegenstand m; (attachment) Zusatzgerät nt. ~**ness** n Eignung f; [physical] ~**ness** Gesundheit f; (Sport) Fitneß f. ~**ted** a eingebaut; ⟨garment⟩ tailliert

fitted: ~ **'carpet** n Teppichboden m. ~ **'cupboard** n Einbauschrank m. ~ **'kitchen** n Einbauküche f. ~ **'sheet** n Spannlaken nt

fitter /'fɪtə(r)/ n Monteur m

fitting /'fɪtɪŋ/ a passend • n (of clothes) Anprobe f; (of shoes) Weite f; (Techn) Zubehörteil nt; ~**s** pl Zubehör nt. ~ **room** n Anprobekabine f

five /faɪv/ a fünf • n Fünf f. ~**r** n Fünfpfundschein m

fix /fɪks/ n (sl: drugs) Fix m; **be in a** ~ (fam) in der Klemme sitzen • vt befestigen (**to an** + dat); (arrange) festlegen; (repair) reparieren; (Phot) fixieren; ~ **a meal** (Amer) Essen machen

fixation /fɪk'seɪʃn/ n Fixierung f

fixed /'fɪkst/ a fest

fixture /'fɪkstʃə(r)/ n (Sport) Veranstaltung f; ~**s and fittings** zu einer Wohnung gehörende Einrichtungen pl

fizz /fɪz/ vi sprudeln

fizzle /'fɪzl/ vi ~ **out** verpuffen

fizzy /'fɪzɪ/ a sprudelnd. ~ **drink** n Brause[limonade] f

flabbergasted /'flæbəgɑːstɪd/ a **be** ~ platt sein (fam)

flabby /'flæbɪ/ a schlaff

flag¹ /flæg/ n Fahne f; (Naut) Flagge f • vt (pt/pp flagged) ~ **down** anhalten ⟨taxi⟩

flag² vi (pt/pp flagged) ermüden

flagon /'flægən/ n Krug m

'flag-pole n Fahnenstange f

flagrant /'fleɪgrənt/ a flagrant

'flagstone n [Pflaster]platte f

flair /fleə(r)/ n Begabung f

flake /fleɪk/ n Flocke f • vi ~**[off]** abblättern

flaky /'fleɪkɪ/ a blättrig. ~ **pastry** n Blätterteig m

flamboyant /flæm'bɔɪənt/ a extravagant

flame /fleɪm/ n Flamme f

flammable /'flæməbl/ a feuergefährlich

flan /flæn/ n [fruit] ~ Obsttorte f

flank /flæŋk/ n Flanke f • vt flankieren

flannel /'flænl/ n Flanell m; (for washing) Waschlappen m

flannelette /flænə'let/ n (Tex) Biber m

flap /flæp/ n Klappe f; **in a** ~ (fam) aufgeregt • v (pt/pp flapped) vi flattern; (fam) sich aufregen • vt ~ **its wings** mit den Flügeln schlagen

flare /fleə(r)/ n Leuchtsignal nt. • vi ~ **up** auflodern; (fam: get angry) aufbrausen. ~**d** a ⟨garment⟩ ausgestellt

flash /flæʃ/ n Blitz m; **in a** ~ (fam) im Nu • vi blitzen; (repeatedly) blinken; ~ **past** vorbeirasen • vt aufleuchten lassen; ~ **one's headlights** die Lichthupe betätigen

flash: ~**back** n Rückblende f. ~**bulb** n (Phot) Blitzbirne f. ~**er** n (Auto) Blinker m. ~**light** n (Phot) Blitzlicht nt; (Amer: torch) Taschenlampe f. ~**y** a auffällig

flask /flɑːsk/ n Flasche f; (Chem) Kolben m; (vacuum~) Thermosflasche (P) f

flat /flæt/ a (**flatter, flattest**) flach; ⟨surface⟩ eben; ⟨refusal⟩ glatt; ⟨beer⟩ schal; ⟨battery⟩ verbraucht;⟨Auto⟩ leer; ⟨tyre⟩ platt; (Mus) **A** ~ As nt; **B** ~ B nt • n Wohnung f; (Mus) Erniedrigungszeichen nt; (fam: puncture) Reifenpanne f

flat: ~ **'feet** npl Plattfüße pl. ~**-fish** n Plattfisch m. ~**ly** adv ⟨refuse⟩ glatt. ~ **rate** n Einheitspreis m

flatten /ˈflætn/ vt platt drücken

flatter /ˈflætə(r)/ vt schmeicheln (+ dat). **~y** n Schmeichelei f

flat 'tyre n Reifenpanne f

flatulence /ˈflætjʊləns/ n Blähungen pl

flaunt /flɔːnt/ vt prunken mit

flautist /ˈflɔːtɪst/ n Flötist(in) m(f)

flavour /ˈfleɪvə(r)/ n Geschmack m ● vt abschmecken. **~ing** n Aroma nt

flaw /flɔː/ n Fehler m. **~less** a tadellos; ⟨complexion⟩ makellos

flax /flæks/ n Flachs m. **~en** a flachsblond

flea /fliː/ n Floh m. **~ market** n Flohmarkt m

fleck /flek/ n Tupfen m

fled /fled/ see **flee**

flee /fliː/ v (pt/pp fled) ● vi fliehen (**from** vor + dat) ● vt flüchten aus

fleec|e /fliːs/ n Vlies nt ● vt (fam) schröpfen. **~y** a flauschig

fleet /fliːt/ n Flotte f; ⟨of cars⟩ Wagenpark m

fleeting /ˈfliːtɪŋ/ a flüchtig

Flemish /ˈflemɪʃ/ a flämisch

flesh /fleʃ/ n Fleisch nt; **in the ~** ⟨fam⟩ in Person. **~y** a fleischig

flew /fluː/ see **fly**[2]

flex[1] /fleks/ vt anspannen ⟨muscle⟩

flex[2] n (Electr) Schnur f

flexib|ility /fleksəˈbɪlətɪ/ n Biegsamkeit f; ⟨fig⟩ Flexibilität f. **~le** a biegsam; ⟨fig⟩ flexibel

'flexitime /ˈfleksɪ-/ n Gleitzeit f

flick /flɪk/ vt schnippen. **~ through** vi schnell durchblättern

flicker /ˈflɪkə(r)/ vi flackern

flier /ˈflaɪə(r)/ n = **flyer**

flight[1] /flaɪt/ n ⟨fleeing⟩ Flucht f; **take ~** die Flucht ergreifen

flight[2] n ⟨flying⟩ Flug m; **~ of stairs** Treppe f

flight: ~ path n Flugschneise f. **~ recorder** n Flugschreiber m

flighty /ˈflaɪtɪ/ a (-ier, -iest) flatterhaft

flimsy /ˈflɪmzɪ/ a (-ier, -iest) dünn; ⟨excuse⟩ fadenscheinig

flinch /flɪntʃ/ vi zurückzucken

fling /flɪŋ/ n **have a ~** ⟨fam⟩ sich austoben ● vt (pt/pp flung) schleudern

flint /flɪnt/ n Feuerstein m

flip /flɪp/ vt/i schnippen; **~ through** durchblättern

flippant /ˈflɪpənt/ a, **-ly** adv leichtfertig

flipper /ˈflɪpə(r)/ n Flosse f

flirt /flɜːt/ n kokette Frau f ● vi flirten

flirtat|ion /flɜːˈteɪʃn/ n Flirt m. **~ious** /-ʃəs/ a kokett

flit /flɪt/ vi (pt/pp flitted) flattern

float /fləʊt/ n Schwimmer m; ⟨in procession⟩ Festwagen m; ⟨money⟩ Wechselgeld nt ● vi ⟨thing:⟩ schwimmen; ⟨person:⟩ sich treiben lassen; ⟨in air⟩ schweben; ⟨Comm⟩ floaten

flock /flɒk/ n Herde f; ⟨of birds⟩ Schwarm m ● vi strömen

flog /flɒg/ vt (pt/pp flogged) auspeitschen; ⟨fam: sell⟩ verkloppen

flood /flʌd/ n Überschwemmung f; ⟨fig⟩ Flut f; **be in ~** ⟨river:⟩ Hochwasser führen ● vt überschwemmen ● vi ⟨river:⟩ über die Ufer treten

'floodlight n Flutlicht nt ● vt (pt/pp floodlit) anstrahlen

floor /flɔː(r)/ n Fußboden m; ⟨storey⟩ Stock m ● vt ⟨baffle⟩ verblüffen

floor: ~board n Dielenbrett nt. **~cloth** n Scheuertuch nt. **~polish** n Bohnerwachs nt. **~ show** n Kabarettvorstellung f

flop /flɒp/ n ⟨fam⟩ ⟨failure⟩ Reinfall m; ⟨Theat⟩ Durchfall m ● vi (pt/pp flopped) ⟨fam⟩ ⟨fail⟩ durchfallen; **~ down** sich plumpsen lassen

floppy /ˈflɒpɪ/ a schlapp. **~ 'disc** n Diskette f

flora /ˈflɔːrə/ n Flora f

floral /ˈflɔːrəl/ a Blumen-

florid /ˈflɒrɪd/ a ⟨complexion⟩ gerötet; ⟨style⟩ blumig

florist /ˈflɒrɪst/ n Blumenhändler(in) m(f)

flounce /flaʊns/ n Volant m ● vi **~ out** hinausstolzieren

flounder[1] /ˈflaʊndə(r)/ vi zappeln

flounder[2] n ⟨fish⟩ Flunder f

flour /ˈflaʊə(r)/ n Mehl nt

flourish /ˈflʌrɪʃ/ n große Geste f; ⟨scroll⟩ Schnörkel m ● vi gedeihen; ⟨fig⟩ blühen ● vt schwenken

floury /ˈflaʊərɪ/ a mehlig

flout /flaʊt/ vt mißachten

flow /fləʊ/ n Fluß m; ⟨of traffic, blood⟩ Strom m ● vi fließen

flower /ˈflaʊə(r)/ n Blume f ● vi blühen

flower: ~-bed n Blumenbeet nt. **~ed** a geblümt. **~pot** n Blumentopf m. **~y** a blumig

flown /fləʊn/ see **fly**[2]

flu /fluː/ n ⟨fam⟩ Grippe f

fluctuat|e /ˈflʌktjʊeɪt/ vi schwanken. **~ion** /-ˈeɪʃn/ n Schwankung f

fluent /'flu:ənt/ a, **-ly** adv fließend

fluff /flʌf/ n Fusseln pl; (down) Flaum m. **~y** a (-ier, -iest) flauschig

fluid /'flu:ɪd/ a flüssig; (fig) veränderlich ● n Flüssigkeit f

fluke /flu:k/ n [glücklicher] Zufall m

flung /flʌŋ/ see **fling**

flunk /flʌŋk/ vt/i (Amer, fam) durchfallen (in + dat)

fluorescent /fluə'resnt/ a fluoreszierend; **~ lighting** Neonbeleuchtung f

fluoride /'fluərad/ n Fluor nt

flurry /'flʌrɪ/ n (snow) Gestöber nt; (fig) Aufregung f

flush /flʌʃ/ n (blush) Erröten nt ● vi rot werden ● vt spülen ● a in einer Ebene (with mit); (fam: affluent) gut bei Kasse

flustered /'flʌstəd/ a nervös

flute /flu:t/ n Flöte f

flutter /'flʌtə(r)/ n Flattern nt ● vi flattern

flux /flʌks/ n **in a state of ~** im Fluß

fly¹ /flaɪ/ n (pl **flies**) Fliege f

fly² v (pt **flew**, pp **flown**) ● vi fliegen; ⟨flag:⟩ wehen; (rush) sausen ● vt fliegen; führen ⟨flag⟩

fly³ ~ & flies pl (on trousers) Hosenschlitz m

flyer /'flaɪə(r)/ n Flieger(in) m(f); (Amer: leaflet) Flugblatt nt

flying: **~ 'buttress** n Strebebogen m. **~ 'saucer** n fliegende Untertasse f. **~ 'visit** n Stippvisite f

fly: **~leaf** n Vorsatzblatt nt. **~over** n Überführung f

foal /fəʊl/ n Fohlen nt

foam /fəʊm/ n Schaum m; (synthetic) Schaumstoff m ● vi schäumen. **~ 'rubber** n Schaumgummi m

fob /fɒb/ vt (pt/pp **fobbed**) **~ sth off** etw andrehen (**on s.o.** jdm); **~ s.o. off** jdn abspeisen (**with** mit)

focal /'fəʊkl/ a Brenn-

focus /'fəʊkəs/ n Brennpunkt m; **in ~** scharf eingestellt ● v (pt/pp **focused** or **focussed**) ● vt einstellen (**on** auf + acc); (fig) konzentrieren (**on** auf + acc) ● vi (fig) sich konzentrieren (**on** auf + acc)

fodder /'fɒdə(r)/ n Futter nt

foe /fəʊ/ n Feind m

foetus /'fi:təs/ n (pl **-tuses**) Fötus m

fog /fɒg/ n Nebel m

foggy /'fɒgɪ/ a (**foggier**, **foggiest**) neblig

'fog-horn n Nebelhorn nt

fogy /'fəʊgɪ/ n **old ~** alter Knacker m

foible /'fɔɪbl/ n Eigenart f

foil¹ /fɔɪl/ n Folie f; (Culin) Alufolie f

foil² vt (thwart) vereiteln

foil³ n (Fencing) Florett nt

foist /fɔɪst/ vt andrehen (**on s.o.** jdm)

fold¹ /fəʊld/ n (for sheep) Pferch m

fold² n Falte f; (in paper) Kniff m ● vt falten; **~ one's arms** die Arme verschränken ● vi sich falten lassen; (fail) eingehen. **~ up** vt zusammenfalten; zusammenklappen ⟨chair⟩ ● vi sich zusammenfalten/-klappen lassen; (fam) ⟨business:⟩ eingehen

fold|er /'fəʊldə(r)/ n Mappe f. **~ing** a Klapp-

foliage /'fəʊlɪɪdʒ/ n Blätter pl; (of tree) Laub nt

folk /fəʊk/ npl Leute pl

folk: **~-dance** n Volkstanz m. **~lore** n Folklore f. **~-song** n Volkslied nt

follow /'fɒləʊ/ vt/i folgen (+ dat); (pursue) verfolgen; (in vehicle) nachfahren (+ dat); **~ suit** (fig) dasselbe tun. **~ up** vt nachgehen (+ dat)

follow|er /'fɒləʊə(r)/ n Anhänger(in) m(f). **~ing** a folgend ● n Folgende(s) nt; (supporters) Anhängerschaft f ● prep im Anschluß an (+ acc)

folly /'fɒlɪ/ n Torheit f

fond /fɒnd/ a (-er, -est), **-ly** adv liebevoll; **be ~ of** gern haben; gern essen ⟨food⟩

fondle /'fɒndl/ vt liebkosen

fondness /'fɒndnɪs/ n Liebe f (**for** zu)

font /fɒnt/ n Taufstein m

food /fu:d/ n Essen nt; (for animals) Futter nt; (groceries) Lebensmittel pl

food: **~ mixer** n Küchenmaschine f. **~ poisoning** n Lebensmittelvergiftung f. **~ processor** n Küchenmaschine f. **~ value** n Nährwert m

fool¹ /fu:l/ n (Culin) Fruchtcreme f

fool² n Narr m; **you are a ~** du bist dumm; **make a ~ of oneself** sich lächerlich machen ● vt hereinlegen ● vi **~ around** herumalbern

'fool|hardy a tollkühn. **~ish** a, **-ly** adv dumm. **~ishness** n Dummheit f. **~proof** a narrensicher

foot /fʊt/ n (pl **feet**) Fuß m; (measure) Fuß m (30,48 cm); (of bed) Fußende nt; **on ~** zu Fuß; **on one's feet** auf den Beinen; **put one's ~ in it** (fam) ins Fettnäpfchen treten

foot: **~-and-'mouth disease** n Maul- und Klauenseuche f. **~ball** n Fußball m. **~baller** n Fußballspieler m.

~**ball pools** *npl* Fußballtoto *nt*. ~**brake** *n* Fußbremse *f*. ~**bridge** *n* Fußgängerbrücke *f*. ~**hills** *npl* Vorgebirge *nt*. ~**hold** *n* Halt *m*. ~**ing** *n* Halt *m*; (*fig*) Basis *f*. ~**lights** *npl* Rampenlicht *nt*. ~**man** *n* Lakai *m*. ~**note** *n* Fußnote *f*. ~**path** *n* Fußweg *m*. ~**print** *n* Fußabdruck *m*. ~**step** *n* Schritt *m*; **follow in s.o.'s** ~**steps** (*fig*) in jds Fußstapfen treten. ~**stool** *n* Fußbank *f*. ~**wear** *n* Schuhwerk *nt*

for /fə(r), *betont* fɔ:(r)/ *prep* für (+ *acc*); ⟨*send, long*⟩ nach; ⟨*ask, fight*⟩ um; **what** ~? wozu? ~ **supper** zum Abendessen; ~ **nothing** umsonst; ~ **all that** trotz allem; ~ **this reason** aus diesem Grund; ~ **a month** einen Monat; **I have lived here** ~ **ten years** ich wohne seit zehn Jahren hier ● *conj* denn

forage /'fɒrɪdʒ/ *n* Futter *nt* ● *vi* ~ **for** suchen nach

forbade /fə'bæd/ *see* **forbid**

forbear|ance /fɔ:'beərəns/ *n* Nachsicht *f*. ~**ing** *a* nachsichtig

forbid /fə'bɪd/ *vt* (*pt* **forbade**, *pp* **forbidden**) verbieten (**s.o.** jdm). ~**ding** *a* bedrohlich; (*stern*) streng

force /fɔ:s/ *n* Kraft *f*; (*of blow*) Wucht *f*; (*violence*) Gewalt *f*; **in** ~ gültig; (*in large numbers*) in großer Zahl; **come into** ~ in Kraft treten; **the** ~**s** *pl* die Streitkräfte *pl* ● *vt* zwingen; (*break open*) aufbrechen; ~ **sth on s.o.** jdm etw aufdrängen

forced /fɔ:st/ *a* gezwungen; ~ **landing** Notlandung *f*

force: ~**-'feed** *vt* (*pt/pp* **-fed**) zwangsernähren. ~**ful** *a*, **-ly** *adv* energisch

forceps /'fɔ:seps/ *n inv* Zange *f*

forcibl|e /'fɔ:səbl/ *a* gewaltsam. ~**y** *adv* mit Gewalt

ford /fɔ:d/ *n* Furt *f* ● *vt* durchwaten; (*in vehicle*) durchfahren

fore /fɔ:(r)/ *a* vordere(r,s) ● *n* **to the** ~ im Vordergrund

fore: ~**arm** *n* Unterarm *m*. ~**boding** /-'bəʊdɪŋ/ *n* Vorahnung *f*. ~**cast** *n* Voraussage *f*; (*for weather*) Vorhersage *f* ● *vt* (*pt/pp* ~**cast**) voraussagen, vorhersagen. ~**court** *n* Vorhof *m*. ~**fathers** *npl* Vorfahren *pl*. ~**finger** *n* Zeigefinger *m*. ~**front** *n* **be in the** ~**front** führend sein. ~**gone** *a* **be a** ~**gone conclusion** von vornherein feststehen. ~**ground** *n* Vordergrund *m*. ~**head** /'fɒrɪd/ *n* Stirn *f*. ~**hand** *n* Vorhand *f*

foreign /'fɒrən/ *a* ausländisch; ⟨*country*⟩ fremd; **he is** ~ er ist Ausländer. ~ **currency** *n* Devisen *pl*. ~**er** *n* Ausländer(in) *m(f)*. ~ **language** *n* Fremdsprache *f*

Foreign: ~ **Office** *n* ≈ Außenministerium *nt*. ~ **'Secretary** *n* ≈ Außenminister *m*

fore: ~**leg** *n* Vorderbein *nt*. ~**man** *n* Vorarbeiter *m*. ~**most** *a* führend ● *adv* **first and** ~**most** zuallererst. ~**name** *n* Vorname *m*

forensic /fə'rensɪk/ *a* ~ **medicine** Gerichtsmedizin *f*

'forerunner *n* Vorläufer *m*

fore'see *vt* (*pt* **-saw**, *pp* **-seen**) voraussehen, vorhersehen. ~**able** /-əbl/ *a* **in the** ~**able future** in absehbarer Zeit

'foresight *n* Weitblick *m*

forest /'fɒrɪst/ *n* Wald *m*. ~**er** *n* Förster *m*

fore'stall *vt* zuvorkommen (+ *dat*)

forestry /'fɒrɪstrɪ/ *n* Forstwirtschaft *f*

'foretaste *n* Vorgeschmack *m*

fore'tell *vt* (*pt/pp* **-told**) vorhersagen

forever /fə'revə(r)/ *adv* für immer

fore'warn *vt* vorher warnen

foreword /'fɔ:wɜ:d/ *n* Vorwort *nt*

forfeit /'fɔ:fɪt/ *n* (*in game*) Pfand *nt* ● *vt* verwirken

forgave /fə'geɪv/ *see* **forgive**

forge¹ /fɔ:dʒ/ *vi* ~ **ahead** (*fig*) Fortschritte machen

forge² *n* Schmiede *f* ● *vt* schmieden; (*counterfeit*) fälschen. ~**r** *n* Fälscher *m*. ~**ry** *n* Fälschung *f*

forget /fə'get/ *vt/i* (*pt* **-got**, *pp* **-gotten**) vergessen; verlernen ⟨*language, skill*⟩. ~**ful** *a* vergeßlich. ~**fulness** *n* Vergeßlichkeit *f*. ~**-me-not** *n* Vergißmeinnicht *nt*

forgive /fə'gɪv/ *vt* (*pt* **-gave**, *pp* **-given**) ~ **s.o. for sth** jdm etw vergeben *od* verzeihen. ~**ness** *n* Vergebung *f*, Verzeihung *f*

forgo /fɔ:'gəʊ/ *vt* (*pt* **-went**, *pp* **-gone**) verzichten auf (+ *acc*)

forgot(ten) /fə'gɒt(n)/ *see* **forget**

fork /fɔ:k/ *n* Gabel *f*; (*in road*) Gabelung *f* ● *vi* ⟨*road:*⟩ sich gabeln; ~ **right** rechts abzweigen. ~ **out** *vt* (*fam*) blechen

fork-lift 'truck *n* Gabelstapler *m*

forlorn /fə'lɔ:n/ *a* verlassen; ⟨*hope*⟩ schwach

form /fɔ:m/ *n* Form *f*; (*document*) Formular *nt*; (*bench*) Bank *f*; (*Sch*) Klasse *f* ● *vt* formen (**into** zu);

(create) bilden ● *vi* sich bilden; *⟨idea:⟩* Gestalt annehmen

formal /'fɔːml/ *a*, **-ly** *adv* formell, förmlich. **~ity** /-'mælətɪ/ *n* Förmlichkeit *f*; *(requirement)* Formalität *f*

format /'fɔːmæt/ *n* Format *nt*

formation /fɔː'meɪʃn/ *n* Formation *f*

formative /'fɔːmətɪv/ *a* **~ years** Entwicklungsjahre *pl*

former /'fɔːmə(r)/ *a* ehemalig; **the ~** der/die/das erstere. **~ly** *adv* früher

formidable /'fɔːmɪdəbl/ *a* gewaltig

formula /'fɔːmjʊlə/ *n* *(pl* **-ae** /-liː/ *or* **-s)** Formel *f*

formulate /'fɔːmjʊleɪt/ *vt* formulieren

forsake /fə'seɪk/ *vt* *(pt* **-sook** /-sʊk/, *pp* **-saken)** verlassen

fort /fɔːt/ *n* *(Mil)* Fort *nt*

forte /'fɔːteɪ/ *n* Stärke *f*

forth /fɔːθ/ *adv* **back and ~** hin und her; **and so ~** und so weiter

forth: **~'coming** *a* bevorstehend; *(fam: communicative)* mitteilsam. **~right** *a* direkt. **~'with** *adv* umgehend

fortieth /'fɔːtɪɪθ/ *a* vierzigste(r,s)

fortification /fɔːtɪfɪ'keɪʃn/ *n* Befestigung *f*

fortify /'fɔːtɪfaɪ/ *vt* *(pt/pp* **-ied)** befestigen; *(fig)* stärken

fortitude /'fɔːtɪtjuːd/ *n* Standhaftigkeit *f*

fortnight /'fɔːt-/ *n* vierzehn Tage *pl.* **~ly** *a* vierzehntäglich ● *adv* alle vierzehn Tage

fortress /'fɔːtrɪs/ *n* Festung *f*

fortuitous /fɔː'tjuːɪtəs/ *a*, **-ly** *adv* zufällig

fortunate /'fɔːtʃʊnət/ *a* glücklich; **be ~** Glück haben. **~ly** *adv* glücklicherweise

fortune /'fɔːtʃuːn/ *n* Glück *nt*; *(money)* Vermögen *nt.* **~-teller** *n* Wahrsagerin *f*

forty /'fɔːtɪ/ *a* vierzig; **have ~ winks** *(fam)* ein Nickerchen machen ● *n* Vierzig *f*

forum /'fɔːrəm/ *n* Forum *nt*

forward /'fɔːwəd/ *adv* vorwärts; *(to the front)* nach vorn ● *a* Vorwärts-; *(presumptuous)* anmaßend ● *n* *(Sport)* Stürmer *m* ● *vt* nachsenden *⟨letter⟩.* **~s** *adv* vorwärts

fossil /'fɒsl/ *n* Fossil *nt.* **~ized** *a* versteinert

foster /'fɒstə(r)/ *vt* fördern; in Pflege nehmen *⟨child⟩.* **~-child** *n* Pflegekind *nt.* **~-mother** *n* Pflegemutter *f*

fought /fɔːt/ *see* **fight**

foul /faʊl/ *a* **(-er, -est)** widerlich; *⟨language⟩* unflätig; **~ play** *(Jur)* Mord *m* ● *n* *(Sport)* Foul *nt* ● *vt* verschmutzen; *(obstruct)* blockieren; *(Sport)* foulen. **~ smelling** *a* übelriechend

found[1] /faʊnd/ *see* **find**

found[2] *vt* gründen

foundation /faʊn'deɪʃn/ *n* *(basis)* Grundlage *f*; *(charitable)* Stiftung *f*; **~s** *pl* Fundament *nt.* **~-stone** *n* Grundstein *m*

founder[1] /'faʊndə(r)/ *n* Gründer(in) *m(f)*

founder[2] *vi* *⟨ship:⟩* sinken; *(fig)* scheitern

foundry /'faʊndrɪ/ *n* Gießerei *f*

fountain /'faʊntɪn/ *n* Brunnen *m.* **~-pen** *n* Füllfederhalter *m*

four /fɔː(r)/ *a* vier ● *n* Vier *f*

four: **~-'poster** *n* Himmelbett *nt.* **~some** /'fɔːsəm/ *n* **in a ~some** zu viert. **~'teen** *a* vierzehn ● *n* Vierzehn *f.* **~'teenth** *a* vierzehnte(r,s)

fourth /fɔːθ/ *a* vierte(r,s)

fowl /faʊl/ *n* Geflügel *nt*

fox /fɒks/ *n* Fuchs *m* ● *vt* *(puzzle)* verblüffen

foyer /'fɔɪeɪ/ *n* Foyer *nt*; *(in hotel)* Empfangshalle *f*

fraction /'frækʃn/ *n* Bruchteil *m*; *(Math)* Bruch *m*

fracture /'fræktʃə(r)/ *n* Bruch *m* ● *vt/i* brechen

fragile /'frædʒaɪl/ *a* zerbrechlich

fragment /'frægmənt/ *n* Bruchstück *nt*, Fragment *nt.* **~ary** *a* bruchstückhaft

fragran|ce /'freɪgrəns/ *n* Duft *m.* **~t** *a* duftend

frail /freɪl/ *a* **(-er, -est)** gebrechlich

frame /freɪm/ *n* Rahmen *m*; *(of spectacles)* Gestell *nt*; *(Anat)* Körperbau *m*; **~ of mind** Gemütsverfassung *f* ● *vt* einrahmen; *(fig)* formulieren; *(sl)* ein Verbrechen anhängen (+ *dat).* **~work** *n* Gerüst *nt*; *(fig)* Gerippe *nt*

franc /fræŋk/ *n* *(French, Belgian)* Franc *m*; *(Swiss)* Franken *m*

France /frɑːns/ *n* Frankreich *nt*

franchise /'fræntʃaɪz/ *n* *(Pol)* Wahlrecht *nt*; *(Comm)* Franchise *nt*

frank[1] /fræŋk/ *vt* frankieren

frank[2] *a*, **-ly** *adv* offen

frankfurter /'fræŋkfɜːtə(r)/ *n* Frankfurter *f*

frantic /'fræntɪk/ a, **-ally** adv verzweifelt; **be ~** außer sich (dat) sein (**with** vor)

fraternal /frə'tɜːnl/ a brüderlich

fraud /frɔːd/ n Betrug m; (person) Betrüger(in) m(f). **~ulent** /-jʊlənt/ a betrügerisch

fraught /frɔːt/ a **~ with danger** gefahrvoll

fray[1] /freɪ/ n Kampf m

fray[2] vi ausfransen

freak /friːk/ n Mißbildung f; (person) Mißgeburt f; (phenomenon) Ausnahmeerscheinung f ● a anormal. **~ish** a anormal

freckle /'frekl/ n Sommersprosse f. **~d** a sommersprossig

free /friː/ a (**freer, freest**) frei; (ticket, copy, time) Frei-; (lavish) freigebig; **~ [of charge]** kostenlos; **set ~** freilassen; (rescue) befreien; **you are ~ to ...** es steht Ihnen frei, zu ... ● vt (pt/pp **freed**) freilassen; (rescue) befreien; (disentangle) freibekommen

free: ~dom n Freiheit f. **~hand** adv aus freier Hand. **~hold** n [freier] Grundbesitz m. **~'kick** n Freistoß m. **~lance** a & adv freiberuflich. **~ly** adv frei; (voluntarily) freiwillig; (generously) großzügig. **F~mason** n Freimaurer m. **F~masonry** n Freimaurerei f. **~-range** a **~-range eggs** Landeier pl. **~ 'sample** n Gratisprobe f. **~style** n Freistil m. **~way** n (Amer) Autobahn f. **~-'wheel** vi im Freilauf fahren

freez|e /friːz/ vt (pt **froze**, pp **frozen**) einfrieren; stoppen (wages) ● vi gefrieren; **it's ~ing** es friert

freez|er /'friːzə(r)/ n Gefriertruhe f; (upright) Gefrierschrank m. **~ing** a eiskalt ● n below **~ing** unter Null

freight /freɪt/ n Fracht f. **~er** n Frachter m. **~ train** n (Amer) Güterzug m

French /frentʃ/ a französisch ● n (Lang) Französisch nt; **the ~** pl die Franzosen

French: ~ 'beans npl grüne Bohnen pl. **~ 'bread** n Stangenbrot nt. **~ 'fries** npl Pommes frites pl. **~man** n Franzose m. **~ 'window** n Terrassentür f. **~woman** n Französin f

frenzied /'frenzɪd/ a rasend

frenzy /'frenzɪ/ n Raserei f

frequency /'friːkwənsɪ/ n Häufigkeit f; (Phys) Frequenz f

frequent[1] /'friːkwənt/ a, **-ly** adv häufig

frequent[2] /frɪ'kwent/ vt regelmäßig besuchen

fresco /'freskəʊ/ n Fresko nt

fresh /freʃ/ a (**-er, -est**), **-ly** adv frisch; (new) neu; (Amer: cheeky) frech

freshen /'freʃn/ vi (wind:) auffrischen. **~ up** vt auffrischen ● vi sich frisch machen

freshness /'freʃnɪs/ n Frische f

'freshwater a Süßwasser-

fret /fret/ vi (pt/pp **fretted**) sich grämen. **~ful** a weinerlich

'fretsaw n Laubsäge f

friar /'fraɪə(r)/ n Mönch m

friction /'frɪkʃn/ n Reibung f; (fig) Reibereien pl

Friday /'fraɪdeɪ/ n Freitag m

fridge /frɪdʒ/ n Kühlschrank m

fried /fraɪd/ see **fry**[2] ● a gebraten; **~ egg** Spiegelei nt

friend /frend/ n Freund(in) m(f). **~liness** n Freundlichkeit f. **~ly** a (**-ier, -iest**) freundlich; **~ly with** befreundet mit. **~ship** n Freundschaft f

frieze /friːz/ n Fries m

fright /fraɪt/ n Schreck m

frighten /'fraɪtn/ vt angst machen (+ dat); (startle) erschrecken; **be ~ed** Angst haben (**of** vor + dat). **~ing** a angsterregend

frightful /'fraɪtfl/ a, **-ly** adv schrecklich

frigid /'frɪdʒɪd/ a frostig; (Psych) frigide. **~ity** /-'dʒɪdətɪ/ n Frostigkeit f; Frigidität f

frill /frɪl/ n Rüsche f; (paper) Manschette f. **~y** a rüschenbesetzt

fringe /frɪndʒ/ n Fransen pl; (of hair) Pony m; (fig: edge) Rand m. **~ benefits** npl zusätzliche Leistungen pl

frisk /frɪsk/ vi herumspringen ● vt (search) durchsuchen, (fam) filzen

frisky /'frɪskɪ/ a (**-ier, -iest**) lebhaft

fritter /'frɪtə(r)/ vt **~ [away]** verplempern (fam)

frivol|ity /frɪ'vɒlətɪ/ n Frivolität f. **~ous** /'frɪvələs/ a, **-ly** adv frivol, leichtfertig

frizzy /'frɪzɪ/ a kraus

fro /frəʊ/ see **to**

frock /frɒk/ n Kleid nt

frog /frɒg/ n Frosch m. **~man** n Froschmann m. **~-spawn** n Froschlaich m

frolic /'frɒlɪk/ vi (pt/pp **frolicked**) herumtollen

from /frɒm/ *prep* von (+ *dat*); (*out of*) aus (+ *dat*); (*according to*) nach (+ *dat*); ~ **Monday** ab Montag; ~ **that day** seit dem Tag

front /frʌnt/ *n* Vorderseite *f*; (*fig*) Fassade *f*; (*of garment*) Vorderteil *nt*; (*sea-*) Strandpromenade *f*; (*Mil, Pol, Meteorol*) Front *f*; **in** ~ **of** vor; **in** *or* **at the** ~ vorne; **to the** ~ nach vorne ● *a* vordere(r,s); ⟨*page, row*⟩ erste(r,s); ⟨*tooth, wheel*⟩ Vorder-

frontal /'frʌntl/ *a* Frontal-

front: ~ **'door** *n* Haustür *f*. ~ **'garden** *n* Vorgarten *m*

frontier /'frʌntɪə(r)/ *n* Grenze *f*

front-wheel 'drive *n* Vorderradantrieb *m*

frost /frɒst/ *n* Frost *m*; (*hoar-*) Raureif *m*; **ten degrees of** ~ zehn Grad Kälte. ~**bite** *n* Erfrierung *f*. ~**bitten** *a* erfroren

frost|ed /'frɒstɪd/ *a* ~**ed glass** Mattglas *nt*. ~**ing** *n* (*Amer Culin*) Zuckerguß *m*. ~**y** *a*, **-ily** *adv* frostig

froth /frɒθ/ *n* Schaum *m* ● *vi* schäumen. ~**y** *a* schaumig

frown /fraʊn/ *n* Stirnrunzeln *nt* ● *vi* die Stirn runzeln; ~ **on** mißbilligen

froze /frəʊz/ *see* **freeze**

frozen /'frəʊzn/ *see* **freeze** ● *a* gefroren; (*Culin*) tiefgekühlt; **I'm** ~ (*fam*) mir ist eiskalt. ~ **food** *n* Tiefkühlkost *f*

frugal /'fru:gl/ *a*, **-ly** *adv* sparsam; ⟨*meal*⟩ frugal

fruit /fru:t/ *n* Frucht *f*; (*collectively*) Obst *nt*. ~ **cake** *n* englischer [Tee]kuchen *m*

fruit|erer /'fru:tərə(r)/ *n* Obsthändler *m*. ~**ful** *a* fruchtbar

fruition /fru:'ɪʃn/ *n* **come to** ~ sich verwirklichen

fruit: ~ **juice** *n* Obstsaft *m*. ~**less** *a*, **-ly** *adv* fruchtlos. ~ **machine** *n* Spielautomat *m*. ~ **'salad** *n* Obstsalat *m*

fruity /'fru:tɪ/ *a* fruchtig

frumpy /'frʌmpɪ/ *a* unmodisch

frustrat|e /frʌ'streɪt/ *vt* vereiteln; (*Psych*) frustrieren. ~**ing** *a* frustrierend. ~**ion** /-eɪʃn/ *n* Frustration *f*

fry¹ /fraɪ/ *n inv* **small** ~ (*fig*) kleine Fische *pl*

fry² *vt/i* (*pt/pp* **fried**) [in der Pfanne] braten. ~**ing-pan** *n* Bratpfanne *f*

fuck /fʌk/ *vt/i* (*vulg*) ficken. ~**ing** *a* (*vulg*) Scheiß-

fuddy-duddy /'fʌdɪdʌdɪ/ *n* (*fam*) verknöcherter Kerl *m*

fudge /fʌdʒ/ *n* weiche Karamellen *pl*

fuel /'fju:əl/ *n* Brennstoff *m*; (*for car*) Kraftstoff *m*; (*for aircraft*) Treibstoff *m*

fugitive /'fju:dʒətɪv/ *n* Flüchtling *m*

fugue /fju:g/ *n* (*Mus*) Fuge *f*

fulfil /fʊl'fɪl/ *vt* (*pt/pp* **-filled**) erfüllen. ~**ment** *n* Erfüllung *f*

full /fʊl/ *a & adv* (**-er, -est**) voll; (*detailed*) ausführlich; ⟨*skirt*⟩ weit; ~ **of** voll von (+ *dat*), voller (+ *gen*); **at** ~ **speed** in voller Fahrt ● *n* **in** ~ vollständig

full: ~ **'moon** *n* Vollmond *m*. ~**-scale** *a* ⟨*model*⟩ in Originalgröße; ⟨*rescue, alert*⟩ großangelegt. ~ **'stop** *n* Punkt *m*. ~**-time** *a* ganztägig ● *adv* ganztags

fully /'fʊlɪ/ *adv* völlig; (*in detail*) ausführlich

fulsome /'fʊlsəm/ *a* übertrieben

fumble /'fʌmbl/ *vi* herumfummeln (**with** an + *dat*)

fume /fju:m/ *vi* vor Wut schäumen

fumes /fju:mz/ *npl* Dämpfe *pl*; (*from car*) Abgase *pl*

fumigate /'fju:mɪgeɪt/ *vt* ausräuchern

fun /fʌn/ *n* Spaß *m*; **for** ~ aus *od* zum Spaß; **make** ~ **of** sich lustig machen über (+ *acc*); **have** ~! viel Spaß!

function /'fʌŋkʃn/ *n* Funktion *f*; (*event*) Veranstaltung *f* ● *vi* funktionieren; (*serve*) dienen (**as** als). ~**al** *a* zweckmäßig

fund /fʌnd/ *n* Fonds *m*; (*fig*) Vorrat *m*; ~**s** *pl* Geldmittel *pl* ● *vt* finanzieren

fundamental /fʌndə'mentl/ *a* grundlegend; (*essential*) wesentlich

funeral /'fju:nərl/ *n* Beerdigung *f*; (*cremation*) Feuerbestattung *f*

funeral: ~ **directors** *pl*, (*Amer*) ~ **home** *n* Bestattungsinstitut *nt*. ~ **march** *n* Trauermarsch *m*. ~ **parlour** *n* (*Amer*) Bestattungsinstitut *nt*. ~ **service** *n* Trauergottesdienst *m*

'funfair *n* Jahrmarkt *m*, Kirmes *f*

fungus /'fʌŋgəs/ *n* (*pl* **-gi** /-gaɪ/) Pilz *m*

funicular /fju:'nɪkjʊlə(r)/ *n* Seilbahn *f*

funnel /'fʌnl/ *n* Trichter *m*; (*on ship, train*) Schornstein *m*

funnily /'fʌnɪlɪ/ *adv* komisch; ~ **enough** komischerweise

funny /'fʌnɪ/ a (-ier, -iest) komisch. ~-bone n (fam) Musikantenknochen m

fur /fɜː(r)/ n Fell nt; (for clothing) Pelz m; (in kettle) Kesselstein m. ~ 'coat n Pelzmantel m

furious /'fjʊərɪəs/ a, -ly adv wütend (with auf + acc)

furnace /'fɜːnɪs/ n (Techn) Ofen m

furnish /'fɜːnɪʃ/ vt einrichten; (supply) liefern. ~ed a ~ed room möbliertes Zimmer nt. ~ings npl Einrichtungsgegenstände pl

furniture /'fɜːnɪtʃə(r)/ n Möbel pl

furred /fɜːd/ a ⟨tongue⟩ belegt

furrow /'fʌrəʊ/ n Furche f

furry /'fɜːrɪ/ a ⟨animal⟩ Pelz-; ⟨toy⟩ Plüsch-

further /'fɜːðə(r)/ a weitere(r,s); at the ~ end am anderen Ende; until ~ notice bis auf weiteres ● adv weiter; ~ off weiter entfernt ● vt fördern

further: ~ edu'cation n Weiterbildung f. ~'more adv überdies

furthest /'fɜːðɪst/ a am weitesten entfernt ● adv am weitesten

furtive /'fɜːtɪv/ a, -ly adv verstohlen

fury /'fjʊərɪ/ n Wut f

fuse¹ /fjuːz/ n (of bomb) Zünder m; (cord) Zündschnur f

fuse² n (Electr) Sicherung f ● vt/i verschmelzen; the lights have ~d die Sicherung [für das Licht] ist durchgebrannt. ~-box n Sicherungskasten m

fuselage /'fjuːzəlɑːʒ/ n (Aviat) Rumpf m

fusion /'fjuːʒn/ n Verschmelzung f, Fusion f

fuss /fʌs/ n Getue nt; make a ~ of verwöhnen; (caress) liebkosen ● vi Umstände machen

fussy /'fʌsɪ/ a (-ier, -iest) wählerisch; (particular) penibel

fusty /'fʌstɪ/ a moderig

futile /'fjuːtaɪl/ a zwecklos. ~ity /-'tɪlətɪ/ n Zwecklosigkeit f

future /'fjuːtʃə(r)/ a zukünftig ● n Zukunft f; (Gram) [erstes] Futur nt; ~ perfect zweites Futur nt; in ~ in Zukunft

futuristic /fjuːtʃə'rɪstɪk/ a futuristisch

fuzz /fʌz/ n the ~ (sl) die Bullen pl

fuzzy /'fʌzɪ/ a (-ier, -iest) ⟨hair⟩ kraus; (blurred) verschwommen

G

gab /gæb/ n (fam) have the gift of the ~ gut reden können

gabble /'gæbl/ vi schnell reden

gable /'geɪbl/ n Giebel m

gad /gæd/ vi (pt/pp gadded) ~ about dauernd ausgehen

gadget /'gædʒɪt/ n [kleines] Gerät nt

Gaelic /'geɪlɪk/ n Gälisch nt

gaffe /gæf/ n Fauxpas m

gag /gæg/ n Knebel m; (joke) Witz m; (Theat) Gag m ● vt (pt/pp gagged) knebeln

gaiety /'geɪətɪ/ n Fröhlichkeit f

gaily /'geɪlɪ/ adv fröhlich

gain /geɪn/ n Gewinn m; (increase) Zunahme f ● vt gewinnen; (obtain) erlangen; ~ weight zunehmen ● vi ⟨clock:⟩ vorgehen. ~ful a ~ful employment Erwerbstätigkeit f

gait /geɪt/ n Gang m

gala /'gɑːlə/ n Fest nt; swimming ~ Schwimmfest nt ● attrib Gala-

galaxy /'gæləksɪ/ n Galaxie f; the G~ die Milchstraße

gale /geɪl/ n Sturm m

gall /gɔːl/ n Galle f; (impudence) Frechheit f

gallant /'gælənt/ a, -ly adv tapfer; (chivalrous) galant. ~ry n Tapferkeit f

'gall-bladder n Gallenblase f

gallery /'gælərɪ/ n Galerie f

galley /'gælɪ/ n (ship's kitchen) Kombüse f; ~ [proof] [Druck]fahne f

gallivant /'gælɪvænt/ vi (fam) ausgehen

gallon /'gælən/ n Gallone f (= 4,5 l; Amer = 3,7 l)

gallop /'gæləp/ n Galopp m ● vi galoppieren

gallows /'gæləʊz/ n Galgen m

'gallstone n Gallenstein m

galore /gə'lɔː(r)/ adv in Hülle und Fülle

galvanize /'gælvənaɪz/ vt galvanisieren

gambit /'gæmbɪt/ n Eröffnungsmanöver nt

gamble /'gæmbl/ n (risk) Risiko nt ● vi [um Geld] spielen; ~ on (rely) sich verlassen auf (+ acc). ~r n Spieler(in) m(f)

game /geɪm/ n Spiel nt; (animals, birds) Wild nt; ~s (Sch) Sport m ● a (brave) tapfer; (willing) bereit (for zu). ~keeper n Wildhüter m

gammon /'gæmən/ n [geräucherter] Schinken m

gamut /'gæmət/ n Skala f

gander /'gændə(r)/ n Gänserich m

gang /gæŋ/ n Bande f; (of workmen) Kolonne f ● vi ~ **up** sich zusammenrotten (**on** gegen)

gangling /'gæŋglɪŋ/ a schlaksig

gangrene /'gæŋgri:n/ n Wundbrand m

gangster /'gæŋstə(r)/ n Gangster m

gangway /'gæŋweɪ/ n Gang m; (Naut, Aviat) Gangway f

gaol /dʒeɪl/ n Gefängnis nt ● vt ins Gefängnis sperren. ~**er** n Gefängniswärter m

gap /gæp/ n Lücke f; (interval) Pause f; (difference) Unterschied m

gap|e /geɪp/ vi gaffen; ~**e at** anstarren. ~**ing** a klaffend

garage /'gærɑ:ʒ/ n Garage f; (for repairs) Werkstatt f; (for petrol) Tankstelle f

garb /gɑ:b/ n Kleidung f

garbage /'gɑ:bɪdʒ/ n Müll m. ~ **can** n (Amer) Mülleimer m

garbled /'gɑ:bld/ a verworren

garden /'gɑ:dn/ n Garten m; [public] ~**s** pl [öffentliche] Anlagen pl ● vi im Garten arbeiten. ~**er** n Gärtner (in) m(f). ~**ing** n Gartenarbeit f

gargle /'gɑ:gl/ n (liquid) Gurgelwasser nt ● vi gurgeln

gargoyle /'gɑ:gɔɪl/ n Wasserspeier m

garish /'geərɪʃ/ a grell

garland /'gɑ:lənd/ n Girlande f

garlic /'gɑ:lɪk/ n Knoblauch m

garment /'gɑ:mənt/ n Kleidungsstück nt

garnet /'gɑ:nɪt/ n Granat m

garnish /'gɑ:nɪʃ/ n Garnierung f ● vt garnieren

garret /'gærɪt/ n Dachstube f

garrison /'gærɪsn/ n Garnison f

garrulous /'gærʊləs/ a geschwätzig

garter /'gɑ:tə(r)/ n Strumpfband nt; (Amer: suspender) Strumpfhalter m

gas /gæs/ n Gas nt; (Amer fam: petrol) Benzin nt ● v (pt/pp **gassed**) ● vt vergasen ● vi (fam) schwatzen. ~**cooker** n Gasherd m. ~ '**fire** n Gasofen m

gash /gæʃ/ n Schnitt m; (wound) klaffende Wunde f ● vt ~ **one's arm** sich (dat) den Arm aufschlitzen

gasket /'gæskɪt/ n (Techn) Dichtung f

gas: ~ **mask** n Gasmaske f. ~**-meter** n Gaszähler m

gasoline /'gæsəli:n/ n (Amer) Benzin nt

gasp /gɑ:sp/ vi keuchen; (in surprise) hörbar die Luft einziehen

'**gas station** n (Amer) Tankstelle f

gastric /'gæstrɪk/ a Magen-. ~ '**flu** n Darmgrippe f. ~ '**ulcer** n Magengeschwür nt

gastronomy /gæ'strɒnəmɪ/ n Gastronomie f

gate /geɪt/ n Tor nt; (to field) Gatter nt; (barrier) Schranke f; (at airport) Flugsteig m

gâteau /'gætəʊ/ n Torte f

gate: ~**crasher** n ungeladener Gast m. ~**way** n Tor nt

gather /'gæðə(r)/ vt sammeln; (pick) pflücken; (conclude) folgern (**from** aus); (Sewing) kräuseln; ~ **speed** schneller werden ● vi sich versammeln; ⟨storm:⟩ sich zusammenziehen. ~**ing** n **family** ~**ing** Familientreffen nt

gaudy /'gɔ:dɪ/ a (-ier, -iest) knallig

gauge /geɪdʒ/ n Stärke f; (Rail) Spurweite f; (device) Meßinstrument nt ● vt messen; (estimate) schätzen

gaunt /gɔ:nt/ a hager

gauntlet /'gɔ:ntlɪt/ n **run the** ~ Spießruten laufen

gauze /gɔ:z/ n Gaze f

gave /geɪv/ see give

gawky /'gɔ:kɪ/ a (-ier, -iest) schlaksig

gawp /gɔ:p/ vi (fam) glotzen; ~ **at** anglotzen

gay /geɪ/ a (-er, -est) fröhlich; (fam) homosexuell, (fam) schwul

gaze /geɪz/ n [langer] Blick m ● vi sehen; ~ **at** ansehen

gazelle /gə'zel/ n Gazelle f

GB abbr of **Great Britain**

gear /gɪə(r)/ n Ausrüstung f; (Techn) Getriebe nt; (Auto) Gang m; **in** ~ mit eingelegtem Gang; **change** ~ schalten ● vt anpassen (**to** dat)

gear: ~**box** n (Auto) Getriebe nt. ~**lever** n, (Amer) ~**-shift** n Schalthebel m

geese /gi:s/ see goose

geezer /'gi:zə(r)/ n (sl) Typ m

gel /dʒel/ n Gel nt

gelatine /'dʒelətɪn/ n Gelatine f

gelignite /'dʒelɪgnaɪt/ n Gelatinedynamit nt

gem /dʒem/ n Juwel nt

Gemini /'dʒemɪnaɪ/ n (Astr) Zwillinge pl

gender /'dʒendə(r)/ n (Gram) Geschlecht nt

gene /dʒiːn/ n Gen nt

genealogy /dʒiːnɪˈælədʒɪ/ n Genealogie f

general /ˈdʒenrəl/ a allgemein ● n General m; **in ∼** im allgemeinen. **∼ e'lection** n allgemeine Wahlen pl

generaliz|ation /dʒenrəlaɪˈzeɪʃn/ n Verallgemeinerung f. **∼e** /ˈdʒenrəlaɪz/ vi verallgemeinern

generally /ˈdʒenrəlɪ/ adv im allgemeinen

general prac'titioner n praktischer Arzt m

generate /ˈdʒenəreɪt/ vt erzeugen

generation /dʒenəˈreɪʃn/ n Generation f

generator /ˈdʒenəreɪtə(r)/ n Generator m

generic /dʒɪˈnerɪk/ a **∼ term** Oberbegriff m

generosity /dʒenəˈrɒsɪtɪ/ n Großzügigkeit f

generous /ˈdʒenərəs/ a, **-ly** adv großzügig

genetic /dʒɪˈnetɪk/ a genetisch. **∼ engineering** n Gentechnologie f. **∼s** n Genetik f

Geneva /dʒɪˈniːvə/ n Genf nt

genial /ˈdʒiːnɪəl/ a, **-ly** adv freundlich

genitals /ˈdʒenɪtlz/ pl [äußere] Geschlechtsteile pl

genitive /ˈdʒenɪtɪv/ a & n **∼ [case]** Genitiv m

genius /ˈdʒiːnɪəs/ n (pl **-uses**) Genie nt; (quality) Genialität f

genocide /ˈdʒenəsaɪd/ n Völkermord m

genre /ˈʒɑːrə/ n Gattung f, Genre nt

gent /dʒent/ n (fam) Herr m; **the ∼s** sg die Herrentoilette f

genteel /dʒenˈtiːl/ a vornehm

gentle /ˈdʒentl/ a (**-r, -st**) sanft

gentleman /ˈdʒentlmən/ n Herr m; (well-mannered) Gentleman m

gent|leness /ˈdʒentlnɪs/ n Sanftheit f. **∼ly** adv sanft

genuine /ˈdʒenjuɪn/ a echt; (sincere) aufrichtig. **∼ly** adv (honestly) ehrlich

genus /ˈdʒiːnəs/ n (Biol) Gattung f

geograph|ical /dʒɪəˈgræfɪkl/ a, **-ly** adv geographisch. **∼y** /dʒɪˈɒgrəfɪ/ n Geographie f, Erdkunde f

geological /dʒɪəˈlɒdʒɪkl/ a, **-ly** adv geologisch

geolog|ist /dʒɪˈɒlədʒɪst/ n Geologe m/ -gin f. **∼y** n Geologie f

geometr|ic(al) /dʒɪəˈmetrɪk(l)/ a geometrisch. **∼y** /dʒɪˈɒmɪtrɪ/ n Geometrie f

geranium /dʒəˈreɪnɪəm/ n Geranie f

geriatric /dʒerɪˈætrɪk/ a geriatrisch ● n geriatrischer Patient m. **∼s** n Geriatrie f

germ /dʒɜːm/ n Keim m; **∼s** pl (fam) Bazillen pl

German /ˈdʒɜːmən/ a deutsch ● n (person) Deutsche(r) m/f; (Lang) Deutsch nt; **in ∼** auf deutsch; **into ∼** ins Deutsche

Germanic /dʒəˈmænɪk/ a germanisch

German: ∼ 'measles n Röteln pl. **∼ 'shepherd [dog]** n [deutscher] Schäferhund m

Germany /ˈdʒɜːmənɪ/ n Deutschland nt

germinate /ˈdʒɜːmɪneɪt/ vi keimen

gesticulate /dʒeˈstɪkjʊleɪt/ vi gestikulieren

gesture /ˈdʒestʃə(r)/ n Geste f

get /get/ v (pt/pp got, pp Amer also gotten, pres p getting) ● vt bekommen, (fam) kriegen; (procure) besorgen; (buy) kaufen; (fetch) holen; (take) bringen; (on telephone) erreichen; (fam: understand) kapieren; machen ⟨meal⟩; **∼ s.o. to do sth** jdn dazu bringen, etw zu tun ● vi (become) werden; **∼ to** kommen zu/ nach ⟨town⟩; (reach) erreichen; **∼ dressed** sich anziehen; **∼ married** heiraten. **∼ at** vt herankommen an (+ acc); **what are you ∼ting at?** worauf willst du hinaus? **∼ away** vi (leave) wegkommen; (escape) entkommen. **∼ back** vi zurückkommen ● vt (recover) zurückbekommen; **∼ one's own back** sich revanchieren. **∼ by** vi vorbeikommen; (manage) sein Auskommen haben. **∼ down** vi heruntersteigen; **∼ down to** sich [heran]machen an (+ acc) ● vt (depress) deprimieren. **∼ in** vi einsteigen ● vt (fetch) hereinholen. **∼ off** vi (dismount) absteigen; (from bus) aussteigen; (leave) wegkommen; (Jur) freigesprochen werden ● vt (remove) abbekommen. **∼ on** vi (mount) aufsteigen; (to bus) einsteigen; (be on good terms) auskommen (with mit); (make progress) Fortschritte machen; **how are you ∼ting on?** wie geht's? **∼ out** vi herauskommen; (of car) aussteigen; **∼ out of** (avoid doing) sich drücken um ● *vt* herausholen; herausbekommen ⟨*cork, stain*⟩. **~ over** *vi* hinübersteigen ● *vt* ⟨*fig*⟩ hinwegkommen über (+ *acc*). **~ round** *vi* herumkommen; ⟨*avoid*⟩ umgehen; **I never ~ round to it** ich komme nie dazu ● *vt* herumkriegen. **~ through** *vi* durchkommen. **~ up** *vi* aufstehen

get: **~away** *n* Flucht *f*. **~-up** *n* Aufmachung *f*

geyser /'giːzə(r)/ *n* Durchlauferhitzer *m*; (*Geol*) Geysir *m*

ghastly /'gɑːstlɪ/ *a* (**-ier, -iest**) gräßlich; (*pale*) blaß

gherkin /'gɜːkɪn/ *n* Essiggurke *f*

ghetto /'getəʊ/ *n* Getto *nt*

ghost /gəʊst/ *n* Geist *m*, Gespenst *nt*. **~ly** *a* geisterhaft

ghoulish /'guːlɪʃ/ *a* makaber

giant /'dʒaɪənt/ *n* Riese *m* ● *a* riesig

gibberish /'dʒɪbərɪʃ/ *n* Kauderwelsch *nt*

gibe /dʒaɪb/ *n* spöttische Bemerkung *f* ● *vi* spotten (**at** über + *acc*)

giblets /'dʒɪblɪts/ *npl* Geflügelklein *nt*

giddiness /'gɪdɪnɪs/ *n* Schwindel *m*

giddy /'gɪdɪ/ *a* (**-ier, -iest**) schwindlig; **I feel ~** mir ist schwindlig

gift /gɪft/ *n* Geschenk *nt*; (*to charity*) Gabe *f*; (*talent*) Begabung *f*. **~ed** /-ɪd/ *a* begabt. **~-wrap** *vt* als Geschenk einpacken

gig /gɪg/ *n* (*fam, Mus*) Gig *m*

gigantic /dʒaɪ'gæntɪk/ *a* riesig, riesengroß

giggle /'gɪgl/ *n* Kichern *nt* ● *vi* kichern

gild /gɪld/ *vt* vergolden

gills /gɪlz/ *npl* Kiemen *pl*

gilt /gɪlt/ *a* vergoldet ● *n* Vergoldung *f*. **~-edged** *a* (*Comm*) mündelsicher

gimmick /'gɪmɪk/ *n* Trick *m*

gin /dʒɪn/ *n* Gin *m*

ginger /'dʒɪndʒə(r)/ *a* rotblond; ⟨*cat*⟩ rot ● *n* Ingwer *m*. **~bread** *n* Pfefferkuchen *m*

gingerly /'dʒɪndʒəlɪ/ *adv* vorsichtig

gipsy /'dʒɪpsɪ/ *n* = **gypsy**

giraffe /dʒɪ'rɑːf/ *n* Giraffe *f*

girder /'gɜːdə(r)/ *n* (*Techn*) Träger *m*

girdle /'gɜːdl/ *n* Bindegürtel *m*; (*corset*) Hüfthalter *m*

girl /gɜːl/ *n* Mädchen *nt*; (*young woman*) junge Frau *f*. **~friend** *n* Freundin *f*. **~ish** *a*, **-ly** *adv* mädchenhaft

giro /'dʒaɪərəʊ/ *n* Giro *nt*; (*cheque*) Postscheck *m*

girth /gɜːθ/ *n* Umfang *m*; (*for horse*) Bauchgurt *m*

gist /dʒɪst/ *n* **the ~** das Wesentliche

give /gɪv/ *n* Elastizität *f* ● *v* (*pt* **gave**, *pp* **given**) ● *vt* geben/(*as present*) schenken (**to** *dat*); (*donate*) spenden; ⟨*lecture*⟩ halten; ⟨*one's name*⟩ angeben ● *vi* geben; (*yield*) nachgeben. **~ away** *vt* verschenken; (*betray*) verraten; (*distribute*) verteilen; **~ away the bride** ≈ Brautführer sein. **~ back** *vt* zurückgeben. **~ in** *vt* einreichen ● *vi* (*yield*) nachgeben. **~ off** *vt* abgeben. **~ up** *vt*/*i* aufgeben; **~ oneself up** sich stellen. **~ way** *vi* nachgeben; (*Auto*) die Vorfahrt beachten

given /'gɪvn/ *see* **give** ● *a* **~ name** Vorname *m*

glacier /'glæsɪə(r)/ *n* Gletscher *m*

glad /glæd/ *a* froh (**of** über + *acc*). **~den** /'glædn/ *vt* erfreuen

glade /gleɪd/ *n* Lichtung *f*

gladly /'glædlɪ/ *adv* gern[e]

glamorous /'glæmərəs/ *a* glanzvoll; ⟨*film star*⟩ glamourös

glamour /'glæmə(r)/ *n* [betörender] Glanz *m*

glance /glɑːns/ *n* [flüchtiger] Blick *m* ● *vi* **~ at** einen Blick werfen auf (+ *acc*). **~ up** *vi* aufblicken

gland /glænd/ *n* Drüse *f*

glandular /'glændjʊlə(r)/ *a* Drüsen-

glare /gleə(r)/ *n* grelles Licht *nt*; (*look*) ärgerlicher Blick *m* ● *vi* **~ at** böse ansehen

glaring /'gleərɪŋ/ *a* grell; ⟨*mistake*⟩ kraß

glass /glɑːs/ *n* Glas *nt*; (*mirror*) Spiegel *m*; **~es** *pl* (*spectacles*) Brille *f*. **~y** *a* glasig

glaze /gleɪz/ *n* Glasur *f* ● *vt* verglasen; (*Culin, Pottery*) glasieren

glazier /'gleɪzɪə(r)/ *n* Glaser *m*

gleam /gliːm/ *n* Schein *m* ● *vi* glänzen

glean /gliːn/ *vi* Ähren lesen ● *vt* (*learn*) erfahren

glee /gliː/ *n* Frohlocken *nt*. **~ful** *a*, **-ly** *adv* frohlockend

glen /glen/ *n* [enges] Tal *nt*

glib /glɪb/ *a*, **-ly** *adv* (*pej*) gewandt

glid|e /glaɪd/ *vi* gleiten; (*through the air*) schweben. **~er** *n* Segelflugzeug *nt*. **~ing** *n* Segelfliegen *nt*

glimmer /'glɪmə(r)/ *n* Glimmen *nt* ● *vi* glimmen

glimpse /glɪmps/ *n* **catch a ~ of** flüchtig sehen ● *vt* flüchtig sehen

glint /glɪnt/ n Blitzen nt ● vi blitzen

glisten /'glɪsn/ vi glitzern

glitter /'glɪtə(r)/ vi glitzern

gloat /gləʊt/ vi schadenfroh sein; ~ over sich weiden an (+ dat)

global /'gləʊbl/ a, **-ly** adv global

globe /gləʊb/ n Kugel f; (map) Globus m

gloom /gluːm/ n Düsterkeit f; (fig) Pessimismus m

gloomy /'gluːmɪ/ a (-ier, -iest), **-ily** adv düster; (fig) pessimistisch

glorif|y /'glɔːrɪfaɪ/ vt (pt/pp **-ied**) verherrlichen; **a ~ied waitress** eine bessere Kellnerin f

glorious /'glɔːrɪəs/ a herrlich; ⟨deed, hero⟩ glorreich

glory /'glɔːrɪ/ n Ruhm m; (splendour) Pracht f ● vi ~ **in** genießen

gloss /glɒs/ n Glanz m ● a Glanz- ● vi ~ **over** beschönigen

glossary /'glɒsərɪ/ n Glossar nt

glossy /'glɒsɪ/ a (-ier, -iest) glänzend

glove /glʌv/ n Handschuh m. ~ **compartment** n (Auto) Handschuhfach nt

glow /gləʊ/ n Glut f; (of candle) Schein m ● vi glühen; ⟨candle:⟩ scheinen. ~**ing** a glühend; ⟨account⟩ begeistert

'glow-worm n Glühwürmchen nt

glucose /'gluːkəʊs/ n Traubenzucker m, Glukose f

glue /gluː/ n Klebstoff m ● vt (pres p **gluing**) kleben (**to** an + acc)

glum /glʌm/ a (glummer, glummest), **-ly** adv niedergeschlagen

glut /glʌt/ n Überfluß m (**of** an + dat); ~ **of fruit** Obstschwemme f

glutton /'glʌtn/ n Vielfraß m. ~**ous** /-əs/ a gefräßig. ~**y** n Gefräßigkeit f

gnarled /nɑːld/ a knorrig; ⟨hands⟩ knotig

gnash /næʃ/ vt ~ **one's teeth** mit den Zähnen knirschen

gnat /næt/ n Mücke f

gnaw /nɔː/ vt/i nagen (**at** an + dat)

gnome /nəʊm/ n Gnom m

go /gəʊ/ n (pl **goes**) Energie f; (attempt) Versuch m; **on the go** auf Trab; **at one go** auf einmal; **it's your go** du bist dran; **make a go of it** Erfolg haben ● vi (pt **went**, pp **gone**) gehen; (in vehicle) fahren; (leave) weggehen; (on journey) abfahren; ⟨time:⟩ vergehen; (vanish) verschwinden; (fail) versagen; (become) werden; (belong) kommen; **go swimming/shopping** schwimmen/

einkaufen gehen; **where are you going?** wo gehst du hin? **it's all gone** es ist nichts mehr übrig; **I am not going to** ich werde es nicht tun; **'to go'** (Amer) 'zum Mitnehmen'. **go away** vi weggehen/-fahren; **go back** vi zurückgehen/-fahren. **go by** vi vorbeigehen/-fahren; ⟨time:⟩ vergehen. **go down** vi hinuntergehen/-fahren; ⟨sun, ship:⟩ untergehen; ⟨prices:⟩ fallen; ⟨temperature, swelling:⟩ zurückgehen. **go for** vt holen; (fam: attack) losgehen auf (+ acc). **go in** vi hineingehen/-fahren; **go in for** teilnehmen an (+ dat) ⟨competition⟩; (take up) sich verlegen auf (+ acc). **go off** vi weggehen/-fahren; ⟨alarm:⟩ klingeln; ⟨gun, bomb:⟩ losgehen; (go bad) schlecht werden; **go off well** gut verlaufen. **go on** vi weitergehen/-fahren; (continue) weitermachen; (talking) fortfahren; (happen) vorgehen; **go on at** (fam) herumnörgeln an (+ dat). **go out** vi ausgehen; (leave) hinausgehen/-fahren. **go over** vi hinübergehen/-fahren ● vt (check) durchgehen. **go round** vi herumgehen/-fahren; (visit) vorbeigehen; (turn) sich drehen; (be enough) reichen. **go through** vi durchgehen/-fahren ● vt (suffer) durchmachen; (check) durchgehen. **go under** vi untergehen; (fail) scheitern. **go up** vi hinaufgehen/-fahren; ⟨lift:⟩ hochfahren; ⟨prices:⟩ steigen. **go without** vt verzichten auf (+ acc) ● vi darauf verzichten

goad /gəʊd/ vt anstacheln (**into** zu); (taunt) reizen

'go-ahead a fortschrittlich; (enterprising) unternehmend ● n (fig) grünes Licht nt

goal /gəʊl/ n Ziel nt; (Sport) Tor nt. ~**keeper** n Torwart m. ~**-post** n Torpfosten m

goat /gəʊt/ n Ziege f

gobble /'gɒbl/ vt hinunterschlingen

'go-between n Vermittler(in) m(f)

goblet /'gɒblɪt/ n Pokal m; (glass) Kelchglas m

goblin /'gɒblɪn/ n Kobold m

God, god /gɒd/ n Gott m

god: ~**child** n Patenkind nt. ~**daughter** n Patentochter f. ~**dess** n Göttin f. ~**father** n Pate m. **G~-forsaken** a gottverlassen. ~**mother** n Patin f. ~**parents** npl Paten pl. ~**send** n Segen m. ~**son** n Patensohn m

goggle /'gɒgl/ vi (fam) ~ at anglotzen. ~s npl Schutzbrille f

going /'gəʊɪŋ/ a ⟨price, rate⟩ gängig; ⟨concern⟩ gutgehend ● n it is hard ~ es ist schwierig; while the ~ is good solange es noch geht. ~s-'on npl [seltsame] Vorgänge pl

gold /gəʊld/ n Gold nt ● a golden

golden /'gəʊldn/ a golden. ~ 'handshake n hohe Abfindungssumme f. ~ 'wedding n goldene Hochzeit f

gold: ~fish n inv Goldfisch m. ~mine n Goldgrube f. ~-plated a vergoldet. ~smith n Goldschmied m

golf /gɒlf/ n Golf m

golf: ~-club n Golfklub m; (implement) Golfschläger m. ~-course n Golfplatz m. ~er m Golfspieler(in) m(f)

gondola /'gɒndələ/ n Gondel f. ~lier /-'lɪə(r)/ n Gondoliere m

gone /gɒn/ see go

gong /gɒŋ/ n Gong m

good /gʊd/ a (better, best) gut; (well-behaved) brav, artig; ~ at gut in (+ dat); a ~ deal ziemlich viel; as ~ as so gut wie; (almost) fast; ~ morning/evening guten Morgen/Abend; ~ afternoon guten Tag; ~ night gute Nacht ● n the ~ das Gute; for ~ für immer; do ~ Gutes tun; do s.o. ~ jdm guttun; it's no ~ es ist nutzlos; (hopeless) da ist nichts zu machen; be up to no ~ nichts Gutes im Schilde führen

goodbye /gʊd'baɪ/ int auf Wiedersehen; (Teleph, Radio) auf Wiederhören

good: ~-for-nothing a nichtsnutzig ● n Taugenichts m. G~ 'Friday n Karfreitag m. ~-'looking a gutaussehend. ~-'natured a gutmütig

goodness /'gʊdnɪs/ n Güte f; my ~! du meine Güte! thank ~! Gott sei Dank!

goods /gʊdz/ npl Waren pl. ~ train n Güterzug m

good'will n Wohlwollen nt; (Comm) Goodwill m

goody /'gʊdɪ/ n (fam) Gute(r) m/f. ~-goody n Musterkind nt

gooey /'guːɪ/ a (fam) klebrig

goof /guːf/ vi (fam) einen Schnitzer machen

goose /guːs/ n (pl geese) Gans f

gooseberry /'gʊzbərɪ/ n Stachelbeere f

goose /guːs/: ~-flesh n, ~pimples npl Gänsehaut f

gore¹ /gɔː(r)/ n Blut nt

gore² vt mit den Hörnern aufspießen

gorge /gɔːdʒ/ n (Geog) Schlucht f ● vt ~ oneself sich vollessen

gorgeous /'gɔːdʒəs/ a prachtvoll; (fam) herrlich

gorilla /gə'rɪlə/ n Gorilla m

gormless /'gɔːmlɪs/ a (fam) doof

gorse /gɔːs/ n inv Stechginster m

gory /'gɔːrɪ/ a (-ier, -iest) blutig; ⟨story⟩ blutrünstig

gosh /gɒʃ/ int (fam) Mensch!

go-'slow n Bummelstreik m

gospel /'gɒspl/ n Evangelium nt

gossip /'gɒsɪp/ n Klatsch m; (person) Klatschbase f ● vi klatschen. ~y a geschwätzig

got /gɒt/ see get; have ~ haben; have ~ to müssen; have ~ to do sth etw tun müssen

Gothic /'gɒθɪk/ a gotisch

gotten /'gɒtn/ see get

gouge /gaʊdʒ/ vt ~ out aushöhlen

goulash /'guːlæʃ/ n Gulasch nt

gourmet /'gʊəmeɪ/ n Feinschmecker m

gout /gaʊt/ n Gicht f

govern /'gʌvn/ vt/i regieren; (determine) bestimmen. ~ess n Gouvernante f

government /'gʌvnmənt/ n Regierung f. ~al /-'mentl/ a Regierungs-

governor /'gʌvənə(r)/ n Gouverneur m; (on board) Vorstandsmitglied nt; (of prison) Direktor m; (fam: boss) Chef m

gown /gaʊn/ n [elegantes] Kleid nt; (Univ, Jur) Talar m

GP abbr of general practitioner

grab /græb/ vt (pt/pp grabbed) ergreifen; ~ [hold of] packen

grace /greɪs/ n Anmut f; (before meal) Tischgebet nt; (Relig) Gnade f; with good ~ mit Anstand; say ~ [vor dem Essen] beten; three days' ~ drei Tage Frist. ~ful a, -ly adv anmutig

gracious /'greɪʃəs/ a gnädig; (elegant) vornehm

grade /greɪd/ n Stufe f; (Comm) Güteklasse f; (Sch) Note f; (Amer, Sch: class) Klasse f; (Amer) = gradient ● vt einstufen; (Comm) sortieren. ~ crossing n (Amer) Bahnübergang m

gradient /'greɪdɪənt/ n Steigung f; (downward) Gefälle nt

gradual /'grædʒʊəl/ a, -ly adv allmählich

graduate¹ /'grædʒʊət/ n Akademiker(in) m(f)

graduate² /'grædʒʊeɪt/ vi (Univ) sein Examen machen. ~d a abgestuft; ⟨container⟩ mit Maßeinteilung

graffiti /grə'fi:ti:/ npl Graffiti pl

graft /grɑ:ft/ n (Bot) Pfropfreis nt; (Med) Transplantat nt; (fam: hard work) Plackerei f ● vt (Bot) aufpfropfen; (Med) übertragen

grain /greɪn/ n (sand, salt, rice) Korn nt; (cereals) Getreide nt; (in wood) Maserung f; **against the** ~ (fig) gegen den Strich

gram /græm/ n Gramm nt

grammar /'græmə(r)/ n Grammatik f. ~ **school** n ≈ Gymnasium nt

grammatical /grə'mætɪkl/ a, -ly adv grammatisch

granary /'grænərɪ/ n Getreidespeicher m

grand /grænd/ a (-er, -est) großartig

grandad /'grændæd/ n (fam) Opa m

'grandchild n Enkelkind nt

'granddaughter n Enkelin f

grandeur /'grændʒə(r)/ n Pracht f

'grandfather n Großvater m. ~ **clock** n Standuhr f

grandiose /'grændɪəʊs/ a grandios

grand: ~**mother** n Großmutter f. ~**parents** npl Großeltern pl. ~ **pi'ano** n Flügel m. ~**son** n Enkel m. ~**stand** n Tribüne f

granite /'grænɪt/ n Granit m

granny /'grænɪ/ n (fam) Oma f

grant /grɑ:nt/ n Subvention f; (Univ) Studienbeihilfe f ● vt gewähren; (admit) zugeben; **take sth for** ~**ed** etw als selbstverständlich hinnehmen

granular /'grænjʊlə(r)/ a körnig

granulated /'grænjʊleɪtɪd/ a ~ **sugar** Kristallzucker m

granule /'grænju:l/ n Körnchen nt

grape /greɪp/ n [Wein]traube f; **bunch of** ~**s** [ganze] Weintraube f

grapefruit /'greɪp-/ n inv Grapefruit f, Pampelmuse f

graph /grɑ:f/ n Kurvendiagramm nt

graphic /'græfɪk/ a, -ally adv grafisch; (vivid) anschaulich. ~**s** n (design) grafische Gestaltung f

'graph paper n Millimeterpapier nt

grapple /'græpl/ vi ringen

grasp /grɑ:sp/ n Griff m ● vt ergreifen; (understand) begreifen. ~**ing** a habgierig

grass /grɑ:s/ n Gras nt; (lawn) Rasen m; **at the** ~ **roots** an der Basis.

~**hopper** n Heuschrecke f. ~**land** n Weideland nt

grassy /'grɑ:sɪ/ a grasig

grate¹ /greɪt/ n Feuerrost m; (hearth) Kamin m

grate² vt (Culin) reiben; ~ **one's teeth** mit den Zähnen knirschen

grateful /'greɪtfl/ a, -ly adv dankbar (**to** dat)

grater /'greɪtə(r)/ n (Culin) Reibe f

gratify /'grætɪfaɪ/ vt (pt/pp -ied) befriedigen. ~**ing** a erfreulich

grating /'greɪtɪŋ/ n Gitter nt

gratis /'grɑ:tɪs/ adv gratis

gratitude /'grætɪtju:d/ n Dankbarkeit f

gratuitous /grə'tju:ɪtəs/ a (uncalled for) überflüssig

gratuity /grə'tju:ətɪ/ n (tip) Trinkgeld nt

grave¹ /greɪv/ a (-r, -st), -ly adv ernst; ~**ly ill** schwer krank

grave² n Grab nt. ~-**digger** n Totengräber m

gravel /'grævl/ n Kies m

grave: ~**stone** n Grabstein m. ~**yard** n Friedhof m

gravitate /'grævɪteɪt/ vi gravitieren

gravity /'grævətɪ/ n Ernst m; (force) Schwerkraft f

gravy /'greɪvɪ/ n [Braten]soße f

gray /greɪ/ a (Amer) = **grey**

graze¹ /greɪz/ vi ⟨animal⟩ weiden

graze² n Schürfwunde f ● vt ⟨car⟩ streifen; ⟨knee⟩ aufschürfen

grease /gri:s/ n Fett nt; (lubricant) Schmierfett nt ● vt einfetten; (lubricate) schmieren. ~-**proof 'paper** n Pergamentpapier nt

greasy /'gri:sɪ/ a (-ier, -iest) fettig

great /greɪt/ a (-er, -est) groß; (fam: marvellous) großartig

great: ~-'**aunt** n Großtante f. **G**~ '**Britain** n Großbritannien nt. ~-'**grandchildren** npl Urenkel pl. ~-'**grandfather** n Urgroßvater m. ~-'**grandmother** n Urgroßmutter f

great|ly /'greɪtlɪ/ adv sehr. ~**ness** n Größe f

great-'uncle n Großonkel m

Greece /gri:s/ n Griechenland nt

greed /gri:d/ n [Hab]gier f

greedy /'gri:dɪ/ a (-ier, -iest), -ily adv gierig; **don't be**~ sei nicht so unbescheiden

Greek /gri:k/ a griechisch ● n Grieche m/Griechin f; (Lang) Griechisch nt

green /gri:n/ a (-er, -est) grün; (fig)
unerfahren ● n Grün nt; (grass)
Wiese f; ~s pl Kohl m; **the G~s** pl
(Pol) die Grünen pl
greenery /'gri:nəri/ n Grün nt
'greenfly n Blattlaus f
greengage /'gri:ngeɪdʒ/ n Reneklode
f
green: ~**grocer** n Obst- und Gemüse-
händler m. ~**house** n Gewächshaus
nt. ~**house effect** n Treibhausef-
fekt m
Greenland /'gri:nlənd/ n Grönland nt
greet /gri:t/ vt grüßen; (welcome)
begrüßen. ~**ing** n Gruß m; (welcome) Begrüßung f. ~**ings card** n
Glückwunschkarte f
gregarious /grɪ'geərɪəs/ a gesellig
grenade /grɪ'neɪd/ n Granate f
grew /gru:/ see **grow**
grey /greɪ/ a (-er, -est) grau ● n Grau
nt ● vi grau werden. ~**hound** n
Windhund m
grid /grɪd/ n Gitter nt; (on map) Git-
ternetz nt; (Electr) Überlandlei-
tungsnetz nt
grief /gri:f/ n Trauer f; **come to** ~
scheitern
grievance /'gri:vəns/ n Beschwerde f
grieve /gri:v/ vt betrüben ● vi
trauern (**for** um)
grievous /'gri:vəs/ a, -**ly** adv schwer
grill /grɪl/ n Gitter nt; (Culin) Grill m;
mixed ~ Gemischtes nt vom Grill
● vt/i grillen; (interrogate) [streng]
verhören
grille /grɪl/ n Gitter nt
grim /grɪm/ a (grimmer, grimmest),
-**ly** adv ernst; ⟨determination⟩
verbissen
grimace /grɪ'meɪs/ n Grimasse f ● vi
Grimassen schneiden
grime /graɪm/ n Schmutz m
grimy /'graɪmɪ/ a (-ier, -iest)
schmutzig
grin /grɪn/ n Grinsen nt ● vi (pt/pp
grinned) grinsen
grind /graɪnd/ n (fam: hard work)
Plackerei f ● vt (pt/pp ground) mahlen; (smooth, sharpen) schleifen;
(Amer: mince) durchdrehen; ~
one's teeth mit den Zähnen
knirschen
grip /grɪp/ n Griff m; (bag) Reise-
tasche f ● vt (pt/pp gripped) ergreifen; (hold) festhalten; fesseln
⟨interest⟩
gripe /graɪp/ vi (sl: grumble)
meckern

gripping /'grɪpɪŋ/ a fesselnd
grisly /'grɪzlɪ/ a (-ier, -iest) grausig
gristle /'grɪsl/ n Knorpel m
grit /grɪt/ n [grober] Sand m; (for
roads) Streugut nt; (courage) Mut m
● vt (pt/pp gritted) streuen ⟨road⟩;
~ **one's teeth** die Zähne
zusammenbeißen
grizzle /'grɪzl/ vi quengeln
groan /grəʊn/ n Stöhnen nt ● vi
stöhnen
grocer /'grəʊsə(r)/ n Lebensmittel-
händler m; ~**'s [shop]** Lebensmittel-
geschäft nt. ~**ies** npl Lebensmittel
pl
groggy /'grɒgɪ/ a schwach;
(unsteady) wackelig [auf den
Beinen]
groin /grɔɪn/ n (Anat) Leiste f
groom /gru:m/ n Bräutigam m; (for
horse) Pferdepfleger(in) m(f) ● vt
striegeln ⟨horse⟩
groove /gru:v/ n Rille f
grope /grəʊp/ vi tasten (**for** nach)
gross /grəʊs/ a (-er, -est) fett; (coarse)
derb; (glaring) grob; (Comm) brutto;
⟨salary, weight⟩ Brutto- ● n inv Gros
nt. ~**ly** adv (very) sehr
grotesque /grəʊ'tesk/ a, -**ly** adv
grotesk
grotto /'grɒtəʊ/ n (pl -es) Grotte f
grotty /'grɒtɪ/ a (fam) mies
ground[1] /graʊnd/ see **grind**
ground[2] n Boden m; (terrain)
Gelände nt; (reason) Grund m;
(Amer, Electr) Erde f; ~s pl (park)
Anlagen pl; (of coffee) Satz m ● vi
⟨ship:⟩ auflaufen ● vt aus dem Verkehr ziehen ⟨aircraft⟩; (Amer,
Electr) erden
ground: ~ **floor** n Erdgeschoß nt.
~**ing** n Grundlage f. ~**less** a grundlos. ~ **'meat** n Hackfleisch nt.
~**sheet** n Bodenplane f. ~**work** n
Vorarbeiten pl
group /gru:p/ n Gruppe f ● vt gruppieren ● vi sich gruppieren
grouse[1] /graʊs/ n inv schottisches
Moorschneehuhn nt
grouse[2] vi (fam) meckern
grovel /'grɒvl/ vi (pt/pp grovelled)
kriechen. ~**ling** a kriecherisch
grow /grəʊ/ v (pt grew, pp grown) ● vi
wachsen; (become) werden; (increase) zunehmen ● vt anbauen; ~
one's hair sich ⟨dat⟩ die Haare wachsen lassen. ~ **up** vi aufwachsen;
⟨town:⟩ entstehen

growl /graʊl/ n Knurren nt ● vi knurren

grown /grəʊn/ see **grow**. ~**-up** a erwachsen ● n Erwachsene(r) m/f

growth /grəʊθ/ n Wachstum nt; (increase) Zunahme f; (Med) Gewächs nt

grub /grʌb/ n (larva) Made f; (fam: food) Essen nt

grubby /'grʌbɪ/ a (-ier, -iest) schmuddelig

grudge /grʌdʒ/ n Groll m; **bear s.o. a** ~**e** einen Groll gegen jdn hegen ● vt ~**e s.o. sth** jdm etw mißgönnen. ~**ing** a, **-ly** adv widerwillig

gruelling /'gru:əlɪŋ/ a strapaziös

gruesome /'gru:səm/ a grausig

gruff /grʌf/ a, **-ly** adv barsch

grumble /'grʌmbl/ vi schimpfen (**at** mit)

grumpy /'grʌmpɪ/ a (-ier, -iest) griesgrämig

grunt /grʌnt/ n Grunzen nt ● vi grunzen

guarant|ee /gærən'ti:/ n Garantie f; (document) Garantieschein m ● vt garantieren; garantieren für ⟨quality, success⟩; **be** ~**eed** ⟨product:⟩ Garantie haben. ~**or** n Bürge m

guard /gɑːd/ n Wache f; (security) Wächter m; (on train) ≈ Zugführer m; (Techn) Schutz m; **be on** ~ Wache stehen; **on one's** ~ auf der Hut ● vt bewachen; (protect) schützen ● vi ~ **against** sich hüten vor (+ dat). ~**-dog** n Wachhund m

guarded /'gɑːdɪd/ a vorsichtig

guardian /'gɑːdɪən/ n Vormund m

guerrilla /gə'rɪlə/ n Guerillakämpfer m. ~ **warfare** n Partisanenkrieg m

guess /ges/ n Vermutung f ● vt erraten ● vi raten; (Amer: believe) glauben. ~**work** n Vermutung f

guest /gest/ n Gast m. ~**-house** n Pension f

guffaw /gʌ'fɔː/ n derbes Lachen nt ● vi derb lachen

guidance /'gaɪdəns/ n Führung f, Leitung f; (advice) Beratung f

guide /gaɪd/ n Führer(in) m(f); (book) Führer m; **[Girl] G**~ Pfadfinderin f ● vt führen, leiten. ~**book** n Führer m

guided /'gaɪdɪd/ a ~ **missile** Fernlenkgeschoß nt; ~ **tour** Führung f

guide: ~**-dog** n Blindenhund m. ~**lines** npl Richtlinien pl

guild /gɪld/ n Gilde f, Zunft f

guile /gaɪl/ n Arglist f

guillotine /'gɪləti:n/ n Guillotine f; (for paper) Papierschneidemaschine f

guilt /gɪlt/ n Schuld f. ~**ily** adv schuldbewußt

guilty /'gɪltɪ/ a (-ier, -iest) a schuldig (**of** gen); ⟨look⟩ schuldbewußt; ⟨conscience⟩ schlecht

guinea-pig /'gɪnɪ-/ n Meerschweinchen nt; (person) Versuchskaninchen nt

guise /gaɪz/ n **in the** ~ **of** in Gestalt (+ gen)

guitar /gɪ'tɑː(r)/ n Gitarre f. ~**ist** n Gitarrist(in) m(f)

gulf /gʌlf/ n (Geog) Golf m; (fig) Kluft f

gull /gʌl/ n Möwe f

gullet /'gʌlɪt/ n Speiseröhre f; (throat) Kehle f

gullible /'gʌlɪbl/ a leichtgläubig

gully /'gʌlɪ/ n Schlucht f; (drain) Rinne f

gulp /gʌlp/ n Schluck m ● vi schlucken ● vt ~ **down** hinunterschlucken

gum¹ /gʌm/ n & **-s** pl (Anat) Zahnfleisch nt

gum² n Gummi[harz] nt; (glue) Klebstoff m; (chewing-gum) Kaugummi m ● vt (pt/pp gummed) kleben (**to** an + acc). ~**boot** n Gummistiefel m

gummed /gʌmd/ see **gum²** a ⟨label⟩ gummiert

gumption /'gʌmpʃn/ n (fam) Grips m

gun /gʌn/ n Schußwaffe f; (pistol) Pistole f; (rifle) Gewehr nt; (cannon) Geschütz nt ● vt (pt/pp gunned) ~ **down** niederschießen

gun: ~**fire** n Geschützfeuer nt. ~**man** bewaffneter Bandit m

gunner /'gʌnə(r)/ n Artillerist m

gun: ~**powder** n Schießpulver nt. ~**shot** n Schuß m

gurgle /'gɜːgl/ vi gluckern; (of baby) glucksen

gush /gʌʃ/ vi strömen; (enthuse) schwärmen (**over** von). ~ **out** vi herausströmen

gusset /'gʌsɪt/ n Zwickel m

gust /gʌst/ n (of wind) Windstoß m; (Naut) Bö f

gusto /'gʌstəʊ/ n **with** ~ mit Schwung

gusty /'gʌstɪ/ a böig

gut /gʌt/ n Darm m; ~**s** pl Eingeweide pl; (fam: courage) Schneid m ● vt (pt/pp gutted) (Culin) ausnehmen; ~**ted by fire** ausgebrannt

gutter /'gʌtə(r)/ n Rinnstein m; (fig) Gosse f; (on roof) Dachrinne f

guttural /'gʌtərəl/ a guttural

guy /gaɪ/ n (fam) Kerl m

guzzle /'gʌzl/ vt/i schlingen; (drink) schlürfen

gym /dʒɪm/ n (fam) Turnhalle f; (gymnastics) Turnen nt

gymnasium /dʒɪm'neɪzɪəm/ n Turnhalle f

gymnast /'dʒɪmnæst/ n Turner(in) m(f). ~ics /-'næstɪks/ n Turnen nt

gym: ~ **shoes** pl Turnschuhe pl. ~-**slip** n (Sch) Trägerkleid nt

gynaecolog|ist /gaɪnɪ'kɒlədʒɪst/ n Frauenarzt m /-ärztin f. ~y n Gynäkologie f

gypsy /'dʒɪpsɪ/ n Zigeuner(in) m(f)

gyrate /dʒaɪə'reɪt/ vi sich drehen

H

haberdashery /'hæbədæʃərɪ/ n Kurzwaren pl; (Amer) Herrenmoden pl

habit /'hæbɪt/ n Gewohnheit f; (Relig: costume) Ordenstracht f; **be in the** ~ die Angewohnheit haben (**of** zu)

habitable /'hæbɪtəbl/ a bewohnbar

habitat /'hæbɪtæt/ n Habitat nt

habitation /hæbɪ'teɪʃn/ n **unfit for human** ~ für Wohnzwecke ungeeignet

habitual /hə'bɪtjʊəl/ a gewohnt; (inveterate) gewohnheitsmäßig. ~ly adv gewohnheitsmäßig; (constantly) ständig

hack¹ /hæk/ n (writer) Schreiberling m; (hired horse) Mietpferd nt

hack² vt hacken; ~ **to pieces** zerhacken

hackneyed /'hæknɪd/ a abgedroschen

'hacksaw n Metallsäge f

had /hæd/ see **have**

haddock /'hædək/ n inv Schellfisch m

haemorrhage /'hemərɪdʒ/ n Blutung f

haemorrhoids /'hemərɔɪdz/ npl Hämorrhoiden pl

hag /hæg/ n old ~ alte Hexe f

haggard /'hægəd/ a abgehärmt

haggle /'hægl/ vi feilschen (**over** um)

hail¹ /heɪl/ vt begrüßen; herbeirufen ⟨taxi⟩ ● vi ~ **from** kommen aus

hail² n Hagel m ● vi hageln. ~**stone** n Hagelkorn nt

hair /heə(r)/ n Haar nt; **wash one's** ~ sich (dat) die Haare waschen

hair: ~**brush** n Haarbürste f. ~**cut** n Haarschnitt m; **have a** ~**cut** sich (dat) die Haare schneiden lassen. ~-**do** n (fam) Frisur f. ~**dresser** n Friseur m/Friseuse f. ~**drier** n Haartrockner m; (hand-held) Fön (P) m. ~**grip** n [Haar]klemme f. ~**pin** n Haarnadel f. ~**pin 'bend** n Haarnadelkurve f. ~-**raising** a haarsträubend. ~**style** n Frisur f

hairy /'heərɪ/ a (-ier, -iest) behaart; (excessively) haarig; (fam: frightening) brenzlig

hake /heɪk/ n inv Seehecht m

hale /heɪl/ a ~ **and hearty** gesund und munter

half /hɑːf/ n (pl **halves**) Hälfte f; **cut in** ~ halbieren; **one and a** ~ eineinhalb, anderthalb; ~ **a dozen** ein halbes Dutzend; ~ **an hour** eine halbe Stunde ● a & adv halb; ~ **past two** halb drei; [**at**]~ **price** zum halben Preis

half: ~**board** n Halbpension f. ~**caste** n Mischling m. ~-'**hearted** a lustlos. ~-'**hourly** a & adv halbstündlich. ~-'**mast** n **at** ~-**mast** auf halbmast. ~-**measure** n Halbheit f. ~-'**term** n schulfreie Tage nach dem halben Trimester. ~-'**timbered** a Fachwerk-. ~-'**time** n (Sport) Halbzeit f. ~-'**way** a the ~-**way mark/stage** die Hälfte ● adv auf halbem Weg; **get** ~-**way** den halben Weg zurücklegen; (fig) bis zur Hälfte kommen. ~-**wit** n Idiot m

halibut /'hælɪbət/ n inv Heilbutt m

hall /hɔːl/ n Halle f; (room) Saal m; (Sch) Aula f; (entrance) Flur m; (mansion) Gutshaus nt; ~ **of residence** (Univ) Studentenheim nt

'hallmark n [Feingehalts]stempel m; (fig) Kennzeichen nt (**of** für) ● vt stempeln

hallo /hə'ləʊ/ int [guten] Tag! (fam) hallo!

Hallowe'en /hæləʊ'iːn/ n der Tag vor Allerheiligen

hallucination /həluːsɪ'neɪʃn/ n Halluzination f

halo /'heɪləʊ/ n (pl -es) Heiligenschein m; (Astr) Hof m

halt /hɔːlt/ n Halt m; **come to a** ~ stehenbleiben; ⟨traffic:⟩ zum Stillstand kommen ● vi haltmachen; ~! halt! ~**ing** a, adv -ly zögernd

halve /hɑːv/ *vt* halbieren; *(reduce)* um die Hälfte reduzieren

ham /hæm/ *n* Schinken *m*

hamburger /'hæmbɜːɡə(r)/ *n* Hamburger *m*

hamlet /'hæmlɪt/ *n* Weiler *m*

hammer /'hæmə(r)/ *n* Hammer *m* ● *vt/i* hämmern (**at** an + *acc*)

hammock /'hæmək/ *n* Hängematte *f*

hamper[1] /'hæmpə(r)/ *n* Picknickkorb *m*; **[gift]**~ Geschenkkorb *m*

hamper[2] *vt* behindern

hamster /'hæmstə(r)/ *n* Hamster *m*

hand /hænd/ *n* Hand *f*; *(of clock)* Zeiger *m*; *(writing)* Handschrift *f*; *(worker)* Arbeiter(in) *m(f)*; *(Cards)* Blatt *nt*; **all** ~**s** *(Naut)* alle Mann; **at** ~ in der Nähe; **on the one/other** ~ einer-/andererseits; **out of** ~ außer Kontrolle; *(summarily)* kurzerhand; **in** ~ unter Kontrolle; *(available)* verfügbar; **give s.o. a** ~ jdm behilflich sein ● *vt* reichen (**to** *dat*). ~ **in** *vt* abgeben. ~ **out** *vt* austeilen. ~ **over** *vt* überreichen

hand: ~**bag** *n* Handtasche *f*. ~**book** *n* Handbuch *nt*. ~**brake** *n* Handbremse *f*. ~**cuffs** *npl* Handschellen *pl*. ~**ful** *n* Handvoll *f*; **be [quite] a** ~**ful** *(fam)* nicht leicht zu haben sein

handicap /'hændɪkæp/ *n* Behinderung *f*; *(Sport & fig)* Handikap *nt*. ~**ped** *a* **mentally/physically** ~**ped** geistig/körperlich behindert

handi|craft /'hændɪkrɑːft/ *n* Basteln *nt*; *(Sch)* Werken *nt*. ~**work** *n* Werk *nt*

handkerchief /'hæŋkətʃɪf/ *n* (*pl* ~**s** & **-chieves**) Taschentuch *nt*

handle /'hændl/ *n* Griff *m*; *(of door)* Klinke *f*; *(of cup)* Henkel *m*; *(of broom)* Stiel *m*; **fly off the** ~ *(fam)* aus der Haut fahren ● *vt* handhaben; *(treat)* umgehen mit; *(touch)* anfassen. ~**bars** *npl* Lenkstange *f*

hand: ~**-luggage** *n* Handgepäck *nt*. ~**made** *a* handgemacht. ~**-out** *n* Prospekt *m*; *(money)* Unterstützung *f*. ~**rail** *n* Handlauf *m*. ~**shake** *n* Händedruck *m*

handsome /'hænsəm/ *a* gutaussehend; *(generous)* großzügig; *(large)* beträchtlich

hand: ~**stand** *n* Handstand *m*. ~**writing** *n* Handschrift *f*. ~**-'written** *a* handgeschrieben

handy /'hændɪ/ *a* (**-ier, -iest**) handlich; *(person)* geschickt; **have/keep**

~ **griffbereit haben/halten.** ~**man** *n* **[home]** ~**man** Heimwerker *m*

hang /hæŋ/ *vt/i* *(pt/pp* hung*)* hängen; ~ **wallpaper** tapezieren ● *vt* *(pt/pp* hanged*)* hängen *(criminal)*; ~ **oneself** sich erhängen ● *n* **get the** ~ **of it** *(fam)* den Dreh herauskriegen. ~ **about** *vi* sich herumdrücken. ~ **on** *vi* sich festhalten (**to** an + *dat*); *(fam: wait)* warten. ~ **out** *vi* heraushängen; *(fam: live)* wohnen ● *vt* draußen aufhängen *(washing)*. ~ **up** *vt/i* aufhängen

hangar /'hæŋə(r)/ *n* Flugzeughalle *f*

hanger /'hæŋə(r)/ *n* [Kleider]bügel *m*

hang: ~**-glider** *n* Drachenflieger *m*. ~**-gliding** *n* Drachenfliegen *nt*. ~**man** *n* Henker *m*. ~**over** *n* *(fam)* Kater *m* *(fam)*. ~**-up** *n* *(fam)* Komplex *m*

hanker /'hæŋkə(r)/ *vi* ~ **after sth** sich *(dat)* etw wünschen

hanky /'hæŋkɪ/ *n* *(fam)* Taschentuch *nt*

hanky-panky /hæŋkɪ'pæŋkɪ/ *n* *(fam)* Mauscheleien *pl*

haphazard /hæp'hæzəd/ *a*, **-ly** *adv* planlos

happen /'hæpn/ *vi* geschehen, passieren; **as it** ~**s** zufälligerweise; **I** ~**ed to be there** ich war zufällig da; **what has** ~**ed to him?** was ist mit ihm los? *(become of)* was ist aus ihm geworden? ~**ing** *n* Ereignis *nt*

happi|ly /'hæpɪlɪ/ *adv* glücklich; *(fortunately)* glücklicherweise. ~**ness** *n* Glück *nt*

happy /'hæpɪ/ *a* (**-ier, -iest**) glücklich. ~**-go-'lucky** *a* sorglos

harass /'hærəs/ *vt* schikanieren. ~**ed** *a* abgehetzt. ~**ment** *n* Schikane *f*; *(sexual)* Belästigung *f*

harbour /'hɑːbə(r)/ *n* Hafen *m* ● *vt* Unterschlupf gewähren (+ *dat*); hegen *(grudge)*

hard /hɑːd/ *a* (**-er, -est**) hart; *(difficult)* schwer; ~ **of hearing** schwerhörig ● *adv* hart; *(work)* schwer; *(pull)* kräftig; *(rain, snow)* stark; **think** ~**!** denk mal nach! **be** ~ **up** *(fam)* knapp bei Kasse sein; **be** ~ **done by** *(fam)* ungerecht behandelt werden

hard: ~**back** *n* gebundene Ausgabe *f*. ~**board** *n* Hartfaserplatte *f*. ~**-boiled** *a* hartgekocht

harden /'hɑːdn/ *vi* hart werden

hard-'hearted *a* hartherzig

hard|ly /'hɑːdlɪ/ adv kaum; ∼**ly ever** kaum [jemals]. ∼**ness** n Härte f. ∼**ship** n Not f

hard: ∼ **'shoulder** n (Auto) Rand-streifen m. ∼**ware** n Haushaltswa-ren pl; (Computing) Hardware f. ∼-**'wearing** a strapazierfähig. ∼-**'working** a fleißig

hardy /'hɑːdɪ/ a (-ier, -iest) abgehär-tet; ⟨plant⟩ winterhart

hare /heə(r)/ n Hase m. ∼**'lip** n Hasenscharte f

hark /hɑːk/ vi ∼! hört! ∼ **back** vi ∼ **back to** (fig) zurückkommen auf (+ acc)

harm /hɑːm/ n Schaden m; out of ∼'s way in Sicherheit; it won't do any∼ es kann nichts schaden ● vt ∼ s.o. jdm etwas antun. ∼**less** a harmlos ∼**ful** a schädlich.

harmonica /hɑː'mɒnɪkə/ n Mundhar-monika f

harmonious /hɑː'məʊnɪəs/ a, -ly adv harmonisch

harmon|ize /'hɑːmənaɪz/ vi (fig) har-monieren. ∼**y** n Harmonie f

harness /'hɑːnɪs/ n Geschirr nt; (of parachute) Gurtwerk m ● vt an-schirren ⟨horse⟩; (use) nutzbar machen

harp /hɑːp/ n Harfe f ● vi ∼ **on** [about] (fam) herumreiten auf (+ dat). ∼**ist** n Harfenist(in) m(f)

harpoon /hɑː'puːn/ n Harpune f

harpsichord /'hɑːpsɪkɔːd/ n Cembalo nt

harrow /'hærəʊ/ n Egge f. ∼**ing** a grauenhaft

harsh /hɑːʃ/ a (-er, -est), -ly adv hart; ⟨voice⟩ rauh; ⟨light⟩ grell. ∼**ness** n Härte f; Rauheit f

harvest /'hɑːvɪst/ n Ernte f ● vt ernten

has /hæz/ see **have**

hash /hæʃ/ n (Culin) Haschee nt; make a ∼ of (fam) verpfuschen

hashish /'hæʃɪʃ/ n Haschisch nt

hassle /'hæsl/ n (fam) Ärger m ● vt schikanieren

hassock /'hæsək/ n Kniekissen nt

haste /heɪst/ n Eile f; make ∼ sich beeilen

hasten /'heɪsn/ vi sich beeilen (to zu); (go quickly) eilen ● vt beschleunigen

hasty /'heɪstɪ/ a (-ier, -iest), -ily adv hastig; ⟨decision⟩ voreilig

hat /hæt/ n Hut m; (knitted) Mütze f

hatch¹ /hætʃ/ n (for food) Durch-reiche f; (Naut) Luke f

hatch² vi ∼ **[out]** ausschlüpfen ● vt ausbrüten

'hatchback n (Auto) Modell nt mit Hecktür

hatchet /'hætʃɪt/ n Beil nt

hate /heɪt/ n Haß m ● vt hassen. ∼**ful** a abscheulich

hatred /'heɪtrɪd/ n Haß m

haughty /'hɔːtɪ/ a (-ier, -iest), -ily adv hochmütig

haul /hɔːl/ n (fish) Fang m; (loot) Beute f ● vt/i ziehen (**on** an + dat). ∼**age** /-ɪdʒ/ n Transport m. ∼**ier** /-ɪə(r)/ n Spediteur m

haunt /hɔːnt/ n Lieblingsaufenthalt m ● vt umgehen in (+ dat); **this house is** ∼**ed** in diesem Haus spukt es

have /hæv/ vt (3 sg pres tense **has**; pt/pp **had**) haben; bekommen ⟨baby⟩; holen ⟨doctor⟩; ∼ **a meal/drink** etwas essen/trinken; ∼ **lunch** zu Mittag essen; ∼ **a walk** spazieren-gehen; ∼ **a dream** träumen; ∼ **a rest** sich ausruhen; ∼ **a swim** schwim-men; ∼ **sth done** etw machen lassen; ∼ **sth made** sich (dat) etw machen lassen; ∼ **to do sth** etw tun müssen; ∼ **it out with** zur Rede stellen; **so I** ∼! tatsächlich! **he has [got] two houses** er hat zwei Häuser; **you have got the money, haven't you?** du hast das Geld, nicht [wahr]? ● v aux haben; (with verbs of motion & some others) sein; **I** ∼ **seen him** ich habe ihn gesehen; **he has never been there** er ist nie da gewesen. ∼ **on** vt (be wearing) anhaben; (dupe) anführen

haven /'heɪvn/ n (fig) Zuflucht f

haversack /'hævə-/ n Rucksack m

havoc /'hævək/ n Verwüstung f; **play** ∼ **with** (fig) völlig durchein-anderbringen

haw /hɔː/ see **hum**

hawk¹ /hɔːk/ n Falke m

hawk² vt hausieren mit. ∼**er** n Hau-sierer m

hawthorn /'hɔː-/ n Hagedorn m

hay /heɪ/ n Heu nt. ∼ **fever** n Heu-schnupfen m. ∼**stack** n Heuschober m

'haywire a (fam) **go** ∼ verrückt spie-len; ⟨plans:⟩ über den Haufen gew-orfen werden

hazard /'hæzəd/ n Gefahr f; (risk) Risiko nt ● vt riskieren. ∼**ous** /-əs/ a gefährlich; (risky) riskant. ∼

[warning] lights npl (Auto) Warnblinkanlage f

haze /heɪz/ n Dunst m

hazel /'heɪzl/ n Haselbusch m. ~**nut** n Haselnuß f

hazy /'heɪzɪ/ a (-ier, -iest) dunstig; (fig) unklar

he /hi:/ pron er

head /hed/ n Kopf m; (chief) Oberhaupt nt; (of firm) Chef(in) m(f); (of school) Schulleiter(in) m(f); (on beer) Schaumkrone f; (of bed) Kopfende nt; **20** ~ **of cattle** 20 Stück Vieh; ~ **first** kopfüber • vt anführen; (Sport) köpfen ⟨ball⟩ • vi ~ **for** zusteuern auf (+ acc). ~**ache** n Kopfschmerzen pl. ~**dress** n Kopfschmuck m

head|er /'hedə(r)/ n Kopfball m; (dive) Kopfsprung m. ~**ing** n Überschrift f

head: ~**lamp** n (Auto) Scheinwerfer m. ~**land** n Landspitze f. ~**light** n (Auto) Scheinwerfer m. ~**line** n Schlagzeile f. ~**long** adv kopfüber. ~'**master** n Schulleiter m. ~'**mistress** n Schulleiterin f. ~-**on** a & adv frontal. ~**phones** npl Kopfhörer m. ~**quarters** npl Hauptquartier nt; (Pol) Zentrale f. ~-**rest** n Kopfstütze f. ~**room** n lichte Höhe f. ~**scarf** n Kopftuch nt. ~**strong** a eigenwillig. ~ '**waiter** n Oberkellner m. ~**way** n make ~**way** Fortschritte machen. ~ **wind** n Gegenwind m. ~**word** n Stichwort nt

heady /'hedɪ/ a berauschend

heal /hi:l/ vt/i heilen

health /helθ/ n Gesundheit f

health: ~ **farm** n Schönheitsfarm f. ~ **foods** npl Reformkost f. ~-**food shop** n Reformhaus nt. ~ **insurance** n Krankenversicherung f

healthy /'helθɪ/ a (-ier, -iest), -ily adv gesund

heap /hi:p/ n Haufen m; ~s (fam) jede Menge • vt ~ [**up**] häufen; ~ed teaspoon gehäufter Teelöffel

hear /hɪə(r)/ vt/i (pt/pp heard) hören; ~,~! hört, hört! **he would not** ~ **of** it er ließ es nicht zu

hearing /'hɪərɪŋ/ n Gehör nt; (Jur) Verhandlung f. ~-**aid** n Hörgerät nt

'**hearsay** n from ~ vom Hörensagen

hearse /hɜ:s/ n Leichenwagen m

heart /hɑ:t/ n Herz nt; (courage) Mut m; ~s pl (Cards) Herz nt; **by** ~ auswendig

heart: ~**ache** n Kummer m. ~ **attack** n Herzanfall m. ~**beat** n Herzschlag

m. ~-**break** n Leid nt. ~-**breaking** a herzzerreißend. ~-**broken** a untröstlich. ~**burn** n Sodbrennen nt. ~**en** vt ermutigen. ~**felt** a herzlich[st]

hearth /hɑ:θ/ n Herd m; (fireplace) Kamin m. ~**rug** n Kaminvorleger m

heart|ily /'hɑ:tɪlɪ/ adv herzlich; ⟨eat⟩ viel. ~**less** a, -ly adv herzlos. ~**y** a herzlich; ⟨meal⟩ groß; ⟨person⟩ burschikos

heat /hi:t/ n Hitze f; (Sport) Vorlauf m • vt heiß machen; heizen ⟨room⟩. ~**ed** a geheizt; ⟨swimming pool⟩ beheizt; ⟨discussion⟩ hitzig. ~**er** n Heizgerät nt; (Auto) Heizanlage f

heath /hi:θ/ n Heide f

heathen /'hi:ðn/ a heidnisch • n Heide m/Heidin f

heather /'heðə(r)/ n Heidekraut nt

heating /'hi:tɪŋ/ n Heizung f

heat: ~-**stroke** n Hitzschlag m. ~**wave** n Hitzewelle f

heave /hi:v/ vt/i ziehen; (lift) heben; (fam: throw) schmeißen; ~ **a sigh** einen Seufzer ausstoßen

heaven /'hevn/ n Himmel m. ~**ly** a himmlisch

heavy /'hevɪ/ a (-ier, -iest), -ily adv schwer; ⟨traffic, rain⟩ stark; ⟨sleep⟩ tief. ~**weight** n Schwergewicht nt

Hebrew /'hi:bru:/ a hebräisch

heckle /'hekl/ vt [durch Zwischenrufe] unterbrechen. ~**r** n Zwischenrufer m

hectic /'hektɪk/ a hektisch

hedge /hedʒ/ n Hecke f • vi (fig) ausweichen. ~**hog** n Igel m

heed /hi:d/ n **pay** ~ **to** Beachtung schenken (+ dat) • vt beachten. ~**less** a ungeachtet (of gen)

heel[1] /hi:l/ n Ferse f; (of shoe) Absatz m; **down at** ~ heruntergekommen; **take to one's** ~s (fam) Fersengeld geben

heel[2] vi ~ **over** (Naut) sich auf die Seite legen

hefty /'heftɪ/ a (-ier, -iest) kräftig; (heavy) schwer

heifer /'hefə(r)/ n Färse f

height /haɪt/ n Höhe f; (of person) Größe f. ~**en** vt (fig) steigern

heir /eə(r)/ n Erbe m. ~**ess** n Erbin f. ~**loom** n Erbstück nt

held /held/ see **hold**[2]

helicopter /'helɪkɒptə(r)/ n Hubschrauber m

hell /hel/ n Hölle f; **go to** ~! (sl) geh zum Teufel! • int verdammt!

hello /hə'ləʊ/ int [guten] Tag! (fam) hallo!

helm /helm/ n [Steuer]ruder nt; **at the ~** (fig) am Ruder

helmet /'helmɪt/ n Helm m

help /help/ n Hilfe f; (employees) Hilfskräfte pl; **that's no ~** das nützt nichts ● vt/i helfen (s.o. jdm); **~ oneself to sth** sich (dat) etw nehmen; **~ yourself** (at table) greif zu; **I could not ~ laughing** ich mußte lachen; **it cannot be ~ed** es läßt sich nicht ändern; **I can't ~ it** ich kann nichts dafür

help|er /'helpə(r)/ n Helfer(in) m(f). **~ful** a, **-ly** adv hilfsbereit; ⟨advice⟩ nützlich. **~ing** n Portion f. **~less** a, **-ly** adv hilflos

helter-skelter /heltə'skeltə(r)/ adv holterdiepolter ● n Rutschbahn f

hem /hem/ n Saum m ● vt (pt/pp hemmed) säumen; **~ in** umzingeln

hemisphere /'hemɪ-/ n Hemisphäre f

'hem-line n Rocklänge f

hemp /hemp/ n Hanf m

hen /hen/ n Henne f; (any female bird) Weibchen nt

hence /hens/ adv daher; **five years ~** in fünf Jahren. **~'forth** adv von nun an

henchman /'hentʃmən/ n (pej) Gefolgsmann m

'henpecked a **~ husband** Pantoffelheld m

her /hɜ:(r)/ a ihr ● pron (acc) sie; (dat) ihr; **I know~** ich kenne sie; **give ~ the money** gib ihr das Geld

herald /'herəld/ vt verkünden. **~ry** n Wappenkunde f

herb /hɜ:b/ n Kraut nt

herbaceous /hɜ:'beɪʃəs/ a krautartig; **~ border** Staudenrabatte f

herd /hɜ:d/ n Herde f ● vt (tend) hüten; (drive) treiben. **~ together** vi sich zusammendrängen ● vt zusammentreiben

here /hɪə(r)/ adv hier; (to this place) hierher; **in ~** hier drinnen; **come/ bring ~** herkommen/herbringen. **~'after** adv im folgenden. **~'by** adv hiermit

heredit|ary /hə'redɪtərɪ/ a erblich. **~y** n Vererbung f

here|sy /'herəsɪ/ n Ketzerei f. **~tic** n Ketzer(in) m(f)

here'with adv (Comm) beiliegend

heritage /'herɪtɪdʒ/ n Erbe nt

hermetic /hɜ:'metɪk/ a, **-ally** adv hermetisch

hermit /'hɜ:mɪt/ n Einsiedler m

hernia /'hɜ:nɪə/ n Bruch m, Hernie f

hero /'hɪərəʊ/ n (pl -es) Held m

heroic /hɪ'rəʊɪk/ a, **-ally** adv heldenhaft

heroin /'herəʊɪn/ n Heroin nt

hero|ine /'herəʊɪn/ n Heldin f. **~ism** n Heldentum nt

heron /'herən/ n Reiher m

herring /'herɪŋ/ n Hering m; **red ~** (fam) falsche Spur f. **~bone** n (pattern) Fischgrätenmuster nt

hers /hɜ:z/ poss pron ihre(r), ihrs; **a friend of ~** ein Freund von ihr; **that is ~** das gehört ihr

her'self pron selbst; (refl) sich; **by ~** allein

hesitant /'hezɪtənt/ a, **-ly** adv zögernd

hesitat|e /'hezɪteɪt/ vi zögern. **~ion** /-'teɪʃn/ n Zögern nt; **without ~ion** ohne zu zögern

het /het/ a **~ up** (fam) aufgeregt

hetero'sexual /hetərəʊ-/ a heterosexuell

hew /hju:/ vt (pt hewed, pp hewed or hewn) hauen

hexagonal /hek'sægənl/ a sechseckig

heyday /'heɪ-/ n Glanzzeit f

hi /haɪ/ int he! (hallo) Tag!

hiatus /haɪ'eɪtəs/ n (pl -tuses) Lücke f

hibernat|e /'haɪbəneɪt/ vi Winterschlaf halten. **~ion** /-'neɪʃn/ n Winterschlaf m

hiccup /'hɪkʌp/ n Hick m; (fam: hitch) Panne f; **have the ~s** den Schluckauf haben ● vi hick machen

hid /hɪd/, **hidden** see hide²

hide¹ /haɪd/ n (Comm) Haut f; (leather) Leder nt

hide² vt (pt hid, pp hidden) verstecken; (keep secret) verheimlichen ● vi sich verstecken. **~-and-'seek** n play **~-and-seek** Versteck spielen

hideous /'hɪdɪəs/ a, **-ly** adv häßlich; (horrible) gräßlich

'hide-out n Versteck nt

hiding¹ /'haɪdɪŋ/ n (fam) **give s.o. a ~** jdn verdreschen

hiding² n **go into ~** untertauchen

hierarchy /'haɪərɑ:kɪ/ n Hierarchie f

hieroglyphics /haɪərə'glɪfɪks/ npl Hieroglyphen pl

higgledy-piggledy /hɪgldɪ'pɪgldɪ/ adv kunterbunt durcheinander

high /haɪ/ a (-er, -est) hoch; attrib hohe(r,s); ⟨meat⟩ angegangen; ⟨wind⟩ stark; (on drugs) high; **it's ~ time** es ist höchste Zeit ● adv hoch;

~ **and low** überall ● *n* Hoch *nt*; (*temperature*) Höchsttemperatur *f*

high: ~**brow** *a* intellektuell. ~ **chair** *n* Kinderhochstuhl *m*. ~-'**handed** *a* selbstherrlich. ~-'**heeled** *a* hochhackig. ~ **jump** *n* Hochsprung *m*

highlight *n* (*fig*) Höhepunkt *m*; ~**s** *pl* (*in hair*) helle Strähnen *pl* ● *vt* (*emphasize*) hervorheben

highly /'haɪlɪ/ *adv* hoch; **speak** ~ **of** loben; **think** ~ **of** sehr schätzen. ~-'**strung** *a* nervös

Highness /'haɪnɪs/ *n* Hoheit *f*

high: ~-**rise** *a* ~-**rise flats** *pl* Wohnturm *m*. ~ **season** *n* Hochsaison *f*. ~ **street** *n* Hauptstraße *f.* ~ '**tide** *n* Hochwasser *nt*. ~**way** *n* **public** ~**way** öffentliche Straße *f*

hijack /'haɪdʒæk/ *vt* entführen. ~**er** *n* Entführer *m*

hike /haɪk/ *n* Wanderung *f* ● *vi* wandern. ~**r** *n* Wanderer *m*

hilarious /hɪ'leərɪəs/ *a* sehr komisch

hill /hɪl/ *n* Berg *m*; (*mound*) Hügel *m*; (*slope*) Hang *m*

hill: ~-**billy** *n* (*Amer*) Hinterwäldler *m*. ~**side** *n* Hang *m*. ~**y** *a* hügelig

hilt /hɪlt/ *n* Griff *m*; **to the** ~ (*fam*) voll und ganz

him /hɪm/ *pron* (*acc*) ihn; (*dat*) ihm; **I know** ~ ich kenne ihn; **give** ~ **the money** gib ihm das Geld. ~'**self** *pron* selbst; (*refl*) sich; **by** ~**self** allein

hind /haɪnd/ *a* Hinter-

hind|er /'hɪndə(r)/ *vt* hindern. ~**rance** /-rəns/ *n* Hindernis *nt*

hindsight /'haɪnd-/ *n* **with** ~ rückblickend

Hindu /'hɪndu:/ *n* Hindu *m* ● *a* Hindu-. ~**ism** *n* Hinduismus *m*

hinge /hɪndʒ/ *n* Scharnier *nt*; (*on door*) Angel *f* ● *vi* ~ **on** (*fig*) ankommen auf (+ *acc*)

hint /hɪnt/ *n* Wink *m*, Andeutung *f*; (*advice*) Hinweis *m*; (*trace*) Spur *f* ● *vi* ~ **at** anspielen auf (+ *acc*)

hip /hɪp/ *n* Hüfte *f*

hippie /'hɪpɪ/ *n* Hippie *m*

hip 'pocket *n* Gesäßtasche *f*

hippopotamus /hɪpə'pɒtəməs/ *n* (*pl* -**muses** *or* -**mi** /-maɪ/) Nilpferd *nt*

hire /'haɪə(r)/ *vt* mieten (*car*); leihen (*suit*); einstellen (*person*); ~[**out**] vermieten; verleihen ● *n* Mieten *nt*; Leihen *nt*. ~-**car** *n* Leihwagen *m*

his /hɪz/ *a* sein ● *poss pron* seine(r), seins; **a friend of** ~ ein Freund von ihm; **that is** ~ das gehört ihm

hiss /hɪs/ *n* Zischen *nt* ● *vt/i* zischen

historian /hɪ'stɔ:rɪən/ *n* Historiker(in) *m*(*f*)

historic /hɪ'stɒrɪk/ *a* historisch. ~**al** *a*, -**ly** *adv* geschichtlich, historisch

history /'hɪstərɪ/ *n* Geschichte *f*

hit /hɪt/ *n* (*blow*) Schlag *m*; (*fam: success*) Erfolg *m*; **direct** ~ Volltreffer *m* ● *vt/i* (*pt/pp* **hit**, *pres p* **hitting**) schlagen; (*knock against, collide with, affect*) treffen; ~ **the target** das Ziel treffen; ~ **on** (*fig*) kommen auf (+ *acc*); ~ **it off** gut auskommen (**with** mit); ~ **one's head on sth** sich (*dat*) den Kopf an etw (*dat*) stoßen

hitch /hɪtʃ/ *n* Problem *nt*; **technical** ~ Panne *f* ● *vt* festmachen (**to** an + *dat*); ~ **up** hochziehen; ~ **a lift** per Anhalter fahren, (*fam*) trampen. ~-**hike** *vi* per Anhalter fahren, (*fam*) trampen. ~-**hiker** *n* Anhalter(in) *m*(*f*)

hither /'hɪðə(r)/ *adv* hierher; ~ **and thither** hin und her. ~'**to** *adv* bisher

hive /haɪv/ *n* Bienenstock *m*. ~ **off** *vt* (*Comm*) abspalten

hoard /hɔ:d/ *n* Hort *m* ● *vt* horten, hamstern

hoarding /'hɔ:dɪŋ/ *n* Bauzaun *m*; (*with advertisements*) Reklamewand *f*

hoar-frost /'hɔ:-/ *n* Rauhreif *m*

hoarse /hɔ:s/ *a* (-**r**, -**st**), -**ly** *adv* heiser. ~**ness** *n* Heiserkeit *f*

hoax /həʊks/ *n* übler Scherz *m*; (*false alarm*) blinder Alarm *m*

hob /hɒb/ *n* Kochmulde *f*

hobble /'hɒbl/ *vi* humpeln

hobby /'hɒbɪ/ *n* Hobby *nt*. ~**horse** *n* (*fig*) Lieblingsthema *nt*

hobnailed /'hɒb-/ *a* ~ **boots** *pl* genagelte Schuhe *pl*

hock /hɒk/ *n* [weißer] Rheinwein *m*

hockey /'hɒkɪ/ *n* Hockey *nt*

hoe /həʊ/ *n* Hacke *f* ● *vt* (*pres p* **hoeing**) hacken

hog /hɒg/ *n* [Mast]schwein *nt* ● *vt* (*pt/pp* **hogged**) (*fam*) mit Beschlag belegen

hoist /hɔɪst/ *n* Lastenaufzug *m* ● *vt* hochziehen; hissen (*flag*)

hold[1] *n* (*Naut, Aviat*) Laderaum *m*

hold[2] /həʊld/ *n* Halt *m*; (*Sport*) Griff *m*; (*fig: influence*) Einfluß *m*; **get** ~ **of** fassen; (*fam: contact*) erreichen ● *v* (*pt/pp* **held**) ● *vt* halten; (*container:*) fassen; (*believe*) meinen; (*possess*) haben; anhalten (*breath*); ~ **one's tongue** den Mund halten ● *vi* (*rope:*)

halten; ⟨weather:⟩ sich halten; **not ~ with** (fam) nicht einverstanden sein mit. **~ back** vt zurückhalten ● vi zögern. **~ on** vi (wait) warten; (on telephone) am Apparat bleiben; **~ on to** (keep) behalten; (cling to) sich festhalten an (+ dat). **~ out** vt hinhalten ● vi (resist) aushalten. **~ up** vt hochhalten; (delay) aufhalten; (rob) überfallen

'hold|all n Reisetasche f. **~er** n Inhaber(in) m(f); (container) Halter m. **~-up** n Verzögerung f; (attack) Überfall m

hole /həʊl/ n Loch nt

holiday /'hɒlədeɪ/ n Urlaub m; (Sch) Ferien pl; (public) Feiertag m; (day off) freier Tag m; **go on ~** in Urlaub fahren. **~-maker** n Urlauber(in) m(f)

holiness /'həʊlɪnɪs/ n Heiligkeit f

Holland /'hɒlənd/ n Holland nt

hollow /'hɒləʊ/ a hohl; ⟨promise⟩ leer ● n Vertiefung f; (in ground) Mulde f. **~ out** vt aushöhlen

holly /'hɒlɪ/ n Stechpalme f

'hollyhock n Stockrose f

hologram /'hɒləgræm/ n Hologramm nt

holster /'həʊlstə(r)/ n Pistolentasche f

holy /'həʊlɪ/ a (-ier, -iest) heilig. **H~ Ghost** or **Spirit** n Heiliger Geist m. **~ water** n Weihwasser nt. **H~ Week** n Karwoche f

homage /'hɒmɪdʒ/ n Huldigung f; **pay ~** to huldigen (+ dat)

home /həʊm/ n Zuhause nt; (house) Haus nt; (institution) Heim nt; (native land) Heimat f ● adv **at ~** zu Hause; **come/go ~** nach Hause kommen/gehen

home: ~ad'dress n Heimatanschrift f. **~ com'puter** n Heimcomputer m. **~ game** n Heimspiel nt. **~ help** n Haushaltshilfe f. **~land** n Heimatland nt. **~less** a obdachlos

homely /'həʊmlɪ/ a (-ier, -iest) a gemütlich; (Amer: ugly) unscheinbar

home: ~-'made a selbstgemacht. **H~ Office** n Innenministerium nt. **H~ 'Secretary** n Innenminister m. **~sick** a be **~sick** Heimweh haben (for nach). **~sickness** n Heimweh nt. **~ 'town** n Heimatstadt f. **~work** n (Sch) Hausaufgaben pl

homicide /'hɒmɪsaɪd/ n Totschlag m; (murder) Mord m

homoeopath|ic /həʊmɪə'pæθɪk/ a homöopathisch. **~y** /-'ɒpəθɪ/ n Homöopathie f

homogeneous /hɒmə'dʒiːnɪəs/ a homogen

homo'sexual a homosexuell ● n Homosexuelle(r) m/f

honest /'ɒnɪst/ a, **-ly** adv ehrlich. **~y** n Ehrlichkeit f

honey /'hʌnɪ/ n Honig m; (fam: darling) Schatz m

honey: ~comb n Honigwabe f. **~moon** n Flitterwochen pl; (journey) Hochzeitsreise f. **~suckle** n Geißblatt nt

honk /hɒŋk/ vi hupen

honorary /'ɒnərərɪ/ a ehrenamtlich; ⟨member, doctorate⟩ Ehren-

honour /'ɒnə(r)/ n Ehre f ● vt ehren; honorieren ⟨cheque⟩. **~able** /-əbl/ a, **-bly** adv ehrenhaft

hood /hʊd/ n Kapuze f; (of pram) [Klapp]verdeck nt; (over cooker) Abzugshaube f; (Auto, Amer) Kühlerhaube f

hoodlum /'huːdləm/ n Rowdy m

'hoodwink vt (fam) reinlegen

hoof /huːf/ n (pl ~s or **hooves**) Huf m

hook /hʊk/ n Haken m; **by ~ or by crook** mit allen Mitteln ● vt festhaken (**to** an + acc)

hook|ed /hʊkt/ a **~ed nose** Hakennase f; **~ed on** (fam) abhängig von; (keen on) besessen von. **~er** n (Amer, sl) Nutte f

hookey /'hʊkɪ/ n **play ~** (Amer, fam) schwänzen

hooligan /'huːlɪgən/ n Rowdy m. **~ism** n Rowdytum nt

hoop /huːp/ n Reifen m

hooray /hʊ'reɪ/ int & n = **hurrah**

hoot /huːt/ n Ruf m; **~s of laughter** schallendes Gelächter nt ● vi ⟨owl:⟩ rufen; ⟨car:⟩ hupen; (jeer) johlen. **~er** n (of factory) Sirene f; (Auto) Hupe f

hoover /'huːvə(r)/ n **H~** (P) Staubsauger m ● vt/i [staub]saugen

hop[1] /hɒp/ n, & **~s** pl Hopfen m

hop[2] n Hüpfer m; **catch s.o. on the ~** (fam) jdm ungelegen kommen ● vi (pt/pp **hopped**) hüpfen; **~ it!** (fam) hau ab! **~ in** vi (fam) einsteigen. **~ out** vi (fam) aussteigen

hope /həʊp/ n Hoffnung f; (prospect) Aussicht f (**of** auf + acc) ● vt/i hoffen (**for** auf + acc); **I ~ so** hoffentlich

hope|ful /'həʊpfl/ a hoffnungsvoll; **be ~ful that** hoffen, daß. **~fully** adv hoffnungsvoll; (*it is hoped*) hoffentlich. **~less** *a*, **-ly** *adv* hoffnungslos; (*useless*) nutzlos; (*incompetent*) untauglich

horde /hɔːd/ *n* Horde *f*

horizon /həˈraɪzn/ *n* Horizont *m*; **on the ~** am Horizont

horizontal /hɒrɪˈzɒntl/ *a*, **-ly** *adv* horizontal. **~ bar** *n* Reck *nt*

horn /hɔːn/ *n* Horn *nt*; (*Auto*) Hupe *f*

hornet /ˈhɔːnɪt/ *n* Hornisse *f*

horny /ˈhɔːnɪ/ *a* schwielig

horoscope /ˈhɒrəskəʊp/ *n* Horoskop *nt*

horrible /ˈhɒrɪbl/ *a*, **-bly** *adv* schrecklich

horrid /ˈhɒrɪd/ *a* gräßlich

horrific /həˈrɪfɪk/ *a* entsetzlich

horrify /ˈhɒrɪfaɪ/ *vt* (*pt/pp* **-ied**) entsetzen

horror /ˈhɒrə(r)/ *n* Entsetzen *nt*. **~ film** *n* Horrorfilm *m*

hors-d'œuvre /ɔːˈdɜːvr/ *n* Vorspeise *f*

horse /hɔːs/ *n* Pferd *nt*

horse: **~back** *n* **on ~back** zu Pferde. **~-ˈchestnut** *n* [Roß]kastanie *f*. **~man** *n* Reiter *m*. **~play** *n* Toben *nt*. **~power** *n* Pferdestärke *f*. **~racing** *n* Pferderennen *nt*. **~radish** *n* Meerrettich *m*. **~shoe** *n* Hufeisen *nt*

horti'cultural /hɔːtɪ-/ *a* Gartenbau-. **'horticulture** *n* Gartenbau *m*

hose /həʊz/ *n* (*pipe*) Schlauch *m* ● *vt* **~ down** abspritzen

hosiery /ˈhəʊzərɪ/ *n* Strumpfwaren *pl*

hospice /ˈhɒspɪs/ *n* Heim *nt*; (*for the terminally ill*) Sterbeklinik *f*

hospitable /hɒˈspɪtəbl/ *a*, **-bly** *adv* gastfreundlich

hospital /ˈhɒspɪtl/ *n* Krankenhaus *nt*

hospitality /hɒspɪˈtælətɪ/ *n* Gastfreundschaft *f*

host¹ /həʊst/ *n* **a ~ of** eine Menge von

host² *n* Gastgeber *m*

host³ *n* (*Relig*) Hostie *f*

hostage /ˈhɒstɪdʒ/ *n* Geisel *f*

hostel /ˈhɒstl/ *n* [Wohn]heim *nt*

hostess /ˈhəʊstɪs/ *n* Gastgeberin *f*

hostile /ˈhɒstaɪl/ *a* feindlich; (*unfriendly*) feindselig

hostilit|y /hɒˈstɪlətɪ/ *n* Feindschaft *f*; **~ies** *pl* Feindseligkeiten *pl*

hot /hɒt/ *a* (**hotter, hottest**) heiß; ⟨*meal*⟩ warm; (*spicy*) scharf; **I am** *or* **feel ~** mir ist heiß

hotbed *n* (*fig*) Brutstätte *f*

hotchpotch /ˈhɒtʃpɒtʃ/ *n* Mischmasch *m*

hotel /həʊˈtel/ *n* Hotel *nt*. **~ier** /-ɪə(r)/ *n* Hotelier *m*

hot: **~head** *n* Hitzkopf *m*. **~ˈheaded** *a* hitzköpfig. **~house** *n* Treibhaus *nt*. **~ly** *adv* (*fig*) heiß, heftig. **~plate** *n* Tellerwärmer *m*; (*of cooker*) Kochplatte *f*. **~ tap** *n* Warmwasserhahn *m*. **~-tempered** *a* jähzornig. **~-ˈwater bottle** *n* Wärmflasche *f*

hound /haʊnd/ *n* Jagdhund *m* ● *vt* (*fig*) verfolgen

hour /ˈaʊə(r)/ *n* Stunde *f*. **~ly** *a & adv* stündlich; **~ly pay** *or* **rate** Stundenlohn *m*

house¹ /haʊs/ *n* Haus *nt*; **at my ~** bei mir

house² /haʊz/ *vt* unterbringen

house /haʊs/: **~boat** *n* Hausboot *nt*. **~breaking** *n* Einbruch *m*. **~hold** *n* Haushalt *m*. **~holder** *n* Hausinhaber(in) *m(f)*. **~keeper** *n* Haushälterin *f*. **~keeping** *n* Hauswirtschaft *f*; (*money*) Haushaltsgeld *nt*. **~plant** *n* Zimmerpflanze *f*. **~-trained** *a* stubenrein. **~-warming** *n* **have a ~-warming party** Einstand feiern. **~wife** *n* Hausfrau *f*. **~work** *n* Hausarbeit *f*

housing /ˈhaʊzɪŋ/ *n* Wohnungen *pl*; (*Techn*) Gehäuse *nt*. **~ estate** *n* Wohnsiedlung *f*

hovel /ˈhɒvl/ *n* elende Hütte *f*

hover /ˈhɒvə(r)/ *vi* schweben; (*be undecided*) schwanken; (*linger*) herumstehen. **~craft** *n* Luftkissenfahrzeug *nt*

how /haʊ/ *adv* wie; **~ do you do?** guten Tag! **~ many** wie viele; **~ much** wieviel; **and ~!** und ob!

how'ever *adv* (*in question*) wie; (*nevertheless*) jedoch, aber; **~ small** wie klein es auch sein mag

howl /haʊl/ *n* Heulen *nt* ● *vi* heulen; ⟨*baby:*⟩ brüllen. **~er** *n* (*fam*) Schnitzer *m*

hub /hʌb/ *n* Nabe *f*; (*fig*) Mittelpunkt *m*

hubbub /ˈhʌbʌb/ *n* Stimmengewirr *nt*

'hub-cap *n* Radkappe *f*

huddle /ˈhʌdl/ *vi* **~ together** sich zusammendrängen

hue¹ /hjuː/ *n* Farbe *f*

hue² *n* **~ and cry** Aufruhr *m*

huff /hʌf/ *n* **in a ~** beleidigt

hug /hʌg/ *n* Umarmung *f* ● *vt* (*pt/pp* **hugged**) umarmen

huge /hjuːdʒ/ *a*, **-ly** *adv* riesig

hulking /'hʌlkɪŋ/ a (fam) ungeschlacht

hull /hʌl/ n (Naut) Rumpf m

hullo /hə'ləʊ/ int = **hallo**

hum /hʌm/ n Summen nt; Brummen nt ● vt/i (pt/pp **hummed**) summen; ⟨motor:⟩ brummen; ~ **and haw** nicht mit der Sprache herauswollen

human /'hju:mən/ a menschlich ● n Mensch m. ~ **'being** n Mensch m

humane /hju:'meɪn/ a, **-ly** adv human

humanitarian /hju:mænɪ'teərɪən/ a humanitär

humanit|y /hju:'mænətɪ/ n Menschheit f; ~**ies** pl (Univ) Geisteswissenschaften pl

humble /'hʌmbl/ a (**-r, -st**), **-bly** adv demütig ● vt demütigen

'humdrum a eintönig

humid /'hju:mɪd/ a feucht. ~**ity** /-'mɪdətɪ/ n Feuchtigkeit f

humilia|te /hju:'mɪlɪeɪt/ vt demütigen. ~**ion** /-'eɪʃn/ n Demütigung f

humility /hju:'mɪlətɪ/ n Demut f

'humming-bird n Kolibri m

humorous /'hju:mərəs/ a, **-ly** adv humorvoll; ⟨story⟩ humoristisch

humour /'hju:mə(r)/ n Humor m; ⟨mood⟩ Laune f; **have a sense of** ~ Humor haben ● vt ~ **s.o.** jdm seinen Willen lassen

hump /hʌmp/ n Buckel m; (of camel) Höcker m ● vt schleppen

hunch /hʌntʃ/ n (idea) Ahnung f

'hunch|back n Bucklige(r) m/f. ~**ed** a ~**ed up** gebeugt

hundred /'hʌndrəd/ a **one/a** ~ [ein]hundert ● n Hundert nt; (written figure) Hundert f. ~**th** a hundertste(r,s) ● n Hundertstel nt. ~**weight** n ≈ Zentner m

hung /hʌŋ/ see **hang**

Hungarian /hʌŋ'geərɪən/ a ungarisch ● n Ungar(in) m(f)

Hungary /'hʌŋgərɪ/ n Ungarn nt

hunger /'hʌŋgə(r)/ n Hunger m. ~**strike** n Hungerstreik m

hungry /'hʌŋgrɪ/ a (**-ier, -iest**), **-ily** adv hungrig; **be** ~ Hunger haben

hunk /hʌŋk/ n [großes] Stück nt

hunt /hʌnt/ n Jagd f; (for criminal) Fahndung f ● vt/i jagen; fahnden nach ⟨criminal⟩; ~ **for** suchen. ~**er** n Jäger m; (horse) Jagdpferd nt. ~**ing** n Jagd f

hurdle /'hɜ:dl/ n (Sport & fig) Hürde f. ~**r** n Hürdenläufer(in) m(f)

hurl /hɜ:l/ vt schleudern

hurrah /hʊ'rɑ:/, **hurray** /hʊ'reɪ/ int hurra! ● n Hurra nt

hurricane /'hʌrɪkən/ n Orkan m

hurried /'hʌrɪd/ a, **-ly** adv eilig; (superficial) flüchtig

hurry /'hʌrɪ/ n Eile f; **be in a** ~ es eilig haben ● vi (pt/pp **-ied**) sich beeilen; (go quickly) eilen. ~ **up** vi sich beeilen ● vt antreiben

hurt /hɜ:t/ n Schmerz m ● vt/i (pt/pp **hurt**) weh tun (+ dat); (injure) verletzen; (offend) kränken. ~**ful** a verletzend

hurtle /'hɜ:tl/ vi ~ **along** rasen

husband /'hʌzbənd/ n [Ehe]mann m

hush /hʌʃ/ n Stille f ● vt ~ **up** vertuschen. ~**ed** a gedämpft. ~**-'hush** a (fam) streng geheim

husk /hʌsk/ n Spelze f

husky /'hʌskɪ/ a (**-ier, -iest**) heiser; (burly) stämmig

hustle /'hʌsl/ vt drängen ● n Gedränge nt; ~ **and bustle** geschäftiges Treiben nt

hut /hʌt/ n Hütte f

hutch /hʌtʃ/ n [Kaninchen]stall m

hybrid /'haɪbrɪd/ a hybrid ● n Hybride f

hydrangea /haɪ'dreɪndʒə/ n Hortensie f

hydrant /'haɪdrənt/ n [**fire**] ~ Hydrant m

hydraulic /haɪ'drɔ:lɪk/ a, **-ally** adv hydraulisch

hydrochloric /haɪdrə'klɔ:rɪk/ a ~ **acid** Salzsäure f

hydroe'lectric /haɪdrəʊ-/ a hydroelektrisch. ~ **power station** n Wasserkraftwerk nt

hydrofoil /'haɪdrə-/ n Tragflügelboot nt

hydrogen /'haɪdrədʒən/ n Wasserstoff m

hyena /haɪ'i:nə/ n Hyäne f

hygien|e /'haɪdʒi:n/ n Hygiene f. ~**ic** /haɪ'dʒi:nɪk/ a, **-ally** adv hygienisch

hymn /hɪm/ n Kirchenlied nt. ~**book** n Gesangbuch nt

hyphen /'haɪfn/ n Bindestrich m. ~**ate** vt mit Bindestrich schreiben

hypno|sis /hɪp'nəʊsɪs/ n Hypnose f. ~**tic** /-'nɒtɪk/ a hypnotisch

hypno|tism /'hɪpnətɪzm/ n Hypnotik f. ~**tist** /-tɪst/ n Hypnotiseur m. ~**tize** vt hypnotisieren

hypochondriac /haɪpə'kɒndrɪæk/ a hypochondrisch ● n Hypochonder m

hypocrisy /hɪ'pɒkrəsɪ/ n Heuchelei f

hypocrit|e /'hɪpəkrɪt/ n Heuchler(in) m(f). **~ical** /-'krɪtɪkl/ a, **-ly** adv heuchlerisch

hypodermic /haɪpə'dɜːmɪk/ a & n ~ **[syringe]** Injektionsspritze f

hypothe|sis /haɪ'pɒθəsɪs/ n Hypothese f. **~tical** /-ə'θetɪkl/ a, **-ly** adv hypothetisch

hyster|ia /hɪ'stɪərɪə/ n Hysterie f. **~ical** /-'sterɪkl/ a, **-ly** adv hysterisch. **~ics** /hɪ'sterɪks/ npl hysterischer Anfall m

I

I /aɪ/ pron ich

ice /aɪs/ n Eis nt ● vt mit Zuckerguß überziehen ⟨cake⟩

ice: ~ **age** n Eiszeit f. **~-axe** n Eispickel m. **~berg** /-bɜːg/ n Eisberg m. **~box** n (Amer) Kühlschrank m. ~ **'cream** n [Speise]eis nt. **~-'cream parlour** n Eisdiele f. **~-cube** n Eiswürfel m

Iceland /'aɪslənd/ n Island nt

ice: ~ **'lolly** n Eis nt am Stiel. ~ **rink** n Eisbahn f

icicle /'aɪsɪkl/ n Eiszapfen m

icing /'aɪsɪŋ/ n Zuckerguß m. ~ **sugar** n Puderzucker m

icon /'aɪkɒn/ n Ikone f

icy /'aɪsɪ/ a (**-ier, -iest**), **-ily** adv eisig; ⟨road⟩ vereist

idea /aɪ'dɪə/ n Idee f; (conception) Vorstellung f; **I have no ~!** ich habe keine Ahnung!

ideal /aɪ'dɪəl/ a ideal ● n Ideal nt. **~ism** n Idealismus m. **~ist** n Idealist (in) m(f). **~istic** /-'lɪstɪk/ a idealistisch. **~ize** vt idealisieren. **~ly** adv ideal; (in ideal circumstances) idealerweise

identical /aɪ'dentɪkl/ a identisch; ⟨twins⟩ eineiig

identi|fication /aɪdentɪfɪ'keɪʃn/ n Identifizierung f; (proof of identity) Ausweispapiere pl. **~fy** /aɪ'dentɪfaɪ/ vt (pt/pp **-ied**) identifizieren

identity /aɪ'dentətɪ/ n Identität f. ~ **card** n [Personal]ausweis m

ideolog|ical /aɪdɪə'lɒdʒɪkl/ a ideologisch. **~y** /aɪdɪ'ɒlədʒɪ/ n Ideologie f

idiom /'ɪdɪəm/ n [feste] Redewendung f. **~atic** /-'mætɪk/ a, **-ally** adv idiomatisch

idiosyncrasy /ɪdɪə'sɪŋkrəsɪ/ n Eigenart f

idiot /'ɪdɪət/ n Idiot m. **~ic** /-'ɒtɪk/ a idiotisch

idle /'aɪdl/ a (**-r, -st**), **-ly** adv untätig; (lazy) faul; (empty) leer; ⟨machine⟩ nicht in Betrieb ● vi faulenzen; ⟨engine:⟩ leer laufen. **~ness** n Untätigkeit f; Faulheit f

idol /'aɪdl/ n Idol nt. **~ize** /'aɪdəlaɪz/ vt vergöttern

idyllic /ɪ'dɪlɪk/ a idyllisch

i.e. abbr (**id est**) d.h.

if /ɪf/ conj wenn; (whether) ob; **as if** als ob

ignite /ɪg'naɪt/ vt entzünden ● vi sich entzünden

ignition /ɪg'nɪʃn/ n (Auto) Zündung f. ~ **key** n Zündschlüssel m

ignoramus /ɪgnə'reɪməs/ n Ignorant m

ignoran|ce /'ɪgnərəns/ n Unwissenheit f. **~t** a unwissend; (rude) ungehobelt

ignore /ɪg'nɔː(r)/ vt ignorieren

ilk /ɪlk/ n (fam) **of that~** von der Sorte

ill /ɪl/ a krank; (bad) schlecht; **feel ~ at ease** sich unbehaglich fühlen ● adv schlecht ● n Schlechte(s) nt; (evil) Übel nt. **~-advised** a unklug. **~-bred** a schlecht erzogen

illegal /ɪ'liːgl/ a, **-ly** adv illegal

illegible /ɪ'ledʒəbl/ a, **-bly** adv unleserlich

illegitima|cy /ɪlɪ'dʒɪtɪməsɪ/ n Unehelichkeit f. **~te** /-mət/ a unehelich; ⟨claim⟩ unberechtigt

illicit /ɪ'lɪsɪt/ a, **-ly** adv illegal

illitera|cy /ɪ'lɪtərəsɪ/ n Analphabetentum nt. **~te** /-rət/ a **be ~te** nicht lesen und schreiben können ● n Analphabet(in) m(f)

illness /'ɪlnɪs/ n Krankheit f

illogical /ɪ'lɒdʒɪkl/ a, **-ly** adv unlogisch

ill-treat /ɪl'triːt/ vt mißhandeln. **~ment** n Mißhandlung f

illuminat|e /ɪ'luːmɪneɪt/ vt beleuchten. **~ing** a aufschlußreich. **~ion** /-'neɪʃn/ n Beleuchtung f

illusion /ɪ'luːʒn/ n Illusion f; **be under the ~ that** sich (dat) einbilden, daß

illusory /ɪ'luːsərɪ/ a illusorisch

illustrat|e /'ɪləstreɪt/ vt illustrieren. **~ion** /-'streɪʃn/ n Illustration f

illustrious /ɪ'lʌstrɪəs/ a berühmt

image /'ɪmɪdʒ/ n Bild nt; (statue) Standbild nt; (figure) Figur f; (exact likeness) Ebenbild nt; **[public]** ~ Image nt

imagin|able /ɪˈmædʒɪnəbl/ a vorstellbar. **~ary** /-ərɪ/ a eingebildet

imaginat|ion /ɪmædʒɪˈneɪʃn/ n Phantasie f; (*fancy*) Einbildung f. **~ive** /ɪˈmædʒɪnətɪv/ a, **-ly** adv phantasievoll; (*full of ideas*) einfallsreich

imagine /ɪˈmædʒɪn/ vt sich (*dat*) vorstellen; (*wrongly*) sich (*dat*) einbilden

im'balance n Unausgeglichenheit f

imbecile /ˈɪmbəsiːl/ n Schwachsinnige(r) m/f; (*pej*) Idiot m

imbibe /ɪmˈbaɪb/ vt trinken; (*fig*) aufnehmen

imbue /ɪmˈbjuː/ vt **be ~d with** erfüllt sein von

imitat|e /ˈɪmɪteɪt/ vt nachahmen, imitieren. **~ion** /-ˈteɪʃn/ n Nachahmung f, Imitation f

immaculate /ɪˈmækjʊlət/ a, **-ly** adv tadellos; (*Relig*) unbefleckt

imma'terial a (*unimportant*) unwichtig, unwesentlich

imma'ture a unreif

immediate /ɪˈmiːdɪət/ a sofortig; (*nearest*) nächste(r,s). **~ly** adv sofort; **~ly next to** unmittelbar neben ● *conj* sobald

immemorial /ɪməˈmɔːrɪəl/ a **from time ~** seit Urzeiten

immense /ɪˈmens/ a, **-ly** adv riesig; (*fam*) enorm; (*extreme*) äußerst

immers|e /ɪˈmɜːs/ vt untertauchen; **be ~ed in** (*fig*) vertieft sein in (+ *acc*). **~ion** /-ˈɜːʃn/ n Untertauchen nt. **~ion heater** n Heißwasserbereiter m

immigrant /ˈɪmɪɡrənt/ n Einwanderer m

immigrat|e /ˈɪmɪɡreɪt/ vi einwandern. **~ion** /-ˈgreɪʃn/ n Einwanderung f

imminent /ˈɪmɪnənt/ a **be ~** unmittelbar bevorstehen

immobil|e /ɪˈməʊbaɪl/ a unbeweglich. **~ize** /-bəlaɪz/ vt (*fig*) lähmen; (*Med*) ruhigstellen

immoderate /ɪˈmɒdərət/ a übermäßig

immodest /ɪˈmɒdɪst/ a unbescheiden

immoral /ɪˈmɒrəl/ a, **-ly** adv unmoralisch. **~ity** /ɪməˈrælətɪ/ n Unmoral f

immortal /ɪˈmɔːtl/ a unsterblich. **~ity** /-ˈtælətɪ/ n Unsterblichkeit f. **~ize** vt verewigen

immovable /ɪˈmuːvəbl/ a unbeweglich; (*fig*) fest

immune /ɪˈmjuːn/ a immun (**to/from** gegen). **~ system** n Abwehrsystem nt

immunity /ɪˈmjuːnətɪ/ n Immunität f

immunize /ˈɪmjʊnaɪz/ vt immunisieren

imp /ɪmp/ n Kobold m

impact /ˈɪmpækt/ n Aufprall m; (*collision*) Zusammenprall m; (*of bomb*) Einschlag m; (*fig*) Auswirkung f

impair /ɪmˈpeə(r)/ vt beeinträchtigen

impale /ɪmˈpeɪl/ vt aufspießen

impart /ɪmˈpɑːt/ vt übermitteln (**to** *dat*); vermitteln (*knowledge*)

im'parti|al a unparteiisch. **~'ality** n Unparteilichkeit f

im'passable a unpassierbar

impasse /æmˈpɑːs/ n (*fig*) Sackgasse f

impassioned /ɪmˈpæʃnd/ a leidenschaftlich

im'passive a, **-ly** adv unbeweglich

im'patien|ce n Ungeduld f. **~t** a, **-ly** adv ungeduldig

impeach /ɪmˈpiːtʃ/ vt anklagen

impeccable /ɪmˈpekəbl/ a, **-bly** adv tadellos

impede /ɪmˈpiːd/ vt behindern

impediment /ɪmˈpedɪmənt/ n Hindernis nt; (*in speech*) Sprachfehler m

impel /ɪmˈpel/ vt (*pt/pp* **impelled**) treiben; **feel ~led** sich genötigt fühlen (**to** zu)

impending /ɪmˈpendɪŋ/ a bevorstehend

impenetrable /ɪmˈpenɪtrəbl/ a undurchdringlich

imperative /ɪmˈperətɪv/ a **be ~** dringend notwendig sein ● n (*Gram*) Imperativ m, Befehlsform f

imper'ceptible a nicht wahrnehmbar

im'perfect a unvollkommen; (*faulty*) fehlerhaft ● n (*Gram*) Imperfekt nt. **~ion** /-ˈfekʃn/ n Unvollkommenheit f; (*fault*) Fehler m

imperial /ɪmˈpɪərɪəl/ a kaiserlich. **~ism** n Imperialismus m

imperil /ɪmˈperəl/ vt (*pt/pp* **imperilled**) gefährden

imperious /ɪmˈpɪərɪəs/ a, **-ly** adv herrisch

im'personal a unpersönlich

impersonat|e /ɪmˈpɜːsəneɪt/ vt sich ausgeben als; (*Theat*) nachahmen, imitieren. **~or** n Imitator m

impertinen|ce /ɪmˈpɜːtɪnəns/ n Frechheit f. **~t** a frech

imperturbable /ɪmpəˈtɜːbəbl/ a unerschütterlich

impervious /ɪmˈpɜːvɪəs/ a **~ to** (*fig*) unempfänglich für

impetuous /im'petjʊəs/ *a*, **-ly** *adv* ungestüm

impetus /'impitəs/ *n* Schwung *m*

impish /'impiʃ/ *a* schelmisch

implacable /im'plækəbl/ *a* unerbittlich

im'plant¹ *vt* einpflanzen

'implant² *n* Implantat *nt*

implement¹ /'impliment/ *n* Gerät *nt*

implement² /'impliment/ *vt* ausführen

implicat|e /'implikeit/ *vt* verwickeln. **∼ion** /-'keiʃn/ *n* Verwicklung *f*; **∼ions** *pl* Auswirkungen *pl*; **by ∼ion** implizit

implicit /im'plisit/ *a*, **-ly** *adv* unausgesprochen; (*absolute*) unbedingt

implore /im'plɔ:(r)/ *vt* anflehen

imply /im'plai/ *vt* (*pt/pp* **-ied**) andeuten; **what are you ∼ing?** was wollen Sie damit sagen?

impo'lite *a*, **-ly** *adv* unhöflich

import¹ /'impɔ:t/ *n* Import *m*, Einfuhr *f*; (*importance*) Wichtigkeit *f*; (*meaning*) Bedeutung *f*

import² /im'pɔ:t/ *vt* importieren, einführen

importan|ce /im'pɔ:tns/ *n* Wichtigkeit *f*. **∼t** *a* wichtig

importer /im'pɔ:tə(r)/ *n* Importeur *m*

impos|e /im'pəʊz/ *vt* auferlegen (**on** *dat*) ● *vi* sich aufdrängen (**on** *dat*). **∼ing** *a* eindrucksvoll. **∼ition** /impə'ziʃn/ *n* **be an ∼ition** eine Zumutung sein

impossi'bility *n* Unmöglichkeit *f*

im'possible *a*, **-bly** *adv* unmöglich

impostor /im'pɒstə(r)/ *n* Betrüger(in) *m(f)*

impoten|ce /'impətəns/ *n* Machtlosigkeit *f*; (*Med*) Impotenz *f*. **∼t** *a* machtlos; (*Med*) impotent

impound /im'paʊnd/ *vt* beschlagnahmen

impoverished /im'pɒvəriʃt/ *a* verarmt

im'practicable *a* undurchführbar

im'practical *a* unpraktisch

impre'cise *a* ungenau

impregnable /im'pregnəbl/ *a* uneinnehmbar

impregnate /'impregneit/ *vt* tränken; (*Biol*) befruchten

im'press *vt* beeindrucken; **∼ sth [up]on s.o.** jdm etw einprägen

impression /im'preʃn/ *n* Eindruck *m*; (*imitation*) Nachahmung *f*; (*imprint*) Abdruck *m*; (*edition*) Auflage *f*. **∼ism** *n* Impressionismus *m*

impressive /im'presiv/ *a* eindrucksvoll

'imprint¹ *n* Abdruck *m*

im'print² *vt* prägen; (*fig*) einprägen (**on** *dat*)

im'prison *vt* gefangenhalten; (*put in prison*) ins Gefängnis sperren

im'probable *a* unwahrscheinlich

impromptu /im'prɒmptju:/ *a* improvisiert ● *adv* aus dem Stegreif

im'proper *a*, **-ly** *adv* inkorrekt; (*indecent*) unanständig

impro'priety *n* Unkorrektheit *f*

improve /im'pru:v/ *vt* verbessern; verschönern ⟨*appearance*⟩ ● *vi* sich bessern; **∼ [up]on** übertreffen. **∼ment** /-mənt/ *n* Verbesserung *f*; (*in health*) Besserung *f*

improvise /'imprəvaiz/ *vt/i* improvisieren

im'prudent *a* unklug

impuden|ce /'impjʊdəns/ *n* Frechheit *f*. **∼t** *a*, **-ly** *adv* frech

impuls|e /'impʌls/ *n* Impuls *m*; **on [an] ∼e** impulsiv. **∼ive** /-'pʌlsiv/ *a*, **-ly** *adv* impulsiv

impunity /im'pju:nəti/ *n* **with ∼** ungestraft

im'pur|e *a* unrein. **∼ity** *n* Unreinheit *f*; **∼ities** *pl* Verunreinigungen *pl*

impute /im'pju:t/ *vt* zuschreiben (**to** *dat*)

in /in/ *prep* in (+ *dat*/(*into*) + *acc*); **sit in the garden** im Garten sitzen; **go in the garden** in den Garten gehen; **in May** im Mai; **in the summer/winter** im Sommer/Winter; **in 1992** [im Jahre] 1992; **in this heat** bei dieser Hitze; **in the rain/sun** im Regen/in der Sonne; **in the evening** am Abend; **in the sky** am Himmel; **in the world** auf der Welt; **in the street** auf der Straße; **deaf in one ear** auf einem Ohr taub; **in the army** beim Militär; **in English/German** auf englisch/deutsch; **in ink/pencil** mit Tinte/Bleistift; **in a soft/loud voice** mit leiser/lauter Stimme; **in doing this, he ...** indem er das tut/tat, ... er ● *adv* (*at home*) zu Hause; (*indoors*) drinnen; **he's not in yet** er ist noch nicht da; **all in** alles inbegriffen; (*fam: exhausted*) kaputt; **day in, day out** tagaus, tagein; **keep in with s.o.** sich mit jdm gut stellen; **have it in for s.o.** (*fam*) es auf jdn abgesehen haben; **let oneself in for sth** sich auf etw (*acc*) einlassen; **send/go in** hineinschicken/-gehen; **come/bring**

in hereinkommen/-bringen ● *a* (*fam: in fashion*) in ● *n* **the ins and outs** alle Einzelheiten *pl*

ina'bility *n* Unfähigkeit *f*

inac'cessible *a* unzugänglich

in'accura|cy *n* Ungenauigkeit *f*. ~**te** *a*, **-ly** *adv* ungenau

in'ac|tive *a* untätig. ~**'tivity** *n* Untätigkeit *f*

in'adequate *a*, **-ly** *adv* unzulänglich; **feel** ~ sich der Situation nicht gewachsen fühlen

inad'missible *a* unzulässig

inadvertently /ɪnəd'vɜːtəntlɪ/ *adv* versehentlich

inad'visable *a* nicht ratsam

inane /ɪ'neɪn/ *a*, **-ly** *adv* albern

in'animate *a* unbelebt

in'applicable *a* nicht zutreffend

inap'propriate *a* unangebracht

inar'ticulate *a* undeutlich; **be** ~ sich nicht gut ausdrücken können

inat'tentive *a* unaufmerksam

in'audible *a*, **-bly** *adv* unhörbar

inaugural /ɪ'nɔːgjʊrl/ *a* Antritts-

inaugurat|e /ɪ'nɔːgjʊreɪt/ *vt* [feierlich] in sein Amt einführen. ~**ion** /-'reɪʃn/ *n* Amtseinführung *f*

inau'spicious *a* ungünstig

inborn /'ɪnbɔːn/ *a* angeboren

inbred /ɪn'bred/ *a* angeboren

incalculable /ɪn'kælkjʊləbl/ *a* nicht berechenbar; (*fig*) unabsehbar

in'capable *a* unfähig; **be** ~ **of doing sth** nicht fähig sein, etw zu tun

incapacitate /ɪnkə'pæsɪteɪt/ *vt* unfähig machen

incarcerate /ɪn'kɑːsəreɪt/ *vt* einkerkern

incarnat|e /ɪn'kɑːnət/ *a* **the devil** ~**e** der leibhaftige Satan. ~**ion** /-'neɪʃn/ *n* Inkarnation *f*

incendiary /ɪn'sendɪərɪ/ *a* & *n* ~ **[bomb]** Brandbombe *f*

incense[1] /'ɪnsens/ *n* Weihrauch *m*

incense[2] /ɪn'sens/ *vt* wütend machen

incentive /ɪn'sentɪv/ *n* Anreiz *m*

inception /ɪn'sepʃn/ *n* Beginn *m*

incessant /ɪn'sesnt/ *a*, **-ly** *adv* unaufhörlich

incest /'ɪnsest/ *n* Inzest *m*, Blutschande *f*

inch /ɪntʃ/ *n* Zoll *m* ● *vi* ~ **forward** sich ganz langsam vorwärtsschieben

inciden|ce /'ɪnsɪdəns/ *n* Vorkommen *nt*. ~**t** *n* Zwischenfall *m*

incidental /ɪnsɪ'dentl/ *a* nebensächlich; ⟨*remark*⟩ beiläufig; ⟨*expenses*⟩ Neben-. ~**ly** *adv* übrigens

incinerat|e /ɪn'sɪnəreɪt/ *vt* verbrennen. ~**or** *n* Verbrennungsofen *m*

incipient /ɪn'sɪpɪənt/ *a* angehend

incision /ɪn'sɪʒn/ *n* Einschnitt *m*

incisive /ɪn'saɪsɪv/ *a* scharfsinnig

incisor /ɪn'saɪzə(r)/ *n* Schneidezahn *m*

incite /ɪn'saɪt/ *vt* aufhetzen. ~**ment** *n* Aufhetzung *f*

inci'vility *n* Unhöflichkeit *f*

in'clement *a* rauh

inclination /ɪnklɪ'neɪʃn/ *n* Neigung *f*

incline[1] /ɪn'klaɪn/ *vt* neigen; **be** ~**d to do sth** dazu neigen, etw zu tun ● *vi* sich neigen

incline[2] /'ɪnklaɪn/ *n* Neigung *f*

inclu|de /ɪn'kluːd/ *vt* einschließen; (*contain*) enthalten; (*incorporate*) aufnehmen (**in** in + *acc*). ~**ding** *a* einschließlich (+ *gen*). ~**sion** /-uːʒn/ *n* Aufnahme *f*

inclusive /ɪn'kluːsɪv/ *a* Inklusiv-; ~ **of** einschließlich (+ *gen*) ● *adv* inklusive

incognito /ɪnkɒg'niːtəʊ/ *adv* inkognito

inco'herent *a*, **-ly** *adv* zusammenhanglos; (*incomprehensible*) unverständlich

income /'ɪnkəm/ *n* Einkommen *nt*. ~ **tax** *n* Einkommensteuer *f*

'incoming *a* ankommend; ⟨*mail*, *call*⟩ eingehend. ~ **tide** *n* steigende Flut *f*

in'comparable *a* unvergleichlich

incom'patible *a* unvereinbar; **be** ~ ⟨*people*:⟩ nicht zueinander passen

in'competen|ce *n* Unfähigkeit *f*. ~**t** *a* unfähig

incom'plete *a* unvollständig

incompre'hensible *a* unverständlich

incon'ceivable *a* undenkbar

incon'clusive *a* nicht schlüssig

incongruous /ɪn'kɒŋgrʊəs/ *a* unpassend

inconsequential /ɪnkɒnsɪ'kwenʃl/ *a* unbedeutend

incon'siderate *a* rücksichtslos

incon'sistent *a*, **-ly** *adv* widersprüchlich; (*illogical*) inkonsequent; **be** ~ nicht übereinstimmen

inconsolable /ɪnkən'səʊləbl/ *a* untröstlich

incon'spicuous *a* unauffällig

incontinen|ce /ɪn'kɒntɪnəns/ *n* Inkontinenz *f*. ~**t** *a* inkontinent

incon'venien|ce n Unannehmlichkeit f; (drawback) Nachteil m; **put s.o. to ∼ce** jdm Umstände machen. **∼t** a, **-ly** adv ungünstig; **be ∼t for s.o.** jdm nicht passen

incorporate /ɪnˈkɔːpəreɪt/ vt aufnehmen; (contain) enthalten

incor'rect a, **-ly** adv inkorrekt

incorrigible /ɪnˈkɒrɪdʒəbl/ a unverbesserlich

incorruptible /ɪnkəˈrʌptɪbl/ a unbestechlich

increase¹ /ˈɪnkriːs/ n Zunahme f; (rise) Erhöhung f; **be on the ∼** zunehmen

increas|e² /ɪnˈkriːs/ vt vergrößern; (raise) erhöhen ● vi zunehmen; (rise) sich erhöhen. **∼ing** a, **-ly** adv zunehmend

in'credible a, **-bly** adv unglaublich

incredulous /ɪnˈkredjʊləs/ a ungläubig

increment /ˈɪnkrɪmənt/ n Gehaltszulage f

incriminate /ɪnˈkrɪmɪneɪt/ vt (Jur) belasten

incubat|e /ˈɪŋkjʊbeɪt/ vt ausbrüten. **∼ion** /-ˈbeɪʃn/ n Ausbrüten nt. **∼ion period** n (Med) Inkubationszeit f. **∼or** n (for baby) Brutkasten m

inculcate /ˈɪnkʌlkeɪt/ vt einprägen (in dat)

incumbent /ɪnˈkʌmbənt/ a **be ∼ on s.o.** jds Pflicht sein

incur /ɪnˈkɜː(r)/ vt (pt/pp incurred) sich (dat) zuziehen; machen ⟨debts⟩

in'curable a, **-bly** adv unheilbar

incursion /ɪnˈkɜːʃn/ n Einfall m

indebted /ɪnˈdetɪd/ a verpflichtet (**to** dat)

in'decent a, **-ly** adv unanständig

inde'cision n Unentschlossenheit f

inde'cisive a ergebnislos; ⟨person⟩ unentschlossen

indeed /ɪnˈdiːd/ adv in der Tat, tatsächlich; **yes ∼!** allerdings! **I am/ do** oh doch! **very much ∼** sehr; **thank you very much ∼** vielen herzlichen Dank

indefatigable /ɪndɪˈfætɪɡəbl/ a unermüdlich

in'definite a unbestimmt. **∼ly** adv unbegrenzt; ⟨postpone⟩ auf unbestimmte Zeit

indelible /ɪnˈdelɪbl/ a, **-bly** adv nicht zu entfernen; (fig) unauslöschlich

indemni|fy /ɪnˈdemnɪfaɪ/ vt (pt/pp -ied) versichern; (compensate) entschädigen. **∼ty** n Versicherung f; Entschädigung f

indent /ɪnˈdent/ vt (Typ) einrücken. **∼ation** /-ˈteɪʃn/ n Einrückung f; (notch) Kerbe f

inde'penden|ce n Unabhängigkeit f; (self-reliance) Selbständigkeit f. **∼t** a, **-ly** adv unabhängig; selbständig

indescribable /ɪndɪˈskraɪbəbl/ a, **-bly** adv unbeschreiblich

indestructible /ɪndɪˈstrʌktəbl/ a unzerstörbar

indeterminate /ɪndɪˈtɜːmɪnət/ a unbestimmt

index /ˈɪndeks/ n Register nt

index: ∼ card n Karteikarte f. **∼ finger** n Zeigefinger m. **∼linked** a ⟨pension⟩ dynamisch

India /ˈɪndɪə/ n Indien nt. **∼n** a indisch; (American) indianisch ● n Inder(in) m(f); (American) Indianer(in) m(f)

Indian: ∼ 'ink n Tusche f. **∼ 'summer** n Nachsommer m

indicat|e /ˈɪndɪkeɪt/ vt zeigen; (point at) zeigen auf (+ acc); (hint) andeuten; (register) anzeigen ● vi (Auto) blinken. **∼ion** /-ˈkeɪʃn/ n Anzeichen nt

indicative /ɪnˈdɪkətɪv/ a **be ∼ of** schließen lassen auf (+ acc) ● n (Gram) Indikativ m

indicator /ˈɪndɪkeɪtə(r)/ n (Auto) Blinker m

indict /ɪnˈdaɪt/ vt anklagen. **∼ment** n Anklage f

in'differen|ce n Gleichgültigkeit f. **∼t** a, **-ly** adv gleichgültig; (not good) mittelmäßig

indigenous /ɪnˈdɪdʒɪnəs/ a einheimisch

indi'gest|ible a unverdaulich; (difficult to digest) schwerverdaulich. **∼ion** n Magenverstimmung f

indigna|nt /ɪnˈdɪɡnənt/ a, **-ly** adv entrüstet, empört. **∼tion** /-ˈneɪʃn/ n Entrüstung f, Empörung f

in'dignity n Demütigung f

indi'rect a, **-ly** adv indirekt

indi'screet a indiskret

indis'cretion n Indiskretion f

indiscriminate /ɪndɪˈskrɪmɪnət/ a, **-ly** adv wahllos

indi'spensable a unentbehrlich

indisposed /ɪndɪˈspəʊzd/ a indisponiert

indisputable /ɪndɪ'spjuːtəbl/ a, **-bly** adv unbestreitbar

indi'stinct a, **-ly** adv undeutlich

indistinguishable /ɪndɪ'stɪŋwɪʃəbl/ a be ~ nicht zu unterscheiden sein; (not visible) nicht erkennbar sein

individual /ɪndɪ'vɪdjʊəl/ a, **-ly** adv individuell; (single) einzeln ● n Individuum m. **~ity** /-'æləti/ n Individualität f

indi'visible a unteilbar

indoctrinate /ɪn'dɒktrɪneɪt/ vt indoktrinieren

indolen|ce /'ɪndələns/ n Faulheit f. **~t** a faul

indomitable /ɪn'dɒmɪtəbl/ a unbeugsam

indoor /'ɪndɔː(r)/ a Innen-; ⟨clothes⟩ Haus-; ⟨plant⟩ Zimmer-; (Sport) Hallen-. **~s** /-'dɔːz/ adv im Haus, drinnen; **go ~s** ins Haus gehen

induce /ɪn'djuːs/ vt dazu bewegen (to zu); (produce) herbeiführen. **~ment** n (incentive) Anreiz m

indulge /ɪn'dʌldʒ/ vt frönen (+ dat); verwöhnen ⟨child⟩ ● vi ~ frönen (+ dat). **~nce** /-əns/ n Nachgiebigkeit f; (leniency) Nachsicht f. **~nt** a [zu] nachgiebig; nachsichtig

industrial /ɪn'dʌstrɪəl/ a Industrie-; **take ~ action** streiken. **~ist** n Industrielle(r) m. **~ized** a industrialisiert

industr|ious /ɪn'dʌstrɪəs/ a, **-ly** adv fleißig. **~y** /'ɪndəstrɪ/ n Industrie f; (zeal) Fleiß m

inebriated /ɪ'niːbrɪeɪtɪd/ a betrunken

in'edible a nicht eßbar

inef'fective a, **-ly** adv unwirksam; ⟨person⟩ untauglich

inef'fectual /ɪnɪ'fektʃʊəl/ a unwirksam; ⟨person⟩ untauglich

inef'ficient a unfähig; ⟨organization⟩ nicht leistungsfähig; ⟨method⟩ nicht rationell

in'eligible a nicht berechtigt

inept /ɪ'nept/ a ungeschickt

ine'quality n Ungleichheit f

inert /ɪ'nɜːt/ a unbeweglich; (Phys) träge. **~ia** /ɪ'nɜːʃə/ n Trägheit f

inescapable /ɪnɪ'skeɪpəbl/ a unvermeidlich

inestimable /ɪn'estɪməbl/ a unschätzbar

inevitab|le /ɪn'evɪtəbl/ a unvermeidlich. **~ly** adv zwangsläufig

ine'xact a ungenau

inex'cusable a unverzeihlich

inexhaustible /ɪnɪg'zɔːstəbl/ a unerschöpflich

inexorable /ɪn'eksərəbl/ a unerbittlich

inex'pensive a, **-ly** adv preiswert

inex'perience n Unerfahrenheit f. **~d** a unerfahren

inexplicable /ɪnɪk'splɪkəbl/ a unerklärlich

in'fallible a unfehlbar

infam|ous /'ɪnfəməs/ a niederträchtig; (notorious) berüchtigt. **~y** n Niederträchtigkeit f

infan|cy /'ɪnfənsɪ/ n frühe Kindheit f; (fig) Anfangsstadium nt. **~t** n Kleinkind nt. **~tile** a kindisch

infantry /'ɪnfəntrɪ/ n Infanterie f

infatuated /ɪn'fætʃʊeɪtɪd/ a vernarrt (with in + acc)

infect /ɪn'fekt/ vt anstecken, infizieren; **become ~ed** ⟨wound:⟩ sich infizieren. **~ion** /-'fekʃn/ Infektion f. **~ious** /-'fekʃəs/ a ansteckend

infer /ɪn'fɜː(r)/ vt (pt/pp **inferred**) folgern (from aus); (imply) andeuten. **~ence** /'ɪnfərəns/ n Folgerung f

inferior /ɪn'fɪərɪə(r)/ a minderwertig; (in rank) untergeordnet ● n Untergebene(r) m/f

inferiority /ɪnfɪərɪ'ɒrətɪ/ n Minderwertigkeit f. **~ complex** n Minderwertigkeitskomplex m

infern|al /ɪn'fɜːnl/ a höllisch. **~o** n flammendes Inferno nt

in'fertile a unfruchtbar. **~'tility** n Unfruchtbarkeit f

infest /ɪn'fest/ vt **be ~ed with** befallen sein von; ⟨place⟩ verseucht sein mit

infi'delity n Untreue f

infighting /'ɪnfaɪtɪŋ/ n (fig) interne Machtkämpfe pl

infiltrate /'ɪnfɪltreɪt/ vt infiltrieren; (Pol) unterwandern

infinite /'ɪnfɪnət/ a, **-ly** adv unendlich

infinitesimal /ɪnfɪnɪ'tesɪml/ a unendlich klein

infinitive /ɪn'fɪnətɪv/ n (Gram) Infinitiv m

infinity /ɪn'fɪnətɪ/ n Unendlichkeit f

infirm /ɪn'fɜːm/ a gebrechlich. **~ary** n Krankenhaus nt. **~ity** n Gebrechlichkeit f

inflame /ɪn'fleɪm/ vt entzünden; **become ~d** sich entzünden. **~d** a entzündet

in'flammable a feuergefährlich

inflammation /ɪnflə'meɪʃn/ n Entzündung f

inflammatory /ɪnˈflæmətrɪ/ a aufrührerisch

inflatable /ɪnˈfleɪtəbl/ a aufblasbar

inflat|e /ɪnˈfleɪt/ vt aufblasen; (with pump) aufpumpen. ∼**ion** /-eɪʃn/ n Inflation f. ∼**ionary** /-eɪʃənərɪ/ a inflationär

in'flexible a starr; ⟨person⟩ unbeugsam

inflexion /ɪnˈflekʃn/ n Tonfall m; (Gram) Flexion f

inflict /ɪnˈflɪkt/ vt zufügen (on dat); versetzen ⟨blow⟩ (on dat)

influen|ce /ˈɪnfluəns/ n Einfluß m ● vt beeinflussen. ∼**tial** /-ˈenʃl/ a einflußreich

influenza /ɪnfluˈenzə/ n Grippe f

influx /ˈɪnflʌks/ n Zustrom m

inform /ɪnˈfɔːm/ vt benachrichtigen; (officially) informieren; ∼ s.o. of sth jdm etw mitteilen; **keep s.o.** ∼**ed** jdn auf dem laufenden halten ● vi ∼ **against** denunzieren

in'for|mal a, -ly adv zwanglos; (unofficial) inoffiziell. ∼'**mality** n Zwanglosigkeit f

informant /ɪnˈfɔːmənt/ n Gewährsmann m

informat|ion /ɪnfəˈmeɪʃn/ n Auskunft f; **a piece of** ∼**ion** eine Auskunft. ∼**ive** /ɪnˈfɔːmətɪv/ a aufschlußreich; (instructive) lehrreich

informer /ɪnˈfɔːmə(r)/ n Spitzel m; (Pol) Denunziant m

infra-'red /ɪnfrə-/ a infrarot

in'frequent a, -ly adv selten

infringe /ɪnˈfrɪndʒ/ vt/i ∼ **[on]** verstoßen gegen. ∼**ment** n Verstoß m

infuriat|e /ɪnˈfjʊərɪeɪt/ vt wütend machen. ∼**ing** a ärgerlich; **he is** ∼**ing** er kann einen zur Raserei bringen

infusion /ɪnˈfjuːʒn/ n Aufguß m

ingenious /ɪnˈdʒiːnɪəs/ a erfinderisch; ⟨thing⟩ raffiniert

ingenuity /ɪndʒɪˈnjuːətɪ/ n Geschicklichkeit f

ingenuous /ɪnˈdʒenjʊəs/ a unschuldig

ingot /ˈɪŋgət/ n Barren m

ingrained /ɪnˈgreɪnd/ a eingefleischt; **be** ∼ ⟨dirt:⟩ tief sitzen

ingratiate /ɪnˈgreɪʃɪeɪt/ vt ∼ **oneself** sich einschmeicheln (**with** bei)

in'gratitude n Undankbarkeit f

ingredient /ɪnˈgriːdɪənt/ n (Culin) Zutat f

ingrowing /ˈɪngrəʊɪŋ/ a ⟨nail⟩ eingewachsen

inhabit /ɪnˈhæbɪt/ vt bewohnen. ∼**ant** n Einwohner(in) m(f)

inhale /ɪnˈheɪl/ vt/i einatmen; (Med & when smoking) inhalieren

inherent /ɪnˈhɪərənt/ a natürlich

inherit /ɪnˈherɪt/ vt erben. ∼**ance** /-əns/ n Erbschaft f, Erbe nt

inhibit /ɪnˈhɪbɪt/ vt hemmen. ∼**ed** a gehemmt. ∼**ion** /-ˈbɪʃn/ n Hemmung f

inho'spitable a ungastlich

in'human a unmenschlich

inimitable /ɪˈnɪmɪtəbl/ a unnachahmlich

iniquitous /ɪˈnɪkwɪtəs/ a schändlich; (unjust) ungerecht

initial /ɪˈnɪʃl/ a anfänglich, Anfangs- ● n Anfangsbuchstabe m; **my** ∼**s** meine Initialen ● vt (pt/pp **initialled**) abzeichnen; (Pol) paraphieren. ∼**ly** adv anfangs, am Anfang

initiat|e /ɪˈnɪʃɪeɪt/ vt einführen. ∼**ion** /-eɪʃn/ n Einführung f

initiative /ɪˈnɪʃətɪv/ n Initiative f

inject /ɪnˈdʒekt/ vt einspritzen, injizieren. ∼**ion** /-ekʃn/ n Spritze f, Injektion f

injunction /ɪnˈdʒʌŋkʃn/ n gerichtliche Verfügung f

injur|e /ˈɪndʒə(r)/ vt verletzen. ∼**y** n Verletzung f

in'justice n Ungerechtigkeit f; **do s.o. an** ∼ jdm unrecht tun

ink /ɪŋk/ n Tinte f

inkling /ˈɪŋklɪŋ/ n Ahnung f

inlaid /ɪnˈleɪd/ a eingelegt

inland /ˈɪnlənd/ a Binnen- ● adv landeinwärts. **I**∼ **Revenue** n ≈ Finanzamt nt

in-laws /ˈɪnlɔːz/ npl (fam) Schwiegereltern pl

inlay /ˈɪnleɪ/ n Einlegearbeit f

inlet /ˈɪnlet/ n schmale Bucht f; (Techn) Zuleitung f

inmate /ˈɪnmeɪt/ n Insasse m

inn /ɪn/ n Gasthaus nt

innards /ˈɪnədz/ npl (fam) Eingeweide pl

innate /ɪˈneɪt/ a angeboren

inner /ˈɪnə(r)/ a innere(r,s). ∼**most** a innerste(r,s)

'innkeeper n Gastwirt m

innocen|ce /ˈɪnəsns/ n Unschuld f. ∼**t** a unschuldig. ∼**tly** adv in aller Unschuld

innocuous /ɪˈnɒkjʊəs/ a harmlos

innovat|e /ˈɪnəveɪt/ vi neu einführen. ∼**ion** /-ˈveɪʃn/ n Neuerung f. ∼**or** n Neuerer m

innuendo /ɪnjuːˈendəʊ/ n (pl -es) [versteckte] Anspielung f

innumerable /ɪˈnjuːmərəbl/ a unzählig

inoculat|e /ɪˈnɒkjʊleɪt/ vt impfen. ~ion /-ˈleɪʃn/ n Impfung f

inof'fensive a harmlos

in'operable a nicht operierbar

in'opportune a unpassend

inordinate /ɪˈnɔːdɪnət/ a, -ly adv übermäßig

inor'ganic a anorganisch

'in-patient n [stationär behandelter] Krankenhauspatient m

input /ˈɪnpʊt/ n Input m & nt

inquest /ˈɪnkwest/ n gerichtliche Untersuchung f

inquir|e /ɪnˈkwaɪə(r)/ vi sich erkundigen (about nach); ~e into untersuchen ● vt sich erkundigen nach. ~y n Erkundigung f; (investigation) Untersuchung f

inquisitive /ɪnˈkwɪzətɪv/ a, -ly adv neugierig

inroad /ˈɪnrəʊd/ n Einfall m; make ~s into sth etw angreifen

in'sane a geisteskrank; (fig) wahnsinnig

in'sanitary a unhygienisch

in'sanity n Geisteskrankheit f

insatiable /ɪnˈseɪʃəbl/ a unersättlich

inscri|be /ɪnˈskraɪb/ vt eingravieren. ~ption /-ˈskrɪpʃn/ n Inschrift f

inscrutable /ɪnˈskruːtəbl/ a ergründlich; ⟨expression⟩ undurchdringlich

insect /ˈɪnsekt/ n Insekt nt. ~icide /-ˈsektɪsaɪd/ n Insektenvertilgungsmittel nt

inse'cur|e a nicht sicher; (fig) unsicher. ~ity n Unsicherheit f

insemination /ɪnsemɪˈneɪʃn/ n Besamung f; (Med) Befruchtung f

in'sensible a (unconscious) bewußtlos

in'sensitive a gefühllos; ~ to unempfindlich gegen

in'separable a untrennbar; ⟨people⟩ unzertrennlich

insert¹ /ˈɪnsɜːt/ n Einsatz m

insert² /ɪnˈsɜːt/ vt einfügen, einsetzen; einstecken ⟨key⟩; einwerfen ⟨coin⟩. ~ion /-ɜːʃn/ n (insert) Einsatz m; (in text) Einfügung f

inside /ɪnˈsaɪd/ n Innenseite f; (of house) Innere(s) nt ● attrib Innen- ● adv innen; (indoors) drinnen; go ~ hineingehen; come ~ hereinkommen; ~ out links [herum]; know sth

~ out etw in und auswendig kennen ● prep ~[of] in (+ dat/ (into) + acc)

insidious /ɪnˈsɪdɪəs/ a, -ly adv heimtückisch

insight /ˈɪnsaɪt/ n Einblick m (into in + acc); (understanding) Einsicht f

insignia /ɪnˈsɪɡnɪə/ npl Insignien pl

insig'nificant a unbedeutend

insin'cere a unaufrichtig

insinuat|e /ɪnˈsɪnjʊeɪt/ vt andeuten. ~ion /-ˈeɪʃn/ n Andeutung f

insipid /ɪnˈsɪpɪd/ a fade

insist /ɪnˈsɪst/ vi darauf bestehen; ~ on bestehen auf (+ dat) ● vt ~ that darauf bestehen, daß. ~ence n Bestehen nt. ~ent a, -ly adv beharrlich; be ~ent darauf bestehen

'insole n Einlegesohle f

insolen|ce /ˈɪnsələns/ n Unverschämtheit f. ~t a, -ly adv unverschämt

in'soluble a unlöslich; (fig) unlösbar

in'solvent a zahlungsunfähig

insomnia /ɪnˈsɒmnɪə/ n Schlaflosigkeit f

inspect /ɪnˈspekt/ vt inspizieren; (test) prüfen; kontrollieren ⟨ticket⟩. ~ion /-ekʃn/ n Inspektion f. ~or n Inspektor m; (of tickets) Kontrolleur m

inspiration /ɪnspəˈreɪʃn/ n Inspiration f

inspire /ɪnˈspaɪə(r)/ vt inspirieren; ~ sth in s.o. jdm etw einflößen

insta'bility n Unbeständigkeit f; (of person) Labilität f

install /ɪnˈstɔːl/ vt installieren; [in ein Amt] einführen ⟨person⟩. ~ation /-stəˈleɪʃn/ n Installation f; Amtseinführung f

instalment /ɪnˈstɔːlmənt/ n (Comm) Rate f; (of serial) Fortsetzung f; (Radio, TV) Folge f

instance /ˈɪnstəns/ n Fall m; (example) Beispiel nt; in the first ~ zunächst; for ~ zum Beispiel

instant /ˈɪnstənt/ a sofortig; (Culin) Instant- ● n Augenblick m, Moment m. ~aneous /-ˈteɪnɪəs/ a unverzüglich, unmittelbar; death was ~aneous der Tod trat sofort ein

instant 'coffee n Pulverkaffee m

instantly /ˈɪnstəntlɪ/ adv sofort

instead /ɪnˈsted/ adv statt dessen; ~ of statt (+ gen), anstelle von; ~ of me an meiner Stelle; ~ of going anstatt zu gehen

'instep n Spann m, Rist m

instigat|e /ˈɪnstɪɡeɪt/ vt anstiften; einleiten ⟨proceedings⟩. ~ion /-ˈɡeɪʃn/ n

Anstiftung f; **at his** ~**ion** auf seine Veranlassung. ~**or** n Anstifter(in) m(f)

instil /ɪn'stɪl/ vt (pt/pp **instilled**) einprägen (**into s.o.** jdm)

instinct /'ɪnstɪŋkt/ n Instinkt m. ~**ive** /ɪn'stɪŋktɪv/ a, -**ly** adv instinktiv

institut|e /'ɪnstɪtjuːt/ n Institut nt ● vt einführen; einleiten ⟨search⟩. ~**ion** /-'tjuːʃn/ n Institution f; (home) Anstalt f

instruct /ɪn'strʌkt/ vt unterrichten; (order) anweisen. ~**ion** /-ʌkʃn/ n Unterricht m; Anweisung f; ~**ions** pl **for use** Gebrauchsanweisung f. ~**ive** /-ɪv/ a lehrreich. ~**or** n Lehrer (in) m(f); (Mil) Ausbilder(in) m(f)

instrument /'ɪnstrʊmənt/ n Instrument nt. ~**al** /-'mentl/ a Instrumental-; **be** ~**al in** eine entscheidende Rolle spielen bei

insu'bordi|nate a ungehorsam. ~**nation** /-'neɪʃn/ n Ungehorsam m; (Mil) Insubordination f

in'sufferable a unerträglich

insuf'ficient a, -**ly** adv nicht genügend

insular /'ɪnsjʊlə(r)/ a (fig) engstirnig

insulat|e /'ɪnsjʊleɪt/ vt isolieren. ~**ing tape** n Isolierband nt. ~**ion** /-'leɪʃn/ n Isolierung f

insulin /'ɪnsjʊlɪn/ n Insulin nt

insult[1] /'ɪnsʌlt/ n Beleidigung f

insult[2] /ɪn'sʌlt/ vt beleidigen

insuperable /ɪn'suːpərəbl/ a unüberwindlich

insur|ance /ɪn'ʃʊərəns/ n Versicherung f. ~**e** vt versichern

insurrection /ɪnsə'rekʃn/ n Aufstand m

intact /ɪn'tækt/ a unbeschädigt; (complete) vollständig

'intake n Aufnahme f

in'tangible a nicht greifbar

integral /'ɪntɪgrl/ a wesentlich

integrat|e /'ɪntɪgreɪt/ vt integrieren ● vi sich integrieren. ~**ion** /-'greɪʃn/ n Integration f

integrity /ɪn'tegrəti/ n Integrität f

intellect /'ɪntəlekt/ n Intellekt m. ~**ual** /-'lektjʊəl/ a intellektuell

intelligen|ce /ɪn'telɪdʒəns/ n Intelligenz f; (Mil) Nachrichtendienst m; (information) Meldungen pl. ~**t** a, -**ly** adv intelligent

intelligentsia /ɪntelɪ'dʒentsɪə/ n Intelligenz f

intelligible /ɪn'telɪdʒəbl/ a verständlich

intend /ɪn'tend/ vt beabsichtigen; **be** ~**ed for** bestimmt sein für

intense /ɪn'tens/ a intensiv; ⟨pain⟩ stark. ~**ly** adv äußerst; ⟨study⟩ intensiv

intensi|fication /ɪntensɪfɪ'keɪʃn/ n Intensivierung f. ~**fy** /-'tensɪfaɪ/ v (pt/pp -**ied**) ● vt intensivieren ● vi zunehmen

intensity /ɪn'tensəti/ n Intensität f

intensive /ɪn'tensɪv/ a, -**ly** adv intensiv; **be in** ~ **care** auf der Intensivstation sein

intent /ɪn'tent/ a, -**ly** adv aufmerksam; ~ **on** (absorbed in) vertieft in (+ acc); **be** ~ **on doing sth** fest entschlossen sein, etw zu tun ● n Absicht f; **to all** ~**s and purposes** im Grunde

intention /ɪn'tenʃn/ n Absicht f. ~**al** a, -**ly** adv absichtlich

inter /ɪn'tɜː(r)/ vt (pt/pp **interred**) bestatten

inter'action n Wechselwirkung f

intercede /ɪntə'siːd/ vi Fürsprache einlegen (**on behalf of** für)

intercept /ɪntə'sept/ vt abfangen

'interchange[1] n Austausch m; (Auto) Autobahnkreuz nt

inter'change[2] vt austauschen. ~**able** a austauschbar

intercom /'ɪntəkɒm/ n [Gegen]sprechanlage f

'intercourse n Verkehr m; (sexual) Geschlechtsverkehr m

interest /'ɪntrəst/ n Interesse nt; (Comm) Zinsen pl; **have an** ~ (Comm) beteiligt sein (**in an** + dat) ● vt interessieren; **be** ~**ed** sich interessieren (**in** für). ~**ing** a interessant. ~ **rate** n Zinssatz m

interfere /ɪntə'fɪə(r)/ vi sich einmischen. ~**nce** /-əns/ n Einmischung f; (Radio, TV) Störung f

interim /'ɪntərɪm/ a Zwischen-; (temporary) vorläufig ● n **in the** ~ in der Zwischenzeit

interior /ɪn'tɪərɪə(r)/ a innere(r,s), Innen- ● n Innere(s) nt

interject /ɪntə'dʒekt/ vt einwerfen. ~**ion** /-ekʃn/ n Interjektion f; (remark) Einwurf m

inter'lock vi ineinandergreifen

interloper /'ɪntələʊpə(r)/ n Eindringling m

interlude /'ɪntəluːd/ n Pause f; (performance) Zwischenspiel nt

inter'marry *vi* untereinander heiraten; ⟨*different groups:*⟩ Mischehen schließen

intermediary /ɪntə'miːdɪərɪ/ *n* Vermittler(in) *m(f)*

intermediate /ɪntə'miːdɪət/ *a* Zwischen-

interminable /ɪn'tɜːmɪnəbl/ *a* endlos [lang]

intermission /ɪntə'mɪʃn/ *n* Pause *f*

intermittent /ɪntə'mɪtənt/ *a* in Abständen auftretend

intern /ɪn'tɜːn/ *vt* internieren

internal /ɪn'tɜːnl/ *a* innere(r,s); ⟨*matter, dispute*⟩ intern. **~ly** *adv* innerlich; ⟨*deal with*⟩ intern

inter'national *a*, **-ly** *adv* international ● *n* Länderspiel *nt*; ⟨*player*⟩ Nationalspieler(in) *m(f)*

internist /ɪn'tɜːnɪst/ *n* (*Amer*) Internist *m*

internment /ɪn'tɜːnmənt/ *n* Internierung *f*

'interplay *n* Wechselspiel *nt*

interpolate /ɪn'tɜːpəleɪt/ *vt* einwerfen

interpret /ɪn'tɜːprɪt/ *vt* interpretieren; auslegen ⟨*text*⟩; deuten ⟨*dream*⟩; ⟨*translate*⟩ dolmetschen ● *vi* dolmetschen. **~ation** /-'teɪʃn/ *n* Interpretation *f*. **~er** *n* Dolmetscher(in) *m(f)*

interre'lated *a* verwandt; ⟨*facts*⟩ zusammenhängend

interrogat|e /ɪn'terəgeɪt/ *vt* verhören. **~ion** /-'geɪʃn/ *n* Verhör *nt*

interrogative /ɪntə'rɒgətɪv/ *a & n* **~** [pronoun] Interrogativpronomen *nt*

interrupt /ɪntə'rʌpt/ *vt/i* unterbrechen; **don't ~!** red nicht dazwischen! **~ion** /-ʌpʃn/ *n* Unterbrechung *f*

intersect /ɪntə'sekt/ *vi* sich kreuzen; (*Geom*) sich schneiden. **~ion** /-ekʃn/ *n* Kreuzung *f*

interspersed /ɪntə'spɜːst/ *a* **~ with** durchsetzt mit

inter'twine *vi* sich ineinanderschlingen

interval /'ɪntəvl/ *n* Abstand *m*; (*Theat*) Pause *f*; (*Mus*) Intervall *nt*; **at hourly ~s** alle Stunde; **bright ~s** *pl* Aufheiterungen *pl*

interven|e /ɪntə'viːn/ *vi* eingreifen; (*occur*) dazwischenkommen. **~tion** /-'venʃn/ *n* Eingreifen *nt*; (*Mil, Pol*) Intervention *f*

interview /'ɪntəvjuː/ *n* (*Journ*) Interview *nt*; (*for job*) Vorstellungsgespräch *nt*; **go for an ~** sich vorstellen ● *vt* interviewen; ein Vorstellungsgespräch führen mit. **~er** *n* Interviewer(in) *m(f)*

intestine /ɪn'testɪn/ *n* Darm *m*

intimacy /'ɪntɪməsɪ/ *n* Vertrautheit *f*; (*sexual*) Intimität *f*

intimate¹ /'ɪntɪmət/ *a*, **-ly** *adv* vertraut; ⟨*friend*⟩ eng; (*sexually*) intim

intimate² /'ɪntɪmeɪt/ *vt* zu verstehen geben; (*imply*) andeuten

intimidat|e /ɪn'tɪmɪdeɪt/ *vt* einschüchtern. **~ion** /-'deɪʃn/ *n* Einschüchterung *f*

into /'ɪntə, *vor einem Vokal* ɪntʊ/ *prep* in (+ *acc*); **go ~ the house** ins Haus [hinein]gehen; **be ~** (*fam*) sich auskennen mit; **7 ~ 21** 21 [geteilt] durch 7

in'tolerable *a* unerträglich

in'toleran|ce *n* Intoleranz *f*. **~t** *a* intolerant

intonation /ɪntə'neɪʃn/ *n* Tonfall *m*

intoxicat|ed /ɪn'tɒksɪkeɪtɪd/ *a* betrunken; (*fig*) berauscht. **~ion** /-'keɪʃn/ *n* Rausch *m*

intractable /ɪn'træktəbl/ *a* widerspenstig; ⟨*problem*⟩ hartnäckig

intransigent /ɪn'trænsɪdʒənt/ *a* unnachgiebig

in'transitive *a*, **-ly** *adv* intransitiv

intravenous /ɪntrə'viːnəs/ *a*, **-ly** *adv* intravenös

intrepid /ɪn'trepɪd/ *a* kühn, unerschrocken

intricate /'ɪntrɪkət/ *a* kompliziert

intrigu|e /ɪn'triːg/ *n* Intrige *f* ● *vt* faszinieren ● *vi* intrigieren. **~ing** *a* faszinierend

intrinsic /ɪn'trɪnsɪk/ *a* **~ value** Eigenwert *m*

introduce /ɪntrə'djuːs/ *vt* vorstellen; (*bring in, insert*) einführen

introduct|ion /ɪntrə'dʌkʃn/ *n* Einführung *f*; (*to person*) Vorstellung *f*; (*to book*) Einleitung *f*. **~ory** /-'təri/ *a* einleitend

introspective /ɪntrə'spektɪv/ *a* in sich (*acc*) gerichtet

introvert /'ɪntrəvɜːt/ *n* introvertierter Mensch *m*

intru|de /ɪn'truːd/ *vi* stören. **~der** *n* Eindringling *m*. **~sion** /-uːʒn/ *n* Störung *f*

intuit|ion /ɪntjuː'ɪʃn/ *n* Intuition *f*. **~ive** /-'tjuːɪtɪv/ *a*, **-ly** *adv* intuitiv

inundate /'ɪnəndeɪt/ vt überschwemmen

invade /ɪn'veɪd/ vt einfallen in (+ acc). ~r n Angreifer m

invalid¹ /'ɪnvəlɪd/ n Kranke(r) m/f

invalid² /ɪn'vælɪd/ a ungültig. ~ate vt ungültig machen

in'valuable a unschätzbar; ⟨person⟩ unersetzlich

in'variab|le a unveränderlich. ~ly adv immer

invasion /ɪn'veɪʒn/ n Invasion f

invective /ɪn'vektɪv/ n Beschimpfungen pl

invent /ɪn'vent/ vt erfinden. ~ion /-enʃn/ n Erfindung f. ~ive /-tɪv/ a erfinderisch. ~or n Erfinder m

inventory /'ɪnvəntrɪ/ n Bestandsliste f; **make an** ~ ein Inventar aufstellen

inverse /ɪn'vɜːs/ a, -ly adv umgekehrt ● n Gegenteil nt

invert /ɪn'vɜːt/ vt umkehren. ~ed **commas** npl Anführungszeichen pl

invest /ɪn'vest/ vt investieren, anlegen; ~ **in** (fam: buy) sich (dat) zulegen

investigat|e /ɪn'vestɪgeɪt/ vt untersuchen. ~ion /-'geɪʃn/ n Untersuchung f

invest|ment /ɪn'vestmənt/ n Anlage f; **be a good** ~ment (fig) sich bezahlt machen. ~or n Kapitalanleger m

inveterate /ɪn'vetərət/ a Gewohnheits-; ⟨liar⟩ unverbesserlich

invidious /ɪn'vɪdɪəs/ a unerfreulich; (unfair) ungerecht

invigilate /ɪn'vɪdʒɪleɪt/ vi (Sch) Aufsicht führen

invigorate /ɪn'vɪgəreɪt/ vt beleben

invincible /ɪn'vɪnsəbl/ a unbesiegbar

inviolable /ɪn'vaɪələbl/ a unantastbar

in'visible a unsichtbar. ~ **mending** n Kunststopfen nt

invitation /ɪnvɪ'teɪʃn/ n Einladung f

invit|e /ɪn'vaɪt/ vt einladen. ~ing a einladend

invoice /'ɪnvɔɪs/ n Rechnung f ● vt ~ **s.o.** jdm eine Rechnung schicken

invoke /ɪn'vəʊk/ vt anrufen

in'voluntary a, -ily adv unwillkürlich

involve /ɪn'vɒlv/ vt beteiligen; (affect) betreffen; (implicate) verwickeln; (entail) mit sich bringen; (mean) bedeuten; **be** ~**d in** beteiligt sein an (+dat); (implicated) verwickelt sein in (+ acc); **get** ~**d with**

s.o. sich mit jdm einlassen. ~**d** a kompliziert

in'vulnerable a unverwundbar; ⟨position⟩ unangreifbar

inward /'ɪnwəd/ a innere(r,s). ~ly adv innerlich. ~s adv nach innen

iodine /'aɪədiːn/ n Jod nt

iota /aɪ'əʊtə/ n Jota nt; (fam) Funke m

IOU abbr (I owe you) Schuldschein m

Iran /ɪ'rɑːn/ n der Iran

Iraq /ɪ'rɑːk/ n der Irak

irascible /ɪ'ræsəbl/ a aufbrausend

irate /aɪ'reɪt/ a wütend

Ireland /'aɪələnd/ n Irland nt

iris /'aɪərɪs/ n (Anat) Regenbogenhaut f, Iris f; (Bot) Schwertlilie f

Irish /'aɪərɪʃ/ a irisch ● **the** ~ pl die Iren. ~**man** n Ire m. ~**woman** n Irin f

irk /ɜːk/ vt ärgern. ~**some** /-səm/ a lästig

iron /'aɪən/ a Eisen-; (fig) eisern ● n Eisen nt; (appliance) Bügeleisen nt ● vt/i bügeln. ~ **out** vt ausbügeln

ironic[al] /aɪ'rɒnɪk[l]/ a ironisch

ironing /'aɪənɪŋ/ n Bügeln nt; (articles) Bügelwäsche f; **do the** ~ bügeln. ~-**board** n Bügelbrett nt

ironmonger /'-mʌŋgə(r)/ n ~'s [shop] Haushaltswarengeschäft nt

irony /'aɪərənɪ/ n Ironie f

irradiate /ɪ'reɪdɪeɪt/ vt bestrahlen

irrational /ɪ'ræʃənl/ a irrational

irreconcilable /ɪ'rekənsaɪləbl/ a unversöhnlich

irrefutable /ɪrɪ'fjuːtəbl/ a unwiderlegbar

irregular /ɪ'regʊlə(r)/ a, -ly adv unregelmäßig; (against rules) regelwidrig. ~**ity** /-'lærətɪ/ n Unregelmäßigkeit f; Regelwidrigkeit f

irrelevant /ɪ'reləvənt/ a irrelevant

irreparable /ɪ'repərəbl/ a unersetzlich; **be** ~ nicht wiedergutzumachen sein

irreplaceable /ɪrɪ'pleɪsəbl/ a unersetzlich

irrepressible /ɪrɪ'presəbl/ a unverwüstlich; **be** ~ ⟨person:⟩ nicht unterzukriegen sein

irresistible /ɪrɪ'zɪstəbl/ a unwiderstehlich

irresolute /ɪ'rezəluːt/ a unentschlossen

irrespective /ɪrɪ'spektɪv/ a ~ **of** ungeachtet (+ gen)

irresponsible /ɪrɪ'spɒnsəbl/ a, -bly adv unverantwortlich; ⟨person⟩ verantwortungslos

irreverent /ɪˈrevərənt/ a, **-ly** adv respektlos

irreversible /ɪrɪˈvɜːsəbl/ a unwiderruflich; (Med) irreversibel

irrevocable /ɪˈrevəkəbl/ a, **-bly** adv unwiderruflich

irrigat|e /ˈɪrɪgeɪt/ vt bewässern. **~ion** /-ˈgeɪʃn/ n Bewässerung f

irritability /ɪrɪtəˈbɪlətɪ/ n Gereiztheit f

irritable /ˈɪrɪtəbl/ a reizbar

irritant /ˈɪrɪtənt/ n Reizstoff m

irritat|e /ˈɪrɪteɪt/ vt irritieren; (Med) reizen. **~ion** /-ˈteɪʃn/ n Ärger m; (Med) Reizung f

is /ɪz/ see **be**

Islam /ˈɪzlɑːm/ n der Islam. **~ic** /-ˈlæmɪk/ a islamisch

island /ˈaɪlənd/ n Insel f. **~er** n Inselbewohner(in) m(f)

isle /aɪl/ n Insel f

isolat|e /ˈaɪsəleɪt/ vt isolieren. **~ed** a (remote) abgelegen; (single) einzeln. **~ion** /-ˈleɪʃn/ n Isoliertheit f; (Med) Isolierung f

Israel /ˈɪzreɪl/ n Israel nt. **~i** /ɪzˈreɪlɪ/ a israelisch ● n Israeli m/f

issue /ˈɪʃuː/ n Frage f; (outcome) Ergebnis nt; (of magazine, stamps) Ausgabe f; (offspring) Nachkommen pl; **what is at ~?** worum geht es? **take ~ with s.o.** jdm widersprechen ● vt ausgeben; ausstellen ⟨passport⟩; erteilen ⟨order⟩; herausgeben ⟨book⟩; **be ~d with sth** etw erhalten ● vi **~ from** herausströmen aus

isthmus /ˈɪsməs/ n (pl **-muses**) Landenge f

it /ɪt/ pron es; (m) er; (f) sie; (as direct object) es; (m) ihn; (f) sie; (as indirect object) ihm; (f) ihr; **it is raining** es regnet; **it's me** ich bin's; **who is it?** wer ist da? **of/from it** davon; **with it** damit; **out of it** daraus

Italian /ɪˈtæljən/ a italienisch ● n Italiener(in) m(f); (Lang) Italienisch nt

italic /ɪˈtælɪk/ a kursiv. **~s** npl Kursivschrift f; **in ~s** kursiv

Italy /ˈɪtəlɪ/ n Italien nt

itch /ɪtʃ/ n Juckreiz m; **I have an ~** es juckt mich ● vi jucken; **I'm ~ing** (fam) es juckt mich (**to** zu). **~y** a **be ~y** jucken

item /ˈaɪtəm/ n Gegenstand m; (Comm) Artikel m; (on agenda) Punkt m; (on invoice) Posten m; (act) Nummer f; **~ [of news]** Nachricht f. **~ize** vt einzeln aufführen; spezifizieren ⟨bill⟩

itinerant /aɪˈtɪnərənt/ a Wander-

itinerary /aɪˈtɪnərərɪ/ n [Reise]route f

its /ɪts/ poss pron sein; (f) ihr

it's = **it is, it has**

itself /ɪtˈself/ pron selbst; (refl) sich; **by ~** von selbst; (alone) allein –

ivory /ˈaɪvərɪ/ n Elfenbein nt ● attrib Elfenbein-

ivy /ˈaɪvɪ/ n Efeu m

J

jab /dʒæb/ n Stoß m; (fam: injection) Spritze f ● vt (pt/pp **jabbed**) stoßen

jabber /ˈdʒæbə(r)/ vi plappern

jack /dʒæk/ n (Auto) Wagenheber m; (Cards) Bube m ● vt **~ up** (Auto) aufbocken

jackdaw /ˈdʒækdɔː/ n Dohle f

jacket /ˈdʒækɪt/ n Jacke f; (of book) Schutzumschlag m. **~ po'tato** n in der Schale gebackene Kartoffel f

'jackpot n **hit the ~** das Große Los ziehen

jade /dʒeɪd/ n Jade m

jaded /ˈdʒeɪdɪd/ a abgespannt

jagged /ˈdʒægɪd/ a zackig

jail /dʒeɪl/ = **gaol**

jalopy /dʒəˈlɒpɪ/ n (fam) Klapperkiste f

jam¹ /dʒæm/ n Marmelade f

jam² n Gedränge nt; (Auto) Stau m; (fam: difficulty) Klemme f ● v (pt/pp **jammed**) vt klemmen (**in** + acc); stören ⟨broadcast⟩ ● vi klemmen

Jamaica /dʒəˈmeɪkə/ n Jamaika nt

jangle /ˈdʒæŋgl/ vi klimpern ● vt klimpern mit

janitor /ˈdʒænɪtə(r)/ n Hausmeister m

January /ˈdʒænjʊərɪ/ n Januar m

Japan /dʒəˈpæn/ n Japan nt. **~ese** /dʒæpəˈniːz/ a japanisch ● n Japaner(in) m(f); (Lang) Japanisch nt

jar¹ /dʒɑː(r)/ n Glas nt; (earthenware) Topf m

jar² v (pt/pp **jarred**) vi stören ● vt erschüttern

jargon /ˈdʒɑːgən/ n Jargon m

jaundice /ˈdʒɔːndɪs/ n Gelbsucht f. **~d** a (fig) zynisch

jaunt /dʒɔːnt/ n Ausflug m

jaunty /ˈdʒɔːntɪ/ a (-ier, -iest), **-ily** adv keck

javelin /ˈdʒævlɪn/ n Speer m

jaw /dʒɔː/ n Kiefer m; **~s** pl Rachen m ● vi (fam) quatschen

jay /dʒeɪ/ n Eichelhäher m. **~-walker**
n achtloser Fußgänger m

jazz /dʒæz/ n Jazz m. **~y** a knallig

jealous /'dʒeləs/ a, **-ly** adv eifersüchtig
(of auf + acc). **~y** n Eifersucht f

jeans /dʒiːnz/ npl Jeans pl

jeer /dʒɪə(r)/ n Johlen nt • vi johlen;
~ at verhöhnen

jell /dʒel/ vi gelieren

jelly /'dʒelɪ/ n Gelee nt; (dessert) Götterspeise f. **~fish** n Qualle f

jemmy /'dʒemɪ/ n Brecheisen nt

jeopar|dize /'dʒepədaɪz/ vt gefähr-
den. **~dy** /-dɪ/ n in **~dy** gefährdet

jerk /dʒɜːk/ n Ruck m • vt stoßen;
(pull) reißen • vi rucken; ⟨limb,
muscle:⟩ zucken. **~ily** adv ruckweise. **~y** a ruckartig

jersey /'dʒɜːzɪ/ n Pullover m; (Sport)
Trikot nt; (fabric) Jersey m

jest /dʒest/ n Scherz m; **in ~** im Spaß
• vi scherzen

jet¹ /dʒet/ n (Miner) Jett m

jet² n (of water) [Wasser]strahl m;
(nozzle) Düse f; (plane) Düsenflug-
zeug nt

jet: **~-'black** a pechschwarz. **~ lag** n
Jet-lag nt. **~-pro'pelled** a mit
Düsenantrieb

jettison /'dʒetɪsn/ vt über Bord
werfen

jetty /'dʒetɪ/ n Landesteg m; (breakwater) Buhne f

Jew /dʒuː/ n Jude m /Jüdin f

jewel /'dʒuːəl/ n Edelstein m; (fig)
Juwel nt. **~ler** n Juwelier m; **~ler's
[shop]** Juweliergeschäft nt. **~lery** n
Schmuck m

Jew|ess /'dʒuːɪs/ n Jüdin f. **~ish** a
jüdisch

jib /dʒɪb/ vi (pt/pp jibbed) (fig) sich
sträuben (at gegen)

jiffy /'dʒɪfɪ/ n (fam) **in a ~** in einem
Augenblick

jigsaw /'dʒɪgsɔː/ n **~ [puzzle]** Puzzlespiel nt

jilt /dʒɪlt/ vt sitzenlassen

jingle /'dʒɪŋgl/ n (rhyme) Versehen nt
• vi klimpern • vt klimpern mit

jinx /dʒɪŋks/ n (fam) **it's got a ~ on it**
es ist verhext

jitter|s /'dʒɪtəz/ npl (fam) **have the ~s**
nervös sein. **~y** a (fam) nervös

job /dʒɒb/ n Aufgabe f; (post) Stelle f;
(fam) Job m; **be a ~** (fam) nicht
leicht sein; **it's a good ~ that** es ist
[nur] gut, daß. **~centre** n Arbeits-
vermittlungsstelle f. **~less** a
arbeitslos

jockey /'dʒɒkɪ/ n Jockei m

jocular /'dʒɒkjʊlə(r)/ a, **-ly** adv
spaßhaft

jog /dʒɒg/ n Stoß m; **at a ~** im
Dauerlauf • v (pt/pp jogged) • vt
anstoßen; **s.o.'s memory** jds Gedächtnis nachhelfen • vi (Sport)
joggen. **~ging** n Jogging nt

john /dʒɒn/ n (Amer, fam) Klo nt

join /dʒɔɪn/ n Nahtstelle f • vt verbinden (**to** mit); sich anschließen (+
dat) ⟨person⟩; (become member of)
beitreten (+ dat); eintreten in (+
acc) ⟨firm⟩ • vi ⟨roads:⟩ sich treffen.
~ in vi mitmachen. **~ up** vi (Mil)
Soldat werden • vt zusammenfügen

joiner /'dʒɔɪnə(r)/ n Tischler m

joint /dʒɔɪnt/ a, **-ly** adv gemeinsam
• n Gelenk nt; (in wood, brickwork)
Fuge f; (Culin) Braten m; (fam: bar)
Lokal nt

joist /dʒɔɪst/ n Dielenbalken m

jok|e /dʒəʊk/ n Scherz m; (funny
story) Witz m; (trick) Streich m • vi
scherzen. **~er** n Witzbold m;
(Cards) Joker m. **~ing apart**
Spaß beiseite. **~ingly** adv im Spaß

jollity /'dʒɒlətɪ/ n Lustigkeit f

jolly /'dʒɒlɪ/ a (-ier, -iest) lustig • adv
(fam) sehr

jolt /dʒəʊlt/ n Ruck m • vt einen Ruck
versetzen (+ dat) • vi holpern

Jordan /'dʒɔːdn/ n Jordanien nt

jostle /'dʒɒsl/ vt anrempeln • vi
drängeln

jot /dʒɒt/ n Jota nt • vt (pt/pp jotted)
~ [down] sich (dat) notieren. **~ter**
n Notizblock m

journal /'dʒɜːnl/ n Zeitschrift f;
(diary) Tagebuch nt. **~ese** /-ə'liːz/ n
Zeitungsjargon m. **~ism** n Journa-
lismus m. **~ist** n Journalist(in) m(f)

journey /'dʒɜːnɪ/ n Reise f

jovial /'dʒəʊvɪəl/ a lustig

joy /dʒɔɪ/ n Freude f. **~ful** a, **-ly** adv
freudig, froh. **~ride** n (fam) Spritz-
tour f [im gestohlenen Auto]

jubil|ant /'dʒuːbɪlənt/ a überglück-
lich. **~ation** /-'leɪʃn/ n Jubel m

jubilee /'dʒuːbɪliː/ n Jubiläum nt

Judaism /'dʒuːdeɪɪzm/ n Judentum nt

judder /'dʒʌdə(r)/ vi rucken

judge /dʒʌdʒ/ n Richter m; (of competition) Preisrichter m • vt beurteilen; (estimate) [ein]schätzen • vi ur-
teilen (**by** nach). **~ment** n Beurtei-
lung f; (Jur) Urteil nt; (fig) Urteils-
vermögen nt

judic|ial /dʒuːˈdɪʃl/ *a* gerichtlich. **~iary** /-ʃərɪ/ *n* Richterstand *m*. **~ious** /-ʃəs/ *a* klug

judo /ˈdʒuːdəʊ/ *n* Judo *nt*

jug /dʒʌg/ *n* Kanne *f*; *(small)* Kännchen *nt*; *(for water, wine)* Krug *m*

juggernaut /ˈdʒʌgənɔːt/ *n* *(fam)* Riesenlaster *m*

juggle /ˈdʒʌgl/ *vi* jonglieren. **~r** *n* Jongleur *m*

juice /dʒuːs/ *n* Saft *m*. **~ extractor** *n* Entsafter *m*

juicy /ˈdʒuːsɪ/ *a* (**-ier, -iest**) saftig; *(fam)* ⟨*story*⟩ pikant

juke-box /ˈdʒuːk-/ *n* Musikbox *f*

July /dʒuˈlaɪ/ *n* Juli *m*

jumble /ˈdʒʌmbl/ *n* Durcheinander *nt* ● *vt* **~[up]** durcheinanderbringen. **~ sale** *n* [Wohltätigkeits]basar *m*

jumbo /ˈdʒʌmbəʊ/ *n* **~ [jet]** Jumbo[-Jet] *m*

jump /dʒʌmp/ *n* Sprung *m*; *(in prices)* Anstieg *m*; *(in horse racing)* Hindernis *nt* ● *vi* springen; *(start)* zusammenzucken; **make s.o. ~** jdn erschrecken; **~ at** *(fig)* sofort zugreifen bei ⟨*offer*⟩; **~ to conclusions** voreilige Schlüsse ziehen ● *vt* überspringen; **~ the gun** *(fig)* vorschnell handeln. **~ up** *vi* aufspringen

jumper /ˈdʒʌmpə(r)/ *n* Pullover *m*, Pulli *m*

jumpy /ˈdʒʌmpɪ/ *a* nervös

junction /ˈdʒʌŋkʃn/ *n* Kreuzung *f*; *(Rail)* Knotenpunkt *m*

juncture /ˈdʒʌŋktʃə(r)/ *n* **at this ~** zu diesem Zeitpunkt

June /dʒuːn/ *n* Juni *m*

jungle /ˈdʒʌŋgl/ *n* Dschungel *m*

junior /ˈdʒuːnɪə(r)/ *a* jünger; *(in rank)* untergeordnet; *(Sport)* Junioren- ● *n* Junior *m*. **~ school** *n* Grundschule *f*

juniper /ˈdʒuːnɪpə(r)/ *n* Wacholder *m*

junk /dʒʌŋk/ *n* Gerümpel *nt*, Trödel *m*

junkie /ˈdʒʌŋkɪ/ *n* (*sl*) Fixer *m*

'junk-shop *n* Trödelladen *m*

juris|diction /dʒʊərɪsˈdɪkʃn/ *n* Gerichtsbarkeit *f*. **~'prudence** *n* Rechtswissenschaft *f*

juror /ˈdʒʊərə(r)/ *n* Geschworene(r) *m/f*

jury /ˈdʒʊərɪ/ *n* **the ~** die Geschworenen *pl*; *(for competition)* die Jury

just /dʒʌst/ *a* gerecht ● *adv* gerade; *(only)* nur; *(simply)* einfach; *(exactly)* genau; **~ as tall** ebenso groß; **~ listen!** hör doch mal! **I'm ~ going**

ich gehe schon; **~ put it down** stell es nur hin

justice /ˈdʒʌstɪs/ *n* Gerechtigkeit *f*; **do ~ to** gerecht werden (+ *dat*); **J~ of the Peace** ≈ Friedensrichter *m*

justifiab|le /ˈdʒʌstɪfaɪəbl/ *a* berechtigt. **~ly** *adv* berechtigterweise

justi|fication /dʒʌstɪfɪˈkeɪʃn/ *n* Rechtfertigung *f*. **~fy** /ˈdʒʌstɪfaɪ/ *vt* (*pt/pp* **-ied**) rechtfertigen

justly /ˈdʒʌstlɪ/ *adv* zu Recht

jut /dʒʌt/ *vi* (*pt/pp* **jutted**) **~ out** vorstehen

juvenile /ˈdʒuːvənaɪl/ *a* jugendlich; *(childish)* kindisch ● *n* Jugendliche(r) *m/f*. **~ delinquency** *n* Jugendkriminalität *f*

juxtapose /dʒʌkstəˈpəʊz/ *vt* nebeneinanderstellen

K

kangaroo /kæŋgəˈruː/ *n* Känguruh *nt*

karate /kəˈrɑːtɪ/ *n* Karate *nt*

kebab /kɪˈbæb/ *n* *(Culin)* Spießchen *nt*

keel /kiːl/ *n* Kiel *m* ● *vi* **~ over** umkippen; *(Naut)* kentern

keen /kiːn/ *a* (**-er, -est**) *(sharp)* scharf; *(intense)* groß; *(eager)* eifrig, begeistert; **~ on** *(fam)* erpicht auf (+ *acc*); **~ on s.o.** von jdm sehr angetan; **be ~ to do sth** etw gerne machen wollen. **~ly** *adv* tief. **~ness** *n* Eifer *m*, Begeisterung *f*

keep /kiːp/ *n* *(maintenance)* Unterhalt *m*; *(of castle)* Bergfried *m*; **for ~s** für immer ● *v* (*pt/pp* **kept**) ● *vt* behalten; *(store)* aufbewahren; *(not throw away)* aufheben; *(support)* unterhalten; *(detain)* aufhalten; freihalten ⟨*seat*⟩; halten ⟨*promise, animals*⟩; führen, haben ⟨*shop*⟩; einhalten ⟨*law, rules*⟩; **~ sth hot** etw warm halten; **~ s.o. from doing sth** jdn davon abhalten, etw zu tun; **~ s.o. waiting** jdn warten lassen; **~ sth to oneself** etw nicht weitersagen; **where do you ~ the sugar?** wo hast du den Zucker? ● *vi* *(remain)* bleiben; ⟨*food:*⟩ sich halten; **~ left/right** sich links/rechts halten; **~ doing sth** etw dauernd machen; **~ on doing sth** etw weitermachen; **~ in with** sich gut stellen mit. **~ up** *vi*

Schritt halten ● *vt* (*continue*) weitermachen

keep|er /'ki:pə(r)/ *n* Wärter(in) *m(f)*. **~ing** *n* Obhut *f*; **be in ~ing with** passen zu. **~sake** *n* Andenken *nt*

keg /keg/ *n* kleines Faß *nt*

kennel /'kenl/ *n* Hundehütte *f*; **~s** *pl* (*boarding*) Hundepension *f*; (*breeding*) Zwinger *m*

Kenya /'kenjə/ *n* Kenia *nt*

kept /kept/ *see* **keep**

kerb /kɜ:b/ *n* Bordstein *m*

kernel /'kɜ:nl/ *n* Kern *m*

kerosene /'kerəsi:n/ *n* (*Amer*) Petroleum *nt*

ketchup /'ketʃʌp/ *n* Ketchup *m*

kettle /'ketl/ *n* [Wasser]kessel *m*; **put the ~ on** Wasser aufsetzen; **a pretty ~ of fish** (*fam*) eine schöne Bescherung *f*

key /ki:/ *n* Schlüssel *m*; (*Mus*) Tonart *f*; (*of piano, typewriter*) Taste *f* ● *vt* **~ in** *vt* eintasten

key: ~board *n* Tastatur *f*; (*Mus*) Klaviatur *f*. **~boarder** *n* Taster(in) *m(f)*. **~hole** *n* Schlüsselloch *nt*. **~ring** *n* Schlüsselring *m*

khaki /'kɑ:kɪ/ *a* khakifarben ● *n* Khaki *nt*

kick /kɪk/ *n* [Fuß]tritt *m*; **for ~s** (*fam*) zum Spaß ● *vt* treten; **~ the bucket** (*fam*) abkratzen ● *vi* ⟨*animal:*⟩ ausschlagen. **~-off** *n* (*Sport*) Anstoß *m*

kid /kɪd/ *n* Kitz *nt*; (*fam: child*) Kind *nt* ● *vt* (*pt/pp* **kidded**) (*fam*) **~ s.o.** jdm etwas vormachen. **~ gloves** *npl* Glacéhandschuhe *pl*

kidnap /'kɪdnæp/ *vt* (*pt/pp* **-napped**) entführen. **~per** *n* Entführer *m*. **~ping** *n* Entführung *f*

kidney /'kɪdnɪ/ *n* Niere *f*. **~ machine** *n* künstliche Niere *f*

kill /kɪl/ *vt* töten; (*fam*) totschlagen ⟨*time*⟩; **~ two birds with one stone** zwei Fliegen mit einer Klappe schlagen. **~er** *n* Mörder(in) *m(f)*. **~ing** *n* Tötung *f*; (*murder*) Mord *m*

'killjoy *n* Spielverderber *m*

kiln /kɪln/ *n* Brennofen *m*

kilo /'ki:ləʊ/ *n* Kilo *nt*

kilo /'kɪlə/: **~gram** *n* Kilogramm *nt*. **~hertz** /-hɜ:ts/ *n* Kilohertz *nt*. **~metre** *n* Kilometer *m*. **~watt** *n* Kilowatt *nt*

kilt /kɪlt/ *n* Schottenrock *m*

kin /kɪn/ *n* Verwandtschaft *f*; **next of ~** nächster Verwandter *m*/nächste Verwandte *f*

kind¹ /kaɪnd/ *n* Art *f*; (*brand, type*) Sorte *f*; **what ~ of car?** was für ein Auto? **~ of** (*fam*) irgendwie

kind² *a* (**-er, -est**) nett; **~ to animals** gut zu Tieren; **~ regards** herzliche Grüße

kindergarten /'kɪndəgɑ:tn/ *n* Vorschule *f*

kindle /'kɪndl/ *vt* anzünden

kind|ly /'kaɪndlɪ/ *a* (**-ier, -iest**) nett ● *adv* netterweise; (*if you please*) gefälligst. **~ness** *n* Güte *f*; (*favour*) Gefallen *m*

kindred /'kɪndrɪd/ *a* **~ spirit** Gleichgesinnte(r) *m/f*

kinetic /kɪ'netɪk/ *a* kinetisch

king /kɪŋ/ *n* König *m*; (*Draughts*) Dame *f*. **~dom** *n* Königreich *nt*; (*fig & Relig*) Reich *nt*

king: ~fisher *n* Eisvogel *m*. **~-sized** *a* extragroß

kink /kɪŋk/ *n* Knick *m*. **~y** *a* (*fam*) pervers

kiosk /'ki:ɒsk/ *n* Kiosk *m*

kip /kɪp/ *n* **have a ~** (*fam*) pennen ● *vi* (*pt/pp* **kipped**) (*fam*) pennen

kipper /'kɪpə(r)/ *n* Räucherhering *m*

kiss /kɪs/ *n* Kuß *m* ● *vt/i* küssen

kit /kɪt/ *n* Ausrüstung *f*; (*tools*) Werkzeug *nt*; (*construction*) ~ Bausatz *m* ● *vt* (*pt/pp* **kitted**) **~ out** ausrüsten. **~bag** *n* Seesack *m*

kitchen /'kɪtʃɪn/ *n* Küche *f* ● *attrib* Küchen-. **~ette** /kɪtʃɪ'net/ *n* Kochnische *f*

kitchen: ~ 'garden *n* Gemüsegarten *m*. **~ 'sink** *n* Spülbecken *nt*

kite /kaɪt/ *n* Drachen *m*

kith /kɪθ/ *n* **with ~ and kin** mit der ganzen Verwandtschaft

kitten /'kɪtn/ *n* Kätzchen *nt*

kitty /'kɪtɪ/ *n* (*money*) [gemeinsame] Kasse *f*

kleptomaniac /kleptə'meɪnɪæk/ *n* Kleptomane *m*/-manin *f*

knack /næk/ *n* Trick *m*, Dreh *m*

knapsack /'næp-/ *n* Tornister *m*

knead /ni:d/ *vt* kneten

knee /ni:/ *n* Knie *nt*. **~cap** *n* Kniescheibe *f*

kneel /ni:l/ *vi* (*pt/pp* **knelt**) knien; **~ [down]** sich [nieder]knien

knelt /nelt/ *see* **kneel**

knew /nju:/ *see* **know**

knickers /'nɪkəz/ *npl* Schlüpfer *m*

knick-knacks /'nɪknæks/ *npl* Nippsachen *pl*

knife /naɪf/ n (pl knives) Messer nt
• vt einen Messerstich versetzen (+
dat); (to death) erstechen

knight /naɪt/ n Ritter m; (Chess)
Springer m • vt adeln

knit /nɪt/ vt/i (pt/pp knitted) stricken;
~ one, purl one eine rechts, eine
links; ~ one's brow die Stirn runzeln. ~ting n Stricken nt; (work)
Strickzeug nt. ~ting-needle n
Stricknadel f. ~wear n Strickwaren
pl

knives /naɪvz/ npl see knife

knob /nɒb/ n Knopf m; (on door)
Knauf m; (small lump) Beule f;
(small piece) Stückchen nt. ~bly a
knorrig; (bony) knochig

knock /nɒk/ n Klopfen nt; (blow)
Schlag m; there was a ~ at the door
es klopfte • vt anstoßen; (at door)
klopfen an (+ acc); (fam: criticize)
heruntermachen; ~ a hole in sth ein
Loch in etw (acc) schlagen; ~ one's
head sich (dat) den Kopf stoßen (on
an + dat) • vi klopfen. ~ about vt
schlagen • vi (fam) herumkommen.
~ down vt herunterwerfen; (with
fist) niederschlagen; (in car) anfahren; (demolish) abreißen; (fam: reduce) herabsetzen. ~ off vt herunterwerfen; (fam: steal) klauen;
(fam: complete quickly) hinhauen
• vi (fam: cease work) Feierabend
machen. ~ out vt ausschlagen;
(make unconscious) bewußtlos
schlagen; (Boxing) k.o. schlagen. ~
over vt umwerfen; (in car) anfahren

knock: ~-down a ~-down prices
Schleuderpreise pl. ~er n Tür-
klopfer m. ~-kneed /-'niːd/ a X-beinig. ~-out n (Boxing) K.o. m

knot /nɒt/ n Knoten m • vt (pt/pp
knotted) knoten

knotty /'nɒtɪ/ a (-ier, -iest) (fam)
verwickelt

know /nəʊ/ vt/i (pt knew, pp known)
wissen; kennen ⟨person⟩; können
⟨language⟩; get to ~ kennenlernen
• n in the ~ (fam) im Bild

know: ~-all n (fam) Alleswisser m.
~-how n (fam) [Sach]kenntnis f.
~ing a wissend. ~ingly adv wissend; (intentionally) wissentlich

knowledge /'nɒlɪdʒ/ n Kenntnis f (of
von/gen); (general) Wissen nt; (specialized) Kenntnisse pl. ~able /-əbl/
a be ~able viel wissen

known /nəʊn/ see know • a bekannt

knuckle /'nʌkl/ n [Finger]knöchel
m; (Culin) Hachse f • vi ~ under
sich fügen; ~ down sich
dahinterklemmen

kosher /'kəʊʃə(r)/ a koscher

kowtow /kaʊ'taʊ/ vi Kotau machen
(to vor + dat)

kudos /'kjuːdɒs/ n (fam) Prestige nt

L

lab /læb/ n (fam) Labor nt

label /'leɪbl/ n Etikett nt • vt (pt/pp
labelled) etikettieren

laboratory /lə'bɒrətrɪ/ n Labor nt

laborious /lə'bɔːrɪəs/ a, -ly adv
mühsam

labour /'leɪbə(r)/ n Arbeit f; (workers)
Arbeitskräfte pl; (Med) Wehen pl;
L~ (Pol) die Labourpartei • attrib
Labour- • vi arbeiten • vt (fig) sich
lange auslassen über (+ acc). ~er n
Arbeiter m

'labour-saving a arbeitssparend

laburnum /lə'bɜːnəm/ n Goldregen m

labyrinth /'læbərɪnθ/ n Labyrinth nt

lace /leɪs/ n Spitze f; (of shoe) Schnürsenkel m • vt schnüren; ~d with
rum mit einem Schuß Rum

lacerate /'læsəreɪt/ vt zerreißen

lack /læk/ n Mangel m (of an + dat)
• vt I ~ the time mir fehlt die Zeit
• vi be ~ing fehlen

lackadaisical /lækə'deɪzɪkl/ a lustlos

laconic /lə'kɒnɪk/ a, -ally adv
lakonisch

lacquer /'lækə(r)/ n Lack m; (for hair)
[Haar]spray m

lad /læd/ n Junge m

ladder /'lædə(r)/ n Leiter f; (in fabric)
Laufmasche f

laden /'leɪdn/ a beladen

ladle /'leɪdl/ n [Schöpf]kelle f • vt
schöpfen

lady /'leɪdɪ/ n Dame f; (title) Lady f

lady: ~bird n, (Amer) ~bug n Marienkäfer m. ~like a damenhaft

lag¹ /læg/ vi (pt/pp lagged) ~ behind
zurückbleiben; (fig) nachhinken

lag² vt (pt/pp lagged) umwickeln
⟨pipes⟩

lager /'lɑːgə(r)/ n Lagerbier nt

lagoon /lə'guːn/ n Lagune f

laid /leɪd/ see lay³

lain /leɪn/ see lie²

lair /leə(r)/ n Lager nt

laity /'leɪətɪ/ n Laienstand m

lake /leɪk/ n See m
lamb /læm/ n Lamm nt
lame /leɪm/ a (-r, -st) lahm
lament /lə'ment/ n Klage f; (song) Klagelied nt ● vt beklagen ● vi klagen. **~able** /'læməntəbl/ a beklagenswert
laminated /'læmɪneɪtɪd/ a laminiert
lamp /læmp/ n Lampe f; (in street) Laterne f. **~post** n Laternenpfahl m. **~shade** n Lampenschirm m
lance /lɑ:ns/ n Lanze f ● vt (Med) aufschneiden. **~·'corporal** n Gefreite(r) m
land /lænd/ n Land nt; plot of ~ Grundstück nt ● vt/i landen; ~ s.o. with sth (fam) jdm etw aufhalsen
landing /'lændɪŋ/ n Landung f; (top of stairs) Treppenflur m. **~stage** n Landesteg m
land: **~lady** n Wirtin f. **~locked** a **~-locked country** Binnenstaat m. **~lord** n Wirt m; (of land) Grundbesitzer m; (of building) Hausbesitzer m. **~mark** n Erkennungszeichen nt; (fig) Meilenstein m. **~owner** n Grundbesitzer m. **~scape** /-skeɪp/ n Landschaft f. **~slide** n Erdrutsch m
lane /leɪn/ n kleine Landstraße f; (Auto) Spur f; (Sport) Bahn f; 'get in ~' (Auto) 'bitte einordnen'
language /'læŋgwɪdʒ/ n Sprache f; (speech, style) Ausdrucksweise f.
laboratory n Sprachlabor nt
languid /'læŋgwɪd/ a, **-ly** adv träge
languish /'læŋgwɪʃ/ vi schmachten
lank /læŋk/ a (hair) strähnig
lanky /'læŋkɪ/ a (-ier, -iest) schlaksig
lantern /'læntən/ n Laterne f
lap¹ /læp/ n Schoß m
lap² n (Sport) Runde f; (of journey) Etappe f ● vi (pt/pp lapped) plätschern (against gegen)
lap³ vt (pt/pp lapped) ~ up aufschlecken
lapel /lə'pel/ n Revers nt
lapse /læps/ n Fehler m; (moral) Fehltritt m; (of time) Zeitspanne f ● vi (expire) erlöschen; ~ into verfallen in (+ acc)
larceny /'lɑ:sənɪ/ n Diebstahl m
lard /lɑ:d/ n [Schweine]schmalz nt
larder /'lɑ:də(r)/ n Speisekammer f
large /lɑ:dʒ/ a (-r, -st) & adv groß; by and ~ im großen und ganzen; at ~ auf freiem Fuß; (in general) im allgemeinen. **~ly** adv großenteils
lark¹ /lɑ:k/ n (bird) Lerche f

lark² n (joke) Jux m ● vi ~ about herumalbern
larva /'lɑ:və/ n (pl **-vae** /-vi:/) Larve f
laryngitis /lærɪn'dʒaɪtɪs/ n Kehlkopfentzündung f
larynx /'lærɪŋks/ n Kehlkopf m
lascivious /lə'sɪvɪəs/ a lüstern
laser /'leɪzə(r)/ n Laser m
lash /læʃ/ n Peitschenhieb m; (eyelash) Wimper f ● vt peitschen; (tie) festbinden (to an + acc). ~ out vi um sich schlagen; (spend) viel Geld ausgeben (on für)
lashings /'læʃɪŋz/ npl ~ of (fam) eine Riesenmenge von
lass /læs/ n Mädchen nt
lasso /lə'su:/ n Lasso nt
last¹ /lɑ:st/ n (for shoe) Leisten m
last² a & n letzte(r,s); ~ night heute od gestern nacht; (evening) abend; at ~ endlich; the ~ time das letztemal; for the ~ time zum letztenmal; the ~ but one der/die/das vorletzte; that's the ~ straw (fam) das schlägt dem Faß den Boden aus ● adv zuletzt; (last time) das letztemal; do sth ~ etw zuletzt od als letztes machen; he/she went ~ er/sie ging als letzter/letzte ● vi dauern; (weather:) sich halten; (relationship:) halten. **~ing** a dauerhaft. **~ly** adv schließlich, zum Schluß
latch /lætʃ/ n [einfache] Klinke f; on the ~ nicht verschlossen
late /leɪt/ a & adv (-r, -st) spät; (delayed) verspätet; (deceased) verstorben; the ~st news die neuesten Nachrichten; stay up ~ bis spät aufbleiben; of ~ in letzter Zeit; arrive ~ zu spät ankommen; I am ~ ich komme zu spät od habe mich verspätet; the train is ~ der Zug hat Verspätung. **~comer** n Zuspätkommende(r) m/f. **~ly** adv in letzter Zeit. **~ness** n Zuspätkommen nt; (delay) Verspätung f
latent /'leɪtnt/ a latent
later /'leɪtə(r)/ a & adv später; ~ on nachher
lateral /'lætərəl/ a seitlich
lathe /leɪð/ n Drehbank f
lather /'lɑ:ðə(r)/ n [Seifen]schaum m ● vt einseifen ● vi schäumen
Latin /'lætɪn/ a lateinisch ● n Latein nt. ~ **A'merica** n Lateinamerika nt
latitude /'lætɪtju:d/ n (Geog) Breite f; (fig) Freiheit f

latter /'lætə(r)/ a & n **the ~** der/die/ das letztere. **~ly** adv in letzter Zeit

lattice /'lætɪs/ n Gitter nt

Latvia /'lætvɪə/ n Lettland nt

laudable /'lɔːdəbl/ a lobenswert

laugh /lɑːf/ n Lachen nt; **with a ~** lachend ● vi lachen (**at/about** über + acc); **~ at s.o.** (mock) jdn auslachen. **~able** /-əbl/ a lachhaft, lächerlich. **~ing-stock** n Gegenstand m des Spottes

laughter /'lɑːftə(r)/ n Gelächter nt

launch¹ /lɔːntʃ/ n (boat) Barkasse f

launch² n Stapellauf m; (of rocket) Abschuß m; (of product) Lancierung f ● vt vom Stapel lassen ⟨ship⟩; zu Wasser lassen ⟨lifeboat⟩; abschießen ⟨rocket⟩; starten ⟨attack⟩; (Comm) lancieren ⟨product⟩

launder /'lɔːndə(r)/ vt waschen. **~ette** /-'dret/ n Münzwäscherei f

laundry /'lɔːndrɪ/ n Wäscherei f; (clothes) Wäsche f

laurel /'lɒrəl/ n Lorbeer m

lava /'lɑːvə/ n Lava f

lavatory /'lævətrɪ/ n Toilette f

lavender /'lævəndə(r)/ n Lavendel m

lavish /'lævɪʃ/ a, **-ly** adv großzügig; (wasteful) verschwenderisch; **on a ~ scale** mit viel Aufwand ● vt **~ sth on s.o.** jdn mit etw überschütten

law /lɔː/ n Gesetz nt; (system) Recht nt; **study ~** Jura studieren; **~ and order** Recht und Ordnung

law: ~-abiding a gesetzestreu. **~court** n Gerichtshof m. **~ful** a rechtmäßig. **~less** a gesetzlos

lawn /lɔːn/ n Rasen m. **~-mower** n Rasenmäher m

'law suit n Prozeß m

lawyer /'lɔːjə(r)/ n Rechtsanwalt m /-anwältin f

lax /læks/ a lax, locker

laxative /'læksətɪv/ n Abführmittel nt

laxity /'læksətɪ/ n Laxheit f

lay¹ /leɪ/ a Laien-

lay² see **lie²**

lay³ vt (pt/pp **laid**) legen; decken ⟨table⟩. **~ a trap** eine Falle stellen. **~ down** vt hinlegen; festlegen ⟨rules, conditions⟩. **~ off** vt entlassen ⟨workers⟩ ● vi (fam: stop) aufhören. **~ out** vt hinlegen; aufbahren ⟨corpse⟩; anlegen ⟨garden⟩; (Typ) gestalten

lay: ~about n Faulenzer m. **~-by** n Parkbucht f; (on motorway) Rastplatz m

layer /'leɪə(r)/ n Schicht f

layette /leɪ'et/ n Babyausstattung f

lay: ~man n Laie m. **~out** n Anordnung f; (design) Gestaltung f; (Typ) Layout nt. **~ 'preacher** n Laienprediger m

laze /leɪz/ vi **~[about]** faulenzen

laziness /'leɪzɪnɪs/ n Faulheit f

lazy /'leɪzɪ/ a (-ier, -iest) faul. **~bones** n Faulenzer m

lb /paʊnd/ abbr (**pound**) Pfd.

lead¹ /led/ n Blei nt; (of pencil) [Bleistift]mine f

lead² /liːd/ n Führung f; (leash) Leine f; (flex) Schnur f; (clue) Hinweis m, Spur f; (Theat) Hauptrolle f; (distance ahead) Vorsprung m; **be in the ~** in Führung liegen ● vt/i (pt/pp **led**) führen; leiten ⟨team⟩; (induce) bringen; (at cards) ausspielen; **~ the way** vorangehen; **~ up to sth** (fig) etw (dat) vorangehen. **~ away** vt wegführen

leaded /'ledɪd/ a verbleit

leader /'liːdə(r)/ n Führer m; (of expedition, group) Leiter(in) m(f); (of orchestra) Konzertmeister m; (in newspaper) Leitartikel m. **~ship** n Führung f; Leitung f

leading /'liːdɪŋ/ a führend; **~ lady** Hauptdarstellerin f; **~ question** Suggestivfrage f

leaf /liːf/ n (pl **leaves**) Blatt nt; (of table) Ausziehplatte f ● vi **~ through sth** etw durchblättern. **~let** n Merkblatt nt; (advertising) Reklameblatt nt; (political) Flugblatt nt

league /liːg/ n Liga f; **be in ~ with** unter einer Decke stecken mit

leak /liːk/ n (hole) undichte Stelle f; (Naut) Leck nt; (of gas) Gasausfluß m ● vi undicht sein; ⟨ship:⟩ leck sein, lecken; ⟨liquid:⟩ auslaufen; ⟨gas:⟩ ausströmen ● vt auslaufen lassen; **~ sth to s.o.** (fig) jdm etw zuspielen. **~y** a undicht; (Naut) leck

lean¹ /liːn/ a (-er, -est) mager

lean² v (pt/pp **leaned** or **leant** /lent/) ● vt lehnen (**against/on** an + acc) ● vi ⟨pers:⟩ sich lehnen (**against/on** an + acc); (not be straight) sich neigen; **be ~ing against** lehnen an (+ dat); **~ on s.o.** (depend) bei jdm festen Halt finden. **~ back** vi sich zurücklehnen. **~ forward** vi sich vorbeugen. **~ out** vi sich hinauslehnen. **~ over** vi sich vorbeugen

leaning /'liːnɪŋ/ a schief ● n Neigung f

leap /liːp/ n Sprung m ● vi (pt/pp **leapt** /lept/ or **leaped**) springen; **he leapt at it** (fam) er griff sofort zu. **~-frog** n Bockspringen nt. **~ year** n Schaltjahr nt

learn /lɜːn/ vt/i (pt/pp **learnt** or **learned**) lernen; (hear) erfahren; **~ to swim** schwimmen lernen

learn|ed /ˈlɜːnɪd/ a gelehrt. **~er** n Anfänger m; **~er [driver]** Fahrschüler(in) m(f). **~ing** n Gelehrsamkeit f

lease /liːs/ n Pacht f; (contract) Mietvertrag m; (Comm) Pachtvertrag m ● vt pachten; **~ [out]** verpachten

leash /liːʃ/ n Leine f

least /liːst/ a geringste(r,s); **have ~ time** am wenigsten Zeit haben ● n **the ~** das wenigste; **at ~** wenigstens, mindestens; **not in the ~** nicht im geringsten ● adv am wenigsten

leather /ˈleðə(r)/ n Leder nt. **~y** a ledern; (tough) zäh

leave /liːv/ n Erlaubnis f; (holiday) Urlaub m; **on ~** auf Urlaub; **take one's ~** sich verabschieden ● v (pt/pp **left**) vt lassen; (go out of, abandon) verlassen; (forget) liegenlassen; (bequeath) vermachen (**to** dat); **~ it to me!** überlassen Sie es mir! **there is nothing left** es ist nichts mehr übrig ● vi [weg]gehen/-fahren; (train, bus:) abfahren. **~ behind** vt zurücklassen; (forget) liegenlassen. **~ out** vt liegenlassen; (leave outside) draußen lassen; (omit) auslassen

leaves /liːvz/ see **leaf**

Lebanon /ˈlebənən/ n Libanon m

lecherous /ˈletʃərəs/ a lüstern

lectern /ˈlektɜːn/ n [Lese]pult nt

lecture /ˈlektʃə(r)/ n Vortrag m; (Univ) Vorlesung f; (reproof) Strafpredigt f ● vi einen Vortrag/eine Vorlesung halten (**on** über + acc) ● vt **~ s.o.** jdm eine Strafpredigt halten. **~r** n Vortragende(r) m/f; (Univ) Dozent(in) m(f)

led /led/ see **lead²**

ledge /ledʒ/ n Leiste f; (shelf, of window) Sims m; (in rock) Vorsprung m

ledger /ˈledʒə(r)/ n Hauptbuch nt

lee /liː/ n (Naut) Lee f

leech /liːtʃ/ n Blutegel m

leek /liːk/ n Stange f Porree; **~s** pl Porree m

leer /lɪə(r)/ n anzügliches Grinsen nt ● vi anzüglich grinsen

lee|ward /ˈliːwəd/ adv nach Lee. **~way** n (fig) Spielraum m

left¹ /left/ see **leave**

left² a linke(r,s) ● adv links; (go) nach links ● n linke Seite f; **on the ~** links; **from/to the ~** von/nach links; **the ~** (Pol) die Linke

left: ~-'handed a linkshändig. **~-'luggage [office]** n Gepäckaufbewahrung f. **~overs** npl Reste pl. **~-'wing** a (Pol) linke(r,s)

leg /leg/ n Bein nt; (Culin) Keule f; (of journey) Etappe f

legacy /ˈlegəsɪ/ n Vermächtnis nt, Erbschaft f

legal /ˈliːgl/ a, **-ly** adv gesetzlich; (matters) rechtlich; (department, position) Rechts-; **be ~** [gesetzlich] erlaubt sein; **take ~ action** gerichtlich vorgehen

legality /lɪˈgælətɪ/ n Legalität f

legalize /ˈliːgəlaɪz/ vt legalisieren

legend /ˈledʒənd/ n Legende f. **~ary** a legendär

legible /ˈledʒəbl/ a, **-bly** adv leserlich

legion /ˈliːdʒn/ n Legion f

legislat|e /ˈledʒɪsleɪt/ vi Gesetze erlassen. **~ion** /-ˈleɪʃn/ n Gesetzgebung f; (laws) Gesetze pl

legislat|ive /ˈledʒɪslətɪv/ a gesetzgebend. **~ure** /-ətʃə(r)/ n Legislative f

legitimate /lɪˈdʒɪtɪmət/ a rechtmäßig; (justifiable) berechtigt; (child) ehelich

leisure /ˈleʒə(r)/ n Freizeit f; **at your ~** wenn Sie Zeit haben. **~ly** a gemächlich

lemon /ˈlemən/ n Zitrone f. **~ade** /-ˈneɪd/ n Zitronenlimonade f

lend /lend/ vt (pt/pp **lent**) leihen; **s.o. sth** jdm etw leihen; **~ a hand** (fam) helfen. **~ing library** n Leihbücherei f

length /leŋθ/ n Länge f; (piece) Stück nt; (of wallpaper) Bahn f; (of time) Dauer f; **at ~** ausführlich; (at last) endlich

length|en /ˈleŋθən/ vt länger machen ● vi länger werden. **~ways** adv der Länge nach, längs

lengthy /ˈleŋθɪ/ a (-ier, -iest) langwierig

lenien|ce /ˈliːnɪəns/ n Nachsicht f. **~t** a, **-ly** adv nachsichtig

lens /lenz/ n Linse f; (Phot) Objektiv nt; (of spectacles) Glas nt

lent /lent/ see **lend**

Lent n Fastenzeit f

lentil /ˈlentl/ n (Bot) Linse f

Leo /'li:əʊ/ n (Astr) Löwe m

leopard /'lepəd/ n Leopard m

leotard /'li:əta:d/ n Trikot nt

leper /'lepə(r)/ n Leprakranke(r) m/f; n (Bible & fig) Aussätzige(r) m/f

leprosy /'leprəsi/ n Lepra f

lesbian /'lezbiən/ a lesbisch ● n Lesbierin f

lesion /'li:ʒn/ n Verletzung f

less /les/ a, adv, n & prep weniger; ~ **and** ~ immer weniger; **not any the** ~ um nichts weniger

lessen /'lesn/ vt verringern ● vi nachlassen; ⟨value:⟩ abnehmen

lesser /'lesə(r)/ a geringere(r,s)

lesson /'lesn/ n Stunde f; (in textbook) Lektion f; (Relig) Lesung f; **teach s.o. a** ~ (fig) jdm eine Lehre erteilen

lest /lest/ conj (liter) damit ... nicht

let /let/ vt (pt/pp let, pres p letting) lassen; (rent) vermieten; ~ **alone** (not to mention) geschweige denn; **'to** ~' 'zu vermieten'; ~ **us go** gehen wir; ~ **me know** sagen Sie mir Bescheid; ~ **him do it** laß ihn das machen; **just** ~ **him!** soll er doch! ~ **s.o. sleep/win** jdn schlafen/gewinnen lassen; ~ **oneself in for sth** (fam) sich (dat) etw einbrocken. ~ **down** vt hinunter-/herunterlassen; (lengthen) länger machen; ~ **s.o. down** (fam) jdn im Stich lassen; (disappoint) jdn enttäuschen. ~ **in** vt hereinlassen. ~ **off** vt abfeuern ⟨gun⟩; hochgehen lassen ⟨firework, bomb⟩; (emit) ausstoßen; (excuse from) befreien von; (not punish) frei ausgehen lassen. ~ **out** vt hinaus-/herauslassen; (make larger) auslassen. ~ **through** vt durchlassen. ~ **up** vi (fam) nachlassen

'let-down n Enttäuschung f, (fam) Reinfall m

lethal /'li:θl/ a tödlich

letharg|ic /lɪ'θa:dʒɪk/ a lethargisch. ~**y** /'leθədʒi/ n Lethargie f

letter /'letə(r)/ n Brief m; (of alphabet) Buchstabe m; **by** ~ brieflich. ~**-box** n Briefkasten m. ~**-head** n Briefkopf m. ~**ing** n Beschriftung f

lettuce /'letis/ n [Kopf]salat m

'let-up n (fam) Nachlassen nt

leukaemia /lu:'ki:mɪə/ n Leukämie f

level /'levl/ a eben; (horizontal) waagerecht; (in height) auf gleicher Höhe; ⟨spoonful⟩ gestrichen; **draw** ~ **with** gleichziehen mit; **one's** ~ **best** sein möglichstes ● n Höhe f; (fig) Ebene f, Niveau nt; (stage)

Stufe f; **on the** ~ (fam) ehrlich ● vt (pt/pp levelled) einebnen; (aim) richten (**at** auf + acc)

level: ~ **'crossing** n Bahnübergang m. ~**-'headed** a vernünftig

lever /'li:və(r)/ n Hebel m ● vt ~ **up** mit einem Hebel anheben. ~**age** /-rɪdʒ/ n Hebelkraft f

levity /'levəti/ n Heiterkeit f; (frivolity) Leichtfertigkeit f

levy /'levi/ vt (pt/pp levied) erheben ⟨tax⟩

lewd /lju:d/ a (-er, -est) anstößig

liabilit|y /laɪə'bɪləti/ n Haftung f; ~**ies** pl Verbindlichkeiten pl

liable /'laɪəbl/ a haftbar; **be** ~ **to do sth** etw leicht tun können

liaise /lɪ'eɪz/ vi (fam) Verbindungsperson sein

liaison /lɪ'eɪzɒn/ n Verbindung f; (affair) Verhältnis nt

liar /'laɪə(r)/ n Lügner(in) m(f)

libel /'laɪbl/ n Verleumdung f ● vt (pt/pp libelled) verleumden. ~**lous** a verleumderisch

liberal /'lɪbərl/ a, -ly adv tolerant; (generous) großzügig. **L~** a (Pol) liberal ● n Liberale(r) m/f

liberat|e /'lɪbəreɪt/ vt befreien. ~**ed** a ⟨woman⟩ emanzipiert. ~**ion** /-'reɪʃn/ n Befreiung f. ~**or** n Befreier m

liberty /'lɪbəti/ n Freiheit f; **take the** ~ **of doing sth** sich (dat) erlauben, etw zu tun; **take liberties** sich (dat) Freiheiten erlauben

Libra /'li:brə/ n (Astr) Waage f

librarian /laɪ'breərɪən/ n Bibliothekar(in) m(f)

library /'laɪbrəri/ n Bibliothek f

Libya /'lɪbɪə/ n Libyen nt

lice /laɪs/ see **louse**

licence /'laɪsns/ n Genehmigung f; (Comm) Lizenz f; (for TV) ≈ Fernsehgebühr f; (for driving) Führerschein m; (for alcohol) Schankkonzession f; (freedom) Freiheit f

license /'laɪsns/ vt eine Genehmigung/(Comm) Lizenz erteilen (+ dat); **be** ~**d** ⟨car:⟩ zugelassen sein; ⟨restaurant:⟩ Schankkonzession haben. ~**-plate** n Nummernschild nt

licentious /laɪ'senʃəs/ a lasterhaft

lichen /'laɪkən/ n (Bot) Flechte f

lick /lɪk/ n Lecken nt; **a** ~ **of paint** ein bißchen Farbe ● vt lecken; (fam: defeat) schlagen

lid /lɪd/ n Deckel m; (of eye) Lid nt

lie¹ /laɪ/ n Lüge f; **tell a ~** lügen ● vi (pt/pp **lied**, pres p **lying**) lügen; **~ to** belügen

lie² vi (pt **lay**, pp **lain**, pres p **lying**) liegen; **here ~s …** hier ruht … **~ down** vi sich hinlegen

Liège /lɪˈeɪʒ/ n Lüttich nt

'lie-in n have a **~** [sich] ausschlafen

lieu /ljuː/ n **in ~ of** statt (+ gen)

lieutenant /lefˈtenənt/ n Oberleutnant m

life /laɪf/ n (pl **lives**) Leben nt; (biography) Biographie f; **lose one's ~** ums Leben kommen

life: ~belt n Rettungsring m. **~boat** n Rettungsboot nt. **~buoy** n Rettungsring m. **~-guard** n Lebensretter m. **~-jacket** n Schwimmweste f. **~less** a leblos. **~like** a naturgetreu. **~line** n Rettungsleine f. **~long** a lebenslang. **~ preserver** n (Amer) Rettungsring m. **~-size(d)** a … in Lebensgröße. **~time** n Leben nt; **in s.o.'s ~time** zu jds Lebzeiten; **the chance of a ~time** eine einmalige Gelegenheit

lift /lɪft/ n Aufzug m, Lift m; **give s.o. a ~** jdn mitnehmen; **get a ~** mitgenommen werden ● vt heben; aufheben ⟨restrictions⟩ ● vi ⟨fog:⟩ sich lichten. **~ up** vt hochheben

'lift-off n Abheben nt

ligament /ˈlɪgəmənt/ n (Anat) Band nt

light¹ /laɪt/ a (**-er, -est**) (not dark) hell; **~ blue** hellblau ● n Licht nt; (lamp) Lampe f; **in the ~ of** (fig) angesichts (+ gen); **have you [got] a ~?** haben Sie Feuer? ● vt (pt/pp **lit** or **lighted**) anzünden ⟨fire, cigarette⟩; anmachen ⟨lamp⟩; (illuminate) beleuchten. **~ up** vi ⟨face:⟩ sich erhellen

light² a (**-er, -est**) (not heavy) leicht; **~ sentence** milde Strafe f ● adv **travel ~** mit wenig Gepäck reisen

'light-bulb n Glühbirne f

lighten¹ /ˈlaɪtn/ vt heller machen ● vi heller werden

lighten² vt leichter machen ⟨load⟩

lighter /ˈlaɪtə(r)/ n Feuerzeug nt

light: ~-'headed a benommen. **~-'hearted** a unbekümmert. **~house** n Leuchtturm m. **~ing** n Beleuchtung f. **~ly** adv leicht; (casually) leichthin; **get off ~ly** glimpflich davonkommen

lightning /ˈlaɪtnɪŋ/ n Blitz m. **~-conductor** n Blitzableiter m

'lightweight a leicht ● n (Boxing) Leichtgewicht nt

like¹ /laɪk/ a ähnlich; (same) gleich ● prep wie; (similar to) ähnlich (+ dat); **~ this** so; **a man ~ that** so ein Mann; **what's he ~?** wie ist er denn? ● conj (fam: as) wie; (Amer: as if) als ob

like² vt mögen; **I should/would ~** ich möchte; **I ~ the car** das Auto gefällt mir; **I ~ chocolate** ich esse gern Schokolade; **~ dancing/singing** gern tanzen/singen; **I ~ that!** (fam) das ist doch die Höhe! ● n **~s and dislikes** pl Vorlieben und Abneigungen pl

like|able /ˈlaɪkəbl/ a sympathisch. **~lihood** /-lɪhʊd/ n Wahrscheinlichkeit f. **~ly** a (**-ier, -iest**) & adv wahrscheinlich; **not ~ly!** (fam) auf gar keinen Fall!

'like-minded a gleichgesinnt

liken /ˈlaɪkən/ vt vergleichen (**to** mit)

like|ness /ˈlaɪknɪs/ n Ähnlichkeit f. **~wise** adv ebenso

liking /ˈlaɪkɪŋ/ n Vorliebe f; **is it to your ~?** gefällt es Ihnen?

lilac /ˈlaɪlək/ n Flieder m ● a fliederfarben

lily /ˈlɪlɪ/ n Lilie f. **~ of the valley** n Maiglöckchen nt

limb /lɪm/ n Glied nt

limber /ˈlɪmbə(r)/ vi **~ up** Lockerungsübungen machen

lime¹ /laɪm/ n (fruit) Limone f; (tree) Linde f

lime² n Kalk m. **~light** n **be in the ~light** im Rampenlicht stehen. **~stone** n Kalkstein m

limit /ˈlɪmɪt/ n Grenze f; (limitation) Beschränkung f; **that's the ~!** (fam) das ist doch die Höhe! ● vt beschränken (**to** auf + acc). **~ation** /-ˈteɪʃn/ n Beschränkung f. **~ed** a beschränkt; **~ed company** Gesellschaft f mit beschränkter Haftung

limousine /ˈlɪməziːn/ n Limousine f

limp¹ /lɪmp/ n Hinken nt; **have a ~** hinken ● vi hinken

limp² a (**-er, -est**), **-ly** adv schlaff

limpet /ˈlɪmpɪt/ n **like a ~** (fig) wie eine Klette

limpid /ˈlɪmpɪd/ a klar

linctus /ˈlɪŋktəs/ n [cough] **~** Hustensirup m

line¹ /laɪn/ n Linie f; (length of rope, cord) Leine f; (Teleph) Leitung f; (of writing) Zeile f; (row) Reihe f; (wrinkle) Falte f; (of business) Branche f; (Amer: queue) Schlange f;

in ~ with gemäß (+ *dat*) ● *vt* säumen ⟨*street*⟩. ~ up *vi* sich aufstellen ● *vt* aufstellen
line² *vt* füttern ⟨*garment*⟩; (*Techn*) auskleiden
lineage /'lɪnɪɪdʒ/ *n* Herkunft *f*
linear /'lɪnɪə(r)/ *a* linear
lined¹ /laɪnd/ *a* (*wrinkled*) faltig; ⟨*paper*⟩ liniert
lined² *a* ⟨*garment*⟩ gefüttert
linen /'lɪnɪn/ *n* Leinen *nt*; (*articles*) Wäsche *f*
liner /'laɪnə(r)/ *n* Passagierschiff *nt*
'linesman *n* (*Sport*) Linienrichter *m*
linger /'lɪŋgə(r)/ *vi* [zurück]bleiben
lingerie /'læʒərɪ/ *n* Damenunterwäsche *f*
linguist /'lɪŋgwɪst/ *n* Sprachkundige(r) *m/f*
linguistic /lɪŋ'gwɪstɪk/ *a*, **-ally** *adv* sprachlich. ~s *n* Linguistik *f*
lining /'laɪnɪŋ/ *n* (*of garment*) Futter *nt*; (*Techn*) Auskleidung *f*
link /lɪŋk/ *n* (*of chain*) Glied *nt*; (*fig*) Verbindung *f* ● *vt* verbinden; ~ **arms** sich unterhaken
links /lɪŋks/ *n or npl* Golfplatz *m*
lino /'laɪnəʊ/ *n*, **linoleum** /lɪ'nəʊlɪəm/ *n* Linoleum *nt*
lint /lɪnt/ *n* Verbandstoff *m*
lion /'laɪən/ *n* Löwe *m*; ~'s **share** (*fig*) Löwenanteil *m*. ~ess *n* Löwin *f*
lip /lɪp/ *n* Lippe *f*; (*edge*) Rand *m*; (*of jug*) Schnabel *m*
lip: ~-**reading** *n* Lippenlesen *nt*. ~-**service** *n* pay ~-**service** ein Lippenbekenntnis ablegen (**to** zu). ~**stick** *n* Lippenstift *m*
liquefy /'lɪkwɪfaɪ/ *vt* (*pt/pp* -**ied**) verflüssigen ● *vi* sich verflüssigen
liqueur /lɪ'kjʊə(r)/ *n* Likör *m*
liquid /'lɪkwɪd/ *n* Flüssigkeit *f* ● *a* flüssig
liquidat|e /'lɪkwɪdeɪt/ *vt* liquidieren. ~**ion** /-'deɪʃn/ *n* Liquidation *f*
liquidize /'lɪkwɪdaɪz/ *vt* [im Mixer] pürieren. ~**r** *n* (*Culin*) Mixer *m*
liquor /'lɪkə(r)/ *n* Alkohol *m*; (*juice*) Flüssigkeit *f*
liquorice /'lɪkərɪs/ *n* Lakritze *f*
'liquor store *n* (*Amer*) Spirituosengeschäft *nt*
lisp /lɪsp/ *n* Lispeln *nt* ● *vt/i* lispeln
list¹ /lɪst/ *n* Liste *f* ● *vt* aufführen
list² *vi* ⟨*ship:*⟩ Schlagseite haben
listen /'lɪsn/ *vi* zuhören (**to** *dat*); ~ **to the radio** Radio hören. ~**er** *n* Zuhörer(in) *m*(*f*); (*Radio*) Hörer(in) *m*(*f*)
listless /'lɪstlɪs/ *a*, -**ly** *adv* lustlos

lit /lɪt/ *see* **light¹**
litany /'lɪtənɪ/ *n* Litanei *f*
literacy /'lɪtərəsɪ/ *n* Lese- und Schreibfertigkeit *f*
literal /'lɪtərəl/ *a* wörtlich. ~**ly** *adv* buchstäblich
literary /'lɪtərərɪ/ *a* literarisch
literate /'lɪtərət/ *a* be ~ lesen und schreiben können
literature /'lɪtrətʃə(r)/ *n* Literatur *f*; (*fam*) Informationsmaterial *nt*
lithe /laɪð/ *a* geschmeidig
Lithuania /lɪθjʊ'eɪnɪə/ *n* Litauen *nt*
litigation /lɪtɪ'geɪʃn/ *n* Rechtsstreit *m*
litre /'li:tə(r)/ *n* Liter *m & nt*
litter /'lɪtə(r)/ *n* Abfall *m*; (*Zool*) Wurf *m* ● *vt* be ~ed **with** übersät sein mit. ~-**bin** *n* Abfalleimer *m*
little /'lɪtl/ *a* klein; (*not much*) wenig ● *adv* & *n* wenig; a ~ ein bißchen/wenig; ~ **by** ~ nach und nach
liturgy /'lɪtədʒɪ/ *n* Liturgie *f*
live¹ /laɪv/ *a* lebendig; ⟨*ammunition*⟩ scharf; ~ **broadcast** Live-Sendung *f*; be ~ (*Electr*) unter Strom stehen ● *adv* (*Radio, TV*) live
live² /lɪv/ *vi* leben; (*reside*) wohnen; ~ **up to** gerecht werden (+ *dat*). ~ **on** *vt* leben von; (*eat*) sich ernähren von ● *vi* weiterleben
liveli|hood /'laɪvlɪhʊd/ *n* Lebensunterhalt *m*. ~**ness** *n* Lebendigkeit *f*
lively /'laɪvlɪ/ *a* (-**ier**, -**iest**) lebhaft, lebendig
liven /'laɪvn/ *v* ~ **up** *vt* beleben ● *vi* lebhaft werden
liver /'lɪvə(r)/ *n* Leber *f*
lives /laɪvz/ *see* **life**
livestock /'laɪv-/ *n* Vieh *nt*
livid /'lɪvɪd/ *a* (*fam*) wütend
living /'lɪvɪŋ/ *a* lebend ● *n* **earn one's** ~ seinen Lebensunterhalt verdienen; **the** ~ *pl* die Lebenden. ~-**room** *n* Wohnzimmer *nt*
lizard /'lɪzəd/ *n* Eidechse *f*
load /ləʊd/ *n* Last *f*; (*quantity*) Ladung *f*; (*Electr*) Belastung *f*; ~**s of** (*fam*) jede Menge ● *vt* laden ⟨*goods, gun*⟩; beladen ⟨*vehicle*⟩; ~ **a camera** einen Film in eine Kamera einlegen. ~**ed** *a* beladen; (*fam: rich*) steinreich; ~**ed question** Fangfrage *f*
loaf¹ /ləʊf/ *n* (*pl* **loaves**) Brot *nt*
loaf² *vi* faulenzen
loan /ləʊn/ *n* Leihgabe *f*; (*money*) Darlehen *nt*; **on** ~ geliehen ● *vt* leihen (**to** *dat*)

loath /ləʊθ/ a be ~ to do sth etw ungern tun
loath|e /ləʊð/ vt verabscheuen. ~ing n Abscheu m. ~some a abscheulich
loaves /ləʊvz/ see loaf
lobby /'lɒbɪ/ n Foyer nt; (anteroom) Vorraum m; (Pol) Lobby f
lobe /ləʊb/ n (of ear) Ohrläppchen nt
lobster /'lɒbstə(r)/ n Hummer m
local /'ləʊkl/ a hiesig; ⟨time, traffic⟩ Orts-; **under ~ anaesthetic** unter örtlicher Betäubung; **I'm not ~** ich bin nicht von hier ● n Hiesige(r) m/f; (fam: public house) Stammkneipe f. ~ au'thority n Kommunalbehörde f. ~ **call** n (Teleph) Ortsgespräch nt
locality /ləʊ'kælətɪ/ n Gegend f
localized /'ləʊkəlaɪzd/ a lokalisiert
locally /'ləʊkəlɪ/ adv am Ort
locat|e /ləʊ'keɪt/ vt ausfindig machen; **be ~ed** sich befinden. ~ion n /-'keɪʃn/ n Lage f; **filmed on ~ion** als Außenaufnahme gedreht
lock¹ /lɒk/ n (hair) Strähne f
lock² n (on door) Schloß nt; (on canal) Schleuse f ● vt abschließen ● vi sich abschließen lassen. ~ **in** vt einschließen. ~ **out** vt ausschließen. ~ **up** vt abschließen; einsperren ⟨person⟩ ● vi zuschließen
locker /'lɒkə(r)/ n Schließfach nt; (Mil) Spind m; (in hospital) kleiner Schrank m
locket /'lɒkɪt/ n Medaillon nt
lock: ~**-out** n Aussperrung f. ~**smith** n Schlosser m
locomotion /ləʊkə'məʊʃn/ n Fortbewegung f
locomotive /ləʊkə'məʊtɪv/ n Lokomotive f
locum /'ləʊkəm/ n Vertreter(in) m(f)
locust /'ləʊkəst/ n Heuschrecke f
lodge /lɒdʒ/ n (porter's) Pförtnerhaus nt; (masonic) Loge f ● vt (submit) einreichen; (deposit) deponieren ● vi zur Untermiete wohnen (**with** bei); (become fixed) steckenbleiben. ~**r** n Untermieter(in) m(f)
lodging /'lɒdʒɪŋ/ n Unterkunft f; ~**s** npl möbliertes Zimmer nt
loft /lɒft/ n Dachboden m
lofty /'lɒftɪ/ a (-ier, -iest) hoch; (haughty) hochmütig
log /lɒg/ n Baumstamm m; (for fire) [Holz]scheit nt; **sleep like a ~** (fam) wie ein Murmeltier schlafen
logarithm /'lɒgərɪðm/ n Logarithmus m

'log-book n (Naut) Logbuch nt
loggerheads /'lɒgə-/ npl **be at ~** (fam) sich in den Haaren liegen
logic /'lɒdʒɪk/ n Logik f. ~**al** a, -ly adv logisch
logistics /lə'dʒɪstɪks/ npl Logistik f
logo /'ləʊgəʊ/ n Symbol nt, Logo nt
loin /lɔɪn/ n (Culin) Lende f
loiter /'lɔɪtə(r)/ vi herumlungern
loll /lɒl/ vi sich lümmeln
loll|ipop /'lɒlɪpɒp/ n Lutscher m. ~**y** n Lutscher m; (fam: money) Moneten pl
London /'lʌndən/ n London nt ● attrib Londoner. ~**er** n Londoner(in) m(f)
lone /ləʊn/ a einzeln. ~**liness** n Einsamkeit f
lonely /'ləʊnlɪ/ a (-ier, -iest) einsam
lone|r /'ləʊnə(r)/ n Einzelgänger m. ~**some** a einsam
long¹ /lɒŋ/ a (-er /'lɒŋgə(r)/, -est /'lɒŋgɪst/) lang; ⟨journey⟩ weit; **a ~ time** lange; **a ~ way** weit; **in the ~ run** auf lange Sicht; (in the end) letzten Endes ● adv lange; **all day ~** den ganzen Tag; **not ~ ago** vor kurzem; **before ~** bald; **no ~er** nicht mehr; **as** or **so ~ as** solange; **so ~!** (fam) tschüs! **will you be ~?** dauert es noch lange [bei dir]? **it won't take ~** es dauert nicht lange
long² vi **~ for** sich sehnen nach
long-'distance a Fern-; (Sport) Langstrecken-
longevity /lɒn'dʒevətɪ/ n Langlebigkeit f
'longhand n Langschrift f
longing /'lɒŋɪŋ/ a, -ly adv sehnsüchtig ● n Sehnsucht f
longitude /'lɒŋgɪtjuːd/ n (Geog) Länge f
long: ~ **jump** n Weitsprung m. ~-**life milk** n H-Milch f. ~-**lived** /-lɪvd/ a langlebig. ~-**range** a (Mil, Aviat) Langstrecken-; ⟨forecast⟩ langfristig. ~-**sighted** a weitsichtig. ~-**sleeved** a langärmelig. ~-**suffering** a langmütig. ~-**term** a langfristig. ~ **wave** n Langwelle f. ~-**winded** /-'wɪndɪd/ a langatmig
loo /luː/ n (fam) Klo nt
look /lʊk/ n Blick m; (appearance) Aussehen nt; [**good**] ~**s** pl [gutes] Aussehen nt; **have a ~ at** sich (dat) ansehen; **go and have a ~** sieh mal nach ● vi sehen; (search) nachsehen; (seem) aussehen; **don't ~** sieh nicht hin; ~ **here!** hören Sie mal! ~

at ansehen; ~ **for** suchen; ~ **for-ward to** sich freuen auf (+ *acc*); ~ **in on** vorbeischauen bei; ~ **into** (*examine*) nachgehen (+ *dat*); ~ **like** aussehen wie; ~ **on to** ⟨*room:*⟩gehen auf (+ *acc*). ~ **after** *vt* betreuen. ~ **down** *vi* hinuntersehen; ~ **down on s.o.** (*fig*) auf jdn herabsehen. ~ **out** *vi* hinaus-/ heraussehen; (*take care*) aufpassen; ~ **out for** Ausschau halten nach; ~ **out!** Vorsicht! ~ **round** *vi* sich umsehen. ~ **up** *vi* aufblicken; ~ **up to s.o.** (*fig*) zu jdm aufsehen • *vt* nachschlagen ⟨*word*⟩

'look-out *n* Wache *f*; (*prospect*) Aussicht *f*; **be on the** ~ **for** Ausschau halten nach

loom¹ /luːm/ *n* Webstuhl *m*

loom² *vi* auftauchen; (*fig*) sich abzeichnen

loony /'luːnɪ/ *a* (*fam*) verrückt

loop /luːp/ *n* Schlinge *f*; (*in road*) Schleife *f*; (*on garment*) Aufhänger *m* • *vt* schlingen. ~**hole** *n* Hintertürchen *nt*; (*in the law*) Lücke *f*

loose /luːs/ *a* (-**r**, -**st**), -**ly** *adv* lose; (*not tight enough*) locker; (*inexact*) frei; **be at a** ~ **end** nichts zu tun haben; **set** ~ freilassen; **run** ~ frei herumlaufen. ~ **'change** *n* Kleingeld *nt*. ~ **'chippings** *npl* Rollsplit *m*

loosen /'luːsn/ *vt* lockern • *vi* sich lockern

loot /luːt/ *n* Beute *f* • *vt/i* plündern. ~**er** *n* Plünderer *m*

lop /lɒp/ *vt* (*pt/pp* **lopped**) stutzen. ~ **off** *vt* abhacken

lop'sided *a* schief

loquacious /lə'kweɪʃəs/ *a* redselig

lord /lɔːd/ *n* Herr *m*; (*title*) Lord *m*; **House of L**~**s** ≈ Oberhaus *nt*; **the L**~**'s Prayer** das Vaterunser; **good L**~**!** du liebe Zeit!

lore /lɔː(r)/ *n* Überlieferung *f*

lorry /'lɒrɪ/ *n* Last[kraft]wagen *m*

lose /luːz/ *v* (*pt/pp* **lost**) • *vt* verlieren; (*miss*) verpassen • *vi* verlieren; ⟨*clock:*⟩ nachgehen; **get lost** verlorengehen; ⟨*person:*⟩ sich verlaufen. ~**r** *n* Verlierer *m*

loss /lɒs/ *n* Verlust *m*; **be at a** ~ nicht mehr weiter wissen; **be at a** ~ **for words** nicht wissen, was man sagen soll

lost /lɒst/ *see* **lose**. ~ **'property office** *n* Fundbüro *nt*

lot¹ /lɒt/ *n* Los *nt*; (*at auction*) Posten *m*; **draw** ~**s** losen (**for** um)

lot² *n* **the** ~ alle; (*everything*) alles; **a** ~ **[of]** viel; (*many*) viele; ~**s of** (*fam*) eine Menge; **it has changed a** ~ es hat sich sehr verändert

lotion /'ləʊʃn/ *n* Lotion *f*

lottery /'lɒtərɪ/ *n* Lotterie *f*. ~ **ticket** *n* Los *nt*

loud /laʊd/ *a* (-**er**, -**est**), -**ly** *adv* laut; ⟨*colours*⟩ grell • *adv* **[out]** ~ laut. ~**'hailer** *n* Megaphon *nt*. ~**'speaker** *n* Lautsprecher *m*

lounge /laʊndʒ/ *n* Wohnzimmer *nt*; (*in hotel*) Aufenthaltsraum *m*. • *vi* sich lümmeln. ~ **suit** *n* Straßenanzug *m*

louse /laʊs/ *n* (*pl* **lice**) Laus *f*

lousy /'laʊzɪ/ *a* (-**ier**, -**iest**) (*fam*) lausig

lout /laʊt/ *n* Flegel *m*, Lümmel *m*. ~**ish** *a* flegelhaft

lovable /'lʌvəbl/ *a* liebenswert

love /lʌv/ *n* Liebe *f*; (*Tennis*) null; **in** ~ verliebt • *vt* lieben; ~ **doing sth** etw sehr gerne machen; **I** ~ **chocolate** ich esse sehr gerne Schokolade. ~**affair** *n* Liebesverhältnis *nt*. ~ **letter** *n* Liebesbrief *m*

lovely /'lʌvlɪ/ *a* (-**ier**, -**iest**) schön; **we had a** ~ **time** es war sehr schön

lover /'lʌvə(r)/ *n* Liebhaber *m*

love: ~ **song** *n* Liebeslied *nt*. ~ **story** *n* Liebesgeschichte *f*

loving /'lʌvɪŋ/ *a*, -**ly** *adv* liebevoll

low /ləʊ/ *a* (-**er**, -**est**) niedrig; ⟨*cloud, note*⟩ tief; ⟨*voice*⟩ leise; (*depressed*) niedergeschlagen • *adv* niedrig; ⟨*fly, sing*⟩ tief; ⟨*speak*⟩ leise; **feel** ~ deprimiert sein • *n* (*Meteorol*) Tief *nt*; (*fig*) Tiefstand *m*

low: ~**brow** *a* geistig anspruchslos. ~**-cut** *a* ⟨*dress*⟩ tief ausgeschnitten

lower /'ləʊə(r)/ *a & adv see* **low** • *vt* niedriger machen; (*let down*) herunterlassen; (*reduce*) senken; ~ **oneself** sich herabwürdigen

low: ~**'fat** *a* fettarm. ~**'grade** *a* minderwertig. ~**lands** /-ləndz/ *npl* Tiefland *nt*. ~ **'tide** *n* Ebbe *f*

loyal /'lɔɪəl/ *a*, -**ly** *adv* treu. ~**ty** *n* Treue *f*

lozenge /'lɒzɪndʒ/ *n* Pastille *f*

Ltd *abbr* (**Limited**) GmbH

lubricant /'luːbrɪkənt/ *n* Schmiermittel *nt*

lubricat|e /'luːbrɪkeɪt/ *vt* schmieren. ~**ion** /-'keɪʃn/ *n* Schmierung *f*

lucid /'luːsɪd/ *a* klar. ~**ity** /-'sɪdətɪ/ *n* Klarheit *f*

luck /lʌk/ n Glück nt; **bad** ~ Pech nt; **good** ~! viel Glück! ~**ily** adv glücklicherweise, zum Glück

lucky /'lʌkɪ/ a (-ier, -iest) glücklich; ⟨day, number⟩ Glücks-; **be** ~ Glück haben; ⟨thing:⟩ Glück bringen. ~ **'charm** n Amulett nt

lucrative /'lu:krətɪv/ a einträglich

ludicrous /'lu:dɪkrəs/ a lächerlich

lug /lʌg/ vt (pt/pp **lugged**) (fam) schleppen

luggage /'lʌgɪdʒ/ n Gepäck nt

luggage: ~-**rack** n Gepäckablage f. ~ **trolley** n Kofferkuli m. ~-**van** n Gepäckwagen m

lugubrious /lu:'gu:brɪəs/ a traurig

lukewarm /'lu:k-/ a lauwarm

lull /lʌl/ n Pause f • vt ~ **to sleep** einschläfern

lullaby /'lʌləbaɪ/ n Wiegenlied nt

lumbago /lʌm'beɪgəʊ/ n Hexenschuß m

lumber /'lʌmbə(r)/ n Gerümpel nt; (Amer: timber) Bauholz nt • vt ~ **s.o. with sth** jdm etw aufhalsen. ~**jack** n (Amer) Holzfäller m

luminous /'lu:mɪnəs/ a leuchtend; **be** ~ leuchten

lump[1] /lʌmp/ n Klumpen m; (of sugar) Stück nt; (swelling) Beule f; (in breast) Knoten m; (tumour) Geschwulst f; **a** ~ **in one's throat** (fam) ein Kloß im Hals • vt ~ **together** zusammentun

lump[2] vt ~ **it** (fam) sich damit abfinden

lump: ~ **sugar** n Würfelzucker m. ~ **'sum** n Pauschalsumme f

lumpy /'lʌmpɪ/ a (-ier, -iest) klumpig

lunacy /'lu:nəsɪ/ n Wahnsinn m

lunar /'lu:nə(r)/ a Mond-

lunatic /'lu:nətɪk/ n Wahnsinnige(r) m/f

lunch /lʌntʃ/ n Mittagessen nt • vi zu Mittag essen

luncheon /'lʌntʃn/ n Mittagessen nt. ~ **meat** n Frühstücksfleisch nt. ~ **voucher** n Essensbon m

lunch: ~-**hour** n Mittagspause f. ~-**time** n Mittagszeit f

lung /lʌŋ/ n Lungenflügel m; ~**s** pl Lunge f. ~ **cancer** n Lungenkrebs m

lunge /lʌndʒ/ vi sich stürzen (**at** auf + acc)

lurch[1] /lɜ:tʃ/ n **leave in the** ~ (fam) im Stich lassen

lurch[2] vi schleudern; ⟨person:⟩ torkeln

lure /lʊə(r)/ n Lockung f; (bait) Köder m • vt locken

lurid /'lʊərɪd/ a grell; (sensational) reißerisch

lurk /lɜ:k/ vi lauern

luscious /'lʌʃəs/ a lecker, köstlich

lush /lʌʃ/ a üppig

lust /lʌst/ n Begierde f • vi ~ **after** gieren nach. ~**ful** a lüstern

lustre /'lʌstə(r)/ n Glanz m

lusty /'lʌstɪ/ a (-ier, -iest) kräftig

lute /lu:t/ n Laute f

luxuriant /lʌg'zʊərɪənt/ a üppig

luxurious /lʌg'zʊərɪəs/ a, -ly adv luxuriös

luxury /'lʌkʃərɪ/ n Luxus m • attrib Luxus-

lying /'laɪɪŋ/ see **lie**[1], **lie**[2]

lymph gland /'lɪmf-/ n Lymphdrüse f

lynch /lɪntʃ/ vt lynchen

lynx /lɪŋks/ n Luchs m

lyric /'lɪrɪk/ a lyrisch. ~**al** a lyrisch; (fam: enthusiastic) schwärmerisch. ~ **poetry** n Lyrik f. ~**s** npl [Lied]text m

M

mac /mæk/ n (fam) Regenmantel m

macabre /mə'kɑ:br/ a makaber

macaroni /mækə'rəʊnɪ/ n Makkaroni pl

macaroon /mækə'ru:n/ n Makrone f

mace[1] /meɪs/ n Amtsstab m

mace[2] n (spice) Muskatblüte f

machinations /mækɪ'neɪʃnz/ pl Machenschaften pl

machine /mə'ʃi:n/ n Maschine f • vt (sew) mit der Maschine nähen; (Techn) maschinell bearbeiten. ~**gun** n Maschinengewehr nt

machinery /mə'ʃi:nərɪ/ n Maschinerie f

machine tool n Werkzeugmaschine f

machinist /mə'ʃi:nɪst/ n Maschinist m; (on sewing machine) Maschinennäherin f

mackerel /'mækrl/ n inv Makrele f

mackintosh /'mækɪntoʃ/ n Regenmantel m

mad /mæd/ a (**madder, maddest**) verrückt; (dog) tollwütig; (fam: angry) böse (**at** auf + acc)

madam /'mædəm/ n gnädige Frau f

madden /'mædən/ vt (make angry) wütend machen

made /meɪd/ *see* **make**; ∼ **to measure** maßgeschneidert

Madeira cake /mə'dɪərə-/ *n* Sandkuchen *m*

mad|ly /'mædlɪ/ *adv* (*fam*) wahnsinnig. ∼**man** *n* Irre(r) *m*. ∼**ness** *n* Wahnsinn *m*

madonna /mə'dɒnə/ *n* Madonna *f*

magazine /mægə'ziːn/ *n* Zeitschrift *f*; (*Mil, Phot*) Magazin *nt*

maggot /'mægət/ *n* Made *f*. ∼**y** *a* madig

Magi /'meɪdʒaɪ/ *npl* **the** ∼ die Heiligen Drei Könige

magic /'mædʒɪk/ *n* Zauber *m*; (*tricks*) Zauberkunst *f* ● *a* magisch; ⟨*word, wand, flute*⟩ Zauber-. ∼**al** *a* zauberhaft

magician /mə'dʒɪʃn/ *n* Zauberer *m*; (*entertainer*) Zauberkünstler *m*

magistrate /'mædʒɪstreɪt/ *n* ≈ Friedensrichter *m*

magnanim|ity /mægnə'nɪmətɪ/ *n* Großmut *f*. ∼**ous** /-'næ nɪməs/ *a* großmütig

magnesia /mæg'niːʃə/ *n* Magnesia *f*

magnet /'mægnɪt/ *n* Magnet *m*. ∼**ic** /-'netɪk/ *a* magnetisch. ∼**ism** *n* Magnetismus *m*. ∼**ize** *vt* magnetisieren

magnification /mægnɪfɪ'keɪʃn/ *n* Vergrößerung *f*

magnificen|ce /mæg'nɪfɪsəns/ *n* Großartigkeit *f*. ∼**t** *a*, **-ly** *adv* großartig

magnify /'mægnɪfaɪ/ *vt* (*pt/pp* **-ied**) vergrößern; (*exaggerate*) übertreiben. ∼**ing glass** *n* Vergrößerungsglas *nt*

magnitude /'mægnɪtjuːd/ *n* Größe *f*; (*importance*) Bedeutung *f*

magpie /'mægpaɪ/ *n* Elster *f*

mahogany /mə'hɒgənɪ/ *n* Mahagoni *nt*

maid /meɪd/ *n* Dienstmädchen *nt*; (*liter: girl*) Maid *f*; **old** ∼ (*pej*) alte Jungfer *f*

maiden /'meɪdn/ *n* (*liter*) Maid *f* ● *a* ⟨*speech, voyage*⟩ Jungfern-. ∼ **'aunt** *n* unverheiratete Tante *f*. ∼ **name** *n* Mädchenname *m*

mail¹ /meɪl/ *n* Kettenpanzer *m*

mail² *n* Post *f* ● *vt* mit der Post schicken; (*send off*) abschicken

mail: ∼**-bag** *n* Postsack *m*. ∼**box** *n* (*Amer*) Briefkasten *m*. ∼**ing list** *n* Postversandliste *f*. ∼**man** *n* (*Amer*) Briefträger *m*. ∼**-order firm** *n* Versandhaus *nt*

maim /meɪm/ *vt* verstümmeln

main¹ *n* (*water, gas, electricity*) Hauptleitung *f*

main² *a* Haupt- ● *n* **in the** ∼ im großen und ganzen

main: ∼**land** /-lənd/ *n* Festland *nt*. ∼**ly** *adv* hauptsächlich. ∼**stay** *n* (*fig*) Stütze *f*. ∼ **street** *n* Hauptstraße *f*

maintain /meɪn'teɪn/ *vt* aufrechterhalten; (*keep in repair*) instand halten; (*support*) unterhalten; (*claim*) behaupten

maintenance /'meɪntənəns/ *n* Aufrechterhaltung *f*; (*care*) Instandhaltung *f*; (*allowance*) Unterhalt *m*

maisonette /meɪzə'net/ *n* Wohnung *f* [auf zwei Etagen]

maize /meɪz/ *n* Mais *m*

majestic /mə'dʒestɪk/ *a*, **-ally** *adv* majestätisch

majesty /'mædʒəstɪ/ *n* Majestät *f*

major /'meɪdʒə(r)/ *a* größer ● *n* (*Mil*) Major *m*; (*Mus*) Dur *nt* ● *vi* (*Amer*) ∼ **in** als Hauptfach studieren

Majorca /mə'jɔːkə/ *n* Mallorca *nt*

majority /mə'dʒɒrətɪ/ *n* Mehrheit *f*; **in the** ∼ in der Mehrzahl

major road *n* Hauptverkehrsstraße *f*

make /meɪk/ *n* (*brand*) Marke *f* ● *v* (*pt/pp* **made**) ● *vt* machen; (*force*) zwingen; (*earn*) verdienen; halten ⟨*speech*⟩; treffen ⟨*decision*⟩; erreichen ⟨*destination*⟩ ● *vi* ∼ **as if to** Miene machen zu. ∼ **do** *vi* zurechtkommen (**with** mit). ∼ **for** *vi* zusteuern auf (+ *acc*). ∼ **off** *vi* sich davonmachen (**with** mit). ∼ **out** *vt* (*distinguish*) ausmachen; (*write out*) ausstellen; (*assert*) behaupten. ∼ **over** *vt* überschreiben (**to** auf + *acc*). ∼ **up** *vt* (*constitute*) bilden; (*invent*) erfinden; (*apply cosmetics to*) schminken; ∼ **up one's mind** sich entschließen ● *vi* sich versöhnen; ∼ **up for sth** etw wiedergutmachen; ∼ **up for lost time** verlorene Zeit aufholen

'make-believe *n* Phantasie *f*

maker /'meɪkə(r)/ *n* Hersteller *m*

make: ∼**shift** *a* behelfsmäßig ● *n* Notbehelf *m*. ∼**-up** *n* Make-up *nt*

making /'meɪkɪŋ/ *n* **have the** ∼**s of** das Zeug haben zu

maladjusted /mælə'dʒʌstɪd/ *a* verhaltensgestört

malaise /mə'leɪz/ *n* (*fig*) Unbehagen *nt*

male /meɪl/ *a* männlich ● *n* Mann *m*; (*animal*) Männchen *nt*. ~ **nurse** *n* Krankenpfleger *m*. ~ **voice 'choir** *n* Männerchor *m*

malevolen|ce /məˈlevələns/ *n* Bosheit *f*. ~**t** *a* boshaft

malfunction /mælˈfʌŋkʃn/ *n* technische Störung *f*; (*Med*) Funktionsstörung *f* ● *vi* nicht richtig funktionieren

malice /ˈmælɪs/ *n* Bosheit *f*; **bear s.o.** ~ einen Groll gegen jdn hegen

malicious /məˈlɪʃəs/ *a*, **-ly** *adv* böswillig

malign /məˈlaɪn/ *vt* verleumden

malignan|cy /məˈlɪgnənsɪ/ *n* Bösartigkeit *f*. ~**t** *a* bösartig

malinger /məˈlɪŋgə(r)/ *vi* simulieren, sich krank stellen. ~**er** *n* Simulant *m*

malleable /ˈmælɪəbl/ *a* formbar

mallet /ˈmælɪt/ *n* Holzhammer *m*

malnu'trition /mæl-/ *n* Unterernährung *f*

mal'practice *n* Berufsvergehen *nt*

malt /mɔːlt/ *n* Malz *nt*

mal'treat /mæl-/ *vt* mißhandeln. ~**ment** *n* Mißhandlung *f*

mammal /ˈmæml/ *n* Säugetier *nt*

mammoth /ˈmæməθ/ *a* riesig ● *n* Mammut *nt*

man /mæn/ *n* (*pl* **men**) Mann *m*; (*mankind*) der Mensch; (*chess*) Figur *f*; (*draughts*) Stein *m* ● *vt* (*pt/pp* **manned**) bemannen ⟨*ship*⟩; bedienen ⟨*pump*⟩; besetzen ⟨*counter*⟩

manacle /ˈmænəkl/ *vt* fesseln (**to** an + *acc*); ~**d** in Handschellen

manage /ˈmænɪdʒ/ *vt* leiten; verwalten ⟨*estate*⟩; (*cope with*) fertig werden mit; ~ **to do sth** es schaffen, etw zu tun ● *vi* zurechtkommen; ~ **on** auskommen mit. ~**able** /-əbl/ *a* ⟨*tool*⟩ handlich; ⟨*person*⟩ fügsam. ~**ment** /-mənt/ *n* **the** ~**ment** die Geschäftsleitung *f*

manager /ˈmænɪdʒə(r)/ *n* Geschäftsführer *m*; (*of bank*) Direktor *m*; (*of estate*) Verwalter *m*; (*Sport*) [Chef] trainer *m*. ~**ess** *n* Geschäftsführer(in) *f*. ~**ial** /-ˈdʒɪərɪəl/ *a* ~**ial staff** Führungskräfte *pl*

managing /ˈmænɪdʒɪŋ/ *a* ~ **director** Generaldirektor *m*

mandarin /ˈmændərɪn/ *n* ~ **[orange]** Mandarine *f*

mandat|e /ˈmændeɪt/ *n* Mandat *nt*. ~**ory** /-dətrɪ/ *a* obligatorisch

mane /meɪn/ *n* Mähne *f*

manful /ˈmænfl/ *a*, **-ly** *adv* mannhaft

manger /ˈmeɪndʒə(r)/ *n* Krippe *f*

mangle[1] /ˈmæŋgl/ *n* Wringmaschine *f*; (*for smoothing*) Mangel *f*

mangle[2] *vt* (*damage*) verstümmeln

mango /ˈmæŋgəʊ/ *n* (*pl* **-es**) Mango *f*

mangy /ˈmeɪndʒɪ/ *a* ⟨*dog*⟩ räudig

man: ~**handle** *vt* grob behandeln ⟨*person*⟩. ~**hole** *n* Kanalschacht *m*. ~**hole cover** *n* Kanaldeckel *m*. ~**hood** *n* Mannesalter *nt*; (*quality*) Männlichkeit *f*. ~**-hour** *n* Arbeitsstunde *f*. ~**-hunt** *n* Fahndung *f*

man|ia /ˈmeɪnɪə/ *n* Manie *f*. ~**iac** /-ɪæk/ *n* Wahnsinnige(r) *m/f*

manicur|e /ˈmænɪkjʊə(r)/ *n* Maniküre *f* ● *vt* maniküren. ~**ist** *n* Maniküre *f*

manifest /ˈmænɪfest/ *a*, **-ly** *adv* offensichtlich ● *vt* ~ **itself** sich manifestieren

manifesto /mænɪˈfestəʊ/ *n* Manifest *nt*

manifold /ˈmænɪfəʊld/ *a* mannigfaltig

manipulat|e /məˈnɪpjuleɪt/ *vt* handhaben; (*pej*) manipulieren. ~**ion** /-ˈleɪʃn/ *n* Manipulation *f*

man'kind *n* die Menschheit

manly /ˈmænlɪ/ *a* männlich

'man-made *a* künstlich. ~ **fibre** *n* Kunstfaser *f*

manner /ˈmænə(r)/ *n* Weise *f*; (*kind*, *behaviour*) Art *f*; **in this** ~ auf diese Weise; **[good/bad]** ~**s** [gute/ schlechte] Manieren *pl*. ~**ism** *n* Angewohnheit *f*

mannish /ˈmænɪʃ/ *a* männlich

manœuvrable /məˈnuːvrəbl/ *a* manövrierfähig

manœuvre /məˈnuːvə(r)/ *n* Manöver *nt* ● *vt/i* manövrieren

manor /ˈmænə(r)/ *n* Gutshof *m*; (*house*) Gutshaus *nt*

man: ~**power** *n* Arbeitskräfte *pl*. ~**servant** *n* (*pl* **menservants**) Diener *m*

mansion /ˈmænʃn/ *n* Villa *f*

'manslaughter *n* Totschlag *m*

mantelpiece /ˈmæntl-/ *n* Kaminsims *m* & *nt*

manual /ˈmænjʊəl/ *a* Hand- ● *n* Handbuch *nt*

manufacture /mænjʊˈfæktʃə(r)/ *vt* herstellen ● *n* Herstellung *f*. ~**r** *n* Hersteller *m*

manure /məˈnjʊə(r)/ *n* Mist *m*

manuscript /ˈmænjʊskrɪpt/ *n* Manuskript *nt*

many /'meni/ a viele; ~ **a time** oft • n **a good/great** ~ sehr viele

map /mæp/ n Landkarte f; (of town) Stadtplan m • vt (pt/pp **mapped**) ~ **out** (fig) ausarbeiten

maple /'meɪpl/ n Ahorn m

mar /mɑ:(r)/ vt (pt/pp **marred**) verderben

marathon /'mærəθən/ n Marathon m

marauding /mə'rɔ:dɪŋ/ a plündernd

marble /'mɑ:bl/ n Marmor m; (for game) Murmel f

March /mɑ:tʃ/ n März m

march n Marsch m • vi marschieren • vt marschieren lassen; ~ **s.o. off** jdn abführen

mare /'meə(r)/ n Stute f

margarine /mɑ:dʒə'ri:n/ n Margarine f

margin /'mɑ:dʒɪn/ n Rand m; (leeway) Spielraum m; (Comm) Spanne f. ~**al** a, **-ly** adv geringfügig

marigold /'mærɪgəʊld/ n Ringelblume f

marijuana /mærɪ'hwɑ:nə/ n Marihuana nt

marina /mə'ri:nə/ n Jachthafen m

marinade /mærɪ'neɪd/ n Marinade f • vt marinieren

marine /mə'ri:n/ a Meeres- • n Marine f; (sailor) Marineinfanterist m

marionette /mærɪə'net/ n Marionette f

marital /'mærɪtl/ a ehelich. ~ **status** n Familienstand m

maritime /'mærɪtaɪm/ a See-

marjoram /'mɑ:dʒərəm/ n Majoran m

mark¹ /mɑ:k/ n (currency) Mark f

mark² n Fleck m; (sign) Zeichen nt; (trace) Spur f; (target) Ziel nt; (Sch) Note f • vt markieren; (spoil) beschädigen; (characterize) kennzeichnen; (Sch) korrigieren; (Sport) decken; ~ **time** (Mil) auf der Stelle treten; (fig) abwarten; ~ **my words** das [eine] will ich dir sagen. ~ **out** vt markieren

marked /mɑ:kt/ a, ~**ly** /-kɪdlɪ/ adv deutlich; (pronounced) ausgeprägt

marker /'mɑ:kə(r)/ n Marke f; (of exam) Korrektor(in) m(f)

market /'mɑ:kɪt/ n Markt m • vt vertreiben; (launch) auf den Markt bringen. ~**ing** n Marketing nt. ~ **re'search** n Marktforschung f

marking /'mɑ:kɪŋ/ n Markierung f; (on animal) Zeichnung f

marksman /'mɑ:ksmən/ n Scharfschütze m

marmalade /'mɑ:məleɪd/ n Orangenmarmelade f

marmot /'mɑ:mət/ n Murmeltier nt

maroon /mə'ru:n/ a dunkelrot

marooned /mə'ru:nd/ a (fig) von der Außenwelt abgeschnitten

marquee /mɑ:'ki:/ n Festzelt nt; (Amer: awning) Markise f

marquetry /'mɑ:kɪtrɪ/ n Einlegearbeit f

marquis /'mɑ:kwɪs/ n Marquis m

marriage /'mærɪdʒ/ n Ehe f; (wedding) Hochzeit f. ~**able** /-əbl/ a heiratsfähig

married /'mærɪd/ see **marry** • a verheiratet. ~ **life** n Eheleben nt

marrow /'mærəʊ/ n (Anat) Mark nt; (vegetable) Kürbis m

marr|y /'mærɪ/ vt/i (pt/pp **married**) heiraten; (unite) trauen; **get** ~**ied** heiraten

marsh /mɑ:ʃ/ n Sumpf m

marshal /'mɑ:ʃl/ n Marschall m; (steward) Ordner m • vt (pt/pp **marshalled**) (Mil) formieren; (fig) ordnen

marshy /'mɑ:ʃɪ/ a sumpfig

marsupial /mɑ:'su:pɪəl/ n Beuteltier nt

martial /'mɑ:ʃl/ a kriegerisch. ~ **'law** n Kriegsrecht nt

martyr /'mɑ:tə(r)/ n Märtyrer(in) m(f) • vt zum Märtyrer machen. ~**dom** /-dəm/ n Martyrium nt

marvel /'mɑ:vl/ n Wunder nt • vi (pt/pp **marvelled**) staunen (**at** über + acc). ~**lous** /-vələs/ a, **-ly** adv wunderbar

Marxis|m /'mɑ:ksɪzm/ n Marxismus m. ~**t** a marxistisch • n Marxist(in) m(f)

marzipan /'mɑ:zɪpæn/ n Marzipan nt

mascara /mæ'skɑ:rə/ n Wimperntusche f

mascot /'mæskət/ n Maskottchen nt

masculin|e /'mæskjʊlɪn/ a männlich • n (Gram) Maskulinum nt. ~**ity** /-'lɪnətɪ/ n Männlichkeit f

mash /mæʃ/ n (fam, Culin) Kartoffelpüree nt • vt stampfen. ~**ed pota-toes** npl Kartoffelpüree nt

mask /mɑ:sk/ n Maske f • vt maskieren

masochis|m /'mæsəkɪzm/ n Masochismus m. ~**t** /-ɪst/ n Masochist m

mason /'meɪsn/ n Steinmetz m

Mason n Freimaurer m. ~**ic** /mə'sɒnɪk/ a freimaurerisch

masonry /'meɪsnrɪ/ n Mauerwerk nt
masquerade /mæskəˈreɪd/ n (fig)
Maskerade f ● vi ~ **as** (pose) sich
ausgeben als
mass¹ /mæs/ n (Relig) Messe f
mass² n Masse f ● vi sich sammeln;
(Mil) sich massieren
massacre /'mæsəkə(r)/ n Massaker
nt ● vt niedermetzeln
massage /'mæsɑːʒ/ n Massage f ● vt
massieren
masseu|r /mæˈsɜː(r)/ n Masseur m.
~se /-'sɜːz/ n Masseuse f
massive /'mæsɪv/ a massiv; (huge)
riesig
mass: ~ **media** npl Massenmedien
pl. **~-pro'duce** vt in Massenproduktion herstellen. ~ **pro-
'duction** n Massenproduktion f
mast /mɑːst/ n Mast m
master /'mɑːstə(r)/ n Herr m;
(teacher) Lehrer m; (craftsman,
artist) Meister m; (of ship) Kapitän
m ● vt meistern; beherrschen
⟨language⟩
master: ~**key** n Hauptschlüssel m.
~**ly** a meisterhaft. ~**mind** n füh-
render Kopf m ● vt der führende
Kopf sein von. ~**piece** n Meister-
werk nt. ~**y** n (of subject) Beherrschung f
masturbat|e /'mæstəbeɪt/ vi mastur-
bieren. ~**ion** /-'beɪʃn/ n Masturba-
tion f
mat /mæt/ n Matte f; (on table) Untersatz m
match¹ /mætʃ/ n Wettkampf m; (in
ball games) Spiel nt; (Tennis) Match
nt; (marriage) Heirat f; **be a good ~**
⟨colours:⟩ gut zusammenpassen; **be
no ~ for s.o.** jdm nicht gewachsen
sein ● vt (equal) gleichkommen (+
dat); (be like) passen zu; (find sth
similar) etwas Passendes finden zu
● vi zusammenpassen
match² n Streichholz nt. ~**box** n
Streichholzschachtel f
matching /'mætʃɪŋ/ a [zusammen]
passend
mate¹ /meɪt/ n Kumpel m; (assistant) Gehilfe m; (Naut) Maat m;
(Zool) Männchen nt; (female) Weibchen nt ● vi sich paaren ● vt paaren
mate² n (Chess) Matt nt
material /məˈtɪərɪəl/ n Material nt;
(fabric) Stoff m; **raw ~s** Rohstoffe pl
● a materiell
material|ism /məˈtɪərɪəlɪzm/ n
Materialismus m. ~**istic** /-'lɪstɪk/ a

materialistisch. ~**ize** /-laɪz/ vi sich
verwirklichen
maternal /məˈtɜːnl/ a mütterlich
maternity /məˈtɜːnətɪ/ n Mutterschaft f. ~ **clothes** npl Umstands-
kleidung f. ~ **ward** n Entbindungs-
station f
matey /'meɪtɪ/ a (fam) freundlich
mathematic|al /mæθəˈmætɪkl/ a, **-ly**
adv mathematisch. ~**ian** /-məˈtɪʃn/ n
Mathematiker(in) m(f)
mathematics /mæθˈmætɪks/ n Ma-
thematik f
maths /mæθs/ n (fam) Mathe f
matinée /'mætɪneɪ/ n (Theat) Nach-
mittagsvorstellung f
matriculat|e /məˈtrɪkjʊleɪt/ vi sich
immatrikulieren. ~**ion** /-'leɪʃn/ n
Immatrikulation f
matrimon|ial /mætrɪˈməʊnɪəl/ a
Ehe-. ~**y** /'mætrɪmənɪ/ n Ehe f
matrix /'meɪtrɪks/ n (pl matrices
/-siːz/) n (Techn: mould) Matrize f
matron /'meɪtrən/ n (of hospital)
Oberin f; (of school) Hausmutter f.
~**ly** a matronenhaft
matt /mæt/ a matt
matted /'mætɪd/ a verfilzt
matter /'mætə(r)/ n (affair) Sache f;
(pus) Eiter m; (Phys: substance) Ma-
terie f; **money ~s** Geldangelegen-
heiten pl; **as a ~ of fact** eigentlich;
what is the ~? was ist los? ● vi
wichtig sein; ~ **to s.o.** jdm etwas
ausmachen; **it doesn't ~** es macht
nichts. ~**-of-fact** a sachlich
matting /'mætɪŋ/ n Matten pl
mattress /'mætrɪs/ n Matratze f
matur|e /məˈtjʊə(r)/ a reif; (Comm)
fällig ● vi reifen; ⟨person:⟩ reifer
werden; (Comm) fällig werden ● vt
reifen lassen. ~**ity** n Reife f; (Comm)
Fälligkeit f
maul /mɔːl/ vt übel zurichten
Maundy /'mɔːndɪ/ n ~ **Thursday**
Gründonnerstag m
mauve /məʊv/ a lila
mawkish /'mɔːkɪʃ/ a rührselig
maxim /'mæksɪm/ n Maxime f
maximum /'mæksɪməm/ a maximal
● n (pl **-ima**) Maximum nt. ~ **speed**
n Höchstgeschwindigkeit f
may /meɪ/ v aux (nur Präsens) (be
allowed to) dürfen; (be possible) können; **may I come in?** darf ich rein-
kommen? **may he succeed** möge es
ihm gelingen; **I may as well stay** am
besten bleibe ich hier; **it may be true**
es könnte wahr sein

May *n* Mai *m*

maybe /'meɪbɪ/ *adv* vielleicht

'May Day *n* der Erste Mai

mayonnaise /meɪə'neɪz/ *n* Mayonnaise *f*

mayor /'meə(r)/ *n* Bürgermeister *m*. **~ess** *n* Bürgermeisterin *f*; (*wife of mayor*) Frau Bürgermeister *f*

maze /meɪz/ *n* Irrgarten *m*; (*fig*) Labyrinth *nt*

me /miː/ *pron* (*acc*) mich; (*dat*) mir; **he knows ~** er kennt mich; **give ~ the money** gib mir das Geld; **it's ~** (*fam*) ich bin es

meadow /'medəʊ/ *n* Wiese *f*

meagre /'miːgə(r)/ *a* dürftig

meal¹ /miːl/ *n* Mahlzeit *f*; (*food*) Essen *nt*

meal² *n* (*grain*) Schrot *m*

mealy-mouthed /miːlɪ'maʊðd/ *a* heuchlerisch

mean¹ /miːn/ *a* (-er, -est) geizig; (*unkind*) gemein; (*poor*) schäbig

mean² *a* mittlere(r,s) ● *n* (*average*) Durchschnitt *m*; **the golden ~** die goldene Mitte

mean³ *vt* (*pt/pp* meant) heißen; (*signify*) bedeuten; (*intend*) beabsichtigen; **I ~ it** das ist mein Ernst; **~ well** es gut meinen; **be meant for** ⟨*present:*⟩ bestimmt sein für; ⟨*remark:*⟩ gerichtet sein an (+ *acc*)

meander /mɪ'ændə(r)/ *vi* sich schlängeln; ⟨*person:*⟩ schlendern

meaning /'miːnɪŋ/ *n* Bedeutung *f*. **~ful** *a* bedeutungsvoll. **~less** *a* bedeutungslos

means /miːnz/ *n* Möglichkeit *f*, Mittel *nt*; **~ of transport** Verkehrsmittel *nt*; **by ~ of** durch; **by all ~!** aber natürlich! **by no ~** keineswegs ● *npl* (*resources*) [Geld]mittel *pl*. **~ test** *n* Bedürftigkeitsnachweis *m*

meant /ment/ *see* mean³

'meantime *n* **in the ~** in der Zwischenzeit ● *adv* inzwischen

'meanwhile *adv* inzwischen

measles /'miːzlz/ *n* Masern *pl*

measly /'miːzlɪ/ *a* (*fam*) mickerig

measurable /'meʒərəbl/ *a* meßbar

measure /'meʒə(r)/ *n* Maß *nt*; (*action*) Maßnahme *f* ● *vt/i* messen; **~ up to** (*fig*) herankommen an (+ *acc*). **~d** *a* gemessen. **~ment** /-mənt/ *n* Maß *nt*

meat /miːt/ *n* Fleisch *nt*. **~ball** *n* (*Culin*) Klops *m*. **~ loaf** *n* falscher Hase *m*

mechan|ic /mɪ'kænɪk/ *n* Mechaniker *m*. **~ical** *a*, **-ly** *adv* mechanisch. **~ical engineering** Maschinenbau *m*. **~ics** *n* Mechanik *f* ● *n pl* Mechanismus *m*

mechan|ism /'mekənɪzm/ *n* Mechanismus *m*. **~ize** *vt* mechanisieren

medal /'medl/ *n* Orden *m*; (*Sport*) Medaille *f*

medallion /mɪ'dælɪən/ *n* Medaillon *nt*

medallist /'medəlɪst/ *n* Medaillengewinner(in) *m(f)*

meddle /'medl/ *vi* sich einmischen (**in** + *acc*); (*tinker*) herumhantieren (**with** an + *acc*)

media /'miːdɪə/ *see* **medium** ● *n pl* **the ~** die Medien *pl*

median /'miːdɪən/ *a* **~ strip** (*Amer*) Mittelstreifen *m*

mediat|e /'miːdɪeɪt/ *vi* vermitteln. **~or** *n* Vermittler(in) *m(f)*

medical /'medɪkl/ *a* medizinisch; ⟨*treatment*⟩ ärztlich ● *n* ärztliche Untersuchung *f*. **~ insurance** *n* Krankenversicherung *f*. **~ student** *n* Medizinstudent *m*

medicat|ed /'medɪkeɪtɪd/ *a* medizinisch. **~ion** /-'keɪʃn/ *n* (*drugs*) Medikamente *pl*

medicinal /mɪ'dɪsɪnl/ *a* medizinisch; ⟨*plant*⟩ heilkräftig

medicine /'medsən/ *n* Medizin *f*; (*preparation*) Medikament *nt*

medieval /medɪ'iːvl/ *a* mittelalterlich

mediocr|e /miːdɪ'əʊkə(r)/ *a* mittelmäßig. **~ity** /-'ɒkrətɪ/ *n* Mittelmäßigkeit *f*

meditat|e /'medɪteɪt/ *vi* nachdenken (**on** über + *acc*); (*Relig*) meditieren. **~ion** /-'teɪʃn/ *n* Meditation *f*

Mediterranean /medɪtə'reɪnɪən/ *n* Mittelmeer *nt* ● *a* Mittelmeer-

medium /'miːdɪəm/ *a* mittlere(r, s); ⟨*steak*⟩ medium; **of ~ size** von mittlerer Größe ● *n* (*pl* media) Medium *nt*; (*means*) Mittel *nt* ● (*pl* -s) (*person*) Medium *nt*

medium: ~-sized *a* mittelgroß. **~ wave** *n* Mittelwelle *f*

medley /'medlɪ/ *n* Gemisch *nt*; (*Mus*) Potpourri *nt*

meek /miːk/ *a* (-er, -est), **-ly** *adv* sanftmütig; (*unprotesting*) widerspruchslos

meet /miːt/ *v* (*pt/pp* met) ● *vt* treffen; (*by chance*) begegnen (+ *dat*); (*at station*) abholen; ⟨*make the acquaintance of*⟩ kennenlernen; stoßen auf (+ *acc*) ⟨*problem*⟩; bezahlen

⟨bill⟩; erfüllen ⟨requirements⟩ ● vi sich treffen; (for the first time) sich kennenlernen; ~ **with** stoßen auf (+ acc) ⟨problem⟩; sich treffen mit ⟨person⟩ ● n Jagdtreffen nt

meeting /ˈmiːtɪŋ/ n Treffen nt; (by chance) Begegnung f; (discussion) Besprechung f; (of committee) Sitzung f; (large) Versammlung f

megalomania /megələˈmeɪnɪə/ n Größenwahnsinn m

megaphone /ˈmegəfəʊn/ n Megaphon nt

melancholy /ˈmelənkəlɪ/ a melancholisch ● n Melancholie f

mellow /ˈmeləʊ/ a (-er, -est) ⟨fruit⟩ ausgereift; ⟨sound, person⟩ sanft ● vi reifer werden

melodic /mɪˈlɒdɪk/ a melodisch

melodious /mɪˈləʊdɪəs/ a melodiös

melodrama /ˈmelə-/ n Melodrama nt. ~**tic** /-drəˈmætɪk/ a, -ally adv melodramatisch

melody /ˈmelədɪ/ n Melodie f

melon /ˈmelən/ n Melone f

melt /melt/ vt/i schmelzen. ~ **down** vt einschmelzen. ~**ing-pot** n (fig) Schmelztiegel m

member /ˈmembə(r)/ n Mitglied nt; (of family) Angehörige(r) m/f; **M**~ **of Parliament** Abgeordnete(r) m/f. ~**ship** n Mitgliedschaft f; (members) Mitgliederzahl f

membrane /ˈmembreɪn/ n Membran f

memento /mɪˈmentəʊ/ n Andenken nt

memo /ˈmeməʊ/ n Mitteilung f

memoirs /ˈmemwɑːz/ n pl Memoiren pl

memorable /ˈmemərəbl/ a denkwürdig

memorandum /meməˈrændəm/ n Mitteilung f

memorial /mɪˈmɔːrɪəl/ n Denkmal nt. ~ **service** n Gedenkfeier f

memorize /ˈmeməraɪz/ vt sich (dat) einprägen

memory /ˈmemərɪ/ n Gedächtnis nt; (thing remembered) Erinnerung f; (of computer) Speicher m; **from** ~ auswendig; **in** ~ **of** zur Erinnerung an (+ acc)

men /men/ see **man**

menac|**e** /ˈmenɪs/ n Drohung f; (nuisance) Plage f ● vt bedrohen. ~**ing** a, -ly adv drohend

mend /mend/ vt reparieren; (patch) flicken; ausbessern ⟨clothes⟩ ● n **on the** ~ auf dem Weg der Besserung

ˈmenfolk n pl Männer pl

menial /ˈmiːnɪəl/ a niedrig

meningitis /menɪnˈdʒaɪtɪs/ n Hirnhautentzündung f, Meningitis f

menopause /ˈmenə-/ n Wechseljahre pl

menstruat|**e** /ˈmenstrʊeɪt/ vi menstruieren. ~**ion** /-ˈeɪʃn/ n Menstruation f

mental /ˈmentl/ a, -ly adv geistig; (fam: mad) verrückt. ~ **aˈrithmetic** n Kopfrechnen nt. ~ **ˈillness** n Geisteskrankheit f

mentality /menˈtælətɪ/ n Mentalität f

mention /ˈmenʃn/ n Erwähnung f ● vt erwähnen; **don't** ~ **it** keine Ursache; bitte

menu /ˈmenjuː/ n Speisekarte f

mercantile /ˈmɜːkəntaɪl/ a Handels-

mercenary /ˈmɜːsɪnərɪ/ a geldgierig ● n Söldner m

merchandise /ˈmɜːtʃəndaɪz/ n Ware f

merchant /ˈmɜːtʃənt/ n Kaufmann m; (dealer) Händler m. ~ **ˈnavy** n Handelsmarine f

merci|**ful** /ˈmɜːsɪfl/ a barmherzig. ~**fully** adv (fam) glücklicherweise. ~**less** a, -ly adv erbarmungslos

mercury /ˈmɜːkjʊrɪ/ n Quecksilber nt

mercy /ˈmɜːsɪ/ n Barmherzigkeit f, Gnade f; **be at s.o.'s** ~ jdm ausgeliefert sein

mere /mɪə(r)/ a, -ly adv bloß

merest /ˈmɪərɪst/ a kleinste(r,s)

merge /mɜːdʒ/ vi zusammenlaufen; (Comm) fusionieren ● vt (Comm) zusammenschließen

merger /ˈmɜːdʒə(r)/ n Fusion f

meridian /məˈrɪdɪən/ n Meridian m

meringue /məˈræŋ/ n Baiser nt

merit /ˈmerɪt/ n Verdienst nt; (advantage) Vorzug m; (worth) Wert m ● vt verdienen

mermaid /ˈmɜːmeɪd/ n Meerjungfrau f

merri|**ly** /ˈmerɪlɪ/ adv fröhlich. ~**ment** /-mənt/ n Fröhlichkeit f; (laughter) Gelächter nt

merry /ˈmerɪ/ a (-ier, -iest) fröhlich; ~ **Christmas!** fröhliche Weihnachten!

merry: ~-**go-round** n Karussell nt. ~-**making** n Feiern nt

mesh /meʃ/ n Masche f; (size) Maschenweite f; (fig: network) Netz nt

mesmerize /'mezməraɪz/ vt hypnotisieren. **~d** a (fig) [wie] gebannt

mess /mes/ n Durcheinander nt; (trouble) Schwierigkeiten pl; (something spilt) Bescherung f (fam); (Mil) Messe f; **make a ~ of** (botch) verpfuschen ● vt **~ up** in Unordnung bringen; (botch) verpfuschen ● vi **~ about** herumalbern; (tinker) herumspielen (with mit)

message /'mesɪdʒ/ n Nachricht f; **give s.o. a ~** jdm etwas ausrichten

messenger /'mesɪndʒə(r)/ n Bote m

Messiah /mɪ'saɪə/ n Messias m

Messrs /'mesəz/ n pl see **Mr**; (on letter) **~ Smith** Firma Smith

messy /'mesɪ/ a (-ier, -iest) schmutzig; (untidy) unordentlich

met /met/ see **meet**

metabolism /mɪ'tæbəlɪzm/ n Stoffwechsel m

metal /'metl/ n Metall nt ● a Metall-. **~lic** /mɪ'tælɪk/ a metallisch. **~lurgy** /mɪ'tælədʒɪ/ n Metallurgie f

metamorphosis /metə'mɔːfəsɪs/ n (pl -phoses /-siːz/) Metamorphose f

metaphor /'metəfə(r)/ n Metapher f. **~ical** /-'fɒrɪkl/ a, **-ly** adv metaphorisch

meteor /'miːtɪə(r)/ n Meteor m. **~ic** /-'ɒrɪk/ a kometenhaft

meteorological /miːtɪərə'lɒdʒɪkl/ a Wetter-

meteorolog|ist /miːtɪə'rɒlədʒɪst/ n Meteorologe m/-gin f. **~y** n Meteorologie f

meter[1] /'miːtə(r)/ n Zähler m

meter[2] n (Amer) = **metre**

method /'meθəd/ n Methode f; (Culin) Zubereitung f

methodical /mɪ'θɒdɪkl/ a, **-ly** adv systematisch, methodisch

Methodist /'meθədɪst/ n Methodist(in) m(f)

meths /meθs/ n (fam) Brennspiritus m

methylated /'meθɪleɪtɪd/ a **~ spirit[s]** Brennspiritus m

meticulous /mɪ'tɪkjʊləs/ a, **-ly** adv sehr genau

metre /'miːtə(r)/ n Meter m & n; (rhythm) Versmaß nt

metric /'metrɪk/ a metrisch

metropolis /mɪ'trɒpəlɪs/ n Metropole f

metropolitan /metrə'pɒlɪtən/ a hauptstädtisch; (international) weltstädtisch

mettle /'metl/ n Mut m

mew /mjuː/ n Miau ● vi miauen

Mexican /'meksɪkən/ a mexikanisch ● n Mexikaner(in) m(f). **'Mexico** n Mexiko nt

miaow /mɪaʊ/ n Miau nt ● vi miauen

mice /maɪs/ see **mouse**

microbe /'maɪkrəʊb/ n Mikrobe f

micro /'maɪkrəʊ/: **~chip** n Mikrochip nt. **~computer** n Mikrocomputer m. **~film** n Mikrofilm m. **~phone** n Mikrophon nt. **~processor** n Mikroprozessor m. **~scope** /-skəʊp/ n Mikroskop nt. **~scopic** /-'skɒpɪk/ a mikroskopisch. **~wave** n Mikrowelle f. **~wave [oven]** n Mikrowellenherd m

mid /mɪd/ a **~ May** Mitte Mai; **in ~ air** in der Luft

midday /mɪd'deɪ/ n Mittag m

middle /'mɪdl/ a mittlere(r, s); **the M~ Ages** das Mittelalter; **the ~ class[es]** der Mittelstand; **the M~ East** der Nahe Osten ● n Mitte f; **in the ~ of the night** mitten in der Nacht

middle: **~-aged** a mittleren Alters. **~-class** a bürgerlich. **~man** n (Comm) Zwischenhändler m

middling /'mɪdlɪŋ/ a mittelmäßig

midge /mɪdʒ/ n [kleine] Mücke f

midget /'mɪdʒɪt/ n Liliputaner(in) m(f)

Midlands /'mɪdləndz/ npl **the ~** Mittelengland n

'midnight n Mitternacht f

midriff /'mɪdrɪf/ n (fam) Taille f

midst /mɪdst/ n **in the ~ of** mitten in (+ dat); **in our ~** unter uns

mid: **~summer** n Hochsommer m; (solstice) Sommersonnenwende f. **~way** adv auf halbem Wege. **~wife** n Hebamme f. **~wifery** /-wɪfrɪ/ n Geburtshilfe f. **~'winter** n Mitte f des Winters

might[1] /maɪt/ v aux **I ~** vielleicht; **it ~ be true** es könnte wahr sein; **I ~ as well stay** am besten bleibe ich hier; **he asked if he ~ go** er fragte, ob er gehen dürfte; **you ~ have drowned** du hättest ertrinken können

might[2] n Macht f

mighty /'maɪtɪ/ a (-ier, -iest) mächtig

migraine /'miːgreɪn/ n Migräne f

migrant /'maɪgrənt/ a Wander● n (bird) Zugvogel m

migrat|e /maɪ'greɪt/ vi abwandern; ⟨birds:⟩ ziehen. **~ion** /-'greɪʃn/ n Wanderung f; (of birds) Zug m

mike /maɪk/ n (fam) Mikrophon nt

mild /maɪld/ a (-er, -est) mild

mildew /'mɪldjuː/ n Schimmel m;
(Bot) Mehltau m

mild|ly /'maɪldlɪ/ adv leicht; **to put it
~ly** gelinde gesagt. **~ness** n Milde f

mile /maɪl/ n Meile f (= 1,6 km); **~s
too big** (fam) viel zu groß

mile|age /-ɪdʒ/ n Meilenzahl f; (of car)
Meilenstand m. **~stone** n Meilenstein m

militant /'mɪlɪtənt/ a militant

military /'mɪlɪtrɪ/ a militärisch. **~
service** n Wehrdienst m

militate /'mɪlɪteɪt/ vi ~ **against** sprechen gegen

militia /mɪ'lɪʃə/ n Miliz f

milk /mɪlk/ n Milch f ● vt melken

milk: **~man** n Milchmann m. **~
shake** n Milchmixgetränk nt

milky /'mɪlkɪ/ a (-ier, -iest) milchig.
M~ Way n (Astr) Milchstraße f

mill /mɪl/ n Mühle f; (factory) Fabrik f
● vt/i mahlen; (Techn) fräsen. **~
about, ~ around** vi umherlaufen

millennium /mɪ'lenɪəm/ n Jahr-
tausend nt

miller /'mɪlə(r)/ n Müller m

millet /'mɪlɪt/ n Hirse f

milli|gram /'mɪlɪ-/ n Milligramm nt.
~metre n Millimeter m & nt

milliner /'mɪlɪnə(r)/ n Modistin f;
(man) Hutmacher m. **~y** n Damen-
hüte pl

million /'mɪljən/ n Million f; **a ~
pounds** eine Million Pfund. **~aire**
/-'neə(r)/ n Millionär(in) m(f)

'millstone n Mühlstein m

mime /maɪm/ n Pantomime f ● vt
pantomimisch darstellen

mimic /'mɪmɪk/ n Imitator m ● vt
(pt/pp mimicked) nachahmen. **~ry** n
Nachahmung f

mimosa /mɪ'məʊzə/ n Mimose f

mince /mɪns/ n Hackfleisch nt ● vt
(Culin) durchdrehen; **not ~ words**
kein Blatt vor den Mund nehmen

mince: **~meat** n Masse f aus Korin-
then, Zitronat usw; **make ~meat of**
(fig) vernichtend schlagen. **~'pie** n
mit 'mincemeat' gefülltes Pastet-
chen nt

mincer /'mɪnsə(r)/ n Fleischwolf m

mind /maɪnd/ n Geist m; (sanity)
Verstand m; **to my ~** meiner Meinung nach; **give s.o. a piece of one's
~** jdm gehörig die Meinung sagen;
make up one's ~ sich entschließen;
be out of one's ~ nicht bei Verstand

sein; **have sth in ~** etw im Sinn
haben; **bear sth in ~** an etw (acc)
denken; **have a good ~ to** große
Lust haben, zu; **I have changed my ~**
ich habe es mir anders überlegt ● vt
aufpassen auf (+ acc); **I don't ~ the
noise** der Lärm stört mich nicht; **~
the step!** Achtung Stufe! ● vi (care)
sich kümmern (about um); **I don't ~**
mir macht es nichts aus; **never ~!**
macht nichts! **do you ~ if?** haben
Sie etwas dagegen, wenn? **~ out** vi
aufpassen

mind|ful a **~ful of** eingedenk (+
gen). **~less** a geistlos

mine¹ /maɪn/ poss pron meine(r),
meins; **a friend of ~** ein Freund von
mir; **that is ~** das gehört mir

mine² n Bergwerk nt; (explosive)
Mine f ● vt abbauen; (Mil) vermi-
nen. **~ detector** n Minensuchgerät
nt. **~field** n Minenfeld nt

miner /'maɪnə(r)/ n Bergarbeiter m

mineral /'mɪnərəl/ n Mineral nt.
~ogy /-'rælədʒɪ/ n Mineralogie f. **~
water** n Mineralwasser nt

minesweeper /'maɪn-/ n Minen-
räumboot nt

mingle /'mɪŋgl/ vi ~ **with** sich mischen unter (+ acc)

miniature /'mɪnɪtʃə(r)/ a Klein- ● n
Miniatur f

mini|bus /'mɪnɪ-/ n Kleinbus m. **~cab**
n Taxi nt

minim /'mɪnɪm/ n (Mus) halbe Note f

minim|al /'mɪnɪməl/ a minimal. **~ize**
vt auf ein Minimum reduzieren.
~um n (pl -ima) Minimum nt ● a
Mindest-

mining /'maɪnɪŋ/ n Bergbau m

miniskirt /'mɪnɪ-/ n Minirock m

minist|er /'mɪnɪstə(r)/ n Minister m;
(Relig) Pastor m. **~erial** /-'stɪərɪəl/ a
ministeriell

ministry /'mɪnɪstrɪ/ n (Pol) Ministerium nt; **the ~** (Relig) das geistliche
Amt

mink /mɪŋk/ n Nerz m

minor /'maɪnə(r)/ a kleiner; (less important) unbedeutend ● n Minder-
jährige(r) m/f; (Mus) Moll nt

minority /maɪ'nɒrətɪ/ n Minderheit f;
(age) Minderjährigkeit f

minor road n Nebenstraße f

mint¹ /mɪnt/ n Münzstätte f ● a
⟨stamp⟩ postfrisch; **in ~ condition**
wie neu ● vt prägen

mint² n (herb) Minze f; (sweet) Pfef-
ferminzbonbon m & nt

minuet /mɪnjʊ'et/ n Menuett nt

minus /'maɪnəs/ prep minus, weniger; (fam: without) ohne ● n ~ [sign] Minuszeichen nt

minute¹ /'mɪnɪt/ n Minute f; **in a** ~ (shortly) gleich; ~**s** pl (of meeting) Protokoll nt

minute² /maɪ'nju:t/ a winzig; (precise) genau

mirac|le /'mɪrəkl/ n Wunder nt. ~**ulous** /-'rækjʊləs/ a wunderbar

mirage /'mɪrɑ:ʒ/ n Fata Morgana f

mire /'maɪə(r)/ n Morast m

mirror /'mɪrə(r)/ n Spiegel m ● vt widerspiegeln

mirth /mɜ:θ/ n Heiterkeit f

misad'venture /mɪs-/ n Mißgeschick nt

misanthropist /mɪ'zænθrəpɪst/ n Menschenfeind m

misappre'hension n Mißverständnis nt; **be under a** ~ sich irren

misbe'hav|e vi sich schlecht benehmen. ~**iour** n schlechtes Benehmen nt

mis'calcu|late vt falsch berechnen ● vi sich verrechnen. ~**'lation** n Fehlkalkulation f

'miscarriage n Fehlgeburt f; ~ **of justice** Justizirrtum m. **mis'carry** vi eine Fehlgeburt haben

miscellaneous /mɪsə'leɪnɪəs/ a vermischt

mischief /'mɪstʃɪf/ n Unfug m; (harm) Schaden m

mischievous /'mɪstʃɪvəs/ a, -**ly** adv schelmisch; (malicious) boshaft

miscon'ception n falsche Vorstellung f

mis'conduct n unkorrektes Verhalten nt; (adultery) Ehebruch m

miscon'strue vt mißdeuten

mis'deed n Missetat f

misde'meanour n Missetat f

miser /'maɪzə(r)/ n Geizhals m

miserable /'mɪzrəbl/ a, -**bly** adv unglücklich; (wretched) elend

miserly /'maɪzəlɪ/ adv geizig

misery /'mɪzərɪ/ n Elend nt; (fam: person) Miesepeter m

mis'fire vi fehlzünden; (go wrong) fehlschlagen

'misfit n Außenseiter(in) m(f)

mis'fortune n Unglück nt

mis'givings npl Bedenken pl

mis'guided a töricht

mishap /'mɪshæp/ n Mißgeschick nt

misin'form vt falsch unterrichten

misin'terpret vt mißdeuten

mis'judge vt falsch beurteilen; (estimate wrongly) falsch einschätzen

mis'lay vt (pt/pp -**laid**) verlegen

mis'lead vt (pt/pp -**led**) irreführen. ~**ing** a irreführend

mis'manage vt schlecht verwalten. ~**ment** n Mißwirtschaft f

misnomer /mɪs'nəʊmə(r)/ n Fehlbezeichnung f

'misprint n Druckfehler m

mis'quote vt falsch zitieren

misrepre'sent vt falsch darstellen

miss /mɪs/ n Fehltreffer m ● vt verpassen; (fail to hit or find) verfehlen; (fail to attend) versäumen; (fail to notice) übersehen; (feel the loss of) vermissen ● vi (fail to hit) nicht treffen. ~ **out** vt auslassen

Miss n (pl -**es**) Fräulein nt

misshapen /mɪs'ʃeɪpən/ a mißgestaltet

missile /'mɪsaɪl/ n [Wurf]geschoß nt; (Mil) Rakete f

missing /'mɪsɪŋ/ a fehlend; (lost) verschwunden; (Mil) vermißt; **be** ~ fehlen

mission /'mɪʃn/ n Auftrag m; (Mil) Einsatz m; (Relig) Mission f

missionary /'mɪʃənrɪ/ n Missionar (in) m(f)

mis'spell vt (pt/pp -**spelt** or -**spelled**) falsch schreiben

mist /mɪst/ n Dunst m; (fog) Nebel m; (on window) Beschlag m ● vi ~ **up** beschlagen

mistake /mɪ'steɪk/ n Fehler m; **by** ~ aus Versehen ● vt (pt mistook, pp mistaken) mißverstehen; ~ **for** verwechseln mit

mistaken /mɪ'steɪkən/ a falsch; **be** ~ sich irren; ~ **identity** Verwechslung f. ~**ly** adv irrtümlicherweise

mistletoe /'mɪsltəʊ/ n Mistel f

mistress /'mɪstrɪs/ n Herrin f; (teacher) Lehrerin f; (lover) Geliebte f

mis'trust n Mißtrauen nt ● vt mißtrauen (+ dat)

misty /'mɪstɪ/ a (-**ier**, -**iest**) dunstig; (foggy) neblig; (fig) unklar

misunder'stand vt (pt/pp -**stood**) mißverstehen. ~**ing** n Mißverständnis nt

misuse¹ /mɪs'ju:z/ vt mißbrauchen

misuse² /mɪs'ju:s/ n Mißbrauch m

mite /maɪt/ n (Zool) Milbe f; **little** ~ (child) kleines Ding nt

mitigat|e /'mɪtɪgeɪt/ vt mildern. **~ing** a mildernd

mitten /'mɪtən/ n Fausthandschuh m

mix /mɪks/ n Mischung f ● vt mischen ● vi sich mischen; **~ with** (associate with) verkehren mit. **~ up** vt mischen; (muddle) durcheinanderbringen; (mistake for) verwechseln (with mit)

mixed /mɪkst/ a gemischt; **be ~ up** durcheinander sein

mixer /'mɪksə(r)/ n Mischmaschine f; (Culin) Küchenmaschine f

mixture /'mɪkstʃə(r)/ n Mischung f; (medicine) Mixtur f; (Culin) Teig m

'mix-up n Durcheinander nt; (confusion) Verwirrung f; (mistake) Verwechslung f

moan /məʊn/ n Stöhnen nt ● vi stöhnen; (complain) jammern

moat /məʊt/ n Burggraben m

mob /mɒb/ n Horde f; (rabble) Pöbel m; (fam: gang) Bande f ● vt (pt/pp **mobbed**) herfallen über (+ acc); belagern ⟨celebrity⟩

mobile /'məʊbaɪl/ a beweglich ● n Mobile nt. **~ 'home** n Wohnwagen m

mobility /mə'bɪlɪtɪ/ n Beweglichkeit f

mobi|lization /məʊbɪlaɪ'zeɪʃn/ n Mobilisierung f. **~lize** /'məʊbɪlaɪz/ vt mobilisieren

mocha /'mɒkə/ n Mokka m

mock /mɒk/ a Schein- ● vt verspotten ● vi spotten. **~ery** n Spott m

'mock-up n Modell nt

modal /'məʊdl/ a **~ auxiliary** Modalverb nt

mode /məʊd/ n [Art und] Weise f; (fashion) Mode f

model /'mɒdl/ n Modell nt; (example) Vorbild nt; [fashion] **~** Mannequin nt ● a Modell-; (exemplary) Muster- ● v (pt/pp **modelled**) ● vt formen, modellieren; vorführen ⟨clothes⟩ ● vi Mannequin sein; (for artist) Modell stehen

moderate¹ /'mɒdəreɪt/ vt mäßigen ● vi sich mäßigen

moderate² /'mɒdərət/ a mäßig; ⟨opinion⟩ gemäßigt ● n (Pol) Gemäßigte(r) m/f. **~ly** adv mäßig; (fairly) einigermaßen

moderation /mɒdə'reɪʃn/ n Mäßigung f; **in ~** mit Maß[en]

modern /'mɒdn/ a modern. **~ize** vt modernisieren. **~ languages** npl neuere Sprachen pl

modest /'mɒdɪst/ a bescheiden; (decorous) schamhaft. **~y** n Bescheidenheit f

modicum /'mɒdɪkəm/ n **a ~ of** ein bißchen

modif|ication /mɒdɪfɪ'keɪʃn/ n Abänderung f. **~y** /'mɒdɪfaɪ/ vt (pt/pp **-fied**) abändern

modulate /'mɒdjʊleɪt/ vt/i modulieren

moist /mɔɪst/ a (**-er**, **-est**) feucht

moisten /'mɔɪsn/ vt befeuchten

moistur|e /'mɔɪstʃə(r)/ n Feuchtigkeit f. **~izer** n Feuchtigkeitscreme f

molar /'məʊlə(r)/ n Backenzahn m

molasses /mə'læsɪz/ n (Amer) Sirup m

mole¹ /məʊl/ n Leberfleck m

mole² n (Zool) Maulwurf m

mole³ n (breakwater) Mole f

molecule /'mɒlɪkjuːl/ n Molekül nt

'molehill n Maulwurfshaufen m

molest /mə'lest/ vt belästigen

mollify /'mɒlɪfaɪ/ vt (pt/pp **-ied**) besänftigen

mollusc /'mɒləsk/ n Weichtier nt

mollycoddle /'mɒlɪkɒdl/ vt verzärteln

molten /'məʊltən/ a geschmolzen

mom /mɒm/ n (Amer fam) Mutti f

moment /'məʊmənt/ n Moment m, Augenblick m; **at the ~** im Augenblick, augenblicklich. **~ary** a vorübergehend

momentous /mə'mentəs/ a bedeutsam

momentum /mə'mentəm/ n Schwung m

monarch /'mɒnək/ n Monarch(in) m(f). **~y** n Monarchie f

monast|ery /'mɒnəstrɪ/ n Kloster nt. **~ic** /mə'næstɪk/ a Kloster-

Monday /'mʌndeɪ/ n Montag m

money /'mʌnɪ/ n Geld nt

money: ~-box n Sparbüchse f. **~-lender** n Geldverleiher m. **~ order** n Zahlungsanweisung f

mongrel /'mʌŋgrəl/ n Promenadenmischung f

monitor /'mɒnɪtə(r)/ n (Techn) Monitor m ● vt überwachen ⟨progress⟩; abhören ⟨broadcast⟩

monk /mʌŋk/ n Mönch m

monkey /'mʌŋkɪ/ n Affe m. **~-nut** n Erdnuß f. **~-wrench** n (Techn) Engländer m

mono /'mɒnəʊ/ n Mono nt

monocle /'mɒnəkl/ n Monokel nt

monogram /'mɒnəgræm/ n Monogramm nt

monologue /'mɒnəlɒg/ n Monolog m

monopol|ize /mə'nɒpəlaɪz/ vt monopolisieren. **~y** n Monopol nt

monosyll|abic /mɒnəsɪ'læbɪk/ a einsilbig. **~able** /'mɒnəsɪləbl/ n einsilbiges Wort nt

monotone /'mɒnətəʊn/ n in a **~** mit monotoner Stimme

monoton|ous /mə'nɒtənəs/ a, **-ly** adv eintönig, monoton; (tedious) langweilig. **~y** n Eintönigkeit f, Monotonie f

monsoon /mɒn'suːn/ n Monsun m

monster /'mɒnstə(r)/ n Ungeheuer nt; (cruel person) Unmensch m

monstrosity /mɒn'strɒsətɪ/ n Monstrosität f

monstrous /'mɒnstrəs/ a ungeheuer; (outrageous) ungeheuerlich

montage /mɒn'tɑːʒ/ n Montage f

month /mʌnθ/ n Monat m. **~ly** a & adv monatlich ● n (periodical) Monatszeitschrift f

monument /'mɒnjʊmənt/ n Denkmal nt. **~al** /-'mentl/ a (fig) monumental

moo /muː/ n Muh nt ● vi (pt/pp mooed) muhen

mooch /muːtʃ/ vi **~ about** (fam) herumschleichen

mood /muːd/ n Laune f; **be in a good/bad ~** gute/schlechte Laune haben

moody /'muːdɪ/ a (-ier, -iest) launisch

moon /muːn/ n Mond m; **over the ~** (fam) überglücklich

moon: ~light n Mondschein m. **~lighting** n (fam) ≈ Schwarzarbeit f. **~lit** a mondhell

moor[1] /mʊə(r)/ n Moor nt

moor[2] vt (Naut) festmachen ● vi anlegen. **~ings** npl (chains) Verankerung f; (place) Anlegestelle f

moose /muːs/ n Elch m

moot /muːt/ a **it's a ~ point** darüber läßt sich streiten ● vt aufwerfen ⟨question⟩

mop /mɒp/ n Mop m; **~ of hair** Wuschelkopf m ● vt (pt/pp mopped) wischen. **~ up** vt aufwischen

mope /məʊp/ vi Trübsal blasen

moped /'məʊped/ n Moped nt

moral /'mɒrəl/ a, **-ly** adv moralisch, sittlich; (virtuous) tugendhaft ● n Moral f; **~s** pl Moral f

morale /mə'rɑːl/ n Moral f

morality /mə'rælətɪ/ n Sittlichkeit f

moralize /'mɒrəlaɪz/ vi moralisieren

morbid /'mɔːbɪd/ a krankhaft; (gloomy) trübe

more /mɔː(r)/ a, adv & n mehr; (in addition) noch; **a few ~** noch ein paar; **any ~** noch etwas; **once ~** noch einmal; **~ or less** mehr oder weniger; **some ~ tea?** noch etwas Tee? **~ interesting** interessanter; **~ [and ~] quickly** [immer] schneller; **no ~, thank you,** nichts mehr, danke; **no ~ bread** kein Brot mehr; **no ~ apples** keine Äpfel mehr

moreover /mɔː'rəʊvə(r)/ adv außerdem

morgue /mɔːg/ n Leichenschauhaus nt

moribund /'mɒrɪbʌnd/ a sterbend

morning /'mɔːnɪŋ/ n Morgen m; **in the ~** morgens, am Morgen; (tomorrow) morgen früh

Morocco /mə'rɒkəʊ/ n Marokko nt

moron /'mɔːrɒn/ n (fam) Idiot m

morose /mə'rəʊs/ a, **-ly** adv mürrisch

morphine /'mɔːfiːn/ n Morphium nt

Morse /mɔːs/ n **~ [code]** Morsealphabet nt

morsel /'mɔːsl/ n (food) Happen m

mortal /'mɔːtl/ a sterblich; (fatal) tödlich ● n Sterbliche(r) m/f. **~ity** /mɔː'tælətɪ/ n Sterblichkeit f. **~ly** adv tödlich

mortar /'mɔːtə(r)/ n Mörtel m

mortgage /'mɔːgɪdʒ/ n Hypothek f ● vt hypothekarisch belasten

mortify /'mɔːtɪfaɪ/ vt (pt/pp -ied) demütigen

mortuary /'mɔːtjʊərɪ/ n Leichenhalle f; (public) Leichenschauhaus nt; (Amer: undertaker's) Bestattungsinstitut nt

mosaic /məʊ'zeɪɪk/ n Mosaik nt

Moscow /'mɒskəʊ/ n Moskau nt

Moselle /məʊ'zel/ n Mosel f; (wine) Moselwein m

mosque /mɒsk/ n Moschee f

mosquito /mɒs'kiːtəʊ/ n (pl **-es**) [Stech]mücke f, Schnake f; (tropical) Moskito m

moss /mɒs/ n Moos nt. **~y** a moosig

most /məʊst/ a der/die/das meiste; (majority) die meisten; **for the ~ part** zum größten Teil ● adv am meisten; (very) höchst; **the ~ interesting day** der interessanteste Tag; **~ unlikely** höchst unwahrscheinlich ● n das meiste; **~ of them** die meisten [von ihnen]; **at [the] ~** höchstens; **~ of the time** die meiste Zeit. **~ly** adv meist

MOT n ≈ TÜV m

motel /məʊˈtel/ n Motel nt

moth /mɒθ/ n Nachtfalter m; [clothes-]~ Motte f

moth: ~**ball** n Mottenkugel f. ~**eaten** a mottenzerfressen

mother /ˈmʌðə(r)/ n Mutter f; **M~'s Day** Muttertag m ● vt bemuttern

mother: ~**hood** n Mutterschaft f. ~**in-law** n (pl ~s-in-law) Schwiegermutter f. ~**land** n Mutterland nt. ~**ly** a mütterlich. ~**of-pearl** n Perlmutter f. ~**to-be** n werdende Mutter f. ~ **tongue** n Muttersprache f

mothproof /ˈmɒθ-/ a mottenfest

motif /məʊˈtiːf/ n Motiv m

motion /ˈməʊʃn/ n Bewegung f; (proposal) Antrag m ● vt/i ~ [to] s.o. jdm ein Zeichen geben (to zu). ~**less** a, **-ly** adv bewegungslos

motivat|e /ˈməʊtɪveɪt/ vt motivieren. ~**ion** /-ˈveɪʃn/ n Motivation f

motive /ˈməʊtɪv/ n Motiv nt

motley /ˈmɒtlɪ/ a bunt

motor /ˈməʊtə(r)/ n Motor m; (car) Auto nt ● a Motor-; (Anat) motorisch ● vi [mit dem Auto] fahren

Motorail /ˈməʊtəreɪl/ n Autozug m

motor: ~ **bike** n (fam) Motorrad nt. ~ **boat** n Motorboot nt. ~**cade** /-keɪd/ n (Amer) Autokolonne f. ~**car** n Auto nt, Wagen m. ~ **cycle** n Motorrad nt. ~**cyclist** n Motorradfahrer m. ~**ing** n Autofahren nt. ~**ist** n Autofahrer(in) m(f). ~**ize** vt motorisieren. ~ **vehicle** n Kraftfahrzeug nt. ~**way** n Autobahn f

mottled /ˈmɒtld/ a gesprenkelt

motto /ˈmɒtəʊ/ n (pl -es) Motto nt

mould¹ /məʊld/ n (fungus) Schimmel m

mould² n Form f ● vt formen (into zu). ~**ing** n (Archit) Fries m

mouldy /ˈməʊldɪ/ a schimmelig; (fam: worthless) schäbig

moult /məʊlt/ vi ⟨bird:⟩ sich mausern; ⟨animal:⟩ sich haaren

mound /maʊnd/ n Hügel m; (of stones) Haufen m

mount¹ /maʊnt/ n Berg m

mount² n (animal) Reittier nt; (of jewel) Fassung f; (of photo, picture) Passepartout nt ● vt (get on) steigen auf (+ acc); (on pedestal) montieren auf (+ acc); besteigen ⟨horse⟩; fassen ⟨jewel⟩; aufziehen ⟨photo, picture⟩ ● vi aufsteigen; ⟨tension:⟩ steigen. ~ **up** vi sich häufen; (add up) sich anhäufen

mountain /ˈmaʊntɪn/ n Berg m

mountaineer /maʊntɪˈnɪə(r)/ n Bergsteiger(in) m(f). ~**ing** n Bergsteigen nt

mountainous /ˈmaʊntɪnəs/ a bergig, gebirgig

mourn /mɔːn/ vt betrauern ● vi trauern (for um). ~**er** n Trauernde(r) m/f. ~**ful** a, **-ly** adv trauervoll. ~**ing** n Trauer f

mouse /maʊs/ n (pl mice) Maus f. ~**trap** n Mausefalle f

mousse /muːs/ n Schaum m; (Culin) Mousse f

moustache /məˈstɑːʃ/ n Schnurrbart m

mousy /ˈmaʊsɪ/ a graubraun; (person) farblos

mouth¹ /maʊð/ vt ~ sth etw lautlos mit den Lippen sagen

mouth² /maʊθ/ n Mund m; (of animal) Maul nt; (of river) Mündung f

mouth: ~**ful** n Mundvoll m; (bite) Bissen m. ~**organ** n Mundharmonika f. ~**piece** n Mundstück nt; (fig: person) Sprachrohr nt. ~**wash** n Mundwasser nt

movable /ˈmuːvəbl/ a beweglich

move /muːv/ n Bewegung f; (fig) Schritt m; (moving house) Umzug m; (in board-game) Zug m; **on the** ~ unterwegs; **get a** ~ **on** (fam) sich beeilen ● vt bewegen; (emotionally) rühren; (move along) rücken; (in board-game) ziehen; (take away) wegnehmen; wegfahren ⟨car⟩; (rearrange) umstellen; (transfer) versetzen ⟨person⟩; verlegen ⟨office⟩; (propose) beantragen; ~ **house** umziehen ● vi sich bewegen; (move house) umziehen; **don't** ~! stillhalten! (stop) stillstehen! ~ **along** vt/i weiterrücken. ~ **away** vt/i wegrücken; (move house) wegziehen. ~ **forward** vt/i vorrücken; ⟨vehicle:⟩ vorwärts fahren. ~ **in** vi einziehen. ~ **off** vi ⟨vehicle:⟩ losfahren. ~ **out** vi ausziehen. ~ **over** vt/i [zur Seite] rücken. ~ **up** vi aufrücken

movement /ˈmuːvmənt/ n Bewegung f; (Mus) Satz m; (of clock) Uhrwerk nt

movie /ˈmuːvɪ/ n (Amer) Film m; **go to the** ~**s** ins Kino gehen

moving /ˈmuːvɪŋ/ a beweglich; (touching) rührend

mow /məʊ/ vt (pt **mowed**, pp **mown** or **mowed**) mähen. **~ down** vt (destroy) niedermähen

mower /'məʊə(r)/ n Rasenmäher m

MP abbr see **Member of Parliament**

Mr /'mɪstə(r)/ n (pl **Messrs**) Herr m

Mrs /'mɪsɪz/ n Frau f

Ms /mɪz/ n Frau f

much /mʌtʃ/ a, adv & n viel; **as ~ as** soviel wie; **very ~ loved/ interested** sehr geliebt/ interessiert

muck /mʌk/ n (fam: filth) Dreck m. **~ about** vi herumalbern; (tinker) herumspielen (**with** mit). **~ in** vi (fam) mitmachen. **~ out** vt ausmisten. **~ up** vt (fam) vermasseln; (make dirty) schmutzig machen

mucky /'mʌkɪ/ a (-ier, -iest) dreckig

mucus /'mju:kəs/ n Schleim m

mud /mʌd/ n Schlamm m

muddle /'mʌdl/ n Durcheinander nt; (confusion) Verwirrung f ● vt **~[up]** durcheinanderbringen

muddy /'mʌdɪ/ a (-ier, -iest) schlammig; ⟨shoes⟩ schmutzig

'mudguard n Kotflügel m; (on bicycle) Schutzblech nt

muesli /'mu:zlɪ/ n Müsli nt

muff /mʌf/ n Muff m

muffle /'mʌfl/ vt dämpfen ⟨sound⟩; **~ [up]** (for warmth) einhüllen (**in** in + acc)

muffler /'mʌflə(r)/ n Schal m; (Amer, Auto) Auspufftopf m

mufti /'mʌftɪ/ n **in ~** in Zivil

mug¹ /mʌg/ n Becher m; (for beer) Bierkrug m; (fam: face) Visage f; (fam: simpleton) Trottel m

mug² vt (pt/pp **mugged**) überfallen. **~ger** n Straßenräuber m. **~ging** n Straßenraub m

muggy /'mʌgɪ/ a (-ier, -iest) schwül

mule¹ /mju:l/ n Maultier nt

mule² n (slipper) Pantoffel m

mull /mʌl/ vt **~ over** nachdenken über (+ acc)

mulled /mʌld/ a **~ wine** Glühwein m

multi /'mʌltɪ/: **~coloured** a vielfarbig, bunt. **~lingual** /-'lɪŋgwəl/ a mehrsprachig. **~'national** a multinational

multiple /'mʌltɪpl/ a vielfach; (with pl) mehrere ● n Vielfache(s) nt

multiplication /mʌltɪplɪ'keɪʃn/ n Multiplikation f

multiply /'mʌltɪplaɪ/ v (pt/pp -ied) ● vt multiplizieren (**by** mit) ● vi sich vermehren

multi-storey a **~ car park** Parkhaus nt

mum¹ /mʌm/ a **keep ~** (fam) den Mund halten

mum² n (fam) Mutti f

mumble /'mʌmbl/ vt/i murmeln

mummy¹ n (fam) Mutti f

mummy² /'mʌmɪ/ n (Archaeol) Mumie f

mumps /mʌmps/ n Mumps m

munch /mʌntʃ/ vt/i mampfen

mundane /mʌn'deɪn/ a banal; (worldly) weltlich

municipal /mju:'nɪsɪpl/ a städtisch

munitions /mju:'nɪʃnz/ npl Kriegsmaterial nt

mural /'mjʊərəl/ n Wandgemälde nt

murder /'mɜ:də(r)/ n Mord m ● vt ermorden; (fam: ruin) verhunzen. **~er** n Mörder m. **~ess** n Mörderin f. **~ous** /-rəs/ a mörderisch

murky /'mɜ:kɪ/ a (-ier, -iest) düster

murmur /'mɜ:mə(r)/ n Murmeln nt ● vt/i murmeln

muscle /'mʌsl/ n Muskel m

muscular /'mʌskjʊlə(r)/ a Muskel-; (strong) muskulös

muse /mju:z/ vi nachsinnen (**on** über + acc)

museum /mju:'zɪəm/ n Museum nt

mush /mʌʃ/ n Brei m

mushroom /'mʌʃrʊm/ n [eßbarer] Pilz m, esp Champignon m ● vi (fig) wie Pilze aus dem Boden schießen

mushy /'mʌʃɪ/ a breiig

music /'mju:zɪk/ n Musik f; (written) Noten pl; **set to ~** vertonen

musical /'mju:zɪkl/ a musikalisch ● n Musical nt. **~ box** n Spieldose f. **~ instrument** n Musikinstrument nt

'music-hall n Varieté nt

musician /mju:'zɪʃn/ n Musiker(in) m(f)

'music-stand n Notenständer m

Muslim /'mʊzlɪm/ a mohammedanisch ● n Mohammedaner(in) m(f)

muslin /'mʌzlɪn/ n Musselin m

mussel /'mʌsl/ n [Mies]muschel f

must /mʌst/ v aux (nur Präsens) müssen; (with negative) dürfen ● n **a ~** (fam) ein Muß nt

mustard /'mʌstəd/ n Senf m

muster /'mʌstə(r)/ vt versammeln; aufbringen ⟨strength⟩ ● vi sich versammeln

musty /'mʌstɪ/ a (-ier, -iest) muffig

mutation /mju:'teɪʃn/ n Veränderung f; (Biol) Mutation f

mute /mju:t/ a stumm

muted /'mju:tɪd/ a gedämpft

mutilat|e /'mju:tɪleɪt/ vt verstümmeln. **~ion** /-'leɪʃn/ n Verstümmelung f

mutin|ous /'mju:tɪnəs/ a meuterisch. **~y** n Meuterei f ● vi (pt/pp **-ied**) meutern

mutter /'mʌtə(r)/ n Murmeln nt ● vt/i murmeln

mutton /'mʌtn/ n Hammelfleisch nt

mutual /'mju:tjʊəl/ a gegenseitig; (fam: common) gemeinsam. **~ly** adv gegenseitig

muzzle /'mʌzl/ n (of animal) Schnauze f; (of firearm) Mündung f; (for dog) Maulkorb m ● vt einen Maulkorb anlegen (+ dat)

my /maɪ/ a mein

myopic /maɪ'ɒpɪk/ a kurzsichtig

myself /maɪ'self/ pron selbst; (refl) mich; **by ~** allein; **I thought to ~** ich habe mir gedacht

mysterious /mɪ'stɪərɪəs/ a, **-ly** adv geheimnisvoll; (puzzling) mysteriös, rätselhaft

mystery /'mɪstərɪ/ n Geheimnis nt; (puzzle) Rätsel nt; **~ [story]** Krimi m

mysti|c[al] /'mɪstɪk[l]/ a mystisch. **~cism** /-sɪzm/ n Mystik f

mystification /mɪstɪfɪ'keɪʃn/ n Verwunderung f

mystified /'mɪstɪfaɪd/ a **be ~** vor einem Rätsel stehen

mystique /mɪ'sti:k/ n geheimnisvoller Zauber m

myth /mɪθ/ n Mythos m; (fam: untruth) Märchen nt. **~ical** a mythisch; (fig) erfunden

mythology /mɪ'θɒlədʒɪ/ n Mythologie f

N

nab /næb/ vt (pt/pp **nabbed**) (fam) erwischen

nag¹ /næg/ n (horse) Gaul m

nag² vt/i (pt/pp **nagged**) herumnörgeln (s.o. an jdm). **~ging** a ⟨pain⟩ nagend ● n Nörgelei f

nail /neɪl/ n (Anat, Techn) Nagel m; **on the ~** (fam) sofort ● vt nageln (**to** an + acc). **~ down** vt festnageln; (close) zunageln

nail: ~-brush n Nagelbürste f. **~-file** n Nagelfeile f. **~ polish** n Nagellack m. **~ scissors** npl Nagelschere f. **~ varnish** n Nagellack m

naïve /naɪ'i:v/ a, **-ly** adv naiv. **~ty** /-ətɪ/ n Naivität f

naked /'neɪkɪd/ a nackt; ⟨flame⟩ offen; **with the ~ eye** mit bloßem Auge. **~ness** n Nacktheit f

name /neɪm/ n Name m; (reputation) Ruf m; **by ~** dem Namen nach; **by the ~ of** namens; **call s.o. ~s** (fam) jdn beschimpfen ● vt nennen; (give a name to) einen Namen geben (+ dat); (announce publicly) den Namen bekanntgeben von. **~less** a namenlos. **~ly** adv nämlich

name: ~-plate n Namensschild nt. **~sake** n Namensvetter m/Namensschwester f

nanny /'nænɪ/ n Kindermädchen nt. **~-goat** n Ziege f

nap /næp/ n Nickerchen nt; **have a ~** ein Nickerchen machen ● vi **catch s.o. ~ping** jdn überrumpeln

nape /neɪp/ n **~ [of the neck]** Nacken m

napkin /'næpkɪn/ n Serviette f; (for baby) Windel f

nappy /'næpɪ/ n Windel f

narcotic /nɑ:'kɒtɪk/ a betäubend ● n Narkotikum nt; (drug) Rauschgift nt

narrat|e /nə'reɪt/ vt erzählen. **~ion** /-eɪʃn/ n Erzählung f

narrative /'nærətɪv/ a erzählend ● n Erzählung f

narrator /nə'reɪtə(r)/ n Erzähler(in) m(f)

narrow /'nærəʊ/ a (**-er, -est**) schmal; (restricted) eng; ⟨margin, majority⟩ knapp; (fig) beschränkt; **have a ~ escape**, adv **~ly escape** mit knapper Not davonkommen ● vi sich verengen. **~-'minded** a engstirnig

nasal /'neɪzl/ a nasal; (Med & Anat) Nasen-

nastily /'nɑ:stɪlɪ/ adv boshaft

nasturtium /nə'stɜ:ʃəm/ n Kapuzinerkresse f

nasty /'nɑ:stɪ/ a (**-ier, -iest**) übel; (unpleasant) unangenehm; (unkind) boshaft; (serious) schlimm; **turn ~** gemein werden

nation /'neɪʃn/ n Nation f; (people) Volk nt

national /'næʃənl/ a national; ⟨newspaper⟩ überregional; ⟨campaign⟩ landesweit ● n Staatsbürger(in) m(f)

national: ~ 'anthem n Nationalhymne f. **N~ 'Health Service** n staatlicher Gesundheitsdienst m. **N~ In-'surance** n Sozialversicherung f

nationalism /'næʃənəlɪzm/ n Natio-nalismus m

nationality /næʃə'nælətɪ/ n Staats-angehörigkeit f

national|ization /næʃənəlaɪ'zeɪʃn/ n Verstaatlichung f. **~ize** /'næʃənə-laɪz/ vt verstaatlichen. **~ly** /'næʃə-nəlɪ/ adv landesweit

'nation-wide a landesweit

native /'neɪtɪv/ a einheimisch; (in-nate) angeboren ● n Eingeborene(r) m/f; (local inhabitant) Ein-heimische(r) m/f; **a ~ of Vienna** ein gebürtiger Wiener

native: **~ 'land** n Heimatland nt. **~ 'language** n Muttersprache f

Nativity /nə'tɪvɪtɪ/ n **the ~** Christi Geburt f. **~ play** n Krippenspiel nt

natter /'nætə(r)/ vi **have a ~** (fam) einen Schwatz halten ● vi (fam) schwatzen

natural /'nætʃrəl/ a, **-ly** adv natür-lich; **~[-coloured]** naturfarben

natural: **~ 'gas** n Erdgas nt. **~ 'his-tory** n Naturkunde f

naturalist /'nætʃrəlɪst/ n Natur-forscher m

natural|ization /nætʃrəlaɪ'zeɪʃn/ n Einbürgerung f. **~ize** /'nætʃrəlaɪz/ vt einbürgern

nature /'neɪtʃə(r)/ n Natur f; (kind) Art f; **by ~** von Natur aus. **~ re-serve** n Naturschutzgebiet nt

naturism /'neɪtʃərɪzm/ n Freikörper-kultur f

naught /nɔːt/ n = **nought**

naughty /'nɔːtɪ/ a (-ier, -iest), **-ily** adv unartig; (slightly indecent) gewagt

nausea /'nɔːzɪə/ n Übelkeit f

nause|ate /'nɔːzɪeɪt/ vt anekeln. **~ating** a ekelhaft. **~ous** /-ɪəs/ a **I feel ~ous** mir ist übel

nautical /'nɔːtɪkl/ a nautisch. **~ mile** n Seemeile f

naval /'neɪvl/ a Marine-

nave /neɪv/ n Kirchenschiff nt

navel /'neɪvl/ n Nabel m

navigable /'nævɪgəbl/ a schiffbar

navigat|e /'nævɪgeɪt/ vi navigieren ● vt befahren ⟨river⟩. **~ion** /-'geɪʃn/ n Navigation f. **~or** n Navigator m

navvy /'nævɪ/ n Straßenarbeiter m

navy /'neɪvɪ/ n [Kriegs]marine f ● a **~ [blue]** marineblau

near /nɪə(r)/ a (-er, -est) nah[e]; **the ~est bank** die nächste Bank ● adv nahe; **~ by** nicht weit weg; **~ at hand** in der Nähe; **draw ~** sich nähern ● prep nahe an (+ dat/acc);

in der Nähe von; **~ to tears** den Tränen nahe; **go ~ [to] sth** nahe an etw (acc) herangehen ● vt sich nä-hern (+ dat)

near: **~by** a nahegelegen. **~ly** adv fast, beinahe; **not ~ly** bei weitem nicht. **~ness** n Nähe f. **~ side** n Beifahrerseite f. **~-sighted** a (Amer) kurzsichtig

neat /niːt/ a (-er, -est), **-ly** adv adrett; (tidy) ordentlich; (clever) geschickt; (undiluted) pur. **~ness** n Ordent-lichkeit f

necessarily /'nesəserəlɪ/ adv notwen-digerweise; **not ~** nicht unbedingt

necessary /'nesəsərɪ/ a nötig, notwendig

necessit|ate /nɪ'sesɪteɪt/ vt notwen-dig machen. **~y** n Notwendigkeit f; **she works from ~y** sie arbeitet, weil sie es nötig hat

neck /nek/ n Hals m; **~ and ~** Kopf an Kopf

necklace /'neklɪs/ n Halskette f

neck: **~line** n Halsausschnitt m. **~tie** n Schlips m

nectar /'nektə(r)/ n Nektar m

neé /neɪ/ a **~** Brett geborene Brett

need /niːd/ n Bedürfnis nt; (misfor-tune) Not f; **be in ~** Not leiden; **be in ~ of** brauchen; **in case of ~** notfalls; **if ~ be** wenn nötig; **there is a ~ for** es besteht ein Bedarf an (+ dat); **there is no ~ for that** das ist nicht nötig; **there is no ~ for you to go** du brauchst nicht zu gehen ● vt brau-chen; **you ~ not go** du brauchst nicht zu gehen; **~ I come?** muß ich kommen? **I ~ to know** ich muß es wissen; **it ~s to be done** es muß gemacht werden

needle /'niːdl/ n Nadel f ● vt (annoy) ärgern

needless /'niːdlɪs/ a, **-ly** adv unnötig; **~ to say** selbstverständlich, natürlich

'needlework n Nadelarbeit f

needy /'niːdɪ/ a (-ier, -iest) bedürftig

negation /nɪ'geɪʃn/ n Verneinung f

negative /'negətɪv/ a negativ ● n Ver-neinung f; (photo) Negativ nt

neglect /nɪ'glekt/ n Vernachlässi-gung f; **state of ~** verwahrloster Zustand m ● vt vernachlässigen; (omit) versäumen (to zu). **~ed** a verwahrlost. **~ful** a nachlässig; **be ~ful of** vernachlässigen

negligen|ce /'neglɪdʒəns/ n Nachläs-sigkeit f; (Jur) Fahrlässigkeit f. **~t**

a, **-ly** *adv* nachlässig; (*Jur*) fahrlässig

negligible /'neglɪdʒəbl/ *a* unbedeutend

negotiable /nɪ'gəʊʃəbl/ *a* ⟨*road*⟩ befahrbar; (*Comm*) unverbindlich; **not** ~ nicht übertragbar

negotiat|e /nɪ'gəʊʃɪeɪt/ *vt* aushandeln; (*Auto*) nehmen ⟨*bend*⟩ ● *vi* verhandeln. ~**ion** /-'eɪʃn/ *n* Verhandlung *f.* ~**or** *n* Unterhändler(in) *m(f)*

Negro /'niːɡrəʊ/ *a* Neger- ● *n* (*pl* -es) Neger *m*

neigh /neɪ/ *vi* wiehern

neighbour /'neɪbə(r)/ *n* Nachbar(in) *m(f).* ~**hood** *n* Nachbarschaft *f;* **in the** ~**hood of** in der Nähe von; (*fig*) um . . . herum. ~**ing** *a* Nachbar-. ~**ly** *a* [gut]nachbarlich

neither /'naɪðə(r)/ *a* & *pron* keine(r,s) [von beiden] ● *adv* ~ . . . **nor** weder . . . noch ● *conj* auch nicht

neon /'niːɒn/ *n* Neon *nt.* ~ **light** *n* Neonlicht *nt*

nephew /'nevjuː/ *n* Neffe *m*

nepotism /'nepətɪzm/ *n* Vetternwirtschaft *f*

nerve /nɜːv/ *n* Nerv *m;* (*fam: courage*) Mut *m;* (*fam: impudence*) Frechheit *f;* **lose one's** ~ den Mut verlieren. ~**-racking** *a* nervenaufreibend

nervous /'nɜːvəs/ *a,* **-ly** *adv* (*afraid*) ängstlich; (*highly-strung*) nervös; (*Anat, Med*) Nerven-; **be** ~ Angst haben. ~ '**breakdown** *n* Nervenzusammenbruch *m.* ~**ness** Ängstlichkeit *f;* (*Med*) Nervosität *f*

nervy /'nɜːvɪ/ *a* (-ier, -iest) nervös; (*Amer: impudent*) frech

nest /nest/ *n* Nest *nt* ● *vi* nisten. ~**egg** *n* Notgroschen *m*

nestle /'nesl/ *vi* sich schmiegen (**against** an + *acc*)

net¹ /net/ *n* Netz *nt;* (*curtain*) Store *m* ● *vt* (*pt/pp* netted) (*catch*) [mit dem Netz] fangen

net² *a* netto; ⟨*salary, weight*⟩ Netto- ● *vt* (*pt/pp* netted) netto einnehmen; (*yield*) einbringen

'**netball** *n* ≈ Korbball *m*

Netherlands /'neðələndz/ *npl* **the** ~ die Niederlande *pl*

netting /'netɪŋ/ *n* **[wire]** ~ Maschendraht *m*

nettle /'netl/ *n* Nessel *f*

'**network** *n* Netz *nt*

neuralgia /njʊə'rældʒə/ *n* Neuralgie *f*

neurolog|ist /njʊə'rɒlədʒɪst/ *n* Neurologe *m*/-gin *f.* ~**y** *n* Neurologie *f*

neur|osis /njʊə'rəʊsɪs/ *n* (*pl* -oses /-siːz/) Neurose *f.* ~**otic** /-'rɒtɪk/ *a* neurotisch

neuter /'njuːtə(r)/ *a* (*Gram*) sächlich ● *n* (*Gram*) Neutrum *nt* ● *vt* kastrieren; (*spay*) sterilisieren

neutral /'njuːtrl/ *a* neutral ● *n* **in** ~ (*Auto*) im Leerlauf. ~**ity** /-'trælətɪ/ *n* Neutralität *f.* ~**ize** *vt* neutralisieren

never /'nevə(r)/ *adv* nie, niemals; (*fam: not*) nicht; ~ **mind** macht nichts; **well I** ~! ja so was! ~**-ending** *a* endlos

nevertheless /nevəðə'les/ *adv* dennoch, trotzdem

new /njuː/ *a* (-er, -est) neu

new: ~**born** *a* neugeboren. ~**comer** *n* Neuankömmling *m.* ~**fangled** /-'fæŋgld/ *a* (*pej*) neumodisch. ~**laid** *a* frisch gelegt

'**newly** *adv* frisch. ~**weds** *npl* jungverheiratetes Paar *nt*

new: ~ '**moon** *n* Neumond *m.* ~**ness** *n* Neuheit *f*

news /njuːz/ *n* Nachricht *f;* (*Radio, TV*) Nachrichten *pl;* **piece of** ~ Neuigkeit *f*

news: ~**agent** *n* Zeitungshändler *m.* ~ **bulletin** *n* Nachrichtensendung *f.* ~**caster** *n* Nachrichtensprecher(in) *m(f).* ~**flash** *n* Kurzmeldung *f.* ~**letter** *n* Mitteilungsblatt *nt.* ~**paper** *n* Zeitung *f;* (*material*) Zeitungspapier *nt.* ~**reader** *n* Nachrichtensprecher(in) *m(f)*

newt /njuːt/ *n* Molch *m*

New: ~ **Year's 'Day** *n* Neujahr *nt.* ~ **Year's 'Eve** *n* Silvester *nt.* ~ **Zealand** /'ziːlənd/ *n* Neuseeland *nt*

next /nekst/ *a* & *n* nächste(r,s); **who's** ~? wer kommt als nächster dran? **the** ~ **best** das nächstbeste; ~ **door** nebenan; **my** ~ **of kin** mein nächster Verwandter; ~ **to nothing** fast gar nichts; **the week after** ~ übernächste Woche ● *adv* als nächstes; ~ **to** neben

NHS *abbr see* **National Health Service**

nib /nɪb/ *n* Feder *f*

nibble /'nɪbl/ *vt/i* knabbern (**at** an + *dat*)

nice /naɪs/ *a* (-r, -st) nett; ⟨*day, weather*⟩ schön; ⟨*food*⟩ gut; ⟨*distinction*⟩ fein. ~**ly** *adv* nett; (*well*) gut. ~**ties** /'naɪsətɪz/ *npl* Feinheiten *pl*

niche /niːʃ/ n Nische f; (fig) Platz m

nick /nɪk/ n Kerbe f; (fam: prison) Knast m; (fam: police station) Revier nt; **in the ~ of time** (fam) gerade noch rechtzeitig; **in good ~** (fam) in gutem Zustand ● vt einkerben; (steal) klauen; (fam: arrest) schnappen

nickel /'nɪkl/ n Nickel nt; (Amer) Fünfcentstück nt

'nickname n Spitzname m

nicotine /'nɪkətiːn/ n Nikotin nt

niece /niːs/ n Nichte f

Nigeria /naɪ'dʒɪərɪə/ n Nigeria nt. **~n** a nigerianisch ● n Nigerianer(in) m(f)

niggardly /'nɪgədlɪ/ a knauserig

niggling /'nɪglɪŋ/ a gering; (petty) kleinlich; ⟨pain⟩ quälend

night /naɪt/ n Nacht f; (evening) Abend m; **at ~** nachts; **Monday ~** Montag nacht/abend

night: **~cap** n Schlafmütze f; (drink) Schlaftrunk m. **~club** n Nachtklub m. **~dress** n Nachthemd nt. **~fall** n **at ~fall** bei Einbruch der Dunkelheit. **~gown** n, (fam) **~ie** /'naɪtɪ/ n Nachthemd nt

nightingale /'naɪtɪŋgeɪl/ n Nachtigall f

night: **~life** n Nachtleben nt. **~ly** a nächtlich ● adv jede Nacht. **~mare** n Alptraum m. **~shade** n (Bot) **deadly ~shade** Tollkirsche f. **~time** n **at ~time** bei Nacht. **~watchman** n Nachtwächter m

nil /nɪl/ n null

nimble /'nɪmbl/ a (-r, -st), **-bly** adv flink

nine /naɪn/ a neun ● n Neun f. **~'teen** a neunzehn. **~'teenth** a neunzehnte(r, s)

ninetieth /'naɪntɪɪθ/ a neunzigste(r,s)

ninety /'naɪntɪ/ a neunzig

ninth /naɪnθ/ a neunte(r, s)

nip /nɪp/ n Kniff m; (bite) Biß m ● vt kneifen; (bite) beißen; **~ in the bud** (fig) im Keim ersticken ● vi (fam: run) laufen

nipple /'nɪpl/ n Brustwarze f; (Amer: on bottle) Sauger m

nippy /'nɪpɪ/ a (-ier, -iest) (fam) (cold) frisch; (quick) flink

nitrate /'naɪtreɪt/ n Nitrat nt

nitrogen /'naɪtrədʒn/ n Stickstoff m

nitwit /'nɪtwɪt/ n (fam) Dummkopf m

no /nəʊ/ adv nein ● n (pl noes) Nein nt ● a kein(e); (pl) keine; **in no time** [sehr] schnell; **no parking/smoking** Parken/Rauchen verboten; **no one** = **nobody**

nobility /nəʊ'bɪlətɪ/ n Adel m

noble /'nəʊbl/ a (-r, -st) edel; (aristocratic) adlig. **~man** n Adlige(r) m

nobody /'nəʊbədɪ/ pron niemand, keiner; **he knows ~** er kennt niemanden od keinen ● n **a ~** ein Niemand m

nocturnal /nɒk'tɜːnl/ a nächtlich; ⟨animal, bird⟩ Nacht-

nod /nɒd/ n Nicken nt ● v (pt/pp nodded) ● vi nicken ● vt **~ one's head** mit dem Kopf nicken. **~ off** vi einnicken

nodule /'nɒdjuːl/ n Knötchen nt

noise /nɔɪz/ n Geräusch nt; (loud) Lärm m. **~less** a, **-ly** adv geräuschlos

noisy /'nɔɪzɪ/ a (-ier, -iest), **-ily** adv laut; ⟨eater⟩ geräuschvoll

nomad /'nəʊmæd/ n Nomade m. **~ic** /-'mædɪk/ a nomadisch; ⟨life, tribe⟩ Nomaden-

nominal /'nɒmɪnl/ a, **-ly** adv nominell

nominat|e /'nɒmɪneɪt/ vt nominieren, aufstellen; (appoint) ernennen. **~ion** /-'neɪʃn/ n Nominierung f; Ernennung f

nominative /'nɒmɪnətɪv/ a & n (Gram) **[case]** Nominativ m

nonchalant /'nɒnʃələnt/ a, **-ly** adv nonchalant; ⟨gesture⟩ lässig

non-com'missioned /nɒn-/ a **~ officer** Unteroffizier m

non-com'mittal a unverbindlich; **be ~** sich nicht festlegen

nondescript /'nɒndɪskrɪpt/ a unbestimmbar; ⟨person⟩ unscheinbar

none /nʌn/ pron keine(r)/keins; **~ of us** keiner von uns; **~ of it/ this** nichts davon ● adv **~ too** nicht gerade; **~ too soon** [um] keine Minute zu früh; **~ the wiser** um nichts klüger; **~ the less** dennoch

nonentity /nɒ'nentətɪ/ n Null f

non-ex'istent a nichtvorhanden; **be ~** nicht vorhanden sein

non-'fiction n Sachliteratur f

non-'iron a bügelfrei

nonplussed /nɒn'plʌst/ a verblüfft

nonsens|e /'nɒnsəns/ n Unsinn m. **~ical** /-'sensɪkl/ a unsinnig

non-'smoker n Nichtraucher m; (compartment) Nichtraucherabteil nt

non-'stop adv ununterbrochen; ⟨fly⟩ nonstop; **~ 'flight** Nonstopflug m

non-'swimmer *n* Nichtschwimmer *m*

non-'violent *a* gewaltlos

noodles /'nuːdlz/ *npl* Bandnudeln *pl*

nook /nʊk/ *n* Eckchen *nt*, Winkel *m*

noon /nuːn/ *n* Mittag *m*; **at ~** um 12 Uhr mittags

noose /nuːs/ *n* Schlinge *f*

nor /nɔː(r)/ *adv* noch ● *conj* auch nicht

Nordic /'nɔːdɪk/ *a* nordisch

norm /nɔːm/ *n* Norm *f*

normal /'nɔːml/ *a* normal. **~ity** /-'mælətɪ/ *n* Normalität *f*. **~ly** *adv* normal; (*usually*) normalerweise

north /nɔːθ/ *n* Norden *m*; **to the ~ of** nördlich von ● *a* Nord-, nord- ● *adv* nach Norden

north: N~ America *n* Nordamerika *nt*. **~-east** *a* Nordost- ● *n* Nordosten *m*

norther|ly /'nɔːðəlɪ/ *a* nördlich. **~n** *a* nördlich. **N~n Ireland** *n* Nordirland *nt*

north: N~ 'Pole *n* Nordpol *m*. **N~ 'Sea** *n* Nordsee *f*. **~ward[s]** /-wəd[z]/ *adv* nach Norden. **~-west** *a* Nordwest- ● *n* Nordwesten *m*

Nor|way /'nɔːweɪ/ *n* Norwegen *nt*. **~wegian** /-'wiːdʒn/ *a* norwegisch ● *n* Norweger(in) *m(f)*

nose /nəʊz/ *n* Nase *f* ● *vi* **~ about** herumschnüffeln

nose: ~bleed *n* Nasenbluten *nt*. **~dive** *n* (*Aviat*) Sturzflug *m*

nostalg|ia /nɒˈstældʒɪə/ *n* Nostalgie *f*. **~ic** *a* nostalgisch

nostril /'nɒstrəl/ *n* Nasenloch *nt*; (*of horse*) Nüster *f*

nosy /'nəʊzɪ/ *a* (**-ier, -iest**) (*fam*) neugierig

not /nɒt/ *adv* nicht; **~ a** kein(e); **if ~** wenn nicht; **~ at all** gar nicht; **~ a bit** kein bißchen; **~ even** nicht mal; **~ yet** noch nicht; **he is ~ a German** er ist kein Deutscher

notab|le /'nəʊtəbl/ *a* bedeutend; (*remarkable*) bemerkenswert. **~ly** *adv* insbesondere

notary /'nəʊtərɪ/ *n* **~ 'public** ≈ Notar *m*

notation /nəʊ'teɪʃn/ *n* Notation *f*; (*Mus*) Notenschrift *f*

notch /nɒtʃ/ *n* Kerbe *f*. **~ up** *vt* (*score*) erzielen

note /nəʊt/ *n* (*written comment*) Notiz *f*, Anmerkung *f*; (*short letter*) Briefchen *nt*, Zettel *m*; (*bank~*) Banknote *f*, Schein *m*; (*Mus*) Note *f*; (*sound*) Ton *m*; (*on piano*) Taste *f*; **eighth/**

quarter ~ (*Amer*) Achtel-/Viertelnote *f*; **half/whole ~** (*Amer*) halbe/ ganze Note *f*; **of ~** von Bedeutung; **make a ~ of** notieren ● *vt* beachten; (*notice*) bemerken (**that** daß). **~ down** *vt* notieren

'notebook *n* Notizbuch *nt*

noted /'nəʊtɪd/ *a* bekannt (**for** für)

note: ~paper *n* Briefpapier *nt*. **~worthy** *a* beachtenswert

nothing /'nʌθɪŋ/ *n*, *pron* & *adv* nichts; **for ~** umsonst; **~ but** nichts als; **~ much** nicht viel; **~ interesting** nichts Interessantes; **it's ~ to do with you** das geht dich nichts an

notice /'nəʊtɪs/ *n* (*on board*) Anschlag *m*, Bekanntmachung *f*; (*announcement*) Anzeige *f*; (*review*) Kritik *f*; (*termination of lease, employment*) Kündigung *f*; [**advance**] **~** Bescheid *m*; **give** [**in one's**] **~** kündigen; **give s.o. ~** jdm kündigen; **take no ~ of** keine Notiz nehmen von; **take no ~!** ignoriere es! ● *vt* bemerken. **~able** /-əbl/ *a*, **-bly** *adv* merklich. **~-board** *n* Anschlagbrett *nt*

noti|fication /nəʊtɪfɪˈkeɪʃn/ *n* Benachrichtigung *f*. **~fy** /'nəʊtɪfaɪ/ *vt* (*pt/pp* **-ied**) benachrichtigen

notion /'nəʊʃn/ *n* Idee *f*; **~s** *pl* (*Amer: haberdashery*) Kurzwaren *pl*

notorious /nəʊ'tɔːrɪəs/ *a* berüchtigt

notwith'standing *prep* trotz (+ *gen*) ● *adv* trotzdem, dennoch

nought /nɔːt/ *n* Null *f*

noun /naʊn/ *n* Substantiv *nt*

nourish /'nʌrɪʃ/ *vt* nähren. **~ing** *a* nahrhaft. **~ment** *n* Nahrung *f*

novel /'nɒvl/ *a* neu[artig] ● *n* Roman *m*. **~ist** *n* Romanschriftsteller(in) *m(f)*. **~ty** *n* Neuheit *f*; **~ties** *pl* kleine Geschenkartikel *pl*

November /nəʊ'vembə(r)/ *n* November *m*

novice /'nɒvɪs/ *n* Neuling *m*; (*Relig*) Novize *m*/Novizin *f*

now /naʊ/ *adv* & *conj* jetzt; **~** [**that**] jetzt, wo; **just ~** gerade, eben; **right ~** sofort; **~ and again** hin und wieder; **now now!** na, na!

'nowadays *adv* heutzutage

nowhere /'nəʊ-/ *adv* nirgendwo, nirgends

noxious /'nɒkʃəs/ *a* schädlich

nozzle /'nɒzl/ *n* Düse *f*

nuance /'njuːɑːs/ *n* Nuance *f*

nuclear /'njuːklɪə(r)/ *a* Kern-. **~ de'terrent** *n* nukleares Abschreckungsmittel *nt*

nucleus /'nju:klɪəs/ n (pl **-lei** /-lɪaɪ/)
Kern m

nude /nju:d/ a nackt ● n (Art) Akt m;
in the ~ nackt

nudge /nʌdʒ/ n Stups m ● vt stupsen

nud|ist /'nju:dɪst/ n Nudist m. **~ity** n
Nacktheit f

nugget /'nʌgɪt/ n [Gold]klumpen m

nuisance /'nju:sns/ n Ärgernis nt;
(pest) Plage f; **be a ~** ärgerlich sein;
⟨person:⟩ lästig sein; **what a ~!** wie
ärgerlich!

null /nʌl/ a **~ and void** null und
nichtig. **~ify** /'nʌlɪfaɪ/ vt (pt/pp **-ied**)
für nichtig erklären

numb /nʌm/ a gefühllos, taub; **~**
with cold taub vor Kälte ● vt
betäuben

number /'nʌmbə(r)/ n Nummer f;
(amount) Anzahl f; (Math) Zahl f
● vt numerieren; (include) zählen
(among zu). **~-plate** n Nummernschild nt

numeral /'nju:mərəl/ n Ziffer f

numerate /'nju:mərət/ a **be ~** rechnen können

numerical /nju:'merɪkl/ a, **-ly** adv
numerisch; **in ~ order** zahlenmäßig
geordnet

numerous /'nju:mərəs/ a zahlreich

nun /nʌn/ n Nonne f

nuptial /'nʌpʃl/ a Hochzeits-. **~s** npl
(Amer) Hochzeit f

nurse /nɜ:s/ n [Kranken]schwester f;
(male) Krankenpfleger m; **children's**
~ Kindermädchen nt ● vt pflegen.
~maid n Kindermädchen nt

nursery /'nɜ:sərɪ/ n Kinderzimmer nt;
(Hort) Gärtnerei f; **[day] ~** Kinder-
tagesstätte f. **~ rhyme** n Kinderreim
m. **~ school** n Kindergarten m

nursing /'nɜ:sɪŋ/ n Krankenpflege f.
~ home n Pflegeheim nt

nurture /'nɜ:tʃə(r)/ vt nähren; (fig)
hegen

nut /nʌt/ n Nuß f; (Techn) [Schrau-
ben]mutter f; (fam: head) Birne f
(fam); **be ~s** (fam) spinnen (fam).
~crackers npl Nußknacker m.
~meg n Muskat m

nutrient /'nju:trɪənt/ n Nährstoff m

nutrit|ion /nju:'trɪʃn/ n Ernährung f.
~ious /-ʃəs/ a nahrhaft

'nutshell n Nußschale f; **in a ~** (fig)
kurz gesagt

nuzzle /'nʌzl/ vt beschnüffeln

nylon /'naɪlɒn/ n Nylon nt; **~s** pl
Nylonstrümpfe pl

nymph /nɪmf/ n Nymphe f

O

O /əʊ/ n (Teleph) null

oaf /əʊf/ n (pl **oafs**) Trottel m

oak /əʊk/ n Eiche f ● attrib Eichen-

OAP abbr (old-age pensioner) Rent-
ner(in) m(f)

oar /ɔ:(r)/ n Ruder nt. **~sman** n
Ruderer m

oasis /əʊ'eɪsɪs/ n (pl **oases** /-si:z/) Oase
f

oath /əʊθ/ n Eid m; (swear-word)
Fluch m

oatmeal /'əʊt-/ n Hafermehl nt

oats /əʊts/ npl Hafer m; (Culin)
[**rolled**] **~** Haferflocken pl

obedien|ce /ə'bi:dɪəns/ n Gehorsam
m. **~t** a, **-ly** adv gehorsam

obes|e /əʊ'bi:s/ a fettleibig. **~ity** n
Fettleibigkeit f

obey /ə'beɪ/ vt/i gehorchen (+ dat);
befolgen ⟨instructions, rules⟩

obituary /ə'bɪtjʊərɪ/ n Nachruf m;
(notice) Todesanzeige f

object¹ /'ɒbdʒɪkt/ n Gegenstand m;
(aim) Zweck m; (intention) Absicht f;
(Gram) Objekt nt; **money is no ~**
Geld spielt keine Rolle

object² /əb'dʒekt/ vi Einspruch erheben (**to** gegen); (be against) etwas
dagegen haben

objection /əb'dʒekʃn/ n Einwand m;
have no ~ nichts dagegen haben.
~able /-əbl/ a anstößig; ⟨person⟩
unangenehm

objectiv|e /əb'dʒektɪv/ a, **-ly** adv
objektiv ● n Ziel nt. **~ity** /-'tɪvətɪ/ n
Objektivität f

objector /əb'dʒektə(r)/ n Gegner m

obligation /ɒblɪ'geɪʃn/ n Pflicht f; **be**
under an ~ verpflichtet sein; **with-**
out ~ unverbindlich

obligatory /ə'blɪgətrɪ/ a obligato-
risch; **be ~** Vorschrift sein

oblig|e /ə'blaɪdʒ/ vt verpflichten;
(compel) zwingen; (do a small service) einen Gefallen tun (+ dat);
much ~ed! vielen Dank! **~ing** a
entgegenkommend

oblique /ə'bli:k/ a schräg; ⟨angle⟩
schief; (fig) indirekt. **~ stroke** n
Schrägstrich m

obliterate /ə'blɪtəreɪt/ vt auslöschen

oblivion /ə'blɪvɪən/ n Vergessenheit f

oblivious /ə'blɪvɪəs/ a **be ~** sich (dat)
nicht bewußt sein (**of** or **to** gen)

oblong /'ɒblɒŋ/ a rechteckig ● n
Rechteck nt

obnoxious /əb'nɒkʃəs/ a widerlich

oboe /'əʊbəʊ/ n Oboe f

obscen|e /əb'si:n/ a obszön; (atrocious) abscheulich. ~ity /-'senətɪ/ n Obszönität f; Abscheulichkeit f

obscur|e /əb'skjʊə(r)/ a dunkel; (unknown) unbekannt ● vt verdecken; (confuse) verwischen. ~ity n Dunkelheit f; Unbekanntheit f

obsequious /əb'si:kwɪəs/ a unterwürfig

observa|nce /əb'zɜ:vns/ n (of custom) Einhaltung f. ~nt a aufmerksam. ~tion /ɒbzə'veɪʃn/ n Beobachtung f; (remark) Bemerkung f

observatory /əb'zɜ:vətrɪ/ n Sternwarte f; (weather) Wetterwarte f

observe /əb'zɜ:v/ vt beobachten; (say, notice) bemerken; (keep, celebrate) feiern; (obey) einhalten. ~r n Beobachter m

obsess /əb'ses/ vt be ~ed by besessen sein von. ~ion /-eʃn/ n Besessenheit f; (persistent idea) fixe Idee f. ~ive /-ɪv/ a, -ly adv zwanghaft

obsolete /'ɒbsəli:t/ a veraltet

obstacle /'ɒbstəkl/ n Hindernis nt

obstetrician /ɒbstə'trɪʃn/ n Geburtshelfer m. **obstetrics** /-'stetrɪks/ n Geburtshilfe f

obstina|cy /'ɒbstɪnəsɪ/ n Starrsinn m. ~te /-nət/ a, -ly adv starrsinnig; (refusal) hartnäckig

obstreperous /əb'strepərəs/ a widerspenstig

obstruct /əb'strʌkt/ vt blockieren; (hinder) behindern. ~ion /-ʌkʃn/ n Blockierung f; Behinderung f; (obstacle) Hindernis nt. ~ive /-ɪv/ a be ~ive Schwierigkeiten bereiten

obtain /əb'teɪn/ vt erhalten, bekommen ● vi gelten. ~able /-əbl/ a erhältlich

obtrusive /əb'tru:sɪv/ a aufdringlich; (thing) auffällig

obtuse /əb'tju:s/ a (Geom) stumpf; (stupid) begriffsstutzig

obviate /'ɒbvɪeɪt/ vt beseitigen

obvious /'ɒbvɪəs/ a, -ly adv offensichtlich, offenbar

occasion /ə'keɪʒn/ n Gelegenheit f; (time) Mal nt; (event) Ereignis nt; (cause) Anlaß m, Grund m; on ~ gelegentlich, hin und wieder; **on the** ~ **of** anläßlich (+ gen) ● vt veranlassen

occasional /ə'keɪʒənl/ a gelegentlich; he has the ~ glass of wine er trinkt

gelegentlich ein Glas Wein. ~ly adv gelegentlich, hin und wieder

occult /ɒ'kʌlt/ a okkult

occupant /'ɒkjʊpənt/ n Bewohner(in) m(f); (of vehicle) Insasse m

occupation /ɒkjʊ'peɪʃn/ n Beschäftigung f; (job) Beruf m; (Mil) Besetzung f; (period) Besatzung f. ~al a Berufs-. ~al therapy n Beschäftigungstherapie f

occupier /'ɒkjʊpaɪə(r)/ n Bewohner(in) m(f)

occupy /'ɒkjʊpaɪ/ vt (pt/pp occupied) besetzen (seat, (Mil) country); einnehmen (space); in Anspruch nehmen (time); (live in) bewohnen; (fig) bekleiden (office); (keep busy) beschäftigen; ~ oneself sich beschäftigen

occur /ə'kɜ:(r)/ vi (pt/pp occurred) geschehen; (exist) vorkommen, auftreten; it ~red to me that es fiel mir ein, daß. **occurrence** /ə'kʌrəns/ n Auftreten nt; (event) Ereignis nt

ocean /'əʊʃn/ n Ozean m

o'clock /ə'klɒk/ adv [at] 7 ~ [um] 7 Uhr

octagonal /ɒk'tægənl/ a achteckig

octave /'ɒktɪv/ n (Mus) Oktave f

October /ɒk'təʊbə(r)/ n Oktober m

octopus /'ɒktəpəs/ n (pl -puses) Tintenfisch m

odd /ɒd/ a (-er, -est) seltsam, merkwürdig; (number) ungerade; (not of set) einzeln; **forty** ~ über vierzig; ~ **jobs** Gelegenheitsarbeiten pl; **the** ~ **one out** die Ausnahme; **at** ~ **moments** zwischendurch; **have the** ~ **glass of wine** gelegentlich ein Glas Wein trinken

odd|ity /'ɒdɪtɪ/ n Kuriosität f. ~**ly** adv merkwürdig; ~**ly enough** merkwürdigerweise. ~**ment** n (of fabric) Rest m

odds /ɒdz/ npl (chances) Chancen pl; **at** ~ uneinig; ~ **and ends** Kleinkram m; **it makes no** ~ es spielt keine Rolle

ode /əʊd/ n Ode f

odious /'əʊdɪəs/ a widerlich, abscheulich

odour /'əʊdə(r)/ n Geruch m. ~**less** a geruchlos

oesophagus /i:'sɒfəgəs/ n Speiseröhre f

of /ɒv, unbetont əv/ prep von (+ dat); (made of) aus (+ dat); **the two of us** wir zwei; **a child of three** ein dreijähriges Kind; **the fourth of January** der vierte Januar; **a pound of butter** ein

Pfund Butter; **a cup of tea/coffee** eine Tasse Tee/Kaffee; **a bottle of wine** eine Flasche Wein; **half of it** die Hälfte davon; **the whole of the room** das ganze Zimmer

off /ɒf/ *prep* von (+ *dat*); **£10 ~ the price** £10 Nachlaß; **~ the coast** vor der Küste; **get ~ the ladder/bus** von der Leiter/aus dem Bus steigen; **take/leave the lid ~ the saucepan** den Topf abdecken/nicht zudecken ● *adv* weg; ⟨*button, lid, handle*⟩ ab; ⟨*light*⟩ aus; ⟨*brake*⟩ los; ⟨*machine*⟩ abgeschaltet; ⟨*tap*⟩ zu; (*on appliance*) **'off' 'aus'; 2 kilometres ~** 2 Kilometer entfernt; **a long way ~** weit weg; (*time*) noch lange hin; **~ and on** hin und wieder; **with his hat/ coat ~** ohne Hut/Mantel; **with the light/lid ~** ohne Licht/Deckel; **20% ~** 20% Nachlaß; **be ~** (*leave*) [weg]- gehen; (*Sport*) starten; ⟨*food:*⟩ schlecht/(*all gone*) alle sein; **be better/worse ~** besser/schlechter dran sein; **be well ~** gut dran sein; (*financially*) wohlhabend sein; **have a day ~** einen freien Tag haben; **go/drive ~** weggehen/ -fahren; **turn/take sth ~** etw abdre- hen/-nehmen

offal /'ɒfl/ *n* (*Culin*) Innereien *pl*

offence /ə'fens/ *n* (*illegal act*) Verge- hen *nt*; **give/take ~** Anstoß erregen/ nehmen (**at** an + *dat*)

offend /ə'fend/ *vt* beleidigen. **~er** *n* (*Jur*) Straftäter *m*

offensive /ə'fensɪv/ *a* anstößig; (*Mil, Sport*) offensiv ● *n* Offensive *f*

offer /'ɒfə(r)/ *n* Angebot *nt*; **on special ~** im Sonderangebot ● *vt* anbieten (**to** *dat*); leisten ⟨*resistance*⟩; **~ s.o. sth** jdm etw anbieten; **~ to** sich anbieten, etw zu tun. **~ing** *n* Gabe *f*

off'hand *a* brüsk; (*casual*) lässig ● *adv* so ohne weiteres

office /'ɒfɪs/ *n* Büro *nt*; (*post*) Amt *nt*; **in ~** im Amt; **~ hours** *pl* Dienststun- den *pl*

officer /'ɒfɪsə(r)/ *n* Offizier *m*; (*offi- cial*) Beamte(r) *m*/Beamtin *f*; (*po- lice*) Polizeibeamte(r) *m*/-beamtin *f*

official /ə'fɪʃl/ *a* offiziell, amtlich ● *n* Beamte(r) *m*/Beamtin *f*; (*Sport*) Funktionär *m*. **~ly** *adv* offiziell

officiate /ə'fɪʃɪeɪt/ *vi* amtieren

officious /ə'fɪʃəs/ *a*, **-ly** *adv* übereifrig

'offing *n* **in the ~** in Aussicht

'off-licence *n* Wein- und Spirituosen- handlung *f*

off-'load *vt* ausladen

'off-putting *a* (*fam*) abstoßend

off'set *vt* (*pt/pp* **-set**, *pres p* **-setting**) ausgleichen

'offshoot *n* Schößling *m*; (*fig*) Zweig *m*

'offshore *a* offshore-. **~ rig** *n* Bohrin- sel *f*

off'side *a* (*Sport*) abseits

'offspring *n* Nachwuchs *m*

off'stage *adv* hinter den Kulissen

off-'white *a* fast weiß

often /'ɒfn/ *adv* oft; **every so ~** von Zeit zu Zeit

ogle /'əʊgl/ *vt* beäugeln

ogre /'əʊgə(r)/ *n* Menschenfresser *m*

oh /əʊ/ *int* oh! ach! **oh dear!** o weh!

oil /ɔɪl/ *n* Öl *nt*; (*petroleum*) Erdöl *nt* ● *vt* ölen

oil: **~cloth** *n* Wachstuch *nt*. **~field** *n* Ölfeld *nt*. **~-painting** *n* Ölgemälde *nt*. **~ refinery** *n* [Erd]ölraffinerie *f*. **~skins** *npl* Ölzeug *nt*. **~-slick** *n* Ölteppich *m*. **~-tanker** *n* Öltanker *m*. **~ well** *n* Ölquelle *f*

oily /'ɔɪlɪ/ *a* (**-ier, -iest**) ölig

ointment /'ɔɪntmənt/ *n* Salbe *f*

OK /əʊ'keɪ/ *a & int* (*fam*) in Ordnung; **okay** ● *adv* (*well*) gut ● *vt* (*auch* **okay**) (*pt/pp* **okayed**) genehmigen

old /əʊld/ *a* (**-er, -est**) alt; (*former*) ehemalig

old: **~ 'age** *n* Alter *nt*. **~-age 'pen- sioner** *n* Rentner(in) *m(f)*. **~ boy** *n* ehemaliger Schüler. **~-'fashioned** *a* altmodisch. **~ girl** ehemalige Schü- lerin *f*. **~ 'maid** *n* alte Jungfer *f*

olive /'ɒlɪv/ *n* Olive *f*; (*colour*) Oliv *nt* ● *a* olivgrün. **~ branch** *n* Ölzweig *m*; (*fig*) Friedensangebot *nt*. **~ 'oil** *n* Olivenöl *nt*

Olympic /ə'lɪmpɪk/ *a* olympisch ● *n* **the ~s** die Olympischen Spiele *pl*

omelette /'ɒmlɪt/ *n* Omelett *nt*

omen /'əʊmən/ *n* Omen *nt*

ominous /'ɒmɪnəs/ *a* bedrohlich

omission /ə'mɪʃn/ *n* Auslassung *f*; (*failure to do*) Unterlassung *f*

omit /ə'mɪt/ *vt* (*pt/pp* **omitted**) aus- lassen; **~ to do sth** es unterlassen, etw zu tun

omnipotent /ɒm'nɪpətənt/ *a* all- mächtig

on /ɒn/ *prep* auf (+ *dat*/(*on to*) + *acc*); (*on vertical surface*) an (+ *dat*/(*on to*) + *acc*); (*about*) über (+ *acc*); **on Monday** [am] Montag; **on Mondays**

montags; **on the first of May** am
ersten Mai; **on arriving** als ich an-
kam; **on one's finger** am Finger; **on
the right/left** rechts/links; **on the
Rhine/Thames** am Rhein/an der
Themse; **on the radio/television** im
Radio/Fernsehen; **on the bus/train**
im Bus/Zug; **go on the bus/train** mit
dem Bus/Zug fahren; **get on the
bus/train** in den Bus/Zug einsteigen;
on me (*with me*) bei mir; **it's on me**
(*fam*) das spendiere ich ● *adv*
(*further on*) weiter; (*switched on*) an;
⟨*brake*⟩ angezogen; ⟨*machine*⟩
angeschaltet; (*on appliance*) 'on'
'ein'; **with/without his hat/coat on**
mit/ohne Hut/Mantel; **with/without
the lid on** mit/ohne Deckel; **be on**
⟨*film:*⟩ laufen; ⟨*event:*⟩ stattfinden;
be on at (*fam*) bedrängen (**zu** to);
it's not on (*fam*) das geht nicht; **on
and on** immer weiter; **on and off** hin
und wieder; **and so on** und so weiter;
later on später; **move/drive on** wei-
tergehen/-fahren; **stick/sew on** an-
kleben/-nähen

once /wʌns/ *adv* einmal; (*formerly*)
früher; **at** ~ sofort; (*at the same
time*) gleichzeitig; ~ **and for all** ein
für allemal ● *conj* wenn; (*with past
tense*) als. ~**-over** *n* (*fam*) **give s.o./
sth the** ~**-over** sich (*dat*) jdn/etw
kurz ansehen

'oncoming *a* ~ **traffic** Gegenverkehr
m

one /wʌn/ *a* ein(e); (*only*) einzig; **not**
~ kein(e); ~ **day/evening** eines Ta-
ges/Abends ● *n* Eins *f* ● *pron* ei-
ne(r)/eins; (*impersonal*) man; **which**
~ welche(r,s); ~ **another** einander;
~ **by** ~ einzeln; ~ **never knows** man
kann nie wissen

one: ~**-eyed** *a* einäugig. ~**-parent
'family** *n* Einelternfamilie *f*. ~**'self**
pron selbst; (*refl*) sich; **by** ~**self** allein. ~**-sided** *a* einseitig. ~**-way** *a*
⟨*street*⟩ Einbahn-; ⟨*ticket*⟩ einfach

onion /'ʌnjən/ *n* Zwiebel *f*

'onlooker *n* Zuschauer(in) *m(f)*

only /'əʊnlɪ/ *a* einzige(r,s); **an** ~ **child**
ein Einzelkind *nt* ● *adv & conj* nur;
~ **just** gerade erst; (*barely*) gerade
noch

'onset *n* Beginn *m*; (*of winter*) Einsetzen *nt*

onslaught /'ɒnslɔːt/ *n* heftiger Angriff *m*

onus /'əʊnəs/ *n* **the** ~ **is on me** es liegt
an mir (**to** zu)

onward[s] /'ɒnwəd[z]/ *adv* vorwärts;
from then ~ von der Zeit an

ooze /uːz/ *vi* sickern

opal /'əʊpl/ *n* Opal *m*

opaque /əʊ'peɪk/ *a* undurchsichtig

open /'əʊpən/ *a*, **-ly** offen; **be** ~
⟨*shop:*⟩ geöffnet sein; **in the** ~ **air** im
Freien ● *n* **in the** ~ im Freien ● *vt*
öffnen, aufmachen; (*start, set up*)
eröffnen ● *vi* sich öffnen; ⟨*flower:*⟩
aufgehen; ⟨*shop:*⟩ öffnen, aufmachen; (*be started*) eröffnet werden.
~ **up** *vt* öffnen, aufmachen; (*fig*)
eröffnen ● *vi* sich öffnen; (*fig*) sich
eröffnen

open: ~**-air 'swimming pool** *n* Freibad *nt*. ~ **day** *n* Tag *m* der offenen
Tür

opener /'əʊpənə(r)/ *n* Öffner *m*

opening /'əʊpənɪŋ/ *n* Öffnung *f*; (*beginning*) Eröffnung *f*; (*job*) Ein-
stiegsmöglichkeit *f*. ~ **hours** *npl*
Öffnungszeiten *pl*

open: ~**-'minded** *a* aufgeschlossen.
~**-plan** *a* ~**-plan office** Großraum-
büro *nt*. ~ **'sandwich** *n* belegtes Brot
nt

opera /'ɒpərə/ *n* Oper *f*

operable /'ɒpərəbl/ *a* operierbar

opera: ~**-glasses** *npl* Opernglas *nt*.
~**-house** *n* Opernhaus *nt*. ~**-singer**
n Opernsänger(in) *m(f)*

operate /'ɒpəreɪt/ *vt* bedienen
⟨*machine, lift*⟩; betätigen ⟨*lever,
brake*⟩; (*fig: run*) betreiben ● *vi*
(*Techn*) funktionieren; (*be in action*)
in Betrieb sein; (*Mil & fig*) operieren; ~ **[on]** (*Med*) operieren

operatic /ɒpə'rætɪk/ *a* Opern-

operation /ɒpə'reɪʃn/ *n* (*see operate*)
Bedienung *f*; Betätigung *f*; Operation *f*; **in** ~ (*Techn*) in Betrieb; **come
into** ~ (*fig*) in Kraft treten; **have an**
~ (*Med*) operiert werden. ~**al** *a* **be**
~**al** in Betrieb sein; ⟨*law:*⟩ in Kraft
sein

operative /'ɒpərətɪv/ *a* wirksam

operator /'ɒpəreɪtə(r)/ *n* (*user*) Bedie-
nungsperson *f*; (*Teleph*) Vermitt-
lung *f*

operetta /ɒpə'retə/ *n* Operette *f*

opinion /ə'pɪnjən/ *n* Meinung *f*; **in my**
~ meiner Meinung nach. ~**ated** *a*
rechthaberisch

opium /'əʊpɪəm/ *n* Opium *nt*

opponent /ə'pəʊnənt/ *n* Gegner(in)
m(f)

opportun|e /'ɒpətjuːn/ a günstig.
~**ist** /-'tjuːnɪst/ a opportunistisch ●
n Opportunist m
opportunity /ɒpə'tjuːnətɪ/ n Gelegenheit f
oppos|e /ə'pəʊz/ vt Widerstand-
leisten (+ dat); (argue against) sprechen gegen; **be ~ed to sth** gegen etw
sein; **as ~ed to** im Gegensatz zu.
~**ing** a gegnerisch; (opposite)
entgegengesetzt
opposite /'ɒpəzɪt/ a entgegengesetzt;
⟨house, side⟩ gegenüberliegend; ~
number (fig) Gegenstück nt; **the ~
sex** das andere Geschlecht ● n Gegenteil nt ● adv gegenüber ● prep
gegenüber (+ dat)
opposition /ɒpə'zɪʃn/ n Widerstand
m; (Pol) Opposition f
oppress /ə'pres/ vt unterdrücken.
~**ion** /-eʃn/ n Unterdrückung f.
~**ive** /-ɪv/ a tyrannisch; ⟨heat⟩
drückend. ~**or** n Unterdrücker m
opt /ɒpt/ vi ~ **for** sich entscheiden
für; ~ **out** ausscheiden (**of** aus)
optical /'ɒptɪkl/ a optisch; ~ **illusion**
optische Täuschung f
optician /ɒp'tɪʃn/ n Optiker m
optics /'ɒptɪks/ n Optik f
optimis|m /'ɒptɪmɪzm/ n Optimis-
mus m. ~**t** /-mɪst/ n Optimist m. ~**tic**
/-'mɪstɪk/ a, **-ally** adv optimistisch
optimum /'ɒptɪməm/ a optimal ● n
(pl **-ima**) Optimum nt
option /'ɒpʃn/ n Wahl f; (Comm)
Option f. ~**al** a auf Wunsch erhältlich; ⟨subject⟩ wahlfrei; ~**al extras**
pl Extras pl
opu|lence /'ɒpjʊləns/ n Prunk m;
(wealth) Reichtum m. ~**lent** a
prunkvoll; (wealthy) sehr reich
or /ɔː(r)/ conj oder; (after negative)
noch; **or [else]** sonst; **in a year or
two** in ein bis zwei Jahren
oracle /'ɒrəkl/ n Orakel nt
oral /'ɔːrəl/ a, **-ly** adv mündlich; (Med)
oral ● n (fam) Mündliche(s) nt
orange /'ɒrɪndʒ/ n Apfelsine f,
Orange f; (colour) Orange nt ● a
orangefarben. ~**ade** /-'dʒeɪd/ n
Orangeade f
oration /ə'reɪʃn/ n Rede f
orator /'ɒrətə(r)/ n Redner m
oratorio /ɒrə'tɔːrɪəʊ/ n Oratorium nt
oratory /'ɒrətərɪ/ n Redekunst f
orbit /'ɔːbɪt/ n Umlaufbahn f ● vt
umkreisen. ~**al** a ~**al road**
Ringstraße f

orchard /'ɔːtʃəd/ n Obstgarten m
orches|tra /'ɔːkɪstrə/ n Orchester nt.
~**tral** /-'kestrəl/ a Orchester-.
~**trate** vt orchestrieren
orchid /'ɔːkɪd/ n Orchidee f
ordain /ɔː'deɪn/ vt bestimmen; (Relig)
ordinieren
ordeal /ɔː'diːl/ n (fig) Qual f
order /'ɔːdə(r)/ n Ordnung f; (sequence) Reihenfolge f; (condition)
Zustand m; (command) Befehl m; (in
restaurant) Bestellung f; (Comm)
Auftrag m; (Relig, medal) Orden m; ~
out of ~ ⟨machine⟩ außer Betrieb;
in ~ **that** damit; **in** ~ **to help** um zu
helfen; **take holy** ~**s** Geistlicher
werden ● vt (put in~) ordnen; (command) befehlen (+ dat); (Comm, in
restaurant) bestellen; (prescribe)
verordnen
orderly /'ɔːdəlɪ/ a ordentlich; (not
unruly) friedlich ● n (Mil, Med) Sanitäter m
ordinary /'ɔːdɪnərɪ/ a gewöhnlich,
normal; ⟨meeting⟩ ordentlich
ordination /ɔːdɪ'neɪʃn/ n (Relig)
Ordination f
ore /ɔː(r)/ n Erz nt
organ /'ɔːgən/ n (Biol & fig) Organ nt;
(Mus) Orgel f
organic /ɔː'gænɪk/ a, **-ally** adv organisch; (without chemicals) biody-
namisch; ⟨crop⟩ biologisch angebaut; ⟨food⟩ Bio-; ~**ally grown** biologisch angebaut. ~ **farm** n Biohof m.
~ **farming** n biologischer Anbau m
organism /'ɔːgənɪzm/ n Organismus
m
organist /'ɔːgənɪst/ n Organist m
organization /ɔːgənaɪ'zeɪʃn/ n Orga-
nisation f
organize /'ɔːgənaɪz/ vt organisieren;
veranstalten ⟨event⟩. ~**r** n Organisa-
tor m; Veranstalter m
orgasm /'ɔːgæzm/ n Orgasmus m
orgy /'ɔːdʒɪ/ n Orgie f
Orient /'ɔːrɪənt/ n Orient m. **o~al**
/-'entl/ a orientalisch; ~**al carpet**
Orientteppich m ● n Orientale m/
Orientalin f
orient|ate /'ɔːrɪənteɪt/ vt ~**ate one-
self** sich orientieren. ~**ation** /-'teɪʃn/
n Orientierung f
orifice /'ɒrɪfɪs/ n Öffnung f
origin /'ɒrɪdʒɪn/ n Ursprung m; (of
person, goods) Herkunft f
original /ə'rɪdʒənl/ a ursprünglich;
(not copied) original; (new) originell

● *n* Original *nt.* ~**ity** /-'næləti/ *n* Originalität *f.* ~**ly** *adv* ursprünglich

originat|e /ə'rɪdʒɪneɪt/ *vi* entstehen ● *vt* hervorbringen. ~**or** *n* Urheber *m*

ornament /'ɔːnəmənt/ *n* Ziergegenstand *m*; (*decoration*) Verzierung *f.* ~**al** /-'mentl/ *a* dekorativ. ~**ation** /-'teɪʃn/ *n* Verzierung *f*

ornate /ɔː'neɪt/ *a* reich verziert

ornithology /ɔːnɪ'θɒlədʒɪ/ *n* Vogelkunde *f*

orphan /'ɔːfn/ *n* Waisenkind *nt*, Waise *f* ● *vt* zur Waise machen; ~**ed** verwaist. ~**age** /-ɪdʒ/ *n* Waisenhaus *nt*

orthodox /'ɔːθədɒks/ *a* orthodox

orthography /ɔː'θɒɡrəfɪ/ *n* Rechtschreibung *f*

orthopaedic /ɔːθə'piːdɪk/ *a* orthopädisch

oscillate /'ɒsɪleɪt/ *vi* schwingen

ostensible /ɒ'stensəbl/ *a*, -**bly** *adv* angeblich

ostentat|ion /ɒsten'teɪʃn/ *n* Protzerei *f* (*fam*). ~**ious** /-ʃəs/ *a* protzig (*fam*)

osteopath /'ɒstɪəpæθ/ *n* Osteopath *m*

ostracize /'ɒstrəsaɪz/ *vt* ächten

ostrich /'ɒstrɪtʃ/ *n* Strauß *m*

other /'ʌðə(r)/ *a, pron & n* andere(r,s); **the** ~ [**one**] der/die/ das andere; **the** ~ **two** die zwei anderen; **two** ~**s** zwei andere; (*more*) noch zwei; **no** ~**s** sonst keine; **any** ~ **questions?** sonst noch Fragen? **every** ~ **day** jeden zweiten Tag; **the** ~ **day** neulich; **the** ~ **evening** neulich abends; **someone/something** ~ irgend jemand/etwas ● *adv* anders; ~ **than** him außer ihm; **somehow/ somewhere or** ~ irgendwie/ irgendwo

'otherwise *adv* sonst; (*differently*) anders

otter /'ɒtə(r)/ *n* Otter *m*

ouch /aʊtʃ/ *int* autsch

ought /ɔːt/ *v aux* **I/we** ~ **to stay** ich sollte/wir sollten eigentlich bleiben; **he** ~ **not to have done it** er hätte es nicht machen sollen; **that** ~ **to be enough** das sollte eigentlich genügen

ounce /aʊns/ *n* Unze *f* (*28,35 g*)

our /'aʊə(r)/ *a* unser

ours /'aʊəz/ *poss pron* unsere(r,s); **a friend of** ~ ein Freund von uns; **that is** ~ das gehört uns

ourselves /aʊə'selvz/ *pron* selbst; (*refl*) uns; **by** ~ allein

oust /aʊst/ *vt* entfernen

out /aʊt/ *adv* (*not at home*) weg; (*outside*) draußen; (*not alight*) aus; (*unconscious*) bewußtlos; **be** ~ ⟨*sun:*⟩ scheinen; ⟨*flower:*⟩ blühen; ⟨*workers:*⟩ streiken; ⟨*calculation:*⟩ nicht stimmen; (*Sport*) aus sein; (*fig: not feasible*) nicht in Frage kommen; ~ **and about** unterwegs; **have it** ~ **with s.o.** (*fam*) jdn zur Rede stellen; **get** ~! (*fam*) raus! ~ **with it!** (*fam*) heraus damit! **go/ send** ~ hinausgehen/-schicken; **come/bring** ~ herauskommen/ -bringen ● *prep* ~ **of** aus (+ *dat*); **go** ~ **of the door** zur Tür hinausgehen; **be** ~ **of bed/the room** nicht im Bett/im Zimmer sein; ~ **of breath/ danger** außer Atem/Gefahr; ~ **of work** arbeitslos; **nine** ~ **of ten** neun von zehn; **be** ~ **of sugar/bread** keinen Zucker/kein Brot mehr haben ● *prep* aus (+ *dat*); **go** ~ **the door** zur Tür hinausgehen

out'bid *vt* (*pt/pp* -**bid**, *pres p* -**bidding**) überbieten

'outboard *a* ~ **motor** Außenbordmotor *m*

'outbreak *n* Ausbruch *m*

'outbuilding *n* Nebengebäude *nt*

'outburst *n* Ausbruch *m*

'outcast *n* Ausgestoßene(r) *m/f*

'outcome *n* Ergebnis *nt*

'outcry *n* Aufschrei *m* [der Entrüstung]

out'dated *a* überholt

out'do *vt* (*pt* -**did**, *pp* -**done**) übertreffen, übertrumpfen

'outdoor *a* ⟨*life, sports*⟩ im Freien; ~ **shoes** *pl* Straßenschuhe *pl*; ~ **swimming pool** Freibad *nt*

out'doors *adv* draußen; **go** ~ nach draußen gehen

'outer *a* äußere(r,s)

'outfit *n* Ausstattung *f*; (*clothes*) Ensemble *nt*; (*fam: organization*) Betrieb *m*; (*fam*) Laden *m.* ~**ter** *n* **men's** ~**ter's** Herrenbekleidungsgeschäft *nt*

'outgoing *a* ausscheidend; ⟨*mail*⟩ ausgehend; (*sociable*) kontaktfreudig. ~**s** *npl* Ausgaben *pl*

out'grow *vt* (*pt* -**grew**, *pp* -**grown**) herauswachsen aus

'outhouse *n* Nebengebäude *nt*

outing /'aʊtɪŋ/ *n* Ausflug *m*

outlandish /aʊt'lændɪʃ/ a un- gewöhnlich

'**outlaw** n Geächtete(r) m/f ● vt ächten

'**outlay** n Auslagen pl

'**outlet** n Abzug m; (for water) Abfluß m; (fig) Ventil nt; (Comm) Absatz- möglichkeit f

'**outline** n Umriß m; (summary) kurze Darstellung f ● vt umreißen

out'**live** vt überleben

'**outlook** n Aussicht f; (future pro- spect) Aussichten pl; (attitude) Ein- stellung f

'**outlying** a entlegen; ~ **areas** pl Außengebiete pl

out'**moded** a überholt

out'**number** vt zahlenmäßig überle- gen sein (+ dat)

'**out-patient** n ambulanter Patient m; ~**s' department** Ambulanz f

'**outpost** n Vorposten m

'**output** n Leistung f, Produktion f

'**outrage** n Greueltat f; (fig) Skandal m; (indignation) Empörung f ● vt empören. ~**ous** /-'reɪdʒəs/ a empörend

'**outright**¹ a völlig, total; ⟨refusal⟩ glatt

out'**right**² adv ganz; (at once) sofort; (frankly) offen

'**outset** n Anfang m; **from the** ~ von Anfang an

'**outside**¹ a äußere(r,s); ~ **wall** Außenwand f ● n Außenseite f; **from the** ~ von außen; **at the** ~ höchstens

out'**side**² adv außen; (out of doors) draußen; **go** ~ nach draußen gehen ● prep außerhalb (+ gen); (in front of) vor (+ dat/acc)

out'**sider** n Außenseiter m

'**outsize** a übergroß

'**outskirts** npl Rand m

out'**spoken** a offen; **be** ~ kein Blatt vor den Mund nehmen

out'**standing** a hervorragend; (con- spicuous) bemerkenswert; (not settled) unerledigt; (Comm) aus- stehend

'**outstretched** a ausgestreckt

out'**strip** vt (pt/pp -**stripped**) davon- laufen (+ dat); (fig) übertreffen

out'**vote** vt überstimmen

'**outward** /-wəd/ a äußerlich; ~ **jour- ney** Hinreise f ● adv nach außen; **be** ~ **bound** ⟨ship:⟩ auslaufen. ~**ly** adv nach außen hin, äußerlich. ~**s** adv nach außen

out'**weigh** vt überwiegen

out'**wit** vt (pt/pp -**witted**) überlisten

oval /'əʊvl/ a oval ● n Oval nt

ovary /'əʊvəri/ n (Anat) Eierstock m

ovation /əʊ'veɪʃn/ n Ovation f

oven /'ʌvn/ n Backofen m. ~-**ready** a bratfertig

over /'əʊvə(r)/ prep über (+ acc/dat); ~ **dinner** beim Essen; ~ **the week- end** übers Wochenende; ~ **the phone** am Telefon; ~ **the page** auf der nächsten Seite; **all** ~ **Germany** in ganz Deutschland; ⟨travel⟩ durch ganz Deutschland; **all** ~ **the place** (fam) überall ● adv (remaining) übrig; (ended) zu Ende; ~ **again** noch einmal; ~ **and** ~ immer wieder; ~ **here/there** hier/da drü- ben; **all** ~ (everywhere) überall; **it's all** ~ es ist vorbei; **I ache all** ~ mir tut alles weh; **go/drive** ~ hinüberge- hen/-fahren; **come/bring** ~ herüberkommen/-bringen; **turn** ~ herumdrehen

overall¹ /'əʊvərɔ:l/ n Kittel m; ~**s** pl Overall m

overall² /əʊvər'ɔ:l/ a gesamt; (gen- eral) allgemein ● adv insgesamt

over'**awe** vt (fig) überwältigen

over'**balance** vi das Gleichgewicht verlieren

over'**bearing** a herrisch

'**overboard** adv (Naut) über Bord

'**overcast** a bedeckt

over'**charge** vt ~ **s.o.** jdm zu viel berechnen ● vi zu viel verlangen

'**overcoat** n Mantel m

over'**come** vt (pt -**came**, pp -**come**) überwinden; **be** ~ **by** überwältigt werden von

over'**crowded** a überfüllt

over'**do** vt (pt -**did**, pp -**done**) über- treiben; (cook too long) zu lange kochen; ~ **it** (fam: do too much) sich übernehmen

'**overdose** n Überdosis f

'**overdraft** n [Konto]überziehung f; **have an** ~ sein Konto überzogen haben

over'**draw** vt (pt -**drew**, pp -**drawn**) (Comm) überziehen

over'**due** a überfällig

over'**estimate** vt überschätzen

'**overflow**¹ n Überschuß m; (outlet) Überlauf m

over'**flow**² vi überlaufen

over'**grown** a ⟨garden⟩ über- wachsen

'**overhang**¹ n Überhang m

over'hang² *vt/i* (*pt/pp* **-hung**) überhängen (über + *acc*)

'overhaul¹ *n* Überholung *f*

over'haul² *vt* (*Techn*) überholen

over'head¹ *adv* oben

'overhead² *a* Ober-; (*ceiling*) Decken-. **~s** *npl* allgemeine Unkosten *pl*

over'hear *vt* (*pt/pp* **-heard**) mit anhören ⟨*conversation*⟩; **I overheard him saying it** ich hörte zufällig, wie er das sagte

over'heat *vi* zu heiß werden ● *vt* zu stark erhitzen

over'joyed *a* überglücklich

'overland *a & adv* /--'-/ auf dem Landweg; **~ route** Landroute *f*

over'lap *v* (*pt/pp* **-lapped**) ● *vi* sich überschneiden ● *vt* überlappen

over'leaf *adv* umseitig

over'load *vt* überladen; (*Electr*) überlasten

'overlook¹ *n* (*Amer*) Aussichtspunkt *m*

over'look² *vt* überblicken; (*fail to see, ignore*) übersehen

overly /'əʊvəlɪ/ *adv* übermäßig

over'night¹ *adv* über Nacht; **stay ~** übernachten

'overnight² *a* Nacht-; **~ stay** Übernachtung *f*

'overpass *n* Überführung *f*

over'pay *vt* (*pt/pp* **-paid**) überbezahlen

over'populated *a* übervölkert

over'power *vt* überwältigen. **~ing** *a* überwältigend

over'priced *a* zu teuer

overpro'duce *vt* überproduzieren

over'rate *vt* überschätzen. **~d** *a* überbewertet

over'reach *vt* **~ oneself** sich übernehmen

overre'act *vi* überreagieren. **~ion** *n* Überreaktion *f*

over'rid|e *vt* (*pt* **-rode**, *pp* **-ridden**) sich hinwegsetzen über (+ *acc*). **~ing** *a* Haupt-

over'rule *vt* ablehnen; **we were ~d** wir wurden überstimmt

over'run *vt* (*pt* **-ran**, *pp* **-run**, *pres p* **-running**) überrennen; überschreiten ⟨*time*⟩; **be ~ with** überlaufen sein von

over'seas¹ *adv* in Übersee; **go ~** nach Übersee gehen

'overseas² *a* Übersee-

over'see *vt* (*pt* **-saw**, *pp* **-seen**) beaufsichtigen

'overseer /-sɪə(r)/ *n* Aufseher *m*

over'shadow *vt* überschatten

over'shoot *vt* (*pt/pp* **-shot**) hinausschießen über (+ *acc*)

'oversight *n* Versehen *nt*

over'sleep *vi* (*pt/pp* **-slept**) [sich] verschlafen

over'step *vt* (*pt/pp* **-stepped**) überschreiten

over'strain *vt* überanstrengen

overt /əʊ'vɜːt/ *a* offen

over'tak|e *vt/i* (*pt* **-took**, *pp* **-taken**) überholen. **~ing** *n* Überholen *nt*; **no ~ing** Überholverbot *nt*

over'tax *vt* zu hoch besteuern; (*fig*) überfordern

'overthrow¹ *n* (*Pol*) Sturz *m*

over'throw² *vt* (*pt* **-threw**, *pp* **-thrown**) (*Pol*) stürzen

'overtime *n* Überstunden *pl* ● *adv* **work ~** Überstunden machen

over'tired *a* übermüdet

'overtone *n* (*fig*) Unterton *m*

overture /'əʊvətjʊə(r)/ *n* (*Mus*) Ouvertüre *f*; **~s** *pl* (*fig*) Annäherungsversuche *pl*

over'turn *vt* umstoßen ● *vi* umkippen

over'weight *a* übergewichtig; **be ~** Übergewicht haben

overwhelm /-'welm/ *vt* überwältigen. **~ing** *a* überwältigend

over'work *n* Überarbeitung *f* ● *vt* überfordern ● *vi* sich überarbeiten

over'wrought *a* überreizt

ovulation /ɒvjʊ'leɪʃn/ *n* Eisprung *m*

ow|e /əʊ/ *vt* schulden/ (*fig*) verdanken (**[to]** s.o. jdm); **~e s.o. sth** jdm etw schuldig sein; **be ~ing** ⟨*money:*⟩ ausstehen. **'~ing to** *prep* wegen (+ *gen*)

owl /aʊl/ *n* Eule *f*

own¹ /əʊn/ *a & pron* eigen; **it's my ~** es gehört mir; **a car of my ~** mein eigenes Auto; **on one's ~** allein; **hold one's ~** sich behaupten; **get one's ~ back** (*fam*) sich revanchieren

own² *vt* besitzen; (*confess*) zugeben; **I don't ~ it** es gehört mir nicht. **~ up** *vi* es zugeben

owner /'əʊnə(r)/ *n* Eigentümer(in) *m(f)*, Besitzer(in) *m(f)*; (*of shop*) Inhaber(in) *m(f)*. **~ship** *n* Besitz *m*

ox /ɒks/ *n* (*pl* **oxen**) Ochse *m*

oxide /'ɒksaɪd/ *n* Oxyd *nt*

oxygen /'ɒksɪdʒən/ *n* Sauerstoff *m*

oyster /'ɔɪstə(r)/ *n* Auster *f*

ozone /'əʊzəʊn/ n Ozon nt. ~-'friendly a ≈ ohne FCKW. ~ layer n Ozonschicht f

P

pace /peɪs/ n Schritt m; (speed) Tempo nt; keep ~ with Schritt halten mit ● vi ~ up and down auf und ab gehen. ~-maker n (Sport & Med) Schrittmacher m

Pacific /pə'sɪfɪk/ a & n the ~ [Ocean] der Pazifik

pacifier /'pæsɪfaɪə(r)/ n (Amer) Schnuller m

pacifist /'pæsɪfɪst/ n Pazifist m

pacify /'pæsɪfaɪ/ vt (pt/pp -ied) beruhigen

pack /pæk/ n Packung f; (Mil) Tornister m; (of cards) [Karten]spiel nt; (gang) Bande f; (of hounds) Meute f; (of wolves) Rudel nt; a ~ of lies ein Haufen Lügen ● vt/i packen; einpacken ⟨article⟩; be ~ed (crowded) [gedrängt] voll sein; send s.o. ~ing (fam) jdn wegschicken. ~ up vt einpacken ● vi (fam) ⟨machine:⟩ kaputtgehen; ⟨person:⟩ einpacken (fam)

package /'pækɪdʒ/ n Paket nt ● vt verpacken. ~ holiday n Pauschalreise f

packed 'lunch n Lunchpaket nt

packet /'pækɪt/ n Päckchen nt; cost a ~ (fam) einen Haufen Geld kosten

packing /'pækɪŋ/ n Verpackung f

pact /pækt/ n Pakt m

pad¹ /pæd/ n Polster nt; (for writing) [Schreib]block m; (fam: home) Wohnung f ● vt (pt/pp padded) polstern

pad² vi (pt/pp padded) tappen

padding /'pædɪŋ/ n Polsterung f; (in written work) Füllwerk nt

paddle¹ /'pædl/ n Paddel nt ● vt (row) paddeln

paddle² vi waten

paddock /'pædək/ n Koppel f

padlock /'pædlɒk/ n Vorhängeschloß nt ● vt mit einem Vorhängeschloß verschließen

paediatrician /piːdɪə'trɪʃn/ n Kinderarzt m/-ärztin f

pagan /'peɪgən/ a heidnisch ● n Heide m/Heidin f

page¹ /peɪdʒ/ n Seite f

page² n (boy) Page m ● vt ausrufen ⟨person⟩

pageant /'pædʒənt/ n Festzug m. ~ry n Prunk m

paid /peɪd/ see pay ● a bezahlt; put ~ to (fam) zunichte machen

pail /peɪl/ n Eimer m

pain /peɪn/ n Schmerz m; be in ~ Schmerzen haben; take ~s sich (dat) Mühe geben; ~ in the neck (fam) Nervensäge f ● vt (fig) schmerzen

pain: ~ful a schmerzhaft; (fig) schmerzlich. ~-killer n schmerzstillendes Mittel nt. ~less a, -ly adv schmerzlos

painstaking /'peɪnzteɪkɪŋ/ a sorgfältig

paint /peɪnt/ n Farbe f ● vt/i streichen; ⟨artist:⟩ malen. ~brush n Pinsel m. ~er n Maler m; (decorator) Anstreicher m. ~ing n Malerei f; (picture) Gemälde nt

pair /peə(r)/ n Paar nt; ~ of trousers Hose f; ~ of scissors Schere f ● vt paaren ● vi ~ off Paare bilden

pajamas /pə'dʒɑːməz/ n pl (Amer) Schlafanzug m

Pakistan /pɑːkɪ'stɑːn/ n Pakistan nt. ~i a pakistanisch ● n Pakistaner(in) m(f)

pal /pæl/ n Freund(in) m(f)

palace /'pælɪs/ n Palast m

palatable /'pælətəbl/ a schmackhaft

palate /'pælət/ n Gaumen m

palatial /pə'leɪʃl/ a palastartig

palaver /pə'lɑːvə(r)/ n (fam: fuss) Theater nt (fam)

pale¹ /peɪl/ n (stake) Pfahl m; beyond the ~ (fam) unmöglich

pale² a (-r, -st) blaß ● vi blaß werden. ~ness n Blässe f

Palestin|e /'pælɪstaɪn/ n Palästina nt. ~ian /pælə'stɪnɪən/ a palästinensisch ● n Palästinenser(in) m(f)

palette /'pælɪt/ n Palette f

pall /pɔːl/ n Sargtuch nt; (fig) Decke f ● vi an Reiz verlieren

pall|id /'pælɪd/ a bleich. ~or n Blässe f

palm /pɑːm/ n Handfläche f; (tree, symbol) Palme f ● vt ~ sth off on s.o. jdm etw andrehen. P~ 'Sunday n Palmsonntag m

palpable /'pælpəbl/ a tastbar; (perceptible) spürbar

palpitat|e /'pælpɪteɪt/ vi klopfen. ~ions /-'teɪʃnz/ npl Herzklopfen nt

paltry /'pɔːltrɪ/ a (-ier, -iest) armselig

pamper /'pæmpə(r)/ vt verwöhnen

pamphlet /'pæmflɪt/ n Broschüre f

pan /pæn/ *n* Pfanne *f*; (*saucepan*) Topf *m*; (*of scales*) Schale *f* ● *vt* (*pt/pp* **panned**) (*fam*) verreißen

panacea /pænə'si:ə/ *n* Allheilmittel *nt*

panache /pə'næʃ/ *n* Schwung *m*

'pancake *n* Pfannkuchen *m*

pancreas /'pæŋkrɪəs/ *n* Bauchspeicheldrüse *f*

panda /'pændə/ *n* Panda *m*. ~ **car** *n* Streifenwagen *m*

pandemonium /pændɪ'məʊnɪəm/ *n* Höllenlärm *m*

pander /'pændə(r)/ *vi* ~ **to s.o.** jdm zu sehr nachgeben

pane /peɪn/ *n* [Glas]scheibe *f*

panel /'pænl/ *n* Tafel *f*, Platte *f*; ~ **of experts** Expertenrunde *f*; ~ **of judges** Jury *f*. ~**ling** *n* Täfelung *f*

pang /pæŋ/ *n* ~**s of hunger** Hungergefühl *nt*; ~**s of conscience** Gewissensbisse *pl*

panic /'pænɪk/ *n* Panik *f* ● *vi* (*pt/pp* **panicked**) in Panik geraten. ~-**stricken** *a* von Panik ergriffen

panorama /pænə'rɑ:mə/ *n* Panorama *nt*. ~**ic** /-'ræmɪk/ *a* Panorama-

pansy /'pænzɪ/ *n* Stiefmütterchen *nt*

pant /pænt/ *vi* keuchen; ⟨*dog*:⟩ hecheln

pantechnicon /pæn'teknɪkən/ *n* Möbelwagen *m*

panther /'pænθə(r)/ *n* Panther *m*

panties /'pæntɪz/ *npl* [Damen]slip *m*

pantomime /'pæntəmaɪm/ *n* [zu Weihnachten aufgeführte] Märchenvorstellung *f*

pantry /'pæntrɪ/ *n* Speisekammer *f*

pants /pænts/ *npl* Unterhose *f*; (*woman's*) Schlüpfer *m*; (*trousers*) Hose *f*

'pantyhose *n* (*Amer*) Strumpfhose *f*

papal /'peɪpl/ *a* päpstlich

paper /'peɪpə(r)/ *n* Papier *nt*; (*wall*~) Tapete *f*; (*newspaper*) Zeitung *f*; (*exam*~) Testbogen *m*; (*exam*) Klausur *f*; (*treatise*) Referat *nt*; ~**s** *pl* (*documents*) Unterlagen *pl*; (*for identification*) [Ausweis]papiere *pl*; **on** ~ schriftlich ● *vt* tapezieren

paper: ~**back** *n* Taschenbuch *nt*. ~**clip** *n* Büroklammer *f*. ~**knife** *n* Brieföffner *m*. ~**weight** *n* Briefbeschwerer *m*. ~**work** *n* Schreibarbeit *f*

par /pɑ:(r)/ *n* (*Golf*) Par *nt*; **on a** ~ gleichwertig (**with** *dat*); **feel below** ~ sich nicht ganz auf der Höhe fühlen

parable /'pærəbl/ *n* Gleichnis *nt*

parachut|e /'pærəʃu:t/ *n* Fallschirm *m* ● *vi* [mit dem Fallschirm] abspringen. ~**ist** *n* Fallschirmspringer *m*

parade /pə'reɪd/ *n* Parade *f*; (*procession*) Festzug *m* ● *vi* marschieren ● *vt* (*show off*) zur Schau stellen

paradise /'pærədaɪs/ *n* Paradies *nt*

paradox /'pærədɒks/ *n* Paradox *nt*. ~**ical** /-'dɒksɪkl/ paradox

paraffin /'pærəfɪn/ *n* Paraffin *nt*

paragon /'pærəgən/ *n* ~ **of virtue** Ausbund *m* der Tugend

paragraph /'pærəgrɑ:f/ *n* Absatz *m*

parallel /'pærəlel/ *a* & *adv* parallel ● *n* (*Geog*) Breitenkreis *m*; (*fig*) Parallele *f*

paralyse /'pærəlaɪz/ *vt* lähmen; (*fig*) lahmlegen

paralysis /pə'ræləsɪs/ *n* (*pl* -**ses** /-si:z/) Lähmung *f*

paramount /'pærəmaʊnt/ *a* überragend; **be** ~ vorgehen

paranoid /'pærənɔɪd/ *a* [krankhaft] mißtrauisch

parapet /'pærəpɪt/ *n* Brüstung *f*

paraphernalia /pærəfə'neɪlɪə/ *n* Kram *m*

paraphrase /'pærəfreɪz/ *n* Umschreibung *f* ● *vt* umschreiben

paraplegic /pærə'pli:dʒɪk/ *a* querschnittsgelähmt ● *n* Querschnittsgelähmte(r) *m/f*

parasite /'pærəsaɪt/ *n* Parasit *m*, Schmarotzer *m*

parasol /'pærəsɒl/ *n* Sonnenschirm *m*

paratrooper /'pærətru:pə(r)/ *n* Fallschirmjäger *m*

parcel /'pɑ:sl/ *n* Paket *nt*

parch /pɑ:tʃ/ *vt* austrocknen; **be** ~**ed** ⟨*person*:⟩ einen furchtbaren Durst haben

parchment /'pɑ:tʃmənt/ *n* Pergament *nt*

pardon /'pɑ:dn/ *n* Verzeihung *f*; (*Jur*) Begnadigung *f*; ~? (*fam*) bitte? **I beg your** ~ wie bitte? (*sorry*) Verzeihung! ● *vt* verzeihen; (*Jur*) begnadigen

pare /peə(r)/ *vt* (*peel*) schälen

parent /'peərənt/ *n* Elternteil *m*; ~**s** *pl* Eltern *pl*. ~**al** /pə'rentl/ *a* elterlich

parenthesis /pə'renθəsɪs/ *n* (*pl* -**ses** /-si:z/) Klammer *f*

parish /'pærɪʃ/ n Gemeinde f. **~ioner** /pə'rɪʃənə(r)/ n Gemeindemitglied nt

parity /'pærətɪ/ n Gleichheit f

park /pɑːk/ n Park m ● vt/i parken

parking /'pɑːkɪŋ/ n Parken nt; 'no **~**' 'Parken verboten'. **~-lot** n (Amer) Parkplatz m. **~-meter** n Parkuhr f. **~ space** n Parkplatz m

parliament /'pɑːləmənt/ n Parlament nt. **~ary** /-'mentərɪ/ a parlamentarisch

parlour /'pɑːlə(r)/ n Wohnzimmer nt

parochial /pə'rəʊkɪəl/ a Gemeinde-; (fig) beschränkt

parody /'pærədɪ/ n Parodie f ● vt (pt/pp **-ied**) parodieren

parole /pə'rəʊl/ n **on ~** auf Bewährung

paroxysm /'pærəksɪzm/ n Anfall m

parquet /'pɑːkeɪ/ n **~ floor** Parkett nt

parrot /'pærət/ n Papagei m

parry /'pærɪ/ vt (pt/pp **-ied**) abwehren ⟨blow⟩; (Fencing) parieren

parsimonious /pɑːsɪ'məʊnɪəs/ a geizig

parsley /'pɑːslɪ/ n Petersilie f

parsnip /'pɑːsnɪp/ n Pastinake f

parson /'pɑːsn/ n Pfarrer m

part /pɑːt/ n Teil m; (Techn) Teil nt; (area) Gegend f; (Theat) Rolle f; (Mus) Part m; **spare ~** Ersatzteil nt; **for my ~** meinerseits; **on the ~ of** von Seiten (+ gen); **take s.o.'s ~** für jdn Partei ergreifen; **take ~ in** teilnehmen an (+ dat) ● adv teils ● vt trennen; scheiteln ⟨hair⟩ ● vi ⟨people:⟩ sich trennen; **~ with** sich trennen von

partake /pɑː'teɪk/ vt (pt **-took**, pp **-taken**) teilnehmen; **~ of** (eat) zu sich nehmen

part-ex'change n **take in ~** in Zahlung nehmen

partial /'pɑːʃl/ a Teil-; **be ~ to** mögen. **~ity** /pɑːʃɪ'ælətɪ/ n Voreingenommenheit f; (liking) Vorliebe f. **~ly** adv teilweise

particip|ant /pɑː'tɪsɪpənt/ n Teilnehmer(in) m(f). **~ate** /-peɪt/ vi teilnehmen (**in** an + dat). **~ation** /-'peɪʃn/ n Teilnahme f

participle /'pɑːtɪsɪpl/ n Partizip nt; **present/past ~** erstes/zweites Partizip nt

particle /'pɑːtɪkl/ n Körnchen nt; (Phys) Partikel nt; (Gram) Partikel f

particular /pə'tɪkjʊlə(r)/ a besondere(r,s); (precise) genau; (fastidious) penibel; **in ~** besonders. **~ly** adv besonders

adv besonders. **~s** npl nähere Angaben pl

parting /'pɑːtɪŋ/ n Abschied m; (in hair) Scheitel m ● attrib Abschieds-

partition /pɑː'tɪʃn/ n Trennwand f; (Pol) Teilung f ● vt teilen. **~ off** vt abtrennen

partly /'pɑːtlɪ/ adv teilweise

partner /'pɑːtnə(r)/ n Partner(in) m(f); (Comm) Teilhaber m. **~ship** n Partnerschaft f; (Comm) Teilhaberschaft f

partridge /'pɑːtrɪdʒ/ n Rebhuhn nt

part-'time a & adv Teilzeit-; **be or work ~** Teilzeitarbeit machen

party /'pɑːtɪ/ n Party f, Fest nt; (group) Gruppe f; (Pol, Jur) Partei f; **be ~ to** sich beteiligen an (+ dat)

'party line¹ n (Teleph) Gemeinschaftsanschluß m

party 'line² n (Pol) Parteilinie f

pass /pɑːs/ n Ausweis m; (Geog, Sport) Paß m; (Sch) ≈ ausreichend; **get a ~** bestehen ● vt vorbeigehen/ -fahren an (+ dat); (overtake) überholen; (hand) reichen; (Sport) abgeben, abspielen; (approve) annehmen; (exceed) übersteigen; bestehen ⟨exam⟩; machen ⟨remark⟩; fällen ⟨judgement⟩; (Jur) verhängen ⟨sentence⟩; **~ water** Wasser lassen; **~ the time** sich (dat) die Zeit vertreiben; **~ sth off as sth** etw als etw ausgeben; **~ one's hand over sth** mit der Hand über etw (acc) fahren ● vi vorbeigehen/-fahren; (get by) vorbeikommen; (overtake) überholen; ⟨time:⟩ vergehen; (in exam) bestehen; **let sth ~** (fig) etw übergehen; **[I] ~!** [ich] passe! **~ away** vi sterben. **~ down** vt herunterreichen; (fig) weitergeben. **~ out** vi ohnmächtig werden. **~ round** vt herumreichen. **~ up** vt heraufreichen; (fam: miss) vorübergehen lassen

passable /'pɑːsəbl/ a ⟨road⟩ befahrbar; (satisfactory) passabel

passage /'pæsɪdʒ/ n Durchgang m; (corridor) Gang m; (voyage) Überfahrt f; (in book) Passage f

passenger /'pæsɪndʒə(r)/ n Fahrgast m; (Naut, Aviat) Passagier m; (in car) Mitfahrer m. **~ seat** n Beifahrersitz m

passer-by /pɑːsə'baɪ/ n (pl **-s-by**) Passant(in) m(f)

'passing place n Ausweichstelle f

passion /'pæʃn/ n Leidenschaft f. **~ate** /-ət/ a, **-ly** adv leidenschaftlich

passive /'pæsɪv/ *a* passiv ● *n* Passiv
nt

Passover /'pɑːsəʊvə(r)/ *n* Passah *nt*

pass: ~**port** *n* [Reise]paß *m*. ~**word**
n Kennwort *nt*; (*Mil*) Losung *f*

past /pɑːst/ *a* vergangene(r,s); (*former*) ehemalig; **in the** ~ **few days** in
den letzten paar Tagen; **that's all** ~
das ist jetzt vorbei ● *n* Vergangen-
heit *f* ● *prep* an (+ *dat*) ... vorbei;
(*after*) nach; **at ten** ~ **two** um zehn
nach zwei ● *adv* vorbei; **go/come** ~
vorbeigehen/-kommen

pasta /'pæstə/ *n* Nudeln *pl*

paste /peɪst/ *n* Brei *m*; (*dough*) Teig
m; (*fish-, meat-*) Paste *f*; (*adhesive*)
Kleister *m*; (*jewellery*) Straß *m* ● *vt*
kleistern

pastel /'pæstl/ *n* Pastellfarbe *f*;
(*crayon*) Pastellstift *m*; (*drawing*)
Pastell *nt* ● *attrib* Pastell-

pasteurize /'pɑːstʃəraɪz/ *vt* pasteurisieren

pastille /'pæstɪl/ *n* Pastille *f*

pastime /'pɑːstaɪm/ *n* Zeitvertreib *m*

pastoral /'pɑːstərəl/ *a* ländlich; ⟨*care*⟩
seelsorgerisch

pastr|y /'peɪstrɪ/ *n* Teig *m*; **cakes and**
~**ies** Kuchen und Gebäck

pasture /'pɑːstʃə(r)/ *n* Weide *f*

pasty[1] /'pæstɪ/ *n* Pastete *f*

pasty[2] /'peɪstɪ/ *a* blaß, (*fam*) käsig

pat /pæt/ *n* Klaps *m*; (*of butter*) Stückchen *nt* ● *adv* **have sth off** ~ etw aus
dem Effeff können ● *vt* (*pt/pp* **pat-
ted**) tätscheln; ~ **s.o. on the back**
jdm auf die Schulter klopfen

patch /pætʃ/ *n* Flicken *m*; (*spot*)
Fleck *m*; **not a** ~ **on** (*fam*) gar nicht
zu vergleichen mit ● *vt* flicken. ~
up *vt* [zusammen]flicken; beilegen
⟨*quarrel*⟩

patchy /'pætʃɪ/ *a* ungleichmäßig

pâté /'pæteɪ/ *n* Pastete *f*

patent /'peɪtnt/ *a*, **-ly** *adv* offensichtlich ● *n* Patent *nt* ● *vt* patentieren.
~ **leather** *n* Lackleder *nt*

patern|al /pə'tɜːnl/ *a* väterlich. ~**ity** *n*
Vaterschaft *f*

path /pɑːθ/ *n* (*pl* ~**s**/pɑːðz/) [Fuß]weg
m, Pfad *m*; (*orbit, track*) Bahn *f*; (*fig*)
Weg *m*

pathetic /pə'θetɪk/ *a* mitleiderregend;
⟨*attempt*⟩ erbärmlich

patholog|ical /pæθə'lɒdʒɪkl/ *a* patho-
logisch. ~**ist** /pə'θɒlədʒɪst/ *n* Patho-
loge *m*

pathos /'peɪθɒs/ *n* Rührseligkeit *f*

patience /'peɪʃns/ *n* Geduld *f*; (*game*)
Patience *f*

patient /'peɪʃnt/ *a*, **-ly** *adv* geduldig
● *n* Patient(in) *m*(*f*)

patio /'pætɪəʊ/ *n* Terrasse *f*

patriot /'pætrɪət/ *n* Patriot(in) *m*(*f*).
~**ic** /-'ɒtɪk/ *a* patriotisch. ~**ism** *n*
Patriotismus *m*

patrol /pə'trəʊl/ *n* Patrouille *f* ● *vt/i*
patrouillieren [in (+ *dat*)]; ⟨*police:*⟩
auf Streife gehen/fahren [in (+
dat)]. ~ **car** *n* Streifenwagen *m*

patron /'peɪtrən/ *n* Gönner *m*; (*of
charity*) Schirmherr *m*; (*of the arts*)
Mäzen *m*; (*customer*) Kunde *m*/Kun-
din *f*; (*Theat*) Besucher *m*. ~**age**
/'pætrənɪdʒ/ *n* Schirmherrschaft *f*

patroniz|e /'pætrənaɪz/ *vt* (*fig*) herab-
lassend behandeln. ~**ing** *a*, **-ly** *adv*
gönnerhaft

patter[1] /'pætə(r)/ *n* Getrippel *nt*; (*of
rain*) Plätschern *nt* ● *vi* trippeln;
plätschern

patter[2] *n* (*speech*) Gerede *nt*

pattern /'pætn/ *n* Muster *nt*

paunch /pɔːntʃ/ *n* [Schmer]bauch *m*

pauper /'pɔːpə(r)/ *n* Arme(r) *m/f*

pause /pɔːz/ *n* Pause *f* ● *vi* innehalten

pave /peɪv/ *vt* pflastern; ~ **the way**
den Weg bereiten (**for** *dat*). ~**ment**
n Bürgersteig *m*

pavilion /pə'vɪljən/ *n* Pavillon *m*;
(*Sport*) Klubhaus *nt*

paw /pɔː/ *n* Pfote *f*; (*of large animal*)
Pranke *f*, Tatze *f*

pawn[1] /pɔːn/ *n* (*Chess*) Bauer *m*; (*fig*)
Schachfigur *f*

pawn[2] *vt* verpfänden ● *n* **in** ~ ver-
pfändet. ~**broker** *n* Pfandleiher *m*.
~**shop** *n* Pfandhaus *nt*

pay /peɪ/ *n* Lohn *m*; (*salary*) Gehalt
nt; **be in the** ~ **of** bezahlt werden
von ● *v* (*pt/pp* **paid**) ● *vt* bezahlen;
zahlen ⟨*money*⟩; ~ **s.o. a visit** jdm
einen Besuch abstatten; ~ **s.o. a
compliment** jdm ein Kompliment
machen ● *vi* zahlen; (*be profitable*)
sich bezahlt machen; (*fig*) sich lohnen; ~ **for sth** etw bezahlen. ~ **back**
vt zurückzahlen. ~ **in** *vt* einzahlen.
~ **off** *vt* abzahlen ⟨*debt*⟩ ● *vi* (*fig*)
sich auszahlen. ~ **up** *vi* zahlen

payable /'peɪəbl/ *a* zahlbar; **make** ~
to ausstellen auf (+ *acc*)

payee /peɪ'iː/ *n* [Zahlungs]empfänger
m

payment /'peɪmənt/ *n* Bezahlung *f*;
(*amount*) Zahlung *f*

pay: ~ **packet** n Lohntüte f; ~ **phone** n Münzfernsprecher m

pea /pi:/ n Erbse f

peace /pi:s/ n Frieden m; **for my ~ of mind** zu meiner eigenen Beruhigung

peace|able /'pi:səbl/ a friedlich. ~**ful** a, -**ly** adv friedlich. ~**maker** n Friedensstifter m

peach /pi:tʃ/ n Pfirsich m

peacock /'pi:kɒk/ n Pfau m

peak /pi:k/ n Gipfel m; (fig) Höhepunkt m. ~**ed 'cap** n Schirmmütze f. ~ **hours** npl Hauptbelastungszeit f; (for traffic) Hauptverkehrszeit f

peaky /'pi:kɪ/ a kränklich

peal /pi:l/ n (of bells) Glockengeläut nt; ~**s of laughter** schallendes Gelächter nt

'**peanut** n Erdnuß f; **for** ~**s** (fam) für einen Apfel und ein Ei

pear /peə(r)/ n Birne f

pearl /pɜ:l/ n Perle f

peasant /'peznt/ n Bauer m

peat /pi:t/ n Torf m

pebble /'pebl/ n Kieselstein m

peck /pek/ n Schnabelhieb m; (kiss) flüchtiger Kuß m ● vt/i picken/(nip) hacken (**at** nach). ~**ing order** n Hackordnung f

peckish /'pekɪʃ/ a **be** ~ (fam) Hunger haben

peculiar /pɪ'kju:lɪə(r)/ a eigenartig, seltsam; ~ **to** eigentümlich (+ dat). ~**ity** /-'ærətɪ/ n Eigenart f

pedal /'pedl/ n Pedal nt ● vt fahren ⟨bicycle⟩ ● vi treten. ~ **bin** n Treteimer m

pedantic /pɪ'dæntɪk/ a, -**ally** adv pedantisch

peddle /'pedl/ vt handeln mit

pedestal /'pedɪstl/ n Sockel m

pedestrian /pɪ'destrɪən/ n Fußgänger(in) m(f) ● a (fig) prosaisch. ~ '**crossing** n Fußgängerüberweg m. ~ '**precinct** n Fußgängerzone f

pedicure /'pedɪkjʊə(r)/ n Pediküre f

pedigree /'pedɪgri:/ n Stammbaum m ● attrib ⟨animal⟩ Rasse-

pedlar /'pedlə(r)/ n Hausierer m

pee /pi:/ vi (pt/pp **peed**) (fam) pinkeln

peek /pi:k/ vi (fam) gucken

peel /pi:l/ n Schale f ● vt schälen ● vi ⟨skin:⟩ sich schälen; ⟨paint:⟩ abblättern. ~**ings** npl Schalen pl

peep /pi:p/ n kurzer Blick m ● vi gucken. ~**hole** n Guckloch nt. **P~ing 'Tom** n (fam) Spanner m

peer[1] /pɪə(r)/ vi ~ **at** forschend ansehen

peer[2] n Peer m; **his** ~**s** pl seinesgleichen

peev|ed /pi:vd/ a (fam) ärgerlich. ~**ish** a reizbar

peg /peg/ n (hook) Haken m; (for tent) Pflock m, Hering m; (for clothes) [Wäsche]klammer f; **off the** ~ (fam) von der Stange ● vt (pt/pp **pegged**) anpflocken; anklammern ⟨washing⟩

pejorative /pɪ'dʒɒrətɪv/ a, -**ly** adv abwertend

pelican /'pelɪkən/ n Pelikan m

pellet /'pelɪt/ n Kügelchen nt

pelt[1] /pelt/ n (skin) Pelz m, Fell nt

pelt[2] vt bewerfen ● vi (fam: run fast) rasen; ~ [**down**] ⟨rain:⟩ [hernieder]prasseln

pelvis /'pelvɪs/ n (Anat) Becken nt

pen[1] /pen/ n (for animals) Hürde f

pen[2] n Federhalter m; (ball-point) Kugelschreiber m

penal /'pi:nl/ a Straf-. ~**ize** vt bestrafen; (fig) benachteiligen

penalty /'penltɪ/ n Strafe f; (fine) Geldstrafe f; (Sport) Strafstoß m; (Football) Elfmeter m

penance /'penəns/ n Buße f

pence /pens/ see **penny**

pencil /'pensɪl/ n Bleistift m ● vt (pt/pp **pencilled**) mit Bleistift schreiben. ~-**sharpener** n Bleistiftspitzer m

pendant /'pendənt/ n Anhänger m

pending /'pendɪŋ/ a unerledigt ● prep bis zu

pendulum /'pendjʊləm/ n Pendel nt

penetrat|e /'penɪtreɪt/ vt durchdringen; ~**e [into]** eindringen in (+ acc). ~**ing** a durchdringend. ~**ion** /-'treɪʃn/ n Durchdringen nt

'**penfriend** n Brieffreund(in) m(f)

penguin /'pengwɪn/ n Pinguin m

penicillin /penɪ'sɪlɪn/ n Penizillin nt

peninsula /pə'nɪnsʊlə/ n Halbinsel f

penis /'pi:nɪs/ n Penis m

peniten|ce /'penɪtəns/ n Reue f. ~**t** a reuig ● n Büßer m

penitentiary /penɪ'tenʃərɪ/ n (Amer) Gefängnis nt

pen: ~**knife** n Taschenmesser nt. ~-**name** n Pseudonym nt

pennant /'penənt/ n Wimpel m

penniless /'penɪlɪs/ a mittellos

penny /'penɪ/ n (pl **pence**; single coins **pennies**) Penny m; (Amer) Centstück nt; **spend a** ~ (fam) mal verschwinden; **the ~'s dropped** (*fam*) der Groschen ist gefallen

pension /'penʃn/ *n* Rente *f*; (*of civil servant*) Pension *f*. **~er** *n* Rentner (in) *m(f)*; Pensionär(in) *m(f)*

pensive /'pensɪv/ *a* nachdenklich

Pentecost /'pentɪkɒst/ *n* Pfingsten *nt*

pent-up /'pentʌp/ *a* angestaut

penultimate /pe'nʌltɪmət/ *a* vorletzte(r,s)

penury /'penjʊrɪ/ *n* Armut *f*

peony /'pɪənɪ/ *n* Pfingstrose *f*

people /'pi:pl/ *npl* Leute *pl*, Menschen *pl*; (*citizens*) Bevölkerung *f*; **the ~** das Volk; **English ~** die Engländer; **~ say** man sagt; **for four ~** für vier Personen ● *vt* bevölkern

pep /pep/ *n* (*fam*) Schwung *m*

pepper /'pepə(r)/ *n* Pfeffer *m*; (*vegetable*) Paprika *m* ● *vt* (*Culin*) pfeffern

pepper: ~corn *n* Pfefferkorn *nt*. **~mint** *n* Pfefferminz *nt*; (*Bot*) Pfefferminze *f*. **~pot** *n* Pfefferstreuer *m*

per /pɜ:(r)/ *prep* pro; **~ cent** Prozent *nt*

perceive /pə'si:v/ *vt* wahrnehmen

percentage /pə'sentɪdʒ/ *n* Prozentsatz *m*; (*part*) Teil *m*

perceptible /pə'septəbl/ *a* wahrnehmbar

percept|ion /pə'sepʃn/ *n* Wahrnehmung *f*. **~ive** /-tɪv/ *a* feinsinnig

perch¹ /pɜ:tʃ/ *n* Stange *f* ● *vi* ⟨*bird:*⟩ sich niederlassen

perch² *n inv* (*fish*) Barsch *m*

percolat|e /'pɜ:kəleɪt/ *vi* durchsickern. **~or** *n* Kaffeemaschine *f*

percussion /pə'kʌʃn/ *n* Schlagzeug *nt*. **~ instrument** *n* Schlaginstrument *nt*

peremptory /pə'remptərɪ/ *a* herrisch

perennial /pə'renɪəl/ *a* ⟨*problem*⟩ immer wiederkehrend ● *n* (*Bot*) mehrjährige Pflanze *f*

perfect¹ /'pɜ:fɪkt/ *a* perfekt, vollkommen; (*fam: utter*) völlig ● *n* (*Gram*) Perfekt *nt*

perfect² /pə'fekt/ *vt* vervollkommnen. **~ion** /-ekʃn/ *n* Vollkommenheit *f*; **to ~ion** perfekt

perfectly /'pɜ:fɪktlɪ/ *adv* perfekt; (*completely*) vollkommen, völlig

perforate /'pɜ:fəreɪt/ *vt* perforieren; (*make a hole in*) durchlöchern. **~d** *a* perforiert

perform /pə'fɔ:m/ *vt* ausführen; erfüllen ⟨*duty*⟩; (*Theat*) aufführen ⟨*play*⟩; spielen ⟨*role*⟩ ● *vi* (*Theat*)

auftreten; (*Techn*) laufen. **~ance** *n* Aufführung *f*; (*at theatre, cinema*) Vorstellung *f*; (*Techn*) Leistung *f*. **~er** *n* Künstler(in) *m(f)*

perfume /'pɜ:fju:m/ *n* Parfüm *nt*; (*smell*) Duft *m*

perfunctory /pə'fʌŋktərɪ/ *a* flüchtig

perhaps /pə'hæps/ *adv* vielleicht

peril /'perəl/ *n* Gefahr *f*. **~ous** /-əs/ *a* gefährlich

perimeter /pə'rɪmɪtə(r)/ *n* [äußere] Grenze *f*; (*Geom*) Umfang *m*

period /'pɪərɪəd/ *n* Periode *f*; (*Sch*) Stunde *f*; (*full stop*) Punkt *m* ● *attrib* ⟨*costume*⟩ zeitgenössisch; ⟨*furniture*⟩ antik. **~ic** /-'ɒdɪk/ *a*, **-ally** *adv* periodisch. **~ical** /-'ɒdɪkl/ *n* Zeitschrift *f*

peripher|al /pə'rɪfərl/ *a* nebensächlich. **~y** *n* Peripherie *f*

periscope /'perɪskəʊp/ *n* Periskop *nt*

perish /'perɪʃ/ *vi* ⟨*rubber:*⟩ verrotten; ⟨*food:*⟩ verderben; (*die*) ums Leben kommen. **~able** /-əbl/ *a* leicht verderblich. **~ing** *a* (*fam: cold*) eiskalt

perjur|e /'pɜ:dʒə(r)/ *vt* **~e oneself** einen Meineid leisten. **~y** *n* Meineid *m*

perk¹ /pɜ:k/ *n* (*fam*) [Sonder]vergünstigung *f*

perk² *vi* **~ up** munter werden

perky /'pɜ:kɪ/ *a* munter

perm /pɜ:m/ *n* Dauerwelle *f* ● *vt* **~ s.o.'s hair** jdm eine Dauerwelle machen

permanent /'pɜ:mənənt/ *a* ständig; ⟨*job, address*⟩ fest. **~ly** *adv* ständig; ⟨*work, live*⟩ dauernd, permanent; ⟨*employed*⟩ fest

permeable /'pɜ:mɪəbl/ *a* durchlässig

permeate /'pɜ:mɪeɪt/ *vt* durchdringen

permissible /pə'mɪsəbl/ *a* erlaubt

permission /pə'mɪʃn/ *n* Erlaubnis *f*

permissive /pə'mɪsɪv/ *a* ⟨*society*⟩ permissiv

permit¹ /pə'mɪt/ *vt* (*pt/pp* **-mitted**) erlauben (**s.o.** jdm); **~ me!** gestatten Sie!

permit² /'pɜ:mɪt/ *n* Genehmigung *f*

pernicious /pə'nɪʃəs/ *a* schädlich; (*Med*) perniziös

perpendicular /pɜ:pən'dɪkjʊlə(r)/ *a* senkrecht ● *n* Senkrechte *f*

perpetrat|e /'pɜ:pɪtreɪt/ *vt* begehen. **~or** *n* Täter *m*

perpetual /pə'petjʊəl/ *a*, **-ly** *adv* ständig, dauernd

perpetuate /pə'petjʊeɪt/ vt bewahren; verewigen ⟨error⟩

perplex /pə'pleks/ vt verblüffen. **~ed** a verblüfft. **~ity** n Verblüffung f

persecut|e /'pɜːsɪkjuːt/ vt verfolgen. **~ion** /-'kjuːʃn/ n Verfolgung f

perseverance /pɜːsɪ'vɪərəns/ n Ausdauer f

persever|e /pɜːsɪ'vɪə(r)/ vi beharrlich weitermachen. **~ing** a ausdauernd

Persia /'pɜːʃə/ n Persien nt

Persian /'pɜːʃn/ a persisch; ⟨cat, carpet⟩ Perser-

persist /pə'sɪst/ vi beharrlich weitermachen; ⟨continue⟩ anhalten; ⟨view:⟩ weiter bestehen; **~ in doing sth** dabei bleiben, etw zu tun. **~ence** n Beharrlichkeit f. **~ent** a, **-ly** adv beharrlich; ⟨continuous⟩ anhaltend

person /'pɜːsn/ n Person f; **in ~** persönlich

personal /'pɜːsənl/ a, **-ly** adv persönlich. **~ 'hygiene** n Körperpflege f

personality /pɜːsə'næləti/ n Persönlichkeit f

personify /pə'sɒnɪfaɪ/ vt (pt/pp **-ied**) personifizieren, verkörpern

personnel /pɜːsə'nel/ n Personal nt

perspective /pə'spektɪv/ n Perspektive f

perspicacious /pɜːspɪ'keɪʃəs/ a scharfsichtig

persp|iration /pɜːspɪ'reɪʃn/ n Schweiß m. **~ire** /-'spaɪə(r)/ vi schwitzen

persua|de /pə'sweɪd/ vt überreden; ⟨convince⟩ überzeugen. **~sion** /-eɪʒn/ n Überredung f; ⟨powers of ~sion⟩ Überredungskunst f; ⟨belief⟩ Glaubensrichtung f

persuasive /pə'sweɪsɪv/ a, **-ly** adv beredsam; ⟨convincing⟩ überzeugend

pert /pɜːt/ a, **-ly** adv keß

pertain /pə'teɪn/ vi **~ to** betreffen; ⟨belong⟩ gehören zu

pertinent /'pɜːtɪnənt/ a relevant (**to** für)

perturb /pə'tɜːb/ vt beunruhigen

peruse /pə'ruːz/ vt lesen

perva|de /pə'veɪd/ vt durchdringen. **~sive** /-sɪv/ a durchdringend

pervers|e /pə'vɜːs/ a eigensinnig. **~ion** /-ɜːʃn/ n Perversion f

pervert¹ /pə'vɜːt/ vt verdrehen; verführen ⟨person⟩

pervert² /'pɜːvɜːt/ n Perverse(r) m

perverted /pə'vɜːtɪd/ a abartig

pessimis|m /'pesɪmɪzm/ n Pessimismus m. **~t** /-mɪst/ n Pessimist m.

~tic /-'mɪstɪk/ a, **-ally** adv pessimistisch

pest /pest/ n Schädling m; ⟨fam: person⟩ Nervensäge f

pester /'pestə(r)/ vt belästigen; **~ s.o. for sth** jdm wegen etw in den Ohren liegen

pesticide /'pestɪsaɪd/ n Schädlingsbekämpfungsmittel nt

pet /pet/ n Haustier nt; ⟨favourite⟩ Liebling m ● vt (pt/pp **petted**) liebkosen

petal /'petl/ n Blütenblatt nt

peter /'piːtə(r)/ vi **~ out** allmählich aufhören; ⟨stream:⟩ versickern

petite /pə'tiːt/ a klein und zierlich

petition /pə'tɪʃn/ n Bittschrift f ● vt eine Bittschrift richten an (+ acc)

pet 'name n Kosename m

petrif|y /'petrɪfaɪ/ vt/i (pt/pp **-ied**) versteinern; **~ied** ⟨frightened⟩ vor Angst wie versteinert

petrol /'petrl/ n Benzin nt

petroleum /pɪ'trəʊlɪəm/ n Petroleum nt

petrol: ~-pump n Zapfsäule f. **~ station** n Tankstelle f. **~ tank** n Benzintank m

'pet shop n Tierhandlung f

petticoat /'petɪkəʊt/ n Unterrock m

petty /'petɪ/ a (**-ier, -iest**) kleinlich. **~ 'cash** n Portokasse f

petulant /'petjʊlənt/ a gekränkt

pew /pjuː/ n [Kirchen]bank f

pewter /'pjuːtə(r)/ n Zinn nt

phantom /'fæntəm/ n Gespenst nt

pharmaceutical /fɑːmə'sjuːtɪkl/ a pharmazeutisch

pharmac|ist /'fɑːməsɪst/ n Apotheker(in) m(f). **~y** n Pharmazie f; ⟨shop⟩ Apotheke f

phase /feɪz/ n Phase f ● vt **~ in/out** allmählich einführen/abbauen

Ph.D. ⟨abbr of **Doctor of Philosophy**⟩ Dr. phil.

pheasant /'feznt/ n Fasan m

phenomen|al /fɪ'nɒmɪnl/ a phänomenal. **~on** n (pl **-na**) Phänomen nt

phial /'faɪəl/ n Fläschchen nt

philanderer /fɪ'lændərə(r)/ n Verführer m

philanthrop|ic /fɪlən'θrɒpɪk/ a menschenfreundlich. **~ist** /fɪ'lænθrəpɪst/ n Philanthrop m

philately /fɪ'lætəlɪ/ n Philatelie f, Briefmarkenkunde f

philharmonic /fɪlɑː'mɒnɪk/ n ⟨orchestra⟩ Philharmoniker pl

Philippines /'fɪlɪpi:nz/ *npl* Philippinen *pl*

philistine /'fɪlɪstaɪn/ *n* Banause *m*

philosoph|er /fɪ'lɒsəfə(r)/ *n* Philosoph *m*. **~ical** /fɪlə'sɒfɪkl/ *a*, **-ly** *adv* philosophisch. **~y** *n* Philosophie *f*

phlegm /flem/ *n* (*Med*) Schleim *m*

phlegmatic /fleg'mætɪk/ *a* phlegmatisch

phobia /'fəʊbɪə/ *n* Phobie *f*

phone /fəʊn/ *n* Telefon *nt*; **be on the ~** Telefon haben; (*be phoning*) telefonieren ● *vt* anrufen ● *vi* telefonieren. **~ back** *vt/i* zurückrufen. **~ book** *n* Telefonbuch *nt*. **~ box** *n* Telefonzelle *f*. **~ card** *n* Telefonkarte *f*. **~-in** *n* (*Radio*) Hörersendung *f*. **~ number** *n* Telefonnummer *f*

phonetic /fə'netɪk/ *a* phonetisch. **~s** *n* Phonetik *f*

phoney /'fəʊnɪ/ *a* (**-ier, -iest**) falsch; (*forged*) gefälscht

phosphorus /'fɒsfərəs/ *n* Phosphor *m*

photo /'fəʊtəʊ/ *n* Foto *nt*, Aufnahme *f*. **~copier** *n* Fotokopiergerät *nt*. **~copy** *n* Fotokopie *f* ● *vt* fotokopieren

photogenic /fəʊtəʊ'dʒenɪk/ *a* fotogen

photograph /'fəʊtəgrɑːf/ *n* Fotografie *f*, Aufnahme *f* ● *vt* fotografieren

photograph|er /fə'tɒgrəfə(r)/ *n* Fotograf(in) *m(f)*. **~ic** /fəʊtə'græfɪk/ *a*, **-ally** *adv* fotografisch. **~y** *n* Fotografie *f*

phrase /freɪz/ *n* Redensart *f* ● *vt* formulieren. **~-book** *n* Sprachführer *m*

physical /'fɪzɪkl/ *a*, **-ly** *adv* körperlich; ⟨*geography, law*⟩ physikalisch. **~ edu'cation** *n* Turnen *nt*

physician /fɪ'zɪʃn/ *n* Arzt *m*/Ärztin *f*

physic|ist /'fɪzɪsɪst/ *n* Physiker(in) *m(f)*. **~s** *n* Physik *f*

physiology /fɪzɪ'ɒlədʒɪ/ *n* Physiologie *f*

physio'therap|ist /fɪzɪəʊ-/ *n* Physiotherapeut(in) *m(f)*. **~y** *n* Physiotherapie *f*

physique /fɪ'ziːk/ *n* Körperbau *m*

pianist /'pɪənɪst/ *n* Klavierspieler(in) *m(f)*; (*professional*) Pianist(in) *m(f)*

piano /pɪ'ænəʊ/ *n* Klavier *nt*

pick[1] /pɪk/ *n* Spitzhacke *f*

pick[2] *n* Auslese *f*; **take one's ~** sich (*dat*) aussuchen ● *vt/i* (*pluck*)

pflücken; (*select*) wählen, sich (*dat*) aussuchen; **~ and choose** wählerisch sein; **~ one's nose** in der Nase bohren; **~ a quarrel** einen Streit anfangen; **~ a hole in sth** ein Loch in etw (*acc*) machen; **~ holes in** (*fam*) kritisieren; **~ at one's food** im Essen herumstochern. **~ on** *vt* wählen; (*fam: find fault with*) herumhacken auf (+ *dat*). **~ up** *vt* in die Hand nehmen; (*off the ground*) aufheben; hochnehmen; (*learn*) lernen; (*acquire*) erwerben; (*buy*) kaufen; (*Teleph*) abnehmen ⟨*receiver*⟩; auffangen ⟨*signal*⟩; (*collect*) abholen; aufnehmen ⟨*passengers*⟩; ⟨*police:*⟩ aufgreifen ⟨*criminal*⟩; sich holen ⟨*illness*⟩; (*fam*) aufgabeln ⟨*girl*⟩. **~ oneself up** aufstehen ● *vi* (*improve*) sich bessern

'pickaxe *n* Spitzhacke *f*

picket /'pɪkɪt/ *n* Streikposten *m* ● *vt* Streikposten aufstellen vor (+ *dat*). **~ line** *n* Streikpostenkette *f*

pickle /'pɪkl/ *n* (*Amer: gherkin*) Essiggurke *f*; **~s** *pl* [Mixed] Pickles *pl* ● *vt* einlegen

pick: **~pocket** *n* Taschendieb *m*. **~-up** *n* (*truck*) Lieferwagen *m*; (*on record-player*) Tonabnehmer *m*

picnic /'pɪknɪk/ *n* Picknick *nt* ● *vi* (*pt/pp* **-nicked**) picknicken

pictorial /pɪk'tɔːrɪəl/ *a* bildlich

picture /'pɪktʃə(r)/ *n* Bild *nt*; (*film*) Film *m*; **as pretty as a ~** bildhübsch; **put s.o. in the ~** (*fig*) jdn ins Bild setzen ● *vt* (*imagine*) sich (*dat*) vorstellen

picturesque /pɪktʃə'resk/ *a* malerisch

pie /paɪ/ *n* Pastete *f*; (*fruit*) Kuchen *m*

piece /piːs/ *n* Stück *nt*; (*of set*) Teil *nt*; (*in game*) Stein *m*; (*Journ*) Artikel *m*; **a ~ of bread/paper** ein Stück Brot/Papier; **a ~ of news/advice** eine Nachricht/ein Rat; **take to ~s** auseinandernehmen ● *vt* **~ together** zusammensetzen; (*fig*) zusammenstückeln. **~meal** *adv* stückweise. **~-work** *n* Akkordarbeit *f*

pier /pɪə(r)/ *n* Pier *m*; (*pillar*) Pfeiler *m*

pierc|e /pɪəs/ *vt* durchstechen; **~e a hole in sth** ein Loch in etw (*acc*) stechen. **~ing** *a* durchdringend

piety /'paɪətɪ/ *n* Frömmigkeit *f*

piffle /'pɪfl/ *n* (*fam*) Quatsch *m*

pig /pɪg/ *n* Schwein *nt*

pigeon /'pɪdʒɪn/ *n* Taube *f*. **~-hole** *n* Fach *nt*

piggy /'pɪgɪ/ n (fam) Schweinchen nt.
~**back** n **a** ~**back** jdn
huckepack tragen. ~ **bank** n Sparschwein nt

pig'headed a (fam) starrköpfig

pigment /'pɪgmənt/ n Pigment nt.
~**ation** /-men'teɪʃn/ n Pigmentie-
rung f

pig: ~**skin** n Schweinsleder nt. ~**sty**
n Schweinestall m. ~**tail** n (fam)
Zopf m

pike /paɪk/ n inv (fish) Hecht m

pilchard /'pɪltʃəd/ n Sardine f

pile¹ /paɪl/ n (of fabric) Flor m

pile² n Haufen m ● vt ~ **sth on to sth**
etw auf etw (acc) häufen. ~ **up** vt
häufen ● vi sich häufen

piles /paɪlz/ npl Hämorrhoiden pl

'pile-up n Massenkarambolage f

pilfer /'pɪlfə(r)/ vt/i stehlen

pilgrim /'pɪlgrɪm/ n Pilger(in) m(f).
~**age** /-ɪdʒ/ n Pilgerfahrt f, Wall-
fahrt f

pill /pɪl/ n Pille f

pillage /'pɪlɪdʒ/ vt plündern

pillar /'pɪlə(r)/ n Säule f. ~**-box** n
Briefkasten m

pillion /'pɪljən/ n Sozius[sitz] m

pillory /'pɪlərɪ/ n Pranger m ● vt (pt/pp
-ied) anprangern

pillow /'pɪləʊ/ n Kopfkissen nt. ~**case**
n Kopfkissenbezug m

pilot /'paɪlət/ n Pilot m; (Naut)
Lotse m ● vt fliegen ⟨plane⟩; lotsen
⟨ship⟩. ~**light** n Zündflamme f

pimp /pɪmp/ n Zuhälter m

pimple /'pɪmpl/ n Pickel m

pin /pɪn/ n Stecknadel f; (Techn) Bolzen m, Stift m; (Med) Nagel m; **I**
have ~**s and needles in my leg** (fam)
mein Bein ist eingeschlafen ● vt
(pt/pp **pinned**) anstecken (**to/on** an
+ acc); (sewing) stecken; (hold
down) festhalten; ~ **sth on s.o.** (fam)
jdm etw anhängen. ~ **up** vt hoch-
stecken; (on wall) anheften,
anschlagen

pinafore /'pɪnəfɔː(r)/ n Schürze f. ~
dress n Kleiderrock m

pincers /'pɪnsəz/ npl Kneifzange f;
(Zool) Scheren pl

pinch /pɪntʃ/ n Kniff m; (of salt) Prise
f; **at a** ~ (fam) zur Not ● vt kneifen,
zwicken; (fam: steal) klauen; ~
one's finger sich (dat) den Finger
klemmen ● vi ⟨shoe:⟩ drücken

'pincushion n Nadelkissen nt

pine¹ /paɪn/ n (tree) Kiefer f

pine² vi ~ **for** sich sehnen nach; ~
away sich verzehren

pineapple /'paɪn-/ n Ananas f

ping /pɪŋ/ n Klingeln nt

'ping-pong n Tischtennis nt

pink /pɪŋk/ a rosa

pinnacle /'pɪnəkl/ n Gipfel m; (on
roof) Turmspitze f

pin: ~**point** vt genau festlegen.
~**stripe** n Nadelstreifen m

pint /paɪnt/ n Pint nt (0,57 l, Amer:
0,47 l)

'pin-up n Pin-up-Girl nt

pioneer /paɪə'nɪə(r)/ n Pionier m ● vt
bahnbrechende Arbeit leisten für

pious /'paɪəs/ a, **-ly** adv fromm

pip¹ /pɪp/ n (seed) Kern m

pip² n (sound) Tonsignal nt

pipe /paɪp/ n Pfeife f; (for water, gas)
Rohr nt ● vt in Rohren leiten; (Cu-
lin) spritzen. ~ **down** vi (fam) den
Mund halten

pipe: ~**-dream** n Luftschloß nt.
~**line** n Pipeline f; **in the** ~**line**
(fam) in Vorbereitung

piper /'paɪpə(r)/ n Pfeifer m

piping /'paɪpɪŋ/ a ~ **hot** kochend heiß

piquant /'piːkənt/ a pikant

pique /piːk/ n **in a fit of** ~ beleidigt

pirate /'paɪərət/ n Pirat m

Pisces /'paɪsiːz/ n (Astr) Fische pl

piss /pɪs/ vi (sl) pissen

pistol /'pɪstl/ n Pistole f

piston /'pɪstən/ n (Techn) Kolben m

pit /pɪt/ n Grube f; (for orchestra)
Orchestergraben m ● vt (pt/pp **pit-
ted**) (fig) messen (**against** mit)

pitch¹ /pɪtʃ/ n (steepness) Schräge f;
(of voice) Stimmlage f; (of sound)
[Ton]höhe f; (Sport) Feld nt; (of
street-trader) Standplatz m; (fig: degree) Grad m ● vt werfen; aufschlagen ⟨tent⟩ ● vi fallen

pitch² n (tar) Pech nt. ~**-'black** a
pechschwarz. ~**-'dark** a stockdunkel

pitcher /'pɪtʃə(r)/ n Krug m

'pitchfork n Heugabel f

piteous /'pɪtɪəs/ a erbärmlich

'pitfall n (fig) Falle f

pith /pɪθ/ n (Bot) Mark nt; (of orange)
weiße Haut f; (fig) Wesentliche(s) nt

pithy /'pɪθɪ/ a (-ier, -iest) (fig)
prägnant

piti|ful /'pɪtɪfl/ a bedauernswert.
~**less** a mitleidslos

pittance /'pɪtns/ n Hungerlohn m

pity /'pɪtɪ/ n Mitleid nt, Erbarmen nt;
[what a] ~! [wie] schade! **take** ~ **on**

sich erbarmen über (+ *acc*) ● *vt*
bemitleiden

pivot /'pɪvət/ *n* Drehzapfen *m*; (*fig*)
Angelpunkt *m* ● *vi* sich drehen (**on**
um)

pixie /'pɪksɪ/ *n* Kobold *m*

pizza /'piːtsə/ *n* Pizza *f*

placard /'plækɑːd/ *n* Plakat *nt*

placate /plə'keɪt/ *vt* beschwichtigen

place /pleɪs/ *n* Platz *m*; (*spot*) Stelle *f*;
(*town, village*) Ort *m*; (*fam: house*)
Haus *nt*; **out of ~** fehl am Platze;
take ~ stattfinden; **all over the ~**
überall ● *vt* setzen; (*upright*) stellen;
(*flat*) legen; (*remember*) unterbringen (*fam*); **~ an order** eine
Bestellung aufgeben; **be ~d** (*in race*)
sich plazieren. **~-mat** *n* Set *nt*

placid /'plæsɪd/ *a* gelassen

plagiar|ism /'pleɪdʒərɪzm/ *n* Plagiat
nt. **~ize** *vt* plagiieren

plague /pleɪg/ *n* Pest *f* ● *vt* plagen

plaice /pleɪs/ *n inv* Scholle *f*

plain /pleɪn/ *a* (**-er, -est**) klar; (*simple*)
einfach; (*not pretty*) nicht hübsch;
(*not patterned*) einfarbig; (*choco-*
late) zartbitter; **in ~ clothes** in Zivil
● *adv* (*simply*) einfach ● *n* Ebene *f*;
(*Knitting*) linke Masche *f*. **~ly** *adv*
klar, deutlich; (*simply*) einfach; (*ob-*
viously) offensichtlich

plaintiff /'pleɪntɪf/ *n* (*Jur*) Kläger(in)
m(f)

plaintive /'pleɪntɪv/ *a*, **-ly** *adv* klagend

plait /plæt/ *n* Zopf *m* ● *vt* flechten

plan /plæn/ *n* Plan *m* ● *vt* (*pt/pp*
planned) planen; (*intend*) vorhaben

plane¹ /pleɪn/ *n* (*tree*) Platane *f*

plane² *n* Flugzeug *nt*; (*Geom & fig*)
Ebene *f*

plane³ *n* (*Techn*) Hobel *m* ● *vt* hobeln

planet /'plænɪt/ *n* Planet *m*

plank /plæŋk/ *n* Brett *nt*; (*thick*)
Planke *f*

planning /'plænɪŋ/ *n* Planung *f*. **~
permission** *n* Baugenehmigung *f*

plant /plɑːnt/ *n* Pflanze *f*; (*Techn*)
Anlage *f*; (*factory*) Werk *nt* ● *vt*
pflanzen; (*place in position*) setzen;
~ oneself in front of s.o. sich vor jdn
hinstellen. **~ation** /plæn'teɪʃn/ *n*
Plantage *f*

plaque /plɑːk/ *n* [Gedenk]tafel *f*; (*on
teeth*) Zahnbelag *m*

plasma /'plæzmə/ *n* Plasma *nt*

plaster /'plɑːstə(r)/ *n* Verputz *m*; (*sticking ~*) Pflaster *nt*; **~ [of Paris]** Gips

m ● *vt* verputzen (*wall*); (*cover*) bedecken mit. **~ed** *a* (*sl*) besoffen.
~er *n* Gipser *m*

plastic /'plæstɪk/ *n* Kunststoff *m*,
Plastik *nt* ● *a* Kunststoff-, Plastik-;
(*malleable*) formbar, plastisch

Plasticine (P) /'plæstɪsiːn/ *n* Knet-
masse *f*

plastic 'surgery *n* plastische Chirurgie *f*

plate /pleɪt/ *n* Teller *m*; (*flat sheet*)
Platte *f*; (*with name, number*) Schild
nt; (*gold and silverware*) vergoldete/
versilberte Ware *f*; (*in book*) Tafel *f*
● *vt* (*with gold*) vergolden; (*with
silver*) versilbern

plateau /'plætəʊ/ *n* (*pl* **-x** /-əʊz/)
Hochebene *f*

platform /'plætfɔːm/ *n* Plattform *f*;
(*stage*) Podium *nt*; (*Rail*) Bahnsteig
m; **~ 5** Gleis 5

platinum /'plætɪnəm/ *n* Platin *nt*

platitude /'plætɪtjuːd/ *n* Platitüde *f*

platonic /plə'tɒnɪk/ *a* platonisch

platoon /plə'tuːn/ *n* (*Mil*) Zug *m*

platter /'plætə(r)/ *n* Platte *f*

plausible /'plɔːzəbl/ *a* plausibel

play /pleɪ/ *n* Spiel *nt*; [Theater]stück
nt; (*Radio*) Hörspiel *nt*; (*TV*) Fern-
sehspiel *nt*; **~ on words** Wortspiel *nt*
● *vt/i* spielen; ausspielen (*card*); **~
safe** sichergehen. **~ down** *vt* herun-
terspielen. **~ up** *vi* (*fam*) Mätzchen
machen

play: ~boy *n* Playboy *m*. **~er** *n*
Spieler(in) *m(f)*. **~ful** *a*, **-ly** *adv*
verspielt. **~ground** *n* Spielplatz *m*;
(*Sch*) Schulhof *m*. **~group** *n* Kindergarten *m*

playing: ~-card *n* Spielkarte *f*. **~-
field** *n* Sportplatz *m*

play: ~mate *n* Spielkamerad *m*. **~-
pen** *n* Laufstall *m*, Laufgitter *nt*.
~thing *n* Spielzeug *nt*. **~wright**
/-raɪt/ *n* Dramatiker *m*

plc *abbr* (**public limited company**) ≈
GmbH

plea /pliː/ *n* Bitte *f*; **make a ~ for**
bitten um

plead /pliːd/ *vt* vorschützen; (*Jur*)
vertreten (*case*) ● *vi* flehen (**for** um);
~ guilty sich schuldig bekennen; **~
with s.o.** jdn anflehen

pleasant /'pleznt/ *a* angenehm; (*person*) nett. **~ly** *adv* angenehm; (*say,
smile*) freundlich

pleas|e /pliːz/ *adv* bitte ● *vt* gefallen
(+ *dat*); **~e s.o.** jdm eine Freude
machen; **~e oneself** tun, was man

will. ~ed *a* erfreut; **be** ~ed **with/ about sth** sich über etw (*acc*) freuen. ~ing *a* erfreulich

pleasurable /'pleʒərəbl/ *a* angenehm

pleasure /'pleʒə(r)/ *n* Vergnügen *nt*; (*joy*) Freude *f*; **with** ~ gern[e]

pleat /pli:t/ *n* Falte *f* • *vt* fälteln. ~ed 'skirt *n* Faltenrock *m*

plebiscite /'plebisit/ *n* Volksabstimmung *f*

pledge /pledʒ/ *n* Pfand *nt*; (*promise*) Versprechen *nt* • *vt* verpfänden; versprechen

plentiful /'plentifl/ *a* reichlich; **be** ~ reichlich vorhanden sein

plenty /'plenti/ *n* eine Menge; (*enough*) reichlich; ~ **of money/ people** viel Geld/viele Leute

pleurisy /'pluərəsi/ *n* Rippenfellentzündung *f*

pliable /'plaɪəbl/ *a* biegsam

pliers /'plaɪəz/ *npl* [Flach]zange *f*

plight /plaɪt/ *n* [Not]lage *f*

plimsolls /'plimsəlz/ *npl* Turnschuhe *pl*

plinth /plɪnθ/ *n* Sockel *m*

plod /plɒd/ *vi* (*pt/pp* **plodded**) trotten; (*work hard*) sich abmühen

plonk /plɒŋk/ *n* (*fam*) billiger Wein *m*

plot /plɒt/ *n* Komplott *nt*; (*of novel*) Handlung *f*; ~ **of land** Stück *nt* Land • *vt* einzeichnen • *vi* ein Komplott schmieden

plough /plaʊ/ *n* Pflug *m* • *vt/i* pflügen. ~ **back** *vt* (*Comm*) wieder investieren

ploy /plɔɪ/ *n* (*fam*) Trick *m*

pluck /plʌk/ *n* Mut *m* • *vt* zupfen; rupfen ⟨*bird*⟩; pflücken ⟨*flower*⟩; ~ **up courage** Mut fassen

plucky /'plʌki/ *a* (-ier, -iest) tapfer, mutig

plug /plʌg/ *n* Stöpsel *m*; (*wood*) Zapfen *m*; (*cotton wool*) Bausch *m*; (*Electr*) Stecker *m*; (*Auto*) Zündkerze *f*; (*fam: advertisement*) Schleichwerbung *f* • *vt* zustopfen; (*fam: advertise*) Schleichwerbung machen für. ~ **in** *vt* (*Electr*) einstecken

plum /plʌm/ *n* Pflaume *f*

plumage /'plu:mɪdʒ/ *n* Gefieder *nt*

plumb /plʌm/ *n* Lot *nt* • *adv* lotrecht • *vt* loten. ~ **in** *vt* installieren

plumb|er /'plʌmə(r)/ *n* Klempner *m*. ~ing *n* Wasserleitungen *pl*

'plumb-line *n* [Blei]lot *nt*

plume /plu:m/ *n* Feder *f*

plummet /'plʌmɪt/ *vi* herunterstürzen

plump /plʌmp/ *a* (-er, -est) mollig, rundlich • *vt* ~ **for** wählen

plunder /'plʌndə(r)/ *n* Beute *f* • *vt* plündern

plunge /plʌndʒ/ *n* Sprung *m*; **take the** ~ (*fam*) den Schritt wagen • *vt/i* tauchen

plu'perfect /plu:-/ *n* Plusquamperfekt *nt*

plural /'pluərl/ *a* pluralisch • *n* Mehrzahl *f*, Plural *m*

plus /plʌs/ *prep* plus (+ *dat*) • *a* Plus- • *n* Pluszeichen *nt*; (*advantage*) Plus *nt*

plush[y] /'plʌʃ[ɪ]/ *a* luxuriös

ply /plaɪ/ *vt* (*pt/pp* **plied**) ausüben ⟨*trade*⟩; ~ **s.o. with drink** jdm ein Glas nach dem anderen eingießen. ~**wood** *n* Sperrholz *nt*

p.m. *adv* (*abbr of post meridiem*) nachmittags

pneumatic /nju:'mætɪk/ *a* pneumatisch. ~ '**drill** *n* Preßlufthammer *m*

pneumonia /nju:'məʊnɪə/ *n* Lungenentzündung *f*

poach /pəʊtʃ/ *vt* (*Culin*) pochieren; (*steal*) wildern. ~**er** *n* Wilddieb *m*

pocket /'pɒkɪt/ *n* Tasche *f*; ~ **of resistance** Widerstandsnest *nt*; **be out of** ~ [an einem Geschäft] verlieren • *vt* einstecken. ~**-book** *n* Notizbuch *nt*; (*wallet*) Brieftasche *f*. ~**money** *n* Taschengeld *nt*

pock-marked /'pɒk-/ *a* pockennarbig

pod /pɒd/ *n* Hülse *f*

podgy /'pɒdʒɪ/ *a* (-ier, -iest) dick

poem /'pəʊɪm/ *n* Gedicht *nt*

poet /'pəʊɪt/ *n* Dichter(in) *m(f)*. ~**ic** /-'etɪk/ *a* dichterisch

poetry /'pəʊɪtrɪ/ *n* Dichtung *f*

poignant /'pɔɪnjənt/ *a* ergreifend

point /pɔɪnt/ *n* Punkt *m*; (*sharp end*) Spitze *f*; (*meaning*) Sinn *m*; (*purpose*) Zweck *m*; (*Electr*) Steckdose *f*; ~**s** *pl* (*Rail*) Weiche *f*; ~ **of view** Standpunkt *m*; **good/bad** ~**s** gute/schlechte Seiten; **what is the** ~? wozu? **the** ~ **is** es geht darum; **I don't see the** ~ das sehe ich nicht ein; **up to a** ~ bis zu einem gewissen Grade; **be on the** ~ **of doing sth** im Begriff sein, etw zu tun • *vt* richten (**at** auf + *acc*); ausfugen ⟨*brickwork*⟩ • *vi* deuten (**at/to** auf + *acc*); (*with finger*) mit dem Finger zeigen. ~ **out** *vt* zeigen auf (+ *acc*); ~ **sth out to s.o.** jdn auf etw (*acc*) hinweisen

point-'blank *a* aus nächster Entfernung; (*fig*) rundweg

point|ed /'pɔɪntɪd/ *a* spitz; ⟨*question*⟩ gezielt. **~er** *n* (*hint*) Hinweis *m*. **~less** *a* zwecklos, sinnlos

poise /pɔɪz/ *n* Haltung *f*. **~d** *a* (*confident*) selbstsicher; **~d to** bereit zu

poison /'pɔɪzn/ *n* Gift *nt* ● *vt* vergiften. **~ous** *a* giftig

poke /pəʊk/ *n* Stoß *m* ● *vt* stoßen; schüren ⟨*fire*⟩; (*put*) stecken; **~ fun at** sich lustig machen über (+ *acc*)

poker[1] /'pəʊkə(r)/ *n* Schüreisen *nt*

poker[2] *n* (*Cards*) Poker *nt*

poky /'pəʊkɪ/ *a* (**-ier, -iest**) eng

Poland /'pəʊlənd/ *n* Polen *nt*

polar /'pəʊlə(r)/ *a* Polar-. **~'bear** *n* Eisbär *m*. **~ize** *vt* polarisieren

Pole /pəʊl/ *n* Pole *m*/Polin *f*

pole[1] *n* Stange *f*

pole[2] *n* (*Geog, Electr*) Pol *m*

'polecat *n* Iltis *m*

'pole-star *n* Polarstern *m*

'pole-vault *n* Stabhochsprung *m*

police /pə'li:s/ *npl* Polizei *f* ● *vt* polizeilich kontrollieren

police: ~man *n* Polizist *m*. **~ state** *n* Polizeistaat *m*. **~ station** *n* Polizeiwache *f*. **~woman** *n* Polizistin *f*

policy[1] /'pɒlɪsɪ/ *n* Politik *f*

policy[2] *n* (*insurance*) Police *f*

polio /'pəʊlɪəʊ/ *n* Kinderlähmung *f*

Polish /'pəʊlɪʃ/ *a* polnisch

polish /'pɒlɪʃ/ *n* (*shine*) Glanz *m*; (*for shoes*) [Schuh]creme *f*; (*for floor*) Bohnerwachs *m*; (*for furniture*) Politur *f*; (*for silver*) Putzmittel *nt*; (*for nails*) Lack *m*; (*fig*) Schliff *m* ● *vt* polieren; bohnern ⟨*floor*⟩. **~ off** *vt* (*fam*) verputzen ⟨*food*⟩; erledigen ⟨*task*⟩

polisher /'pɒlɪʃə(r)/ *n* (*machine*) Poliermaschine *f*; (*for floor*) Bohnermaschine *f*

polite /pə'laɪt/ *a*, **-ly** *adv* höflich. **~ness** *n* Höflichkeit *f*

politic /'pɒlɪtɪk/ *a* ratsam

politic|al /pə'lɪtɪkl/ *a*, **-ly** *adv* politisch. **~ian** /pɒlɪ'tɪʃn/ *n* Politiker(in) *m(f)*

politics /'pɒlətɪks/ *n* Politik *f*

polka /'pɒlkə/ *n* Polka *f*

poll /pəʊl/ *n* Abstimmung *f*; (*election*) Wahl *f*; **[opinion] ~** [Meinungs]umfrage *f*; **go to the ~s** wählen ● *vt* erhalten ⟨*votes*⟩

pollen /'pɒlən/ *n* Blütenstaub *m*, Pollen *m*

polling /'pəʊlɪŋ/ **:~-booth** *n* Wahlkabine *f*. **~-station** *n* Wahllokal *nt*

'poll tax *n* Kopfsteuer *f*

pollutant /pə'lu:tənt/ *n* Schadstoff *m*

pollut|e /pə'lu:t/ *vt* verschmutzen. **~ion** /-u:ʃn/ *n* Verschmutzung *f*

polo /'pəʊləʊ/ *n* Polo *nt*. **~-neck** *n* Rollkragen *m*. **~ shirt** *n* Polohemd *nt*

polyester /pɒlɪ'estə(r)/ *n* Polyester *m*

polystyrene (P) /pɒlɪ'staɪri:n/ *n* Polystyrol *nt*; (*for packing*) Styropor (P) *nt*

polytechnic /pɒlɪ'teknɪk/ *n* ≈ technische Hochschule *f*

polythene /'pɒlɪθi:n/ *n* Polyäthylen *nt*. **~ bag** *n* Plastiktüte *f*

polyun'saturated *a* mehrfachungesättigt

pomegranate /'pɒmɪgrænɪt/ *n* Granatapfel *m*

pomp /pɒmp/ *n* Pomp *m*

pompon /'pɒmpɒn/ *n* Pompon *m*

pompous /'pɒmpəs/ *a*, **-ly** *adv* großspurig

pond /pɒnd/ *n* Teich *m*

ponder /'pɒndə(r)/ *vi* nachdenken

ponderous /'pɒndərəs/ *a* schwerfällig

pong /pɒŋ/ *n* (*fam*) Mief *m*

pony /'pəʊnɪ/ *n* Pony *nt*. **~-tail** *n* Pferdeschwanz *m*. **~-trekking** *n* Ponyreiten *nt*

poodle /'pu:dl/ *n* Pudel *m*

pool[1] /pu:l/ *n* [Schwimm]becken *nt*; (*pond*) Teich *m*; (*of blood*) Lache *f*

pool[2] *n* (*common fund*) [gemeinsame] Kasse *f*; **~s** *pl* (*Fußball*)toto *nt* ● *vt* zusammenlegen

poor /pʊə(r)/ *a* (**-er, -est**) arm; (*not good*) schlecht; **in ~ health** nicht gesund ● *npl* **the ~** die Armen. **~ly** *a* **be ~ly** krank sein ● *adv* ärmlich; (*badly*) schlecht

pop[1] /pɒp/ *n* Knall *m*; (*drink*) Brause *f* ● *v* (*pt/pp* **popped**) ● *vt* (*fam:* **put**) stecken (**in** in + *acc*) ● *vi* knallen; (*burst*) platzen. **~ in** *vi* (*fam*) reinschauen. **~ out** *vi* (*fam*) kurz rausgehen

pop[2] *n* (*fam*) Popmusik *f*, Pop *m* ● *attrib* Pop-

'popcorn *n* Puffmais *m*

pope /pəʊp/ *n* Papst *m*

poplar /'pɒplə(r)/ *n* Pappel *f*

poppy /'pɒpɪ/ *n* Mohn *m*

popular /'pɒpjʊlə(r)/ *a* beliebt, populär; ⟨*belief*⟩ volkstümlich. **~ity** /-'lærətɪ/ *n* Beliebtheit *f*, Popularität *f*

populat|e /'pɒpjʊleɪt/ *vt* bevölkern. **~ion** /-'leɪʃn/ *n* Bevölkerung *f*

porcelain /'pɔːsəlɪn/ *n* Porzellan *nt*

porch /pɔːtʃ/ *n* Vorbau *m*; (*Amer*) Veranda *f*

porcupine /'pɔːkjʊpaɪn/ *n* Stachelschwein *nt*

pore¹ /pɔː(r)/ *n* Pore *f*

pore² *vi* **~ over** studieren

pork /pɔːk/ *n* Schweinefleisch *nt*

porn /pɔːn/ *n* (*fam*) Porno *m*

pornograph|ic /pɔːnə'græfɪk/ *a* pornographisch. **~y** /-'nɒgrəfɪ/ *n* Pornographie *f*

porous /'pɔːrəs/ *a* porös

porpoise /'pɔːpəs/ *n* Tümmler *m*

porridge /'pɒrɪdʒ/ *n* Haferbrei *m*

port¹ /pɔːt/ *n* Hafen *m*; (*town*) Hafenstadt *f*

port² *n* (*Naut*) Backbord *nt*

port³ *n* (*wine*) Portwein *m*

portable /'pɔːtəbl/ *a* tragbar

porter /'pɔːtə(r)/ *n* Portier *m*; (*for luggage*) Gepäckträger *m*

portfolio /pɔːt'fəʊlɪəʊ/ *n* Mappe *f*; (*Comm*) Portefeuille *nt*

'porthole *n* Bullauge *nt*

portion /'pɔːʃn/ *n* Portion *f*; (*part, share*) Teil *nt*

portly /'pɔːtlɪ/ *a* (**-ier, -iest**) beleibt

portrait /'pɔːtrɪt/ *n* Porträt *nt*

portray /pɔː'treɪ/ *vt* darstellen. **~al** *n* Darstellung *f*

Portug|al /'pɔːtjʊgl/ *n* Portugal *nt*. **~uese** /-'giːz/ *a* portugiesisch ● *n* Portugiese *m*/-giesin *f*

pose /pəʊz/ *n* Pose *f* ● *vt* aufwerfen ⟨*problem*⟩; stellen ⟨*question*⟩ ● *vi* posieren; (*for painter*) Modell stehen; **~ as** sich ausgeben als

posh /pɒʃ/ *a* (*fam*) feudal

position /pə'zɪʃn/ *n* Platz *m*; (*posture*) Haltung *f*; (*job*) Stelle *f*; (*situation*) Lage *f*, Situation *f*; (*status*) Stellung *f* ● *vt* plazieren; **~ oneself** sich stellen

positive /'pɒzətɪv/ *a*, **-ly** *adv* positiv; (*definite*) eindeutig; (*real*) ausgesprochen ● *n* Positiv *nt*

possess /pə'zes/ *vt* besitzen. **~ion** /pə'zeʃn/ *n* Besitz *m*; **~ions** *pl* Sachen *pl*

possess|ive /pə'zesɪv/ *a* Possessiv-; **be ~ive** zu sehr an jdm hängen. **~or** *n* Besitzer *m*

possibility /pɒsə'bɪlətɪ/ *n* Möglichkeit *f*

possib|le /'pɒsəbl/ *a* möglich. **~ly** *adv* möglicherweise; **not ~ly** unmöglich

post¹ /pəʊst/ *n* (*pole*) Pfosten *m* ● *vt* anschlagen ⟨*notice*⟩

post² *n* (*place of duty*) Posten *m*; (*job*) Stelle *f* ● *vt* postieren; (*transfer*) versetzen

post³ *n* (*mail*) Post *f*; **by ~** mit der Post ● *vt* aufgeben ⟨*letter*⟩; (*send by ~*) mit der Post schicken; **keep s.o. ~ed** jdn auf dem laufenden halten

postage /'pəʊstɪdʒ/ *n* Porto *nt*. **~ stamp** *n* Briefmarke *f*

postal /'pəʊstl/ *a* Post-. **~ order** *n* ≈ Geldanweisung *f*

post: ~-box *n* Briefkasten *m*. **~card** *n* Postkarte *f*; (*picture*) Ansichtskarte *f*. **~code** *n* Postleitzahl *f*. **~-'date** *vt* vordatieren

poster /'pəʊstə(r)/ *n* Plakat *nt*

posterior /pɒ'stɪərɪə(r)/ *a* hintere(r,s) ● *n* (*fam*) Hintern *m*

posterity /pɒ'sterətɪ/ *n* Nachwelt *f*

posthumous /'pɒstjʊməs/ *a*, **-ly** *adv* postum

post: ~man *n* Briefträger *m*. **~mark** *n* Poststempel *m*

post-mortem /-'mɔːtəm/ *n* Obduktion *f*

'post office *n* Post *f*

postpone /pəʊst'pəʊn/ *vt* aufschieben; **~ until** verschieben auf (+ *acc*). **~ment** *n* Verschiebung *f*

postscript /'pəʊstskrɪpt/ *n* Nachschrift *f*

posture /'pɒstʃə(r)/ *n* Haltung *f*

post-'war *a* Nachkriegs-

posy /'pəʊzɪ/ *n* Sträußchen *nt*

pot /pɒt/ *n* Topf *m*; (*for tea, coffee*) Kanne *f*; **~s of money** (*fam*) eine Menge Geld; **go to ~** (*fam*) herunterkommen

potassium /pə'tæsɪəm/ *n* Kalium *nt*

potato /pə'teɪtəʊ/ *n* (*pl* **-es**) Kartoffel *f*

poten|cy /'pəʊtənsɪ/ *n* Stärke *f*. **~t** *a* stark

potential /pə'tenʃl/ *a*, **-ly** *adv* potentiell ● *n* Potential *nt*

pot: ~-hole *n* Höhle *f*; (*in road*) Schlagloch *nt*. **~-holer** *n* Höhlenforscher *m*. **~-shot** *n* **take a ~-shot at** schießen auf (+ *acc*)

potted /'pɒtɪd/ *a* eingemacht; (*shortened*) gekürzt. **~ 'plant** *n* Topfpflanze *f*

potter¹ /'pɒtə(r)/ *vi* **~ [about]** herumwerkeln

potter² n Töpfer(in) m(f). ~y n Töpferei f; (articles) Töpferwaren pl

potty /'pɒtɪ/ a (-ier, -iest) (fam) verrückt ● n Töpfchen nt

pouch /paʊtʃ/ n Beutel m

pouffe /puːf/ n Sitzkissen nt

poultry /'pəʊltrɪ/ n Geflügel nt

pounce /paʊns/ vi zuschlagen; ~ **on** sich stürzen auf (+ acc)

pound¹ /paʊnd/ n (money & 0,454 kg) Pfund nt

pound² vt hämmern ● vi ⟨heart:⟩ hämmern; (run heavily) stampfen

pour /pɔː(r)/ vt gießen; einschenken ⟨drink⟩ ● vi strömen; (with rain) gießen. ~ **out** vi ausströmen ● vt ausschütten; einschenken ⟨drink⟩

pout /paʊt/ vi einen Schmollmund machen

poverty /'pɒvətɪ/ n Armut f

powder /'paʊdə(r)/ n Pulver nt; (cosmetic) Puder m ● vt pudern. ~y a pulverig

power /'paʊə(r)/ n Macht f; (strength) Kraft f; (Electr) Strom m; (nuclear) Energie f; (Math) Potenz f. ~ **cut** n Stromsperre f. ~ed a betrieben (by mit); ~ed by electricity mit Elektroantrieb. ~ful a mächtig; (strong) stark. ~less a machtlos. ~station n Kraftwerk nt

practicable /'præktɪkəbl/ a durchführbar, praktikabel

practical /'præktɪkl/ a, -ly adv praktisch. ~ 'joke n Streich m

practice /'præktɪs/ n Praxis f; (custom) Brauch m; (habit) Gewohnheit f; (exercise) Übung f; (Sport) Training nt; in ~ (in reality) in der Praxis; out of ~ außer Übung; put into ~ ausführen

practise /'præktɪs/ vt üben; (carry out) praktizieren; ausüben ⟨profession⟩ ● vi üben; ⟨doctor:⟩ praktizieren. ~d a geübt

pragmatic /præg'mætɪk/ a, ~ally adv pragmatisch

praise /preɪz/ n Lob nt ● vt loben. ~worthy a lobenswert

pram /præm/ n Kinderwagen m

prance /prɑːns/ vi herumhüpfen; ⟨horse:⟩ tänzeln

prank /præŋk/ n Streich m

prattle /'prætl/ vi plappern

prawn /prɔːn/ n Garnele f, Krabbe f. ~ 'cocktail n Krabbencocktail m

pray /preɪ/ vi beten. ~er /preə(r)/ n Gebet nt; ~ers pl (service) Andacht f

preach /priːtʃ/ vt/i predigen. ~er n Prediger m

preamble /priː'æmbl/ n Einleitung f

pre-ar'range /priː-/ vt im voraus arrangieren

precarious /prɪ'keərɪəs/ a, -ly adv unsicher

precaution /prɪ'kɔːʃn/ n Vorsichtsmaßnahme f; as a ~ zur Vorsicht. ~ary a Vorsichts-

precede /prɪ'siːd/ vt vorangehen (+ dat)

preceden|ce /'presɪdəns/ n Vorrang m. ~t n Präzedenzfall m

preceding /prɪ'siːdɪŋ/ a vorhergehend

precinct /'priːsɪŋkt/ n Bereich m; (traffic-free) Fußgängerzone f; (Amer: district) Bezirk m

precious /'preʃəs/ a kostbar; ⟨style⟩ preziös ● adv (fam) ~ little recht wenig

precipice /'presɪpɪs/ n Steilabfall m

precipitate¹ /prɪ'sɪpɪtət/ a voreilig

precipitat|e² /prɪ'sɪpɪteɪt/ vt schleudern; (fig: accelerate) beschleunigen. ~ion /-'teɪʃn/ n (Meteorol) Niederschlag m

précis /'preɪsiː/ n (pl précis /-siːz/) Zusammenfassung f

precis|e /prɪ'saɪs/ a, -ly adv genau. ~ion /-'sɪʒn/ n Genauigkeit f

preclude /prɪ'kluːd/ vt ausschließen

precocious /prɪ'kəʊʃəs/ a frühreif

pre|con'ceived /priː-/ a vorgefaßt. ~con'ception n vorgefaßte Meinung f

precursor /priː'kɜːsə(r)/ n Vorläufer m

predator /'predətə(r)/ n Raubtier nt

predecessor /'priːdɪsesə(r)/ n Vorgänger(in) m(f)

predicament /prɪ'dɪkəmənt/ n Zwangslage f

predicat|e /'predɪkət/ n (Gram) Prädikat nt. ~ive /prɪ'dɪkətɪv/ a, -ly adv prädikativ

predict /prɪ'dɪkt/ vt voraussagen. ~able /-əbl/ a voraussehbar; ⟨person⟩ berechenbar. ~ion /-'dɪkʃn/ n Voraussage f

pre'domin|ant /prɪ-/ a vorherrschend. ~antly adv hauptsächlich, überwiegend. ~ate vi vorherrschen

pre-'eminent /priː-/ a hervorragend

pre-empt /priː'empt/ vt zuvorkommen (+ dat)

preen /priːn/ vt putzen; ~ oneself (fig) selbstgefällig tun

pre|fab /'priː:fæb/ n (fam) [einfaches] Fertighaus nt. ~**'fabricated** a vorgefertigt

preface /'prefɪs/ n Vorwort nt

prefect /'priː:fekt/ n Präfekt m

prefer /prɪ'fɜː:(r)/ vt (pt/pp **preferred**) vorziehen; I ~ **to walk** ich gehe lieber zu Fuß; I ~ **wine** ich trinke lieber Wein

prefera|ble /'prefərəbl/ a be ~**ble** vorzuziehen sein (**to** dat). ~**bly** adv vorzugsweise

preferen|ce /'prefərəns/ n Vorzug m. ~**tial** /-'renʃl/ a bevorzugt

prefix /'priː:fɪks/ n Vorsilbe f

pregnan|cy /'pregnənsɪ/ n Schwangerschaft f. ~**t** a schwanger; ⟨animal⟩ trächtig

prehi'storic /priː-/ a prähistorisch

prejudice /'predʒʊdɪs/ n Vorurteil nt; (bias) Voreingenommenheit f ● vt einnehmen (**against** gegen). ~**d** a voreingenommen

preliminary /prɪ'lɪmɪnərɪ/ a Vor-

prelude /'prelju:d/ n Vorspiel nt

pre-'marital a vorehelich

premature /'premətjʊə(r)/ a vorzeitig; ⟨birth⟩ Früh-. ~**ly** adv zu früh

pre'meditated /priː-/ a vorsätzlich

premier /'premɪə(r)/ a führend ● n (Pol) Premier[minister] m

première /'premɪeə(r)/ n Premiere f

premises /'premɪsɪz/ npl Räumlichkeiten pl; **on the** ~ im Haus

premiss /'premɪs/ n Prämisse f

premium /'priː:mɪəm/ n Prämie f; **be at a** ~ hoch im Kurs stehen

premonition /premə'nɪʃn/ n Vorahnung f

preoccupied /prɪ'ɒkjʊpaɪd/ a [in Gedanken] beschäftigt

prep /prep/ n (Sch) Hausaufgaben pl

pre-'packed /priː-/ a abgepackt

preparation /prepə'reɪʃn/ n Vorbereitung f; (substance) Präparat nt

preparatory /prɪ'pærətrɪ/ a Vor- ● adv ~ **to** vor (+ dat)

prepare /prɪ'peə(r)/ vt vorbereiten; anrichten ⟨meal⟩ ● vi sich vorbereiten (**for** auf + acc); ~**d to** bereit zu

pre'pay /priː-/ vt (pt/pp -**paid**) im voraus bezahlen

preposition /prepə'zɪʃn/ n Präposition f

prepossessing /priː:pə'zesɪŋ/ a ansprechend

preposterous /prɪ'pɒstərəs/ a absurd

prerequisite /priː'rekwɪzɪt/ n Voraussetzung f

prerogative /prɪ'rɒgətɪv/ n Vorrecht nt

Presbyterian /prezbɪ'tɪərɪən/ a presbyterianisch ● n Presbyterianer(in) m(f)

prescribe /prɪ'skraɪb/ vt vorschreiben; (Med) verschreiben

prescription /prɪ'skrɪpʃn/ n (Med) Rezept nt

presence /'prezns/ n Anwesenheit f, Gegenwart f; ~ **of mind** Geistesgegenwart f

present[1] /'preznt/ a gegenwärtig; **be** ~ anwesend sein; (occur) vorkommen ● n Gegenwart f; (Gram) Präsens nt; **at** ~ zur Zeit; **for the** ~ vorläufig

present[2] n (gift) Geschenk nt

present[3] /prɪ'zent/ vt überreichen; (show) zeigen; vorlegen ⟨cheque⟩; (introduce) vorstellen; ~ **s.o. with sth** jdm etw überreichen. ~**able** /-əbl/ a **be** ~**able** sich zeigen lassen können

presentation /prezn'teɪʃn/ n Überreichung f. ~ **ceremony** n Verleihungszeremonie f

presently /'prezntlɪ/ adv nachher; (Amer: now) zur Zeit

preservation /prezə'veɪʃn/ n Erhaltung f

preservative /prɪ'zɜː:vətɪv/ n Konservierungsmittel nt

preserve /prɪ'zɜː:v/ vt erhalten; (Culin) konservieren; (bottle) einmachen ● n (Hunting & fig) Revier nt; (jam) Konfitüre f

preside /prɪ'zaɪd/ vi den Vorsitz haben (**over** bei)

presidency /'prezɪdənsɪ/ n Präsidentschaft f

president /'prezɪdnt/ n Präsident m; (Amer: chairman) Vorsitzende(r) m/f. ~**ial** /-'denʃl/ a Präsidenten-; ⟨election⟩ Präsidentschafts-

press /pres/ n Presse f ● vt/i drücken; drücken auf (+ acc) ⟨button⟩; pressen ⟨flower⟩; (iron) bügeln; (urge) bedrängen; ~ **for** drängen auf (+ acc); **be** ~**ed for time** in Zeitdruck sein. ~ **on** vi weitergehen/-fahren; (fig) weitermachen

press: ~ **cutting** n Zeitungsausschnitt m. ~**ing** a dringend. ~**-stud** n Druckknopf m. ~**-up** n Liegestütz m

pressure /'preʃə(r)/ n Druck m ● vt
= **pressurize**. **~-cooker** n Schnell-
kochtopf m. **~ group** n Interessen-
gruppe f

pressurize /'preʃəraɪz/ vt Druck
ausüben auf (+ acc). **~d** a Druck-

prestig|e /pre'stiːʒ/ n Prestige nt.
~ious /-'stɪdʒəs/ a Prestige-

presumably /prɪ'zjuːməblɪ/ adv vermutlich

presume /prɪ'zjuːm/ vt vermuten; **~
to do sth** sich (dat) anmaßen, etw zu
tun ● vi **~ on** ausnutzen

presumpt|ion /prɪ'zʌmpʃn/ n Ver-
mutung f; (boldness) Anmaßung f.
~uous /-'zʌmptjʊəs/ a, **-ly** adv
anmaßend

presup'pose /priː-/ vt voraussetzen

pretence /prɪ'tens/ n Verstellung f;
(pretext) Vorwand m; **it's all ~** das
ist alles gespielt

pretend /prɪ'tend/ vt (claim) vorgeben; **~ that** so tun, als ob; **~ to be**
sich ausgeben als

pretentious /prɪ'tenʃəs/ a protzig

pretext /'priːtekst/ n Vorwand m

pretty /'prɪtɪ/ a (-ier, -iest), **~ily** adv
hübsch ● adv (fam: fairly) ziemlich

pretzel /'pretsl/ n Brezel f

prevail /prɪ'veɪl/ vi siegen; ⟨custom:⟩
vorherrschen; **~ on s.o. to do sth**
jdn dazu bringen, etw zu tun

prevalen|ce /'prevələns/ n Häufig-
keit f. **~t** a vorherrschend

prevent /prɪ'vent/ vt verhindern,
verhüten; **~ s.o. [from] doing sth**
jdn daran hindern, etw zu tun.
~able /-əbl/ a vermeidbar. **~ion**
/-enʃn/ n Verhinderung f, Verhü-
tung f. **~ive** /-ɪv/ a vorbeugend

preview /'priːvjuː/ n Voraufführung f

previous /'priːvɪəs/ a vorhergehend;
~ to vor (+ dat). **~ly** adv vorher,
früher

pre-'war /priː-/ a Vorkriegs-

prey /preɪ/ n Beute f; **bird of ~** Raub-
vogel m ● vi **~ on** Jagd machen auf
(+ acc); **~ on s.o.'s mind** jdm schwer
auf der Seele liegen

price /praɪs/ n Preis m ● vt (Comm)
auszeichnen. **~less** a unschätzbar;
(fig) unbezahlbar

prick /prɪk/ n Stich m ● vt/i stechen;
~ up one's ears die Ohren spitzen

prickl|e /'prɪkl/ n Stachel m; (thorn)
Dorn m. **~y** a stachelig; ⟨sensation⟩
stechend

pride /praɪd/ n Stolz m; (arrogance)
Hochmut m; (of lions) Rudel nt ● vt
~ oneself on stolz sein auf (+ acc)

priest /priːst/ n Priester m

prig /prɪg/ n Tugendbold m

prim /prɪm/ a (primmer, primmest)
prüde

primarily /'praɪmərɪlɪ/ adv hauptsächlich, in erster Linie

primary /'praɪmərɪ/ a Haupt-. **~
school** n Grundschule f

prime[1] /praɪm/ a Haupt-; (first-rate)
erstklassig ● n **be in one's ~** in den
besten Jahren sein

prime[2] vt scharf machen ⟨bomb⟩;
grundieren ⟨surface⟩; (fig) in-
struieren

Prime Minister /praɪ'mɪnɪstə(r)/ n
Premierminister(in) m(f)

primeval /praɪ'miːvl/ a Ur-

primitive /'prɪmɪtɪv/ a primitiv

primrose /'prɪmrəʊz/ n gelbe Schlüs-
selblume f

prince /prɪns/ n Prinz m

princess /prɪn'ses/ n Prinzessin f

principal /'prɪnsəpl/ a Haupt- ● n
(Sch) Rektor(in) m(f)

principality /prɪnsɪ'pælɪtɪ/ n Für-
stentum nt

principally /'prɪnsəplɪ/ adv hauptsächlich

principle /'prɪnsəpl/ n Prinzip nt,
Grundsatz m; **in/on ~** im/aus
Prinzip

print /prɪnt/ n Druck m; (Phot)
Abzug m; **in ~** gedruckt; (available)
erhältlich; **out of ~** vergriffen ● vt
drucken; (write in capitals) in
Druckschrift schreiben; (Computing) ausdrucken; (Phot) abziehen.
~ed matter n Drucksache f

print|er /'prɪntə(r)/ n Drucker m.
~ing n Druck m

'printout n (Computing) Ausdruck m

prior /'praɪə(r)/ a frühere(r,s); **~ to**
vor (+ dat)

priority /praɪ'ɒrətɪ/ n Priorität f, Vor-
rang m; (matter) vordringliche
Sache f

prise /praɪz/ vt **~ open/up**
aufstemmen/hochstemmen

prism /'prɪzm/ n Prisma nt

prison /'prɪzn/ n Gefängnis nt. **~er** n
Gefangene(r) m/f

pristine /'prɪstiːn/ a tadellos

privacy /'prɪvəsɪ/ n Privatsphäre f;
have no ~ nie für sich sein

private /'praɪvət/ *a*, **-ly** *adv* privat; (*confidential*) vertraulich; ⟨*car, secretary, school*⟩ Privat- ● *n* (*Mil*) [einfacher] Soldat *m*; **in ~** privat; (*confidentially*) vertraulich

privation /praɪ'veɪʃn/ *n* Entbehrung *f*

privatize /'praɪvətaɪz/ *vt* privatisieren

privilege /'prɪvəlɪdʒ/ *n* Privileg *nt*. **~d** *a* privilegiert

privy /'prɪvɪ/ *a* **be ~ to** wissen

prize /praɪz/ *n* Preis *m* ● *vt* schätzen. **~-giving** *n* Preisverleihung *f*. **~-winner** *n* Preisgewinner(in) *m(f)*

pro /prəʊ/ *n* (*fam*) Profi *m*; **the ~s and cons** das Für und Wider

probability /prɒbə'bɪlətɪ/ *n* Wahrscheinlichkeit *f*

probable /'prɒbəbl/ *a*, **-bly** *adv* wahrscheinlich

probation /prə'beɪʃn/ *n* (*Jur*) Bewährung *f*. **~ary** *a* Probe-; **~ary period** Probezeit *f*

probe /prəʊb/ *n* Sonde *f*; (*fig: investigation*) Untersuchung *f* ● *vt/i* **~ [into]** untersuchen

problem /'prɒbləm/ *n* Problem *nt*; (*Math*) Textaufgabe *f*. **~atic** /-'mætɪk/ *a* problematisch

procedure /prə'si:dʒə(r)/ *n* Verfahren *nt*

proceed /prə'si:d/ *vi* gehen; (*in vehicle*) fahren; (*continue*) weitergehen/-fahren; (*speaking*) fortfahren; (*act*) verfahren ● *vt* **~ to do sth** anfangen, etw zu tun

proceedings /prə'si:dɪŋz/ *npl* Verfahren *nt*; (*Jur*) Prozeß *m*

proceeds /'prəʊsi:dz/ *npl* Erlös *m*

process /'prəʊses/ *n* Prozeß *m*; (*procedure*) Verfahren *nt*; **in the ~** dabei ● *vt* verarbeiten; (*Admin*) bearbeiten; (*Phot*) entwickeln

procession /prə'seʃn/ *n* Umzug *m*, Prozession *f*

proclaim /prə'kleɪm/ *vt* ausrufen

proclamation /prɒklə'meɪʃn/ *n* Proklamation *f*

procure /prə'kjʊə(r)/ *vt* beschaffen

prod /prɒd/ *n* Stoß *m* ● *vt* stoßen; (*fig*) einen Stoß geben (+ *dat*)

prodigal /'prɒdɪgl/ *a* verschwenderisch

prodigious /prə'dɪdʒəs/ *a* gewaltig

prodigy /'prɒdɪdʒɪ/ *n* **[infant] ~** Wunderkind *nt*

produce¹ /'prɒdju:s/ *n* landwirtschaftliche Erzeugnisse *pl*

produce² /prə'dju:s/ *vt* erzeugen, produzieren; (*manufacture*) herstellen; (*bring out*) hervorholen; (*cause*) hervorrufen; inszenieren ⟨*play*⟩; (*Radio, TV*) redigieren. **~r** *n* Erzeuger *m*, Produzent *m*; Hersteller *m*; (*Theat*) Regisseur *m*; (*Radio, TV*) Redakteur(in) *m(f)*

product /'prɒdʌkt/ *n* Erzeugnis *nt*, Produkt *nt*. **~ion** /prə'dʌkʃn/ *n* Produktion *f*; (*Theat*) Inszenierung *f*

productiv|e /prə'dʌktɪv/ *a* produktiv; ⟨*land, talks*⟩ fruchtbar. **~ity** /-'tɪvətɪ/ *n* Produktivität *f*

profan|e /prə'feɪn/ *a* weltlich; (*blasphemous*) [gottes]lästerlich. **~ity** /-'fænətɪ/ *n* (*oath*) Fluch *m*

profess /prə'fes/ *vt* behaupten; bekennen ⟨*faith*⟩

profession /prə'feʃn/ *n* Beruf *m*. **~al** *a*, **-ly** *adv* beruflich; (*not amateur*) Berufs-; (*expert*) fachmännisch; (*Sport*) professionell ● *n* Fachmann *m*; (*Sport*) Profi *m*

professor /prə'fesə(r)/ *n* Professor *m*

proficien|cy /prə'fɪʃnsɪ/ *n* Können *nt*. **~t** *a* **be ~t in** beherrschen

profile /'prəʊfaɪl/ *n* Profil *nt*; (*character study*) Porträt *nt*

profit /'prɒfɪt/ *n* Gewinn *m*, Profit *m* ● *vi* **~ from** profitieren von. **~able** /-əbl/ *a*, **-bly** *adv* gewinnbringend; (*fig*) nutzbringend

profound /prə'faʊnd/ *a*, **-ly** *adv* tief

profus|e /prə'fju:s/ *a*, **-ly** *adv* üppig; (*fig*) überschwenglich. **~ion** /-ju:ʒn/ *n* **in ~ion** in großer Fülle

progeny /'prɒdʒənɪ/ *n* Nachkommenschaft *f*

program /'prəʊgræm/ *n* Programm *nt* ● *vt* (*pt/pp* **programmed**) programmieren

programme /'prəʊgræm/ *n* Programm *nt*; (*Radio, TV*) Sendung *f*. **~r** *n* (*Computing*) Programmierer (in) *m(f)*

progress¹ /'prəʊgres/ *n* Vorankommen *nt*; (*fig*) Fortschritt *m*; **in ~** im Gange; **make ~** (*fig*) Fortschritte machen

progress² /prə'gres/ *vi* vorankommen; (*fig*) fortschreiten. **~ion** /-eʃn/ *n* Folge *f*; (*development*) Entwicklung *f*

progressive /prə'gresɪv/ *a* fortschrittlich; ⟨*disease*⟩ fortschreitend. **~ly** *adv* zunehmend

prohibit /prə'hɪbɪt/ vt verbieten (s.o. jdm). ~**ive** /-ɪv/ a unerschwinglich

project¹ /'prɒdʒekt/ n Projekt nt; (Sch) Arbeit f

project² /prə'dʒekt/ vt projizieren ⟨film⟩; (plan) planen ● vi (jut out) vorstehen

projectile /prə'dʒektaɪl/ n Geschoß nt

projector /prə'dʒektə(r)/ n Projektor m

proletariat /prəʊlɪ'teərɪət/ n Proletariat nt

prolific /prə'lɪfɪk/ a fruchtbar; (fig) produktiv

prologue /'prəʊlɒg/ n Prolog m

prolong /prə'lɒŋ/ vt verlängern

promenade /prɒmə'nɑːd/ n Promenade f ● vi spazierengehen

prominent /'prɒmɪnənt/ a vorstehend; (important) prominent; (conspicuous) auffällig; ⟨place⟩ gut sichtbar

promiscu|ity /prɒmɪ'skjuːətɪ/ n Promiskuität f. ~**ous** /prə'mɪskjʊəs/ a be ~**ous** häufig den Partner wechseln

promis|e /'prɒmɪs/ n Versprechen nt ● vt/i versprechen (s.o. jdm); the P~ed Land das Gelobte Land. ~**ing** a vielversprechend

promot|e /prə'məʊt/ vt befördern; (advance) fördern; (publicize) Reklame machen für; be ~ed (Sport) aufsteigen. ~**ion** /-əʊʃn/ n Beförderung f; (Sport) Aufstieg m; (Comm) Reklame f

prompt /prɒmpt/ a prompt, unverzüglich; (punctual) pünktlich ● adv pünktlich ● vt/i veranlassen (to zu); (Theat) soufflieren (+ dat). ~**er** n Souffleur m/Souffleuse f. ~**ly** adv prompt

prone /prəʊn/ a be/lie ~ auf dem Bauch liegen; be ~ to neigen zu; be ~ to do sth dazu neigen, etw zu tun

prong /prɒŋ/ n Zinke f

pronoun /'prəʊnaʊn/ n Fürwort nt, Pronomen nt

pronounce /prə'naʊns/ vt aussprechen; (declare) erklären. ~**d** a ausgeprägt; (noticeable) deutlich. ~**ment** n Erklärung f

pronunciation /prənʌnsɪ'eɪʃn/ n Aussprache f

proof /pruːf/ n Beweis m; (Typ) Korrekturbogen m ● a ~ **against** water/theft wasserfest/diebessicher. ~**-reader** n Korrektor m

prop¹ /prɒp/ n Stütze f ● vt (pt/pp propped) ~ **open** offenhalten; ~ **against** (lean) lehnen an (+ acc). ~ **up** vt stützen

prop² n (Theat, fam) Requisit nt

propaganda /prɒpə'gændə/ n Propaganda f

propagate /'prɒpəgeɪt/ vt vermehren; (fig) verbreiten, propagieren

propel /prə'pel/ vt (pt/pp propelled) [an]treiben. ~**ler** n Propeller m. ~**ling 'pencil** n Drehbleistift m

propensity /prə'pensətɪ/ n Neigung f (for zu)

proper /'prɒpə(r)/ a, -**ly** adv richtig; (decent) anständig. ~ '**name**, ~ '**noun** n Eigenname m

property /'prɒpətɪ/ n Eigentum nt; (quality) Eigenschaft f; (Theat) Requisit nt; (land) [Grund]besitz m; (house) Haus nt. ~ **market** n Immobilienmarkt m

prophecy /'prɒfəsɪ/ n Prophezeiung f

prophesy /'prɒfɪsaɪ/ vt (pt/pp -ied) prophezeien

prophet /'prɒfɪt/ n Prophet m. ~**ic** /prə'fetɪk/ a prophetisch

proportion /prə'pɔːʃn/ n Verhältnis nt; (share) Teil m; ~**s** pl Proportionen; (dimensions) Maße. ~**al** a, -**ly** adv proportional

proposal /prə'pəʊzl/ n Vorschlag m; (of marriage) [Heirats]antrag m

propose /prə'pəʊz/ vt vorschlagen; (intend) vorhaben; einbringen ⟨motion⟩; ausbringen ⟨toast⟩ ● vi einen Heiratsantrag machen

proposition /prɒpə'zɪʃn/ n Vorschlag m

propound /prə'paʊnd/ vt darlegen

proprietor /prə'praɪətə(r)/ n Inhaber(in) m(f)

propriety /prə'praɪətɪ/ n Korrektheit f; (decorum) Anstand m

propulsion /prə'pʌlʃn/ n Antrieb m

prosaic /prə'zeɪɪk/ a prosaisch

prose /prəʊz/ n Prosa f

prosecut|e /'prɒsɪkjuːt/ vt strafrechtlich verfolgen. ~**ion** /-'kjuːʃn/ n strafrechtliche Verfolgung f; the ~**ion** die Anklage. ~**or** n [Public] P~**or** Staatsanwalt m

prospect¹ /'prɒspekt/ n Aussicht f

prospect² /prə'spekt/ vi suchen (for nach)

prospect|ive /prə'spektɪv/ a (future) zukünftig. ~**or** n Prospektor m

prospectus /prə'spektəs/ n Prospekt m

prosper /'prɒspə(r)/ *vi* gedeihen, florieren; ⟨*person*⟩ Erfolg haben. **~ity** /-'sperəti/ *n* Wohlstand *m*

prosperous /'prɒspərəs/ *a* wohlhabend

prostitut|e /'prɒstɪtjuːt/ *n* Prostituierte *f.* **~ion** /-'tjuːʃn/ *n* Prostitution *f*

prostrate /'prɒstreɪt/ *a* ausgestreckt; **~ with grief** (*fig*) vor Kummer gebrochen

protagonist /prəʊ'tægənɪst/ *n* Kämpfer *m*; (*fig*) Protagonist *m*

protect /prə'tekt/ *vt* schützen (**from** vor + *dat*); beschützen ⟨*person*⟩. **~ion** /-ekʃn/ *n* Schutz *m.* **~ive** /-ɪv/ *a* Schutz-; (*fig*) beschützend. **~or** *n* Beschützer *m*

protégé /'prɒtɪʒeɪ/ *n* Schützling *m*, Protegé *m*

protein /'prəʊtiːn/ *n* Eiweiß *nt*

protest¹ /'prəʊtest/ *n* Protest *m*

protest² /prə'test/ *vi* protestieren

Protestant /'prɒtɪstənt/ *a* protestantisch, evangelisch ● *n* Protestant(in) *m*(*f*), Evangelische(r) *m*/*f*

protester /prə'testə(r)/ *n* Protestierende(r) *m*/*f*

protocol /'prəʊtəkɒl/ *n* Protokoll *nt*

prototype /'prəʊtə-/ *n* Prototyp *m*

protract /prə'trækt/ *vt* verlängern. **~or** *n* Winkelmesser *m*

protrude /prə'truːd/ *vi* [her]vorstehen

proud /praʊd/ *a*, **-ly** *adv* stolz (**of** auf + *acc*)

prove /pruːv/ *vt* beweisen ● *vi* **~to be** sich erweisen als

proverb /'prɒvɜːb/ *n* Sprichwort *nt.* **~ial** /prə'vɜːbɪəl/ *a* sprichwörtlich

provide /prə'vaɪd/ *vt* zur Verfügung stellen; spenden ⟨*shade*⟩; **~ s.o. with sth** jdn mit etw versorgen *od* versehen ● *vi* **~ for** sorgen für

provided /prə'vaɪdɪd/ *conj* **~ [that]** vorausgesetzt [daß]

providen|ce /'prɒvɪdəns/ *n* Vorsehung *f.* **~tial** /-'denʃl/ *a* **be ~tial** ein Glück sein

providing /prə'vaɪdɪŋ/ *conj* = **provided**

provinc|e /'prɒvɪns/ *n* Provinz *f*; (*fig*) Bereich *m.* **~ial** /prə'vɪnʃl/ *a* provinziell

provision /prə'vɪʒn/ *n* Versorgung *f* (**of** mit); **~s** *pl* Lebensmittel *pl.* **~al** *a*, **-ly** *adv* vorläufig

proviso /prə'vaɪzəʊ/ *n* Vorbehalt *m*

provocat|ion /prɒvə'keɪʃn/ *n* Provokation *f.* **~ive** /prə'vɒkətɪv/ *a*, **-ly** *adv* provozierend; (*sexually*) aufreizend

provoke /prə'vəʊk/ *vt* provozieren; (*cause*) hervorrufen

prow /praʊ/ *n* Bug *m*

prowess /'praʊɪs/ *n* Kraft *f*

prowl /praʊl/ *vi* herumschleichen ● *n* **be on the ~** herumschleichen

proximity /prɒk'sɪmətɪ/ *n* Nähe *f*

proxy /'prɒksɪ/ *n* Stellvertreter(in) *m*(*f*); (*power*) Vollmacht *f*

prude /pruːd/ *n* **be a ~** prüde sein

pruden|ce /'pruːdns/ *n* Umsicht *f.* **~t** *a*, **-ly** *adv* umsichtig; (*wise*) klug

prudish /'pruːdɪʃ/ *a* prüde

prune¹ /pruːn/ *n* Backpflaume *f*

prune² *vt* beschneiden

pry /praɪ/ *vi* (*pt*/*pp* **pried**) neugierig sein

psalm /sɑːm/ *n* Psalm *m*

pseudonym /'sjuːdənɪm/ *n* Pseudonym *nt*

psychiatric /saɪkɪ'ætrɪk/ *a* psychiatrisch

psychiatr|ist /saɪ'kaɪətrɪst/ *n* Psychiater(in) *m*(*f*). **~y** *n* Psychiatrie *f*

psychic /'saɪkɪk/ *a* übersinnlich; **I'm not ~** ich kann nicht hellsehen

psycho|'analyse /saɪkəʊ-/ *vt* psychoanalysieren. **~a'nalysis** *n* Psychoanalyse *f.* **~'analyst** Psychoanalytiker(in) *m*(*f*)

psychological /saɪkə'lɒdʒɪkl/ *a*, **-ly** *adv* psychologisch; ⟨*illness*⟩ psychisch

psycholog|ist /saɪ'kɒlədʒɪst/ *n* Psychologe *m*/ -login *f.* **~y** *n* Psychologie *f*

psychopath /'saɪkəpæθ/ *n* Psychopath(in) *m*(*f*)

PTO *abbr* (**please turn over**) b.w.

pub /pʌb/ *n* (*fam*) Kneipe *f*

puberty /'pjuːbətɪ/ *n* Pubertät *f*

public /'pʌblɪk/ *a*, **-ly** *adv* öffentlich; **make ~** publik machen ● *n* **the ~** die Öffentlichkeit; **in ~** in aller Öffentlichkeit

publican /'pʌblɪkən/ *n* [Gast]wirt *m*

publication /pʌblɪ'keɪʃn/ *n* Veröffentlichung *f*

public: ~ con'venience *n* öffentliche Toilette *f.* **~ 'holiday** *n* gesetzlicher Feiertag *m.* **~ 'house** *n* [Gast]wirtschaft *f*

publicity /pʌb'lɪsətɪ/ *n* Publicity *f*; (*advertising*) Reklame *f*

publicize /'pʌblɪsaɪz/ vt Reklame machen für

public: ~ **'library** n öffentliche Bücherei f. ~ **'school** n Privatschule f; (Amer) staatliche Schule f. ~**'spirited** a be ~spirited Gemeinsinn haben. ~ **'transport** n öffentliche Verkehrsmittel pl

publish /'pʌblɪʃ/ vt veröffentlichen. ~**er** n Verleger(in) m(f); (firm) Verlag m. ~**ing** n Verlagswesen nt

pucker /'pʌkə(r)/ vt kräuseln

pudding /'pʊdɪŋ/ n Pudding m; (course) Nachtisch m

puddle /'pʌdl/ n Pfütze f

puerile /'pjʊəraɪl/ a kindisch

puff /pʌf/ n (of wind) Hauch m; (of smoke) Wölkchen nt; (for powder) Quaste f ● vt blasen, pusten; ~ **out** ausstoßen. ● vi keuchen; ~ **at** paffen an (+ dat) ⟨pipe⟩. ~**ed** a (out of breath) aus der Puste. ~ **pastry** n Blätterteig m

puffy /'pʌfɪ/ a geschwollen

pugnacious /pʌg'neɪʃəs/ a, -ly adv aggressiv

pull /pʊl/ n Zug m; (jerk) Ruck m; (fam: influence) Einfluß m ● vt ziehen; ziehen an (+ dat) ⟨rope⟩; ~ **a muscle** sich (dat) einen Muskel zerren; ~ **oneself together** sich zusammennehmen; ~ **one's weight** tüchtig mitarbeiten; ~ **s.o.'s leg** (fam) jdn auf den Arm nehmen. ~ **down** vt herunterziehen; (demolish) abreißen. ~ **in** vt hereinziehen ● vi (Auto) einscheren. ~ **off** vt abziehen; (fam) schaffen. ~ **out** vt herausziehen ● vi (Auto) ausscheren. ~ **through** vt durchziehen ● vi (recover) durchkommen. ~ **up** vt heraufziehen; ausziehen ⟨plant⟩; (reprimand) zurechtweisen ● vi (Auto) anhalten

pulley /'pʊlɪ/ n (Techn) Rolle f

pullover /'pʊləʊvə(r)/ n Pullover m

pulp /pʌlp/ n Brei m; (of fruit) [Frucht]fleisch nt

pulpit /'pʊlpɪt/ n Kanzel f

pulsate /pʌl'seɪt/ vi pulsieren

pulse /pʌls/ n Puls m

pulses /'pʌlsɪz/ npl Hülsenfrüchte pl

pulverize /'pʌlvəraɪz/ vt pulverisieren

pumice /'pʌmɪs/ n Bimsstein m

pummel /'pʌml/ vt (pt/pp pummelled) mit den Fäusten bearbeiten

pump /pʌmp/ n Pumpe f ● vt pumpen; (fam) aushorchen. ~ **up** vt hochpumpen; (inflate) aufpumpen

pumpkin /'pʌmpkɪn/ n Kürbis m

pun /pʌn/ n Wortspiel nt

punch¹ /pʌntʃ/ n Faustschlag m; (device) Locher m ● vt boxen; lochen ⟨ticket⟩; stanzen ⟨hole⟩

punch² n (drink) Bowle f

punch: ~ **line** n Pointe f. ~**-up** n Schlägerei f

punctual /'pʌŋktjʊəl/ a, -ly adv pünktlich. ~**ity** /-'ælətɪ/ n Pünktlichkeit f

punctuat|e /'pʌŋktjʊeɪt/ vt mit Satzzeichen versehen. ~**ion** /-'eɪʃn/ n Interpunktion f. ~**ion mark** n Satzzeichen nt

puncture /'pʌŋktʃə(r)/ n Loch nt; (tyre) Reifenpanne f ● vt durchstechen

pundit /'pʌndɪt/ n Experte m

pungent /'pʌndʒənt/ a scharf

punish /'pʌnɪʃ/ vt bestrafen. ~**able** /-əbl/ a strafbar. ~**ment** n Strafe f

punitive /'pjuːnɪtɪv/ a Straf-

punnet /'pʌnɪt/ n Körbchen nt

punt /pʌnt/ n (boat) Stechkahn m

punter /'pʌntə(r)/ n (gambler) Wetter m; (client) Kunde m

puny /'pjuːnɪ/ a (-ier, -iest) mickerig

pup /pʌp/ n = puppy

pupil /'pjuːpl/ n Schüler(in) m(f); (of eye) Pupille f

puppet /'pʌpɪt/ n Puppe f; (fig) Marionette f

puppy /'pʌpɪ/ n junger Hund m

purchase /'pɜːtʃəs/ n Kauf m; (leverage) Hebelkraft f ● vt kaufen. ~**r** n Käufer m

pure /pjʊə(r)/ a (-r, -st), -ly adv rein

purée /'pjʊəreɪ/ n Püree nt, Brei m

purgatory /'pɜːgətrɪ/ n (Relig) Fegefeuer nt; (fig) Hölle f

purge /pɜːdʒ/ n (Pol) Säuberungsaktion f ● vt reinigen; (Pol) säubern

puri|fication /pjʊərɪfɪ'keɪʃn/ n Reinigung f. ~**fy** /'pjʊərɪfaɪ/ vt (pt/pp -ied) reinigen

puritanical /pjʊərɪ'tænɪkl/ a puritanisch

purity /'pjʊərɪtɪ/ n Reinheit f

purl /pɜːl/ n (Knitting) linke Masche f ● vt/i links stricken

purple /'pɜːpl/ a [dunkel]lila

purport /pə'pɔːt/ vt vorgeben

purpose /'pɜːpəs/ n Zweck m; (intention) Absicht f; (determination)

Entschlossenheit *f*; **on** ~ absichtlich; **to no** ~ unnützerweise. ~**ful** *a*, **-ly** *adv* entschlossen. ~**ly** *adv* absichtlich

purr /pɜː(r)/ *vi* schnurren

purse /pɜːs/ *n* Portemonnaie *nt*; (*Amer: handbag*) Handtasche *f* ● *vt* schürzen ⟨*lips*⟩

pursue /pə'sjuː/ *vt* verfolgen; (*fig*) nachgehen (+ *dat*). ~**r** /-ə(r)/ *n* Verfolger *m*

pursuit /pə'sjuːt/ *n* Verfolgung *f*; Jagd *f*; (*pastime*) Beschäftigung *f*; **in** ~ hinterher

pus /pʌs/ *n* Eiter *m*

push /pʊʃ/ *n* Stoß *m*, (*fam*) Schubs *m*; **get the** ~ (*fam*) hinausfliegen ● *vt/i* schieben; (*press*) drücken; (*roughly*) stoßen; **be** ~**ed for time** (*fam*) unter Zeitdruck stehen. ~ **off** *vt* hinunterstoßen ● *vi* (*fam: leave*) abhauen. ~ **on** *vi* (*continue*) weitergehen/-fahren; (*with activity*) weitermachen. ~ **up** *vt* hochschieben; hochtreiben ⟨*price*⟩

push: ~**-button** *n* Druckknopf *m*. ~**chair** *n* [Kinder]sportwagen *m*. ~**over** *n* (*fam*) Kinderspiel *nt*. ~**up** *n* (*Amer*) Liegestütz *m*

pushy /'pʊʃi/ *a* (*fam*) aufdringlich

puss /pʊs/ *n*, **pussy** /'pʊsi/ *n* Mieze *f*

put /pʊt/ *vt* (*pt/pp* put, *pres p* putting) tun; (*place*) setzen; (*upright*) stellen; (*flat*) legen; (*express*) ausdrücken; (*say*) sagen; (*estimate*) schätzen (**at** auf + *acc*); ~ **aside** *or* **by** beiseite legen; ~ **one's foot down** (*fam*) energisch werden; (*Auto*) Gas geben ● *vi* ~ **to sea** auslaufen ● *a* **stay** ~ dableiben. ~ **away** *vt* wegräumen. ~ **back** *vt* wieder hinsetzen/-stellen/-legen; zurückstellen ⟨*clock*⟩. ~ **down** *vt* hinsetzen/-stellen/-legen; (*suppress*) niederschlagen; (*kill*) töten; (*write*) niederschreiben; (*attribute*) zuschreiben (**to** *dat*). ~ **forward** *vt* vorbringen; vorstellen ⟨*clock*⟩. ~ **in** *vt* hineinsetzen/-stellen/-legen; (*insert*) einstecken; (*submit*) einreichen ● *vi* ~ **in for** beantragen. ~ **off** *vt* ausmachen ⟨*light*⟩; (*postpone*) verschieben; ~ **s.o. off** jdn abbestellen; (*disconcert*) jdn aus der Fassung bringen; ~ **s.o. off sth** jdm etw verleiden. ~ **on** *vt* anziehen ⟨*clothes, brake*⟩; sich (*dat*) aufsetzen ⟨*hat*⟩; (*Culin*) aufsetzen; anmachen ⟨*light*⟩; aufführen ⟨*play*⟩; annehmen ⟨*accent*⟩; ~ **on weight** zunehmen. ~

out *vt* hinaussetzen/-stellen/-legen; ausmachen ⟨*fire, light*⟩; ausstrecken ⟨*hand*⟩; (*disconcert*) aus der Fassung bringen; ~ **s.o./oneself out** jdm/sich Umstände machen. ~ **through** *vt* durchstecken; (*Teleph*) verbinden (**to** mit). ~ **up** *vt* errichten ⟨*building*⟩; aufschlagen ⟨*tent*⟩; aufspannen ⟨*umbrella*⟩; anschlagen ⟨*notice*⟩; erhöhen ⟨*price*⟩; unterbringen ⟨*guest*⟩; ~ **s.o. up to sth** jdn zu etw anstiften ● *vi* (*at hotel*) absteigen in (+ *dat*); ~ **up with sth** sich (*dat*) etw bieten lassen

putrefy /'pjuːtrɪfaɪ/ *vi* (*pt/pp* -ied) verwesen

putrid /'pjuːtrɪd/ faulig

putty /'pʌti/ *n* Kitt *m*

put-up /'pʊtʌp/ *a* **a** ~ **job** ein abgekartetes Spiel *nt*

puzzl|e /'pʌzl/ *n* Rätsel *nt*; (*jig-saw*) Puzzlespiel *nt* ● *vt* **it** ~**es me** es ist mir rätselhaft ● *vi* ~**e over** sich (*dat*) den Kopf zerbrechen über (+ *acc*). ~**ing** *a* rätselhaft

pyjamas /pə'dʒɑːməz/ *npl* Schlafanzug *m*

pylon /'paɪlən/ *n* Mast *m*

pyramid /'pɪrəmɪd/ *n* Pyramide *f*

python /'paɪθn/ *n* Pythonschlange *f*

Q

quack¹ /kwæk/ *n* Quaken *nt* ● *vi* quaken

quack² *n* (*doctor*) Quacksalber *m*

quad /kwɒd/ *n* (*fam: court*) Hof *m*; ~**s** *pl* = **quadruplets**

quadrangle /'kwɒdræŋgl/ *n* Viereck *nt*; (*court*) Hof *m*

quadruped /'kwɒdrʊped/ *n* Vierfüßer *m*

quadruple /'kwɒdrʊpl/ *a* vierfach ● *vt* vervierfachen ● *vi* sich vervierfachen. ~**ts** /-plɪts/ *npl* Vierlinge *pl*

quagmire /'kwɒgmaɪə(r)/ *n* Sumpf *m*

quaint /kweɪnt/ *a* (-er, -est) malerisch; (*odd*) putzig

quake /kweɪk/ *n* (*fam*) Erdbeben *nt* ● *vi* beben; (*with fear*) zittern

Quaker /'kweɪkə(r)/ *n* Quäker(in) *m(f)*

qualif|ication /kwɒlɪfɪ'keɪʃn/ *n* Qualifikation *f*; (*reservation*) Einschränkung *f*. ~**ied** /-faɪd/ *a* qualifiziert; (*trained*) ausgebildet; (*limited*) bedingt

qualify /'kwɒlɪfaɪ/ v (pt/pp -ied) ● vt qualifizieren; (entitle) berechtigen; (limit) einschränken ● vi sich qualifizieren

quality /'kwɒlətɪ/ n Qualität f; (characteristic) Eigenschaft f

qualm /kwɑːm/ n Bedenken pl

quandary /'kwɒndərɪ/ n Dilemma nt

quantity /'kwɒntɪtɪ/ n Quantität f, Menge f; **in** ~ in großen Mengen

quarantine /'kwɒrəntiːn/ n Quarantäne f

quarrel /'kwɒrl/ n Streit m ● vi (pt/pp **quarrelled**) sich streiten. ~**some** a streitsüchtig

quarry[1] /'kwɒrɪ/ n (prey) Beute f

quarry[2] n Steinbruch m

quart /kwɔːt/ n Quart nt

quarter /'kwɔːtə(r)/ n Viertel nt; (of year) Vierteljahr nt; (Amer) 25-Cent-Stück nt; ~**s** pl Quartier nt; **at [a]** ~ **to six** um Viertel vor sechs; **from all** ~**s** aus allen Richtungen ● vt vierteln; (Mil) einquartieren (**on** bei). ~-'**final** n Viertelfinale nt

quarterly /'kwɔːtəlɪ/ a & adv vierteljährlich

quartet /kwɔː'tet/ n Quartett nt

quartz /kwɔːts/ n Quarz m. ~ **watch** n Quarzuhr f

quash /kwɒʃ/ vt aufheben; niederschlagen ⟨rebellion⟩

quaver /'kweɪvə(r)/ n (Mus) Achtelnote f ● vi zittern

quay /kiː/ n Kai m

queasy /'kwiːzɪ/ a **I feel** ~ mir ist übel

queen /kwiːn/ n Königin f; (Cards, Chess) Dame f

queer /kwɪə(r)/ a (-er, -est) eigenartig; (dubious) zweifelhaft; (ill) unwohl; (fam: homosexual) schwul ● n (fam) Schwule(r) m

quell /kwel/ vt unterdrücken

quench /kwentʃ/ vt löschen

query /'kwɪərɪ/ n Frage f; (question mark) Fragezeichen nt ● vt (pt/pp -ied) in Frage stellen; reklamieren ⟨bill⟩

quest /kwest/ n Suche f (**for** nach)

question /'kwestʃn/ n Frage f; (for discussion) Thema nt; **out of the** ~ ausgeschlossen; **without** ~ ohne Frage; **the person in** ~ die fragliche Person ● vt in Frage stellen; ~ **s.o.** jdn ausfragen; ⟨police:⟩ jdn verhören. ~**able** /-əbl/ a zweifelhaft. ~ **mark** n Fragezeichen nt

questionnaire /kwestʃə'neə(r)/ n Fragebogen m

queue /kjuː/ n Schlange f ● vi ~ [up] Schlange stehen, sich anstellen (**for** nach)

quibble /'kwɪbl/ vi Haarspalterei treiben

quick /kwɪk/ a (-er, -est), -ly adv schnell; **be** ~**!** mach schnell! **have a** ~ **meal** schnell etwas essen ● adv schnell ● n **cut to the** ~ (fig) bis ins Mark getroffen. ~**en** vt beschleunigen ● vi sich beschleunigen

quick: ~**sand** n Treibsand m. ~-**tempered** a aufbrausend

quid /kwɪd/ n inv (fam) Pfund nt

quiet /'kwaɪət/ a (-er, -est), -ly adv still; (calm) ruhig; (soft) leise; **keep** ~ **about** (fam) nichts sagen von ● n Stille f; Ruhe f; **on the** ~ heimlich

quiet|en /'kwaɪətn/ vt beruhigen ● vi ~**en down** ruhig werden. ~**ness** n (see quiet) Stille f; Ruhe f

quill /kwɪl/ n Feder f; (spine) Stachel m

quilt /kwɪlt/ n Steppdecke f. ~**ed** a Stepp-

quince /kwɪns/ n Quitte f

quins /kwɪnz/ npl (fam) = **quintuplets**

quintet /kwɪn'tet/ n Quintett nt

quintuplets /'kwɪntjʊplɪts/ npl Fünflinge pl

quip /kwɪp/ n Scherz m ● vi (pt/pp **quipped**) scherzen

quirk /kwɜːk/ n Eigenart f

quit /kwɪt/ v (pt/pp **quitted** or **quit**) vt verlassen; (give up) aufgeben; ~ **doing sth** aufhören, etw zu tun ● vi gehen; **give s.o. notice to** ~ jdm die Wohnung kündigen

quite /kwaɪt/ adv ganz; (really) wirklich; ~ **[so]!** genau! ~ **a few** ziemlich viele

quits /kwɪts/ a quitt

quiver /'kwɪvə(r)/ vi zittern

quiz /kwɪz/ n Quiz nt ● vt (pt/pp **quizzed**) ausfragen. ~**zical** a, -ly adv fragend

quorum /'kwɔːrəm/ n **have a** ~ beschlußfähig sein

quota /'kwəʊtə/ n Anteil m; (Comm) Kontingent nt

quotation /kwəʊ'teɪʃn/ n Zitat nt; (price) Kostenvoranschlag m; (of shares) Notierung f. ~ **marks** npl Anführungszeichen pl

quote /kwəʊt/ n (fam) = **quotation**; **in** ~**s** in Anführungszeichen ● vt/i zitieren

R

rabbi /'ræbaɪ/ n Rabbiner m; (title) Rabbi m

rabbit /'ræbɪt/ n Kaninchen nt

rabble /'ræbl/ n the ~ der Pöbel

rabid /'ræbɪd/ a fanatisch; ⟨animal⟩ tollwütig

rabies /'reɪbi:z/ n Tollwut f

race[1] /reɪs/ n Rasse f

race[2] n Rennen nt; (fig) Wettlauf m ● vi [am Rennen] teilnehmen; ⟨athlete, horse:⟩ laufen; (fam: rush) rasen ● vt um die Wette laufen mit; an einem Rennen teilnehmen lassen ⟨horse⟩

race: ~course n Rennbahn f. **~horse** n Rennpferd nt. **~-track** n Rennbahn f

racial /'reɪʃl/ a, **-ly** adv rassisch; ⟨discrimination, minority⟩ Rassen-

racing /'reɪsɪŋ/ n Rennsport m; (horse-) Pferderennen nt. ~ **car** n Rennwagen m. ~ **driver** n Rennfahrer m

racis|m /'reɪsɪzm/ n Rassismus m. ~**t** /-ɪst/ a rassistisch ● n Rassist m

rack[1] /ræk/ n Ständer m; (for plates) Gestell nt ● vt ~ **one's brains** sich (dat) den Kopf zerbrechen

rack[2] n go to ~ **and ruin** verfallen; (fig) herunterkommen

racket[1] /'rækɪt/ n (Sport) Schläger m

racket[2] n (din) Krach m; (swindle) Schwindelgeschäft nt

racy /'reɪsɪ/ a (**-ier, -iest**) schwungvoll; (risqué) gewagt

radar /'reɪdɑ:(r)/ n Radar m

radian|ce /'reɪdɪəns/ n Strahlen nt. ~**t** a, **-ly** adv strahlend

radiat|e /'reɪdɪeɪt/ vt ausstrahlen ● vi ⟨heat:⟩ ausgestrahlt werden; ⟨roads:⟩ strahlenförmig ausgehen. ~**ion** /-'eɪʃn/ n Strahlung f

radiator /'reɪdɪeɪtə(r)/ n Heizkörper m; (Auto) Kühler m

radical /'rædɪkl/ a, **-ly** adv radikal ● n Radikale(r) m/f

radio /'reɪdɪəʊ/ n Radio nt; **by** ~ über Funk ● vt funken ⟨message⟩

radio|'active a radioaktiv. ~**ac-'tivity** n Radioaktivität f

radiography /'reɪdɪ'ɒgrəfɪ/ n Röntgenographie f

'radio ham n Hobbyfunker m

radio'therapy n Strahlenbehandlung f

radish /'rædɪʃ/ n Radieschen nt

radius /'reɪdɪəs/ n (pl **-dii** /-dɪaɪ/) Radius m, Halbmesser m

raffle /'ræfl/ n Tombola f ● vt verlosen

raft /rɑ:ft/ n Floß nt

rafter /'rɑ:ftə(r)/ n Dachsparren m

rag[1] /ræg/ n Lumpen m; (pej: newspaper) Käseblatt nt; **in** ~**s** in Lumpen

rag[2] vt (pt/pp **ragged**) (fam) aufziehen

rage /reɪdʒ/ n Wut f; **all the** ~ (fam) der letzte Schrei ● vi rasen; ⟨storm:⟩ toben

ragged /'rægɪd/ a zerlumpt; ⟨edge⟩ ausgefranst

raid /reɪd/ n Überfall m; (Mil) Angriff m; (police) Razzia f ● vt überfallen; (Mil) angreifen; ⟨police:⟩ eine Razzia durchführen in (+ dat); (break in) eindringen in (+ acc). ~**er** n Eindringling m; (of bank) Bankräuber m

rail /reɪl/ n Schiene f; (pole) Stange f; (hand~) Handlauf m; (Naut) Reling f; **by** ~ mit der Bahn

railings /'reɪlɪŋz/ npl Geländer nt

'railroad n (Amer) = railway

'railway n [Eisen]bahn f. ~**man** n Eisenbahner m. ~ **station** n Bahnhof m

rain /reɪn/ n Regen m ● vi regnen

rain: ~bow n Regenbogen m. ~**check** n (Amer) **take a ~check** on aufschieben. ~**coat** n Regenmantel m. ~**fall** n Niederschlag m

rainy /'reɪnɪ/ a (**-ier, -iest**) regnerisch

raise /reɪz/ n (Amer) Lohnerhöhung f ● vt erheben; (upright) aufrichten; (make higher) erhöhen; (lift) [hoch]heben; lüften ⟨hat⟩; [auf]ziehen ⟨children, animals⟩; aufwerfen ⟨question⟩; aufbringen ⟨money⟩

raisin /'reɪzn/ n Rosine f

rake /reɪk/ n Harke f, Rechen m ● vt harken, rechen. ~ **up** vt zusammenharken; (fam) wieder aufrühren

'rake-off n (fam) Prozente pl

rally /'rælɪ/ n Versammlung f; (Auto) Rallye f; (Tennis) Ballwechsel m ● vt sammeln ● vi sich sammeln; (recover strength) sich erholen

ram /ræm/ n Schafbock m; (Astr) Widder m ● vt (pt/pp **rammed**) rammen

rambl|e /'ræmbl/ n Wanderung f ● vi wandern; (in speech) irrereden. ~**er** n Wanderer m; (rose) Kletterrose f.

~ing *a* weitschweifig; ⟨*club*⟩ Wander-

ramp /ræmp/ *n* Rampe *f*; (*Aviat*) Gangway *f*

rampage¹ /'ræmpeɪdʒ/ *n* **be/go on the ~** randalieren

rampage² /ræm'peɪdʒ/ *vi* randalieren

rampant /'ræmpənt/ *a* weit verbreitet; (*in heraldry*) aufgerichtet

rampart /'ræmpɑ:t/ *n* Wall *m*

ramshackle /'ræmʃækl/ *a* baufällig

ran /ræn/ *see* **run**

ranch /rɑ:ntʃ/ *n* Ranch *f*

rancid /'rænsɪd/ *a* ranzig

rancour /'ræŋkə(r)/ *n* Groll *m*

random /'rændəm/ *a* willkürlich; **a ~ sample** eine Stichprobe ● **n at ~** aufs Geratewohl; ⟨*choose*⟩ willkürlich

randy /'rændɪ/ *a* (**-ier, -iest**) (*fam*) geil

rang /ræŋ/ *see* **ring²**

range /reɪndʒ/ *n* Serie *f*, Reihe *f*; (*Comm*) Auswahl *f*, Angebot *nt* (**of** an + *dat*); (*of mountains*) Kette *f*; (*Mus*) Umfang *m*; (*distance*) Reichweite *f*; (*for shooting*) Schießplatz *m*; (*stove*) Kohlenherd *m*; **at a ~ of** auf eine Entfernung von ● *vi* reichen; **~ from ... to** gehen von ... bis. **~r** *n* Aufseher *m*

rank¹ /ræŋk/ *n* (*row*) Reihe *f*; (*Mil*) Rang *m*; (*social position*) Stand *m*; **the ~ and file** die breite Masse; **the ~s** *pl* die gemeinen Soldaten ● *vt/i* einstufen; **~ among** zählen zu

rank² *a* (*bad*) übel; ⟨*plants*⟩ üppig; (*fig*) kraß

ransack /'rænsæk/ *vt* durchwühlen; (*pillage*) plündern

ransom /'rænsəm/ *n* Lösegeld *nt*; **hold s.o. to ~** Lösegeld für jdn fordern

rant /rænt/ *vi* rasen

rap /ræp/ *n* Klopfen *nt*; (*blow*) Schlag *m* ● *v* (*pt/pp* **rapped**) ● *vt* klopfen auf (+ *acc*) ● *vi* **~ at/on** klopfen an/auf (+ *acc*)

rape¹ /reɪp/ *n* (*Bot*) Raps *m*

rape² *n* Vergewaltigung *f* ● *vt* vergewaltigen

rapid /'ræpɪd/ *a*, **-ly** *adv* schnell. **~ity** /rə'pɪdətɪ/ *n* Schnelligkeit *f*

rapids /'ræpɪdz/ *npl* Stromschnellen *pl*

rapist /'reɪpɪst/ *n* Vergewaltiger *m*

rapport /ræ'pɔ:(r)/ *n* [innerer] Kontakt *m*

rapt /ræpt/ *a*, **-ly** *adv* gespannt; ⟨*look*⟩ andächtig; **~ in** versunken in (+ *acc*)

rapture /'ræptʃə(r)/ *n* Entzücken *nt*. **~ous** /-rəs/ *a*, **-ly** *adv* begeistert

rare¹ /reə(r)/ *a* (**-r, -st**), **-ly** *adv* selten

rare² *a* (*Culin*) englisch gebraten

rarefied /'reərɪfaɪd/ *a* dünn

rarity /'reərətɪ/ *n* Seltenheit *f*

rascal /'rɑ:skl/ *n* Schlingel *m*

rash¹ /ræʃ/ *n* (*Med*) Ausschlag *m*

rash² *a* (**-er, -est**), **-ly** *adv* voreilig

rasher /'ræʃə(r)/ *n* Speckscheibe *f*

rasp /rɑ:sp/ *n* Raspel *f*

raspberry /'rɑ:zberɪ/ *n* Himbeere *f*

rat /ræt/ *n* Ratte *f*; (*fam: person*) Schuft *m*; **smell a ~** (*fam*) Lunte riechen

rate /reɪt/ *n* Rate *f*; (*speed*) Tempo *nt*; (*of payment*) Satz *m*; (*of exchange*) Kurs *m*; **~s** *pl* (*taxes*) ≈ Grundsteuer *f*; **at any ~** auf jeden Fall; **at this ~** auf diese Weise ● *vt* einschätzen; **~ among** zählen zu ● *vi* **~ as** gelten als

rather /'rɑ:ðə(r)/ *adv* lieber; (*fairly*) ziemlich; **~!** und ob!

rati|fication /rætɪfɪ'keɪʃn/ *n* Ratifizierung *f*. **~fy** /'rætɪfaɪ/ *vt* (*pt/pp* **-ied**) ratifizieren

rating /'reɪtɪŋ/ *n* Einschätzung *f*; (*class*) Klasse *f*; (*sailor*) [einfacher] Matrose *m*; **~s** *pl* (*Radio, TV*) ≈ Einschaltquote *f*

ratio /'reɪʃɪəʊ/ *n* Verhältnis *nt*

ration /'ræʃn/ *n* Ration *f* ● *vt* rationieren

rational /'ræʃənl/ *a*, **-ly** *adv* rational. **~ize** *vt/i* rationalisieren

'rat race *n* (*fam*) Konkurrenzkampf *m*

rattle /'rætl/ *n* Rasseln *nt*; (*of china, glass*) Klirren *nt*; (*of windows*) Klappern *nt*; (*toy*) Klapper *f* ● *vi* rasseln; klirren; klappern ● *vt* rasseln mit; (*shake*) schütteln. **~ off** *vt* herunterrasseln

'rattlesnake *n* Klapperschlange *f*

raucous /'rɔ:kəs/ *a* rauh

ravage /'rævɪdʒ/ *vt* verwüsten, verheeren

rave /reɪv/ *vi* toben; **~ about** schwärmen von

raven /'reɪvn/ *n* Rabe *m*

ravenous /'rævənəs/ *a* heißhungrig

ravine /rə'vi:n/ *n* Schlucht *f*

raving /'reɪvɪŋ/ *a* **~ mad** (*fam*) total verrückt

ravishing /'rævɪʃɪŋ/ *a* hinreißend

raw /rɔ:/ a (-er, -est) roh; (not processed) Roh-; ⟨skin⟩ wund; ⟨weather⟩ naßkalt; (inexperienced) unerfahren; **get a ~ deal** (fam) schlecht wegkommen. **~ ma'terials** npl Rohstoffe pl

ray /reɪ/ n Strahl m; **~ of hope** Hoffnungsschimmer m

raze /reɪz/ vt **~ to the ground** dem Erdboden gleichmachen

razor /'reɪzə(r)/ n Rasierapparat m. **~ blade** n Rasierklinge f

re /ri:/ prep betreffs (+ gen)

reach /ri:tʃ/ n Reichweite f; (of river) Strecke f; **within/out of ~** in/außer Reichweite; **within easy ~** leicht erreichbar • vt erreichen; (arrive at) ankommen in (+ dat); (~ as far as) reichen bis zu; kommen zu ⟨decision, conclusion⟩; (pass) reichen • vi reichen (**to** bis zu); **~ for** greifen nach; **I can't ~** ich komme nicht daran

re'act /rɪ-/ vi reagieren

re'action /rɪ-/ n Reaktion f. **~ary** a reaktionär

reactor /rɪ'æktə(r)/ n Reaktor m

read /ri:d/ vt/i (pt/pp **read** /red/) lesen; (aloud) vorlesen (**to** dat); (Univ) studieren; ablesen ⟨meter⟩. **~ out** vt vorlesen

readable /'ri:dəbl/ a lesbar

reader /'ri:də(r)/ n Leser(in) m(f); (book) Lesebuch nt

readi|ly /'redɪlɪ/ adv bereitwillig; (easily) leicht. **~ness** n Bereitschaft f; **in ~ness** bereit

reading /'ri:dɪŋ/ n Lesen nt; (Pol, Relig) Lesung f

rea'djust /ri:-/ vt neu einstellen • vi sich umstellen (**to** auf + acc)

ready /'redɪ/ a (-ier, -iest) fertig; (willing) bereit; (quick) schnell; **get ~** sich fertigmachen; (prepare to) sich bereitmachen

ready: ~'made a fertig. **~ 'money** n Bargeld nt. **~-to-'wear** a Konfektions-

real /rɪəl/ a wirklich; (genuine) echt; (actual) eigentlich • adv (Amer, fam) echt. **~ estate** n Immobilien pl

realis|m /'rɪəlɪzm/ n Realismus m. **~t** /-lɪst/ n Realist m. **~tic** /-'lɪstɪk/ a, **-ally** adv realistisch

reality /rɪ'ælətɪ/ n Wirklichkeit f, Realität f

realization /rɪəlaɪ'zeɪʃn/ n Erkenntnis f

realize /'rɪəlaɪz/ vt einsehen; (become aware) gewahr werden; verwirklichen ⟨hopes, plans⟩; (Comm) realisieren; einbringen ⟨price⟩; **I didn't ~** das wußte ich nicht

really /'rɪəlɪ/ adv wirklich; (actually) eigentlich

realm /relm/ n Reich nt

realtor /'ri:əltə(r)/ n (Amer) Immobilienmakler m

reap /ri:p/ vt ernten

reap'pear /ri:-/ vi wiederkommen

rear¹ /rɪə(r)/ a Hinter-; (Auto) Heck- • n **the ~** der hintere Teil; **from the ~** von hinten

rear² vt aufziehen • vi **~ [up]** ⟨horse:⟩ sich aufbäumen

'rear-light n Rücklicht nt

re'arm /ri:-/ vi wieder aufrüsten

rear'range /ri:-/ vt umstellen

rear-view 'mirror n (Auto) Rückspiegel m

reason /'ri:zn/ n Grund m; (good sense) Vernunft f; (ability to think) Verstand m; **within ~** in vernünftigen Grenzen • vi argumentieren; **~ with** vernünftig reden mit. **~able** /-əbl/ a vernünftig; (not expensive) preiswert. **~ably** /-əblɪ/ adv (fairly) ziemlich

reas'sur|ance /ri:-/ n Beruhigung f; Versicherung f. **~e** vt beruhigen; **~e s.o. of sth** jdm etw (gen) versichern

rebate /'ri:beɪt/ n Rückzahlung f; (discount) Nachlaß m

rebel¹ /'rebl/ n Rebell m

rebel² /rɪ'bel/ vi (pt/pp **rebelled**) rebellieren. **~lion** /-lən/ n Rebellion f. **~lious** /-ləs/ a rebellisch

re'bound¹ /rɪ-/ vi abprallen

'rebound² /ri:-/ n Rückprall m

rebuff /rɪ'bʌf/ n Abweisung f • vt abweisen; eine Abfuhr erteilen (**s.o.** jdm)

re'build /ri:-/ vt (pt/pp **-built**) wieder aufbauen; (fig) wiederaufbauen

rebuke /rɪ'bju:k/ n Tadel m • vt tadeln

rebuttal /rɪ'bʌtl/ n Widerlegung f

re'call /rɪ-/ n Erinnerung f; **beyond ~** unwiderruflich • vt zurückrufen; abberufen ⟨diplomat⟩; vorzeitig einberufen ⟨parliament⟩; (remember) sich erinnern an (+ acc)

recant /rɪ'kænt/ vi widerrufen

recap /'ri:kæp/ vt/i (fam) = **recapitulate**

recapitulate /ri:kə'pɪtjʊleɪt/ *vt/i* zusammenfassen; rekapitulieren

re'capture /ri:-/ *vt* wieder gefangennehmen ⟨*person*⟩; wieder einfangen ⟨*animal*⟩

reced|e /rɪ'si:d/ *vi* zurückgehen. ~**ing** *a* ⟨*forehead, chin*⟩ fliehend; ~**ing hair** Stirnglatze *f*

receipt /rɪ'si:t/ *n* Quittung *f*; (*receiving*) Empfang *m*; ~**s** *pl* (*Comm*) Einnahmen *pl*

receive /rɪ'si:v/ *vt* erhalten, bekommen; empfangen ⟨*guests*⟩. ~**r** *n* (*Teleph*) Hörer *m*; (*Radio, TV*) Empfänger *m*; (*of stolen goods*) Hehler *m*

recent /'ri:snt/ *a* kürzlich erfolgte(r,s). ~**ly** *adv* in letzter Zeit; (*the other day*) kürzlich, vor kurzem

receptacle /rɪ'septəkl/ *n* Behälter *m*

reception /rɪ'sepʃn/ *n* Empfang *m*; ~ **[desk]** (*in hotel*) Rezeption *f*. ~**ist** *n* Empfangsdame *f*

receptive /rɪ'septɪv/ *a* aufnahmefähig; ~ **to** empfänglich für

recess /rɪ'ses/ *n* Nische *f*; (*holiday*) Ferien *pl*; (*Amer, Sch*) Pause *f*

recession /rɪ'seʃn/ *n* Rezession *f*

re'charge /ri:-/ *vt* [wieder] aufladen

recipe /'resəpɪ/ *n* Rezept *nt*

recipient /rɪ'sɪpɪənt/ *n* Empfänger *m*

recipro|cal /rɪ'sɪprəkl/ *a* gegenseitig. ~**cate** /-keɪt/ *vt* erwidern

recital /rɪ'saɪtl/ *n* (*of poetry, songs*) Vortrag *m*; (*on piano*) Konzert *nt*

recite /rɪ'saɪt/ *vt* aufsagen; (*before audience*) vortragen; (*list*) aufzählen

reckless /'reklɪs/ *a*, **-ly** *adv* leichtsinnig; (*careless*) rücksichtslos. ~**ness** *n* Leichtsinn *m*; Rücksichtslosigkeit *f*

reckon /'rekən/ *vt* rechnen; (*consider*) glauben ● *vi* ~ **on/with** rechnen mit

re'claim /rɪ-/ *vt* zurückfordern; zurückgewinnen ⟨*land*⟩

reclin|e /rɪ'klaɪn/ *vi* liegen. ~**ing seat** *n* Liegesitz *m*

recluse /rɪ'klu:s/ *n* Einsiedler(in) *m*(*f*)

recognition /rekəg'nɪʃn/ *n* Erkennen *nt*; (*acknowledgement*) Anerkennung *f*; **in** ~ als Anerkennung (**of** *gen*); **be beyond** ~ nicht wiederzuerkennen sein

recognize /'rekəgnaɪz/ *vt* erkennen; (*know again*) wiedererkennen; (*acknowledge*) anerkennen

re'coil /rɪ-/ *vi* zurückschnellen; (*in fear*) zurückschrecken

recollect /rekə'lekt/ *vt* sich erinnern an (+ *acc*). ~**ion** /-ekʃn/ *n* Erinnerung *f*

recommend /rekə'mend/ *vt* empfehlen. ~**ation** /-'deɪʃn/ *n* Empfehlung *f*

recompense /'rekəmpens/ *n* Entschädigung *f* ● *vt* entschädigen

recon|cile /'rekənsaɪl/ *vt* versöhnen; ~**cile oneself to** sich abfinden mit. ~**ciliation** /-sɪlɪ'eɪʃn/ *n* Versöhnung *f*

recon'dition /ri:-/ *vt* generalüberholen. ~**ed engine** *n* Austauschmotor *m*

reconnaissance /rɪ'kɒnɪsns/ *n* (*Mil*) Aufklärung *f*

reconnoitre /rekə'nɔɪtə(r)/ *vi* (*pres p* -**tring**) auf Erkundung ausgehen

recon'sider /ri:-/ *vt* sich (*dat*) noch einmal überlegen

recon'struct /ri:-/ *vt* wieder aufbauen; rekonstruieren ⟨*crime*⟩. ~**ion** *n* Wiederaufbau *m*; Rekonstruktion *f*

record[1] /rɪ'kɔ:d/ *vt* aufzeichnen; (*register*) registrieren; (*on tape*) aufnehmen

record[2] /'rekɔ:d/ *n* Aufzeichnung *f*; (*Jur*) Protokoll *nt*; (*Mus*) [Schall]platte *f*; (*Sport*) Rekord *m*; ~**s** *pl* Unterlagen *pl*; **keep a** ~ **of** sich (*dat*) notieren; **off the** ~ inoffiziell; **have a [criminal]** ~ vorbestraft sein

recorder /rɪ'kɔ:də(r)/ *n* (*Mus*) Blockflöte *f*

recording /rɪ'kɔ:dɪŋ/ *n* Aufzeichnung *f*, Aufnahme *f*

'record-player *n* Plattenspieler *m*

recount /rɪ'kaʊnt/ *vt* erzählen

re-'count[1] /ri:-/ *vt* nachzählen

're-count[2] /ri:-/ *n* (*Pol*) Nachzählung *f*

recoup /rɪ'ku:p/ *vt* wiedereinbringen; ausgleichen ⟨*losses*⟩

recourse /rɪ'kɔ:s/ *n* **have** ~ **to** Zuflucht nehmen zu

re-'cover /ri:-/ *vt* neu beziehen

recover /rɪ'kʌvə(r)/ *vt* zurückbekommen; bergen ⟨*wreck*⟩ ● *vi* sich erholen. ~**y** *n* Wiedererlangung *f*; Bergung *f*; (*of health*) Erholung *f*

recreation /rekrɪ'eɪʃn/ *n* Erholung *f*; (*hobby*) Hobby *nt*. ~**al** *a* Freizeit-; **be** ~**al** erholsam sein

recrimination /rɪkrɪmɪ'neɪʃn/ *n* Gegenbeschuldigung *f*

recruit /rɪ'kru:t/ *n* (*Mil*) Rekrut *m*; **new** ~ (*member*) neues Mitglied *nt*; (*worker*) neuer Mitarbeiter *m* ● *vt* rekrutieren; anwerben ⟨*staff*⟩.

~**ment** n Rekrutierung f; Anwerbung f

rectang|le /'rektæŋgl/ n Rechteck nt. ~**ular** /-'tæŋgjʊlə(r)/ a rechteckig

rectify /'rektɪfaɪ/ vt (pt/pp -ied) berichtigen

rector /'rektə(r)/ n Pfarrer m; (Univ) Rektor m. ~**y** n Pfarrhaus nt

recuperat|e /rɪ'kju:pəreɪt/ vi sich erholen. ~**ion** /-'reɪʃn/ n Erholung f

recur /rɪ'kɜ:(r)/ vi (pt/pp recurred) sich wiederholen; ⟨illness:⟩ wiederkehren

recurren|ce /rɪ'kʌrəns/ n Wiederkehr f. ~**t** a wiederkehrend

recycle /ri:'saɪkl/ vt wiederverwerten. ~**d paper** n Umweltschutzpapier nt

red /red/ a (redder, reddest) rot ● n Rot nt. ~'**currant** n rote Johannisbeere f

redd|en /'redn/ vt röten ● vi rot werden. ~**ish** a rötlich

re'decorate /ri:-/ vt renovieren; (paint) neu streichen; (wallpaper) neu tapezieren

redeem /rɪ'di:m/ vt einlösen; (Relig) erlösen

redemption /rɪ'dempʃn/ n Erlösung f

rede'ploy /ri:-/ vt an anderer Stelle einsetzen

red: ~-**haired** a rothaarig. ~-'**handed** a catch s.o. ~-'**handed** jdn auf frischer Tat ertappen. ~ '**herring** n falsche Spur f. ~-**hot** a glühend heiß. **R~**'**Indian** n Indianer(in) m(f)

redi'rect /ri:-/ vt nachsenden ⟨letter⟩; umleiten ⟨traffic⟩

red: ~ '**light** n (Auto) rote Ampel f. ~**ness** n Röte f

re'do /ri:-/ vt (pt -did, pp -done) noch einmal machen

re'double /ri:-/ vt verdoppeln

redress /rɪ'dres/ n Entschädigung f ● vt wiedergutmachen; wiederherstellen ⟨balance⟩

red 'tape n (fam) Bürokratie f

reduc|e /rɪ'dju:s/ vt verringern, vermindern; (in size) verkleinern; ermäßigen ⟨costs⟩; herabsetzen ⟨price, goods⟩; (Culin) einkochen lassen. ~**tion** /-'dʌkʃn/ n Verringerung f; (in price) Ermäßigung f; (in size) Verkleinerung f

redundan|cy /rɪ'dʌndənsɪ/ n Beschäftigungslosigkeit f; (payment) Abfindung f. ~**t** a überflüssig;

make ~**t** entlassen; **be made** ~**t** beschäftigungslos werden

reed /ri:d/ n [Schilf]rohr nt; ~**s** pl Schilf nt

reef /ri:f/ n Riff nt

reek /ri:k/ vi riechen (**of** nach)

reel /ri:l/ n Rolle f, Spule f ● vi (stagger) taumeln ● vt ~ **off** (fig) herunterrasseln

refectory /rɪ'fektərɪ/ n Refektorium nt; (Univ) Mensa f

refer /rɪ'fɜ:(r)/ v (pt/pp referred) ● vt verweisen (**to** an + acc); übergeben, weiterleiten ⟨matter⟩ (**to** an + acc) ● vi ~ **to** sich beziehen auf (+ acc); (mention) erwähnen; (concern) betreffen; (consult) sich wenden an (+ acc); nachschlagen in (+ dat) ⟨book⟩; **are you** ~**ring to me?** meinen Sie mich?

referee /refə'ri:/ n Schiedsrichter m; (Boxing) Ringrichter m; (for job) Referenz f ● vt/i (pt/pp refereed) Schiedsrichter/Ringrichter sein (bei)

reference /'refərəns/ n Erwähnung f; (in book) Verweis m; (for job) Referenz f; (Comm) '**your** ~' 'Ihr Zeichen'; **with** ~ **to** in bezug auf (+ acc); (in letter) unter Bezugnahme auf (+ acc); **make** [**a**] ~ **to** erwähnen. ~ **book** n Nachschlagewerk nt. ~ **number** n Aktenzeichen nt

referendum /refə'rendəm/ n Volksabstimmung f

re'fill¹ /ri:-/ vt nachfüllen

'**refill**² /ri:-/ n (for pen) Ersatzmine f

refine /rɪ'faɪn/ vt raffinieren. ~**d** a fein, vornehm. ~**ment** n Vornehmheit f; (Techn) Verfeinerung f. ~**ry** /-ərɪ/ n Raffinerie f

reflect /rɪ'flekt/ vt reflektieren; ⟨mirror:⟩ [wider]spiegeln; **be** ~**ed in** sich spiegeln in (+ dat) ● vi nachdenken (**on** über + acc); ~ **badly upon s.o.** (fig) jdn in ein schlechtes Licht stellen. ~**ion** /-ekʃn/ n Reflexion f; (image) Spiegelbild nt; **on** ~**ion** nach nochmaliger Überlegung. ~**ive** /-ɪv/ a, -**ly** adv nachdenklich. ~**or** n Rückstrahler m

reflex /'ri:fleks/ a Reflex m ● attrib Reflex-

reflexive /rɪ'fleksɪv/ a reflexiv

reform /rɪ'fɔ:m/ n Reform f ● vt reformieren ● vi sich bessern. **R~ation** /refə'meɪʃn/ n (Relig) Reformation f. ~**er** n Reformer m; (Relig) Reformator m

refract /rɪˈfrækt/ vt (Phys) brechen

refrain¹ /rɪˈfreɪn/ n Refrain m

refrain² vi ~ from doing sth etw nicht tun

refresh /rɪˈfreʃ/ vt erfrischen. ~ing a erfrischend. ~ments npl Erfrischungen pl

refrigerat|e /rɪˈfrɪdʒəreɪt/ vt kühlen. ~or n Kühlschrank m

re'fuel /riː-/ v (pt/pp -fuelled) vt/i auftanken

refuge /ˈrefjuːdʒ/ n Zuflucht f; take ~ in Zuflucht nehmen in (+ dat)

refugee /refjʊˈdʒiː/ n Flüchtling m

'refund¹ /riː-/ get a ~ sein Geld zurückbekommen

re'fund² /rɪ-/ vt zurückerstatten

refurbish /riːˈfɜːbɪʃ/ vt renovieren

refusal /rɪˈfjuːzl/ n (see **refuse¹**) Ablehnung f; Weigerung f

refuse¹ /rɪˈfjuːz/ vt ablehnen; (not grant) verweigern; ~ to do sth sich weigern, etw zu tun ● vi ablehnen; sich weigern

refuse² /ˈrefjuːs/ n Müll m, Abfall m. ~ collection n Müllabfuhr f

refute /rɪˈfjuːt/ vt widerlegen

re'gain /rɪ-/ vt wiedergewinnen

regal /ˈriːgl/ a, **-ly** adv königlich

regalia /rɪˈgeɪlɪə/ npl Insignien pl

regard /rɪˈgɑːd/ n (heed) Rücksicht f; (respect) Achtung f; ~s pl Grüße pl; with ~ to in bezug auf (+ acc) ● vt ansehen, betrachten (as als); as ~s in bezug auf (+ acc). ~ing prep bezüglich (+ gen). ~less adv ohne Rücksicht (of auf + acc)

regatta /rɪˈgætə/ n Regatta f

regenerate /rɪˈdʒenəreɪt/ vt regenerieren ● vi sich regenerieren

regime /reɪˈʒiːm/ n Regime nt

regiment /ˈredʒɪmənt/ n Regiment nt. ~al /-ˈmentl/ a Regiments-. ~ation /-ˈteɪʃn/ n Reglementierung f

region /ˈriːdʒən/ n Region f; in the ~ of (fig) ungefähr. ~al a, **-ly** adv regional

register /ˈredʒɪstə(r)/ n Register nt; (Sch) Anwesenheitsliste f ● vt registrieren; (report) anmelden; einschreiben ⟨letter⟩; aufgeben ⟨luggage⟩ ● vi (report) sich anmelden; it didn't ~ (fig) ich habe es nicht registriert

registrar /redʒɪˈstrɑː(r)/ n Standesbeamte(r) m

registration /redʒɪˈstreɪʃn/ n Registrierung f; Anmeldung f. ~ number n Autonummer f

registry office /ˈredʒɪstrɪ-/ n Standesamt nt

regret /rɪˈgret/ n Bedauern nt ● vt (pt/pp **regretted**) bedauern. ~fully adv mit Bedauern

regrettab|le /rɪˈgretəbl/ a bedauerlich. ~ly adv bedauerlicherweise

regular /ˈregjʊlə(r)/ a, **-ly** adv regelmäßig; (usual) üblich; (Mil) Berufs- ● n Berufssoldat m; (in pub) Stammgast m; (in shop) Stammkunde m. ~ity /-ˈlærətɪ/ n Regelmäßigkeit f

regulat|e /ˈregjʊleɪt/ vt regulieren. ~ion /-ˈleɪʃn/ n (rule) Vorschrift f

rehabilitat|e /riːhəˈbɪlɪteɪt/ vt rehabilitieren. ~ion /-ˈteɪʃn/ n Rehabilitation f

rehears|al /rɪˈhɜːsl/ n (Theat) Probe f. ~e vt proben

reign /reɪn/ n Herrschaft f ● vi herrschen, regieren

reimburse /riːɪmˈbɜːs/ vt ~ s.o. for sth jdm etw zurückerstatten

rein /reɪn/ n Zügel m

reincarnation /riːɪnkɑːˈneɪʃn/ n Reinkarnation f, Wiedergeburt f

reindeer /ˈreɪndɪə(r)/ n inv Rentier nt

reinforce /riːɪnˈfɔːs/ vt verstärken. ~d 'concrete n Stahlbeton m. ~ment n Verstärkung f; send ~ments Verstärkung schicken

reinstate /riːɪnˈsteɪt/ vt wiedereinstellen; (to office) wiedereinsetzen

reiterate /riːˈɪtəreɪt/ vt wiederholen

reject /rɪˈdʒekt/ vt ablehnen. ~ion /-ekʃn/ n Ablehnung f

rejects /ˈriːdʒekts/ npl (Comm) Ausschußware f

rejoic|e /rɪˈdʒɔɪs/ vi (liter) sich freuen. ~ing n Freude f

re'join /rɪ-/ vt sich wieder anschließen (+ dat); wieder beitreten (+ dat) ⟨club, party⟩; (answer) erwidern

rejuvenate /rɪˈdʒuːvəneɪt/ vt verjüngen

relapse /rɪˈlæps/ n Rückfall m ● vi einen Rückfall erleiden

relate /rɪˈleɪt/ vt (tell) erzählen; (connect) verbinden ● vi zusammenhängen (to mit). ~d a verwandt (to mit)

relation /rɪˈleɪʃn/ n Beziehung f; (person) Verwandte(r) m/f. ~ship n Beziehung f; (link) Verbindung f; (blood tie) Verwandtschaft f; (affair) Verhältnis nt

relative /ˈrelətɪv/ n Verwandte(r) m/f ● a relativ; (Gram) Relativ-. ~ly adv relativ, verhältnismäßig

relax /rɪˈlæks/ vt lockern, entspannen ● vi sich lockern, sich entspannen. ~ation /-ˈseɪʃn/ n Entspannung f. ~ing a entspannend

relay¹ /riːˈleɪ/ vt (pt/pp -laid) weitergeben; (Radio, TV) übertragen

relay² /ˈriːleɪ/ n (Electr) Relais nt; **work in ~s** sich bei der Arbeit ablösen. ~ [race] n Staffel f

release /rɪˈliːs/ n Freilassung f, Entlassung f; (Techn) Auslöser m ● vt freilassen; (let go of) loslassen; (Techn) auslösen; veröffentlichen ⟨information⟩

relegate /ˈrelɪgeɪt/ vt verbannen; **be ~d** (Sport) absteigen

relent /rɪˈlent/ vi nachgeben. ~less a, -ly adv erbarmungslos; (unceasing) unaufhörlich

relevan|ce /ˈreləvəns/ n Relevanz f. ~t a relevant (**to** für)

reliab|ility /rɪlaɪəˈbɪlətɪ/ n Zuverlässigkeit f. ~le /-ˈlaɪəbl/ a, -ly adv zuverlässig

relian|ce /rɪˈlaɪəns/ n Abhängigkeit f (**on** von). ~t a angewiesen (**on** auf + acc)

relic /ˈrelɪk/ n Überbleibsel nt; (Relig) Reliquie f

relief /rɪˈliːf/ n Erleichterung f; (assistance) Hilfe f; (distraction) Abwechslung f; (replacement) Ablösung f; (Art) Relief nt; **in ~** im Relief. ~ **map** n Reliefkarte f. ~ **train** n Entlastungszug m

relieve /rɪˈliːv/ vt erleichtern; (take over from) ablösen; ~ **of** entlasten von

religion /rɪˈlɪdʒən/ n Religion f

religious /rɪˈlɪdʒəs/ a religiös. ~ly adv (conscientiously) gewissenhaft

relinquish /rɪˈlɪŋkwɪʃ/ vt loslassen; (give up) aufgeben

relish /ˈrelɪʃ/ n Genuß m; (Culin) Würze f ● vt genießen

relo'cate /riː-/ vt verlegen

reluctan|ce /rɪˈlʌktəns/ n Widerstreben nt. ~t a widerstrebend; **be ~t** zögern (**to** zu). ~tly adv ungern, widerstrebend

rely /rɪˈlaɪ/ vi (pt/pp -ied) ~ **on** sich verlassen auf (+ acc); (be dependent on) angewiesen sein auf (+ acc)

remain /rɪˈmeɪn/ vi bleiben; (be left) übrigbleiben. ~**der** n Rest m. ~**ing** a restlich. ~s npl Reste pl; **[mortal] ~s** [sterbliche] Überreste pl

remand /rɪˈmɑːnd/ n **on ~** in Untersuchungshaft ● vt ~ **in custody** in Untersuchungshaft schicken

remark /rɪˈmɑːk/ n Bemerkung f ● vt bemerken. ~**able** /-əbl/ a, -**bly** adv bemerkenswert

re'marry /riː-/ vi wieder heiraten

remedial /rɪˈmiːdɪəl/ a Hilfs-; (Med) Heil-

remedy /ˈremədɪ/ n [Heil]mittel nt (**for** gegen); (fig) Abhilfe f ● vt (pt/pp -ied) abhelfen (+ dat); beheben ⟨fault⟩

rememb|er /rɪˈmembə(r)/ vt sich erinnern an (+ acc); ~**er to do sth** daran denken, etw zu tun; ~**er me to him** grüßen Sie ihn von mir ● vi sich erinnern. ~**rance** n Erinnerung f

remind /rɪˈmaɪnd/ vt erinnern (**of** an + acc). ~**er** n Andenken nt; (letter, warning) Mahnung f

reminisce /remɪˈnɪs/ vi sich seinen Erinnerungen hingeben. ~**nces** /-ənsɪs/ npl Erinnerungen pl. ~**nt** a **be ~nt of** erinnern an (+ acc)

remiss /rɪˈmɪs/ a nachlässig

remission /rɪˈmɪʃn/ n Nachlaß m; (of sentence) [Straf]erlaß m; (Med) Remission f

remit /rɪˈmɪt/ vt (pt/pp **remitted**) überweisen ⟨money⟩. ~**tance** n Überweisung f

remnant /ˈremnənt/ n Rest m

remonstrate /ˈremənstreɪt/ vi protestieren; ~ **with s.o.** jdm Vorhaltungen machen

remorse /rɪˈmɔːs/ n Reue f. ~**ful** a, -**ly** adv reumütig. ~**less** a, -**ly** adv unerbittlich

remote /rɪˈməʊt/ a fern; (isolated) abgelegen; (slight) gering. ~ **con'trol** n Fernsteuerung f; (for TV) Fernbedienung f. ~-**con'trolled** a ferngesteuert; fernbedient

remotely /rɪˈməʊtlɪ/ adv entfernt; **not ~** nicht im entferntesten

re'movable /rɪ-/ a abnehmbar

removal /rɪˈmuːvl/ n Entfernung f; (from house) Umzug m. ~ **van** n Möbelwagen m

remove /rɪˈmuːv/ vt entfernen; (take off) abnehmen; (take out) herausnehmen

remunerat|e /rɪˈmjuːnəreɪt/ vt bezahlen. ~**ion** /-ˈreɪʃn/ n Bezahlung f. ~**ive** /-ətɪv/ a einträglich

render /ˈrendə(r)/ vt machen; erweisen ⟨service⟩; (translate) wiedergeben; (Mus) vortragen

renegade /'renɪgeɪd/ n Abtrünnige(r) m/f

renew /rɪ'njuː/ vt erneuern; verlängern ⟨contract⟩. **~al** n Erneuerung f; Verlängerung f

renounce /rɪ'naʊns/ vt verzichten auf (+ acc); (Relig) abschwören (+ dat)

renovat|e /'renəveɪt/ vt renovieren. **~ion** /-'veɪʃn/ n Renovierung f

renown /rɪ'naʊn/ n Ruf m. **~ed** a berühmt

rent /rent/ n Miete f • vt mieten; (hire) leihen; **~ [out]** vermieten; verleihen. **~al** n Mietgebühr f; Leihgebühr f

renunciation /rɪnʌnsɪ'eɪʃn/ n Verzicht m

re'open /riː-/ vt/i wieder aufmachen

re'organize /riː-/ vt reorganisieren

rep /rep/ n (fam) Vertreter m

repair /rɪ'peə(r)/ n Reparatur f; **in good/bad ~** in gutem/schlechtem Zustand • vt reparieren

repartee /repɑː'tiː/ n **piece of ~** schlagfertige Antwort f

repatriat|e /riː'pætrɪeɪt/ vt repatriieren. **~ion** /-'eɪʃn/ n Repatriierung f

re'pay /riː-/ vt (pt/pp -paid) zurückzahlen; **~ s.o. for sth** jdm etw zurückzahlen. **~ment** n Rückzahlung f

repeal /rɪ'piːl/ n Aufhebung f • vt aufheben

repeat /rɪ'piːt/ n Wiederholung f • vt/i wiederholen; **~ after me** sprechen Sie mir nach. **~ed** a, **-ly** adv wiederholt

repel /rɪ'pel/ vt (pt/pp **repelled**) abwehren; (fig) abstoßen. **~lent** a abstoßend

repent /rɪ'pent/ vi Reue zeigen. **~ance** n Reue f. **~ant** a reuig

repercussions /riːpə'kʌʃnz/ npl Auswirkungen pl

repertoire /'repətwɑː(r)/ n Repertoire nt

repertory /'repətrɪ/ n Repertoire nt

repetit|ion /repɪ'tɪʃn/ n Wiederholung f. **~ive** /rɪ'petɪtɪv/ a eintönig

re'place /rɪ-/ vt zurücktun; (take the place of) ersetzen; (exchange) austauschen, auswechseln. **~ment** n Ersatz m. **~ment part** n Ersatzteil nt

'replay /riː-/ n (Sport) Wiederholungsspiel nt; **[action] ~** Wiederholung f

replenish /rɪ'plenɪʃ/ vt auffüllen ⟨stocks⟩; (refill) nachfüllen

replete /rɪ'pliːt/ a gesättigt

replica /'replɪkə/ n Nachbildung f

reply /rɪ'plaɪ/ n Antwort f (**to** auf + acc) • vt/i (pt/pp **replied**) antworten

report /rɪ'pɔːt/ n Bericht m; (Sch) Zeugnis nt; (rumour) Gerücht nt; (of gun) Knall m • vt berichten; (notify) melden; **~ s.o. to the police** jdn anzeigen • vi berichten (**on** über + acc); (present oneself) sich melden (**to** bei). **~er** n Reporter(in) m(f)

repose /rɪ'pəʊz/ n Ruhe f

repos'sess /riː-/ vt wieder in Besitz nehmen

reprehensible /reprɪ'hensəbl/ a tadelnswert

represent /reprɪ'zent/ vt darstellen; (act for) vertreten, repräsentieren. **~ation** /-'teɪʃn/ n Darstellung f; **make ~ations to** vorstellig werden bei

representative /reprɪ'zentətɪv/ a repräsentativ (**of** für) • n Bevollmächtigte(r) m/f; (Comm) Vertreter (in) m(f); (Amer, Pol) Abgeordnete(r) m/f

repress /rɪ'pres/ vt unterdrücken. **~ion** /-eʃn/ n Unterdrückung f. **~ive** /-ɪv/ a repressiv

reprieve /rɪ'priːv/ n Begnadigung f; (postponement) Strafaufschub m; (fig) Gnadenfrist f • vt begnadigen

reprimand /'reprɪmɑːnd/ n Tadel m • vt tadeln

'reprint[1] /riː-/ n Nachdruck m

re'print[2] /riː-/ vt neu auflegen

reprisal /rɪ'praɪzl/ n Vergeltungsmaßnahme f

reproach /rɪ'prəʊtʃ/ n Vorwurf m • vt Vorwürfe pl machen (+ dat). **~ful** a, **-ly** adv vorwurfsvoll

repro'duc|e /riː-/ vt wiedergeben, reproduzieren • vi sich fortpflanzen. **~tion** /-'dʌkʃn/ n Reproduktion f; (Biol) Fortpflanzung f. **~tion furniture** n Stilmöbel pl. **~tive** /-'dʌktɪv/ a Fortpflanzungs-

reprove /rɪ'pruːv/ vt tadeln

reptile /'reptaɪl/ n Reptil nt

republic /rɪ'pʌblɪk/ n Republik f. **~an** a republikanisch • n Republikaner (in) m(f)

repudiate /rɪ'pjuːdɪeɪt/ vt zurückweisen

repugnan|ce /rɪ'pʌgnəns/ n Widerwille m. **~t** a widerlich

repuls|e /rɪ'pʌls/ vt abwehren; (fig) abweisen. **~ion** /-ʌlʃn/ n Widerwille m. **~ive** /-ɪv/ a abstoßend, widerlich

reputable /'repjʊtəbl/ a ⟨firm⟩ von gutem Ruf; (respectable) anständig

reputation /repjʊ'teɪʃn/ n Ruf m

repute /rɪ'pju:t/ n Ruf m. **~d** /-ɪd/ a, -ly adv angeblich

request /rɪ'kwest/ n Bitte f ● vt bitten. **~ stop** n Bedarfshaltestelle f

require /rɪ'kwaɪə(r)/ vt (need) brauchen; (demand) erfordern; **be ~d to do sth** etw tun müssen. **~ment** n Bedürfnis nt; (condition) Erfordernis nt

requisite /'rekwɪzɪt/ a erforderlich ● n **toilet/travel ~s** pl Toiletten/ Reiseartikel pl

requisition /rekwɪ'zɪʃn/ n ~ **[order]** Anforderung f ● vt anfordern

re'sale /ri:-/ n Weiterverkauf m

rescind /rɪ'sɪnd/ vt aufheben

rescue /'reskju:/ n Rettung f ● vt retten. **~r** n Retter m

research /rɪ'sɜ:tʃ/ n Forschung f ● vt erforschen; (Journ) recherchieren ● vi ~ **into** erforschen. **~er** n Forscher m; (Journ) Rechercheur m

resem|blance /rɪ'zembləns/ n Ähnlichkeit f. **~ble** /-bl/ vt ähneln (+ dat)

resent /rɪ'zent/ vt übelnehmen; einen Groll hegen gegen ⟨person⟩. **~ful** a, -ly adv verbittert. **~ment** n Groll m

reservation /rezə'veɪʃn/ n Reservierung f; (doubt) Vorbehalt m; (enclosure) Reservat nt

reserve /rɪ'zɜ:v/ n Reserve f; (for animals) Reservat nt; (Sport) Reservespieler(in) m(f) ● vt reservieren; ⟨client:⟩ reservieren lassen; (keep) aufheben; sich (dat) vorbehalten ⟨right⟩. **~d** a reserviert

reservoir /'rezəvwɑ:(r)/ n Reservoir nt

re'shape /ri:-/ vt umformen

re'shuffle /ri:-/ n (Pol) Umbildung f ● vt (Pol) umbilden

reside /rɪ'zaɪd/ vi wohnen

residence /'rezɪdəns/ n Wohnsitz m; (official) Residenz f; (stay) Aufenthalt m. **~ permit** n Aufenthaltsgenehmigung f

resident /'rezɪdənt/ a ansässig (**in** in + dat); ⟨housekeeper, nurse⟩ im Haus wohnend ● n Bewohner(in) m(f); (of street) Anwohner m. **~ial** /-'denʃl/ a Wohn-

residue /'rezɪdju:/ n Rest m; (Chem) Rückstand m

resign /rɪ'zaɪn/ vt ~ **oneself to** sich abfinden mit ● vi kündigen; (from public office) zurücktreten. **~ation** /rezɪg'neɪʃn/ n Resignation f; (from job) Kündigung f; Rücktritt m. **~ed** a, -ly adv resigniert

resilient /rɪ'zɪlɪənt/ a federnd; (fig) widerstandsfähig

resin /'rezɪn/ n Harz nt

resist /rɪ'zɪst/ vt/i sich widersetzen (+ dat); (fig) widerstehen (+ dat). **~ance** n Widerstand m. **~ant** a widerstandsfähig

resolut|e /'rezəlu:t/ a, -ly adv entschlossen. **~ion** /-'lu:ʃn/ n Entschlossenheit f; (intention) Vorsatz m; (Pol) Resolution f

resolve /rɪ'zɒlv/ n Entschlossenheit f; (decision) Beschluß m ● vt beschließen; (solve) lösen. **~d** a entschlossen

resonan|ce /'rezənəns/ n Resonanz f. **~t** a klangvoll

resort /rɪ'zɔ:t/ n (place) Urlaubsort m; **as a last ~** wenn alles andere fehlschlägt ● vi ~ **to** (fig) greifen zu

resound /rɪ'zaʊnd/ vi widerhallen. **~ing** a widerhallend; (loud) laut; (notable) groß

resource /rɪ'sɔ:s/ n **~s** pl Ressourcen pl. **~ful** a findig. **~fulness** n Findigkeit f

respect /rɪ'spekt/ n Respekt m, Achtung f (**for** vor + dat); (aspect) Hinsicht f; **with ~ to** in bezug auf (+ acc) ● vt respektieren, achten

respectability /rɪspektə'bɪlətɪ/ n (see respectable) Ehrbarkeit f; Anständigkeit f

respect|able /rɪ'spektəbl/ a, -bly adv ehrbar; (decent) anständig; (considerable) ansehnlich. **~ful** a, -ly adv respektvoll

respective /rɪ'spektɪv/ a jeweilig. **~ly** adv beziehungsweise

respiration /respə'reɪʃn/ n Atmung f

respite /'respaɪt/ n [Ruhe]pause f; (delay) Aufschub m

resplendent /rɪ'splendənt/ a glänzend

respond /rɪ'spɒnd/ vi antworten; (react) reagieren (**to** auf + acc); ⟨patient:⟩ ansprechen (**to** auf + acc)

response /rɪ'spɒns/ n Antwort f; Reaktion f

responsibility /rɪspɒnsɪ'brɪlətɪ/ *n* Verantwortung *f*; (*duty*) Verpflichtung *f*

responsib|le /rɪ'spɒnsəbl/ *a* verantwortlich; (*trustworthy*) verantwortungsvoll. **~ly** *adv* verantwortungsbewußt

responsive /rɪ'spɒnsɪv/ *a* **be ~** reagieren

rest[1] /rest/ *n* Ruhe *f*; (*holiday*) Erholung *f*; (*interval & Mus*) Pause *f*; **have a ~** eine Pause machen; (*rest*) sich ausruhen ● *vt* ausruhen; (*lean*) lehnen (**on** an/auf + *acc*) ● *vi* ruhen; (*have a rest*) sich ausruhen

rest[2] *n* **the ~** der Rest; (*people*) die Übrigen *pl* ● *vi* **it ~s with you** es ist an Ihnen (**to** zu)

restaurant /'restərɒnt/ *n* Restaurant *nt*, Gaststätte *f*. **~ car** *n* Speisewagen *m*

restful /'restfl/ *a* erholsam

restitution /restɪ'tju:ʃn/ *n* Entschädigung *f*; (*return*) Rückgabe *f*

restive /'restɪv/ *a* unruhig

restless /'restlɪs/ *a*, **-ly** *adv* unruhig

restoration /restə'reɪʃn/ *n* (*of building*) Restaurierung *f*

restore /rɪ'stɔ:(r)/ *vt* wiederherstellen; restaurieren ⟨*building*⟩; (*give back*) zurückgeben

restrain /rɪ'streɪn/ *vt* zurückhalten; **~ oneself** sich beherrschen. **~ed** *a* zurückhaltend. **~t** *n* Zurückhaltung *f*

restrict /rɪ'strɪkt/ *vt* einschränken; **~ to** beschränken auf (+ *acc*). **~ion** /-ɪkʃn/ *n* Einschränkung *f*; Beschränkung *f*. **~ive** /-ɪv/ *a* einschränkend

'**rest room** *n* (*Amer*) Toilette *f*

result /rɪ'zʌlt/ *n* Ergebnis *nt*, Resultat *nt*; (*consequence*) Folge *f*; **as a ~** als Folge (**of** *gen*) ● *vi* sich ergeben (**from** aus); **~ in** enden in (+ *dat*); (*lead to*) führen zu

resume /rɪ'zju:m/ *vt* wiederaufnehmen; wieder einnehmen ⟨*seat*⟩ ● *vi* wieder beginnen

résumé /'rezʊmeɪ/ *n* Zusammenfassung *f*

resumption /rɪ'zʌmpʃn/ *n* Wiederaufnahme *f*

resurgence /rɪ'sɜ:dʒəns/ *n* Wiederaufleben *nt*

resurrect /rezə'rekt/ *vt* (*fig*) wiederbeleben. **~ion** /-ekʃn/ *n* **the R~ion** (*Relig*) die Auferstehung

resuscitat|e /rɪ'sʌsɪteɪt/ *vt* wiederbeleben. **~ion** /-'teɪʃn/ *n* Wiederbelebung *f*

retail /'ri:teɪl/ *n* Einzelhandel *m* ● *a* Einzelhandels- ● *adv* im Einzelhandel ● *vt* im Einzelhandel verkaufen ● *vi* **~ at** im Einzelhandel kosten. **~er** *n* Einzelhändler *m*. **~ price** *n* Ladenpreis *m*

retain /rɪ'teɪn/ *vt* behalten

retaliat|e /rɪ'tælɪeɪt/ *vi* zurückschlagen. **~ion** /-ɪ'eɪʃn/ *n* Vergeltung *f*; **in ~ion** als Vergeltung

retarded /rɪ'tɑ:dɪd/ *a* zurückgeblieben

retentive /rɪ'tentɪv/ *a* ⟨*memory*⟩ gut

reticen|ce /'retɪsns/ *n* Zurückhaltung *f*. **~t** *a* zurückhaltend

retina /'retɪnə/ *n* Netzhaut *f*

retinue /'retɪnju:/ *n* Gefolge *nt*

retire /rɪ'taɪə(r)/ *vi* in den Ruhestand treten; (*withdraw*) sich zurückziehen. **~d** *a* im Ruhestand. **~ment** *n* Ruhestand *m*; **since my ~ment** seit ich nicht mehr arbeite

retiring /rɪ'taɪərɪŋ/ *a* zurückhaltend

retort /rɪ'tɔ:t/ *n* scharfe Erwiderung *f*; (*Chem*) Retorte *f* ● *vt* scharf erwidern

re'touch /ri:-/ *vt* (*Phot*) retuschieren

re'trace /rɪ-/ *vt* zurückverfolgen; **~ one's steps** denselben Weg zurückgehen

retract /rɪ'trækt/ *vt* einziehen; zurücknehmen ⟨*remark*⟩ ● *vi* widerrufen

re'train /ri:-/ *vt* umschulen ● *vi* umgeschult werden

retreat /rɪ'tri:t/ *n* Rückzug *m*; (*place*) Zufluchtsort *m* ● *vi* sich zurückziehen

re'trial /ri:-/ *n* Wiederaufnahmeverfahren *nt*

retribution /retrɪ'bju:ʃn/ *n* Vergeltung *f*

retrieve /rɪ'tri:v/ *vt* zurückholen; (*from wreckage*) bergen; (*Computing*) wiederauffinden; ⟨*dog*:⟩ apportieren

retrograde /'retrəgreɪd/ *a* rückschrittlich

retrospect /'retrəspekt/ *n* **in ~** rückblickend. **~ive** /-ɪv/ *a*, **-ly** *adv* rückwirkend; (*looking back*) rückblickend

return /rɪ'tɜ:n/ *n* Rückkehr *f*; (*giving back*) Rückgabe *f*; (*Comm*) Ertrag *m*; (*ticket*) Rückfahrkarte *f*; (*Aviat*) Rückflugschein *m*; **by ~ [of post]**

postwendend; **in** ~ dafür; **in** ~ **for**
für; **many happy** ~**s!** herzlichen
Glückwunsch zum Geburtstag! ● *vi*
zurückgehen/-fahren; (*come back*)
zurückkommen ● *vt* zurückgeben;
(*put back*) zurückstellen/-legen;
(*send back*) zurückschicken; (*elect*)
wählen

return: ~ **flight** *n* Rückflug *m*. ~
match *n* Rückspiel *nt*. ~ **ticket** *n*
Rückfahrkarte *f*; (*Aviat*) Rückflugschein *m*

reunion /riː'juːnɪən/ *n* Wiedervereini-
gung *f*; (*social gathering*) Treffen *nt*

reunite /riːjuː'naɪt/ *vt* wiedervereinigen ● *vi* sich wiedervereinigen

re'us|able /riː-/ *a* wiederverwendbar.
~**e** *vt* wiederverwenden

rev /rev/ *n* (*Auto*, *fam*) Umdrehung *f*
● *vt*/*i* ~ **[up]** den Motor auf Touren
bringen

reveal /rɪ'viːl/ *vt* zum Vorschein
bringen; (*fig*) enthüllen. ~**ing** *a*
(*fig*) aufschlußreich

revel /'revl/ *vi* (*pt*/*pp* **revelled**) ~ **in**
sth etw genießen

revelation /revə'leɪʃn/ *n* Offen-
barung *f*, Enthüllung *f*

revelry /'revlrɪ/ *n* Lustbarkeit *f*

revenge /rɪ'vendʒ/ *n* Rache *f*; (*fig* &
Sport) Revanche *f* ● *vt* rächen

revenue /'revənjuː/ *n* [Staats]einnah-
men *pl*

reverberate /rɪ'vɜːbəreɪt/ *vi* nachhallen

revere /rɪ'vɪə(r)/ *vt* verehren. ~**nce**
/'revərəns/ *n* Ehrfurcht *f*

Reverend /'revərənd/ *a* the ~ **X** Pfarrer X; (*Catholic*) Hochwürden X

reverent /'revərənt/ *a*, **-ly** *adv*
ehrfürchtig

reverie /'revərɪ/ *n* Träumerei *f*

revers /rɪ'vɪə/ *n* (*pl* **revers** /-z/) Revers
nt

reversal /rɪ'vɜːsl/ *n* Umkehrung *f*

reverse /rɪ'vɜːs/ *a* umgekehrt ● *n*
Gegenteil *nt*; (*back*) Rückseite *f*;
(*Auto*) Rückwärtsgang *m* ● *vt* umkehren; (*Auto*) zurücksetzen; ~ **the
charges** (*Teleph*) ein R-Gespräch
führen ● *vi* zurücksetzen

revert /rɪ'vɜːt/ *vi* ~ **to** zurückfallen
an (+ *acc*); zurückkommen auf (+
acc) ⟨*topic*⟩

review /rɪ'vjuː/ *n* Rückblick *m* (**of** auf
+ *acc*); (*re-examination*) Überprüfung *f*; (*Mil*) Truppenschau *f*; (*of
book, play*) Kritik *f*, Rezension *f* ● *vt*

zurückblicken auf (+ *acc*); überprüfen ⟨*situation*⟩; (*Mil*) besichtigen;
kritisieren, rezensieren ⟨*book*,
play⟩. ~**er** *n* Kritiker *m*, Rezensent
m

revile /rɪ'vaɪl/ *vt* verunglimpfen

revis|e /rɪ'vaɪz/ *vt* revidieren; (*for
exam*) wiederholen. ~**ion** /-'vɪʒn/ *n*
Revision *f*; Wiederholung *f*

revival /rɪ'vaɪvl/ *n* Wiederbelebung *f*

revive /rɪ'vaɪv/ *vt* wiederbeleben;
(*fig*) wieder aufleben lassen ● *vi*
wieder aufleben

revoke /rɪ'vəʊk/ *vt* aufheben; widerrufen ⟨*command*, *decision*⟩

revolt /rɪ'vəʊlt/ *n* Aufstand *m* ● *vi*
rebellieren ● *vt* anwidern. ~**ing** *a*
widerlich, eklig

revolution /revə'luːʃn/ *n* Revolution
f; (*Auto*) Umdrehung *f*. ~**ary** /-ərɪ/
a revolutionär. ~**ize** *vt* revo-
lutionieren

revolve /rɪ'vɒlv/ *vi* sich drehen; ~
around kreisen um

revolv|er /rɪ'vɒlvə(r)/ *n* Revolver *m*.
~**ing** *a* Dreh-

revue /rɪ'vjuː/ *n* Revue *f*; (*satirical*)
Kabarett *nt*

revulsion /rɪ'vʌlʃn/ *n* Abscheu *m*

reward /rɪ'wɔːd/ *n* Belohnung *f* ● *vt*
belohnen. ~**ing** *a* lohnend

re'write /riː-/ *vt* (*pt* **rewrote**, *pp* **re-
written**) noch einmal [neu] schrei-
ben; (*alter*) umschreiben

rhapsody /'ræpsədɪ/ *n* Rhapsodie *f*

rhetoric /'retərɪk/ *n* Rhetorik *f*. ~**al**
/rɪ'tɒrɪkl/ *a* rhetorisch

rheuma|tic /ruː'mætɪk/ *a* rheuma-
tisch. ~**tism** /'ruːmətɪzm/ *n* Rheuma-
tismus *m*, Rheuma *nt*

Rhine /raɪn/ *n* Rhein *m*

rhinoceros /raɪ'nɒsərəs/ *n* Nashorn
nt, Rhinozeros *nt*

rhubarb /'ruːbɑːb/ *n* Rhabarber *m*

rhyme /raɪm/ *n* Reim *m* ● *vt* reimen
● *vi* sich reimen

rhythm /'rɪðm/ *n* Rhythmus *m*.
~**ic[al]** *a*, **-ally** *adv* rhythmisch

rib /rɪb/ *n* Rippe *f* ● *vt* (*pt*/*pp* **ribbed**)
(*fam*) aufziehen (*fam*)

ribald /'rɪbld/ *a* derb

ribbon /'rɪbən/ *n* Band *nt*; (*for typewriter*) Farbband *nt*; **in** ~**s** in Fetzen

rice /raɪs/ *n* Reis *m*

rich /rɪtʃ/ *a* (**-er**, **-est**), **-ly** *adv* reich;
⟨*food*⟩ gehaltvoll; (*heavy*) schwer ● *n*
the ~ *pl* die Reichen; ~**es** *pl* Reichtum *m*

rickets /'rɪkɪts/ *n* Rachitis *f*

rickety /'rɪkətɪ/ a wackelig

ricochet /'rɪkəʃeɪ/ vi abprallen

rid /rɪd/ vt (pt/pp rid, pres p ridding)
befreien (**of** von); **get ~ of**
loswerden

riddance /'rɪdns/ n **good ~!** auf
Nimmerwiedersehen!

ridden /'rɪdn/ see ride

riddle /'rɪdl/ n Rätsel nt

riddled /'rɪdld/ a **~ with** durchlöchert mit

ride /raɪd/ n Ritt m; (in vehicle) Fahrt
f; **take s.o. for a ~** (fam) jdn reinlegen ● v (pt rode, pp ridden) ● vt
reiten ⟨horse⟩; fahren mit ⟨bicycle⟩
● vi reiten; (in vehicle) fahren. **~r** n
Reiter(in) m(f); (on bicycle) Fahrer
(in) m(f); (in document) Zusatzklau-
sel f

ridge /rɪdʒ/ n Erhebung f; (on roof)
First m; (of mountain) Grat m,
Kamm m; (of high pressure) Hoch-
druckkeil m

ridicule /'rɪdɪkjuːl/ n Spott m ● vt
verspotten, spotten über (+ acc)

ridiculous /rɪ'dɪkjʊləs/ a, **-ly** adv
lächerlich

riding /'raɪdɪŋ/ n Reiten nt ● attrib
Reit-

rife /raɪf/ a **be ~** weit verbreitet sein

riff-raff /'rɪfræf/ n Gesindel nt

rifle /'raɪfl/ n Gewehr nt ● vt plündern; **~ through** durchwühlen

rift /rɪft/ n Spalt m; (fig) Riß m

rig[1] /rɪg/ n Ölbohrturm m; (at sea)
Bohrinsel f ● vt (pt/pp rigged) **~ out**
ausrüsten; **~ up** aufbauen

rig[2] vt (pt/pp rigged) manipulieren

right /raɪt/ a richtig; (not left)
rechte(r,s); **be ~** ⟨person:⟩ recht haben; ⟨clock:⟩ richtig gehen; **put ~**
wieder in Ordnung bringen; (fig)
richtigstellen; **that's ~!** das stimmt!
● adv richtig; (directly) direkt; (completely) ganz; (not left) rechts; ⟨go⟩
nach rechts; **~ away** sofort ● n
Recht nt; (not left) rechte Seite f; **on
the ~** rechts; **from/to the ~** von/
nach rechts; **be in the ~** recht haben; **by ~s** eigentlich; **the R~** (Pol)
die Rechte. **~ angle** n rechter Winkel m

righteous /'raɪtʃəs/ a rechtschaffen

rightful /'raɪtfl/ a, **-ly** adv rechtmäßig

right: **~-'handed** a rechtshändig. **~-
hand 'man** n (fig) rechte Hand f

rightly /'raɪtlɪ/ adv mit Recht

right: **~ of way** n Durchgangsrecht
nt; (path) öffentlicher Fußweg m;

(Auto) Vorfahrt f. **~-'wing** a (Pol)
rechte(r,s)

rigid /'rɪdʒɪd/ a starr; (strict) streng.
~ity /-'dʒɪdətɪ/ n Starrheit f;
Strenge f

rigmarole /'rɪgmərəʊl/ n Geschwätz
nt; (procedure) Prozedur f

rigorous /'rɪgərəs/ a, **-ly** adv streng

rigour /'rɪgə(r)/ n Strenge f

rile /raɪl/ vt (fam) ärgern

rim /rɪm/ n Rand m; (of wheel) Felge f

rind /raɪnd/ n (on fruit) Schale f; (on
cheese) Rinde f; (on bacon) Schwarte
f

ring[1] /rɪŋ/ n Ring m; (for circus)
Manege f; **stand in a ~** im Kreis
stehen ● vt umringen; **~ in red** rot
einkreisen

ring[2] n Klingeln nt; **give s.o. a ~**
(Teleph) jdn anrufen ● v (pt rang, pp
rung) ● vt läuten; **~ [up]** (Teleph)
anrufen ● vi läuten, klingeln. **~
back** vt/i (Teleph) zurückrufen. **~
off** vi (Teleph) auflegen

ring: **~leader** n Rädelsführer m. **~
road** n Umgehungsstraße f

rink /rɪŋk/ n Eisbahn f

rinse /rɪns/ n Spülung f; (hair colour)
Tönung f ● vt spülen; tönen ⟨hair⟩.
~ off vt abspülen

riot /'raɪət/ n Aufruhr m; **~s** pl Unruhen pl; **~ of colours** bunte Farben-
pracht f; **run ~** randalieren ● vi
randalieren. **~er** n Randalierer m.
~ous /-əs/ a aufrührerisch; (boisterous) wild

rip /rɪp/ n Riß m ● vt/i (pt/pp ripped)
zerreißen; **~ open** aufreißen. **~ off**
vt (fam) neppen

ripe /raɪp/ a (-r, -st) reif

ripen /'raɪpn/ vi reifen ● vt reifen
lassen

ripeness /'raɪpnɪs/ n Reife f

'rip-off n (fam) Nepp m

ripple /'rɪpl/ n kleine Welle f ● vt
kräuseln ● vi sich kräuseln

rise /raɪz/ n Anstieg m; (fig) Aufstieg
m; (increase) Zunahme f; (in wages)
Lohnerhöhung f; (in salary) Gehalts-
erhöhung f; **give ~ to** Anlaß geben
zu ● vi (pt rose, pp risen) steigen;
⟨ground:⟩ ansteigen; ⟨sun, dough:⟩
aufgehen; ⟨river:⟩ entspringen; (get
up) aufstehen; (fig) aufsteigen (**to**
zu); ⟨rebel⟩ sich erheben; ⟨court:⟩
sich vertagen. **~r** n **early ~r** Früh-
aufsteher m

rising /'raɪzɪŋ/ a steigend; ⟨sun⟩ aufgehend; **the ~ generation** die heranwachsende Generation ● n (revolt) Aufstand m

risk /rɪsk/ n Risiko nt; **at one's own ~** auf eigene Gefahr ● vt riskieren

risky /'rɪskɪ/ a (-ier, -iest) riskant

risqué /'rɪskeɪ/ a gewagt

rissole /'rɪsəʊl/ n Frikadelle f

rite /raɪt/ n Ritus m; **last ~s** Letzte Ölung f

ritual /'rɪtjʊəl/ a rituell ● n Ritual nt

rival /'raɪvl/ a rivalisierend ● n Rivale m/Rivalin f; **~s** pl (Comm) Konkurrenten pl ● vt (pt/pp rivalled) gleichkommen (+ dat); (compete with) rivalisieren mit. **~ry** n Rivalität f; (Comm) Konkurrenzkampf m

river /'rɪvə(r)/ n Fluß m. **~-bed** n Flußbett nt

rivet /'rɪvɪt/ n Niete f ● vt [ver]nieten; **~ed by** ⟨fig⟩ gefesselt von

road /rəʊd/ n Straße f; ⟨fig⟩ Weg m

road: ~-block n Straßensperre f. **~-hog** n (fam) Straßenschreck m. **~-map** n Straßenkarte f. **~ safety** n Verkehrssicherheit f. **~ sense** n Verkehrssinn m. **~side** n Straßenrand m. **~way** n Fahrbahn f. **~works** npl Straßenarbeiten pl. **~worthy** a verkehrssicher

roam /rəʊm/ vi wandern

roar /rɔː(r)/ n Gebrüll nt; **~s of laughter** schallendes Gelächter nt ● vi brüllen; (with laughter) schallend lachen. **~ing** a ⟨fire⟩ prasselnd; **do a ~ing trade** (fam) ein Bombengeschäft machen

roast /rəʊst/ a gebraten, Brat-; **~ beef/pork** Rinder-/Schweinebraten m ● n Braten m ● vt/i braten; rösten ⟨coffee, chestnuts⟩

rob /rɒb/ vt (pt/pp robbed) berauben (of gen); ausrauben ⟨bank⟩. **~ber** n Räuber m. **~bery** n Raub m

robe /rəʊb/ n Robe f; (Amer: bathrobe) Bademantel m

robin /'rɒbɪn/ n Rotkehlchen nt

robot /'rəʊbɒt/ n Roboter m

robust /rəʊ'bʌst/ a robust

rock¹ /rɒk/ n Fels m; **stick of ~** Zuckerstange f; **on the ~s** ⟨ship⟩ aufgelaufen; ⟨marriage⟩ kaputt; ⟨drink⟩ mit Eis

rock² vt/i schaukeln

rock³ n (Mus) Rock m

rock-'bottom n Tiefpunkt m

rockery /'rɒkərɪ/ n Steingarten m

rocket /'rɒkɪt/ n Rakete f ● vi in die Höhe schießen

rocking: ~-chair n Schaukelstuhl m. **~-horse** n Schaukelpferd nt

rocky /'rɒkɪ/ a (-ier, -iest) felsig; (unsteady) wackelig

rod /rɒd/ n Stab m; (stick) Rute f; (for fishing) Angel[rute] f

rode /rəʊd/ see **ride**

rodent /'rəʊdnt/ n Nagetier nt

roe¹ /rəʊ/ n Rogen m; (soft) Milch f

roe² n (pl roe or roes) **~[-deer]** Reh nt

rogue /rəʊg/ n Gauner m

role /rəʊl/ n Rolle f

roll /rəʊl/ n Rolle f; (bread) Brötchen nt; (list) Liste f; (of drum) Wirbel m ● vi rollen; **be ~ing in money** (fam) Geld wie Heu haben ● vt rollen; walzen ⟨lawn⟩; ausrollen ⟨pastry⟩. **~ over** vi sich auf die andere Seite rollen. **~ up** vt aufrollen; hochkrempeln ⟨sleeves⟩ ● vi (fam) auftauchen

'roll-call n Namensaufruf m; (Mil) Appell m

roller /'rəʊlə(r)/ n Rolle f; (lawn, road) Walze f; (hair) Lockenwickler m. **~ blind** n Rollo nt. **~-coaster** n Berg-und-Talbahn f. **~-skate** n Rollschuh m

'rolling-pin n Teigrolle f

Roman /'rəʊmən/ a römisch ● n Römer(in) m(f)

romance /rə'mæns/ n Romantik f; (love-affair) Romanze f; (book) Liebesgeschichte f

Romania /rəʊ'meɪnɪə/ n Rumänien nt. **~n** a rumänisch ● n Rumäne m/-nin f

romantic /rəʊ'mæntɪk/ a, **-ally** adv romantisch. **~ism** /-tɪsɪzm/ n Romantik f

Rome /rəʊm/ n Rom nt

romp /rɒmp/ n Tollen nt ● vi [herum]tollen. **~ers** npl Strampelhöschen nt

roof /ruːf/ n Dach nt; (of mouth) Gaumen m ● vt **~ over** überdachen. **~-rack** n Dachgepäckträger m. **~-top** n Dach nt

rook /rʊk/ n Saatkrähe f; (Chess) Turm m ● vt (fam: swindle) schröpfen

room /ruːm/ n Zimmer nt; (for functions) Saal m; (space) Platz m. **~y** a geräumig

roost /ruːst/ n Hühnerstange f ● vi schlafen

root¹ /ruːt/ n Wurzel f; **take ∼** anwachsen ● vi Wurzeln schlagen. **∼ out** vt (fig) ausrotten

root² vi **∼ about** wühlen; **∼ for s.o.** (Amer, fam) für jdn sein

rope /rəup/ n Seil nt; **know the ∼s** (fam) sich auskennen. **∼ in** vt (fam) einspannen

rope-'ladder n Strickleiter f

rosary /'rəuzəri/ n Rosenkranz m

rose¹ /rəuz/ n Rose f; (of watering-can) Brause f

rose² see **rise**

rosemary /'rəuzməri/ n Rosmarin m

rosette /rəu'zet/ n Rosette f

roster /'rɒstə(r)/ n Dienstplan m

rostrum /'rɒstrəm/ n Podest nt, Podium nt

rosy /'rəuzi/ a (-ier, -iest) rosig

rot /rɒt/ n Fäulnis f; (fam: nonsense) Quatsch m ● vi (pt/pp rotted) [ver]faulen

rota /'rəutə/ n Dienstplan m

rotary /'rəutəri/ a Dreh-; (Techn) Rotations-

rotat|e /rəu'teɪt/ vt drehen; im Wechsel anbauen (crops) ● vi sich drehen; (Techn) rotieren. **∼ion** /-eɪʃn/ n Drehung f; (of crops) Fruchtfolge f; **in ∼ion** im Wechsel

rote /rəut/ n **by ∼** auswendig

rotten /'rɒtn/ a faul; (fam) mies; ⟨person⟩ fies

rotund /rəu'tʌnd/ a rundlich

rough /rʌf/ a (-er, -est) rauh; (uneven) uneben; (coarse, not gentle) grob; (brutal) roh; (turbulent) stürmisch; (approximate) ungefähr ● adv **sleep ∼** im Freien übernachten; **play ∼** holzen ● n **do sth in ∼** etw ins unreine schreiben ● vt **∼ it** primitiv leben. **∼ out** vt im Groben entwerfen

roughage /'rʌfɪdʒ/ n Ballaststoffe pl

rough 'draft n grober Entwurf m

rough|ly /'rʌflɪ/ adv (see **rough**) rauh; grob; roh; ungefähr. **∼ness** n Rauheit f

'rough paper n Konzeptpapier nt

round /raund/ a (-er, -est) rund ● n Runde f; (slice) Scheibe f; **do one's ∼s** seine Runde machen ● prep um (+ acc); **∼ the clock** rund um die Uhr ● adv **all ∼** ringsherum; **∼ and ∼** im Kreis; **ask s.o. ∼** jdn einladen; **turn/ look ∼** sich umdrehen/umsehen ● vt biegen um ⟨corner⟩ ● vi **∼ on**

s.o. jdn anfahren. **∼ off** vt abrunden. **∼ up** vt aufrunden; zusammentreiben ⟨animals⟩; festnehmen ⟨criminals⟩

roundabout /'raundəbaut/ a **∼ route** Umweg m ● n Karussell nt; (for traffic) Kreisverkehr m

round: ∼-'shouldered a mit einem runden Rücken. **∼ 'trip** n Rundreise f

rous|e /rauz/ vt wecken; (fig) erregen. **∼ing** a mitreißend

route /ruːt/ n Route f; (of bus) Linie f

routine /ruː'tiːn/ a, **-ly** adv routinemäßig ● n Routine f; (Theat) Nummer f

roux /ruː/ n Mehlschwitze f

rove /rəuv/ vi wandern

row¹ /rəu/ n (line) Reihe f; **in a ∼** (one after the other) nacheinander

row² vt/i rudern

row³ /rau/ n (fam) Krach m ● vi (fam) sich streiten

rowan /'rəuən/ n Eberesche f

rowdy /'raudi/ a (-ier, -iest) laut

rowing boat /'rəuɪŋ-/ n Ruderboot nt

royal /'rɔɪəl/ a, **-ly** adv königlich

royal|ty /'rɔɪəltɪ/ n Königtum nt; (persons) Mitglieder pl der königlichen Familie; **-ies** pl (payments) Tantiemen pl

rub /rʌb/ n **give sth a ∼** etw reiben/ (polish) polieren ● vt (pt/pp rubbed) reiben; (polish) polieren; **don't ∼ it in** (fam) reib es mir nicht unter die Nase. **∼ off** vt abreiben ● vi abgehen; **∼ off on** abfärben auf (+ acc). **∼ out** vt ausradieren

rubber /'rʌbə(r)/ n Gummi m; (eraser) Radiergummi m. **∼ band** n Gummiband nt. **∼y** a gummiartig

rubbish /'rʌbɪʃ/ n Abfall m, Müll m; (fam: nonsense) Quatsch m; (fam: junk) Plunder m, Kram m ● vt (fam) schlechtmachen. **∼ bin** n Mülleimer m, Abfalleimer m. **∼ dump** n Abfallhaufen m; (official) Müllhalde f

rubble /'rʌbl/ n Trümmer pl, Schutt m

ruby /'ruːbɪ/ n Rubin m

rucksack /'rʌksæk/ n Rucksack m

rudder /'rʌdə(r)/ n [Steuer]ruder nt

ruddy /'rʌdɪ/ a (-ier, -iest) rötlich; (sl) verdammt

rude /ruːd/ a (-r, -st), **-ly** adv unhöflich; (improper) unanständig. **∼ness** n Unhöflichkeit f

rudiment /'ru:dɪmənt/ n ~s pl Anfangsgründe pl. ~ary /-'mentərɪ/ a elementar; (Biol) rudimentär

rueful /'ru:fl/ a, -ly adv reumütig

ruffian /'rʌfɪən/ n Rüpel m

ruffle /'rʌfl/ n Rüsche f ● vt zerzausen

rug /rʌg/ n Vorleger m, [kleiner] Teppich m; (blanket) Decke f

rugged /'rʌgɪd/ a ⟨coastline⟩ zerklüftet

ruin /'ru:ɪn/ n Ruine f; (fig) Ruin m ● vt ruinieren. ~ous /-əs/ a ruinös

rule /ru:l/ n Regel f; (control) Herrschaft f; (government) Regierung f; (for measuring) Lineal nt; **as a** ~ in der Regel ● vt regieren, herrschen über (+ acc); (fig) beherrschen; (decide) entscheiden; ziehen ⟨line⟩ ● vi regieren, herrschen. ~ **out** vt ausschließen

ruled /ru:ld/ a ⟨paper⟩ liniert

ruler /'ru:lə(r)/ n Herrscher(in) m(f); (measure) Lineal nt

ruling /'ru:lɪŋ/ a herrschend; ⟨factor⟩ entscheidend; (Pol) regierend ● n Entscheidung f

rum /rʌm/ n Rum m

rumble /'rʌmbl/ n Grollen nt ● vi grollen; ⟨stomach:⟩ knurren

ruminant /'ru:mɪnənt/ n Wiederkäuer m

rummage /'rʌmɪdʒ/ vi wühlen; ~ **through** durchwühlen

rummy /'rʌmɪ/ n Rommé nt

rumour /'ru:mə(r)/ n Gerücht nt ● vt **is is ~ed that** es geht das Gerücht, daß

rump /rʌmp/ n Hinterteil nt. ~ **steak** n Rumpsteak nt

rumpus /'rʌmpəs/ n (fam) Spektakel m

run /rʌn/ n Lauf m; (journey) Fahrt f; (series) Serie f, Reihe f; (Theat) Laufzeit f; (Skiing) Abfahrt f; (enclosure) Auslauf m; (Amer: ladder) Laufmasche f; **at a** ~ im Laufschritt; ~ **of bad luck** Pechsträhne f; **be on the** ~ flüchtig sein; **have the** ~ **of sth** etw zu seiner freien Verfügung haben; **in the long** ~ auf lange Sicht ● v (pt ran, pp run, pres p running) ● vi laufen; (flow) fließen; ⟨eyes:⟩ tränen; ⟨bus:⟩ verkehren, fahren; ⟨butter, ink:⟩ zerfließen; ⟨colours:⟩ [ab]färben; (in election) kandidieren;

~ **across s.o./sth** auf jdn/ etw stoßen ● vt laufen lassen; einlaufen lassen ⟨bath⟩; (manage) führen, leiten; (drive) fahren; eingehen ⟨risk⟩; (Journ) bringen ⟨article⟩; ~ **one's hand over sth** mit der Hand über etw (acc) fahren. ~ **away** vi weglaufen. ~ **down** vi hinunter-/herunterlaufen; ⟨clockwork:⟩ ablaufen; ⟨stocks:⟩ sich verringern ● vt (run over) überfahren; (reduce) verringern; (fam: criticize) heruntermachen. ~ **in** vi hinein-/ hereinlaufen. ~ **off** vi weglaufen ● vt abziehen ⟨copies⟩. ~ **out** vi hinaus-/herauslaufen; ⟨supplies, money:⟩ ausgehen; **I've** ~ **out of sugar** ich habe keinen Zucker mehr. ~ **over** vi hinüber-/herüberlaufen; (overflow) überlaufen ● vt überfahren. ~ **through** vi durchlaufen. ~ **up** vi hinauf-/herauflaufen; (towards) hinlaufen ● vt machen ⟨debts⟩; auflaufen lassen ⟨bill⟩; (sew) schnell nähen

'runaway n Ausreißer m

run-'down a ⟨area⟩ verkommen

rung¹ /rʌŋ/ n (of ladder) Sprosse f

rung² see ring²

runner /'rʌnə(r)/ n Läufer m; (Bot) Ausläufer m; (on sledge) Kufe f. ~ **bean** n Stangenbohne f. ~-**up** n Zweite(r) m/f

running /'rʌnɪŋ/ a laufend; ⟨water⟩ fließend; **four times** ~ viermal nacheinander ● n Laufen nt; (management) Führung f, Leitung f; **be/not be in the** ~ eine/keine Chance haben. ~ '**commentary** n fortlaufender Kommentar m

runny /'rʌnɪ/ a flüssig

run:~-**of-the-'mill** a gewöhnlich. ~-**up** n (Sport) Anlauf m; (to election) Zeit f vor der Wahl. ~**way** n Start- und Landebahn f, Piste f

rupture /'rʌptʃə(r)/ n Bruch m ● vt/i brechen; ~ **oneself** sich (dat) einen Bruch heben

rural /'rʊərəl/ a ländlich

ruse /ru:z/ n List f

rush¹ /rʌʃ/ n (Bot) Binse f

rush² n Hetze f; **in a** ~ in Eile ● vi sich hetzen; (run) rasen; ⟨water:⟩ rauschen ● vt hetzen, drängen; ~ **s.o. to hospital** jdn schnellstens ins Krankenhaus bringen. ~-**hour** n Hauptverkehrszeit f, Stoßzeit f

rusk /rʌsk/ n Zwieback m

Russia /'rʌʃə/ n Rußland nt. **~n** a russisch ● n Russe m/Russin f; (Lang) Russisch nt

rust /rʌst/ n Rost m ● vi rosten

rustic /'rʌstɪk/ a bäuerlich; ⟨furniture⟩ rustikal

rustle /'rʌsl/ vi rascheln ● vt rascheln mit; (Amer) stehlen ⟨cattle⟩. **~ up** vt (fam) improvisieren

'rustproof a rostfrei

rusty /'rʌstɪ/ a (-ier, -iest) rostig

rut /rʌt/ n Furche f; **be in a ~** (fam) aus dem alten Trott nicht herauskommen

ruthless /'ru:θlɪs/ a, **-ly** adv rücksichtslos. **~ness** n Rücksichtslosigkeit f

rye /raɪ/ n Roggen m

S

sabbath /'sæbəθ/ n Sabbat m

sabbatical /sə'bætɪkl/ n (Univ) Forschungsurlaub m

sabot|age /'sæbəta:ʒ/ n Sabotage f ● vt sabotieren. **~eur** /-'tɜ:(r)/ n Saboteur m

sachet /'sæʃeɪ/ n Beutel m; (scented) Kissen nt

sack¹ /sæk/ vt (plunder) plündern

sack² n Sack m; **get the ~** (fam) rausgeschmissen werden ● vt (fam) rausschmeißen. **~ing** n Sackleinen nt; (fam: dismissal) Rausschmiß m

sacrament /'sækrəmənt/ n Sakrament nt

sacred /'seɪkrɪd/ a heilig

sacrifice /'sækrɪfaɪs/ n Opfer nt ● vt opfern

sacrilege /'sækrɪlɪdʒ/ n Sakrileg nt

sad /sæd/ a (sadder, saddest) traurig; ⟨loss, death⟩ schmerzlich. **~den** vt traurig machen

saddle /'sædl/ n Sattel m ● vt satteln; **~ s.o. with sth** (fam) jdm etw aufhalsen

sadis|m /'seɪdɪzm/ n Sadismus m. **~t** /-dɪst/ n Sadist m. **~tic** /sə'dɪstɪk/ a, **-ally** adv sadistisch

sad|ly /'sædlɪ/ adv traurig; (unfortunately) leider. **~ness** n Traurigkeit f

safe /seɪf/ a (-r, -st) sicher; ⟨journey⟩ gut; (not dangerous) ungefährlich; **~ and sound** gesund und wohlbehalten ● n Safe m. **~guard** n Schutz m ● vt schützen. **~ly** adv sicher; ⟨arrive⟩ gut

safety /'seɪftɪ/ n Sicherheit f. **~-belt** n Sicherheitsgurt m. **~-pin** n Sicherheitsnadel f. **~-valve** n [Sicherheits]ventil nt

sag /sæg/ vi (pt/pp sagged) durchhängen

saga /'sɑ:gə/ n Saga f; (fig) Geschichte f

sage¹ /seɪdʒ/ n (herb) Salbei m

sage² a weise ● n Weise(r) m

Sagittarius /sædʒɪ'teərɪəs/ n (Astr) Schütze m

said /sed/ see say

sail /seɪl/ n Segel nt; (trip) Segelfahrt f ● vi segeln; (on liner) fahren; (leave) abfahren (for nach) ● vt segeln mit

'sailboard n Surfbrett nt. **~ing** n Windsurfen nt

sailing /'seɪlɪŋ/ n Segelsport m. **~-boat** n Segelboot nt. **~-ship** n Segelschiff nt

sailor /'seɪlə(r)/ n Seemann m; (in navy) Matrose m

saint /seɪnt/ n Heilige(r) m/f. **~ly** a heilig

sake /seɪk/ n **for the ~ of** ... um ... (gen) willen; **for my/your ~** um meinet-/deinetwillen

salad /'sæləd/ n Salat m. **~ cream** n ≈ Mayonnaise f. **~-dressing** n Salatsoße f

salary /'sælərɪ/ n Gehalt nt

sale /seɪl/ n Verkauf m; (event) Basar m; (at reduced prices) Schlußverkauf m; **for ~** zu verkaufen

sales|man n Verkäufer m. **~woman** n Verkäuferin f

salient /'seɪlɪənt/ a wichtigste(r,s)

saliva /sə'laɪvə/ n Speichel m

sallow /'sæləʊ/ a (-er, -est) bleich

salmon /'sæmən/ n Lachs m. **~-pink** a lachsrosa

saloon /sə'lu:n/ n Salon m; (Auto) Limousine f; (Amer: bar) Wirtschaft f

salt /sɔ:lt/ n Salz nt ● a salzig; ⟨water, meat⟩ Salz- ● vt salzen; (cure) pökeln; streuen ⟨road⟩. **~-cellar** n Salzfaß nt. **~ 'water** n Salzwasser nt. **~y** a salzig

salutary /'sæljʊtərɪ/ a heilsam

salute /sə'lu:t/ n (Mil) Gruß m ● vt/i (Mil) grüßen

salvage /'sælvɪdʒ/ n (Naut) Bergung f ● vt bergen

salvation /sæl'veɪʃn/ n Rettung f; (Relig) Heil nt. **S~ 'Army** n Heilsarmee f

salvo /'sælvəʊ/ n Salve f

same /seɪm/ a & pron the ~ der/die/
das gleiche; (pl) die gleichen; (identical) der-/die-/dasselbe; (pl) dieselben ● adv the ~ gleich; all the ~
trotzdem; the ~ to you gleichfalls
sample /'sɑːmpl/ n Probe f; (Comm)
Muster nt ● vt probieren, kosten
sanatorium /sænə'tɔːrɪəm/ n Sanatorium nt
sanctify /'sæŋktɪfaɪ/ vt (pt/pp -fied)
heiligen
sanctimonious /sæŋktɪ'məʊnɪəs/ a,
-ly adv frömmlerisch
sanction /'sæŋkʃn/ n Sanktion f ● vt
sanktionieren
sanctity /'sæŋktətɪ/ n Heiligkeit f
sanctuary /'sæŋktjʊərɪ/ n (Relig) Heiligtum nt; (refuge) Zuflucht f; (for
wildlife) Tierschutzgebiet nt
sand /sænd/ n Sand m ● vt ~ [down]
[ab]schmirgeln
sandal /'sændl/ n Sandale f
sand: ~bank n Sandbank f. ~paper
n Sandpapier nt ● vt [ab]schmir-
geln. ~-pit n Sandkasten m
sandwich /'sænwɪdʒ/ n ≈ belegtes
Brot nt; Sandwich m ● vt ~ed between eingeklemmt zwischen
sandy /'sændɪ/ a (-ier, -iest) sandig;
⟨beach, soil⟩ Sand-; ⟨hair⟩ rotblond
sane /seɪn/ a (-r, -st) geistig normal;
(sensible) vernünftig
sang /sæŋ/ see sing
sanitary /'sænɪtərɪ/ a hygienisch;
⟨system⟩ sanitär. ~ napkin n
(Amer), ~ towel n [Damen]binde f
sanitation /sænɪ'teɪʃn/ n Kanalisation und Abfallbeseitigung pl
sanity /'sænətɪ/ n [gesunder] Verstand m
sank /sæŋk/ see sink
sap /sæp/ n (Bot) Saft m ● vt (pt/pp
sapped) schwächen
sapphire /'sæfaɪə(r)/ n Saphir m
sarcas|m /'sɑːkæzm/ n Sarkasmus m.
~tic /-'kæstɪk/ a, -ally adv
sarkastisch
sardine /sɑː'diːn/ n Sardine f
Sardinia /sɑː'dɪnɪə/ n Sardinien nt
sardonic /sɑː'dɒnɪk/ a, -ally adv höhnisch; ⟨smile⟩ sardonisch
sash /sæʃ/ n Schärpe f
sat /sæt/ see sit
satanic /sə'tænɪk/ a satanisch
satchel /'sætʃl/ n Ranzen m
satellite /'sætəlaɪt/ n Satellit m. ~
dish n Satellitenschüssel f. ~ television n Satellitenfernsehen nt
satin /'sætɪn/ n Satin m

satire /'sætaɪə(r)/ n Satire f
satirical /sə'tɪrɪkl/ a, -ly adv satirisch
satir|ist /'sætərɪst/ n Satiriker(in)
m(f). ~ize vt satirisch darstellen;
⟨book:⟩ eine Satire sein auf (+ acc)
satisfaction /sætɪs'fækʃn/ n Befrie-
digung f; to my ~ zu meiner
Zufriedenheit
satisfactory /sætɪs'fæktərɪ/ a, -ily
adv zufriedenstellend
satisf|y /'sætɪsfaɪ/ vt (pt/pp -fied)
befriedigen; zufriedenstellen ⟨cus-
tomer⟩; (convince) überzeugen; be
~ied zufrieden sein. ~ying a befriedigend; ⟨meal⟩ sättigend
saturat|e /'sætʃəreɪt/ vt durchträn-
ken; (Chem & fig) sättigen. ~ed a
durchnäßt; ⟨fat⟩ gesättigt
Saturday /'sætədeɪ/ n Samstag m,
Sonnabend m
sauce /sɔːs/ n Soße f; (cheek) Frechheit f. ~pan n Kochtopf m
saucer /'sɔːsə(r)/ n Untertasse f
saucy /'sɔːsɪ/ a (-ier, -iest) frech
Saudi Arabia /saʊdɪə'reɪbɪə/ n Saudi-
Arabien nt
sauna /'sɔːnə/ n Sauna f
saunter /'sɔːntə(r)/ vi schlendern
sausage /'sɒsɪdʒ/ n Wurst f
savage /'sævɪdʒ/ a wild; (fierce)
scharf; (brutal) brutal ● n Wilde(r)
m/f ● vt anfallen. ~ry n Brutalität f
save /seɪv/ n (Sport) Abwehr f ● vt
retten (from vor + dat); (keep) aufheben; (not waste) sparen; (collect)
sammeln; (avoid) ersparen; (Sport)
verhindern ⟨goal⟩ ● vi ~ [up] sparen ● prep außer (+ dat), mit Ausnahme (+ gen)
saver /'seɪvə(r)/ n Sparer m
saving /'seɪvɪŋ/ n (see save) Rettung
f; Sparen nt; Ersparnis f; ~s pl
(money) Ersparnisse pl. ~s account
n Sparkonto nt. ~s bank n Sparkasse f
saviour /'seɪvjə(r)/ n Retter m
savour /'seɪvə(r)/ n Geschmack m
● vt auskosten. ~y a herzhaft, würzig; (fig) angenehm
saw¹ /sɔː/ see see¹
saw² n Säge f ● v (pt sawed, pp sawn
or sawed) sägen. ~dust n Sägemehl
nt
saxophone /'sæksəfəʊn/ n Saxophon
nt
say /seɪ/ n Mitspracherecht nt; have
one's ~ seine Meinung sagen ● vt/i
(pt/pp said) sagen; sprechen
⟨prayer⟩; that is to ~ das heißt; that

goes without ~ing das versteht sich von selbst; **when all is said and done** letzten Endes; **I** ~! (*attracting attention*) hallo! ~ing *n* Redensart *f*

scab /skæb/ *n* Schorf *m*; (*pej*) Streikbrecher *m*

scaffold /'skæfəld/ *n* Schafott *nt*. ~ing *n* Gerüst *nt*

scald /skɔːld/ *vt* verbrühen

scale[1] /skeɪl/ *n* (*of fish*) Schuppe *f*

scale[2] *n* Skala *f*; (*Mus*) Tonleiter *f*; (*ratio*) Maßstab *m*; **on a grand** ~ in großem Stil ● *vt* (*climb*) erklettern. ~ **down** *vt* verkleinern

scales /skeɪlz/ *npl* (*for weighing*) Waage *f*

scalp /skælp/ *n* Kopfhaut *f* ● *vt* skalpieren

scalpel /'skælpl/ *n* Skalpell *nt*

scam /skæm/ *n* (*fam*) Schwindel *m*

scamper /'skæmpə(r)/ *vi* huschen

scan /skæn/ *n* (*Med*) Szintigramm *nt* ● *v* (*pt/pp* scanned) ● *vt* absuchen; (*quickly*) flüchtig ansehen; (*Med*) szintigraphisch untersuchen ● *vi* ⟨*poetry:*⟩ das richtige Versmaß haben

scandal /'skændl/ *n* Skandal *m*; (*gossip*) Skandalgeschichten *pl*. ~ize /-dəlaɪz/ *vt* schockieren. ~ous /-əs/ *a* skandalös

Scandinavia /skændɪ'neɪvɪə/ *n* Skandinavien *nt*. ~n *a* skandinavisch ● *n* Skandinavier(in) *m(f)*

scant /skænt/ *a* wenig

scanty /'skæntɪ/ *a* (-ier, -iest), -ily *adv* spärlich; ⟨*clothing*⟩ knapp

scapegoat /'skeɪp-/ *n* Sündenbock *m*

scar /skɑː(r)/ *n* Narbe *f* ● *vt* (*pt/pp* scarred) eine Narbe hinterlassen auf (+ *dat*)

scarc|e /skeəs/ *a* (-r, -st) knapp; **make oneself** ~**e** (*fam*) sich aus dem Staub machen. ~**ely** *adv* kaum. ~**ity** *n* Knappheit *f*

scare /skeə(r)/ *n* Schreck *m*; (*panic*) [allgemeine] Panik *f*; (*bomb* ~) Bombendrohung *f* ● *vt* Angst machen (+ *dat*); **be** ~**d** Angst haben (**of** vor + *dat*)

'**scarecrow** *n* Vogelscheuche *f*

scarf /skɑːf/ *n* (*pl* scarves) Schal *m*; (*square*) Tuch *nt*

scarlet /'skɑːlət/ *a* scharlachrot. ~ '**fever** *n* Scharlach *m*

scary /'skeərɪ/ *a* unheimlich

scathing /'skeɪðɪŋ/ *a* bissig

scatter /'skætə(r)/ *vt* verstreuen; (*disperse*) zerstreuen ● *vi* sich zerstreuen. ~-**brained** *a* (*fam*) schusselig. ~**ed** *a* verstreut; ⟨*showers*⟩ vereinzelt

scatty /'skætɪ/ *a* (-ier, -iest) (*fam*) verrückt

scavenge /'skævɪndʒ/ *vi* [im Abfall] Nahrung suchen; ⟨*animal:*⟩ Aas fressen. ~**r** *n* Aasfresser *m*

scenario /sɪ'nɑːrɪəʊ/ *n* Szenario *nt*

scene /siːn/ *n* Szene *f*; (*sight*) Anblick *m*; (*place of event*) Schauplatz *m*; **behind the** ~**s** hinter den Kulissen; ~ **of the crime** Tatort *m*

scenery /'siːnərɪ/ *n* Landschaft *f*; (*Theat*) Szenerie *f*

scenic /'siːnɪk/ *a* landschaftlich schön; (*Theat*) Bühnen-

scent /sent/ *n* Duft *m*; (*trail*) Fährte *f*; (*perfume*) Parfüm *nt*. ~**ed** *a* parfümiert

sceptic|al /'skeptɪkl/ *a*, -**ly** *adv* skeptisch. ~**ism** /-tɪsɪzm/ *n* Skepsis *f*

schedule /'ʃedjuːl/ *n* Programm *nt*; (*of work*) Zeitplan *m*; (*timetable*) Fahrplan *m*; **behind** ~ im Rückstand; **according to** ~ planmäßig ● *vt* planen. ~**d flight** *n* Linienflug *m*

scheme /skiːm/ *n* Programm *nt*; (*plan*) Plan *m*; (*plot*) Komplott *nt* ● *vi* Ränke schmieden

schizophren|ia /skɪtsə'friːnɪə/ *n* Schizophrenie *f*. ~**ic** /-'frenɪk/ *a* schizophren

scholar /'skɒlə(r)/ *n* Gelehrte(r) *m/f*. ~**ly** *a* gelehrt. ~**ship** *n* Gelehrtheit *f*; (*grant*) Stipendium *f*

school /skuːl/ *n* Schule *f*; (*Univ*) Fakultät *f* ● *vt* schulen; dressieren ⟨*animal*⟩

school: ~**boy** *n* Schüler *m*. ~**girl** *n* Schülerin *f*. ~**ing** *n* Schulbildung *f*. ~**master** *n* Lehrer *m*. ~**mistress** *n* Lehrerin *f*. ~**teacher** *n* Lehrer(in) *m(f)*

sciatica /saɪ'ætɪkə/ *n* Ischias *m*

scien|ce /'saɪəns/ *n* Wissenschaft *f*. ~**tific** /-'tɪfɪk/ *a* wissenschaftlich. ~**tist** *n* Wissenschaftler *m*

scintillating /'sɪntɪleɪtɪŋ/ *a* sprühend

scissors /'sɪzəz/ *npl* Schere *f*; **a pair of** ~ eine Schere

scoff[1] /skɒf/ *vi* ~ **at** spotten über (+ *acc*)

scoff[2] *vt* (*fam*) verschlingen

scold /skəʊld/ *vt* ausschimpfen

scoop /sku:p/ n Schaufel f; (Culin) Portionierer m; (Journ) Exklusivmeldung f ● vt ~ out aushöhlen; (remove) auslöffeln; ~ up schaufeln; schöpfen ⟨liquid⟩

scoot /sku:t/ vi (fam) rasen. ~er n Roller m

scope /skəʊp/ n Bereich m; (opportunity) Möglichkeiten pl

scorch /skɔ:tʃ/ vt versengen. ~ing a glühend heiß

score /skɔ:(r)/ n [Spiel]stand m; (individual) Punktzahl f; (Mus) Partitur f; (Cinema) Filmmusik f; a ~ [of] (twenty) zwanzig; keep [the] ~ zählen; (written) aufschreiben; on that ~ was das betrifft ● vt erzielen; schießen ⟨goal⟩; (cut) einritzen vi Punkte erzielen; (Sport) ein Tor schießen; (keep score) Punkte zählen. ~r n Punktezähler m; (of goals) Torschütze m

scorn /skɔ:n/ n Verachtung f ● vt verachten. ~ful a, -ly adv verächtlich

Scorpio /'skɔ:pɪəʊ/ n (Astr) Skorpion m

scorpion /'skɔ:pɪən/ n Skorpion m

Scot /skɒt/ n Schotte m/Schottin f

Scotch /skɒtʃ/ a schottisch ● n (whisky) Scotch m

scotch vt unterbinden

scot-'free a get off ~ straffrei ausgehen

Scot|land /'skɒtlənd/ n Schottland nt. ~s, ~tish a schottisch

scoundrel /'skaʊndrl/ n Schurke m

scour¹ /'skaʊə(r)/ vt (search) absuchen

scour² vt (clean) scheuern

scourge /skɜ:dʒ/ n Geißel f

scout /skaʊt/ n (Mil) Kundschafter m ● vi ~ for Ausschau halten nach

Scout n [Boy] ~ Pfadfinder m

scowl /skaʊl/ n böser Gesichtsausdruck m ● vi ein böses Gesicht machen

scraggy /'skrægɪ/ a (-ier, -iest) (pej) dürr, hager

scram /skræm/ vi (fam) abhauen

scramble /'skræmbl/ n Gerangel nt ● vi klettern; ~ for sich drängen nach ● vt (Teleph) verschlüsseln. ~d 'egg[s] n[pl] Rührei nt

scrap¹ /skræp/ n (fam: fight) Rauferei f ● vi sich raufen

scrap² n Stückchen nt; (metal) Schrott m; ~s pl Reste; not a ~ kein

bißchen ● vt (pt/pp **scrapped**) aufgeben

'scrap-book n Sammelalbum nt

scrape /skreɪp/ vt schaben; (clean) abkratzen; (damage) [ver]schrammen. ~ through vi gerade noch durchkommen. ~ together vt zusammenkriegen

scraper /'skreɪpə(r)/ n Kratzer m

'scrap iron n Alteisen nt

scrappy /'skræpɪ/ a lückenhaft

'scrap-yard n Schrottplatz m

scratch /skrætʃ/ n Kratzer m; start from ~ von vorne anfangen; not be up to ~ zu wünschen übriglassen ● vt/i kratzen; (damage) zerkratzen

scrawl /skrɔ:l/ n Gekrakel nt ● vt/i krakeln

scrawny /'skrɔ:nɪ/ a (-ier, -iest) (pej) dürr, hager

scream /skri:m/ n Schrei m ● vt/i schreien

screech /skri:tʃ/ n Kreischen nt ● vt/i kreischen

screen /skri:n/ n Schirm m; (Cinema) Leinwand f; (TV) Bildschirm m ● vt schützen; (conceal) verdecken; vorführen ⟨film⟩; (examine) überprüfen; (Med) untersuchen. ~ing n (Med) Reihenuntersuchung f. ~play n Drehbuch nt

screw /skru:/ n Schraube f ● vt schrauben. ~ up vt festschrauben; (crumple) zusammenknüllen; zusammenkneifen ⟨eyes⟩; (sl: bungle) vermasseln; ~ up one's courage seinen Mut zusammennehmen

'screwdriver n Schraubenzieher m

screwy /'skru:ɪ/ a (-ier, -iest) (fam) verrückt

scribble /'skrɪbl/ n Gekritzel nt ● vt/i kritzeln

script /skrɪpt/ n Schrift f; (of speech, play) Text m; (Radio, TV) Skript nt; (of film) Drehbuch nt

Scripture /'skrɪptʃə(r)/ n (Sch) Religion f; the ~s pl die Heilige Schrift f

scroll /skrəʊl/ n Schriftrolle f; (decoration) Volute f

scrounge /skraʊndʒ/ vt/i schnorren. ~r n Schnorrer m

scrub¹ /skrʌb/ n (land) Buschland nt, Gestrüpp nt

scrub² vt/i (pt/pp **scrubbed**) schrubben; (fam: cancel) absagen; fallenlassen ⟨plan⟩

scruff /skrʌf/ n by the ~ of the neck beim Genick

scruffy /'skrʌfɪ/ a (-ier, -iest) vergammelt

scrum /skrʌm/ n Gedränge nt

scruple /'skru:pl/ n Skrupel m

scrupulous /'skru:pjʊləs/ a, -ly adv gewissenhaft

scrutin|ize /'skru:tɪnaɪz/ vt [genau] ansehen. ~y n (look) prüfender Blick m

scuff /skʌf/ vt abstoßen

scuffle /'skʌfl/ n Handgemenge nt

scullery /'skʌlərɪ/ n Spülküche f

sculpt|or /'skʌlptə(r)/ n Bildhauer(in) m(f). ~ure /-tʃə(r)/ n Bildhauerei f; (piece of work) Skulptur f, Plastik f

scum /skʌm/ n Schmutzschicht f; (people) Abschaum m

scurrilous /'skʌrɪləs/ a niederträchtig

scurry /'skʌrɪ/ vi (pt/pp -ied) huschen

scuttle¹ /'skʌtl/ n Kohleneimer m

scuttle² vt versenken ⟨ship⟩

scuttle³ vi schnell krabbeln

scythe /saɪð/ n Sense f

sea /si:/ n Meer nt, See f; at ~ auf See; by ~ mit dem Schiff. ~board n Küste f. ~food n Meeresfrüchte pl. ~gull n Möwe f

seal¹ /si:l/ n (Zool) Seehund m

seal² n Siegel nt; (Techn) Dichtung f ● vt versiegeln; (Techn) abdichten; (fig) besiegeln. ~ off vt abriegeln

'sea-level n Meeresspiegel m

seam /si:m/ n Naht f; (of coal) Flöz nt

'seaman n Seemann m; (sailor) Matrose m

seamless /'si:mlɪs/ a nahtlos

seance /'seɪɑ:ns/ n spiritistische Sitzung f

sea: ~plane n Wasserflugzeug nt. ~port n Seehafen m

search /sɜ:tʃ/ n Suche f; (official) Durchsuchung f ● vt durchsuchen; absuchen ⟨area⟩ ● vi suchen (for nach). ~ing a prüfend, forschend

search: ~light n [Such]scheinwerfer m. ~-party n Suchmannschaft f

sea: ~sick a seekrank. ~side n at/to the ~side am/ans Meer

season /'si:zn/ n Jahreszeit f; (social, tourist, sporting) Saison f ● vt (flavour) würzen. ~able /-əbl/ a der Jahreszeit gemäß. ~al a Saison-. ~ing n Gewürze pl

'season ticket n Dauerkarte f

seat /si:t/ n Sitz m; (place) Sitzplatz m; (bottom) Hintern m; take a ~ Platz nehmen ● vt setzen; (have seats for) Sitzplätze bieten (+ dat); remain

~ed sitzen bleiben. ~-belt n Sicherheitsgurt m; fasten one's ~-belt sich anschnallen

sea: ~weed n [See]tang m. ~worthy a seetüchtig

secateurs /sekə'tɜ:z/ npl Gartenschere f

seclu|de /sɪ'klu:d/ vt absondern. ~ded a abgelegen. ~sion /-ʒn/ n Zurückgezogenheit f

second¹ /sɪ'kɒnd/ vt (transfer) [vorübergehend] versetzen

second² /'sekənd/ a zweite(r,s); on ~ thoughts nach weiterer Überlegung ● n Sekunde f; (Sport) Sekundant m; ~s pl (goods) Waren zweiter Wahl; the ~ der/die/das zweite ● adv (in race) an zweiter Stelle ● vt unterstützen ⟨proposal⟩

secondary /'sekəndrɪ/ a zweitrangig; (Phys) Sekundär-. ~ school n höhere Schule f

second: ~-best a zweitbeste(r,s). ~ 'class adv ⟨travel, send⟩ zweiter Klasse. ~-class a zweitklassig

'second hand n (on clock) Sekundenzeiger m

second-'hand a gebraucht ● adv aus zweiter Hand

secondly /'sekəndlɪ/ adv zweitens

second-'rate a zweitklassig

secrecy /'si:krəsɪ/ n Heimlichkeit f

secret /'si:krɪt/ a geheim; ⟨agent, police⟩ Geheim-; ⟨drinker, lover⟩ heimlich ● n Geheimnis nt

secretarial /sekrə'teərɪəl/ a Sekretärinnen-; ⟨work, staff⟩ Sekretariats-

secretary /'sekrətərɪ/ n Sekretär(in) m(f)

secret|e /sɪ'kri:t/ vt absondern. ~ion /-i:ʃn/ n Absonderung f

secretive /'si:krətɪv/ a geheimtuerisch. ~ness n Heimlichtuerei f

secretly /'si:krɪtlɪ/ adv heimlich

sect /sekt/ n Sekte f

section /'sekʃn/ n Teil m; (of text) Abschnitt m; (of firm) Abteilung f; (of organization) Sektion f

sector /'sektə(r)/ n Sektor m

secular /'sekjʊlə(r)/ a weltlich

secure /sɪ'kjʊə(r)/ a, -ly adv sicher; (firm) fest; (emotionally) geborgen ● vt sichern; (fasten) festmachen; (obtain) sich (dat) sichern

securit|y /sɪ'kjʊərətɪ/ n Sicherheit f; (emotional) Geborgenheit f; ~ies Wertpapiere pl; (Fin) Effekten pl

sedan /sɪ'dæn/ n (Amer) Limousine f

sedate¹ /sɪ'deɪt/ *a*, **-ly** *adv* gesetzt
sedate² *vt* sedieren
sedation /sɪ'deɪʃn/ *n* Sedierung *f*; **be under ~** sediert sein
sedative /'sedətɪv/ *a* beruhigend ● *n* Beruhigungsmittel *nt*
sedentary /'sedəntərɪ/ *a* sitzend
sediment /'sedɪmənt/ *n* [Boden]satz *m*
seduce /sɪ'dju:s/ *vt* verführen
seduct|ion /sɪ'dʌkʃn/ *n* Verführung *f*. **~ive** /-tɪv/ *a*, **-ly** *adv* verführerisch
see¹ /si:/ *v* (*pt* **saw**, *pp* **seen**) ● *vt* sehen; (*understand*) einsehen; (*imagine*) sich (*dat*) vorstellen; (*escort*) begleiten; **go and ~** nachsehen; (*visit*) besuchen; **~ you later!** bis nachher! **~ing that** da ● *vi* sehen; (*check*) nachsehen; **~ about** sich kümmern um. **~ off** *vt* verabschieden; (*chase away*) vertreiben. **~ through** *vi* durchsehen ● *vt* (*fig*) **~ through s.o.** jdn durchschauen
see² *n* (*Relig*) Bistum *nt*
seed /si:d/ *n* Samen *m*; (*of grape*) Kern *m*; (*fig*) Saat *f*; (*Tennis*) gesetzter Spieler *m*; **go to ~** Samen bilden; (*fig*) heruntergekommen. **~ed** *a* (*Tennis*) gesetzt. **~ling** *n* Sämling *m*
seedy /'si:dɪ/ *a* (**-ier**, **-iest**) schäbig; (*area*) heruntergekommen
seek /si:k/ *vt* (*pt/pp* **sought**) suchen
seem /si:m/ *vi* scheinen. **~ingly** *adv* scheinbar
seemly /'si:mlɪ/ *a* schicklich
seen /si:n/ *see* **see¹**
seep /si:p/ *vi* sickern
see-saw /'si:sɔː/ *n* Wippe *f*
seethe /si:ð/ *vi* **~ with anger** vor Wut schäumen
'see-through *a* durchsichtig
segment /'segmənt/ *n* Teil *m*; (*of worm*) Segment *nt*; (*of orange*) Spalte *f*
segregat|e /'segrɪgeɪt/ *vt* trennen. **~ion** /-'geɪʃn/ *n* Trennung *f*
seize /si:z/ *vt* ergreifen; (*Jur*) beschlagnahmen; **~ s.o. by the arm** jdn am Arm packen. **~ up** *vi* (*Techn*) sich festfressen
seizure /'si:ʒə(r)/ *n* (*Jur*) Beschlagnahme *f*; (*Med*) Anfall *m*
seldom /'seldəm/ *adv* selten
select /sɪ'lekt/ *a* ausgewählt; (*exclusive*) exklusiv ● *vt* auswählen; aufstellen (*team*). **~ion** /-ekʃn/ *n* Auswahl *f*. **~ive** /-ɪv/ *a*, **-ly** *adv* selektiv; (*choosy*) wählerisch
self /self/ *n* (*pl* **selves**) Ich *nt*

self: **~-ad'dressed** *a* adressiert. **~-ad'hesive** *a* selbstklebend. **~-as'surance** *n* Selbstsicherheit *f*. **~-as'sured** *a* selbstsicher. **~-'catering** *n* Selbstversorgung *f*. **~-'centred** *a* egozentrisch. **~-'confidence** *n* Selbstbewußtsein *nt*, Selbstvertrauen *nt*. **~-'confident** *a* selbstbewußt. **~-'conscious** *a* befangen. **~-con'tained** *a* (*flat*) abgeschlossen. **~-con'trol** *n* Selbstbeherrschung *f*. **~-de'fence** *n* Selbstverteidigung *f*; (*Jur*) Notwehr *f*. **~-de'nial** *n* Selbstverleugnung *f*. **~-determi'nation** *n* Selbstbestimmung *f*. **~-em'ployed** selbständig. **~-e'steem** *n* Selbstachtung *f*. **~-'evident** *a* offensichtlich. **~-'governing** *a* selbstverwaltet. **~-'help** *n* Selbsthilfe *f*. **~-in'dulgent** *a* maßlos. **~-'interest** *n* Eigennutz *m*
self|ish /'selfɪʃ/ *a*, **-ly** *adv* egoistisch, selbstsüchtig. **~less** *a*, **-ly** *adv* selbstlos
self: **~-'pity** *n* Selbstmitleid *nt*. **~-'portrait** *n* Selbstporträt *nt*. **~-pos'sessed** *a* selbstbeherrscht. **~-preser'vation** *n* Selbsterhaltung *f*. **~-re'spect** *n* Selbstachtung *f*. **~-'righteous** *a* selbstgerecht. **~-'sacrifice** *n* Selbstaufopferung *f*. **~-'satisfied** *a* selbstgefällig. **~-'service** *n* Selbstbedienung *f* ● *attrib* Selbstbedienungs-. **~-suf'ficient** *a* selbständig. **~-'willed** *a* eigenwillig
sell /sel/ *v* (*pt/pp* **sold**) ● *vt* verkaufen; **be sold out** ausverkauft sein ● *vi* sich verkaufen. **~ off** *vt* verkaufen
seller /'selə(r)/ *n* Verkäufer *m*
Sellotape (P) /'seləʊ-/ *n* ≈ Tesafilm (P) *m*
'sell-out *n* **be a ~** ausverkauft sein; (*fam: betrayal*) Verrat sein
selves /selvz/ *see* **self**
semblance /'sembləns/ *n* Anschein *m*
semen /'si:mən/ *n* (*Anat*) Samen *m*
semester /sɪ'mestə(r)/ *n* (*Amer*) Semester *nt*
semi|breve /'semɪbri:v/ *n* (*Mus*) ganze Note *f*. **~circle** *n* Halbkreis *m*. **~'circular** *a* halbkreisförmig. **~'colon** *n* Semikolon *nt*. **~-de'tached** *a* & *n* **~-detached [house]** Doppelhaushälfte *f*. **~'final** *n* Halbfinale *nt*
seminar /'semɪnɑː(r)/ *n* Seminar *nt*. **~y** /-nərɪ/ *n* Priesterseminar *nt*
'semitone *n* (*Mus*) Halbton *m*
semolina /semə'li:nə/ *n* Grieß *m*

senat|e /'senət/ n Senat m. ~**or** n
Senator m
send /send/ vt/i (pt/pp **sent**) schicken;
~ **one's regards** grüßen lassen; ~
for kommen lassen ⟨person⟩; sich
⟨dat⟩ schicken lassen ⟨thing⟩. ~**er** n
Absender m. ~**off** n Verabschie-
dung f
senil|e /'si:naɪl/ a senil. ~**ity** /sɪ'nɪlətɪ/
n Senilität f
senior /'si:nɪə(r)/ a älter; (in rank)
höher ● n Ältere(r) m/f; (in rank)
Vorgesetzte(r) m/f. ~ '**citizen** n Se-
nior(in) m(f)
seniority /si:nɪ'ɒrətɪ/ n höheres Alter
nt; (in rank) höherer Rang m
sensation /sen'seɪʃn/ n Sensation f;
(feeling) Gefühl nt. ~**al** a, -**ly** adv
sensationell
sense /sens/ n Sinn m; (feeling)
Gefühl nt; (common~) Verstand m;
in a ~ in gewisser Hinsicht; **make** ~
Sinn ergeben ● vt spüren. ~**less** a,
-**ly** adv sinnlos; (unconscious)
bewußtlos
sensible /'sensəbl/ a, -**bly** adv vernünftig; ⟨suitable⟩ zweckmäßig
sensitiv|e /'sensətɪv/ a, -**ly** adv emp-
findlich; (understanding) einfühl-
sam. ~**ity** /-'tɪvətɪ/ Empfindlichkeit f
sensory /'sensərɪ/ a Sinnes-
sensual /'sensjʊəl/ a sinnlich. ~**ity**
/-'ælətɪ/ n Sinnlichkeit f
sensuous /'sensjʊəs/ a sinnlich
sent /sent/ see **send**
sentence /'sentəns/ n Satz m; (Jur)
Urteil nt; (punishment) Strafe f ● vt
verurteilen
sentiment /'sentɪmənt/ n Gefühl nt;
(opinion) Meinung f; (sentimentality) Sentimentalität f. ~**al**
/-'mentl/ a sentimental. ~**ality**
/-'tælətɪ/ n Sentimentalität f
sentry /'sentrɪ/ n Wache f
separable /'sepərəbl/ a trennbar
separate[1] /'sepərət/ a, -**ly** adv getrennt, separat
separat|e[2] /'sepəreɪt/ vt trennen ● vi
sich trennen. ~**ion** /-'reɪʃn/ n Trennung f
September /sep'tembə(r)/ n September m
septic /'septɪk/ a vereitert; **go** ~
vereitern
sequel /'si:kwəl/ n Folge f; (fig)
Nachspiel m
sequence /'si:kwəns/ n Reihenfolge f
sequin /'si:kwɪn/ n Paillette f

serenade /serə'neɪd/ n Ständchen nt
● vt ... **s.o.** jdm ein Ständchen
bringen
seren|e /sɪ'ri:n/ a, -**ly** adv gelassen.
~**ity** /-'renətɪ/ n Gelassenheit f
sergeant /'sɑ:dʒənt/ n (Mil) Feldwe-
bel m; (in police) Polizeimeister m
serial /'sɪərɪəl/ n Fortsetzungsge-
schichte f; (Radio, TV) Serie f. ~**ize**
vt in Fortsetzungen veröffentlichen;
(Radio, TV) senden
series /'sɪəriːz/ n Serie f
serious /'sɪərɪəs/ a, -**ly** adv ernst; ⟨ill-
ness, error⟩ schwer. ~**ness** n Ernst
m
sermon /'sɜ:mən/ n Predigt f
serpent /'sɜ:pənt/ n Schlange f
serrated /se'reɪtɪd/ a gezackt
serum /'sɪərəm/ n Serum nt
servant /'sɜ:vənt/ n Diener(in) m(f)
serve /sɜ:v/ n (Tennis) Aufschlag m
● vt dienen (+ dat); bedienen ⟨cus-
tomer, guest⟩; servieren ⟨food⟩;
(Jur) zustellen (**on s.o.** jdm); verbüßen ⟨sentence⟩; ~ **its purpose** seinen Zweck erfüllen; **it** ~**s you right!**
das geschieht dir recht! ~**s two** für
zwei Personen ● vi dienen; (Tennis)
aufschlagen
service /'sɜ:vɪs/ n Dienst m; (Relig)
Gottesdienst m; (in shop, restaurant) Bedienung f; (transport) Verbindung f; (maintenance) Wartung
f; (set of crockery) Service nt; (Tennis) Aufschlag m; ~**s** pl Dienstleis-
tungen pl; (on motorway) Tankstelle
und Raststätte f; **in the** ~**s** beim
Militär; **be of** ~ nützlich sein; **out
of/in** ~ ⟨machine:⟩ außer/ in Betrieb
● vt (Techn) warten. ~**able** /-əbl/
a nützlich; (durable) haltbar
service: ~ **area** n Tankstelle und
Raststätte f. ~ **charge** n Bedie-
nungszuschlag m. ~**man** n Soldat
m. ~ **station** n Tankstelle f
serviette /sɜ:vɪ'et/ n Serviette f
servile /'sɜ:vaɪl/ a unterwürfig
session /'seʃn/ n Sitzung f; (Univ)
Studienjahr nt
set /set/ n Satz m; (of crockery) Service nt; (of cutlery) Garnitur f; (TV,
Radio) Apparat m; (Math) Menge f;
(Theat) Bühnenbild nt; (Cinema)
Szenenaufbau m; (of people) Kreis m;
shampoo and ~ Waschen und Legen ● a (ready) fertig, bereit; (rigid)
fest; ⟨book⟩ vorgeschrieben; **be** ~
on doing sth entschlossen sein, etw
zu tun; **be** ~ **in one's ways** in seinen

Gewohnheiten festgefahren sein ● *v*
(*pt/pp* **set**, *pres p* **setting**) ● *vt* setzen; (*adjust*) einstellen; stellen
⟨*task, alarm clock*⟩; festsetzen, festlegen ⟨*date, limit*⟩; aufgeben ⟨*homework*⟩; zusammenstellen ⟨*questions*⟩; [ein]fassen ⟨*gem*⟩; einrichten
⟨*bone*⟩; legen ⟨*hair*⟩; decken ⟨*table*⟩
● *vi* ⟨*sun:*⟩ untergehen; (*become
hard*) fest werden; ∼ **about sth** sich
an etw (*acc*) machen; ∼ **about doing
sth** sich daranmachen, etw zu tun.
∼ **back** *vt* zurücksetzen; (*hold up*)
aufhalten; (*fam: cost*) kosten. ∼ **off**
vi losgehen; (*in vehicle*) losfahren
● *vt* auslösen ⟨*alarm*⟩, explodieren
lassen ⟨*bomb*⟩. ∼ **out** *vi* losgehen;
(*in vehicle*) losfahren ● ∼ **out to do
sth** sich vornehmen, etw zu tun ● *vt*
auslegen; (*state*) darlegen. ∼ **up** *vt*
aufbauen; (*fig*) gründen
set 'meal *n* Menü *nt*
settee /se'tiː/ *n* Sofa *nt*, Couch *f*
setting /'setɪŋ/ *n* Rahmen *m*; (*surroundings*) Umgebung *f*; (*of sun*)
Untergang *m*; (*of jewel*) Fassung *f*
settle /'setl/ *vt* (*decide*) entscheiden;
(*agree*) regeln; (*fix*) festsetzen;
(*calm*) beruhigen; (*pay*) bezahlen
● *vi* sich niederlassen; ⟨*snow, dust:*⟩
liegenbleiben; (*subside*) sich senken; ⟨*sediment:*⟩ sich absetzen. ∼
down *vi* sich beruhigen; (*perma-
nently*) seßhaft werden. ∼ **up** *vi*
abrechnen
settlement /'setlmənt/ *n* (*see* **settle**)
Entscheidung *f*; Regelung *f*; Bezahlung *f*; (*Jur*) Vergleich *m*; (*colony*)
Siedlung *f*
settler /'setlə(r)/ *n* Siedler *m*
'set-to *n* (*fam*) Streit *m*
'set-up *n* System *nt*
seven /'sevn/ *a* sieben. ∼**'teen** *a* sieb-
zehn. ∼**'teenth** *a* siebzehnte(r,s)
seventh /'sevnθ/ *a* siebte(r,s)
seventieth /'sevntɪɪθ/ *a* sieb-
zigste(r,s)
seventy /'sevntɪ/ *a* siebzig
sever /'sevə(r)/ *vt* durchtrennen;
abbrechen ⟨*relations*⟩
several /'sevrl/ *a & pron* mehrere,
einige
sever|e /sɪ'vɪə(r)/ *a* (**-r, -st**), **-ly** *adv*
streng; ⟨*pain*⟩ stark; ⟨*illness*⟩
schwer. ∼**ity** /-'verətɪ/ *n* Strenge *f*;
Schwere *f*
sew /səʊ/ *vt/i* (*pt* **sewed**, *pp* **sewn** *or*
sewed) nähen. ∼ **up** *vt* zunähen
sewage /'suːɪdʒ/ *n* Abwasser *nt*

sewer /'suːə(r)/ *n* Abwasserkanal *m*
sewing /'səʊɪŋ/ *n* Nähen *nt*; (*work*)
Näharbeit *f*. ∼ **machine** *n* Nähma-
schine *f*
sewn /səʊn/ *see* **sew**
sex /seks/ *n* Geschlecht *nt*; (*sexuality,
intercourse*) Sex *m*. ∼**ist** *a* sexis-
tisch. ∼ **offender** *n* Triebver-
brecher *m*
sexual /'seksjʊəl/ *a*, **-ly** *adv* sexuell. ∼
'**intercourse** *n* Geschlechtsverkehr
m
sexuality /seksjʊ'ælətɪ/ *n* Sexualität *f*
sexy /'seksɪ/ *a* (**-ier, -iest**) sexy
shabby /'ʃæbɪ/ *a* (**-ier, -iest**), **-ily** *adv*
schäbig
shack /ʃæk/ *n* Hütte *f*
shackles /'ʃæklz/ *npl* Fesseln *pl*
shade /ʃeɪd/ *n* Schatten *m*; (*of colour*)
[Farb]ton *m*; (*for lamp*) [Lampen]-
schirm *m*; (*Amer: window-blind*) Jalousie *f* ● *vt* beschatten; (*draw lines
on*) schattieren
shadow /'ʃædəʊ/ *n* Schatten *m* ● *vt*
(*follow*) beschatten. ∼**y** *a* schat-
tenhaft
shady /'ʃeɪdɪ/ *a* (**-ier, -iest**) schattig;
(*fam: disreputable*) zwielichtig
shaft /ʃɑːft/ *n* Schaft *m*; (*Techn*) Welle
f; (*of light*) Strahl *m*; (*of lift*) Schacht
m; ∼**s** *pl* (*of cart*) Gabeldeichsel *f*
shaggy /'ʃægɪ/ *a* (**-ier, -iest**) zottig
shake /ʃeɪk/ *n* Schütteln *nt* ● *v* (*pt*
shook, *pp* **shaken**) ● *vt* schütteln;
(*cause to tremble, shock*) erschüttern; ∼ **hands with s.o.** jdm die Hand
geben ● *vi* wackeln; (*tremble*) zittern. ∼ **off** *vt* abschütteln
shaky /'ʃeɪkɪ/ *a* (**-ier, -iest**) wackelig;
⟨*hand, voice*⟩ zittrig
shall /ʃæl/ *v aux* **I** ∼ **go** ich werde
gehen; **we** ∼ **see** wir werden sehen;
what ∼ **I do?** was soll ich machen?
I'll come too, ∼ **I?** ich komme mit, ja?
thou shalt not kill (*liter*) du sollst
nicht töten
shallow /'ʃæləʊ/ *a* (**-er, -est**) seicht;
⟨*dish*⟩ flach; (*fig*) oberflächlich
sham /ʃæm/ *a* unecht ● *n* Heuchelei
f; (*person*) Heuchler(in) *m(f)* ● *vt*
(*pt/pp* **shammed**) vortäuschen
shambles /'ʃæmblz/ *n* Durcheinander *nt*
shame /ʃeɪm/ *n* Scham *f*; (*disgrace*)
Schande *f*; **be a** ∼ schade sein; **what
a** ∼! wie schade! ∼**-faced** *a* betreten
shame|ful /'ʃeɪmfl/ *a*, **-ly** *adv* schänd-
lich. ∼**less** *a*, **-ly** *adv* schamlos

shampoo /ʃæm'puː/ n Shampoo nt
● vt schamponieren

shandy /'ʃændɪ/ n Radler m

shan't /ʃɑːnt/ = **shall not**

shape /ʃeɪp/ n Form f; (figure) Gestalt f; **take ~** Gestalt annehmen
● vt formen (**into** zu) ● vi ~ **up** sich entwickeln. **~less** a formlos; ⟨clothing⟩ unförmig

shapely /'ʃeɪplɪ/ a (-ier, -iest) wohlgeformt

share /ʃeə(r)/ n [An]teil m; (Comm) Aktie f ● vt/i teilen. **~holder** n Aktionär(in) m(f)

shark /ʃɑːk/ n Hai[fisch] m

sharp /ʃɑːp/ a (-er, -est), **-ly** adv scharf; (pointed) spitz; (severe) heftig; (sudden) steil; (alert) clever; (unscrupulous) gerissen ● adv scharf; (Mus) zu hoch; **at six o'clock ~** Punkt sechs Uhr; **look ~!** beeil dich!
● n (Mus) Kreuz nt. **~en** vt schärfen; [an]- spitzen ⟨pencil⟩

shatter /'ʃætə(r)/ vt zertrümmern; (fig) zerstören; **be ~ed** ⟨person:⟩ erschüttert sein ● vi zersplittern

shave /ʃeɪv/ n Rasur f; **have a ~** sich rasieren ● vt rasieren ● vi sich rasieren. **~r** n Rasierapparat m

shaving /'ʃeɪvɪŋ/ n Rasieren nt. **~brush** n Rasierpinsel m

shawl /ʃɔːl/ n Schultertuch nt

she /ʃiː/ pron sie

sheaf /ʃiːf/ n (pl **sheaves**) Garbe f; (of papers) Bündel nt

shear /ʃɪə(r)/ vt (pt **sheared**, pp **shorn** or **sheared**) scheren

shears /ʃɪəz/ npl [große] Schere f

sheath /ʃiːθ/ n (pl **~s** /ʃiːðz/) Scheide f

sheaves /ʃiːvz/ see **sheaf**

shed[1] /ʃed/ n Schuppen m; (for cattle) Stall m

shed[2] vt (pt/pp **shed**, pres p **shedding**) verlieren; vergießen ⟨blood, tears⟩; **~ light on** Licht bringen in (+ acc)

sheen /ʃiːn/ n Glanz m

sheep /ʃiːp/ n inv Schaf nt. **~-dog** n Hütehund m

sheepish /'ʃiːpɪʃ/ a, **-ly** adv verlegen

sheepskin n Schaffell nt

sheer /ʃɪə(r)/ a rein; (steep) steil; (transparent) hauchdünn ● adv steil

sheet /ʃiːt/ n Laken nt, Bettuch nt; (of paper) Blatt nt; (of glass, metal) Platte f

sheikh /ʃeɪk/ n Scheich m

shelf /ʃelf/ n (pl **shelves**) Brett nt, Bord nt; (set of shelves) Regal nt

shell /ʃel/ n Schale f; (of snail) Haus nt; (of tortoise) Panzer m; (on beach) Muschel f; (of unfinished building) Rohbau m; (Mil) Granate f ● vt pellen; enthülsen ⟨peas⟩; (Mil) [mit Granaten] beschießen. **~ out** vi (fam) blechen

shellfish n inv Schalentiere pl; (Culin) Meeresfrüchte pl

shelter /'ʃeltə(r)/ n Schutz m; (air-raid ~) Luftschutzraum m ● vt schützen (**from** vor + dat) ● vi sich unterstellen. **~ed** a geschützt; ⟨life⟩ behütet

shelve /ʃelv/ vt auf Eis legen; (abandon) aufgeben ● vi ⟨slope:⟩ abfallen

shelves /ʃelvz/ see **shelf**

shelving /'ʃelvɪŋ/ n (shelves) Regale pl

shepherd /'ʃepəd/ n Schäfer m; (Relig) Hirte m ● vt führen. **~ess** n Schäferin f. **~'s pie** n Auflauf m aus mit Kartoffelbrei bedecktem Hackfleisch

sherry /'ʃerɪ/ n Sherry m

shield /ʃiːld/ n Schild m; (for eyes) Schirm m; (Techn & fig) Schutz m ● vt schützen (**from** vor + dat)

shift /ʃɪft/ n Verschiebung f; (at work) Schicht f; **make ~** sich (dat) behelfen (**with** mit) ● vt rücken; (take away) wegnehmen; (rearrange) umstellen; schieben ⟨blame⟩ (**on to** auf + acc) ● vi sich verschieben; (fam: move quickly) rasen

shift work n Schichtarbeit f

shifty /'ʃɪftɪ/ a (-ier, -iest) (pej) verschlagen

shilly-shally /'ʃɪlɪʃælɪ/ vi fackeln (fam)

shimmer /'ʃɪmə(r)/ n Schimmer m ● vi schimmern

shin /ʃɪn/ n Schienbein nt

shine /ʃaɪn/ n Glanz m ● v (pt/pp **shone**) ● vi leuchten; (reflect light) glänzen; ⟨sun:⟩ scheinen ● vt ~ **a light on** beleuchten

shingle /'ʃɪŋgl/ n (pebbles) Kiesel pl

shingles /'ʃɪŋglz/ n (Med) Gürtelrose f

shiny /'ʃaɪnɪ/ a (-ier, -iest) glänzend

ship /ʃɪp/ n Schiff nt ● vt (pt/pp **shipped**) verschiffen

ship: **~building** n Schiffbau m. **~ment** n Sendung f. **~per** n Spediteur m. **~ping** n Versand m; (traffic)

Schiffahrt f. ∼**shape** a & adv in Ordnung. ∼**wreck** n Schiffbruch m. ∼**wrecked** a schiffbrüchig. ∼**yard** n Werft f

shirk /ʃɜːk/ vt sich drücken vor (+ dat). ∼**er** n Drückeberger m

shirt /ʃɜːt/ n [Ober]hemd nt; (for woman) Hemdbluse f

shit /ʃɪt/ n (vulg) Scheiße f ● vi (pt/pp shit) (vulg) scheißen

shiver /'ʃɪvə(r)/ n Schauder m ● vi zittern

shoal /ʃəʊl/ n (of fish) Schwarm m

shock /ʃɒk/ n Schock m; (Electr) Schlag m; (impact) Erschütterung f ● vt einen Schock versetzen (+ dat); (scandalize) schockieren. ∼**ing** a schockierend; (fam: dreadful) fürchterlich

shod /ʃɒd/ see shoe

shoddy /'ʃɒdɪ/ a (-ier, -iest) minderwertig

shoe /ʃuː/ n Schuh m; (of horse) Hufeisen nt ● vt (pt/pp shod, pres p shoeing) beschlagen ⟨horse⟩

shoe: ∼**horn** n Schuhanzieher m. ∼**lace** n Schnürsenkel m. ∼**maker** n Schuhmacher m. ∼**string** n on a ∼**string** (fam) mit ganz wenig Geld

shone /ʃɒn/ see shine

shoo /ʃuː/ vt scheuchen ● int sch!

shook /ʃʊk/ see shake

shoot /ʃuːt/ n (Bot) Trieb m; (hunt) Jagd f ● v (pt/pp shot) ● vt schießen; (kill) erschießen; drehen ⟨film⟩ ● vi schießen. ∼ **down** vt abschießen. ∼ **out** vi (rush) herausschießen. ∼ **up** vi (grow) in die Höhe schießen; ⟨prices:⟩ schnellen

'**shooting-range** n Schießstand m

shop /ʃɒp/ n Laden m, Geschäft nt; (workshop) Werkstatt f; **talk** ∼ (fam) fachsimpeln ● vi (pt/pp shopped, pres p shopping) einkaufen; **go** ∼**ping** einkaufen gehen

shop: ∼ **assistant** n Verkäufer(in) m(f). ∼**keeper** n Ladenbesitzer(in) m(f). ∼**lifter** n Ladendieb m. ∼**lifting** n Ladendiebstahl m

shopping /'ʃɒpɪŋ/ n Einkaufen nt; (articles) Einkäufe pl; **do the** ∼ einkaufen. ∼ **bag** n Einkaufstasche f. ∼ **centre** n Einkaufszentrum nt. ∼ **trolley** n Einkaufswagen m

shop: ∼**steward** n [gewerkschaftlicher] Vertrauensmann m. ∼'**window** n Schaufenster nt

shore /ʃɔː(r)/ n Strand m; (of lake) Ufer nt

shorn /ʃɔːn/ see shear

short /ʃɔːt/ a (-er, -est) kurz; ⟨person⟩ klein; (curt) schroff; **a** ∼ **time ago** vor kurzem; **be** ∼ **of** ... zuwenig ... haben; **be in** ∼ **supply** knapp sein ● adv kurz; (abruptly) plötzlich; (curtly) kurz angebunden; **in** ∼ kurzum; ∼ **of** (except) außer; **go** ∼ Mangel leiden; **stop** ∼ **of doing sth** davor zurückschrecken, etw zu tun

shortage /'ʃɔːtɪdʒ/ n Mangel m (**of** an + dat); (scarcity) Knappheit f

short: ∼**bread** n ≈ Mürbekekse pl. ∼ '**circuit** n Kurzschluß m. ∼**coming** n Fehler m. ∼ '**cut** n Abkürzung f

shorten /'ʃɔːtn/ vt [ab]kürzen; kürzer machen ⟨garment⟩

short: ∼**hand** n Kurzschrift f, Stenographie f. ∼-'**handed** a **be** ∼**handed** zuwenig Personal haben. ∼**hand** '**typist** n Stenotypistin f. ∼ **list** n engere Auswahl f. ∼-**lived** /-lɪvd/ a kurzlebig

short|ly /'ʃɔːtlɪ/ adv in Kürze; ∼**ly before/after** kurz vorher/danach. ∼**ness** n Kürze f; (of person) Kleinheit f

shorts /ʃɔːts/ npl kurze Hose f, Shorts pl

short: ∼-'**sighted** a kurzsichtig. ∼-**sleeved** a kurzärmelig. ∼-'**staffed** a **be** ∼-**staffed** zuwenig Personal haben. ∼ '**story** n Kurzgeschichte f. ∼-'**tempered** a aufbrausend. ∼-**term** a kurzfristig. ∼ **wave** n Kurzwelle f

shot /ʃɒt/ see shoot ● n Schuß m; (pellets) Schrot m; (person) Schütze m; (Phot) Aufnahme f; (injection) Spritze f; (fam: attempt) Versuch m; **like a** ∼ (fam) sofort. ∼**gun** n Schrotflinte f. ∼-**putting** n (Sport) Kugelstoßen nt

should /ʃʊd/ v aux **you** ∼ **go** du solltest gehen; **I** ∼ **have seen him** ich hätte ihn sehen sollen; **I** ∼ **like** ich möchte; **this** ∼ **be enough** das müßte eigentlich reichen; **if he** ∼ **be there** falls er da sein sollte

shoulder /'ʃəʊldə(r)/ n Schulter f ● vt schultern; (fig) auf sich (acc) nehmen. ∼**blade** n Schulterblatt nt. ∼**strap** n Tragriemen m; (on garment) Träger m

shout /ʃaʊt/ n Schrei m ● vt/i schreien. ∼ **down** vt niederschreien

shouting /'ʃaʊtɪŋ/ n Geschrei nt

shove /ʃʌv/ n Stoß m; (fam) Schubs m ● vt stoßen; (fam) schubsen;

(*fam: put*) tun ● *vi* drängeln. ~ **off** *vi* (*fam*) abhauen

shovel /'ʃʌvl/ *n* Schaufel *f* ● *vt* (*pt/pp* **shovelled**) schaufeln

show /ʃəʊ/ *n* (*display*) Pracht *f*; (*exhibition*) Ausstellung *f*, Schau *f*; (*performance*) Vorstellung *f*; (*Theat, TV*) Show *f*; **on** ~ ausgestellt ● *v* (*pt* **showed**, *pp* **shown**) ● *vt* zeigen; (*put on display*) ausstellen; vorführen ⟨*film*⟩ ● *vi* sichtbar sein; ⟨*film*:⟩ gezeigt werden. ~ **in** *vt* hereinführen. ~ **off** *vi* (*fam*) angeben ● *vt* vorführen; (*flaunt*) angeben mit. ~ **up** *vi* [deutlich] zu sehen sein; (*fam: arrive*) auftauchen ● *vt* deutlich zeigen; (*fam: embarrass*) blamieren

'**show-down** *n* Entscheidungskampf *m*

shower /'ʃaʊə(r)/ *n* Dusche *f*; (*of rain*) Schauer *m*; **have a** ~ duschen ● *vt* ~ **with** überschütten mit ● *vi* duschen. ~**proof** *a* regendicht. ~**y** *a* regnerisch

'**show-jumping** *n* Springreiten *nt*

shown /ʃəʊn/ *see* **show**

show: ~**-off** *n* Angeber(in) *m(f)*. ~**piece** *n* Paradestück *nt*. ~**room** *n* Ausstellungsraum *m*

showy /'ʃəʊɪ/ *a* protzig

shrank /ʃræŋk/ *see* **shrink**

shred /ʃred/ *n* Fetzen *m*; (*fig*) Spur *f* ● *vt* (*pt/pp* **shredded**) zerkleinern; (*Culin*) schnitzeln. ~**der** *n* Reißwolf *m*; (*Culin*) Schnitzelwerk *nt*

shrewd /ʃruːd/ *a* (**-er**, **-est**), **-ly** *adv* klug. ~**ness** *n* Klugheit *f*

shriek /ʃriːk/ *n* Schrei *m* ● *vt/i* schreien

shrift /ʃrɪft/ *n* **give s.o. short** ~ jdn kurz abfertigen

shrill /ʃrɪl/ *a*, **-y** *adv* schrill

shrimp /ʃrɪmp/ *n* Garnele *f*, Krabbe *f*

shrine /ʃraɪn/ *n* Heiligtum *nt*

shrink /ʃrɪŋk/ *vi* (*pt* **shrank**, *pp* **shrunk**) schrumpfen; ⟨*garment*:⟩ einlaufen; (*draw back*) zurückschrecken (**from** vor + *dat*)

shrivel /'ʃrɪvl/ *vi* (*pt/pp* **shrivelled**) verschrumpeln

shroud /ʃraʊd/ *n* Leichentuch *nt*; (*fig*) Schleier *m*

Shrove /ʃrəʊv/ *n* ~'**Tuesday** Fastnachtsdienstag *m*

shrub /ʃrʌb/ *n* Strauch *m*

shrug /ʃrʌg/ *n* Achselzucken *nt* ● *vt/i* (*pt/pp* **shrugged**) ~ **[one's shoulders]** die Achseln zucken

shrunk /ʃrʌŋk/ *see* **shrink**. ~**en** *a* geschrumpft

shudder /'ʃʌdə(r)/ *n* Schauder *m* ● *vi* schaudern; (*tremble*) zittern

shuffle /'ʃʌfl/ *vi* schlurfen ● *vt* mischen ⟨*cards*⟩

shun /ʃʌn/ *vt* (*pt/pp* **shunned**) meiden

shunt /ʃʌnt/ *vt* rangieren

shush /ʃʊʃ/ *int* sch!

shut /ʃʌt/ *v* (*pt/pp* **shut**, *pres p* **shutting**) ● *vt* zumachen, schließen; ~ **one's finger in the door** sich (*dat*) den Finger in der Tür einklemmen ● *vi* sich schließen; ⟨*shop*:⟩ schließen, zumachen. ~ **down** *vt* schließen; stillegen ⟨*factory*⟩ ● *vi* schließen; ⟨*factory*:⟩ stillgelegt werden. ~ **up** *vt* abschließen; (*lock*) einsperren ● *vi* (*fam*) den Mund halten

'**shut-down** *n* Stillegung *f*

shutter /'ʃʌtə(r)/ *n* [Fenster]laden *m*; (*Phot*) Verschluß *m*

shuttle /'ʃʌtl/ *n* (*Tex*) Schiffchen *nt* ● *vi* pendeln

shuttle: ~**cock** *n* Federball *m*. ~ **service** *n* Pendelverkehr *m*

shy /ʃaɪ/ *a* (**-er**, **-est**), **-ly** *adv* schüchtern; (*timid*) scheu ● *vi* (*pt/pp* **shied**) ⟨*horse*:⟩ scheuen. ~**ness** *n* Schüchternheit *f*

Siamese /saɪə'miːz/ *a* siamesisch

siblings /'sɪblɪŋz/ *npl* Geschwister *pl*

Sicily /'sɪsɪlɪ/ *n* Sizilien *nt*

sick /sɪk/ *a* krank; ⟨*humour*⟩ makaber; **be** ~ (*vomit*) sich übergeben; **be** ~ **of sth** (*fam*) etw satt haben; **I feel** ~ mir ist schlecht

sicken /'sɪkn/ *vt* anwidern ● *vi* **be** ~**ing for something** krank werden

sickle /'sɪkl/ *n* Sichel *f*

sick|ly /'sɪklɪ/ *a* (**-ier**, **-iest**) kränklich. ~**ness** *n* Krankheit *f*; (*vomiting*) Erbrechen *nt*

'**sick-room** *n* Krankenzimmer *nt*

side /saɪd/ *n* Seite *f*; **on the** ~ (*as sideline*) nebenbei; ~ **by** ~ nebeneinander; (*fig*) Seite an Seite; **take** ~**s** Partei ergreifen (**with** für); **to be on the safe** ~ vorsichtshalber ● *attrib* Seiten- ● *vi* ~ **with** Partei ergreifen für

side: ~**board** *n* Anrichte *f*. ~**burns** *npl* Koteletten *pl*. ~**-effect** *n* Nebenwirkung *f*. ~**lights** *npl* Standlicht *nt*. ~**line** *n* Nebenbeschäftigung *f*. ~**show** *n* Nebenattraktion *f*. ~**step** *vt* ausweichen (+ *dat*). ~**-track** *vt* ablenken. **~walk** n (*Amer*) Bürgersteig m. **~ways** adv seitwärts

siding /'saɪdɪŋ/ n Abstellgleis nt

sidle /'saɪdl/ vi sich heranschleichen (**up to** an + acc)

siege /siːdʒ/ n Belagerung f; (*by police*) Umstellung f

sieve /sɪv/ n Sieb nt ● vt sieben

sift /sɪft/ vt sieben; (*fig*) durchsehen

sigh /saɪ/ n Seufzer m ● vi seufzen

sight /saɪt/ n Sicht f; (*faculty*) Sehvermögen nt; (*spectacle*) Anblick m; (*on gun*) Visier nt; **~s** pl Sehenswürdigkeiten pl; **at first** ~ auf den ersten Blick; **within/out of** ~ in/außer Sicht; **lose** ~ **of** aus dem Auge verlieren; **know by** ~ vom Sehen kennen; **have bad** ~ schlechte Augen haben ● vt sichten

'sightseeing n **go** ~ die Sehenswürdigkeiten besichtigen

sign /saɪn/ n Zeichen nt; (*notice*) Schild nt ● vt/i unterschreiben; (*author, artist:*) signieren. ~ **on** vi (*as unemployed*) sich arbeitslos melden; (*Mil*) sich verpflichten

signal /'sɪɡnl/ n Signal nt ● vt/i (pt/pp **signalled**) signalisieren; ~ **to s.o.** jdm ein Signal geben (**to** zu). **~-box** n Stellwerk nt

signature /'sɪɡnətʃə(r)/ n Unterschrift f; (*of artist*) Signatur f. ~ **tune** n Kennmelodie f

signet-ring /'sɪɡnɪt-/ n Siegelring m

significance /sɪɡ'nɪfɪkəns/ n Bedeutung f. **~t** a, **-ly** adv bedeutungsvoll; (*important*) bedeutend

signify /'sɪɡnɪfaɪ/ vt (pt/pp **-ied**) bedeuten

signpost /'saɪn-/ n Wegweiser m

silence /'saɪləns/ n Stille f; (*of person*) Schweigen nt ● vt zum Schweigen bringen. **~r** n (*on gun*) Schalldämpfer m; (*Auto*) Auspufftopf m

silent /'saɪlənt/ a, **-ly** adv still; (*without speaking*) schweigend; **remain** ~ schweigen. ~ **film** n Stummfilm m

silhouette /sɪluː'et/ n Silhouette f; (*picture*) Schattenriß m ● vt **be ~d** sich als Silhouette abheben

silicon /'sɪlɪkən/ n Silizium nt

silk /sɪlk/ n Seide f ● attrib Seiden-. **~worm** n Seidenraupe f

silky /'sɪlkɪ/ a (**-ier, -iest**) seidig

sill /sɪl/ n Sims m & nt

silly /'sɪlɪ/ a (**-ier, -iest**) dumm, albern

silo /'saɪləʊ/ n Silo m

silt /sɪlt/ n Schlick m

silver /'sɪlvə(r)/ a silbern; (*coin, paper*) Silber- ● n Silber nt

silver: **~-plated** a versilbert. **~ware** n Silber nt. ~ **'wedding** n Silberhochzeit f

similar /'sɪmɪlə(r)/ a, **-ly** adv ähnlich. **~ity** /-'lærətɪ/ n Ähnlichkeit f

simile /'sɪmɪlɪ/ n Vergleich m

simmer /'sɪmə(r)/ vi leise kochen, ziehen ● vt ziehen lassen

simple /'sɪmpl/ a (**-r, -st**) einfach; (*person*) einfältig. **~ton** /'sɪmpltən/ n Einfaltspinsel m

simplicity /sɪm'plɪsətɪ/ n Einfachheit f

simplification /sɪmplɪfɪ'keɪʃn/ n Vereinfachung f. **~fy** /'sɪmplɪfaɪ/ vt (pt/pp **-ied**) vereinfachen

simply /'sɪmplɪ/ adv einfach

simulate /'sɪmjʊleɪt/ vt vortäuschen; (*Techn*) simulieren. **~ion** /-'leɪʃn/ n Vortäuschung f; Simulation f

simultaneous /sɪml'teɪnɪəs/ a, **-ly** adv gleichzeitig; (*interpreting*) Simultan-

sin /sɪn/ n Sünde f ● vi (pt/pp **sinned**) sündigen

since /sɪns/ prep seit (+ dat) ● adv seitdem ● conj seit; (*because*) da

sincere /sɪn'sɪə(r)/ a aufrichtig; (*heartfelt*) herzlich. **~ly** adv aufrichtig; **Yours ~ly** Mit freundlichen Grüßen

sincerity /sɪn'serətɪ/ n Aufrichtigkeit f

sinew /'sɪnjuː/ n Sehne f

sinful /'sɪnfl/ a sündhaft

sing /sɪŋ/ vt/i (pt **sang**, pp **sung**) singen

singe /sɪndʒ/ vt (pres p **singeing**) versengen

singer /'sɪŋə(r)/ n Sänger(in) m(f)

single /'sɪŋgl/ a einzeln; (*one only*) einzig; (*unmarried*) ledig; (*ticket*) einfach; (*room, bed*) Einzel- ● n (*ticket*) einfache Fahrkarte f; (*record*) Single f; **~s** pl (*Tennis*) Einzel nt ● vt **~out** auswählen

single: **~-breasted** a einreihig. **~-handed** a & adv allein. **~-minded** a zielstrebig. ~ **'parent** n Alleinerziehende(r) m/f

singlet /'sɪŋglɪt/ n Unterhemd nt

singly /'sɪŋglɪ/ adv einzeln

singular /'sɪŋgjʊlə(r)/ a eigenartig; (*Gram*) im Singular ● n Singular m. **~ly** adv außerordentlich

sinister /'sɪnɪstə(r)/ a finster

sink /sɪŋk/ n Spülbecken nt ● v (pt sank, pp sunk) ● vi sinken ● vt versenken ⟨ship⟩; senken ⟨shaft⟩. ~ **in** vi einsinken; (fam: be understood) kapiert werden

'sink unit n Spüle f

sinner /'sɪnə(r)/ n Sünder(in) m(f)

sinus /'saɪnəs/ n Nebenhöhle f

sip /sɪp/ n Schlückchen nt ● vt (pt/pp sipped) in kleinen Schlucken trinken

siphon /'saɪfn/ n (bottle) Siphon m. ~ **off** vt mit einem Saugheber ablassen

sir /sɜ:(r)/ n mein Herr; S~ (title) Sir; **Dear S~s** Sehr geehrte Herren

siren /'saɪrən/ n Sirene f

sissy /'sɪsɪ/ n Waschlappen m

sister /'sɪstə(r)/ n Schwester f; (nurse) Oberschwester f. ~**in-law** n (pl ~s-in-law) Schwägerin f. ~**ly** a schwesterlich

sit /sɪt/ v (pt/pp sat, pres p sitting) ● vi sitzen; (sit down) sich setzen; ⟨committee:⟩ tagen ● vt setzen; machen ⟨exam⟩. ~ **back** vi sich zurücklehnen. ~ **down** vi sich setzen. ~ **up** vi [aufrecht] sitzen; (rise) sich aufsetzen; (not slouch) gerade sitzen; (stay up) aufbleiben

site /saɪt/ n Gelände nt; (for camping) Platz m; (Archaeol) Stätte f ● vt legen

sitting /'sɪtɪŋ/ n Sitzung f; (for meals) Schub m

situat|e /'sɪtjʊeɪt/ vt legen; **be** ~**ed** liegen. ~**ion** /-'eɪʃn/ n Lage f; (circumstances) Situation f; (job) Stelle f

six /sɪks/ a sechs. ~**teen** a sechzehn. ~**teenth** a sechzehnte(r,s)

sixth /sɪksθ/ a sechste(r,s)

sixtieth /'sɪkstɪɪθ/ a sechzigste(r,s)

sixty /'sɪkstɪ/ a sechzig

size /saɪz/ n Größe f ● vt ~ **up** (fam) taxieren

sizeable /'saɪzəbl/ a ziemlich groß

sizzle /'sɪzl/ vi brutzeln

skate[1] /skeɪt/ n inv (fish) Rochen m

skate[2] n Schlittschuh m; (roller-) Rollschuh m ● vi Schlittschuh/ Rollschuh laufen. ~**r** n Eisläufer(in) m(f); Rollschuhläufer(in) m(f)

skating /'skeɪtɪŋ/ n Eislaufen nt. ~**rink** n Eisbahn f

skeleton /'skelɪtn/ n Skelett nt. ~ **'key** n Dietrich m. ~ **'staff** n Minimalbesetzung f

sketch /sketʃ/ n Skizze f; (Theat) Sketch m ● vt skizzieren

sketchy /'sketʃɪ/ a (-ier, -iest), -**ily** adv skizzenhaft

skew /skju:/ n on the ~ schräg

skewer /'skjʊə(r)/ n [Brat]spieß m

ski /ski:/ n Ski m ● vi (pt/pp skied, pres p skiing) Ski fahren or laufen

skid /skɪd/ n Schleudern nt ● vi (pt/pp skidded) schleudern

skier /'ski:ə(r)/ n Skiläufer(in) m(f)

skiing /'ski:ɪŋ/ n Skilaufen nt

skilful /'skɪlfl/ a, -**ly** adv geschickt

skill /skɪl/ n Geschick nt. ~**ed** a geschickt; (trained) ausgebildet

skim /skɪm/ vt (pt/pp skimmed) entrahmen ⟨milk⟩. ~ **off** vt abschöpfen. ~ **through** vt überfliegen

skimp /skɪmp/ vt sparen an (+ dat)

skimpy /'skɪmpɪ/ a (-ier, -iest) knapp

skin /skɪn/ n Haut f; (on fruit) Schale f ● vt (pt/pp skinned) häuten; schälen ⟨fruit⟩

skin: ~**-deep** a oberflächlich. ~**diving** n Sporttauchen nt

skinflint /'skɪnflɪnt/ n Geizhals m

skinny /'skɪnɪ/ a (-ier, -iest) dünn

skip[1] /skɪp/ n Container m

skip[2] n Hüpfer m ● v (pt/pp skipped) vi hüpfen; (with rope) seilspringen ● vt überspringen

skipper /'skɪpə(r)/ n Kapitän m

'skipping-rope n Sprungseil nt

skirmish /'skɜ:mɪʃ/ n Gefecht nt

skirt /skɜ:t/ n Rock m ● vt herumgehen um

skit /skɪt/ n parodistischer Sketch m

skittle /'skɪtl/ n Kegel m

skive /skaɪv/ vi (fam) blaumachen

skulk /skʌlk/ vi lauern

skull /skʌl/ n Schädel m

skunk /skʌŋk/ n Stinktier nt

sky /skaɪ/ n Himmel m. ~**light** n Dachluke f. ~**scraper** n Wolkenkratzer m

slab /slæb/ n Platte f; (slice) Scheibe f; (of chocolate) Tafel f

slack /slæk/ a (-er, -est) schlaff, locker; ⟨person⟩ nachlässig; (Comm) flau ● vi bummeln

slacken /'slækn/ vi sich lockern; (diminish) nachlassen; ⟨speed:⟩ sich verringern ● vt lockern; (diminish) verringern

slacks /slæks/ npl Hose f

slag /slæg/ n Schlacke f

slain /sleɪn/ see **slay**

slake /sleɪk/ vt löschen

slam /slæm/ v (pt/pp slammed) ● vt zuschlagen; (put) knallen (fam);

(*fam: criticize*) verreißen ● *vi*
zuschlagen

slander /'slɑːndə(r)/ *n* Verleumdung
f ● *vt* verleumden. **~ous** /-rəs/ *a*
verleumderisch

slang /slæŋ/ *n* Slang *m*. **~y** *a* salopp

slant /slɑːnt/ *n* Schräge *f*; **on the ~**
schräg ● *vt* abschrägen; (*fig*) färben
⟨*report*⟩ ● *vi* sich neigen

slap /slæp/ *n* Schlag *m* ● *vt* (*pt/pp*
slapped) schlagen; (*put*) knallen
(*fam*) ● *adv* direkt

slap: ~dash *a* (*fam*) schludrig. **~-up**
a (*fam*) toll

slash /slæʃ/ *n* Schlitz *m* ● *vt* aufschlitzen; [drastisch] reduzieren ⟨*prices*⟩

slat /slæt/ *n* Latte *f*

slate /sleɪt/ *n* Schiefer *m* ● *vt* (*fam*)
heruntermachen; verreißen ⟨*per-
formance*⟩

slaughter /'slɔːtə(r)/ *n* Schlachten *nt*;
(*massacre*) Gemetzel *nt* ● *vt*
schlachten; abschlachten. **~house**
n Schlachthaus *nt*

Slav /slɑːv/ *a* slawisch ● *n* Slawe *m*/
Slawin *f*

slave /sleɪv/ *n* Sklave *m*/ Sklavin *f*
● *vi* **~ [away]** schuften. **~driver** *n*
Leuteschinder *m*

slav|ery /'sleɪvərɪ/ *n* Sklaverei *f*. **~ish**
a, **-ly** *adv* sklavisch

Slavonic /slə'vɒnɪk/ *a* slawisch

slay /sleɪ/ *vt* (*pt* **slew**, *pp* **slain**)
ermorden

sleazy /'sliːzɪ/ *a* (**-ier, -iest**) schäbig

sledge /sledʒ/ *n* Schlitten *m*. **~ham-
mer** *n* Vorschlaghammer *m*

sleek /sliːk/ *a* (**-er, -est**) seidig; (*well-
fed*) wohlgenährt

sleep /sliːp/ *n* Schlaf *m*; **go to ~**
einschlafen; **put to ~** einschläfern
● *v* (*pt/pp* **slept**) ● *vi* schlafen ● *vt*
(*accommodate*) Unterkunft bieten
für. **~er** *n* Schläfer(in) *m(f)*; (*Rail*)
Schlafwagen *m*; (*on track*) Schwelle *f*

sleeping: ~-bag *n* Schlafsack *m*. **~-
car** *n* Schlafwagen *m*. **~-pill** *n*
Schlaftablette *f*

sleep: ~less *a* schlaflos. **~-walking**
n Schlafwandeln *nt*

sleepy /'sliːpɪ/ *a* (**-ier, -iest**), **-ily** *adv*
schläfrig

sleet /sliːt/ *n* Schneeregen *m* ● *vi* **it is
~ing** es gibt Schneeregen

sleeve /sliːv/ *n* Ärmel *m*; (*for record*)
Hülle *f*. **~less** *a* ärmellos

sleigh /sleɪ/ *n* [Pferde]schlitten *m*

sleight /slaɪt/ *n* **~ of hand**
Taschenspielerei *f*

slender /'slendə(r)/ *a* schlank; (*fig*)
gering

slept /slept/ *see* **sleep**

sleuth /sluːθ/ *n* Detektiv *m*

slew[1] /sluː/ *vi* schwenken

slew[2] *see* **slay**

slice /slaɪs/ *n* Scheibe *f* ● *vt* in Scheiben schneiden; **~d bread** Schnitt-
brot *nt*

slick /slɪk/ *a* clever ● *n* (*of oil*) Ölteppich *m*

slid|e /slaɪd/ *n* Rutschbahn *f*; (*for
hair*) Spange *f*; (*Phot*) Dia *nt* ● *v*
(*pt/pp* **slid**) ● *vi* rutschen ● *vt* schieben. **~ing** *a* gleitend; ⟨*door, seat*⟩
Schiebe-

slight /slaɪt/ *a* (**-er, -est**), **-ly** *adv*
leicht; ⟨*importance*⟩ gering; ⟨*acquaintance*⟩ flüchtig; (*slender*)
schlank; **not in the ~est** nicht im
geringsten; **~ly better** ein bißchen
besser ● *vt* kränken, beleidigen ● *n*
Beleidigung *f*

slim /slɪm/ *a* (**slimmer, slimmest**)
schlank; ⟨*volume*⟩ schmal; (*fig*) gering ● *vi* eine Schlankheitskur
machen

slim|e /slaɪm/ *n* Schleim *m*. **~y** *a*
schleimig

sling /slɪŋ/ *n* (*Med*) Schlinge *f* ● *vt*
(*pt/pp* **slung**) (*fam*) schmeißen

slip /slɪp/ *n* (*mistake*) Fehler *m*, (*fam*)
Patzer *m*; (*petticoat*) Unterrock *m*;
(*for pillow*) Bezug *m*; (*paper*) Zettel
m; **give s.o. the ~** (*fam*) jdm entwischen; **~ of the tongue** Versprecher
m ● *v* (*pt/pp* **slipped**) ● *vi* rutschen;
(*fall*) ausrutschen; (*go quickly*)
schlüpfen; (*decline*) nachlassen ● *vt*
schieben; **~ s.o.'s mind** jdm entfallen. **~ away** *vi* sich fortschleichen;
⟨*time:*⟩ verfliegen. **~ up** *vi* (*fam*)
einen Schnitzer machen

slipped 'disc *n* (*Med*) Bandscheiben-
vorfall *m*

slipper /'slɪpə(r)/ *n* Hausschuh *m*

slippery /'slɪpərɪ/ *a* glitschig; ⟨*surface*⟩ glatt

slipshod /'slɪpʃɒd/ *a* schludrig

'slip-up *n* (*fam*) Schnitzer *m*

slit /slɪt/ *n* Schlitz *m* ● *vt* (*pt/pp* **slit**)
aufschlitzen

slither /'slɪðə(r)/ *vi* rutschen

sliver /'slɪvə(r)/ *n* Splitter *m*

slobber /'slɒbə(r)/ *vi* sabbern

slog /slɒg/ *n* [**hard**] **~** Schinderei *f*
● *v* (*pt/pp* **slogged**) ● *vi* schuften
● *vt* schlagen

slogan /'sləʊgən/ n Schlagwort nt; (advertising) Werbespruch m

slop /slɒp/ v (pt/pp slopped) ● vt verschütten ● vi ∼ over überschwappen. ∼s npl Schmutzwasser nt

slop|e /sləʊp/ n Hang m; (inclination) Neigung f ● vi sich neigen. ∼ing a schräg

sloppy /'slɒpɪ/ a (-ier, -iest) schludrig; (sentimental) sentimental

slosh /slɒʃ/ vi (fam) platschen; ⟨water:⟩ schwappen ● vt (fam: hit) schlagen

slot /slɒt/ n Schlitz m; (TV) Sendezeit f ● v (pt/pp slotted) ● vt einfügen ● vi sich einfügen (in in + acc)

sloth /sləʊθ/ n Trägheit f

'slot-machine n Münzautomat m; (for gambling) Spielautomat m

slouch /slaʊtʃ/ vi sich schlecht halten

slovenly /'slʌvnlɪ/ a schlampig

slow /sləʊ/ a (-er, -est), -ly adv langsam; be ∼ ⟨clock:⟩ nachgehen; in ∼ motion in Zeitlupe ● adv langsam ● vt verlangsamen ● vi ∼ down, ∼up langsamer werden

slow: ∼coach n (fam) Trödler m. ∼ness n Langsamkeit f

sludge /slʌdʒ/ n Schlamm m

slug /slʌg/ n Nacktschnecke f

sluggish /'slʌgɪʃ/ a, -ly adv träge

sluice /sluːs/ n Schleuse f

slum /slʌm/ n (house) Elendsquartier nt; ∼s pl Elendsviertel nt

slumber /'slʌmbə(r)/ n Schlummer m ● vi schlummern

slump /slʌmp/ n Sturz m ● vi fallen; (crumple) zusammensacken; ⟨prices:⟩ stürzen; ⟨sales:⟩ zurückgehen

slung /slʌŋ/ see sling

slur /slɜː(r)/ n (discredit) Schande f ● vt (pt/pp slurred) undeutlich sprechen

slurp /slɜːp/ vt/i schlürfen

slush /slʌʃ/ n [Schnee]matsch m; (fig) Kitsch m. ∼ fund n Fonds m für Bestechungsgelder

slushy /'slʌʃɪ/ a matschig; (sentimental) kitschig

slut /slʌt/ n Schlampe f (fam)

sly /slaɪ/ a (-er, -est), -ly adv verschlagen ● n on the ∼ heimlich

smack¹ /smæk/ n Schlag m, Klaps m ● vt schlagen; ∼ one's lips mit den Lippen schmatzen ● adv (fam) direkt

smack² vi ∼ of (fig) riechen nach

small /smɔːl/ a (-er, -est) klein; in the ∼ hours in den frühen Morgenstunden ● adv chop up ∼ kleinhacken ● n ∼ of the back Kreuz nt

small: ∼ ads npl Kleinanzeigen pl. ∼ 'change n Kleingeld nt. ∼-holding n landwirtschaftlicher Kleinbetrieb m. ∼pox n Pocken pl. ∼ talk n leichte Konversation f

smarmy /'smɑːmɪ/ a (-ier, -iest) (fam) ölig

smart /smɑːt/ a (-er, -est), -ly adv schick; (clever) schlau, clever; (brisk) flott; (Amer fam: cheeky) frech ● vi brennen

smarten /'smɑːtn/ vt ∼ oneself up mehr auf sein Äußeres achten

smash /smæʃ/ n Krach m; (collision) Zusammenstoß m; (Tennis) Schmetterball m ● vt zerschlagen; (strike) schlagen; (Tennis) schmettern ● vi zerschmettern; (crash) krachen (into gegen). ∼ing a (fam) toll

smattering /'smætərɪŋ/ n a ∼ of German ein paar Brocken Deutsch

smear /smɪə(r)/ n verschmierter Fleck m; (Med) Abstrich m; (fig) Verleumdung f ● vt schmieren; (coat) beschmieren (with mit); (fig) verleumden ● vi schmieren

smell /smel/ n Geruch m; (sense) Geruchssinn m ● v (pt/pp smelt or smelled) ● vt riechen; (sniff) riechen an (+ dat) ● vi riechen (of nach)

smelly /'smelɪ/ a (-ier, -iest) übelriechend

smelt¹ /smelt/ see smell

smelt² vt schmelzen

smile /smaɪl/ n Lächeln nt ● vi lächeln; ∼ at anlächeln

smirk /smɜːk/ vi feixen

smith /smɪθ/ n Schmied m

smithereens /smɪðə'riːnz/ npl smash to ∼ in tausend Stücke schlagen

smitten /'smɪtn/ a ∼ with sehr angetan von

smock /smɒk/ n Kittel m

smog /smɒg/ n Smog m

smoke /sməʊk/ n Rauch m ● vt/i rauchen; (Culin) räuchern. ∼less a rauchfrei; ⟨fuel⟩ rauchlos

smoker /'sməʊkə(r)/ n Raucher m; (Rail) Raucherabteil nt

'smoke-screen n [künstliche] Nebelwand f

smoking /'sməʊkɪŋ/ n Rauchen nt; 'no ∼' 'Rauchen verboten'

smoky /'sməʊkɪ/ a (-ier, -iest) verraucht; ⟨taste⟩ rauchig

smooth /smu:ð/ a (-er, -est), -ly adv glatt ● vt glätten. ~ **out** vt glattstreichen

smother /'smʌðə(r)/ vt ersticken; (cover) bedecken; (suppress) unterdrücken

smoulder /'sməʊldə(r)/ vi schwelen

smudge /smʌdʒ/ n Fleck m ● vt verwischen ● vi schmieren

smug /smʌg/ a (smugger, smuggest), -ly adv selbstgefällig

smuggl|e /'smʌgl/ vt schmuggeln. ~er n Schmuggler m. ~ing n Schmuggel m

smut /smʌt/ n Rußflocke f; (mark) Rußfleck m; (fig) Schmutz m

smutty /'smʌtɪ/ a (-ier, -iest) schmutzig

snack /snæk/ n Imbiß m. ~-bar n Imbißstube f

snag /snæg/ n Schwierigkeit f, (fam) Haken m

snail /sneɪl/ n Schnecke f; at a ~'s pace im Schneckentempo

snake /sneɪk/ n Schlange f

snap /snæp/ n Knacken nt; (photo) Schnappschuß m ● attrib ⟨decision⟩ plötzlich ● v (pt/pp snapped) ● vi [entzwei]brechen; ~ **at** (bite) schnappen nach; (speak sharply) [scharf] anfahren ● vt zerbrechen; (say) fauchen; (Phot) knipsen. ~ **up** vt wegschnappen

snappy /'snæpɪ/ a (-ier, -iest) bissig; (smart) flott; make it ~! ein bißchen schnell!

'snapshot n Schnappschuß m

snare /sneə(r)/ n Schlinge f

snarl /snɑ:l/ vi [mit gefletschten Zähnen] knurren

snatch /snætʃ/ n (fragment) Fetzen pl; (theft) Raub m; make a ~ at greifen nach ● vt schnappen; (steal) klauen; entführen ⟨child⟩; ~ **sth from s.o.** jdm etw entreißen

sneak /sni:k/ n (fam) Petze f ● vi schleichen; (fam: tell tales) petzen ● vt (take) mitgehen lassen ● vi ~ **in/out** sich hinein-/hinausschleichen

sneakers /'sni:kəz/ npl (Amer) Turnschuhe pl

sneaking /'sni:kɪŋ/ a heimlich; ⟨suspicion⟩ leise

sneaky /'sni:kɪ/ a hinterhältig

sneer /snɪə(r)/ vi höhnisch lächeln; (mock) spotten

sneeze /sni:z/ n Niesen nt ● vi niesen

snide /snaɪd/ a (fam) abfällig

sniff /snɪf/ vi schnüffeln ● vt schnüffeln an (+ dat); schnüffeln ⟨glue⟩

snigger /'snɪgə(r)/ vi [boshaft] kichern

snip /snɪp/ n Schnitt m; (fam:~bargain) günstiger Kauf m ● vt/i ~ [at] schnippeln an (+ dat)

snipe /snaɪp/ vi ~ **at** aus dem Hinterhalt schießen auf (+ acc); (fig) anschießen. ~r n Heckenschütze m

snippet /'snɪpɪt/ n Schnipsel m; (of information) Bruchstück nt

snivel /'snɪvl/ vi (pt/pp snivelled) flennen

snob /snɒb/ n Snob m. ~**bery** n Snobismus m. ~**bish** a snobistisch

snoop /snu:p/ vi (fam) schnüffeln

snooty /'snu:tɪ/ a (fam) hochnäsig

snooze /snu:z/ n Nickerchen nt ● vi dösen

snore /snɔ:(r)/ vi schnarchen

snorkel /'snɔ:kl/ n Schnorchel m

snort /snɔ:t/ vi schnauben

snout /snaʊt/ n Schnauze f

snow /snəʊ/ n Schnee m ● vi schneien; ~**ed under with** (fig) überhäuft mit

snow: ~**ball** n Schneeball m ● vi lawinenartig anwachsen. ~**drift** n Schneewehe f. ~**drop** n Schneeglöckchen nt. ~**fall** n Schneefall m. ~**flake** n Schneeflocke f. ~**flurry** n Schneegestöber nt. ~**man** n Schneemann m. ~ **-plough** n Schneepflug m. ~**storm** n Schneesturm m

snub /snʌb/ n Abfuhr f ● vt (pt/pp snubbed) brüskieren

'snub-nosed a stupsnasig

snuff¹ /snʌf/ n Schnupftabak m

snuff² vt ~[out] löschen

snuffle /'snʌfl/ vi schnüffeln

snug /snʌg/ a (snugger, snuggest) behaglich, gemütlich

snuggle /'snʌgl/ vi sich kuscheln (up to an + acc)

so /səʊ/ adv so; not so fast nicht so schnell; so am I ich auch; so does he er auch; so I see das sehe ich; that is so das stimmt; so much the better um so besser; so it is tatsächlich; if so wenn ja; so as to um zu; so long! (fam) tschüs! ● pron I hope so hoffentlich; I think so ich glaube schon; I told you so ich hab's dir gleich gesagt; because I say so weil ich es sage; I'm afraid so leider ja; so saying/doing, he/she ... indem er/sie das sagte/tat, . . .; **an hour or so** eine Stunde oder so; **very much so** durchaus ● *conj (therefore)* also; **so that** damit; **so there!** fertig! **so what!** na und! **so you see** wie du siehst; **so where have you been?** wo warst du denn?

soak /səʊk/ *vt* naß machen; *(steep)* einweichen; *(fam: fleece)* schröpfen ● *vi* weichen; ⟨*liquid:*⟩ sickern. **~ up** *vt* aufsaugen

soaking /'səʊkɪŋ/ *a & adv* **~ [wet]** patschnaß *(fam)*

soap /səʊp/ *n* Seife *f*. **~ opera** *n* Seifenoper *f*. **~ powder** *n* Seifenpulver *nt*

soapy /'səʊpɪ/ *a* (-ier, -iest) seifig

soar /sɔː(r)/ *vi* aufsteigen; ⟨*prices:*⟩ in die Höhe schnellen

sob /sɒb/ *n* Schluchzer *m* ● *vi (pt/pp sobbed)* schluchzen

sober /'səʊbə(r)/ *a*, **-ly** *adv* nüchtern; *(serious)* ernst; ⟨*colour*⟩ gedeckt. **~ up** *vi* nüchtern werden

'so-called *a* sogenannt

soccer /'sɒkə(r)/ *n (fam)* Fußball *m*

sociable /'səʊʃəbl/ *a* gesellig

social /'səʊʃl/ *a* gesellschaftlich; *(Admin, Pol, Zool)* sozial

socialism /'səʊʃəlɪzm/ *n* Sozialismus *m*. **~t** /-ɪst/ *a* sozialistisch ● *n* Sozialist *m*

socialize /'səʊʃəlaɪz/ *vi* [gesellschaftlich] verkehren

socially /'səʊʃəlɪ/ *adv* gesellschaftlich; **know ~** privat kennen

social: **~ se'curity** *n* Sozialhilfe *f*. **~ work** *n* Sozialarbeit *f*. **~ worker** *n* Sozialarbeiter(in) *m(f)*

society /sə'saɪətɪ/ *n* Gesellschaft *f*; *(club)* Verein *m*

sociologist /səʊsɪ'ɒlədʒɪst/ *n* Soziologe *m*. **~y** *n* Soziologie *f*

sock[1] /sɒk/ *n* Socke *f*; *(knee-length)* Kniestrumpf *m*

sock[2] *n (fam)* Schlag *m* ● *vt (fam)* hauen

socket /'sɒkɪt/ *n (of eye)* Augenhöhle *f*; *(of joint)* Gelenkpfanne *f*; *(wall plug)* Steckdose *f*; *(for bulb)* Fassung *f*

soda /'səʊdə/ *n* Soda *nt*; *(Amer)* Limonade *f*. **~ water** *n* Sodawasser *nt*

sodden /'sɒdn/ *a* durchnäßt

sodium /'səʊdɪəm/ *n* Natrium *nt*

sofa /'səʊfə/ *n* Sofa *nt*. **~ bed** *n* Schlafcouch *f*

soft /sɒft/ *a* (-er, -est), **-ly** *adv* weich; *(quiet)* leise; *(gentle)* sanft; *(fam:*

silly) dumm; **have a ~ spot for s.o.** jdn mögen. **~ drink** *n* alkoholfreies Getränk *nt*

soften /'sɒfn/ *vt* weich machen; *(fig)* mildern ● *vi* weich werden

soft: **~ toy** *n* Stofftier *nt*. **~ware** *n* Software *f*

soggy /'sɒgɪ/ *a* (-ier, -iest) aufgeweicht

soil[1] /sɔɪl/ *n* Erde *f*, Boden *m*

soil[2] *vt* verschmutzen

solace /'sɒləs/ *n* Trost *m*

solar /'səʊlə(r)/ *a* Sonnen-

sold /səʊld/ *see* **sell**

solder /'səʊldə(r)/ *n* Lötmetall *nt* ● *vt* löten

soldier /'səʊldʒə(r)/ *n* Soldat *m* ● *vi* **~ on** [unbeirrbar] weitermachen

sole[1] /səʊl/ *n* Sohle *f*

sole[2] *n (fish)* Seezunge *f*

sole[3] *a* einzig. **~ly** *adv* einzig und allein

solemn /'sɒləm/ *a*, **-ly** *adv* feierlich; *(serious)* ernst. **~ity** /sə'lemnətɪ/ *n* Feierlichkeit *f*; Ernst *m*

solicit /sə'lɪsɪt/ *vt* bitten um ● *vi* ⟨*prostitute:*⟩ sich an Männer heranmachen

solicitor /sə'lɪsɪtə(r)/ *n* Rechtsanwalt *m*/-anwältin *f*

solicitous /sə'lɪsɪtəs/ *a* besorgt

solid /'sɒlɪd/ *a* fest; *(sturdy)* stabil; *(not hollow, of same substance)* massiv; *(unanimous)* einstimmig; *(complete)* ganz ● *n (Geom)* Körper *m*; **~s** *pl (food)* feste Nahrung *f*

solidarity /sɒlɪ'dærətɪ/ *n* Solidarität *f*

solidify /sə'lɪdɪfaɪ/ *vi (pt/pp -ied)* fest werden

soliloquy /sə'lɪləkwɪ/ *n* Selbstgespräch *nt*

solitary /'sɒlɪtərɪ/ *a* einsam; *(sole)* einzig. **~ con'finement** *n* Einzelhaft *f*

solitude /'sɒlɪtjuːd/ *n* Einsamkeit *f*

solo /'səʊləʊ/ *n* Solo *nt* ● *a* Solo-; ⟨*flight*⟩ Allein- ● *adv* solo. **~ist** *n* Solist(in) *m(f)*

solstice /'sɒlstɪs/ *n* Sonnenwende *f*

soluble /'sɒljʊbl/ *a* löslich; *(solvable)* lösbar

solution /sə'luːʃn/ *n* Lösung *f*

solvable /'sɒlvəbl/ *a* lösbar

solve /sɒlv/ *vt* lösen

solvent /'sɒlvənt/ *a* zahlungsfähig; *(Chem)* lösend ● *n* Lösungsmittel *nt*

sombre /'sɒmbə(r)/ *a* dunkel; ⟨*mood*⟩ düster

some /sʌm/ *a & pron* etwas; *(a little)* ein bißchen; *(with pl noun)* einige; *(a* *few*) ein paar; (*certain*) manche(r,s); (*one or the other*) [irgend]ein; ~ **day** eines Tages; **I want** ~ ich möchte etwas/ (*pl*) welche; **will you have** ~ **wine?** möchten Sie Wein? **I need** ~ **money/books** ich brauche Geld/ Bücher; **do** ~ **shopping** einkaufen

some: ~**body** /-bədɪ/ *pron & n* jemand; (*emphatic*) irgend jemand. ~**how** *adv* irgendwie. ~**one** *pron & n* = somebody

somersault /'sʌməsɔːlt/ *n* Purzelbaum *m* (*fam*); (*Sport*) Salto *m*; **turn a** ~ einen Purzelbaum schlagen/ einen Salto springen

'**something** *pron & adv* etwas; (*emphatic*) irgend etwas; ~ **different** etwas anderes; ~ **like** so etwas wie; **see** ~ **of s.o.** jdn mal sehen

some: ~**time** *adv* irgendwann ● *a* ehemalig. ~**times** *adv* manchmal. ~**what** *adv* ziemlich. ~**where** *adv* irgendwo; ⟨*go*⟩ irgendwohin

son /sʌn/ *n* Sohn *m*

sonata /sə'nɑːtə/ *n* Sonate *f*

song /sɒŋ/ *n* Lied *nt*. ~**bird** *n* Singvogel *m*

sonic /'sɒnɪk/ *a* Schall-. ~ '**boom** *n* Überschallknall *m*

'**son-in-law** *n* (*pl* ~**s-in-law**) Schwiegersohn *m*

soon /suːn/ *adv* (**-er, -est**) bald; (*quickly*) schnell; **too** ~ zu früh; **as** ~ **as sobald;** **as** ~ **as possible** so bald wie möglich; ~**er or later** früher oder später; **no** ~**er had I arrived than . . .** kaum war ich angekommen, da . . .; **I would** ~**er stay** ich würde lieber bleiben

soot /sʊt/ *n* Ruß *m*

sooth|e /suːð/ *vt* beruhigen; lindern ⟨*pain*⟩. ~**ing** *a*, **-ly** *adv* beruhigend; lindernd

sooty /'sʊtɪ/ *a* rußig

sop /sɒp/ *n* Beschwichtigungsmittel *nt*

sophisticated /sə'fɪstɪkeɪtɪd/ *a* weltgewandt; (*complex*) hochentwickelt

soporific /sɒpə'rɪfɪk/ *a* einschläfernd

sopping /'sɒpɪŋ/ *a & adv* ~ [**wet**] durchnäßt

soppy /'sɒpɪ/ *a* (**-ier, -iest**) (*fam*) rührselig

soprano /sə'prɑːnəʊ/ *n* Sopran *m*; (*woman*) Sopranistin *f*

sordid /'sɔːdɪd/ *a* schmutzig

sore /sɔː(r)/ *a* (**-r, -st**) wund; (*painful*) schmerzhaft; **have a** ~ **throat**

Halsschmerzen haben ● *n* wunde Stelle *f*. ~**ly** *adv* sehr

sorrow /'sɒrəʊ/ *n* Kummer *m*, Leid *nt*. ~**ful** *a* traurig

sorry /'sɒrɪ/ *a* (**-ier, -iest**) (*sad*) traurig; (*wretched*) erbärmlich; **I am** ~ es tut mir leid; **she is** *or* **feels** ~ **for him** er tut ihr leid; **I am** ~ **to say** leider; ~**! Entschuldigung!**

sort /sɔːt/ *n* Art *f*; (*brand*) Sorte *f*; **he's a good** ~ (*fam*) er ist in Ordnung; **be out of** ~**s** (*fam*) nicht auf der Höhe sein ● *vt* sortieren. ~ **out** *vt* sortieren; (*fig*) klären

sought /sɔːt/ *see* **seek**

soul /səʊl/ *n* Seele *f*. ~**ful** *a* gefühlvoll

sound[1] /saʊnd/ *a* (**-er, -est**) gesund; (*sensible*) vernünftig; (*secure*) solide; (*thorough*) gehörig ● *adv* **be** ~ **asleep** fest schlafen

sound[2] *vt* (*Naut*) loten. ~ **out** *vt* (*fig*) aushorchen

sound[3] *n* (*strait*) Meerenge *f*

sound[4] *n* Laut *m*; (*noise*) Geräusch *nt*; (*Phys*) Schall *m*; (*Radio, TV*) Ton *m*; (*of bells, music*) Klang *m*; **I don't like the** ~ **of it** (*fam*) das hört sich nicht gut an ● *vi* [er]tönen; (*seem*) sich anhören ● *vt* (*pronounce*) aussprechen; schlagen ⟨*alarm*⟩; (*Med*) abhorchen ⟨*chest*⟩. ~ **barrier** *n* Schallmauer *f*. ~**less** *a*, **-ly** *adv* lautlos

soundly /'saʊndlɪ/ *adv* solide; ⟨*sleep*⟩ fest; ⟨*defeat*⟩ vernichtend

'**soundproof** *a* schalldicht

soup /suːp/ *n* Suppe *f*. ~**ed-up** *a* (*fam*) ⟨*engine*⟩ frisiert

soup: ~**-plate** *n* Suppenteller *m*. ~**spoon** *n* Suppenlöffel *m*

sour /'saʊə(r)/ *a* (**-er, -est**) sauer; (*bad-tempered*) griesgrämig, verdrießlich

source /sɔːs/ *n* Quelle *f*

south /saʊθ/ *n* Süden *m*; **to the** ~ **of** südlich von ● *a* Süd-, süd- ● *adv* nach Süden

south: S~ '**Africa** *n* Südafrika *nt*. **S**~ **A'merica** *n* Südamerika *nt*. ~**-'east** *n* Südosten *m*

southerly /'sʌðəlɪ/ *a* südlich

southern /'sʌðən/ *a* südlich

South 'Pole *n* Südpol *m*

'**southward[s]** /-wəd[z]/ *adv* nach Süden

souvenir /suːvə'nɪə(r)/ *n* Andenken *nt*, Souvenir *nt*

sovereign /'sɒvrɪn/ *a* souverän ● *n* Souverän *m*. ~**ty** *n* Souveränität *f*

Soviet /'səʊvɪət/ a sowjetisch; ~ Union Sowjetunion f

sow¹ /saʊ/ n Sau f

sow² /səʊ/ vt (pt **sowed**, pp **sown** or **sowed**) säen

soya /'sɔɪə/ n ~ **bean** Sojabohne f

spa /spɑ:/ n Heilbad nt

space /speɪs/ n Raum m; (gap) Platz m; (Astr) Weltraum m; **leave/clear a** ~ Platz lassen/schaffen ● vt ~ **[out]** [in Abständen] verteilen

space: ~**craft** n Raumfahrzeug nt. ~**ship** n Raumschiff nt

spacious /'speɪʃəs/ a geräumig

spade /speɪd/ n Spaten m; (for child) Schaufel f; ~**s** pl (Cards) Pik nt; **call a** ~ **a** ~ das Kind beim rechten Namen nennen. ~**work** n Vorarbeit f

Spain /speɪn/ n Spanien nt

span¹ /spæn/ n Spanne f; (of arch) Spannweite f ● vt (pt/pp **spanned**) überspannen; umspannen ⟨time⟩

span² see **spick**

Span|iard /'spænjəd/ n Spanier(in) m(f). ~**ish** a spanisch ● n (Lang) Spanisch nt; **the** ~**ish** pl die Spanier

spank /spæŋk/ vt verhauen

spanner /'spænə(r)/ n Schraubenschlüssel m

spar /spɑ:(r)/ vi (pt/pp **sparred**) (Sport) sparren; (argue) sich zanken

spare /speə(r)/ a (surplus) übrig; (additional) zusätzlich; ⟨seat, time⟩ frei; ⟨room⟩ Gäste-; ⟨bed, cup⟩ Extra- ● n (part) Ersatzteil nt ● vt ersparen; (not hurt) verschonen; (do without) entbehren; (afford to give) erübrigen; **to** ~ (surplus) übrig. ~ 'wheel n Reserverad nt

sparing /'speərɪŋ/ a, **-ly** adv sparsam

spark /spɑ:k/ n Funke m ● vt ~ **off** zünden; (fig) auslösen. ~**ing-plug** n (Auto) Zündkerze f

sparkl|e /'spɑ:kl/ n Funkeln nt ● vi funkeln. ~**ing** a funkelnd; ⟨wine⟩ Schaum-

sparrow /'spærəʊ/ n Spatz m

sparse /spɑ:s/ a spärlich. ~**ly** adv spärlich; ⟨populated⟩ dünn

Spartan /'spɑ:tn/ a spartanisch

spasm /'spæzm/ n Anfall m; (cramp) Krampf m. ~**odic** /-'mɒdɪk/ a, **-ally** adv sporadisch; (Med) krampfartig

spastic /'spæstɪk/ a spastisch [gelähmt] ● n Spastiker(in) m(f)

spat /spæt/ see **spit²**

spate /speɪt/ n Flut f; (series) Serie f; **be in full** ~ Hochwasser führen

spatial /'speɪʃl/ a räumlich

spatter /'spætə(r)/ vt spritzen; ~ **with** bespritzen mit

spatula /'spætjʊlə/ n Spachtel m; (Med) Spatel m

spawn /spɔ:n/ n Laich m ● vi laichen ● vt (fig) hervorbringen

spay /speɪ/ vt sterilisieren

speak /spi:k/ v (pt **spoke**, pp **spoken**) ● vi sprechen (**to** mit); ~**ing!** (Teleph) am Apparat! ● vt sprechen; sagen ⟨truth⟩. ~ **up** vi lauter sprechen; ~ **up for oneself** seine Meinung äußern

speaker /'spi:kə(r)/ n Sprecher(in) m(f); (in public) Redner(in) m(f); (loudspeaker) Lautsprecher m

spear /spɪə(r)/ n Speer m ● vt aufspießen. ~**head** vt (fig) anführen

spec /spek/ n **on** ~ (fam) auf gut Glück

special /'speʃl/ a besondere(r,s), speziell. ~**ist** n Spezialist m; (Med) Facharzt m/-ärztin f. ~**ity** /-'ʃr'æləti/ n Spezialität f

special|ize /'speʃəlaɪz/ vi sich spezialisieren (**in** auf + acc). ~**ly** adv speziell; (particularly) besonders

species /'spi:ʃi:z/ n Art f

specific /spə'sɪfɪk/ a bestimmt; (precise) genau; (Phys) spezifisch. ~**ally** adv ausdrücklich

specification /spesɪfɪ'keɪʃn/ n & ~**s** pl genaue Angaben pl

specify /'spesɪfaɪ/ vt (pt/pp **-ied**) [genau] angeben

specimen /'spesɪmən/ n Exemplar nt; (sample) Probe f; (of urine) Urinprobe f

speck /spek/ n Fleck m; (particle) Teilchen nt

speckled /'spekld/ a gesprenkelt

specs /speks/ npl (fam) Brille f

spectacle /'spektəkl/ n (show) Schauspiel nt; (sight) Anblick m. ~**s** npl Brille f

spectacular /spek'tækjʊlə(r)/ a spektakulär

spectator /spek'teɪtə(r)/ n Zuschauer(in) m(f)

spectre /'spektə(r)/ n Gespenst nt; (fig) Schreckgespenst nt

spectrum /'spektrəm/ n (pl **-tra**) Spektrum nt

speculat|e /'spekjʊleɪt/ vi spekulieren. ~**ion** /-'leɪʃn/ n Spekulation f. ~**or** n Spekulant m

sped /sped/ see **speed**

speech /spiːtʃ/ n Sprache f; (address) Rede f. **~less** a sprachlos

speed /spiːd/ n Geschwindigkeit f; (rapidity) Schnelligkeit f; (gear) Gang m; **at ~** mit hoher Geschwindigkeit ● vi (pt/pp **sped**) schnell fahren ● (pt/pp **speeded**) (go too fast) zu schnell fahren. **~ up** (pt/pp **speeded up**) ● vt beschleunigen ● vi schneller werden; ⟨vehicle:⟩ schneller fahren

speed: ~boat n Rennboot nt. **~ing** n Geschwindigkeitsüberschreitung f. **~ limit** n Geschwindigkeitsbeschränkung f

speedometer /spiː'dɒmɪtə(r)/ n Tachometer m

speedy /'spiːdɪ/ a (-ier, -iest), **-ily** adv schnell

spell¹ /spel/ n Weile f; (of weather) Periode f

spell² v (pt/pp **spelled** or **spelt**) ● vt schreiben; (aloud) buchstabieren; (fig: mean) bedeuten ● vi richtig schreiben; (aloud) buchstabieren. **~ out** vt buchstabieren; (fig) genau erklären

spell³ n Zauber m; (words) Zauberspruch m. **~bound** a wie verzaubert

spelling /'spelɪŋ/ n Schreibweise f; (orthography) Rechtschreibung f

spelt /spelt/ see **spell²**

spend /spend/ vt/i (pt/pp **spent**) ausgeben; verbringen ⟨time⟩

spent /spent/ see **spend**

sperm /spɜːm/ n Samen m

spew /spjuː/ vt speien

spher|e /sfɪə(r)/ n Kugel f; (fig) Sphäre f. **~ical** /'sferɪkl/ a kugelförmig

spice /spaɪs/ n Gewürz nt; (fig) Würze f

spick /spɪk/ a **~ and span** blitzsauber

spicy /'spaɪsɪ/ a würzig, pikant

spider /'spaɪdə(r)/ n Spinne f

spik|e /spaɪk/ n Spitze f; (Bot, Zool) Stachel m; (on shoe) Spike m. **~y** a stachelig

spill /spɪl/ v (pt/pp **spilt** or **spilled**) ● vt verschütten; vergießen ⟨blood⟩ ● vi überlaufen

spin /spɪn/ v (pt/pp **spun**, pres p **spinning**) ● vt drehen; spinnen ⟨wool⟩; schleudern ⟨washing⟩ ● vi sich drehen. **~ out** vt in die Länge ziehen

spinach /'spɪnɪdʒ/ n Spinat m

spinal /'spaɪnl/ a Rückgrat-. **~ 'cord** n Rückenmark nt

spindl|e /'spɪndl/ n Spindel f. **~y** a spindeldürr

spin-'drier n Wäscheschleuder f

spine /spaɪn/ n Rückgrat nt; (of book) [Buch]rücken m; (Bot, Zool) Stachel m. **~less** a (fig) rückgratlos

spinning /'spɪnɪŋ/ n Spinnen nt. **~-wheel** n Spinnrad nt

'spin-off n Nebenprodukt nt

spinster /'spɪnstə(r)/ n ledige Frau f

spiral /'spaɪrl/ a spiralig ● n Spirale f ● vi (pt/pp **spiralled**) sich hochwinden; ⟨smoke:⟩ in einer Spirale aufsteigen. **~ 'staircase** n Wendeltreppe f

spire /'spaɪə(r)/ n Turmspitze f

spirit /'spɪrɪt/ n Geist m; (courage) Mut m; **~s** pl (alcohol) Spirituosen pl; **in high ~s** in gehobener Stimmung; **in low ~s** niedergedrückt. **~ away** vt verschwinden lassen

spirited /'spɪrɪtɪd/ a lebhaft; (courageous) beherzt

spirit: ~-level n Wasserwaage f. **~ stove** n Spirituskocher m

spiritual /'spɪrɪtjʊəl/ a geistig; (Relig) geistlich. **~ism** /-ɪzm/ n Spiritismus m. **~ist** /-ɪst/ a spiritistisch ● n Spiritist m

spit¹ /spɪt/ n (for roasting) [Brat]-spieß m

spit² n Spucke f ● vt/i (pt/pp **spat**, pres p **spitting**) spucken; ⟨cat:⟩ fauchen; ⟨fat:⟩ spritzen; **it's ~ting with rain** es tröpfelt; **be the ~ting image of s.o.** jdm wie aus dem Gesicht geschnitten sein

spite /spaɪt/ n Boshaftigkeit f; **in ~ of** trotz (+ gen) ● vt ärgern. **~ful** a, **-ly** adv gehässig

spittle /'spɪtl/ n Spucke f

splash /splæʃ/ n Platschen nt; (fam: drop) Schuß m; **~ of colour** Farbfleck m ● vt spritzen; **~ s.o. with sth** jdn mit etw bespritzen ● vi spritzen. **~ about** vi planschen

spleen /spliːn/ n Milz f

splendid /'splendɪd/ a herrlich, großartig

splendour /'splendə(r)/ n Pracht f

splint /splɪnt/ n (Med) Schiene f

splinter /'splɪntə(r)/ n Splitter m ● vi zersplittern

split /splɪt/ n Spaltung f; (Pol) Bruch m; (tear) Riß m ● v (pt/pp **split**, pres p **splitting**) ● vt spalten; (share) teilen; (tear) zerreißen; **~ one's sides** sich kaputtlachen ● vi sich spalten; (tear) zerreißen; **~ on s.o.** (fam) jdn

verpfeifen. ~ **up** vt aufteilen ● vi
⟨couple:⟩ sich trennen
splutter /'splʌtə(r)/ vi prusten
spoil /spɔɪl/ n ~s pl Beute f ● v (pt/pp
spoilt or spoiled) ● vt verderben;
verwöhnen ⟨person⟩ ● vi verderben.
~**sport** n Spielverderber m
spoke[1] /spəʊk/ n Speiche f
spoke[2], **spoken** /spəʊkn/ see **speak**
'**spokesman** n Sprecher m
sponge /spʌndʒ/ n Schwamm m ● vt
abwaschen ● vi ~ **on** schmarotzen
bei. ~**bag** n Waschbeutel m. ~**cake** n Biskuitkuchen m
spong|er /'spʌndʒə(r)/ n Schmarotzer
m. ~**y** a schwammig
sponsor /'spɒnsə(r)/ n Sponsor m;
⟨god-parent⟩ Pate m/Patin f; ⟨for
membership⟩ Bürge m ● vt sponsern; bürgen für
spontaneous /spɒn'teɪnɪəs/ a, -ly
adv spontan
spoof /spu:f/ n ⟨fam⟩ Parodie f
spooky /'spu:kɪ/ a (-ier, -iest) ⟨fam⟩
gespenstisch
spool /spu:l/ n Spule f
spoon /spu:n/ n Löffel m ● vt löffeln.
~**-feed** vt (pt/pp -fed) ⟨fig⟩ alles
vorkauen (+ dat). ~**ful** n Löffel m
sporadic /spə'rædɪk/ a, -ally adv
sporadisch
sport /spɔ:t/ n Sport m; ⟨amusement⟩
Spaß m ● vt [stolz] tragen. ~**ing** a
sportlich; a ~**ing chance** eine faire
Chance
sports: ~ **car** n Sportwagen m. ~
coat n, ~ **jacket** n Sakko m. ~**man** n
Sportler m. ~**woman** n Sportlerin f
sporty /'spɔ:tɪ/ a (-ier, -iest) sportlich
spot /spɒt/ n Fleck m; ⟨place⟩ Stelle f;
⟨dot⟩ Punkt m; ⟨drop⟩ Tropfen m;
⟨pimple⟩ Pickel m; ~s pl ⟨rash⟩
Ausschlag m; a ~ **of** ⟨fam⟩ ein bißchen; on the ~ auf der Stelle; be in a
tight ~ ⟨fam⟩ in der Klemme sitzen
● vt (pt/pp spotted) entdecken
spot: ~'**check** n Stichprobe f. ~**less** a
makellos; ⟨fam: very clean⟩ blitz-
sauber. ~**light** n Scheinwerfer m;
⟨fig⟩ Rampenlicht m
spotted /'spɒtɪd/ a gepunktet
spotty /'spɒtɪ/ a (-ier, -iest) fleckig;
⟨pimply⟩ pickelig
spouse /spaʊz/ n Gatte m/Gattin f
spout /spaʊt/ n Schnabel m, Tülle f
● vi schießen (from aus)
sprain /spreɪn/ n Verstauchung f ● vt
verstauchen
sprang /spræŋ/ see **spring**[2]

sprat /spræt/ n Sprotte f
sprawl /sprɔ:l/ vi sich ausstrecken;
⟨fall⟩ der Länge nach hinfallen
spray[1] /spreɪ/ n ⟨of flowers⟩ Strauß m
spray[2] n Sprühnebel m; ⟨from sea⟩
Gischt m; ⟨device⟩ Spritze f; ⟨container⟩ Sprühdose f; ⟨preparation⟩
Spray nt ● vt spritzen; ⟨with aero-
sol⟩ sprühen
spread /spred/ n Verbreitung f;
⟨paste⟩ Aufstrich m; ⟨fam: feast⟩
Festessen nt ● v (pt/pp spread) ● vt
ausbreiten; streichen ⟨butter, jam⟩;
bestreichen ⟨bread, surface⟩;
streuen ⟨sand, manure⟩; verbreiten
⟨news, disease⟩; verteilen ⟨pay-
ments⟩ ● vi sich ausbreiten. ~ **out**
vt ausbreiten; ⟨space out⟩ verteilen
● vi sich verteilen
spree /spri:/ n ⟨fam⟩ **go on a shopping** ~ groß einkaufen gehen
sprig /sprɪg/ n Zweig m
sprightly /'spraɪtlɪ/ a (-ier, -iest)
rüstig
spring[1] /sprɪŋ/ n Frühling m ● attrib
Frühlings-
spring[2] n ⟨jump⟩ Sprung m; ⟨water⟩
Quelle f; ⟨device⟩ Feder f; ⟨elasticity⟩
Elastizität f ● v (pt sprang, pp
sprung) ● vi springen; ⟨arise⟩
entspringen (from dat) ● vt ~ **sth
on s.o.** jdn mit etw überfallen
spring: ~**board** n Sprungbrett nt. ~
'**cleaning** n Frühjahrsputz m.
~**time** n Frühling m
sprinkl|e /'sprɪŋkl/ vt sprengen;
⟨scatter⟩ streuen; bestreuen ⟨sur-
face⟩. ~**er** n Sprinkler m; ⟨Hort⟩
Sprenger m. ~**ing** n dünne Schicht f
sprint /sprɪnt/ n Sprint m ● vi rennen; ⟨Sport⟩ sprinten. ~**er** n Kurz-
streckenläufer(in) m(f)
sprout /spraʊt/ n Trieb m; [Brussels]
~s pl Rosenkohl m ● vi sprießen
spruce /spru:s/ a gepflegt ● n Fichte f
sprung /sprʌŋ/ see **spring**[2] ● a
gefedert
spry /spraɪ/ a (-er, -est) rüstig
spud /spʌd/ n ⟨fam⟩ Kartoffel f
spun /spʌn/ see **spin**
spur /spɜ:(r)/ n Sporn m; ⟨stimulus⟩
Ansporn m; ⟨road⟩ Nebenstraße f;
on the ~ **of the moment** ganz spontan ● vt (pt/pp spurred) ~ [**on**] ⟨fig⟩
anspornen
spurious /'spjʊərɪəs/ a, -ly adv falsch
spurn /spɜ:n/ vt verschmähen
spurt /spɜ:t/ n Strahl m; ⟨Sport⟩ Spurt
m; **put on a** ~ spurten ● vi spritzen

spy /spaɪ/ n Spion(in) m(f) ● vi spionieren ● vt (fam: see) sehen. ~ **on** vt nachspionieren (**s.o.** jdm). ~ **out** vt auskundschaften

spying /'spaɪɪŋ/ n Spionage f

squabble /'skwɒbl/ n Zank m ● vi sich zanken

squad /skwɒd/ n Gruppe f; (Sport) Mannschaft f

squadron /'skwɒdrən/ n (Mil) Geschwader nt

squalid /'skwɒlɪd/ a, **-ly** adv schmutzig

squall /skwɔːl/ n Bö f ● vi brüllen

squalor /'skwɒlə(r)/ n Schmutz m

squander /'skwɒndə(r)/ vt vergeuden

square /skweə(r)/ a quadratisch; ⟨metre, mile⟩ Quadrat-; ⟨meal⟩ anständig; **all** ~ (fam) quitt ● n Quadrat nt; (area) Platz m; (on chessboard) Feld nt ● vt (settle) klären; (Math) quadrieren ● vi (agree) übereinstimmen

squash /skwɒʃ/ n Gedränge nt; (drink) Fruchtsaftgetränk nt; (Sport) Squash nt ● vt zerquetschen; (suppress) niederschlagen. ~**y** a weich

squat /skwɒt/ a gedrungen ● n (fam) besetztes Haus nt ● vi (pt/pp **squatted**) hocken; ~ **in a house** ein Haus besetzen. ~**ter** n Hausbesetzer m

squawk /skwɔːk/ vi krächzen

squeak /skwiːk/ n Quieken nt; (of hinge, brakes) Quietschen nt ● vi quieken; quietschen

squeal /skwiːl/ n Schrei m; (screech) Kreischen nt ● vi schreien; kreischen

squeamish /'skwiːmɪʃ/ a empfindlich

squeeze /skwiːz/ n Druck m; (crush) Gedränge nt ● vt drücken; (to get juice) ausdrücken; (force) zwängen; (fam: extort) herauspressen (**from** aus) ● vi ~ **in/out** sich hinein-/hinauszwängen

squelch /skweltʃ/ vi quatschen

squid /skwɪd/ n Tintenfisch m

squiggle /'skwɪgl/ n Schnörkel m

squint /skwɪnt/ n Schielen nt ● vi schielen

squire /'skwaɪə(r)/ n Gutsherr m

squirm /skwɜːm/ vi sich winden

squirrel /'skwɪrl/ n Eichhörnchen nt

squirt /skwɜːt/ n Spritzer m ● vt/i spritzen

St abbr (**Saint**) St.; (**Street**) Str.

stab /stæb/ n Stich m; (fam: attempt) Versuch m ● vt (pt/pp **stabbed**) stechen; (to death) erstechen

stability /stə'bɪlətɪ/ n Stabilität f

stabilize /'steɪbɪlaɪz/ vt stabilisieren ● vi sich stabilisieren

stable¹ /'steɪbl/ a (**-r, -st**) stabil

stable² n Stall m; (establishment) Reitstall m

stack /stæk/ n Stapel m; (of chimney) Schornstein m; (fam: large quantity) Haufen m ● vt stapeln

stadium /'steɪdɪəm/ n Stadion nt

staff /stɑːf/ n (stick & Mil) Stab m (● & pl) (employees) Personal nt; (Sch) Lehrkräfte pl ● vt mit Personal besetzen. ~**room** n (Sch) Lehrerzimmer nt

stag /stæg/ n Hirsch m

stage /steɪdʒ/ n Bühne f; (in journey) Etappe f; (in process) Stadium nt; **by or in** ~**s** in Etappen ● vt aufführen; (arrange) veranstalten

stage: ~ **door** n Bühneneingang m. ~ **fright** n Lampenfieber nt

stagger /'stægə(r)/ vi taumeln ● vt staffeln ⟨holidays⟩; versetzt anordnen ⟨seats⟩; **I was** ~**ed** es hat mir die Sprache verschlagen. ~**ing** a unglaublich

stagnant /'stægnənt/ a stehend; (fig) stagnierend

stagnat|e /stæg'neɪt/ vi (fig) stagnieren. ~**ion** /-'neɪʃn/ n Stagnation f

staid /steɪd/ a gesetzt

stain /steɪn/ n Fleck m; (for wood) Beize f ● vt färben; beizen ⟨wood⟩; (fig) beflecken; ~**ed glass** farbiges Glas nt. ~**less** a fleckenlos; ⟨steel⟩ rostfrei. ~ **remover** n Fleckentferner m

stair /steə(r)/ n Stufe f; ~**s** pl Treppe f. ~**case** n Treppe f

stake /steɪk/ n Pfahl m; (wager) Einsatz m; (Comm) Anteil m; **be at** ~ auf dem Spiel stehen ● vt [an einem Pfahl] anbinden; (wager) setzen; ~ **a claim to sth** Anspruch auf etw (acc) erheben

stale /steɪl/ a (**-r, -st**) alt; ⟨air⟩ verbraucht. ~**mate** n Patt nt

stalk¹ /stɔːk/ n Stiel m, Stengel m

stalk² vt pirschen auf (+ acc) ● vi stolzieren

stall /stɔːl/ n Stand m; ~**s** pl (Theat) Parkett nt ● vi ⟨engine:⟩ stehenbleiben; (fig) ausweichen ● vt abwürgen ⟨engine⟩

stallion /'stæljən/ n Hengst m

stalwart /'stɔːlwət/ a treu ● n treuer Anhänger m

stamina /'stæmɪnə/ n Ausdauer f

stammer /'stæmə(r)/ n Stottern nt ● vt/i stottern

stamp /stæmp/ n Stempel m; (postage ~) [Brief]marke f ● vt stempeln; (impress) prägen; (put postage on) frankieren; ~ one's feet mit den Füßen stampfen ● vi stampfen. ~ out [aus]stanzen; (fig) ausmerzen

stampede /stæm'piːd/ n wilde Flucht f; (fam) Ansturm m ● vi in Panik fliehen

stance /stɑːns/ n Haltung f

stand /stænd/ n Stand m; (rack) Ständer m; (pedestal) Sockel m; (Sport) Tribüne f; (fig) Einstellung f ● v (pt/pp **stood**) ● vi stehen; (rise) aufstehen; (be candidate) kandidieren; (stay valid) gültig bleiben; ~ still stillstehen; ~ firm (fig) festbleiben; ~ together zusammenhalten; ~ to lose / gain gewinnen / verlieren können; ~ to reason logisch sein; ~ in for vertreten; ~ for (mean) bedeuten; I won't ~ for that das lasse ich mir nicht bieten ● vt stellen; (withstand) standhalten (+ dat); (endure) ertragen; vertragen ⟨climate⟩; (put up with) aushalten; haben ⟨chance⟩; ~ one's ground nicht nachgeben; ~ the test of time sich bewähren; ~ s.o. a beer jdm ein Bier spendieren; I can't ~ her (fam) ich kann sie nicht ausstehen. ~ by vi danebenstehen; (be ready) sich bereithalten ● vt ~ by s.o. (fig) zu jdm stehen. ~ down vi (retire) zurücktreten. ~ out vi hervorstehen; (fig) herausragen. ~ up vi aufstehen; ~ up for eintreten für; ~ up to sich wehren gegen

standard /'stændəd/ a Normal-; be ~ practice allgemein üblich sein ● n Maßstab m; (Techn) Norm f; (level) Niveau nt; (flag) Standarte f; ~s pl (morals) Prinzipien pl; ~ of living Lebensstandard m. ~ize vt standardisieren; (Techn) normen

'standard lamp n Stehlampe f

'stand-in n Ersatz m

standing /'stændɪŋ/ a (erect) stehend; (permanent) ständig ● n Rang m; (duration) Dauer f. ~ 'order n Dauerauftrag m. ~-room n Stehplätze pl

stand: ~-**offish** /stænd'ɒfɪʃ/ a distanziert. ~**point** n Standpunkt m. ~**still** n Stillstand m; come to a ~**still** zum Stillstand kommen

stank /stæŋk/ see **stink**

staple¹ /'steɪpl/ a Grund- ● n (product) Haupterzeugnis nt

staple² n Heftklammer f ● vt heften. ~**r** n Heftmaschine f

star /stɑː(r)/ n Stern m; (asterisk) Sternchen nt; (Theat, Sport) Star m ● vi (pt/pp **starred**) die Hauptrolle spielen

starboard /'stɑːbəd/ n Steuerbord nt

starch /stɑːtʃ/ n Stärke f ● vt stärken. ~**y** a stärkehaltig; (fig) steif

stare /steə(r)/ n Starren nt ● vi starren; ~ at anstarren

'starfish n Seestern m

stark /stɑːk/ a (-er, -est) scharf; ⟨contrast⟩ kraß ● adv ~ naked splitternackt

starling /'stɑːlɪŋ/ n Star m

'starlit a sternhell

starry /'stɑːrɪ/ a sternklar

start /stɑːt/ n Anfang m, Beginn m; (departure) Aufbruch m; (Sport) Start m; from the ~ von Anfang an; for a ~ erstens ● vi anfangen, beginnen; (set out) aufbrechen; ⟨engine:⟩ anspringen; (Auto, Sport) starten; (jump) aufschrecken; to ~ with zuerst ● vt anfangen, beginnen; (cause) verursachen; (found) gründen; starten ⟨car, race⟩; in Umlauf setzen ⟨rumour⟩. ~**er** n (Culin) Vorspeise f; (Auto, Sport) Starter m. ~**ing-point** n Ausgangspunkt m

startle /'stɑːtl/ vt erschrecken

starvation /stɑː'veɪʃn/ n Verhungern nt

starve /stɑːv/ vi hungern; (to death) verhungern ● vt verhungern lassen

stash /stæʃ/ vt (fam) ~ [away] beiseite schaffen

state /steɪt/ n Zustand m; (grand style) Prunk m; (Pol) Staat m; ~ of play Spielstand m; be in a ~ ⟨person:⟩ aufgeregt sein; lie in ~ feierlich aufgebahrt sein ● attrib Staats-, staatlich ● vt erklären; (specify) angeben. ~-aided a staatlich gefördert. ~less a staatenlos

stately /'steɪtlɪ/ a (-ier, -iest) stattlich. ~ 'home n Schloß nt

statement /'steɪtmənt/ n Erklärung f; (Jur) Aussage f; (Banking) Auszug m

'statesman n Staatsmann m

static /'stætɪk/ a statisch; **remain ~** unverändert bleiben

station /'steɪʃn/ n Bahnhof m; (police) Wache f; (radio) Sender m; (space, weather) Station f; (Mil) Posten m; (status) Rang m ● vt stationieren; (post) postieren. **~ary** /-ərɪ/ a stehend; **be ~ary** stehen

stationer /'steɪʃənə(r)/ n **~'s [shop]** Schreibwarengeschäft nt. **~y** n Briefpapier nt; (writing-materials) Schreibwaren pl

'station-wagon n (Amer) Kombi[wagen] m

statistic /stə'tɪstɪk/ n statistische Tatsache f. **~al** a, **-ly** adv statistisch. **~s** n & pl Statistik f

statue /'stætju:/ n Statue f

stature /'stætʃə(r)/ n Statur f; (fig) Format nt

status /'steɪtəs/ n Status m, Rang m. **~ symbol** n Statussymbol nt

statut|e /'stætju:t/ n Statut nt. **~ory** a gesetzlich

staunch /stɔ:ntʃ/ a (-er, -est), **-ly** adv treu

stave /steɪv/ vt **~ off** abwenden

stay /steɪ/ n Aufenthalt m ● vi bleiben; (reside) wohnen; **~ the night** übernachten; **~ put** dableiben ● vt **~ the course** durchhalten. **~ away** vi wegbleiben. **~ behind** vi zurückbleiben. **~ in** vi zu Hause bleiben; (Sch) nachsitzen. **~ up** vi oben bleiben; (upright) stehen bleiben; (on wall) hängen bleiben; ⟨person:⟩ aufbleiben

stead /sted/ n in his **~** an seiner Stelle; **stand s.o. in good ~** jdm zustatten kommen. **~fast** a, **-ly** adv standhaft

steadily /'stedɪlɪ/ adv fest; (continually) stetig

steady /'stedɪ/ a (-ier, -iest) fest; (not wobbly) stabil; ⟨hand⟩ ruhig; (regular) regelmäßig; (dependable) zuverlässig

steak /steɪk/ n Steak nt

steal /sti:l/ vt/i (pt stole, pp stolen) stehlen (from dat). **~ in/out** vi sich hinein-/hinausstehlen

stealth /stelθ/ n Heimlichkeit f; **by ~** heimlich. **~y** a heimlich

steam /sti:m/ n Dampf m; **under one's own ~** (fam) aus eigener Kraft ● vt (Culin) dämpfen, dünsten ● vi dampfen. **~ up** vi beschlagen

'steam-engine n Dampfmaschine f; (Rail) Dampflokomotive f

steamer /'sti:mə(r)/ n Dampfer m

'steamroller n Dampfwalze f

steamy /'sti:mɪ/ a dampfig

steel /sti:l/ n Stahl m ● vt **~ oneself** allen Mut zusammennehmen

steep¹ /sti:p/ vt (soak) einweichen

steep² a, **-ly** adv steil; (fam: exorbitant) gesalzen

steeple /'sti:pl/ n Kirchturm m. **~chase** n Hindernisrennen nt

steer /stɪə(r)/ vt/i steuern; **~ clear of s.o./sth** jdm/ etw aus dem Weg gehen. **~ing** n (Auto) Steuerung f. **~ing-wheel** n Lenkrad nt

stem¹ /stem/ n Stiel m; (of word) Stamm m ● vi (pt/pp stemmed) **~ from** zurückzuführen sein auf (+ acc)

stem² vt (pt/pp stemmed) eindämmen; stillen ⟨bleeding⟩

stench /stentʃ/ n Gestank m

stencil /'stensl/ n Schablone f; (for typing) Matrize f

step /step/ n Schritt m; (stair) Stufe f; **~s** pl (ladder) Trittleiter f; **in ~** im Schritt; **~ by ~** Schritt für Schritt; **take ~s** (fig) Schritte unternehmen ● vi (pt/pp stepped) treten; **~ in** (fig) eingreifen; **~ into s.o.'s shoes** an jds Stelle treten; **~ out of line** aus der Reihe tanzen. **~ up** vi hinaufsteigen ● vt (increase) erhöhen, steigern; verstärken ⟨efforts⟩

step: **~brother** n Stiefbruder m. **~child** n Stiefkind nt. **~daughter** n Stieftochter f. **~father** n Stiefvater m. **~ladder** n Trittleiter f. **~mother** n Stiefmutter f

'stepping-stone n Trittstein m; (fig) Sprungbrett nt

step: **~sister** n Stiefschwester f. **~son** n Stiefsohn m

stereo /'sterɪəʊ/ n Stereo nt; (equipment) Stereoanlage f; **in ~** stereo. **~phonic** /-'fɒnɪk/ a stereophon

stereotype /'sterɪətaɪp/ n stereotype Figur f. **~d** a stereotyp

steril|e /'steraɪl/ a steril. **~ity** /stə'rɪlətɪ/ n Sterilität f

steriliz|ation /steralaɪ'zeɪʃn/ n Sterilisation f. **~e** vt sterilisieren

sterling /'stɜ:lɪŋ/ a Sterling-; (fig) gediegen ● n Sterling m

stern¹ /stɜ:n/ a (-er, -est), **-ly** adv streng

stern² n (of boat) Heck nt

stew /stju:/ n Eintopf m; **in a ~** (fam) aufgeregt ● vt/i schmoren; **~ed fruit** Kompott nt

steward /'stju:əd/ n Ordner m; (on ship, aircraft) Steward m. ~ess n Stewardeß f

stick[1] /stɪk/ n Stock m; (of chalk) Stück nt; (of rhubarb) Stange f; (Sport) Schläger m

stick[2] v (pt/pp stuck) ● vt stecken; (stab) stechen; (glue) kleben; (fam: put) tun; (fam: endure) aushalten ● vi stecken; (adhere) kleben, haften (to an + dat); (jam) klemmen; ~ to sth (fig) bei etw bleiben; ~ at it (fam) dranbleiben; ~ at nothing (fam) vor nichts zurückschrecken; ~ up for (fam) eintreten für; be stuck nicht weiterkönnen; (vehicle:) festsitzen, festgefahren sein; (drawer:) klemmen; be stuck with sth (fam) etw am Hals haben. ~ out vi abstehen; (project) vorstehen ● vt (fam) hinausstrecken; herausstrecken (tongue).

sticker /'stɪkə(r)/ n Aufkleber m

'sticking plaster n Heftpflaster nt

stickler /'stɪklə(r)/ n be a ~ for es sehr genau nehmen mit

sticky /'stɪkɪ/ a (-ier, -iest) klebrig; (adhesive) Klebe-

stiff /stɪf/ a (-er, -est), -ly adv steif; (brush) hart; (dough) fest; (difficult) schwierig; (penalty) schwer; be bored ~ (fam) sich zu Tode langweilen. ~en vt steif machen ● vi steif werden. ~ness n Steifheit f

stifl|e /'staɪfl/ vt ersticken; (fig) unterdrücken. ~ing a be ~ing zum Ersticken sein

stigma /'stɪgmə/ n Stigma nt

stile /staɪl/ n Zauntritt m

stiletto /stɪ'letəʊ/ n Stilett nt; (heel) Bleistiftabsatz m

still[1] /stɪl/ n Destillierapparat m

still[2] a still; (drink) ohne Kohlensäure; keep ~ stillhalten; stand ~ stillstehen ● n Stille f ● adv noch; (emphatic) immer noch; (nevertheless) trotzdem; ~ not immer noch nicht

'stillborn a totgeboren

still 'life n Stilleben nt

stilted /'stɪltɪd/ a gestelzt, geschraubt

stilts /stɪlts/ npl Stelzen pl

stimulant /'stɪmjʊlənt/ n Anregungsmittel nt

stimulat|e /'stɪmjʊleɪt/ vt anregen. ~ion /-'leɪʃn/ n Anregung f

stimulus /'stɪmjʊləs/ n (pl -li /-laɪ/) Reiz m

sting /stɪŋ/ n Stich m; (from nettle, jellyfish) Brennen nt; (organ) Stachel m ● v (pt/pp stung) ● vt stechen ● vi brennen; (insect:) stechen. ~ing nettle n Brennessel f

stingy /'stɪndʒɪ/ a (-ier, -iest) geizig, (fam) knauserig

stink /stɪŋk/ n Gestank m ● vi (pt stank, pp stunk) stinken (of nach)

stint /stɪnt/ n Pensum nt ● vi ~ on sparen an (+ dat)

stipulat|e /'stɪpjʊleɪt/ vt vorschreiben. ~ion /-'leɪʃn/ n Bedingung f

stir /stɜ:(r)/ n (commotion) Aufregung f ● v (pt/pp stirred) vt rühren ● vi sich rühren

stirrup /'stɪrəp/ n Steigbügel m

stitch /stɪtʃ/ n Stich m; (Knitting) Masche f; (pain) Seitenstechen nt; be in ~es (fam) sich kaputtlachen ● vt nähen

stoat /stəʊt/ n Hermelin nt

stock /stɒk/ n Vorrat m (of an + dat); (in shop) [Waren]bestand m; (livestock) Vieh nt; (lineage) Abstammung f; (Finance) Wertpapiere pl; (Culin) Brühe f; (plant) Levkoje f; in/out of ~ vorrätig/nicht vorrätig; take ~ (fig) Bilanz ziehen ● a Standard● vt (shop:) führen; auffüllen (shelves). ~ up vi sich eindecken (with mit)

stock: ~broker n Börsenmakler m. ~ cube n Brühwürfel m. S~ Exchange n Börse f

stocking /'stɒkɪŋ/ n Strumpf m

stockist /'stɒkɪst/ n Händler m

stock: ~market n Börse f. ~pile vt horten; anhäufen (weapons). ~-'still a bewegungslos. ~taking n (Comm) Inventur f

stocky /'stɒkɪ/ a (-ier, -iest) untersetzt

stodgy /'stɒdʒɪ/ a pappig [und schwer verdaulich]

stoical /'stəʊɪkl/ a, -ly adv stoisch

stoke /stəʊk/ vt heizen

stole[1] /stəʊl/ n Stola f

stole[2], **stolen** /stəʊln/ see steal

stolid /'stɒlɪd/ a, -ly adv stur

stomach /'stʌmək/ n Magen m ● vt vertragen. ~ache n Magenschmerzen pl

stone /stəʊn/ n Stein m; (weight) 6,35 kg ● a steinern; (wall, Age) Stein- ● vt mit Steinen bewerfen; entsteinen (fruit). ~-cold a eiskalt. ~-'deaf n (fam) stocktaub

stony /'stəʊnɪ/ a steinig

stood /stʊd/ see stand

stool /stu:l/ n Hocker m

stoop /stu:p/ n **walk with a ~** gebeugt gehen ● vi sich bücken; (fig) sich erniedrigen

stop /stɒp/ n Halt m; (break) Pause f; (for bus) Haltestelle f; (for train) Station f; (Gram) Punkt m; (on organ) Register nt; **come to a ~** stehenbleiben; **put a ~ to sth** etw unterbinden ● v (pt/pp **stopped**) ● vt anhalten, stoppen; (switch off) abstellen; (plug, block) zustopfen; (prevent) verhindern; **~ s.o. doing sth** jdn daran hindern, etw zu tun; **~ doing sth** aufhören, etw zu tun; **~ that!** hör auf damit! laß das sein! ● vi anhalten; (cease) aufhören; ⟨clock:⟩ stehenbleiben; (fam: stay) bleiben (with bei) ● int halt! stopp!

stop: **~gap** n Notlösung f. **~over** n Zwischenaufenthalt m; (Aviat) Zwischenlandung f

stoppage /'stɒpɪdʒ/ n Unterbrechung f; (strike) Streik m; (deduction) Abzug m

stopper /'stɒpə(r)/ n Stöpsel m

stop: **~-press** n letzte Meldungen pl. **~-watch** n Stoppuhr f

storage /'stɔ:rɪdʒ/ n Aufbewahrung f; (in warehouse) Lagerung f; (Computing) Speicherung f

store /stɔ:(r)/ n (stock) Vorrat m; (shop) Laden m; (department ~) Kaufhaus nt; (depot) Lager nt; **in ~** auf Lager; **put in ~** lagern; **set great ~ by** großen Wert legen auf (+ acc); **be in ~ for s.o.** (fig) jdm bevorstehen ● vt aufbewahren; (in warehouse) lagern; (Computing) speichern. **~-room** n Lagerraum m

storey /'stɔ:rɪ/ n Stockwerk nt

stork /stɔ:k/ n Storch m

storm /stɔ:m/ n Sturm m; (with thunder) Gewitter nt ● vt/i stürmen. **~y** a stürmisch

story /'stɔ:rɪ/ n Geschichte f; (in newspaper) Artikel m; (fam: lie) Märchen nt

stout /staʊt/ a (-er, -est) beleibt; (strong) fest

stove /stəʊv/ n Ofen m; (for cooking) Herd m

stow /stəʊ/ vt verstauen. **~away** n blinder Passagier m

straddle /'strædl/ vt rittlings sitzen auf (+ dat); (standing) mit gespreizten Beinen stehen über (+ dat)

straggl|e /'strægl/ vi hinterherhinken. **~er** n Nachzügler m. **~y** a strähnig

straight /streɪt/ a (-er, -est) gerade; (direct) direkt; (clear) klar; ⟨hair⟩ glatt; ⟨drink⟩ pur; **be ~** (tidy) in Ordnung sein ● adv gerade; (directly) direkt, geradewegs; (clearly) klar; **~ away** sofort; **~ on** or **ahead** geradeaus; **~ out** (fig) geradeheraus; **go ~** (fam) ein ehrliches Leben führen; **put sth ~** etw in Ordnung bringen; **sit/stand up ~** geradesitzen/-stehen

straighten /'streɪtn/ vt gerademachen; (put straight) geraderichten ● vi gerade werden; **~ [up]** ⟨person:⟩ sich aufrichten. **~ out** vt geradebiegen

straight'forward a offen; (simple) einfach

strain¹ /streɪn/ n Rasse f; (Bot) Sorte f; (of virus) Art f

strain² n Belastung f; **~s** pl (of music) Klänge pl ● vt belasten; (overexert) überanstrengen; (injure) zerren ⟨muscle⟩; (Culin) durchseihen; abgießen ⟨vegetables⟩ ● vi sich anstrengen. **~ed** a ⟨relations⟩ gespannt. **~er** n Sieb nt

strait /streɪt/ n Meerenge f; **in dire ~s** in großen Nöten. **~-jacket** n Zwangsjacke f. **~-'laced** a puritanisch

strand¹ /strænd/ n (of thread) Faden m; (of beads) Kette f; (of hair) Strähne f

strand² vt **be ~ed** festsitzen

strange /streɪndʒ/ a (-r, -st) fremd; (odd) seltsam, merkwürdig. **~r** n Fremde(r) m/f

strangely /'streɪndʒlɪ/ adv seltsam, merkwürdig; **~ enough** seltsamerweise

strangle /'stræŋgl/ vt erwürgen; (fig) unterdrücken

strangulation /stræŋgjʊ'leɪʃn/ n Erwürgen nt

strap /stræp/ n Riemen m; (for safety) Gurt m; (to grasp in vehicle) Halteriemen m; (of watch) Armband nt; (shoulder-) Träger m ● vt (pt/pp **strapped**) schnallen; **~ in** or **down** festschnallen

strapping /'stræpɪŋ/ a stramm

strata /'strɑ:tə/ npl see **stratum**

stratagem /'strætədʒəm/ n Kriegslist f

strategic /strə'ti:dʒɪk/ a, **-ally** adv strategisch

strategy /'strætədʒɪ/ n Strategie f

stratum /'strɑ:təm/ n (pl **strata**) Schicht f

straw /strɔ:/ n Stroh nt; (single piece, drinking) Strohhalm m; **that's the last ~** jetzt reicht's aber

strawberry /'strɔ:bərɪ/ n Erdbeere f

stray /streɪ/ a streunend ● n streunendes Tier nt ● vi sich verirren; (deviate) abweichen

streak /stri:k/ n Streifen m; (in hair) Strähne f; (fig: trait) Zug m ● vi flitzen. **~y** a streifig; ⟨bacon⟩ durchwachsen

stream /stri:m/ n Bach m; (flow) Strom m; (current) Strömung f; (Sch) Parallelzug m ● vi strömen; **in/out** hinaus-/herausströmen

streamer /'stri:mə(r)/ n Luftschlange f; (flag) Wimpel m

'streamline vt (fig) rationalisieren. **~d** a stromlinienförmig

street /stri:t/ n Straße f. **~car** n (Amer) Straßenbahn f. **~ lamp** n Straßenlaterne f

strength /streŋθ/ n Stärke f; (power) Kraft f; **on the ~ of** auf Grund (+ gen). **~en** vt stärken; (reinforce) verstärken

strenuous /'strenjʊəs/ a anstrengend

stress /stres/ n (emphasis) Betonung f; (strain) Belastung f; (mental) Streß m ● vt betonen; (put a strain on) belasten. **~ful** a stressig (fam)

stretch /stretʃ/ n (of road) Strecke f; (elasticity) Elastizität f; **at a ~** ohne Unterbrechung; **a long ~** eine lange Zeit; **have a ~** sich strecken ● vt strecken; (widen) dehnen; (spread) ausbreiten; fordern ⟨person⟩; **~ one's legs** sich (dat) die Beine vertreten ● vi sich erstrecken; (become wider) sich dehnen; ⟨person:⟩ sich strecken. **~er** n Tragbahre f

strew /stru:/ vt (pp **strewn** or **strewed**) streuen

stricken /'strɪkn/ a betroffen; **~ with** heimgesucht von

strict /strɪkt/ a (-er, -est), **-ly** adv streng; **~ly speaking** strenggenommen

stride /straɪd/ n [großer] Schritt m; **make great ~s** (fig) große Fortschritte machen; **take sth in one's ~** mit etw gut fertig werden ● vi (pt **strode**, pp **stridden**) [mit großen Schritten] gehen

strident /'straɪdnt/ a, **-ly** adv schrill; ⟨colour⟩ grell

strife /straɪf/ n Streit m

strike /straɪk/ n Streik m; (Mil) Angriff m; **be on ~** streiken ● v (pt/pp **struck**) ● vt schlagen; (knock against, collide with) treffen; prägen ⟨coin⟩; anzünden ⟨match⟩; stoßen auf (+ acc) ⟨oil, gold⟩; abbrechen ⟨camp⟩; (delete) streichen; (impress) beeindrucken; (occur to) einfallen (+ dat); (Mil) angreifen; **~ s.o. a blow** jdm einen Schlag versetzen ● vi treffen; ⟨lightning:⟩ einschlagen; ⟨clock:⟩ schlagen; (attack) zuschlagen; ⟨workers:⟩ streiken; **~ lucky** Glück haben. **~-breaker** n Streikbrecher m

striker /'straɪkə(r)/ n Streikende(r) m/f

striking /'straɪkɪŋ/ a auffallend

string /strɪŋ/ n Schnur f; (thin) Bindfaden m; (of musical instrument, racket) Saite f; (of bow) Sehne f; (of pearls) Kette f; **the ~s** (Mus) die Streicher pl; **pull ~s** (fam) seine Beziehungen spielen lassen, Fäden ziehen ● vt (pt/pp **strung**) (thread) aufziehen ⟨beads⟩. **~ed** a (Mus) Saiten-; (played with bow) Streich-

stringent /'strɪndʒnt/ a streng

strip /strɪp/ n Streifen m ● v (pt/pp **stripped**) ● vt ablösen; ausziehen ⟨clothes⟩; abziehen ⟨bed⟩; abbeizen ⟨wood, furniture⟩; auseinandernehmen ⟨machine⟩; (deprive) berauben (of gen); **~ sth off** etw von etw entfernen ● vi (undress) sich ausziehen. **~ club** n Stripteaselokal nt

stripe /straɪp/ n Streifen m. **~d** a gestreift

'striplight n Neonröhre f

stripper /'strɪpə(r)/ n Stripperin f; (male) Stripper m

strip-'tease n Striptease m

strive /straɪv/ vi (pt **strove**, pp **striven**) sich bemühen (to zu); **~ for** streben nach

strode /strəʊd/ see **stride**

stroke[1] /strəʊk/ n Schlag m; (of pen) Strich m; (Swimming) Zug m; (style) Stil m; (Med) Schlaganfall m; **~ of luck** Glücksfall m; **put s.o. off his ~** jdn aus dem Konzept bringen

stroke[2] ● vt streicheln

stroll /strəʊl/ n Spaziergang m, (fam) Bummel m ● vi spazieren, (fam) bummeln. **~er** n (Amer: push-chair) [Kinder]sportwagen m

strong /strɒŋ/ a (-er /-gə(r)/, -est /-gɪst/), -ly adv stark; (powerful, healthy) kräftig; (severe) streng; (sturdy) stabil; (convincing) gut

strong: ~-box n Geldkassette f. ~hold n Festung f; (fig) Hochburg f. ~-'minded a willensstark. ~-room n Tresorraum m

stroppy /'strɒpɪ/ a widerspenstig

strove /strəʊv/ see strive

struck /strʌk/ see strike

structural /'strʌktʃərl/ a, -ly adv baulich

structure /'strʌktʃə(r)/ n Struktur f; (building) Bau m

struggle /'strʌgl/ n Kampf m; with a ~ mit Mühe ● vi kämpfen; ~ for breath nach Atem ringen; ~ to do sth sich abmühen, etw zu tun; ~ to one's feet mühsam aufstehen

strum /strʌm/ v (pt/pp strummed) ● vt klimpern auf (+ dat) ● vi klimpern

strung /strʌŋ/ see string

strut¹ /strʌt/ n Strebe f

strut² vi (pt/pp strutted) stolzieren

stub /stʌb/ n Stummel m; (counterfoil) Abschnitt m ● vt (pt/pp stubbed) ~ one's toe sich (dat) den Zeh stoßen (on an + dat). ~ out vt ausdrücken ⟨cigarette⟩

stubb|le /'stʌbl/ n Stoppeln pl. ~ly a stoppelig

stubborn /'stʌbən/ a, -ly adv starrsinnig; ⟨refusal⟩ hartnäckig

stubby /'stʌbɪ/ a (-ier, -iest) kurz und dick

stucco /'stʌkəʊ/ n Stuck m

stuck /stʌk/ see stick². ~-'up a (fam) hochnäsig

stud¹ /stʌd/ n Nagel m; (on clothes) Niete f; (for collar) Kragenknopf m; (for ear) Ohrstecker m

stud² n (of horses) Gestüt nt

student /'stju:dnt/ n Student(in) m(f); (Sch) Schüler(in) m(f). ~ nurse n Lernschwester f

studied /'stʌdɪd/ a gewollt

studio /'stju:dɪəʊ/ n Studio nt; (for artist) Atelier nt

studious /'stju:dɪəs/ a lerneifrig; (earnest) ernsthaft

stud|y /'stʌdɪ/ n Studie f; (room) Studierzimmer nt; (investigation) Untersuchung f; ~ies pl Studium nt ● v (pt/pp studied) ● vt studieren; (examine) untersuchen ● vi lernen; (at university) studieren

stuff /stʌf/ n Stoff m; (fam: things) Zeug nt ● vt vollstopfen; (with padding, Culin) füllen; ausstopfen ⟨animal⟩; ~ sth into sth etw in etw (acc) [hinein]stopfen. ~ing n Füllung f

stuffy /'stʌfɪ/ a (-ier, -iest) stickig; (old-fashioned) spießig

stumbl|e /'stʌmbl/ vi stolpern; ~e across zufällig stoßen auf (+ acc). ~ing-block n Hindernis nt

stump /stʌmp/ n Stumpf m ● ~ up vt/i (fam) blechen. ~ed a (fam) überfragt

stun /stʌn/ vt (pt/pp stunned) betäuben; ~ned by ⟨fig⟩ wie betäubt von

stung /stʌŋ/ see sting

stunk /stʌŋk/ see stink

stunning /'stʌnɪŋ/ a (fam) toll

stunt¹ /stʌnt/ n (fam) Kunststück nt

stunt² vt hemmen. ~ed a verkümmert

stupendous /stju:'pendəs/ a, -ly adv enorm

stupid /'stju:pɪd/ a dumm. ~ity /-'pɪdətɪ/ n Dummheit f. ~ly adv dumm; ~ly [enough] dummerweise

stupor /'stju:pə(r)/ n Benommenheit f

sturdy /'stɜ:dɪ/ a (-ier, -iest) stämmig; ⟨furniture⟩ stabil; ⟨shoes⟩ fest

stutter /'stʌtə(r)/ n Stottern nt ● vt/i stottern

sty¹ /staɪ/ n (pl sties) Schweinestall m

sty², stye n (pl styes) (Med) Gerstenkorn nt

style /staɪl/ n Stil m; (fashion) Mode f; (sort) Art f; (hair~) Frisur f; in ~ in großem Stil

stylish /'staɪlɪʃ/ a, -ly adv stilvoll

stylist /'staɪlɪst/ n Friseur m/Friseuse f. ~ic /-'lɪstɪk/ a, -ally adv stilistisch

stylized /'staɪlaɪzd/ a stilisiert

stylus /'staɪləs/ n (on record-player) Nadel f

suave /swɑ:v/ a (pej) gewandt

sub'conscious /sʌb-/ a, -ly adv unterbewußt ● n Unterbewußtsein nt

subcon'tract vt [vertraglich] weitervergeben (to an + acc)

'subdivi|de vt unterteilen. ~sion n Unterteilung f

subdue /səb'dju:/ vt unterwerfen; (make quieter) beruhigen. ~d a gedämpft; ⟨person⟩ still

subject¹ /'sʌbdʒɪkt/ a be ~ to sth etw (dat) unterworfen sein ● n. Staatsbürger(in) m(f); (of ruler) Untertan *m*; (*theme*) Thema *nt*; (*of investiga-tion*) Gegenstand *m*; (*Sch*) Fach *nt*; (*Gram*) Subjekt *nt*

subject² /səb'dʒekt/ *vt* unterwerfen (**to** *dat*); (*expose*) aussetzen (**to** *dat*)

subjective /səb'dʒektɪv/ *a*, **-ly** *adv* subjektiv

subjugate /'sʌbdʒʊgeɪt/ *vt* unter-jochen

subjunctive /səb'dʒʌŋktɪv/ *n* Kon-junktiv *m*

sub'let *vt* (*pt/pp* **-let**) untervermieten

sublime /sə'blaɪm/ *a*, **-ly** *adv* erhaben

subliminal /sʌ'blɪmɪnl/ *a* unter-schwellig

sub-ma'chine-gun *n* Maschinenpi-stole *f*

subma'rine *n* Unterseeboot *nt*

submerge /səb'mɜːdʒ/ *vt* untertau-chen; **be** ∼**d** unter Wasser stehen ● *vi* tauchen

submiss|ion /səb'mɪʃn/ *n* Unterwer-fung *f*. ∼**ive** /-sɪv/ *a* gehorsam; (*pej*) unterwürfig

submit /səb'mɪt/ *v* (*pt/pp* **-mitted**, *pres p* **-mitting**) ● *vt* vorlegen (**to** *dat*); (*hand in*) einreichen ● *vi* sich unterwerfen (**to** *dat*)

subordinate¹ /sə'bɔːdɪnət/ *a* unter-geordnet ● *n* Untergebene(r) *m/f*

subordinate² /sə'bɔːdɪneɪt/ *vt* unter-ordnen (**to** *dat*)

subscribe /səb'skraɪb/ *vi* spenden; ∼ **to** (*fig*) sich anschließen (+ *dat*); abonnieren ⟨*newspaper*⟩. ∼**r** *n* Spender *m*; Abonnent *m*

subscription /səb'skrɪpʃn/ *n* (*to club*) [Mitglieds]beitrag *m*; (*to newspaper*) Abonnement *nt*; **by** ∼ mit Spenden

subsequent /'sʌbsɪkwənt/ *a*, **-ly** *adv* folgend; (*later*) später

subservient /səb'sɜːvɪənt/ *a*, **-ly** *adv* untergeordnet; (*servile*) unter-würfig

subside /səb'saɪd/ *vi* sinken; ⟨*ground:*⟩ sich senken; ⟨*storm:*⟩ nachlassen

subsidiary /səb'sɪdɪərɪ/ *a* untergeord-net ● *n* Tochtergesellschaft *f*

subsid|ize /'sʌbsɪdaɪz/ *vt* subventio-nieren. ∼**y** *n* Subvention *f*

subsist /səb'sɪst/ *vi* leben (**on** von). ∼**ence** *n* Existenz *f*

substance /'sʌbstəns/ *n* Substanz *f*

sub'standard *a* unzulänglich; ⟨*goods*⟩ minderwertig

substantial /səb'stænʃl/ *a* solide; ⟨*meal*⟩ reichhaltig; (*considerable*)

beträchtlich. ∼**ly** *adv* solide; (*essen-tially*) im wesentlichen

substantiate /səb'stænʃɪeɪt/ *vt* erhärten

substitut|e /'sʌbstɪtjuːt/ *n* Ersatz *m*; (*Sport*) Ersatzspieler(in) *m(f)* ● *vt* ∼**e A for B** B durch A ersetzen ● *vi* ∼**e for s.o.** jdn vertreten. ∼**ion** /-'tjuːʃn/ *n* Ersetzung *f*

subterfuge /'sʌbtəfjuːdʒ/ *n* List *f*

subterranean /sʌbtə'reɪnɪən/ *a* unterirdisch

'subtitle *n* Untertitel *m*

subtle /'sʌtl/ *a* (**-r, -st**), **-tly** *adv* fein; (*fig*) subtil

subtract /səb'trækt/ *vt* abziehen, subtrahieren. ∼**ion** /-ækʃn/ *n* Sub-traktion *f*

suburb /'sʌbɜːb/ *n* Vorort *m*; **in the** ∼**s** am Stadtrand. ∼**an** /sə'bɜːbən/ *a* Vorort-; (*pej*) spießig. ∼**ia** /sə'bɜːbɪə/ *n* die Vororte *pl*

subversive /səb'vɜːsɪv/ *a* subversiv

'subway *n* Unterführung *f*; (*Amer: railway*) U-Bahn *f*

succeed /sək'siːd/ *vi* Erfolg haben; ⟨*plan:*⟩ gelingen; (*follow*) nachfol-gen (+ *dat*); **I** ∼**ed** es ist mir gelun-gen; **he** ∼**ed in escaping** es gelang ihm zu entkommen ● *vt* folgen (+ *dat*). ∼**ing** *a* folgend

success /sək'ses/ *n* Erfolg *m*. ∼**ful** *a*, **-ly** *adv* erfolgreich

succession /sək'seʃn/ *n* Folge *f*; (*series*) Serie *f*; (*to title, office*) Nach-folge *f*; (*to throne*) Thronfolge *f*; **in** ∼ hintereinander

successive /sək'sesɪv/ *a* aufeinander-folgend. ∼**ly** *adv* hintereinander

successor /sək'sesə(r)/ *n* Nachfol-ger(in) *m(f)*

succinct /sək'sɪŋkt/ *a*, **-ly** *adv* prägnant

succulent /'sʌkjʊlənt/ *a* saftig

succumb /sə'kʌm/ *vi* erliegen (**to** *dat*)

such /sʌtʃ/ *a* solche(r,s); ∼ **a book** ein solches *od* solch ein Buch; ∼ **a thing** so etwas; ∼ **a long time** so lange; **there is no** ∼ **thing** das gibt es gar nicht; **there is no** ∼ **person** eine solche Person gibt es nicht ● *pron* **as** ∼ als solche(r,s); (*strictly speak-ing*) an sich; ∼ **as** wie [zum Beispiel]; **and** ∼ und dergleichen. ∼**like** *pron* (*fam*) dergleichen

suck /sʌk/ *vt/i* saugen; lutschen ⟨*sweet*⟩. ∼ **up** *vt* aufsaugen ● *vi* ∼ **up to s.o.** (*fam*) sich bei jdm einschmeicheln

sucker /'sʌkə(r)/ n (Bot) Ausläufer m; (fam: person) Dumme(r) m/f

suckle /'sʌkl/ vt säugen

suction /'sʌkʃn/ n Saugwirkung f

sudden /'sʌdn/ a, -ly adv plötzlich; (abrupt) jäh ● n all of a ~ auf einmal

sue /su:/ vt (pres p suing) verklagen (for auf + acc) ● vi klagen

suede /sweid/ n Wildleder nt

suet /'su:it/ n [Nieren]talg m

suffer /'sʌfə(r)/ vi leiden (from an + dat) ● vt erleiden; (tolerate) dulden. ~ance /-əns/ n on ~ance bloß geduldet. ~ing n Leiden nt

suffice /sə'fais/ vi genügen

sufficient /sə'fiʃnt/ a, -ly adv genug, genügend; be ~ genügen

suffix /'sʌfiks/ n Nachsilbe f

suffocat|e /'sʌfəkeit/ vt/i ersticken. ~ion /-'keiʃn/ n Ersticken nt

sugar /'ʃʊgə(r)/ n Zucker m ● vt zuckern; (fig) versüßen. ~ basin, ~-bowl n Zuckerschale f. ~y a süß; (fig) süßlich

suggest /sə'dʒest/ vt vorschlagen; (indicate, insinuate) andeuten. ~ion /-estʃən/ n Vorschlag m; Andeutung f; (trace) Spur f. ~ive /-iv/ a, -ly adv anzüglich; be ~ive of schließen lassen auf (+ acc)

suicidal /su:i'saidl/ a selbstmörderisch

suicide /'su:isaid/ n Selbstmord m

suit /su:t/ n Anzug m; (woman's) Kostüm nt; (Cards) Farbe f; (Jur) Prozeß m; follow ~ (fig) das Gleiche tun ● vt (adapt) anpassen (to dat); (be convenient for) passen (+ dat); (go with) passen zu; (clothing:) stehen (s.o. jdm); be ~ed for geeignet sein für; ~ yourself! wie du willst!

suit|able /'su:təbl/ a geeignet; (convenient) passend; (appropriate) angemessen; (for weather, activity) zweckmäßig. ~ably adv angemessen; zweckmäßig

'suitcase n Koffer m

suite /swi:t/ n Suite f; (of furniture) Garnitur f

sulk /sʌlk/ vi schmollen. ~y a schmollend

sullen /'sʌlən/ a, -ly adv mürrisch

sulphur /'sʌlfə(r)/ n Schwefel f. ~ic /-'fju:rik/ a ~ic acid Schwefelsäure f

sultana /sʌl'tɑ:nə/ n Sultanine f

sultry /'sʌltri/ a (-ier, -iest) (weather) schwül

sum /sʌm/ n Summe f; (Sch) Rechenaufgabe f ● vt/i (pt/pp summed) ~ up zusammenfassen; (assess) einschätzen

summar|ize /'sʌməraiz/ vt zusammenfassen. ~y n Zusammenfassung f ● a, -ily adv summarisch; (dismissal) fristlos

summer /'sʌmə(r)/ n Sommer m. ~-house n [Garten]laube f. ~time n Sommer m

summery /'sʌməri/ a sommerlich

summit /'sʌmit/ n Gipfel m. ~ conference n Gipfelkonferenz f

summon /'sʌmən/ vt rufen; holen (help); (Jur) vorladen. ~ up vt aufbringen

summons /'sʌmənz/ n (Jur) Vorladung f ● vt vorladen

sump /sʌmp/ n (Auto) Ölwanne f

sumptuous /'sʌmptjʊəs/ a, -ly adv prunkvoll; (meal) üppig

sun /sʌn/ n Sonne f ● vt (pt/pp sunned) ~ oneself sich sonnen

sun: ~bathe vi sich sonnen. ~-bed n Sonnenbank f. ~burn n Sonnenbrand m

sundae /'sʌndei/ n Eisbecher m

Sunday /'sʌndei/ n Sonntag m

'sundial n Sonnenuhr f

sundry /'sʌndri/ a verschiedene pl; all and ~ alle pl

'sunflower n Sonnenblume f

sung /sʌŋ/ see sing

'sun-glasses npl Sonnenbrille f

sunk /sʌŋk/ see sink

sunken /'sʌŋkn/ a gesunken; (eyes) eingefallen

sunny /'sʌni/ a (-ier, -iest) sonnig

sun: ~rise n Sonnenaufgang m. ~roof n (Auto) Schiebedach nt. ~set n Sonnenuntergang m. ~shade n Sonnenschirm m. ~shine n Sonnenschein m. ~stroke n Sonnenstich m. ~tan n [Sonnen]bräune f. ~-tanned a braun[gebrannt]. ~-tan oil n Sonnenöl nt

super /'su:pə(r)/ a (fam) prima, toll

superb /sʊ'pɜ:b/ a erstklassig

supercilious /su:pə'siliəs/ a überlegen

superficial /su:pə'fiʃl/ a, -ly adv oberflächlich

superfluous /sʊ'pɜ:flʊəs/ a überflüssig

super'human a übermenschlich

superintendent /su:pərin'tendənt/ n (of police) Kommissar m

superior /su:'piəriə(r)/ a überlegen; (in rank) höher ● n Vorgesetzte(r) m/f. ~ity /-'ɒrəti/ n Überlegenheit f

superlative /su:'pɜːlətɪv/ a unübertrefflich ● n Superlativ m

'**superman** n Übermensch m

'**supermarket** n Supermarkt m

super'natural a übernatürlich

'**superpower** n Supermacht f

supersede /su:pə'si:d/ vt ersetzen

super'sonic a Überschall-

superstiti|on /su:pə'stɪʃn/ n Aberglaube m. ~ous /-'stɪʃəs/ a, -ly adv abergläubisch

supervis|e /'su:pəvaɪz/ vt beaufsichtigen; überwachen ⟨work⟩. ~ion /-'vɪʒn/ n Aufsicht f; Überwachung f. ~or n Aufseher(in) m(f)

supper /'sʌpə(r)/ n Abendessen nt

supple /'sʌpl/ a geschmeidig

supplement /'sʌplɪmənt/ n Ergänzung f; (addition) Zusatz m; (to fare) Zuschlag m; (book) Ergänzungsband m; (to newspaper) Beilage f ● vt ergänzen. ~ary /-'mentəri/ a zusätzlich

supplier /sə'plaɪə(r)/ n Lieferant m

supply /sə'plaɪ/ n Vorrat m; supplies pl (Mil) Nachschub m ● vt (pt/pp -ied) liefern; ~ s.o. with sth jdn mit etw versorgen

support /sə'pɔːt/ n Stütze f; (fig) Unterstützung f ● vt stützen; (bear weight of) tragen; (keep) ernähren; (give money to) unterstützen; (speak in favour of) befürworten; (Sport) Fan sein von. ~er n Anhänger(in) m(f); (Sport) Fan m. ~ive /-ɪv/ a be ~ive [to s.o.] [jdm] eine große Stütze sein

suppose /sə'pəʊz/ vt annehmen; (presume) vermuten; (imagine) sich (dat) vorstellen; be ~d to do sth etw tun sollen; not be ~d to (fam) nicht dürfen; I ~ so vermutlich. ~dly /-ɪdlɪ/ adv angeblich

supposition /sʌpə'zɪʃn/ n Vermutung f

suppository /sʌ'pɒzɪtrɪ/ n Zäpfchen nt

suppress /sə'pres/ vt unterdrücken. ~ion /-eʃn/ n Unterdrückung f

supremacy /su:'preməsɪ/ n Vorherrschaft f

supreme /su:'pri:m/ a höchste(r,s); ⟨court⟩ oberste(r,s)

surcharge /'sɜːtʃɑːdʒ/ n Zuschlag m

sure /ʃʊə(r)/ a (-r, -st) sicher; make ~ sich vergewissern (of gen); (check) nachprüfen; be ~ to do it sieh zu, daß du es tust ● adv (Amer, fam) klar; ~ enough tatsächlich. ~ly adv

sicher; (for emphasis) doch; (Amer: gladly) gern

surety /'ʃʊərətɪ/ n Bürgschaft f; stand ~ for bürgen für

surf /sɜːf/ n Brandung f

surface /'sɜːfɪs/ n (of sea) Oberfläche f ● vi (emerge) auftauchen. ~ mail n by ~ mail auf dem Land-/Seeweg

'**surfboard** n Surfbrett nt

surfeit /'sɜːfɪt/ n Übermaß nt

surfing /'sɜːfɪŋ/ n Surfen nt

surge /sɜːdʒ/ n (of sea) Branden nt; (fig) Welle f ● vi branden; ~ forward nach vorn drängen

surgeon /'sɜːdʒən/ n Chirurg(in) m(f)

surgery /'sɜːdʒərɪ/ n Chirurgie f; (place) Praxis f; (room) Sprechzimmer nt; (hours) Sprechstunde f; have ~ operiert werden

surgical /'sɜːdʒɪkl/ a, -ly adv chirurgisch

surly /'sɜːlɪ/ a (-ier, -iest) mürrisch

surmise /sə'maɪz/ vt mutmaßen

surmount /sə'maʊnt/ vt überwinden

surname /'sɜːneɪm/ n Nachname m

surpass /sə'pɑːs/ vt übertreffen

surplus /'sɜːpləs/ a überschüssig; be ~ to requirements nicht benötigt werden ● n Überschuß m (of an + dat)

surpris|e /sə'praɪz/ n Überraschung f ● vt überraschen; be ~ed sich wundern (at über + acc). ~ing a, -ly adv überraschend

surrender /sə'rendə(r)/ n Kapitulation f ● vi sich ergeben; (Mil) kapitulieren ● vt aufgeben

surreptitious /sʌrəp'tɪʃəs/ a, -ly adv heimlich, verstohlen

surrogate /'sʌrəgət/ n Ersatz m. ~ 'mother n Leihmutter f

surround /sə'raʊnd/ vt umgeben; (encircle) umzingeln; ~ed by umgeben von. ~ing a umliegend. ~ings npl Umgebung f

surveillance /sə'veɪləns/ n Überwachung f; be under ~ überwacht werden

survey[1] /'sɜːveɪ/ n Überblick m; (poll) Umfrage f; (investigation) Untersuchung f; (of land) Vermessung f; (of house) Gutachten nt

survey[2] /sə'veɪ/ vt betrachten; vermessen ⟨land⟩; begutachten ⟨building⟩. ~or n Landvermesser m; Gutachter m

survival /sə'vaɪvl/ n Überleben nt; (of tradition) Fortbestand m

surviv|e /sə'vaɪv/ vt überleben ● vi überleben; ⟨tradition:⟩ erhalten bleiben. **~or** n Überlebende(r) m/f; **be a ~or** (fam) nicht unterzukriegen sein

susceptible /sə'septəbl/ a empfänglich/ (Med) anfällig (**to** für)

suspect¹ /sə'spekt/ vt verdächtigen; (assume) vermuten; **he ~s nothing** er ahnt nichts

suspect² /'sʌspekt/ a verdächtig ● n Verdächtige(r) m/f

suspend /sə'spend/ vt aufhängen; (stop) [vorläufig] einstellen; (from duty) vorläufig beurlauben. **~er belt** n Strumpfbandgürtel m. **~ers** npl Strumpfbänder pl; (Amer: braces) Hosenträger pl

suspense /sə'spens/ n Spannung f

suspension /sə'spenʃn/ n (Auto) Federung f. **~ bridge** n Hängebrücke f

suspici|on /sə'spɪʃn/ n Verdacht m; (mistrust) Mißtrauen nt; (trace) Spur f. **~ous** /-ɪʃəs/ a, **-ly** adv mißtrauisch; (arousing suspicion) verdächtig

sustain /sə'steɪn/ vt tragen; (fig) aufrechterhalten; erhalten ⟨life⟩; erleiden ⟨injury⟩

sustenance /'sʌstɪnəns/ n Nahrung f

swab /swɒb/ n (Med) Tupfer m; (specimen) Abstrich m

swagger /'swægə(r)/ vi stolzieren

swallow¹ /'swɒləʊ/ vt/i schlucken. **~ up** vt verschlucken; verschlingen ⟨resources⟩

swallow² n (bird) Schwalbe f

swam /swæm/ see **swim**

swamp /swɒmp/ n Sumpf m ● vt überschwemmen. **~y** a sumpfig

swan /swɒn/ n Schwan m

swank /swæŋk/ vi (fam) angeben

swap /swɒp/ n (fam) Tausch m ● vt/i (pt/pp **swapped**) (fam) tauschen (**for** gegen)

swarm /swɔːm/ n Schwarm m ● vi schwärmen; **be ~ing with** wimmeln von

swarthy /'swɔːðɪ/ a (**-ier, -iest**) dunkel

swastika /'swɒstɪkə/ n Hakenkreuz nt

swat /swɒt/ vt (pt/pp **swatted**) totschlagen

sway /sweɪ/ n (fig) Herrschaft f ● vi schwanken; (gently) sich wiegen ● vt wiegen; (influence) beeinflussen

swear /sweə(r)/ v (pt **swore**, pp **sworn**) ● vt schwören ● vi schwören (**by** auf

+ acc); (curse) fluchen. **~-word** n Kraftausdruck m

sweat /swet/ n Schweiß m ● vi schwitzen

sweater /'swetə(r)/ n Pullover m

sweaty /'swetɪ/ a verschwitzt

swede /swiːd/ n Kohlrübe f

Swed|e n Schwede m /-din f. **~en** n Schweden nt. **~ish** a schwedisch

sweep /swiːp/ n Schornsteinfeger m; (curve) Bogen m; (movement) ausholende Bewegung f; **make a clean ~** (fig) gründlich aufräumen ● v (pt/pp **swept**) ● vt fegen, kehren ● vi (go swiftly) rauschen; ⟨wind:⟩ fegen. **~ up** vt zusammenfegen/-kehren

sweeping /'swiːpɪŋ/ a ausholend; ⟨statement⟩ pauschal; ⟨changes⟩ weitreichend

sweet /swiːt/ a (**-er, -est**) süß; **have a ~ tooth** gern Süßes mögen ● n Bonbon m & nt; (dessert) Nachtisch m. **~ corn** n [Zucker]mais m

sweeten /'swiːtn/ vt süßen. **~er** n Süßstoff m; (fam: bribe) Schmiergeld nt

sweet: ~heart n Schatz m. **~-shop** n Süßwarenladen m. **~ness** n Süße f. **~ 'pea** n Wicke f

swell /swel/ n Dünung f ● v (pt **swelled**, pp **swollen** or **swelled**) ● vi [an]schwellen; ⟨sails:⟩ sich blähen; ⟨wood:⟩ aufquellen ● vt anschwellen lassen; (increase) vergrößern. **~ing** n Schwellung f

swelter /'sweltə(r)/ vi schwitzen

swept /swept/ see **sweep**

swerve /swɜːv/ vi einen Bogen machen

swift /swɪft/ a (**-er, -est**), **-ly** adv schnell

swig /swɪg/ n (fam) Schluck m, Zug m ● vt (pt/pp **swigged**) (fam) [herunter]kippen

swill /swɪl/ n (for pigs) Schweinefutter nt ● vt ~ [**out**] [aus]spülen

swim /swɪm/ n **have a ~** schwimmen ● vi (pt **swam**, pp **swum**) schwimmen; **my head is ~ming** mir dreht sich der Kopf. **~mer** n Schwimmer m(f)

swimming /'swɪmɪŋ/ n Schwimmen nt. **~-baths** npl Schwimmbad nt. **~-pool** n Schwimmbecken nt; (private) Swimmingpool m

'swim-suit n Badeanzug m

swindle /'swɪndl/ n Schwindel m, Betrug m ● vt betrügen. **~r** n Schwindler m

swine /swaɪn/ n Schwein nt

swing /swɪŋ/ n Schwung m; (shift) Schwenk m; (seat) Schaukel f; in **full** ~ in vollem Gange ● v (pt/pp **swung**) ● vi schwingen; (on swing) schaukeln; (sway) schwanken; (dangle) baumeln; (turn) schwenken ● vt schwingen; (influence) beeinflussen. ~'**door** n Schwingtür f

swingeing /'swɪndʒɪŋ/ a hart; (fig) drastisch

swipe /swaɪp/ n (fam) Schlag m ● vt (fam) knallen; (steal) klauen

swirl /swɜːl/ n Wirbel m ● vt/i wirbeln

swish /swɪʃ/ a (fam) schick ● vi zischen

Swiss /swɪs/ a Schweizer, schweizerisch ● n Schweizer(in) m(f); **the** ~ pl die Schweizer. ~ '**roll** n Biskuitrolle f

switch /swɪtʃ/ n Schalter m; (change) Wechsel m; (Amer, Rail) Weiche f ● vt wechseln; (exchange) tauschen ● vi wechseln; ~ **to** umstellen auf (+ acc). ~ **off** vt ausschalten; abschalten ⟨engine⟩. ~ **on** vt einschalten, anschalten

switch: ~**back** n Achterbahn f. ~**board** n [Telefon]zentrale f

Switzerland /'swɪtsələnd/ n die Schweiz

swivel /'swɪvl/ v (pt/pp **swivelled**) ● vt drehen ● vi sich drehen

swollen /'swəʊlən/ see **swell** ● a geschwollen. ~**'headed** a eingebildet

swoop /swuːp/ n Sturzflug m; (by police) Razzia f ● vi ~ **down** herabstoßen

sword /sɔːd/ n Schwert nt

swore /swɔː(r)/ see **swear**

sworn /swɔːn/ see **swear**

swot /swɒt/ n (fam) Streber m ● vt/i (pt/pp **swotted**) (fam) büffeln

swum /swʌm/ see **swim**

swung /swʌŋ/ see **swing**

syllable /'sɪləbl/ n Silbe f

syllabus /'sɪləbəs/ n Lehrplan m; (for exam) Studienplan m

symbol /'sɪmbəl/ n Symbol nt (of für). ~**ic** /-'bɒlɪk/ a, -**ally** adv symbolisch. ~**ism** /-ɪzm/ n Symbolik f. ~**ize** vt symbolisieren

symmetr|ical /sɪ'metrɪkl/ a, -**ly** adv symmetrisch. ~**y** /'sɪmətrɪ/ n Symmetrie f

sympathetic /sɪmpə'θetɪk/ a, -**ally** adv mitfühlend; (likeable) sympathisch

sympathize /'sɪmpəθaɪz/ vi mitfühlen. ~**r** n (Pol) Sympathisant m

sympathy /'sɪmpəθɪ/ n Mitgefühl nt; (condolences) Beileid nt

symphony /'sɪmfənɪ/ n Sinfonie f

symptom /'sɪmptəm/ n Symptom nt. ~**atic** /-'mætɪk/ a symptomatisch (of für)

synagogue /'sɪnəgɒg/ n Synagoge f

synchronize /'sɪŋkrənaɪz/ vt synchronisieren

syndicate /'sɪndɪkət/ n Syndikat nt

syndrome /'sɪndrəʊm/ n Syndrom nt

synonym /'sɪnənɪm/ n Synonym nt. ~**ous** /-'nɒnɪməs/ a, -**ly** adv synonym

synopsis /sɪ'nɒpsɪs/ n (pl -**opses** /-siːz/) Zusammenfassung f; (of opera, ballet) Inhaltsangabe f

syntax /'sɪntæks/ n Syntax f

synthesis /'sɪnθəsɪs/ n (pl -**ses** /-siːz/) Synthese f

synthetic /sɪn'θetɪk/ a synthetisch ● n Kunststoff m

Syria /'sɪrɪə/ n Syrien nt

syringe /sɪ'rɪndʒ/ n Spritze f ● vt spritzen; ausspritzen ⟨ears⟩

syrup /'sɪrəp/ n Sirup m

system /'sɪstəm/ n System nt. ~**atic** /-'mætɪk/ a, -**ally** adv systematisch

T

tab /tæb/ n (projecting) Zunge f; (with name) Namensschild nt; (loop) Aufhänger m; **keep** ~**s on** (fam) [genau] beobachten; **pick up the** ~ (fam) bezahlen

tabby /'tæbɪ/ n getigerte Katze f

table /'teɪbl/ n Tisch m; (list) Tabelle f; **at [the]** ~ bei Tisch ● vt einbringen. ~**-cloth** n Tischdecke f, Tischtuch nt. ~**spoon** n Servierlöffel m

tablet /'tæblɪt/ n Tablette f; (of soap) Stück nt; (slab) Tafel f

'table tennis n Tischtennis nt

tabloid /'tæblɔɪd/ n kleinformatige Zeitung f; (pej) Boulevardzeitung f

taboo /tə'buː/ a tabu ● n Tabu nt

tacit /'tæsɪt/ a, -**ly** adv stillschweigend

taciturn /'tæsɪtɜːn/ a wortkarg

tack /tæk/ n (nail) Stift m; (stitch) Heftstich m; (Naut & fig) Kurs m ● vt festnageln; (sew) heften ● vi (Naut) kreuzen

tackle /'tækl/ n Ausrüstung f ● vt angehen

tacky /'tækɪ/ a klebrig

tact /tækt/ n Takt m, Taktgefühl nt. **~ful** a, **-ly** adv taktvoll

tactic|al /'tæktɪkl/ a, **-ly** adv taktisch. **~s** npl Taktik f

tactless /'tæktlɪs/ a, **-ly** adv taktlos. **~ness** n Taktlosigkeit f

tadpole /'tædpəʊl/ n Kaulquappe f

tag¹ /tæg/ n (label) Schild nt ● vi (pt/pp tagged) **~ along** mitkommen

tag² n (game) Fangen nt

tail /teɪl/ n Schwanz m; **~s** pl (tail-coat) Frack m; **heads or ~s?** Kopf oder Zahl? ● vt (fam: follow) beschatten ● vi **~ off** zurückgehen

tail: **~back** n Rückstau m. **~coat** n Frack m. **~-end** n Ende nt. **~ light** n Rücklicht nt

tailor /'teɪlə(r)/ n Schneider m. **~-made** a maßgeschneidert

'tail wind n Rückenwind m

taint /teɪnt/ vt verderben

take /teɪk/ v (pt took, pp taken) ● vt nehmen; (with one) mitnehmen; (take to a place) bringen; (steal) stehlen; (win) gewinnen; (capture) einnehmen; (require) brauchen; (last) dauern; (teach) geben; machen ⟨exam, subject, holiday, photograph⟩; messen ⟨pulse, temperature⟩; **~ s.o. home** jdn nach Hause bringen; **~ sth to the cleaner's** etw in die Reinigung bringen; **~ s.o. prisoner** jdn gefangennehmen; **be ~n ill** krank werden; **~ sth calmly** etw gelassen aufnehmen ● vi ⟨plant:⟩ angehen. **~ after s.o.** jdm nachschlagen; (in looks) jdm ähnlich sehen; **~ to** (like) mögen; (as a habit) sich (dat) angewöhnen. **~ away** vt wegbringen; (remove) wegnehmen; (subtract) abziehen; **'to ~ away'** 'zum Mitnehmen'. **~ back** vt zurücknehmen; (return) zurückbringen. **~ down** vt herunternehmen; (remove) abnehmen; (write down) aufschreiben. **~ in** vt hineinbringen; (bring indoors) hereinholen; (to one's home) aufnehmen; (understand) begreifen; (deceive) hereinlegen; (make smaller) enger machen. **~ off** vt ablegen; (coat); sich (dat) ausziehen

⟨clothes⟩; (deduct) abziehen; (mimic) nachmachen; **~ time off** sich (dat) frei nehmen; **~ oneself off** [fort]gehen ● vi (Aviat) starten. **~ on** vt annehmen; (undertake) übernehmen; (engage) einstellen; (as opponent) antreten gegen. **~ out** vt hinausbringen; (for pleasure) ausgehen mit; ausführen ⟨dog⟩; (remove) herausnehmen; (withdraw) abheben ⟨money⟩; (from library) ausleihen; **~ out a subscription to sth** etw abonnieren; **~ it out on s.o.** (fam) seinen Ärger an jdm auslassen. **~ over** vt hinüberbringen; übernehmen ⟨firm, control⟩ ● vi **~ over from s.o.** jdn ablösen. **~ up** vt hinaufbringen; annehmen ⟨offer⟩; ergreifen ⟨profession⟩; sich (dat) zulegen ⟨hobby⟩; in Anspruch nehmen ⟨time⟩; einnehmen ⟨space⟩; aufreißen ⟨floorboards⟩; **~ sth up with s.o.** mit jdm über etw (acc) sprechen ● vi **~ up with s.o.** sich mit jdm einlassen

take: **~-away** n Essen nt zum Mitnehmen; (restaurant) Restaurant nt mit Straßenverkauf. **~-off** n (Aviat) Start m, Abflug m. **~-over** n Übernahme f

takings /'teɪkɪnz/ npl Einnahmen pl

talcum /'tælkəm/ n **~ [powder]** Körperpuder m

tale /teɪl/ n Geschichte f

talent /'tælənt/ n Talent nt. **~ed** a talentiert

talk /tɔːk/ n Gespräch nt; (lecture) Vortrag m; **make small ~** Konversation machen ● vi reden, sprechen (to/with mit) ● vt reden; **~ s.o. into sth** jdn zu etw überreden. **~ over** vt besprechen

talkative /'tɔːkətɪv/ a gesprächig

'talking-to n Standpauke f

tall /tɔːl/ a (-er, -est) groß; ⟨building, tree⟩ hoch; **that's a ~ order** das ist ziemlich viel verlangt. **~boy** n hohe Kommode f. **~ 'story** n übertriebene Geschichte f

tally /'tælɪ/ n **keep a ~ of** Buch führen über (+ acc) ● vi übereinstimmen

talon /'tælən/ n Klaue f

tambourine /tæmbə'riːn/ n Tamburin nt

tame /teɪm/ a (-r, -st), **-ly** adv zahm; (dull) lahm (fam) ● vt zähmen. **~r** n Dompteur m

tamper /'tæmpə(r)/ vi **~ with** sich (dat) zu schaffen machen an (+ dat)

tampon /'tæmpɒn/ n Tampon m

tan /tæn/ a gelbbraun ● n Gelbbraun nt; (from sun) Bräune f ● v (pt/pp tanned) ● vt gerben ⟨hide⟩ ● vi braun werden

tang /tæŋ/ n herber Geschmack m; (smell) herber Geruch m

tangent /'tændʒənt/ n Tangente f; **go off at a ~** (fam) vom Thema abschweifen

tangible /'tændʒɪbl/ a greifbar

tangle /'tæŋgl/ n Gewirr nt; (in hair) Verfilzung f ● vt ~**[up]** verheddern ● vi sich verheddern

tango /'tæŋgəʊ/ n Tango m

tank /tæŋk/ n Tank m; (Mil) Panzer m

tankard /'tæŋkəd/ n Krug m

tanker /'tæŋkə(r)/ n Tanker m; (lorry) Tank[last]wagen m

tantaliz|e /'tæntəlaɪz/ vt quälen. ~**ing** n verlockend

tantamount /'tæntəmaʊnt/ a **be ~ to** gleichbedeutend sein mit

tantrum /'tæntrəm/ n Wutanfall m

tap /tæp/ n Hahn m; (knock) Klopfen nt; **on ~** zur Verfügung ● (pt/pp tapped) ● vt klopfen an (+ acc); anzapfen ⟨barrel, tree⟩; erschließen ⟨resources⟩; abhören ⟨telephone⟩ ● vi klopfen. ~**dance** n Step[tanz] m ● vi Step tanzen, steppen

tape /teɪp/ n Band nt; (adhesive) Klebstreifen m; (for recording) Tonband nt ● vt mit Klebstreifen zukleben; (record) auf Band aufnehmen

'**tape-measure** n Bandmaß nt

taper /'teɪpə(r)/ n dünne Wachskerze f ● vi sich verjüngen

'**tape recorder** n Tonbandgerät nt

tapestry /'tæpɪstrɪ/ n Gobelinstickerei f

'**tapeworm** n Bandwurm m

'**tap water** n Leitungswasser nt

tar /tɑː(r)/ n Teer m ● vt (pt/pp tarred) teeren

tardy /'tɑːdɪ/ a (-ier, -iest) langsam; (late) spät

target /'tɑːgɪt/ n Ziel nt; (board) [Ziel]scheibe f

tariff /'tærɪf/ n Tarif m; (duty) Zoll m

tarnish /'tɑːnɪʃ/ vi anlaufen

tarpaulin /tɑː'pɔːlɪn/ n Plane f

tarragon /'tærəgən/ n Estragon m

tart¹ /tɑːt/ a (-er, -est) sauer; (fig) scharf

tart² n ≈ Obstkuchen m; (individual) Törtchen nt; (sl: prostitute) Nutte f

● vt ~ **oneself up** (fam) sich auftakeln

tartan /'tɑːtn/ n Schottenmuster nt; (cloth) Schottenstoff m ● attrib schottisch kariert

tartar /'tɑːtə(r)/ n (on teeth) Zahnstein m

tartar 'sauce /tɑːtə-/ n ≈ Remouladensoße f

task /tɑːsk/ n Aufgabe f; **take s.o. to ~** jdm Vorhaltungen machen. ~ **force** n Sonderkommando nt

tassel /'tæsl/ n Quaste f

taste /teɪst/ n Geschmack m; (sample) Kostprobe f ● vt kosten, probieren; schmecken ⟨flavour⟩ ● vi schmecken (**of** nach). ~**ful** a, **-ly** adv (fig) geschmackvoll. ~**less** a, **-ly** adv geschmacklos

tasty /'teɪstɪ/ a (-ier, -iest) lecker, schmackhaft

tat /tæt/ see **tit²**

tatter|ed /'tætəd/ a zerlumpt; ⟨pages⟩ zerfleddert. ~**s** npl **in ~s** in Fetzen

tattoo¹ /tə'tuː/ n Tätowierung f ● vt tätowieren

tattoo² n (Mil) Zapfenstreich m

tatty /'tætɪ/ a (-ier, -iest) schäbig; ⟨book⟩ zerfleddert

taught /tɔːt/ see **teach**

taunt /tɔːnt/ n höhnische Bemerkung f ● vt verhöhnen

Taurus /'tɔːrəs/ n (Astr) Stier m

taut /tɔːt/ a straff

tavern /'tævən/ n (liter) Schenke f

tawdry /'tɔːdrɪ/ a (-ier, -iest) billig und geschmacklos

tawny /'tɔːnɪ/ a gelbbraun

tax /tæks/ n Steuer f ● vt besteuern; (fig) strapazieren; ~ **with** beschuldigen (+ gen). ~**able** /-əbl/ a steuerpflichtig. ~**ation** /-'seɪʃn/ n Besteuerung f. ~**-free** a steuerfrei

taxi /'tæksɪ/ n Taxi nt ● vi (pt/pp taxied, pres p taxiing) ⟨aircraft:⟩ rollen. ~ **driver** n Taxifahrer m. ~ **rank** n Taxistand m

'**taxpayer** n Steuerzahler m

tea /tiː/ n Tee m. ~**-bag** n Teebeutel m. ~**-break** n Teepause f

teach /tiːtʃ/ vt/i (pt/pp taught) unterrichten; ~ **s.o. sth** jdm etw beibringen. ~**er** n Lehrer(in) m(f)

tea: ~**-cloth** n (for drying) Geschirrtuch nt. ~**cup** n Teetasse f

teak /tiːk/ n Teakholz nt

team /tiːm/ n Mannschaft f; (fig) Team nt; (of animals) Gespann nt ● vi ~ **up** sich zusammentun

'team-work n Teamarbeit f
'teapot n Teekanne f
tear¹ /teə(r)/ n Riß m ● v (pt **tore,** pp **torn**) ● vt reißen; (damage) zerreißen; **~ open** aufreißen; **~ oneself away** sich losreißen ● vi [zer]-reißen; (run) rasen. **~ up** vt zerreißen
tear² /tɪə(r)/ n Träne f. **~ful** a weinend. **~fully** adv unter Tränen. **~gas** n Tränengas nt
tease /ti:z/ vt necken
tea: ~-set n Teeservice nt. **~ shop** n Café nt. **~spoon** n Teelöffel m. **~strainer** n Teesieb nt
teat /ti:t/ n Zitze f; (on bottle) Sauger m
'tea-towel n Geschirrtuch nt
technical /'teknɪkl/ a technisch; (specialized) fachlich. **~ity** /-'kælətɪ/ n technisches Detail nt; (Jur) Formfehler m. **~ly** adv technisch; (strictly) streng genommen. **~ term** n Fachausdruck m
technician /tek'nɪʃn/ n Techniker m
technique /tek'ni:k/ n Technik f
technological /teknə'lɒdʒɪkl/ a, **-ly** adv technologisch
technology /tek'nɒlədʒɪ/ n Technologie f
teddy /'tedɪ/ n **~ [bear]** Teddybär m
tedious /'ti:dɪəs/ a langweilig
tedium /'ti:dɪəm/ n Langeweile f
teem /ti:m/ vi (rain) in Strömen gießen; **be ~ing with** (full of) wimmeln von
teenage /'ti:neɪdʒ/ a Teenager-; **~ boy/girl** Junge m/Mädchen nt im Teenageralter. **~r** n Teenager m
teens /ti:nz/ npl **the ~** die Teenagerjahre pl
teeny /'ti:nɪ/ a (**-ier, -iest**) winzig
teeter /'ti:tə(r)/ vi schwanken
teeth /ti:θ/ see **tooth**
teeth|e /ti:ð/ vi zahnen. **~ing troubles** npl (fig) Anfangsschwierigkeiten pl
teetotal /ti:'təʊtl/ a abstinent. **~ler** n Abstinenzler m
telecommunications /telɪkəmju:-nɪ'keɪʃnz/ npl Fernmeldewesen nt
telegram /'telɪgræm/ n Telegramm nt
telegraph /'telɪgrɑːf/ n Telegraf m. **~ic** /-'græfɪk/ a telegrafisch. **~ pole** n Telegrafenmast m
telepathy /tɪ'lepəθɪ/ n Telepathie f; **by ~** telepathisch

telephone /'telɪfəʊn/ n Telefon nt; **be on the ~** Telefon haben; (be telephoning) telefonieren ● vt anrufen ● vi telefonieren
telephone: ~ book n Telefonbuch nt. **~ booth** n, **~ box** n Telefonzelle f. **~ directory** n Telefonbuch nt. **~ number** n Telefonnummer f
telephonist /tɪ'lefənɪst/ n Telefonist(in) m(f)
tele'photo /telɪ-/ a **~ lens** Teleobjektiv nt
teleprinter /'telɪ-/ n Fernschreiber m
telescop|e /'telɪskəʊp/ n Teleskop nt, Fernrohr nt. **~ic** /-'skɒpɪk/ a teleskopisch; (collapsible) ausziehbar
televise /'telɪvaɪz/ vt im Fernsehen übertragen
television /'telɪvɪʒn/ n Fernsehen nt; **watch ~** fernsehen. **~ set** n Fernsehapparat m, Fernseher m
telex /'teleks/ n Telex nt ● vt telexen
tell /tel/ vt/i (pt/pp **told**) sagen (**s.o.** jdm); (relate) erzählen; (know) wissen; (distinguish) erkennen; **~ the time** die Uhr lesen; **time will ~** das wird man erst sehen; **his age is beginning to ~** sein Alter macht sich bemerkbar; **don't ~ me** sag es mir nicht; **you mustn't ~** du darfst nichts sagen. **~ off** vt ausschimpfen
teller /'telə(r)/ n (cashier) Kassierer(in) m(f)
telly /'telɪ/ n (fam) = **television**
temerity /tɪ'merətɪ/ n Kühnheit f
temp /temp/ n (fam) Aushilfssekretärin f
temper /'tempə(r)/ n (disposition) Naturell nt; (mood) Laune f; (anger) Wut f; **lose one's ~** wütend werden ● vt (fig) mäßigen
temperament /'temprəmənt/ n Temperament nt. **~al** /-'mentl/ a temperamentvoll; (moody) launisch
temperance /'temprəns/ n Mäßigung f; (abstinence) Abstinenz f
temperate /'tempərət/ a gemäßigt
temperature /'temprətʃə(r)/ n Temperatur f; **have** or **run a ~** Fieber haben
tempest /'tempɪst/ n Sturm m. **~uous** /-'pestjʊəs/ a stürmisch
template /'templɪt/ n Schablone f
temple¹ /'templ/ n Tempel m
temple² n (Anat) Schläfe f
tempo /'tempəʊ/ n Tempo nt
temporary /'tempərərɪ/ a, **-ily** adv vorübergehend; (measure, building) provisorisch

tempt /tempt/ *vt* verleiten; (*Relig*) versuchen; herausfordern ⟨*fate*⟩; (*entice*) [ver]locken; **be ∼ed** versucht sein (**to** zu); **I am ∼ed by it** es lockt mich. **∼ation** /-'teɪʃn/ *n* Versuchung *f*. **∼ing** *a* verlockend

ten /ten/ *a* zehn

tenable /'tenəbl/ *a* (*fig*) haltbar

tenaci|ous /tɪ'neɪʃəs/ *a*, **-ly** *adv* hartnäckig. **∼ty** /-'næsətɪ/ *n* Hartnäckigkeit *f*

tenant /'tenənt/ *n* Mieter(in) *m(f)*; (*Comm*) Pächter(in) *m(f)*

tend[1] /tend/ *vt* (*look after*) sich kümmern um

tend[2] *vi* ∼ **to do sth** dazu neigen, etw zu tun

tendency /'tendənsɪ/ *n* Tendenz *f*; (*inclination*) Neigung *f*

tender[1] /'tendə(r)/ *n* (*Comm*) Angebot *nt*; **legal ∼** gesetzliches Zahlungsmittel ● *vt* anbieten; einreichen ⟨*resignation*⟩

tender[2] *a* zart; (*loving*) zärtlich; (*painful*) empfindlich. **∼ly** *adv* zärtlich. **∼ness** *n* Zartheit *f*; Zärtlichkeit *f*

tendon /'tendən/ *n* Sehne *f*

tenement /'tenəmənt/ *n* Mietshaus *nt*

tenet /'tenɪt/ *n* Grundsatz *m*

tenner /'tenə(r)/ *n* (*fam*) Zehnpfundschein *m*

tennis /'tenɪs/ *n* Tennis *nt*. **∼-court** *n* Tennisplatz *m*

tenor /'tenə(r)/ *n* Tenor *m*

tense[1] /tens/ *n* (*Gram*) Zeit *f*

tense[2] *a* (**-r**, **-st**) gespannt ● *vt* anspannen ⟨*muscle*⟩

tension /'tenʃn/ *n* Spannung *f*

tent /tent/ *n* Zelt *nt*

tentacle /'tentəkl/ *n* Fangarm *m*

tentative /'tentətɪv/ *a*, **-ly** *adv* vorläufig; (*hesitant*) zaghaft

tenterhooks /'tentəhʊks/ *npl* **be on ∼** wie auf glühenden Kohlen sitzen

tenth /tenθ/ *a* zehnte(r,s) ● *n* Zehntel *nt*

tenuous /'tenjʊəs/ *a* (*fig*) schwach

tepid /'tepɪd/ *a* lauwarm

term /tɜːm/ *n* Zeitraum *m*; (*Sch*) Halbjahr *nt*; (*Univ*) ≈ Semester *nt*; (*expression*) Ausdruck *m*; **∼s** *pl* (*conditions*) Bedingungen *pl*; **∼ of office** Amtszeit *f*; **in the short/long ∼** kurz-/langfristig; **be on good/bad ∼s** gut/nicht gut miteinander auskommen; **come to ∼s with** sich abfinden mit

terminal /'tɜːmɪnl/ *a* End-; (*Med*) unheilbar ● *n* (*Aviat*) Terminal *m*; (*of bus*) Endstation *f*; (*on battery*) Pol *m*; (*Computing*) Terminal *nt*

terminat|e /'tɜːmɪneɪt/ *vt* beenden; lösen ⟨*contract*⟩; unterbrechen ⟨*pregnancy*⟩ ● *vi* enden. **∼ion** /-'neɪʃn/ *n* Beendigung *f*; (*Med*) Schwangerschaftsabbruch *m*

terminology /tɜːmɪ'nɒlədʒɪ/ *n* Terminologie *f*

terminus /'tɜːmɪnəs/ *n* (*pl* **-ni** /-naɪ/) Endstation *f*

terrace /'terəs/ *n* Terrasse *f*; (*houses*) Häuserreihe *f*; **the ∼s** (*Sport*) die [Steh]ränge *pl*. **∼d house** *n* Reihenhaus *nt*

terrain /te'reɪn/ *n* Gelände *nt*

terrible /'terəbl/ *a*, **-bly** *adv* schrecklich

terrier /'terɪə(r)/ *n* Terrier *m*

terrific /tə'rɪfɪk/ *a* (*fam*) (*excellent*) sagenhaft; (*huge*) riesig

terri|fy /'terɪfaɪ/ *vt* (*pt/pp* **-ied**) angst machen (+ *dat*); **be ∼fied** Angst haben. **∼fying** *a* furchterregend

territorial /terɪ'tɔːrɪəl/ *a* Territorial-

territory /'terɪtərɪ/ *n* Gebiet *nt*

terror /'terə(r)/ *n* [panische] Angst *f*; (*Pol*) Terror *m*. **∼ism** /-ɪzm/ *n* Terrorismus *m*. **∼ist** /-ɪst/ *n* Terrorist *m*. **∼ize** *vt* terrorisieren

terse /tɜːs/ *a*, **-ly** *adv* kurz, knapp

test /test/ *n* (*Sch*) Klassenarbeit *f*; **put to the ∼** auf die Probe stellen ● *vt* prüfen; (*examine*) untersuchen (**for** auf + *acc*)

testament /'testəmənt/ *n* Testament *nt*; **Old/New T∼** Altes/Neues Testament *nt*

testicle /'testɪkl/ *n* Hoden *m*

testify /'testɪfaɪ/ *v* (*pt/pp* **-ied**) ● *vt* beweisen; **∼ that** bezeugen, daß ● *vi* aussagen; **∼ to** bezeugen

testimonial /testɪ'məʊnɪəl/ *n* Zeugnis *nt*

testimony /'testɪmənɪ/ *n* Aussage *f*

'test-tube *n* Reagenzglas *nt*. **∼ 'baby** *n* (*fam*) Retortenbaby *nt*

testy /'testɪ/ *a* gereizt

tetanus /'tetənəs/ *n* Tetanus *m*

tetchy /'tetʃɪ/ *a* gereizt

tether /'teðə(r)/ *n* **be at the end of one's ∼** am Ende seiner Kraft sein ● *vt* anbinden

text /tekst/ *n* Text *m*. **∼book** *n* Lehrbuch *nt*

textile /'tekstaɪl/ *a* Textil- ● *n* **∼s** *pl* Textilien *pl*

texture /'tekstʃə(r)/ n Beschaffenheit f; (Tex) Struktur f

Thai /taɪ/ a thailändisch. **~land** n Thailand nt

Thames /temz/ n Themse f

than /ðən, betont ðæn/ conj als; **older ~ me** älter als ich

thank /θæŋk/ vt danken (+ dat); **~ you [very much]** danke [schön]. **~ful** a, **-ly** adv dankbar. **~less** a undankbar

thanks /θæŋks/ npl Dank m; **~!** (fam) danke! **~ to** dank (+ dat or gen)

that /ðæt/ a & pron (pl those) der/die/ das; (pl) die; **~ one** der/die/das da; **I'll take ~** ich nehme den/die/das; **I don't like those** die mag ich nicht; **~ is** das heißt; **is ~ you?** bist du es? **who is ~?** wer ist da? **with/after ~** damit/danach; **like ~** so; **a man like ~** so ein Mann; **~ is why** deshalb; **~'s it!** genau! **all ~ I know** alles was ich weiß; **the day ~ I saw him** an dem Tag, als ich ihn sah ● adv so; **~ good/hot** so gut/heiß ● conj daß

thatch /θætʃ/ n Strohdach nt. **~ed** a strohgedeckt

thaw /θɔ:/ n Tauwetter nt ● vt/i auftauen; **it's ~ing** es taut

the /ðə, vor einem Vokal ðɪ:/ def art der/die/das; (pl) die; **play ~ piano/ violin** Klavier/Geige spielen ● adv **~ more ~ better** je mehr, desto besser; **all ~ better** um so besser

theatre /'θɪətə(r)/ n Theater nt; (Med) Operationssaal m

theatrical /θɪ'ætrɪkl/ a Theater-; (showy) theatralisch

theft /θeft/ n Diebstahl m

their /ðeə(r)/ a ihr

theirs /ðeəz/ poss pron ihre(r), ihrs; **a friend of ~** ein Freund von ihnen; **those are ~** die gehören ihnen

them /ðem/ pron (acc) sie; (dat) ihnen; **I know ~** ich kenne sie; **give ~ the money** gib ihnen das Geld

theme /θi:m/ n Thema nt

them'selves pron selbst; (refl) sich; **by ~** allein

then /ðen/ adv dann; (at that time in past) damals; **by ~** bis dahin; **since ~** seitdem; **before ~** vorher; **from ~ on** von da an; **now and ~** dann und wann; **there and ~** auf der Stelle ● a damalig

theolog|ian /θɪə'ləʊdʒɪən/ n Theologe m. **~y** /-'ɒlədʒɪ/ n Theologie f

theorem /'θɪərəm/ n Lehrsatz m

theoretical /θɪə'retɪkl/ a, **-ly** adv theoretisch

theory /'θɪərɪ/ n Theorie f; **in ~** theoretisch

therapeutic /θerə'pju:tɪk/ a therapeutisch

therap|ist /'θerəpɪst/ n Therapeut(in) m(f). **~y** n Therapie f

there /ðeə(r)/ adv da; (with movement) dahin, dorthin; **down/up ~** da unten/oben; **~ is/are** da ist/sind; (in existence) es gibt; **~ he/she is** da ist er/sie; **send/take ~** hinschicken/ -bringen ● int there, there! nun, nun!

there: ~abouts adv da [in der Nähe]; **or ~abouts** (roughly) ungefähr. **~'after** adv danach. **~by** adv dadurch. **~fore** /-fɔ:(r)/ adv deshalb, also

thermal /'θɜ:ml/ a Thermal-; **~ 'underwear** n Thermowäsche f

thermometer /θə'mɒmɪtə(r)/ n Thermometer nt

Thermos (P) /'θɜ:məs/ n **~ [flask]** Thermosflasche (P) f

thermostat /'θɜ:məstæt/ n Thermostat m

these /ði:z/ see this

thesis /'θi:sɪs/ n (pl -ses /-si:z/) Dissertation f; (proposition) These f

they /ðeɪ/ pron sie; **~ say** (generalizing) man sagt

thick /θɪk/ a (-er, -est), **-ly** adv dick; (dense) dicht; ⟨liquid⟩ dickflüssig; (fam: stupid) dumm ● adv dick ● n **in the ~ of** mitten in (+ dat). **~en** vt dicker machen; eindicken ⟨sauce⟩ ● vi dicker werden; ⟨fog:⟩ dichter werden; ⟨plot:⟩ kompliziert werden. **~ness** n Dicke f; Dichte f; Dickflüssigkeit f

thick: ~set a untersetzt. **~-'skinned** a (fam) dickfellig

thief /θi:f/ n (pl thieves) Dieb(in) m(f)

thieving /'θi:vɪŋ/ a diebisch ● n Stehlen nt

thigh /θaɪ/ n Oberschenkel m

thimble /'θɪmbl/ n Fingerhut m

thin /θɪn/ a (thinner, thinnest), **-ly** adv dünn ● adv dünn ● v (pt/pp thinned) ● vt verdünnen ⟨liquid⟩ ● vi sich lichten. **~ out** vt ausdünnen

thing /θɪŋ/ n Ding nt; (subject, affair) Sache f; **~s** pl (belongings) Sachen pl; **for one ~** erstens; **the right ~** das Richtige; **just the ~!** genau das Richtige! **how are ~s?** wie geht's? **the latest ~** (fam) der letzte Schrei; **the best ~ would be** am besten wäre es

think /θɪŋk/ *vt/i* (*pt/pp* **thought**) denken (**about/of** an + *acc*); (*believe*) meinen; (*consider*) nachdenken; (*regard as*) halten für; **I ~ so** ich glaube schon; **what do you ~?** was meinen Sie? **what do you ~ of it?** was halten Sie davon? **~ better of it** es sich (*dat*) anders überlegen. **~ over** *vt* sich (*dat*) überlegen. **~ up** *vt* sich (*dat*) ausdenken

third /θɜːd/ *a* dritte(r,s) ● *n* Drittel *nt*. **~ly** *adv* drittens. **~-rate** *a* drittrangig

thirst /θɜːst/ *n* Durst *m*. **~y** *a*, **-ily** *adv* durstig; **be ~y** Durst haben

thirteen /θɜːˈtiːn/ *a* dreizehn. **~th** *a* dreizehnte(r,s)

thirtieth /ˈθɜːtiːθ/ *a* dreißigste(r,s)

thirty /ˈθɜːtɪ/ *a* dreißig

this /ðɪs/ *a* (*pl* **these**) diese(r,s); (*pl*) diese; **~ one** diese(r,s) da; **I'll take ~** ich nehme diesen/ diese/ dieses; **~ evening/morning** heute abend/morgen; **these days** heutzutage ● *pron* (*pl* **these**) das, dies[es]; (*pl*) die, diese; **~ and that** dies und das; **~ or that** dieses oder das da; **like ~** so; **~ is Peter** das ist Peter; (*Teleph*) hier [spricht] Peter; **who is ~** wer ist das? (*Teleph, Amer*) wer ist am Apparat?

thistle /ˈθɪsl/ *n* Distel *f*

thorn /θɔːn/ *n* Dorn *m*. **~y** *a* dornig

thorough /ˈθʌrə/ *a* gründlich

thorough: **~bred** *n* reinrassiges Tier *nt*; (*horse*) Rassepferd *nt*. **~fare** *n* Durchfahrtsstraße *f*; **'no ~fare'** 'keine Durchfahrt'

thorough|ly /ˈθʌrəlɪ/ *adv* gründlich; (*completely*) völlig; (*extremely*) äußerst. **~ness** *n* Gründlichkeit *f*

those /ðəʊz/ *see* **that**

though /ðəʊ/ *conj* obgleich, obwohl; **as ~** als ob ● *adv* (*fam*) doch

thought /θɔːt/ *see* **think** ● *n* Gedanke *m*; (*thinking*) Denken *nt*. **~ful** *a*, **-ly** *adv* nachdenklich; (*considerate*) rücksichtsvoll. **~less** *a*, **-ly** *adv* gedankenlos

thousand /ˈθaʊznd/ *a* **one/a ~** [ein]tausend ● *n* Tausend *nt*; **~s of** Tausende von. **~th** *a* tausendste(r,s) ● *n* Tausend- stel *nt*

thrash /θræʃ/ *vt* verprügeln; (*defeat*) [vernichtend] schlagen. **~ about** *vi* sich herumwerfen; (*fish:*) zappeln. **~ out** *vt* ausdiskutieren

thread /θred/ *n* Faden *m*; (*of screw*) Gewinde *nt* ● *vt* einfädeln; auffädeln (*beads*); **~ one's way through** sich

schlängeln durch. **~bare** *a* fadenscheinig

threat /θret/ *n* Drohung *f*; (*danger*) Bedrohung *f*

threaten /ˈθretn/ *vt* drohen (+ *dat*); (*with weapon*) bedrohen; **~ to do sth** drohen, etw zu tun; **~ s.o.** **with sth** jdm etw androhen ● *vi* drohen. **~ing** *a*, **-ly** *adv* drohend; (*ominous*) bedrohlich

three /θriː/ *a* drei. **~fold** *a* & *adv* dreifach. **~some** /-səm/ *n* Trio *nt*

thresh /θreʃ/ *vt* dreschen

threshold /ˈθreʃəʊld/ *n* Schwelle *f*

threw /θruː/ *see* **throw**

thrift /θrɪft/ *n* Sparsamkeit *f*. **~y** *a* sparsam

thrill /θrɪl/ *n* Erregung *f*; (*fam*) Nervenkitzel *m* ● *vt* (*excite*) erregen; **be ~ed with** sich sehr freuen über (+ *acc*). **~er** *n* Thriller *m*. **~ing** *a* erregend

thrive /θraɪv/ *vi* (*pt* **thrived** *or* **throve**, *pp* **thrived** *or* **thriven** /ˈθrɪvn/) gedeihen (**on** bei); (*business:*) florieren

throat /θrəʊt/ *n* Hals *m*; **sore ~** Halsschmerzen *pl*; **cut s.o.'s ~** jdm die Kehle durchschneiden

throb /θrɒb/ *n* Pochen *nt* ● *vi* (*pt/pp* **throbbed**) pochen; (*vibrate*) vibrieren

throes /θrəʊz/ *npl* **in the ~ of** (*fig*) mitten in (+ *dat*)

thrombosis /θrɒmˈbəʊsɪs/ *n* Thrombose *f*

throne /θrəʊn/ *n* Thron *m*

throng /θrɒŋ/ *n* Menge *f*

throttle /ˈθrɒtl/ *vt* erdrosseln

through /θruː/ *prep* durch (+ *acc*); (*during*) während (+ *gen*); (*Amer: up to & including*) bis einschließlich ● *adv* durch; **all ~** die ganze Zeit; **~ and ~** durch und durch; **wet ~** durch und durch naß; **read sth ~** etw durchlesen; **let/walk ~** durchlassen/-gehen ● *a* (*train*) durchgehend; **be ~** (*finished*) fertig sein; (*Teleph*) durch sein

throughout /θruːˈaʊt/ *prep* **~ the country** im ganzen Land; **~ the night** die Nacht durch ● *adv* ganz; (*time*) die ganze Zeit

throve /θrəʊv/ *see* **thrive**

throw /θrəʊ/ *n* Wurf *m* ● *vt* (*pt* **threw**, *pp* **thrown**) werfen; schütten (*liquid*); betätigen (*switch*); abwerfen (*rider*); (*fam: disconcert*) aus der Fassung bringen; (*fam*) geben

⟨party⟩; ~ sth to s.o. jdm etw zuwer-
fen; ~ sth at s.o. etw nach jdm
werfen; (pelt with) jdn mit etw bewerfen. ~ away vt wegwerfen. ~
out vt hinauswerfen; (~ away) wegwerfen; verwerfen ⟨plan⟩. ~ up vt
hochwerfen ● vi (fam) sich
übergeben

'throw-away a Wegwerf-

thrush /θrʌʃ/ n Drossel f

thrust /θrʌst/ n Stoß m; (Phys) Schub
m ● vt (pt/pp thrust) stoßen; (insert)
stecken; ~ [up]on aufbürden (s.o.
jdm)

thud /θʌd/ n dumpfer Schlag m

thug /θʌg/ n Schläger m

thumb /θʌm/ n Daumen m; rule of ~
Faustregel f; under s.o.'s ~ unter jds
Fuchtel ● vt ~ a lift (fam) per Anhalter fahren. ~-index n Daumen-
register nt. ~tack n (Amer) Reißzwecke f

thump /θʌmp/ n Schlag m; (noise)
dumpfer Schlag m ● vt schlagen ● vi
hämmern (on an/auf + acc); ⟨heart:⟩
pochen

thunder /'θʌndə(r)/ n Donner m ● vi
donnern. ~clap n Donnerschlag m.
~storm n Gewitter nt. ~y a
gewittrig

Thursday /'θɜːzdeɪ/ n Donnerstag m

thus /ðʌs/ adv so

thwart /θwɔːt/ vt vereiteln; ~ s.o. jdm
einen Strich durch die Rechnung
machen

thyme /taɪm/ n Thymian m

thyroid /'θaɪrɔɪd/ n Schilddrüse f

tiara /tɪ'ɑːrə/ n Diadem nt

tick¹ /tɪk/ n on~ (fam) auf Pump

tick² n (sound) Ticken nt; (mark)
Häkchen nt; (fam: instant) Sekunde
f ● vi ticken ● vt abhaken. ~ off vt
abhaken; (fam) rüffeln. ~ over vi
⟨engine:⟩ im Leerlauf laufen

ticket /'tɪkɪt/ n Karte f; (for bus,
train) Fahrschein m; (Aviat) Flugschein m; (for lottery) Los nt; (for
article deposited) Schein m; (label)
Schild nt; (for library) Lesekarte f;
(fine) Strafzettel m. ~-collector n
Fahrkartenkontrolleur m. ~-office
n Fahrkartenschalter m; (for entry)
Kasse f

tick|le /'tɪkl/ n Kitzeln nt ● vt/i kit-
zeln. ~lish /'tɪklɪʃ/ a kitzlig

tidal /'taɪdl/ a ⟨river, harbour⟩ Tide-.
~ wave n Flutwelle f

tiddly-winks /'tɪdlɪwɪŋks/ n Floh-
spiel nt

tide /taɪd/ n Gezeiten pl; (of events)
Strom m; the ~ is in/out es ist
Flut/Ebbe ● vt ~ s.o. over jdm über
die Runden helfen

tidiness /'taɪdɪnɪs/ n Ordentlichkeit f

tidy /'taɪdɪ/ a (-ier, -iest), -ily adv
ordentlich ● vt ~ [up] aufräumen;
~ oneself up sich zurechtmachen

tie /taɪ/ n Krawatte f, Schlips m;
(cord) Schnur f; (fig: bond) Band nt;
(restriction) Bindung f; (Sport) Unentschieden nt; (in competition)
Punktgleichheit f ● v (pres p tying)
● vt binden; machen ⟨knot⟩ ● vi
(Sport) unentschieden spielen;
(have equal scores, votes) punkt-
gleich sein; ~ in with passen zu. ~
up vt festbinden; verschnüren ⟨par-
cel⟩; fesseln ⟨person⟩; be ~d up
(busy) beschäftigt sein

tier /tɪə(r)/ n Stufe f; (of cake) Etage f;
(in stadium) Rang m

tiff /tɪf/ n Streit m, (fam) Krach m

tiger /'taɪgə(r)/ n Tiger m

tight /taɪt/ a (-er, -est), -ly adv fest;
(taut) straff; ⟨clothes⟩ eng; ⟨control⟩
streng; (fam: drunk) blau; in a ~
corner (fam) in der Klemme ● adv
fest

tighten /'taɪtn/ vt festerziehen; straffen ⟨rope⟩; anziehen ⟨screw⟩; verschärfen ⟨control⟩ ● vi sich spannen

tight: ~-'fisted a knauserig. ~rope
n Hochseil nt

tights /taɪts/ npl Strumpfhose f

tile /taɪl/ n Fliese f; (on wall) Kachel f;
(on roof) [Dach]ziegel m ● vt mit
Fliesen auslegen; kacheln ⟨wall⟩;
decken ⟨roof⟩

till¹ /tɪl/ prep & conj = until

till² n Kasse f

tiller /'tɪlə(r)/ n Ruderpinne f

tilt /tɪlt/ n Neigung f; at full ~ mit
voller Wucht ● vt kippen; [zur Seite]
neigen ⟨head⟩ ● vi sich neigen

timber /'tɪmbə(r)/ n [Nutz]holz nt

time /taɪm/ n Zeit f; (occasion) Mal nt;
(rhythm) Takt m; ~s (Math) mal; at
any ~ jederzeit; this ~ dieses Mal,
diesmal; at ~s manchmal; ~ and
again immer wieder; two at a ~ zwei
auf einmal; on ~ pünktlich; in ~
rechtzeitig; (eventually) mit der Zeit;
in no ~ im Handumdrehen; in a
year's ~ in einem Jahr; behind ~
verspätet; behind the ~s rückständig; for the ~ being vorläufig; what
is the ~? wie spät ist es? wieviel Uhr
ist es? by the ~ we arrive bis wir

ankommen; **did you have a nice ∼?** hat es dir gut gefallen? **have a good ∼!** viel Vergnügen! ● *vt* stoppen ⟨*race*⟩; **be well ∼d** gut abgepaßt sein
time: ∼ **bomb** *n* Zeitbombe *f*. ∼**lag** *n* Zeitdifferenz *f*. ∼**less** *a* zeitlos. ∼**ly** *a* rechtzeitig. ∼**-switch** *n* Zeitschalter *m*. ∼**table** *n* Fahrplan *m*; (*Sch*) Stundenplan *m*
timid /'tɪmɪd/ *a*, **-ly** *adv* scheu; (*hesitant*) zaghaft
timing /'taɪmɪŋ/ *n* Wahl *f* des richtigen Zeitpunkts; (*Sport, Techn*) Timing *nt*
tin /tɪn/ *n* Zinn *nt*; (*container*) Dose *f* ● *vt* (*pt/pp* **tinned**) in Dosen *od* Büchsen konservieren. ∼ **foil** *n* Stanniol *nt*; (*Culin*) Alufolie *f*
tinge /tɪndʒ/ *n* Hauch *m* ● *vt* ∼**d with** mit einer Spur von
tingle /'tɪŋgl/ *vi* kribbeln
tinker /'tɪŋkə(r)/ *vi* herumbasteln (**with** an + *dat*)
tinkle /'tɪŋkl/ *n* Klingeln *nt* ● *vi* klingeln
tinned /tɪnd/ *a* Dosen-, Büchsen-
'tin opener *n* Dosen-/Büchsenöffner *m*
'tinpot *a* (*pej*) ⟨*firm*⟩ schäbig
tinsel /'tɪnsl/ *n* Lametta *nt*
tint /tɪnt/ *n* Farbton *m* ● *vt* tönen
tiny /'taɪnɪ/ *a* (**-ier, -iest**) winzig
tip¹ /tɪp/ *n* Spitze *f*
tip² *n* (*money*) Trinkgeld *nt*; (*advice*) Rat *m*, (*fam*) Tip *m*; (*for rubbish*) Müllhalde *f* ● *v* (*pt/pp* **tipped**) ● *vt* (*tilt*) kippen; (*reward*) Trinkgeld geben (s.o. jdm) ● *vi* kippen. ∼ **off** *vt* ∼ **s.o. off** jdm einen Hinweis geben. ∼ **out** *vt* auskippen. ∼ **over** *vt/i* umkippen
'tip-off *n* Hinweis *m*
tipped /tɪpt/ *a* Filter-
tipsy /'tɪpsɪ/ *a* (*fam*) beschwipst
tiptoe /'tɪptəʊ/ *n* **on** ∼ auf Zehenspitzen
tiptop /tɪp'tɒp/ *a* (*fam*) erstklassig
tire /'taɪə(r)/ *vt/i* ermüden. ∼**d** *a* müde; **be ∼d of sth** etw satt haben; ∼**d out** [völlig] erschöpft. ∼**less** *a*, **-ly** *adv* unermüdlich. ∼**some** /-səm/ *a* lästig
tiring /'taɪrɪŋ/ *a* ermüdend
tissue /'tɪʃu:/ *n* Gewebe *nt*; (*handkerchief*) Papiertaschentuch *nt*. ∼**paper** *n* Seidenpapier *nt*
tit¹ /tɪt/ *n* (*bird*) Meise *f*
tit² *n* ∼ **for tat** wie du mir, so ich dir
'titbit *n* Leckerbissen *m*

titillate /'tɪtɪleɪt/ *vt* erregen
title /'taɪtl/ *n* Titel *m*. ∼**-role** *n* Titelrolle *f*
tittle-tattle /'tɪtltætl/ *n* Klatsch *m*
titular /'tɪtjʊlə(r)/ *a* nominell
to /tu:, *unbetont* tə/ *prep* zu (+ *dat*); (*with place, direction*) nach; (*to cinema, theatre*) in (+ *acc*); (*to wedding, party*) auf (+ *acc*); ⟨*address, send, fasten*⟩ an (+ *acc*); (*per*) pro; (*up to, until*) bis; **to the station** zum Bahnhof; **to Germany/Switzerland** nach Deutschland/in die Schweiz; **to the toilet/one's room** auf die Toilette/ sein Zimmer; **to the office/an exhibition** ins Büro/ in eine Ausstellung; **to university** auf die Universität; **twenty/quarter to eight** zwanzig/Viertel vor acht; **5 to 6 pounds** 5 bis 6 Pfund; **to the end** bis zum Schluß; **to this day** bis heute; **to the best of my knowledge** nach meinem besten Wissen; **give/say sth to s.o.** jdm etw geben/sagen; **go/ come to s.o.** zu jdm gehen/kommen; **I've never been to Berlin** ich war noch nie in Berlin; **there's nothing to it** es ist nichts dabei ● *verbal constructions* **to go** gehen; **to stay** bleiben; **learn to swim** schwimmen lernen; **want to/have to go** gehen wollen/müssen; **be easy/difficult to forget** leicht/schwer zu vergessen sein; **too ill/tired to go** zu krank/ müde, um zu gehen; **he did it to annoy me** er tat es, um mich zu ärgern; **you have to** du mußt; **I don't want to** ich will nicht; **I'd love to** gern; **I forgot to** ich habe es vergessen; **he wants to be a teacher** er will Lehrer werden; **live to be 90** 90 werden; **he was the last to arrive** er kam als letzter; **to be honest** ehrlich gesagt ● *adv* **pull to** anlehnen; **to and fro** hin und her
toad /təʊd/ *n* Kröte *f*. ∼**stool** *n* Giftpilz *m*
toast /təʊst/ *n* Toast *m* ● *vt* toasten ⟨*bread*⟩; (*drink a ∼ to*) trinken auf (+ *acc*). ∼**er** *n* Toaster *m*
tobacco /tə'bækəʊ/ *n* Tabak *m*. ∼**nist's [shop]** *n* Tabakladen *m*
toboggan /tə'bɒgən/ *n* Schlitten *m* ● *vi* Schlitten fahren
today /tə'deɪ/ *n & adv* heute; ∼ **week** heute in einer Woche; ∼**'s paper** die heutige Zeitung
toddler /'tɒdlə(r)/ *n* Kleinkind *nt*

to-do /tə'du:/ n (fam) Getue nt, Theater nt

toe /təʊ/ n Zeh m; (of footwear) Spitze f ● vt ~ **the line** spuren. **~nail** n Zehennagel m

toffee /'tɒfɪ/ n Karamelbonbon m & nt

together /tə'geðə(r)/ adv zusammen; (at the same time) gleichzeitig

toil /tɔɪl/ n [harte] Arbeit f ● vi schwer arbeiten

toilet /'tɔɪlɪt/ n Toilette f. ~ **bag** n Kulturbeutel m. ~ **paper** n Toilettenpapier nt

toiletries /'tɔɪlɪtrɪz/ npl Toilettenartikel pl

toilet: ~ **roll** n Rolle f Toilettenpapier. ~ **water** n Toilettenwasser nt

token /'təʊkən/ n Zeichen nt; (counter) Marke f; (voucher) Gutschein m ● attrib symbolisch

told /təʊld/ see **tell** ● a **all** ~ insgesamt

tolerable /'tɒlərəbl/ a, **-bly** adv erträglich; (not bad) leidlich

toleran|ce /'tɒlərəns/ n Toleranz f. ~t a, **-ly** adv tolerant

tolerate /'tɒləreɪt/ vt dulden, tolerieren; (bear) ertragen

toll¹ /təʊl/ n Gebühr f; (for road) Maut f (Aust); ~ **death** = Zahl f der Todesopfer; **take a heavy** ~ einen hohen Tribut fordern

toll² vi läuten

tom /tɒm/ n (cat) Kater m

tomato /tə'mɑːtəʊ/ n (pl **-es**) Tomate f. ~ **purée** n Tomatenmark nt

tomb /tu:m/ n Grabmal nt

'tomboy n Wildfang m

'tombstone n Grabstein m

'tom-cat n Kater m

tome /təʊm/ n dicker Band m

tomfoolery /tɒm'fu:lərɪ/ n Blödsinn m

tomorrow /tə'mɒrəʊ/ n & adv morgen; ~ **morning** morgen früh; **the day after** ~ übermorgen; **see you** ~! bis morgen!

ton /tʌn/ n Tonne f; ~**s of** (fam) jede Menge

tone /təʊn/ n Ton m; (colour) Farbton m ● vt ~ **down** dämpfen; (fig) mäßigen. ~ **up** vt kräftigen; straffen ⟨muscles⟩

tongs /tɒŋz/ npl Zange f

tongue /tʌŋ/ n Zunge f; ~ **in cheek** (fam) nicht ernst. ~**-twister** n Zungenbrecher m

tonic /'tɒnɪk/ n Tonikum nt; (for hair) Haarwasser nt; (fig) Wohltat f; ~ **[water]** Tonic nt

tonight /tə'naɪt/ n & adv heute nacht; (evening) heute abend

tonne /tʌn/ n Tonne f

tonsil /'tɒnsl/ n (Anat) Mandel f. ~**litis** /-sə'laɪtɪs/ n Mandelentzündung f

too /tu:/ adv zu; (also) auch; ~ **much/little** zuviel/zuwenig

took /tʊk/ see **take**

tool /tu:l/ n Werkzeug nt; (for gardening) Gerät nt

toot /tu:t/ n Hupsignal nt ● vi tuten; (Auto) hupen

tooth /tu:θ/ n (pl **teeth**) Zahn m

tooth: ~**ache** n Zahnschmerzen pl. ~**brush** n Zahnbürste f. ~**less** a zahnlos. ~**paste** n Zahnpasta f. ~**pick** n Zahnstocher m

top¹ /tɒp/ n (toy) Kreisel m

top² n oberer Teil m; (apex) Spitze f; (summit) Gipfel m; (Sch) Erste(r) m/f; (top part or half) Oberteil nt; (head) Kopfende nt; (of road) oberes Ende nt; (upper surface) Oberfläche f; (lid) Deckel m; (of bottle) Verschluß m; (garment) Top nt; **at the/ on** ~ oben; **on** ~ **of** oben auf (+ dat/acc); **on** ~ **of that** (besides) obendrein; **from** ~ **to bottom** von oben bis unten ● a oberste(r,s); (highest) höchste(r,s); (best) beste(r,s) ● vt (pt/pp **topped**) an erster Stelle stehen auf (+ dat) ⟨list⟩; (exceed) übersteigen; (remove the ~ of) die Spitze abschneiden. ~ **up** vt nachfüllen, auffüllen

top: ~ **'hat** n Zylinder[hut] m. ~**heavy** a kopflastig

topic /'tɒpɪk/ n Thema nt. ~**al** a aktuell

top: ~**less** a & adv oben ohne. ~**most** a oberste(r,s)

topple /'tɒpl/ vt/i umstürzen. ~ **off** vi stürzen

top-'secret a streng geheim

topsy-turvy /tɒpsɪ'tɜːvɪ/ adv völlig durcheinander

torch /tɔːtʃ/ n Taschenlampe f; (flaming) Fackel f

tore /tɔː(r)/ see **tear¹**

torment¹ /'tɔːment/ n Qual f

torment² /tɔː'ment/ vt quälen

torn /tɔːn/ see **tear¹** ● a zerrissen

tornado /tɔː'neɪdəʊ/ n (pl **-es**) Wirbelsturm m

torpedo /tɔːˈpiːdəʊ/ n (pl -es) Torpedo m ● vt torpedieren

torrent /ˈtɒrənt/ n reißender Strom m. **∼ial** /təˈrenʃl/ a ⟨rain⟩ wolkenbruchartig

torso /ˈtɔːsəʊ/ n Rumpf m; (Art) Torso m

tortoise /ˈtɔːtəs/ n Schildkröte f. **∼shell** n Schildpatt nt

tortuous /ˈtɔːtjʊəs/ a verschlungen; (fig) umständlich

torture /ˈtɔːtʃə(r)/ n Folter f; (fig) Qual f ● vt foltern; (fig) quälen

toss /tɒs/ vt werfen; (into the air) hochwerfen; (shake) schütteln; (unseat) abwerfen; mischen ⟨salad⟩; wenden ⟨pancake⟩; **∼ a coin** mit einer Münze losen ● vi **∼ and turn** (in bed) sich [schlaflos] im Bett wälzen. **∼ up** vi [mit einer Münze] losen

tot[1] /tɒt/ n kleines Kind nt; (fam: of liquor) Gläschen nt

tot[2] vt (pt/pp totted) **∼ up** (fam) zusammenzählen

total /ˈtəʊtl/ a gesamt; (complete) völlig, total ● n Gesamtzahl f; (sum) Gesamtsumme f ● vt (pt/pp totalled) zusammenzählen; (amount to) sich belaufen auf (+ acc)

totalitarian /təʊtælɪˈteərɪən/ a totalitär

totally /ˈtəʊtəlɪ/ adv völlig, total

totter /ˈtɒtə(r)/ vi taumeln; (rock) schwanken. **∼y** a wackelig

touch /tʌtʃ/ n Berührung f; (sense) Tastsinn m; (Mus) Anschlag m; (contact) Kontakt m; (trace) Spur f; (fig) Anflug m; **get/be in ∼** sich in Verbindung setzen/in Verbindung stehen (with mit) ● vt berühren; (get hold of) anfassen; (lightly) tippen auf/an (+ acc); (brush against) streifen [gegen]; (reach) erreichen; (equal) herankommen an (+ acc); (fig: move) rühren; anrühren ⟨food, subject⟩; **don't ∼ that!** faß das nicht an! ● vi sich berühren; **∼ on** (fig) berühren. **∼ down** vi (Aviat) landen. **∼ up** vt ausbessern

touch|ing /ˈtʌtʃɪŋ/ a rührend. **∼y** a empfindlich; ⟨subject⟩ heikel

tough /tʌf/ a (-er, -est) zäh; (severe, harsh) hart; (difficult) schwierig; (durable) strapazierfähig

toughen /ˈtʌfn/ vt härten; **∼ up** abhärten

tour /tʊə(r)/ n Reise f, Tour f; (of building, town) Besichtigung f; (Theat, Sport) Tournee f; (of duty) Dienstzeit f ● vt fahren durch; besichtigen ⟨building⟩ ● vi herumreisen

touris|m /ˈtʊərɪzm/ n Tourismus m, Fremdenverkehr m. **∼t** /-rɪst/ n Tourist(in) m(f) ● attrib Touristen-. **∼t office** n Fremdenverkehrsbüro nt

tournament /ˈtʊənəmənt/ n Turnier nt

'tour operator n Reiseveranstalter m

tousle /ˈtaʊzl/ vt zerzausen

tout /taʊt/ n Anreißer m; (ticket ∼) Kartenschwarzhändler m ● vi **∼ for customers** Kunden werben

tow /təʊ/ n **give s.o./a car a ∼** jdn/ein Auto abschleppen; **'on ∼'** 'wird geschleppt'; **in ∼** (fam) im Schlepptau ● vt schleppen; ziehen ⟨trailer⟩. **∼ away** vt abschleppen

toward[s] /təˈwɔːd(z)/ prep zu (+ dat); (with time) gegen (+ acc); (with respect to) gegenüber (+ dat)

towel /ˈtaʊəl/ n Handtuch nt. **∼ling** n (Tex) Frottee nt

tower /ˈtaʊə(r)/ n Turm m ● vi **∼ above** überragen. **∼ block** n Hochhaus nt. **∼ing** a hochragend

town /taʊn/ n Stadt f. **∼ 'hall** n Rathaus nt

tow: ∼-path n Treidelpfad m. **∼-rope** n Abschleppseil nt

toxic /ˈtɒksɪk/ a giftig. **∼ 'waste** n Giftmüll m

toxin /ˈtɒksɪn/ n Gift nt

toy /tɔɪ/ n Spielzeug nt ● vi **∼ with** spielen mit; stochern in (+ dat) ⟨food⟩. **∼shop** n Spielwarengeschäft nt

trac|e /treɪs/ n Spur f ● vt folgen (+ dat); (find) finden; (draw) zeichnen; (with tracing-paper) durchpausen. **∼ing-paper** n Pauspapier nt

track /træk/ n Spur f; (path) [unbefestigter] Weg m; (Sport) Bahn f; (Rail) Gleis nt; **keep ∼ of** im Auge behalten ● vt verfolgen. **∼ down** vt aufspüren; (find) finden

'tracksuit n Trainingsanzug m

tract[1] /trækt/ n (land) Gebiet nt

tract[2] n (pamphlet) [Flug]schrift f

tractor /ˈtræktə(r)/ n Traktor m

trade /treɪd/ n Handel m; (line of business) Gewerbe nt; (business) Geschäft nt; (craft) Handwerk nt; **by ∼** von Beruf ● vt tauschen; **∼ in** (give in part exchange) in Zahlung geben ● vi handeln (in mit)

'**trade mark** n Warenzeichen nt
trader /'treɪdə(r)/ n Händler m
trade: ~ **'union** n Gewerkschaft f. ~
  '**unionist** n Gewerkschaftler(in)
  m(f)
trading /'treɪdɪŋ/ n Handel m. ~
  estate n Gewerbegebiet nt. ~ **stamp**
  n Rabattmarke f
tradition /trə'dɪʃn/ n Tradition f.
  ~**al** a, **-ly** adv traditionell
traffic /'træfɪk/ n Verkehr m; (trading) Handel m ● vi handeln (**in** mit)
traffic: ~ **circle** n (Amer) Kreisverkehr m. ~ **jam** n [Verkehrs]stau m.
  ~ **lights** npl [Verkehrs]ampel f. ~
  warden n ≈ Hilfspolizist m; (woman) Politesse f
tragedy /'trædʒədɪ/ n Tragödie f
tragic /'trædʒɪk/ a, **-ally** adv tragisch
trail /treɪl/ n Spur f; (path) Weg m,
  Pfad m ● vi schleifen; ⟨plant:⟩ sich
  ranken; ~ [**behind**] zurückbleiben;
  (Sport) zurückliegen ● vt verfolgen,
  folgen (+ dat); (drag) schleifen
trailer /'treɪlə(r)/ n (Auto) Anhänger
  m; (Amer: caravan) Wohnwagen m;
  (film) Vorschau f
train /treɪn/ n Zug m; (of dress)
  Schleppe f; ~ **of thought** Gedanken-
  gang m ● vt ausbilden; (Sport) trainieren; (aim) richten auf (+ acc);
  erziehen ⟨child⟩; abrichten/(to do
  tricks) dressieren ⟨animal⟩; ziehen
  ⟨plant⟩ ● vi eine Ausbildung machen; (Sport) trainieren. ~**ed** a
  ausgebildet
trainee /treɪ'niː/ n Auszubildende(r)
  m/f; (Techn) Praktikant(in) m(f)
train|er /'treɪnə(r)/ n (Sport) Trainer
  m; (in circus) Dompteur m; ~**ers** pl
  Trainingsschuhe pl. ~**ing** n Ausbildung f; (Sport) Training nt; (of
  animals) Dressur f
traipse /treɪps/ vi (fam) latschen
trait /treɪt/ n Eigenschaft f
traitor /'treɪtə(r)/ n Verräter m
tram /træm/ n Straßenbahn f. ~
  lines npl Straßenbahnschienen pl
tramp /træmp/ n Landstreicher m;
  (hike) Wanderung f ● vi stapfen;
  (walk) marschieren
trample /'træmpl/ vt/i trampeln (**on**
  auf + acc)
trampoline /'træmpəliːn/ n Trampo-
  lin nt
trance /trɑːns/ n Trance f
tranquil /'træŋkwɪl/ a ruhig. ~**lity**
  /-'kwɪlətɪ/ n Ruhe f

tranquillizer /'træŋkwɪlaɪzə(r)/ n
  Beruhigungsmittel nt
transact /træn'zækt/ vt abschließen.
  ~**ion** /-ækʃn/ n Transaktion f
transcend /træn'send/ vt übersteigen
transcript /'trænskrɪpt/ n Abschrift
  f; (of official proceedings) Protokoll
  nt. ~**ion** /-'skrɪpʃn/ n Abschrift f
transept /'trænsept/ n Querschiff nt
transfer[1] /'trænsfɜː(r)/ n (see
  transfer[2]) Übertragung f; Verlegung
  f; Versetzung f; Überweisung f;
  (Sport) Transfer m; (design) Abzieh-
  bild nt
transfer[2] /træns'fɜː(r)/ v (pt/pp trans-
  ferred) ● vt übertragen; verlegen
  ⟨firm, prisoners⟩; versetzen ⟨em-
  ployee⟩; überweisen ⟨money⟩;
  (Sport) transferieren ● vi [über]-
  wechseln; (when travelling) umsteigen. ~**able** /-əbl/ a übertragbar
transform /træns'fɔːm/ vt verwandeln. ~**ation** /-fə'meɪʃn/ n Verwand-
  lung f. ~**er** n Transformator m
transfusion /træns'fjuːʒn/ n Transfusion f
transient /'trænzɪənt/ a kurzlebig;
  ⟨life⟩ kurz
transistor /træn'zɪstə(r)/ n Transistor m
transit /'trænsɪt/ n Transit m; (of
  goods) Transport m; **in** ~ ⟨goods⟩
  auf dem Transport
transition /træn'sɪʒn/ n Übergang m.
  ~**al** a Übergangs-
transitive /'trænsɪtɪv/ a, **-ly** adv
  transitiv
transitory /'trænsɪtərɪ/ a vergänglich; ⟨life⟩ kurz
translat|e /træns'leɪt/ vt übersetzen.
  ~**ion** /-'leɪʃn/ n Übersetzung f. ~**or**
  n Übersetzer(in) m(f)
translucent /trænz'luːsnt/ a durchscheinend
transmission /trænz'mɪʃn/ n Übertragung f
transmit /trænz'mɪt/ vt (pt/pp trans-
  mitted) übertragen. ~**ter** n Sender
  m
transparen|cy /træns'pærənsɪ/ n
  (Phot) Dia nt. ~**t** a durchsichtig
transpire /træn'spaɪə(r)/ vi sich herausstellen; (fam: happen) passieren
transplant[1] /'trænsplɑːnt/ n Ver-
  pflanzung f, Transplantation f
transplant[2] /træns'plɑːnt/ vt umpflanzen; (Med) verpflanzen

transport[1] /'trænspɔːt/ *n* Transport *m*

transport[2] /træn'spɔːt/ *vt* transportieren. **~ation** /-'teɪʃn/ *n* Transport *m*

transpose /træns'pəʊz/ *vt* umstellen

transvestite /træns'vestaɪt/ *n* Transvestit *m*

trap /træp/ *n* Falle *f*; (*fam: mouth*) Klappe *f*; **pony and** ~ Einspänner *m* ● *vt* (*pt/pp* **trapped**) [mit einer Falle] fangen; (*jam*) einklemmen; **be ~ped** festsitzen; (*shut in*) eingeschlossen sein; (*cut off*) abgeschnitten sein. **~'door** *n* Falltür *f*

trapeze /trə'piːz/ *n* Trapez *nt*

trash /træʃ/ *n* Schund *m*; (*rubbish*) Abfall *m*; (*nonsense*) Quatsch *m*. **~can** *n* (*Amer*) Mülleimer *m*. **~y** *a* Schund-

trauma /'trɔːmə/ *n* Trauma *nt*. **~tic** /-'mætɪk/ *a* traumatisch

travel /'trævl/ *n* Reisen *nt* ● *v* (*pt/pp* **travelled**) ● *vi* reisen; (*go in vehicle*) fahren; ⟨*light, sound:*⟩ sich fortpflanzen; (*Techn*) sich bewegen ● *vt* bereisen; fahren ⟨*distance*⟩. **~ agency** *n* Reisebüro *nt*. **~ agent** *n* Reisebürokaufmann *m*

traveller /'trævələ(r)/ *n* Reisende(r) *m*|*f*; (*Comm*) Vertreter *m*; **~s** *pl* (*gypsies*) Zigeuner *pl*. **~'s cheque** *n* Reisescheck *m*

trawler /'trɔːlə(r)/ *n* Fischdampfer *m*

tray /treɪ/ *n* Tablett *nt*; (*for baking*) [Back]blech *nt*; (*for documents*) Ablagekorb *m*

treacher|ous /'tretʃərəs/ *a* treulos; (*dangerous, deceptive*) tückisch. **~y** *n* Verrat *m*

treacle /'triːkl/ *n* Sirup *m*

tread /tred/ *n* Schritt *m*; (*step*) Stufe *f*; (*of tyre*) Profil *nt* ● *v* (*pt* **trod**, *pp* **trodden**) ● *vi* (*walk*) gehen; ~ **on/in** treten auf/ in (+ *acc*) ● *vt* treten

treason /'triːzn/ *n* Verrat *m*

treasure /'treʒə(r)/ *n* Schatz *m* ● *vt* in Ehren halten. **~r** *n* Kassenwart *m*

treasury /'treʒərɪ/ *n* Schatzkammer *f*; **the T~** das Finanzministerium

treat /triːt/ *n* [besonderes] Vergnügen *nt*; **give s.o. a** ~ jdm etwas Besonderes bieten ● *vt* behandeln; ~ **s.o. to sth** jdm etw spendieren

treatise /'triːtɪz/ *n* Abhandlung *f*

treatment /'triːtmənt/ *n* Behandlung *f*

treaty /'triːtɪ/ *n* Vertrag *m*

treble /'trebl/ *a* dreifach; ~ **the amount** dreimal soviel ● *n* (*Mus*) Diskant *m*; (*voice*) Sopran *m* ● *vt* verdreifachen ● *vi* sich verdreifachen. ~ **clef** *n* Violinschlüssel *m*

tree /triː/ *n* Baum *m*

trek /trek/ *n* Marsch *m* ● *vi* (*pt/pp* **trekked**) latschen

trellis /'trelɪs/ *n* Gitter *nt*

tremble /'trembl/ *vi* zittern

tremendous /trɪ'mendəs/ *a*, **-ly** *adv* gewaltig; (*fam: excellent*) großartig

tremor /'tremə(r)/ *n* Zittern *nt*; [**earth**] ~ Beben *nt*

trench /trentʃ/ *n* Graben *m*; (*Mil*) Schützengraben *m*

trend /trend/ *n* Tendenz *f*; (*fashion*) Trend *m*. **~y** *a* (**-ier, -iest**) (*fam*) modisch

trepidation /trepɪ'deɪʃn/ *n* Beklommenheit *f*

trespass /'trespəs/ *vi* ~ **on** unerlaubt betreten. **~er** *n* Unbefugte(r) *m*|*f*

trial /'traɪəl/ *n* (*Jur*) [Gerichts]verfahren *nt*, Prozeß *m*; (*test*) Probe *f*; (*ordeal*) Prüfung *f*; **be on** ~ auf Probe sein; (*Jur*) angeklagt sein (**for** wegen); **by** ~ **and error** durch Probieren

triang|le /'traɪæŋgl/ *n* Dreieck *nt*; (*Mus*) Triangel *m*. **~ular** /-'æŋgjʊlə(r)/ *a* dreieckig

tribe /traɪb/ *n* Stamm *m*

tribulation /trɪbjʊ'leɪʃn/ *n* Kummer *m*

tribunal /traɪ'bjuːnl/ *n* Schiedsgericht *nt*

tributary /'trɪbjʊtərɪ/ *n* Nebenfluß *m*

tribute /'trɪbjuːt/ *n* Tribut *m*; **pay** ~ Tribut zollen (**to** *dat*)

trice /traɪs/ *n* **in a** ~ im Nu

trick /trɪk/ *n* Trick *m*; (*joke*) Streich *m*; (*Cards*) Stich *m*; (*feat of skill*) Kunststück *nt*; **that should do the** ~ (*fam*) damit dürfte es klappen ● *vt* täuschen, (*fam*) hereinlegen

trickle /'trɪkl/ *vi* rinnen

trick|ster /'trɪkstə(r)/ *n* Schwindler *m*. **~y** *a* (**-ier, -iest**) *a* schwierig

tricycle /'traɪsɪkl/ *n* Dreirad *nt*

tried /traɪd/ *see* **try**

trifl|e /'traɪfl/ *n* Kleinigkeit *f*; (*Culin*) Trifle *nt*. **~ing** *a* unbedeutend

trigger /'trɪgə(r)/ *n* Abzug *m*; (*fig*) Auslöser *m* ● *vt* ~ [**off**] auslösen

trigonometry /trɪgə'nɒmɪtrɪ/ *n* Trigonometrie *f*

trim /trɪm/ *a* (**trimmer, trimmest**) gepflegt ● *n* (*cut*) Nachschneiden *nt*;

(*decoration*) Verzierung *f*; (*condition*) Zustand *m* ● *vt* schneiden; (*decorate*) besetzen; (*Naut*) trimmen. ~**ming** *n* Besatz *m*; ~**mings** *pl* (*accessories*) Zubehör *nt*; (*decorations*) Verzierungen *pl*; **with all the** ~**mings** mit allem Drum und Dran

Trinity /'trɪnɪtɪ/ *n* **the [Holy]** ~ **die** [Heilige] Dreieinigkeit *f*

trinket /'trɪŋkɪt/ *n* Schmuckgegenstand *m*

trio /'triːəʊ/ *n* Trio *nt*

trip /trɪp/ *n* Reise *f*; (*excursion*) Ausflug *m* ● *v* (*pt/pp* **tripped**) ● *vt* ~ **s.o.** **up** jdm ein Bein stellen ● *vi* stolpern (**on/over** über + *acc*)

tripe /traɪp/ *n* Kaldaunen *pl*; (*nonsense*) Quatsch *m*

triple /'trɪpl/ *a* dreifach ● *vt* verdreifachen ● *vi* sich verdreifachen

triplets /'trɪplɪts/ *npl* Drillinge *pl*

triplicate /'trɪplɪkət/ *n* **in** ~ in dreifacher Ausfertigung

tripod /'traɪpɒd/ *n* Stativ *nt*

tripper /'trɪpə(r)/ *n* Ausflügler *m*

trite /traɪt/ *a* banal

triumph /'traɪʌmf/ *n* Triumph *m* ● *vi* triumphieren (**over** über + *acc*). ~**ant** /-'ʌmfnt/ *a*, **-ly** *adv* triumphierend

trivial /'trɪvɪəl/ *a* belanglos. ~**ity** /-'ælɪtɪ/ *n* Belanglosigkeit *f*

trod, trodden /trɒd, 'trɒdn/ *see* **tread**

trolley /'trɒlɪ/ *n* (*for serving food*) Servierwagen *m*; (*for shopping*) Einkaufswagen *m*; (*for luggage*) Kofferkuli *m*; (*Amer: tram*) Straßenbahn *f*. ~ **bus** *n* O-Bus *m*

trombone /trɒm'bəʊn/ *n* Posaune *f*

troop /truːp/ *n* Schar *f*; ~**s** *pl* Truppen *pl* ● *vi* ~ **in/out** hinein-/hinausströmen

trophy /'trəʊfɪ/ *n* Trophäe *f*; (*in competition*) ≈ Pokal *m*

tropic /'trɒpɪk/ *n* Wendekreis *m*; ~**s** *pl* Tropen *pl*. ~**al** *a* tropisch; 〈*fruit*〉 Süd-

trot /trɒt/ *n* Trab *m* ● *vi* (*pt/pp* **trotted**) traben

trouble /'trʌbl/ *n* Ärger *m*; (*difficulties*) Schwierigkeiten *pl*; (*inconvenience*) Mühe *f*; (*conflict*) Unruhe *f*; (*Med*) Beschwerden *pl*; (*Techn*) Probleme *pl*; **get into** ~ Ärger bekommen; **take** ~ sich (*dat*) Mühe geben ● *vt* (*disturb*) stören; (*worry*) beunruhigen ● *vi* sich bemühen. ~-

maker *n* Unruhestifter *m*. ~**some** /-səm/ *a* schwierig; 〈*flies, cough*〉 lästig

trough /trɒf/ *n* Trog *m*

trounce /traʊns/ *vt* vernichtend schlagen; (*thrash*) verprügeln

troupe /truːp/ *n* Truppe *f*

trousers /'traʊzəz/ *npl* Hose *f*

trousseau /'truːsəʊ/ *n* Aussteuer *f*

trout /traʊt/ *n inv* Forelle *f*

trowel /'traʊəl/ *n* Kelle *f*; (*for gardening*) Pflanzkelle *f*

truant /'truːənt/ *n* **play** ~ die Schule schwänzen

truce /truːs/ *n* Waffenstillstand *m*

truck /trʌk/ *n* Last[kraft]wagen *m*; (*Rail*) Güterwagen *m*

truculent /'trʌkjʊlənt/ *a* aufsässig

trudge /trʌdʒ/ *n* [mühseliger] Marsch *m* ● *vi* latschen

true /truː/ *a* (**-r, -st**) wahr; (*loyal*) treu; (*genuine*) echt; **come** ~ in Erfüllung gehen; **is that** ~? stimmt das?

truism /'truːɪzm/ *n* Binsenwahrheit *f*

truly /'truːlɪ/ *adv* wirklich; (*faithfully*) treu; **Yours** ~ Hochachtungsvoll

trump /trʌmp/ *n* (*Cards*) Trumpf *m* ● *vt* übertrumpfen. ~ **up** *vt* (*fam*) erfinden

trumpet /'trʌmpɪt/ *n* Trompete *f*. ~**er** *n* Trompeter *m*

truncheon /'trʌntʃn/ *n* Schlagstock *m*

trundle /'trʌndl/ *vt/i* rollen

trunk /trʌŋk/ *n* [Baum]stamm *m*; (*body*) Rumpf *m*; (*of elephant*) Rüssel *m*; (*for travelling*) [Übersee]koffer *m*; (*for storage*) Truhe *f*; (*Amer: of car*) Kofferraum *m*; ~**s** *pl* Badehose *f*

truss /trʌs/ *n* (*Med*) Bruchband *nt*

trust /trʌst/ *n* Vertrauen *nt*; (*group of companies*) Trust *m*; (*organization*) Treuhandgesellschaft *f*; (*charitable*) Stiftung *f* ● *vt* trauen (+ *dat*), vertrauen (+ *dat*); (*hope*) hoffen ● *vi* vertrauen (**in/to** auf + *acc*)

trustee /trʌs'tiː/ *n* Treuhänder *m*

'trustful /'trʌstfl/ *a*, **-ly** *adv* vertrauensvoll. ~**ing** *a* vertrauensvoll. ~**worthy** *a* vertrauenswürdig

truth /truːθ/ *n* (*pl* **-s** /truːðz/) Wahrheit *f*. ~**ful** *a*, **-ly** *adv* ehrlich

try /traɪ/ *n* Versuch *m* ● *v* (*pt/pp* **tried**) ● *vt* versuchen; (*sample, taste*) probieren; (*be a strain on*) anstrengen; (*Jur*) vor Gericht stellen; verhandeln 〈*case*〉 ● *vi* versuchen; (*make an* *effort*) sich bemühen. ~ **on** *vt* anprobieren; aufprobieren ⟨*hat*⟩. ~ **out** *vt* ausprobieren

trying /'traɪɪŋ/ *a* schwierig

T-shirt /'tiː-/ *n* T-Shirt *nt*

tub /tʌb/ *n* Kübel *m*; (*carton*) Becher *m*; (*bath*) Wanne *f*

tuba /'tjuːbə/ *n* (*Mus*) Tuba *f*

tubby /'tʌbɪ/ *a* (**-ier, -iest**) rundlich

tube /tjuːb/ *n* Röhre *f*; (*pipe*) Rohr *nt*; (*flexible*) Schlauch *m*; (*of tooth-paste*) Tube *f*; (*Rail, fam*) U-Bahn *f*

tuber /'tjuːbə(r)/ *n* Knolle *f*

tuberculosis /tjuːbɜːkjʊ'ləʊsɪs/ *n* Tuberkulose *f*

tubing /'tjuːbɪŋ/ *n* Schlauch *m*

tubular /'tjuːbjʊlə(r)/ *a* röhrenförmig

tuck /tʌk/ *n* Saum *m*; (*decorative*) Biese *f* ● *vt* (*put*) stecken. ~ **in** *vt* hineinstecken; ~ **s.o. in** jdn zudecken ● *vi* (*fam: eat*) zulangen. ~ **up** *vt* hochkrempeln ⟨*sleeves*⟩; (*in bed*) zudecken

Tuesday /'tjuːzdeɪ/ *n* Dienstag *m*

tuft /tʌft/ *n* Büschel *nt*

tug /tʌg/ *n* Ruck *m*; (*Naut*) Schleppdampfer *m* ● *v* (*pt/pp* **tugged**) ● *vt* ziehen ● *vi* zerren (**at** an + *dat*). ~ **of war** *n* Tauziehen *nt*

tuition /tjuː'ɪʃn/ *n* Unterricht *m*

tulip /'tjuːlɪp/ *n* Tulpe *f*

tumble /'tʌmbl/ *n* Sturz *m* ● *vi* fallen; ~ **to sth** (*fam*) etw kapieren. ~**down** *a* verfallen. ~**-drier** *n* Wäschetrockner *m*

tumbler /'tʌmblə(r)/ *n* Glas *nt*

tummy /'tʌmɪ/ *n* (*fam*) Magen *m*; (*abdomen*) Bauch *m*

tumour /'tjuːmə(r)/ *n* Geschwulst *f*, Tumor *m*

tumult /'tjuːmʌlt/ *n* Tumult *m*. ~**uous** /-'mʌltjʊəs/ *a* stürmisch

tuna /'tjuːnə/ *n* Thunfisch *m*

tune /tjuːn/ *n* Melodie *f*; **out of** ~ ⟨*instrument*⟩ verstimmt; **to the** ~ **of** (*fam*) in Höhe von ● *vt* stimmen; (*Techn*) einstellen. ~ **in** *vt* einstellen ● *vi* ~ **in to a station** einen Sender einstellen. ~ **up** *vi* (*Mus*) stimmen

tuneful /'tjuːnfl/ *a* melodisch

tunic /'tjuːnɪk/ *n* (*Mil*) Uniformjacke *f*; (*Sch*) Trägerkleid *nt*

Tunisia /tjuː'nɪzɪə/ *n* Tunesien *nt*

tunnel /'tʌnl/ *n* Tunnel *m* ● *vi* (*pt/pp* **tunnelled**) einen Tunnel graben

turban /'tɜːbən/ *n* Turban *m*

turbine /'tɜːbaɪn/ *n* Turbine *f*

turbot /'tɜːbət/ *n* Steinbutt *m*

turbulen|ce /'tɜːbjʊləns/ *n* Turbulenz *f*. ~**t** *a* stürmisch

tureen /tjʊə'riːn/ *n* Terrine *f*

turf /tɜːf/ *n* Rasen *m*; (*segment*) Rasenstück *nt*. ~ **out** *vt* (*fam*) rausschmeißen

'**turf accountant** *n* Buchmacher *m*

Turk /tɜːk/ *n* Türke *m*/Türkin *f*

turkey /'tɜːkɪ/ *n* Pute *f*, Truthahn *m*

Turk|ey *n* die Türkei. ~**ish** *a* türkisch

turmoil /'tɜːmɔɪl/ *n* Aufruhr *m*; (*confusion*) Durcheinander *nt*

turn /tɜːn/ *n* (*rotation*) Drehung *f*; (*in road*) Kurve *f*; (*change of direction*) Wende *f*; (*short walk*) Runde *f*; (*Theat*) Nummer *f*; (*fam: attack*) Anfall *m*; **do s.o. a good** ~ jdm einen guten Dienst erweisen; **take** ~**s** sich abwechseln; **in** ~ der Reihe nach; **out of** ~ außer der Reihe; **it's your** ~ du bist an der Reihe ● *vt* drehen; (~ *over*) wenden; (*reverse*) umdrehen; (*Techn*) drechseln ⟨*wood*⟩; ~ **the page** umblättern; ~ **the corner** um die Ecke biegen ● *vi* sich drehen; (~ *round*) sich umdrehen; ⟨*car:*⟩ wenden; ⟨*leaves:*⟩ sich färben; ⟨*weather:*⟩ umschlagen; (*become*) werden; ~ **right/left** nach rechts/ links abbiegen; ~ **to s.o.** sich an jdn wenden; **have** ~**ed against s.o.** gegen jdn sein. ~ **away** *vt* abweisen ● *vi* sich abwenden. ~ **down** *vt* herunterschlagen ⟨*collar*⟩; herunterdrehen ⟨*heat, gas*⟩; leiser stellen ⟨*sound*⟩; (*reject*) ablehnen; abweisen ⟨*person*⟩. ~ **in** *vt* einschlagen ⟨*edges*⟩ ● *vi* ⟨*car:*⟩ einbiegen; (*fam: go to bed*) ins Bett gehen. ~ **off** *vt* zudrehen ⟨*tap*⟩; ausschalten ⟨*light, radio*⟩; abstellen ⟨*water, gas, engine, machine*⟩ ● *vi* abbiegen. ~ **on** *vt* aufdrehen ⟨*tap*⟩; einschalten ⟨*light, radio*⟩; anstellen ⟨*water, gas, engine, machine*⟩. ~ **out** *vt* (*expel*) vertreiben, (*fam*) hinauswerfen; ausschalten ⟨*light*⟩; abdrehen ⟨*gas*⟩; (*produce*) produzieren; (*empty*) ausleeren; [gründlich] aufräumen ⟨*room, cupboard*⟩ ● *vi* (*go out*) hinausgehen; (*transpire*) sich herausstellen; ~ **out well/badly** gut/schlecht gehen. ~ **over** *vt* umdrehen ● *vi* sich umdrehen. ~ **up** *vt* hochschlagen ⟨*collar*⟩; aufdrehen ⟨*heat, gas*⟩; lauter stellen ⟨*sound, radio*⟩ ● *vi* auftauchen

turning /'tɜːnɪŋ/ *n* Abzweigung *f*. ~**point** *n* Wendepunkt *m*

turnip /'tɜːnɪp/ n weiße Rübe f

turn: ~**out** n (of people) Teilnahme f, Beteiligung f; (of goods) Produktion f. ~**over** n (Comm) Umsatz m; (of staff) Personalwechsel m. ~**pike** n (Amer) gebührenpflichtige Autobahn f. ~**stile** n Drehkreuz nt. ~**table** n Drehscheibe f; (on record-player) Plattenteller m. ~**up** n [Hosen]aufschlag m

turpentine /'tɜːpəntaɪn/ n Terpentin nt

turquoise /'tɜːkwɔɪz/ a türkis[farben] ● n (gem) Türkis m

turret /'tʌrɪt/ n Türmchen nt

turtle /'tɜːtl/ n Seeschildkröte f

tusk /tʌsk/ n Stoßzahn m

tussle /'tʌsl/ n Balgerei f; (fig) Streit m ● vi sich balgen

tutor /'tjuːtə(r)/ n [Privat]lehrer m

tuxedo /tʌk'siːdəʊ/ n (Amer) Smoking m

TV abbr of **television**

twaddle /'twɒdl/ n Geschwätz nt

twang /twæŋ/ n (in voice) Näseln nt ● vt zupfen

tweed /twiːd/ n Tweed m

tweezers /'twiːzəz/ npl Pinzette f

twelfth /twelfθ/ a zwölfte(r,s)

twelve /twelv/ a zwölf

twentieth /'twentɪɪθ/ a zwanzigste(r,s)

twenty /'twentɪ/ a zwanzig

twerp /twɜːp/ n (fam) Trottel m

twice /twaɪs/ adv zweimal

twiddle /'twɪdl/ vt drehen an (+ dat)

twig¹ /twɪg/ n Zweig m

twig² vt/i (pt/pp **twigged**) (fam) kapieren

twilight /'twaɪ-/ n Dämmerlicht nt

twin /twɪn/ n Zwilling m ● attrib Zwillings-. ~ **beds** npl zwei Einzelbetten pl

twine /twaɪn/ n Bindfaden m ● vi sich winden; ⟨plant:⟩ sich ranken

twinge /twɪndʒ/ n Stechen nt; ~ of conscience Gewissensbisse pl

twinkle /'twɪŋkl/ n Funkeln nt ● vi funkeln

twin 'town n Partnerstadt f

twirl /twɜːl/ vt/i herumwirbeln

twist /twɪst/ n Drehung f; (curve) Kurve f; (unexpected occurrence) überraschende Wendung f ● vt drehen; (distort) verdrehen; (fam: swindle) beschummeln; ~ **one's ankle** sich (dat) den Knöchel verrenken ● vi sich drehen; ⟨road:⟩ sich winden. ~**er** n (fam) Schwindler m

twit /twɪt/ n (fam) Trottel m

twitch /twɪtʃ/ n Zucken nt ● vi zucken

twitter /'twɪtə(r)/ n Zwitschern nt ● vi zwitschern

two /tuː/ a zwei

two: ~**-faced** a falsch. ~**-piece** a zweiteilig. ~**some** /-səm/ n Paar nt. ~**-way** a ~**-way traffic** Gegenverkehr m

tycoon /taɪ'kuːn/ n Magnat m

tying /'taɪɪŋ/ see **tie**

type /taɪp/ n Art f, Sorte f; (person) Typ m; (printing) Type f ● vt mit der Maschine schreiben, (fam) tippen ● vi maschineschreiben, (fam) tippen. ~**writer** n Schreibmaschine f. ~**written** a maschinegeschrieben

typhoid /'taɪfɔɪd/ n Typhus m

typical /'tɪpɪkl/ a, **-ly** adv typisch (of für)

typify /'tɪpɪfaɪ/ vt (pt/pp **-ied**) typisch sein für

typing /'taɪpɪŋ/ n Maschineschreiben nt. ~ **paper** n Schreibmaschinenpapier nt

typist /'taɪpɪst/ n Schreibkraft f

typography /taɪ'pɒgrəfɪ/ n Typographie f

tyrannical /tɪ'rænɪkl/ a tyrannisch

tyranny /'tɪrənɪ/ n Tyrannei f

tyrant /'taɪrənt/ n Tyrann m

tyre /'taɪə(r)/ n Reifen m

U

ubiquitous /juː'bɪkwɪtəs/ a allgegenwärtig; **be** ~ überall zu finden sein

udder /'ʌdə(r)/ n Euter nt

ugl|iness /'ʌglɪnɪs/ n Häßlichkeit f. ~**y** a (**-ier, -iest**) häßlich; (nasty) übel

UK abbr see **United Kingdom**

ulcer /'ʌlsə(r)/ n Geschwür nt

ulterior /ʌl'tɪərɪə(r)/ a ~ **motive** Hintergedanke m

ultimate /'ʌltɪmət/ a letzte(r,s); (final) endgültig; (fundamental) grundlegend, eigentlich. ~**ly** adv schließlich

ultimatum /ʌltɪ'meɪtəm/ n Ultimatum nt

ultrasound /'ʌltrə-/ n (Med) Ultraschall m

ultra'violet a ultraviolett

umbilical /ʌm'bɪlɪkl/ a ~ **cord** Nabelschnur f

umbrella /ʌm'brelə/ n [Regen]schirm m

umpire /'ʌmpaɪə(r)/ n Schiedsrichter m • vt/i Schiedsrichter sein (bei)

umpteen /ʌmp'ti:n/ a (fam) zig. ~th a (fam) zigste(r,s); for the ~th time zum zigsten Mal

un'able /ʌn-/ a be ~ to do sth etw nicht tun können

una'bridged a ungekürzt

unac'companied a ohne Begleitung; ⟨luggage⟩ unbegleitet

unac'countabl|e a unerklärlich. ~y adv unerklärlicherweise

unac'customed a ungewohnt; be ~ to sth etw nicht gewohnt sein

una'dulterated a unverfälscht, rein; (utter) völlig

un'aided a ohne fremde Hilfe

unalloyed /ʌnə'lɔɪd/ a (fig) ungetrübt

unanimity /ju:nə'nɪmətɪ/ n Einstimmigkeit f

unanimous /ju:'nænɪməs/ a, -ly adv einmütig; ⟨vote, decision⟩ einstimmig

un'armed a unbewaffnet; ~ combat Kampf m ohne Waffen

unas'suming a bescheiden

unat'tached a nicht befestigt; ⟨person⟩ ungebunden

unat'tended a unbeaufsichtigt

un'authorized a unbefugt

una'voidable a unvermeidlich

una'ware a be ~ of sth sich (dat) etw (gen) nicht bewußt sein. ~s /-eəz/ adv catch s.o. ~s jdn überraschen

un'balanced a unausgewogen; (mentally) unausgeglichen

un'bearable a, -bly adv unerträglich

unbeat|able /ʌn'bi:təbl/ a unschlagbar. ~en a ungeschlagen; ⟨record⟩ ungebrochen

unbeknown /ʌnbɪ'nəʊn/ a (fam) ~ to me ohne mein Wissen

unbe'lievable a unglaublich

un'bend vi (pt/pp -bent) (relax) aus sich herausgehen

un'biased a unvoreingenommen

un'block vt frei machen

un'bolt vt aufriegeln

un'breakable a unzerbrechlich

unbridled /ʌn'braɪdld/ a ungezügelt

un'burden vt ~ oneself (fig) sich aussprechen

un'button vt aufknöpfen

uncalled-for /ʌn'kɔ:ldfɔ:(r)/ a unangebracht

un'canny a unheimlich

un'ceasing a unaufhörlich

uncere'monious a, -ly adv formlos; (abrupt) brüsk

un'certain a (doubtful) ungewiß; ⟨origins⟩ unbestimmt; be ~ nicht sicher sein; in no ~ terms ganz eindeutig. ~ty n Ungewißheit f

un'changed a unverändert

un'charitable a lieblos

uncle /'ʌŋkl/ n Onkel m

un'comfortable a, -bly adv unbequem; feel ~ (fig) sich nicht wohl fühlen

un'common a ungewöhnlich

un'compromising a kompromißlos

uncon'ditional a, -ly adv bedingungslos

un'conscious a bewußtlos; (unintended) ungewollt; be ~ of sth sich (dat) etw (gen) nicht bewußt sein. ~ly adv unbewußt

uncon'ventional a unkonventionell

unco'operative a nicht hilfsbereit

un'cork vt entkorken

uncouth /ʌn'ku:θ/ a ungehobelt

un'cover vt aufdecken

unctuous /'ʌŋktjʊəs/ a, -ly adv salbungsvoll

unde'cided a unentschlossen; (not settled) nicht entschieden

undeniable /ʌndɪ'naɪəbl/ a, -bly adv unbestreitbar

under /'ʌndə(r)/ prep unter (+ dat/acc); ~ it darunter; ~ there da drunter; ~ repair in Reparatur; ~ construction im Bau; ~ age minderjährig; ~ way unterwegs; (fig) im Gange • adv darunter

'undercarriage n (Aviat) Fahrwerk nt, Fahrgestell nt

'underclothes npl Unterwäsche f

under'cover a geheim

'undercurrent n Unterströmung f; (fig) Unterton m

under'cut vt (pt/pp -cut) (Comm) unterbieten

'underdog n Unterlegene(r) m

under'done a nicht gar; (rare) nicht durchgebraten

under'estimate vt unterschätzen

under'fed a unterernährt

under'foot adv am Boden; trample ~ zertrampeln

under'go vt (pt -went, pp -gone) durchmachen; sich unterziehen (+ dat) ⟨operation, treatment⟩; ~ repairs repariert werden

under'graduate n Student(in) m(f)

under'ground¹ adv unter der Erde; ⟨mining⟩ unter Tage

'**underground**² *a* unterirdisch; (*secret*) Untergrund- ● *n* (*railway*) U-Bahn *f*. ~ **car park** *n* Tiefgarage *f*
'**undergrowth** *n* Unterholz *nt*
'**underhand** *a* hinterhältig
'**underlay** *n* Unterlage *f*
under'lie *vt* (*pt* -**lay**, *pp* -**lain**, *pres p* -**lying**) (*fig*) zugrundeliegen (+ *dat*)
under'line *vt* unterstreichen
underling /'ʌndəlɪŋ/ *n* (*pej*) Untergebene(r) *m/f*
under'lying *a* (*fig*) eigentlich
under'mine *vt* (*fig*) unterminieren, untergraben
underneath /ʌndə'niːθ/ *prep* unter (+ *dat/acc*); ~ **it** darunter ● *adv* darunter
'**underpants** *npl* Unterhose *f*
'**underpass** *n* Unterführung *f*
under'privileged *a* unterprivilegiert
under'rate *vt* unterschätzen
'**underseal** *n* (*Auto*) Unterbodenschutz *m*
'**undershirt** *n* (*Amer*) Unterhemd *nt*
understaffed /-'staːft/ *a* unterbesetzt
under'stand *vt/i* (*pt/pp* -**stood**) verstehen; **I** ~ **that** . . . (*have heard*) ich habe gehört, daß . . . ~**able** /-əbl/ *a* verständlich. ~**ably** /-əblɪ/ *adv* verständlicherweise
under'standing *a* verständnisvoll ● *n* Verständnis *nt*; (*agreement*) Vereinbarung *f*; **reach an** ~ sich verständigen; **on the** ~ **that** unter der Voraussetzung, daß
'**understatement** *n* Untertreibung *f*
'**understudy** *n* (*Theat*) Ersatzspieler(in) *m(f)*
under'take *vt* (*pt* -**took**, *pp* -**taken**) unternehmen; ~ **to do sth** sich verpflichten, etw zu tun
'**undertaker** *n* Leichenbestatter *m*; [**firm of**] ~**s** Bestattungsinstitut *nt*
under'taking *n* Unternehmen *nt*; (*promise*) Versprechen *nt*
'**undertone** *n* (*fig*) Unterton *m*; **in an** ~ mit gedämpfter Stimme
under'value *vt* unterbewerten
'**underwater**¹ *a* Unterwasser-
under'water² *adv* unter Wasser
'**underwear** *n* Unterwäsche *f*
under'weight *a* untergewichtig; **be** ~ Untergewicht haben
'**underworld** *n* Unterwelt *f*
'**underwriter** *n* Versicherer *m*
unde'sirable *a* unerwünscht
undies /'ʌndɪz/ *npl* (*fam*) [Damen]unterwäsche *f*

un'dignified *a* würdelos
un'do *vt* (*pt* -**did**, *pp* -**done**) aufmachen; (*fig*) ungeschehen machen; (*ruin*) zunichte machen
un'done *a* offen; (*not accomplished*) unerledigt
un'doubted *a* unzweifelhaft. ~**ly** *adv* zweifellos
un'dress *vt* ausziehen; **get** ~**ed** sich ausziehen ● *vi* sich ausziehen
un'due *a* übermäßig
undulating /'ʌndjʊleɪtɪŋ/ *a* Wellen-; ⟨*country*⟩ wellig
un'duly *adv* übermäßig
un'dying *a* ewig
un'earth *vt* ausgraben; (*fig*) zutage bringen. ~**ly** *a* unheimlich; **at an** ~**ly hour** (*fam*) in aller Herrgottsfrühe
un'eas|e *n* Unbehagen *nt*. ~**y** *a* unbehaglich; **I feel** ~**y** mir ist unbehaglich zumute
un'eatable *a* ungenießbar
uneco'nomic *a*, -**ally** *adv* unwirtschaftlich
uneco'nomical *a* verschwenderisch
unem'ployed *a* arbeitslos ● *npl* **the** ~ die Arbeitslosen
unem'ployment *n* Arbeitslosigkeit *f*. ~ **benefit** *n* Arbeitslosenunterstützung *f*
un'ending *a* endlos
un'equal *a* unterschiedlich; ⟨*struggle*⟩ ungleich; **be** ~ **to a task** einer Aufgabe nicht gewachsen sein. ~**ly** *adv* ungleichmäßig
unequivocal /ʌnɪ'kwɪvəkl/ *a*, -**ly** *adv* eindeutig
unerring /ʌn'ɜːrɪŋ/ *a* unfehlbar
un'ethical *a* unmoralisch; **be** ~ gegen das Berufsethos verstoßen
un'even *a* uneben; (*unequal*) ungleich; (*not regular*) ungleichmäßig; ⟨*number*⟩ ungerade. ~**ly** *adv* ungleichmäßig
unex'pected *a*, -**ly** *adv* unerwartet
un'failing *a* nie versagend
un'fair *a*, -**ly** *adv* ungerecht, unfair. ~**ness** *n* Ungerechtigkeit *f*
un'faithful *a* untreu
unfa'miliar *a* ungewohnt; (*unknown*) unbekannt
un'fasten *vt* aufmachen; (*detach*) losmachen
un'favourable *a* ungünstig
un'feeling *a* gefühllos
un'finished *a* unvollendet; ⟨*business*⟩ unerledigt

un'fit a ungeeignet; (*incompetent*) unfähig; (*Sport*) nicht fit; ~ **for work** arbeitsunfähig

unflinching /ʌnˈflɪntʃɪŋ/ a unerschrocken

un'fold vt auseinanderfalten, entfalten; (*spread out*) ausbreiten ● vi sich entfalten

unfore'seen a unvorhergesehen

unforgettable /ʌnfəˈgetəbl/ a unvergeßlich

unforgivable /ʌnfəˈgɪvəbl/ a unverzeihlich

un'fortunate a unglücklich; (*unfavourable*) ungünstig; (*regrettable*) bedauerlich; **be** ~ ⟨person:⟩ Pech haben. ~**ly** adv leider

un'founded a unbegründet

unfurl /ʌnˈfɜːl/ vt entrollen ● vi sich entrollen

un'furnished a unmöbliert

ungainly /ʌnˈgeɪnlɪ/ a unbeholfen

ungodly /ʌnˈgɒdlɪ/ a gottlos; **at an** ~ **hour** (*fam*) in aller Herrgottsfrühe

un'grateful a, **-ly** adv undankbar

un'happi|**ly** adv unglücklich; (*unfortunately*) leider. ~**ness** n Kummer m

un'happy a unglücklich; (*not content*) unzufrieden

un'harmed a unverletzt

un'healthy a ungesund

un'hook vt vom Haken nehmen; aufhaken ⟨dress⟩

un'hurt a unverletzt

unhy'gienic a unhygienisch

unicorn /ˈjuːnɪkɔːn/ n Einhorn nt

unification /juːnɪfɪˈkeɪʃn/ n Einigung f

uniform ● /ˈjuːnɪfɔːm/ a, **-ly** adv einheitlich ● n Uniform f

unify /ˈjuːnɪfaɪ/ vt (pt/pp **-ied**) einigen

uni'lateral /juːnɪ-/ a, **-ly** adv einseitig

uni'maginable a unvorstellbar

unim'portant a unwichtig

unin'habited a unbewohnt

unin'tentional a, **-ly** adv unabsichtlich

union /ˈjuːnɪən/ n Vereinigung f; (*Pol*) Union f; (*trade* ~) Gewerkschaft f. ~**ist** n (*Pol*) Unionist m

unique /juːˈniːk/ a einzigartig. ~**ly** adv einmalig

unison /ˈjuːnɪsn/ n in ~ einstimmig

unit /ˈjuːnɪt/ n Einheit f; (*Math*) Einer m; (*of furniture*) Teil nt, Element nt

unite /juːˈnaɪt/ vt vereinigen ● vi sich vereinigen

united /juːˈnaɪtɪd/ a einig. **U**~ **'Kingdom** n Vereinigtes Königreich nt. **U**~ **'Nations** n Vereinte Nationen pl. **U**~ **States [of America]** n Vereinigte Staaten pl [von Amerika]

unity /ˈjuːnətɪ/ n Einheit f; (*harmony*) Einigkeit f

universal /juːnɪˈvɜːsl/ a, **-ly** adv allgemein

universe /ˈjuːnɪvɜːs/ n [Welt]all nt, Universum nt

university /juːnɪˈvɜːsətɪ/ n Universität f ● attrib Universitäts-

un'just a, **-ly** adv ungerecht

unkempt /ʌnˈkempt/ a ungepflegt

un'kind a, **-ly** adv unfreundlich; (*harsh*) häßlich. ~**ness** n Unfreundlichkeit f; Häßlichkeit f

un'known a unbekannt

un'lawful a, **-ly** adv gesetzwidrig

unleaded /ʌnˈledɪd/ a bleifrei

un'leash vt (*fig*) entfesseln

unless /ənˈles/ conj wenn ... nicht; ~ **I am mistaken** wenn ich mich nicht irre

un'like a nicht ähnlich, unähnlich; (*not the same*) ungleich ● prep im Gegensatz zu (+ dat)

un'likely a unwahrscheinlich

un'limited a unbegrenzt

un'load vt entladen; ausladen ⟨luggage⟩

un'lock vt aufschließen

un'lucky a unglücklich; ⟨day, number⟩ Unglücks-; **be** ~ Pech haben; ⟨thing:⟩ Unglück bringen

un'manned a unbemannt

un'married a unverheiratet. ~ **'mother** n ledige Mutter f

un'mask vt (*fig*) entlarven

unmistakable /ʌnmɪˈsteɪkəbl/ a, **-bly** adv unverkennbar

un'mitigated a vollkommen

un'natural a, **-ly** adv unnatürlich; (*not normal*) nicht normal

un'necessary a, **-ily** adv unnötig

un'noticed a unbemerkt

unob'tainable a nicht erhältlich

unob'trusive a, **-ly** adv unaufdringlich; ⟨thing⟩ unauffällig

unof'ficial a, **-ly** adv inoffiziell

un'pack vt/i auspacken

un'paid a unbezahlt

un'palatable a ungenießbar

un'paralleled a beispiellos

un'pick vt auftrennen

un'pleasant a, **-ly** adv unangenehm. ~**ness** n (*bad feeling*) Ärger m

un'plug vt (pt/pp **-plugged**) den Stecker herausziehen von

un'popular a unbeliebt

un'precedented a beispiellos

unpre'dictable a unberechenbar

unpre'meditated a nicht vorsätzlich

unpre'pared a nicht vorbereitet

unprepos'sessing a wenig attraktiv

unpre'tentious a bescheiden

un'principled a skrupellos

unpro'fessional a be ~ gegen das Berufsethos verstoßen; (Sport) unsportlich sein

un'profitable a unrentabel

un'qualified a unqualifiziert; (fig: absolute) uneingeschränkt

un'questionable a unbezweifelbar; ⟨right⟩ unbestreitbar

unravel /ʌnˈrævl/ vt (pt/pp **-ravelled**) entwirren; (Knitting) aufziehen

un'real a unwirklich

un'reasonable a unvernünftig; be ~ zuviel verlangen

unre'lated a unzusammenhängend; be ~ nicht verwandt sein; ⟨events:⟩ nicht miteinander zusammenhängen

unre'liable a unzuverlässig

unrequited /ʌnrɪˈkwaɪtɪd/ a unerwidert

unreservedly /ʌnrɪˈzɜːvɪdlɪ/ adv uneingeschränkt; (frankly) offen

un'rest n Unruhen pl

un'rivalled a unübertroffen

un'roll vt aufrollen ● vi sich aufrollen

unruly /ʌnˈruːlɪ/ a ungebärdig

un'safe a nicht sicher

un'said a ungesagt

un'salted a ungesalzen

unsatis'factory a unbefriedigend

un'savoury a unangenehm; (fig) unerfreulich

unscathed /ʌnˈskeɪðd/ a unversehrt

un'screw vt abschrauben

un'scrupulous a skrupellos

un'seemly a unschicklich

un'selfish a selbstlos

un'settled a ungeklärt; ⟨weather⟩ unbeständig; ⟨bill⟩ unbezahlt

unshakeable /ʌnˈʃeɪkəbl/ a unerschütterlich

unshaven /ʌnˈʃeɪvn/ a unrasiert

unsightly /ʌnˈsaɪtlɪ/ a unansehnlich

un'skilled a ungelernt; ⟨work⟩ unqualifiziert

un'sociable a ungesellig

unso'phisticated a einfach

un'sound a krank, nicht gesund; ⟨building⟩ nicht sicher; ⟨advice⟩ unzuverlässig; ⟨reasoning⟩ nicht stichhaltig; **of ~ mind** unzurechnungsfähig

unspeakable /ʌnˈspiːkəbl/ a unbeschreiblich

un'stable a nicht stabil; (mentally) labil

un'steady a, **-ily** adv unsicher; (wobbly) wackelig

un'stuck a come ~ sich lösen; (fam: fail) scheitern

unsuc'cessful a, **-ly** adv erfolglos; be ~ keinen Erfolg haben

un'suitable a ungeeignet; (inappropriate) unpassend; (for weather, activity) unzweckmäßig

unsu'specting a ahnungslos

un'sweetened a ungesüßt

unthinkable /ʌnˈθɪŋkəbl/ a unvorstellbar

un'tidiness n Unordentlichkeit f

un'tidy a, **-ily** adv unordentlich

un'tie vt aufbinden; losbinden ⟨person, boat, horse⟩

until /ənˈtɪl/ prep bis (+ acc); **not ~** erst; **~ the evening** bis zum Abend; **~ his arrival** bis zu seiner Ankunft ● conj bis; **not ~** erst wenn; (in past) erst als

untimely /ʌnˈtaɪmlɪ/ a ungelegen; (premature) vorzeitig

un'tiring a unermüdlich

un'told a unermeßlich

unto'ward a ungünstig; (unseemly) ungehörig; **if nothing ~ happens** wenn nichts dazwischenkommt

un'true a unwahr; **that's ~** das ist nicht wahr

unused¹ /ʌnˈjuːzd/ a unbenutzt; (not utilized) ungenutzt

unused² /ʌnˈjuːst/ a be ~ **to sth** etw nicht gewohnt sein

un'usual a, **-ly** adv ungewöhnlich

un'veil vt enthüllen

un'versed a nicht bewandert (**in** in + dat)

un'wanted a unerwünscht

un'warranted a ungerechtfertigt

un'welcome a unwillkommen

un'well a be or feel ~ sich nicht wohl fühlen

unwieldy /ʌnˈwiːldɪ/ a sperrig

un'willing a, **-ly** adv widerwillig; be ~ **to do sth** etw nicht tun wollen

un'wind v (pt/pp **unwound**) ● vt abwickeln ● vi sich abwickeln; (fam: relax) sich entspannen

un'wise *a*, **-ly** *adv* unklug

unwitting /ʌn'wɪtɪŋ/ *a*, **-ly** *adv* unwissentlich

un'worthy *a* unwürdig

un'wrap *vt* (*pt/pp* **-wrapped**) auswickeln; auspacken ⟨*present*⟩

un'written *a* ungeschrieben

up /ʌp/ *adv* oben; (*with movement*) nach oben; (*not in bed*) auf; ⟨*collar*⟩ hochgeklappt; ⟨*road*⟩ aufgerissen; ⟨*price*⟩ gestiegen; ⟨*curtains*⟩ aufgehängt; ⟨*shelves*⟩ angebracht; ⟨*notice*⟩ angeschlagen; ⟨*tent*⟩ aufgebaut; ⟨*building*⟩ gebaut; **be up for sale** zu verkaufen sein; **up there** da oben; **up to** (*as far as*) bis; **time's up** die Zeit ist um; **what's up?** (*fam*) was ist los? **what's he up to?** (*fam*) was hat er vor? **I don't feel up to it** ich fühle mich dem nicht gewachsen; **be one up on s.o.** (*fam*) jdm etwas vorolaushaben; **go up** hinaufgehen; **come up** heraufkommen ● *prep* **be up on sth** [oben] auf etw (*dat*) sein; **up the mountain** oben am Berg; (*movement*) den Berg hinauf; **be up the tree** oben im Baum sein; **up the road** die Straße entlang; **up the river** stromaufwärts; **go up the stairs** die Treppe hinaufgehen; **be up the pub** (*fam*) in der Kneipe sein

'upbringing *n* Erziehung *f*

up'date *vt* auf den neuesten Stand bringen

up'grade *vt* aufstufen

upheaval /ʌp'hi:vl/ *n* Unruhe *f*; (*Pol*) Umbruch *m*

up'hill *a* (*fig*) mühsam ● *adv* bergauf

up'hold *vt* (*pt/pp* **upheld**) unterstützen; bestätigen ⟨*verdict*⟩

upholster /ʌp'həʊlstə(r)/ *vt* polstern. **~er** *n* Polsterer *m*. **~y** *n* Polsterung *f*

'upkeep *n* Unterhalt *m*

up-'market *a* anspruchsvoll

upon /ə'pɒn/ *prep* auf (+ *dat/acc*)

upper /'ʌpə(r)/ *a* obere(r,s); ⟨*deck, jaw, lip*⟩ Ober-; **have the ~ hand** die Oberhand haben ● *n* (*of shoe*) Obermaterial *nt*

upper: **~ circle** *n* zweiter Rang *m*. **~ class** *n* Oberschicht *f*. **~most** *a* oberste(r,s)

'upright *a* aufrecht ● *n* Pfosten *m*

'uprising *n* Aufstand *m*

'uproar *n* Aufruhr *m*

up'root *vt* entwurzeln

up'set[1] *vt* (*pt/pp* **upset**, *pres p* **upsetting**) umstoßen; (*spill*) verschütten; durcheinanderbringen ⟨*plan*⟩; (*distress*) erschüttern; ⟨*food:*⟩ nicht bekommen (+ *dat*); **get ~ about sth** sich über etw (*acc*) aufregen; **be very ~** sehr bestürzt sein

'upset[2] *n* Aufregung *f*; **have a stomach ~** einen verdorbenen Magen haben

'upshot *n* Ergebnis *nt*

upside 'down *adv* verkehrt herum; **turn ~** umdrehen

up'stairs[1] *adv* oben; ⟨*go*⟩ nach oben

'upstairs[2] *a* im Obergeschoß

'upstart *n* Emporkömmling *m*

up'stream *adv* stromaufwärts

'upsurge *n* Zunahme *f*

'uptake *n* **slow on the ~** schwer von Begriff; **be quick on the ~** schnell begreifen

up'tight *a* nervös

'upturn *n* Aufschwung *m*

upward /'ʌpwəd/ *a* nach oben; ⟨*movement*⟩ Aufwärts-; **~ slope** Steigung *f* ● **~[s]** *adv* aufwärts, nach oben

uranium /jʊ'reɪnɪəm/ *n* Uran *nt*

urban /'ɜ:bən/ *a* städtisch

urbane /ɜ:'beɪn/ *a* weltmännisch

urge /ɜ:dʒ/ *n* Trieb *m*, Drang *m* ● *vt* drängen; **~ on** antreiben

urgen|cy /'ɜ:dʒənsɪ/ *n* Dringlichkeit *f*. **~t** *a*, **-ly** *adv* dringend

urinate /'jʊərɪneɪt/ *vi* urinieren

urine /'jʊərɪn/ *n* Urin *m*, Harn *m*

urn /ɜ:n/ *n* Urne *f*; (*for tea*) Teemaschine *f*

us /ʌs/ *pron* uns; **it's us** wir sind es

US[A] *abbr* USA *pl*

usable /'ju:zəbl/ *a* brauchbar

usage /'ju:zɪdʒ/ *n* Brauch *m*; (*of word*) [Sprach]gebrauch *m*

use[1] /ju:s/ *n* (*see* **use**[2]) Benutzung *f*; Verwendung *f*; Gebrauch *m*; **be of ~** nützlich sein; **be of no ~** nichts nützen; **make ~ of** Gebrauch machen von; (*exploit*) ausnutzen; **it is no ~** es hat keinen Zweck; **what's the ~?** wozu?

use[2] /ju:z/ *vt* benutzen ⟨*implement, room, lift*⟩; verwenden ⟨*ingredient, method, book, money*⟩; gebrauchen ⟨*words, force, brains*⟩; **~ [up]** aufbrauchen

used[1] /ju:zd/ *a* benutzt; ⟨*car*⟩ Gebraucht-

used[2] /ju:st/ *pt* **be ~ to sth** an etw (*acc*) gewöhnt sein; **get ~ to** sich gewöhnen an (+ *acc*); **he ~ to say** hat immer gesagt; **he ~ to live here** er hat früher hier gewohnt

useful /'ju:sfl/ *a* nützlich. **~ness** *n*
Nützlichkeit *f*

useless /'ju:slıs/ *a* nutzlos; (*not
usable*) unbrauchbar; (*pointless*)
zwecklos

user /'ju:zə(r)/ *n* Benutzer(in) *m(f)*.
~-'friendly *a* benutzerfreundlich

usher /'ʌʃə(r)/ *n* Platzanweiser *m*; (*in
court*) Gerichtsdiener *m* ● *vt* ~ **in**
hineinführen

usherette /ʌʃə'ret/ *n* Platzanweise-
rin *f*

USSR *abbr* UdSSR *f*

usual /'ju:ʒʊəl/ *a* üblich. **~ly** *adv*
gewöhnlich

usurp /ju:'zɜ:p/ *vt* sich (*dat*) wider-
rechtlich aneignen

utensil /ju:'tensl/ *n* Gerät *nt*

uterus /'ju:tərəs/ *n* Gebärmutter *f*

utilitarian /ju:tılı'teərıən/ *a* zweckmäßig

utility /ju:'tılətı/ *a* Gebrauchs- ● *n*
Nutzen *m*. ~ **room** *n* ≈ Waschküche
f

utiliz|ation /ju:tılaı'zeıʃn/ *n* Nutzung
f. **~e** /'ju:tılaız/ *vt* nutzen

utmost /'ʌtməʊst/ *a* äußerste(r,s),
größte(r,s) ● *n* **do one's** ~ sein möglichstes tun

utter¹ /'ʌtə(r)/ *a*, **-ly** *adv* völlig

utter² *vt* von sich geben 〈*sigh,
sound*〉; sagen 〈*word*〉. **~ance** /-əns/ *n*
Äußerung *f*

U-turn /'ju:-/ *n* (*fig*) Kehrtwendung *f*;
'no ~s' (*Auto*) 'Wenden verboten'

V

vacan|cy /'veıkənsı/ *n* (*job*) freie
Stelle *f*; (*room*) freies Zimmer *nt*;
'no ~cies' 'belegt'. **~t** *a* frei; 〈*look*〉
[gedanken]leer

vacate /və'keıt/ *vt* räumen

vacation /və'keıʃn/ *n* (*Univ & Amer*)
Ferien *pl*

vaccinat|e /'væksıneıt/ *vt* impfen.
~ion /-'neıʃn/ *n* Impfung *f*

vaccine /'væksi:n/ *n* Impfstoff *m*

vacuum /'vækjʊəm/ *n* Vakuum *nt*,
luftleerer Raum *m* ● *vt* saugen. **~
cleaner** *n* Staubsauger *m*. **~ flask** *n*
Thermosflasche (P) *f*. **~-packed** *a*
vakuumverpackt

vagaries /'veıgərız/ *npl* Launen *pl*

vagina /və'dʒaınə/ *n* (*Anat*) Scheide *f*

vagrant /'veıgrənt/ *n* Landstreicher
m

vague /veıg/ *a* (**-r, -st**), **-ly** *adv* vage;
〈*outline*〉 verschwommen

vain /veın/ *a* (**-er, -est**) eitel; 〈*hope,
attempt*〉 vergeblich; **in ~** vergeblich. **~ly** *adv* vergeblich

vale /veıl/ *n* (*liter*) Tal *nt*

valet /'væleı/ *n* Kammerdiener *m*

valiant /'vælıənt/ *a*, **-ly** *adv* tapfer

valid /'vælıd/ *a* gültig; 〈*claim*〉berech-
tigt; 〈*argument*〉 stichhaltig; 〈*reason*〉 triftig. **~ate** *vt* (*confirm*) bestätigen. **~ity** /və'lıdətı/ *n* Gültigkeit *f*

valley /'vælı/ *n* Tal *nt*

valour /'vælə(r)/ *n* Tapferkeit *f*

valuable /'væljʊəbl/ *a* wertvoll. **~s**
npl Wertsachen *pl*

valuation /vælju'eıʃn/ *n* Schätzung *f*

value /'vælju:/ *n* Wert *m*; (*usefulness*)
Nutzen *m* ● *vt* schätzen. ~ **'added
tax** *n* Mehrwertsteuer *f*

valve /vælv/ *n* Ventil *nt*; (*Anat*)
Klappe *f*; (*Electr*) Röhre *f*

vampire /'væmpaıə(r)/ *n* Vampir *m*

van /væn/ *n* Lieferwagen *m*

vandal /'vændl/ *n* Rowdy *m*. **~ism**
/-ızm/ *n* mutwillige Zerstörung *f*.
~ize *vt* demolieren

vanilla /və'nılə/ *n* Vanille *f*

vanish /'vænıʃ/ *vi* verschwinden

vanity /'vænətı/ *n* Eitelkeit *f*. ~ **bag** *n*
Kosmetiktäschchen *nt*

vantage-point /'va:ntıdʒ-/ *n* Aussichtspunkt *m*

vapour /'veıpə(r)/ *n* Dampf *m*

variable /'veərıəbl/ *a* unbeständig;
(*Math*) variabel; (*adjustable*)
regulierbar

variance /'veərıəns/ *n* **be at** ~ nicht
übereinstimmen

variant /'veərıənt/ *n* Variante *f*

variation /veərı'eıʃn/ *n* Variation *f*;
(*difference*) Unterschied *m*

varicose /'værıkəʊs/ *a* ~ **veins** *pl*
Krampfadern *pl*

varied /'veərıd/ *a* vielseitig; 〈*diet*〉
abwechslungsreich

variety /və'raıətı/ *n* Abwechslung *f*;
(*quantity*) Vielfalt *f*; (*Comm*) Auswahl *f*; (*type*) Art *f*; (*Bot*) Abart *f*;
(*Theat*) Varieté *nt*

various /'veərıəs/ *a* verschiedene.
~ly *adv* unterschiedlich

varnish /'va:nıʃ/ *n* Lack *m* ● *vt*
lackieren

vary /'veərı/ *vi* (*pt/pp* **-ied**) sich
ändern; (*be different*) verschieden
sein ● *vt* [ver]ändern; (*add variety
to*) abwechslungsreicher gestalten.

~ing *a* wechselnd; *(different)* unterschiedlich

vase /vɑːz/ *n* Vase *f*

vast /vɑːst/ *a* riesig; ⟨*expanse*⟩ weit. **~ly** *adv* gewaltig

vat /væt/ *n* Bottich *m*

VAT /viːeˈtiː, væt/ *abbr* (**value added tax**) Mehrwertsteuer *f*, MwSt.

vault[1] /vɔːlt/ *n* (*roof*) Gewölbe *nt*; (*in bank*) Tresor *m*; (*tomb*) Gruft *f*

vault[2] *n* Sprung *m* ● *vt/i* **~ [over]** springen über

VDU *abbr* (**visual display unit**) Bildschirmgerät *nt*

veal /viːl/ *n* Kalbfleisch *nt* ● *attrib* Kalbs-

veer /vɪə(r)/ *vi* sich drehen; (*Naut*) abdrehen; (*Auto*) ausscheren

vegetable /ˈvedʒtəbl/ *n* Gemüse *nt*; **~s** *pl* Gemüse *nt* ● *attrib* Gemüse-; ⟨*oil, fat*⟩ Pflanzen-

vegetarian /vedʒɪˈteərɪən/ *a* vegetarisch ● *n* Vegetarier(in) *m(f)*

vegetat|e /ˈvedʒɪteɪt/ *vi* dahinvegetieren. **~ion** /-ˈteɪʃn/ *n* Vegetation *f*

vehemen|ce /ˈviːəməns/ *n* Heftigkeit *f*. **~t** *a*, **-ly** *adv* heftig

vehicle /ˈviːɪkl/ *n* Fahrzeug *nt*; (*fig: medium*) Mittel *nt*

veil /veɪl/ *n* Schleier *m* ● *vt* verschleiern

vein /veɪn/ *n* Ader *f*; (*mood*) Stimmung *f*; (*manner*) Art *f*; **~s and arteries** Venen und Arterien. **~ed** *a* geädert

Velcro (P) /ˈvelkrəʊ/ *n* **~ fastening** Klettverschluß *m*

velocity /vɪˈlɒsətɪ/ *n* Geschwindigkeit *f*

velvet /ˈvelvɪt/ *n* Samt *m*. **~y** *a* samtig

vending-machine /ˈvendɪŋ-/ *n* [Verkaufs]automat *m*

vendor /ˈvendə(r)/ *n* Verkäufer(in) *m(f)*

veneer /vəˈnɪə(r)/ *n* Furnier *nt*; (*fig*) Tünche *f*. **~ed** *a* furniert

venerable /ˈvenərəbl/ *a* ehrwürdig

venereal /vɪˈnɪərɪəl/ *a* **~ disease** Geschlechtskrankheit *f*

Venetian /vəˈniːʃn/ *a* venezianisch. **v~ blind** *n* Jalousie *f*

vengeance /ˈvendʒəns/ *n* Rache *f*; **with a ~** (*fam*) gewaltig

Venice /ˈvenɪs/ *n* Venedig *nt*

venison /ˈvenɪsn/ *n* (*Culin*) Wild *nt*

venom /ˈvenəm/ *n* Gift *nt*; (*fig*) Haß *m*. **~ous** /-əs/ *a* giftig

vent[1] /vent/ *n* Öffnung *f*; (*fig*) Ventil *nt*; **give ~ to** Luft machen (+*dat*) ● *vt* Luft machen (+*dat*)

vent[2] *n* (*in jacket*) Schlitz *m*

ventilat|e /ˈventɪleɪt/ *vt* belüften. **~ion** /-ˈleɪʃn/ *n* Belüftung *f*; (*installation*) Lüftung. *f*. **~or** *n* Lüftungsvorrichtung *f*; (*Med*) Beatmungsgerät *nt*

ventriloquist /venˈtrɪləkwɪst/ *n* Bauchredner *m*

venture /ˈventʃə(r)/ *n* Unternehmung *f* ● *vt* wagen ● *vi* sich wagen

venue /ˈvenjuː/ *n* Treffpunkt *m*; (*for event*) Veranstaltungsort *m*

veranda /vəˈrændə/ *n* Veranda *f*

verb /vɜːb/ *n* Verb *nt*. **~al** *a*, **-ly** *adv* mündlich; (*Gram*) verbal

verbatim /vɜːˈbeɪtɪm/ *a* & *adv* [wort]wörtlich

verbose /vɜːˈbəʊs/ *a* weitschweifig

verdict /ˈvɜːdɪkt/ *n* Urteil *nt*

verge /vɜːdʒ/ *n* Rand *m*; **be on the ~ of doing sth** im Begriff sein, etw zu tun ● *vi* **~ on** (*fig*) grenzen an (+ *acc*)

verger /ˈvɜːdʒə(r)/ *n* Küster *m*

verify /ˈverɪfaɪ/ *vt* (*pt/pp* **-ied**) überprüfen; (*confirm*) bestätigen

vermin /ˈvɜːmɪn/ *n* Ungeziefer *nt*

vermouth /ˈvɜːməθ/ *n* Wermut *m*

vernacular /vəˈnækjʊlə(r)/ *n* Landessprache *f*

versatil|e /ˈvɜːsətaɪl/ *a* vielseitig. **~ity** /-ˈtɪlətɪ/ *n* Vielseitigkeit *f*

verse /vɜːs/ *n* Strophe *f*; (*of Bible*) Vers *m*; (*poetry*) Lyrik *f*

version /ˈvɜːʃn/ *n* Version *f*; (*translation*) Übersetzung *f*; (*model*) Modell *nt*

versus /ˈvɜːsəs/ *prep* gegen (+ *acc*)

vertebra /ˈvɜːtɪbrə/ *n* (*pl* **-brae** /-briː/) (*Anat*) Wirbel *m*

vertical /ˈvɜːtɪkl/ *a*, **-ly** *adv* senkrecht ● *n* Senkrechte *f*

vertigo /ˈvɜːtɪgəʊ/ *n* (*Med*) Schwindel *m*

verve /vɜːv/ *n* Schwung *m*

very /ˈverɪ/ *adv* sehr; **~ much** sehr; (*quantity*) sehr viel; **~ little** sehr wenig; **~ probably** höchstwahrscheinlich; **at the ~ most** allerhöchstens ● *a* (*mere*) bloß; **the ~ first** der/die/das allererste; **the ~ thing** genau das Richtige; **at the ~ end/ beginning** ganz am Ende/Anfang; **only a ~ little** nur ein ganz kleines bißchen

vessel /'vesl/ n Schiff nt; (receptacle & Anat) Gefäß nt

vest /vest/ n [Unter]hemd nt; (Amer: waistcoat) Weste f ● vt ~ sth in s.o. jdm etw verleihen; **have a ~ed interest in sth** ein persönliches Interesse an etw (dat) haben

vestige /'vestɪdʒ/ n Spur f

vestment /'vestmənt/ n (Relig) Gewand nt

vestry /'vestrɪ/ n Sakristei f

vet /vet/ n Tierarzt m /-ärztin f ● vt (pt/pp **vetted**) überprüfen

veteran /'vetərən/ n Veteran m. ~**car** n Oldtimer m

veterinary /'vetərɪnərɪ/ a tierärztlich. ~ **surgeon** n Tierarzt m /-ärztin f

veto /'viːtəʊ/ n (pl **-es**) Veto nt ● vt sein Veto einlegen gegen

vex /veks/ vt ärgern. ~**ation** /-'seɪʃn/ n Ärger m. ~**ed** a verärgert; ~**ed question** vieldiskutierte Frage f

VHF abbr (**very high frequency**) UKW

via /'vaɪə/ prep über (+ acc)

viable /'vaɪəbl/ a lebensfähig; (fig) realisierbar; ⟨firm⟩ rentabel

viaduct /'vaɪədʌkt/ n Viadukt nt

vibrant /'vaɪbrənt/ a (fig) lebhaft

vibrat|e /vaɪ'breɪt/ vi vibrieren. ~**ion** /-'breɪʃn/ n Vibrieren nt

vicar /'vɪkə(r)/ n Pfarrer m. ~**age** /-rɪdʒ/ n Pfarrhaus nt

vicarious /vɪ'keərɪəs/ a nachempfunden

vice[1] /vaɪs/ n Laster nt

vice[2] n (Techn) Schraubstock m

vice 'chairman n stellvertretender Vorsitzender m

vice 'president n Vizepräsident m

vice versa /vaɪsɪ'vɜːsə/ adv umgekehrt

vicinity /vɪ'sɪnɪtɪ/ n Umgebung f; **in the ~ of** in der Nähe von

vicious /'vɪʃəs/ a, **-ly** adv boshaft; ⟨animal⟩ bösartig. ~ **'circle** n Teufelskreis m

victim /'vɪktɪm/ n Opfer nt. ~**ize** vt schikanieren

victor /'vɪktə(r)/ n Sieger m

victor|ious /vɪk'tɔːrɪəs/ a siegreich. ~**y** /'vɪktərɪ/ n Sieg m

video /'vɪdɪəʊ/ n Video nt; (recorder) Videorecorder m ● **attrib** Video- ● vt [auf Videoband] aufnehmen

video: ~ **cas'sette** n Videokassette f. ~ **game** n Videospiel nt. ~ **'nasty** n Horrorvideo nt. ~ **recorder** n Videorecorder m

vie /vaɪ/ vi (pres p **vying**) wetteifern

Vienn|a /vɪ'enə/ n Wien nt. ~**ese** /vɪə'niːz/ a Wiener

view /vjuː/ n Sicht f; (scene) Aussicht f, Blick m; (picture, opinion) Ansicht f; **in my ~** meiner Ansicht nach; **in ~ of** angesichts (+ gen); **keep/have sth in ~** etw im Auge behalten/haben; **be on ~** besichtigt werden können ● vt sich (dat) ansehen; besichtigen ⟨house⟩; (consider) betrachten ● vi (TV) fernsehen. ~**er** n (TV) Zuschauer(in) m(f); (Phot) Diabetrachter m

view: ~**finder** n (Phot) Sucher m. ~**point** n Standpunkt m

vigil /'vɪdʒɪl/ n Wache f

vigilan|ce /'vɪdʒɪləns/ n Wachsamkeit f. ~**t** a, **-ly** adv wachsam

vigorous /'vɪgərəs/ a, **-ly** adv kräftig; (fig) heftig

vigour /'vɪgə(r)/ n Kraft f; (fig) Heftigkeit f

vile /vaɪl/ a abscheulich

villa /'vɪlə/ n (for holidays) Ferienhaus nt

village /'vɪlɪdʒ/ n Dorf nt. ~**r** n Dorfbewohner(in) m(f)

villain /'vɪlən/ n Schurke m; (in story) Bösewicht m

vim /vɪm/ n (fam) Schwung m

vindicat|e /'vɪndɪkeɪt/ vt rechtfertigen. ~**ion** /-'keɪʃn/ n Rechtfertigung f

vindictive /vɪn'dɪktɪv/ a nachtragend

vine /vaɪn/ n Weinrebe f

vinegar /'vɪnɪgə(r)/ n Essig m

vineyard /'vɪnjɑːd/ n Weinberg m

vintage /'vɪntɪdʒ/ a erlesen ● n (year) Jahrgang m. ~ **'car** n Oldtimer m

viola /vɪ'əʊlə/ n (Mus) Bratsche f

violat|e /'vaɪəleɪt/ vt verletzen; (break) brechen; (disturb) stören; (defile) schänden. ~**ion** /-'leɪʃn/ n Verletzung f; Schändung f

violen|ce /'vaɪələns/ n Gewalt f; (fig) Heftigkeit f. ~**t** a gewalttätig; (fig) heftig. ~**tly** adv brutal; (fig) heftig

violet /'vaɪələt/ a violett ● n (flower) Veilchen n

violin /vaɪə'lɪn/ n Geige f, Violine f. ~**ist** n Geiger(in) m(f)

VIP abbr (**very important person**) Prominente(r) m(f)

viper /'vaɪpə(r)/ n Kreuzotter f; (fig) Schlange f

virgin /'vɜːdʒɪn/ a unberührt ● n Jungfrau f. ~**ity** /-'dʒɪnɪtɪ/ n Unschuld f

Virgo /'vɜːɡəʊ/ n (*Astr*) Jungfrau f

viril|e /'vɪraɪl/ a männlich. ~**ity** /-'rɪlətɪ/ n Männlichkeit f

virtual /'vɜːtjʊəl/ a a ~ ... praktisch ein ... ~**ly** adv praktisch

virtu|e /'vɜːtjuː/ n Tugend f; (*advantage*) Vorteil m; **by** or **in** ~**e of** auf Grund (+ *gen*)

virtuoso /vɜːtʊ'əʊzəʊ/ n (*pl* **-si** /-ziː/) Virtuose m

virtuous /'vɜːtjʊəs/ a tugendhaft

virulent /'vɪrʊlənt/ a bösartig; ⟨poison⟩ stark; (*fig*) scharf

virus /'vaɪərəs/ n Virus nt

visa /'viːzə/ n Visum nt

vis-à-vis /viːzɑː'viː/ adv & prep gegenüber (+ *dat*)

viscous /'vɪskəs/ a dickflüssig

visibility /vɪzə'bɪlətɪ/ n Sichtbarkeit f; (*Meteorol*) Sichtweite f

visible /'vɪzəbl/ a, **-bly** adv sichtbar

vision /'vɪʒn/ n Vision f; (*sight*) Sehkraft f; (*foresight*) Weitblick m

visit /'vɪzɪt/ n Besuch m ● vt besuchen; besichtigen ⟨town, building⟩. ~**ing hours** npl Besuchszeiten pl. ~**or** n Besucher(in) m(f); (*in hotel*) Gast m; **have** ~**ors** Besuch haben

visor /'vaɪzə(r)/ n Schirm m; (*on helmet*) Visier nt; (*Auto*) [Sonnen] blende f

vista /'vɪstə/ n Aussicht f

visual /'vɪzjʊəl/ a, **-ly** adv visuell; ~**ly handicapped** sehbehindert. ~ **aids** npl Anschauungsmaterial nt. ~ **display unit** n Bildschirmgerät nt

visualize /'vɪzjʊəlaɪz/ vt sich (*dat*) vorstellen

vital /'vaɪtl/ a unbedingt notwendig; (*essential to life*) lebenswichtig. ~**ity** /vaɪ'tælətɪ/ n Vitalität f. ~**ly** /'vaɪtəlɪ/ adv äußerst

vitamin /'vɪtəmɪn/ n Vitamin nt

vitreous /'vɪtrɪəs/ a glasartig; ⟨enamel⟩ Glas-

vivaci|ous /vɪ'veɪʃəs/ a, **-ly** adv lebhaft. ~**ty** /-'væsətɪ/ n Lebhaftigkeit f

vivid /'vɪvɪd/ a, **-ly** adv lebhaft; ⟨description⟩ lebendig

vixen /'vɪksn/ n Füchsin f

vocabulary /və'kæbjʊlərɪ/ n Wortschatz m; (*list*) Vokabelverzeichnis nt; **learn** ~ Vokabeln lernen

vocal /'vəʊkl/ a, **-ly** adv stimmlich; (*vociferous*) lautstark. ~ **cords** npl Stimmbänder pl

vocalist /'vəʊkəlɪst/ n Sänger(in) m(f)

vocation /və'keɪʃn/ n Berufung f. ~**al** a Berufs-

vociferous /və'sɪfərəs/ a lautstark

vodka /'vɒdkə/ n Wodka m

vogue /vəʊɡ/ n Mode f; **in** ~ in Mode

voice /vɔɪs/ n Stimme f ● vt zum Ausdruck bringen

void /vɔɪd/ a leer; (*not valid*) ungültig; ~ **of** ohne ● n Leere f

volatile /'vɒlətaɪl/ a flüchtig; ⟨person⟩ sprunghaft

volcanic /vɒl'kænɪk/ a vulkanisch

volcano /vɒl'keɪnəʊ/ n Vulkan m

volition /və'lɪʃn/ n **of one's own** ~ aus eigenem Willen

volley /'vɒlɪ/ n (*of gunfire*) Salve f; (*Tennis*) Volley m

volt /vəʊlt/ n Volt nt. ~**age** /-ɪdʒ/ n (*Electr*) Spannung f

voluble /'vɒljʊbl/ a, **-bly** adv redselig; ⟨protest⟩ wortreich

volume /'vɒljuːm/ n (*book*) Band m; (*Geom*) Rauminhalt m; (*amount*) Ausmaß nt; (*Radio, TV*) Lautstärke f. ~ **control** n Lautstärkeregler m

voluntary /'vɒləntərɪ/ a, **-ily** adv freiwillig

volunteer /vɒlən'tɪə(r)/ n Freiwillige(r) m/f ● vt anbieten; geben ⟨information⟩ ● vi sich freiwillig melden

voluptuous /və'lʌptjʊəs/ a sinnlich

vomit /'vɒmɪt/ n Erbrochene(s) nt ● vt erbrechen ● vi sich übergeben

voracious /və'reɪʃəs/ a gefräßig; ⟨appetite⟩ unbändig

vot|e /vəʊt/ n Stimme f; (*ballot*) Abstimmung f; (*right*) Wahlrecht nt; **take a** ~**e on** abstimmen über (+ *acc*) ● vi abstimmen; (*in election*) wählen ● vt ~**e s.o. president** jdn zum Präsidenten wählen. ~**er** n Wähler(in) m(f)

vouch /vaʊtʃ/ vi ~ **for** sich verbürgen für. ~**er** n Gutschein m

vow /vaʊ/ n Gelöbnis nt; (*Relig*) Gelübde nt ● vt geloben

vowel /'vaʊəl/ n Vokal m

voyage /'vɔɪɪdʒ/ n Seereise f; (*in space*) Reise f, Flug m

vulgar /'vʌlɡə(r)/ a vulgär, ordinär. ~**ity** /-'ɡærətɪ/ n Vulgarität f

vulnerable /'vʌlnərəbl/ a verwundbar

vulture /'vʌltʃə(r)/ n Geier m

vying /'vaɪɪŋ/ *see* **vie**

W

wad /wɒd/ n Bausch m; (bundle) Bündel nt. **~ding** n Wattierung f

waddle /'wɒdl/ vi watscheln

wade /weɪd/ vi waten; **~ through** (fam) sich durchackern durch ⟨book⟩

wafer /'weɪfə(r)/ n Waffel f; (Relig) Hostie f

waffle[1] /'wɒfl/ vi (fam) schwafeln

waffle[2] n (Culin) Waffel f

waft /wɒft/ vt/i wehen

wag /wæg/ v (pt/pp **wagged**) ● vt wedeln mit; **~ one's finger at s.o.** jdm mit dem Finger drohen ● vi wedeln

wage[1] /weɪdʒ/ vt führen

wage[2] n, & **~s** pl Lohn m. **~ packet** n Lohntüte f

wager /'weɪdʒə(r)/ n Wette f

waggle /'wægl/ vt wackeln mit ● vi wackeln

wagon /'wægən/ n Wagen m; (Rail) Waggon m

wail /weɪl/ n [klagender] Schrei m ● vi heulen; (lament) klagen

waist /weɪst/ n Taille f. **~coat** /'weɪskəʊt/ n Weste f. **~line** n Taille f

wait /weɪt/ n Wartezeit f; **lie in ~ for** auflauern (+ dat) ● vi warten (**for** auf + acc); (at table) servieren; **~ on** bedienen ● vt **~ one's turn** warten, bis man an der Reihe ist

waiter /'weɪtə(r)/ n Kellner m; **~!** Herr Ober!

waiting: **~-list** n Warteliste f. **~-room** n Warteraum m; (doctor's) Wartezimmer nt

waitress /'weɪtrɪs/ n Kellnerin f

waive /weɪv/ vt verzichten auf (+ acc)

wake[1] /weɪk/ n Totenwache f ● v (pt **woke**, pp **woken**) **~ [up]** ● vt [auf]wecken ● vi aufwachen

wake[2] n (Naut) Kielwasser nt; **in the ~ of** im Gefolge (+ gen)

waken /'weɪkn/ vt [auf]wecken ● vi aufwachen

Wales /weɪlz/ n Wales nt

walk /wɔːk/ n Spaziergang m; (gait) Gang m; (path) Weg m; **go for a ~** spazierengehen ● vi gehen; (not ride) laufen, zu Fuß gehen; (ramble) wandern; **learn to ~** laufen lernen ● vt ausführen ⟨dog⟩. **~ out** vi hinausgehen; ⟨workers:⟩ in den Streik treten; **~ out on s.o.** jdn verlassen

walker /'wɔːkə(r)/ n Spaziergänger(in) m(f); (rambler) Wanderer m/Wanderin f

walking /'wɔːkɪŋ/ n Gehen nt; (rambling) Wandern nt. **~-stick** n Spazierstock m

walk: **~-out** n Streik m. **~-over** n (fig) leichter Sieg m

wall /wɔːl/ n Wand f; (external) Mauer f; **go to the ~** (fam) eingehen; **drive s.o. up the ~** (fam) jdn auf die Palme bringen ● vt **~ up** zumauern

wallet /'wɒlɪt/ n Brieftasche f

'wallflower n Goldlack m

wallop /'wɒləp/ n (fam) Schlag m ● vt (pt/pp **walloped**) (fam) schlagen

wallow /'wɒləʊ/ vi sich wälzen; (fig) schwelgen

'wallpaper n Tapete f ● vt tapezieren

walnut /'wɔːlnʌt/ n Walnuß f

waltz /wɔːlts/ n Walzer m ● vi Walzer tanzen; **come ~ing up** (fam) angetanzt kommen

wan /wɒn/ a bleich

wand /wɒnd/ n Zauberstab m

wander /'wɒndə(r)/ vi umherwandern, (fam) bummeln; (fig: digress) abschweifen. **~ about** vi umherwandern. **~lust** n Fernweh nt

wane /weɪn/ n **be on the ~** schwinden; ⟨moon:⟩ abnehmen ● vi schwinden; abnehmen

wangle /'wæŋgl/ vt (fam) organisieren

want /wɒnt/ n Mangel m (**of** an + dat); (hardship) Not f; (desire) Bedürfnis nt ● vt wollen; (need) brauchen; **~ [to have] sth** etw haben wollen; **~ to do sth** etw tun wollen; **we ~ to stay** wir wollen bleiben; **I ~ you to go** ich will, daß du gehst; **it ~s painting** es müßte gestrichen werden; **you ~ to learn to swim** du solltest schwimmen lernen ● vi **he doesn't ~ for anything** ihm fehlt es an nichts. **~ed** a gesucht. **~ing** a **be ~ing** fehlen; **he is ~ing in** ihm fehlt es an (+ dat)

wanton /'wɒntən/ a, **-ly** adv mutwillig

war /wɔː(r)/ n Krieg m; **be at ~** sich im Krieg befinden

ward /wɔːd/ n [Kranken]saal m; (unit) Station f; (of town) Wahlbezirk m; (child) Mündel nt ● vt **~ off** abwehren

warden /ˈwɔːdn/ n Heimleiter(in) m(f); (of youth hostel) Herbergsvater m; (supervisor) Aufseher(in) m(f)

warder /ˈwɔːdə(r)/ n Wärter(in) m(f)

wardrobe /ˈwɔːdrəʊb/ n Kleiderschrank m; (clothes) Garderobe f

warehouse /ˈweəhaʊs/ n Lager nt; (building) Lagerhaus nt

wares /weəz/ npl Waren pl

war: ~**fare** n Krieg m. ~**head** n Sprengkopf m. ~**like** a kriegerisch

warm /wɔːm/ a (-er, -est), -ly adv warm; (welcome) herzlich; **I am** ~ mir ist warm ● vt wärmen. ~ **up** vt aufwärmen ● vi warm werden; (Sport) sich aufwärmen. ~**-hearted** a warmherzig

warmth /wɔːmθ/ n Wärme f

warn /wɔːn/ vt warnen (**of** vor + dat). ~**ing** n Warnung f; (advance notice) Vorwarnung f; (caution) Verwarnung f

warp /wɔːp/ vt verbiegen ● vi sich verziehen

'war-path n **on the** ~ auf dem Kriegspfad

warrant /ˈwɒrənt/ n (for arrest) Haftbefehl m; (for search) Durchsuchungsbefehl m ● vt (justify) rechtfertigen; (guarantee) garantieren

warranty /ˈwɒrəntɪ/ n Garantie f

warrior /ˈwɒrɪə(r)/ n Krieger m

'warship n Kriegsschiff nt

wart /wɔːt/ n Warze f

'wartime n Kriegszeit f

wary /ˈweərɪ/ a (-ier, -iest), -ily adv vorsichtig; (suspicious) mißtrauisch

was /wɒz/ see **be**

wash /wɒʃ/ n Wäsche f; (Naut) Wellen pl; **have a** ~ sich waschen ● vt waschen; spülen (dishes); aufwischen (floor); (flow over) bespülen; ~ **one's hands** sich (dat) die Hände waschen ● vi sich waschen; (fabric:) sich waschen lassen. ~ **out** vt auswaschen; ausspülen (mouth). ~ **up** vt abwaschen, spülen ● vi (Amer) sich waschen

washable /ˈwɒʃəbl/ a waschbar

wash: ~**basin** n Waschbecken nt. ~**cloth** n (Amer) Waschlappen m

washed 'out a (faded) verwaschen; (tired) abgespannt

washer /ˈwɒʃə(r)/ n (Techn) Dichtungsring m; (machine) Waschmaschine f

washing /ˈwɒʃɪŋ/ n Wäsche f. ~**machine** n Waschmaschine f. ~**powder** n Waschpulver nt. ~**-up** n Abwasch m; **do the** ~**-up** abwaschen, spülen. ~**-up liquid** n Spülmittel nt

wash: ~**-out** n Pleite f; (person) Niete f. ~**-room** n Waschraum m

wasp /wɒsp/ n Wespe f

wastage /ˈweɪstɪdʒ/ n Schwund m

waste /weɪst/ n Verschwendung f; (rubbish) Abfall m; ~**s** pl Öde f; ~ **of time** Zeitverschwendung f ● a (product) Abfall-; **lay** ~ verwüsten ● vt verschwenden ● vi ~ **away** immer mehr abmagern

waste: ~**-di'sposal unit** n Müllzerkleinerer m. ~**ful** a verschwenderisch. ~**land** n Ödland nt. ~ **'paper** n Altpapier nt. ~**-'paper basket** n Papierkorb m

watch /wɒtʃ/ n Wache f; (timepiece) [Armband]uhr f; **be on the** ~ aufpassen ● vt beobachten; sich (dat) ansehen (film, match); (be careful of, look after) achten auf (+ acc); ~ **television** fernsehen ● vi zusehen. ~ **out** vi Ausschau halten (**for** nach); (be careful) aufpassen

watch: ~**dog** n Wachhund m. ~**ful** a, -ly adv wachsam. ~**maker** n Uhrmacher m. ~**man** n Wachmann m. ~**-strap** n Uhrarmband nt. ~**tower** n Wachturm m. ~**word** n Parole f

water /ˈwɔːtə(r)/ n Wasser nt; ~**s** pl Gewässer nt ● vt gießen (garden, plant); (dilute) verdünnen; (give drink to) tränken ● vi (eyes:) tränen; **my mouth was** ~**ing** mir lief das Wasser im Munde zusammen. ~ **down** vt verwässern

water: ~**-colour** n Wasserfarbe f; (painting) Aquarell nt. ~**cress** n Brunnenkresse f. ~**fall** n Wasserfall m

'watering-can n Gießkanne f

water: ~**-lily** n Seerose f. ~**logged** a **be** ~**logged** (ground:) unter Wasser stehen. ~**-main** n Hauptwasserleitung f. ~**mark** n Wasserzeichen nt. ~ **polo** n Wasserball m. ~**-power** n Wasserkraft f. ~**proof** a wasserdicht. ~**shed** n Wasserscheide f; (fig) Wendepunkt m. ~**-skiing** n Wasserskilaufen nt. ~**tight** a wasserdicht. ~**way** n Wasserstraße f

watery /ˈwɔːtərɪ/ a wäßrig

watt /wɒt/ n Watt nt

wave /weɪv/ n Welle f; (gesture)
Handbewegung f; (as greeting) Winken nt ● vt winken mit; (brandish)
schwingen; (threateningly) drohen
mit; wellen ⟨hair⟩; ~ one's hand
winken ● vi winken (to dat); ⟨flag:⟩
wehen. ~length n Wellenlänge f

waver /'weɪvə(r)/ vi schwanken

wavy /'weɪvɪ/ a wellig

wax¹ /wæks/ vi ⟨moon:⟩ zunehmen;
(fig: become) werden

wax² n Wachs nt; (in ear) Schmalz nt
● vt wachsen. ~works n Wachs-
figurenkabinett nt

way /weɪ/ n Weg m; (direction) Richtung f; (respect) Hinsicht f; (manner) Art f; (method) Art und Weise f;
~s pl Gewohnheiten pl; in the ~ im
Weg; on the ~ auf dem Weg (to
nach/zu); (under way) unterwegs; a
little/long ~ ein kleines/ganzes
Stück; a long ~ off weit weg; this ~
hierher; (like this) so; which ~ in
welche Richtung; (how) wie; by the
~ übrigens; in some ~s in gewisser
Hinsicht; either ~ so oder so; in this
~ auf diese Weise; in a ~ in gewisser
Weise; in a bad ~ ⟨person⟩ in
schlechter Verfassung; lead the ~
vorausgehen; make ~ Platz machen
(for dat); 'give ~' (Auto) 'Vorfahrt
beachten'; go out of one's ~ (fig)
sich (dat) besondere Mühe geben
(to zu); get one's [own] ~ seinen
Willen durchsetzen ● adv weit; ~
behind weit zurück. ~ 'in n Eingang
m

way'lay vt (pt/pp -laid) überfallen;
(fam: intercept) abfangen

way 'out n Ausgang m; (fig) Ausweg
m

way-'out a (fam) verrückt

wayward /'weɪwəd/ a eigenwillig

WC abbr WC nt

we /wiː/ pron wir

weak /wiːk/ a (-er, -est), -ly adv
schwach; ⟨liquid⟩ dünn. ~en vt
schwächen ● vi schwächer werden.
~ling n Schwächling m. ~ness n
Schwäche f

wealth /welθ/ n Reichtum m; (fig)
Fülle f (of an + dat). ~y a (-ier, -iest)
reich

wean /wiːn/ vt entwöhnen

weapon /'wepən/ n Waffe f

wear /weə(r)/ n (clothing) Kleidung f;
~ and tear Abnutzung f, Verschleiß
m ● v (pt wore, pp worn) ● vt tragen;
(damage) abnutzen; ~ a hole in sth

etw durchsetzen; what shall I ~?
was soll ich anziehen? ● vi sich abnutzen; (last) halten. ~ off vi abgehen; ⟨effect:⟩ nachlassen. ~ out vt
abnutzen; (exhaust) erschöpfen ● vi
sich abnutzen

wearable /'weərəbl/ a tragbar

weary /'wɪərɪ/ a (-ier, -iest), -ily adv
müde ● v (pt/pp wearied) ● vt ermüden ● vi ~ of sth etw (gen) überdrüssig werden

weasel /'wiːzl/ n Wiesel nt

weather /'weðə(r)/ n Wetter nt; in this
~ bei diesem Wetter; under the ~
(fam) nicht ganz auf dem Posten
● vt abwettern ⟨storm⟩; (fig)
überstehen

weather: ~-beaten a verwittert;
wettergegerbt ⟨face⟩. ~cock n Wet-
terhahn m. ~ forecast n Wettervor-
hersage f. ~-vane n Wetterfahne f

weave¹ /wiːv/ vi (pt/pp weaved) sich
schlängeln (through durch)

weave² n (Tex) Bindung f ● vt (pt
wove, pp woven) weben; (plait)
flechten; (fig) einflechten (in in +
acc). ~r n Weber m

web /web/ n Netz nt. ~bed feet npl
Schwimmfüße pl

wed /wed/ vt/i (pt/pp wedded)
heiraten. ~ding n Hochzeit f; (ceremony) Trauung f

wedding: ~ day n Hochzeitstag m.
~ dress n Hochzeitskleid nt. ~-ring
n Ehering m, Trauring m

wedge /wedʒ/ n Keil m; (of cheese)
[keilförmiges] Stück nt ● vt
festklemmen

wedlock /'wedlɒk/ n (liter) Ehe f; in/
out of ~ ehelich/unehelich

Wednesday /'wenzdeɪ/ n Mittwoch m

wee /wiː/ a (fam) klein ● vi Pipi
machen

weed /wiːd/ n & ~s pl Unkraut nt
● vt/i jäten. ~ out vt (fig) aussieben

'weed-killer n Unkrautvertilgungs-
mittel nt

weedy /'wiːdɪ/ a (fam) spillerig

week /wiːk/ n Woche f. ~day n
Wochentag m. ~end n Wochenende
nt

weekly /'wiːklɪ/ a & adv wöchentlich
● n Wochenzeitschrift f

weep /wiːp/ vi (pt/pp wept) weinen.
~ing 'willow n Trauerweide f

weigh /weɪ/ vt/i wiegen; ~ anchor
den Anker lichten. ~ down vt (fig)
niederdrücken. ~ up vt (fig)
abwägen

weight /weɪt/ n Gewicht nt; **put on/ lose** ~ zunehmen/abnehmen. ~**ing** n (allowance) Zulage f

weight: ~**lessness** n Schwere- losigkeit f. ~**lifting** n Gewicht- heben nt

weighty /'weɪtɪ/ a (-ier, -iest) schwer; (important) gewichtig

weir /wɪə(r)/ n Wehr nt

weird /wɪəd/ a (-er, -est) unheimlich; (bizarre) bizarr

welcome /'welkəm/ a willkommen; **you're** ~! nichts zu danken! **you're** ~ **to have it** das können Sie gerne haben ● n Willkommen nt ● vt begrüßen

weld /weld/ vt schweißen. ~**er** n Schweißer m

welfare /'welfeə(r)/ n Wohl nt; (Admin) Fürsorge f. **W**~ **State** n Wohlfahrtsstaat m

well¹ /wel/ n Brunnen m; (oil ~) Quelle f; (of staircase) Treppenhaus nt

well² adv (better, best) gut; **as** ~ auch; **as** ~ **as** (in addition) sowohl ... als auch; ~ **done!** gut gemacht! ● a gesund; **he is not** ~ es geht ihm nicht gut; **get** ~ **soon!** gute Besse- rung! ● int nun, na

well: ~-**behaved** a artig. ~-**being** n Wohl nt. ~-**bred** a wohlerzogen. ~- **heeled** a (fam) gut betucht

wellingtons /'welɪŋtənz/ npl Gummistiefel pl

well: ~-**known** a bekannt. ~-**mean- ing** a wohlmeinend. ~-**meant** a gut- gemeint. ~-**off** a wohlhabend; **be** ~-**off** gut dran sein. ~-**read** a bele- sen. ~-**to-do** a wohlhabend

Welsh /welʃ/ a walisisch ● n (Lang) Walisisch nt; **the** ~ pl die Waliser. ~**man** n Waliser m. ~ **rabbit** n überbackenes Käsebrot nt

went /went/ see **go**

wept /wept/ see **weep**

were /wɜ:(r)/ see **be**

west /west/ n Westen m; **to the** ~ **of** westlich von ● a West-, west- ● adv nach Westen; **go** ~ (fam) flötenge- hen. ~**erly** a westlich. ~**ern** a west- lich ● n Western m

West: ~ **'Germany** n Westdeutsch- land nt. ~ **'Indian** a westindisch ● n Westinder(in) m(f). ~ **'Indies** /-ɪndɪz/ npl Westindische Inseln pl

'westward[s] /-wəd[z]/ adv nach Westen

wet /wet/ a (**wetter, wettest**) naß; ⟨fam: person⟩ weichlich, lasch; '~ **paint**' 'frisch gestrichen' ● vt (pt/pp **wet** or **wetted**) naß machen. ~ **'blanket** n Spaßverderber m

whack /wæk/ n (fam) Schlag m ● vt (fam) schlagen. ~**ed** a (fam) kaputt

whale /weɪl/ n Wal m; **have a** ~ **of a time** (fam) sich toll amüsieren

wharf /wɔ:f/ n Kai m

what /wɒt/ pron & int was; ~ **for?** wozu? ~ **is it like?** wie ist es? ~ **is your name?** wie ist Ihr Name? ~ **is the weather like?** wie ist das Wetter? ~'**s he talking about?** wovon redet er? ● a welche(r,s); ~ **kind of a** was für ein(e); **at** ~ **time?** um wieviel Uhr?

what'ever a [egal] welche(r,s) ● pron was ... auch; ~ **is it?** was ist das bloß? ~ **he does** was er auch tut; ~ **happens** was auch geschieht; **nothing** ~ überhaupt nichts

whatso'ever pron & a ≈ **whatever**

wheat /wi:t/ n Weizen m

wheedle /'wi:dl/ vt gut zureden (+ dat); ~ **sth out of s.o.** jdm etw ablocken

wheel /wi:l/ n Rad nt; (pottery) Töp- ferscheibe f; (steering ~) Lenkrad nt; **at the** ~ am Steuer ● vt (push) schieben ● vi kehrtmachen; (circle) kreisen

wheel: ~**barrow** n Schubkarre f. ~**chair** n Rollstuhl m. ~-**clamp** n Parkkralle f

wheeze /wi:z/ vi keuchen

when /wen/ adv wann; **the day** ~ der Tag, an dem ● conj wenn; (in the past) als; (although) wo ... doch; ~ **swimming/reading** beim Schwim- men/Lesen

whence /wens/ adv (liter) woher

when'ever conj & adv [immer] wenn; (at whatever time) wann im- mer; ~ **did it happen?** wann ist das bloß passiert?

where /weə(r)/ adv & conj wo; ~ **[to]** wohin; ~**[from]** woher

whereabouts¹ /weərə'baʊts/ adv wo

'whereabouts² n Verbleib m; (of per- son) Aufenthaltsort m

where'as conj während; (in contrast) wohingegen

where'by adv wodurch

whereu'pon adv worauf[hin]

wher'ever conj & adv wo immer; (to whatever place) wohin immer; (from *whatever place)* woher immer; *(every-where)* überall wo; ~ **is he?** wo ist er bloß? ~ **possible** wenn irgend möglich

whet /wet/ *vt* *(pt/pp* **whetted)** wetzen; anregen *⟨appetite⟩*

whether /'weðə(r)/ *conj* ob

which /wɪtʃ/ *a & pron* welche(r,s); ~ **one** welche(r,s) ● *rel pron* der/die/das, *(pl)* die; *(after clause)* was; **after** ~ wonach; **on** ~ worauf

which'ever *a & pron* [egal] welche(r, s); ~ **it is** was es auch ist

whiff /wɪf/ *n* Hauch *m*

while /waɪl/ *n* Weile *f*; **a long** ~ lange; **be worth** ~ sich lohnen; **it's worth my** ~ es lohnt sich für mich ● *conj* während; *(as long as)* solange; *(al-though)* obgleich ● *vt* ~ **away** sich *(dat)* vertreiben

whilst /waɪlst/ *conj* während

whim /wɪm/ *n* Laune *f*

whimper /'wɪmpə(r)/ *vi* wimmern; *⟨dog:⟩* winseln

whimsical /'wɪmzɪkl/ *a* skurril

whine /waɪn/ *n* Winseln *nt* ● *vi* winseln

whip /wɪp/ *n* Peitsche *f*; *(Pol)* Einpeitscher *m* ● *vt* *(pt/pp* **whipped)** peitschen; *(Culin)* schlagen; *(snatch)* reißen; *(fam: steal)* klauen. ~ **up** *vt* *(incite)* anheizen; *(fam)* schnell hinzaubern *⟨meal⟩*. ~**ped 'cream** *n* Schlagsahne *f*

whirl /wɜ:l/ *n* Wirbel *m*; **I am in a** ~ mir schwirrt der Kopf ● *vt/i* wirbeln. ~**pool** *n* Strudel *m*. ~**wind** *n* Wirbelwind *m*

whirr /wɜ:(r)/ *vi* surren

whisk /wɪsk/ *n* *(Culin)* Schneebesen *m* ● *vt* *(Culin)* schlagen. ~ **away** *vt* wegreißen

whisker /'wɪskə(r)/ *n* Schnurrhaar *nt*; ~**s** *pl* *(on man's cheek)* Backenbart *m*

whisky /'wɪskɪ/ *n* Whisky *m*

whisper /'wɪspə(r)/ *n* Flüstern *nt*; *(rumour)* Gerücht *nt*; **in a** ~ im Flüsterton ● *vt/i* flüstern

whistle /'wɪsl/ *n* Pfiff *m*; *(instrument)* Pfeife *f* ● *vt/i* pfeifen

white /waɪt/ *a* (**-r, -st)** weiß ● *n* Weiß *nt*; *(of egg)* Eiweiß *nt*; *(person)* Weiße(r) *m/f*

white: ~ **'coffee** *n* Kaffee *m* mit Milch. ~**'collar worker** *n* Angestellte(r) *m*. ~ **'lie** *n* Notlüge *f*

whiten /'waɪtn/ *vt* weiß machen ● *vi* weiß werden

whiteness /'waɪtnɪs/ *n* Weiß *nt*

'whitewash *n* Tünche *f*; *(fig)* Schönfärberei *f* ● *vt* tünchen

Whitsun /'wɪtsn/ *n* Pfingsten *nt*

whittle /'wɪtl/ *vt* ~ **down** reduzieren; kürzen *⟨list⟩*

whiz[z] /wɪz/ *vi* *(pt/pp* **whizzed)** zischen. ~**-kid** *n* *(fam)* Senkrechtstarter *m*

who /hu:/ *pron* wer; *(acc)* wen; *(dat)* wem ● *rel pron* der/die/das, *(pl)* die

who'ever *pron* wer [immer]; ~ **he is** wer er auch ist; ~ **is it?** wer ist das bloß?

whole /həʊl/ *a* ganz; *⟨truth⟩* voll ● *n* Ganze(s) *nt*; **as a** ~ als Ganzes; **on the** ~ im großen und ganzen; **the** ~ **lot** alle; *(everything)* alles; **the** ~ **of Germany** ganz Deutschland; **the** ~ **time** die ganze Zeit

whole: ~**food** *n* Vollwertkost *f*. ~**'hearted** *a* rückhaltlos. ~**meal** *a* Vollkorn-

'wholesale *a* Großhandels- ● *adv* en gros; *(fig)* in Bausch und Bogen. ~**r** *n* Großhändler *m*

wholesome /'həʊlsəm/ *a* gesund

wholly /'həʊlɪ/ *adv* völlig

whom /hu:m/ *pron* wen; **to** ~ wem ● *rel pron* den/die/das, *(pl)* die; *(dat)* dem/der/dem, *(pl)* denen

whooping cough /'hu:pɪŋ-/ *n* Keuchhusten *m*

whopping /'wɒpɪŋ/ *a* *(fam)* Riesen-

whore /hɔ:(r)/ *n* Hure *f*

whose /hu:z/ *pron* wessen; ~ **is that?** wem gehört das? ● *rel pron* dessen/deren/dessen, *(pl)* deren

why /waɪ/ *adv* warum; *(for what purpose)* wozu; **that's** ~ darum ● *int* na

wick /wɪk/ *n* Docht *m*

wicked /'wɪkɪd/ *a* böse; *(mischievous)* frech, boshaft

wicker /'wɪkə(r)/ *n* Korbgeflecht *nt* ● *attrib* Korb-

wide /waɪd/ *a* (**-r, -st)** weit; *(broad)* breit; *(fig)* groß; **be** ~ *(far from target)* danebengehen ● *adv* weit; *(off target)* daneben; ~ **awake** hellwach; **far and** ~ weit und breit. ~**ly** *adv* weit; *⟨known, accepted⟩* weithin; *⟨differ⟩* stark

widen /'waɪdn/ *vt* verbreitern; *(fig)* erweitern ● *vi* sich verbreitern

'widespread *a* weitverbreitet

widow /'wɪdəʊ/ *n* Witwe *f*. ~**ed** *a* verwitwet. ~**er** *n* Witwer *m*

width /wɪdθ/ n Weite f; (breadth) Breite f

wield /wiːld/ vt schwingen; ausüben ⟨power⟩

wife /waɪf/ n (pl wives) [Ehe]frau f

wig /wɪg/ n Perücke f

wiggle /ˈwɪgl/ vi wackeln ● vt wackeln mit

wild /waɪld/ a (-er, -est), **-ly** adv wild; ⟨animal⟩ wildlebend; ⟨flower⟩ wild-wachsend; (furious) wütend; **be ~ about** (keen on) wild sein auf (+ acc) ● adv wild; **run ~** frei herumlaufen ● n **in the ~** wild; **the ~s** pl die Wildnis f

'wildcat strike n wilder Streik m

wilderness /ˈwɪldənɪs/ n Wildnis f; (desert) Wüste f

wild: ~-'goose chase n aussichtslose Suche f. **~life** n Tierwelt f

wilful /ˈwɪlfl/ a, **-ly** adv mutwillig; (self-willed) eigenwillig

will[1] /wɪl/ v aux wollen; (forming future tense) werden; **he ~ arrive tomorrow** er wird morgen kommen; **~ you go?** gehst du? **you ~ be back soon, won't you?** du kommst doch bald wieder, nicht? **he ~ be there, won't he?** er wird doch da sein? **she ~ be there by now** sie wird jetzt schon da sein: **~ you be quiet!** willst du wohl ruhig sein! **~ you have some wine?** möchten Sie Wein? **the engine won't start** der Motor will nicht anspringen

will[2] n Wille m; (document) Testament nt

willing /ˈwɪlɪŋ/ a willig; (eager) bereit-willig; **be ~** bereit sein. **~ly** adv bereitwillig; (gladly) gern. **~ness** n Bereitwilligkeit f

willow /ˈwɪləʊ/ n Weide f

'will-power n Willenskraft f

willy-'nilly adv wohl oder übel

wilt /wɪlt/ vi welk werden, welken

wily /ˈwaɪlɪ/ a (-ier, -iest) listig

wimp /wɪmp/ n Schwächling m

win /wɪn/ n Sieg m; **have a ~** gewin-nen ● v (pt/pp won; pres p winning) ● vt gewinnen; bekommen ⟨scholar-ship⟩ ● vi gewinnen; (in battle) sie-gen. **~ over** vt auf seine Seite bringen

wince /wɪns/ vi zusammenzucken

winch /wɪntʃ/ n Winde f ● vt **~ up** hochwinden

wind[1] /wɪnd/ n Wind m; (breath) Atem m; (fam: flatulence) Blähun-gen pl; **have the ~ up** (fam) Angst

haben ● vt **~ s.o.** jdm den Atem nehmen

wind[2] /waɪnd/ v (pt/pp wound) ● vt (wrap) wickeln; (move by turning) kurbeln; aufziehen ⟨clock⟩ ● vi ⟨road:⟩ sich winden. **~ up** vt aufzie-hen ⟨clock⟩; schließen ⟨proceedings⟩

wind /wɪnd/ : **~fall** n unerwarteter Glücksfall m; **~falls** pl (fruit) Fal-lobst nt. **~ instrument** n Blasinstrument nt. **~mill** n Wind-mühle f

window /ˈwɪndəʊ/ n Fenster nt; (of shop) Schaufenster nt

window: ~-box n Blumenkasten m. **~-cleaner** n Fensterputzer m. **~-dresser** n Schaufensterdekorateur (in) m(f). **~-dressing** n Schaufen-sterdekoration f; (fig) Schönfärbe-rei f. **~-pane** n Fensterscheibe f. **~-shopping** n Schaufensterbummel m. **~-sill** n Fensterbrett nt

'windpipe n Luftröhre f

'windscreen n, (Amer) **'windshield** n Windschutzscheibe f. **~ washer** n Scheibenwaschanlage f. **~-wiper** n Scheibenwischer m

wind: ~surfing n Windsurfen nt. **~swept** a windgepeitscht; ⟨person⟩ zersaust

windy /ˈwɪndɪ/ a (-ier, -iest) windig; **be ~** (fam) Angst haben

wine /waɪn/ n Wein m

wine: ~-bar n Weinstube f. **~glass** n Weinglas nt. **~-list** n Weinkarte f

winery /ˈwaɪnərɪ/ n (Amer) Weingut nt

'wine-tasting n Weinprobe f

wing /wɪŋ/ n Flügel m; (Auto) Kotflü-gel m; **~s** pl (Theat) Kulissen pl

wink /wɪŋk/ n Zwinkern nt; **not sleep a ~** kein Auge zutun ● vi zwinkern; ⟨light:⟩ blinken

winner /ˈwɪnə(r)/ n Gewinner(in) m(f); (Sport) Sieger(in) m(f)

winning /ˈwɪnɪŋ/ a siegreich; ⟨smile⟩ gewinnend. **~-post** n Zielpfosten m. **~s** npl Gewinn m

wint|er /ˈwɪntə(r)/ n Winter m. **~ry** a winterlich

wipe /waɪp/ n **give sth a ~** etw abwi-schen ● vt abwischen; aufwischen ⟨floor⟩; (dry) abtrocknen. **~ off** vt abwischen; (erase) auslöschen. **~ out** vt (cancel) löschen; (destroy) ausrotten. **~ up** vt aufwischen; ab-trocknen ⟨dishes⟩

wire /ˈwaɪə(r)/ n Draht m. **~-haired** a rauhhaarig

wireless /'waɪəlɪs/ n Radio nt
wire 'netting n Maschendraht m
wiring /'waɪərɪŋ/ n [elektrische] Leitungen pl
wiry /'waɪərɪ/ a (**-ier, -iest**) drahtig
wisdom /'wɪzdəm/ n Weisheit f; (prudence) Klugheit f. **∼ tooth** n Weisheitszahn m
wise /waɪz/ a (**-r, -st**), **-ly** adv weise; (prudent) klug
wish /wɪʃ/ n Wunsch m ● vt wünschen; **∼ s.o. well** jdm alles Gute wünschen; **I ∼ you could stay** ich wünschte, du könntest hierbleiben ● vi sich (dat) etwas wünschen. **∼ful** a **∼ful thinking** Wunschdenken nt
wishy-washy /'wɪʃɪwɒʃɪ/ a labberig; ⟨colour⟩ verwaschen; ⟨person⟩ lasch
wisp /wɪsp/ n Büschel nt; (of hair) Strähne f; (of smoke) Fahne f
wisteria /wɪs'tɪərɪə/ n Glyzinie f
wistful /'wɪstfl/ a, **-ly** adv wehmütig
wit /wɪt/ n Geist m, Witz m; (intelligence) Verstand m; (person) geistreicher Mensch m; **be at one's ∼s' end** sich (dat) keinen Rat mehr wissen; **scared out of one's ∼s** zu Tode erschrocken
witch /wɪtʃ/ n Hexe f. **∼craft** n Hexerei f. **∼-hunt** n Hexenjagd f
with /wɪð/ prep mit (+ dat); **∼ fear/ cold** vor Angst/Kälte; **∼ it** damit; **I'm going ∼ you** ich gehe mit; **take it ∼ you** nimm es mit; **I haven't got it ∼ me** ich habe es nicht bei mir; **I'm not ∼ you** (fam) ich komme nicht mit
with'draw v (pt **-drew**, pp **-drawn**) ● vt zurückziehen; abheben ⟨money⟩ ● vi sich zurückziehen. **∼al** n Zurückziehen nt; (of money) Abhebung f; (from drugs) Entzug m. **∼al symptoms** npl Entzugserscheinungen pl
with'drawn see withdraw ● a ⟨person⟩ verschlossen
wither /'wɪðə(r)/ vi [ver]welken
with'hold vt (pt/pp **-held**) vorenthalten (**from s.o.** jdm)
with'in prep innerhalb (+ gen); **∼ the law** im Rahmen des Gesetzes ● adv innen
with'out prep ohne (+ acc); **∼ my noticing it** ohne daß ich es merkte
with'stand vt (pt/pp **-stood**) standhalten (+ dat)
witness /'wɪtnɪs/ n Zeuge m/Zeugin f; (evidence) Zeugnis nt ● vt Zeuge/

Zeugin sein (+ gen); bestätigen ⟨signature⟩. **∼-box** n, (Amer) **∼-stand** n Zeugenstand m
witticism /'wɪtɪsɪzm/ n geistreicher Ausspruch m
wittingly /'wɪtɪŋlɪ/ adv wissentlich
witty /'wɪtɪ/ a (**-ier, -iest**) witzig, geistreich
wives /waɪvz/ see wife
wizard /'wɪzəd/ n Zauberer m. **∼ry** n Zauberei f
wizened /'wɪznd/ a verhutzelt
wobb|le /'wɒbl/ vi wackeln. **∼ly** a wackelig
woe /wəʊ/ n (liter) Jammer m; **∼ is me!** wehe mir!
woke, woken /wəʊk, 'wəʊkn/ see wake¹
wolf /wʊlf/ n (pl wolves /wʊlvz/) Wolf m ● vt **∼[down]** hinunterschlingen
woman /'wʊmən/ n (pl women) Frau f. **∼izer** n Schürzenjäger m. **∼ly** a fraulich
womb /wuːm/ n Gebärmutter f
women /'wɪmɪn/ npl see woman; **W∼'s Libber** /'lɪbə(r)/ n Frauenrechtlerin f. **W∼'s Liberation** n Frauenbewegung f
won /wʌn/ see win
wonder /'wʌndə(r)/ n Wunder nt; (surprise) Staunen nt ● vt/i sich fragen; (be surprised) sich wundern; **I ∼ da** frage ich mich; **I ∼ whether she is ill** ob sie wohl krank ist? **∼ful** a, **-ly** adv wunderbar
won't /wəʊnt/ = will not
woo /wuː/ vt (liter) werben um; (fig) umwerben
wood /wʊd/ n Holz nt; (forest) Wald m; **touch ∼!** unberufen!
wood: ∼cut n Holzschnitt m. **∼ed** /-ɪd/ a bewaldet. **∼en** a Holz-; (fig) hölzern. **∼pecker** n Specht m. **∼wind** n Holzbläser pl. **∼work** n (wooden parts) Holzteile pl; (craft) Tischlerei f. **∼worm** n Holzwurm m. **∼y** a holzig
wool /wʊl/ n Wolle f ● attrib Woll-. **∼len** a wollen. **∼lens** npl Wollsachen pl
woolly /'wʊlɪ/ a (**-ier, -iest**) wollig; (fig) unklar
word /wɜːd/ n Wort nt; (news) Nachricht f; **by ∼ of mouth** mündlich; **have a ∼ with** sprechen mit; **have ∼s** einen Wortwechsel haben. **∼ing** n Wortlaut m. **∼ processor** n Textverarbeitungssystem nt
wore /wɔː(r)/ see wear

work /wɜːk/ n Arbeit f; (Art, Literature) Werk nt; ~s pl (factory, mechanism) Werk nt; at ~ bei der Arbeit;
out of ~ arbeitslos ● vi arbeiten;
⟨machine, system:⟩ funktionieren;
(have effect) wirken; (study) lernen;
it won't ~ (fig) es klappt nicht
● vt arbeiten lassen; bedienen
⟨machine⟩; betätigen ⟨lever⟩; ~
one's way through sth sich durch
etw hindurcharbeiten. ~ off vt
abarbeiten. ~ out vt ausrechnen;
(solve) lösen ● vi gutgehen, (fam)
klappen. ~ up vt aufbauen; sich
(dat) holen ⟨appetite⟩; get ~ed up
sich aufregen
workable /'wɜːkəbl/ a (feasible)
durchführbar
workaholic /wɜːkə'hɒlɪk/ n arbeits-
wütiger Mensch m
worker /'wɜːkə(r)/ n Arbeiter(in)
m(f)
working /'wɜːkɪŋ/ a berufstätig; ⟨day,
clothes⟩ Arbeits-; be in ~ order funktionieren. ~'class n Arbeiterklasse
f. ~-class a Arbeiter-; be ~-class zur
Arbeiterklasse gehören
work: ~man n Arbeiter m; (craftsman) Handwerker m. ~manship n
Arbeit f. ~-out n [Fitneß]training
nt. ~shop n Werkstatt f
world /wɜːld/ n Welt f; in the ~ auf
der Welt; a ~ of difference ein him-
melweiter Unterschied; think the ~
of s.o. große Stücke auf jdn halten.
~ly a weltlich; ⟨person⟩ weltlich
gesinnt. ~-wide a & adv /-'-/
weltweit
worm /wɜːm/ n Wurm m ● vi ~
one's way into s.o.'s confidence sich
in jds Vertrauen einschleichen. ~-
eaten a wurmstichig
worn /wɔːn/ see wear ● a abgetragen.
~-out a abgetragen; ⟨carpet⟩ abgenutzt; ⟨person⟩ erschöpft
worried /'wʌrɪd/ a besorgt
worry /'wʌrɪ/ n Sorge f ● v (pt/pp
worried) ● vt beunruhigen, Sorgen
machen (+ dat); (bother) stören ● vi
sich beunruhigen, sich (dat) Sorgen
machen. ~ing a beunruhigend
worse /wɜːs/ a & adv schlechter;
(more serious) schlimmer ● n
Schlechtere(s) nt; Schlimmere(s) nt
worsen /'wɜːsn/ vt verschlechtern
● vi sich verschlechtern
worship /'wɜːʃɪp/ n Anbetung f; (service) Gottesdienst m; Your/His W~
Euer/Seine Ehren ● v (pt/pp

-shipped) ● vt anbeten ● vi am Gottesdienst teilnehmen
worst /wɜːst/ a schlechteste(r,s);
(most serious) schlimmste(r,s) ● adv
am schlechtesten; am schlimmsten
● n the ~ das Schlimmste; get the
~ of it den kürzeren ziehen
worsted /'wʊstɪd/ n Kammgarn m
worth /wɜːθ/ n Wert m; £10's ~ of
petrol Benzin für £10 ● a be ~ £5 £5
wert sein; be ~ it (fig) sich lohnen.
~less a wertlos. ~while a lohnend
worthy /'wɜːðɪ/ a würdig
would /wʊd/ v aux I ~ do it ich würde
es tun, ich täte es; ~ you go? wür-
dest du gehen? he said he ~n't er
sagte, er würde es nicht tun; what
~ you like? was möchten Sie?
wound¹ /wuːnd/ n Wunde f ● vt
verwunden
wound² /waʊnd/ see wind²
wove, woven /wəʊv, 'wəʊvn/ see
weave²
wrangle /'ræŋgl/ n Streit m ● vi sich
streiten
wrap /ræp/ n Umhang m ● vt (pt/pp
wrapped) ~[up] wickeln; einpacken
⟨present⟩ ● vi ~ up warmly sich
warm einpacken; be ~ped up in
(fig) aufgehen in (+ dat). ~per n
Hülle f. ~ping n Verpackung f.
~ping paper n Einwickelpapier nt
wrath /rɒθ/ n Zorn m
wreak /riːk/ vt ~ havoc Verwüstun-
gen anrichten
wreath /riːθ/ n (pl ~s /-ðz/) Kranz m
wreck /rek/ n Wrack nt ● vt zerstören; zunichte machen ⟨plans⟩;
zerrütten ⟨marriage⟩. ~age /-ɪdʒ/ n
Wrackteile pl; (fig) Trümmer pl
wren /ren/ n Zaunkönig m
wrench /rentʃ/ n Ruck m; (tool)
Schraubenschlüssel m; be a ~ (fig)
weh tun ● vt reißen; ~ sth from s.o.
jdm etw entreißen
wrest /rest/ vt entwinden (from s.o.
jdm)
wrestl|e /'resl/ vi ringen. ~er n
Ringer m. ~ing n Ringen nt
wretch /retʃ/ n Kreatur f. ~ed /-ɪd/ a
elend; (very bad) erbärmlich
wriggle /'rɪgl/ n Zappeln nt ● vi zappeln; (move forward) sich schlängeln; ~ out of sth (fam) sich vor etw
(dat) drücken
wring /rɪŋ/ vt (pt/pp wrung) wringen;
(~ out) auswringen; umdrehen
⟨neck⟩; ringen ⟨hands⟩; be ~ing wet
tropfnaß sein

wrinkle /'rɪŋkl/ n Falte f; (on skin) Runzel f ● vt kräuseln ● vi sich kräuseln, sich falten. **~d** a runzlig

wrist /rɪst/ n Handgelenk nt. **~watch** n Armbanduhr f

writ /rɪt/ n (Jur) Verfügung f

write /raɪt/ vt/i (pt **wrote**, pp **written**, pres p **writing**) schreiben. **~ down** vt aufschreiben. **~ off** vt abschreiben; zu Schrott fahren ⟨car⟩

'write-off n ≈ Totalschaden m

writer /'raɪtə(r)/ n Schreiber(in) m(f); (author) Schriftsteller(in) m(f)

'write-up n Bericht m; (review) Kritik f

writhe /raɪð/ vi sich winden

writing /'raɪtɪŋ/ n Schreiben nt; (handwriting) Schrift f; in **~** schriftlich. **~-paper** n Schreibpapier nt

written /'rɪtn/ see **write**

wrong /rɒŋ/ a, -**ly** adv falsch; (morally) unrecht; (not just) ungerecht; **be ~** nicht stimmen; ⟨person:⟩ unrecht haben; **what's ~?** was ist los? ● adv falsch; **go ~** ⟨person:⟩ etwas falsch machen; ⟨machine:⟩ kaputtgehen; ⟨plan:⟩ schiefgehen ● n Unrecht nt ● vt Unrecht tun (+ dat). **~ful** a ungerechtfertigt. **~fully** adv ⟨accuse⟩ zu Unrecht

wrote /rəʊt/ see **write**

wrought 'iron /rɔːt-/ n Schmiedeeisen nt ● attrib schmiedeeisern

wrung /rʌŋ/ see **wring**

wry /raɪ/ a (-er, -est) ironisch; ⟨humour⟩ trocken

X

xerox (P) /'zɪərɒks/ vt fotokopieren

Xmas /'krɪsməs, 'eksməs/ n (fam) Weihnachten nt

'X-ray n (picture) Röntgenaufnahme f; **~s** pl Röntgenstrahlen pl; **have an ~** geröntgt werden ● vt röntgen; durchleuchten ⟨luggage⟩

Y

yacht /jɒt/ n Jacht f; (for racing) Segelboot nt. **~ing** n Segeln nt

yank /jæŋk/ vt (fam) reißen

Yank n (fam) Amerikaner(in) m(f), (fam) Ami m

yap /jæp/ vi (pt/pp **yapped**) ⟨dog:⟩ kläffen

yard¹ /jɑːd/ n Hof m; (for storage) Lager nt

yard² n Yard nt (= 0,91 m). **~stick** n (fig) Maßstab m

yarn /jɑːn/ n Garn nt; (fam: tale) Geschichte f

yawn /jɔːn/ n Gähnen nt ● vi gähnen. **~ing** a gähnend

year /jɪə(r)/ n Jahr nt; (of wine) Jahrgang m; **for ~s** jahrelang. **~-book** n Jahrbuch nt. **~ly** a & adv jährlich

yearn /jɜːn/ vi sich sehnen (**for** nach). **~ing** n Sehnsucht f

yeast /jiːst/ n Hefe f

yell /jel/ n Schrei m ● vi schreien

yellow /'jeləʊ/ a gelb ● n Gelb nt. **~ish** a gelblich

yelp /jelp/ vi jaulen

yen /jen/ n Wunsch m (**for** nach)

yes /jes/ adv ja; (contradicting) doch ● n Ja nt

yesterday /'jestədeɪ/ n & adv gestern; **~'s paper** die gestrige Zeitung; **the day before ~** vorgestern

yet /jet/ adv noch; (in question) schon; (nevertheless) doch; **as ~** bisher; **not ~** noch nicht; **the best ~** das bisher beste ● conj doch

yew /juː/ n Eibe f

Yiddish /'jɪdɪʃ/ n Jiddisch nt

yield /jiːld/ n Ertrag m ● vt bringen; abwerfen ⟨profit⟩ ● vi nachgeben; (Amer, Auto) die Vorfahrt beachten

yodel /'jəʊdl/ vi (pt/pp **yodelled**) jodeln

yoga /'jəʊgə/ n Yoga m

yoghurt /'jɒgət/ n Joghurt m

yoke /jəʊk/ n Joch nt; (of garment) Passe f

yokel /'jəʊkl/ n Bauerntölpel m

yolk /jəʊk/ n Dotter m, Eigelb nt

yonder /'jɒndə(r)/ adv (liter) dort drüben

you /juː/ pron du; (acc) dich; (dat) dir; (pl) ihr; (acc, dat) euch; (formal) (nom & acc, sg & pl) Sie; (dat, sg & pl) Ihnen; (one) man; (acc) einen; (dat) einem; **all of ~** ihr/Sie alle; **I know ~** ich kenne dich/euch/Sie; **I'll give ~ the money** ich gebe dir/euch/Ihnen das Geld; **it does ~ good** es tut gut; **it's bad for ~** es ist ungesund

young /jʌŋ/ a (-er /-gə(r)/, -est /-gɪst/) jung ● npl (animals) Junge pl; **the ~** die Jugend f. **~ster** n Jugendliche(r) m/f; (child) Kleine(r) m/f

your /jɔ:(r)/ a dein; (pl) euer; (formal) Ihr

yours /jɔ:z/ poss pron deine(r), deins; (pl) eure(r), euers; (formal, sg & pl) Ihre(r), Ihr[e]s; **a friend of** ∼ ein Freund von dir/Ihnen/euch; **that is** ∼ das gehört dir/Ihnen/euch

your'self pron (pl -selves) selbst; (refl) dich; (dat) dir; (pl) euch; (formal) sich; **by** ∼ allein

youth /ju:θ/ n (pl youths /-ðz/ Jugend f; (boy) Jugendliche(r) m. ∼ful a jugendlich. ∼ **hostel** n Jugendherberge f

Yugoslav /'ju:gəslɑ:v/ a jugoslawisch. ∼**ia** /-'slɑ:vɪə/ n Jugoslawien nt

Z

zany /'zeɪnɪ/ a (-ier, -iest) närrisch, verrückt

zeal /zi:l/ n Eifer m

zealous /'zeləs/ a, **-ly** adv eifrig

zebra /'zebrə/ n Zebra nt. ∼'**crossing** n Zebrastreifen m

zenith /'zenɪθ/ n Zenit m; (fig) Gipfel m

zero /'zɪərəʊ/ n Null f

zest /zest/ n Begeisterung f

zigzag /'zɪgzæg/ n Zickzack m • vi (pt/pp -zagged) im Zickzack laufen/ (in vehicle) fahren

zinc /zɪŋk/ n Zink nt

zip /zɪp/ n ∼ **[fastener]** Reißverschluß m • vt ∼ **[up]** den Reißverschluß zuziehen an (+ dat)

'**Zip code** n (Amer) Postleitzahl f

zipper /'zɪpə(r)/ n Reißverschluß m

zither /'zɪðə(r)/ n Zither f

zodiac /'zəʊdɪæk/ n Tierkreis m

zombie /'zɒmbɪ/ n (fam) **like a** ∼ ganz benommen

zone /zəʊn/ n Zone f

zoo /zu:/ n Zoo m

zoological /zəʊə'lɒdʒɪkl/ a zoologisch

zoolog|ist /zəʊ'ɒlədʒɪst/ n Zoologe m/ -gin f. ∼**y** Zoologie f

zoom /zu:m/ vi sausen. ∼ **lens** n Zoomobjektiv nt

Englische unregelmäßige Verben

Ein Sternchen (*) weist darauf hin, daß die korrekte Form von der jeweiligen Bedeutung abhängt.

Infinitive *Infinitiv*	Past Tense *Präteritum*	Past Participle *2. Partizip*
arise	arose	arisen
awake	awoke	awoken
be	was *sg*, were *pl*	been
bear	bore	borne
beat	beat	beaten
become	became	become
begin	began	begun
behold	beheld	beheld
bend	bent	bent
beseech	beseeched, besought	beseeched, besought
bet	bet, betted	bet, betted
bid	*bade, bid	*bidden, bid
bind	bound	bound
bite	bit	bitten
bleed	bled	bled
blow	blew	blown
break	broke	broken
breed	bred	bred
bring	brought	brought
build	built	built
burn	burnt, burned	burnt, burned
burst	burst	burst
bust	busted, bust	busted, bust
buy	bought	bought
cast	cast	cast
catch	caught	caught
choose	chose	chosen
cling	clung	clung
come	came	come
cost	*cost, costed	*cost, costed
creep	crept	crept
cut	cut	cut
deal	dealt	dealt
dig	dug	dug
do	did	done
draw	drew	drawn
dream	dreamt, dreamed	dreamt, dreamed
drink	drank	drunk
drive	drove	driven
dwell	dwelt	dwelt
eat	ate	eaten
fall	fell	fallen
feed	fed	fed
feel	felt	felt
fight	fought	fought
find	found	found

Infinitive *Infinitiv*	Past Tense *Präteritum*	Past Participle *2. Partizip*
flee	fled	fled
fling	flung	flung
fly	flew	flown
forbid	forbade	forbidden
forget	forgot	forgotten
forgive	forgave	forgiven
forsake	forsook	forsaken
freeze	froze	frozen
get	got	got, (*Amer also*) gotten
give	gave	given
go	went	gone
grind	ground	ground
grow	grew	grown
hang	*hung, hanged	*hung, hanged
have	had	had
hear	heard	heard
hew	hewed	hewed, hewn
hide	hid	hidden
hit	hit	hit
hold	held	held
hurt	hurt	hurt
keep	kept	kept
kneel	knelt	knelt
know	knew	known
lay	laid	laid
lead	led	led
lean	leaned, lent	leaned, lent
leap	leapt, leaped	leapt, leaped
learn	learnt, learned	learnt, learned
leave	left	left
lend	lent	lent
let	let	let
lie[2]	lay	lain
light	lit, lighted	lit, lighted
lose	lost	lost
make	made	made
mean	meant	meant
meet	met	met
mow	mowed	mown, mowed
overhang	overhung	overhung
pay	paid	paid
put	put	put
quit	quitted, quit	quitted, quit
read /riːd/	read /red/	read /red/
rid	rid	rid
ride	rode	ridden
ring[2]	rang	rung
rise	rose	risen
run	ran	run
saw	sawed	sawn, sawed

Infinitive	Past Tense	Past Participle
Infinitiv	*Präteritum*	*2. Partizip*
say	said	said
see	saw	seen
seek	sought	sought
sell	sold	sold
send	sent	sent
set	set	set
sew	sewed	sewn, sewed
shake	shook	shaken
shear	sheared	shorn, sheared
shed	shed	shed
shine	shone	shone
shit	shit	shit
shoe	shod	shod
shoot	shot	shot
show	showed	shown
shrink	shrank	shrunk
shut	shut	shut
sing	sang	sung
sink	sank	sunk
sit	sat	sat
slay	slew	slain
sleep	slept	slept
slide	slid	slid
sling	slung	slung
slit	slit	slit
smell	smelt, smelled	smelt, smelled
sow	sowed	sown, sowed
speak	spoke	spoken
speed	*sped, speeded	*sped, speeded
spell	spelled, spelt	spelled, spelt
spend	spent	spent
spill	spilt, spilled	spilt, spilled
spin	spun	spun
spit	spat	spat
split	split	split
spoil	spoilt, spoiled	spoilt, spoiled
spread	spread	spread
spring	sprang	sprung
stand	stood	stood
steal	stole	stolen
stick	stuck	stuck
sting	stung	stung
stink	stank	stunk
strew	strewed	strewn, strewed
stride	strode	stridden
strike	struck	struck
string	strung	strung
strive	strove	striven
swear	swore	sworn
sweep	swept	swept
swell	swelled	swollen, swelled

Infinitive *Infinitiv*	Past Tense *Präteritum*	Past Participle *2. Partizip*
swim	swam	swum
swing	swung	swung
take	took	taken
teach	taught	taught
tear	tore	torn
tell	told	told
think	thought	thought
thrive	thrived, throve	thrived, thriven
throw	threw	thrown
thrust	thrust	thrust
tread	trod	trodden
understand	understood	understood
undo	undid	undone
wake	woke	woken
wear	wore	worn
weave[2]	wove	woven
weep	wept	wept
wet	wet, wetted	wet, wetted
win	won	won
wind[2] /waɪnd/	wound /waʊnd/	wound /waʊnd/
wring	wrung	wrung
write	wrote	written

Phonetic symbols used for German words

a	Hand	hant	ŋ	lang	laŋ	
aː	Bahn	baːn	o	moral	moˈraːl	
ɐ	Ober	ˈoːbɐ	oː	Boot	boːt	
ɐ̯	Uhr	uːɐ̯	ǫ	Foyer	fǫaˈjeː	
ã	Conférencier	kõferãˈsi̯eː	õ	Konkurs	kõˈkʊrs	
ãː	Abonnement	abɔnəˈmãː	õː	Ballon	baˈlõː	
ai̯	weit	vai̯t	ɔ	Post	pɔst	
au̯	Haut	hau̯t	ø	Ökonom	økoˈnoːm	
b	Ball	bal	øː	Öl	øːl	
ç	ich	ɪç	œ	göttlich	ˈgœtlɪç	
d	dann	dan	ɔy	heute	ˈhɔytə	
dʒ	Gin	dʒɪn	p	Pakt	pakt	
e	Metall	meˈtal	r	Rast	rast	
eː	Beet	beːt	s	Hast	hast	
ɛ	mästen	ˈmɛstən	ʃ	Schal	ʃaːl	
ɛː	wählen	ˈvɛːlən	t	Tal	taːl	
ɛ̃ː	Cousin	kuˈzɛ̃ː	ts	Zahl	tsaːl	
ə	Nase	ˈnaːzə	tʃ	Couch	kau̯tʃ	
f	Faß	fas	u	kulant	kuˈlant	
g	Gast	gast	uː	Hut	huːt	
h	haben	ˈhaːbən	u̯	aktuell	akˈtu̯ɛl	
i	Rivale	riˈvaːlə	ʊ	Pult	pʊlt	
iː	viel	fiːl	v	was	vas	
i̯	Aktion	akˈtsi̯oːn	x	Bach	bax	
ɪ	Birke	ˈbɪrkə	y	Physik	fyˈziːk	
j	ja	jaː	yː	Rübe	ˈryːbə	
k	kalt	kalt	ỹ	Nuance	ˈnỹãːsə	
l	Last	last	ʏ	Fülle	ˈfʏlə	
m	Mast	mast	z	Nase	ˈnaːzə	
n	Naht	naːt	ʒ	Regime	reˈʒiːm	

ˀ Glottal stop, e.g. Koordination /koˀɔrdinaˈtsi̯oːn/.
ː Length sign after a vowel, e.g. Chrom /kroːm/.
ˈ Stress mark before stressed syllable, e.g. Balkon /balˈkõː/.

Die für das Englische verwendeten Zeichen der Lautschrift

ɑː	barn	bɑːn		l	lot	lɒt
ɑ̃	nuance	ˈnjuːɑ̃s		m	mat	mæt
æ	fat	fæt		n	not	nɒt
æ̃	lingerie	ˈlæ̃ʒərɪ		ŋ	sing	sɪŋ
aɪ	fine	faɪn		ɒ	got	gɒt
aʊ	now	naʊ		ɔː	paw	pɔː
b	bat	bæt		ɔɪ	boil	bɔɪl
d	dog	dɒg		p	pet	pet
dʒ	jam	dʒæm		r	rat	ræt
e	met	met		s	sip	sɪp
eɪ	fate	feɪt		ʃ	ship	ʃɪp
eə	fairy	ˈfeərɪ		t	tip	tɪp
əʊ	goat	gəʊt		tʃ	chin	tʃɪn
ə	ago	əˈgəʊ		θ	thin	θɪn
ɜː	fur	fɜː(r)		ð	the	ðə
f	fat	fæt		uː	boot	buːt
g	good	gʊd		ʊ	book	bʊk
h	hat	hæt		ʊə	tourism	ˈtʊərɪzm
ɪ	bit, happy	bɪt, ˈhæpɪ		ʌ	dug	dʌg
ɪə	near	nɪə(r)		v	van	væn
iː	meet	miːt		w	win	wɪn
j	yet	jet		z	zip	zɪp
k	kit	kɪt		ʒ	vision	ˈvɪʒn

ː bezeichnet Länge des vorhergehenden Vokals, z. B. boot [buːt].

ˈ Betonung, steht unmittelbar vor einer betonten Silbe, z. B. ago [əˈgəʊ].

(r) Ein „r" in runden Klammern wird nur gesprochen, wenn im Textzusammenhang ein Vokal unmittelbar folgt, z. B. fire /ˈfaɪə(r); fire at /ˈfaɪər æt/.

Guide to German pronunciation

Consonants are pronounced as in English with the following exceptions:

b	as	p	*at the end of a word or*
d	as	t	*syllable*
g	as	k	

ch	as in Scottish lo<u>ch</u> *after a, o, u, au*		
	like an exaggerated h as in <u>h</u>uge		
	after i, e, ä, ö, ü, eu, ei		

-chs	as	x	(as in bo<u>x</u>)
-ig	as	-ich /ɪç/	*when a suffix*
j	as	y	(as in <u>y</u>es)
ps ⎫			the p is pronounced
pn ⎭			
qu	as	k + v	
s	as	z	(as in <u>z</u>ero) *at the beginning of a word*
	as	s	(as in bu<u>s</u>) *at the end of a word or syllable, before a consonant, or when doubled*
sch	as	sh	
sp	as	shp	*at the beginning of a*
st	as	sht	*word*
v	as	f	(as in <u>f</u>or)
	as	v	(as in <u>v</u>ery) *within a word*
w	as	v	(as in <u>v</u>ery)
z	as	ts	

Vowels are approximately as follows:

a	short	as	u	(as in b<u>u</u>t)
	long	as	a	(as in c<u>a</u>r)
e	short	as	e	(as in p<u>e</u>n)
	long	as	a	(as in p<u>a</u>per)
i	short	as	i	(as in b<u>i</u>t)
	long	as	ee	(as in qu<u>ee</u>n)
o	short	as	o	(as in h<u>o</u>t)
	long	as	o	(as in p<u>o</u>pe)

u	short	as	oo	(as in f<u>oo</u>t)
	long	as	oo	(as in b<u>oo</u>t)

Vowels are always short before a double consonant, and long when followed by an h or when double

ie	is pronounced ee	(as in k<u>ee</u>p)

Diphthongs

au		as	ow	(as in h<u>ow</u>)
ei		as	y	(as in m<u>y</u>)
ai				
eu		as	oy	(as in b<u>oy</u>)
äu				

German irregular verbs

1st, 2nd and 3rd person present are given after the infinitive, and past subjunctive after the past indicative, where there is a change of vowel or any other irregularity.

Compound verbs are only given if they do not take the same forms as the corresponding simple verb, e.g. *befehlen*, or if there is no corresponding simple verb, e.g. *bewegen*.

An asterisk (*) indicates a verb which is also conjugated regularly.

Infinitive *Infinitiv*	Past Tense *Präteritum*	Past Participle *2. Partizip*
abwägen	wog (wöge) ab	abgewogen
ausbedingen	bedang (bedänge) aus	ausbedungen
*backen (du bäckst, er bäckt)	buk (büke)	gebacken
befehlen (du befiehlst, er befiehlt)	befahl (beföhle, befähle)	befohlen
beginnen	begann (begänne)	begonnen
beißen (du/er beißt)	biß (bisse)	gebissen
bergen (du birgst, er birgt)	barg (bärge)	geborgen
bersten (du/er birst)	barst (bärste)	geborsten
bewegen[2]	bewog (bewöge)	bewogen
biegen	bog (böge)	gebogen
bieten	bot (böte)	geboten
binden	band (bände)	gebunden
bitten	bat (bäte)	gebeten
blasen (du/er bläst)	blies	geblasen
bleiben	blieb	geblieben
*bleichen	blich	geblichen
braten (du brätst, er brät)	briet	gebraten
brechen (du brichst, er bricht)	brach (bräche)	gebrochen
brennen	brannte (brennte)	gebrannt
bringen	brachte (brächte)	gebracht
denken	dachte (dächte)	gedacht
dreschen (du drischst, er drischt)	drosch (drösche)	gedroschen
dringen	drang (dränge)	gedrungen
dürfen (ich/er darf, du darfst)	durfte (dürfte)	gedurft
empfehlen (du empfiehlst, er empfiehlt)	empfahl (empföhle)	empfohlen
erlöschen (du erlischst, er erlischt)	erlosch (erlösche)	erloschen
*erschallen	erscholl (erschölle)	erschollen
*erschrecken (du erschrickst, er erschrickt)	erschrak (erschräke)	erschrocken

Infinitive *Infinitiv*	Past Tense *Präteritum*	Past Participle 2. *Partizip*
erwägen	erwog (erwöge)	erwogen
essen (du/er ißt)	aß (äße)	gegessen
fahren (du fährst, er fährt)	fuhr (führe)	gefahren
fallen (du fällst, er fällt)	fiel	gefallen
fangen (du fängst, er fängt)	fing	gefangen
fechten (du fichtst, er ficht)	focht (föchte)	gefochten
finden	fand (fände)	gefunden
flechten (du flichtst, er flicht)	flocht (flöchte)	geflochten
fliegen	flog (flöge)	geflogen
fliehen	floh (flöhe)	geflohen
fließen (du/er fließt)	floß (flösse)	geflossen
fressen (du/er frißt)	fraß (fräße)	gefressen
frieren	fror (fröre)	gefroren
*gären	gor (göre)	gegoren
gebären (du gebierst, sie gebiert)	gebar (gebäre)	geboren
geben (du gibst, er gibt)	gab (gäbe)	gegeben
gedeihen	gedieh	gediehen
gehen	ging	gegangen
gelingen	gelang (gelänge)	gelungen
gelten (du giltst, er gilt)	galt (gölte, gälte)	gegolten
genesen (du/er genest)	genas (genäse)	genesen
genießen (du/er genießt)	genoß (genösse)	genossen
geschehen (es geschieht)	geschah (geschähe)	geschehen
gewinnen	gewann (gewönne, gewänne)	gewonnen
gießen (du/er gießt)	goß (gösse)	gegossen
gleichen	glich	geglichen
gleiten	glitt	geglitten
glimmen	glomm (glömme)	geglommen
graben (du gräbst, er gräbt)	grub (grübe)	gegraben
greifen	griff	gegriffen
haben (du hast, er hat)	hatte (hätte)	gehabt
halten (du hältst, er hält)	hielt	gehalten
hängen[2]	hing	gehangen
hauen	haute	gehauen
heben	hob (höbe)	gehoben
heißen (du/er heißt)	hieß	geheißen
helfen (du hilfst, er hilft)	half (hülfe)	geholfen
kennen	kannte (kennte)	gekannt
klingen	klang (klänge)	geklungen
kneifen	kniff	gekniffen
kommen	kam (käme)	gekommen
können (ich/er kann, du kannst)	konnte (könnte)	gekonnt
kriechen	kroch (kröche)	gekrochen
laden (du lädst, er lädt)	lud (lüde)	geladen
lassen (du/er läßt)	ließ	gelassen
laufen (du läufst, er läuft)	lief	gelaufen

Infinitive *Infinitiv*	Past Tense *Präteritum*	Past Participle *2. Partizip*
leiden	litt	gelitten
leihen	lieh	geliehen
lesen (du/er liest)	las (läse)	gelesen
liegen	lag (läge)	gelegen
lügen	log (löge)	gelogen
mahlen	mahlte	gemahlen
meiden	mied	gemieden
melken	molk (mölke)	gemolken
messen (du/er mißt)	maß (mäße)	gemessen
mißlingen	mißlang (mißlänge)	mißlungen
mögen (ich/er mag, du magst)	mochte (möchte)	gemocht
müssen (ich/er muß, du mußt)	mußte (müßte)	gemußt
nehmen (du nimmst, er nimmt)	nahm (nähme)	genommen
nennen	nannte (nennte)	genannt
pfeifen	pfiff	gepfiffen
preisen (du/er preist)	pries	gepriesen
quellen (du quillst, er quillt)	quoll (quölle)	gequollen
raten (du rätst, er rät)	riet	geraten
reiben	rieb	gerieben
reißen (du/er reißt)	riß	gerissen
reiten	ritt	geritten
rennen	rannte (rennte)	gerannt
riechen	roch (röche)	gerochen
ringen	rang (ränge)	gerungen
rinnen	rann (ränne)	geronnen
rufen	rief	gerufen
*salzen (du/er salzt)	salzte	gesalzen
saufen (du säufst, er säuft)	soff (söffe)	gesoffen
*saugen	sog (söge)	gesogen
schaffen[1]	schuf (schüfe)	geschaffen
scheiden	schied	geschieden
scheinen	schien	geschienen
scheißen (du/er scheißt)	schiß	geschissen
schelten (du schiltst, er schilt)	schalt (schölte)	gescholten
scheren[1]	schor (schöre)	geschoren
schieben	schob (schöbe)	geschoben
schießen (du/er schießt)	schoß (schösse)	geschossen
schinden	schindete	geschunden
schlafen (du schläfst, er schläft)	schlief	geschlafen
schlagen (du schlägst, er schlägt)	schlug (schlüge)	geschlagen
schleichen	schlich	geschlichen
schleifen[2]	schliff	geschliffen
schließen (du/er schließt)	schloß (schlösse)	geschlossen
schlingen	schlang (schlänge)	geschlungen

Infinitive *Infinitiv*	Past Tense *Präteritum*	Past Participle *2. Partizip*
schmeißen (du/er schmeißt)	schmiß (schmisse)	geschmissen
schmelzen (du/er schmilzt)	schmolz (schmölze)	geschmolzen
schneiden	schnitt	geschnitten
*schrecken (du schrickst, er schrickt)	schrak (schräke)	geschreckt
schreiben	schrieb	geschrieben
schreien	schrie	geschrie[e]n
schreiten	schritt	geschritten
schweigen	schwieg	geschwiegen
schwellen (du schwillst, er schwillt)	schwoll (schwölle)	geschwollen
schwimmen	schwamm (schwömme)	geschwommen
schwinden	schwand (schwände)	geschwunden
schwingen	schwang (schwänge)	geschwungen
schwören	schwor (schwüre)	geschworen
sehen (du siehst, er sieht)	sah (sähe)	gesehen
sein (ich bin, du bist, er ist, wir sind, ihr seid, sie sind)	war (wäre)	gewesen
senden[1]	sandte (sendete)	gesandt
sieden	sott (sötte)	gesotten
singen	sang (sänge)	gesungen
sinken	sank (sänke)	gesunken
sinnen	sann (sänne)	gesonnen
sitzen (du/er sitzt)	saß (säße)	gesessen
sollen (ich/er soll, du sollst)	sollte	gesollt
*spalten	spaltete	gespalten
speien	spie	gespie[e]n
spinnen	spann (spönne, spänne)	gesponnen
sprechen (du sprichst, er spricht)	sprach (spräche)	gesprochen
sprießen (du/er sprießt)	sproß (sprösse)	gesprossen
springen	sprang (spränge)	gesprungen
stechen (du stichst, er sticht)	stach (stäche)	gestochen
stehen	stand (stünde, stände)	gestanden
stehlen (du stiehlst, er stiehlt)	stahl (stähle)	gestohlen
steigen	stieg	gestiegen
sterben (du stirbst, er stirbt)	starb (stürbe)	gestorben
stinken	stank (stänke)	gestunken
stoßen (du/er stößt)	stieß	gestoßen
streichen	strich	gestrichen
streiten	stritt	gestritten
tragen (du trägst, er trägt)	trug (trüge)	getragen
treffen (du triffst, er trifft)	traf (träfe)	getroffen
treiben	trieb	getrieben
treten (du trittst, er tritt)	trat (träte)	getreten

Infinitive *Infinitiv*	Past Tense *Präteritum*	Past Participle *2. Partizip*
*triefen	troff (tröffe)	getroffen
trinken	trank (tränke)	getrunken
trügen	trog (tröge)	getrogen
tun (du tust, er tut)	tat (täte)	getan
verderben (du verdirbst, er verdirbt)	verdarb (verdürbe)	verdorben
vergessen (du/er vergißt)	vergaß (vergäße)	vergessen
verlieren	verlor (verlöre)	verloren
verschleißen (du/er verschleißt)	verschliß	verschlissen
verzeihen	verzieh	verziehen
wachsen[1] (du/er wächst)	wuchs (wüchse)	gewachsen
waschen (du wäschst, er wäscht)	wusch (wüsche)	gewaschen
weichen[2]	wich	gewichen
weisen (du/er weist)	wies	gewiesen
*wenden[2]	wandte (wendete)	gewandt
werben (du wirbst, er wirbt)	warb (würbe)	geworben
werden (du wirst, er wird)	wurde (würde)	geworden
werfen (du wirfst, er wirft)	warf (würfe)	geworfen
wiegen[1]	wog (wöge)	gewogen
winden	wand (wände)	gewunden
wissen (ich/er weiß, du weißt)	wußte (wüßte)	gewußt
wollen (ich/er will, du willst)	wollte	gewollt
wringen	wrang (wränge)	gewrungen
ziehen	zog (zöge)	gezogen
zwingen	zwang (zwänge)	gezwungen

OXFORD

MORE OXFORD PAPERBACKS

This book is just one of nearly 1000 Oxford Paperbacks currently in print. If you would like details of other Oxford Paperbacks, including titles in the World's Classics, Oxford Reference, Oxford Books, OPUS, Past Masters, Oxford Authors, and Oxford Shakespeare series, please write to:

UK and Europe: Oxford Paperbacks Publicity Manager, Arts and Reference Publicity Department, Oxford University Press, Walton Street, Oxford OX2 6DP.

Customers in UK and Europe will find Oxford Paperbacks available in all good bookshops. But in case of difficulty please send orders to the Cash-with-Order Department, Oxford University Press Distribution Services, Saxon Way West, Corby, Northants NN18 9ES. Tel: 0536 741519; Fax: 0536 746337. Please send a cheque for the total cost of the books, plus £1.75 postage and packing for orders under £20; £2.75 for orders over £20. Customers outside the UK should add 10% of the cost of the books for postage and packing.

USA: Oxford Paperbacks Marketing Manager, Oxford University Press, Inc., 200 Madison Avenue, New York, N.Y. 10016.

Canada: Trade Department, Oxford University Press, 70 Wynford Drive, Don Mills, Ontario M3C 1J9.

Australia: Trade Marketing Manager, Oxford University Press, G.P.O. Box 2784Y, Melbourne 3001, Victoria.

South Africa: Oxford University Press, P.O. Box 1141, Cape Town 8000.

OXFORD REFERENCE

Oxford is famous for its superb range of dictionaries and reference books. The Oxford Reference series offers the most up-to-date and comprehensive paperbacks at the most competitive prices, across a broad spectrum of subjects.

THE CONCISE OXFORD COMPANION
TO ENGLISH LITERATURE

Edited by Margaret Drabble and Jenny Stringer

Based on the immensely popular fifth edition of the *Oxford Companion to English Literature* this is an indispensable, compact guide to the central matter of English literature.

There are more than 5,000 entries on the lives and works of authors, poets, playwrights, essayists, philosophers, and historians; plot summaries of novels and plays; literary movements; fictional characters; legends; theatres; periodicals; and much more.

The book's sharpened focus on the English literature of the British Isles makes it especially convenient to use, but there is still generous coverage of the literature of other countries and of other disciplines which have influenced or been influenced by English literature.

From reviews of *The Oxford Companion to English Literature Fifth Edition:*

'a book which one turns to with constant pleasure . . . a book with much style and little prejudice' Iain Gilchrist, *TLS*

'it is quite difficult to imagine, in this genre, a more useful publication' Frank Kermode, *London Review of Books*

'incarnates a living sense of tradition . . . sensitive not to fashion merely but to the spirit of the age' Christopher Ricks, *Sunday Times*

Also available in Oxford Reference:

The Concise Oxford Dictionary of Art and Artists
edited by Ian Chilvers
A Concise Oxford Dictionary of Mathematics
Christopher Clapham
The Oxford Spelling Dictionary   compiled by R. E. Allen
A Concise Dictionary of Law   edited by Elizabeth A. Martin